Encyclopedia of
Behavior Modification and Cognitive Behavior Therapy

Encyclopedia of
Behavior Modification and Cognitive Behavior Therapy
volume two

Child Clinical Applications

Michel Hersen Editor-in-Chief
Pacific University

Alan M. Gross | **Ronald S. Drabman**
University of Mississippi | *University of Mississippi Medical Center*

Editors

A SAGE Reference Publication

SAGE Publications
Thousand Oaks ▪ London ▪ New Delhi

For information:

 Sage Publications, Inc.
2455 Teller Road
Thousand Oaks, California 91320

Sage Publications Ltd.
1 Oliver's Yard
55 City Road
London EC1Y 1SP
United Kingdom

Sage Publications India Pvt. Ltd.
B-42, Panchsheel Enclave
Post Box 4109
New Delhi 110 017 India

Printed in the United States of America.

ISBN 0-7619-2747-6

Acquiring Editor:	Jim Brace-Thompson
Editorial Assistant:	Karen Ehrmann
Project Editor:	Claudia A. Hoffman
Copy Editor:	Barbara Coster
Typesetter:	C&M Digitals (P) Ltd.
Indexer:	Molly Hall
Cover Designer:	Ravi Balasuriya

Contents

Editorial Board, *vi*

List of Entries, *vii*

Reader's Guide, *ix*

About the Editors, *xi*

Contributors, *xii*

Preface, *xvii*

Introduction, *xix*

Entries

A–Z *653–1096*

Master Bibliography, *1097*

Index, *I-1*

Editors

Alan M. Gross
University of Mississippi

Ronald S. Drabman
University of Mississippi Medical Center

Advisory Board Members

List of Entries

Editors' Note: This list of entries is for Volume II: Child Clinical Applications only. For Volume I: Adult Clinical Applications and Volume III: Educational Applications, please see the List of Entries in the respective volumes.

Adolescent Anger Management
Antecedent Control Procedures
Anxiety Management
Applied Behavior Analysis
Aromatic Ammonia
Assertiveness Training
Attention Training Procedures
Aversive Conditioning
Avoidance Training

Baer, Donald M.
Beat the Buzzer
Behavior Management for
   Improving Academic and
   Classroom Behavior
Behavior Therapy
Behavioral Assessment
Behavioral Consultation
Behavioral Contracting
Behavioral Family Therapy
Behavioral Group Therapy With
   Children and Youth
Behavioral Interview
Behavioral Pediatrics
Behavioral Rehearsal
Behavioral Weight Control
   Therapy With Children
Bell and Pad Bladder
   Training
Biofeedback

Case Conceptualization
Chore and Allowance Program
   for Children
Classical Conditioning

Cognitive Behavior Therapy:
   Child Clinical Applications
Cognitive Restructuring
Competing Response Training
Compliance Training
Contingency Management
Contingent Exercise
Contingent Restraint
Correspondence Training
Counterconditioning
Covert Conditioning With
   Children and Adolescents

Differential Reinforcement of
   Incompatible Behavior
Differential Reinforcement of
   Low Rates of Responding
Differential Reinforcement of
   Other Behavior
Discrete Trial Therapy
Discrimination Training
Drug Abuse Prevention Strategies

Empirically Supported
   Treatments for Childhood
   Disorders
Errorless Compliance Training
Escape Training
Event Recording
Exposure and Response
   Prevention
Extinction

Facial Screening
Fading

Feedback
Five-Step Procedure
   for Stealing
Flooding
Full-Spectrum Home Training
   for Simple Bed-Wetting
Function Communication
   Training
Functional Analysis

Generalization
Generalized Conditioned
   Punisher
Generalized Conditioned
   Reinforcer
Goal Setting
Good Behavior Game
Graduated Extinction
Group Contingency

Habit Reversal
Habituation
Home-Based Reinforcement
Homework

Imaginal Procedures
In Vivo Desensitization

Lemon Juice Therapy
Life Skills Training
Lovaas, O. Ivar

Maintenance
Manualized Behavior Therapy
Marking Time-Out

Massed Practice
Modeling
Multisystemic Therapy

Negative Practice
Negative Reinforcement
Noncontingent Reward
    (Reinforcement)

Operant Conditioning
Overcorrection

Pain Management
Paradigmatic Behavior Therapy
Parent-Child Interaction
    Therapy
Parent Training
Peer Intervention
Pharmacotherapy
Point System
Positive Practice
Positive Reinforcement
Premack Principle
Problem-Solving Training
Prompt
Public Posting
Punishment

Regulated Breathing
Reinforced Practice
Reinforcer Sampling/Assessment
Relapse Prevention
Relaxation Training in Children
Research Designs
Response Blocking
Response Cost
Restitution
Retention Control Training
Ritual Prevention
Role Playing

Schedules of Reinforcement
Self-Injury and Suicide
Self-Instruction Training
Self-Monitoring
Self-Praise
Sensory Extinction
Shaping
Skinner, Burrhus Frederic
Social and Interpersonal Skills
    Training
Social Competence Treatment:
    Externalizing Disorders
Somatic Control Strategies
Spontaneous Recovery

Sport Skill Training
Sticker/Star Chart
Stimulus Control
Stimulus Discrimination
    Training
Systematic Desensitization With
    Children and Adolescents

Task Analysis
Thought Stopping
3-5-10-15 Method
    for Spelling
Time-Out
Token Economy
Transfer of Stimulus
    Control

Vicarious Conditioning
Vicarious Extinction
Vicarious Punishment
Vicarious Reinforcement
Virtual Reality Therapy
    With Children

Water Misting
Watson, John Broadus
Write-Say Method

Reader's Guide

We provide this list to assist readers in locating entries on related topics. It classifies entries into general categories. Some entry titles appear in more than one category.

MAJOR TECHNIQUES

Adolescent Anger Management
Antecedent Control Procedures
Anxiety Management
Assertiveness Training
Aversive Conditioning
Avoidance Training
Behavior Management for
   Improving Academic and
   Classroom Behavior
Behavioral Consultation
Behavioral Contracting
Behavioral Family Therapy
Behavioral Group Therapy With
   Children and Youth
Behavioral Weight Control
   Therapy With Children
Bell and Pad Bladder Training
Biofeedback
Cognitive Restructuring
Contingency Management
Counterconditioning
Discrete Trial Therapy
Drug Abuse Prevention Strategies
Exposure and Response
   Prevention
Extinction
Flooding
Full-Spectrum Home Training for
   Simple Bed-Wetting
Function Communication
   Training
Habit Reversal
In Vivo Desensitization
Life Skills Training

Manualized Behavior Therapy
Modeling
Multisystemic Therapy
Negative Reinforcement
Overcorrection
Pain Management
Parent-Child Interaction Therapy
Parent Training
Peer Intervention
Pharmacotherapy
Point System
Positive Reinforcement
Premack Principle
Punishment
Relapse Prevention
Relaxation Training in Children
Response Blocking
Response Cost
Self-Injury and Suicide
Shaping
Social and Interpersonal
   Skills Training
Social Competence Treatment:
   Externalizing Disorders
Sport Skill Training
Systematic Desensitization With
   Children and Adolescents
Time-Out
Token Economy

MINOR TECHNIQUES

Aromatic Ammonia
Attention Training Procedures
Beat the Buzzer
Behavioral Rehearsal

Chore and Allowance Program
   for Children
Competing Response Training
Compliance Training
Contingent Exercise
Contingent Restraint
Correspondence Training
Covert Conditioning With
   Children and Adolescents
Differential Reinforcement of
   Incompatible Behavior
Differential Reinforcement of
   Low Rates of Behavior
Differential Reinforcement of
   Other Behavior
Discrimination Training
Errorless Compliance Training
Escape Training
Facial Screening
Fading
Feedback
Five-Step Procedure for Stealing
Generalized Conditioned
   Punisher
Generalized Conditioned
   Reinforcer
Goal Setting
Good Behavior Game
Graduated Extinction
Group Contingency
Habituation
Home-Based Reinforcement
Homework
Imaginal Procedures
Lemon Juice Therapy
Marking Time-Out

Massed Practice
Negative Practice
Noncontingent Reward
  (Reinforcement)
Positive Practice
Problem-Solving Training
Prompt
Public Posting
Regulated Breathing
Reinforced Practice
Restitution
Retention Control Training
Ritual Prevention
Role Playing
Self-Instruction Training
Self-Monitoring
Self-Praise
Sensory Extinction
Somatic Control Strategies
Spontaneous Recovery
Sticker/Star Chart
Stimulus Control
Stimulus Discrimination Training
Task Analysis

Thought Stopping
3-5-10-15 Method for Spelling
Transfer of Stimulus Control
Vicarious Conditioning
Vicarious Extinction
Vicarious Punishment
Vicarious Reinforcement
Virtual Reality Therapy
  With Children
Water Misting
Write-Say Method

ASSESSMENT

Behavioral Assessment
Behavioral Interview
Event Recording
Reinforcer Sampling/Assessment

RESEARCH AND THEORETICAL

Applied Behavior Analysis
Behavior Therapy

Behavioral Pediatrics
Case Conceptualization
Classical Conditioning
Cognitive Behavior Therapy:
  Child Clinical Applications
Empirically Supported
  Treatments for Childhood
  Disorders
Functional Analysis
Generalization
Maintenance
Operant Conditioning
Paradigmatic Behavior
  Therapy
Research Designs
Schedules of
  Reinforcement

BIOGRAPHIES

Baer, Donald M.
Lovaas, O. Ivar
Skinner, Burrhus Frederic
Watson, John Broadus

About the Editors

Dr. Ronald S. Drabman, Diplomate in Clinical Psychology of the American Board of Professional Psychology, is Professor of Psychiatry and Human Behavior (Psychology), Director of the Psychology Residency and Post Doctoral Training Programs, and Supervisor of the child community rotation at the University of Mississippi Medical Center. He received his PhD in 1972 from the State University of New York at Stony Brook. He then accepted a position as Assistant Professor at Central Florida University. In 1975, he joined the faculty of the University of Mississippi Medical Center as Associate Professor. His clinical and research interests include all aspects of child behavior. He has published in the areas of child behavior modification, the effects of television violence, behavioral pediatrics, and psychometrics. His research has been supported by several grants from the National Institute of Mental Health. He is a Fellow of the American Psychological Association (Divisions 25 and 12) and served as member-at-large and Secretary-Treasurer to the Division 25 Council. He has also served as finance chairperson, member of the publications board, and Secretary-Treasurer of the Association for the Advancement of Behavior Therapy. He has been Executive Secretary of the Mississippi State Board of Psychological Examiners and an Associate Editor of the *Journal of Applied Behavior Analysis and Behavior Therapy*. He has been on the editorial board of *Research in Developmental Disabilities, Journal of Applied Behavior Analysis, Behavior Modification, Child and Family Behavioral Therapy, Analysis and Intervention in Developmental Disabilities*, and *Children's Health Care*. In 1999, he won the distinguished Educator Award from the Association of Medical School Psychologists.

Alan M. Gross, PhD, is Professor of Psychology and Director of Clinical Training at the University of Mississippi. He is a graduate of Washington State University. He is the former Editor of *The Behavior Therapist*, and served as Associate Editor for the *Journal of Clinical Child Psychology*. He currently serves on the editorial boards of several scientific journals, including *Behavior Therapy, Journal of Clinical Child and Adolescent Psychology, Behavior Modification, Journal of Family Violence, Aggression and Violent Behavior*, and *Clinical Case Studies*. He has been the recipient of several grants from the National Institute of Mental Health as well as research funding from the Alcoholic Beverage Medical Research Foundation. He has published numerous scientific journal articles and book chapters in the areas of behavior problems in children, self-management, and dating violence.

Contributors

Ron Acierno
Medical University of South Carolina

J. Scott Allen Jr.
Oakland County Court Psychological Clinic,
*   Pontiac, Michigan*

Keith D. Allen
Nebraska Medical Center

Krisann Alvarez
University of Nevada, Las Vegas

Frank Andrasik
University of West Florida

Heather Applegate
Louden County Schools, Virginia

Kevin J. Armstrong
Mississippi State University

Ruth A. Baer
University of Kentucky

Alisa B. Bahl-Long
Towson University

Heidi Bechtoldt Baldacci
University of Toledo

Erin McNaughton Barlos
Nova Southeastern University

Gezim Begolli
University of Central Florida

Debora J. Bell
University of Missouri-Columbia

Christine M. Bennett
Western Michigan University

Elliott Bonem
Eastern Michigan University

Marilyn K. Bonem
Eastern Michigan University

Gilbert J. Botvin
Weill Medical College,
*   Cornell University*

Nataly Bovopoulos
Macquarie University

Elizabeth V. Brestan
Auburn University

Christopher M. Browne
Mississippi State University

James E. Carr
Western Michigan University

Timothy A. Cavell
University of Arkansas

Yi-Chuen Chen
West Virginia University

Bruce F. Chorpita
University of Hawaii at Minoa

Karen A. Christoff
University of Mississippi

Andrea M. Chronis
University of Maryland

Jean Clore
Western Michigan University

Natalie M. Costa
University of New Orleans

Richard J. Cowan
University of Nebraska Medical Center

Eric L. Daleiden
Hawaii Department of Health

Jeffrey S. Danforth
Eastern Connecticut State University

Christopher Dehon
University of Vermont

Katherine M. Dollar
Jackson State University

Brad Donohue
University of Nevada, Las Vegas

Ronald S. Drabman
*University of Mississippi
    Medical Center*

Kelly Drake
University of Nevada, Las Vegas

Amy K. Drayton
Eastern Michigan University

Joseph M. Ducharme
University of Toronto

V. Mark Durand
University of South Florida

Raymond L. Eastman
Stephen F. Austin State University

Dikla Eckshtain
Western Michigan University

Jill T. Ehrenreich
University of Central Florida

T. David Elkin
*University of Mississippi
    Medical Center*

Ian M. Evans
Massey University

Sheila M. Eyberg
University of Florida

Gregory A. Fabiano
University of Buffalo, SUNY

Eva L. Feindler
Long Island University, C. W. Post Campus

Clinton Field
*Father Flanagan's Boys' Home, University of
    Nebraska School of Medicine*

Brian J. Fisak Jr.
University of Central Florida

William C. Follette
University of Nevada, Reno

Beverly L. Fortson
West Virginia University

Tawnya J. Fraizer
Western Michigan University

Sarah E. Francis
University of Hawaii at Minoa

Kurt A. Freeman
Oregon Health & Science University

Stacy B. Fried
Towson University

Patrick C. Friman
*Father Flanagan's Boys' Home, University of
    Nebraska School of Medicine*

Scott T. Gaynor
Western Michigan University

Jennifer M. Gillis
SUNY at Binghamton

Leilani Greening
University of Alabama

Kenneth W. Griffin
Weill Medical College, Cornell University

Amie E. Grills
*Virginia Polytechnic Institute and
    State University*

Alan M. Gross
University of Mississippi

Colleen A. Halliday-Boykins
Medical University of South Carolina

Amanda Harris
Western Michigan University

Stephen N. Haynes
University of Hawaii

Scott W. Henggeler
Medical University of South Carolina

Martin Herbert
Exeter University, United Kingdom

Charmaine K. Higa
University of Tulsa

Sarah J. Hildebrand
University of Toledo

Kellie A. Hilker
University of Mississippi Medical Center

Arthur C. Houts
West Clinic, Memphis, Tennessee

Jennifer L. Hudson
Macquarie University

Hillary Hunt
University of Mississippi

Stephen D. A. Hupp
Southern Illinois University-Edwardsville

Nichole Jurbergs
Louisiana State University

Christopher A. Kearney
University of Nevada, Las Vegas

Mary Lou Kelley
Louisiana State University

Angela Walter Keyes
University of New Orleans

Jeffrey L. Kibler
Jackson State University

Neil M. Kirkpatrick
University of Vermont

Tiffany Kyle-Linkovich
University of Central Florida

Steven R. Lawyer
Medical University of South Carolina

Linda A. LeBlanc
Western Michigan University

Craig W. LeCroy
University of Wisconsin

Lisa Linning
University of Nevada, Las Vegas

Thomas R. Linscheid
*Columbus Children's Hospital,
  Ohio State University*

Miranda Loeper
Auburn University

Thomas W. Lombardo
University of Mississippi

Christopher J. Lonigan
Florida State University

Barbara Lopez
Florida International University

Amanda Lords
University of West Florida

Richard W. Malott
Western Michigan University

Corby K. Martin
Pennington Biomedical Research Center

Eric J. Mash
University of Calgary, Canada

Carrie Masia-Warner
New York University

Greta M. Massetti
University of Buffalo, SUNY

Jessica M. Matthews
University of Maine

James F. McCoy
Auburn University

Melanie D. McDiarmid
University of Florida

Cliff McKinney
University of Central Florida

Michael W. Mellon
*Mayo Clinic-Dana Child Development
  and Learning Disorders Program,
  Rochester, Minnesota*

Raymond G. Miltenberger
North Dakota State University

Tracy L. Morris
West Virginia University

Larry L. Mullins
Oklahoma State University

Douglas W. Nangle
University of Maine

Shari K. Neul
Texas Children's Hospital

Larissa N. Niec
Central Michigan University

Matthew K. Nock
Harvard University

William H. O'Brien
Bowling Green State University

Patrick M. O'Callaghan
Louisiana State University

Thomas H. Ollendick
*Virginia Polytechnic Institute and
    State University*

Brian Rabian
Pennsylvania State University

Mark D. Rapport
University of Central Florida

Ruth Anne Rehfeldt
Southern Illinois University

David Reitman
Nova Southeastern University

Michelle S. Rivera
University of Maine

Mark W. Roberts
Idaho State University

Angela Rojas-Vilches
University of Central Florida

Jonathan P. Roland
Western Michigan University

Raymond G. Romanczyk
SUNY at Binghamton

Sheldon D. Rose
University of Wisconsin

Barbara O. Rothbaum
Emory University School of Medicine

Kenneth J. Ruggiero
Medical University of South Carolina

Dennis C. Russo
The May Institute, Norwood, Massachusetts

Mohamed Sabaawi
ONE Research Institute, Midlothian, Virginia

Sarah-Jeanne Salvy
*Columbus Children's Hospital,
    Ohio State University*

Kelly J. Sandor
Eastern Michigan University

Rachael A. Sautter
Western Michigan University

Joseph R. Scotti
West Virginia University

Laura D. Seligman
University of Toledo

Daniel B. Shabani
Western Michigan University

William Sharp
University of Mississippi

Daniel T. Shea
Jackson State University

Elizabeth J. Shepherd
University of Maine

Wendy K. Silverman
Florida International University

Persephanie Silverthorn
University of New Orleans

Sharon M. Simpson
Oklahoma Health Sciences Center

Nirbhay N. Singh
ONE Research Institute, Midlothian, Virginia

Jeffrey Skowron
The May Institute, Norwood, Massachusetts

Karen E. Starr
Long Island University, C. W. Post Campus

Timothy R. Stickle
University of Vermont

Laura Stoppelbein
University of Mississippi Medical Center

Eric A. Storch
University of Florida

Stephanie Stowman
University of Nevada, Las Vegas

Paul S. Strand
Washington State University

Sara E. Sytsma-Jordan
University of Mississippi Medical Center

Andrew M. Terranova
University of Vermont

Emily Thomas-Johnson
University of Mississippi

Thomas M. Timko Jr.
University of Central Florida

James T. Todd
Eastern Michigan University

George C. Tremblay
Antioch New England Graduate School

Sarah Valley-Gray
Nova Southeastern University

Jill Van Pelt
Oklahoma State University

Jennifer Vecchio
University of Nevada, Las Vegas

Katy I. Vidler
Macquarie University

Angela Waguespack
Nova Southeastern University

Elizabeth Seeley Wait
Macquarie University

Michael E. Walker
Stephen F. Austin State University

Carl F. Weems
University of New Orleans

Jonathan Weinand
Great River Mental HealthCare Associates, West Burlington, Iowa

Donald Williamson
Pennington Biomedical Research Center, Baton Rouge, Louisiana

Lisa A. Wuyek
University of Toledo

Brian T. Wymbs
University of Buffalo-SUNY

Karen R. Zeff
University of Maine

Elana Zimand
Virtually Better, Inc., Decatur, Georgia

Preface

We hope that the *Encyclopedia of Behavior Modification and Cognitive Behavior Therapy: Child Clinical Applications* (Volume II) will be useful to a great variety of individuals. Practitioners, professors, schoolteachers, and, most important, students will find material in it that can make their tasks easier. We have included short and medium-length articles written by prominent scholars in the field of child clinical psychology. All authors were asked to provide an encyclopedia-like entry concerning a subject with which they are extremely familiar. We also asked our authors to write biographies of some of the field's luminaries. In selecting topics and authors, we made use of the indexes from various child clinical psychology journals, our own experience, and the experiences of our students and the encyclopedia's editorial board. We apologize for any topics left out, but with 141 entries, we sincerely hope they are few. As for the biographies, the conundrum of who to include and the more difficult one of who to leave out was one on which we knew we could never be close to perfect. So for those left out, please understand that space was the main limiting factor.

One of the aspects of editing this volume of the encyclopedia that we enjoyed most was the format.

There are short, concisely written articles that give a quick, useful definition of a term, concept, or procedure, and there are also more major entries. In the major entries, the authors were asked to include sections on complications of the procedure as well as a case illustration. Reading the case illustration provides interesting insights into how our expert clinicians conceive of the practice of child clinical psychology. Perusing the complications sections allows one to look into the question of what can go wrong, an area of child clinical psychology that is not often discussed in scientific articles.

There are many individuals to thank for their part in making this volume a reality. First, Michel Hersen, who conceived the project and convinced us of its potential contribution. Second, the authors who gave of their time and intellect so the book could come to fruition. Finally, we would like to thank our wives, Jeannie and Marj, for putting up with us while we spent time working on this project.

—*Alan M. Gross*
University of Mississippi

—*Ronald S. Drabman*
University of Mississippi Medical Center

Introduction

The *Encyclopedia of Behavior Modification and Cognitive Behavior Therapy* was designed to enhance the resources available to scholars, practitioners, students, and other interested social science readers. The fact that this three-volume work is needed at this time is a testimonial to the pioneers in this field, who, only three or four decades ago, were fighting the therapeutic establishment to have a voice. Now, of course, behavior modification, behavior therapy, and cognitive behavior therapy are part of the daily lexicon for all. Over the ensuing years, the range of application of all of these therapeutic and modification strategies has proliferated to a point where it literally is difficult to keep abreast of the field. One of the objectives of this encyclopedia, then, is to bring all of the most relevant aspects of the field together in readable, albeit brief, format.

This three-volume work provides a thorough examination of components comprising behavior modification, behavior therapy, cognitive behavior therapy, and applied behavior analysis for both adult and child populations in a variety of settings (e.g., outpatient, institutional, and classroom). The specific volumes are as follows: Volume I: Adult Clinical Applications, Volume II: Child Clinical Applications, Volume III: Educational Applications. Although the focus is on technical applications, the hundreds of entries also provide historical context to apprise readers of the parameters in which behavior therapists have worked, including research issues and strategies. Entries also contain descriptions of assessment, ethical concerns, theoretical differences, and the unique contributions of key figures in the field. In so doing, there are both biographical sketches and autobiographical sketches for the interested reader.

The entries in this encyclopedia have been written at a level that is appropriate for the educated clinical and social science reader. Indeed, entries have been written in jargon-free fashion, with explanations provided for specialized terminology. Rather than burdening the reader with a plethora of citations within the text, contributors were asked to simply present clear descriptions but include suggestions for further reading at the end of each entry. The objective here has been to make this work as readable as possible for an interdisciplinary audience.

Most of the major entries for specific strategies have followed a similar format:

1. Description of the Strategy

2. Research Basis

3. Relevant Target Populations and Exceptions

4. Complications

5. Case Illustration

6. Suggested Readings

Biographical sketches have included the following:

1. Birthplace and date

2. Early influences

3. Education history

4. Professional models

5. Major contributions to the field

6. Current work and views

7. Future plans

Many individuals have contributed to the fruition of this labor-intensive project. First, I thank my fellow editors, Johan Rosqvist, Alan Gross, Ronald Drabman, George Sugai, and Robert Horner, for their excellent work on this encyclopedia. Second, all of us thank the Advisory Board for their helpful suggestions throughout the process. Third, I thank all of the contributors for taking time out to share their expertise with us and to write in a clear fashion so that all can understand. Fourth, I thank Carole Londerée, my very able editorial assistant (who has made me swear to never again undertake such a complicated project), for keeping things on track. And fifth, but hardly least of all, thank you, James Brace-Thompson and the terrific staff at Sage, for shepherding us through the process. Your wise guidance has been much appreciated.

—*Michel Hersen, PhD, ABPP*
Forest Grove, Oregon

ADOLESCENT ANGER MANAGEMENT

DESCRIPTION OF THE STRATEGY

In a variety of clinical, educational, and residential treatment settings, adolescents exhibiting oppositional defiant and conduct disorders show patterns of irritability and aggressive behavior, including anger outbursts, that result in poor conflict resolution, poor interpersonal skills, and a host of compliance problems. Although behavior modification interventions that use a combination of contingency management and punishment strategies have been successfully implemented to reduce occurrences of aggressive behavior in a controlled setting, these approaches are somewhat limited. Often, when the adolescent returns to the natural environment and is outside the control of the contingencies and the purview of adults, the aggressive behavior returns. Problems with maintenance and generalization of behavior change indicate that aggression management self-control skills are not being learned.

Cognitive behavioral anger management technology, on the other hand, emphasizes the cognitive and physiological components of anger and focuses on teaching arousal reduction skills within that context. It is based on the hypothesis that aggressive behavior is elicited by an aversive "trigger" stimulus that is followed by both physiological arousal and distorted cognitive responses, which result in the emotional experience of anger. Children and adolescents who behave impulsively and aggressively often react to the trigger and fail to solve interpersonal conflict in an appropriate manner. Research has shown that hostile attributions and expectations of negative outcome influence negative behavioral responses to interpersonal interactions. Aggressive youth seem to lack a prosocial reasoning process, and instead engage in distorted thinking that intensifies their perceptions of injustice, fuels their rage, and justifies their use of aggression. They have trouble regulating their emotions and understanding their emotional states, perhaps due to early family experiences or an innate physiological dysynchrony. They seem unable to cope with even mild levels of anger in a constructive way. The irritability or annoyance resulting from minor interpersonal conflict or having a goal blocked often expresses itself in intensified anger and explosive rage.

To prevent an aggressive reaction to a triggering stimulus, it is necessary for adolescents to learn to manage their anger arousal and to process the interpersonal exchange so that they can exhibit a more prosocial response. The anger management treatment protocol focuses on the three components of the anger experience: physiological, cognitive, and behavioral. It is designed to help young people develop self-control skills in each of these areas.

To manage the physiological component, the anger management protocol first directs the client to identify the experience of anger, to label the various intensities of the emotion, and to recognize the early warning signs, such as a flushed feeling or quickened heart rate. The therapist validates the experience of anger as a normal and frequently occurring emotion having an intensity range that is under the adolescent's control. Clients are then asked to identify and track common triggers of their anger using a self-monitoring assessment called a Hassle Log. Charting daily occurrences of anger (whether handled well or not) helps the youth to recognize idiosyncratic patterns of anger loss and control and to increase awareness of external triggers and internal physiological and cognitive reactions. Finally, they are taught arousal management skills such as deep breathing, imagery, and relaxation in order to reduce the accumulated physical tension and to increase the probability that they will think through the interpersonal event in a more rational fashion.

The cognitive component of anger management targets both the cognitive deficiencies and distortions that are characteristic of those who respond aggressively and impulsively to perceived provocation. Aggressive youth lack specific problem-solving skills. They generate few possible solutions to interpersonal problems and seem unable to generate future consequences for their aggressive behavior. Furthermore, their assumptions, expectations, beliefs, and attributions are distorted in distinct ways that actually increase their anger experience. In particular, they perceive triggering stimuli to be intentional and unjust acts on the part of others—direct insults that are meant to be hostile. They believe that responding aggressively is optimal in terms of outcome, ego protection, and perceived power in the eyes of others. They expect themselves to behave aggressively and believe that others expect them to as well. Then they do not take responsibility for their actions. In fact, they blame others for their own misbehavior. These cognitive distortions combine to confirm that aggression is completely justified because it is the only way to resolve a conflict.

Cognitive restructuring strategies are used to help adolescents identify their distorted thinking styles and to encourage them to substitute a series of self-instructions that will enable them to solve problems effectively. Strategies that assist in examining the irrational and narrow focus of their cognitions help them to develop alternative causal attributions and a nonaggressive perspective. They are encouraged to engage in self-coaching of attributions that protect their self-esteem while allowing them to de-escalate conflict and create mental distance from the trigger. This type of cognitive work is difficult for aggressive and impulsive adolescents to do, but it is the most critical element of the anger management intervention. Altering these internal processes is essential to help youth to better manage their anger experience, rethink

their possible responses to provocation, and select a more prosocial behavioral response.

The final component of the anger reaction is behavioral. Once adolescents are able to manage their physiological arousal and cognitive process, they still need to respond to the situation and achieve some level of social competence. Withdrawal patterns and verbal and nonverbal aggression are the most typical responses to interpersonal conflicts and perceived provocation. They need training in solving problems, being assertive, and learning to communicate to resolve conflict. The probability that they can exhibit these skills effectively is enhanced by successful management of emotional arousal. Arousal management and cognitive restructuring should precede the behavioral skills training.

The anger control program uses a modeling technique of role play with actual scenarios generated from completed Hassle Logs. The role plays are arranged for the youth so that they are gradually exposed to greater levels of provocation and conflict as their skills grow. Each treatment session includes a variety of graded homework assignments designed so that the adolescents can practice their newly acquired skills and generalize them to the natural environment. Many of the cognitive restructuring strategies are transformed into games, to which the adolescents seem to be quite receptive. Role play with coaching helps them to practice these improved cognitive responses. They are able to learn how to solve problems and to develop nonhostile attributions in response to hypothetical conflict situations. Repeated practice once the "package" of skills has been taught is necessary not only to reinforce the newly acquired responses but also to help the adolescent make appropriate social judgments in response to the triggering event, to maximize successful outcome.

Anger management groups usually consist of six to eight adolescents between the ages of 14 and 18. Ideally, the group should be facilitated by two therapists, who can model a social interaction in a role play. The program consists of a minimum of 10 sessions. If it is implemented in a residential facility, the sessions may be held as frequently as deemed necessary. In a nonresidential setting, one or two sessions a week are recommended.

RESEARCH BASIS

Research has shown that anger control training results in specific behavioral changes in children and adolescents, assessed via self-report and changes in cognitions. However, few of the published anger control studies have produced directly observable and reliably recorded change in actual rates and intensities of aggressive behavior. Most studies are too brief to adequately assess maintenance.

The following data are offered to show the relative effectiveness of implementation versus nonimplementation of the anger management program.

A field study testing the effectiveness of the program on antisocial behaviors of adolescents in a runaway shelter showed a decrease in antisocial behavior compared with pretreatment weeks. Interestingly, there was a greater decrease for females residing at the shelter. They represented 54% of the total sample of 522 adolescents.

The effectiveness of an 18-session treatment package for adolescents in a long-term state psychiatric facility was evaluated, and results indicated that adolescents receiving treatment increased their use of anger control skills and received fewer consequences for aggressive behavior on the treatment ward when compared to adolescents not receiving the anger management training.

A condensed program implemented in a short-term psychiatric facility indicated change in aggressive behaviors during hospitalization, as well as 4 to 6 weeks after the adolescents were discharged.

In a day school setting, counts of the number of incidents of physical aggression by the subjects were compared for 6 months prior to and for 6 months after the intervention. Reductions in physical aggression approached a statistically significant change, based on parent and teacher reports.

RELEVANT TARGET POPULATIONS AND EXCEPTIONS

The anger management program was designed primarily for adolescents but can be tailored to younger children. Younger children and clients with developmental delays may struggle with the cognitive restructuring strategies and may need greater emphasis on the behavioral skills training. Adolescents experiencing extreme depression and/or suicidal thoughts may not have the motivation to participate. Also, adolescents who are currently abusing substances will not benefit from the program, since the substances reduce their motivation and dampen their cognitive functioning. Finally, adolescents with thought disorders or delusions will be unable to glean much from the program, since they will have difficulty understanding the cognitive restructuring components.

CASE ILLUSTRATION

"Jordan," a 17-year-old Caucasian male, was referred to individual therapy by a school counselor following several months of disruptive school behavior (cutting classes, disrespect toward teachers, and several temper explosions toward authority figures). Upon intake, it was revealed that Jordan had almost daily blowups with his mother and had been physically violent toward his younger brother, who suffered from serious emotional difficulties. There had been several brushes with the police involving minor accidents and speeding tickets. Jordan had also verbally acted out toward these officers and thus had to appear in court. There was some concern about substance use as well as failing grades, which, when combined with his poor behavioral performance, might have reduced the likelihood that he would be able to complete his senior year of high school.

A brief review of his family history revealed early exposure to domestic violence, resulting in the eventual divorce of his parents. Although Jordan idolized his father (as they both shared a tremendous passion for hockey, which Jordan had played for the past 10 years), he rarely saw him since his remarriage and move out of state. Jordan's younger brother was often in psychiatric settings and, at the time of intake, had experienced another suicide attempt and was placed in a residential treatment facility. This left Jordan and his mother living together in an almost quasi marital setting, in which he was responsible for much of the upkeep of the house and demanded his meals, clothing, and money from his mother.

The first three sessions were spent gathering information in order to understand Jordan's anger eruptions and to help form with him an understandable functional hypothesis regarding his temper problem. Using self-recording data sheets, Jordan was asked to identify triggering events and accompanying cognitive responses for each incident in which he experienced a groundswell of anger. Analysis of these data suggested that his most proximal trigger event for temper loss were adults who he perceived were "disrespecting him" and perhaps undermining his high school graduation and subsequent move away to college. Some of these incidents involved a teacher who failed him for a marking period, a parking guard who indicated he couldn't park in a certain school lot, his mother who accused him of taking the car without permission, and so on. Each of these triggers resulted in an emotional rush felt quite viscerally by Jordan and a desire to both verbally and physically attack the other so as to right the perceived "social injustice" that was thrust upon him. Jordan felt sincerely that he was entitled to lots of resources and maintained that anger as an appropriate response to adults who thwarted his attempts to get what he wanted.

The anger management portion of his therapy focused on restructuring these faulty assumptions, his blame of the other, and his core belief that he "deserved despite his behavior," as well as on specific anger management skills that he could use in these daily interpersonal interactions with adults in his life. Although not initially motivated for treatment, a strong therapeutic alliance was established by joining with him in his goal to reach independence (graduate high school and move away to college). Each encounter that would potentially sabotage his plan was reframed as "inevitable given that adults don't seem to understand what you need." Jordan was able to develop a "new" expectation that adults may disrespect him as well as a new perspective on his anger eruptions. In contrast to his prior sense that his temper explosions enabled him to establish control and respect, these anger eruptions were reconstrued as self-sabotage of his attempts to reach his own goals. Thus, he came to believe that the use of anger control strategies would actually empower him to reach toward his future.

Once these cognitive premises had been restructured, Jordan was receptive to learning the skills of anger control. In particular, he learned to monitor his physiological cues of impending anger arousal and to invoke some self-calming strategies (deep breathing, self-imposed psychological time-outs, and releasing his tension through physical pursuits). Further, he was taught how to ignore the "annoying" things that others did or said by focusing his attention elsewhere and responding to them in a neutral and controlled fashion. He was encouraged to be "smarter" than those around him and head off confrontation using a range of assertive communications. In particular, he was able to use seemingly honest empathic responses to discern adults who were attempting to "disrespect" him. Finally, he was given a tremendous amount of positive feedback for his successive approximation toward anger control as well as for his movement

toward reaching his own goals. After approximately six sessions, it seemed probable that he would graduate with sufficient credits and that his acceptance into college, perhaps to play hockey, was confirmed.

With Jordan's permission, two individual sessions were held with his mother, who needed to fully understand her own anger triggers and her role in the anger explosions between them. Jordan's anger was reframed as in part due to his anxiety about major life transitions and in part due to his family history. This helped her become more receptive to trying to prevent confrontations with him. Two mediation sessions were also conducted with Jordan and his mother in order to work out equitable behavioral contracts concerning the use of the car, money, and household responsibilities. In each of these sessions, anger management methods were interwoven with conflict negotiation and communication skills training, and specific contracts were written and signed.

Along with a final wrap-up session, the treatment process as described above lasted 14 sessions and was quite successful in reducing Jordan's anger outbursts. He graduated high school and as we speak is packing for college.

—Eva L. Feindler and Karen E. Starr

See also: *Anger (Vol. III), Anger Management (Vol. I), Behavioral Treatment for Aggression in Couples (Vol. I)*

Suggested Readings

Beck, R., & Fernandez, E. (1998). Cognitive-behavioral therapy in the treatment of anger. *Cognitive Therapy and Research, 22,* 63–74.

Deffenbacher, J. L. (1999). Cognitive-behavioral conceptualization and treatment of anger. *JCLP/In Session: Psychotherapy in Practice, 55,* 295–309.

Feindler, E. L. (1995). An ideal treatment package for children and adolescents with anger disorders. In H. Kassinove (Ed.), *Anger disorders: Definition, diagnosis, and treatment* (pp. 173–194). New York: Taylor & Francis.

Feindler, E. L., & Ecton, R. B. (1990). Anger control training for temper control disorders. In E. L. Feindler & G. R. Kalfus (Eds.), *Adolescent behavior therapy handbook* (pp. 351–371). New York: Springer.

Feindler, E. L., & Guttman, J. (1994). Cognitive-behavioral anger control training for groups of adolescents: A treatment manual. In C. W. LeCroy (Ed.), *Handbook of child and adolescent treatment manuals* (pp. 170–199). New York: Lexington Books.

Keenan, K. (2000). Emotion dysregulation as a risk factor for child psychopathology. *Clinical Psychology: Science and Practice, 7,* 418–434.

Larson, J. D., Calamari, J. E., West, J. G., & Frevert, T. A. (1998). Aggression management in the residential setting: Integration of a cognitive-behavioral component. *Residential Treatment for Children and Youth, 15,* 1–9.

Lochman, J. E., & Dodge, K. A. (1994). Social-cognitive processes of severely violent, moderately aggressive, and non-aggressive boys. *Journal of Child Clinical Psychology, 62,* 366–374.

Novoco, R. (1979). The cognitive regulation of anger and stress. In P. C. Kendell & S. C. Hollon (Eds.), *Cognitive-behavioral interventions: Theory, research and procedures* (pp. 241–285). New York: Academic Press.

Sukhodolsky, D. G., Solomon, R. M., & Perine, J. (2000). Cognitive-behavioral, anger-control intervention for elementary school children: A treatment-outcome study. *Journal of Child and Adolescent Group Therapy, 10,* 159–170.

ANTECEDENT CONTROL PROCEDURES

DESCRIPTION OF THE STRATEGY

Antecedent control procedures are environmental changes implemented prior to the behavior in order to control the frequency of that behavior—usually the reduction of challenging behavior, often with clients requiring pervasive support.

The Law of Effect

Antecedent control procedures started with a cat in a box. In 1898, Edward L. Thorndike published the following observation concerning a cat placed in a cage (puzzle box) containing dangling ropes, levers, and latches: When the cat made the proper response with these manipulanda, the cage door would open and the cat would exit and eat the food placed just outside. Over the following trials, the cat would less and less frequently make irrelevant responses and more and more quickly make the door-opening response, exit, and eat the food.

Over the following decades, Thorndike would develop and evolve his famous law of effect. Here is a modern statement of that law of effect: The results of our actions determine whether we will repeat those actions; some results will cause the frequency of those actions to increase, and other results will cause that frequency to decrease. (The cat will more and more frequently make a response that results in food, and it will less and less frequently make a response that results in water mist sprayed in its face or results in nothing.)

Thorndike's simple but profound law of effect now serves as the foundation of essentially all behavior analysis, including applied behavior analysis (behavior modification): To increase the frequency of desirable behavior, make sure that behavior results in a reinforcer (reward) or the removal of an aversive condition. (When the autistic child properly completes a puzzle, give him or her a hug. When the disruptive child properly asks permission to take a break from a difficult task, allow him or her to escape that task.) And to decrease the frequency of undesirable behavior, make sure that behavior results in an aversive condition, the loss of a reinforcer, or the withholding of a reinforcer. (When the child plays violently with a toy, briefly remove the toy.) The traditional applied behavior analysis intervention has been to apply the law of effect in a very straightforward manner, by directly reinforcing or punishing the behavior of interest, either to increase or to decrease the frequency of that behavior. However, in recent years, behavior analysts have been developing two related, integrated approaches that provide some alternatives to this traditional, straightforward application of the law of effect.

Two New Approaches

Primarily, these two new approaches address the reduction in the frequency of challenging behavior for clients classified as autistic, mentally handicapped, or emotionally impaired. Challenging behavior (problem, dysfunctional, maladaptive, inappropriate behavior) includes self-injury, aggression, property destruction, inappropriate or interfering self-stimulation, and disruptions. However, the goal is not just to reduce challenging behavior but to do so in a way that will also increase functional, adaptive, appropriate behavior, including behavior that facilitates learning, behavior such as orienting toward the trainer or the instructional materials. (Giving a sedative to a disruptive child might reduce the frequency of disruptive behavior, but it might also interfere with increases in the frequency of functional behavior.)

One of these two new behavior-analytic approaches is positive behavioral support. A major goal of this approach is to reduce challenging behavior without using aversive control procedures (punishment and penalties).

And the other new approach, antecedent control, provides some procedures for accomplishing that goal of reducing challenging behavior in a nonaversive way. Antecedent control procedures emphasize changing conditions prior to the occurrence of the behavior of interest; they contrast with consequence control procedures, which emphasize changing conditions following a behavior. Therefore, when using antecedent control procedures to reduce problem behavior, *behavior analysts tend to provide positive behavioral support by concentrating on the conditions prior to the problem behavior, rather than by adding aversive consequences after the problem behavior.*

Antecedent control procedures do not involve a rejection of the law of effect. (The frequency of Thorndike's cat's exiting the cage is not only a function of the consequence of that response—the food but also of the conditions antecedent to that response—how food-deprived the cat is and perhaps how cramped the cage is.) Rather than a rejection of the law of effect, antecedent control procedures are a more subtle application of that law than traditionally has been practiced by applied behavior analysts. (Instead of punishing the disruptive behavior of a child, the behavior analyst using antecedent control procedures would assess the function of the disruptive behavior. If the assessment revealed that the behavior was reinforced [rewarded] by escape from an aversively difficult task, then the behavior analyst might reduce the difficulty of that task, a condition antecedent to the behavior.)

How New Are Antecedent Control Procedures?

In a sense, antecedent control procedures are nothing new. From the time of B. F. Skinner's 1930s research with rats in his Skinner box, experimental behavior analysts have paid careful attention to the antecedent control procedure of food deprivation, to ensure that the food would be an effective reinforcer for the rat's lever-pressing behavior. Since Theodore Ayllon and Jack Michael's 1950s research with back ward mental patients, applied behavior analysts have paid careful attention to the antecedent control procedure of reinforcer deprivation, to ensure that the snack or whatever preferred reinforcer would be an effective reinforcer for the client's appropriate behavior.

Nonetheless, the emphasis on antecedent control procedures as an intervention of choice is new. Traditionally, when challenging behavior would occur, the first intervention would often be the implementation of a consequence control procedure (punishment,

penalty, or extinction). However, with this new emphasis on positive behavioral support and antecedent control procedures, when challenging behavior occurs, the first intervention often follows an assessment of the function and causes of that behavior. Based on that assessment, the behavior analyst implements an antecedent control procedure, for example, a procedure involving the reduction of the aversiveness of the setting or an increase in the reinforcing value of the setting. Thus, the antecedent control approach often addresses the challenging behavior itself only indirectly, whereas the consequence control approach usually involves applying an added performance-management procedure directly to the challenging behavior.

Consequence Control Procedures for Challenging Behavior

The traditional behavior-analytic approach to challenging behavior is to implement a consequence control procedure that decreases the frequency of the challenging behavior. The first step is to perform a functional assessment or functional analysis to determine the function of the behavior (i.e., to determine what consequence of that behavior is reinforcing it).

Extinction

Perhaps staff attention is reinforcing the challenging behavior. In that case, a consequence control intervention would involve being especially careful to ignore that behavior (an extinction procedure—the withholding of the reinforcer).

Extinction and DRA

Perhaps escape from an aversive condition is reinforcing the challenging behavior, for example, a difficult learning task. In that case, a consequence intervention would be to take care that the client not succeed in escaping from the learning task (also an extinction procedure). Another consequence intervention would be to reinforce a more appropriate alternative behavior such as asking or signaling for permission to take a break (differential reinforcement of alternative behavior or DRA).

Punishment

Perhaps performing tasks that are too difficult for the client's skill level may generate too few reinforcers and too many aversive stimuli. This frustrating circumstance may be a motivating operation (formerly called establishing operation) that increases the value of intrinsic aggression reinforcers that support aggression to others or to physical property or that support self-injury. In that case, a consequence intervention could be to implement some sort of punishment or penalty procedure that decreases the frequency of the challenging behavior.

Or it might be that the challenging behavior is some form of self-stimulation such as hand flapping that is automatically or intrinsically reinforcing. In that case, a consequence intervention again could be to implement some sort of punishment or penalty procedure.

Antecedent Control Procedures for Challenging Behavior

In contrast, the antecedent control approach would be for the behavior analyst to view the challenging behavior as a warning that the environment is too aversive for the client or that the environment does not contain procedures that effectively reinforce (strengthen) positive behavior.

The first step is to perform an antecedent conditions assessment to determine the sources of aversive stimulation, the frequency of reinforcers, and the effectiveness of those reinforcers. In addition, the behavior analyst will often do a functional assessment of the challenging behavior to determine how that behavior functions to produce consequences that are reinforcing it (e.g., is the behavior producing reinforcing attention or allowing the client to escape a difficult task?). These assessments will allow the behavior analyst to change the conditions antecedent to the challenging behavior, in an effort to decrease the frequency of that behavior.

Decreasing the Aversiveness of Antecedent Conditions

Task Difficulty. Often the training tasks or activities of daily living are too difficult for the client to perform with reliable success. As a result, the tasks become sufficiently aversive that the client will refuse to do them or will engage in challenging escape behavior. For example, a man with Down syndrome was noncompliant and aggressive when instructed to bathe using a bar of soap with graduated physical assistance. However, when the difficulty was reduced

by pouring liquid soap in his hand, the challenging behaviors essentially stopped.

Direct Sources of Aversive Stimulation. It may be possible to remove the source of the aversive stimulation that evokes aggressive behavior. For example, a child with autism aggressed against an infant sibling when the sibling made aversive noise by banging a metal plate on the high chair. Both the aversive noise and the subsequent aggression were reduced when the parents replaced the metal plate with a plastic one.

Cumulating Aversive Conditions. Sometimes a slightly difficult task or activity of only mild aversiveness will evoke challenging escape or aggressive behavior only when combined with other sources of aversive stimulation such as sleep deprivation, constipation, noise, heat, and/or medical problems. When those sources of additional aversive stimulation are decreased, the challenging behavior will also decrease.

Increasing Reinforcer Frequency

Challenging behavior often decreases and appropriate behavior often increases when the frequency of reinforcement is high in a training or work setting.

Reinforcing Approximations to the Desired Response. When a client is acquiring a new skill, it is important to reinforce approximations to the desired response, rather than reinforcing only perfect responses. This is true for language skills as well as motor skills. In so doing, it is easier to maintain a frequency of reinforcer delivery high enough to prevent challenging behavior. As the client becomes more skilled, closer approximations to the desired response can be required before giving the reinforcer.

Interspersing Maintenance Tasks. The frequency of overall reinforcer delivery can also be increased by interspersing previously mastered tasks in sessions where a new, difficult task is being trained. This can increase task involvement and decrease challenging behavior.

Reinforcer Latency. The quicker the reinforcer, the more effective the reinforcer; the quicker the response acquisition, the higher the frequency of reinforcers and the lower the frequency of challenging behavior. One way to decrease the latency between the response and the reinforcer is to train tasks with automatic, built-in, intrinsic reinforcers (e.g., computer games, music boxes, and toy pianos immediately reinforce the appropriate responses).

Free (Noncontingent) Reinforcers. Presenting occasional free reinforcers independent of the desired behavior also increases the reinforcer frequency in the training or work setting and can thereby decrease the frequency of challenging behavior such as inappropriate escape responses.

Reinforcement of Alternative Behavior. Sometimes it is easier to prevent an inappropriate behavior if at the same time a more appropriate alternative behavior is provided. For example, a child with neurological impairment was grabbing objects and mouthing them. But when given a more appropriate object to chew, she got the sensory-stimulation reinforcer in a much less disruptive manner and could work on her educational tasks more effectively. Another example: Grade school children were being disruptive and noisy throughout the class, but when allowed brief, periodic opportunities to create chaos in the classroom, the teacher was more able to prevent the disruptions during the remainder of time. And still another example: To further reduce the autistic child's aggression against his noisy infant sibling, the child was taught to give the infant a pacifier or bottle and also to say "Baby needs help" to a parent when the infant was crying.

Rate of Task Presentation. A high rate of task presentation can increase the reinforcer frequency when the task has some intrinsic reinforcing value or when completing the task often leads to immediate reinforcers. In fact, often challenging behavior is most frequent during the intertrial (intertask) intervals and also during transition intervals and while waiting for staff to begin a new activity.

Increasing Reinforcer Effectiveness

Motivating Operations. Reinforcer effectiveness is most frequently discussed in terms of motivating operations (previously called motivating operations), for example, making sure the client has not just eaten a large meal, if you are planning to use food as a reinforcer in a training session. In so doing, you will not only get more appropriate learning and performance but also less challenging behavior.

In addition, the concept of motivation operation has recently been applied to training children to make requests (mand training): The trainer uses response blocking to make sure a strong reinforcer is not readily available (e.g., a preferred toy might be out of reach on a shelf). An appropriate form of request would then be reinforced with the presentation of that preferred toy.

Reinforcer Assessment. The lack of effective reinforcers is one of the biggest causes of failure of performance management and failure of instructional programs, and the lack of effective reinforcers is also one of the biggest causes of challenging behavior. Often what the trainer assumes is an effective reinforcer isn't. And what was effective yesterday isn't today. Prior to the training or task maintenance sessions, assessing which potential reinforcers the client most frequently looks at, approaches, reaches for, or interacts with can allow the behavior analyst to use the reinforcers that are currently most effective. But even what was most reinforcing a few minutes ago might not be now, so allowing the client to select from among an array of reinforcers, throughout the training and maintenance sessions, can also increase the likelihood that an effective reinforcer is being used.

However, sometimes it is necessary to select among options that are not currently present. In that case, for example, the client might select from pictures of lunch options. Being allowed such options decreased the challenging behavior of a young man with autism.

In addition, some tasks themselves may be less aversive or more inherently reinforcing. So, being allowed to select from among vocational tasks can result in the client spending more time engaged in functional activities. And children with autism and mental retardation less frequently emitted serious problem behavior when given the opportunity to select their instructional tasks as well as their reinforcers. However, the opportunity for choice does not always reduce the frequency of challenging behavior.

Choice. In addition, simply the choice of the task and of the reinforcer may reduce the frequency of challenging behavior, even when the choices are among highly preferred tasks and reinforcers. This may be because choosing, itself, has become a learned reinforcer, and thus the overall reinforcer density is higher when given the opportunity to choose.

RESEARCH BASIS

Most of the antecedent control procedures have a strong research base, starting with the basic animal laboratory Skinner box research, proceeding through applied behavior-analysis research using expert behavior analysts working with real clients with real problems, but in somewhat restricted settings, to more practical systems-oriented research with the actual technicians working with their clients in typical settings. Like most areas of applied behavior analysis, though, much more research is needed to determine if typical technicians with typical clients in typical settings actually can and actually will implement these procedures properly and reliably.

RELEVANT TARGET POPULATIONS AND EXCEPTIONS

Though antecedent control procedures are potentially applicable to any population with any behavior, most of the research has addressed the reduction of challenging behavior (the issue of most concern to most staff), especially for clients who need pervasive support (probably the population with the highest frequency of challenging behavior). No particular population has been reported for which antecedent control procedures are inappropriate, nor is there any reason why there should be such populations.

COMPLICATIONS

Antecedent control procedures should be conducted in a context where there are reinforcement procedures for appropriate behavior; however, reinforcer assessment may not reveal any effective reinforcers for the client. Alternatively, in the absence of reinforcer assessment, the staff may erroneously assume they are using effective reinforcers, though it is common for staff to implement reinforcement procedures where the presumed reinforcer clearly is not functional. And even given an effective reinforcer, the frequency of challenging behavior may be so high that it is difficult to reinforce appropriate behavior, especially if the staff is not highly skilled. Also, functional assessments and analyses may fail to reveal the motivation operations and reinforcement and escape options causing self-injurious, aggressive, and violent behavior for mentally handicapped clients.

Although essentially all of these antecedent procedures have a solid research base, any specific application may require careful expert analysis, implementation, evaluation, and recycling before success is achieved.

Implementing applied behavior analysis procedures in general and antecedent control procedures in particular not only requires considerable technical expertise on the part of the staff, but it also requires a client-centered philosophy and gut reaction that is not easy to establish and maintain, even among those with the best intentions. For example, having just been the recipient of violent aggression from a client, it is difficult for the staff to resist violent retribution, let alone to stop and think how to make antecedent conditions more reinforcing and less aversive for the person who just perpetrated the violent aggression. Having just been attacked, it is hard to "coddle" the client rather than to "teach him a lesson for his own good" and to "prepare him for what the real world will be like."

In fact, in spite of our best efforts, many of our clients will never be ready for the real world or even a traditionally sheltered world, without considerable added positive behavioral support with great concern for the antecedent conditions of life.

CASE ILLUSTRATION

A mentally handicapped woman showed extremely challenging behavior when instructed to take her morning shower. She would tantrum and resist staff efforts to help her, in spite of the use of consequence control procedures—reinforcement of compliance and time-out for challenging behavior (which actually might have been reinforcement of escape behavior). Functional assessment (antecedent assessment) showed that challenging behavior was infrequent during the rest of the day. So on the assumption that the woman was not enough of a "morning person" to cope with the rush of demanding morning activities, the behavior analyst rescheduled the shower for the evening, with a resulting elimination of challenging behavior at shower time and without the need of complex consequence control procedures needing skilled staff and staff monitoring.

A functional assessment suggested that escape from instructional demands might be reinforcing the aggression, screaming, and self-injury of a child with autism. The overall demand level (and presumably the aversiveness) of the instructional sessions was decreased by interspersing many less difficult tasks among the demanding tasks. In addition, the child was allowed to select from among the training tasks and, when behaving inappropriately during a task, was encouraged to select from among more appropriate activities. Challenging behavior was almost eliminated, and correct responding to the demanding instructional tasks increased from zero to 75%.

—*Richard W. Malott*

See also: *Behavioral Analytic Approach to Gambling (Vol. III), Behavioral Treatment in Natural Environments (Vols. I & III), Changes in Behavior (Vol. I), Stimulus Control (Vol. II)*

Suggested Readings

Anderson, C. M., & Long, E. S. (2002). Use of a structured descriptive assessment methodology to identify variables affecting problem behavior. *Journal of Applied Behavior Analysis, 35,* 137–154.

Asmus, J. M., Wacker, D. P., Harding, J., Berg, W. K., Derby, K. M., & Kocis, E. (1999). Evaluation of antecedent stimulus parameters for the treatment of escape-maintained aberrant behavior. *Journal of Applied Behavior Analysis, 32,* 495–513.

Chandler, L. K., & Dahlquist, C. M. (2002). *Functional assessment: Strategies to prevent and remediate challenging behavior in school settings.* Upper Saddle River, NJ: Prentice Hall.

Iwata, B. A., Smith, R. G., & Michael, J. L. (2000). Current research on the influence of establishing operations on behavior in applied settings. *Journal of Applied Behavior Analysis, 33,* 411–418.

Koegel, L. K., Koegel, R. L., & Dunlap, G. (1996). *Positive behavioral support: Including people with difficult behavior in the community.* Baltimore: Paul H. Brookes.

Laraway, S., Snycerski, S., Michael, J., & Poling, A. (2003). Motivating variables and terms to describe them: Some further refinements. *Journal of Applied Behavior Analysis, 36,* 407–414.

Luiselli, J. K., & Cameron, M. J. (1998). *Antecedent control: Innovative approaches to behavioral support.* Baltimore: Paul H. Brookes.

Mueller, M. M., Wilczynski, S. M., Moore, J. W., Fusilier, I., & Trahant, D. (2001). Antecedent manipulations in a tangible condition: The effects of stimulus preference on aggression. *Journal of Applied Behavior Analysis, 34,* 237–240.

Singh, N. N., & Singh, J. (1984). Antecedent control of oral reading errors and self-corrections by mentally retarded children. *Journal of Applied Behavior Analysis, 17,* 111–119.

Smith, R. G., & Iwata, B. A. (1997). Antecedent influences on behavior disorders. *Journal of Applied Behavior Analysis, 30,* 343–375.

ANXIETY MANAGEMENT

DESCRIPTION OF THE STRATEGY

Anxiety management training (AMT) is a form of coping skills training that teaches applied relaxation as a means of anxiety control. AMT was first designed for the treatment of generalized anxiety disorder in adults and has been conceptualized as a treatment for any problem in which anxiety plays a central role. Although AMT was initially developed for adults, researchers have also suggested a modified set of AMT procedures for children. AMT alone does not appear to be the current treatment of choice for childhood anxiety disorders; however, components of AMT seem to be incorporated into a number of well-accepted treatment protocols for childhood anxiety.

In AMT, clients are taught to identify and respond to both physiological and cognitive signals of anxiety with a specific coping behavior. More specifically, clients learn to respond to their anxiety symptoms through the implementation of a relaxation response. As sessions progress, clients are instructed in how to recognize physiological and cognitive cues that signal the onset of anxiety. This enables the client to prevent even higher levels of anxiety from developing by responding to early anxiety cues with the execution of relaxation behaviors.

There are several subtle distinctions that differentiate AMT from other behavioral treatments for anxiety, such as systematic desensitization or flooding techniques. In AMT, the clients take an active role in their anxiety reduction by selectively applying a coping skill (i.e., relaxation training) to reduce anxiety symptoms evoked during imaginal exposure exercises. During systematic desensitization, relaxation training and exposure are also employed, although the usage of such skills differs from AMT procedures, as a relaxed state is optimally maintained from the start of a systematic desensitization session and imaginal exposure episodes are typically brief and terminated by the therapist before high levels of fear or anxiety fully disrupt the client's relaxed state. In addition, AMT uses only two levels of anxiety (moderate and high) for exposure tasks, whereas systematic desensitization utilizes a gradual, stepwise hierarchy of stimuli intensity that induces a range of anticipated responding spanning from very low levels of anxiety to much higher levels of anxiety. Flooding procedures, unlike AMT, do not include active coping skills training, such as the learning of relaxation exercises. In flooding, adaptation to feared stimuli is more of a passive process that focuses on habituation to such stimuli, whereby clients are usually exposed to highly feared stimuli without any previous, incremental presentation of less fear-evoking stimuli.

AMT treatment protocols usually consist of five structured sessions. However, more than five sessions are often implemented, as particular sessions may be repeated. The sessions typically take place once a week for approximately 1 hour at a time. The therapist begins the first session with an overview of the treatment structure and rationale. The reason for this overview is that client understanding of the therapeutic process is considered an important component of AMT. Therapy is described to clients as a type of skill acquisition, learned primarily through extensive practice. Furthermore, AMT is discussed as a method to train clients in the early identification of anxiety and the elimination of anxiety through relaxation. The therapist also emphasizes the importance of active involvement on the part of the clients during the course of their AMT treatment. The therapist may also describe how relaxation will be taught, and clients are informed that imagery will be used as a way for the clients to induce anxiety in session.

In addition to an overview of the treatment rationale, the client also begins relaxation training during the first session. A relaxation scene to be used during this session is constructed with the assistance of the client. The relaxation scene should be an event that the client has actually experienced, should contain as many concrete details as possible, and should include as many sensory cues as possible. The therapist typically explains that relaxation is a skill that needs to be practiced outside of session for generalization of such skills to occur. For this reason, the importance of homework is emphasized. During the first session, this homework consists of practicing relaxation skills on a daily basis and monitoring the level of tension experienced before and after relaxation sessions. During homework, the degree of relaxation obtained may be monitored on a scale of 1–100 (where low scores indicate a relaxed state, middle numbers indicate moderate levels of anxiety, and higher numbers indicate more intense levels of anxiety).

Notably, the original procedures for relaxation training in AMT were designed for adults, and these procedures may be difficult for children to follow. Clinicians using AMT in their work with children should be mindful regarding the possible selection of alternative relaxation procedures that have been especially developed for use with this population. These alternative relaxation procedures may include imagery and fantasy strategies that facilitate learning about how to relax particular muscle groups. For instance, the child can visualize squeezing an orange as a way to learn to tense and relax muscles in the arm. When working with children using AMT, it is recommended that relaxation training be limited to 15-minute intervals, using a maximum of three muscle groups per interval.

The second AMT session begins with identification of an anxiety-evoking scene of moderate intensity (i.e., a rating of 60 on a scale of 1–100). Through use of imagery, exposure to the anxiety-evoking scene is then induced in session, with the goal of making the imagined situation as vivid as possible. Once the anxiety-evoking scene is introduced, the therapist instructs the client to begin relaxation. After a relaxed state has been achieved, anxiety-evoking imagery is used in order to obtain another anxious state. When the client reports that he or she feels sufficiently anxious, imaginal exposure is terminated, and the therapist signals for the client to begin the relaxation procedure again. This process teaches the client to quickly respond to an anxious state with induction of a relaxation response. Therefore, this same procedure of anxiety induction, followed by implementation of the relaxation procedure, is practiced a number of times throughout the second session. As homework, the client is instructed to practice using relaxation skills in a number of locations. For example, the client may be instructed to practice the training while riding on the school bus or before attending a social gathering.

In the third session, the therapist begins to give increased responsibility for the initiation of relaxation to the client. Procedurally, an anxiety-evoking scene of moderate intensity (i.e., level 60) is presented and the client is asked to pay particular attention to any early symptoms indicative of an anxious response. The scene is then terminated, and the client is instructed to implement the relaxation process. This cycle is repeated several times throughout the session in order to facilitate improved identification of anxiety-related cues. As homework, the client continues to practice relaxation independently, with the specific instruction of implementing the procedure in response to a novel situation that produces mild anxiety.

In the fourth AMT session, the intensity of the anxiety-evoking scene utilized in session is increased through the use of an imaginal scene with a discomfort level of 90 or above. The cycle of anxiety induction followed by implementation of relaxation is repeated several times throughout the session, with the level of scene intensity varied between scenes that produce moderate levels of anxiety and those that produce higher levels of anxiety. In addition, the therapist continues to give increased responsibility for initiation of relaxation to the client. Homework includes practicing detection of early anxiety signals and independently responding to such cues with relaxation strategies.

In the fifth session, the client has most of the responsibility for induction of relaxation procedures. The therapist helps to present a highly anxiety-evoking scene; however, all other activities are controlled by the client. Once anxiety is induced, the client responds to the anxiety elicited by self-initiating the relaxation procedure. In this session, relaxation is initiated without termination of the anxiety scene. Once the client obtains a stable state of relaxation, moderate and high intensity scenes are presented in alternating orders, with each scene followed by client initiation of the relaxation procedure.

RESEARCH BASIS

AMT has been systematically researched over the last 30 years. Originally, AMT was used to treat manifestations of generalized anxiety disorder in adults; however, AMT also appears effective for the treatment of several other problems among adults, including test anxiety, social anxiety, and anger difficulties. AMT may decrease symptoms associated with a number of medical conditions, including hypertension, diabetes, ulcers, and asthma. AMT was not developed as a treatment for child anxiety, and limited research has been forwarded to examine the implementation of AMT as a specific intervention for child populations. One reason for this limited amount of research on the effectiveness of AMT in child and adolescent populations may be that components and variations of AMT appear to be embedded in current research-based treatment protocols for child and adolescent anxiety disorders. As a result, AMT is not generally used as an intervention, independent of other treatment components, with child and adolescent populations.

Support exists for the efficacy of approaches similar to AMT in the treatment of childhood fears and phobias. Researchers have suggested that AMT, with the incorporation of cognitive restructuring and other behavior management skills, may be effective in the treatment of children and adolescents with generalized anxiety disorder, social phobia, and separation anxiety disorder. AMT is also a component of a manualized treatment for obsessive-compulsive disorder (OCD). In this empirically supported treatment procedure, AMT is used in conjunction with exposure and response prevention (Ex/RP) techniques. Although AMT is often used concurrently with Ex/RP, at least one research study has found that Ex/RP treatment components are more effective than AMT alone in the treatment of childhood OCD.

RELEVANT TARGET POPULATIONS AND EXCEPTIONS

As noted, components and variations of AMT are found within a number of current treatment protocols for child anxiety, such as a treatment protocol for OCD. In the course of this treatment for OCD, AMT is defined by the combination of relaxation training, breathing exercises, and cognitive restructuring skills that can be used during implementation of Ex/RP tasks. Research on the use of AMT within treatment protocols for OCD has indicated that AMT may be effective in making exposure more predictable and controllable by decreasing the level of anxiety related to exposure activities and by targeting co-occurring anxiety disorders that may interfere with the treatment of OCD.

As noted, treatment components similar to those in AMT also appear within an empirically supported treatment designed to treat a variety of childhood anxiety disorders including social phobia, generalized anxiety disorder, and separation anxiety disorder. Components of this treatment that seem consistent with AMT include teaching children to recognize internal cues associated with anxiety, relaxation training, and self-monitoring.

COMPLICATIONS

There are a number of potential complications when conducting AMT or related treatment strategies with children. For instance, researchers have noted that clinicians should pay particular attention to the motivation level and cognitive capability of children and adolescents when asking them to self-monitor. The age and developmental level of certain childhood populations may also limit the utility of AMT and related cognitive-behavioral strategies. In particular, recognition of cognitive or physiological cues signaling anxiety, a necessary feature of AMT and many related cognitive-behavioral strategies, may require a degree of insight or cognitive skill on the part of the child that may not be fully developed among all children. Consequently, most of the anxiety-focused interventions for children are targeted at school-aged children (ages 7–12), as younger children may be relatively limited in their ability to understand themselves, self-monitor, and regulate their own behavior. A child's cognitive ability and level of metacognition may also be important regarding the ability to adequately comprehend terminology associated with AMT or similar treatment strategies.

The anxiety-evoking exposure exercises typical of AMT and other behavioral treatments for anxiety disorders may be inherently stressful to the child. Therefore, a child may be reluctant to participate in exposure activities or may use alternative cognitive strategies in order to prevent arousal from occurring in the session, such as distraction. As a result, it is important to clearly articulate the rationale of this treatment to the child and to seek the child's collaboration in treatment procedures. To whatever degree possible, it is also important to make sure that the child is actually experiencing sufficient anxiety during imaginal exposure exercises. At the same time, the clinician must take careful steps to make sure that exposure is presented in such a way that the child does not endure extremely high levels of anxiety in session. If exposure progresses too quickly or if it leads to the induction of overly intense anxiety symptoms, the clinician runs the risk of the child experiencing some trauma in session. For many of the same reasons, it is also important to make sure that when imaginal exposure is conducted within the session, anxiety is fully reduced before the session is terminated.

CASE ILLUSTRATION

"Jared" was an 11-year-old male who presented to a community mental health clinic, accompanied by his parents, due to difficulties with swallowing pills, both at home and at school, that were prescribed by his psychiatrist for the treatment of attention-deficit/hyperactivity disorder (ADHD). Upon consultation, Jared's psychiatrist indicated no medical etiology for this problem and reported his belief that the cause of Jared's swallowing difficulties was anxiety-related in nature. During initial assessment, Jared and his parents completed several questionnaire measures assessing a range of internalizing and externalizing difficulties, in addition to a detailed history of the problem behavior and a semi-structured interview to assess for diagnostically relevant symptomatology. Jared's school nurse (who administered medications to him in that environment) also completed a questionnaire measure regarding his behavior, and Jared's parents were instructed to keep a frequency count of his compliance with swallowing medications during the week following the initial assessment.

Results of this assessment indicated that while Jared had no prior history of swallowing difficulties

during infancy or childhood, his tolerance of psychostimulant medications was poor from the start of its usage, 2 months ago, resulting in recurrent feelings of nausea, headache, and sleeplessness, though his mother and psychiatrist believed that these side effects seemed to steadily improve throughout the 1st week of treatment. Nonetheless, during the 2nd week of treatment, Jared began refusing to take his pills either at home or at school. Changes in the type and dosing of psychostimulant medication failed to remediate his medication compliance problems. Jared reported that he felt "embarrassed" about taking psychostimulant medications, especially at school, and further indicated a particular concern that he would "throw up" in front of family or peers after swallowing his pill. Jared failed to meet full diagnostic criteria for any clinical disorder, other than ADHD. However, he did report mild to moderate symptoms of social anxiety, oppositional defiant disorder, and specific phobia (vomiting) that appeared consistent with his medication compliance issues.

AMT was administered to Jared over six treatment sessions. During an initial assessment feedback session in which the antecedent and consequent conditions that seemed to be associated with Jared's current swallowing difficulties were reviewed, commitment was obtained to participate in a brief course of AMT. In the first AMT session, the rationale for this treatment approach was extensively reviewed with Jared and his family members, a method for identifying Jared's level of anxiety in session (using Subjective Units of Discomfort [SUDS] levels) was introduced, and Jared helped to design his relaxation paradigm. Jared then assisted in teaching his parents the relaxation paradigm he created, and the family practiced relaxation skills together. In Session 2, a moderately anxiety-evoking situation was identified (swallowing a psychostimulant pill and feeling nauseous) and imaginal exposure was utilized to induce anxiety at a SUDS level of 60. Upon attainment of this SUDS level, Jared was instructed to begin his relaxation paradigm. This exposure-relaxation cycle was then repeated several times in session. At the start of Session 3, Jared's parents reported a significant increase in his medication compliance, up from compliance during 7 of 21 administration attempts during Week 1 of treatment, to 15 of 21 administration attempts at the start of Week 3, with increasing compliance observed throughout the previous week. Jared also reported that he was feeling "a little" less anxious about potentially vomiting after taking his medication. In Session 3, Jared was encouraged to report "how his body felt" and any negative self-talk that occurred each time his SUDS levels increased during imaginal exposure to his moderately intense anxiety-evoking situation. Discussion of how to use the physiological and cognitive cues that Jared reported during exposure activities to prompt relaxation use was also conducted. For homework, Jared indicated that he would try to use his relaxation skills when he noticed any of these anxiety-related cues following medication usage at school.

Session 4's content was virtually identical to Session 3's, with a more specific focus on alternately imagining a slightly expanded scene that involved Jared taking his medication in school and feeling nauseous afterward, as this situation continued to present difficulty to him, and his regular moderately intense scene. In Session 5, the therapist discussed induction of Jared's high-intensity anxiety-evoking situation (taking his psychostimulant medication in school and vomiting in the classroom) and the possible side effects of reviewing such highly emotional imagery with him and his family. Jared strongly indicated that he was "ready" for the imaginal presentation of this situation but agreed to allow his mother to remain in the room during initial exposure to this imagery, in case of any adverse effects. Jared repeatedly and successfully induced anxiety at a SUDS level of approximately 80 during this session to his high-intensity scene (with alternating presentation of his moderately anxiety-evoking scene), and appropriate use of relaxation in session. At the start of Session 6, Jared's parents reported that he appeared to no longer exhibit problems with medication compliance and had not refused to take his medication at any point during the previous week. Jared proudly self-initiated both imaginal exposure and relaxation to his high-intensity situation and announced to the therapist that he was ready to discontinue treatment. A follow-up phone call from Jared's psychiatrist indicated that he continued to evidence full compliance with swallowing medications 3 months after AMT was completed.

—*Jill T. Ehrenreich and Brian J. Fisak Jr.*

See also: *AMT: Anxiety/Anger Management Training (Vols. I & III), Barlow, David H. (Vols. I & III), Cognitive Behavior Therapy: Child Clinical Applications (Vol. II), Foa, Edna B. (Vols. I & III), Stress Inoculation Training (Vols. I & III)*

Suggested Readings

Grace, N., Spirito, A., Finch, A. J., & Ott, E. S. (1993). Coping skills for anxiety control in children. In A. J. Finch, M. W. Nelson, & E. S. Ott (Eds.), *Cognitive-behavioral procedures with children and adolescents: A practical guide* (pp. 257–288). Boston: Allyn & Bacon.

Kendall, P. C. (1992). *Coping cat workbook.* Ardmore, PA: Workbook.

Kendall, P. C., Chansky, T. E., Friedman, M., Kim, R., Kortlander, E., Sessa, F. M., & Siqueland, L. (1991). Treating anxiety disorders in children and adolescents. In P. C. Kendall (Ed.), *Child and adolescent therapy: Cognitive-behavioral procedures* (pp. 131–164). New York: Guilford Press.

Koeppen, A. S. (1974). Relaxation training for children. *Elementary School Guidance and Counseling,* October, 14–21.

March, J. S., & Mulle, K. (1998). *OCD in children and adolescents: A cognitive-behavioral treatment manual.* New York: Guilford Press.

Suinn, R. M. (1990). *Anxiety management training.* New York: Plenum.

APPLIED BEHAVIOR ANALYSIS

DESCRIPTION AND THEORETICAL ASSUMPTIONS

Applied behavior analysis (ABA) is the systematic application of basic behavioral principles to the solving of individual and societal problems. ABA has emerged as a preeminent perspective in the treatment of childhood disorders and disabilities, particularly problems associated with severely challenging behavior and significant skill deficits. It is a scientific school of thought rather than a specific method. Children come to professional attention because of a social judgment: Their behavior does not conform to certain adult expectations. From the ABA perspective, intervention requires modification of the social and ecological influences that define as well as regulate the child's behavior.

Behavior means anything an individual can do, including thinking and feeling, as long as these can be directly observed. Because the approach is internally consistent, applying both to the explanation and remediation of behavior problems, the principles defining behavior analysis are quite few in number, and these will be outlined. And because the deductions from these principles are infinitely variable, the strategies that can be applied are essentially unlimited. However, the theoretical assumptions and conventions of ABA constrain which procedures currently fall within the accepted rubric of ABA.

Historically, ABA evolved from the body of laboratory research carried out by B. F. Skinner and colleagues, experimentally analyzing the environmental influences and learning histories that predictably control an organism's behavior. The explanation for why an individual is acting a certain way is sought in the current and past environmental contingencies. This stands in contrast to the hypothesized and not directly observable internal mechanisms (traits, dispositions, or psychiatric syndromes) that are often considered causal in both psychology and everyday understanding. Most of Skinner's work dealt with what he called "operant" behavior. An operant is an overt action that impacts on the environment in some way—in the artificial research setting this was the familiar pressing of a lever that mechanically activated the delivery of food. Rate of responding was the most commonly used measure, but any characteristic of behavioral dynamics can be brought under control, such as interresponse interval, force exerted, or the particular form of how the lever is pressed. If its consequences are beneficial (food for a hungry individual), the operant response will become strengthened ("reinforced")—will more probably reoccur in that particular context. In the natural environment, consequences typically reflect physical realities: putting on a sweater is intrinsically reinforced by warmth and protection from the cold weather outside. However, the contingencies between an action and its consequences can also be extrinsic—planfully arranged within social environments, such as a parent praising a child for independently putting on a sweater before ever going outside into the cold. Such contingency relationships are inevitably reciprocal: The parent's positive reaction will in turn be reinforced by the child's increased compliance with future requests.

It is the deliberate arrangement of environmental contingencies to shape socially desired behavior that defines *applied* behavior analysis. Thus, terms such as behavior *management* or *engineering* (implying manipulation for the benefit of the controlling individual), although still in use, have given way to the more neutral ABA label. The emphasis on *analysis* shifts the focus toward explaining behavior rather than simply trying to change it.

ABA, in keeping with its radical behavioral roots, eschews intervening and internal explanatory mechanisms, whether biological or cognitive. Cognitive explanations of a child's behavior are particularly suspect, since the fundamental principle is the contextual analysis in which behavior must be explained by the current environmental circumstances and the learning history of the child. As a professional discipline, this encourages the design of interventions based on what can be done to change conditions, whereas if a behavior problem is seen as being derived from biology (e.g., overactive behavior is due to a deficit in brain chemistry), then there is a tendency to seek biological remedies (e.g., prescribing Ritalin). Similarly, explanations that rely on cognitive causes, such as the child's expectations or beliefs, again suggest that interventions need not focus on altering social environments but on trying to change the child's understanding.

FUNDAMENTAL PRINCIPLES

Reinforcement

It is a basic principle of survival and evolution that actions resulting in benefits for the organism will be repeated, and actions resulting in discomfort, harm, or social disadvantage will become less probable. The environmental consequences that strengthen or weaken behavior are thus called reinforcers (or reinforcements). Traditional behavioral theories tended to distinguish between primary reinforcements that satisfy some biological need (such as food and water) and secondary reinforcements that acquire their reward value through social learning (such as money or compliments). Behavior analysts prefer to think of reinforcement not in the sense of hedonistic or motivational principles (outcomes the individual enjoys or that someone else defines as rewarding) but more neutrally in terms of any event that actually leads to a repetition of the behavior.

While this logic results in a rather circular definition and reduces the explanatory power of the reinforcement concept, it has the advantage of allowing the practitioner to understand that if a child is repeatedly engaging in a behavior that appears to have negative consequences (resulting, for example, in loss of privileges from a parent or teacher), it must in fact be receiving positive reinforcement of some kind (perhaps by the attention he or she is getting from the adult). Logically, many reinforcing events are themselves behaviors (watching TV, going swimming).

Therefore, one could argue that any behavior that is highly likely to occur, if the opportunity is presented, will serve as a reinforcer for any other behavior that is less probable (doing homework, walking to the swimming pool)—a concept known as the Premack principle.

As a rule, immediate consequences are more likely to strengthen behavior than distant or delayed ones, so that threats and promises regarding future outcomes tend to have only a weak influence on children. A major component of early social learning within families involves teaching children to be more influenced by larger, delayed rewards (achieving good grades) than by smaller, more immediate gratifications (playing outside rather than doing homework). Because of different socialization experiences, and possibly constitutional factors, individual children differ greatly in their responsiveness to immediate versus delayed reinforcement, resulting in some being described loosely as impulsive, or reward dominant.

Partial Reinforcement

In order for behavior to be maintained (be repeated in appropriate contexts), it does not need to receive reinforcement every time it occurs. Reinforcement might be delivered on a *partial* basis after a specific number of responses (fixed ratio schedule, e.g., "if you tidy your room every day this week, we will go to McDonalds on Sunday"), or after a varying time delay (variable interval schedule, e.g., "I'm not sure what days your grandma is coming over this month, but if your room is tidy when she comes, I'll give you a dollar each time"). Different schedules of reinforcement produce different patterns of responding. However, these complex relationships that have been worked out in the laboratory have minimal relevance to everyday behaviors, which occur in sequences of actions largely dictated by available time and physically circumscribed activities or routines (going to school, doing homework, watching TV, preparing a snack, texting a friend).

Behavior that has only been partially reinforced is more resistant to extinction (takes longer to decrease), as illustrated in real life by the persistence of gambling or a child showing off long after everyone has stopped laughing at him or her or paying attention. The reasons for this phenomenon, known as the partial reinforcement effect, are still not clearly understood, but a possible explanation is that the child can less easily discriminate between the conditions under which a behavior will be rewarded and when it will no longer be rewarded. The partial reinforcement effect has some interesting practical implications. One is that if you want a positive behavior to continue (be maintained) in situations where specific reinforcement might not be available, such as outside the therapy context, it would be useful to reinforce the behavior in the treatment context on a partial basis. Another implication is that if you want an inappropriate behavior to decrease, it will be important not to occasionally forget and reinforce the behavior sporadically. Thus, consistency in responding to a child's negative behavior has important implications for parenting.

Shaping and Chaining

One of the earliest demonstrations in the operant laboratory was that a given response could be shaped through the reinforcement of successive approximations to the desired behavior. This is the essential principle that is used by animal trainers to teach animals to perform complicated tricks. A spontaneously occurring behavior that is similar in form to the desired behavior (such as a dolphin naturally arching out of the water) is selectively reinforced so that minor variations (rising slightly higher) meeting the criteria for the new behavior (leaping through a hoop) are progressively reinforced. Since this allows nonverbal organisms to be instructed in what is required of them, its relevance to children with severe disabilities and limited communication became immediately obvious. The principle can be used to teach new behaviors to children unable to follow a verbal command or repeat a behavior through imitation; this was one of the first applications to show the potential of behavior analysis.

Systematically raising the standard for what will be reinforced means that teaching within the ABA paradigm tends to be positive, with high levels of reinforcement, and errors minimized. A good coach will praise a child's improvement in a task (such as hitting the tennis ball without bending the elbow, even if the shot itself went into the net) but will expect a slight further improvement before praising again. Chaining is a somewhat similar process, except that a fairly complex task, like teaching a child with mental retardation to tie a shoelace, can be broken down into a sequence of small actions. These are reinforced separately at first, and gradually the reinforcement is delivered only as combinations of actions are completed, eventually ending with the reinforcement only occurring for the completion of the entire sequence. Breaking down complex tasks into their major component parts is known as a task analysis. It is helpful, following the principle that immediate reinforcement is most powerful, to sometimes use a backward chaining approach in teaching a skill. In shoelace tying, one might perform most of the sequence for the child (providing full physical assistance), leaving only the final step of pulling the bow tight for the child to be prompted to do independently, which is then followed by the reinforcement of task completion ("well done, now you can run off and play").

Extinction

If behavior is maintained by its consequences, it follows that behaviors no longer receiving reinforcement will decrease in probability and eventually stop occurring altogether. Both the deliberate removal of reinforcement and the resultant phenomenon of a decrease in frequency of the behavior are known as extinction. It should be noted that if a behavior has been regularly reinforced and then suddenly subjected to extinction, the response will not start to decrease immediately. In fact there is typically a burst of more rapid responding: Imagine that if you have been working a slot machine at a casino that has been paying out quite regularly but now has suddenly stopped doing so, you will engage in a burst of lever pulling before you finally walk away.

The extinction principle has great importance clinically when a child is actively engaging in an "excess" behavior that is judged socially undesirable. To reduce that behavior the practitioner needs to ascertain what reinforcement is maintaining it (an assessment process known as a functional analysis) and then try to remove that reinforcement. Since the reinforcement might be something of importance to the child, such as social attention or a feeling of security, simply removing the reinforcement is often not desirable. Furthermore, if a behavior is intrinsically reinforced, such as the positive sensory feedback a child might obtain from some undesirable habit (such as smoking), it is difficult to remove such consequences.

In these situations it is necessary to define an alternative, appropriate response and ensure that this behavior receives the reinforcement and the undesired behavior does not. Clearly, if this alternative behavior is also incompatible (cannot physically be performed at the same time as the undesirable one), then its acquisition will further interfere with the occurrence of the negative behavior. An example of this might be reinforcing play skills with peers in a child who is normally aggressive. You can see that this is also a type of differential reinforcement, and indeed if instead of specifying the alternative positive behavior one simply reinforces any acceptable thing the child is doing that is *not* the undesired behavior, the strategy is known as the differential reinforcement of other behavior (DRO). In everyday home or classroom settings, trying to simply extinguish a behavior by ignoring it or putting the child into a "time-out" room is often unsuccessful. This is because the function of the undesirable behavior may be to obtain social attention or reduce boredom. The adult does not really have control over these other potential reinforcers in the environment, such as approval from peers or the excitement of being noticed. Thus, reinforcing positive alternative behaviors is an essential component of the application of the extinction principle.

Punishment

A somewhat similar argument can be made regarding the practical use of punishment in controlling behavior. By definition, a punishment contingency is one in which a consequence causes a behavior to decrease in frequency. Typically, the sorts of consequences that serve as punishers are the ones one would expect in the everyday use of the word, namely loss of privileges (e.g., being grounded) or aversive (e.g., being reprimanded) and painful experiences (e.g., spanking). Note that if a behavior results in the *termination* of an aversive event, that behavior will tend to *increase* in probability. Thus, the behavior of annoying a teacher might be reinforced by the reduction of boredom from an uninteresting class activity. Such a contingency is known as negative reinforcement, a phrase often confused with punishment. A more elaborate illustration might be if a parent yells at a child who is engaging in an ongoing, annoying behavior. The temporary ending of the child's behavior negatively reinforces the parent's use of harsh discipline, but the action may have merely interrupted the child's activities, and the yelling, rather than serving as a punishing event, is reinforcing to the child who is seeking some sort of parental reaction. These negative cycles of ineffective parenting have been labeled "coercive traps."

Obviously, for a punishment contingency to effectively reduce a behavior, that behavior must not be being simultaneously reinforced. Unfortunately, in everyday situations this is rarely the case. Children may be punished by a parent for an action that actually has a significant positive function for the child, such as getting attention from peers, obtaining some desirable object, or reducing feelings of powerlessness. Theoretically, it is also debatable as to whether a punishing consequence ever leads to a permanent reduction in the behavior (new learning of a replacement skill) or whether the behavior is simply temporarily suppressed in the individual while the punishment contingency is in effect. When the contingency is removed (such as when the teacher leaves the room or the child is far away from the parental authority), the negative behavior may reoccur. For these reasons, it is more effective to teach a positive alternative to the undesired behavior than simply try to eliminate it. Furthermore, in everyday life, what we typically refer to as "punishment" for a child is rarely a formal punishment contingency. In families, for example, the aversive consequence is often delivered long after the behavior has occurred ("you were such a bad boy this morning, you are not going to watch TV this evening").

On these and other empirical grounds, applied behavior analysts tend to recommend against any reliance on punishment procedures, either as a method of social control (punishing criminal behavior occurs too long after the transgression to be contingent and thus influential), parental discipline (spanking), or deliberate professional intervention. The use of painful, aversive contingencies has, however, been a matter of major controversy when applied to very difficult behaviors, such as severe self-injury in an autistic child. The consensus of contemporary professional opinion is that the potential short-term effectiveness of such methods is outweighed by the ethical restrictions, and that alternative strategies for dealing with very challenging behaviors exist. The collection of alternative methods is now often referred to as "positive behavior support" and includes such procedures as (a) a very careful analysis of the challenging behavior to see what function it serves the child, (b) the teaching and differential reinforcement of alternative, more socially appropriate behaviors, particularly communication skills, (c) the removal of boring, frustrating, and coercive situations in the child's life, and (d) an emphasis on allowing choice of activities and generally a more client-centered assessment of the child's entire life circumstances.

Stimulus Control

A fundamental principle of ABA is that behavior is contextual, which means that discrete behaviors occur in specific contexts. This is because in one setting (playing outside with friends), a certain behavior (running around) will be readily reinforced (social interaction of an exciting game). The physically similar behavior of running around in a different situation, such as a preschool classroom, will result in a very different outcome, including being labeled as hyperactive. A stimulus or a cue becomes a controlling antecedent for behavior when a discriminative contingency exists—in, and only in, the presence of a specific cue a given behavior is reinforced. It is the stimulus that actually sets the occasion for (controls) the behavior. To claim that behavior is determined by its consequences is actually tautological, since the consequences happen only after the current behavior has already occurred. It is the next occurrence of the behavior, in the presence of the relevant cue or antecedent event, that is made more likely by a reinforcement.

A rather useful procedure can be derived from this basic principle. Once a behavior is reliably occurring in the presence of a stimulus cue, and not occurring in its absence (i.e., it is under discriminative stimulus control), we immediately have a way for the child to communicate in the absence of any formal language. If a nonverbal child is reinforced with candy for picking up a block and dropping it in a box only when a loud tone is presented as a cue, we can vary the intensity or pitch of the tone and see whether he or she responds to the new sounds. In this way, we could assess the auditory acuity of a deaf, nonverbal child, or we could assess stimulus generalization (responding the same way to slightly different cues) by seeing whether a child taught to pick up a block when shown a picture of a dog will do the same when shown a picture of a cat. Using such methods, children with no communication can inform us as to exactly what they do or do not see, hear, smell, or conceptualize. Following this same logic, we realize that any socially undesirable behavior is also "communicating" something about the child's needs.

Because of this relationship between antecedent, behavior, and its consequence (A-B-C), Skinner described their interaction as the "three-term contingency." This leads to important behavior analytic principles for assessment in applied settings. To understand a child's behavior, it is necessary to know the context in which it occurred, exactly what the child did, and what the consequences were. Thus, two children might both be described by their preschool teacher as "aggressive" and referred for treatment. By careful observation in the classroom, we might discover that Child A would typically see another child with a toy (cue), go over and grab it (behavior), and have fun playing with it himself or herself (consequence—obtained something desirable). Child B might be playing with a toy when another child comes over and sits next to him or her (cue). Child B then pulls this other child's hair (behavior) and the other child goes away and plays with the others (consequence—avoided stressful social interaction by being left alone). It is clear from these simple interactions that the form of the behavior, its eliciting context, and its function (what it achieves for the child) are all very different, so that treatment of Child A and Child B would also be completely different, despite their having a similar label (diagnosis) of aggressiveness.

IMPLICATIONS FOR PRACTICE

Early in ABA's history, the principles and procedures developed in the animal laboratory were translated quite literally into practice. If an operant lever press or key peck could be shaped by food for a hungry rat or pigeon, then presumably the behaviors of a child with mental retardation could equally be shaped by the contingent presentation of food, such as candy. The original demonstrations of the potential of reinforcement now in hindsight look like laboratory demonstrations: getting a child with autism to raise his hand by reinforcing successive approximations with small bites of candy, for instance.

The successes achieved, however, did have the very positive effect of helping practitioners recognize that behaviors in child clients, even those interpreted as the symptoms of some kind of psychiatric "illness," could be shaped by the social environment. This recognition profoundly impacted the development of a general psychological model for understanding and treating mental illness, and in particular provided intensive teaching methods for young people with the most severe disabilities. But the needs of children and families are very different from the controlled environment of the research laboratory, and this has gradually come to be recognized through the following critical concerns.

Target Behavior Selection

"Be still, be quiet, be docile" were the words used by two leading behavior analysts to emphasize that many early ABA programs, especially those dealing with disruptive children in classroom settings, were providing contingent reinforcement for the students staying quietly in their seats but not for engaging in the required, more important, academic activities. The concern that ABA provided a possible way of managing behavior, but did not help the practitioner identify which were the most important behaviors to target, was pointed out by Robert Hawkins in a provocative paper titled "Who Decided *That* Was the Behavior?" This led to a number of behavior analysts addressing criteria for identifying the crucial behaviors to work with and for deciding when a meaningful outcome had been achieved. In an essay subtitled "How Applied Behavior Analysis Is Finding Its Heart," Mont Wolf suggested the relevance of *social validity* criteria, such as the normative behavior by children of the same age and cultural group. Other clinicians have suggested educative validity criteria, such as emphasizing the behaviors that will facilitate friendship and acceptance by other children or generate new learning opportunities.

Another way of thinking about the focus for behavioral intervention is to understand that children have many behaviors in their repertoire that are interlinked in a systemic way. This means that changing one "keystone" behavior might influence a child's entire repertoire of inappropriate behavior. For example, reducing a child's bullying behavior might increase peer interaction, which would teach new interaction skills, which would reduce sibling conflict at home, resulting in more homework behavior, which would result in higher grades. Discovering how specific behaviors are organized within a given individual's repertoire (i.e., personality) could thus lead to the design of interventions that affect not just one operant but a whole class of behaviors. Children's developmental progress is not a matter of fixed stages but a behavioral hierarchy: One class of behaviors (playing soccer, for instance) is dependent on the prior acquisition of more basic skills (kicking a ball, standing on one leg, cooperating with a team).

Natural Contexts

Controversy has also arisen from the fact that ABA programs can be quite unnatural and artificial. Should the consequences for reading a book at school be a monetary payoff, or should reading be reinforced by the enjoyment derived from the story itself? Is it appropriate to give children snacks and other material rewards for behaviors such as sharing or being polite that are usually reinforced by social contingencies such as praise or affection? Once an artificial contingency of reinforcement is removed, such as at the end of treatment, are the natural consequences of the behavior going to be strong enough to allow the desired behavior change to continue? Modern ABA interventions pay careful attention to *maintenance,* the natural environmental contingencies that will sustain desirable behavior, and to *generalization,* ensuring that natural cues will regulate the behavior in other settings, not just the context of the office or classroom where the original intervention took place.

A similar issue arises when teaching natural routines to children. These need to be functional and fit into the social ecology. In the operant laboratory, *rate* of responding is the primary measure used, and behavioral baselines (records) typically illustrate changes in response rate over time. But with the exception of factory work, human behaviors need to be performed in their proper context. Early ABA teaching programs followed a "discrete trials" procedure, practicing one behavior over and over again. Contemporary approaches embed the instruction in household or school routines. If a child is being reinforced for helping around the home, it is not expected that he or she will repeatedly wash the dishes over and over again in the same way as the pigeon might peck at a key switch. The *routine* of washing dishes (one that has a clear beginning, and ends when the desired goal has been accomplished) should be initiated spontaneously by the child (without the parent having to nag), should be performed on the cue that there are dirty dishes in the sink, has to be done with quality (taking care not to break anything) and fluency (reasonably quickly), and the task ended when all the dishes have been washed. Quality and fluency are properties of behavior that can be shaped by contingencies, some of which can be self-imposed. Taking pride in one's work is another way of saying that one self-reinforces for meeting one's own performance standard.

Closely related to this complexity regarding the performance of a skill is the degree to which an activity is functional for the child. If the child has an intellectual disability, learning to match colored shapes to the correct hole in an octagonal ball is neither a useful activity nor any fun to do with friends. Conversely, learning to match a plate with the correct place in a dishwasher could be a valuable life skill, or learning to operate a Playstation could enhance social opportunities. Early ABA programs that were criticized for focusing on nonfunctional, repetitive, isolated behaviors have now given way to an emphasis on activities with secondary payoffs, such as being a valuable leisure pursuit, helping the child to interact socially, or enhancing employability.

Analysis of Complex Behavior Such as Language and Emotion

How does ABA deal with the fact that children have complex repertoires of thought and other cognitive processes? The simple strategy for dealing with cognition is to presume that these events are behaviors like any other, controlled by the same set of contextual principles, and therefore cannot be used as valid explanations for overt actions. On the other hand, it is widely recognized in ABA that as humans differ from other animals by having a symbolic communication system, there are "rule-governed" behaviors in which verbal descriptions of contingencies can be substituted for the actual contingencies. To train a dog to fetch your slippers would take hours of shaping, which is completely unnecessary in the case of a verbal child, for whom one simply says "Be a honey and run upstairs and get my shoes." Hundreds of social learning trials will have created the conditions whereby compliance has become a response class (all exemplars of following a parental instruction have been reinforced), whereby specific words have become mands or cues for action ("run upstairs . . ."), and spoken words ("shoes") have become tacts or labels. Words, mental images, pictures, and the real objects themselves achieve what is known as *stimulus equivalence*—they all have the same function in controlling behavior as they are all equivalent discriminative stimuli for a particular overt response.

In defining overt, operant behavior, Skinner also recognized and identified another class of behaviors called respondents, characterized as those responses that were reflexively elicited by certain stimuli and which usually did not act upon the environment to change it. Emotional responses such as fear, anger, and joy are examples of respondent behaviors, and it is now accepted that these initially unlearned emotional responses are easily modified by both Pavlovian conditioning procedures and by operant contingencies. Thus, emotional responses in children can be conditioned to previously neutral stimuli (fear conditioned to a harmless puppy after a child has been bitten by a snarling dog), as well as shaped by the sorts of consequences they achieve for the child—social attention and sympathy, avoidance of unpleasant situations, and so on. If certain stimuli can evoke emotions such as anxiety in children, and since that is an uncomfortable emotional experience, the child will be motivated to avoid such stimuli. To the extent that this active avoidance reduces anxiety, that reduction in discomfort will reinforce the avoidance behavior.

DATA AND THE NATURE OF EVIDENCE

Early studies demonstrating the clinical effectiveness of ABA relied exclusively on the single-subject methodology of the animal operant laboratory. Baseline (preintervention) frequencies of the target behavior were recorded and compared to the frequencies following the intervention. In the lab, experimental control is demonstrated directly by altering contingencies and recording the responsiveness of the behavior to these changes. In applied settings, it is impractical to reverse a treatment and return to previous conditions, and so various designs have been developed in an attempt to show that it was the specific planned intervention contingency that brought about a favorable change in behavior, not some extraneous influence occurring at the same time.

The basic value of these designs is that they allow the clinician to monitor the effectiveness of the intervention, to correct the intervention strategy on the basis of this behavioral feedback, and to provide a direct measure of the nature of the outcome. But as already pointed out, an increase or decrease in some behavior is not the same as a clinically meaningful outcome for the child, and so numerous other criteria have been introduced, such as a probe trial in which the child is given the opportunity to perform the desired behavior. An important way to judge behaviors such as new independent living skills like dressing, making a snack, or making a purchase is to record

the degree of assistance that is still required, such as a prompt, some level of physical assistance, or fully independently. For children with very severe physical or motor disabilities, full independence may not be a possible goal; in such instances, autonomy might be defined by the child being able to signal the initiation of a behavior, or exercise choice.

Despite these complexities, one of the hallmarks of ABA is that behavior change will be carefully recorded and monitored and that by keeping systematic data, better informed practical decisions can be made and interventions adjusted according to objective feedback. These values have generated interesting repercussions when the individuals carrying out the intervention are not the same as the ABA professional who designed it. Thus, nonprofessional caregivers, teachers, parents, and other relevant participants have been taught to observe the antecedent, behaviors, and consequences, to assist with a functional analysis, have been taught to record the frequency of behavioral occurrences, and have been asked to exercise social judgments in the evaluation of meaningful change.

CONCLUSION AND IMPLICATIONS

ABA has evolved as a distinctive framework for practice that is united by the use of common language and terminology from the experimental analysis of behavior that endorses certain philosophical assumptions and that both unifies the approach and restricts its development and integration with other psychological forms of treatment. The ABA tradition in professional interventions with children provides an extensive and empirically supported alternative to the dominant biomedical paradigm for understanding children's disabilities and behavioral disorders. The perspective is an optimistic one that examines actual behavior in context and avoids labels and fictitious explanations that might diminish the tendency to take action. This has been true even when a disability has an obvious biological cause, such as traumatic brain injury or some genetically based syndrome. In ABA the approach to such children would not be to assess their limitations, but to think about how the environment might be modified to enable desirable behaviors to take place. A child with a low tested IQ would be seen as an individual for whom special behavioral supports would need to be introduced so that he or she could participate actively in society. This positive, optimistic emphasis on what can be done is one of the most significant contributions of ABA.

Avoiding labels and diagnoses that gloss over important details of the form and function of behavior has the benefit of challenging fictitious explanations. Isolate play does not occur because a child has Asperger's Disorder, nor can a child's distractibility be accounted for because he has a syndrome of attention deficit disorder (ADD). On the other hand, some concepts are considered taboo in ABA, whereas in fact they are reasonable summaries of very complex patterns of behavior. By recognizing that learning histories have shaped different patterns of behavior in children or produced deficits in their repertoires, when individual children enter ostensibly the same environment, such as the same preschool classroom, their subsequent interactions with the contingencies operating in those environments are going to be fundamentally different. A behavioral perspective should not mean that the emotional experiences of children and their motivational needs can not be considered. Thus, important developmental concepts that relate to complex experiences, such as attachment or emotion regulation, are in serious need of integration with the powerful principles of applied behavior analysis.

The design of an effective intervention for children within ABA requires appreciation of social expectations (what behaviors will be reinforced within the child's natural environment?). Arbitrary social criteria determine whether a behavior will be tolerated and reinforced or disapproved of and punished within a system where adults have most of the control. For children this means that the contingencies they experience at home, in their local community, and at school are likely to be different. A child's adaptation to a classroom environment will at least partially be a function of the synchrony between home and school contingencies or, if very discrepant, mediated by general behaviors such as the child's ability to discriminate that different contingencies are in effect.

Planned behavioral interventions cannot be delivered according to a formula. This truism results in the best ABA programs being highly individualistic forms of treatment that must be evaluated through the monitoring of outcomes. Recently the need to also monitor unintended outcomes has become clear. The empirical justification for a given intervention plan is not based on some prior assumption that a standardized method or intervention protocol will be effective. It comes from whether a valid assessment has been carried out, whether principles are being appropriately applied, and whether expected results are being achieved. At one level, ABA interpretations of problems are nonjudgmental. A given environment is neither good nor bad, healthy or unhealthy, right or wrong, and although in this essay some behaviors have been labeled inappropriate or undesirable, behavior analysis is particularly clear in defining these as social judgments, not intrinsic properties of any behavior. At another level, however, ABA cannot escape the need to make value judgments about intervention strategies: Simply because some procedure is possible or empirically validated in the experimental context, it does not mean it is desirable in the applied context. The ABA field now widely accepts that there is an ethical and professional responsibility to design interventions that are socially acceptable, safe, and do not have unknown side effects.

—*Ian M. Evans*

See also: *Applied Behavior Analysis (Vols. I & III), Azrin, Nathan H. (Vols. I & III), Functional Analysis (Vol. II), Goldiamond, Israel (Vols. I & III), Operant Conditioning (Vols. I, II, & III), Single-Case Research (Vols. I & III), Skinner, Burrhus Frederic (Vols. I, II, & III)*

Suggested Readings

Baer, D. M., Wolf, M. M., & Risley, T. R. (1968). Some current dimensions of applied behavior analysis. *Journal of Applied Behavior Analysis, 1,* 91–97.

Kazdin, A. E. (2001). *Behavior modification in applied settings* (6th ed.). Belmont, CA: Wadsworth.

Malott, R. W., Whaley, D. L., & Malott, M. E. (1991). *Elementary principles of behavior* (2nd ed.). Englewood Cliffs, NJ: Prentice Hall.

Scotti, J. R., & Meyer, L. H. (1999). *Behavioral intervention: Principles, models, and practices.* Baltimore: Paul H. Brookes.

Sidman, M. (1960). *Tactics of scientific research.* New York: Basic Books.

Skinner, B. F. (1953). *Science and human behavior.* New York: Macmillan.

Sulzer-Azaroff, B., & Mayer, G. R. (1991). *Behavior analysis for lasting change.* Fort Worth, TX: Holt, Rinehart, & Winston.

AROMATIC AMMONIA

Response-contingent aromatic ammonia is an aversive olfactory treatment procedure that has been shown to be effective in suppressing aggressive and self-injurious behaviors that have proven unresponsive to other approaches. The underlying principle for its efficacy is the punishing effect of the ammonia's noxious odor. Treatment involves applying a crushed capsule of 0.33 cc alcohol 36% (Burroughs Wellcome Co.) or a small handheld vial of ammonia under the child's nose immediately after the child exhibits the undesirable response. Exposure is limited to approximately 3 seconds or until the child exhibits evidence of inhalation, for example, coughing. Medical consultations are necessary before and during treatment to safeguard against possible side effects, including mucous membrane irritation and allergic reactions. The therapist may need to hold the child's head securely during administrations to help ensure inhalation and to prevent the child from coming in direct contact with the ammonia. Using a vial may be preferred over the capsule to further reduce the risk of the child and others coming in direct contact with any ammonia residue after the capsule is broken. The capsules or vial should be readily available for immediate contingent exposure. In addition, the therapist should conceal the ammonia in the palm of his or her hand so that the child is unable to discriminate when punishment contingencies are in effect. Administrations can begin during designated treatment sessions with the child or during the child's normal routine. Treatment may be restricted to as few as two 10-minute sessions a day with successful results. Restricted administrations should be considered for cases exhibiting high rates of the target behavior because of the risks associated with excessive and prolonged exposure. As the response rate declines, the relative frequency of the contingency is increased so that every response is punished. If longer durations of administrations are necessary to achieve effects, then this may indicate a poor prognosis for complete suppression, and a revised treatment plan or other clinical options may be considered.

Research on treatment outcome has revealed rapid and sustainable suppression of self-injurious behaviors with developmentally delayed children. Complete elimination of the response has been achieved but is not always observed. Treatment gains tend to be situation specific, thus requiring that contingencies be applied across settings and caretakers. In addition to being effective alone, ammonia is effective in strengthening the effects of milder forms of aversive treatment such as facial screening and in reducing the recovery of target behaviors when treatment is discontinued. Although observed to be effective primarily with developmentally delayed children in institutionalized

settings, aromatic ammonia has been successfully applied in laboratory settings with nondevelopmentally delayed cases. In addition to being effective, aromatic ammonia is simple to use, easy to obtain, economical, portable, concealable, can be implemented quickly without removing the child from the immediate context in which the response occurs, and is more acceptable than more intense aversive procedures such as shock. Family members, teachers, and other caregivers can be trained easily in the procedure. However, as with all aversive procedures, contingent ammonia should only be used when positive reinforcement and less restrictive approaches such as differential reinforcement of other behavior (DRO), overcorrection, and time-out have been tried unsuccessfully. Approval from ethical boards and the family is needed before initiating treatment, and staff/child care workers should agree that the aversive procedure is less harmful than providing no treatment at all because of the dangerousness of the child's behavior problem either to the child or others.

—*Laura Stoppelbein and Leilani Greening*

See also: *Aversion Relief (Vols. I & III), Classical Conditioning (Vols. I, II, & III), Extinction and Habituation (Vol. III), Punishment (Vol. II)*

Suggested Readings

Bell, K. E., & Stein, D. M. (1992). Behavioral treatments for pica: A review of empirical studies. *International Journal of Eating Disorders, 11,* 377–389.

Rojahn, J., McGonigle, J. J., Curcio, C., & Dixon, M. J. (1987). Suppression of pica by water mist and aromatic ammonia: A comparative analysis. *Behavior Modification, 11,* 65–74.

ASSERTIVENESS TRAINING

DESCRIPTION OF THE STRATEGY

Assertiveness can be defined in a variety of ways, though perhaps most simply as the honest and appropriate expression of one's thoughts, feelings, and beliefs without violating the rights of others. As such, assertiveness training (AT) is a cognitive-behavioral technique that has been primarily used to teach children appropriate ways to express anger. AT is also often used to help children overcome individual forms of inhibited expression, including difficulty making requests or expressing opinions. AT is often used as a part of a broader treatment program (e.g., for impulsive or anxious children) and has also been used in bullying programs in schools and other settings.

Used alone or in conjunction with other forms of treatment, AT is based on the assumption that children have personal rights and responsibilities, including, for example, the right to express their feelings and the responsibility to behave in a way that does not violate the rights of others. The child is taught alternate responses to situations that have previously resulted in aggressive or unassertive behaviors. The first step in AT involves increasing the child's awareness of his or her personal rights and responsibilities toward others. For example, children learn that they have the right to be safe and not be hurt, to make mistakes, to experience and express their feelings, to be treated with respect, to say no to others and not feel guilty, to change their minds, and to ask for what they need. Children also learn that they have responsibilities, such as to treat others with respect, to allow others to make mistakes, and to allow others to have ideas and opinions that differ from their own.

The next step in AT is to learn how to exercise these rights and responsibilities in a nonaggressive and nonpassive manner. Paying attention to both verbal and nonverbal behavior, children are taught to distinguish between aggressive, passive, and assertive responses. The child first develops proficiency in identifying the different responses. With repeated rehearsal and subsequent feedback from the therapist (or via video feedback), the child develops competency at responding assertively.

Typically, cognitive restructuring techniques are included in the instruction of assertiveness to address unhelpful beliefs that the child might have, such as "No one will be interested in hearing what I have to say" or "If I don't yell at the other kids, they won't listen to me." Teaching children problem solving may also be a necessary part of AT, to enable children to consider alternative ways of managing a situation.

AT includes a range of specific techniques used to promote behavior change: direct instruction of the skill, modeling, and behavior rehearsal. The skills can be refined through self-evaluation, self-monitoring, homework assignments, naturalist experiments, therapist or video feedback, and reinforcement. Structured role plays can be employed to create opportunities for

modeling and behavior rehearsal. In a role play, the therapist and child act out scenarios to practice the child's newly acquired skills in increasingly difficult situations. Once a level of proficiency is acquired by the child, assertiveness skills can be practiced within real contexts, beginning with less stressful situations to optimize successful outcomes, then continuing with increasingly stressful situations. Practice between sessions (i.e., homework) is assigned to foster generalization of treatment effects to the real world.

RESEARCH BASIS

Through numerous case studies and controlled trials, AT has been found to be effective in increasing assertive behavior, decreasing aggressive behavior and anxiety, as well as improving self-esteem and self-concept. The outcomes of AT on the adaptive social functioning of children and adolescents are also encouraging: children who receive AT have demonstrated improvements in school behavior, popularity, and academic achievement.

Research suggests that utilizing a combination of training techniques to teach assertiveness produces the best outcome. The efficacy of providing assertiveness education is enhanced with the inclusion of training techniques such as behavioral rehearsal, feedback, and modeling (overt and covert). With respect to modeling, studies have shown that covert modeling, that is, having the child imagine someone else acting assertively in situations, has been as effective as overt modeling. Research has also suggested that models perceived to be similar to the observer (e.g., in age and competence) may enhance learning. Therefore, using models (live or video/audio) that are similar in age to the child and have similar competence levels may improve the efficacy of AT. This is one argument for running AT in a group format. Although both individual and group format have been shown to produce good outcomes, there are many advantages to the group format, as it provides multiple opportunities for rehearsal and modeling with same-aged peers. Finally, there has been some evidence suggesting that observing a coping model produces better learning and self-efficacy then observing a mastery model. That is, a therapist presenting a mastery model (completes the task perfectly) may result in poorer outcomes than a therapist presenting a coping model (performs the task while handling difficulties that arise).

RELEVANT TARGET POPULATIONS AND EXCEPTIONS

The rationale for AT is based on a social skills deficit model, that is, the child does not possess the skills to be appropriately assertive. However, some children who do not act assertively may do so not because of a skills deficit but instead because their emotions (anxiety, depression, or anger) play a role in preventing the expression of appropriate feelings and adaptive acts. When this is the case, an intervention that focuses on anxiety, depression, or anger management is the preferred treatment option. For many children, however, the lack of assertiveness may come about as a combination of emotional difficulties and a skills deficit. AT is recommended for children with a skills deficit when it occurs alone or with emotional difficulties.

AT has been successfully used with a wide range of child problems and disorders, including school-related stress, anxiety, depression, autism, aggression, eating disorders, and substance abuse. AT has also gained popularity as an intervention for the reduction of bullying in schools for both the victims and aggressors of such behaviors. It has been shown to improve the self-esteem and coping skills of children who have been sexually abused and children going through a parental divorce. Programs for specialized populations, such as children with disabilities, have also been shown to enhance social efficacy and interpersonal skills. AT has been employed in programs for children with communication impairments (speech, visual, and hearing), asthma, diabetes, and spinal cord injuries. AT has also been found to be more pertinent in improving the social functioning of children with physical impairments (e.g., cleft palate) than has physical rehabilitation.

COMPLICATIONS

Some children, particularly anxious or depressed children, may fear the consequences of employing their assertiveness skills. Children may fear they will be rejected by others if they stand up for themselves. Aggressive children may fear that if they act assertively, they will be perceived as weak. In these instances, cognitive restructuring may prove useful. The therapist may also encourage the child to test out the child's belief by using new skills and evaluating the actual consequences of acting assertively.

Changes in the child's assertiveness may come as a surprise to others in the child's environment. It is possible that a previously unassertive child may be perceived as aggressive when he or she employs more assertive behavior. While it may be important to inform family members to expect some changes in the child's behavior, it is also important to inform the child that the child is not responsible for the way in which others respond to his or her assertiveness. Reinforcing the child's right to present his or her opinions in an assertive way and restructuring beliefs regarding the consequences of being perceived as aggressive may prove beneficial.

AT is reliant upon a Western ideal and is therefore not necessarily appropriate with all ethnic groups. For some cultural groups, assertive behavior, based on the definition provided here, may be perceived as aggressive and inappropriate when directed toward older or more powerful members of society. While AT has its basis on a Western (Euro-American) perspective of social competence, the extent to which this bias is perpetuated does, however, vary, depending on individual therapists' sensitivity to diverse perspectives.

CASE EXAMPLE

"Mira," a 14-year-old girl, reported a number of social situations in which she experienced moderate to severe anxiety. These situations included answering questions in class, making conversations with other kids at lunchtime, and doing class presentations. Mira and her parents reported that she does not like being the center of attention and so avoids many social situations. She has only a few friends with which she feels comfortable and rarely goes out with these friends outside of school. Mira's parents described her as a shy and sensitive girl. During therapy, Mira was taught a number of skills to manage her social anxiety and began to face a number of situations that she had been avoiding. Mira was working through a gradual exposure hierarchy of her social fears.

It became clear during the exposure component of the treatment program that Mira was experiencing difficulties with one of the other girls in her English class. The girl in her class had asked to borrow one of her favorite markers. Mira had loaned the marker to her friend but the friend had not returned it. Mira was very upset about the marker and angry that it had not been returned. Mira did not feel comfortable asking for it back. The therapist had noticed a pattern of unassertive behavior with Mira and noticed also in therapy that she was very eager to please the therapist and did not like to make requests. Mira and the therapist agreed that the issue with the marker provided a good opportunity to learn a new skill—assertiveness—to assist Mira in working through her exposure hierarchy and improve her confidence. In previous sessions, the therapist had also included a social skills training component to the therapy. Mira had begun to work on specific social skills, including maintaining eye contact, using a loud, confident voice, standing up straight, and keeping her hands relaxed beside her body (rather than fiddling with her hands).

To begin, the therapist described Mira's rights and responsibilities. They constructed a poster of Mira's rights and responsibilities that she could put up on her bedroom wall. The poster included the following: Mira had the right to express her feelings and opinions, to have her opinions heard by others, and the responsibility to listen to other people's opinions and treat others with respect. Second, the therapist provided an overview of the difference between passive, assertive, and aggressive responses. The therapist made use of a number of examples from Mira's life to demonstrate these three response styles. For example, the therapist used an example where three children were hurt by something that their friend had said about them behind their back. Passive Patricia responded by becoming really upset and cried. She decided not to talk about it with her friend at all. Aggressive Angela responded by shouting in a nasty tone of voice, "I hate you. I don't want to be your friend anymore. I am going to tell everyone something nasty about you!" Assertive Ailsa responded by confidently and calmly saying, "I feel hurt by what you said to me. I wish you had talked to me about it first and then maybe we could have worked it out."

The therapist acted out each of these three responses in a role play, asking Mira to identify the three different response styles. The therapist then invited Mira to participate in the role plays, first of all to play the friend and then to play the roles of Patricia, Angela, and Ailsa. The therapist provided feedback and positive reinforcement to Mira regarding her use of assertiveness, aggression, and passivity. Mira was asked to keep track of her assertive and unassertive responses during the week on a monitoring form for homework. From her homework it was clear that Mira was frequently passive with her friends and teachers at school.

In the next session, the therapist and Mira decided to act out increasingly difficult situations to practice her assertiveness. This time Mira was encouraged to remember her social skills (eye contact, not fiddling, strong voice, good posture) when she practiced the assertive responses. After a couple of practices, the therapist and Mira decided to videotape the role plays to assist in providing feedback. The therapist went first, modeling an assertive response to the situation. The therapist made sure to include a number of obstacles to overcome, such as feeling really nervous and wanting to get out of the situation. Mira and the therapist then looked at the recording, providing both positive feedback and constructive criticism. The therapist modeled the situation again, this time integrating the feedback into the role play. Next, it was Mira's turn to act out the scenario with the camera. When they watched the recording of Mira's role play, the therapist provided positive feedback and constructive criticism. Mira was improving in regard to her use of assertive statements and her eye contact but was having difficulties using a strong voice and standing up straight without fiddling with her hands. Mira and the therapist rehearsed the scenario again so that Mira could focus on her body language and her voice quality.

After a week of continued practice at home, Mira felt ready to practice her assertiveness skills in real-life situations. In particular, Mira was keen to ask her friend to return her favorite marker. The therapist discussed any fears or worries Mira might have about putting the skills into practice. Mira revealed that she was not sure what she would say if her friend ignored her or was nasty in return. The therapist and Mira together tackled each of these thoughts. First of all, they discussed what she was concerned would happen if her friend ignored her or was nasty. Mira replied that she believed this would mean her friend did not like her or did not care about her. Mira and the therapist were able to generate evidence for these thoughts: It was more likely that her friend would just return the marker rather than ignore her; her friend was not a nasty person; Mira recalled other occasions when friends had asked for things back and nothing bad had happened. Mira considered the worse case scenario: What if she deliberately ignored her or become nasty, what would happen then? First, if this was to happen, there might be many other reasons that her friend was being nasty other than because she did not like Mira. For example, Mira's friend could have had a fight with someone else or she could have lost the marker and felt guilty about it. But, worst case scenario, if she really did not like Mira anymore, although Mira would feel hurt, she had other friends with which she could play, and it was not the end of the world if this one girl did not like her.

The therapist and child brainstormed all the things she could say to herself and all the things she could do that could help her feel less anxious in the situation, such as doing a lot of practice beforehand, taking a friend with her, making sure she goes up to her friend when she was not too busy with something else, and reminding herself that she can handle this. Mira and the therapist rehearsed the scenario a number of times in the session. The following week Mira bravely approached her friend and asked for her marker back. Her friend said "Oh yeah, sure. I forgot I had it. I will bring it tomorrow." The friend forgot to bring it in the next day, so Mira had the opportunity to ask for her marker again. Mira was pleased she was able to face her fears and act assertively. Mira continued to apply her assertiveness skills and face her fears in increasingly anxiety-provoking situations.

—Jennifer L. Hudson, Katy I. Vidler,
Elizabeth Seeley Wait, and Nataly Bovopoulos

See also: *Behavioral Marital Therapy (Vols. I & III), Behavioral Treatment for Aggression in Couples (Vol. III), Social and Interpersonal Skills Training (Vol. II), Social Competence Treatment: Externalizing Disorders (Vol. II), Social Effectiveness Training (Vols. I & III), Social Skills Training (Vols. I & III)*

Suggested Readings

Lange, A. J., & Jakubowski, P. (1976). *Responsible assertive behavior.* Champaign, IL: Research Press.

Nelson, W. M., III & Finch, A. J., Jr. (1996). Managing anger in youth: A cognitive-behavioral intervention approach. In P. C. Kendall (Ed.), *Child and adolescent therapy: Cognitive-behavioral procedures* (2nd ed.). New York: Guilford Press.

Rapee, R. M., Wignall, A., Hudson, J. L., & Schniering, C. A. (2000). *Evidence-based treatment of child and adolescent anxiety disorders.* Oakland, CA: New Harbinger.

Rakos, R. F. (1991). *Assertive behavior: Theory, research and training.* London: Routledge.

ATTENTION TRAINING PROCEDURES

DESCRIPTION OF THE STRATEGY

Children with developmental disabilities often have difficulties attending to important features of environmental stimuli. These attentional deficits are most keenly experienced during preacademic and academic skills teaching for some children. For example, a child may show difficulties distinguishing between the printed words *bat* and *cat* because he or she fails to attend to the first letter of each of the words. In this example, the beginning letters can be regarded as the critical, relevant, or distinctive features of the two stimuli, as it is based on those letters that a distinction between the two words can be drawn. A similar difficulty is when the child attends to only a restricted number of relevant stimulus features, such as overattending to a person's eyeglasses and subsequently failing to recognize the person without his or her eyeglasses. Failures to attend to relevant features of stimuli can impede a child's progress in acquiring any number of rudimentary scholastic and daily living skills.

Attending to only a restricted number of relevant stimulus features, or stimulus overselectivity, is a common barrier for children with autism. Stimulus overselectivity may in part account for several learning deficits that children with autism often exhibit. First, overselectivity may account for the difficulties that some children with autism have in social situations where the child must attend to many important social cues in order for the social interaction to be successful (i.e., the other person's facial expression, eye contact, gestures, speech inflection, pitch, volume, etc., and the particular situation). Second, stimulus overselectivity may contribute to a child's failure to generalize new skills to novel settings where those cues that were selectively attended to during training are absent. Third, stimulus overselectivity may explain the limitations some children have when external prompts (i.e., gestures or physical guidance) are used to facilitate skill acquisition, as the child may selectively attend to the prompt and not the relevant features of the training stimuli. Children with autism, mental retardation, and other developmental disabilities, as well as young typically developing children, have been shown to demonstrate attentional deficits such as those described. Although such failures in stimulus control are often described in terms of attentional failures, a behavior analytic account of these and other learning difficulties assumes that the source of the difficulties is the learning environment that has been arranged for the child. The challenge, then, is for the child's environment to be arranged in such a way that the critical features of stimuli are identified and enhanced.

Several attention training procedures fall under the rubric of *within-stimulus prompting*. Within-stimulus prompting involves enhancing the critical features of a training stimulus so that a prompt is presented *within* that critical feature. In other words, an inherent characteristic of the stimulus itself is magnified, and as the child's responding comes under discriminative control, the prompt is faded. Within-stimulus prompting requires that physical modifications are made to the training stimuli. For example, in teaching a child to discriminate between the printed words *bat* and *cat*, the critical features of the stimuli might be enhanced by enlarging the beginning letter of each of the two words. As the child's accuracy in discriminating between the two words improves, the size of the two letters is gradually reduced across successive trials, until the letters in each word are all the same size. This is known as size fading. Another possibility is to exaggerate the intensity of the first letter of each of the words. The beginning letter of each word might be prepared in a dark, heavy font relative to the other letters of each word. As the child's accuracy improves, the intensity of the two letters is gradually reduced across successive trials, until all the letters are of the same intensity. This is known as intensity fading. Within-stimulus prompts are effective in teaching children who show attentional deficits such as overselective responding because the prompt cannot distract their attention from the critical feature of the stimulus; the prompt *is* the critical feature.

Other attention training procedures fall under the rubric of *extra-stimulus prompting*. Extra-stimulus prompts are prompts that are presented external to the training stimulus so as to magnify its relevant feature or features. The use of some but not all extra-stimulus prompting procedures requires that physical modifications are made to the training stimulus. For example, in teaching a child to discriminate between road signs, making the shapes of different representations of road signs more salient is likely to improve the child's discrimination. One possibility would be to superimpose a brightly colored outline surrounding the perimeter of each sign, and as the child's accuracy in identifying the road signs improves, the size of the outline is gradually reduced across successive trials until the child can identify the road signs in its absence. In the word discrimination task described previously, examples of extra-stimulus prompts would involve underlining the first letter of the word or embedding a relevant picture behind the first letter of the word (such as embedding a picture of a cat behind the letter *c* in the printed word *cat*) and then gradually eliminating the prompt as the child's accuracy in discriminating between the two words improves. These procedures involve what is known as *superimposition and fading. Superimposition and shaping* strategies also employ extra-stimulus prompts and are similar to superimposition and fading strategies in that a prompt is superimposed upon the training stimulus. However, the configuration of the extra-stimulus prompt is gradually changed so that it ultimately takes the form of the relevant stimulus feature. For example, we might present a picture of a cat in place of the letter *c* in the printed word *cat*. As the child's accuracy in reading the word improves, we gradually change the configuration of the picture so that it eventually is shown as the letter *c*.

The use of extra-stimulus prompts does not always require that physical modifications are made to the training stimuli. Rather, response prompting procedures also make use of extra-stimulus prompts. Physical, positional, gestural, and modeled prompts are all examples of extra-stimulus prompts that can be used to guide correct responding during discrimination tasks. For example, the teacher might physically guide the child to the picture of the correct road sign during a receptive identification discrimination task, or model the correct expressive labeling of a particular road sign.

When extra-stimulus prompts are used, attention must be granted toward the most efficient way to transfer control from the prompt to the relevant feature of the stimulus. This is not a concern with within-stimulus prompting because the prompt itself is a magnification along some dimension of a particular feature of the stimulus. With extra-stimulus prompts, however, it is important to ensure that the prompt facilitates attention to the relevant feature rather than distracting from it. One way to transfer stimulus control from the extra-stimulus prompt to the training stimulus is to introduce a time delay between the instructions that are given to a child and the presentation of prompt. In a graduated time delay procedure, the length of the time delay is gradually increased as the child's accuracy improves, while in a constant time delay procedure, the length of the time delay is held constant. In the road sign discrimination task, a graduated time delay procedure would involve physically guiding the child to the correct sign immediately after instructing the child to "show me the stop sign," for example. As the child's accuracy improves, we would gradually increase the delay between our instructions and the presentation of our physical prompt. The ultimate goal is that eventually we would observe the child anticipating the correct response during the delay between the instructions and our prompt. Other transfer of control procedures include the system of most-to-least prompts, which requires progressing from the most intrusive to the least intrusive prompts as the child's accuracy improves, and the system of least-to-most prompts, which requires progressing from the least intrusive to the most intrusive prompts as the child's accuracy decreases. Regardless of which transfer of control procedure is selected, the most desirable strategy is one in which the prompt facilitates, rather than distracts, the child's attention.

With all of the procedures described so far, the child's attention to the relevant stimulus feature will also be facilitated if known effective reinforcement procedures are used. At each fading step, it is important that correct responses first be reinforced continuously and then intermittently. Then, as the child moves onto the next fading step, correct responses must first be reinforced continuously and then intermittently, and so on. This way, the child's accuracy will be sustained.

RESEARCH BASIS

A large body of results illustrates the efficacy of within-stimulus prompts in teaching children with autism and related disabilities such skills as color, shape, object, and number discriminations, as well as prepositions, body positions, and rudimentary arithmetic and reading skills. Comparisons of within-stimulus and extra-stimulus prompts have shown that children with autism rarely master discrimination tasks when extra-stimulus prompts are used to facilitate attention to the relevant stimulus feature, but do so when within-stimulus prompts are used instead. At the same time, other studies have shown that extra-stimulus prompts do facilitate attention when graduated time delay procedures are used to transfer stimulus control from the prompt to the relevant stimulus feature; in fact, instructional time may be minimal and errors few. Thus, extra-stimulus prompts may be effective when faded along a temporal dimension, but not other dimensions. Extra-stimulus prompts may also be more effective the higher the child's overall level of functioning.

Research has also shown that overselective attention in general is not an inherent characteristic of autism or mental retardation, but can be reduced using behavioral strategies. Exposing a child to discrimination tasks in which reinforcement is provided contingent upon attending to multiple stimulus cues (the color, shape, and lettering of road signs, for example) has been shown to improve overselective responding. Overtraining the child on such tasks may improve the child's attention to important features of stimuli in many situations.

Requiring the child to make specific orienting responses to the relevant stimulus features (such as naming the shape or color of a road sign, for example) has also been shown to facilitate attention.

Transfer of control procedures that favor the child's emission of anticipatory responses has been shown to be most effective in fading extra-stimulus prompts, particularly if the overall percentage of reinforcement is reduced at each fading step.

RELEVANT TARGET POPULATIONS AND EXCEPTIONS

The attention training strategies discussed have been used primarily with individuals with autism, mental retardation, and young children without disabilities. Because some literature suggests that extra-stimulus prompts are most effective with individuals with higher overall levels of functioning, it may be desirable to use within-stimulus prompts with learners with more severely impaired intellectual functioning, such as children with severe or profound mental retardation.

COMPLICATIONS

An important practical issue to consider is the fact that many of the attention training procedures described require the physical modification of training stimuli. Many instructors or therapists will find the preparation of numerous stimuli to be time consuming and laborious. For this reason, procedures that require the prompt to be embedded within or superimposed upon the training stimuli may be effective, but not efficient. Response prompting strategies do not present this same complication. Computer-assisted or computer-based instruction may provide a possible solution to this barrier. Moreover, computer-based discrimination tasks may correct for human error that is an inherent aspect of tabletop discrete trial teaching. Several discrete trial software packages are currently commercially available. Some instructors and therapists may prefer the human contact that the child receives during tabletop teaching. One possibility is to control stimulus presentation and prompt fading by computer but have reinforcer deliveries mediated by the teacher or therapist. It may also be desirable to supplement tabletop teaching with computer-based discrimination training, particularly when teachers or therapists lack the behavioral expertise required to use prompt fading and transfer of control procedures effectively.

CASE ILLUSTRATION

"Cassandra" was a 4-year-old female diagnosed with autism and moderate mental retardation. She exhibited a wide range of attentional deficits, including her inability to recognize others by characteristics other than their hair. If Cassandra's therapist would wear her hair back or her uncle would cover his hair with a hat, for example, Cassandra would have difficulties recognizing each person. Cassandra was receiving in-home behavior therapy for children with autism, which consisted of approximately 10 hours of structured teaching in preacademic skills each week. Cassandra's attentional deficits also presented themselves during the discrimination tasks that she works on with her therapist. Cassandra's therapist programmed tasks that would help facilitate Cassandra's attention to the critical features of stimuli. Recently, Cassandra was working on category matching using pictures. In one problem, reinforcement was provided contingent upon matching a picture of toothpaste to a picture of a toothbrush when pictures of a pencil and a fork are the incorrect options. Likewise, reinforcement was provided contingent upon matching a picture of a dish to the picture of the fork, and a picture of a notebook to the picture of the pencil. Despite the fact that Cassandra could expressively label the objects, her accuracy in matching was at chance levels, for she attended only to the length of the toothbrush, fork, and pencil, which is approximately the same for each object. Thus, Cassandra's failure to discriminate between the stimuli on the basis of their other critical features (i.e., the brush, the fork prongs, the eraser, etc.) impeded her mastery of this task.

Cassandra's therapist's first job was to identify what prompting strategy would facilitate Cassandra's attention without distracting her from the stimuli. The therapist was a college student who didn't have the time or resources to prepare multiple pictures of the same stimuli. Knowing that physical guidance was typically effective with Cassandra, she opted to use extra-stimulus prompts in the form of physical guidance. The therapist was aware that physical prompts are the most intrusive, yet was also aware of the efficacy of physical prompts using graduated time delay procedures to transfer control. The onset of each trial was marked by the therapist's handing Cassandra a picture with the instructions to "match." Immediately after handing the picture to Cassandra, the therapist took her hand and gently guided her to place the picture of the bowl in front of the picture of the fork. She then verbally praised Cassandra for good matching. Ten trials were conducted at this prompt level, with reinforcement delivered immediately for each correct response. After 10 correct (albeit prompted) responses, reinforcement was reduced to every 2 correct (prompted) responses, followed by every 3 correct (prompted) responses. Following two consecutive blocks of 8–9 correct responses, the prompt level was increased from immediate to a 1-second delay: Following the therapist's instructions to "match" on each trial, a 1-second delay preceded the presentation of the physical prompt. During the first block of 10 trials at this prompt level, correct prompted or anticipatory responses were continuously reinforced with verbal praise. During the second block, every two correct prompted or anticipatory responses produced verbal praise, and during the third block, every three correct prompted or anticipatory responses produced verbal praise. Following two consecutive blocks of 8 to 9 correct prompted or anticipatory responses, the prompt level was increased from 1 second to 2 seconds. The same procedure for thinning reinforcement as was used at the prior fading steps was again used. It was at this prompt level that the therapist began to notice that Cassandra regularly anticipated correct responses during the delays preceding the prompts. Following two consecutive blocks of 8 to 9 correct prompted or anticipatory responses, the delay was increased to 3 seconds. At the 1-, 2-, and 3-second prompt levels, the therapist always returned to the previous prompt level should Cassandra make incorrect anticipatory responses on three consecutive trials. While this procedure might seem overly tedious, by the final prompt level Cassandra reliably anticipated correct responses during the delays, to the point where physical prompts were no longer necessary; the task is mastered.

Following mastery, Cassandra continued to work on this and other similar tasks. Her therapist programmed discrimination tasks in which reinforcement was provided contingent upon matching stimuli along more than one dimension. Examples included matching identical objects along the dimensions of color, size, and shape (such as matching a large red triangle to the same when other options include a large red square, a small red triangle, a large blue triangle). Improvements in Cassandra's attention abilities were not only observed during her therapy program but also during everyday naturalistic activities. For example, she began to attend to other critical features of people's appearances rather than overselecting upon their hair.

—*Ruth Anne Rehfeldt*

See also: *Behavioral Assessment (Vols. I, II, & III), Behavior Therapy and Neuropsychology (Vol. III), Private Events (Vol. III)*

Suggested Readings

Green, G. (2001). Behavior analytic instruction for learners with autism: Advances in stimulus control technology. *Focus on Autism and Other Developmental Disabilities, 16,* 72–85.

Koegel, R. L., Dunlap, G., Richman, G. S., & Dyer, K. (1981). The use of specific orienting cues for teaching discrimination tasks. *Analysis and Intervention in Developmental Disabilities, 1,* 187–198.

Lancioni, G. E., & Smeets, P. M. (1986). Procedures and parameters of errorless discrimination training with developmentally impaired individuals. *International Review of Research in Mental Retardation, 14,* 135–164.

Lovaas, O. I., Koegel, R. L., & Schreibman, L. (1979). Stimulus overselectivity in autism: A review of research. *Psychological Bulletin, 86,* 1236–1254.

Matthews, B., Shute, R., & Rees, R. (2001). An analysis of stimulus overselectivity in adults with autism. *Journal of Intellectual & Developmental Disability, 26,* 161–176.

Schreibman, L. (1975). Effects of within-stimulus and extra-stimulus prompting on discrimination learning in autistic children. *Journal of Applied Behavior Analysis, 8,* 91–112.

Schreibman, L., Charlop, M. H., & Koegel, R. L. (1982). Teaching autistic children to use extra-stimulus prompts. *Journal of Experimental Child Psychology, 33,* 475–491.

Touchette, P. E., & Howard, J. S. (1984). Errorless learning: Reinforcement contingencies and stimulus control transfer in delayed prompting. *Journal of Applied Behavior Analysis, 17,* 175–188.

Wolery, M., Gast, D. L., Kirk, K., & Schuster, J. (1988). Fading extra-stimulus prompts with autistic children using time delay. *Education and Treatment of Children, 11,* 29–44.

AVERSIVE CONDITIONING

DESCRIPTION OF THE STRATEGY

Aversive conditioning, also referred to as aversion therapy when applied in clinical settings, involves the systematic pairing of an aversive stimulus with some undesired behavior. For example, taste-aversion conditioning involves the pairing of food ingestion with the subsequent onset of nausea or sickness. As a result of the pairing, the food item is avoided in the future. Similarly, shock may be systematically paired with sexual arousal that arises from some prohibited stimulus (i.e., children), in the hopes that the fear elicited by the shock interferes with the original emotion and behavior elicited by the prohibited stimulus.

Aversive conditioning, a technique arising out of the classical conditioning literature, is typically distinguished from *punishment,* which is a technique arising out of the operant conditioning literature. While both techniques involve the onset of an aversive stimulus following the performance of some behavior, in the case of aversive conditioning, the therapist does not directly modify the client's instrumental behavior by simply providing punishment. Rather, some aspect of the stimulus is paired with aversive sensations such that the resulting emotional state inhibits the instrumental behavior. Referring to the above examples, the allure of the taste of a certain food, or the image of children, is modified as a result of becoming associated with illness or shock, respectively.

Aversive conditioning is sometimes referred to as counterconditioning. That is because the response one makes to a stimulus is reversed, or "countered," as a result of a subsequent pairing. That is, via a process of classical conditioning, a stimulus that initially elicits approach behavior may come to elicit withdrawal. In a classic example, a child who originally approached small furry animals became fearful and avoidant of them as a result of their being repeatedly paired with an aversive noise. When used clinically, the goal of aversive conditioning is to establish (through classical conditioning) an emotional state that will inhibit or counter the initial response.

RESEARCH BASIS

Aversive conditioning derives from laboratory studies in classical conditioning dating back to Pavlov. The most fundamental empirical base for aversive conditioning concerns research on food aversion. This research illustrates several important parameters of aversive conditioning. For instance, the pairing of food and illness may result in subsequent avoidance of the food even if the onset of illness is delayed by several hours. On the other hand, the pairing procedure is ineffective if stimuli such as sounds or lights are substituted for food. Therefore, animals appear to have a biological *preparedness* to respond to pairings between illness and the taste or smell of stimuli, but not between illness and the sight or sound of stimuli. Consistent with these laboratory findings, the clinical effectiveness of aversive conditioning procedures depends, in part, on the relevance or *belongingness* between the conditioned stimulus (e.g., food or shock) and the unconditioned stimulus (e.g., illness).

In addition to being grounded in basic laboratory research, aversive conditioning also has an applied legacy. As will be discussed in the following section, aversive conditioning is a procedure that has been utilized in an attempt to reduce a wide range of undesired behaviors in both adults and children. The procedure has proved to be more effective for certain child-specific problems such as thumb-sucking and bed-wetting, and less effective for many adult-specific problems such as addictive and fetishistic behavior. With respect to adults, the results of early studies were frequently interpreted as supportive of the effectiveness of aversive conditioning procedures. However, longer-term follow-up studies often proved less encouraging. Those studies illustrated that the behavior changes resulting from aversive conditioning procedures in adults frequently do not generalize to nontraining settings and are short-lived when they do. Enthusiasm for aversive conditioning has also been reduced due to ethical concerns about deliberately exposing individuals to aversive stimuli.

RELEVANT TARGET POPULATIONS AND EXCEPTIONS

Aversive conditioning techniques have been used with respect to bed-wetting, thumb-sucking, alcohol consumption, cigarette smoking, fetishistic sexual behaviors, pedophilia, changing sexual orientation, and other unwanted behaviors. A characteristic aversive conditioning technique for a shoe fetish would be to give a shock to the hands or feet or to ingest an emetic drug that produces nausea, upon the presentation of a shoe. In theory, subsequent fetishistic behavior should be reduced owing to the reciprocal inhibition derived from the new learning. Similarly, in the case of children, thumb-sucking has been paired with an aversive stimulus by placing a foul-tasting substance on the child's thumb. The aversive stimulus is administered each time the child places the thumb in the mouth. Via

this pairing, the aversive experience comes to compete with the previously positive experience of thumb-sucking, generating an avoidance of the behavior. Finally, an aversive conditioning technique for quitting smoking is rapid smoking. In this procedure, participants smoke cigarettes as fast as they can, one after the other or multiply, to the point of becoming nauseous or sick. They are encouraged and facilitated to continue smoking in this manner until it is no longer physically possible to do so. In this way, the act of smoking, along with the substances to which one is exposed as a result (e.g., nicotine), are paired with the aversive physical sensations of becoming sick. The pairing of smoking with nausea should reduce the appeal of smoking.

Aversive conditioning techniques have been shown to reduce undesired habitual behavior in ways predicted by theory, and thereby provide patients with a greater degree of control. However, the effects of such procedures are sometimes highly context-specific, meaning that although behavior change occurs in the setting in which training occurred, it may not generalize to other settings. Therefore, an individual exposed to a rapid smoking intervention may avoid smoking in the clinic in which training occurred or in the presence of the therapist, but will show little or no differences in smoking behavior elsewhere. Similarly, an individual may avoid alcohol after having ingested anabuse—a drug that induces nausea and vomiting when paired with alcohol—but only for the time period during which the drug is thought to be in effect. Moreover, alcoholics sometimes refuse to take anabuse in anticipation of subsequently drinking alcohol.

Limited generalization of the conditioned behavior seriously reduces the utility of avoidance conditioning techniques as methods for effective and long-lasting behavior change.

COMPLICATIONS

In addition to problems of generalization discussed above, aversive conditioning techniques raise ethical questions related to the appropriateness of inflicting pain and discomfort on people—even if they consent to it. Because of these concerns, such procedures are often used as a last resort or as "default" treatments to temporarily reduce some aberrant behavior while other methods are used to generate new ways of coping.

When aversive conditioning techniques are used, it is usually within the context of a larger program that incorporates other interventions as well. This is illustrated in a program for eliminating thumb-sucking in children. The application of an aversive-tasting substance to the thumb of the youngster is only one element of a comprehensive intervention that involves (a) educating parents about the habitual rather than purposeful nature of the behavior, (b) increasing the number of brief, positive, nonverbal contacts with the child (i.e., pats on the head, brief back rubs, mussing the hair, etc.) prior to and during the treatment, (c) informing the child of the age inappropriateness of the thumb-sucking and the negative effects on one's teeth and peer relationships that may result from it, and (d) eliminating lectures, reprimands, and reasoning about the issue.

CASE ILLUSTRATION

"Jack," age 7, was taken by his parents to see a psychologist because of nightly bed-wetting. The psychological consultation was prompted by the inconvenience of this behavior and also because of embarrassment experienced by Jack at a recent sleepover with friends. It was clear from the initial consultation that both Jack and his parents were highly motivated to rectify Jack's nighttime enuresis.

Following up on the advice of the psychologist, Jack's parents purchased a battery-operated bell and pad device. When installed, this device produces a loud and aversive sound as soon as a child urinates into the bed, due to the closing of an electrical circuit by the liquid. Consistent with aversive conditioning principles, the bell and pad device results in the pairing of an aversive stimulus (i.e., loud sound) and the onset of urination. In addition to being startled by the loud noise, the procedure also calls for the child to get out of bed, change the sheets, and reset the alarm, following a bed-wetting incident. Within 4 to 12 weeks, children generally become more aware of the sensation of a full bladder and begin to preempt the aversive stimulus by getting up and urinating in the toilet.

In Jack's case, the introduction of the bell and pad system into his bed was welcomed due to his motivation to quit wetting the bed. Initially, however, Jack required help from his parents to fully awaken and get out of bed and change the sheets when the alarm sounded. This ritual was resisted by Jack and taxing to his parents. After 2 weeks with no noticeable change, the family was less enthusiastic about the treatment.

However, after the 5th week, the frequency of Jack's bed-wetting began to decline. On several occasions, Jack was heard by his parents getting up at night to use the toilet and then returning to bed. By the 10th week, Jack had put together a string of 2 weeks of nights in which he did not urinate in the bed. It was then decided that the bell and pad would be removed.

Within 3 days, Jack and his parents were disappointed to find that Jack had urinated in his bed again. Bed-wetting, once again, became frequent. The family was alerted by the psychologist that such a relapse is common, and may be tied to the change in the stimulus condition arising from the removal of the system. That is, Jack's learning had not generalized to an environment in which the bell and pad was not hooked up. Therefore, the alarm system was reinstalled, and within 2 weeks Jack was consistently making it through the night without urinating in his bed. Although upset with the reintroduction of the device, Jack was motivated to "be dry," and consented to an agreement that the system would be removed after 8 consecutive dry nights. At the same time, Jack became less insistent about drinking water or soda after dinner.

After 8 dry days, the bell and pad was removed. Over the next 4 months, Jack had only 2 instances of bed-wetting, and was consistently asking to have sleepovers with friends.

—Paul S. Strand

See also: *Aversion Relief (Vols. I & III), Avoidance Training (Vol. II), Electrical Aversion (Vols. I & III), Operant Conditioning (Vols. I, II, & III)*

Suggested Readings

Christophersen, E. R., & Mortweet. S. L. (1999). *Treatments that work with children.* Washington, D.C.: American Psychological Association.

Mace, C. F., & Roberts, M. L. (1993). Factors affecting selection of behavioral interventions. In J. Reichle & D. P. Wacker (Eds.), *Communicative alternatives to challenging behavior: Integrating functional assessment and intervention strategies* (3rd ed., pp. 113–133). Baltimore, MD: Paul H. Brookes.

McConaghy, N. (1994). Paraphilias and gender identity disorders. In M. Hersen and R. T. Ammerman (Eds.), *Handbook of prescriptive treatments for adults* (pp. 317–346). New York: Plenum.

Pavlov, I. P. (1927). *Conditioned reflexes* (G. V. Anrep, Trans.). London: Oxford University Press.

Rachman, S. J., & Teasdale, J. (1969). *Aversion therapy and behavior disorders: An analysis.* Coral Gables, FL: University of Miami Press.

Wolpe, J. (1958). *Psychotherapy by reciprocal inhibition.* Stanford, CA: Stanford University Press.

Wolpe, J. (1990). *The practice of behavior therapy* (4th ed.). New York: Pergamon.

AVOIDANCE TRAINING

Avoidance training is a procedure for maintaining or increasing the future likelihood of a behavior. In avoidance training, a behavior that delays or cancels the onset of an aversive stimulus becomes more likely to occur in the future (i.e., the behavior is reinforced). The procedure is based on the principle of negative reinforcement. It is similar to escape training, in that negative reinforcement strengthens an operant response. However, the discriminative stimulus (S^D) in avoidance training, which may be neutral or arbitrary, produces its effect through pairing with the aversive stimulus. Over trials, direct exposure to the aversive stimulus is not necessary to maintain avoidance responses.

The avoidance training procedure produces increases in the frequency of the trained behavior within the training context. Because the behavior avoids aversive stimulation, the procedure can be quite durable and long lasting. Quicker, longer-lasting, and more generalized changes in the behavior may occur when avoidance training is combined with positive reinforcement-based procedures. Combining avoidance training with antecedent control procedures has been shown to be more effective than using either procedure alone.

Avoidance training is a basic paradigm of behavioral science and has been well studied in animals as well as humans. The procedure can be effective with children and adults with a wide range of intellectual, medical, and behavioral disorders. It has been used effectively in a variety of clinical populations, including individuals diagnosed with autism and other pervasive developmental disorders, mild to severe mental retardation, disruptive behavior disorders, and schizophrenia. Interventions employing avoidance training have been used as part of procedures to teach behaviors such as work compliance, social interaction skills, eye contact, incontinence care, compliance with medical procedures, and compliance with therapeutic exercise routines.

In a common variation on avoidance training, known as signaled avoidance, a nonaversive or less aversive stimulus is presented a period of time before the aversive stimuli. Displaying the target behavior in the presence of the signal delays or cancels the onset of the aversive stimuli. For example, a relatively quiet alarm may be used to signal the impending onset of a relatively louder alarm. Such a procedure is commonly used as part of a treatment for enuresis in young children.

As with other aversive-based procedures, avoidance has potential negative side effects. Avoidance training may occasion aggression, particularly when artificial aversives are introduced by the trainer. The effects may be less likely to generalize than if positive reinforcement-based procedures are used. Avoidance training also raises ethical concerns due to the use of aversive stimuli, particularly when used with young children or those with severe disabilities.

—*Dennis C. Russo and Jeffrey Skowron*

See also: *Aversion Relief (Vols. I & III), Aversive Conditioning (Vol. II), Electrical Aversion (Vols. I & III), Extinction and Habituation (Vol. III), Operant Conditioning (Vols. I, II, & III)*

Suggested Readings

Cooper, J. O., Heron, T. E., & Heward, W. L. (1987). *Applied behavior analysis.* Upper Saddle River, NJ: Prentice Hall.

White, G. W., Mathews, R. M., & Fawcett, S. B. (1989). Reducing risk of pressure sores: Effects of watch prompts and alarm avoidance on wheelchair push-ups. *Journal of Applied Behavior Analysis, 22,* 287–295.

B

DONALD M. BAER

Donald M. Baer was born on October 25, 1931, in St. Louis, Missouri. He was the second child of Russian immigrants who had not completed high school and who believed that in the United States, education was essential for success. Baer learned in early childhood that school was the most important thing in his life, that he should learn everything that was taught, and that he would go on to college. His mother supervised his homework, but Baer noticed that she and his teachers often disagreed about the correct answers to questions and solutions to problems. His curiosity about how these two sources of great authority could disagree on matters of fact caused him to wonder how people knew what was true and sparked his early interest in scientific proof.

By the age of 15, Baer was bored with high school and longed for the intellectual excitement of a university environment. His greatest dream was to go immediately to the University of Chicago, whose undergraduate college sometimes accepted students who had not finished high school. Baer's father, who earned a modest income as a union organizer, refused. He expected Baer to complete high school and go to the local state university, where the tuition was affordable. Baer's strong-willed mother immediately applied for and was offered three sales jobs in local department stores and announced that the money was needed to send Baer to Chicago. Baer's father could not permit his wife to work, as this violated the middle-class norms of the time (as his mother well knew). On the condition that she decline these offers, he agreed to pay the expenses, and Baer went to Chicago at the age of 16. He deeply loved the University of Chicago and never forgot his parents' sacrifices in sending him there. Within a week, he knew that he wanted to spend the rest of his life in universities. Decades later, he also enjoyed telling people that he did not have a high school diploma.

Baer spent 9 years at the University of Chicago, earning a bachelor's degree and a doctorate. Although he did not study psychology until graduate school, his undergraduate curriculum taught him the differences between experimental and other methods of study, and he soon realized that he was an experimentalist. Leon Nedelski, a physics professor and outstanding undergraduate teacher, was a powerful influence on Baer's later work in psychology, because he taught him experimental logic, operationism, and logical positivism.

As a graduate student, Baer initially studied mathematics but found it dull. One day, a friend who was studying psychology showed Baer the formula for the Weber-Fechner law in his textbook and asked Baer to explain the mathematics. Baer was intrigued and borrowed the book. Until then, he had thought that psychology was primarily Freudian and unscientific. He was surprised to see a mathematical formula in a psychology text and stayed up all night reading this book, amazed to discover the world of experimental psychology, where propositions about how behavior works required strong evidence from controlled experiments. As the sun rose the next morning, Baer finished the book and decided to study experimental psychology.

His new adviser was Jacob Gewirtz, who had been trained in experimental child psychology and Hullian theory and was beginning to study Skinner. Baer and Gewirtz recognized in each other a commitment to experimental logic. Behaviorism quickly became Baer's preferred paradigm, as it was the most empirical and laboratory-based of the paradigms he studied, and its statements were nearly always subject to proof or disproof. With Gewirtz, Baer studied social deprivation as a motivational variable in young children. Gewirtz's colleague, Howard Hunt, ran an operant rat lab, where Baer learned to use a Skinner box. Baer concluded that behavioral principles could be clearly demonstrated in controlled laboratory environments, but that application in the real world, where conditions were less well controlled, would be the acid test of their soundness. Thus, he became interested in the application of behavioral principles as an exercise in proof.

As Baer was nearing completion of his doctorate, the APA convention was held in Chicago. On the last day of the convention, he had returned to the lab and was cleaning rat cages. Gewirtz called, annoyed with Baer for leaving the convention hotel, and said that Dr. Sidney Bijou was there, but he was leaving in 2 hours and wanted to interview Don for a faculty position at the University of Washington. In the August heat, Baer ran back to the hotel, arrived gasping for breath and soaked with sweat, and was introduced to Bijou. To his surprise, he got the job and spent the next 8 years at the University of Washington, where he and several colleagues established a program of research in the experimental analysis of child behavior. He and Bijou also wrote several books articulating a behavior analytic approach to child development. Baer often described Bijou as the perfect senior colleague, who provided him with space, equipment, and freedom and taught him how to function in academia.

In 1965, Baer moved to the University of Kansas, where he and Frances Horowitz began building the Department of Human Development and Family Life. With Mont Wolf and Todd Risley, he cofounded the *Journal of Applied Behavior Analysis* and wrote the seminal article defining this new field as a natural science approach to intervention in problematic behaviors of individual, social, and cultural importance. In the following decades, Baer published widely in the areas of developmental theory, social and language development, developmental disabilities and mental retardation, experimental methods and research design, generalization, self-instruction, creativity, and social policy. He had numerous federal research grants and supervised over 100 doctoral dissertations.

Although Baer said that his work was motivated more by scientific understanding than by a desire to help people, he was committed to applied research and believed that science provides the most promising methods for addressing the problems of humanity. His work, and the work of his former students, has improved the lives of countless children and adults in mental health, educational, medical, and legal settings. Though best known for his research and teaching, on several occasions Baer served as an advocate for disadvantaged members of society. In the late 1970s, he testified in the *Wyatt vs. Stickney* case that persons with severe disabilities could benefit from treatment. In recent years, he served as an expert witness in several lawsuits by parents seeking funding for applied behavior analysis programs for their autistic children. He found this work so important that he charged no fee other than expenses, a fact that appeared to bewilder some of the attorneys who cross-examined him.

Behaviorists are sometimes accused of thinking narrowly, but Baer thought broadly. He was optimistic that a natural science approach to human behavior could solve a wide range of significant problems and improve the quality of life for all members of society. He was bold and creative in exploring new territory, eloquent and articulate in persuading others to join him. He also listened carefully to the ideas of colleagues and students, was receptive to novel applications, and would consider seriously the merits of any argument. This combination of characteristics was perfectly suited to the task of guiding the new field of applied behavior analysis toward maturity. Baer died on April 28, 2002. However, his contributions will be remembered for a long time.

—Ruth A. Baer

See also: *Applied Behavior Analysis (Vols. I, II, & III), Azrin, Nathan H. (Vols. I & III), Behavioral Treatment in Natural Environments (Vols. I & III), Correspondence Training (Vol. II), Operant Conditioning (Vols. I, II, & III) Single Case Research (Vols. I & III)*

Suggested readings

Baer, D. M. (1981). A flight of behavior analysis. *The Behavior Analyst, 4,* 85–91.

Baer, D. M., Wolf, M. M., & Risley, T. R. (1968). Some current dimensions of applied behavior analysis. *Journal of Applied Behavior Analysis, 1,* 91–97.

Bijou, S. W., & Baer, D. M. (1978). *Behavior analysis of child development.* Englewood Cliffs, NJ: Prentice Hall.

BEAT THE BUZZER

DESCRIPTION OF THE STRATEGY

Beat the Buzzer is a simple contingency management procedure most frequently used to reduce morning dawdling in children and decrease conflict between children and their parents. Beat the Buzzer involves setting a timer for a reasonable time limit by which the child must complete a set list of responsibilities. The night before implementing the program, the parent must explain the procedure to the child and make a list of duties the child is expected to complete in the morning before leaving the home. Typical duties include getting dressed, eating breakfast, and brushing teeth. The list is posted in a location the child can easily reference, such as on the refrigerator door or bathroom mirror. Next, the parent explains that a timer will be set each morning and that the child must have completed all duties and be ready to leave before the timer rings. The parent also explains what will happen if the child does or does not complete all duties on the list prior to this time and encourages the child to "beat the buzzer."

The standard procedure indicates that if the child is ready on time or earlier (i.e., beats the buzzer), he or she is permitted to stay up 30 minutes past the usual bedtime that evening. For each minute or portion of a minute the child is late, he or she loses 30 minutes of television time that afternoon (younger child) or is put to bed 30 minutes early (older children). So a child who is 61 seconds late would lose an hour of television or go to bed an hour earlier that night.

When the child wakes up in the morning, the parent sets the timer for a specific time. The child is responsible for beating the buzzer, and the parent is only permitted to remind the child once of any particular duty. Arguing with the child is strictly prohibited.

A critical feature of this procedure is that parents adhere to stated consequences. Children who are not ready on time must lose the stated privilege (e.g., television time) and not access any other enjoyable activities during that time period. (Although one study has shown that children can successfully beat the buzzer without systematic consequences, it is important to note that in that particular study, *no consequences* were ever set forth for beating the buzzer.)

This technique has typically been used to help children learn to get ready on time in the morning with minimal parent-child conflict. However, it has also been used to reduce dawdling at cleanup time in a kindergarten classroom. It is conceivable that the procedure could be adapted for use at other problematic times prone to dawdling, such as at bedtime or during chore completion. Furthermore, modifications to the standard procedure, including use of child-selected rewards and token rewards, have been effective.

RESEARCH BASIS

More than 20 years of clinical use and several published research studies back the effectiveness of this procedure. Studies using Beat the Buzzer have consisted of single-case and small *n* studies. This procedure has been shown to reduce time needed to get ready, dawdling, negative parent-child interactions, and parent reminders while subsequently increasing on-time behavior and compliance. Furthermore, treatment gains have been maintained, in some cases, for more than 6 months.

RELEVANT TARGET POPULATIONS AND EXCEPTIONS

Beat the Buzzer has been used successfully with preschool and school-age children as well as with children with developmental disabilities and multiple handicaps. The procedure has also been effective in parents with a history of abusive discipline. In fact, this method has even been successful in reducing cleanup time in a kindergarten classroom *without* providing systematic consequences for beating the buzzer (e.g., no rewards were given or privileges removed). Notably, not only was the procedure effective, but the improvements were maintained for the remainder of the school year.

This procedure can be easily modified to address individual needs. For instance, additional training in task completion may be needed in young children. A picture-based list of tasks can be provided for young children or those with reading difficulties. Children with attentional difficulties can be trained to check off individual tasks as they are completed on a reusable white board. Children with developmental delays or physical handicaps may require physical assistance to complete listed tasks, but may still do so within a time limit and without conflict.

COMPLICATIONS

In general, Beat the Buzzer is a very straightforward, simple, and effective procedure. However, researchers and clinicians have identified a few situations that may complicate implementation of this procedure. For instance, some researchers have suggested that parents may have difficulty accurately tracking exactly how late the child is in completing the list of tasks, correctly calculating time of privilege loss, and making sure lost time is properly enforced. Since some parents may find this confusing, it has been suggested that an all-or-none system be used. For example, if the child were ready on time, the reward would be earned for that day (e.g., permitted to watch television), and if the child were not ready on time, the reward would be lost for that day (e.g., not permitted to watch television).

Another potential problem identified in the literature is the delay between the buzzer and delivery of the consequence. Researchers have raised concerns that some children may fail to beat the buzzer because the consequences are too delayed to motivate a change in their behavior. To address this problem, researchers have suggested immediate delivery of a token reward by placing a sticker or stamp on a chart following completion of each task, which can be traded in for a backup reward upon completion of all tasks.

Clinically, we have found some difficulty using this procedure in households with irregular schedules and limited structure. For instance, in order to use an earlier or later bedtime as a consequence, the child must first have a regular bedtime. In these situations, a general increase in structure or modified procedures may be necessary prior to implementing this procedure.

—*Sara E. Sytsma-Jordan*
and Ronald S. Drabman

See also: *Behavioral Treatment in Natural Environments (Vols. I & III), Good Behavior Game (Vol. II), Positive Reinforcement (Vol. II), Setting Events (Vols. I & III), Reinforcement (Vols. I & III)*

Suggested Readings

Adams, C. D., & Drabman, R. S. (1996). Improving morning interactions: Beat-the-buzzer with a boy having multiple handicaps. *Child & Family Behavior Therapy, 17,* 13–26.

Drabman, R. S., & Creedon, D. L. (1979). Beat the buzzer. *Child Behavior Therapy, 1,* 295–296.

Hudson, A., Vincent, J., Wilks, R., & Drabman, R. (1986). "Beat the Buzzer" for early morning dawdling: Two case illustrations. *Behaviour Change, 2,* 136–142.

Wolfe, D. A., Kelly, J. A., & Drabman, R. S. (1981). "Beat the Buzzer": A method for training an abusive mother to decrease recurrent child conflicts. *Journal of Clinical Child Psychology, 10,* 114–116.

BEHAVIOR MANAGEMENT FOR IMPROVING ACADEMIC AND CLASSROOM BEHAVIOR

Many educational and behavioral interventions have been designed to increase appropriate classroom behavior and academic performance in school-age children. Teachers, psychologists, and other professionals have implemented a number of classroom management techniques to improve students' academic and social behavior. For example, teachers have altered children's behavior through the contingent application of praise, reprimands, rewards, time-out, or withdrawal of privileges. The procedures have been applied to single students in the classroom as well as classwide. Also, students have been trained to implement self-managed interventions by observing, monitoring, evaluating, and/or rewarding their performance of target behavior. Common targets of intervention include on-task, work completion, work accuracy, homework completion, adherence to classroom rules, and following directions. Disruptive behaviors such as talking, being out of a seat, playing with classroom materials, aggression, and destruction of property are also common targets. A very heterogeneous sample of children have been the recipients of behavioral interventions for improving classroom behavior. For example, classroom management procedures have been used with children in preschool through high school as well as those with mental retardation, attention-deficit/hyperactivity disorder (ADHD), learning disabled, emotionally disturbed, and of average intelligence and skills. Treatments have been implemented in regular and special needs classrooms. Interventions have involved modifying setting variables, antecedents, and consequences. Many problems that present at school require intervention outside of the classroom as well. Often parent education and training, pharmacotherapy, and other external resources may be necessary to optimize treatment. Below we review interventions and techniques to be used within the classroom setting to improve classroom behavior and attention as well as academic performance. We begin with a brief review of functional assessment and linking assessment to treatment. Specific classroom interventions are described in two sections: the first will focus on the antecedents to behavior and the second on altering the consequences for behavior.

LINKING TREATMENT TO ASSESSMENT: FUNCTIONAL ASSESSMENT

Assessment of the contingencies maintaining problem behavior should always precede treatment. Assessment may include a combination of academic, observational, and interview measures. A well-established yet contemporary model of assessment whose results directly lead to treatment recommendations is functional assessment. Functional assessment methods attempt to identify the antecedents and consequences that maintain or suppress behavior, in other words, the factors that determine the occurrence or nonoccurrence of a behavior. If conducted prior to treatment, interventions with increased probability of success may be designed. Treatments based on the functions of behavior are more effective and enduring than arbitrarily chosen treatments. These interventions should incorporate naturally occurring contingencies, which gives them a greater likelihood of fitting into the natural classroom.

Functional assessment may include three major components: indirect data, descriptive data, and a functional analysis. Indirect data include interview data and information from rating scales. Indirect data are the easiest to collect, though the least reliable. They are useful for identifying the problems to be further assessed. For example, interviewing the teacher regarding the situations in which the target behavior does or does not occur is a common method for obtaining information about a behavior function using the indirect method. Descriptive data include direct observation and recording of the antecedents and consequences of behavior in the natural environment. They are necessary to look for patterns in the child's behavior. A functional analysis is the experimental manipulation of test conditions in order to determine the function of a target behavior. The common conditions tested are escape, attention, tangibles, and control. That is, some behaviors occur in order for the child to escape a demand, gain attention, or to receive a reward. Functional analyses typically are conducted in analogue settings outside the natural classroom. They are cumbersome and time consuming but offer

the most definitive results as compared to the other components of a functional assessment. A functional analysis is not possible or even necessary for every behavior (single-occurrence behavior) or every child (older elementary student and adolescents). When appropriate, however, the functional analysis can pinpoint the function of the child's misbehavior. The teacher or psychologist is then ready to design an intervention using this information. Children should be taught new ways to achieve the same outcome, for example, raising their hand to get the teacher's attention rather than talking out of turn, or asking for a break to escape a task demand briefly rather than throwing their book across the room.

SETTING AND ANTECEDENT INTERVENTIONS

Setting and antecedent variables are often overlooked in the classroom literature with greater emphasis placed on treatments that alter consequences. However, manipulations of antecedent conditions can be quite effective and usually place emphasis on changing the setting or teacher behavior in order to increase desired classroom behavior, and may serve to prevent behavior problems. For example, the single most important classroom variable related to academic achievement are the amount of time the child spends actively engaged in academic responding. Many classroom settings have very little time set aside for actually practicing academic skills. In addition, increased academic responding and academic achievement are dependent on effective teaching. According to research in the area, effective teaching is focused, has clear goals, provides extensive coverage of content, monitors student performance, asks questions at levels that produce frequent correct responses, and provides immediate and frequent feedback to students. This type of teaching leads to increased academic responding and academic achievement.

A number of environmental variables in the classroom may also be manipulated to act as antecedent control interventions. Desks may be arranged in a number of different configurations to decrease the likelihood of talking, or, alternatively, to increase cooperative learning. Outside noise and distractions such as classroom visitors should be kept to a minimum to avoid disruption. Repetitive tasks should be kept novel to keep the students interested. This may be achieved through a number of creative variations of the same task. Each classroom should have a structured schedule for the school day so that there is very little free time, transitions go smoothly, and students know what they should be doing at all times. The rules of the classroom and responsibilities of the students, both academic and behavioral, should be clearly explained to the children so that there is no confusion. Consequences for misbehavior should also be outlined explicitly.

Antecedent strategies for controlling the classroom are simple ways to optimize effective instruction and reduce the likelihood of behavior problems. These techniques are both time and cost efficient, take little training to implement, and may benefit the entire class rather than target students alone. Few behavioral interventions have focused on altering these variables despite their importance to achievement.

Peer tutoring is another method that can greatly increase engaged time and academic responding. Pairing students and training them to provide feedback and correctives to each other enhances the skills of both the tutor and the tutee. Peer tutoring programs have been designed to teach spelling, math, reading, and other skills for children as young as kindergarten and as advanced as high school.

CONSEQUENCE INTERVENTIONS

No matter how structured and organized a classroom is, there is no way to prevent all disruptive behavior. Each classroom should be outfitted with a number of predetermined consequences to deal with problematic behavior as it arises. Furthermore, many students require increased, salient, and immediate consequences in order to maintain appropriate behavior and attention. For example, children with ADHD often require considerable increased consequences along with medication in order for satisfactory learning to take place.

TEACHER ATTENTION

Teacher attention is an important, naturally occurring, and frequently used consequence that can be effective in increasing appropriate classroom behavior. Teacher attention may be reinforcing or punishing, depending on its effect on behavior. Feedback is one form of teacher attention that has been found to decrease disruptive behavior in ADHD students. Feedback is given to students regarding their classroom behavior at set intervals throughout the day. It is usually delivered verbally in some sort of structured manner such as numerical ratings. A small number of studies have shown that such attention with no additional contingencies may be effective in treating behavior problems. Unfortunately, the literature is limited.

Teacher attention often is delivered in the form of praise. Common forms of praise include a verbal statement, a facial expression such as a smile or wink, and physical contact such as a high five or hug. Verbal praise is most effective when it is specific, sincere, and delivered immediately following the desirable behavior. For example, "Good work" at the end of the school day is far less powerful than "Jenny, I like the way you are working quietly at your desk" while the behavior is occurring. Before implementing praise as a treatment, the effect of the attention should be evaluated to determine its function for the individual student. For example, teacher praise may actually increase rather than reduce disruptive behavior in a middle school student. Praising one or more children in order to reduce the disruptive or disobedient behavior in another child may improve behavior.

Differential reinforcement involves praising desired behavior and ignoring undesired behavior. Differential attention may be delivered in a number of different forms. A child might be praised provided that during a specific time period the rate of the target behavior is less than a specified criteria or not at all. For example, kindergartners might receive praise if they do not leave their seat more than two times during story time. A child may be praised for engaging in a behavior incompatible with the undesirable behavior, rather than the undesirable behavior's absence alone. For example, children may be praised for completing work accurately instead of walking away from their desk without permission. A second grade student may be praised for playing appropriately with a toy if the target behavior is throwing toys. Most commonly in a natural classroom setting, a teacher will deliver praise contingent upon any positive behaviors, not necessarily those incompatible with the problem behavior. For example, a teacher may praise a student for remaining on task in order to decrease disruptive behavior.

The pace of teacher attention has been the focus of a number of studies. Results suggest that a large amount of praise delivered earlier in the school day is more effective than evenly distributing attention throughout the day.

Beat the Buzzer is a technique that has been used to decrease the time between a teacher's request and a student's response. Often, children dawdle during classroom transition, for example, on the way inside from recess or when getting books out of their desks. Beat the Buzzer requires that the teacher set a timer and the children complete the request or transition before the buzzer goes off. Praise is then delivered upon completion of the task within the set time period.

There are, however, a number of problems with using teacher attention as a consequence strategy for classroom management. As mentioned earlier, some students may not find teacher praise to be reinforcing. Also, there is a growing body of research that suggests that positive consequences alone are not sufficient to control behavior, especially in children with ADHD. Most studies show that both positive and negative consequences combined in an intervention are far superior to praise alone.

Teachers often employ negative attention in the form of reprimands. Research has indicated that reprimands can be very effective in reducing a wide range of disruptive behaviors, if delivered properly. Calm, firm, consistent reprimands appear to be superior to emotionally delivered or delayed reprimands. A teacher's reprimand is more effective if eye contact is established in close proximity to the child. Touching the child's shoulder may also increase the student's attention and responsiveness to the corrective feedback. Short, specific reprimands appear to be more effective than longer ones. Reprimands have consistently been found to be effective regardless of the presence or quality of positive consequences in some samples of children. A series of studies by Susan O'Leary demonstrated the importance of reprimands and other negative consequences to maintaining the appropriate behavior of ADHD children. Reprimands, appropriately delivered, are important to effective classroom management and should be included in a comprehensive behavior management program.

ACCELERATIVE PROCEDURES

Research on classroom management generally finds that teacher praise and reprimands are insufficient to maintain appropriate classroom behavior. Generally, additional consequences are necessary for optimal classroom functioning. A variety of rewards have been employed to increase the potency of teacher attention.

For example, teachers have provided a variety of rewards to single or groups of students who performed well in the classroom. A number of studies have shown that academic skills are operants and therefore modified through contingent reinforcement. Academic success may be rewarded with praise, tangibles, or special privileges in the classroom. Even simple, inexpensive, easily delivered rewards increase academic skill acquisition and performance. Teachers may reward middle school students' correct responses during class lectures with candy. Elementary school students may be provided with the opportunity to earn extra recess time after lunch for following classroom rules during the morning.

Rewards often are earned through a variant of a token economy. This involves children earning points or chips based on their performance of desired behavior. The point values for behavior are determined ahead of time. Then children trade in a predetermined number of points or chips in exchange for desired rewards. Token economies have been used with single students or an entire classroom. Dr. William Jenson used a variant of a token economy to promote academic performance. Students connected two numbers on a dot-to-dot figure each time they completed an assignment. Some of the dots were circled and indicated that the students could spin for a reward. Children turned a spinner that landed on unequal pie sections, with each section representing a different reward. More desired rewards were associated with the smallest pie sections.

REDUCTIVE PROCEDURES

As many disruptive behaviors that are seen in the classroom are maintained either by teacher or peer attention, sometimes simply ignoring the misbehavior can help reduce its occurrence. It is important that both teacher and classmates consistently ignore all occurrences of the behavior. Active ignoring is difficult to achieve in a classroom, however, as the target behavior may be too disruptive to learning to ignore. This intervention is not always appropriate, for example, with aggressive behavior.

Time-out refers to a period of time in which students have no positive reinforcement, social or tangible, available to them. A number of studies that have utilized time-out to treat disruptive behavior have enjoyed significant reductions in target behaviors, at times to near zero levels. It has been shown to be effective with ADHD children, both on and off psychostimulant medication. Time-out in the classroom typically requires the child to remain quiet and cooperative throughout the duration of the time-out in order to be released. This process can be time consuming for the teachers, taking their attention away from the other students in the classroom, making time-out an inefficient intervention for punishing misbehavior. It is also ineffective if the behavior being performed by the child is reinforced by escape. If a child's goal in acting out is to escape a task, then time-out as a consequence is actually reinforcing rather than punishing, thus increasing the likelihood that the child will misbehave in such a way in the future.

Time-out may consist of nonexclusion, exclusion, or isolation. Nonexclusion time-out is basically a form of active ignoring. The child is simply denied peer and teacher attention for a set period of time contingent on the misbehavior. Classmates can be trained to move away from the target child in response to inappropriate behavior, therefore removing the possibility of peer reinforcement. Another form of nonexclusion time-out requires that the child move to the edge of the activity immediately after misbehaving, told what he or she did wrong, and told to observe the good behavior of classmates for a set period of time. Exclusion time-out involves removing the child from the activity to a less reinforcing area of the room, for example, a designated time-out chair. Isolation time-out is the contingent removal of a student from the classroom to an isolated room. This is not a preferred form of punishment, as the dangers of abuse are inflated. Rarely is the staff in a school prepared to physically remove children from the class and supervise them appropriately while in isolation. Isolation time-out has been used as a last resort punishment for serious, recurrent behavior problems such as aggression and destruction.

Response cost involves the loss of positive reinforcement (privileges, points, rewards) contingent on misbehavior or failure to meet specified behavioral or academic criteria. Conditioned positive reinforcers may be removed in response to inappropriate behavior. Tokens, smiley faces, points, and colorful slips of paper may be exchanged for backup reinforcers that may vary widely, depending upon the setting. It is important to select the specific reinforcers based on the individual preferences of the students.

A number of studies have shown response cost to be a socially valid treatment, as judged by both parents and teachers. Such treatments are easy to use and highly effective at suppressing behaviors such as rule violation and increasing behaviors such as on-task performance and academic responding. Response cost does not require constant monitoring or recording of behavior by the teacher. As previously mentioned, response cost components are often added to token economies. Response cost procedures have been applied to single students and to entire classrooms.

OVERCORRECTION

Overcorrection is a punishment applied when students misbehave. There are two types of overcorrection, restitution and positive practice. Restitution is having individuals overcorrect the environmental effects of their inappropriate acts. This natural consequence forces children to compensate for inappropriate actions. Examples include cleaning all the desks in the classroom after putting gum on their desks, replacing an entire book if they tore one page, or performing a prosocial act for a classmate they hit. Positive practice requires the individual to repeatedly practice correct forms of the relevant behavior in situations in which the targeted misbehavior commonly occurs. A child may be forced to practice hand-raising during recess after talking out of turn during class, standing in line for 5 extra minutes after skipping ahead, asking for help nicely 10 times after addressing the teacher rudely, or sharing after grabbing a toy from a classmate. Mediational essays and apology letters may be assigned for less physical events such as lying or cheating. The practiced behavior should be topographically similar to the misbehavior in order to prevent the misbehavior from occurring during practice. Positive practice may target academic mistakes as well as behavior problems. Children may be asked to practice misspelled words or incorrect math problems.

Overcorrection consequences should be designed to have the following characteristics. They should be directly related to the misbehavior (require topographically similar responses), which should decrease the likelihood of their being used in a punitive or arbitrary fashion, as well as preventing the misbehavior from reoccurring. The student should be required to use the effort normally required of the appropriately behaving individuals to correct the products of the misbehavior. That is, they should not be allowed to escape what is expected of the others and get off easily. Like all punishments, overcorrection should occur immediately following the infraction. The individual should be instructed and manually guided through the overcorrection with the least intrusive guidance necessary.

These are the general procedures to use when implementing overcorrection. Inform the student of the misbehavior in a neutral tone. Give verbal instructions for the consequences and wait 3 to 5 seconds. If they do not comply, initiate graduated guidance. Terminate guidance when they begin to perform the response on their own.

As briefly mentioned earlier, one specific overcorrection procedure is the mediational essay. Students may be given a written assignment after breaking a rule or behaving disruptively. The essay requires that students verbalize not only their misbehavior and why it was wrong but describe the appropriate behavior they should have been engaged in at the time and why they should behave appropriately in the future. The use of mediational essays has been compared to traditional punish work such as writing lines and copying from textbooks. It seems that the essays are more effective; perhaps it is the act of writing about the behavior and not just the act of writing that makes it a potent punishment.

Directed rehearsal is a term thought to more accurately describe uses of overcorrection with academic problems. Specifically, reviews of the literature led some authors to conclude that when positive practice is applied to errors in spelling, mathematics, reading, or writing, the consequence rarely contained all key components. The term *directed rehearsal* was thought to more accurately label the intervention. Directed rehearsal involves having the student practice the correct version of an academic error a number of times. Like positive practice, the intervention should occur immediately after the mistake is made, if possible. The procedure has been shown to increase spelling accuracy and reading accuracy. For example, directed rehearsal applied to reading errors involves saying the correct version of the word several times and then repeating the entire sentence containing the word. Another version of this procedure, called "cover-copy-compare," has been shown to promote learning of math facts, spelling words, and geography facts.

GROUP CONTINGENCIES

Group contingencies may be based on both reward and response cost systems. They tend to be more efficient than individual contingencies. Peers become an important source of control over each other. There are three types of group contingencies: dependent, interdependent, and independent. In a dependent group contingency, the behavior of an individual or of several select group members earns consequences for the whole group. A target subject whose behavior is especially disruptive is usually selected. This type of intervention is most useful when the child is likely to respond to combined teacher and peer control. Studies have shown group contingencies to be effective in decreasing out-of-seat time, noisy behavior, and noncompliance both in the target students and their classmates, who were not targeted by the intervention. In an interdependent group contingency, the overall behavior of the entire class determines the consequences, that is, group rewards are based on group behavior. This technique is especially useful when disruptive behavior is common in all or most of the group members. Independent group contingencies are similar to a traditional token economy. The same contingencies are applied to each member of the group, but each individual's behavior earns his or her own consequences.

A teacher must make several considerations when deciding whether to implement individual or group consequences. Unfortunately, the literature comparing the two types of interventions is not consistent. One consideration is the behavior to be targeted. An ideal target behavior for group reinforcement is one that is normally under the control of peer influence, for example, behavior that is maintained by peer attention. Another good use of the group contingency is when the individual responsible for the disruption is difficult to pinpoint, for example, a group of students that sit near each other and frequently get in trouble together.

The behavioral goals must also be considered. Group contingencies are particularly useful in promoting social interaction, for example, peer tutoring and situations in which individual motivation is absent. Individuals are less likely to be singled out and teased if they fail. Teachers must be wary, however, as a group contingency should not be implemented in a situation where the predominant form of interaction is negative.

Group contingencies are best used with low-status children who are disruptive in a group whose other members are reasonably well behaved. Group reinforcement for the behavior of the individual child is likely to produce the appropriate peer control without increasing the disruptiveness of the class. High status children, however, may be more disruptive under a group contingency because of their attempts to influence others. The effectiveness of group consequences may also be compromised by children who find it so reinforcing to misbehave that the group is denied rewards.

Once teachers have decided that a group contingency is right for the classroom, the problem behavior, and the target students, they must ensure several things to increase the likelihood of success. Teacher characteristics that positively influence a treatment outcome include enthusiasm and fairness. They must also be sure that they possess a number of highly valued consequences with which to reward the students. Considerations must also be made about practicality, cost of consequences, and time required to implement the group contingency in the classroom. Teachers may run into a problem with some students when peer attention is perceived as more potent than the rewards being offered. Another disadvantage is having to keep extensive records on point totals, which is time consuming.

An all-positive form of group contingency intervention is the token economy. Many classrooms contain token economies designed to reward students for appropriate behavior. Tokens, points, or chips may be earned for good behavior and redeemed for tangible rewards such as candy and prizes or privileges such as extra recess time or playing a special game. Token economies have been established to target a wide range of behaviors. Early studies showed dramatic increases in appropriate behavior with the implementation of token systems in the classroom.

More recently, response cost components have been added to token systems in order to increase their effectiveness. In a response cost lottery, all students begin each day with a designated number of paper slips labeled with his or her name. These slips are removed throughout the day after each instance of rule breaking. At the end of the day, all remaining slips are put in a lottery and one is drawn out. Students are aware that their chance of getting chosen and winning the prize is greater if they have behaved and kept their slips to be entered into the lottery.

HOME-BASED PROCEDURES

Recent literature has begun to stress the importance of parent involvement in the management of the academic and behavioral performance of disruptive children at school. Parents have an important role in their children's education, and home-school communication has been shown to lead to better educational outcomes. One way to facilitate such a relationship is to involve both parent and teacher in home-based interventions for classroom problems. A school-home note is a home-based classroom intervention that allows parents to receive daily feedback of their child's behavior in school. Notes are completed and sent home daily by the teacher. The notes contain information rating the student's performance on that day. Parents are responsible for providing rewards for the child's appropriate behavior. Home-based intervention has many advantages over school-based intervention. School-home notes provide increased communication between parent and teacher and encourage greater parent involvement. School-home notes allow parents to offer powerful reinforcers that may not be available to teachers at school. Also, school-home notes are a quick and simple intervention, making them more likely to be utilized by teachers. The use of the note relieves teachers of the duty to discover effective reinforcers for students and puts the responsibility on the parents of each individual student. The simplicity, ease, and nontime-consuming nature of school-home notes are valuable advantages of this home-based intervention.

General guidelines for the application of school-home notes have been outlined. Parents and teachers should be trained in the use of basic contingency management procedures. Specific target behaviors that are relevant and socially valid should be selected and stated positively. The note should evaluate behavior during several different time intervals throughout the day, giving frequent, time-specific feedback about student performance. Parents, students, and teachers should collaborate when developing performance goals and appropriate reinforcement.

The majority of school-home note interventions require that parents positively reinforce all good notes that are brought home. Typically, parents are not instructed which specific reinforcers to utilize, but common suggestions in the literature include special snacks, TV time, late bedtime, verbal praise, and freedom from chores. The effectiveness of parent-provided positive reinforcement in school-home note interventions has been well documented. Several recent studies suggest that a response cost component would be a beneficial addition to school-home note systems. In this type of school-home note, parents are instructed to reward good notes with positive reinforcement according to a contract that outlines contingencies for reinforcement, just as in an all-positive school-home note. In addition, the response cost component requires that parents provide negative consequences contingent on the loss of response cost points.

SELF-MANAGEMENT TECHNIQUES

Several cognitive-based approaches to controlling disruptive classroom behavior have also been developed, although they are far less supported in the literature than behavioral techniques. These interventions are based on the idea of teaching the child to become his or her own behavior change agent. The major methods for achieving this are through self-monitoring, self-reinforcement, and goal setting. Self-monitoring involves having the student monitor the occurrence of specific behaviors for change. Typically, it is more effective when positive behaviors rather than negative behaviors are monitored. For example, it is considered more effective to monitor students raising their hand before speaking rather than talking without permission. Goal setting requires the students to set goals and evaluate whether goals are achieved. Often children are rewarded for goal achievement, although the use of rewards is not always essential to effectiveness. For example, children have been taught to set goals for how many problems they were to complete within a given period of time and then rewarded for reaching the goal. Self-reinforcement involves the children evaluating whether they behaved appropriately and then to reward themselves based on their determination. Although self-management interventions can be very effective, they work best with students who are motivated to change their behavior and who have a history of self-control and consistently delivered consequences from adults. Also, children must be taught to effectively use the self-management strategies and given feedback on their use of the procedure. Although not always effective, self-management interventions may be particularly useful with motivated, older students and with behaviors that are not within the control of adults.

CONSIDERATIONS

Numerous factors must be considered when implementing a behavior management program for increasing the student's academic performance or classroom behavior. We recommend that a functional assessment be conducted to determine the antecedents and consequences maintaining or suppressing behavior. It is both practical and, in our opinion, ethically important to determine what classroom setting variables or teacher behaviors should be targets of intervention. Keep in mind that academic achievement is the most important classroom behavior and that efforts to maximize academic responding through effective teaching and altering the setting should always be considered. Chosen interventions should be those judged to be socially valid by the student, teacher, and parents. Interventions should be based on socially valid treatment goals and procedures. It may be difficult to target behaviors and use treatment procedures judged to be acceptable to both parents and teachers. For example, teachers tend to emphasize decreasing disruptive behavior, whereas parents tend to emphasize academic behaviors. We recommend including academic behaviors such as work completion and accuracy, despite whatever social behaviors are targeted as improved academic productivity is associated with improvements in classroom behavior.

Although it may seem obvious, children must possess the necessary skills to perform the desired behaviors as to implement the intervention components required of them.

Another important consideration is the inclusion of parents in the intervention. Although many effective classroom management procedures have not involved parent participation, optimal effectiveness is often accomplished by providing parents with information about daily behavior so that they may support the classroom management procedure or be an active participant in the behavior change process. Finally, it is very important to monitor the implementation and effectiveness of any behavioral intervention. To help ensure success, behavioral procedures need to be implemented with integrity and adjusted or replaced if ineffective.

—Mary Lou Kelley and Nichole Jurbergs

See also: *Applied Behavior Analysis (Vols. I, II, & III), Behavioral Treatment in Natural Environments (Vols. I & III), Motor Activity and Behavioral Assessment (Vol. III), Token Economy (Vols. I, II, & III)*

Suggested Readings

Ervin, R. (2002). School based interventions for ADHD. In K. Lane, F. Gresham, & T. O'Shaughnessy (Eds.),

Interventions for students with or at-risk for emotional and behavior disorders. Needham Heights, MA: Allyn & Bacon.

Kelley, M. L. (1990). *School-home notes: Promoting children's classroom success.* New York: Guilford Press.

McKee, W., & Witt, J. (1990). Effective teaching: A review of instructional and environmental variables. In T. Gutkin & C. R. Reynolds (Eds.), *The handbook of school psychology.* New York: John Wiley & Sons.

Noell, G. H. (2003). Functional assessment of school-based concerns. In M. L. Kelley, D. Reitman, and G. H. Noell (Eds.), *Practitioner's guide to empirically based measures of school behavior* (pp. 37–61). New York: Kluwer Academic/Plenum.

Shapiro, E. S. (1996). Interventions for academic problems II: Specific skill areas. In E. Shapiro (Ed.), *Academic skills problems: Direct assessment and intervention* (2nd ed., pp. 146–167). New York: Guilford Press.

BEHAVIOR THERAPY

DESCRIPTION OF THE STRATEGY

The term *behavior therapy* is said to have been coined by Hans Eysenck in 1952. The term, intended as a means of describing therapeutic strategies derived from learning theory, did not come into widespread usage until the late 1950s. Joseph Wolpe later defined behavior therapy as the systematic application of principles derived from learning theory to the rational modification of abnormal or undesirable behavior. In the most inclusive sense, *behavior* refers to both overt (directly observable) and covert (cognition, emotion, and physiological) responses. Behavior therapy encompasses a vast rubric of techniques designed to modify behavior—perhaps the most widely recognized of which being relaxation training, systematic desensitization, extinction, modeling, and contingency management. Although there has been debate among certain authors, therapeutic approaches derived from research on operant as well as respondent (classical) conditioning research are generally included under the label *behavior therapy*.

The publication of B. F. Skinner's *Science and Human Behavior* in 1953 and Joseph Wolpe's *Psychotherapy by Reciprocal Inhibition* in 1958 did much to advance the integration of clinical psychology and learning theory and set the stage for behavior therapy to take hold as a powerful and efficient approach to improving the lives of adults and children evincing all manner of dysfunction. In 1963, the journal *Behaviour, Research, and Therapy* began circulation. The Association for Advancement of Behavior Therapy was formed in 1966 and remains the predominant professional organization within the field.

Behavior therapy differed from earlier psychotherapeutic approaches in its deemphasis on unconscious and/or cognitive processes potentially underlying maladaptive behavior. The medical or "disease" model of psychological symptoms was rejected in favor of functional analysis of antecedents and consequences related to the establishment, maintenance, and generalization of specific behavioral responses. The symptoms of psychological disorders were seen as following the same principles of learning as any adaptive behavior. The influence of the environment on the functioning of the individual was considered paramount. For many, this approach was hailed as a powerful positive force in that sufficient environmental manipulation could lead to profound changes in behavior that previously may have been considered intractable. Behavior therapy emphasizes the setting of clearly defined treatment goals, the objective of the therapist often being to establish specific stimulus-response relationships under which behavior is brought under functional control.

Behavior therapy is a highly individualized approach. Traditional psychotherapeutic approaches often espoused an invariable sequence of treatment, regardless of the specific presenting complaint or individual learning history. Behavior therapy focuses decidedly on the present. The child's behavior is assumed to be maintained by current conditions. The focus is on the child's current environment rather than past conditions to identify factors relevant to the demonstration of problem behavior. Behavior therapy is an action-oriented approach. Necessary changes in the environment are made to produce changes in behavior. Behavior therapy does not rely merely on "talking," that the clients develop "insight," or that the "root cause" of the symptoms be uncovered in order for the client to improve.

A pivotal defining feature of behavior therapy that differentiated it from earlier psychotherapeutic approaches was the emphasis placed on empirical validation. The value of behavior therapy techniques was not drawn merely from theoretical association but from scientific evidence. Behavior therapy is intimately tied to the scientific method.

A cognitive revolution in psychology took place throughout the 1960s–1970s, and the term *cognitive behavior therapy* came into use. Essentially, cognitive behavior therapists were interested in extending therapeutic strategies based on learning theory into the realm of cognitive mediators. Cognitive behaviorists stressed that maladaptive behavior often results from faulty or distorted thinking. They argued that human conditioning is not automatic and direct but is mediated by the individual's verbal and cognitive abilities. The cognitive behavior therapists argued that animal learning models were inadequate for the study of human learning because animal models neglected to address the unique verbal abilities of humans. Cognitive behavior therapists focused on changing an individual's thought processes in order to influence behavior and emotional states. More traditional behavior therapists countered that the cognitive revolution was a retreat to folk psychology, rather than a progressive scientific movement. Philosophical arguments regarding mechanisms and terminology continue to abound. For many therapists in practice, however, the terms *behavior therapy* and *cognitive behavior therapy* are considered synonymous. Clearly, when it comes to the treatment of young children, we must recognize the limits of cognitive strategies. As such, more traditional behavioral approaches tend to hold sway when attempting to modify the behavior of young children with limited verbal ability.

BEHAVIORAL EXCESSES AND DEFICITS

In behavior therapy, the assessment process leads to the identification of specific environment-behavior functional relations. These targets typically can be characterized as either behavioral excesses or behavioral deficits. Excess behaviors consist of exhibiting a certain class of response too frequently, too intensely, or in too many stimulus contexts (with "too" most often defined by the adults in the environment). Behaviors are considered excessive when they occur at a rate or intensity that is maladaptive, in that they ultimately lead to aversive consequences. Examples of excess behavior include tantrumming at bedtime, physical aggression with peers, lying, or stealing.

Behavioral deficits consist of exhibiting a certain class of response too infrequently, at too low intensity, or in too few stimulus contexts, such as a child's failure to learn to read, social withdrawal from peers, failure to do homework, selective mutism, or lack of assertiveness. Again, these deficits are considered to warrant intervention only if they are deemed maladaptive.

The vast majority of child clinical referrals fall in the category of behavioral excesses. Clinical referrals almost invariably are initiated by adults—not children. It is the adults' dissatisfaction—not the child's—that begins the assessment and intervention process. Parents and teachers are far more likely to be dissatisfied by behavioral excesses than by behavioral deficits. The presence of a behavior—especially one that is annoying or destructive—is more readily noticeable than the absence or insufficiency of a behavior. Unfortunately, the disproportionate focus on behavioral excesses leads to a situation in which many children demonstrating behavioral deficits do not receive the professional attention and intervention they need. Most children experiencing mild to moderate levels of anxiety or depression never receive treatment. Only when the difficulties reach the point of behavioral excess (e.g., hand wringing, crying in class, suicidal verbalizations) do many adults notice that a problem exists.

RESPONDENT-BASED APPROACHES

From a respondent or classical conditioning perspective, clinical anxiety results from the association of neutral with nonneutral (fear-inducing) stimuli. The widely cited case of Little Albert illustrates the processes in the respondent conditioning of fear. Although initially unafraid of white, furry animals, Albert acquired fear through a process of repeated pairings of a white rabbit with an unexpected, loud noise, resulting in a startle-and-fear response. Following conditioning of fear to the white rabbit, Albert also became fearful of other furry animals and objects. Generalization of fear may occur to similar stimuli, such that direct conditioning of fear to these secondary stimuli is unnecessary. In general, respondent conditioning is useful for explaining the development of many fears and anxieties. However, a number of criticisms have been noted. For example, anxiety and phobias may develop in the absence of any direct contact with a particular stimulus. Moreover, respondent conditioning assumes, at least in part, that all neutral stimuli have equal potential to become feared through the process of association. This notion of equipotentiality does not address the possibility of a biological predisposition (presumably related to survival mechanisms) toward more ready acquisition of fear of certain stimuli.

The behavioral treatment of fear and anxiety in children dates back to the classic work of Mary Cover

Jones and the elimination of a fear of rabbits in a small boy referred to as "Peter." Treatment consisted of progressive exposure of the rabbit to the child while the child was engaged in a pleasurable response (eating) incompatible with fear. Following treatment, Peter's fear dissipated to the rabbit, as well as to other similar stimuli to which the fear had generalized. The case of Peter is typically presented as an example of "deconditioning" through principles of respondent conditioning.

SYSTEMATIC DESENSITIZATION

Expanding upon the work of Mary Cover Jones, Joseph Wolpe developed a graduated deconditioning technique he termed "systematic desensitization." The rationale for systematic desensitization is that anxiety is a set of conditioned responses that can be unlearned or counterconditioned through associative pairing with anxiety-incompatible stimuli and responses. In systematic desensitization, anxiety-arousing stimuli are gradually and systematically paired (imaginally or in vivo) with cues generated from muscular relaxation or with other competing stimuli such as praise or food. In the initial work with systematic desensitization, imagery was the predominant presentation modality. However, in vivo strategies are becoming increasingly common.

There are three basic steps to conducting systematic desensitization with children: (1) progressive muscle relaxation training, (2) rank ordering of fear and anxiety-producing situations from lowest to highest, and (3) hierarchical presentation of fear stimuli while the child is in a relaxed state. Systematic desensitization has demonstrated success in reducing fear responses for older children and adolescents. Younger children, however, often have trouble obtaining vivid imagery and acquiring the incompatible muscular relaxation responses necessary for systematic desensitization. It is crucial that any attempts at imagery be developmentally appropriate. Furthermore, ancillary strategies such as use of graphically illustrated (e.g., cartoon) workbooks may enhance the effectiveness of relaxation training and deconditioning procedures with young children.

Even though systematic desensitization is widely regarded as an effective treatment for reducing fear responses, considerable disagreement exists regarding the exact mechanism of effect. Systematic desensitization is assumed to work through a process of reciprocal inhibition in which fear (sympathetic arousal) is inhibited by an incompatible response (relaxation). An alternative explanation is that rather than counterconditioning, the effective mechanism in systematic desensitization is extinction. In extinction, repeated pairing of conditioned fear stimuli in the absence of any adverse consequences is said to result in decay of the conditioned response. With sufficient trials, the fear responses are reduced to the point of virtual nonoccurrence and the anxiety is considered extinguished.

EXPOSURE

Exposure-based interventions include flooding (with response prevention) and graduated exposure. These approaches are based on respondent conditioning and the classic extinction paradigm. In general, fearful individuals do not remain in the presence of anxiety-arousing stimuli for a sufficient length of time to allow for extinction to occur in the natural environment. In addition, escape and avoidance behaviors are negatively reinforced by cessation of the aversive fear response. Exposure-based techniques require extended presentation of fear stimuli with concurrent prevention of escape and avoidance behaviors for the extinction of the conditioned responses to occur, thus addressing both components of two-factor theory (discussed below).

Flooding involves sustained exposure (imaginally or in vivo) to fear stimuli. Within the flooding paradigm, the child is required to remain in the presence of the feared stimuli until the fear dissipates. Graduated exposure refers to progressive in vivo exposure to hierarchically presented fear stimuli. Unlike systematic desensitization, stimulus presentation is not accompanied by progressive muscle relaxation. Reinforced practice often is used in conjunction with graduated exposure whereby positive reinforcement is provided for progressively longer exposure to fear stimuli. Graduated exposure generally is considered to be less stressful for the child (and therapist) and thus is often preferred over flooding with younger children.

OPERANT-BASED APPROACHES

From an operant perspective, behavior is learned as a function of its consequences. Accordingly, positive consequences will increase the frequency of a behavior, whereas negative consequences or lack of positive reinforcement will decrease the frequency of a behavior. All behavior is considered subject to contingencies of reinforcement.

Behavioral models of depression emphasize the issue of insufficient positive reinforcement from the environment. Depressed individuals often are seen as lacking adequate social skills necessary for accessing reinforcement from others, resulting in low rates of response-contingent positive reinforcement.

Since depressed children often display deficient ability to deliver positive reinforcement to others, the rate of reciprocal social reinforcement is further diminished—thus a vicious cycle may ensue. Depression also is accompanied by low energy and activity levels, resulting in decreased participation in pleasurable events or activities and diminished capacity to experience pleasure from such activities. The degree to which the child's behavior is followed by contingent reinforcement is assumed to be a critical factor, rather than the total amount of positive experience. This accounts for the fact that noncontingent praise (or delivery of tangible rewards) does not decrease depression. The occurrence of contingent reinforcement is vital. Depression is said to occur when the probability that the child's behavior will be followed by reinforcement is low, and when the probability that the child will be reinforced in the absence of appropriate behavior is high. Such conditions contribute to a reduction in the likelihood of the child engaging in appropriate social behavior.

The operant conditioning paradigm also has been applied to formulations of the development and maintenance of anxiety disorders in youth. All children experience normal, developmentally appropriate fears that are relatively circumscribed, of short duration, and dissipate with time. A range of behaviors, including whining, crying, or attempts to avoid the feared stimulus or situation, may be displayed in response to fears. In an effort to comfort the child, parents inadvertently may reinforce inappropriate behavior on the part of their children, resulting in the development of persistent fear and anxiety. For example, sporadic requests to sleep with the parents can develop into consistent patterns indicative of separation anxiety disorder, parents who order food in restaurants for their adolescents may be reinforcing social anxiety, and allowing a fearful child to stay home from school when he or she complains may lead to serious school refusal behavior. The operant paradigm, similar to the respondent model, cannot explain the development of all fears and anxieties. This is particularly evident in cases where anxieties and phobias persist in the absence of direct reinforcement. Even so, the utility of this approach cannot be understated, especially when considering the role of reinforcement in the maintenance of anxiety.

INTEGRATING RESPONDENT AND OPERANT APPROACHES

Two-factor theory is an integrative approach formulated by O. H. Mowrer that reflects the fact that both respondent and operant conditioning often are involved in the development and maintenance of anxious and avoidant behavior. Two-factor theory states that in the face of an aversive event, the individual experiences increased physiological reactivity and subjective distress. These fear responses then become associated with otherwise neutral stimuli present at the time of the aversive event. Subsequently, fear generalizes to multiple associated stimuli. Escape from, or avoidance of, these conditioned stimuli is negatively reinforced (through removal of the aversive arousal state). For example, in the case of social anxiety, a child may learn to associate social performance situations with increased physiological reactivity (fear). Subsequent avoidance of social performance situations (e.g., public speaking, parties) results in reduction of aversive physiological arousal, which in turn serves to maintain avoidant behavior.

REPRESENTATIVE BEHAVIOR THERAPY TREATMENT PROGRAMS

Philip Kendall and his colleagues have developed a comprehensive cognitive-behavioral protocol for anxious youth. The "Coping Cat" program was designed to teach coping skills to anxious youth. The program is based on the principle that anxious children view the world through a template of threat and behavioral avoidance. Intervention is focused on providing children with new educational experiences to build a more adaptive coping template. Therapists assist children in reconceptualizing anxiety-provoking situations as problems to be solved. Various cognitive-behavioral techniques are used, including relaxation training, imagery, disputation of maladaptive self-talk, problem-solving skills training, and contingency management. Therapists use modeling, role plays, and in vivo exposure to facilitate treatment gains.

Social Effectiveness Therapy for Children

Deborah Beidel and her colleagues have designed a multicomponent behavioral treatment program for children with social anxiety disorder. Social effectiveness therapy is designed to reduce social anxiety, enhance social skill, increase participation in social activities, and improve self-confidence. Components include parent education, social skills training and peer generalization, graduated in vivo exposure, and programmed practice. Strategies used to teach and reinforce appropriate social behavior include instruction, modeling, behavior rehearsal, feedback, and social reinforcement. Social effectiveness therapy for children targets six major topic areas: nonverbal social skills, initiating and maintaining conversations, joining groups of children, friendship establishment and maintenance, positive assertion, and negative assertion. A unique and essential component of the program is the use of formalized peer interaction experiences to assist in the generalization of social skills to situations outside the clinic. Socially skilled child volunteers are recruited from the community to serve as peer facilitators in the peer generalization experiences (developmentally appropriate group recreational activities).

Family Anxiety Management

Family anxiety management, developed by Mark Dadds, Paula Barrett, and their colleagues, is based on behavioral family intervention strategies found effective for the treatment of disruptive behavior disorders in youth. Following the completion of each child therapy session (along the lines as that presented in Kendall's Coping Cat program), the child and parent(s) participate in a family anxiety management session with the therapist. The main goal of the program is to empower parents and children by forming an expert team to overcome anxiety. Parents are trained in reinforcement strategies, with emphasis on differential reinforcement and systematic ignoring of anxious complaints and fearful behavior. Contingency management, communication, and problem-solving strategies are taught in an effort to reduce parent-child conflict and increase cooperation and communication within the family. Family anxiety management has proven to be effective in reducing fear responses—particularly for younger children.

NATURALISTIC INTERVENTION

Behavior therapists stress the importance of intervening in the child's natural environment whenever possible. This philosophy is an outgrowth of the recognition of three basic points: (1) children acquire behavior (adaptive and maladaptive) from their natural environment, (2) behavior remains malleable throughout life, and (3) teaching a child to behave adaptively in a clinic setting does not necessarily produce generalization to natural contexts—settings that often continue to reinforce maladaptive behavior. In recent years, there have been important innovations based on the perspective that intervention should be conducted in the most natural environment feasible. These innovations primarily have been directed at treating conduct problems.

One of the most exciting innovations has been the development of the teaching-family model, used at Boys' Town (a renowned leader in the treatment of severe conduct problems in youth). The model is enacted in a setting that resembles a natural home environment. A maximum of eight youth reside in each home with "teaching parents" who work 24 hours a day, 7 days a week. Teaching parents receive intensive training in which they must be certified in key skills before taking responsibility for youth. After the teaching parents begin working with the children, they receive targeted consultation, are directly observed at certain intervals, and must meet on-the-job performance criteria. An extensive point system is used with the children so that desirable behaviors are consistently reinforced (primarily with commonplace privileges) and undesirable behaviors consistently punished (with loss of points). The teaching parents also are involved with each child's school system in an effort to support the child's academic progress. The advantages of this approach—in terms of consistent rules and consequences—compared to traditional outpatient treatment or standard residential treatment with 8-hour-shift staff may seem obvious, even to the relatively uninformed.

A somewhat related approach to the treatment of severe disruptive behavior is that of foster-family-based treatment (also known as therapeutic foster care). In this approach, couples are recruited from the community who are willing to learn a set of therapeutic skills and accept a disruptive or emotionally disturbed child into their family. The goal of foster-family-based treatment is to provide an alternative to institutional placement, with the hope that the child eventually may return to the family of origin, or alternatively to transition to independent living when he or she reaches the age of 18.

Another alternative approach to the treatment of conduct problems in more naturalistic settings is that of family preservation. Although it seems to have begun with the Homebuilders program in Tacoma, Washington, family preservation is now a nationwide movement with many variations. The general concept is that many children who have been removed from their homes as a consequence of parental neglect and/or abuse (and consequently placed in foster care at great public expense) could be kept at home and their family provided services that would enable them to function more effectively. This not only would save considerable tax dollars but also would preserve family integrity, considered crucial to children's optimal long-term development.

With respect to behavioral deficits in social functioning, a variety of social programs have been implemented in school settings. Peer-pairing is one strategy that has been used to increase the social interaction of peer acceptance of socially isolated children. Peer interaction plays a fundamental role in children's social and emotional development, and disturbances in peer relationships constitute an important risk factor for the development of subsequent psychopathology. In a typical peer-pairing paradigm, shy or socially withdrawn children would be paired with more outgoing and socially facile children from their classrooms. The peer-pairs would then engage in a series of joint-task activities requiring one-on-one interaction.

Peer-pairing interventions have been shown to result in substantial improvement in peer acceptance and positive interaction rate. Peer-pairing interventions may be conceptualized as the provision and structuring of a facilitative environment conducive to mutually reinforcing social interaction influences. Changes in behavior follow from changes in social reinforcement contingencies. Improvements in observed behavior may be explained by reinforcement mechanisms operating in the peer-pairing condition. In addition, changes in peer perceptions may derive largely from the altered perceptions and behavior of the peer partners as a result of social interaction effects. Such processes may lead to the ultimate integration of the formerly socially isolated child into the more outgoing peer partner's social group.

DEVELOPMENTAL ISSUES

Contemporary child behavior therapy reflects an understanding of the unique developmental and family contexts relevant to the design and implementation of treatment programs for children, in contrast to mere downward extensions of interventions designed for adults. Child behavior therapists intervene in developmentally appropriate ways, attending to the unique developmental and familial factors present in the specific situation. Developmental factors have important implications for behavioral treatment. Age-by-treatment interactions are one example. An oft cited assumption is that treatment tends to be more effective when initiated earlier, as opposed to later, in the lifespan of the individual. It is commonly regarded that behavior patterns in young children are less entrenched and thus more susceptible to change. While positive therapeutic change, in general, may be more rapid the younger the individual, certain change strategies may be more effective with older children. Age differences have been reported for the efficacy of self-instructional training across a range of problems, and ability to engage in imagery has been found to vary as a function of age.

Integrating classic developmental and behavioral approaches may enhance the assessment process and may lead to more effective intervention. Child behavior therapists recognize the importance of identifying specific age-related developmental skills and incorporating those skills into specific intervention strategies. Some approaches will be more effective within certain age periods than will others. Identification of developmentally appropriate target goals and modes of behavior change ultimately will increase treatment success.

—Tracy L. Morris

See also: *Behavioral Approaches to Gambling (Vol. I), Behavioral Approaches to Schizophrenia (Vol. I), Behavioral Family Therapy (Vol. II), Behavior Therapy Theory (Vols. I & III), Dialectical Behavior Therapy (Vols. I & III), Multimodal Behavior Therapy (Vol. III)*

Suggested Readings

Beidel, D. C., Turner, S. M., & Morris, T. L. (2000). Behavioral treatment of childhood social phobia. *Journal of Consulting and Clinical Psychology, 68,* 1072–1080.

Dadds, M. R., & Barrett, P. M. (1996). Family processes in child and adolescent anxiety and depression. *Behaviour Change, 13,* 231–239.

Eysenck, H. J. (1952). The effects of psychotherapy: An evaluation. *Journal of Consulting Psychology, 16,* 319–324.

Henggeler, S. W., Melton, G. B., & Smith, L. A. (1992). Family preservation using multisystemic therapy: An effective alternative to incarcerating serious juvenile offenders. *Journal of Consulting and Clinical Psychology, 60,* 953–961.

Hersen, M. (Ed.). (2002). *Clinical behavior therapy: Adults and children.* New York: John Wiley.

Jones, M. C. (1924). The elimination of children's fears. *Journal of Experimental Psychology, 7,* 382–390.

Kendall, P. C., Chansky, T. E., Kane, M. T., Kim, R., Kortlander, E., Ronan, K. R., et al. (1992). *Anxiety disorders in youth: Cognitive-behavioral interventions.* Needham Heights, MA: Allyn & Bacon.

Mowrer, O. H. (1956). Two-factor learning theory reconsidered, with special reference to secondary reinforcement and the concept of habit. *Psychological Review, 63,* 114–128.

O'Donohue, W. T., & Henderson, D. A. (Eds.). (2001). *A history of the behavioral therapies: Founders' personal histories.* Reno, NV: Context Press.

Skinner, B. F. (1953). *Science and human behavior.* New York: Macmillan.

Watson, J. B., & Rayner, R. (1920). Conditioned emotional reactions. *Journal of Experimental Psychology, 3,* 1–14.

Wolpe, J. (1958). *Psychotherapy by reciprocal inhibition.* Stanford, CA: Stanford University Press.

BEHAVIORAL ASSESSMENT

CONCEPTUAL FOUNDATIONS AND KEY CHARACTERISTICS

The distinguishing characteristics of behavioral assessment are made more clear when they are contrasted against psychodynamic and personality assessment systems (e.g., those that use projective and personality assessment instruments such as the Rorschach and MMPI). These assessment systems assume that behavioral problems arise mostly from stable, internal, psychological processes such as unconscious conflicts, impaired object relations, and dysfunctional personality characteristics. Because internal and stable psychological processes are considered to be the main determinant of behavior problems, personality and projective assessment methods emphasize the measurement of internal experiences and personality characteristics. In addition, external environmental factors that can influence problem behavior (e.g., social relationships, how others respond to a problem behavior) are minimally evaluated.

In contrast, behavioral assessment emphasizes the measurement of external environmental factors (e.g., the social setting and how others respond to the person's behaviors), cognitive processes (e.g., thoughts, beliefs), and behavior (how a person acts in a particular environment). Behavioral assessment is closely tied to well-established models of learning such as operant conditioning, classical conditioning, and social learning. It is also strongly influenced by research—many studies have shown that people's environment, particularly their social environment, can influence the onset, maintenance, and cessation of behavior problems and how well treatment goals are achieved.

There are several conceptual foundations of behavioral assessment. The first, as suggested above, is *environmental determinism.* Environmental determinism stresses that how people behave, for example, the likelihood that an adult will experience anxiety when meeting a new person or that children with developmental delays will injure themselves, is affected by the situation they are in and how others have responded to that behavior in the past. It is assumed that learning principles (e.g., reinforcement, punishment, classical conditioning, modeling) can help us understand these behavior-environment relations. Thus, behavior problems and positive behaviors are thought of as logical responses to specific environmental events that precede, co-occur, and/or follow their occurrence.

A second foundation underlying behavioral assessment is an emphasis on *empiricism:* the idea that behavior problems can best be understood by the application of scientific methods. When applied to behavioral assessment, empiricism emphasizes the use of systematic observation, careful measurement and definitions of behaviors and environmental events, the use of well-validated assessment instruments, and control or monitoring of the assessment environment to learn about the form and function of behavior.

In addition to the two aforementioned conceptual foundations, there are several additional characteristics of behavioral assessment. First is an endorsement of the *hypothetico-deductive* method of learning about a client. In this method of inquiry, an assessor develops hypotheses about the behavior of a client and designs assessment strategies to test those hypotheses. For example, based on the hypothesis that a child is injuring himself or herself in order to escape from demanding learning situations, the assessor might systematically change how a teacher responds to the self-injury, to see if this hypothesis is correct.

Another characteristic is an emphasis on the *context of behavior:* the idea that behavior is often influenced by an interaction between the environment and individual differences (e.g., the unique biological characteristics, culture, and learning history of a person). Thus, the form and causes of the same behavior problem can differ across persons and can differ across settings for one person.

An emphasis on the contexts of behavior problems naturally leads to a *sensitivity to individual differences*. Behavioral assessment is sensitive to the notion that each client presents with a unique history, physiology, and context. There can be important differences across clients with the same behavior problem as a result of ethnic and cultural differences, age, sex, sexual orientation, religion, and many other sources of individual differences. To reflect these important differences across clients, assessment strategies are often individualized.

Behavioral assessment also emphasizes *multiple and differing causes* for behavior problems. There can be many possible causes for a single behavior problem. For example, depressed mood can be a consequence of negative life events such as loss of a loved one, negative thoughts about oneself and the future, biochemical changes, and genetic factors. The causes of depressed mood can differ across persons, and there are often multiple causal factors operating at once.

Reciprocal causation can also be important—the idea that a person can affect his or her environment, which can, in turn, affect the person's behavior. For example, a child with chronic headache may make dramatic expressions of pain to the parent, which elicit comfort and nurturance from a parent, which may increase the likelihood that the child will experience headache in the future.

Behavioral assessment also assumes that there can be *temporal variability* in behavior problems and their causes. That is, the characteristics of a behavior problem and the things that cause it can change over time. This is often observed in differences between factors leading to the onset of a problem (e.g., social stimuli for early instances of smoking) and factors that maintain a problem once it is established (e.g., physiological withdrawal effects when a person tries to stop smoking).

Although many types of causes can fit within a behavioral assessment system (e.g., biological, cognitive, early learning, genetic), events in *close temporal relations* to behavior problems are stressed. Immediate responses by others to a behavior problem, responses to positive alternatives to a behavior problem, the setting in which the person finds himself or herself, stimuli that trigger a response, and what the person thinks in challenging situations are examples of the kind of contemporaneous causal events that are emphasized in behavioral assessment.

Behavioral assessment also emphasizes the importance of the *social systems* surrounding a behavior problem. In cases of childhood behavior problems, for example, we know that how well a parent can attend to and help a child develop healthy behaviors can be affected by the parent's mood, physical health, marital and family relationships, economic and other life stressors, and relationships with supervisors on the job.

The aforementioned conceptual foundations and characteristics have a number of implications for persons who adopt a behavioral assessment approach. They must be familiar with learning principles and how they apply to the onset, maintenance, and cessation of behavior problems. Second, they must have the skills required to carefully define and measure behavior and situations. Finally, they must know how to design assessment procedures that will permit accurate identification and measurement of complex relations among behaviors and contextual factors. Finally, behavioral assessors must be familiar with the empirical research relevant to their clients. As outlined below, behavioral assessment focuses on the identification of functional relations between behavior problems and their causes.

THE GOALS AND APPLICATIONS OF BEHAVIORAL ASSESSMENT

A primary goal of behavioral assessment is to obtain accurate information about a client's behavior problems and treatment goals and the factors that affect those behavior problems and goals. This primary goal can be divided into two subgoals: (1) specific measurement of behavior problems, treatment goals, and causal variables (i.e., *description*), and (2) specific measurement of the relations between problems, goals, and causal factors (i.e., *functional analysis*). In treatment applications, the overarching goal of behavioral assessment is to help the clinician make better judgments regarding treatment design and the factors that affect clients' responses to treatment.

To attain the two subordinate goals, the therapist must define and specify behavior problems and potential causal factors. Following this, strategies for collecting data about the relations among target behaviors and casual factors must be designed. In the following sections, strategies used to achieve these subordinate goals are presented.

Description: The Definition, Specification, and Quantification of Behaviors and Causal Variables

Once a behavior problem (or treatment goal) has been broadly identified, typically by the client or a referring person (there are usually multiple problems and treatment goals), the behavioral assessor must identify and measure its key characteristics. A specific description will include the qualities of a target behavior as well as its quantitative dimensions (e.g., rate, duration, intensity). This specification helps the clinician identify the causal variables associated with the behavior problem and helps the clinician track the effects of treatment.

Behavior problems can often be composed of three interrelated *modes:* verbal-cognitive, physiological-affective, and overt-motor. The verbal-cognitive mode includes spoken words as well as thoughts, self-statements, memories, and internal imagery. The physiological-affective mode includes physical responses (e.g., physiological responses, physical sensations) and perceived emotional states. Finally, the overt-motor mode includes observable behavioral responses.

Behavior problems can be complex and difficult to define. For example, children with a school phobia may present with many cognitive, emotional, and overt-motor behaviors such as persistent thoughts about their inability to manage their emotions in school and thoughts that harm will occur if they enter the school, and anxious activation (e.g., accelerated heart rate, muscle tension) when approaching the school. They may also do things at home to avoid being sent to school. However, other children with a school phobia may present with a different configuration of verbal-cognitive, physiological-affective, and overt-motor behaviors.

Once a behavior problem has been described, the best *measurement dimensions* must be selected. Although there are many ways to measure a behavior problem, the most common dimensions are frequency, duration, and intensity. The dimension that is selected depends on which is more relevant for the client. For example, some clients may report infrequent but long-lasting manic periods while for others, manic periods may be frequent but short-lasting.

Following the definition and specification of a behavior problem, the causal variables that affect the client's behavior problems must be identified. As noted earlier, important causal variables can often fall into two broad modes: social/environmental factors and intrapersonal factors. Social/environmental factors include interactions with other people as well as the physical characteristics of an environment (e.g., temperature, noise levels, lighting levels). Intrapersonal factors include verbal-cognitive, affective-physiological, and overt-motor behaviors that may exert significant causal effects on a client's behavior. The causal factor measurement dimensions are similar to those used with target behaviors. Specifically, frequency, duration, and intensity of contextual factor occurrence are most often measured. Important causal factors may also include systems factors, as noted above.

Defining, specifying, and quantifying behavior problems and causal factors have important implications. First, this process requires that the behavioral assessor think carefully and objectively about the nature of the client's behavior problems and about the factors that might influence their occurrence. This careful approach reduces the likelihood that the behavioral assessor will oversimplify, bias, or omit important variables in case formulation. The description and specification process will make it possible for the behavioral assessor to evaluate the social significance of the behavior problem. Finally, this process will permit the behavioral assessor to evaluate whether the pattern of behaviors presented meets formal diagnostic criteria, using the *American Psychiatric Association Diagnostic and Statistical Manual (DSM-IV)* or other diagnostic systems.

The Functional Analysis of the Client's Behavior Problems

Once target behaviors and causal variables have been defined, specified, and quantified, the behavioral assessor develops a *case formulation* that depicts the functional relations among these variables. This explanatory model of target behavior-causal variable interrelations is known as the *functional analysis.* The functional analysis is the identification of all important, modifiable, causal variables associated with the client's behavior problems. It is the primary guide for the development of individualized treatment for a client.

Several variables are included in a functional analysis. First, the assessor must estimate which of many possible causal relations are most important for treatment design. The assessor will seek to identify the most important and modifiable causal relations for the client's behavior problems. Some functional relations are noncausal or correlational. Others are unmodifiable (consider the causal role of spinal cord damage for a client's depressed mood). Some causal variables exert a very limited impact on the behavior problem. The assessor is interested in making these distinctions, because most interventions are aimed at modifying important causal variables in order to reduce behavior problems or approach treatment goals.

The behavioral assessor looks at several factors to identify important causal relations. First, the assessor looks for covariation between a possible causal event and the behavior. However, covariation alone does not imply causality. Thus, the behavioral assessor also seeks to establish (a) temporal order—the changes in the causal variable should precede effects on the target behavior, (b) a logical explanation for the relation (often based on empirical research and theory), and (c) the exclusion of plausible alternative explanations for the observed relation.

Several methods can be used to identify causal functional relations in behavioral assessment. Each method also has strengths and limitations in relation to causal inference and suitability for clinical settings. These assessment methods are presented in the section below titled Methods Used to Identify Causal Functional Relations.

Additional Goals and Applications

Behavioral assessment has additional goals. These include (a) diagnosis and treatment outcome evaluation with clients, (b) the evaluation of mental health delivery systems, (c) informing clients about the assessment and treatment process, (d) conducting research on the causes and covariates of behavior problems, and (e) controlled treatment outcome research.

Behavioral assessment is a conceptually based paradigm—it is based on ideas about behavior and its assessment rather than specific methods of assessment. Therefore, it is adaptable to the assessment in many contexts. In addition to the individual children, adolescents, and adults described above, it has been used in the assessment of marital relationships, families, classrooms and schools, community service agencies, psychiatric units, medical services, and for psychometric evaluation of new assessment instruments.

BEHAVIORAL ASSESSMENT METHODS

Several methods of assessment can be used to identify, specify, and quantify behavior problems and causal variables. Recent surveys of behavior therapists indicate that the most commonly used behavioral assessment methods are behavioral assessment interviewing, behavioral observation, self-monitoring, and rating scales and questionnaires.

Behavioral Assessment Interviewing

Behavioral assessment interviewing differs in structure and focus from other forms of interviewing. Structurally, behavioral interviewing tends to conform with the goals of behavioral assessment in that the assessor structures questions that prompt the client to provide information about the topography of behavior problems and relevant functional relations. Descriptive queries in the interview direct the client to describe the mode and dimensions of behavior problems and to identify possible causal relations (e.g., "About how many times per week do you have panic episodes? How long do they last? Can you describe the situations in which they are most likely to occur?").

In terms of focus, client verbalizations are interpreted in two ways. When viewed as a "marker variable," client verbalizations are interpreted as indicators of behavior problems and casual factor occurrences. That is, they are viewed as self-report measures of the form of behavior problems and possible functional relations. Sometimes client behaviors during an interview are treated as a direct occurrence of the target behavior that arose as a function of some causal event present during that moment of the interview. For example, the assessor might note the discussion topics that elicit anger or paranoid ideation by the client. Important functions of the behavioral assessment interview also include (a) maintenance of a positive, supportive client-assessor relationship and (b) ensuring that clients are fully informed about and agree with the methods and goals of the assessment.

Despite the fact that the interview is a commonly used method of assessment, its psychometric properties are infrequently evaluated. Among the research findings published to date, it appears that low to moderate levels of agreement are observed when two different judges listen to interviews and subsequently generate a list of what they perceive to be the most important target behaviors and causal variables. How the interviewer responds to the client's reports, and similarity between the assessor and client on race, ethnicity, and sex, can sometimes affect the validity of the client's reports.

Behavioral Observation

Behavioral observations can be conducted by nonparticipant and participant observers. Nonparticipant observers are persons who are not normally part of the client's environment but who have been trained to record the occurrence of behaviors and causal variables. Because nonparticipant observers are hired and trained to conduct observations, they are often able to collect data on many complex behaviors, causal variables, and behavior-casual variable sequences. Although nonparticipant observation is a versatile assessment method, it is infrequently used in clinical settings due to the costs associated with hiring trained personnel.

Participant observers are persons who are normally in the client's natural environment. In most cases, participant observers are family members, coworkers, teachers and aides, hospital staff members, or caregivers. Because participant observers are already involved in the client's life, they are able to conduct observations in many different settings and across longer periods of time. The major drawback associated with participant observation is limited focus: Because participant observers have multiple responsibilities, they are usually only able to record a small number of events.

Behavioral observations can occur in the natural environment, such as at home or in the school, or they can occur in controlled clinical situations. Naturalistic observation is consistent with the emphasis of understanding clients' behavior problems in the environment in which they naturally occur, but it is expensive. Observation in controlled clinical situations, called *analogue observation,* is less costly, but the generalizability of the resultant clinical judgments to the natural environment can sometimes be a problem.

Self-Monitoring

Self-monitoring is an assessment method where clients systematically sample and record their own behavior and sometimes the behavior of others. Because clients can access all three modes of responding (cognitive, affective, overt-motor) in multiple settings, self-monitoring has become a very popular and sophisticated assessment method. To increase accuracy, target behaviors must be clearly defined so that clients can validly record their occurrence. Self-monitoring often uses paper-and-pencil recordings but can also occur through the use of small handheld computers. These computers can be prompted to query the client at specific times, with specific prompts, questions to be answered, or ratings to be given.

One of the principal limitations of self-monitoring is observer bias. That is, a client may not accurately record target behaviors due to a number of factors, including expectations for positive or negative consequences, lack of awareness of target behavior occurrence, and application of a criteria for target behavior occurrence that is different from the assessor's. Finally, noncompliance with self-monitoring can be a problem.

Rating Scales and Self-Report Questionnaires

Self-report questionnaires and rating scales are paper-and-pencil or computer-administered inventories that the client completes at various points in time. Rating scales often ask the respondent to describe the behavior of another person, such as a teacher or parent, the rating scales of children. As an assessment method, rating scales and self-report questionnaires have several strengths. First, they are easily administered and interpreted. Second, there are many self-report questionnaires and rating scales that can be used to evaluate a wide array of behavior problems. Finally, questionnaires can be used for several important behavioral assessment goals, including identification of client behavior problems and strengths, identification of functional relations, and treatment design.

The most significant problem with questionnaires is that they are often without reference to settings or other important environmental factors. For example, many questionnaire items ask a client to rate agreement (e.g., "strongly agree . . ." "strongly disagree") with setting-free statements about a target behavior (e.g., "I often feel angry"). They may not ask about situations in which anger is most likely to occur and how others respond to angry behaviors. A second important problem is that many questionnaires and rating scales sum different behaviors, thoughts, and affective states to form a global score. This aggregation of behavioral information is, of course, not consistent with the emphasis in behavioral assessment on the individualized modes, dimensions, and forms of behavior problems.

Sampling

Several behavioral assessment methods, particularly observation and self-monitoring, involve sampling. Clients' behaviors can change, across time and settings, often because of variation in causal variables. Because one cannot realistically measure all behaviors, in all settings, and at all times, sampling strategies must be used—we measure some behaviors, in some settings, and at some times.

A major consideration in deciding upon a sampling strategy is generalizability—to what degree can the measures be presumed to be indicative of how things really are. The behavioral assessor aims to gather data that will permit reasonable inferences about how a client behaves at different points in time (generalizability across time), settings (generalizability across settings), often by measuring a few of many possible behaviors (generalizability across behaviors). Thus, the behavioral assessor must carefully consider what, when, and where to measure behaviors in order to maximize generalizability. Sampling can occur in several ways, as described below.

Event Sampling. Event sampling refers to a strategy wherein the occurrence of a behavior or other event is recorded whenever it is detected. For example, when conducting a classroom observation, the teacher might record each occurrence of an aggressive act by a child and how the teacher responded to it. It would then be possible to calculate the rate of the behavior and possible causal event to help in its specification, to identify possible causal relations for treatment design, and to monitor changes associated with treatment.

Duration Sampling. Duration sampling measures the amount of time that elapses between the beginning and end of a behavior or causal variable. For example, a client who is experiencing anxiety episodes might self-monitor the duration of each episode.

Interval Sampling. Interval sampling involves dividing an observation session into specific intervals, which can span seconds to hours. In partial-interval sampling, an entire interval is recorded as an occurrence if the event is observed during *any* portion of the interval. For example, if the child emits any aggressive act within a 1-minute observation period, the complete interval is recorded as an occurrence of the behavior. In whole-interval sampling, the event must be observed for the entire period before the interval is recorded as an occurrence. One of the main difficulties with interval sampling is that target behavior and causal variable frequency can be underestimated or overestimated as a function of the duration and frequency of the event.

Real-time Sampling. Real-time sampling involves measuring time at the beginning and ending of a behavior and causal variable occurrence. Real-time recording can provide information about the frequency and duration of target behaviors and causal variables. However, like event and duration sampling, real-time sampling requires that the target behaviors and causal variables have discrete beginning and end points.

Setting Sampling. In addition to time sampling, the behavioral assessor must decide in which settings the behaviors and causal variables should be sampled. Settings selected are often those in which the events of interest are most likely to occur. That is, if we are interested in observing difficult parent-child interactions, we might sample homework or bedtime settings, rather than afternoon free play settings.

Subject Sampling. Sometimes we can observe only a few out of many possible assessment subjects. For example, in a classroom with many aggressive children, we may choose to observe only a few of them. In this case, we presume that our clinical inferences from the observed children, such as how well they respond to a classroom behavioral intervention, will be generalizable to other aggressive children in that classroom.

METHODS USED TO IDENTIFY CAUSAL FUNCTIONAL RELATIONS

The assessment methods described above can provide information about the form of behavior problems and causal variables. They can also provide information about functional relations, an important component of the functional analysis. There are several strategies for estimating functional relations for clients' behavior problems.

Marker Variable Strategy

A marker variable is an easily obtained measure that is reliably associated with the strength of a functional relation in the natural environment. For example, a client's psychophysiological reaction to a short laboratory speaking task can serve as a marker for his or her psychophysiological reaction to real-world speaking tasks (e.g., giving a lecture to a class). Empirically validated marker variables can be derived from self-report inventories specifically designed to identify functional relations, structured interviews, psychophysiological assessments, and role-playing exercises. A major advantage of the marker variable strategy is ease of application. A behavior assessor can identify many potential causal functional relations with a very limited investment of time and effort. For example, many markers of potential causal relations can be identified through a single behavioral interview.

Generalizability and validity are the most significant problems with the use of marker variables. The extent to which unvalidated marker variables such as client reports during an interview or responses to a self-report inventory, responses to laboratory stressors, and observations of in-session setting-behavior interactions correlate with "real-life" causal relations is often unknown. In addition, for those situations in which empirically validated marker variables are available, the magnitude of correlation between the marker variable and real-life causal relations can vary substantially across clients.

Concurrent Administration of Different Assessment Instruments

Concurrent administration of different assessment instruments is a second method that can be used to derive hypotheses about potential functional relations. For example, an assessor may observe that an adolescent reports (a) several negative life events (e.g., death of a sibling) occurred within the past year on a self-report inventory, (b) high daily levels of family conflict on self-monitoring forms, and (c) symptoms of depression during a behavioral interview. Given these data, it may be plausible to hypothesize that the child's depression is caused by family conflict and increased life stressors.

As with the marker variable strategy, concurrent administration of different assessment devices permits the behavior assessor to identify many potential causal functional relations with a minimal investment of clinical resources. Causal inferences derived from this method must be held very tentatively, however, because the data are only correlational and it can be hard to tell which events came first.

Behavioral Observation and Self-Monitoring of Naturally Occurring Context-Behavior Interactions

A third procedure to estimate causal relations is systematic observation of naturally occurring context-behavior interactions. Most commonly, clients are observed or self-monitor some dimension (e.g., frequency or magnitude) of a behavior problem along with one or more contextual or response contingency factors that are hypothesized to affect the target behavior.

Self-monitoring and direct observation of naturally occurring functional relations can yield data that are relevant to causal hypotheses. However, these methods have three practical limitations. First, clients or observers must be adequately trained so that all events are accurately and reliably recorded. Second, as the number and/or complexity of events to be observed increase, accuracy and reliability often decrease. Third, it is difficult to exclude the possibility that other variables may be affecting the data. Taken together, these limitations suggest that systematic observation methods are best suited for situations in which the behavior and contextual variables are easily quantified and few in number.

Experimental Manipulation

The fourth method that can be used to estimate casual relations is experimental manipulation. Experimental manipulations involve systematically modifying hypothesized causal variables and observing consequent changes in behavior in the clinic or naturalistic settings. Experimental manipulation has received renewed interest in recent years because it can be an effective strategy for identifying response contingencies that may strengthen, and settings and stimuli that can elicit, behavior problems. Despite the potential treatment utility of experimental manipulations, several questions remain unanswered. First, the reliability and validity of some experimental analog observation methods are unexplored. Second, the incremental benefits of experimental analog observation for treatment design and outcome have not been adequately estimated. Finally, most demonstrations of the treatment utility of analog observation have been limited to a very restricted population of clients who were presenting with a restricted number of behavior problems.

—*William H. O'Brien and Stephen N. Haynes*

See also: Behavioral Assessment (Vols. I & III), Behavior Therapy and Neuropsychology (Vol. III), Functional Analysis (Vol. II), Motor Activity and Behavioral Assessment (Vols. I & III)

Suggested Readings

Bellack, A. S., & Hersen, M. (Eds.). (1998). *Behavioral assessment: A practical handbook.* Boston: Allyn & Bacon.

Crone, D. A., & Horner, R. H. (2003). *Building positive behavior support systems in schools: Functional behavioral assessment.* New York: Guilford Press.

Garb, H. N. (1996). *Studying the clinician: Judgment research and psychological assessment.* Washington, DC: American Psychological Association.

Haynes, S. N., & Heiby, E. M. (Eds.). (2003). *Behavioral assessment.* New York: Wiley.

Haynes, S. N., & O'Brien, W. H. (2000). *Principles and practice of behavioral assessment.* New York: Kluwer.

O'Brien, W. H. (1995). Inaccuracies in the estimation of functional relations using self-monitoring data. *Journal of Behavior Therapy and Experimental Psychiatry, 26,* 351–357.

O'Brien, W. H., & Haynes, S. N. (1995). A functional analytic approach to the assessment and treatment of a child with frequent migraine headaches. *In Session: Psychotherapy in Practice,1,* 65–80.

Shapiro, E. S., & Kratochwill, T. R. (Eds.). (2000). *Behavioral assessment in schools: Theory, research, and clinical foundations* (2nd ed., pp. 3–15). New York: Guilford Press.

Watson, T. S., & Steege, M. (2003). *Conducting school-based functional behavioral assessments: A practitioner's guide.* New York: Guilford Press.

BEHAVIORAL CONSULTATION

DESCRIPTION OF THE STRATEGY

Behavioral consultation evolved out of the need for professionals with expertise in behavior modification to efficiently address the individual concerns of their clients across a variety of treatment settings. Over the last two decades, behavioral consultation has become increasingly researched, and advances in the definitions, standardization, psychometric criteria, training, generalizability of consultation research, methodology, and outcomes for this type of consultation are now documented. Although many models of behavioral consultation have been developed, most models include components that strive to accurately analyze the presenting problem in behavioral terms (i.e., using a functional analysis of behavior), creating a behavioral

intervention that will correct the problem, and evaluating the efficacy of the intervention developed.

In a broader sense, the behavioral consultation model may be conceptualized as a problem-solving process involving a triadic relationship comprised of the client (i.e., a child), the consultee (i.e., teacher or parent), and the consultant (i.e., social worker or psychologist). Throughout this relationship, the consultant concentrates on targeting specific behavioral objectives in the client's environment and providing the necessary skills to the consultee in order to maintain the behavioral objectives or modifications established for the client. The ultimate goal of this model is to produce a behavior change in the client, which may be accomplished via a five-phase process that includes (1) gathering information and baseline data about the client, (2) selecting intervention objectives for the client, (3) designing a behavior plan for the client, (4) teaching specific management skills to the consultee, and (5) conducting a progress evaluation and/or follow-up sessions.

The first phase of the behavioral consultation process is to collect data on the problem behaviors of interest. Assessment of behavior is both an initial step and ongoing process in which specific problem behaviors are identified, a history of the client's behavior is gathered, rates of target behaviors are estimated or observed, previous attempts to ameliorate those problem behaviors are documented, and baseline rates of behaviors are gathered. To identify specific problem behaviors, consultants may interview consultees and clients, use behavior rating scales, and/or conduct a functional analysis in which the relationships of antecedents and consequences to the problem behavior are identified. Many methods exist for measurement of specific problem behaviors, including activity occurrence (determining if the target behavior occurred within a certain period of time), spot checks (randomly checking to observe whether or not the client is engaging in the target behavior), and frequency (recording each occurrence of the target behavior). To gain a history of problem behaviors, consultants may also use interview questions focusing on the age at which the problem behavior began, how long the problem behavior has been present, and changes in the rate and severity of the problem behavior over time. Next, the current rate of the problem behavior may be estimated through direct questioning of the consultee. This allows the consultant to quickly gain basic information about the severity and frequency of the problem behaviors, although this estimation is likely to be somewhat inaccurate. Gathering history about previously attempted strategies allows the consultant to understand what was both previously effective and ineffective for the client and what modifications may be made to previously ineffective strategies, in order to improve their efficacy.

The second phase of behavioral consultation involves selecting objectives and interventions on the basis of data collected. A list of behavioral objectives is created from which the consultant and consultee determine what objectives seem most important to focus on, based on the severity and chronicity of the behavior problems observed. Once priority has been given to the behavioral objectives, the third phase of consultation involves the establishment of a behavior plan designed by the consultant. Based on previously gathered data, the consultant determines which strategies may be most effective in altering the frequency, severity, or pervasiveness of identified problem behaviors. During this phase, the consultee must be taught to modify the consequences of problem behavior. For instance, the consultee may be instructed to alter his or her behavior so that positive consequences do not follow the problem behavior (i.e., the client gaining attention or tangible reinforcers after engaging in the problem behavior) but *do* follow when the client *does not* demonstrate the problem behavior in a situation that may have previously evoked such behavior (i.e., the client receiving a reinforcer for not engaging in the problem behavior when the opportunity is available).

The fourth phase of behavioral consultation entails the consultant, typically someone with expertise in behavior management strategies, teaching the consultee, usually a teacher or parent, the skills to manage a behavior plan for the client, usually a child, once the consultant is phased out of the behavior plan implementation process. In doing so, the consultant provides a detailed explanation about the specific skills required to maintain the behavior plan for the client over time. Implementation of the plan rests with the consultee and must be consistently implemented in order to bring about the most efficacious changes in behaviors. Finally, Phase 5 includes following up on the progress of the behavior plan. This step is highly important, as one-session consultations often have a high rate of failure. During this phase, data on the client's problem behavior(s) are reviewed and monitored in order to discover if the behavior plan is effective or needs additional modifications. In addition,

integrity checks are performed with the consultee to determine whether he or she is continuing to properly implement the behavior plan. The major goals of this phase, therefore, are to collect information regarding client progress and parent/teacher implementation, as well as address necessary modifications to the behavior plan and/or consultee concerns about the plan.

The main purpose of behavioral consultation is to deliver efficient and effective services. To accomplish this, several assumptions must be met. First, measurement of the problem behavior must be conducted with direct, valid, and reliable methods in order to obtain a more accurate conceptualization of what a behavior plan should include. Second, assessment and intervention must be continually conducted and revised throughout the consultation process so that behavior change can be accomplished as efficiently as possible. Third, consultees must be trained in the implementation of the behavior plan so that positive behavioral changes may be maintained once the consultant leaves the client's environment. Fourth, the implementation of the behavior plan must be consistent across time and environments in order to generalize behavior change. Finally, the behavior plan needs to produce an observable behavior change over a short period of time that may be effectively maintained through the contingencies presented. Without these parameters, behavioral consultation may lack in both effectiveness and efficiency.

RESEARCH BASIS

When specific behavior problems can be readily identified and need to be quickly corrected, behavioral consultation, an indirect service model, has been shown to be superior to some other forms of direct intervention, such as counseling. Behavioral consultation appears to lead to positive outcomes for those involved. In addition, behavioral consultation may even be more efficient than direct interventions, in that it requires less time to implement, it permits delivery of services in the client's own environment via the consultee, and it may be the only feasible alternative in some situations, considering the large volume of responsibilities handled by some consultants such as school psychologists. Behavioral consultation is most effective when it is carried out in the client's environment and conducted collaboratively between the consultant and consultee. This maximizes the generalizability and consistency of the behavioral consultation plans developed. Although behavioral consultation may lack the overall efficacy that more direct services offer, behavioral consultation's great strength is that it allows for an efficient, pragmatic intervention when more extensive interventions are not feasible.

RELEVANT TARGET POPULATIONS AND EXCEPTIONS

Behavioral consultation is primarily used in schools, with teachers serving as consultees and students serving as clients. Behavioral consultation, however, can be applied to a variety of settings, including households where parents wish to bring about behavioral changes with their children, work settings where employers may want to bring about behavioral changes to facilitate higher productivity in their employees, or even in sports where coaches may want to make behavioral changes that lead to better performances among their players. In addition, this process can be applied to community and residential care settings, such as foster care or group homes, where child behavior may need to be modified quickly. In sum, behavioral consultation can be applied to most situations in which a behavioral change is the desired outcome and resources are lacking to the extent that more comprehensive interventions are not feasible.

COMPLICATIONS

Many studies demonstrating the efficacy of behavioral consultation lack adequate experimental control, and therefore the generalizability and interpretability of results are limited. Although the research methodology in behavioral consultation has become more rigorous over time, many studies only demonstrate that behavioral consultation is better than no treatment instead of directly comparing it to other treatments, thereby failing to clearly demonstrate greater efficacy versus other methods of intervention. In addition, a large amount of behavioral consultation research relies on teacher-report data instead of direct observation of behavior, leading some to criticize that behavioral consultation may lack an assessment-related behavioral emphasis. One major problem with reliance on questionnaire measures is that teachers often report changes in behavior due to their expectations that students may improve with treatment, even though no change in behavior has occurred. Many

behavioral consultation studies also fail to investigate differences in outcomes associated with having the consultee collaborate on the implementation of the behavior plan with the consultant versus having the consultant alone direct the behavior plan. Although a majority of models stress a collaborative process between the consultant and consultee, recent studies have demonstrated the effectiveness of a more directive style of behavioral consultation.

Other limitations of behavioral consultation involve the consultee failing to properly implement the consultant's behavior plan for the client after the consultant has left the intervention environment. In addition, the consultant may not always be adequately trained to properly identify problem behaviors, as some training programs fail to emphasize the applied aspects of behavior analysis. Another limitation of behavioral consultation research is that an overwhelming majority of this research focuses on school settings and pays little attention to other settings. Some research has also demonstrated that even though behavioral consultation may be cost effective and efficient, a wider range of assessment techniques may be more useful in identifying and treating problems. A possible direct result of inconsistent research design methodologies is that some research clearly demonstrates behavioral consultation to be efficacious in ameliorating behavior problems while other research disputes that finding.

CASE ILLUSTRATION

"Andre" is a 5-year-old African American male evidencing an array of disruptive behavior problems in his preschool classroom. His classroom teacher, Ms. M. (the consultee), characterizes Andre's most problematic behaviors as aggressive in nature, with physical fighting being the most common form of aggressive action described to the preschool's behavioral consultant. Ms. M. also indicates that Andre recurrently displays oppositional and defiant behaviors in the classroom, such as refusing to follow classroom rules or stated instructions, arguing with teachers, blaming other children for his own mistakes, and evidencing temper tantrums in the classroom when denied a preferred object or activity. These disruptive behaviors appear to significantly impair Andre's social, behavioral, and academic functioning in his school environment. Similar problem behaviors are also reportedly a source of stress and concern in

Andre's home. However, Andre's parents were unable to participate in any intervention program for these behaviors in the preschool setting, owing to scheduling conflicts.

Following initial discussion of Andre's problem behaviors with Ms. M. and gathering of historical information regarding both Andre's behavior and previous classroom-based intervention attempts, the consultant conducted a functional analysis of Andre's behavior in the classroom setting. In doing so, the consultant detailed the antecedents (or setting events), overt behavioral actions, and consequences (or events/actions that followed a given behavior) for each of the following actions: (a) physical fighting with peers, (b) refusing to comply with stated rules, (c) arguing with teachers or other adults in the classroom, (d) verbally assigning blame to another child for inappropriate behavior, and (e) evidencing a temper tantrum in the classroom setting. Prior to the onset of this functional analysis, each of the five problem behaviors was operationally defined to ensure consistency in the coding of observed actions. Next, the consultant observed Andre's behavior during a set number of 30-minute intervals, occurring over a week-long span, with careful attention paid to making observations at a variety of points during the school day. Assessing disruptive behavior across different time periods and levels of task demand allowed the consultant to determine the full range of antecedent and consequent conditions that may be maintaining behavior. This same functional analysis procedure was also repeated postintervention, to allow for the assessment of behavioral change.

Following this functional analysis, a list of behavioral objectives was generated with the assistance and continual feedback of the consultee. In this case, the consultant concluded that the consultee appeared to assign a relatively high amount of attention and reinforcement to Andre, as a consequence, when he engaged in disruptive actions. While most of Andre's problem behaviors appeared to be preceded by a relatively mild psychosocial stressor, the consultant observed classroom activity to come to a virtual standstill after Andre became aggressive or defiant, due in part to Ms. M.'s high level of attention and responsiveness to his behaviors. Ms. M. frequently appeared to try and reason with Andre during temper tantrums or aggressive behavioral actions, often resulting in further exacerbation of problem behaviors. Therefore, a behavior plan was established to allow for initiation of alternative teacher responses to Andre's disruptive actions in the classroom. Following education about the function of Ms. M.'s observed behavior during and after Andre's disruptive actions, Ms. M. and the consultant worked together to generate a listing of alternative consequences for Andre's disruptive actions. Prominent components of the resulting behavior plan included use of planned ignoring strategies during tantrums, redirection strategies for more minor disruptive responses, increased positive reinforcement for appropriate behavior, and the introduction of a brief time-out strategy in the classroom. The consultant remained in the classroom setting to assist the consultee in the implementation of this behavior plan for several days, with the consultant providing both oral and written feedback to Ms. M. regarding her progress and the consultee also providing daily oral feedback about her satisfaction with the behavior plan.

To ensure maintenance of the behavior plan provided, a feedback meeting was held with Ms. M. prior to the consultant's departure from the classroom setting, with the objective of discussing any additional frustrations with or desired revisions of the stated behavior plan. The consultant also indicated that she would be available to Ms. M. on a recurrent basis to allow for any needed assistance or further modifications of the existent behavior plan. Finally, several weeks after the consultee took over full management of Andre's behavior plan, the consultant returned to the classroom to complete a follow-up functional assessment to observe whether the implementation of this behavior plan resulted in the occurrence and maintenance of positive behavioral changes.

—*Jill T. Ehrenreich and Cliff McKinney*

See also: *Behavioral Consultation (Vols. I & III), Private Practice of Behavioral Treatment (Vol. III)*

Suggested Readings

Kratchowill, T. R., Bergan, J. R., Sheridan, S. M., & Elliot, S. N. (1998). Assumptions of behavioral consultation: After all is said and done, more has been done than said. *School Psychology Quarterly, 13,* 63–80.

Noell, G. H., Gresham, F. M., & Duhon, G. (1998). Fundamental agreements and epistemological differences in differentiating what was said from what was done in behavioral consultation. *School Psychology Quarterly, 13,* 81–88.

Noell, G. H., & Witt, J. C. (1996). A critical re-evaluation of five fundamental assumptions underlying behavioral consultation. *School Psychology Quarterly, 11,* 189–203.

BEHAVIORAL CONTRACTING

DESCRIPTION OF THE STRATEGY

A hallmark of the earliest forms of behavioral research and therapy was the rapid and repeated manipulation of potent stimuli in experimental or clinical settings. Indeed, early learning research conducted by Pavlov, Watson, Cover Jones, and others showed that the repeated pairing of evolutionarily significant events such as intense auditory stimuli or food (e.g., unconditioned stimuli) with previously neutral events (conditioned stimuli) under certain conditions (e.g., deprivation) could have a powerful effect on learning, including the acquisition and extinction of fear responses. As Skinner began to formulate his own brand of behaviorism, a new term, *contingency,* was introduced. Although initially the term described relations between antecedents, behaviors, and their consequences, it became apparent that the verbal specification of relations between behaviors had special importance. The theoretical significance of verbalizing contingency relations was partly responsible for Skinner's writing an important text about the phenomenon (*Verbal Behavior*). However, the practical significance of verbalizing contingency relations has arguably been even more powerful.

For present purposes, behavioral contracting will refer to written descriptions of contingency relations (defined here as antecedents, behaviors, and consequences) that are intended to modify or influence behavior. Antecedents (also known as discriminative stimuli or cues) are defined as events that precede a behavior that, when specified as part of a contingency contract, indicate that a given behavior should be performed. Behaviors are actions specified in the contingency relation. If successful, the contingency contract will alter some characteristic of the behavior, given the onset of the conditions specified in the contract. Behaviors should be defined in such a way that their occurrence can be unambiguously inferred and agreed upon by well-informed persons. Consequences are events that should reliably follow the performance of the behavior. Often, the performance of the behavior will signal the delivery of both immediate consequences and progress toward long-term, larger rewards.

In fact, any "contract" can be analyzed in terms of the conditions requiring the performance of the behavior, a description of the behavior to be performed, and a specification of outcomes that will follow. Problems that arise in the performance (or failure to perform) behavior specified in a contract can frequently be traced to flaws in one of these areas (e.g., antecedents, behaviors, or consequences). As in our lay understanding of the term, behavioral contracts imply the existence of a contractor and a contractee. By and large, the terms used to describe behavioral contracting—contingency contracting, token economy, or school-home note—refer to the many possible variations of contractor and contractee relations and the degree of formal attention given to details of the contracting process.

The following elements seem to be consistent features of well-formulated behavioral contracts. These elements are described from the perspective of a practitioner seeking to develop an intervention for a prospective client. First, both parties should clarify the anticipated outcomes of the contract. To accomplish this end, the target behaviors should be specified in readily observable terms. Second, rewards for achievement and sanctions for failure to accomplish goals (if applicable) should be clearly specified. Third, the performance of the target behaviors must be monitored frequently, and consequences should be delivered consistent with the terms specified in the contract. Finally, terms of renegotiation and procedures for doing so should be clearly delineated in the contract. Most important, behavioral contracting is a formal process that requires the *collaboration* of two parties and the production of a written contract and formal monitoring processes. Informal agreements or promises made in passing do not constitute instances of behavioral contracting. Thus, whether an agreement between a parent and child would meet the formal definition of contracting described here would depend upon the extent to which these elements noted above are present.

Contracts may involve one or more parties and are typically negotiated with the assistance of a helping professional. Two-party contracts have been used most extensively and are the focus of this entry. In this arrangement, the helping professional assists the parties in negotiating behaviors for change, as well as consequences for meeting the terms of the contract. This type of contracting often involves mediating conflict between parents or teachers and children or adolescents. In these contexts, each party agrees to engage (or not engage) in certain behaviors to facilitate the achievement of specific behavioral objectives. A secondary but important goal involves empowering the dyad to negotiate future contracts, thereby reducing conflict and the need for continued outside assistance. Toward this end, communication and conflict resolution skills training are often included as part of the treatment package provided by the helping professional.

RESEARCH BASIS

Research indicates that behavioral contracting is an effective procedure for promoting behavioral change for adults and children. Several factors influence treatment outcomes associated with behavioral contracting. First, target behaviors should be clearly defined, demonstrated to be within the behavioral repertoire of the child (or taught prior to contract implementation), and stated positively. Relatedly, when target behaviors are difficult to perform or require considerable effort, stronger reinforcers may be necessary to elicit desired responses. Second, consequences must be negotiated by each party, clearly delineated, and strong enough to bring about behavior change. Reinforcer surveys ensure that specified rewards for compliance with contracted goals are salient enough to produce desired outcomes. Some data suggest that positive consequences alone may serve to bring about treatment gains. However, for more serious behavioral problems or behaviors that produce reinforcement that is difficult to regulate, some form of punishment (response cost) must often be added to achieve desired outcomes. Third, monitoring of the performance of target behaviors should be frequent and consequences provided as specified. When a contract is monitored by someone other than a helping professional (i.e., a parent or teacher), the contractor may require instruction in monitoring and the delivery of consequences. School-home notes have been effective in producing change in academic performance. Finally, it may be necessary to manipulate a number of components of behavioral contracts (e.g., problem behavior definitions, methods of performance monitoring, or schedules of reinforcement) to maximize effectiveness. Planning for the maintenance and generalization of behaviors by explicit programming appears necessary for long-term benefits to be realized.

Research suggests many advantages of using behavioral contracts. First, behavioral contracting increases independence and feelings of control over the problem behavior. Each success appears to enhance treatment acceptability, thus increasing the likelihood that participants will continue to implement the contract as planned. Second, the use of behavioral contracting frequently reduces conflict and appears to foster healthier styles of communication between participants. Third-party assistance facilitates modeling of negotiation skills that seem to promote the maintenance and generalization of skills. Through guided practice and feedback, third party assistance can be faded to promote independent implementation. In the best case scenario, behaviors learned as part of the contracting process begin to generate their own "natural" sources of reinforcement (e.g., reduced conflict). Third, with children and adolescents, home-school collaboration can be significantly increased through the use of behavioral contracting. Research indicates that parent-child contracts can impact many school-related behaviors that affect the overall functioning of a child. Collaboration between stakeholders in a child's environment may result in significant improvements in academic performance and behavior.

RELEVANT TARGET POPULATIONS AND EXCEPTIONS

Behavioral contracting has been used in a variety of settings to target symptoms associated with almost every *DSM* category. Significant variation has been observed in the types of consequences selected (reinforcers and sanctions), the identity of the contractor (helping professional, parent, teacher, peer, sibling, or, with older individuals, the children themselves), and intervention settings (school, mental health clinic, and hospital). Even within a particular diagnostic category, the scope of intervention may be broad. For example, for a child diagnosed with attention-deficit/hyperactivity disorder (ADHD), contracting may target a number of different behaviors such as medication compliance, completion of academic tasks, and following through on household chores.

Contingency contracting is similarly utilized at school and at home with children and adolescents in the completion of everyday life activities. This includes behaviors that are targets for improvement, but would not necessarily be indicative of a psychiatric disorder. Examples include increasing behaviors such as social interaction among withdrawn children, school attendance, academic productivity and accuracy, and sustaining attention to task.

Last, the principles of contingency contracting have been applied extensively within health care settings to increase adherence to medical or rehabilitative regimens. Compliance with a range of health promoting behaviors may be targeted, including chronic illnesses and handicapping conditions such as diabetes, obesity, and physical disabilities. Often, the formulation of a contingency contract necessitates breaking down complex regimens of medical care into smaller components, which may be beneficial in and of itself.

COMPLICATIONS

A number of difficulties confront users of contracting procedures. First, individuals may engage in problem behaviors when a contract is not in effect. This difficulty can be minimized by targeting functional behaviors that are linked to naturally occurring reinforcers and by pairing social reinforcers with tangible reinforcers so that consequences can be faded. It should be noted that this "no cure" criticism can be leveled with equal measure to pharmaceutical remedies regarded as having a high degree of efficacy (e.g., stimulant medication).

A second potential complication associated with the use of behavioral contracting arises from preexisting power imbalances. Undoubtedly, there is the potential for children and adolescents to be taken advantage of in negotiation or to have the terms of a contract altered by the parent or teacher. While failure to negotiate or execute a contract in good faith will most assuredly undermine the process, sophisticated professionals will seek to minimize this risk by fostering a collaborative process in which both parties actively participate. In families where severe parent-child conflict is evident, the use of other intervention approaches may be indicated, prior to or concurrent with attempts to utilize contracting.

Parents often require significant support and education surrounding the skills necessary to maintain and follow through on a behavioral contract. For example, they may overreact to instances of noncompliance regarding tasks specified in a given contract. This may inadvertently reinforce noncompliance (assuming the child's behavior to be motivated by attention seeking) and thereby increase the probability of future noncompliance. Because adhering to behavioral contracts may require parents to endure significant antisocial behavior and commit material resources to fulfilling their obligations, some parents may be unable or unwilling to participate in a contracting intervention. For example, it may require considerable restraint for a parent to remove points or privileges following back talk rather than lecture or retaliate, as might have been the case prior to the development of the contract. In cases where a caregiver or teacher is overwhelmed, eliciting support from others in the child's environment, such as relatives, counselors, or school support staff, may be warranted.

Contingency contracting requires prerequisite skills in organization, communication, and negotiation. Thus, as with other behavioral interventions, it is the helper's responsibility to assess for and teach needed prerequisite skills, or alternately, to modify the intervention to accommodate deficits. Significant modifications of these procedures would be needed for children whose developmental age is less than 3 years, as well as for individuals with significant language or cognitive impairments. When adaptations are made, such as when adults with developmental disabilities are explicitly taught contingency relations (i.e., how certain tasks may earn tokens such as money), these variations of behavioral contracting have been highly successful.

CASE ILLUSTRATION

"Max," a 12-year-old adolescent male, was referred for treatment by his mother, Mrs. Sharon Rosen, due to persistent teacher reports of a decline in his academic and behavioral performance. Since school began approximately 2 months ago, Max has earned failing grades in math and social studies and is receiving a grade of D in art. Teachers have further indicated that Max impulsively calls out answers, is frequently out of his seat, and is not completing his independent seatwork. In contrast, his performance during the first three periods of the school day is considered satisfactory. Review of educational records indicates that Max earned average to above average grades in all subject areas during elementary school. This is his first year in middle school.

Mrs. Rosen reported that Max was diagnosed with ADHD, Combined Type, at the age of 7 by his pediatrician. He was prescribed a stimulant medication, and his family was provided education about the disorder. He has continued on stimulant medication since that time, and his symptoms have been controlled to the extent that he did not require psychological or educational assistance until this time.

Approximately 3 weeks ago, the school nurse indicated that Max had not been reporting to the main office to receive his afternoon dose of medication. When confronted, Max explained to his mother that he could not leave class to take his medication because the other students ridiculed him and called him names. Despite his mother's encouragement, use of verbal reprimands, and removal of privileges, Max's noncompliance continued. In contrast, he took his morning dose of medication without difficulty.

An interview was conducted with Max to facilitate a functional assessment of the variables maintaining his noncompliant behavior. Max verbalized an awareness of his academic and behavioral difficulties when his morning dose of medication wore off. He acknowledged that the ridicule he endured for taking his medication was far worse than the academic and behavioral difficulties that resulted. Specifically, to take his medication he was required to raise his hand in the middle of art class and request a pass, cueing his classmates to begin teasing him about his "crazy medicine" and make other jokes at his expense. Max stated that his art teacher is often so busy that she forgets to remind him, thus immediate negative consequences for his lack of compliance are often absent. In summary, medication noncompliance appeared to be maintained by avoidance of peer ridicule (negative reinforcement). Also, while he received negative consequences from his mother when she periodically became aware of his difficulties, these consequences were delayed and not of sufficient magnitude to change Max's behavior.

An intervention plan that included two components was developed by the therapist. First, a social skills intervention enhancing Max's ability to respond to teasing was developed in collaboration with the therapist. The second component of the plan included the development of a behavioral contract to target Max's compliance with his afternoon dose of medication. The contract specified that during his art class, Max would raise his hand at 12:55 P.M., request a pass from his teacher, report to the school nurse, take his medication, and have his monitoring form initialed by the nurse. When he was picked up from school, he would produce the form for his mother. A reinforcer survey was completed by Max to assess potential rewards for medication compliance. In accordance with the contract, Mrs. Rosen agreed that if Max demonstrated the target behavior, he would be allowed 30 minutes to play video games upon arrival home from school. If he did not demonstrate the target behavior, Max would not be allowed to play video games that

evening. As an added incentive, if Max complied with the terms of his contract for 5 out of 5 days per week, Mrs. Rosen would allow him to have a friend over on Friday night, transport them to the local movie store to rent a video game of their choice, and extend the usual bedtime by 1 hour. Both parties signed and dated the contract.

For weekly Sessions 2 to 4, the therapist met with both parties to assess progress. The monitoring sheet and the integrity of contract implementation were assessed each time. Max also continued to receive skills training to improve his response to teasing.

By the fifth session, Max had met his targeted goal of compliance with his medication regimen for 5 of 5 days for 2 weeks in a row. All parties indicated a belief that this level of behavior could be maintained; thus, a plan for fading the procedure was initiated. A new contract was generated that extended the time required for monitoring and delivering consequences on a weekly rather than daily basis. Max and his mother were instructed to use the in-session contract as a guide for negotiating future revisions of the contract. A follow-up session was scheduled for 2 weeks later.

During the follow-up session, the therapist assessed progress and treatment integrity. Performance of the target behavior had been maintained at 100% for the past 2 weeks. Max reported that although his peers continued to tease him when he requested his pass to leave art class, he was better able to cope with the teasing. He indicated that he was doing much better, both academically and behaviorally, and was pleased with his performance. Mrs. Rosen indicated that Max's grades had improved to average or above in all afternoon subjects and his interim report indicated improved behavioral performance as well. Both parties were satisfied with Max's progress and agreed to continue contract negotiations using the 3-week interim report as the basis for continued monitoring and the delivery of continuing incentives. Treatment was terminated at this time. Although it was not necessary in this case, Max's behavioral contract could also have targeted increases in the use of the ignoring technique (compliance with psychosocial treatment). In addition, in collaboration with the teacher, this therapist could have developed a group contingency contract to facilitate reductions in the likelihood of teasing in the classroom environment.

—David Reitman, Angela Waguespack,
and Sarah Valley-Gray

See also: *Behavioral Consultation (Vols. I, II, & III),
Behavioral Contracting (Vols. I & III), Behavioral
Marital Therapy (Vols. I & III), Contingency
Management (Vol. II)*

Suggested Readings

Miltenberger, R. G. (2001). *Behavior modification: Principles
and procedures* (2nd ed.). Belmont, CA: Wadsworth.

Ruth, W. J. (1996). Goal setting and behavior contracting for
students with emotional and behavioral difficulties: An
analysis of daily, weekly, and total goal attainment.
Psychology in the Schools, 33, 153–158.

BEHAVIORAL FAMILY THERAPY

DESCRIPTION OF THE STRATEGY

The intervention known as behavioral family therapy
(BFT) has its origins in the convergence of two broad
theoretical traditions: the behavior and family therapies. The plural *behavioral therapies* indicates an intellectual journey of increasing theoretical sophistication
and range of applications during the half century or so
since operant and classical conditioning principles of
learning were first applied systematically to children's
clinical problems. Applied behavior analysis, behavior
modification and therapy, cognitive behavior therapy,
marital behavior therapy, and behavioral play therapy
have all contributed to present-day BFT. Among the
seminal influences (described later) on the development of its theoretical and practical foundations are
those of Albert Bandura at Stanford University and
Gerald Patterson at the Oregon Social Learning Center.

The systemic family therapy influence in the development of BFT is difficult to specify precisely. There
is no one therapeutic entity that defines family therapy; there are several models or schools. The structural school, which had its origins in the work of
Salvador Minuchin in the 1960s, and strategic family
therapy, which had its beginnings in the Palo Alto
research group led by Gregory Bateson in the early
1950s, have elements of philosophy and methodology
in common with behavioral approaches to childhood
and adult psychopathology. Given the rich but diverse
theoretical and applied origins of BFT, it is not surprising that marking out clear conceptual boundaries
is so difficult. Perhaps the best way of describing BFT
is as a behaviorally orientated therapeutic endeavor
that (a) focuses on changing the interactions between

or among family members, (b) seeks to improve the
functioning of individual members, also (c) the relationships within particular groupings (subsystems
such as parent and child, husband and wife), or (d) the
interactions within the family as a unit. What unites
most family therapies as they engage in their diver-
gent treatment strategies is a perspective that requires
that children's problems be understood as the consequence of the pattern of recursive behavioral sequences
that occur in dysfunctional families.

This perspective, influenced by a general systems
or cybernetic paradigm, was originally conceived by
Von Bertalanffy in the late 1920s in an attempt to
understand living organisms in a holistic way. It was
many years later, in the 1950s, that practitioners applied
his ideas to work with families. These ideas embrace
the concept of reciprocal/circular causation in which
each action can be considered as the consequence of
the action preceding it and the cause of the action following it. No single element in the sequence controls
the operation of the sequence as a whole because it is
itself governed by the operation of the other elements
in the system. Thus, any individual in a family system
is affected by the activities of other members of the
family, activities which the individual's actions or
decisions, in turn, determine.

Similarly, in the behavior therapy idiom, an individual's behavior functions as both stimulus and response.
The ABC analysis (at the core of the learning equation
in behavior therapy) is elaborated into a nonlinear recursive sequence. *A* stands for antecedent events, *B* stands
for the target behaviors or beliefs (the child's and/or
parent's interpretation of events), *C* stands for the consequences that flow from these behaviors/beliefs. *C*s (in
their turn) become *A*s (triggers), which generate new
*C*s (outcomes), and thus generalize to affect the actions
of others in the vicinity of the main protagonists (e.g.,
siblings, parents, and child).

This sequence is called a functional analysis, and in
BFT is directed toward the precise identification of the
conditions that control the targeted behavior problems
and the effects that follow. At its simplest, the important
questions are, What events trigger (elicit) the phobic
fear? or What reinforcement or payoff does the child get
for behaving in an aggressive manner? or What are the
overall ramifications of these events? At a more inter-
pretive level, the child's behavior may have the function
of solving (or attempting to solve) a developmental or
family problem. They serve a purpose, and in this sense
are functional (though they may appear dysfunctional to

the parent or professional) for the individual. An example of this is to be seen in the case illustrated below where a child would rather provoke negative attention than receive no attention at all.

One of the basic premises of BFT is that behavior is precipitated by particular setting events and maintained by its consequences. Another is that much abnormal behavior and cognition is on a continuum with normal behavior and thinking, and as such, is subject, with some important exceptions, to the same laws of learning. Unfortunately, the very processes that help a child adapt to life can, under certain circumstances, contribute self-defeating behaviors. An immature child who learns by imitating an adult does not necessarily comprehend when it is undesirable (deviant) behavior or distorted thinking that is being modeled. The youngster who learns adaptively to avoid a dangerous situation (and ones that are similar) on the basis of a traumatic fear reaction and the relief of escaping from it can also learn by the same processes (classical and operant conditioning, respectively) to avoid school or social gatherings. A caregiver may also unwittingly reinforce inappropriate behavior by attending or giving in to it.

BFT practitioners—professionals with specialist training from mainly the mental health and social services—typically engage more than one family member (whole families, marital or cohabiting partners, or parents and child) in face-to-face treatment. Therapy could also involve a single person for all the sessions. Patients are encouraged by a variety of therapeutic strategies to understand the alliances, conflicts, and attachments that operate within their family unit. They are encouraged to seek alternative solutions to their dilemmas and to feel and act differently in order to see themselves from a new perspective. BFT interventions with children and adolescents make use of techniques drawn from behavior therapy: operant procedures, desensitization, exposure training, social skills training, role play, behavior rehearsal, modeling, relaxation, homework exercises, and self-monitoring. Other methods have their roots in cognitive-behavioral and cognitive therapy: "Socratic questioning," persuasion, challenging, debate, hypothesizing, cognitive restructuring (reframing), verbal self-instruction, and internal dialogues. Given the intimate relationship between BFT and social learning theory, there is a strong focus on social influence, social cognitions, and early attachments.

Behavioral parent training (BPT) is a highly effective group-based intervention that comes under the rubric of BFT. It addresses parents' or other caregivers' difficulties in managing seriously disruptive behavior. Parents of youngsters with conduct problems give more frequent, negative, and ineffectual commands than parents of nonproblematic children. They tend to flounder because they provide attention following deviant behavior or are unlikely to perceive it as unacceptable; they get embroiled in extended coercive hostile interchanges and fail to monitor their children's activities or communicate effectively with them.

Parent training programs are designed to reduce confrontations among members of the family, increase their positive interactions, and moderate the intensity of punishment meted out by parents. Parents are guided in the implementation of brief, mild, nonphysical sanctions such as planned ignoring, time-out, loss of privileges, and logical consequences. Parents' own experiences of being parented and of being children in their own right are discussed and related to their beliefs (attributions) about child rearing and their attitudes to their children.

RESEARCH BASIS

Research on social learning theory, central to BFT, indicates that rewards and punishments, and the adoption of modeled behaviors and attitudes, are not simply the impersonal consequences of behavior. They are mediated by human agents and within attachment and social systems. The result is that children do not simply respond to stimuli; they interpret them. They relate to, interact with, and learn from people who have meaning and value for them. They feel antipathetic to some, attached by respect and/or affection to others, and thus may perceive an encouraging word from the latter as rewarding (i.e., positively reinforcing), but from the former as valueless, perhaps even aversive. Stimuli influence the likelihood of particular behaviors through their predictive function. Salient (contingent) experiences create expectations rather than simple stimulus-response connections.

Patterson's research has highlighted a critical feature of the interactions in families with disruptive children, namely coercion. In a coercive interaction, the aversive behavior of each person is terminated or reduced in frequency by the aversive behavior of the other person, but the long-term effect is to increase the likelihood that the original aversive behavior will occur again. For example, a parent orders a child to go to bed and she or he objects by whining incessantly. If the frustrated parent takes the line of least resistance and stops insisting, the child's whining is reinforced by the removal of the unwanted demand. The parent's reaction of dropping the demand is also (negatively) reinforced when the child stops the aversive whining. The net result of this commonplace scene from everyday life is that both the bedtime whining and the parent's retreat are more likely to be repeated on future occasions. If left unchanged, these coercive patterns of interaction may continue in magnified form into school life and adulthood.

It has been found that a collaborative style of working in BFT that gives parents responsibility for developing solutions alongside a therapist is more likely to increase their sense of confidence (perceived self-efficacy) and self-sufficiency than are therapies that do not. Support for this approach comes from Bandura's research literature on self-efficacy, which has been shown to be a critical causal (mediating) link between knowledge and behavior. Thus, people who own outcomes and feel self-confident are more likely to persist in the face of difficulties until success is achieved. They are also less likely to experience the debilitating effects of stress. Collaboration implies a nonjudgmental, supportive, reciprocal relationship based on combining the therapists' knowledge and the patients' unique strengths and perspectives; it implies respect for his or her contribution to the treatment programs. In a collaborative relationship, the therapist works with parents by actively soliciting their ideas and feelings, understanding their cultural context, involving them in the joint process of setting goals, sharing their experience, discussing and debating ideas, and problem solving together. The collaborative process has the advantage of reducing attrition (dropout) rates during treatment, increasing motivation and commitment, and reducing resistance by giving both patient and the therapist a stake in the outcome of the intervention efforts.

Rigorously designed evaluations of BFT and BPT, which are more numerous than those supporting any other approach, indicate their high level of effectiveness for treating a wide variety of the psychological problems that affect children and families.

RELEVANT TARGET POPULATIONS AND EXCEPTIONS

BFT has been applied to a comprehensive list of adult disorders (ranging from schizophrenia and depression to postcombat trauma and substance abuse), life problems (e.g., marital and personal difficulties), and child and adolescent problems (including anxiety conditions, oppositional behavior, disruptive disorders, and delinquency). A survey of family therapists' primary treatment goals for families produced the following list: improved communication, improved autonomy and individuation, improved empathy, more flexible leadership, improved role agreement, reduced conflict, individual symptomatic improvement, and improved individual task performance.

Because the frontiers of BFT are still expanding, it is difficult to say which problems are not amenable to the method. The range of problems has been broadened by an informed (as opposed to ragbag) eclecticism, which, for many practitioners, encompasses behavioral play therapy, functional and strategic therapy, and cognitive-behavioral approaches. The adjunctive role of marital behavior therapy enhances parent training outcomes and represents a further widening of the BFT repertoire.

COMPLICATIONS

The question of how to adopt a standard by which to evaluate functional ("healthy") as opposed to dysfunctional ("unhealthy") patterns of individual behavior or family organization, boundaries, strategies, rules, roles, decision-making processes, communications, or any of the other attributes family therapists believe to be significant, remains unresolved. Clearly, there are diverse cultural norms and subjective personal values that complicate professional judgments in these matters. There have also been disagreements over the years about the appropriate unit of focus (whole family vs. subsystems) in family therapy. The choice today, for most behavioral family therapists, is likely to be whichever is relevant to a problem at any one time. Its composition may vary over time and is best decided collaboratively by negotiation between the therapist and patient(s).

CASE ILLUSTRATION

"Louise," when brought to the clinic, was a bright, assertive child approaching 4 years of age. She was notorious among her mother's friends for her frightening temper tantrums. Jane, a quiet, shy woman in her late 20s, was feeling increasingly "helpless" at her inability to cope with Louise's aggression, and depressed about her unsatisfactory marital relationship, feelings which she had not dared communicate openly to her husband.

The assessment at the clinic utilizes a multimethod, problem-solving approach to obtain as complete a picture of the child and the family as is possible. The strategy is to begin with a broad-based assessment (measures of behavioral, cognitive, and emotional functioning) of the child and her environment (e.g., family, school, peers) and then to obtain information regarding specific stimulus features, response modes, antecedents, and consequences, severity, duration, and pervasiveness of the particular problems. The family, as a small group, is observed and assessed on a variety of dimensions: patterns of communication, cohesion, and processes of decision making.

Assessment revealed that Jane had no self-confidence and a very poor self-image, particularly with regard to her parenting. Her own mother (siding with her son-in-law) was scathing (as we were soon to discover in conjoint interviews) about the way she "spoiled" Louise, giving in to her on bedtime and table rules. A visit to the play school indicated a "different" child, well liked and cooperative, except when in her mother's presence. Observations of mother and child at play indicated that Jane was nervously intrusive in their interactions and missed opportunities to praise her daughter's clever use of drawing materials. Home observations of the three of them showed Louise continuously seeking attention, the father being remote, and the mother responding inappropriately when Louise was demanding, or ineffectually when she was being defiant. The important assessments of positives in Louise and her parents revealed many assets on which to build change.

The clinical formulation of the clients' problem (all members of a family, in this instance) bridges the assessment, the treatment plan, and its implementation. The contemporary causes of problem behavior may exist in the clients' environment or in their thoughts and feelings. They may exert their influence in several ways: as triggers that are direct in their effects and close in time to the actions they influence, or as outcomes (consequences) of a reinforcing kind. The identification of the current problem may be assisted by information about the patients' past (e.g., early attachments, health, reinforcement history, attitudes, life events). The past may haunt the present in the sense that it may influence current attitudes and thus, in turn, actions. It may be necessary before work can begin on a behavioral program to lay such ghosts to rest by discussing past traumatic events and their meaning.

In the present formulation, it was hypothesized (inter alia) that much of Louise's incessant demanding was attention seeking, and associated with the relative absence of warm and responsive attention she experienced. The lack of clear rules or limits, combined with inconsistent parental reactions to her defiance and tempers, contributed to her lack of self-control at home. These difficulties seemed to suggest the need for a parent training intervention. Discussions with Jane alone revealed a person who had received little in the way of confidence-boosting encouragement as she grew up. Although she loved her husband and appreciated much that he did for her, his lack of emotional support over Louise depressed her. Following a conjoint session with his wife, he expressed shock at her despair and low morale and stated that he was prepared to change if it would save their marriage, something he very much wished for.

Louise had a high score on the Richman & Graham Behavior Screening Questionnaire, but as she was no problem whatsoever at play school, it was decided not to work directly with her. Treatment for the parents began with three conjoint counseling sessions that addressed a variety of issues (e.g., quality time and its importance, child development, and their own personal backgrounds) of concern to them. Following these sessions, it was arranged for them to begin two courses: the group-based Child-Wise Parenting Skills (CWPS) course and a behavioral marital therapy (BMT) program that they attended as a couple on their own. Their ratings after 10 weekly sessions of the CWPS indicated improvements at home, in skills, confidence, and child care outcomes (managing Louise's behavior and enjoying her company). The results of six BMT sessions at the clinic were monitored on rating forms and evaluated qualitatively by means of diaries and written narratives. The program was evaluated as successful in terms of criteria involving their own relationship and an effective alliance in managing their daughter.

—*Martin Herbert*

See also: *Behavioral Contracting (Vols. I, II, & III), Behavioral Marital Therapy (Vols. I & III), Behavioral Treatment in Natural Environments (Vols. I & III)*

Suggested Readings

Alexander J. F., & Parsons, B.V. (1982). *Functional family therapy.* Monterey, CA: Brooks/Cole.

Bandura A. (1977). Self-efficacy: Towards a unifying theory of behavioral change. *Psychological Review, 84,* 191–215.

Bateson, G., Jackson, D. D., Haley, J., & Weakland, J. (1956). Toward a theory of schizophrenia. *Behavioral Science, 1,* 251–264.

Brestan, E. V., & Eyberg, S. M. (1998). Effective psychosocial treatment of conduct-disordered children and adolescents: 29 years, 82 studies, 5275 children. *Journal of Clinical Child Psychology, 27,* 180–189.

Dadds, H. R. (1995). *Families, children and the development of dysfunction.* Thousand Oaks, CA: Sage.

Griest, D. L., & Wells, K. C. (1983). Behavioral family therapy with conduct disorders in children. *Behavior Therapy, 14,* 37–53.

Herbert, M. (2003). *Typical and atypical development: From conception to adolescence.* Oxford, UK: BPS-Blackwell.

Herbert, M., & Wookey, J. (2003). *Managing disruptive behavior: The Child-Wise approach.* Chichester, UK: Wiley.

Minuchin, S. (1974). *Families and family therapy.* Cambridge: Harvard University Press.

Mueser, K. T., & Glynn, S. M. (1999). *Behavioral family therapy for psychiatric disorder.* New York: New Harbinger.

Patterson, G. (1982*). Coercive family process.* Eugene, OR: Castalia.

Sanders, M. R., & James, J. E. (1983). The modification of parent behavior: A review of generalization and maintenance. *Behavior Modification, 7,* 3–27.

Von Bertalanffy, L. (1968). *General systems theory.* Harmondsworth, UK: Penguin.

BEHAVIORAL GROUP THERAPY WITH CHILDREN AND YOUTH

DESCRIPTION OF THE STRATEGY

Behavioral group therapy (BGT) is a major vehicle for the delivery of cognitive-behavioral treatment to children and adolescents. There are a number of advantages of working with children in groups. The peer group is a natural part of child and adolescent development, and as such, the treatment more nearly simulates their real world than the client-adult dyad. Groups also represent a more efficient way of delivering interventions than in dyads. Group membership commonly ends the sense of isolation and lack of understanding many clients experience, since they are surrounded by other children who are dealing with similar issues and problems. Groups may be divided into subgroups for certain exercises and as a way of increasing the amount and breadth of interaction in the group. Certain interventions are more accessible or more effective in the small group, for example, the

use of brainstorming in teaching problem-solving skills. Feedback from other members following role playing and designing extra-group tasks and goals is another. Groups are an effective way of delivering information. Games and other recreational activities in groups are more challenging and cohesion building and can be adapted to encourage trying out new behaviors. Finally, groups enhance generalization of change, since each member observes and helps solve a diversity of problems manifested by the other clients as well as his or her own.

Most therapy groups range in size from 5 to 15 members, although the norm is about 6 to 9. They range in duration from 6 to 20 sessions, depending on the complexity of the presenting problems. Most sessions last from 45 minutes to one and one half hours. There are either one or two therapists. One experienced therapist is more efficient, but two provide an opportunity for therapist training and provide the members with multiple adult roles. Most groups are closed and time limited with a fixed beginning and ending time ranging from 4 to 16 sessions. Open groups in which members are added and dropped periodically are more common in institutions. Most of these decisions regarding the above issues are made for practical reasons. However, there is some data to support smaller groups versus larger groups as well as for providing group structure that permits intense interaction by everyone in the group. The more complex the problems, the longer the length of time in each session and the larger the number of sessions required.

BGT is guided by several principles unique to group context. The first is that there is broad and active participation if the above advantages are to be realized. The interaction should be characterized by its provision of support and reinforcement or mutual aid for each other. The second principle is gradual progress toward independence and autonomy. The therapist initially provides structure and gradually delegates or encourages responsibility for that structure to the members. The third principle is that the goals of treatment ultimately are formulated in terms of generalization of the behaviors and attitudes learned in the group. The fourth principle is that of gradually increased demand for self-disclosure. We begin with introductory interviews in pairs and then describe one's interviewee to the group, the analysis of a case in terms of how each is similar and different from that case, and ultimately in formulating problems with which each client is confronted. It is the behavior and cognitions in these problem situations that become the target of the interventions. Interrelated to the above principles is building the cohesion of the group. With children and youth, the therapy group should be both a work and a fun experience.

In this entry, the focus is on the unique application of behavioral treatment using groups in assessment, the treatment process, and generalization planning. Since most of the intervention and treatment strategies are discussed elsewhere in this encyclopedia, we shall focus primarily on the use of the group in these three processes.

Assessment in Groups

One important early step in the process of treatment is assessment of the presenting problems and the resources the child has for resolving them. In assessment, BGT takes into consideration the environment in which the behavior and emotions occur. This includes each person's social support network. Most BGT models teach specific skills for coping with and resolving unique problem situations. Individual assessment and pregroup interviews are used for treatment planning within groups. But the group itself is also used for assessment by having the members observe each others' interactions, having members interview each other, and by members' observing role plays of others.

As part of assessment, long- and short-term goals are formulated. Each member negotiates his or her own goals with suggestions from the other group members and the therapist. Interviews with parent and teachers may contribute to the formulation of significant goals. For example, the goal of a child with a problem of excessive anger when criticized was to express his disagreement in a matter-of-fact tone of voice or for a child whose long-term goal was to make new friends, his short-term goal might be during the following week to ask another child to play with him. Extra-group tasks (which are often the same as short-term goals) to try out these behaviors are negotiated during the session with each member, and each reports back the results at the subsequent session. Success or failure provides evidence of progress or lack of it.

Principles of Effective Treatment

To provide a better sense of how the group is conducted with children and adolescents, some of the key group strategies for effective treatment are reviewed. These include building group cohesion, identifying and correcting group problems and using effective group interventions, and using individual treatment procedures in a way that is compatible with a group environment.

Building Group Cohesion

Group therapy research has supported the principle of group cohesion as an effective ingredient of group treatment. Especially since most groups for children and adolescents are often involuntary, building cohesion can be a needed process in obtaining motivation and compliance with group tasks. Cohesion refers to the mutual liking of members for each other and the group therapist and their attraction to the program of the group. High cohesion tends to be correlated with high motivation to work on significant problems. The level of cohesion can be monitored by the postsession questionnaire (see Table 1). In groups, the cohesion of the group can be enhanced by the use of group introductory exercises in which members interview each other in pairs, and partners introduce their partner to the group. It is also a safe way of increasing broad participation and is the first step in self-disclosure. With children and youth, the use of games and other recreational activities at the end of a session dramatically increases the cohesion of the group. Cohesion is also enhanced by creating opportunities for continued broad participation, protecting members from premature and/or too harsh confrontation, keeping the interaction positive, using variation in the program, using humor, and developing opportunities for choice and self-decision making by the members. Finally, cohesion is enhanced by training the members in giving and receiving both positive and critical feedback.

Identifying and Dealing With Group Problems

To ascertain group problems, a postsession questionnaire is administered periodically to the members of the group, as shown in Table 1. The scaled items represent member perception of satisfaction with the group, involvement in group activities, degree of self-disclosure, mutual helpfulness, and group cohesion. Additional items may reveal group autonomy and emotional states in the group. Means, discrepancies among the members, and discrepancies between the mean of the members and the group therapist's observations

Table 1   An Example of Questions and Format of a Postsession Questionnaire

1. How useful was this session?

1	2	3	4	5	6	7	8	9
not at all		very little		somewhat		quite a bit		extremely

2. How actively involved were the members in today's session?

1	2	3	4	5	6	7	8	9
not at all		very little		somewhat		quite a bit		extremely

3. How helpful were members to each other during this session?

1	2	3	4	5	6	7	8	9
not at all		very little		somewhat		quite a bit		extremely

4. How much did the members reveal about themselves (their real thoughts, feelings, motivations, and/or concerns) during this session?

1	2	3	4	5	6	7	8	9
not at all		very little		somewhat		quite a bit		extremely

5. How close did the members feel to each other during this session?

1	2	3	4	5	6	7	8	9
not at all		very little		somewhat		quite a bit		extremely

provide a rough estimate of some of the group phenomena as perceived by the members and group therapists.

The summarized data and member comments are discussed at the beginning of the subsequent session. An extreme average on any one or more items represents a potential group problem, as do individuals who have extreme scores relative to their peers. These scores are discussed with the group members, and if a problem is noted, a plan is developed with the group by means of group problem-solving techniques.

Converting Individual to Group Interventions

As mentioned earlier, individual interventions such as reinforcement and cognitive restructuring are administered in such a way as to encourage members to take active roles in helping one another. For example, based on earlier self-descriptions, each member described a cognitive distortion of the member on the left and how that person has changed it and, with the given client's permission, reported his or her observations back to the group. The other members responded to the accuracy of this perception. Similarly, each member will describe in behaviorally specific terms one social skill her or his neighbor has demonstrated in the group. The other members verified the accuracy of this observation.

Group Interventions

Modeling and rehearsal by group members is a major group intervention because it involves many members in each role play. Although used in dyadic treatment, the group provides multiple roles and multiple models for each client. Modeling rehearsal is a form of role playing used to demonstrate new behaviors by leaders or members (modeling) and to practice these behaviors (behavioral rehearsal). These plus group feedback and extra-group tasks are the core of social skills training. In most children groups, group social skill training is a major component.

Brainstorming is conducted by all the group members to help an individual discover alternative strategies for appraising situations, as well as identifying possible interventions for resolving specific situations or difficulties. Because it involves all the members of the group, it is a true group procedure. It is an intrinsic part of systematic problem solving, in which, in contrast with the treatment dyad, the group provides a richness of ideas based on the wide experience of all the members and the therapist.

Group exercises refer to the use of structured interactive activities as ways of teaching clients the skills that mediate the achievement of therapeutic goals. Introductory exercises to gradually increase group self-disclosure and to enhance cohesion have already been mentioned, as have exercises in the use of positive and critical feedback in analyzing problematic situations. Some of the more commonly used group therapy exercises with children and adolescents include analyzing interactive situations, identifying anger-producing events, determining the social network, solving problems systematically, identifying self-defeating behaviors, identifying coping responses, modeling and rehearsing overt behavior, and generalizing and maintaining change.

RESEARCH BASIS

Since 1985, over 30 published control group studies have for the most part provided support for the effectiveness of behavior group therapy with children and youth across a diverse array of problems. Several studies indicated that group therapy is as effective and more cost beneficial than dyadic therapy. The results of group treatment of severe disorders such as severe depression have been mixed. Several examples of group research are provided in the suggested readings.

RELEVANT TARGET POPULATIONS AND EXCEPTIONS

Behavioral group therapy has been used with children and youth with social skill deficiencies, anger control problems, substance abuse, attention-deficit/hyperactivity disorder, trauma recovery, anxiety, coping with divorce of parents, pregnancy prevention, school dropout, stress, grief and loss, obsessive-compulsive disorder, and many combinations of these themes. In most cases, the problems have not been severe. All of these problems are associated with social interaction and informational deficits. Behavior group therapy may have its largest impact when targeting these types of difficulties.

COMPLICATIONS

Groups are not without disadvantages. In contrast to individual or family therapy, it is more difficult in group therapy to individualize treatment plans for each child in the group. It should be noted that group therapy is not one strategy but many strategies that operate within the context of the group and makes use of the group as an additional set of interventions. Stigma associated with therapy group membership can be a barrier to obtaining a child's interest in

joining a group or in obtaining parental permission for a child to participate in group therapy. Concerns about confidentiality are common, especially among older children and adolescents, and can be a barrier to recruitment of members to groups. Confidentiality and the consequences of breaches need to be dealt with by the group therapist in pregroup screening and early in treatment. In addition, problems in groups include clique formation, select member dominance, and distracting behaviors.

CASE ILLUSTRATION

The following is an example of a typical group session in which many of the principles and techniques discussed above are demonstrated. In particular, note how cognitive and behavioral treatment components were integrated into group procedures, as well as the use of feedback reinforcement and behavioral examples.

At the beginning of the third group treatment session for seven girls with social anxiety, the therapist asked each member to describe the extra-group tasks (homework) designed the previous week. Evie had agreed to bring in a problem that had involved peer pressure. She described a situation in which her school friends, as a joke, urged her to hide Lisa's sweater, which was lying on the playground. Lisa was an extremely shy girl who was often scapegoated. Evie initially said she didn't want to hide the sweater because it was a mean act. However, fearing that the other girls wouldn't like her anymore if she didn't do what they suggested, she hid the sweater. Lisa was predictably upset and searched everywhere before she found the sweater. The group treatment members agreed that this was an example of a social behavior that could be worked on, since it was clear what had happened, where it happened, who was involved, and the fact that Evie was dissatisfied with her behavior at the moment she agreed to hide the sweater. The group members pointed out a distortion in the way Evie evaluated the situation, namely her fear that the others wouldn't like her anymore.

In answer to the therapist's question as to the accuracy of her fear, Evie agreed that there were a lot of situations in which others didn't comply with the pressure of the group, and that there were no negative consequences. Evie admitted that she could have refused their request because it was mean, and she need not be afraid of rejection.

In answer to the therapist's question of how else she might have handled the situation, the group members brainstormed ideas. A list of alternative responses was generated. After evaluating most of them, Evie chose to remind herself that she was not the slave of her friends and that it was all right to trust her own judgment in such instances. She saw herself as nice and not a mean person. She also decided, at several members' prompting, that it would have been better to have refused outright to obey the demands of the others and to suggest it was a bad idea, even though it might have resulted in temporary rejection. She would have liked herself better.

The situation of refusing when Evie was pressured was modeled for her by Marion, an older girl in the group who played Evie's role, while several other girls put pressure on Marion (in the role of Lisa). Then Evie rehearsed the situation and received feedback from the group as to what she did well and what she might have done differently. After role playing a second time, the members complimented her and applauded her success. The therapist noted that apologizing for rudeness or an unkindness is not easy, and both Marion and Evie did a good job.

At the end of the process, the therapist noted that this was an example of negative group pressure and encouraged a general discussion of the topic. After several others had presented the results of their homework, pairs of group members designed a task for the following week or agreed to continue working on last week's task. The session was concluded with a game. They then filled out the postsession questionnaire, which reflected their satisfaction with the group, high involvement of the members, and level of cohesion.

—*Sheldon D. Rose and Craig W. LeCroy*

See also: *Behavioral Group Work (Vols. I & III), Group Behavioral Therapy for Depression (Vol. III), Social Effectiveness Training (Vols. I & III), Social and Interpersonal Skills Training (Vol. II), Social Competence Treatment: Externalizing Disorders (Vol. II), Social Skills Training (Vols. I & III)*

Suggested Readings

Kazdin, A. E. (2000). *Psychotherapy for children and adolescents.* New York: Oxford University Press.

Khalsa, S. S. (1996). *Group exercises for enhancing social skills and self-esteem.* Sarasota, FL: Professional Resource Exchange.

LeCroy, C. W. (1994). *Handbook of child and adolescent treatment manuals.* New York: Free Press.

Rose, S. D. (1998). *Group therapy with troubled youth: A cognitive-behavioral interactive approach.* Thousand Oaks, CA: Sage.

Swenson, C. C., & Brown, E. J. (1999). Cognitive behavioral group treatment for physically abused children. *Cognitive and Behavioral Practice, 6,* 212–220.

Vickers, B. (2002). Cognitive behaviour therapy for adolescents with psychological disorders: A group treatment programme. *Clinical Child Psychology and Psychiatry, 7,* 249–262.

BEHAVIORAL INTERVIEW

DESCRIPTION OF THE STRATEGY

The behavioral interview is a hallmark among assessment measures in children. Indeed, most clinicians initiate the assessment process with the implementation of the behavioral interview, as the results of this procedure often act to guide the decision-making process involved in choosing which strategies will be included in the assessment battery. The content and general tone of the interview will vary depending on the nature of the presenting problem, the child's developmental level, and overall purpose of the interview, among other factors. Along these lines, most interviews can be classified as unstructured, semistructured, and structured.

In the unstructured interview with the target child, or significant other, the content and guidelines dictating the interviewer's method of responding are at the discretion of the interviewer. The initial stages of most unstructured interviews focus on identifying and broadly understanding problematic behavior, whereas the latter stages focus on reviewing general life domains that are not directly related to the presenting problem. It is common for the interviewer to assess reasons for the referral, history of the presenting problem, the client's mental status, medical history, social and academic history, hobbies, family background, mental health diagnosis, strengths, and goals for therapy. However, it is within the interviewer's discretion to choose the domains that are to be assessed, as well as the specific content to be assessed within each of the selected domains. The interviewer is also free to record interviewee responses that appear most relevant. Many behavioral unstructured interviews usually include the results of a functional analysis, which depict an understanding of the factors that maintain the problematic behavior. In the functional analysis, the interviewer assesses the onset, frequency, intensity, and duration of the problematic behavior, as well as stimuli that precede (i.e., antecedents), follow (consequences), and co-occur (concomitants) with the problem behavior. Interviewers also assess stimuli that occur when the problem behavior is absent. In this way, interviewers are able to determine stimuli that are incompatible with the problem behavior, which may assist in treatment planning. The unstructured interview is relatively unreliable because interviewers will vary in the questions they ask and the responses they record.

Structured interviews tend to yield global indices concerning the presence or absence of a disorder, as opposed to more specific information about the child, family, and behavioral circumstances that are typically obtained during an unstructured interview. In the structured interview, the interviewer is restricted to asking a priori questions that are generically applied to all interviewees. That is, the questions are predetermined and usually focused on the assessment of a specific behavioral problem (e.g., substance abuse). The interviewer is also trained to record responses according to a prescribed response format (e.g., 1 = criterion met, 2 = unsure, 3 = criterion not met). In this manner, structured interviews tend to be reliable and valid assessment tools. Semistructured interviews often include a list of questions that are relevant to the assessment of a specific problem area. However, unlike the structured interview format, the interviewer is free to choose which questions to ask from the list. Similarly, clinical guidelines are available to assist in scoring or interpreting interviewee responses, although these rules allow greater subjective input from the interviewer. Interviewers who solely rely upon structured and semistructured interview approaches risk missing important information that the interview protocol did not cover. Although the prescribed nature of the semistructured and structured interviews may interfere with the establishment of rapport, this problem is usually avoided with extended training and experience. Moreover, structured interviews do not prohibit interviewers from formulating their own questions to clarify responses, but rather provide detailed rules that tell interviewers what to do in certain situations. Recently, there has been an increase in the use of semistructured and structured interviews in clinical practice due to their adaptability to computerized administration and scoring procedures.

RESEARCH BASIS

Research has shown that although unstructured interviews appear to be necessary in the effective assessment of children, they are relatively unreliable diagnostic tools due to lack of clarity concerning decision rules, confirmatory biases, and errors in judgment. Semistructured and structured interviews are more reliable than unstructured interviews, although reliability coefficients vary depending on the interview, clinical characteristics of the population being interviewed, age of the child, and interviewer experience, among other factors. Similarly, the validity of the structured, and semistructured, interviews is generally good.

RELEVANT TARGET POPULATIONS AND EXCEPTIONS

Unlike most assessment measures that may be relevant only to particular clinical populations, the unstructured behavioral interview, to some extent, is helpful in the assessment of all clinical problems evidenced by children and adolescents. However, these interviews are often limited to nonresearch practice settings (e.g., private practice) because they are relatively unreliable. On the other hand, semistructured and structured interviews are often limited to clinical practice and research settings that depend upon reliable diagnostic assessment (e.g., treatment outcome studies, forensic practices).

In conducting behavioral interviews, multiple informants should be interviewed in separate sessions, whenever feasible, to assess differing perspectives relevant to the presenting problem(s), assist in understanding inconsistencies in reporting by interviewees, and provide additional information to assist in treatment planning. Although the target child and target child's caregivers are typically interviewed, other interviewees often include the target child's caregivers, teacher(s), friends, and relevant relatives. When children are unavailable or not appropriate to be interviewed (e.g., too young, developmentally handicapped), significant others may be relied upon as the chief interviewees. The child's age will assist in determining the appropriate interview format to utilize during the assessment process. For instance, studies have indicated that children younger than 5 years are typically unreliable informants, and their attention is difficult to maintain. Thus, interviews with these children should be informal and should integrate interactive games into the interview format. Older children (i.e., 5 to 11 years) are capable of participating in structured interviews. However, breaks should be frequently scheduled, and the interviewer should use developmentally appropriate vocabulary.

COMPLICATIONS

Behavioral interviews are influenced by reporting biases, as are all self-report measures. Some of these include reporting of memory events that did not occur, positive and negative distortions of memory events, as well as exaggerating, denying, and lying. To assist in the solicitation of accurate information, interviewers must be careful to avoid leading questions (e.g., "Did he touch you in your private area?") that may influence children in particular to provide answers that they perceive to be more acceptable to the interviewer. Instead, interviewers should utilize open-ended questions (e.g., "Where did he touch you?"), especially when the content area is sensitive and the child is more vulnerable to be biased in responding. The interviewer should also avoid asking the same question repeatedly, as research has shown that this will lead children to erroneously change their responses to be more affirmative. Interviewers need to be aware of environmental circumstances (divorce, arrests, work-related injuries) that may contribute to inaccurate reporting behavior during interviews. In these cases, multiple informants may be utilized during unstructured interviews to assist in identifying inaccurate information. Interviewees may also provide inaccurate information because they misunderstand the question. Thus, interviewers need to be appropriately audible and clear in their queries, as well as use developmentally appropriate vocabulary.

CASE ILLUSTRATION

"Billy," a 12-year-old Caucasian male, was referred to a clinical psychologist by his school counselor consequent to his beating up a classmate. Billy and his mother participated in their first assessment session after they completed all program intake forms, including treatment assent and consent. The psychologist decided to begin the assessment process with an unstructured behavioral interview to gather information relevant to treatment planning and to assist in determining other assessment measures to administer.

The behavioral interview began with the psychologist informally making some notes about Billy's presentation (e.g., unkempt hair, poor eye contact, wearing rock concert T shirt and torn blue jeans, walked with head looking down) and interactions with his mother (i.e., argument about who would sit in the reclining chair and who should talk first). Both were informed about the purpose of the interview, including what general information would be assessed. It was explained that the school psychologist had reported that Billy might benefit from therapy and that the purpose of the interview would be to gather information that might assist the psychologist's understanding of the presenting problem, including circumstances relevant to the presenting problem, friends, hobbies, social, academic, and medical history, family background, conduct at school and home, diagnostic issues, strengths, and goals for therapy. Upon being asked if there were any issues he felt should be addressed, Billy responded, "Just leave me alone. Talk to my mother. She's got the problem, not me." Billy's mother retorted, "Billy told me he would come today if he didn't have to talk." The therapist explained that it would be important to gain his perspective and that separate interviews could be arranged. However, Billy reported that today he would commit only to listening. Given Billy's apparent lack of motivation to be interviewed, the psychologist decided to interview his mother while her son was present. In this way, the psychologist believed Billy might learn that the psychologist was nonjudgmental and present opportunities for Billy to respond if he desired.

Billy's mother was asked to describe her understanding of the presenting problem. She indicated that the fistfight leading to the referral was consequent to her son being teased at school by several boys for more than a month. She indicated that her son had moved to his present school and was having a "tough time" making friends. She was succinct, and her responses were pertinent. Therefore, the interviewer asked open-ended questions relevant to antecedents (e.g., "What type of things happen before he gets into fistfights?") and consequences (e.g., "What usually happens to him after he fights?") of his fistfighting behavior. Although motivated to provide answers, Billy's mom was not a good informant, as she was unaware of specific immediate circumstances relevant to this behavior. Billy was quiet throughout this discussion.

To elicit commentary from Billy, the psychologist decided to focus on Billy's friends and hobbies, and return to a behavioral assessment of the presenting problem with Billy at a later time. This strategy was successful, as Billy began speaking liberally, thus allowing the therapist to provide empathy and praise more easily to assist in gaining rapport. Billy reported that he enjoyed competitive games that did not involve physical exercise, such as computer games, darts, and cards. He mentioned that the friends he had at school were good friends, and that the kids at his current school were "troublemakers." When asked to elaborate, Billy mentioned that the kids did not like him, and that they spent much of their time teasing him and trying to get him in trouble. Billy no longer appeared to be inhibited in his responses, and his mother seemed to provide additional perspective without criticizing her son. Therefore, the psychologist did not excuse his mother to the waiting room, as might typically be done to assist in establishing an environment for Billy that would enhance confidentiality and disclosure. The psychologist asked Billy questions relevant to validating information that was provided by his mother, as well as other information relevant to antecedent, concomitant, and consequential thoughts and feelings regarding fistfighting behavior. The psychologist also attempted to elicit information relevant to the onset, frequency, duration, and severity of fistfighting behavior ("Tell me about the first fistfight you experienced at school," "How many fistfights have you experienced?" "How long do the fistfights last?"), as well as situations that had not been associated with arguments or fistfights with students enrolled in his current school.

A transition was then made to discuss general life domains to gain an understanding of the context in which the presenting problem occurs. Both agreed that prior to moving to their new home, Billy was an honor roll student in school, but that he now was getting C's and D's on his report cards. The move was reported to occur consequent to a divorce between his biological parents. Billy was very close to his father. However, the judge awarded custody to Billy's mother because of his father's "problems with alcohol abuse." When asked to specifically elaborate on these problems, Billy's mother stated that his father did not spend much time with Billy, and that when he was available, he was often critical. She added that his father no longer visits Billy. Billy disagreed and said his father was "nice" to him and that he did not visit with his father because his mother influenced him to leave. The therapist quickly conceptualized the onset of Billy's behavioral problems as potentially a result of upset due to the absence of a significant primary reinforcer (i.e., father), and hypothesized that this behavior was being performed, in part, to show others that he was dissatisfied with the current living arrangements. Indeed, Billy appeared to demonstrate no deficits in social skills, particularly conflict resolution, prior to the divorce.

The psychologist then switched topics to an examination of Billy's social network by asking Billy and his mother to talk about things he liked, and disliked, about each of the people living in his home. Billy discussed his relationship with his older brother and younger sister and mother as generally good. However, he said that he was angry that his mother left his father. The psychologist noticed that his mother was upset, and decided to assess his anger at a later time without the presence of his mother. He switched topics to less emotionally charged content, that is, Billy's medical history. Billy's mother reported that Billy had never experienced significant medical or physical problems. Given Billy's expressed irritability in the context of significant loss of reinforcement (i.e., father's absence, problems adjusting to new classmates), the psychologist hypothesized that Billy might be experiencing a depressive disorder. Therefore, he asked a series of diagnostic questions relevant to a depressive disorder. Responses to these questions indicated that Billy met *DSM-IV* criteria for major depression.

The psychologist then assessed significant strengths of Billy, which included being intelligent, empathic, hard working, and sincere. Running out of session time, the therapist decided to end the interview by asking both persons to provide their goals for therapy, including their expectations of meeting these goals. Billy said he wanted to make friends and be able to "deal" with the kids at school. His mother reported that she would like to know how best to help Billy adjust to his school and improve his grades. The psychologist informed them that next week they would have time to define these goals into specific actions and determine target dates in which to realistically accomplish these actions to their satisfaction. The psychologist ended the session by obtaining a commitment from both to attend the next session.

—*Brad Donohue and Stephanie Stowman*

See also: *Behavioral Assessment (Vols. I, II, & III), Dialectical Behavior Therapy (Vol. III), Multimodal Behavior Therapy (Vol. III)*

Suggested Readings

Bellack, A. S., & Hersen, M. (Eds.). (1998). *Behavioral assessment: A practical handbook* (3rd ed.). Boston: Allyn & Bacon.

Ciminero, A. R., Calhoun K. S., & Adams, H. E. (Eds.). (1986). *Handbook of behavioral assessment* (2nd ed.). New York: John Wiley.

Greenspan, S. I. (1981). *The clinical interview of the child.* New York: McGraw-Hill.

BEHAVIORAL PEDIATRICS

DESCRIPTION OF THE STRATEGY

Behavioral pediatrics (BP) is a branch of pediatrics that integrates behavioral and pediatric sciences to promote the health of children. A unique aspect of BP is that competencies for practice can be met by physicians or psychologists, and thus its practitioners include both. Most typically, however, the physician and psychologist work in partnership whether the task at hand involves a particular case or a promising area of research. Another unique aspect is that BP plays a significant role across the three levels of care in medicine: primary (e.g., routine, preventive), secondary (e.g., therapeutic, curative), and tertiary (e.g., rehabilitative, palliative). Historically, there have been three general areas of inquiry and application in BP: (1) common behavior problems that present in outpatient pediatric medical settings (e.g., bedtime problems), (2) behavior problems with significant biological components (e.g., soiling), and (3) biological (i.e., medical) problems with a significant behavioral component (e.g., enuresis). More recently, a fourth general area of BP has emerged, one that more strongly emphasizes the interaction between biological and behavioral factors (e.g., attention-deficit/hyperactivity disorder—ADHD). In addition, there are two general forms of treatment supplied in BP: (1) supportive counseling, usually involving the delivery of health education (e.g., extended crying is normal in early infancy) but no specific action and (2) prescriptive behavioral treatment, usually involving the provision of specific procedures for remediation of presenting problems to caregivers (e.g., motivational programs). This entry will primarily emphasize the latter. Recognition of the high prevalence of behavioral problems that initially and often only present in pediatric settings as well as the reciprocal nature of interactions between medical and behavioral factors in child health has led to dramatic growth in BP over the past 30 years. In addition, the range of behavioral treatments that have been shown to eliminate or at least reduce the severity of problems seen by BP practitioners has also expanded greatly. This entry elaborates on the four general areas of BP, includes examples of problems representative of each, and, where relevant, describes methods that have been utilized for successful treatment.

Behavior Problems Presenting in Pediatric Settings

Twenty to 30% of children seen in primary care exhibit behaviors that meet criteria for a behavioral or emotional disorder, and another 40% or more exhibit behaviors or emotions that cause their parents concern and/or cause some functional impairment for the child but do not meet criteria for a disorder. The types of concerns commonly seen in pediatric settings vary with the age of the child. Parents of infants are most often concerned about excessive crying and sleep problems, parents of preschool children mostly worry about oppositional behaviors, toileting, attentional problems, selective eating, and fears, and parents of school-aged children are mostly concerned about academic, school behavior, and peer relationship problems.

Minor behavior problems will often resolve without the direct intervention of a professional. Thus, pediatric advice about behavior problems is frequently limited to recommending that parents let their child "grow out of it." However, this "tincture of time" approach ignores the substantial stress that child behavior problems can place on a family, a fact highlighted by the increased risk of child abuse that occurs in association with many problem behaviors (e.g., crying and incontinence are leading causes of abuse). In addition, not all children grow out of their behavior problems, and currently there is no reliable means of determining those who will from those who will not. Poorly managed oppositional behaviors can devolve into much more serious problem behaviors that require extraordinary therapeutic interventions for remission (e.g., conduct disorder, delinquency). Unresolved toileting problems can lead to serious medical problems (e.g., megacolon, urinary tract infection). Untreated sleep problems can lead to habitually disrupted sleep patterns, family discord, and child maltreatment. Unsolved school problems can lead to incomplete education and school failure that, in turn, set the stage for drug use, delinquency, and crimes against others. There are many other examples. The upshot is that children with routine behavior problems and their families can benefit substantively from the provision of brief, problem-specific, prescriptive advice. The range of problems initially presenting in primary care settings for which such advice can ultimately be beneficial is broad, and complete coverage is well beyond the scope of this entry. By way of illustration, a very common pediatric complaint, sleep disturbance, and five problem specific interventions that have been used for treatment in pediatric settings will be described.

Bedtime Problems

Learning to go to bed, go to sleep, and stay asleep throughout the night is difficult for many children, and as many as 30% of parents contend with sleep problems three or more nights a week. The problems include resistance to going to bed, fussing and crying while in bed, and night waking with fussing, crying, and/or unauthorized departures from the bedroom. These problems are important because they disrupt the parents' and child's sleep, increasing the likelihood of child irritability during the day and decreasing the parents' ability to cope with that irritability.

A key component of the sleep process involves sleep associations. Children associate what happens before and while they fall asleep with the actual act of falling asleep. Unaware of the power of these associations, parents attempting to help their child sleep can create and perpetuate the very problems the parental efforts are intended to solve. For example, most children fall asleep easily in response to parent presence, cuddling, and soothing. Unfortunately, sleep cycling often results in periodic waking throughout the night, and those children who have learned to fall asleep only in the presence of a parent will call out or cry until a parent arrives to aid the return to sleep. Two common responses by the arriving parent are additional soothing and angry warnings. But the soothing can strengthen the associations further, and the warnings can provoke more intense crying. A self-perpetuating system is thus established. There are many variations on this theme. Although there are several established procedures for treatment of bedtime problems, virtually all of the effective ones include some combination of a nurturing bedtime ritual and modification of parental attention delivered after the child is in bed.

Ignoring. The simplest attentional treatment involves outright ignoring that lasts from the moment the parent leaves the child's bedroom until morning. In effect, the child is left to cry it out. If the child leaves the bedroom, a silent parent physically returns him or her. Generally, ignoring works more rapidly than other approaches, but it can also cause problems that mitigate its overall effectiveness, including stress due to extended crying, alarm in neighbors that hear the crying, and uncertainty and discord between parents.

Graduated Ignoring. This treatment involves advising parents to gradually increase the amount of time they ignore their child's crying (e.g., 5 minutes on the first episode, 10 on the second). These intervals increase over the course of a week, ending with 35 minutes for the first episode on Night 7, 40 for the second, and 45 minutes for all subsequent episodes and nights. Although children can tantrum longer than 45 minutes at night, very few do.

Positive Routines. This procedure involves a hybrid of ignoring and a programmed momentum leading to bedtime. Starting just before the time their child typically falls asleep, parents initiate a few fun activities (lasting no longer than 20 minutes total), and during them issue several simple instructions that the child is highly likely to follow and praise compliance with each. The procedure ends with a terminal instruction that is always a variation on "and now it is time for you to go to bed." If after being placed in bed the child leaves the bedroom, the parent returns the child to bed, explaining that the routine is over and it is time for bed. Crying or verbalizations are ignored. At specified intervals (e.g., 1 week), the parents move the positive routine back in time 5 to 10 minutes. They continue this backward movement until they arrive at a preferred bedtime.

Self-Quieting Skills. In this procedure, the self-quieting skills necessary for a child to manage bedtime upset are taught through the combined use of structured ignoring (e.g., time-out) and high-density nurturing (e.g., time in) during the day. The nurturing establishes the effectiveness of the ignoring by increasing and thus making more salient the contrast between the two conditions. The ignoring teaches the self-quieting by establishing periods of quiet as the criteria that must be met for the ignoring to end and nurturing to begin. Once a self-quieting skill set is established during the day, the parents teach a version of it at night. Specifically, parents provide an extended period of nurturing at bedtime (20–30 minutes of stories, hugs, etc.), then wish their child well, leave the bedroom, and ignore what follows. The ignoring sets the occasion for the child to apply the newly learned self-quieting skills.

Bedtime Pass. In the bedtime pass program, parents provide their child with a pass (e.g., laminated card) at bedtime that the child can use in exchange for a trip out of the bedroom by the child or a summoned visit to the bedroom by parent. The trip or the visit can be used to satisfy a simple request (e.g., drink, hug, visit to the bathroom, reassurance), following which the pass is surrendered until the following night. After the pass is surrendered, the ignoring program is implemented.

This brief discussion of child sleep problems and their treatment is by no means complete, nor is it meant to be. It is merely provided as an illustration of a BP target area. Infant and child sleep disturbance is a very important and common presenting complaint in pediatric settings, but its treatment is unlikely to be part of conventional medical training. As with many other behavior problems, the tincture of time will work for some but by no means all. BP contends with this gap in care by developing brief, problem-specific, prescriptive procedures, all of which can be easily applied by psychologists with their extended clinic visit times, and some of which can be applied by physicians, even though their visits are typically much briefer. Expanding this aspect of BP will involve continued research on common problems presenting in pediatric settings (e.g., opposition, habit disorders, disruptive morning routine, excessive fears, sibling rivalry, picky eating) and development of brief, problem-specific, prescriptive procedures for their treatment.

BIOLOGICAL AND ENVIRONMENTAL INFLUENCES ON BEHAVIOR

Biological and environmental variables both influence behavior, and determining which influence is more important can easily lead to a chicken versus egg type of debate. In fact, few conflicts in behavioral science have been as enduring or as acrimonious as the debate between those who see human development and behavior as determined by internal biologic forces (nature) and those who view human development and behavior as determined by environmental forces

(nurture). The tension between the two is mirrored by a tension between medical and psychological perspectives on behavior, especially the kind of behavior that leads to a medical referral. Similarly, there is differential emphasis placed on either the behavioral or the pediatric side of behavioral pediatrics, depending on the perspective of the BP practitioner. Increasingly, however, the relationship between biology and environment/behavior is seen as bidirectional rather than unidirectional; biology affects behavior and behavior affects biology. This view has led to biobehavioral models in medicine, and a major portion of BP is based on those models. Still, although biology and behavior are necessarily in a reciprocal relationship, at times it makes sense to emphasize the role of one as the influencing agent and the role of the other as the condition to be influenced. In the three sections to follow, the first will emphasize the role of biological influences on BP-relevant behavior (i.e., behavior problems), the second the role of behavioral influences on biology (i.e., medical conditions), and the third will place more emphasis on the interaction of the two influences.

Biological Influences on Behavior

Providing examples of behavior that occurs as a result of, or is strongly influenced by, biological variables is not a difficult assignment. Fever leads to fluid ingestion, rash to itching, nausea to anorexia, bleeding to panic, hypotension to sitting, cramping to reclining, and the list of potential other examples is prohibitively long. Relatedly, in pediatric settings, a large array of presenting behavior problems are caused or exacerbated by biological conditions. A frequently seen example involves fecal incontinence that meets criteria for functional encopresis.

Functional Encopresis

Definition and Etiology. Functional encopresis, a common presenting complaint in pediatrics (3%–5% of all referrals), involves fecal accidents occurring after the age of 4, not due to a general medical condition. As many as 95% of encopresis cases can be traced to a causal biological variable, constipation. Although definitions for constipation vary, children who frequently go 2 or more days without a bowel movement are probably prone to constipation. A common complaint by the parents of encopretic children is that the children deliberately soil their clothing, but this type of accusation is usually false. The primary cause of the soiling is fecal retention, which in the vast majority of cases is the result of a biological predisposition (i.e., constipation), diet, insufficient leverage for passage of hard stools, and occasional or frequent painful bowel movements that basically teach children to hold their stools. For some children, especially those with extreme constipation and/or treatment failure, there is reduced awareness of rectal fullness and sometimes a paradoxical contraction, rather than relaxation of the external rectal muscles during the act of defecation. The combined effect of all these factors is a lowered probability of voluntary stool passage and a heightened probability of fecal retention.

Chronic fecal retention results in fecal impaction, which results in enlargement of the colon. Colon enlargement results in decreased motility of the bowel system and occasionally in involuntary passage of large stools and frequent soiling due to seepage of soft fecal matter. The seepage is often referred to as paradoxical diarrhea because the children retain large masses of stool and thus are functionally constipated, but their colon allows passage of soft stool around the mass, which results in diarrhea. Between 80% and 90% of cases of encopresis are believed to be accompanied by fecal impaction. Successful BP treatment requires some knowledge of the physiology of defecation.

Physiology of Defecation. The large intestine or colon is the distal end of the alimentary tract, which is sequentially composed of the esophagus, stomach, small intestines, and colon. The colon is a tubular-shaped organ with a muscular wall that connects the small intestine to the rectum and anus, and it has three primary functions: fluid absorption, storage, and evacuation. Extended storage and planned evacuation are the defining features of fecal continence. Movement of waste through the colon is achieved through muscular contractions called peristalsis that produce a wavelike motion of the colonic walls. As the waste moves through the colon, water is absorbed, creating semisolid feces. Movement through the colon is potentiated by a variety of external events that instigate muscular contractions in the colonic wall. For example, eating a meal increases colonic contractions (referred to as the gastrocolonic reflex) and moving about will have a similar effect (referred to as the orthocolonic reflex). Most of the time, the rectum, the

distal end of the colon, contains little or no feces, but prior to defecation peristalsis moves feces into it, resulting in rectal distension, stimulation of sensory receptors in the rectal mucosa and in a group of muscles just above the pelvis, relaxation of internal rectal muscles (i.e., internal sphincter), and imminent defecation. This process is involuntary, but the child can inhibit the impending defecation by contracting external rectal muscles (i.e., external sphincter).

Differential Diagnosis. There are rare anatomic and neurologic problems that can lead to fecal retention and soiling. Anatomic problems include a variety of unusual formations and locations of the anus, which are detectable on physical exam and require medical management. Hirschsprung's disease or congenital aganglionosis is a disorder in which the nerves that control the muscles in the wall of part or the entire colon are absent, causing severe constipation. Its incidence is approximately 1 in 25,000, and it usually causes symptoms in infancy.

Evaluation. As with all BP conditions with a medical presentation, an initial examination by a physician (preferably a pediatrician) is critical. The encopresis exam usually includes a routine check of patient history, an abdominal palpation, a rectal examination, and sometimes an X-ray of the abdomen to determine the extent of fecal impaction. A barium enema is rarely necessary unless features of the exam suggest Hirschsprung's disease.

In addition to routine behavior and psychological assessments, the behavioral interview for encopresis should include questions related to constipation. These include asking whether there is ever a long period between bowel movements, bowel movements are atypically large (stop up the toilet), fecal matter ever has an unusually foul odor, fecal matter is ever hard, difficult, or painful to pass, and whether the child ever complains of not being able to feel the movement or make it to the toilet on time. An additional question that pertains more to treatment history than to pathogenesis is whether the child ever hides soiled underwear. Affirmative answers to any or all of these questions are highly suggestive of retentive encopresis, and hiding underwear indicates a history that includes some form of punishment.

The encopresis evaluation is the first step in treatment. Encopresis is not well understood outside the medical community, and the child's parents are likely to be under the influence of the characterological and psychopathological interpretations that are prevalent in Western culture. The parents' interpretation of the condition is also likely to influence how the children view their problem. Thus, the encopresis evaluation can actually begin treatment by providing accurate information that demystifies the problem. Last, the evaluation should include questions about diet and timing of meals. Low-fiber diets and irregular meals can be contributing factors in encopresis.

BP Treatment for Encopresis. During the past 15 years, several descriptive and controlled experimental studies have supported a multicomponent approach to treatment of chronic retentive encopresis. As indicated above, the first component can be addressed within the evaluation. Specifically, the entire elimination process, including its disordered manifestations, should be demystified. Generally, this means providing information about bowel dynamics and the relationship of the problem to constipation. Second, if there is a fecal impaction, it should be removed with enemas and/or laxatives. Third, the child should sit on the toilet for about 5 minutes one or two times a day. Fourth, the parents should promote proper toileting with encouragement and not with coercion. In addition, they should not reserve all their praise and affection for proper elimination; a child should be praised just for sitting on the toilet. Fifth, a stool softener such as mineral oil or glycerin suppositories should be used in order to ease the passage of hard stools. Sixth, dietary fiber should be increased in the child's diet. Seventh, in order to increase and maintain motility in the child's colon, the child's activity levels and fluid intake should be increased. Eighth, during toileting episodes, the child's feet should be on a flat surface. Foot placement is crucial for the abdominal push necessary to produce a bowel movement. And ninth, the child should be rewarded for all bowel movements in the toilet.

This section has emphasized the influence of a biological variable, constipation, on a behavioral problem, encopresis. As indicated above, emphasizing biology or behavior typically involves some degree of arbitrariness. Nonetheless, an emphasis on biology has not only produced a much more benign interpretation of encopresis (e.g., constipation) than had been the case with the historical emphasis on psychology (e.g., psychopathology), but it also has also led to effective treatment and a profoundly more optimistic

view of the prognosis. There are a variety of other behavior problems that present in pediatric settings that also reward a biological emphasis. For example, extremely fussy babies are not necessarily the victims of ineffective parenting. Results of neonatal assessments and BP research on behavioral style indicates that extreme fussiness can be the result of difficult temperament, a construct composed of mostly biological variables. Fussiness can also be the result of harmful intrauterine events or toxic elements in the mother's blood. As another example, evidence suggesting biological predispositions to addiction is growing. In addition, extreme self-injury has been shown to result from diverse biological variables ranging from genetic anomalies (e.g., Tay-Sachs syndrome) to abdominal problems (e.g., ulcer). That the tics of Tourette's syndrome have a biological basis is well established. There are many other examples. The point, though, is not to show that biology trumps behavior in BP, but rather that in some conditions, emphasizing biology can yield a more productive interpretation of a behavior problem and a more successful approach to treatment.

Behavioral Influences on Biology

Just as there are many behavior problems whose assessment and treatment benefit from biological considerations, there are also many medical problems whose assessment and treatment benefit from behavioral considerations. Relatedly, this section discusses problems wherein BP assessment and treatment targets behavior change in order to alter physiologic processes involved in medical problems. Examples of the influential relationship behavior has on disease have been emerging from the scientific literature steadily since the benefits of hand washing on the prevention of infection were noted many years ago. Thus, the direction of influence emphasized in this section, from behavior to presenting medical problem, is well established in the minds of scientists and laypeople alike. There are many examples that could be showcased here to underscore the potential value of the emphasis. In fact, health results produced through changes in behavior have been widely documented in all three levels of medical care: primary care (e.g., preventive benefit of hand washing), secondary (e.g., healthful effects of diet and exercise on cardiovascular conditions), and tertiary (e.g., rehabilitative and the benefit of stretching and range of motion exercises on the tonicity and restricted movement in conditions such as cerebral palsy). Obviously, complete coverage of this area of BP is well beyond the scope of this entry.

Biofeedback and Nocturnal Enuresis

Biofeedback, however, is a prototypical behavioral application that has been used effectively across the three levels of medical care and the four general areas of BP. Generally, biofeedback involves use of electrical or electromechanical instruments to measure and increase the salience of stimuli associated with pertinent biological processes and training patients to discriminate them. The penultimate goal of biofeedback is to train individuals to alter the biological processes in healthful directions, and the ultimate goal is to train them to do so without biofeedback. A common BP intervention that illustrates the principles and goals involved is urine alarm treatment for nocturnal enuresis (NE). Although not commonly characterized as such, alarm treatment is one of the earliest forms of biofeedback treatment procedure. NE is also an exemplary problem for this section because it (a) is a very common presenting problem in pediatric settings, (b) responds readily to biofeedback (alarm-based) treatment, and (c) can lead to unhealthful outcomes if left untreated.

Definition and Etiology of NE. NE involves nocturnal incontinence past the age of 5 years without a medical cause, and it is common (e.g., estimates of first grade children affected range as high as 20%). The exact cause of enuresis is unknown. Early accounts linked it to causal psychopathology, but this connection has been disproved. More current accounts link it to causal physiopathology. This link is based on evidence that some children may have difficulty concentrating their urine during the night and thus produce more than their nonenuretic peers. The evidence is scant, however, as it is based on studies with a very small number of children. In addition, pharmacological treatment (e.g., Desmopressin) that increases nocturnal urine concentration is only minimally effective in eliminating or decreasing accidents, and the effects are usually lost when the treatment is withdrawn. A more cogent, general, and empirically sustainable view is that NE results from a deficit in the behavioral skills necessary to prevent urination while asleep. A critical aspect of the deficit is the salience of imminent urination as a psychological event for children with

NE. To understand the latter view and the role of the urine alarm, it is necessary to briefly review some of the physiology of the systems that govern urination.

Physiology of Urination. The bladder (detrusor) is an elastic hollow organ with a muscular wall. Its shape resembles an upside-down balloon with a long narrow neck; it has two primarily mechanical functions, storage and release of urine. Extended storage and volitional release are the defining properties of urinary continence. In infancy, distension of the bladder leads to contraction of the bladder and automatic (nonvolitional) evacuation of urine. As children mature, the capacity of the central nervous system inhibition of bladder contraction increases during early childhood, which typically coincides with the development of continence. The components of the urogenital system that are under volitional control and that can be used to establish continence include a group of muscles just above the pelvic region (e.g., levator ani, diaphragm). Except during imminent or actual urination, these muscles remain in a state of involuntary partial contraction, which maintains the bladder neck in an elevated and closed position. Even after initiation of urination has begun, contraction of the pelvic floor muscles can abruptly raise the bladder neck and terminate urination. But for children with nocturnal enuresis, these urinary inhibitory responses are either not present or are sporadic at night.

Alarm-Based Biofeedback. The enuresis alarm is a moisture-sensitive switching system, the closing of which (when the child wets the bed) rings the alarm. Repeated pairing of awakening by the alarm with episodes of wetting has consistently been shown to be the single most effective treatment for enuresis by a wide margin. How the alarm produces its results is not specifically known, but the primary effect of the alarm is to increase the salience of biological events involved in nocturnal urination so that the child can act upon them. Early explanations described the mechanism as classical conditioning, with the alarm as the unconditioned stimulus, bladder distention the conditioned stimulus, and waking as the conditioned response. Subsequent explanations emphasized a negative reinforcement paradigm wherein children repeatedly awakened by the alarm gradually learn to avoid it by waking prior to its onset and urinating in the toilet (initially) and (ultimately) holding their urine until a more convenient time. The current prevailing account involves a combination of the two previous accounts with classical conditioning of pelvic floor muscles and reinforcement of volitional behaviors related to continence. Cures are obtained slowly, and during the first few weeks of alarm use, the child often awakens only after voiding completely. The aversive properties of the alarm, however, steadily strengthen the skills necessary to avoid it. These skills include sensory awareness of urinary need, waking to urinate in the bathroom, or contraction of the pelvic floor muscles that offset urination.

Other Examples of Biofeedback

Biofeedback devices much more sophisticated than the enuresis alarm are now widely available. Physiologic processes that can be monitored include muscle tension, skin temperature, respiratory rate, blood pressure, and skin moisture (sweating). These devices have been used in the treatment of a wide variety of disorders, including headaches, anxiety disorders, sleep disorders, and dysfunction of the autonomic nervous system. The influence of intentional behavior on various physiologic processes such as skin temperature and blood pressure that have not been thought to be under volitional control is also being increasingly demonstrated. Other behaviors capable of altering physiologic processes are being researched. For example, awareness enhancement techniques have been used to alter the level of mediators of the immune system in saliva and to decrease the recurrence rate of mouth ulcers.

Interaction Between Biology and Behavior

As implied above, biology and behavior do not represent separate processes within individuals but are interacting systems that could no more function independently than the heart and the brain. As the reciprocal capacity of biologic and behavioral variables to influence each other becomes increasingly clear, decisions about selecting appropriate treatments become more complex. One reason for the complexity is that there are a rapidly growing number of medical and behavioral problems for which there are both clearly effective behavioral and clearly effective medical treatments. How to proceed is thus usually guided by the training and orientation of providers with medical treatments typical of physicians and behavioral treatments typical of psychologists. The BP approach, however,

often employs a combined approach, and a partnership between physician and psychologist is a hallmark of the field.

There are many examples reflecting the benefit from the combined approach to treatment and the related partnership of BP-oriented psychologists and physicians. For example, although the most effective single-mode treatment for NE involves the alarm, a major BP study has shown that combining the most typical pharmacological intervention (Desmopressin) with urine alarm treatment was more effective than either treatment alone. There are many other types of problems that benefit from a combined approach, ranging from relatively common conditions such as feeding problems to very rare conditions such as Tourette's syndrome. Presently, however, a serious and increasingly prevalent problem that almost always initially presents in pediatric settings and whose treatment is virtually emblematic of the value of combined medical and psychological approaches and partnerships between physicians and psychologists is ADHD. Stimulant medications such as methylphenidate (Ritalin) have been demonstrated to decrease disruptive behaviors and improve the off-task behaviors that are typical of the condition. In addition, a variety of behavior modification types of interventions (e.g., reinforcement, extinction, stimulus control) have also been shown to decrease disruptive behaviors and improve on-task behavior. Thus, optimal treatment for ADHD is currently widely considered to involve combining behavioral and pharmacologic treatment. A brief case example reveals this point well.

CASE ILLUSTRATION

An 11-year-old boy in sixth grade was brought to an outpatient behavioral pediatric clinic by his parents for assessment and treatment of behavior problems at home and behavior and academic problems at school. In addition to his biological parents, he lived at home with his 13-year-old sister. His medical and psychiatric histories were unremarkable. His parents had, however, intermittently sought advice about overactivity and oppositional behavior from the boy's pediatrician from the age of 3 years on. His educational history was also unremarkable, with the exception of occasional complaints from teachers about drifting attention and overactivity. These complaints emerged in preschool, where they were sporadic, and continued to the time of the referral, when they had become chronic. At that time, he was receiving Ds and Fs in all his classes and was placed on detention at least three times a week. The parents reported attempting a variety of interventions, including withdrawal of privileges, confinement to his bedroom, and time-based grounding. None of these had produced any discernible effect.

After meeting with the parents, the attending psychologist met with the boy's pediatrician and then his schoolteacher to develop a plan for assessment and subsequent treatment. The assessment included a physical examination by the pediatrician and a variety of tests and observations obtained by the psychologist. The tests included the Diagnostic Interview Schedule for Children, a highly regarded computerized structured interview with an exhaustive section devoted to ADHD, and some paper and pencil behavior problem checklists (e.g., Eyberg Child Behavior Inventory, Connors Parent and Teacher Rating Scales). The observations included his school desk (children with ADHD routinely have very messy desks), his handwriting (children with ADHD typically have fine motor problems), his behavior in class, on the playground, in the clinic waiting room, and at home (during dinner, playtime, and homework). The results of the physical exam showed the boy to be in good health and above average for height and weight. The results of the tests and observations indicated a significantly high level of inattentive, impulsive, and overactive behavior occurring across home and school situations. In fact, the only times when these problems were not manifest were when he was engaged in an absorbing passive activity (e.g., television, computer games) or in a situation that allowed high levels of activity with relatively low levels of sustained attention (e.g., on the playground).

The pediatrician, teacher, and psychologist agreed upon a solely psychological intervention at first. The home portion included an incentive system for appropriate behavior (e.g., reward jar, motivational gaming), a job jar for misbehavior, a task-based grounding system, daily delivery of special time (30 minutes from at least one parent), modified parental communications (e.g., simplified commands in terms of steps, reduction in use of extended temporal concepts, proscription against nagging), and an intensive effort to catch him at, and praise him for, engaging in appropriate behavior. The home program also included a reduced bedtime that could be reclaimed with homework. His bedtime prior to treatment was

9:00 P.M. On weekdays it was reset to 8:00 P.M., but he could stay up until 9 if he sat at the kitchen table and did homework. If he completed his homework or worked steadily until 9:00, he was allowed to stay up an extra half hour as a reward. The school portion included a home-school note system relaying feedback about performance at school so it could be dealt with at home, a change in his seating (nearer the front of the class and studious classmates), decomposing his assignments into smaller parts, a point-based reward system with a privilege menu that involved out-of-seat activities (e.g., delivery of attendance sheets to office). Initial results were positive at home and school, but attentional and impulsivity problems remained, and thus a prescription for Cylert was sought from the pediatrician. Within 4 weeks, the attention and impulsivity problems improved substantially, and his grades had risen to B and C levels. However, during a clinic visit with the psychologist, the boy appeared to exhibit facial tics (blinking, grimacing), and the parents reported they had not seen these previously. A group of medical studies and case reports suggest that in some children, psychostimulant medication (especially Cylert) can produce ticlike responses. Consultation with the physician resulted in a change in medication from Cylert to Adderral. Within 2 weeks, the tic behaviors had disappeared and additional improvements in behavior and academic performance emerged. The psychologist and pediatrician continue to work in partnership on the case and currently are working with the boy's new seventh grade teacher. The success obtained in this case reflects the benefits that can be obtained from approaching some problems that present in BP from the perspective of an interaction between the medical and psychological aspects of a case rather than from the unidirectional perspective of one versus the other.

CONCLUSION

Behavioral pediatrics is a growing field of research and practice that is notable, if not unique, for its integration of medical and behavioral perspectives on problem behavior presenting in pediatric settings. Generally, BP focuses on common behavior problems and on the complex interactions between biology and behavior that affect health. The former focus, common behavior problems, includes a vast number and array of presenting complaints that, although not representative of true psychopathology, do pose psychological risks for the children who exhibit them and their families. The latter, the interactions, can be viewed in three ways: influence of biology on behavior, influence of behavior on biology, and the interactive influence of each on the other. Although the sample of problems discussed (or merely mentioned) in this entry is by necessity very limited, it is representative of the range and diversity of the field. Serious diagnostic conditions such as major depression, suicide, or delinquency represent boundary conditions for BP. BP is a multidisciplinary specialty, but its practice is largely confined to psychologists and physicians. However, limitations on time for, and training on, behavior problems can reduce the physician's ability to deliver complex biobehavioral treatment procedures or modify treatment in accord with unexpected responses. But because the physician is usually the first professional to whom behavior problems are reported, and because there often are medical considerations that emerge in the evaluation of behavior problems, a partnership between psychologist and physician operating in a biobehavioral context is optimal for BP practice.

—*Patrick C. Friman*

See also: *Applied Behavior Analysis (Vol. II), Behavioral Consultation (Vol. II), Behavioral Medicine (Vols. I & III), Memory Rehabilitation After Brain Injury (Vol. I), Psychoneuroimmunology (Vols. I & III)*

Suggested Readings

Blum, N., & Friman, P. C. (2000). Behavioral pediatrics: The confluence of applied behavior analysis and pediatric medicine. In J. Carr and J. Austin (Eds.), *Handbook of applied behavior analysis* (pp. 161–186). Reno, NV: Context Press.

Blum, N., Williams, G., Friman, P. C., & Christophersen, E. R. (1995). Disciplining young children: The role of reason. *Pediatrics, 96,* 336–341.

Christophersen, E. R. (1982). Behavioral pediatrics. *Pediatric Clinics of North America, 29*(2).

Christophersen, E. R., Finney, J. W., & Friman, P. C. (Eds.). (1986). Prevention in primary care. *Pediatric Clinics of North America, 33*(4).

Christophersen, E. R., & Friman, P. C. (2003). Elimination disorders. In R. Brown (Ed.), *Handbook of pediatric psychology in school settings* (pp. 467–487). Mahwah, NJ: Erlbaum.

Friman, P. C., & Blum, N. J. (2003). Behavioral pediatrics: Primary care behavioral pediatrics. In M. Hersen and W. Sledge (Eds.), *Encyclopedia of psychotherapy* (pp. 379–399). New York: Academic Press.

Friman, P. C., & Jones, K. M. (1998). Elimination disorders in children. In S. Watson & F. Gresham (Eds.), *Handbook of child behavior therapy* (pp. 239–260). New York: Plenum.

BEHAVIORAL REHEARSAL

DESCRIPTION OF THE STRATEGY

According to the tenets underlying social learning theory, social skills may be markedly improved through observation and practice of relevant target behaviors, particularly when accompanied by accurate feedback. In behavioral rehearsal, the primary method for improving social skills in children, a facilitator first assists the child in identifying the social skill deficit to be addressed. This is usually accomplished by asking the child, or significant others who have observed the child in social situations, to report problems the child had experienced during social situations. Social skill deficits are also identified by observing the child in naturalistic settings (e.g., school playground, classroom, family dinner, basketball game) or during simulated social scenarios with a confederate. Deficits vary widely but are often related to problems in (a) responding appropriately to others who are rude or socially offensive in some way (i.e., negative assertion) and (b) initiating positive interactions (i.e., positive assertion).

Once the behavioral deficits are determined, the facilitator assists the child in generating behaviors that are likely to be socially effective (e.g., speaking clearly, providing a compliment, engaging other person in small talk) in the identified problem social situation (e.g., asking a girl for a date). Relevant social skills may be identified from outcome studies, brainstorming sessions with the child during an individual session, or from other children in a group setting. The facilitator models the identified skills with the child, portraying the other person in the scenario (e.g., girl to be asked for the date). Subsequent to this interaction, the child should be asked to first report the skills performed by the facilitator that were admired. The child should be given an opportunity to provide suggestions that might improve the facilitator's performance or that might be idiosyncratically effective for the child. The child is instructed to attempt the skills that were modeled while the facilitator enacts the role of the other person in the scenario. Immediately after the child's performance, the facilitator descriptively praises the specific skills that were performed well and asks the child to state what was liked about the performance. Feedback should also be provided that is relevant to improving the child's performance.

In this process, it is best to ask the child what improvements could be performed, praise the child for these suggestions, and offer feedback relevant to further improvements that could be performed, if any. Last, the child should be assigned homework to practice the skills at home or school, including recording of the date, time, situation, behaviors that were practiced effectively, response of others to the practiced target behaviors, and experienced feelings consequent to the interaction.

The initial target skill should be a behavioral repertoire that the child will have the ability to acquire fairly quickly. As the child becomes accustomed to the procedures of behavioral rehearsal, additional skills should be taught. The complexity of the situations being rehearsed should be tailored to the developmental level of the child and should also generally increase in difficulty with practice and consequent skill development. Although the training may occur in group or individual sessions, the format is essentially the same.

There are three forms of behavioral rehearsal. Covert rehearsal requires the child to imagine a scene that involves a social interaction. The child then imagines performing a social skill and the response of others to the performance. The child also imagines alternative behaviors that could be performed. Verbal rehearsal involves a social situation being presented to the child, and the child subsequently identifying each step involved in performing the social skill. It is important that the child verbally arranges these steps in the proper sequence. Children should also be told to describe situations in which the skill would be appropriate, as well as likely consequences of performing the skill. Alternative behaviors are also elicited in this form of rehearsal. Overt rehearsal involves a role play in which the child actually performs the social skill. These three forms of behavioral rehearsal can be used alone or in combination. Overt behavioral rehearsal utilizes structured role-playing exercises to teach children social skills and is probably the most frequently employed of the three methods.

RESEARCH BASIS

Although the relative effectiveness of behavioral rehearsal or social skills training varies, depending on the skills being taught, these programs have generally been found to be effective in controlled clinical trials with children and adolescents. For instance, relevant to negative assertion, social skills training has improved behaviors associated with responding to rude people, and resolving conflicts. Improvements in positive assertion skills (e.g., introducing oneself, eliciting a date, answering the telephone, maintaining a conversation, appropriate disclosure, interviewing skills) have also been shown to improve consequent to the implementation of social skills training. Interestingly, improved social skills have been shown to be positively associated with pleasant mood (e.g., happiness), problem-solving abilities, improved relationships with others, employment, and reductions in conduct problems. Most important, improvements gained from social skills programs have generally been maintained across time, and the utilization of acquired skills by children has been shown to generalize to environmental settings that were not targeted during training.

RELEVANT TARGET POPULATIONS AND EXCEPTIONS

Behavioral rehearsal is appropriate for use across a wide spectrum of problem behaviors and developmental levels in children and adolescents. This intervention has demonstrated effectiveness in treating children and adolescents with social skill deficits, depression, mental retardation, visual and hearing impairments, and social phobia and other anxiety disorders. Behavioral rehearsal may also be used to enhance social skills with children and adolescents who have not evidenced significant deficits, that is, prevention of future problems. For instance, social skills training/behavioral rehearsal may be used to teach children in elementary schools to avoid strangers or to refuse offers to use drugs. Behavioral rehearsal may be used to improve relationships through the teaching of skills related to giving compliments, providing appropriate disclosure of personal information, responding to upset individuals, and effective use of anger management strategies.

COMPLICATIONS

Complications (e.g., refusal of the child to rehearse the modeled behavior, generalizability of acquired skills to environments other than the therapy office) sometimes occur when behavioral rehearsal is implemented, particularly when initiated by inexperienced therapists. Fortunately, these problems are easily prevented. First, it is important to appreciate that role playing provokes anxiety for some children, as they have often been judged negatively in past social situations and thus often lack confidence in their social skills. When children are nervous about their performance, they may refuse to engage in behavioral rehearsal. Children may also be less likely to attempt behavioral rehearsal when the therapist does not model the target skill. Indeed, the therapist should not assume that the child knows how to perform skills that were emphasized in discussion.

To increase compliance to the role-play format, several strategies should be performed, including *instructing* children to perform target behaviors instead of *asking* them to perform target behaviors, always modeling target skills before children are instructed to do so, and praising children during (and immediately after) their performance. If a delay between the instruction to perform the target behavior and the child's participation is evident, the clinician should immediately prompt the child to perform the behavior (e.g., "What were you saying to me?"). While skills may be effectively demonstrated during role-play scenarios, they may fail to generalize to the child's natural environment (i.e., home, school, work). The latter problem is usually ameliorated by encouraging greater practice in the natural environment, monitoring the practice experiences carefully (ideally through direct observation or the observation of a responsible party), and gradually increasing complexity, variability, and difficulty of role-play scenarios to resemble in vivo experiences. While the child may wish to start with the most pressing problem, it will be beneficial for the child to begin with less emotionally charged problem areas that may act to impede new learning.

CASE ILLUSTRATION

"Valerie," a 16-year-old Hispanic female, was referred to the outpatient behavioral treatment program by her school guidance counselor due to problems relating with other youth her age. During the intake examination, her mother reported that Valerie experiences "problems knowing what to say with other children and has only one friend." Valerie reported that she avoids children her age because she "gets nervous." During a behavioral role-play test with the therapist, Valerie evidenced poor social skills, as compared with other children her age. Specific deficits were found in her ability to initiate and maintain conversation, react appropriately to an upset friend, initiate a date, as well as conflict resolution.

After two assessment sessions, Valerie constructed a hierarchy of trouble situations with the therapist during the first intervention session. This hierarchy outlined age-appropriate social situations from most to least intimidating and anxiety producing. The least anxiety-provoking situation consisted of her initiating and maintaining a conversation with one of her friends at school. Her most anxiety-provoking situation was relevant to confronting boys at school who tease her. After the least anxiety-provoking situation was fully described by Valerie, the therapist solicited important skills that would be needed to initiate a conversation. Valerie mentioned that it would be important to start the conversation with a salutation and subsequently discuss the weather and ask the child what she liked to do for fun. The therapist added that it would be important to discuss something she liked about the activity that was mentioned by the other youth. The therapist then instructed Valerie to act just like she thought the other girl might act, while he attempted to perform the specified actions. As might be expected, during the role play Valerie made it difficult for the therapist to maintain a conversation. She answered tersely and failed to volunteer information. However, the therapist persisted with questions and was praiseworthy throughout the interaction. When the conversation was finished, the therapist asked Valerie what she liked about his skills, and she reported that she liked how he kept smiling and telling her "good things" about her responses. The therapist added that he was proud of the way he was able to take a few seconds after her responses to think of a new topic to discuss instead of blurting out the first thing that came to his mind. Valerie agreed, and the therapist asked her if there was anything that she would do differently if she were the person attempting to initiate the conversation. She stated that she would not ask the girl what courses at school she liked, because she thought that was "nerdy." The therapist praised her for her social etiquette and subsequently instructed her to initiate a conversation with him. The therapist answered Valerie's questions in great detail to make it easier for her to think of relevant topics. The latter strategy was performed to increase the likelihood that her first performance would be a successful one. Valerie struggled to come up with questions and comments initially, but as she grew more comfortable toward the end of the role play, her responses became more fluid and relevant. After the role play the therapist immediately praised her "wonderful" performance and asked her what she liked about her performance. Valerie stated, "I thought I asked a lot of good questions and was able to listen carefully to what you were saying so I could tell you what I liked about what you said." The therapist agreed and mentioned that her smile toward the end of the role play was "illuminating." Valerie sheepishly smiled. The therapist asked Valerie if there was anything she would do differently if she were to initiate a similar conversation, and Valerie mentioned that she would probably do "more of the talking." The therapist told Valerie that he thought it was a great first try, and that if she wanted to look at his face a little more the next time, it might help her to focus on what he was saying so she could be even more engaged in the conversation. She agreed, and the therapist subsequently instructed her to practice these skills during a second role-play scenario.

After the second role play, for homework the therapist asked Valerie to identify two students that she could attempt to initiate and maintain conversations with during the next week at school. She mentioned that although Marilyn and Alisha were not her friends, they had been kind to her in the past. Therefore, she was instructed to attempt to initiate and maintain at least one conversation with each of these students prior to her next intervention session. She was given a homework sheet that included the days of the week in the columns and several actions in the rows (i.e., time of the interaction, friend's name, demonstrated skills during the conversation, reaction of friend, experienced feelings). To assist in homework compliance and ensure that Valerie understood the assignment, she was instructed to complete the rows for the second role play under the present day (i.e., Monday). The therapist subsequently praised her for completing the form accurately, and the next session was scheduled.

Valerie received seven more intervention sessions. The format for these sessions was similar to the first session, although role-play scenarios gradually increased in difficulty consistent with her hierarchy. Commensurate with her improved social skills demonstrated during the role plays was Valerie's confidence. Indeed, she enjoyed talking with the therapist about her social accomplishments throughout the preceding week and reported that she was making new friends at school. During the 5th week, Valerie was able to successfully initiate a movie date with one of

the girls in her class. The last session consisted of Valerie reviewing the specific skills that she had acquired throughout intervention.

—*Brad Donohue and Stephanie Stowman*

See also: *Behavioral Rehearsal (Vols. I & III), Modeling (Vols. I, II, & III), Role Playing (Vols. I, II, & III)*

Suggested Readings

Becker, R. E., Heimberg, R. G., & Bellack, A. S. (1987). *Social skills training treatment for depression.* New York: Pergamon Press.

Gresham, F. M. (1998). Social skills training with children: Social learning and applied behavioral analytic approaches. In T. S. Watson & F. S. Gresham (Eds.), *Handbook of child behavior therapy* (pp. 475–497). New York: Plenum.

Matson, J. L., & Ollendick, T. H. (1988). *Enhancing children's social skills: Assessment and training.* New York: Pergamon Press.

BEHAVIORAL WEIGHT CONTROL THERAPY WITH CHILDREN

DESCRIPTION OF THE STRATEGY

Lifestyle behavior modification for obesity is based upon changing eating habits and physical activity to yield negative energy balance, that is, burning more energy than is consumed via eating. During the initial phase of intervention, weight loss occurs at a rate of approximately 1 to 2 pounds (0.5 to 1 kg) per week and gradually tapers to a weight plateau. After this initial weight loss, the goal of treatment is weight maintenance, where the person learns to balance energy intake and energy expenditure.

There is a genetic component to the development of obesity. The interaction of genetics and environment may predispose selected persons to gain weight. Behavioral weight control is based upon basic laws of learning. Classical conditioning refers to the set of circumstances by which cues in an individual's environment become associated with a particular behavior. When an environmental stimulus is repeatedly paired with a behavior, the stimulus itself becomes a trigger to elicit a behavioral reaction. In the case of eating behavior, many aspects of the environment may become associated with hunger sensations and with eating. The smell or sight of food may become conditioned stimuli to eating and therefore trigger hunger sensations. This association is conditioned because the smell and sight of food are repeatedly paired with eating behavior. However, additional stimuli, when paired with eating, may become associated with feelings of hunger. If, for example, an individual habitually eats while watching television, then hunger sensations can be elicited by watching television. Behavioral treatment methods are designed to use the laws of learning to modify eating and exercise habits to produce negative energy balance, where more energy is expended through physical activity than is consumed via eating.

Behavioral Treatment Methods

Components of Behavioral Weight Loss Interventions

Self-Monitoring. A central feature of behavioral weight loss interventions is self-monitoring of eating and exercise habits. Self-monitoring involves recording food intake and intentional efforts to increase physical activity. This monitoring should occur at the time of a behavioral event, that is, at each meal or snack or immediately after a bout of exercise. Self-monitoring by children generally involves recording food intake and environmental events associated with eating and exercise. Children and adolescents can learn to monitor eating and exercise, but parents must assist by reminding and reinforcing self-monitoring that is performed by the child. It is also helpful for the parents to self-monitor their behavior with the child.

Stimulus Control. Stimulus control procedures are designed to alter the relationship between antecedent stimuli and eating and exercise habits. Commonly used stimulus control procedures are (a) eating at the same time and place at each meal, (b) eating slowly, by putting utensils down between bites, (c) eating on small plates, (d) resisting the urge to have seconds, (e) eating while seated, (f) leaving a small amount of food on one's plate, (g) serving small portions of food, and (h) exercising at the same time each day. These procedures serve several functions: (a) extinction of the conditioned association between certain environmental events and unhealthy eating or exercise habits, (b) conditioning of a three meal per day eating pattern that is associated with specific environmental cues, (c) slowing the pace of eating, and (d) developing a consistent pattern of physical activity that becomes

habitual. Parents must enforce the rules of stimulus control by rewarding adherence to the program.

Reinforcement/Shaping. Natural consequences of eating, for example, the good taste of food and reduction of hunger, promote the development of overeating habits, whereas the natural consequences of exercise, for example, fatigue and muscle soreness, promote the development of a sedentary lifestyle. Furthermore, as a person gains weight, the natural consequences of exercise become even more aversive, resulting in less physical activity as obesity increases. Finally, the natural consequences of eating and exercise make conditioning of these habits highly probable. Unfortunately, alteration of the natural consequences of eating is essentially impossible without pharmacological or surgical intervention. The development of healthy physical activity habits makes some of the natural consequences of exercise less aversive over time.

The principle of shaping is generally employed when reinforcement contingencies are formulated. Shaping refers to setting small but reasonable goals at first, and then gradually making them more challenging over the course of therapy.

Behavioral Contracting. To enhance the person's motivation for achieving these goals, a procedure called behavioral contracting is often used. Parents are trained to use behavioral contracting to modify the child's behavior. Behavioral contracting involves clearly specifying behavioral goals in terms of frequency, duration, or intensity, for example, "I will walk at least 20 minutes per day for at least 5 days per week." A behavioral contract generally includes some type of reinforcement contingency for successful attainment of the goal, for example, "If I meet my exercise goal for this week, I will be rewarded by going on an outing with one parent."

Meal Planning. Research with children and parents has shown that explicit meal plans are most effective for compliance. An explicit meal plan might include an actual menu to be followed each day or it may involve a very simplified exchange diet plan. The use of portion-controlled foods that are prepackaged for use in diets can be quite useful for persons who have difficulty following a more general meal plan.

Modification of Physical Activity. Programs to increase physical activity generally include increasing exercise and decreasing sedentary behavior. Research on children has found that reducing sedentary behavior, such as watching television, is one of the most effective forms of exercise prescription.

Problem Solving. This type of training involves training parents and children to (a) identify problems that are obstacles to successful weight management, (b) define the problem in objective behavioral terms, (c) brainstorm about potential solutions to the problem, (d) conduct a cost/benefit analysis for each solution, (e) select a solution and develop a plan of action, and (e) evaluate the success or failure of the plan of action and revise it, based upon this evaluation.

Social Support. Enhancement of social support for behavior change has been found to be a very important factor in successful weight management for children. Social support is primarily derived from parents. Enhancement of social support is best accomplished by inviting parents to attend the therapy sessions and being actively involved in therapy. In these sessions, parents learn to reinforce healthy behavior change and are discouraged from engaging in actions that sabotage progress toward behavior change.

RESEARCH BASIS

Effective weight control in children consists of three components: (1) modification of diet, (2) modification of physical activity habits, and (3) behavior therapy to foster behavior change. Parent training is an important aspect of therapy, especially for promoting behavior change. Parental involvement in therapy promotes weight change, and, in fact, parental involvement alone can produce weight change in individuals who are not the focus of therapy. One reason for the dramatic impact of parental involvement on weight change may be control over the home environment, including the amount and types of foods that are available, method of food preparation, and activities to which children have access and in which the family participates. Adolescents, on the other hand, spend more time away from home and may have more control over the foods that they eat and the activities in which they engage.

A number of diet programs have been used in weight control interventions for children. The majority of these diets rely on moderate calorie restriction to promote weight loss. Consequently, children in these programs typically consume 800 to 1,000 kilocalories per day. The traffic-light diet categorizes foods into "green" or "go" foods, "yellow" or "caution" foods, and "red" or "stop" foods. These foods differ in energy density. The traffic-light diet, when combined with exercise, behavioral techniques, and family involvement, has been found to promote weigh change at 5 and 10 years posttreatment. When engaged in a weight control intervention for a child, both the child and the parents that are participating in therapy are encouraged to self-monitor food intake.

Protein sparing modified fasts (PSMF) are more restrictive diets of 600 to 900 kilocalories per day, and they have been used to treat pediatric obesity. PSMF diets are short in duration, require medical monitoring, and are not used in prepubertal children. The more restrictive PSMF produce greater weight loss in the short term compared to less restrictive diets, but in the long term (e.g., 15 months), weight loss is commensurate with less restrictive diets.

Physical activity alone does not appear to promote weight loss in children, but when used in combination with dietary changes, physical activity facilitates weight loss and long-term weight loss maintenance. Research suggests that lifestyle activity, that is, burning more energy in daily activities, in addition to bouts of physical activity, promotes greater weight loss compared to programmed aerobic physical activity. In addition, the method of promoting physical activity or less sedentary behavior appears to impact weight loss. When children are reinforced for less sedentary behavior, they lose more weight and maintain weight loss better than children who were reinforced for increasing physical activity or who were reinforced for increasing physical activity and reducing sedentary behavior. Once again, children and parents involved in therapy are encouraged to self-monitor the duration and intensity of physical activity.

Research on weight control in children suggests that frequent or daily reinforcement facilitates behavior change and weight loss. In addition, weight loss is promoted by gradual or extended therapeutic contact, where the pace at which didactic content is presented to the child remains flexible. It is important to allow children to gain mastery of a concept or a behavior before continuing therapy. Providing children with perceived choices in therapy also promotes weight loss, and longer therapy is associated with greater weight loss, though data on the association between length of therapy and maintenance of weight loss is lacking. Self-control training and cognitive therapy have not been found to promote weight loss in children.

RELEVANT TARGET
POPULATIONS AND EXCEPTIONS

Most studies on behavioral weight control interventions for children focus upon moderately overweight children who are white, middle class, and 8 to 12 years of age, though some studies have examined weight loss in children as young as 5 years of age. Therefore, little data are available to guide weight loss interventions in children younger than 5 years of age. In addition, the impact of ethnic and cultural factors on weight control interventions for children is unclear and understudied, and ethnic and cultural factors should be considered when making recommendations. For example, dietary plans should take into consideration religious events or special dietary needs (e.g., keeping kosher).

The term *obesity* refers to excess body fat. In adults, body mass index (BMI; kg/m²) is used as an index of adiposity to classify body weight and define obesity. For children and adolescents, however, a statistical approach is used to classify weight status, and the term *obesity* is not applied to children or adolescents. Alternatively, children and adolescents whose BMIs are between the 85th and 95th percentiles of age- and sex-specific population BMIs, measured in the National Health Examination surveys (NHES) II and III, are classified as "at risk for overweight." Children and adolescents whose BMIs are equal to or greater than the 95th percentile are classified as "overweight" or "at risk for obesity."

Overweight children are more likely to experience comorbidity (e.g., diabetes) associated with overweight compared to their normal weight counterparts. In addition, overweight children are likely to become overweight adults, and the association between adiposity and medical conditions such as hypertension in adulthood is well established. Consequently, children who have BMIs equal to or greater than the 85th percentile of their age- and sex-specific population BMIs are appropriate for behavioral weight control interventions. In addition, children who are below the 85th percentile but who are gaining weight that is inconsistent with their level of physical development may be appropriate for a weight control intervention to slow or eliminate weight gain, consequently keeping their body weight out of the at-risk range.

Once a child has been identified for weight control treatment, a medical evaluation is necessary to determine if a medical condition is contributing to body weight or weight gain (e.g., hypothyroidism). In addition, a child should receive medical clearance before increasing physical activity, a primary component of behavioral weight control interventions.

COMPLICATIONS

Children from families in conflict are more likely to drop out of weight control interventions and are more likely to engage in poor dietary habits. In addition, the presence of child or parental psychopathology negatively affects weight loss and maintenance. Given these findings, it is important to assess family conflict and the presence of psychopathology in the child and the child's parents prior to initiating a weight control intervention. Should psychopathology or family conflict be present, referrals to address these problems prior to initiating weight loss treatment may be appropriate. Such decisions should be made on a case-by-case basis, since some children may experience diminished psychological problems following weight loss. For example, children suffering from depressed mood will likely experience improved mood with successful weight loss treatment. Finally, family support may not be universal, and not all family members will support the behavioral changes necessary to promote weight loss for the individual who is the focus of therapy. For example, family members may offer poor food choices to the person in therapy, tease them, or inadvertently reinforce them with food.

One of the concerns about dieting by children and adolescents is the development of eating disorder symptoms. Moderate calorie restriction and increased physical activity in children and adolescents, however, has not been strongly associated with the development of disturbed eating behavior. Another concern is the effect of dieting on the growth and development of children and adolescents. Although this concern is frequently voiced, it appears that moderate calorie restriction might temporary reduce growth rate, but there is no effect on long-term growth.

Motivation for behavior change and adherence to recommendations are particularly problematic for children and adolescents, especially in an environment conducive to sedentary behavior and ingestion of large portions of energy-dense/high-calorie foods. In addition, motivation for lifestyle behavior change can be strongly impacted by culture. For example, some overweight African American girls are relatively unconcerned about their weight status and may have fatalistic attitudes about the health risks associated with obesity.

Frequent or daily reinforcement is necessary to foster motivation and adherence, and this reinforcement most commonly comes from parents. From a behavioral viewpoint, positive reinforcement for good behavior is absolutely necessary to establish sustained behavior change. However, over time parents are likely to revert to punishment to influence children's behavior, which promotes negative parent-child interactions. In addition, adherence to recommendations such as self-monitoring of diet and physical activity habits is extremely difficult for both the child and parent, and these records are frequently inaccurate. Therefore, the child and parent should work with the therapist to establish small attainable goals and behavioral contracts, and upon successful attainment of the goals, rewards should be provided.

CASE ILLUSTRATION

"Mary" was a 13-year-old African American girl who was 5 feet 4 inches tall and weighed 192 pounds. This height and weight can be converted to a BMI of 33, which is at the 99th percentile for Mary's height, weight, age, and sex. Mary was very overweight for her age. Her biological mother, Brenda, was obese, with a body weight of 247 pounds at a height of 5 feet 6 inches. Her BMI was 40. Brenda was married to her husband of 15 years; he was normal weight and had very limited interest in providing support for Mary's weight management program. Brenda reported that her daughter had always been overweight but had gained at least 50 pounds over the last 2 years since the onset of puberty. Mary was mildly concerned about her weight status and expressed some desire to lose weight. Mary and her mother were enrolled in a family-oriented behavioral weight management program that used face-to-face contact and the Internet to modify the eating and exercise habits of the family. During the first 12 weeks of the program, the family met with a counselor on four occasions and learned to follow a simplified dietary exchange program. The mother and daughter began to walk together in the afternoons, and they made a hobby of trying new recipes that they found in the Internet program. Initially, both lost 15 pounds and were making good progress. During the second 12 weeks, Mary started having difficulty in school and gained 2 pounds, while her mother lost another 10 pounds. After the end of

school, they were able to attend several face-to-face sessions and began to make good progress. After 9 months of treatment, Mary had lost 22 pounds and Brenda had lost 30 pounds. At 2-year follow-up, they had maintained these weight losses.

—Donald Williamson and Corby K. Martin

See also: *Behavioral Group Work (Vols. I & III), Group Behavioral Therapy for Depression (Vol. III), Social and Interpersonal Skills Training (Vol. II), Social Competence Treatment: Externalizing Disorders (Vol. II), Social Effectiveness Training (Vols. I & III), Social Skills Training (Vols. I & III)*

Suggested Readings

Berkowitz, R. I., & Stunkard, A. J. (2002). Development of childhood obesity. In T. A. Wadden & A. J. Stunkard (Eds.), *Handbook of obesity treatment* (pp. 515–531). New York: Guilford Press.

Epstein, L. H., Myers, M. D., Raynor, H. A., & Saelens, B. E. (1998). Treatment of pediatric obesity. *Pediatrics, 101,* 554–570.

Goldfield, G. S., Raynor, H. A., & Epstein, L. H. (2002). Treatment of pediatric obesity. In T. A. Wadden, & A. J. Stunkard (Eds.), *Handbook of obesity treatment* (pp. 532–555). New York: Guilford Press.

Wisniewski, L., & Marcus, M. D. (1998). Childhood obesity. In V. B. Van Hasselt & M. Hersen (Eds.), *Handbook of psychological treatment protocols for children and adolescents* (pp. 179–201). Mahwah, NJ: Erlbaum.

BELL AND PAD BLADDER TRAINING

DESCRIPTION OF THE STRATEGY

The problem of nocturnal enuresis or bed-wetting has been written about since ancient times, dating back to the Egyptian papyrus papers in 1550 B.C. This disorder has led to a number of attempts to correct the problem with treatments ranging from medicinal concoctions involving swamp root and juniper berries to using early "medical devices" that included attaching a frog to the waist of the boy who dared to wet his sleeping area. The mystery of why a child would wet in bed has also activated the process of scientific investigation and subsequently spawned as many as 80 years of systematic investigation to identify the causes of bed-wetting and how to eliminate the problem (the incidence of enuresis is twice as common in males up to puberty). Although much science has yet to be done regarding the etiology of bed-wetting and the mechanisms of action that account for effective interventions, psychology as a science has identified a proven treatment: bell and pad bladder training, or the urine alarm.

Perhaps the most widely investigated method to treating bed-wetting is the method of bell and pad bladder training. This method was initially described in the professional literature in 1938 by Mowrer and Mowrer in their practical efforts to deal with the offensive smell of urine in an orphanage for boys, many of which had a problem with wetting their beds. Being early pioneers in learning theory, they approached the problem from the perspective that the boys had failed to learn how to achieve a dry bed and must be taught how to do so. What they basically devised was a method to provide immediate feedback, in the form of punishment, as the wetting accident occurred. Their final design included a moisture-sensitive pad placed on the child's bed that was connected to an alarm box. Once the urine contacted the pad, a circuit was completed in the alarm box and a rather loud auditory stimulus would be activated. The alarm was loud enough to rouse the bed wetter from sleep and eventually interrupt the wetting episode. The Mowrers discovered that over multiple weeks of providing this immediate feedback to the child who wet the bed, the child would eventually remain dry for the entire sleeping period or wake up to visit the toilet. This basic design in the bell and pad method has varied little in the last 50 years other than including body-worn devices (that are considerably smaller) as opposed to the pad.

The bell and pad method (also referred to as urine alarm treatment or conditioning treatment) has proven to be an effective treatment for simple bed-wetting. However, the exact mechanisms that control what is actually occurring in the sleeping bed wetter as he or she progresses to complete remission of the wetting is still not established. Mowrer originally proposed that the change in the child's bed-wetting behavior could best be accounted for through a respondent-conditioning paradigm. The release of urine onto the pad (UCS) would activate the alarm, which would in turn trigger a startle response in the child in the form of a bladder sphincter contraction (UCR), disrupting urination. As treatment progressed and included multiple pairings of the act of urination (UCS) with the alarm (CS), it was thought that all internal bodily sensations in the act of urinating became the signal (CS) that would elicit the bladder sphincter contraction (CR) that would prevent wetting the bed. This was a theoretical explanation that appeared to account for the outcome of this treatment. Unfortunately, Mowrer's respondent conditioning explanation failed to explain why the bladder sphincter contraction did not extinguish when the alarm was withdrawn following successful treatment.

Lovibond provided a more complete account of the apparent learning processes involved with the bell and pad method in the early 1960s. He proposed that the changes that occurred in the child who remitted the bed-wetting with the bell and pad method demonstrated "dual process" learning. The necessary response (i.e., bladder sphincter contraction) to inhibit urination once it has started, or to prevent the onset entirely, was certainly conditioned by pairing the alarm with the act of wetting in a classically conditioned manner. However, Lovibond proposed that most children remained dry once the bell and pad were removed because of negative reinforcement or avoidance learning, which is a form of operant conditioning. Lovibond explained that children who produced a bladder sphincter contraction as a response to their recognition of the internal sensations of the need to urinate would successfully avoid the activation of the alarm. It was this successful avoidance of the aversive experience of a sounding alarm that strengthened the bladder sphincter contraction and maintained dryness in the absence of the alarm.

RESEARCH BASIS

Decades of randomized controlled investigations have been completed to determine the efficacy of the bell and pad method as a treatment for nocturnal enuresis. These studies have consistently demonstrated that the bell and pad method is significantly more likely to lead to complete remission of the wetting compared to various medicines specifically utilized for bed-wetting, psychological treatments that do not include the urine alarm, and compared to no treatment at all. These findings have been reported in several qualitative reviews of the literature and in a meta-analysis of the published randomized clinical studies up to 1989. In general, the research has conservatively reported that, of the children who finish urine alarm treatment, 75% will completely stop bed-wetting, although the number of children beginning to wet once again can be as high as 30% to 40%.

An additional component to basic urine alarm treatment, designed to reduce relapse, includes systematically increasing the water the child drinks at bedtime toward the latter stages of treatment. This component of treatment is referred to as overlearning. With the inclusion of overlearning, the reported number of children beginning to wet again is reduced to 15% to 20%. Length of treatment varies considerably but usually takes 12 to 16 weeks in order to achieve the typical success criteria of 14 consecutive days without bed-wetting. In treatments that include overlearning, the success criteria is required during the period in which fluids are being pushed. Even when children are not successfully treated or if they drop out early, the weekly frequency of bed-wetting is reduced by approximately 50%.

RELEVANT TARGET POPULATIONS AND EXCEPTIONS

The majority of children who present with mono-symptomatic nocturnal enuresis are essentially healthy (physically and emotionally) children who happen to wet the bed. In addition, clinical experience suggests that a child should be motivated and mature enough to complete 12 to 16 weeks of urine alarm treatment. Most children are not treated until approximately 6 years of age.

The primary medical screening task is to rule out disorders that might account for the symptom of bed-wetting and/or excessive or painful urination. These medical disorders might include infections of the urinary tract, endocrine disorders that might produce frequent urination, structural anomalies of the urinary tract, or functional disorders such as constipation. Although medical problems account for less than 10% of children referred for treatment, a basic medical assessment is warranted prior to initiating the bell and pad method.

Research has also identified psychosocial factors that can interfere with completion of urine alarm treatment. Externalizing behavioral disorders in the referred child, which may contribute to problems with compliance with parental requests, will often present themselves in the course of 12 to 16 weeks of treatment. The use of harsh parenting techniques, marital problems, and psychiatric problems in parents all contribute to chaos in the family system that may interfere with proper implementation of the bell and pad method.

Typical psychosocial screening methods to identify these issues will often be helpful to the clinician in determining whether the child and the child's family are capable of implementing the bell and pad method long enough for the child to benefit from the treatment. If it is concluded that the identified psychosocial issues are significant, initially prioritizing treatment of these problems over the bed-wetting is appropriate.

COMPLICATIONS

Although a child may have been medically and psychosocially assessed and deemed to be an appropriate candidate for the bell and pad method, other complications may arise over the course of treatment that will require additional care and management. These complications can lead to unnecessary treatment failure as a result of a family attempting to go it alone with the bell and pad method and argue for the need of at least a minimal amount of professional guidance during treatment.

Generally speaking, the younger children are at the start of treatment, the more frequently they will wet. It is not uncommon for younger children to be wetting the bed twice each night and 7 nights each week. The greater frequency of bed-wetting, and subsequent awakenings with the bell and pad method, can overwhelm a child and the parents, especially during the first several weeks of treatment. Informing the child and parents of this challenge, identifying subtle indicators of progress, and establishing a sensible sleep schedule to ensure enough rest often will be enough clinical support to tolerate the treatment demands at the beginning.

A second complication that can be encountered during bell and pad method is a child who fails to awaken from sleep when the alarm is activated. This child will fail to learn to be dry. Very little is known about how to intervene effectively with this problem. Common sense has led clinicians to obtain the loudest alarm available or ask the parent to awaken the child by providing enough stimulation to do so. Ensuring that the child is fully awakened can be accomplished by washing the child's face. The steps chosen by the parent should be approved by the clinician to prevent the use of any harsh methods.

At times the greatest challenge to children's successful completion of the bell and pad method are their own unrealistic expectations. Children who expect to remit bed-wetting after a few weeks of treatment become disappointed with a wet night after a period of dryness can become so discouraged that they may be at risk of dropping out of treatment before an adequate attempt has been made. The clinician, in concert with parental support, must help the child establish realistic expectations and provide emotional support and reassurance to help the child complete an adequate amount of treatment. Simply establishing an incentive plan that targets reinforcement of compliance with the treatment demands can be helpful in this regard.

Finally, the problem of a child relapsing from successful treatment is considered an additional complication. Research has suggested that preventing relapse is more helpful than attempting to retreat a child who has relapsed. Prevention of relapse can be successful with the use of the previously mentioned component of treatment called overlearning. Overlearning involves the systematic increase of ingested fluids at bedtime by the child after a period of dryness has been achieved. The initial amount consumed should be small, and increased to no more than the estimated functional bladder capacity of the child. If the child continues to maintain dryness during the fluid push, the chance of relapse is significantly reduced. It is as though the learning mechanisms that have accounted for dryness with the bell and pad method have been reinforced or overlearned by the child and act as an inoculation against relapse. In contrast, starting overlearning with too much of a fluid push can completely overwhelm a child who has learned to be dry with the basic urine alarm alone, and can result in a complete relapse. This delicate process of overlearning often requires guidance by the clinician.

CASE ILLUSTRATION

"Willie" was a 6-year-old boy with a history of primary nocturnal enuresis who was wetting approximately 6 to 7 nights per week with typically one wet each of those evenings. Willie's pediatrician completed a medical examination prior to referring him to the enuresis clinic and found him to be generally healthy and evidencing no symptoms of urinary tract infection based on urine screening.

Psychosocial screening indicated that Willie came from an intact and unstressed family, he was the oldest of three children, and his father also wet the bed until about 12 years old. Willie was reported to be a good student, quite popular among his peers, and well behaved at home. However, Willie indicated that he was reluctant to participate in sleepovers with friends, as he feared they would find out he wore pull-up diapers for the bed-wetting. Willie's mother indicated that she worried about his self-esteem because of the bed-wetting. Willie and his parents were informed about the nature of enuresis and the components of urine alarm treatment. Willie was considered an appropriate candidate for bell and pad method. Willie had 5 wet nights in a week of baseline recording. On the 2 nights he was dry, he slept through without waking.

As can be seen in Figure 1, Willie immediately responded to the bell and pad method and eventually achieved his first week of dryness after 4 weeks of treatment and 14 consecutive dry nights after 5 weeks. Overlearning was initiated at this point, with Willie drinking 4 ounces of water at bedtime. However, Willie had a wet the next 3 nights, and overlearning was suspended until a period of dryness could be reestablished. The clinician also reassured Willie that wetting sometimes occurs with overlearning and that he could easily be dry again with additional practice using the urine alarm alone. A period of 21 consecutive dry nights was obtained at 19 weeks of treatment.

Overlearning was reinitiated with gradual increases up to a maximum of 8 ounces of water at bedtime. The reader will also notice an increase in self-awakening to visit the toilet at this time as Willie was challenged with greater levels of hydration. Willie was able to continue to stay dry even with the fluid push, and treatment was discontinued after 32 weeks. Because of Willie's difficulty with managing the fluid push early in treatment, a gradual progression to the maximum fluid load at bedtime was recommended in order to prevent a loss of treatment gains. This gradual approach extended the amount of time in treatment but most likely led to a better outcome. Willie was quite pleased with his progress and was looking forward to a sleepover with his friend and not having to worry about a wet bed.

—*Michael W. Mellon*

See also: *Behavioral Treatment in Natural Environments (Vols. I & III), Biofeedback (Vol. II), Classical Conditioning (Vols. I, II, & III), Full-Spectrum Home Training for Simple Bed-Wetting (Vol. II), Operant Conditioning (Vols. I & III), Retention Control Training (Vol. II)*

Suggested Readings

Houts, A. C., Berman, J. S., & Abramson, H. A. (1994). The effectiveness of psychological and pharmacological

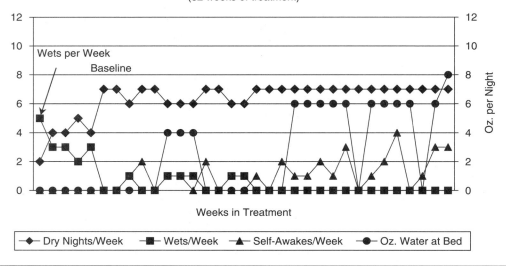

Figure 1   Course of treatment for 6-year-old boy with bell and pad method in which weekly wets and dry nights, self-awakes to visit toilet, and ounces of water intake during the overlearning phase of treatment are tracked.

treatments for nocturnal enuresis. *Journal of Consulting and Clinical Psychology, 62,* 737–745.

Mellon, M. W., and Houts, A. C. (1998). Home-based treatment for primary enuresis. In C. E. Schaefer and J. Briesmeister (Eds.), *Handbook of parent training: Parents as co-therapists for children's behavior problems* (Rev. ed.). New York: Wiley.

Mellon, M. W., & McGrath, M. (2000). Empirically supported treatments in pediatric psychology: Nocturnal enuresis. *Journal of Pediatric Psychology, 25,* 193–214.

BIOFEEDBACK

DESCRIPTION OF THE STRATEGY

Feedback is a process in which the factors that produce a result are themselves modified, corrected, or strengthened by the result. *Bio* is commonly referred to as pertaining to self. Hence, biofeedback is a technique in which information about the self is used to modify, correct, or strengthen processes within the self. More specifically, biofeedback is a therapeutic or research technique that involves monitoring an individual's physiological processes or responses, such as muscular contraction or heart rate, and providing information about that physiological process back to

the individual in a meaningful way so that he or she can modify the physiological process. In pediatric therapeutic settings, the goal is to help children alter their physiology to a healthier standard. We all use biofeedback every day. Looking into a mirror to guide how makeup is applied or how our hair is combed are examples of elementary uses of biofeedback.

A practical example may be helpful at this point for illustration. One of the causes of pain in children is overactivity of muscles (commonly, muscles in the shoulder, neck, head, or facial area). Increased contractions typically occur in response to stressors encountered in daily life (as if one is guarding or bracing against the stress). Stressors can be mental, physical, or both (the more likely case). When faced with a school deadline that is mentally taxing, a child may end up working frantically on the computer and holding the body in somewhat rigid positions for extended time periods. Before long, it would not be surprising to find the child experiencing muscle aches (and impaired thinking). A pediatrician might prescribe a muscle relaxant, while a physical therapist might use heat, massage, or exercise. A biofeedback approach would begin by monitoring muscles suspected to be involved. Once identified, the therapist would instruct or coach the child in ways to prevent muscle tension from building to excessively high levels in the first place and teach strategies to use when tension levels become high and in need of immediate reduction to alleviate the problem once it has occurred. Many of the problems being experienced by children involve the complex interplay of mind and body, as this situation illustrates. For these (and other) problems, biofeedback may be especially useful.

Biofeedback involves three operations: (1) detection and amplification of a biological response by using certain measurement devices (applied to the skin surface) and electronic amplifiers, (2) conversion of these bioelectrical signals to a form that the child can easily understand (the unprocessed muscle tension signal, for example, sounds much like static on the radio, and changes are nearly impossible to decipher without special signal processing), and (3) immediate feedback of or information about the signal to the child. Nowadays, the information obtained from the sensors is most often relayed to a computer for sophisticated analysis. Using special software, the computer is able to massage the physiological information and display it back on a monitor in a meaningful manner so that the child can learn to modulate the physiological process. Because children are used to watching high-quality video graphics (on TV, in video games, and in movies), biofeedback manufacturers have created similarly high-tech and engaging biofeedback displays to capture and hold interest and to enhance intrinsic motivation. These gamelike formats focus on fantasy, curiosity, and challenge.

The top portion of the figure shows a therapist explaining to a child how information about bodily responding is displayed on the computer screen (a feedback tone is also provided via speakers connected to the computer). The lower portions of the figure reveal typical sensor placements for hand warming and forehead muscle tension training (to be discussed later).

The feedback is most often auditory or visual and is presented in either binary or continuous proportional fashion. Binary feedback uses a signal that comes on or goes off at a specified value, and is used when the trainer is having the child strive for a specific target level. Many applications involve lowering overall arousal, and these use continuous feedback to shape every increasing degree of relaxation (e.g., a tone is provided that decreases in pitch or volume as relaxation occurs). The information that is presented to the child has reinforcing or rewarding qualities when the desired response is produced. Typically, the information is presented to the child in real time, so that the child can immediately see the results of his or her actions. The child will eventually cultivate a greater awareness of his or her physiological processes that are ordinarily beyond conscious control, and eventually develop greater voluntary control over the processes. Voluntary control is developed initially through trial and error, then by successively getting closer and closer to the desired training goal and repeated practice. Some have called this process "discern-control-generalize."

There are two basic approaches to biofeedback— *general* and *specific*. The *general approach* is designed for children experiencing conditions that involve excessive or heightened arousal; conditions wherein the child is physiologically stuck in the fight-or-flight mode. This simple phrase adequately explains what happens to a person in an acutely stressful situation; the person's physiology prepares it to run away (flight) or fight. Muscles become tense for action, pulse rate quickens, sweating increases, blood flow in the extremities reduces, pupils dilate, digestion slows, and so on. Biofeedback teaches children how to prevent this exaggerated bodily reaction from occurring in the first place and how to tone it down when it does occur.

Three chief modalities are used to help promote general relaxation, and we term them the therapeutic workhorses of biofeedback. They consist of muscle tension (or electromyographic or EMG), temperature or thermal, and sweat gland activity or skin conductance biofeedback. When used for general relaxation, EMG biofeedback is typically provided from the forehead area (see Figure 1); reductions in this site are believed to spread to other sections of the body and to promote an overall state of muscle relaxation. Relaxation can also be cultivated by teaching children how to warm up their hands using thermal biofeedback. It is not the hand warming per se that is important. In order for hand warming to occur, nervous system activity needs to quiet down, which allows blood vessels in the hands to open up and blood flow to increase. The increased blood flow in the extremities causes the hands to warm. Thus, the temperature increase is a mere marker that relaxation is occurring. Skin conductance, or sweat gland activity, is often an indication of arousal. Part of the fight-or-flight response causes the sweat glands of the

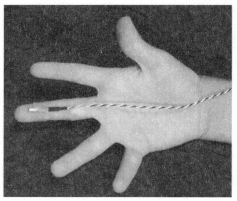

Biofeedback provides concrete evidence that relaxation is actually occurring, so it can be viewed as instrument-aided relaxation. Feedback is a critical link and an additional distinguishing feature of this approach. Imagine how difficult it would be to learn to play tennis if you were blindfolded and were not told when a ball would be served your way. Should you happen to hit the ball, you would have little idea where it went. Removing the blindfold establishes a feedback loop that allows learning to take place more quickly.

What we call the general practice (GP) biofeedback clinician typically uses one or more of the three workhorse techniques to treat conditions that have some association with anxiety or stress. Examples include anxiety disorders, recurrent headaches, sleep problems, and irritable bowel syndrome. For these types of conditions, other behavioral (and medical) approaches have been attempted with similar success. In fact, in practice, GP biofeedback practitioners regularly augment treatments by adding some of the collateral arousal reduction techniques mentioned earlier.

hands to become active (and elsewhere, as all have experienced). By monitoring the amount of sweat gland activity, children can also learn strategies to decrease their arousal.

Biofeedback shares a close kinship with the diverse approaches that employ relaxation as a way to combat life stresses (meditation, mindfulness, yoga, autogenic training, progressive muscle relaxation training, diaphragmatic or paced breathing, and guided imagery). In fact, biofeedback typically combines one or more of these allied relaxation-based approaches. The goal of biofeedback, in its most common application, is quite complementary to these procedures. The distinguishing characteristic is that biofeedback uses instruments that record information about a child's body as a way of gauging targets for treatment and evaluating progress.

Treatments to reduce autonomic arousal range from 8 to 12 sessions on average.

Biofeedback specialists, on the other hand, use applications that require more advanced training, more expensive or specialized equipment, or use the standard equipment but in a more specialized manner. These specialized approaches often require extended training trials (the number of treatment sessions can range from 30 to 80). Examples include modifying certain brain rhythm activity (termed electroencephalographic, or EEG, biofeedback, or neurotherapy) for deterring epilepsy and enhancing attention and concentration in children who are diagnosed with attention-deficit/hyperactivity disorder or who have learning disabilities. Specialized EMG biofeedback is used in various ways. The first is for conditions characterized by an imbalance between muscles

Table 1   Biofeedback and Self-Regulation Skills: Review of Evidence for Pediatric Applications

Disorder	BF Treatment	Modalities
Pain		
Headache	primary or adjunctive	EMG, TMP
Other chronic pain	adjunctive	PNG, EMG
Acute pain & needle phobia	adjunctive	EDA, PNG
Anxiety/Stress-Related Disorders	*adjunctive*	*PNG, EDA, HRV*
Sleep Disorders	*primary or adjunctive*	*EMG, PNG*
Enuresis	primary	EMG, manometric, alarm
Encopresis	primary or adjunctive	EMG, manometric
ANS Dysregulation		
Raynaud's	adjunctive	TMP, EDA
RSD (CRPS)	adjunctive	TMP, EDA
Hypertension	adjunctive	EDA, PNG, HRV, BP
IBS	adjunctive	EDA, PNG, TMP, HRV
Hyperhidrosis	adjunctive	EDA, HRV
Neuromuscular Rehabilitation	*primary or adjunctive*	*EMG*
Attention-Deficit/Hyperactivity Disorder	*adjunctive*	*EEG, EMG*
Learning disorders	*adjunctive*	*EEG, EMG*
Seizure disorders	*adjunctive*	*EEG*
Repetitive Behaviors		
Tics/Tourette's	adjunctive	EEG, EMG, EDA
Habit disorders	adjunctive	EMG, PNG
Impulse control problems	adjunctive	EDA, HRV, PNG
Chronic Illness		
Asthma	adjunctive	EMG, PNG, HRV
Heme/Onc	adjunctive	TMP, PNG
Peak Performance Training	*adjunctive*	*EMG, EEG, HRV*

Key: TMP (peripheral temperature), EMG (electromyography), PNG (pneumography), EEG (electroencephalography), EDA (electrodermal activity), HRV (heart rate variability), BP (blood pressure)

SOURCE: From Culbert, T. P., & Banez, G. A., "Pediatric applications other than headache," in M. S. Schwartz & F. Andrasik (Eds.), *Biofeedback: A practitioner's guide,* 3rd edition, Copyright © 2003. Reprinted with permission from Guilford Press.

or where muscle tone or coordination is compromised (as with back injuries). Muscle tension readings taken from the back can reveal areas with abnormally high readings, abnormally low readings, and sites where asymmetries exist (right- versus left-side differences). These findings may be suggestive of bracing or favoring of a position or posture. Muscle tension biofeedback may also be used to enhance muscle tone and coordination for people having disorders of intestinal motility (fecal incontinence). Heart rate variability biofeedback is another somewhat new and specialized application. Stress and anxiety may or may not be involved in the clinical presentation, and there is little evidence that relaxation or arousal reduction plays a large role in the clinical gains obtained in these latter conditions.

RESEARCH BASIS

Biofeedback owes its development to scientific findings from animal studies (showing early on that animals could control bodily responses that previously were thought to be automatic and not subject to deliberate attempts at control), the cultural revolution (which set the stage for investigations of altered states of consciousness, which eventually provided support that brain waves could be voluntarily controlled; also, the physiological effects of meditation such as were being investigated and eventually became a culturally appealing method of relaxation), and the technological advances that occurred in the 1960s.

These trends led a group of young and energetic researchers and clinicians to form the Biofeedback Society of America in 1968. This group was dedicated to providing the empirical support for the practice of biofeedback. Now known as the Association for Applied Psychophysiology and Biofeedback (AAPB), this group remains as the main professional home for individuals interested in investigating the efficacy of biofeedback for clinical applications, determining the parameters of biofeedback, and identifying new clinical applications and for those clinicians who use biofeedback in their day-to-day practice (see www.aapb.org for further information). AAPB also sponsors a journal, *Applied Psychophysiology and Biofeedback,* and a newsletter, *Biofeedback.*

Recently, members from both AAPB and the Society for Neuronal Regulation (see www.isnr.org) developed guidelines to use when evaluating the clinical efficacy of biofeedback and psychophysiological interventions. A subsequent panel comprehensively searched the available research literature and evaluated the level of support for nearly 40 diverse disorders, rating each on a scale from Level 1 (no empirical support) to Level 5 (strong empirical support and superior to other treatments). The majority of the studies examined by this panel focused on adults, illustrating that work with child populations is lagging far behind. The accompanying table lists the childhood conditions that are currently being addressed in the literature and indicates whether they can be considered as a primary treatment (effective and/or a legitimate treatment alternative) or as an adjunctive treatment (used in conjunction with other approaches to augment or enhance effects).

The research base concerning biofeedback is continuing to grow as new applications and treatment modalities are investigated. Heart rate variability biofeedback is emerging as an additional approach to cultivate lower arousal and relaxation. It is likely that biofeedback will play an increased role in medical settings, to promote well-child care; in school settings, to buffer stress, prevent difficulties, and enhance learning opportunities; and in settings not typically thought of as in need of intervention, to optimize performance overall (music and athletics, for example).

RELEVANT TARGET POPULATIONS AND EXCEPTIONS

Evidence is mounting that biofeedback can be efficacious for children experiencing a number of problems (refer back to Table 1). Although many of the conditions listed in the table respond well to medical treatment (and most are treated mainly by medication), some children do not respond optimally to these approaches. In addition, many parents have concerns about overreliance on medication treatments and the possible adverse effects they may have during development. Furthermore, long-term use of certain medications can actually exacerbate problems due to

dependence and tolerance effects. Thus, biofeedback can be an especially desired alternative for children.

For children to benefit from biofeedback, they must be active rather than passive recipients. Some prefer the term biofeedback *training* as opposed to biofeedback *treatment*, as treatment implies a passive patient receiving something of therapeutic value from the practitioner. It is quite the opposite for biofeedback. Some therapists who work with children refer to themselves as biofeedback teachers, as all children understand the role that teachers play—they teach skills and ideas, they like to ask questions, and they in turn like to be asked questions. This emphasizes the interactive learning approach.

It is of critical importance that children be capable of understanding the biofeedback process (how physiological dysfunction relates to the present condition; why certain aspects of physiology will be monitored; how they will be attempting to alter the functioning of their physiology) and that they possess the motivation to try and learn the desired response. It is interesting to note that after biofeedback is explained to children, they often do particularly well, learning the needed skills at a quicker rate. Children are more enthusiastic, are less skeptical about self-control procedures, and have greater confidence in their "special abilities or powers" (such as the force or magic) to produce the desired response.

COMPLICATIONS

Certain medications that act on the central and autonomic nervous system may complicate biofeedback. For instance, the use of muscle relaxants may so relax the targeted muscle groups that no response can be elicited during training. Some medicines, such as asthma inhalers, act on the autonomic nervous system and cause blood vessels to constrict. The blood vessel constriction decreases blood flow to the hands and feet and could inhibit an individual from learning how to increase blood flow to the periphery. In addition, the use of stimulants, such as methylphenidate (Ritalin), has been found to alter certain brain rhythms, which during EEG biofeedback could impede learning. Also, a favorable response to biofeedback may necessitate medication adjustments. Significant improvement may leave a person overmedicated and in need of a lower drug dose. Prudent biofeedback practitioners maintain a close working relationship with medical colleagues.

Few difficulties have been reported when using biofeedback. When working with very young children, explanations need to be tailored to their comprehension and developmental levels. Session length may need to be adjusted, rest periods may need to be added, and contingency management strategies may be needed to sustain performance when motivation lags or when treatment is not of sufficient intrinsic interest. Parent involvement may be needed as well. Finally, a very small portion of individuals may experience a sudden increase in anxiety as they become deeply relaxed, primarily because this is a foreign state to them. These reactions are typically short lived and easily overcome with the help of a skilled therapist.

BIOFEEDBACK THERAPISTS: TRAINING AND CREDENTIALS

The growing popularity of biofeedback in treating a variety of disorders has led to a significant increase in the number of professionals providing this service to the public. Biofeedback clinicians are employed in a variety of settings: mental health centers, universities, medical schools, hospitals, rehabilitation clinics, and private practice. These clinicians hold degrees in psychology, social work, mental health, medicine, physical therapy, occupational therapy, nursing, and related disciplines. Their training may have been formal, such as at one of the few professional training programs in the country, or as informal as a self-directed literature review. Biofeedback providers are moving toward more formal training and credentialing, as the issue of reimbursement for services has become increasingly important. Insurance companies and other reimbursement agencies are beginning to require credentialing in biofeedback, in line with their expectations for other modes of treatment. Credentialing for biofeedback service delivery, for basic as well as EEG or neurotherapy applications, exists through the Biofeedback Certification Institute of America (see www.bcia.org). Although credentials are not always required to deliver biofeedback, the extended training and knowledge that is acquired through the credentialing process can only add to a practitioner's competence.

When selecting a biofeedback therapist, consider the following: Is the provider credentialed? Has the provider received extended training (attendance at workshops or at a structured program)? Does the provider engage in academic pursuits involving biofeedback (present or teach courses on the topic)? Is the person licensed or certified in his or her specific field? Is the provider familiar with the diagnosis you are seeking to have treated? A list of certified providers may be found at the BCIA Web site. Further information may be found at the following Web sites: www.aapb.org and www.biofeedback.org.

CASE ILLUSTRATION

"Jack" was a typical 15-year-old high school student, but his school performance was below normal and both parents felt that he was working well below his potential. For example, he could not remain on a task longer than a few minutes, even if it was one he found interesting. He subsequently was diagnosed with attention-deficit/hyperactivity disorder (ADHD), primarily inattentive type.

Children with ADHD/ADD often have an EEG brain wave pattern that is different from children who do not experience attention problems. Certain children have excessive amounts of slow brain wave activity (termed theta; 4–7 hertz range) that is associated with inattentiveness. At the same time, they have a deficit of fast brain wave activity (termed beta; 13–30 hertz range), which is associated with attention and concentration. This brain wave pattern is similar to that seen in children who do not have ADHD/ADD when they are inattentive or perhaps even dozing off. Stimulant medication helps the brain to "wake up" and the child to remain alert and more attentive. Neurotherapy attempts to do the same thing (as medication) by altering the child's brain waves to a more awake and alert state.

At the initial assessment, Jack's EEG was monitored while he was exposed to various conditions (sitting quietly, being read to, reading aloud, working difficult mathematical problems, etc.). Of primary concern was the ratio between EEG activity in the theta range to that in the beta range (or the extent to which slow wave activity predominated over fast wave activity). Jack's ratio was about 3:2. EEG biofeedback was used to reduce this ratio to as close to 1:1. Jack resided approximately 3 hours away from the clinic, so treatment was provided in "massed practice" sessions over a long weekend, where Jack would receive three to four sessions within a short period of time.

One biofeedback sensor (the active electrode) was placed directly on top of his head (Cz location over the sensorimotor strip), while the other (reference) was attached to his ear lobe. Each session began with a brief adaptation period of approximately 5 minutes. This period was extended if Jack had problems settling into the session. During biofeedback, Jack was instructed to try and increase beta activity and simultaneously decrease theta activity. Thresholds were set so that he received a reward approximately 80% of the time. As Jack became proficient at reducing theta and increasing beta, the thresholds were set to a more difficult setting, thus shaping his response. In addition, during biofeedback he was asked to listen to or read different types of material to simulate school conditions. Initially, reading material was selected that was of high interest to him, such as articles about tennis players. As Jack became more proficient at biofeedback, actual school material, which was less inherently interesting to him, served as the focus. At various times, Jack was asked to produce the response without the aid of feedback. This gave an idea of how well Jack might be able to perform his biofeedback skills outside the treatment session. The first several sessions lasted roughly 20–25 minutes total. However, as Jack began to learn greater control of his EEG, sessions sometimes lasted over an hour.

Jack was seen for 35 total sessions. At about the 30th session, Jack's parents reported significant changes in his behavior. Jack was now able to maintain attention and concentration with both school and personal tasks that he enjoyed. Jack had always wanted but never had the patience to restring a tennis racket. Now he could do so. Several months following the completion of training, Jack was still able to produce the biofeedback response and was still doing well in school.

—Frank Andrasik and Amanda Lords

See also: *Applied Relaxation and Tension (Vol. III), Biofeedback (Vols. I & III), Progressive Muscular Relaxation (Vols. I & III), Relaxation Strategies (Vol. III), Relaxation Training With Children (Vol. II)*

Suggested Readings

Andrasik, F., & Lords, A. O. (2003). Biofeedback. In L. Freeman (Ed.), *Mosby's complementary and alternative medicine (CAM): A research-based approach* (2nd ed.). Philadelphia: Elsevier Science.

Attanasio, V., Andrasik, F., Burke, E. J., Blake, D. D., Kabela, E., & McCarran, M. S. (1985). Clinical issues in utilizing biofeedback with children. *Clinical Biofeedback and Health, 8,* 134–141.

Culbert, T. P., & Banez, G. A. (2003). Pediatric applications other than headache. In M. S. Schwartz & F. Andrasik (Eds.), *Biofeedback: A practitioner's guide* (3rd ed., pp. 696–724). New York: Guilford Press.

Gilbert, C., & Moss, D. (2003). Biofeedback. In D. Moss, A. McGrady, T. Davies, & I. Wickramasekera (Eds.), *Handbook of mind body medicine for primary care* (pp. 109–122). Thousand Oaks, CA: Sage.

La Vaque, T. J., Hammond, C., Trudeau, D., Monastra, V., Perry, J., Lehrer, P., et al. (2002). Template for developing guidelines for the evaluation of the clinical efficacy of psychophysiological interventions. *Applied Psychophysiology and Biofeedback, 27,* 273–281.

Schwartz, M. S., & Andrasik, F. (Eds.). (2003). *Biofeedback: A practitioner's guide* (3rd ed.). New York: Guilford Press.

Yucha, C., & Gilbert, C. (in press). *The clinical efficacy of biofeedback and neurofeedback.* Wheat Ridge, CO: Association for Applied Psychophysiology and Biofeedback.

CASE CONCEPTUALIZATION

DESCRIPTION OF THE STRATEGY

Case conceptualization is the process of utilizing the abundance of information learned about a client to develop hypotheses about the causal, maintaining, exacerbating, and mitigating variables that directly and indirectly influence clinical problems. A clinically useful case conceptualization includes two essential components. The first is basic information about presenting concerns (e.g., topographical description, frequency of occurrence, when they began) as well as details regarding the etiology and factors currently maintaining clinical problems. Based on this information, the second component is developed and includes information about the interventions thought to be most helpful for that particular client.

Case conceptualization does not exist as a specified strategy or technique with clear guidelines on effective implementation but instead is an activity that can be accomplished in multiple ways. As such, the process is not unique to behavior modification or cognitive behavior therapy with children, and instead is central to clinical endeavors pursued from any theoretical orientation. However, the variables of focus will differ based on theoretical perspective. Furthermore, case conceptualization is particularly important when operating from behavioral or cognitive-behavioral perspectives, given the idiographic nature of these schools of psychological practice.

The theoretical underpinnings of behavior modification and cognitive behavior therapy with children has led to the adoption of functional assessment as the predominant method of case conceptualization for practitioners operating from these psychological orientations. Functional assessment has been defined in various ways but essentially involves an analysis of "act-in-context." In other words, functional assessment involves identifying contextual (i.e., environmental) variables that directly influence the emotional, cognitive, and behavioral experiences of a child or adolescent. To conduct an effective behavioral case conceptualization, clinicians focus on several relevant factors. Each is described next.

Components of a Case Conceptualization

To initiate the case conceptualization process, one must have an adequate definition of the presenting concerns. Presenting problems are typically analyzed based on a tripartite model, in that clinical problems of interest may be cognitive, physiological, and/or overt behavioral. Based on this model, both overt (e.g., crying, hitting) and covert (e.g., thoughts, heart rate) are of import. Definition involves more than simply description, which may include diagnosis, and includes quantifying the presenting complaints in some form (e.g., frequency, duration, intensity). As such, both an adequate description of the problem and an understanding of the impact of the problem on the person's functioning are obtained.

To analyze presenting problems with a focus on contextual variables, information regarding environmental factors most significantly impacting the occurrence of the clinical problems is gathered. At the simplest form, this involves an antecedent-behavior-consequence, or A-B-C, analysis. Such an analysis requires that the clinician investigate the contextual variables antecedent to the clinical problems that seem to trigger their occurrence. Specifically, investigation of antecedent variables involves searching through the myriad possible triggers to understand those that seem directly related to the increase in the problem behavior. In addition, clinicians must investigate consequent variables that occur in response to the clinical behaviors that appear to be maintaining or exacerbating them.

Given the theoretical underpinnings of behavioral case conceptualization, the focus of the contextual analysis is grounded in functionalism versus structuralism. That is, the process involves identifying the antecedent variables that functionally predict the increase in problem behaviors, as well as consequent variables that functionally serve as reinforcing stimuli. For example, assuming that verbal reprimands that occur consequent to child misbehavior are punishing is a structural approach. It is equally as likely that, for a given child, such a consequence may serve as a reinforcing event, thus inadvertently increasing the likelihood that misbehavior will continue.

Comprehensive behavioral case conceptualization goes beyond the A-B-C analysis and also includes an analysis of behavior-behavior relations—that is, how presenting concerns are interrelated. Take, for example, a child who is anxious in social situations. The child might present with a variety of concerns, including shaking, sweating, thoughts of embarrassment, and actually fleeing situations. To understand the act-in-context, one must also understand each act in relation to each other. Is it the case that thoughts of embarrassment precipitate shaking and sweating? Does the child experience the physiological and overt behavioral (i.e., fleeing) symptoms in tandem, but in the absence of cognitive concerns? This analysis helps determine the interrelatedness of clinical problems and serves a useful purpose in treatment hypothesis generation. Continuing with the example, if one knows that cognitive and physiological variables almost always co-occur, then it may be possible to indirectly affect one by treating the other.

In addition to analyzing the act-in-context, which includes an analysis of behavior-behavior relations, behavioral/cognitive-behavioral case conceptualization includes other important "background" or "historical" variables. Information included in these categories typically consists of the early developmental history of the child (i.e., pre-, peri-, and postnatal development), medical history (e.g., illnesses, injuries, surgeries, medications), and family functioning (e.g., cohesion, relationship between parents). In addition, family history of similar clinical concerns is assessed, to provide information on biological or environmental predispositions. These variables are a useful part of the analysis because they help to understand historical experiences (e.g., extended periods of hospitalization when a toddler), developmental complications (e.g., delays in speech development related to the use of aggressive behavior as a form of communication), and familial variables (e.g., maternal history of anxiousness in a child with social phobia) that may be related to the initial cause and maintenance of clinical problems.

Methods of Gathering Information

The various functional assessment methods are divided into two general categories: indirect and direct. Indirect strategies include interview- and questionnaire-based methods of gathering information about contextual variables influencing a child's presenting concerns. Clinicians typically gather information with these methods by contacting relevant care providers (e.g., parents, teachers) who have sufficient history with the client. These methods are beneficial, as they are typically less cost prohibitive and may facilitate gathering information from a variety of people. They can be limited, however, by factors such as recall bias and opportunities to observe occurrence of presenting problems, for example.

In contrast, as the name implies, direct methods of functional assessment involve observing the child to determine the correlation between contextual events and the occurrence of clinical concerns. Direct methods are further divided into unstructured and structured approaches. Unstructured direct methods typically involve a watch-and-wait approach whereby the clinician simply observes the client and documents when problematic behaviors occur, as well as the antecedents and consequences that surrounded them. These types of observations may occur in session, at home, at school, or in other relevant environments (e.g., a child who is afraid of swimming could be observed at a local pool). Structured approaches involve somehow manipulating the child's environment by altering contextual cues and documenting whether those manipulations result in changes in problematic behavior. For example, to evaluate the influence of task difficulty on a student's classroom disruptive behavior problems, one could create situations that vary based on this dimension (i.e., hard versus easy). Comparing rates of disruptive behavior across those conditions would help the clinician understand which type of task is more significantly related to the targeted behavior.

Direct methods of functional assessment are beneficial in that they allow for observation of environment-behavior relations, decreasing reliance on inference. Furthermore, structured approaches allow clinicians to empirically test the influences of specific contextual variables. This increases the confidence in one's understanding of the contextual variables directly influencing targeted behaviors. They are limited, however, due to financial, time, and training constraints.

RESEARCH BASIS

Behavioral case conceptualization has been a focus in the literature for some time. In fact, the processes of developing an understanding of causal contextual mechanisms for a client's presenting problems has traditionally been central to behavioral and cognitive-behavioral therapies. Use of specific functional assessment as a foundational basis for case conceptualization has emerged within the past 20 years. Currently, there is a significant amount of research demonstrating the utility of functional assessment strategies as methods of case conceptualization for youth with disruptive behavior problems and cognitive/developmental delays. Furthermore, there is emerging research assessing the utility of these approaches with typically developing youth with behavioral problems.

In contrast, little research has been done on utilizing specific functional assessment strategies with other child clinical problems (e.g., anxiousness, depressed mood). That said, however, analysis of most behavior modification and/or cognitive-behavioral interventions for children and adolescents reveals that conceptualization is based on the model of act-in-context and relies heavily on understanding the interplay of environmental variables and clinical problems. As such, while *specific* strategies of functional assessment other than a thorough interview may not be available for all childhood disorders, it is clear from existing research that behavioral modification and cognitive-behavioral therapies for children

incorporate functional assessment concepts as part of conceptualization.

RELEVANT TARGET POPULATIONS AND EXCEPTIONS

Given the essential nature of case conceptualization to understanding a particular client's clinical concerns, completion of the process is necessary with each client, regardless of age, gender, and presenting problem. Thus, unlike particular behavioral/cognitive-behavioral interventions that may be applicable to certain populations and/or clinical problems, case conceptualization is a critical ingredient to effective therapy, and thus should be included with all clients. In other words, if the goal of the behaviorally oriented clinician is to select and implement effective interventions, there are no clinically indicated exceptions to the completion of the process of case conceptualization.

While completing a case conceptualization for each child client is an essential component to behavior management and cognitive behavior therapy with children, the processes/strategies used may vary depending on the child's developmental level and/or presenting concerns, as well as on pragmatic constraints (e.g., time to conduct observations). It is the responsibility of the clinician to determine the most effective (i.e., pragmatic) way to gather pertinent information to complete the case conceptualization process. Particular complications are described in more detail below.

COMPLICATIONS

Case conceptualization can be a difficult endeavor, and the clinician may experience one or several complications. One complication is that of difficulty accessing relevant contextual information. If the clinician is relying primarily on interview- and questionnaire-based methods, it is possible that informants may have particular reasons to present information in a certain way (e.g., a parent who overreports clinical problems because he or she feels helpless). Or perhaps respondents are not able to recall associations between clinical problems and environmental variables, thus limiting the analysis of act-in-context. Given that most respondents are not trained observers, this scenario is plausible. As a related issue, personal biases (e.g., a parent who feels a child is noncompliant to anger the parent) may limit the ability to recall other outcomes that occurred in relation to the problem (e.g., escape from completing a request).

Attempting to avoid problems that can occur when relying on recall, clinicians may turn to observational methods to gather information about case conceptualization. However, these strategies are not without complications as well. Specifically, observational methods are limited by a host of pragmatic constraints. Difficulties creating analog situations in the office so as to evoke the clinical problems, inability to travel to a child's home or school to conduct observations, and reactivity to the presence of the observer are but a few of the complications that can emerge when trying to analyze the clinical problems from a contextual perspective through observational methods.

Given the complications of both indirect and direct methods of gathering information about clinical problems to be used in case conceptualization, relying on a combination of approaches may serve as the best approach. That is, gathering information via interview, questionnaire, and through observation, and then synthesizing that information while taking into account limitations of each approach, may serve the clinician well.

CASE ILLUSTRATION

"Craig," a 10-year-old boy, demonstrated significant separation anxiety (e.g., crying, complaining of fear that his mother would be harmed, becoming inconsolable) when his mother, "Ms. P.," attempted to leave him with another care provider (e.g., baby sitter) or send him to school. Craig had been demonstrating these symptoms for approximately 9 months, and they appeared to be getting progressively worse. Their severity had increased such that Craig's mother rarely left him with another adult, and she was contemplating homeschooling him because of his excessive absences from school.

To conduct a thorough case conceptualization, information about background/historical and environmental/contextual variables was gathered to understand better the causal and maintaining variables impacting his behavior. Clinical interviews with Craig's mother indicated that he had no developmental concerns and was generally a healthy child. No emotional problems were present for Craig prior to approximately 1 year ago. In addition, there was no family history of similar concerns or other emotional disorders.

Because structured functional assessment approaches do not exist for analyzing most emotional conditions,

a clinical interview designed to gather information about etiological factors and current variables influencing Craig's anxiousness (i.e., A-B-C analysis) was conducted. This revealed that Craig experienced a mildly upsetting incident prior to the onset of his anxiousness. Specifically, Craig's mother was in a traffic accident resulting in injuries that required a 2-day hospitalization. Although Craig was neither involved in nor witnessed the accident, he reportedly was somewhat upset by seeing his mother in the hospital. However, he was described as not excessively frightened or scared.

The interview revealed that approximately 2 weeks after the accident, Craig started displaying symptoms of anxiousness by repeatedly questioning his mother about where she was going when she left the house and if she would be okay without him with her while he was at school. Ms. P. reported that this prompted her to discuss with Craig the fact that she was all right and to reassure him that everything was fine. She also reported that she stopped using any baby sitters at this time, so as to be with Craig and help him feel "more comfortable and safer."

Within 2 months, Craig reportedly started resisting going to school out of fear of something happening to his mother if he was not with her. Ms. P. indicated that she finally let him stay home one day when he was crying so that they could spend time together. Ms. P. reported that she felt that doing so one time would not cause harm and might help Craig feel more comfortable. However, by 5 months later (approximately 8 months after the initial accident), Craig's symptoms had progressively escalated until he was typically refusing to stay with any adults other than his mother and was so inconsolable in the morning before school that he was staying home approximately two to three days per week. Ms. P. reported that Craig's anxiousness had become so severe that he would not spend the night at friends' houses, would resist going to school, and even became uncomfortable if she wanted to leave for short periods of time (e.g., to go for a walk in the neighborhood).

Craig reported that he often had thoughts that harm would come to his mother if she was not with him. He indicated that he felt guilty about the initial accident because his mom had been on her way to the store to buy his birthday present. He also was able to describe that typically he had thoughts of worry or fear that occurred prior to his outward signs of upset (e.g., crying) and that the worry was difficult to control.

Ms. P. reported using a variety of approaches to help Craig overcome his fears. She indicated that she had tried "forcing" him to leave her side (e.g., send him to school even when he was crying), but that he often became so upset that eventually she would need to go get him. She indicated that she and Craig spent many hours talking about his fears, about her safety, and about the previous accident. She also reported that she asked Craig to "log" in a journal when he started to worry, so that at bedtime they could discuss what was making him feel upset.

Utilizing the above information, the following behavioral case conceptualization was developed. Craig's initial fear response was appropriate to the situation. However, this event likely was the initial cause of the anxiousness. That is, it provided the impetus for a change in the mother-child interaction that has served to exacerbate Craig's healthy anxiety and to maintain increasingly excessive anxiousness. Specific immediate antecedents that appeared directly related to the occurrence of Craig's intense anxiety were situations in which he needed to separate from his mother. These produced increased thoughts of worry, which precipitated other physiological and overt behavioral symptoms of anxiety (i.e., behavior-behavior relations). Environmental consequences that appeared to be maintaining separation anxiety included Craig being able to avoid separation, frequent reassurance from his mother that she is "all right," and discussions about what was worrying him. Based on this conceptualization, several treatment strategies were indicated to alter Craig's anxiety. Specifically, an exposure-based paradigm whereby Craig was exposed to separation from his mother after learning specific relaxation strategies (e.g., diaphragmatic breathing, progressive muscle relaxation) to cope with this distressing experience seemed relevant. Furthermore, treatment involving decreased discussions/reassurance on the part of Craig's mother appeared appropriate. Thus, a combination of both family and individual therapy was pursued.

—*Kurt A. Freeman*

See also: *Behavioral Case Formulation (Vols. I & III), Behavioral Treatment in Natural Environments (Vols. I & III), Operant Conditioning (Vols. I, II, & III), Single-Case Research (Vols. I & III)*

Suggested Readings

Freeman, K. A., & Miller, C. O. (2003). Behavioral case conceptualization for children and adolescents. In M. Hersen (Ed.), *Clinical behavior therapy: Adults and children.* New York: John Wiley.

Persons, J. B., & Tompkins, M. A. (1997). Cognitive-behavioral case formulation. In T. D. Eells (Ed.). *Handbook of psychotherapy case formulation* (pp. 314–339). New York: Guilford Press.

CHORE AND ALLOWANCE PROGRAM FOR CHILDREN

Doing chores and getting an allowance are ways to teach children responsibility, how money and work are related, and to help with household duties. However, family "chore and allowance programs" are often unsuccessful due to frustration, lack of clearly defined rules, inadequate parental supervision, unclear guidelines for "acceptable" completion of duties, and inconsistent or delayed distribution of allowance. Successful chore and allowance programs need to be easy to understand for both child and parent, easy to administer, and able to be reliably monitored for quality control. They also need to ensure a method for immediately granting income contingent upon successful completion of duties.

Why should children be paid to do things that they will eventually need to do as adults? Children should be paid for their work, as payment is an incentive or reward that will extrinsically reinforce their likelihood of performing chores. Payment also teaches the link between completed work and salary. Adults perform household chores for a variety of reinforcers (e.g., approval of neighbors). These reinforcers are not generally developmentally appropriate for children, so money is substituted. When children become adults, they too will be paid by nonmonetary means for their household work.

Creation of the chore and allowance program involves the following:

Step 1: Specific duties and details regarding the completion of chores should be discussed as a family and outlined in a formal family contract:
   a. What chores are to be completed by each child
   b. Days of week each chore should be completed and by which child
   c. Time by which each chore must be completed for each day

Table 1   Sample of a child's chore and allowance chart with rules

JOBS	Sun	Mon	Tues	Wed	Thurs	Fri	Sat
Wash dishes	$ .50 7 p.m.	+$ .50 7 p.m.	$ .50 7 p.m.		$ .50 7 p.m.	+$ .50 7 p.m.	
Collect garbage		$ .25 8 p.m.		Trash +$.75 7 a.m.		$ .25 8 p.m.	
Clean room	$1.00 5 p.m.				$1.00 5 p.m.		
Walk dog in morning		$ .25 7 a.m.	Night +$ .25 6 p.m.	$.25 7 a.m.	Night +$ .25 6 p.m.	$ .25 7 a.m.	

d. How-to steps and criteria for proper completion for each chore

e. Amount of allowance to be earned for each chore's completion.

Step 2: This information should be transferred into a chart format so that each child has a separate chart detailing the above information. Colored pens can be used by each child and parent to indicate which chores were completed and at what time. The parent can then initial each job that has been successfully completed on time.

Determining allowance amounts and how to dispense it can be best accomplished by considering the child's age, developmental level, spending needs, and number of chores assigned. Parents should approximate the total cost of the items they would like their child to purchase with the allowance and then add a little more money so that the child can save, if desired. For younger children, the allowance should be given *immediately* following successful completion of the job in order to effectively demonstrate the relationship between work and pay. Over time, the child's allowance should be faded to weekly payments. At first, parents should verbally praise the child by providing constructive feedback about what the child did correctly and what can be done differently the next time, if necessary, to improve performance.

Step 3: When more than one child is part of the program, rules can be instituted to allow a sibling to complete a chore if the initial child did not do so correctly or was not finished by the assigned completion time. In this case, parents would ask siblings if they would like to do that child's chore. If "yes," then a sibling does the job and receives that portion of the initial child's allowance. If "no," the initial child must immediately complete the chore and does not get paid. If the child refuses, he or she is sent to unlimited time-out until he or she is willing to complete the job. The parent should never complete the chore for the child, as this will teach the child to refuse, thereby allowing the child to avoid completing chores.

Other guidelines include (a) no sharing of chores, such as washing and drying the dishes, as sharing may provide a child an excuse for not working (e.g., "Mom, I can't dry the dishes now because John hasn't washed them yet."); (b) switching jobs with sibling. This is allowed, but the parents do not become involved in the negotiations. The model is similar to the parents having a contractor and subcontractor. If the sibling agrees to switch and completes the chore correctly, then the *original* child gets paid. (That child can pay the sibling who actually did the work.) However, if the sibling agrees but does not complete the job by the assigned time, it is treated in the same manner as if the originally assigned child had not completed the chore. That is, a sibling can complete the task and get the original child's allowance *or* the original child will be made to complete the job for free. This contingency teaches children to be responsible for their duties and to ensure that they are completed (by themselves, or another reliable person) to receive their allowance. Scheduling conflicts can be discussed with parents to allow for changing completion times and days on the weekly chart.

Table 2   Investment chart with sample calculations demonstrating how investing principles can be applied to allowance savings

Date	$ Amt. Earned	$ Amt. Spent	$ Amt. Invested	$ Total Invested	$ Earning on Total Invested	$ Total
[Date]	5.00	2.00	3.00	3.00	0.30	3.30
[Date]	4.00	1.00	3.00	6.30	0.63	6.93
[Date]	4.00	1.00	3.00	9.93	0.99	10.92
[Date]	4.00	8.00	0.00	6.92	0.69	7.61
[Date]	3.00	1.00	2.00	9.61	0.96	10.57

Another important function of an allowance program is its application as a method for teaching children the concepts and how-to's of money management and investing. With the exception of legal and health limits, parents do not dictate how children spend their allowance, nor should parents provide a cash advance before the work is completed.

An easy way to incorporate investing in the chore and allowance program is to do the following:

Step 1: When the first allowance is received, explain to the child, "Any money that you have saved from your previous allowance [i.e., have money left over at the time the next week's allowance is to be paid], I will add 10% to that amount." It is key that the child understands that interest can only be earned on money that has been saved, *not* on money that has just been received (i.e., when the allowance is first given). Apply this process each time the allowance is given by asking the child how much has been saved for the investment.

Step 2: The parent, in front of the child, should perform the calculations (in an easy-to-understand manner) to determine the amount to be added to the child's investment. Create an investment chart that shows the original amount the child put into the mutual fund, the amount withdrawn (spent) from the weekly amount, the amount added to the investment (e.g., 10%), and the total value to visually teach the child how the money *grows* and that the more invested, the more earned.

The above details a practical and easy-to-use plan for instituting and maintaining a successful chore and allowance program for children. Use of the investment steps allows for additional learning experiences and practice in real-life skill development.

—*Shari K. Neul and Ronald S. Drabman*

See also: Behavioral Contracting (Vols. I, II, & III), Behavioral Treatment in Natural Environments (Vols. I & III), Extinction and Habituation (Vol. I)

Suggested Readings

Pastore, D. R., & Friedman, S. B. (1992). Allowances, household chores, and curfews. In S. B. Friedman & M. Fisher (Eds.), *Comprehensive adolescent health care* (pp. 643–673). St. Louis, MO: Quality Medical Publishing

CLASSICAL CONDITIONING

DESCRIPTION OF THE STRATEGY

The clinical applications of classical conditioning techniques have been widely accepted for both children and adult populations. However, treatment emphasis has often focused only on fear and anxiety reduction, an expectable consequence, given the historical development of classical conditioning theory. While a classical approach is effective with anxiety-based disorders, the clinical application of classical conditioning has a variety of uses. Moreover, classical conditioning procedures are significantly enhanced when used in conjunction with approaches based on operant learning theory.

Classical conditioning theory is most often related to the work of Ivan Petrovitch Pavlov. Pavlov worked on three research problems during his life: the function of the heart nerves, the primary digestive glands—which won him the Nobel Prize in 1904—and the analysis of conditioned reflexes. His work on conditioned reflexes followed a serendipitous discovery while investigating the digestive system of dogs.

When he noted, during this study, that an unlearned reflexive response to food, salivation, began to occur outside the presence of food, Pavlov became interested in the effects of external stimuli on reflexive behavior. He defined an unconditioned response as an innate function, which requires no learning to occur (e.g., placing food in a dog's mouth evokes salivation). Pavlov was fascinated by how a seemingly unrelated stimulus could come to elicit a reflexive response.

In Pavlov's original study, food served as the evoking stimulus, or unconditioned stimulus (US), and salivation was the unconditioned response (UR). This represented an unlearned reflexive relationship. Conditioning, then, required the systematic pairing of a neutral stimulus (an NS) with the US. A bell served as the NS and was presented immediately prior to the presentation of the food (US). Following a number of pairings of the bell (NS) and food (US), the bell came to elicit salivation. The bell comes to represent a conditioned stimulus (CS), which elicits the conditioned response (CR), salivation. While nothing is necessarily inherently different about this salivation, the CR salivation reflects the conditioning effects of the eliciting stimulus.

This paradigm serves as the basis for understanding how environmental stimuli may gain control over many reflexive behaviors. Once conditioned, however, these CS-CR relationships will only be maintained if the CS is occasionally paired with the US. In Pavlov's study, the newly acquired CS, the bell, had to be followed occasionally by the US, food. Without these occasional maintenance pairings, the bell lost its ability to elicit salivation. The process of specifically preventing these repeated pairings of the CS and US is referred to as extinction. Pavlov demonstrated the effects of extinction with his dogs by terminating the pairings of the bell and food. Over time, the CR (salivation) diminished until the bell no longer had any effect on salivation. Despite undergoing an extinction procedure, however, the CS would occasionally, again, elicit the CR, a phenomenon known as spontaneous recovery. Notably, this reappearing CS-CR can still be eliminated if the extinction procedure continues.

In addition to the basic conditioning and extinction procedures, Pavlov also demonstrated the effects of stimulus generalization and higher-order conditioning. Stimulus generalization refers to that situation in which stimuli similar to the training stimuli are presented and elicit the same CR. Obviously, the more closely the stimuli are related, the more likely stimulus generalization is to occur. Higher-order conditioning refers to using a previously conditioned stimulus to condition other stimuli to elicit responses.

The most striking historical example in human application of classical conditioning associated with fear and anxiety-based responses is Watson's conditioning of a fear of rats in "Little Albert." When Little Albert was originally presented a rat (an NS), he showed no fear. Later, the rat was paired with a loud noise (a US), which elicited a fear response (a UR). After only a few pairings, the rat (now a CS) began to elicit fear (a CR), a classically conditioned fear response.

Despite the literature's focus on anxiety and fear, classically conditioned responses can take many forms. Generally, the responses will involve some physiological state, such as fear, pain, comfort, or other somatic sensation. In many clinical applications, the goal is to reverse the effects of a classically conditioned response (like fear), while at other times the goal is to establish a conditioned stimulus (e.g., a distended bladder for enuresis). Thus, clinical applications will involve either direct conditioning or extinction procedures. It is widely recognized that operant procedures (reinforcement and punishment) can have a profound impact on the effects of any classically conditioned response. This interaction of classical and operant learning, which is often impossible to separate, has been referred to by O. H. Mowrer as two-factor learning.

RESEARCH BASIS

The clinical application of classical conditioning procedures in children is well documented, with much of the literature focusing on fear reduction and medically related interventions such as enuresis and painful medical procedures. Other applications involve various conditions such as nausea, inappropriate sexual behavior, and self-abusive behavior. Beyond traditional clinical interventions, classical conditioning effects can be readily found in everyday life, usually by carefully examining an individual's learning history. For example, consider the calm feeling one gets when exposed to the smell of freshly baked bread or the sound of ocean waves. These forms of classical conditioning have recently found a market in self-help circles.

Fear reduction techniques derive from extinction procedures. The most basic form of intervention involves direct exposure to the feared stimuli (the CS) without exposure to the US. Over time, the fear response subsides and the CS loses its power to elicit fear. This procedure is commonly referred to as flooding.

Flooding is exemplified by the admonition to "get right back on the horse, after being thrown, to face your fear." Research supports the efficacy of flooding procedures. However, clients are generally reluctant to experience the fear directly (it is hard to get them to climb back on the horse).

Joseph Wolpe developed a more client-friendly procedure, based on the notion of reciprocal inhibition. Using reciprocal inhibition extends simple extinction (the cessation of pairing the CS with the US) to include a counterconditioning procedure, which relies on the fact that feeling anxiety and fear is mutually exclusive to feeling calm and relaxed. Wolpe utilized this to his advantage by pairing relaxation with graduated increments of a feared stimulus.

Wolpe formalized this procedure in a clinical intervention known as systematic desensitization, which calls for developing a hierarchy of feared stimuli and training the individual in relaxation techniques. The procedure begins by exposing the client to the least fear-producing stimulus on the hierarchy while maintaining a state of relaxation. As a level of the hierarchy is mastered, that is, exposure to a fear stimulus engenders no fear, the client moves on to the next level. With this technique, the client never has to experience fear. Systematic desensitization has much greater appeal to individuals than does flooding. Again, many studies support this procedure for treating a variety of fears and anxiety, particularly in children, and for helping reduce the anxiety related to painful medical procedures.

With regard to direct conditioning, the most researched example is the treatment of enuresis. A number of studies examining the effects of various buzzer and pad systems to reduce bed-wetting support this procedure as an effective intervention for enuresis. The goal is to condition the full bladder (an NS) to elicit a waking response (a CR) by pairing it with a buzzer (a US) that "automatically" evokes waking (a UR). Still, it should be noted that this procedure does not occur in isolation and that a number of operant factors will also enhance the desired response. Along with reduced bed-wetting comes escape from a wet bed (negative reinforcement) and praise from parents (positive reinforcement).

RELEVANT TARGET POPULATIONS AND EXCEPTIONS

Classical conditioning interventions are applicable across the lifespan. Children who are experiencing,

for example, separation anxiety, adolescents suffering phobic reactions, or adults enduring certain sexual dysfunctions or troubled by paraphilias involving sexual arousal or sexual desire may all be likely candidates for treatment using classical conditioning techniques. The point is that it may not be specific subpopulations that might be targeted for such treatments, but rather certain diagnosable conditions, those involving a clearly reflexive emotional or somatic response, which should respond best.

COMPLICATIONS

The most serious complication is the fear that results from direct exposure during the flooding procedure. This concern is easily avoided by utilizing the systematic desensitization procedure. A more common complication is the difficulty that often attends recognizing the context in which conditioning occurs. The context or the environment in which conditioning will occur, or has occurred, is not necessarily overtly problematic. The context can include additional stimuli, which may have an unintentional impact on conditioning or extinction. In addition, the context may also provide other forms of reinforcement, consistent with Mowrer's two-factor learning. With appropriate planning, any contextual confounds can generally be corrected, or utilized, to enhance the conditioning procedure.

CASE ILLUSTRATION

Anecdotal evidence abounds that children almost always behave better at their grandparents' house than in their own. Wesley Becker offers "Grandma's Rule," contingency management of the first order, as one very probable reason, and an approach attributed to B. F. Skinner, "catch 'em being good" (although Skinner would most certainly have said it as "catch 'em behaving well") would represent another. While these are clearly operantly oriented, it has already been noted that what occurs between grandchildren and grandparents often involves both *operant conditioning* and *classical conditioning*.

Separating operant conditioning from classical conditioning is rather difficult because we are actually learning in both ways all the time. Generally speaking, motoric behavior is more visibly influenced by operant conditioning, and emotions and somatic sensations seem to be affected, probably effected, more by classical conditioning. This distinction, which shouldn't be seen as hard and fast, appears in the story of how one grandmother encouraged good behavior in her grandchildren.

There were few things one of the authors of this chapter and his siblings enjoyed more than visiting their grandmother's home in northwest Ft. Worth, Texas. They knew there would be many enjoyable things to do—listen to a St. Louis Cardinals' baseball game, sing gospel hymns with a quartet on the radio, or explore her backyard and all its wonders—but whatever they would be doing, they would be well behaved when they did it.

Their grandmother used the results of classical conditioning to effect their good behavior. First, remember that classical conditioning's signature feature is the gaining of control over some response by a previously neutral stimulus, a stimulus that, before the conditioning, had essentially no power to effect anything.

To begin, the very elegant, dynamic grandmother used to ensure that her grandchildren behaved well by always addressing, or referring to, them by their full given names. It wasn't "Bill" or "Little Bill"; it was always "William Porter." It was never "Jan" or (our favorite name for her) "Janabeth"; it was always "Jan Elizabeth." While the tone with which she said her grandchildren's names might have varied a bit, what Grandmother called them never did.

To understand how this works, we must go back in the learning history and begin by recognizing that no one is born automatically responding to one's name. This only occurs with time and particular circumstances. In other words, a person's name begins as a *neutral stimulus.* As with any instance of classical conditioning, one's name must be paired with stimuli that "automatically" evoke a response before it comes to have the power to do so. In most people's lives, the first associations with their names occur in situations for which there is some emotional response. As a baby is being fed, or comforted after encountering something fearful, or calmed before going to sleep, it is not uncommon at all for the caregiver to coo and talk to that baby, often addressing the child by name. At the very least, such occasions could give rise to feelings of relief, a sense of comfort and security, or a feeling of warmth. The caregiver's mere presence can become associated with such feelings (higher-order conditioning), and that is the way we would want it.

Alternatively, just as feelings of comfort and safety can become associated with one's name and the person who calls it, other feelings that aren't so pleasant can also be conditioned. But, think about it—when during your life did your parents, or a teacher or a coach, ever address you by your full given name? It probably wasn't long in your learning history before something happened for which your full name was used to arrest your attention, and probably to interrupt what you were doing.

Therein lies the tale. As we encounter the world and the other people in it, we constantly learn to make discriminations between those situations in which we will find comfort and those in which we had better exercise caution. As long as what we are doing or saying isn't displeasing to someone important to us, the way they address us should be casual, comforting, and inclusive. Should we be doing something or saying something that a significant other thinks we shouldn't, or not doing or saying something that a significant other thinks we should, we are likely to be addressed in way that gives either message clearly.

For most of us, that way of being addressed was by our full given names. If someone addressed you this way, wasn't your first noticeable reaction at least an "orienting response"? Didn't you almost immediately begin to attend carefully to see what was going to happen next? Wasn't that because in times past when someone called you by your full name, you had learned that some rebuke or criticism or punishment was going to follow? How were you addressed the first time, and every time thereafter, you were about to run out into traffic? Didn't your full name precede the direction to climb very carefully down out of that tree? The likelihood was that you weren't addressed so formally unless there were consequences, and not necessarily consequences you would enjoy, that you were about to meet.

In classical conditioning terms, your full name (a CS) had come to be associated with less than pleasant consequences (some USs), the kind of consequences that almost automatically invoked feelings of distress or discomfort (some URs). Once these associations had had their conditioning effects, it is very probable that the use of your full name would come to elicit some sense of apprehension, even anxiousness (some CRs) about what would be coming soon. Almost invariably, then, our behavior was likely to have been interrupted as we endeavored to deal with those unpleasant emotions.

Here, then, was Grandmother's secret. She was elegantly taking advantage of the learning histories. By immediately and consistently addressing her grandchildren by their full names, she was invoking in her grandchildren those feelings of watchfulness and caution even before they had done anything wrong. She turned them into self-monitors of their own behavior, and they were always on their best behavior in her presence.

—*Michael E. Walker*
and Raymond L. Eastman

See also: *Classical Conditioning (Vols. I & III), Historical Antecedents of Behavior Modification and Therapy (Vols. I & III), Pavlov, Ivan P. (Vols. I & III)*

Suggested Readings

Albano, A. M., & Morris, T. L. (1998). Childhood anxiety, obsessive-compulsive disorder, and depression. In J. J. Plaud & G. H. Eifert (Eds.), *From behavior theory to behavior therapy.* Needham Heights, MA: Allyn & Bacon.

Allan, R. W. (1998). Operant-respondent interactions. In W. O'Donohue (Ed.), *Learning and behavior therapy.* Needham Heights, MA: Allyn & Bacon.

Ammerman, R. T., Hersen, M., & Last, C. G. (1999). *Handbook of prescriptive treatments for children and adolescents* (2nd ed.). Needham Heights, MA: Allyn & Bacon.

Barrios, B. A., & O'Dell, S. L. (1989). Fears and anxiety. In E. J. Mash & R. A. Barkley (Eds.), *Treatment of childhood disorders.* New York: Guilford Press.

Boutin, M. E., & Nelson, J. B. (1998). The role of context in classical conditioning: Some implications for cognitive behavioral therapy. In W. O'Donohue (Ed.). *Learning and behavior therapy.* Needham Heights, MA: Allyn & Bacon.

Brem, C. (1993). *A comprehensive guide to child psychotherapy.* Needham Heights, MA: Allyn & Bacon.

Thorpe, G. L. & Olson, S. L. (1997). *Behavior therapy: Concepts, procedures, and applications.* Needham Heights, MA: Allyn & Bacon.

Walker, C. E., Kenning, M., & Faust-Campanile, J. (1989). Enuresis and encopresis. In E. J. Mash & R. A. Barkley (Eds.), *Treatment of childhood disorders.* New York: Guilford Press.

Wolpe, J. (1995). Reciprocal inhibition: Major agent of behavior change. In W. O'Donohue & L. Kransner (Eds.) *Theories of behavior change: Exploring behavior change.* Washington, DC: American Psychological Association.

COGNITIVE BEHAVIOR THERAPY: CHILD CLINICAL APPLICATIONS

DESCRIPTION OF THE STRATEGY

Definition

Cognitive behavior therapy (CBT) has become one of the most widely used therapeutic protocols with child, adolescent, and adult populations. The diversity of treatment components emerging from cognitive and behavioral theories makes it somewhat difficult to define CBT as a single entity. In general, this treatment approach combines techniques from cognitive and behavioral principles, unified by the perspective that psychopathology development and maintenance is associated with reciprocal relations between maladaptive cognitions, learned behaviors, physiological signals, and emotional responding. This mode of treatment holds that interdependent relationships between cognitions, emotions, and behavior are also central to the eventual efficacy of any CBT procedure. Briefly, CBT may best be summarized as a therapeutic attempt to change undesirable emotions using strategies to alter both the behaviors and maladaptive cognitions associated with those emotions. CBT protocols for child populations typically focus on teaching children how to (a) recognize and monitor their own behaviors, thoughts, and feelings associated with psychopathology, (b) recognize the relationships between these three components of psychopathology, (c) examine the evidence supporting or refuting distorted thoughts, and (d) replace distorted thinking and maladaptive behaviors with more flexible and positive coping mechanisms.

History and Development of CBT

Although consideration of cognitive processes was evident in the writings of William James and other early psychologists, such covert processes were of little appeal to early behavior theorists and clinicians who generally preferred to focus upon the observable and more easily definable aspects of behavior. This school of behaviorism evolved from the combined influences of many scientists, including the initial work of Ivan Pavlov in the 1900s, as well as Edward Thorndike, John Watson, B. F. Skinner, and George Miller, among others. However, with the notable exception of vivid demonstrations regarding the evolution and reduction of childhood fears by John Watson and Mary Cover Jones, behaviorally informed interventions for children, largely based upon a well-developed set of classical and operant conditioning techniques, were not particularly popular prior to the 1950s.

In the meantime, CBT was born in the midst of an era when psychoanalytic principles appeared to be falling out of favor and behavior therapy techniques were being challenged for potential weaknesses in the treatment of psychological disorders with prominent, covert features. Important to the evolution of CBT, Albert Bandura and his research on vicarious learning and self-efficacy assisted in a shift around this time from a primary focus on purely behavioral techniques to acknowledgment of some greater cognitive influence in behavior change. In addition to the contributions of Bandura, several distinct treatment approaches and the theoretical views of their developers fueled an increasing interest and focus on CBT as a viable therapeutic alternative for clinicians, including Albert Ellis's rational-emotive therapy, Aaron Beck's cognitive therapy, the behavior modification contributions of Michael Mahoney's personal science, and Donald Meichenbaum's stress inoculation training. Cognitive models, such as Beck's and Ellis's, emphasized the role of irrational, distorted cognitions in the development and maintenance of psychological disorders. More behaviorally oriented researchers adapted existing behavioral strategies such as graduated task assignment, reinforcement, and modeling to modify both overt and covert problem behaviors. Although not often mentioned, the schools of psychoanalysis, phenomenology, philosophy, and neuroscience are also conceptual contributors to CBT as we know it today.

As noted, CBT evolved mainly from the convergence of behaviorism and cognitive theory. CBT theories generally recognize the influence of the environment on psychopathology and judiciously utilize behavioral techniques. However, these models also recognize that it is both the mental representation of external stimuli and its objective properties that often elicit behavior change, rather than just the objective stimuli itself. Cognitive therapy techniques complement behavioral techniques, and as an integrated treatment, this approach may be more successful in treating a wider variety of psychological disorders than either approach alone.

Description of Major Therapeutic Techniques and Procedures

An extensive selection of treatment components is available for use in childhood CBT protocols. The selection of specific techniques is dependent on the problem being treated, the developmental capabilities of the child, and the social resources available to the child. Although an exhaustive listing and discussion of all possible CBT-related therapeutic techniques is

beyond the scope of this entry, many of the most widely used CBT techniques and procedures may best be described in the context of an actual childhood CBT protocol. To this end, several of the major therapeutic techniques and procedures associated with CBT will be presented below via discussion of a single CBT protocol for childhood anxiety disorders.

The Coping Cat Workbook, a manualized CBT protocol developed by Phillip C. Kendall, PhD, is widely used in the treatment of several forms of childhood anxiety and has demonstrated efficacy with diverse groups of children exhibiting diagnoses such as separation anxiety disorder, generalized anxiety disorder, and social phobia. The objective of the Coping Cat protocol is to provide children with adaptive skills to cope with anxiety-provoking situations through the application of a developmentally sensitive protocol that actively encourages children's participation in their treatment. *The Coping Cat Workbook* offers treatment guidelines that can be individualized to the specific client. The treatment is typically 16 to 20 sessions in length and composed of two main segments. The first of these segments focuses on psychoeducation and skill building, while the second segment focuses on a more specific application and practice of learned coping skills. The goal of the first treatment segment is to teach the anxious child how to recognize the cognitive, somatic, and behavioral symptoms that accompany anxiety, and to develop cognitive-behavioral strategies that will enable the child to cope more effectively during anxiety-provoking situations. The steps toward mastering unwanted anxious arousal are presented to the child in a four-step plan, utilizing the acronym FEAR, where *F* is "Feeling frightened?" *E* stands for "Expecting bad things to happen?" *A* is "Actions and attitudes that help," and *R* stands for "Rate and reward."

In the first step of the FEAR plan, children learn to ask themselves the question, Feeling frightened? They are taught how to recognize differing signals associated with emotions and to identify physiological sensations associated with anxiety. In addition, the children are trained in the use of relaxation exercises to help them cope with such somatic sensations. Among the relaxation techniques taught in this phase is progressive muscle relaxation, where the children learn to relax two to three muscle groups at a time. During the next step of the FEAR plan, children are taught to ask the question, Expecting bad things to happen? The focus of this step is on helping children identify their anxious cognitions or catastrophic thoughts and to modify any negative thoughts or expectations. The therapist educates the child on the ways in which self-talk might influence both non-threatening and anxiety-related experiences. A common exercise during this phase is to have the child complete thought bubbles for various cartoon characters. The child fills in the same cartoon bubble with both worry-related and coping thoughts, thereby teaching the child to differentiate between these ways of thinking. In the third step of the FEAR plan, children are provided with an array of "actions and attitudes that help" to reduce and manage unwanted anxiety symptoms. In this phase, children develop a plan to manage their anxiety by learning how to produce alternative solutions for changing a situation, contemplating the consequences of each solution, and following through with the selected plan. In the fourth step of the FEAR plan, children learn to "rate and reward" themselves by self-monitoring their coping responses in order to both assess the outcome of their anxiety management plan and reward themselves for progress made toward coping goals. To that end, children are instructed in the use of a "performance barometer" to help them rate their perceptions of how well they coped during a particular event.

The second segment of the Coping Cat treatment program focuses on the actual in vivo applications of the FEAR plan and the practice of learned coping skills. During this phase, the child is initially exposed to anxiety-provoking situations of a lower intensity, using techniques such as in-session imaginal exercises, with the child gradually progressing to exposure to higher intensity anxiety-provoking situations. The child is also given homework assignments called Show-That-I-Can (STIC) tasks throughout the treatment, which allow for structured practice of skills learned during therapeutic sessions. Homework assignments in the second phase of treatment usually involve some form of practice exposure activity, and children are rewarded for completion of assignments. To maintain therapeutic gains after treatment is completed, the children are also encouraged to continuously practice the FEAR plan in a variety of everyday situations.

Additional treatment components associated with CBT for children can generally be divided into behavioral and cognitive technique categories. Behavioral interventions are based on learning principles and can be classified as either those aiming to increase a desired target behavior through techniques such as modeling or shaping, or those aimed at decreasing the frequency, intensity, or duration of specific target behaviors via extinction, punishment, response cost, or time-out. Additional cognitive treatment components typically target modification and reduction of maladaptive cognitions with interventions such as disputing automatic thoughts, thought stopping, and self-instructional training.

Children being treated with CBT protocols may also receive additional training in social skills or problem-solving skills development. Social skills training usually focuses on improving awareness of interpersonal circumstances, increasing assertiveness, teaching conversation skills, developing strategies for making friends, and working on concepts such as compromise and bargain. Problem-solving skills training usually centers on increasing awareness of problems, generating lists of possible solutions, considering consequences, and producing step-by-step plans for interaction with specific problems. In addition, CBT protocols frequently take into consideration the child's larger social context through the inclusion of additional treatment components focusing on family circumstances or other environmental contingencies, such as particular school or peer-related concerns.

Specialized CBT Protocols

CBT protocols have been developed for several forms of childhood psychopathology. Protocol manuals typically include fun, concrete activities and examples that help therapists communicate occasionally complex CBT concepts to children. Aside from *The Coping Cat Workbook* and other CBT protocols for a broad spectrum of anxiety disorders, specialized cognitive-behavioral treatments for children and adolescents are available for obsessive-compulsive disorder (OCD), impulsive behavior, and adolescent depression, among other difficulties. In addition, treatment protocols for social skills training, problem-solving skills training, self-control training, assertiveness training, and family-based interventions are widely available for use with childhood and adolescent populations.

RESEARCH BASIS

CBT is one of the most widely investigated and efficacious treatments for adults and children with internalizing difficulties. Various studies have observed positive outcomes following CBT, in comparison to other therapies and, more often, in comparison to wait-list groups, in the treatment of several childhood disorders. CBT has also been found to have some better outcomes than pharmacotherapy in the treatment of both OCD and adolescent depression. CBT is often described as the psychotherapy of choice for children and adolescents with OCD and anxiety. Moreover, CBT, with the addition of a structured family component, may improve child anxiety treatment outcomes beyond the use of CBT alone, for some families. CBT may be helpful in the treatment of children with conduct disorder and aggressive behaviors, though it is usually not the primary form of intervention for such issues. CBT, administered in a group setting, has also demonstrated superior efficacy in the treatment of childhood anxiety disorders and in comparison to supportive therapies in the treatment of young children with a sexual abuse history. The specific contributions of the cognitive and behavioral components to the positive outcomes found across research studies are starting to be investigated more closely.

LIMITATIONS AND COMPLICATIONS ASSOCIATED WITH THE USE OF CBT WITH CHILDREN

Complexity of Treatment

Treatments that have demonstrated efficacy but are developed and tested with adult populations alone may not always be of utility when working with children. Therefore, it is important to use CBT interventions that have been adapted to match a child's comprehension level. Currently, treatments for children under the age of 7 tend to use more behavioral strategies and concentrate cognitive components on parent contributions to the therapeutic process. Most cognitive tasks in CBT do not require abstract reasoning, as ability to reason about concrete matters is often sufficient. Since the concrete operational stage of cognitive development usually occurs between 7 to 12 years of age, children in this age group typically possess adequate cognitive skills for understanding many of the basic CBT concepts and activities. Nonetheless, some investigations support the notion that CBT is more effective with children above the age of 11, indicating that not all children between 7 and 11 have adequate resources to ensure the success of an individually focused CBT protocol.

The effectiveness of CBT with children may be dependent on the therapist's ability to communicate concepts at an appropriate developmental level. School-aged children, between the ages of 7 and 12, are less likely to automatically utilize a rational style of thinking and may be more likely to use a more emotional reasoning in some circumstances. Therefore, they will benefit from more concrete language directly related to their specific experiences. Coping strategies suggested to young children should be specific, clear, and simple, using appropriate metaphors to introduce such techniques to them. Therapists should also use language that the child uses and examples based on the child's interests, while listening for an understanding of the child's day-to-day experience, in order to draw associations between the skills being taught in session and the child's familiar environment. In addition, the use of charts and graphs can make feedback about progress more concrete and understandable. As a child ages, cognitions shift from concrete to abstract. Children above the age of 12 become more capable of understanding rational arguments and abstract, general concepts. Therefore, most sophisticated cognitive restructuring techniques may best be reserved for older children and adolescents, unless they are adequately translated to a more simplified format. Ability to use various treatment concepts develops as children age and the expression of symptoms changes as well. For example, although younger children tend to fear more concrete and immediate stimuli, older children, with more sophisticated metacognitive abilities, typically have more generalized worries that are often anticipatory and socially based. Therefore, therapists are advised to always consider the cognitive development level of their individual child client when assessing and treating child psychopathology using CBT techniques.

Individual Differences in Speed of Development

The skills necessary to regulate emotions and behavior continue to evolve during childhood. While basic emotion recognition skills have an adaptive, evolutionary element to them, the accuracy of such recognition and the eventual regulation of emotion develops over time, with children usually having lesser developed emotional or behavioral regulation skills than adults. Some children develop such skills rapidly, while development in other children may be relatively delayed. Problematic behavior often spontaneously remits without intervention as a child develops such emotion regulation skills, and it may be difficult, at times, to distinguish developmentally normal emotional and behavioral mismanagement from more enduring psychopathology. Therefore, treatments using adult rationality as a benchmark for successful cognitive restructuring may be misdirected. Moreover, additional investigation of what constitutes developmentally healthy cognitive processing in children could inform the advancement of age-appropriate CBT interventions.

Systemic Influences

Child psychopathology cannot be effectively treated by considering the child in isolation. Children impact and are impacted by their surrounding environment. Therefore, the context in which the psychopathology develops and is maintained must be considered. Parents, other caregivers, teachers, and peers frequently, and often accidentally, reinforce a child's maladaptive functioning. Very young children typically depend on parents for signals that cue emotional and behavioral regulation. Often, problems in self-control originate with or are exacerbated by parents who are less competent at assisting in necessary skill development. While evidence is notably missing on the treatment of very young children, it often appears that the younger the child, the more treatment involves training parents to teach their children self-control strategies. Even with older children, it is often advantageous to include parents in educational sessions designed to help parents facilitate treatment outside the therapist's office. When the success of treatment elements, such as exposure techniques in the treatment of OCD, is relatively dependent on their practice in the child's natural environment, the involvement of parents in ensuring compliance with such activities seems all the more valuable. In some cases, it may also be helpful to engage parents in concurrent individual counseling for their own mood regulation or skill development to facilitate appropriate parent management of child psychopathology.

The necessary acknowledgment of systemic influences can make CBT more challenging with children than with adults. This is particularly true when elements of the system fail to recognize their contributions to the child's psychopathology or

when adults, educators, and peers are less willing or unavailable to participate in the intervention. Many times, however, parents and educators are more motivated for therapeutic intervention than the child, as it is clear that children typically do not refer themselves for treatment and parents or educators often initiate contact with a therapist. When designing CBT treatment plans, therapists should also consider the specific source of that initial therapeutic contact and their involvement with the child's daily management of symptoms and motivation for participating in treatment processes.

Moreover, in CBT, the child is considered an equal partner in the development of treatment goals and implementation of intervention strategies. Consequently, determining treatment objectives can be difficult if the parent and child disagree on the targeted goals. Parental expectations of how the child should behave may exceed the normal limits for children in their age group, and developmentally normal behavior may appear pathological to the parent, especially those coping with their own mood or environmental difficulties. Assessment of the problem can be further biased by parents' tendency to report symptoms that they find to be irritating, such as impulsivity and hyperactivity, rather than more covert behaviors, such as depression or low self-esteem. Therefore, it is important to gather information from multiple sources, including the child, in this treatment planning effort.

Treatment plans are developed upon careful consideration of cognitive, emotional, behavioral, and environmental contributions to the problem behavior. Depending on the needs of the child, treatment may focus on altering the environment by training teachers and parents. However, a strength of CBT is that it recapitulates the developmental process of increasing autonomy. Therapists often collaborate with children to develop treatment strategies and, commensurate with the child's developmental level, transfer the source of behavioral control from adults to the child. Therefore, it is particularly important for a therapist to engage children and adolescents in treatment. To this end, it can be beneficial for the therapist to discuss the pros and cons of treatment strategies and to encourage clients to experiment with the strategies to find out for themselves whether a particular approach will assist with their problem behaviors, keeping in mind that treatment should be an enjoyable and empowering experience for the child or adolescent.

Limits of Treatment Manuals

Most CBT treatment protocols target and have been tested on clients with one disorder. Efficacy trials using participants with comorbidities are rare. Therefore, it is difficult to determine which interventions are most appropriate for configurations of multiple disorders. Furthermore, most CBT treatment manuals target children aged 7 to 12 years. There are relatively fewer CBT manuals targeting adolescents. When treating adolescents, it can be difficult to decide whether to use interventions designed to treat children or to use treatments intended for adults. Adolescents have unique characteristics that necessitate the development and testing of treatments specifically designed for this age group. Moreover, some evidence has suggested that parent and family components that appear to improve the efficacy of CBT for school-aged children appear to have a potentially lesser impact on adolescents, given their comparative autonomy and the increased influence of peers on their environment. Thus, additional research certainly appears warranted to more effectively address the CBT needs of adolescents.

Characteristics of Clients That Limit the Use of CBT

CBT is less useful for children below 7 years of age, children with cognitive delays or learning disabilities, and children with more external attribution styles. Younger children and less cognitively able children find it difficult to generalize abstract concepts to multiple situations. However, modifications of CBT that target specific behaviors, employ parents more fundamentally in the treatment process, and use more concrete strategies and examples have been successfully used with younger and less cognitively able individuals. Repetition and modeling should be used to a greater extent with these populations than is used with older children or children of average or above intelligence. Furthermore, younger children are more likely to express emotion in the form of overt behaviors, rather than engage in maladaptive self-talk. Children below the age of 5 years may have not developed the more conventionally considered use of covert, verbal self-talk. Therefore, modification of covert self-instruction should be reserved for older children. Typically, therapy with children younger than 5 involves educating parents. Between the ages of 5 to 7, therapy could involve both the parents and the child, with an emphasis on parenting skills development. Usually, individual CBT approaches should not be attempted until after 7 years of age, and even then only children of this age with higher intelligence and motivation levels will likely benefit from an approach that doesn't have a higher parent involvement content. Children with external attribution styles are also more likely to benefit from more behavioral control strategies and environmental change. Children with internal attribution styles, on the other hand, are better suited for self-control skill development. Nonetheless, a component of CBT may involve increasing internal attribution and internal locus of control.

Generalization of Skills

Lack of skill generalization outside the therapeutic setting is not limited to younger or learning-disabled children. Transfer of learned skills to other settings is a problem for almost all CBT clients. The more that children are actively involved in the selection of their own self-regulatory strategies and the more examples from multiple situations within the child's greater environment that are used in training, the more likely it seems that skills will generalize across multiple situations. It is also important that the child actively try new skills in multiple settings. Training the child to self-monitor, evaluate, and reward himself or herself can increase the use of new skills in situations in which the therapist or parent are not present.

CASE ILLUSTRATION

"Mandy M." was a 15-year-old Hispanic female seen for both an initial evaluation and treatment at a university-based childhood anxiety disorders clinic. During the initial telephone contact with the clinic, Mandy's mother, "Mrs. M.," indicated that she was primarily concerned about a sudden increase in the frequency of what she termed "anxiety attacks" that Mandy appeared to be experiencing. Mrs. M. also indicated that while, in the past, similar but more minor attacks appeared to be precipitated by Mandy's worry or anticipation of social or school stressors, lately they seemed to happen "just out of the blue" and appeared to have increased not only in frequency but also in the intensity of occurrence. In addition, Mrs. M. noted that she personally feared that Mandy was now beginning to avoid or attempting to avoid several situations in which her more severe anxiety attacks had occurred. Her biggest concern in this regard was that despite a long history of positive interaction and success in the school environment, Mandy was frequently attempting to stay home from school, where she recently experienced her most severe attack to date, following an after-school yearbook staff meeting. Mrs. M. reported that although Mandy was a valued yearbook staff member who had previously enjoyed such work, she recently noted to her mother that she would prefer to stop working on the yearbook from now on because it "stressed" her too much.

The initial assessment session with Mandy and her family consisted of the completion of several anxiety, mood, and family-related questionnaires about her symptomatology and a more structured, diagnostic interview, conducted first with Mandy alone, then with her parents together. This diagnostic interview measure provided ample time for both less structured discussions regarding Mandy's current functioning and more focused questions that enabled the examiner to accurately diagnose Mandy's difficulties. During this interview, Mandy and her parents reported that she experienced panic attacks approximately five to nine times per week, with a more than threefold increase in the frequency of panic attacks over the last month. During such panic attacks, Mandy reported that she felt nausea, a racing heart, sweating, chills, difficulty breathing, and thoughts that either someone could tell she was panicking or, more frequently, that she might be "going crazy." She also endorsed several social fears during this interview, including fears about public speaking, assertiveness during interactions, and dating. However, her social fears appeared to be of a lesser intensity and impairment than her panic-related concerns. Based on these interviews and the questionnaires completed, the examiner assigned Mandy a diagnosis of panic disorder without agoraphobia (severity rating of 6 [0–8 scale, where 8 = the most severe symptom presentation rating]) and a secondary diagnosis of social phobia (severity rating = 4).

Although Mandy's social fears were noted and recurrently addressed by the treating clinician, the clinician elected to focus on the panic symptoms more intensely at the start of treatment, since they were of primary concern to Mandy and her parents. The therapist elected to treat panic symptoms using panic control treatment for adolescents (PCT-A), a manualized treatment developed by Sara Mattis, PhD, and an adolescent adaptation of an efficacious cognitive-behavioral treatment for panic disorder in adults, originally developed by David H. Barlow, PhD, and his colleagues. Prior to the first session, a meeting was held with Mandy and her parents to discuss this treatment option, along with the nature and treatment-relevant features of both panic disorder and social phobia. Most important, the family was told that the aim of PCT-A was to directly influence the three aspects of panic disorder and related anxiety: the cognitive misinterpretation aspect, the hyperventilation response, and conditioned responses that had developed in response to physical sensations experienced during panic attacks. Mandy and her parents agreed to this course of treatment, and a first appointment was scheduled with the clinician.

The goals of the first session with Mandy were to provide a more detailed description of the cognitive, behavioral, and physiological aspects of anxiety to her, gain more specific information about her particular pattern of panic, and have Mandy learn to describe some recent panic attacks in terms of their cognitive, behavioral, and physiological aspects. In this session, Mandy also began completion of a fear avoidance hierarchy (FAH) by rank-ordering 10 situations that she tended to avoid due to fear of having a panic attack. Among the situations ranked by Mandy were both social situations and situations in which panic had previously occurred, including entering her yearbook staff room, being alone in a car (where she also had a previous panic attack), talking to boys in her school hallways, and using the bathrooms in her school while other girls were in it. In the second session, the rationale for interoceptive exposure, a technique that assists clients in exposing themselves to physiological symptoms associated with panic, was successfully introduced. Sessions 3, 4, and 5 consisted of learning breathing retraining techniques to modify physiological responding during panic attacks and the introduction of cognitive restructuring exercises aimed at common misinterpretations of threat that occur during panic episodes. Specifically, Mandy indicated that she frequently *overestimated the probability* of a panic attack occurring and *catastrophized* the consequences of any panic symptoms that she might be experiencing. During discussions of these cognitive processes, Mandy came to realize that she was actually exacerbating her experience of panic symptoms via her cognitive responding. Such cognitive errors were generally addressed by having Mandy learn to be a detective and investigate the clues that tell her whether her panic thought was realistic or not, then reassessing the likelihood of her panic thoughts, among other techniques. Also during these sessions, situational or in vivo exposure practice assignments were given as homework, to allow for successful mastery of situations low on Mandy's FAH. Sessions 6 and 7 continued and expanded upon cognitive restructuring activities by discussing beliefs about Mandy's worst panic beliefs and using *hypothesis testing* exercises to evaluate the validity of panic-related thoughts and beliefs. These sessions also introduced regular interoceptive exposure practice in session and as homework assignments. Mandy responded extremely well to these interoceptive exercises, particularly an exercise involving spinning in a chair, which created sensations of nausea similar to those experienced during panic, and running in place, which produced sensations associated with rapid breathing and a faster heartbeat. During Session 8, both Mandy and her parents reported that the frequency of panic attacks had dramatically reduced to two or fewer per week. Mandy and her therapist discussed termination at that time, and decided to spend two additional sessions on interoceptive and situational exposures, in addition to further cognitive restructuring exercises, in order to further reduce symptom severity. Following this 10th session, a shorter version of the diagnostic interview completed during the initial assessment was administered to Mandy and her parents. Both parties indicated during this interview that panic disorder symptoms were no longer of a clinically significant nature (severity rating = 2), and that, although not an explicit target of treatment, social phobia symptoms were also no longer clinically significant (severity rating = 3).

—Jill T. Ehrenreich, Tiffany Kyle-Linkovich, and Angela Rojas-Vilches

See also: *Cognitive-Behavioral Approach to Bipolar Disorder (Vol. III), Cognitive Behavior Therapy (Vols. I & III), Cognitive Behavior Therapy With Religious Beliefs and Practices (Vols. I & III), Cognitive Restructuring (Vols. I, II, & III), Self-Instruction Training (Vol. II)*

Suggested Readings

Bond, F. W., & Dryden, W. (2002). *Handbook of brief cognitive behaviour therapy.* New York: John Wiley.

Craighead, L. W., Craighead, W. E., Kazdin, A. E., & Mahoney, M. J. (1994). *Cognitive and behavioral interventions: An empirical approach to mental health problems.* Boston: Allyn & Bacon.

Craighead, W. E., Meyers, A. W., & Craighead, L. W. (1985). A conceptual model for cognitive-behavior therapy with children. *Journal of Abnormal Child Psychology, 13,* 331–342.

Deblinger, E., Stauffer, L. B., & Steer, R. A. (2001). Comparative efficacies of supportive and cognitive behavioral group therapies for young children who have been sexually abused and their nonoffending mothers. *Child Maltreatment, 6,* 332–343.

Dobson, K. S. (2001). *Handbook of cognitive-behavioral therapies* (2nd ed.). New York: Guilford Press.

France, R., & Robson, M. (1997). *Cognitive behavioral therapy in primary care: A practical guide.* Bristol, PA: Jessica Kingsley.

Kendall, P. C. (1991). *Child and adolescent therapy: Cognitive-behavioral procedures.* New York: Guilford Press.

Kendall, P. C. (2000). *Cognitive-behavioral treatment for anxious children: Therapist's manual* (2nd ed.). Ardmore, PA.: Workbook.

Kendall, P. C., & Braswell, L. (1993). *Cognitive-behavioral therapy for impulsive children.* New York: Guilford Press.

Kendall, P. C., Chu, B., Gifford, A., Hayes, C., & Nauta, M. (1998). Breathing life into a manual: Flexibility and creativity with manual-based treatments. *Cognitive & Behavioral Practice, 5,* 177–198.

Kendall, P. C., & Treadwell, K. R. H. (1996). Cognitive-behavioral treatment for childhood anxiety disorders. In E. O. Hibbs and P. S. Jensen (Eds.), *Psychosocial treatments for child and adolescent disorders: Empirically based strategies for clinical practice* (pp. 23–42). Washington, DC: American Psychological Association.

March, J. S. (1995). Cognitive-behavioral psychotherapy for children and adolescents with OCD: A review and recommendation for treatment. *Journal of the American Academy of Child and Adolescent Psychiatry, 34,* 7–18.

March, J. S., Franklin, M., Nelson, A., & Foa, E. (2001). Cognitive-behavioral psychotherapy for pediatric obsessive-compulsive disorder. *Journal of Clinical Child Psychopathology, 30,* 8–18.

March, J. S., and Mulle, K. (1996). Banishing OCD: Cognitive-behavioral psychotherapy for obsessive-compulsive disorders. In E. O. Hibbs and P. S. Jensen (Eds.), *Psychosocial treatments for child and adolescent disorders: Empirically based strategies for clinical practice* (pp. 83–102). Washington, DC: American Psychological Association.

March, J. S., Mulle, K., & Herbel, B. (1994). Behavioral psychotherapy for children and adolescents with obsessive-compulsive disorder: An open trial of a new protocol-driven treatment package. *Journal of the American Academy of Child and Adolescent Psychiatry, 33,* 333–341.

Muris, P., Meesters, C., & Melick, M. V. (2002). Treatment of childhood anxiety disorders: A preliminary comparison between cognitive-behavioral group therapy and a psychological placebo intervention. *Journal of Behavior Therapy and Experimental Psychiatry, 33,* 143–158.

Ronen, T. (1998). Linking developmental and emotional elements into child and family cognitive-behavioural therapy. In P. Graham (Ed.), *Cognitive-behaviour therapy for children and families* (pp. 1–17). New York: Cambridge University Press.

Stallard, P. (2002). Cognitive behaviour therapy with children and young people: A selective review of key issues. *Behavioural and Cognitive Psychotherapy, 30*, 297–309.

Waters, T. L., Barrett, P. M., & March, J. S. (2001). Cognitive-behavioral family treatment of childhood obsessive-compulsive disorder. *American Journal of Psychotherapy, 55*, 372–388.

COGNITIVE RESTRUCTURING

DESCRIPTION OF THE STRATEGY

Cognitive restructuring is a broad term encompassing a variety of procedures designed to eliminate maladaptive thinking patterns and increase the frequency of constructive thoughts and beliefs. The roots of cognitive restructuring may be traced to cognitive psychology. Cognitive theorists proposed that most learning in humans is cognitively mediated (i.e., thoughts influence perceptions and behavior). A major tenet of cognitive therapy is that through the modification of clients' thought processes, their belief systems will be altered, and this ultimately will result in changes in overt behavior and emotional processing.

The work of Albert Ellis was quite influential with respect to the development and proliferation of cognitive and cognitive-behavioral therapies. Ellis termed his approach "rational emotive therapy (RET)." According to Ellis, psychological disorders are the product of irrational thinking patterns. For Ellis, irrational thoughts are those that could be considered self-defeating in that they reduce opportunities for fulfillment and adaptive functioning. Categories of irrational thoughts include thinking that one must receive approval from everyone—all the time, one must succeed in every task, that it is catastrophic when something does not go one's way; and that things will always be the same, nothing will ever get better. Treatment involves the therapist challenging these faulty beliefs and assisting the client in substituting more rational thoughts.

Other theorists whose work was highly influential in setting the stage for the development of cognitive restructuring procedures included Aaron Beck and Donald Meichenbaum. Each emphasized the importance of cognitive processes to socioemotional functioning and the need to address maladaptive cognitions in an effort to reduce symptoms of psychological disorders. In 1974, Goldfried and colleagues detailed a more structured form of RET, which they referred to as systematic rational restructuring (SRR). Essentially, SRR was a set of specific operational procedures for obtaining the type of cognitive change noted as essential within RET. Subsequently, in their text on therapeutic strategies, Cormier and Cormier classified strategies designed to effect cognitive change under the umbrella term "cognitive restructuring." The term has been used since that time to refer to various techniques intended to enhance more adaptive thinking on the part of clients.

A typical cognitive restructuring procedure includes the following elements: the therapist provides the client with the theoretical rationale underlying the procedure and outlines how the therapy will take place; through formal assessment and discussion, the therapist identifies the client's maladaptive thoughts, perceptions, and beliefs; the therapist models more adaptive coping thoughts; the client practices adaptive coping thoughts when faced with the occurrence of irrational thoughts; and ultimately the client is taught to go beyond coping, to the induction of more pervasive positive self-talk intended to enhance self-concept. Imagery and role play may be used to facilitate cognitive rehearsal. Homework assignments typically are a routine part of cognitive restructuring therapy in an effort to increase generalization and maintenance. Self-monitoring logs or diaries assist the client in identifying irrational thoughts as well as antecedents and consequences. Two complementary goals of cognitive restructuring are (a) to help clients learn to cope more effectively when in stressful situations and (b) to alter clients' belief systems so that situations that once would have been perceived as stressful will no longer be seen as such, should they arise in the future. It is the second goal that would be indicative of successful "restructuring" per se.

RESEARCH BASIS

Numerous research studies have been conducted on the efficacy of cognitive restructuring procedures. In general, cognitive restructuring strategies have demonstrated success in the treatment of a diverse array of psychological symptom states, including depression, test anxiety, speech anxiety, social anxiety, panic, assertiveness problems, and posttraumatic stress. However, it should be noted that within most treatment outcome studies, cognitive restructuring was used as a component in a treatment package rather than the sole therapeutic strategy. A limited number of studies have attempted to compare the effectiveness of cognitive restructuring versus exposure-based strategies in isolation. With respect to the treatment of anxiety disorders, cognitive restructuring techniques have tended to yield similar results in terms of symptom reduction as have exposure-based strategies. Mixed results have been found regarding potential enhanced benefit of using exposure and cognitive restructuring in combination. Furthermore, the positive benefits of cognitive restructuring tend to be more pronounced for self-report data than for measures of behavioral change (e.g., direct observation, behavioral performance tasks).

RELEVANT TARGET POPULATION

Theoretically, cognitive restructuring procedures would seem to be most appropriate for psychological disorders in which cognition plays a substantial part. The negative thinking patterns characteristic of individuals suffering from depression and anxiety perhaps would suggest that these populations would be among those who would benefit most from cognitive restructuring procedures. Persons experiencing phase-of-life and adjustment reactions also may benefit from promotion of more rational-based modes of thought.

COMPLICATIONS

Implicit in the successful conduct of cognitive therapy is that clients have the capacity for sufficient metacognition (thinking about thinking). Clients must be able to identify (and report to the therapist) how they think, feel, and behave. Clients must possess sufficient logical reasoning skills to engage in formal problem solving. Memory must not be impaired to any significant degree. Clients must be oriented to reality and not actively psychotic. Furthermore, the therapeutic process requires that clients be motivated to change (limited success will be effected for clients ordered to therapy under duress, as in the case of criminal offenders or parents referred for issues of abuse and neglect).

It should be apparent that cognitive restructuring should be used with young children only under limited and highly structured situations—if at all. Young children do not possess sufficient metacognitive ability to be active participants in the cognitive restructuring process. More efficient behavioral strategies should be considered when working with preadolescent children.

CASE ILLUSTRATION

"Alex" was a 16-year-old boy who was referred by his school counselor for treatment of social anxiety. He reported (and his parents confirmed) that he has felt "shy" most of his life. Over the past 2 years, however, his social anxiety had become much more pronounced. Alex did not want to attend school on days he was expected to participate in public speaking tasks. He would have liked to obtain a part-time job after school but was unable to make phone calls to inquire about positions and was terrified of undergoing a job interview. Most of his friends had begun dating. Alex very much liked to date and participate in social activities, but the very thought of asking a girl out made his stomach churn, his head spin, and his palms sweat. Alex was convinced that his peers thought he was a "dork," and he felt utterly incompetent.

Comprehensive assessment was conducted following intake. Alex obtained extreme elevations on self-report measures of social anxiety. Parent reports and teacher reports corroborated Alex's self-reports—and all measures indicated social anxiety as the primary concern. Structured diagnostic interview confirmed that Alex met criteria for social anxiety disorder. While Alex did not meet full criteria for any other disorders, he was experiencing symptoms of mild depression that seemed to be a consequence of his increasing social isolation. Behavioral performance tasks indicated that Alex possessed the basic social skills required to be a functional teenager but was inhibited in engaging in certain social behaviors in the natural context due to severe anxiety.

Treatment involved targeting and disputing Alex's irrational beliefs regarding his level of social competence and how others perceived him. Alex experienced intense fear of negative evaluation. The therapist helped him see that all individuals make a social faux pas from time to time, that these mishaps are rarely catastrophic, and that what is important is that he learn to roll with these situations when they occur and not retreat socially. Since not all teenagers are as gracious with their peers as we would like them to be, Alex and the therapist role-played situations in which he was made fun of by others. This allowed Alex to practice positive coping statements, which later helped him to handle real-world stressors—which were never as bad as he had expected them to be. Over the course of 14 weekly sessions (and accompanying homework assignments), Alex learned to hold more realistic expectations and to see himself in the way that others saw him: a bright, funny young man with a positive future. His scores on social anxiety measures fell within normal limits, and the symptoms of depression had all but abated. While therapy was considered a success, Alex and his parents were informed that symptoms of social anxiety might reoccur with certain developmental transitions (e.g., going away to college), and if that were to happen, it should not be looked upon as a failure; instead, it should serve as an impetus for a brief booster course of therapy. Once clients gain skill in disputing irrational thinking, they tend to progress through subsequent courses of therapy with even greater ease.

—*Tracy L. Morris*

See also: *Cognitive Behavioral Approach to Bipolar Disorder (Vol. III), Cognitive Behavior Therapy (Vols. I & III), Cognitive Behavior Therapy: Child Clinical Applications (Vol. II), Cognitive Behavior Therapy With Religious Beliefs and Practices (Vols. I & III), Cognitive Restructuring (Vols. I & III)*

Suggested Readings

Beck, A. T. (1970). Cognitive therapy: Nature and relation to behavior therapy. *Behavior Therapy, 1,* 184–200.

Ellis, A. (1973). *Humanistic psychotherapy: The rational-emotive approach.* New York: Julian Press.

Goldfried, M. R., Decenteceo, E. T., & Weinberg, L. (1974). Systematic rational restructuring as a self-control technique. *Behavior Therapy, 5,* 247–254.

Meichenbaum, D. (1977). *Cognitive-behavior modification: An integrative approach.* New York: Plenum.

Prins, P. J. M., & Ollendick, T. H. (2003). Cognitive change and enhanced coping: Missing mediational links in cognitive behavior therapy with anxiety-disordered children. *Clinical Child and Family Psychology Review, 6,* 87–105.

COMPETING RESPONSE TRAINING

DESCRIPTION OF THE STRATEGY

Competing response training (CRT; also, competing reaction training) is a primary component of habit reversal training (HRT), a treatment package most commonly used to reduce undesirable or maladaptive repetitive behaviors, including tics, stuttering, and habit disorders. CRT consists of teaching a competing response, which is applied contingent upon occurrence of the target behavior or any urge to engage in the target behavior for 1 to 3 minutes. Historically, the competing response has been an alternative behavior incompatible with production of the target behavior, involving isometric tensing of the same muscles in the opposite direction used to produce the target behavior. For example, CRT may consist of teaching a client to replace an undesirable response such as hair pulling with a more desirable alternative, "competing" response, such as clenching fists for 2 minutes. More recent applications have been less strict, deemphasizing tensing of opposite muscles and occasionally selecting unrelated alternative behaviors, particularly in treatment of young children. Common competing responses include such actions as clenching fists, opening and closing hands, tensing neck muscles, regulated deep breathing, crossing arms, placing hands in pockets, and sitting on hands.

HRT was developed in the 1970s and was originally comprised of 9 to 13 separate procedures categorized into four core components: (1) awareness training, (2) CRT, (3) motivational procedures, and (4) generalization procedures. The first component consisted of a set of procedures designed to help the client notice instances of the target behavior. The second component was as described above. The third component involved a set of procedures designed to motivate the client to eliminate the target behavior and to facilitate adherence to recommended treatment components. The final component was aimed at enhancing generalization through symbolic rehearsal of common habit-evoking situations (i.e., imagining a high-risk situation and practicing the competing response).

More recently, studies using habit reversal in the treatment of childhood habit and tic disorders have increasingly applied simplified habit-reversal procedures, generally including three components: awareness training, CRT, and social support procedures. Social support procedures are designed to promote generalization and maintenance efforts by having the child's parents praise the absence of the target behavior, praise independent completion of the competing response, and prompt the child to engage in the competing response (physically assisting as needed) when the target behavior is observed.

Habit reversal and its simplified variants have effectively treated a variety of repetitive behaviors, including various motor tics, stuttering, hair pulling, finger and thumb sucking, fingernail biting, scratching, and destructive oral habits (e.g., lip, mouth, and tongue biting), as well as comorbid habit disorders such as concurrent hair pulling and thumb sucking. Habit reversal has been effective in as little as one 2-hour session. Although studies with young children typically require at least one treatment session followed by two to four shorter booster sessions to obtain desired reductions in the target behavior(s), more intractable problems, such as Tourette's disorder, often require many more sessions to achieve desired outcomes.

RESEARCH BASIS

CRT, as a standard component of HRT, is backed by 30 years of research across a wide range of clinical problems and a variety of target populations. Several variations of habit reversal have been effective in treating children and adolescents. Nearly all successful variants have included awareness training and CRT, which are considered to be essential components. Yet research focused on treatment of children indicates that social support efforts may also be required to obtain positive outcomes, particularly with young children.

The research literature has begun to identify important aspects of CRT. First, studies with both children and adults have shown that dissimilar alternative competing responses (i.e., clenching knees in place of thumb sucking) can be equally effective as similar competing responses (i.e., those using the same muscle group) in reducing the target behavior. In fact, some researchers have begun allowing children to participate in selecting their competing responses. This has important implications, because children may find certain competing responses easier to implement or more acceptable than others.

Furthermore, research with adults suggests that the competing response should be conducted for at least 1 minute per occurrence to maintain long-term reductions in the target behavior. It also has shown that contingent application of the competing response (e.g., use following occurrence of the target behavior) is more effective than noncontingent use.

RELEVANT TARGET POPULATIONS AND EXCEPTIONS

CRT has been used with children as young as 2½ years, individuals with developmental disabilities, and adult populations, although outcomes with young children and individuals with developmental disabilities

have been mixed. Young children under the age of 7 using only habit reversal components tend to have more difficulty attaining successful outcomes.

COMPLICATIONS

Researchers have proposed that limitations of habit reversal with young children and developmentally disabled individuals result from poor treatment integrity. This may be related to stimulus control (i.e., failing to use the competing response when the therapist is not present) or motivational issues (i.e., failure to experience negative social consequences for engaging in the target behavior).

Augmenting HRT methods using strategies designed to facilitate awareness of the target behavior (e.g., external prompting devices, surreptitious observation and prompting) have been effective in reminding these individuals to use the competing response, resulting in better outcomes. Furthermore, adding contingency management components such as differential reinforcement or response cost can lead to a successful reduction of repetitive behaviors even in young children and individuals with developmental disabilities. Finally, parent involvement in standard social support procedures (e.g., prompting and praising completion of competing responses), physically assisting children who either will not or cannot complete the competing response independently, and helping children count or otherwise track the duration of the competing response may greatly enhance treatment adherence.

Finally, despite its success, little is known about the function of repetitive behaviors and the mechanism underlying the effectiveness of CRT. Some early research suggests that repetitive behaviors serving different functions (e.g., tension reduction, contingent escape) may be more or less amenable to treatment using habit reversal techniques. Future research in this area should help delineate circumstances under which CRT may be most beneficial.

—*Sara E. Sytsma-Jordan*

See also: *Competing Response Training (Vols. I & III), Differential Reinforcement of Other Behavior (Vols. I, II, & III), Operant Conditioning (Vols. I, II, & III)*

Suggested Readings

Azrin, N. H., & Nunn, R. G. (1973). Habit-reversal: A method of eliminating nervous habits and tics. *Behaviour, Research, and Therapy, 11,* 619–628.

Miltenberger, R. G., Fuqua, R. W., & Woods, D. W. (1998). Applying behavior analysis to clinical problems: Review and analysis of habit reversal. *Journal of Applied Behavior Analysis, 31,* 447–469.

Rapp, J. T., Miltenberger, R. G., Galensky, T. L., Roberts, J., & Ellington, S. A. (1999). Brief functional analysis and simplified habit reversal of thumb sucking in fraternal twin brothers. *Child & Family Behavior Therapy, 21,* 1–17.

Woods, D. W., & Miltenberger, R. G. (1995). Habit reversal: A review of applications and variations. *Journal of Behavior Therapy and Experimental Psychiatry, 26,* 123–131.

Woods, D. W., & Miltenberger, R. G. (1996). A review of habit reversal with childhood habit disorders. *Education and Treatment of Children, 19,* 197–214.

COMPLIANCE TRAINING

DESCRIPTION OF THE STRATEGY

A child's reaction to adult instructions has always been viewed through a developmental lens. If the child is an infant, one assumes that receptive language levels are insufficient to equate nonresponsiveness with willful defiance; a year later, American parents often view the same child's indifference as an annoying yet age-appropriate manifestation of the "terrible twos"; in contrast, a 4-year-old child who angrily shouts "No" and physically resists adult guidance may find himself or herself referred to a professional for treatment. Indeed, there is a point in the social development of children where even the most patient parent can no longer tolerate child disobedience. Consequently, child noncompliance is one of the most common referral problems among parents seeking professional help for their preadolescent children, and for good reason. Developmental psychopathologists have identified sustained child noncompliance as a foundation for serious future misconduct, including oppositional defiant disorder and conduct disorder.

Constance Hanf introduced a breakthrough treatment for noncompliant children in the 1960s at the University of Oregon Medical Center. Hanf's pioneering work conceptualized child noncompliance as a family systems problem, rather than an intrapsychic disorder. Drawing on the behaviorism of B. F. Skinner, the interpersonal emphasis of Harry Stack Sullivan, and the social learning orientation of Julian Rotter, Hanf proposed to "reprogram" the young child's social environment, much as her influential colleague in nearby Eugene, Oregon, Gerald Patterson, was

treating 6- to 12-year-old children with well-established aggressive and predelinquent behavior patterns. Reprogramming the social environment meant teaching the child's parents how to promote compliance. Hanf conceptualized two distinct stages of parent training. First, she believed that parents needed to become better at recognizing and socially reinforcing prosocial child behavior. She hypothesized that parent-delivered social reinforcers would become more valued by the child, given an expanded parent repertoire and greater frequency of use, leading to increased frequencies of child prosocial functions, including compliance. Stage 1, or The Child's Game, still forms a substantive component of modern parent-child interaction therapy. In her Stage 1 pilot work with a small set of referred preschool children, Hanf observed that noncompliance often persisted, despite good improvement by parents in child's game skills. Moreover, ignoring noncompliance seemed ineffectual, since many children reacted to parent instructions with unignorable, intense anger. Therefore, Hanf constructed Stage 2, or The Parent's Game, to target noncompliance directly. She defined a set of contingent, increasingly aversive consequences for noncompliance. Specifically, were the child to disobey an instruction, a warning was issued; if the warning was defied, a brief time-out was required; if the child refused to sit on the time-out chair, a spanking was administered.

Although modern parent-child interaction therapy (PCIT) has evolved since the 1960s, the cornerstones are clearly etched with Hanf's two-stage protocol. Two generations of child clinical researchers have chipped away at the many questions implied by the Hanf protocol, yielding some clear answers to many of the apparent research questions. Two among them, Rex Forehand at the University of Georgia and Sheila Eyberg at the University of Florida, produced a generation of students who diligently pursued controlled, empirical strategies to tease out the many effects of Stage 1 and Stage 2 parent training on a variety of dependent variables. A prototype of modern PCIT procedures is as follows:

Training Parents

Parents are provided with a rationale for the treatment strategy, which focuses on the interactional nature of noncompliance and the logical necessity of adjusting adult responses. Since one implication of such a rationale is that parents are partially to blame for the child's misbehavior, clinicians emphasize the role of parent as teacher, which seems to resonate well with parent consumers. Written materials provide objective descriptions of the parenting skills to be used, data to be collected at home, relevant exemplars, and so on. Therapists model specific parenting skills using an assistant (or a doll manipulated by an assistant) in a child role. Commercial videotapes are also available for this purpose. Parents often role-play skills with a therapist in the child's role. Role playing allows the therapist precise control over the stimulus event to which the parent must react. Such control allows for the gradual introduction of increasingly complex skills (e.g., a time-out resistance sequence or a community management protocol) at a pace commensurate with a parent's acquisition rate. Guided in vivo practice with the child in a play or task analog is a hallmark of PCIT. The clinician can provide social reinforcement and corrective feedback as the parent-child interaction unfolds. Feedback can be immediate if the clinician uses a bug-in-the-ear device. These tiny radio receivers are worn by the parent, much like a hearing aid, and allow the clinician to provide support and information without being physically present. Presumably, the social context of the clinic analog is more ecologically valid, since the parent interacts directly with the child in the absence of the therapist. PCIT therapists usually provide home record cards that prompt the use of new parenting skills, in addition to providing natural setting outcome data. Phone support is a routine component of PCIT, especially during initial use of a difficult routine, such as time-out. Parenting groups can be developed to provide social support, as well as continuing education.

Stage 1 Training

During the Child's Game (also called "child-directed interaction"), parents are instructed to allow the child to choose the game or activity. The parent is encouraged to play as if he or she had some free time at home. The key is active acceptance and support for child play and child signals. If the child is engaged in a motoric activity with the toys, the parent is encouraged to verbally describe that activity (e.g., "You're building a castle with those blocks"), positively evaluate that activity (e.g., "You're really good at that"), or physically imitate the child (i.e., parallel play). If the child talks about his or her activity, parents are

encouraged to paraphrase the child's utterances (i.e., imitation with reduction). If the child asks a question or gives an instruction, parents are instructed to react with at least acknowledgment. In addition, parents are specifically counseled to inhibit questioning, criticizing, or instructing the child, since that is believed to be incompatible with the goals of social reinforcement for child prosocial behavior. From an attachment theory perspective, the responsive play skills taught to parents during Stage 1 resemble those of a sensitive caregiver who accurately interprets infant signals and modulates her or his reaction accordingly. Clinicians assess parent acquisition of Stage 1 skills by observing frequencies of positive parenting (e.g., descriptions, praise, imitations) and unnecessary intrusions (e.g., instructions, questions, criticisms). Some criterion level of performance is sought, such as four or more positive initiations per minute and one or fewer intrusive verbalizations per minute. Probabilistic measures of parent responsiveness, given child signals, can also be quantified.

Stage 2 Training

During clinic task analogs (also called "parent-directed interaction"), a series of age-appropriate chores are provided for the child to perform under parent direction. Instruction-giving skills are introduced first. Parents are trained to emit direct, comprehensible instructions ("Please do X.") rather than indirect instructions ("Why don't you start cleaning up?") or vague instructions ("C'mon! Do it right."). Effective instructions must also be consistent with the child's receptive language and behavioral repertoire. Inhibition of instruction repetition and the insertion of a clear postinstruction pause are recommended to render the instruction salient from the background, similar to a signal-to-noise enhancement strategy. For 2- and 3-year-old children, gaining proximity, making eye contact, and providing a relevant gesture may be important instruction qualities. If the child makes any effort to comply during the postinstruction interval (i.e., the next 5 seconds), parents are to praise that effort. If the child makes no effort, a warning is announced (e.g., "If you don't start putting the blocks away right now, you will have to go to time-out."). Parents are trained to socially reinforce compliance with warnings and to use a time-out procedure for noncompliance with warnings. Time-out is a complex and varied protocol that has its own detailed entry in this encyclopedia. Once time-out has been successfully implemented, parents are taught to return to the original task, thereby preventing the child from simply exchanging time-out for noncompliance. As in Stage 1 training, the clinician observes the dyad interact in a clinic task analog for both assessment and training purposes. Typical performance criteria are a compliance ratio of 75% or higher (i.e., compliance initiations relative to instructions issued) and a social reinforcement ratio of 50% or higher (i.e., contingent attention relative to compliance initiations).

RESEARCH BASIS

Parent training for the treatment of child noncompliance meets criteria for an empirically supported treatment. Randomized clinical trials have shown effects attributable to the parent training, rather than alternative treatments, measurements, or time. Effects generalize from the clinic to the home setting and persist across time. Consumer satisfaction with the program is high. See the scholarly reviews of compliance training in the three volumes listed in the suggested readings (Barkley, Hembree-Kigin & McNeil, and McMahon & Forehand).

Different methods of training parents have been studied, suggesting that more interactive techniques, like role playing and guided practice, are probably necessary for the acquisition of complex routines, such as time-out administration. Nevertheless, videotape models of specific PCIT skills, including compliance training, have been very effective, even without the more costly and time-consuming therapist-directed role playing and guided practice.

The components of Hanf's two-stage model have been examined empirically. Instructional skills alone enhance child compliance, but instructional skills plus time-out for noncompliance increase compliance even more. For preschool children who overtly defy viable instructions, the time-out component of the Hanf program is necessary for behavior to change at all. The spanking component proved unnecessary, but the enforcement of time-out conditions for at least 1 minute via one of several options is necessary. The warning component decreases the number of time-outs needed to induce compliance acquisition and does not interfere with that process. In contrast, the social reinforcement component does not appear to contribute to compliance acquisition or compliance maintenance in previously noncompliant preschool children. Noncompliance

seems maintained by task avoidance, rather than attention seeking. Consequently, social reinforcement for compliance fails to adequately compete with negative reinforcement for task avoidance. Noncompliant children learn to obey with or without the social reinforcement component, as long as the effective components (instruction giving, time-out, and warnings) are in place. Moreover, there is no evidence that Stage 1 responsiveness skills enhance a parent's social reinforcer effectiveness. Child-directed interaction, however, may enhance child and/or parent self-esteem, promote a positive social interactional style, and/or contribute to the compliance training program's high acceptability ratings with consumers.

RELEVANT TARGET POPULATIONS AND EXCEPTIONS

From its onset in the 1960s, compliance training research has focused almost exclusively on the externalizing disorders of 2- to 7-year-old children. Once middle childhood is clearly under way, facets of both Stage 1 and Stage 2 training become problematic. First, responsive play between parent and child gives way to structured games and peer activities. Consequently, the mechanism for inducing responsive parenting skills is largely lost, although a skillful parent can still maintain responsiveness to child signals and social reinforcement of prosocial child behavior, despite the absence of unstructured play formats. Second, managing resistance to time-out during middle childhood is difficult. What to do when one's physically powerful 10-year-old male child chooses to escalate coercive behavior with a mother attempting to send him to a room time-out? Fines, privilege losses, and work chores have all been suggested, but none have been empirically tested, and all can provoke increasingly intense coercive outbursts. Therefore, compliance training as currently formulated does not map on well to middle childhood and requires adaptations. Furthermore, the compliance training protocol was not designed for teenagers. Finally, many childhood forms of coercion require interventions well beyond compliance training, which include aggression, tantrums, rude talk, and all the covert problems of delinquent patterns such as stealing, vandalism, and fire setting.

COMPLICATIONS

Determining a functional time-out protocol is the most complicated aspect of compliance training.

There are many parameters of time-out to consider (e.g., time-out location, duration, enforcement). Since noncompliant children are likely to resist time-out, clinicians need to monitor and adjust the time-out protocol, based on idiosyncratic child reactions.

An additional issue arises over the unsolved case of "Don't" instructions. Most PCIT research is based on child compliance with instructions to initiate a response, quite possibly because it is much easier to create a chore analog based on an active response than a temptation analog that requires child inhibition. Compliance with "Don't" instructions appears to be qualitatively different from compliance with "Do" instructions, involving such complexities as the number and quality of available response options, the child's developmental level, and the quality of the reinforcers provoked by the misbehavior. Many can identify with the futility of using Stage 2 skills to stop preschool-age siblings from bickering during a lengthy car trip. Response options are low, self-regulatory skills are absent, sibling reactivity to tease/touch is high, and time-outs are easy to avoid by simply complying with father each time he bellows "Stop touching your sister!" Notably, it is also true that many times "Don't" instructions stop misbehavior that is not subsequently repeated. Clearly, we need to know a lot more about the basic parameters of compliance with "Don't" instructions.

CASE ILLUSTRATION

"Ms. Thompson" was desperate. "Nathan," her 6-year-old son, had just been "dis-enrolled" from his third after-school program because of his repeated aggressive episodes. As a single mother with an afternoon job and no local relatives, she could not afford to stay home with Nathan. Moreover, he was just as defiant and aggressive at home as in his latchkey program. An interview with Ms. Thompson indicated cross-situational coercive behavior whenever Nathan was frustrated (e.g., by instructions, denied requests, waiting, peer conflicts). Nathan's Child Behavior Checklist Scales and Eyberg Child Behavior Inventory were both elevated on social aggression dimensions. In the Child's Game analog, Ms. Thompson revealed a very high rate of intrusive verbalizations (7.2 instructions + questions + criticisms per minute). In the Clinic Task Analog, Ms. Thompson's praise ratio was 0% and Nathan's compliance ratio was 15%, but it was noted that the mother's poor instruction index (i.e., repeated +

vague instructions ÷ total instructions) was so high (87%) that it was unclear what Nathan would do if given viable instructions. Consequently, the Compliance Test was also administered, yielding 4% compliance, with 40% of the instructions provoking rude talk or angry yelling ("You're not my boss," Nathan frequently shouted at his mother). Home record data revealed 4.5 angry outbursts and 2.1 aggressive bouts with his mother per day during a 7-day period between clinic sessions. Nathan met all *DSM-IV* criteria for a diagnosis of oppositional defiant disorder.

Responsive play skills were introduced first. Ms. Thompson was assigned homework to arrange a 10- to 15-minute period each weekday evening after dinner and at least two periods a day each weekend to play the Child's Game with Nathan. By the third session, her positive verbalization rate was good (over 4.0 per minute), although she still tended to ask a lot questions. Her therapist was very pleased, however, with Ms. Thompson's responsiveness index, which was consistently at 100% for all Nathan's questions and instructions. Nathan clearly enjoyed being the "boss" during special time with Mom.

Instruction-praise skills were introduced next. The therapist modeled direct, comprehensible instructions of three varieties: discrete Do X tasks (e.g., "Come here"), sustained Do X tasks (e.g., "Please put all the blocks in the toy box"), and Stop X tasks (e.g., "Don't jump on the couch"). Ms. Thompson role-played a series of such tasks, praising a doll (manipulated by the therapist) for compliance initiations and contingently helping the doll during the sustained tasks. Since Nathan's Compliance Test indicated he would disobey even viable instructions, warning time-out skills were introduced during the same session. With children who display decent scores on the Compliance Test (e.g., over 50%), a PCIT therapist can legitimately postpone the warning time-out component a week, since the child is likely to obey many parental instructions simply as a function of good instruction-giving skills.

Modeling and role playing were used first to teach Ms. Thompson to issue warnings if the doll made no effort to comply within 5 seconds of the instruction ("If you don't do X right now, you will have to go to time-out"). Nathan observed his mother issue warnings to the doll and praise the doll for compliance initiations to warnings. Next the doll disobeyed a warning and was sent to a time-out chair positioned in a corner of the clinic playroom. Since Nathan was only 6 years old, a 2-minute chair time-out with a 10-second quiet release rule was selected. Disruptive behavior on the time-out chair extended time-out beyond the 2-minute minimum and until 10 seconds of quiet were observed. Time-out escape efforts were punished with 60-second room backups. At home, if Nathan left the time-out chair without permission, he was escorted to his bedroom, the door held shut for 60 seconds, and then returned to the time-out chair. A maximum of three escape efforts per time-out was allowed, resulting in completion of the time-out in his bedroom for any third escape. In the clinic, a 4-foot-high barrier substituted for a door, allowing full visual access during room backup procedures. Each step was modeled for Nathan as the mother role-played with the therapist-manipulated doll. Occasionally, the therapist probed Nathan's comprehension as he watched, asking such questions as, "Why did that doll have to go to timeout?"; "How come she got sent to her room?"; and so on. Nathan refused to speak to the therapist. Guided practice began immediately thereafter. Ms. Thompson wore a bug-in-the-ear to receive support and advice throughout the initial exposure to time-out. A small set of discrete and sustained Do *X* tasks were defined for Nathan to practice "listening to Mom." Nathan's response to initial time-outs was typical: he did not like it at all. He had to be sent to the backup room three times during the first time-out, one time for the second time-out, and one time on the third time-out, prior to meeting the compliance criteria of 10 compliance initiations in a row. His first time-out lasted 5 minutes, but the second two were both closer to 2 minutes, since he quieted down much faster. Home data were maintained for the next 4 weeks, charting each occurrence of time-out for a disobeyed warning and each trip to the backup room. As is typical of children this age with Nathan's assessment profile, his acceptance of his mother's authority to issue reasonable instructions was clearly present within 1 month. Once compliance training had been initiated, the therapist was able to address fighting at the day care, tantrums, and community-setting misbehavior with additional PCIT skills.

—*Mark W. Roberts*

See also: *Behavioral Contracting (Vols. II & III), Behavioral Treatment in Natural Environments (Vols. I & III), Contingency Management (Vol. II), Differential Reinforcement of Other Behavior (Vols. I, II, & III), Generalization (Vols. I & III), Time-Out (Vols. II & III)*

Suggested Readings

Barkley, R. A. (1997). *Defiant children* (2nd ed.). New York: Guilford Press.

Hembree-Kigin, T. L., & McNeil, C. B. (1995). *Parent-child interaction therapy.* New York: Plenum.

McMahon, R. J., & Forehand, R. L. (2003). *Helping the noncompliant child: Family-based treatment for oppositional behavior* (2nd ed.). New York: Guilford Press.

Roberts, M. W. (1982). The effects of warned versus unwarned time-out procedures on child noncompliance. *Child and Family Behavior Therapy, 4,* 37–53.

Roberts, M. W. (1985). Praising child compliance: Reinforcement or ritual? *Journal of Abnormal Child Psychology, 13,* 611–629.

Roberts, M. W., Hatzenbuehler, L. C., & Bean, A. W. (1981). The effects of differential attention and timeout on child noncompliance. *Behavior Therapy, 12,* 93–99.

Roberts, M. W., McMahon, R. J., Forehand, R., & Humphreys, L. (1978). The effect of parental instruction-giving on child compliance. *Behavior Therapy, 9,* 793–798.

Roberts, M. W., & Powers, S. W. (1988). The compliance test. *Behavioral Assessment, 10,* 257-271.

CONTINGENCY MANAGEMENT

DESCRIPTION OF THE STRATEGY

The origins of contingency management lie within the work of B. F. Skinner, the pioneer of behavior analysis. In the early 1950s, Skinner proposed that the same learning principles used as a paradigm for animal research could be adapted to human applications. By the mid 1960s, behavior modification was applied to children with mental retardation, hyperactive behavior, delinquency, and autism. These populations previously were thought of as "resistant" to treatment, and the use of behavior modification greatly improved the quality of care for these children. By the late 1960s, several texts regarding the application of contingency management to education and parenting applications were published, and contingency management has been a key feature of behavioral treatments targeting childhood disorders since that time.

Contingency management can be defined as a process through which the reinforcement and punishment of child behavior are assessed and the environment's responses to the child's behavior (i.e., the contingency structure) are altered to effect behavior change. The dual purpose of contingency management is to decrease maladaptive behavior and increase adaptive behavior. Behaviorists suggest that a breakdown in the environmental contingency structure underlies a child's maladaptive behavior or absence of appropriate behavior. The goal, then, of contingency management is to restructure the child's environment to include consistent consequences so that the child can learn how to behave appropriately as a result of the new environmental structure. Intervention can target any aspect of the child's environment but most often involves the child's home, school, and the clinic setting.

Contingency management can be a component of a larger treatment protocol or can be used on its own to effect behavior change. One of the unique aspects of contingency management is that the therapist can teach a number of individuals in the child's environment (parent, teacher, sibling, peer, nurse, community volunteer) to serve as contingency managers. Behavior therapists typically serve as consultants regarding children's behaviors, and contingency managers (usually a parent or teacher) implement the plan under the advisement of a therapist. The plan may include contingent rewards, punishment, or a combination of these techniques. Older children may serve as their own contingency managers; however, parents and teachers are more frequently chosen as the managers. The design and implementation components most common to contingency management plans include (a) reinforcement assessment, (b) measurement of the target behavior, (c) contingency contracting, and (d) implementation of the contingency management plan.

Reinforcer Assessment

According to behavioral principles, reinforcement is key to the behavior change process. *Reinforcement* can be defined as any response from the environment that increases the probability of a behavior occurring in the future. *Positive reinforcement* occurs when the probability of the desired behavior occurring in the future increases when something is added to the environment (or an already present thing is increased). According to operant conditioning, child behavior increases or is maintained as a function of positive reinforcement provided to the child after performing the behavior. In contrast to positive reinforcement, negative reinforcement occurs when something is removed from the environment (or an already present thing is decreased) in order to increase an adaptive

behavior. In addition, a useful by-product of this method is that often the increase in adaptive behavior renders incompatible undesirable behavior less likely (not to be confused with punishment, a process applied directly to the undesirable behavior).

There are several selection issues that need to be taken into account when introducing a reinforcer into the environment. First, it is important to select consequences that are of value to the child, because not all stimuli and events are reinforcing to every child. Gender and developmental level should be considered, as well as the child's individual preferences. For example, what is reinforcing for a 6-year-old male (e.g., time playing games on a computer) may not be what is reinforcing for a 14-year-old adolescent female (e.g., time talking on the phone). Reinforcers must be individually based, as contingent consequences with no value to the child will be ineffective in increasing behavior. In addition, because children's reinforcer sensitivities can change, it is important to assess these preferences periodically. Booklets listing sample reinforcers for different age ranges and different settings are available to assist with reinforcer selection, as are structured reinforcer rating scales and menus. Second, the therapist and contingency manager must determine the reinforcement schedule, that is, the frequency with which the reinforcer will be delivered. Finally, the reward must be provided contingent upon the performance of the target behavior. A reinforcer is most effective when it is not available at any time other than following performance of an adaptive behavior.

Baseline Measurement

Assessment should be an ongoing process in the development and implementation of a contingency management plan. The first step in developing any contingency management program is to establish clearly which of the child's behaviors are targeted to increase or decrease. Clear behavioral goals help the therapist and contingency manager determine whether the child is on track and behaving appropriately. These goals can include the addition of new behaviors to the child's repertoire, the increased frequency of already present positive behavior, or the decreased frequency of already present negative behavior. A contingency management plan also can target the reduction of negative parent or teacher behavior (e.g., criticism, authoritarian commands, attention to maladaptive child behavior). However, the focus of this entry is on child behavior.

Accurate assessment of the baseline rate for maladaptive behavior, the intensity of the behavior, and the naturally occurring environmental stimuli and reinforcers that serve to maintain the maladaptive behavior is important for the design of the contingency management plan. This assessment should be conducted at the beginning of therapy and should include a thorough evaluation of the antecedents to the behavioral event, the nature of the behavior, and the consequences of the child's behavior. Assessment methods can include parent report, child self-report, child self-monitoring, and direct observation. A parent, teacher, trained observer, or therapist can conduct direct observations of child behavior, and the resultant data should be plotted on a behavior chart. This ongoing monitoring can serve as a motivator for the manager and child as they document behavioral progress, but the monitoring is also practical in that it can help determine when the goals of therapy have been met. In addition to the pretreatment assessment, posttreatment and follow-up assessments are valuable tools for measuring the maintenance of treatment gains.

Contingency Contracting

Contingency contracts can include behavioral contracts, daily report cards, and group contingencies. *Behavioral contracts* are the most frequently used form of contingency contracting. When designing a behavioral contract, the child and contingency manager agree upon one or more specific behaviors to target. It is important for the child and manager to set realistic goals and specific consequences, because if the goal is too large, the child will become less motivated to work on the target behavior and the contract will fail. In addition to agreeing upon the target behaviors, the dyad decides when the contract has been fulfilled and what to do should the contract fail. Renegotiation may be needed if the terms of the contract are met too easily or if the contract proves too difficult for the child.

Daily report cards can be used with children who have disruptive classroom behavior and typically involve a child, parent, and teacher working together. Several target behaviors are selected, phrased in positive terms (i.e., letting the child know what behaviors are expected), and rated on their presence or absence during the school day by the teacher. If the child performs the behavior during a specific time period, he or she receives positive feedback on the daily report card. This report is sent home to the child's parent, who reads it, signs it, and provides at-home rewards contingent upon demonstrated performance of the adaptive classroom behavior. In addition to motivating a child to perform adaptive classroom behavior, daily report cards can be a valuable communication tool between parents and teachers.

Group contingencies are especially useful in settings including more than one child (classroom, sibling group, day care, extracurricular group). When using group contingencies, the consequences (reinforcing or punishing) for group members depend on the behavior of other members. For example, in consequence sharing, an entire group of children receives a reward contingent on the good behavior of one child. Alternatively, interdependent group contingency involves a group of children receiving a reward contingent on the good behavior of the entire group.

Implementing the Contingency Management Plan

Manualized treatments are available for many parent-training protocols and are the gold standard of contingency management training because they provide standard training that includes identification of the behavioral concerns to be addressed and assessment of the environment. The didactic training included in most manualized treatment provides the terms, procedures, and goals of treatment. In conjunction with the manualized treatment, the therapist monitors the execution of the program and provides frequent feedback about the execution of the contingency management plan to the parent.

The use of a bug-in-the-ear microphone device also can enhance greatly the training of contingency managers. The bug-in-the-ear device allows therapists to give directions to parents while they play with their children, allowing parents in vivo practice of contingency management techniques. This is an excellent training tool, as the therapist can direct the parent in using reinforcement or punishment contingent on the behaviors displayed by the child in session. Over time, parents learn to rely less and less on the therapist for direction as their knowledge of contingency management application increases.

Contingency management can include a number of specific techniques (e.g., successive approximations, selective attention, discrimination training, and extinction), but the most frequently used techniques are contingent punishment, time-out, response cost, and differential reinforcement of other behavior (DRO). Booklets that provide step-by-step procedures for implementing these techniques are available to the interested reader.

RESEARCH BASIS

Contingency management is a hallmark of empirically based treatments for childhood disorders. Specifically, research supports the use of contingency management for attention-deficit/hyperactivity disorder, anxiety disorders, chronic pain, conduct disorder, depression, distress due to medical procedures, encopresis, enuresis, obesity, oppositional defiant disorder, phobias, and pervasive developmental disorders. Taken together, there is more research evidence to support the efficacy of behavioral treatments of childhood disorders than any other treatment modality.

Most evidence-based treatments for children with disruptive behavior problems (oppositional defiant disorder, attention-deficit/hyperactivity disorder, and conduct disorder) involve parent training, and research suggests that parents can be trained as successful contingency managers. It is common for contingency management techniques to be imbedded in a larger program such as parent management training (PMT), which typically targets processes such as parent-child interactions and structuring the home environment. Research shows that PMT programs that include contingency management as a component are the most effective treatment modality for disruptive behavior disorders.

There has been a relative dearth of research focusing on measures that specifically assess contingency management in the home. However, in-session techniques, such as in-session drills, can be used to assess parental use and understanding of contingency management skills. Successful completion of homework and in-session performance of skills can point to parental understanding of contingency management.

RELEVANT TARGET
POPULATIONS AND EXCEPTIONS

Contingency management can be used to treat virtually any child population. It has been used successfully with infants, young children, and adolescents.

Contingency management has been implemented with normal children to successfully increase intelligence, creativity, and vocabulary. Children with physical disabilities, developmental delays, chronic illnesses, learning disorders, communication disorders, behavioral problems, and emotional problems have all been treated successfully with contingency management. Contingency management has been used in a number of settings, including the home, classroom, workplace, medical clinics, and in the community.

There are some populations that may not be appropriate for specific contingency management techniques. For example, time-out is not an appropriate technique for children who engage in self-stimulation behaviors, as they will find it reinforcing to sit by themselves on a time-out chair. Also, most teenagers are too developmentally advanced for traditional time-out, so techniques such as response cost or a behavioral contract are better contingency management choices for this age group. Finally, parents who cannot understand the contingency management plan (e.g., because of severe cognitive impairments) or who cannot consistently implement the plan (e.g., because of individual psychopathology) may not be adequate managers.

COMPLICATIONS

Some complications from contingency management techniques are possible. When parents and teachers serve as contingency managers, consequences can become ineffective if they are not consistently implemented in accordance with behavioral principles. For this reason it is helpful for families to work with a behavior therapist initially to decrease the likelihood of complications. Time-out is one technique that parents often have difficulty implementing without the help of a behavior therapist. For example, parents often make time-out too long for children. When this happens, the child may have difficulty staying on the chair and the parent may decide that time-out does not work. Another common time-out mistake is when parents talk to the child when the child is on the time-out chair. Unfortunately, popular media sources such as parenting magazines often provide erroneous advice regarding the purpose of time-out (e.g., it is a time to reason with the child), and contingency managers may have difficulty obtaining behavior change if they rely solely on these sources.

Another contingency management complication may arise from using punishment when a less aversive method (extinction, DRO, cognitive therapy techniques) is available and more appropriate. Punishment can have unintended side effects that include avoidance behavior on the part of the child. For example, a child may lie about a behavioral event in order to avoid the contingent punishment that would follow if the manager were to learn that the child performed a maladaptive behavior. Thus, lying could be a side effect of a contingency management plan.

Finally, some techniques (e.g., extinction) will cause a temporary increase in the maladaptive behavior (i.e., extinction burst) as the child reacts to the new contingency structure in the environment. Parents may fail to persist with the treatment as the child's increased behavior problems become too aversive for them.

CASE ILLUSTRATION

"Samuel" was a 5-year-old boy referred by his mother, "Ms. M.," to a university-based outpatient clinic for the treatment of disruptive behavior problems. At the time of intake, Samuel exhibited severe noncompliance, verbal aggression, and physical aggression toward his parents, siblings, and peers. The severity of his behavior problems had resulted in Samuel's expulsion from one day care program, and he was close to being released from a second program.

The therapist completed a comprehensive assessment of the presenting problems that included a clinical interview, parent and teacher reports of Samuel's behavioral functioning on standardized behavior rating scales, and a behavioral observation of Samuel's interactions with his mother in the clinic. The assessment revealed that Samuel's disruptive behaviors were in the clinical range on standardized measures. In addition, the therapist observed a pattern of interactions between Samuel and his mother that was consistent with the pattern frequently observed between parents and their children with disruptive behavior disorders: (a) Samuel's mother intermittently reinforced Samuel's negative behaviors (e.g., giving in to his demands during tantrums), (b) she infrequently reinforced Samuel's positive behavior (e.g., ignoring him when he complied with a direction), and (c) Samuel used increasingly aversive behaviors (e.g., whining, then crying, then hitting) as a means to escape demands placed on him by caregivers.

Samuel and his mother were referred for parent-child interaction therapy (PCIT), a behavioral family intervention developed to reduce young children's disruptive behaviors, increase their adaptive behaviors, and increase the effective use of contingency management strategies by parents. During the first phase of treatment, the therapist and Ms. M. set specific behavioral goals for Samuel and for herself. Ms. M. was taught to use selective attention to increase Samuel's adaptive behaviors. Through didactic and in vivo coaching, Ms. M. increased her social reinforcement of Samuel's positive behavior (e.g., labeled praise) and used strategic ignoring of negative behaviors intended to get her attention. To assist with skill generalization, Ms. M. practiced these strategies in daily interactions with Samuel. Weekly assessment of Samuel's behaviors by parent report and therapist observation revealed a decrease in attention-seeking behaviors (e.g., whining) but no decrease in incidents of aggression. During the second phase of treatment, Ms. M. was taught to use time-out in a consistent manner appropriate for a 5-year-old child. In the clinic, the therapist coached Ms. M. in the use of negative reinforcement to increase Samuel's compliance with time-out. As Ms. M.'s skills and Samuel's compliance increased, Ms. M. required less direction from the therapist. To facilitate the development of Samuel's adaptive behavior, the therapist consulted with Samuel's day care to implement the behavior plan already being implemented in the clinic and at home. At treatment termination, Samuel's disruptive behaviors had moved from the clinical range to within the normal range compared to other children his age. Ms. M. demonstrated consistent use of positive reinforcement for Samuel's adaptive behavior, clear and consistent use of negative punishment (e.g., removal of privileges contingent on the occurrence of targeted undesirable behavior), and consistent use of time-out.

—Elizabeth V. Brestan,
Miranda Loeper, and Larissa N. Niec

See also: *Applied Behavior Analysis (Vols. I, II, & III), Azrin, Nathan H. (Vols. I & III), Operant Conditioning (Vols. I, II, & III), Single-Case Research (Vol. I), Skinner, Burrhus Frederic (Vols. II & III)*

Suggested Readings

Axelrod, S. (1998). How to use group contingencies. In R. V. Hall & M. L. Hall (Series Eds.), *How to manage behavior series.* Austin, TX: Pro-ed.

Axelrod, S., & Hall, R. V. (1999). *Behavior modification: Basic principles* (2nd ed.). Austin, TX: Pro-ed.

Hall, R. V., & Hall, M. L. (1998). How to negotiate a behavioral contract. In R. V. Hall & M. L. Hall (Series Eds.), *How to manage behavior series.* Austin, TX: Pro-ed.

Hall, R. V., & Hall, M. L. (1998). How to select reinforcers (2nd ed.). In R. V. Hall & M. L. Hall (Series Eds.), *How to manage behavior series.* Austin, TX: Pro-ed.

Hall, R. V., & Hall, M. L. (1998). How to use time-out (2nd ed.). In R. V. Hall & M. L. Hall (Series Eds.), *How to manage behavior series.* Austin, TX: Pro-ed.

CONTINGENT EXERCISE

DESCRIPTION OF THE STRATEGY

Contingent exercise is a positive punishment procedure sometimes used to decrease problem behaviors. In positive punishment, aversive events or activities are "added" or applied contingent on the occurrence of a behavior. Aversive activities are defined as low probability behaviors that a person typically would not choose to engage in. By definition, positive punishment procedures reduce the future probability of a behavior by requiring an individual to engage in low probability behavior (aversive activity) contingent on the occurrence of a high probability behavior (problem behavior). Since many individuals attempt to avoid or escape contingent exercise, the change agent must often use another positive punishment procedure, guided compliance, to compel the person to complete the aversive activity. Other positive punishment procedures include overcorrection, physical restraint, and physical discipline.

In contingent exercise, the client is required to engage in some form of physical exercise immediately contingent on the display of problem behavior. Several aspects of implementing the procedure are critical. First, the client must be capable of carrying out the physical activity without harm. Second, the exercise should be sufficiently effortful and/or tedious (e.g., push ups, sit ups, running laps). Where an attempt is made to make the "punishment fit the crime," a child who frequently kicks may be required to run, or a child who hits or slaps might be required to engage in vigorous arm exercises. Contingent exercise can also be applied more arbitrarily.

RESEARCH BASIS

Research has shown that physical exercise in the form of jogging or vigorous athletic activity has beneficial effects on the classroom behaviors of behaviorally disordered children. In a study by Luce and colleagues, contingent exercise was utilized with two emotionally disturbed children displaying autistic and aggressive behaviors. Contingent exercise resulted in a rapid decrease in aggressive behaviors. They concluded that contingent exercise may be utilized as an alternative procedure by therapists confronted with seriously disruptive behaviors. Other studies have shown that contingent exercise may be effective in reducing problem behaviors among children with developmental delay, autism, and hyperactivity. Notwithstanding studies showing effectiveness, the use of contingent exercise in general clinical and nonclinical populations has not been extensively researched.

COMPLICATIONS

As with all forms of intervention, contingent exercise could potentially be misused or be harmful. To minimize potential risks, a functional assessment of factors contributing to problem behavior might first be conducted. These efforts could result in an intervention that eliminates the need for the problem behavior or treatment that promotes the display of behavior incompatible with the problem behavior. Second, milder forms of punishment (e.g., response cost or time-out) should be attempted prior to the introduction of contingent exercise. If reinforcement-based efforts fail and intervention is still deemed necessary, helpers should be careful to avoid exercises that are too strenuous. Medical evaluations may also be required prior to implementing a program. Thus, contingent exercise should be implemented with the caveats and restrictions as other aversive consequences. Finally, contingent exercise procedures must be carefully explained to adults responsible for the care of the child and may require extensive training of parents, direct care staff, and teachers. In many cases, the use of contingent exercise may be explicitly prohibited by regulatory agencies. In other cases, parents or administrators may be philosophically opposed to its implementation, thus limiting its applicability. Nevertheless, with appropriate safeguards, contingent exercise could merit wider use and study. On a positive note, one could argue that in comparison to other forms of punishment (e.g., physical discipline, restraint), contingent exercise promotes healthy activity, may reduce conflict, and poses less risk of humiliation and injury to the child.

CASE ILLUSTRATION

The client was a 7-year-old boy who engaged in antisocial behaviors. When school staff reported that the client's frequency of aggressive behavior toward others had increased, hitting was selected as the target behavior. Contingent exercise consisted of standing up and sitting down on the floor 10 times. Initially, graduated guidance was required to prompt the client to perform the exercises. Following training, a verbal prompt from the nearest adult such as "No hitting. Stand up and sit down 10 times" was all that was necessary for compliance. The result was a reduction in the daily frequency of hitting, and 2 months of continued monitoring indicated only three episodes of hitting during the entire follow-up period.

—David Reitman and
Erin McNaughton Barlos

See also: *Aversion Relief (Vols. I & III), Behavioral Treatment in Natural Environments (Vols. I & III), Operant Conditioning (Vols. I, II, & III)*

Suggested Readings

Luce, S. C., Delquadri, J., & Hall, R. V. (1980). Contingent exercise: A mild but powerful procedure for suppressing inappropriate verbal and aggressive behavior. *Journal of Applied Behavior Analysis, 13,* 583–584.

Miltenberger, R. G. (2001). Positive punishment procedures. In R. G. Miltenburger, *Behavior modification: Principles and procedures* (2nd ed., pp. 343–360). Belmont, CA: Wadsworth.

CONTINGENT RESTRAINT

Contingent restraint is a procedure typically used to decrease or eliminate self-injurious behavior (SIB) or aggressive behavior in individuals with developmental disabilities. It has also been successfully used in the treatment of pica and in combination with biofeedback relaxation training. Contingent restraint involves physically preventing an individual from engaging in the maladaptive target behavior. The most frequent population of individuals it is used with are children with autism or mental retardation. It is best used in combination with other procedures, most notably reinforcement procedures. Differential reinforcement of alternative behavior (DRA) and differential reinforcement of other behavior (DRO) are two reinforcement procedures most commonly combined with contingent restraint. Because contingent restraint involves physically restraining the target individual, it is used as a method of last resort when other, less restrictive procedures have failed to eliminate or reduce SIB/aggression to acceptable levels. The procedure is highly effective in reducing SIB/aggression when used in conjunction with other procedures designed to reinforce alternative behaviors and when procedures are designed to teach the target individual adaptive skills that replace SIB/aggression. The amount of time contingent restraint is implemented may vary depending on the situation, but the procedure is most effective when used after every instance of SIB/aggression.

The function or purpose of the SIB/aggression must be taken into account when using contingent restraint. Researchers have demonstrated that some individuals will increase SIB/aggression as a means of being physically restrained, particularly when contingent restraint has been used for extended periods of time. In these situations, the function of the SIB/aggression must be carefully evaluated before an appropriate procedure is implemented to decrease SIB/aggression.

There are four categories of contingent restraint: personal restraint, mechanical restraint, planned restraint, and emergency restraint. Personal restraint involves holding the individual in a physical hold for a specified amount of time contingent upon the target behavior. Mechanical restraint, on the other hand, involves the use of mechanical devices (frequently leather straps placed on the wrists and ankles) that limit the individual's range of motion, inhibiting an individual's ability to engage in the target behaviors. Planned restraint involves a careful analysis of the antecedents, consequences, setting events, and topography of the target behavior. Furthermore, when using planned restraint, contingent restraint is used as one part of an overall behavioral plan to decrease the target behavior and increase adaptive behaviors. All individuals involved in the care of the target individual are trained in the proper use of restraint, and everyone is aware of his or her role in its implementation. Emergency restraint is unplanned and involves the use of either mechanical or personal restraint when SIB/aggression has become so severe that intervention is necessary for safety reasons. Research has demonstrated that planned, mechanical restraint is the safest form of contingent restraint for both the target individual and caregivers, while emergency restraint results in the most injuries.

—Heather Applegate

See also: *Aversion Relief (Vols. I & III), Behavioral Treatment in Natural Environments (Vols. I & III), Operant Conditioning (Vols. I, II, & III)*

Suggested Readings

Altmeyer, B. K., Williams, D. E., & Sams, V. (1985). Treatment of severe self-injurious and aggressive biting. *Journal of Behavior Therapy and Experimental Psychiatry, 16,* 159–167.

Matson, J. L., & Keyes, J. B. (1988). Contingent reinforcement and contingent restraint to treat severe aggression and self-injury in mentally retarded and autistic adults. *Journal of the Multihandicapped Person, 12,* 141–153.

Persel, C. S., Persel, C. H., Ashley, M. J., & Krych, D. K. (1997). The use of noncontingent reinforcement and contingent restraint to reduce physical aggression and self-injurious behaviour in a traumatically brain-injured adult. *Brain Injury, 11,* 751–760.

Schroeder, S. R., Rojahn, J., Mulick, J. A., & Schroeder, C. S. (1990). Self-injurious behavior. In J. L. Matson (Ed.), *Handbook of behavior modification with the mentally retarded* (2nd ed., pp. 141–180). New York: Plenum.

Spreat, S., Lipinski, D., Hill, J., & Halpin, M. E. (1986). Safety indices associated with the use of contingent restraint procedures. *Applied Research in Mental Retardation, 7,* 475–481.

CORRESPONDENCE TRAINING

DESCRIPTION OF THE STRATEGY

The term *correspondence* refers to congruence between verbal and nonverbal behavior. For example, if a child says that he or she is going to play with Legos later in the morning and actually plays with Legos when the time comes, then a specific instance of correspondence between saying and doing has occurred. Correspondence may also occur if an accurate verbal report follows the behavior. For example, if the child played with Legos in the morning and then in the afternoon said that he or she played with Legos that morning, then a specific instance of correspondence between doing and saying has occurred. Thus, correspondence involves agreement between verbal and nonverbal behaviors that may follow two temporal sequences: saying-then-doing and doing-then-saying.

If individuals typically do what they say for many different behaviors across different environmental settings, then verbal-nonverbal correspondence is well established and generalized. Generalized correspondence is an important skill for a number of reasons.

First, if people promise to do something, you can usually have confidence that they will fulfill their promise. Second, if you ask people about past behaviors, their answers are usually accurate. In many ways, important human traits such as trustworthiness, honesty, dependability, reliability, and so on are judged by high levels of verbal-nonverbal correspondence. An equally important function of correspondence is its potential use as a behavior change strategy for nonverbal target behaviors that are less accessible for direct modification. Another important function of well-established correspondence is the role that verbalizations may have in mediating generalizations. That is, verbalizations (i.e., covertly talking to yourself) can occur at any time in nontreatment settings and serve as cues for the generalized performance of nonverbal target behaviors.

Most young children do not engage in high levels of verbal-nonverbal correspondence. Correspondence training was developed to teach children increased convergence between saying and doing. The most effective procedures for correspondence training consist of positive reinforcement, modeling-imitation, and chaining. Reinforcement seems to be a critical procedural component, and in order to be maximally effective, it must be contingent upon *correspondence* between saying and doing. That is, if children say they will play with blocks, then they receive a reinforcer after they play with blocks and do not receive a reinforcer if they do not play with blocks. Since reinforcement must be arranged contingent upon both the verbal and nonverbal behavior (often in different settings as well as temporally separated), a very practical concern in correspondence training is direct access to both the verbal and nonverbal behavior so that observational data can be used to determine when reinforcement should occur. Reinforcement of the verbal behavior without verifying that the nonverbal behavior occurred or vice versa does not increase verbal-nonverbal correspondence.

Modeling both the verbal and nonverbal behavior for children and having them imitate correctly can facilitate specific instances of correspondence that then can be reinforced. If the verbal behavior is simple, modeling is usually unnecessary. For example, if the verbal behavior is answering the question, "Are you going to play with the soccer ball at recess?" and the child says "Yes" and the nonverbal behavior is a simple selection of a toy or activity, then modeling probably would not be necessary. If either behavior is more complex, though (e.g., social behaviors such as sharing or making a new friend), then modeling-imitation could be critical.

Chaining procedures involve breaking a complex behavior into sequences of smaller behaviors or steps. Correspondence may be thought of as two chains, one for say-do and the other for do-say. In the say-do sequence, the steps are (a) a verbal promise to engage in a behavior, (b) intermediate behaviors (behaviors that are necessary to perform the promised behavior, such as requesting a toy), and (c) performing the promised behavior. In the do-say sequence, the steps are (a) preceding behaviors (behaviors that are necessary to perform a specific nonverbal behavior, such as requesting a toy), (b) performing the behavior of playing with the toy, and (c) accurately reporting about the previous nonverbal behavior, such as playing with a particular toy. The usual procedure is reinforcement for successful completion of the last step in each of these chains. In the say-do sequence, reinforcers are given after completion of the nonverbal behavior, and in the do-say sequence after completion of the verbal behavior. Rather than reinforcement for a say-do or a do-say chain, the two chains could be combined to form a say (promise)-do-say (report) sequence. For example, a child from whom greater frequency of peer interaction is the goal could receive correspondence training consisting of making the promise, "I'll play with Bill at recess," then actually playing with Bill at recess and finally reporting, "I played with Bill," with reinforcement immediately after the last report.

In order for correspondence training to produce well-generalized verbal-nonverbal correspondence for a large number of responses, across many different situations, and with widely varied time intervals between saying (promising)-doing and doing-saying (reporting), considerable training must occur. At a minimum, training should be conducted across several behaviors, settings, time intervals, and with both chains. After verbal-nonverbal correspondence is broadly established, it is often referred to as rule-governed behavior.

RESEARCH BASIS

Much of the research on verbal-nonverbal correspondence has used single-subject research designs, which allow analysis of an individual's behavior over time, under several experimental conditions. Most studies have employed an initial condition where verbal reports of future or past behavior were obtained and even reinforced, regardless of their accuracy. A consistent finding has been the lack of any change in the nonverbal target behaviors with this contingency. Usually, the next condition involves reinforcement contingent upon correspondence between verbal reports and the nonverbal target behaviors. Correspondence training has produced consistent increases in nonverbal target behaviors. After exposure to correspondence training, most studies employ a third condition, where the verbal reports are reinforced and changes occur in the nonverbal target behaviors. This often reported finding (of changing nonverbal target behavior by reinforcing verbal statements) following correspondence training has led to the recognition of the potential value correspondence training has in the control over inaccessible behaviors or behaviors that occur elsewhere at remote times. A few studies, however, have found that verbalizations may not be necessary to obtain changes in nonverbal behaviors. For example, a teacher may provide the verbalization instead of the child, and changes in the child's nonverbal behavior occurs. Another finding is equal effectiveness of reinforcement for say-do correspondence and reinforcement of do-only in an experimental arrangement where the structure could easily lead to the acquisition of an implicit rule by subjects.

RELEVANT TARGET POPULATIONS AND EXCEPTIONS

Children and adolescents, as well as adults with developmental disabilities, have usually been the participants in investigations and clinical applications of correspondence training. There are two basic conditions necessary to conduct correspondence training. First, a lack of verbal-nonverbal correspondence must exist that is common for children and those with developmental disabilities. Second, there must be convenient access to the nonverbal target behavior. Children and adults with developmental disabilities often are in situations such as day care centers, schools, or treatment programs where their behaviors can easily be observed on a daily basis.

In order for correspondence training to be appropriate, the individual must have some basic language skills. At a minimum, they should have the ability to accurately answer questions regarding nonverbal target behaviors with "Yes" or "No." Thus, very young typically developing children (under 3 years of age) and individuals with severe disabilities, such as adults with mental retardation in the profound range, would not be appropriate for correspondence training.

COMPLICATIONS

Severe language disturbances can interfere with correspondence training. Extreme levels of noncompliant behavior on the part of a child with oppositional defiant disorder may substantially interfere with correspondence training. Direct contingency management of compliance and cooperation may be necessary before correspondence training could be effective.

CASE ILLUSTRATION

"Bob" was an 8-year-old second grade boy with attention-deficit/hyperactivity disorder combined type. Bob was prescribed stimulant medications by his pediatrician that, according to Bob's teachers, have helped reduce his disruptive classroom behavior somewhat, with little if any improvement in his academic performance. With Bob's teachers' recommendation, Bob's parents requested a consultation from a psychologist with expertise in applied behavior analysis for an assessment and possible school-based program. Since the school system had already completed psychological tests and found Bob to have slightly above average intelligence and to be performing at grade level or slightly below in all areas of educational achievement, a functional assessment was conducted. First, the teacher was asked to complete some rating scales (Conner's Teacher Rating Scale, Academic Performance Rating Scale, and School Situation Questionnaires). Second, the teacher was interviewed with a focus on problem behaviors that were disruptive or incompatible with learning as well as academic deficiencies (e.g., not completing assignments). After clear identification of behaviors, the teacher provided information concerning the potential antecedents and consequences for each behavior. The major problem behavior consisted of Bob leaving his desk during individual seat work assignments (which were routinely scheduled three to four times each day) and roaming around the classroom talking with peers, sharpening his pencil repeatedly, looking up and down the hall, and so on. Rarely did he complete more than half of his assignments. To confirm his teacher's impression, several classroom observations were conducted by an assistant unfamiliar to Bob.

Treatment involved correspondence training conducted by the teacher, which initially was limited to the first session of seat work assignment of the day (arithmetic drill). A say-do-say chain was used consisting of the teacher briefly meeting individually with Bob and giving the assignment (e.g., "Here is a sheet with problems you need to work. What are you going to do?"), to which Bob responded, "I am going to stay at my desk until I finish all of these," following by the arithmetic period. At the end of the period, the teacher met again with Bob and asked, "What did you just do?" Bob then reported, "I stayed at my desk and finished all of the problems." When his performance matched his promise and then his report, he was reinforced with points that were exchanged at the end of the day for privileges, such as extra computer time to play games. The teacher was careful to consistently observe during the work period to make sure that reinforcement was provided only for correspondence. After a couple of weeks, correspondence was consistent in the arithmetic drill and the second seat work assignment of the day was added, using the same correspondence training package for several weeks, and then the third seat work assignment was added. By that time, Bob almost always did what he said he would in the brief meeting with the teacher, and reinforcement for correspondence was not necessary for him to stay in his seat and do all the assignments. Reinforcement of his promise or report in the say-do-say chain was sufficient to maintain his in-seat, on-task, and assignment completion nonverbal target behaviors.

—*James F. McCoy*

See also: *Behavioral Case Formulation (Vol. I), Behavioral Treatment in Natural Environments (Vol. I), Setting Events (Vols. I & III), Stimulus Control (Vol. II)*

Suggested Readings

Baer, R. A., Detrich, R., & Weninger, J. M. (1988). On the functional role of the verbalization in correspondence training procedures. *Journal of Applied Behavior Analysis, 21,* 345–356.

Deacon, J. R., & Konarski, E. A. (1987). Correspondence training: An example of rule-governed behavior? *Journal of Applied Behavior Analysis, 20,* 391–400.

Guevremont, D. C., Osnes, P. G., & Stokes, T. F. (1986). Programming maintenance after correspondence training interventions with children. *Journal of Applied Behavior Analysis, 19,* 215–219.

Israel, A. C., & O'Leary, K. D. (1973). Developing correspondence between children's words and deeds. *Child Development, 44,* 577–581.

Luciano-Soriano, M. C., Molina-Lobos, F. J., & Gomez-Becerra, I. (2000). Say-do report training to change chronic behaviors in mentally retarded subjects. *Research in Developmental Disabilities, 21,* 355–366.

Osnes, P. G., Guevremont, D. C., & Stokes, T. F. (1986). If I say I'll talk more then I will. *Behavior Modification, 10,* 287–299.

Paniagua, F. A., & Baer, D. M. (1982). The analysis of correspondence training as a chain reinforceable at any point. *Child Development, 53,* 786–798.

Paniagua, F. A., & Black, S. A. (1990). Management and prevention of hyperactivity and conduct disorders in 8–10-year-old boys through correspondence training procedures. *Child and Family Behavior Therapy, 12,* 23–56.

Risly, T. R., & Hart, B. (1968). Developing correspondence between the nonverbal and verbal behavior of preschool children. *Journal of Applied Behavior Analysis, 1,* 267–281.

Rogers-Warren, A., & Baer, D. M. (1976). Correspondence between saying and doing: Teaching children to share and praise. *Journal of Applied Behavior Analysis, 9,* 335–354.

COUNTERCONDITIONING

DESCRIPTION OF THE STRATEGY

Counterconditioning, as a behavioral intervention for emotional or behavioral problems in children, involves the reduction of a target behavior (CR_1) through the introduction competing response (CR_2). This may be accomplished by presenting a conditioned stimulus (CS_2) for the competing response at the same time as the previously conditioned stimulus (CS_1) for the target behavior. Alternatively, the target behavior may be ignored while the competing response is reinforced. In other words, an undesired emotional response or behavior is reduced over time by the repeated practice of an incompatible emotion or behavior. For example, it has been demonstrated that anger can be eliminated with the use of humor, presumably because humor induces an incompatible emotion state to that of anger. Unwanted behaviors can also be extinguished through the use of counterconditioning principles. For instance, an undesired habit such as nail biting can be eliminated with the induction of an incompatible response (e.g., sitting on one's hands).

Historically, the term *counterconditioning* is derived from Pavlovian or higher-order classical conditioning principles. In 1912, one of Ivan Pavlov's students, M. N. Erofeeva, discovered that if a mild electric shock (CS_1) was applied to one part of a dog's body in temporal contiguity with food delivery (CS_2), defensive behaviors (CR_1) were eliminated and replaced by a conditioned salivary response (CR_2). This effect was termed *counterconditioning* and it appeared that conditioning methods could neutralize the effects of aversive stimulation when paired with an appetitive response. In 1942, Edwin R. Guthrie described two methods for producing associative inhibition or counterconditioning. He first suggested that stimuli (CS_1) could be presented in a weakened form so that they did not evoke the undesired established response (CR_1), but rather elicited some alternative or antagonistic behavior (CR_2). He argued that gradually increasing the strength of the stimuli would lead to the associative inhibition of the former response to these stimuli. Similar to other theorists, Guthrie's second proposed method for producing counterconditioning was to deliberately elicit an antagonistic response (CR_2) for the subject in the presence of the stimulus (CS_1) so that the old response (CR_1) could not be called forth.

In 1958, Joseph Wolpe used the concept of counterconditioning to rationalize the positive effects observed from systematic desensitization. He described systematic desensitization as the reduction of anxious responding through reciprocal inhibition whereby a response incompatible with anxiety (e.g., deep muscle relaxation) can be made to occur in the presence of anxiety-eliciting stimuli. As a result of this incompatible response, the bond between the anxiety response and its eliciting stimuli is weakened or eliminated. Hence, extinction of the fear response occurs as associative inhibition or the learning of an incompatible response proceeds. Wolpe argued that exposure to the feared stimuli alone (i.e., without replacing the anxious response with an incompatible response) is sometimes not an effective therapeutic method of its own accord. Although counterconditioning techniques in behavior therapy have been used for a variety of disorders, they are most commonly discussed in the treatment of anxiety.

In the treatment of anxiety, counterconditioning procedures are used to extinguish anxious-over responding to a particular stimulus. For example, in the treatment of a dog phobia, the goal is to decrease anxious responses (CR_1) in the presence of dogs (CS_1). To recondition or countercondition the fear response, an incompatible response (CR_2) is elicited by a new stimulus (CS_2). A relaxed state is incompatible with anxiety because it is impossible to be both relaxed (i.e., muscles relaxed, slow heart rate) and anxious (i.e., muscles tense, fast heart rate) at the same time. Thus, with the aim of decreasing fear to dogs, the child would first be taught how to achieve deep relaxation. Then when in a relaxed state, the child would be exposed to dog-related stimuli. Typically, initial exposure consists of less anxiety-provoking stimuli (e.g., pictures of dogs) with later exposure consisting of intensely anxiety-provoking stimuli (e.g., petting a large dog). As a result of repeated exposure to the previously feared stimuli (dogs; CS_1) when in a relaxed state (CR_2), the original fear response (CR_1) is replaced.

Counterconditioning is also discussed in the context of operant extinction. Operant extinction is a procedure for reducing the frequency with which a target behavior occurs by consistently withholding reinforcement following the occurrence of the target behavior. In this context, counterconditioning is related to the procedure of differential reinforcement of incompatible behavior (DRI). DRI refers to selectively ignoring a target behavior to produce operant extinction while simultaneously providing reinforcement upon occurrences of an alternative behavior. For example, unwanted stereotypic behaviors such as body rocking or hand flapping can be eliminated by rewarding the occurrence of an alternative response (e.g., sitting still or clasping one's hands) that is incompatible to the unwanted target behavior.

RESEARCH BASIS

Although it is unusual to see counterconditioning used as a stand-alone treatment for psychological problems, many empirically supported treatment packages contain components that involve counterconditioning. As noted elsewhere, the primary exception is that the treatment of simple phobias often involves exposure to the feared stimulus paired with alternative responses or therapist praise.

Experimental evidence has also supported the positive role of counterconditioning in operant extinction. Studies have demonstrated that a target behavior decreases in frequency more rapidly when an alternative behavior is simultaneously reinforced rather than solely withholding contingent reinforcement. However, some clinic studies have suggested that counterconditioning procedures do not increase overall therapeutic benefits up and beyond those achieved through exposure alone.

Finally, with regard to systematic desensitization, research has demonstrated that the client must be able to engage in some degree of vivid imagery for the procedure to be effective. Vivid imagery is the reenactment of a scene in one's imagination with some sense of realness and clarity. It is also important that the client be able to experience the affect that usually accompanies these scenes in real life during vivid imagery. Research suggests that patients who have had psychotic episodes and are in remission or who have a schizoid personality type are less capable of vivid imagery than others.

RELEVANT TARGET POPULATIONS AND EXCEPTIONS

Theoretically, counterconditioning procedures can be used for all populations and disorders in which there is an unwanted classically conditioned behavior or a positively reinforced behavior targeted for operant extinction. In the last five decades, researchers have examined the therapeutic effects of counterconditioning procedures for a wide range of problem behaviors and psychological disorders, including undesired habits, elimination disorders, drug abuse, chronic pain, and self-mutilation. However, as stated above, counterconditioning procedures are most often used in the treatment of anxiety disorders, including specific phobias, panic disorder, posttraumatic stress disorder (PTSD), obsessive-compulsive disorder, and generalized anxiety disorder.

Some recent applications of counterconditioning procedures in treatment include the treatment of comorbid PTSD-depression as well as the treatment of behavioral distress for invasive pediatric procedures. For comorbid PTSD-depression, in addition to the standard well-established treatment of relaxation and exposure to feared stimuli, counterconditioning was used wherein the client was instructed to recall past happy events during exposure to the traumatic stimuli. Another recent application of counterconditioning procedures is in the treatment of behavioral distress for invasive pediatric procedures. Preferred activities were paired with medical stimuli, and differential positive reinforcement was provided contingent on engagement with the preferred activities. As described, the counterconditioning procedures used in these recent applications were supplemental to the already well-established treatment.

COMPLICATIONS

Although counterconditioning procedures have been found effective in the treatment of numerous disorders, generally as part of a more comprehensive treatment package, there are several problems or complications a therapist will want to be aware of before instituting these procedures in treatment. One complication of counterconditioning techniques occurs when the client is a poor reporter. In other words, if a child or his or her caregiver is unable to accurately define what, where, and when the identified problem occurs, it is very difficult for the therapist to assemble an appropriate and effective counterconditioning procedure. Moreover, if the child has several diffuse problems such as multiple fears or a comorbid problem such as depression, counterconditioning techniques may be less effective for one specific problem.

Another complication of counterconditioning procedures is the choice of inappropriate or inadequate replacement responses. For example, some clients may feel tense, uncomfortable, or unnatural when relaxation is induced as a replacement response to fear. There are a number of clients who associate becoming relaxed in front of another person with being more vulnerable to being attacked or compromised in some way. Thus, it is important that the therapist find an appropriate incompatible response for the client. For instance, some researchers have found that inducing anger as opposed to relaxation can help alleviate anxious responding.

A third complication of counterconditioning techniques is the importance of the context in which the conditioning occurs. In other words, if treatment takes place in one specific context such as a psychologist's office, generalization of treatment effects to other contexts may not occur unless the therapist is careful to conduct conditioning sessions in several contexts.

Finally, although research has found that it is important to reinforce the child for employing the incompatible response (e.g., maintaining a relaxed state when presented with a feared stimulus), the therapist must be conscious that the child is truly reinforcing the desired behavior. For example, a therapist may accidentally reinforce a child for not reporting distress due to a desire to please the therapist rather than reinforce the positive performance of the alternative behavior. New technological advancements in the measurement of physiological states and biofeedback may help prevent this kind of false reporting. Physiological measures such as heart rate and galvanic skin response can be used to determine whether or not therapeutic activities effectively induce relaxation. Biofeedback-assisted relaxation training was developed as a therapeutic technique designed to help clients become better aware of their own arousal state as well as provide an accurate reading of the client's true arousal state to the therapist, thus decreasing the possibility of reinforcing nonreporting.

CASE ILLUSTRATION

"Dagny" was a 9-year-old female from a traditional, middle-class, suburban family. Her mother sought individual treatment for Dagny at an outpatient psychology clinic for increased family conflict, stubborn refusal to participate in family events, and periodic bouts of temper. Clinical assessment revealed that the family conflict was of recent onset, within 4 to 6 weeks, and initially focused upon the relationship of Dagny with her older brother, "Howard." These problems had persisted somewhat longer than was typical when the two siblings were fighting, and the stress was beginning to increase irritation among other family members. Antecedent assessment found that the conflict centered on Dagny's refusal to attend Howard's soccer games. When Dagny was required to attend the soccer games, she would refuse to get out of the family car and "throw tantrums" during which she would cry, kick, and scream. This tantrumming was viewed as embarrassing and frustrating to other family members.

Behavioral assessment with Dagny uncovered that Dagny's avoidance and agitation were associated with a fear of bees. Dagny noted that during one of Howard's earlier soccer games, she had witnessed multiple bees circling around a nearby garbage can. She did not report any history of being stung by bees but noted that she experienced intense negative emotion with a physiological reaction when she saw them. Since witnessing the bees at the soccer game, Dagny sought to avoid further encounters with the bees by avoiding the soccer games or refusing to leave the car at the games. Dagny's negative emotion and arousal were conceptualized as conditioned fear responses (CR_1) associated with the presence of bees (CS_1) and anything associated with bees (e.g., garbage cans on the soccer field, attending soccer games).

Treatment for Dagny involved several components that included psychoeducation about fear and anxiety, education about bees and their behavior, training with Dagny's parents about strategies for managing her noncompliance while supporting her efforts to cope with her fear, and systematic desensitization. The systematic desensitization component involved counterconditioning Dagny's fear through the use of relaxation as an alternative response (CR_2).

A hierarchy of fear situations was constructed of Dagny's fears. Roughly speaking, Dagny presented relatively little fear response to insects other than bees, wasps, and hornets, and noted that when looking at still photographs of bees, she thought that they were "gross" but did not experience fear. Videos demonstrating bees buzzing and in motion produced a stronger sense of discomfort and "gave her the creeps" but did not elicit fear or behavioral avoidance. Next in the hierarchy was watching another individual holding a jar with a live bee from a distance, which was associated with some fear and mild efforts to escape or avoid the situation. Even more intense fear resulted from the prospect of being in close proximity to a bee in a jar, watching another person in a room with a bee with its stinger removed, being in a room with a bee with its stinger removed, and being near a live bee in an uncontrolled situation.

Once the fear hierarchy was constructed, Dagny was trained in progressive muscle relaxation. This involved teaching Dagny to contract and relax various muscles groups and to learn to discriminate the tense from the relaxed states. Relaxation training also involved a guided imagery procedure to incorporate visualization skills and to condition images of situations that Dagny found relaxing. Once Dagny demonstrated skills in relaxation, she then practiced maintaining relaxation while she progressively imagined the increasingly arousing situations from her fear hierarchy. Prior to proceeding to the next more distressing situation, Dagny demonstrated the capacity to remain relaxed while imagining the fearful situation. Once Dagny demonstrated relaxation mastery during imaginal exposure, she then practiced remaining relaxed while she was actually exposed to the feared situations.

Dagny made considerable progress in managing her fear of bees, although she remained apprehensive about uncontrolled situations where she was close enough to bees to hear them buzzing or see the details of their body. The family conflict improved fairly rapidly, once her family understood that Dagny's reaction was associated with her fear of bees, not with a refusal to support and participate in family activities.

Dagny's parents were also able to take short-term steps to manage Dagny's potential exposure to bees (e.g., park the car a reasonable distance from bee-infested garbage cans, watch the soccer games from a place on the field with little bee exposure) until her fear was mastered. These steps reduced experiences of embarrassment and direct defiance of parental authority.

—*Eric L. Daleiden and Charmaine K. Higa*

See also: *Classical Conditioning (Vols. I, II, & III), Paul, Gordon L. (Vols. I & III), Systematic Desensitization (Vols. I, II, & III) Wolpe, Joseph (Vols. I & III)*

Suggested Readings

Guthrie, E. R. (1952). *The psychology of learning.* New York: Harper.

Hersen, M. (2002). *Clinical behavior therapy: Adults and children.* New York: John Wiley.

Jones, R. S., & Baker, L. J. (1990). Differential reinforcement and challenging behaviour: A critical review of the DRI schedule. *Behavioural Psychotherapy, 18,* 35–47.

Paunovic, N. (1999). Exposure counterconditioning (EC) as a treatment for severe PTSD and depression with an illustrative case. *Journal of Behavior Therapy and Experimental Psychiatry, 30,* 105–117.

Slifer, K. J., Babbit, R. L., & Cataldo, M. D. (1995). Simulation and counterconditioning as adjuncts to pharmacotherapy for invasive pediatric procedures. *Developmental and Behavioral Pediatrics, 16,* 133–141.

Wolpe, J. (1958). *Psychotherapy by reciprocal inhibition.* Stanford, CA: Stanford University Press.

Wolpe, J. (1990). *The practice of behavior therapy* (4th ed.). New York: Pergamon Press.

Wolpe, J., & Plaud, J. J. (1997). Pavlov's contributions to behavior therapy: The obvious and the not so obvious. *American Psychologist, 52,* 966–972.

Zaichkowsky, L. B., Zaichkowsky, L. D., & Yeager, J. (1986). Biofeedback-assisted relaxation training in the elementary classroom. *Elementary School Guidance & Counseling, 20,* 261–267.

COVERT CONDITIONING WITH CHILDREN AND ADOLESCENTS

DESCRIPTION OF THE STRATEGY

Covert conditioning refers to a set of procedures that share a common basis in the use of imagery as the means of altering response frequency. The term *covert* is utilized because clients are asked to use unobservable, imagined processes to establish new, adaptive responses. Such imaginal processes can include thinking or talking to oneself, imaging, feeling, or reproduction of sensations or bodily cues. A variety of types of imagined scenes can be utilized in covert conditioning, including scenes based on actual experience, the experiences of others, perceived "ideal" situations, and painful or feared situations. The term *conditioning* refers to the fact that the behavioral change being addressed is theoretically governed by the laws of learning, primarily operant conditioning. Basic reinforcement principles, and concepts of punishment, extinction, and habituation, thus apply equally to overt and covert events in this paradigm.

A number of theoretical assumptions have been set forth by Cautela concerning the nature of covert conditioning. First, it is assumed that behavioral processes can be classified as (a) overt or observable behavior, (b) covert behavior or coverants (i.e., imaginal processes, self-talk, affective states) and, (c) physiological processes. Second, continuity exists between overt, observable behaviors and covert behaviors, and there is an interaction between these two sets of events. In this regard, covert events can potentially affect overt behavior and, in turn, overt behavior can impact covert behavior.

Specific covert conditioning procedures include covert sensitization, covert extinction, covert positive reinforcement, covert negative reinforcement, covert response cost, covert modeling, and what is referred to as a "self-control triad." Covert sensitization, covert extinction, covert response cost, and the self-control triad are used to decrease the frequency with which certain target behaviors occur. In *covert sensitization,* clients are asked to first imagine performing a given undesirable target behavior (e.g., excessive hair pulling) and then imagine a negative or aversive consequence (e.g., having a large bald spot and being teased by peers). In *covert extinction,* clients are asked to imagine a given target behavior (e.g., telling tall tales to friends at school) and then to imagine that the reinforcer maintaining the behavior does not occur (e.g., their friends pay no attention to their stories). *Covert cost response* refers to the process by which clients are asked to first imagine a given target behavior (e.g., getting out of their seats in class without permission) and then imagine that they are deprived of a specific reinforcer (removal of recess privileges). The *self-control triad* involves asking a client to yell (stop), take a deep breath, exhale, and relax, and then to imagine a pleasant scene whenever the target behavior occurs.

Covert positive reinforcement and covert negative reinforcement are typically utilized as a means of increasing desirable or positive behaviors. In *covert positive reinforcement,* a client is instructed to imagine a given target behavior (e.g., giving a successful speech in class) and then asked to subsequently imagine a pleasant scene, which serves as a reinforcer (e.g., having the teacher and peers congratulate the client). In a *covert negative reinforcement paradigm,* a client is asked to imagine a very negative or aversive stimulus; the aversive scene is then terminated and a new image is immediately created. Notably, this procedure is inherently difficult with children and is rarely utilized in clinical practice. In *covert modeling,* a client is asked to imagine a model performing a given target behavior (e.g., a favorite peer who engages in a piano competition with little anxiety) and then subsequently imagines a highly reinforcing consequence (winning an award for the performance). Covert modeling can be used to either increase a desired behavior or decrease an undesirable one. In general, clinical use of covert conditioning procedures with children and adolescents is limited to covert reinforcement, covert modeling, and covert extinction, while the use of covert aversive procedures is avoided.

In keeping with the behavioral tradition, a functional analysis of behavior is typically undertaken before a covert conditioning treatment approach is utilized. Antecedent conditions and consequences are identified as are any skill deficits on the part of the child. In addition, it is recommended that an "imagery assessment" be conducted. In this manner, the clinician can identify any difficulties the child might have in successfully engaging in covert conditioning procedures. There are several indicators the clinician may use to determine if a child is able to effectively engage in imagery, including the ability to (a) carry out verbal instructions, (b) learn by watching a model, (c) use accurate details to describe past or future experiences, (d) use language to make attributions and express emotions, (e) engage in pretend play, and (f) describe dreams in detail. Clinical experience reveals that children often show much more bodily expression when engaged in imagery than adults. Physical signs that a child is effectively engaged in imagery might include facial expressions, throat and mouth movements, body movement and posture, and either a relaxed or tense physical state. Verbal indicators that the child is engrossed in the scene include the child being able to narrate the scene, answer questions about the scene, and rate the quality/intensity of the scene.

A typical covert conditioning session involves asking the child to imagine the target scene. When working with children, it is often necessary for the therapist to keep the scenes short and to provide many details, as well as orient the scene to the child's preferences and experiences. The child is asked to rate how pleasant, fearful, or disgusting (depending on the type of conditioning being employed) the scene is, using either a 1 to 3 (for children under age 8) or 1 to 5 (for children older than age 8) scale, with higher numbers indicating greater vividness. After the imagined scene, the child is reinforced for engaging in the scene either in vivo or using imagined reinforcement. Often, the child is rewarded in vivo after engaging in every scene. The in vivo reward is then given after increasing numbers of responses and is eventually faded from in vivo reinforcement to imagined reinforcement. Fewer trials are recommended when working with children compared to adults; therefore, between trials the child and therapist may play a game or draw pictures before the next covert trial. Children often are given audiotapes of the conditioning scenes to practice with at night for 15 to 20 minutes before bed. Parents should be instructed to reinforce the child for practicing with the tapes.

Most important, covert conditioning procedures are often placed within a self-control or self-management framework. In other words, a primary therapeutic goal is to teach the child client a set of skills that can be utilized in everyday situations. Homework assignments are given, and the client is instructed as to which procedures to engage in and under what circumstances. Parents or caregivers are typically instructed in how to cue their child to engage in particular strategies and reinforce their efforts. Clients are also reinforced for their use of these tools in session and encouraged to conceptualize these skills as resources they can use in a variety of situations with a range of difficulties they may encounter. As termination approaches, clients are asked to anticipate future problem situations, establish a plan for solving such problems, and rehearse intervention strategies in advance.

RESEARCH BASIS

The very nature of covert conditioning, that is, the utilization of unobservable or "private" events to effect behavior change, has made research on these procedures

somewhat difficult. The situation is complicated by the fact that single covert conditioning procedures are rarely utilized in practice. Typically, a *set* of covert procedures are implemented, often in combination with other adjunctive procedures from other theoretical models. Thus, it is often difficult or impossible to attribute successful behavior change to a given covert conditioning procedure. Finally, it is safe to say that little research currently exists that compares the efficacy of covert procedures to other types of intervention for specific problems using random group assignment.

At the same time, a fair amount of evidence, the majority of which is case study, single-subject design, or anecdotal, exists that demonstrates the efficacy of a variety of covert conditioning procedures with children. Experimental evidence demonstrating the efficacy of these procedures with children generally is limited to the use of covert reinforcement, covert sensitization, and covert modeling. Clinical experience, however, suggests that all of the covert procedures can be used successfully with children.

RELEVANT TARGET POPULATIONS AND EXCEPTIONS

A vast range of problems of childhood have been addressed with the use of covert conditioning procedures. These problems range from generalized anxiety and depression to the treatment of obsessive-compulsive disorder, trichotillomania, specific phobias and fears, aggressive behavior, self-injurious behavior, and emotional dyscontrol. More discrete problematic behaviors have also been targeted, including head dropping, nose picking, nail biting, and tics. In addition, covert conditioning procedures have been utilized in the field of child health psychology, including problems of pain management, coping with cancer, stress-induced asthma, conditioned nausea and vomiting secondary to chemotherapy, and adherence to medical regimens. Notably, these procedures have been effective with children as young as 3 years of age and in populations experiencing developmental disabilities (e.g., Down syndrome, autism). Thus, it would appear that covert conditioning has wide applicability. In addition, covert conditioning procedures are readily integrated with other behavioral procedures (e.g., relaxation training, in vivo desensitization) and strategies from other theoretical frameworks.

It is notable, however, that younger children and those with severe cognitive impairment may not be able to successfully engage in the imagery-based procedures. Child clients may not always understand the rationale behind such procedures, nor are some of them able to develop clear, meaningful scenes, which is essential for successful treatment. It is often helpful to teach younger children the process of how to engage in successful imagery. This may be done by asking children to use superheroes or movie idols as part of their scene development. Audiotapes, cartoons, actual pictures of scenes, or videos can also be incorporated into sessions as a means of giving children ideas of appropriate target images.

COMPLICATIONS

Significant levels of anxiety, fear, and depression may indeed interfere with a child's ability to successfully engage in covert conditioning procedures and should be monitored carefully. In those cases where excessive affective responses exist, the initiation of alternative therapeutic strategies (e.g., supportive therapy, reassurance, medication management) may be necessary before a child can be taught covert conditioning strategies.

It is also critical that the therapist take considerable time to explain the rationale and purpose of covert procedures and their implementation to ensure that the child has sufficient understanding and motivation to engage in such procedures. Obviously, children who do not practice such procedures between sessions are unlikely to see substantial therapeutic gains. Equally important are the parents' understanding and support for the use of covert conditioning procedures. To the extent that they are indifferent to or do not support their child's treatment regimen, therapy is likely to be undermined.

Finally, it should be noted that treatment failures have been linked to inadequate assessments (i.e., the failure to obtain a valid functional analysis of behavior) and to the inappropriate application of learning principles. Certainly, careful and thorough assessment is critical to identify the antecedent and consequences of a given problem behavior as is an understanding of the basic learning principles and their clinical implementation.

CASE ILLUSTRATION

"Charlie," a 7-year-old boy, was brought to treatment by his parents due to his refusal to have water run over his head or to have his head immersed in water. Reportedly, when Charlie was about 5 years old, he was swimming in the family pool with his brothers when they held him underwater in an attempt to tease Charlie for not being a proficient swimmer. The incident so frightened Charlie that he refused to put his head underwater in the pool. Quite rapidly, Charlie's fear of the water began generalizing to many situations, including refusal to go in the pool at all, refusal to take a shower, refusal to have water poured over his head in the bathtub in order to wash his hair, refusal to sit in the bathtub with more than 1 inch of water in it, and refusal to go outside whenever it rained. At the time he presented for treatment, Charlie was bathing only one time per week and endured this with great distress. His lack of hygiene was creating considerable problems for the family and Charlie's peer relationships.

The treatment rationale provided to Charlie indicated that he would be asked to "use his imagination" to help himself overcome his fear of water, which would help make it easier for him to take showers and be in the pool. Being able to take a shower and be in the pool would make it easier for him to spend time with his friends and brothers and to "have a lot more fun." Treatment began by determining what objects and activities Charlie found reinforcing. Charlie particularly enjoyed playing baseball and collecting baseball cards. Charlie also had a favorite professional baseball player whom he admired immensely. Charlie also enjoyed playing with his dog, Max, and getting to decide what dessert the family would have after dinner. After establishing a set of reinforcing objects and activities, Charlie was taught basic relaxation skills such as how to make himself go limp like a rag doll and how to take deep breaths. A hierarchy of fearful scenes was created that ranged from Charlie's least fearful scene (having a few drops of rain on his head) to a moderately fearful scene (having to have a cup of water poured over his head while having his hair shampooed) to his most feared scenes (swimming underwater from one end of the pool to the other).

Covert modeling and positive covert reinforcement were used initially. Charlie first imagined his baseball hero engaging in each scene, followed by the hero hitting a home run in a championship game. Following covert modeling, Charlie was asked to imagine himself in each scene. The therapist described the scene in detail until Charlie indicated that his image was clear enough that his fear level was at a 3 on scale from 1 to 3.

Initially, Charlie was reinforced in vivo with a baseball card when he engaged in each scene. Over time, in vivo reinforcement was changed to imagined reinforcement by having Charlie imagine himself in a pleasant scene such as playing baseball or playing with Max. If Charlie became excessively distressed during the covert procedures, he was reminded to become "limp like a rag doll" or to take a deep breath. Charlie was given audiotapes of his imagined scenes that he practiced with for 15 to 20 minutes before bed each night. His parents rewarded him with baseball cards or the chance to pick a dessert after dinner for practicing with his tapes.

The use of the covert procedures facilitated Charlie engaging in normal showering behavior and tolerating being in the rain with little to no distress. The remainder of Charlie's fears, those related to being in the pool, were addressed with in vivo gradual exposure by having the therapist visit the family home and engage in exposure at the pool. Eventually, Charlie was able to swim in the pool, including putting his head underwater, with no distress. Therapy was terminated at this time. Three- and 6-month follow-up revealed no reemergence of Charlie's symptoms.

—*Larry L. Mullins and Jill Van Pelt*

See also: *Cautela, Joseph R. (Vols. I & III), Classical Conditioning (Vols. I, II, & III), Covert Control (Vol. III), Covert Positive Reinforcement (Vols. I & III), Covert Reinforcer Sampling (Vol. III), Covert Sensitization Conditioning (Vols. I & III), Imaginal Procedures (Vol. II)*

Suggested Readings

Baron, G., & Cautela, J. (1983). Imagery assessment with normal and special needs children. *Imagination, Cognition, and Personality, 3,* 17–30.

Cautela, J. R. (1982). Covert conditioning in children. *Journal of Behavior Therapy and Experimental Psychiatry, 13,* 209–214.

Cautela, J. R. (1983). The self-control triad. *Behavior Modification, 7,* 299–315.

Cautela, J. R. (1986). Covert conditioning and the control of pain. *Behavior Modification, 10,* 205–217.

Cautela, J. R., & Kearney, A. J. (1986). *The covert conditioning handbook.* New York: Springer.

Cautela, J. R., & Kearney, A. J. (1993). *Covert conditioning handbook.* Pacific Grove, CA: Brooks Cole.

Corbett, L. O., & Corbett, N. J. (1996). Covert conditioning in behavioral medicine. In J. R. Cautela & W. Ishaq (Eds.), *Contemporary issues in behavior therapy: Improving the human condition* (pp. 23–43). New York: Plenum.

Kanfer, F. H., & Gaelick-Buys, L. (1991). Self-management methods. In F. H. Kanfer & A. P. Goldstein (Eds.), *Helping people change* (pp. 305–360). New York: Pergamon Press.

DIFFERENTIAL REINFORCEMENT OF INCOMPATIBLE BEHAVIOR

DESCRIPTION OF THE STRATEGY

Differential reinforcement of incompatible behavior (DRI) is one of several procedures used to decrease the frequency of a problem response (e.g., tantrums), but it is unique in also increasing another response (e.g., appropriate play). Central to understanding differential reinforcement are the principles of reinforcement and extinction as related to the concepts of response differentiation and differential reinforcement, first explicated in the Skinner classics *The Behavior of Organisms: An Experimental Analysis* and *Science and Human Behavior,* respectively. When only responses with particular properties are selectively reinforced, other operating principles being equal, all responses in that class increase in probability, decreasing the probability of all other responses. In DRI, purported reinforcers are delivered contingent on response topographies that are physically impossible to emit simultaneously with a response excess. For instance, completion of a manipulation task cannot occur simultaneously with hand flapping, body rocking, or aggressive behavior, nor can peer tutoring occur during disruptive behavior. The incompatible response competes with the maladaptive response in that increases in the frequency of the incompatible response reduce the opportunity to emit the maladaptive response. Other responses, particularly the target response excess, are on extinction, further reducing the future probability of the behavior excess.

The reinforcer is usually first delivered for each incompatible response and may be any stimulus that will strengthen that response. But use of the functional reinforcer that had maintained the response excess would further decrease the frequency of the behavior excess through satiation, reducing its momentary probability. This defines differential reinforcement of alternative behavior (DRA), also called differential reinforcement of functionally equivalent behavior (DRFE). Therefore, functional reinforcement of an incompatible response combines DRI and DRA contingencies.

An advantage of DRI over punishment is avoiding undesirable effects such as emotional responses and conditioned aversions. In contrast to punishment, extinction, and differential reinforcement of other behavior, DRI can potentially be constructive in building the appropriate response repertoire and avoiding reinforcer deprivation.

RESEARCH BASIS

It has been demonstrated in basic research that specific response properties, including topography, can be strengthened through reinforcement. The result is response differentiation, an increase in the probability of the reinforced response class and a simultaneous decrease in all nonreinforced responses. Studies in applied behavior analysis have shown reduction of a wide variety of unwanted responses via reinforcement of various incompatible behaviors. Representative examples include reinforcement of lying still to reduce disruptive activity during medical treatment, signing "please" to reduce grabbing or self-injury, task compliance to reduce oppositional responses, appropriate verbal responses to reduce inappropriate verbal responses, articulated speech to reduce inarticulate speech, and completion of academic tasks to reduce sleeping or disruptive classroom behavior.

DRI is effective using both positive and negative reinforcement, such as delivery of tokens and escape and avoidance of shock, respectively. Both reinforcers have shown to be effective in reducing self-injury when contingent on toy play. DRI is also effective in utilizing either arbitrary or functional reinforcers. The examples of positive and negative reinforcement described above illustrate arbitrary reinforcers. Examples effectively incorporating a functional (DRA) contingency include reinforcing toy play with the positive reinforcer of staff interaction or the negative reinforcer of escape from demands, depending on the reinforcer previously maintaining self-injury.

Factors that enhance the effectiveness of DRI include extinction of the inappropriate response, functional reinforcement, prompting and instructions, and matching reinforcer density with baseline levels.

Noncontinuous reinforcement and extinction can effectively reduce the response, and thinning to intermittent schedules enhances maintenance.

Since their development in the 1980s, functional assessment and functional analysis are considered an indispensable prerequisite for differential reinforcement. Functional analysis enables extinction of the maladaptive response and reinforcement of an incompatible response to replace the maladaptive response function, combining DRI with DRA. When a communication response is reinforced, DRA is termed *functional communication training*. For example, if a functional analysis indicates that hand biting is reinforced by staff interactions, treatment would reinforce an incompatible alternative response (such as hand raising) to access the same reinforcer, creating a functionally equivalent behavior. In fact, application of DRA strategies derived from functional analyses are currently so much the mainstay in applied behavioral research that even when the replacement response is also incompatible (which it need not), the procedure is rarely identified as a DRI.

Differential reinforcement, explicitly stipulating conditions for reinforcement, is usually associated with behavior analysis. However, the concept of DRI is implicitly incorporated in effective behavior therapy interventions. These include assertiveness training, increasing activities to treat depression, social skills training, relaxation training, rational emotive therapy, habit reversal, approach of or exposure to phobic or obsessive stimuli, and training coping skills. The response to be reduced may be respondent, but the incompatible behavior often involves some implicit reinforcement of an operant, usually incorporating other techniques such as modeling, rehearsal, and feedback.

RELEVANT TARGET POPULATIONS

DRI can be used to reduce any inappropriate response, provided it is possible to identify an appropriate incompatible response and control a powerful reinforcer. It is ideally suited when the goal is to not only to reduce a problem behavior but also to expand the appropriate response repertoire, especially relevant in education settings.

COMPLICATIONS

It may not be possible to find an appropriate incompatible response, or the response selected may not be as appropriate as a more functionally typical response. For example, a response incompatible with head banging is clenching the hands behind the back. However, if the reinforcer had been physical affection, it would be more constructive to teach appropriate manding of affection, that is, by adding a DRA contingency.

—*Marilyn K. Bonem*

See also: *Differential Reinforcement of Other Behavior (Vols. I, II, & III), Operant Conditioning (Vols. I, II, & III), Schedule-Induced Behavior (Vol. III), Schedules of Reinforcement (Vols. I, II, & III), Skinner, Burrhus Frederic (Vols. I, II, & III)*

Suggested readings

Day, R., Rea, J., Schussler, N., Larsen, S., & Johnson, W. (1988). A functionally based approach to the treatment of self-injurious behavior. *Behavior Modification, 12,* 565–589.

Leslie, J. C., & O'Reilly, M. F. (1999). *Behavior analysis: Foundations and applications to psychology.* Amsterdam: Harwood Academic.

Lockwood, K., & Bourland, G. (1982). Reduction of self-injurious behavior by reinforcement of toy use. *Mental Retardation, 20,* 169–173.

Martin, G., & Pear, J. (2003). *Behavior modification: What it is and how to do it.* Upper Saddle River, NJ: Prentice Hall.

Mulick, J., Hoyt, P., Rojahn, J., & Schroeder, S. (1978). Reduction of a "nervous habit" in a profoundly retarded youth by increasing toy play. *Journal of Behavior Therapy and Experimental Psychiatry, 9,* 381–385.

Richman, D. M., Wacker, D. P., Cooper-Brown, L. J., Kayser, K., Crosland, K., Stephens, T. J., et al. (2001). Stimulus characteristics within directives: Effects on accuracy of task completion. *Journal of Applied Behavior Analysis, 34,* 289–312.

Shukla, S., & Albin, R. W. (1996). Effects of extinction alone and extinction plus functional communication training on covariation of problem behaviors. *Journal of Applied Behavior Analysis, 29,* 565–568.

Slifer, K. J., Koontz, K. L., & Cataldo, M. F. (2002). Operant-contingency-based preparation of children for functional magnetic resonance imaging. *Journal of Applied Behavior Analysis, 35,* 191–194.

Steen, P., & Zuriff, G. (1977). The use of relaxation in the treatment of self-injurious behavior. *Journal of Behavior Therapy and Experimental Psychiatry, 8,* 447–448.

Vollmer, T. R., Roan, H. S., Ringdahl, J. E., & Marcus, B. A. (1999). Evaluating treatment challenges with differential reinforcement of alternative behavior. *Journal of Applied Behavior Analysis, 32,* 9–23.

DIFFERENTIAL REINFORCEMENT OF LOW RATES OF BEHAVIOR

DESCRIPTION OF THE STRATEGY

Differential reinforcement of low rates of behavior (DRL) is one of a family of reinforcement schedules that offer an alternative to using punishment to decrease a target behavior. When a DRL schedule is in effect, a response is reinforced after a specific time period elapses since a response last occurred. An increase in interresponse time (IRT > t) reduces response rate. An increase in interresponse time reduces but may not eliminate the rate of the incompatible response. Thus, the DRL contingency is useful when the overall frequency of behavior needs to be reduced, not eliminated. Children are not required to be "perfect"; they can improve and thereby earn reinforcement.

RESEARCH BASIS AND TARGET POPULATION

Laboratory studies with animals have demonstrated that the time between responses (the interresponse time or IRT) is a property of behavior that can be reinforced. The DRL schedule most frequently used in applied settings is full session DRL. Under the full session DRL contingency, reinforcement is delivered at the end of a session if less than a prescribed number of responses occur (the DRL limit). The session might be at home, work, school, or wherever the problem behavior occurs. For example, two students with autism were exposed to a DRL schedule to reduce gazing at the ceiling and inappropriate vocalizing. For one student, the opportunity to look through a gyroscope (the reinforcer) was contingent on ceiling gazing below the criterion set for the session. The DRL procedure for one student was programmed to progressively lower the rate of gazing (longer intervals between instances of gazing), until the behavior no longer interfered with classroom instruction. For the other student, the opportunity to listen to music was contingent on a gradually decreased rate of inappropriate vocalizing. Full session DRL has also been used to reduce the rate of speech (in a student who spoke too rapidly), to decrease the rate of off-task talking, to reduce self-stimulatory behaviors, and to reduce noise levels among groups of school children.

A second DRL variation that is frequently used in laboratory research is spaced responding DRL. In spaced responding DRL, a behavior is reinforced if it has been separated from a previous instance of that behavior by a minimum amount of time (the IRT). It is most effectively used with behaviors that are primarily a problem because of their high rate. A DRL procedure was used to decrease rapid eating in four individuals with severe disabilities. Interresponse times between food bites were reinforced and systematically increased. The eating rate was reduced from 10 to 12 bites per 30 seconds to 3 to 4 bites per 30 seconds. This schedule has been reported to reduce inappropriate classroom questions and stereotypical behaviors of normal and intellectually challenged children. The primary problem is its limited usefulness in settings that don't permit constant monitoring of the behavior.

A final variation of interval DRL specifies that reinforcement will only occur if fewer than a specified number of responses are emitted during the interval. If more than the criterion number of responses occur prior to the end of the interval, the DRL interval resets and reinforcement is delayed. For example, an interval DRL procedure was used to reduce the number of times a child interrupted other children. A DRL interval of 2 minutes was initially implemented.

Reinforcement at the end of the interval was contingent on the emission of fewer than two interruptions. When a second interruption occurred prior to the end of the interval, the 2-minute interval was reset and the reinforcer was delayed. Similarly, a teacher gradually reduced a student's teeth grinding by initially reinforcing the student when no more than four grindings occurred during a specific time period. When the student met this criterion, reinforcement was next contingent upon grinding teeth no more than three times. This criterion was systematically lowered until the behavior was at an acceptable rate. Other classroom behaviors such as excessive question asking, talking out, and leaving one's seat have also been effectively reduced with interval DRL procedures.

COMPLICATIONS

The effectiveness of the DRL procedure depends on the establishment of a response requirement that ensures sufficient reinforcement. For all versions of DRL, selection of the initial DRL duration should be based on an examination of baseline response rates. If the response occurs about once every minute during baseline assessment and the session duration was one hour, the full-session DRL limit would initially be set at 60, and both the spaced responding DRL and the interval DRL would be set at 1 minute. Once reinforcement is reliably delivered, the full session DRL limit should be gradually decreased (the spaced responding and interval durations gradually increased) until an acceptable rate of the behavior is established. A change in the response requirement that is too abrupt (thinned too rapidly) will make reinforcement unlikely, thereby decreasing the effectiveness of the procedure. The reinforcer must be delivered frequently enough to avoid extinction, but not so frequently as to bring on satiation. Complications may also arise if the target behavior has not been specified or assessed well (must be a countable behavior). It must be ensured that the putative reinforcer functions as a reinforcing event. In addition, it should be empirically demonstrated that an acceptable other behavior is part of the student's repertoire. The program should continue even after the student has mastered a new, appropriate behavior so that the student's access to reinforcement is increased.

While adverse side effects have not been described with any of the forms of DRL, some restrictions should be placed on their adoption. None of the DRL procedures should be used for serious self-injurious behavior or aggressive behavior because those behaviors should be eliminated. In addition, full-session DRL may not be a suitable procedure for individuals from populations with a variety of learning difficulties, because some misbehaviors receive no consequence during the full-session or interval DRL schedules. The technique is not appropriate for reducing the likelihood of dangerous behaviors because of the gradually improving nature of the technique. This may also be true in cases of aggressive, destructive, or extremely disruptive behaviors that, because of their severity, need to be eliminated immediately.

—*Elliott Bonem*

See also: Differential Reinforcement of Other Behavior (Vols. I, II, & III), Operant Conditioning (Vols. I, II, & III), Schedule-Induced Behavior (Vol. III), Schedules of Reinforcement (Vols. I, II, & III), Skinner, Burrhus Frederic (Vols. I, II, & III)

Suggested Readings

Deitz, S. M. (1977). An analysis of programming DRL schedules in educational settings. *Behavior Research and Therapy, 15,* 103–111.

Lentz, F. E. (1988). Reductive procedures. In J. C. Witt, S. N. Elliott, & F. M. Gresham (Eds.), *Handbook of behavior therapy in education* (pp. 439–468). New York: Plenum.

Leslie, J. C., & O'Reilly, M. F. (1999). *Behavior analysis: Foundations and applications to psychology.* Amsterdam: Harwood Academic.

DIFFERENTIAL REINFORCEMENT OF OTHER BEHAVIOR

DESCRIPTION OF THE STRATEGY

A reinforcement schedule designed to differentially reinforce other behavior (DRO) is useful when the goal is to gradually eliminate a behavior. When a DRO schedule is in effect, a reinforcer is presented only if an unwanted response does not occur during a predetermined period of time. Reinforcing an increase in the time without the behavior produces a decrease in the rate of the behavior. Because reinforcement is not contingent on the emission of any particular response, any response other than the specified response may be reinforced (e.g., sitting still, sleeping, or doing "nothing"). The DRO schedule is also described as differential reinforcement of zero rates or as omission training because reinforcement is delivered for a zero rate (the omission) of the specified response. It is sometimes combined with punishment. For example, if no response occurs during the DRO interval, reinforcement is delivered; if a response does occur, the punishment procedure (i.e., response cost, time-out) would be immediately applied and a new interval would begin.

There are two variations of the DRO schedule. Under whole-interval DRO, the selected behavior must be absent for the entire interval for the reinforcer to be delivered. For example, if a response (whining behavior) occurs about once every 5 minutes during baseline, the initial interval would be set at 5 minutes and reinforcement would be delivered after each 5-minute period that did not include whining. Under whole-interval DRO, the occurrence of the unwanted response before the interval elapses either resets the interval or cancels the reinforcer programmed at the end of the interval. Thus, whining during the interval could either reset the period to 5 minutes or simply not deliver reinforcement at the end of the 5-minute period.

The other variation is momentary DRO. With this contingency, the problem behavior must be absent at the end of the interval for the reinforcer to be delivered. For example, reinforcement at the end of each 5-minute interval would occur if the whining behavior was absent when the interval ended. If whining continued for 4 minutes but was absent when the interval ended, reinforcement would be presented. Similarly, if whining had been absent for more than 4 minutes but occurred just as the interval ended, the reinforcer would be cancelled. The primary advantage of momentary DRO is that it is easy to monitor because evaluation need only take place at the end of the DRO interval. The disadvantage is that the target behavior may be adventitiously reinforced if it occurs at times other than the end of the DRO interval.

RESEARCH BASIS

A protocol should be followed when implementing the DRO procedure. First, it is essential to identify the reinforcer that is maintaining the problem behavior. This necessitates a functional assessment prior to implementing the DRO procedure. Research indicates that extinction is an essential component of the DRO procedure. That is, the effectiveness of the DRO contingency is dependent upon eliminating the reinforcing

consequence that maintains the problem behavior. Second, a functional assessment should empirically identify a consequence that functions as a reinforcer for the individual. Of course, one consequence that is certain to function as a reinforcer is the consequence (identified through a functional assessment) that is targeted for extinction. When self-injurious behavior (SIB) is maintained by contingent attention, procedures such as DRO (using attention) are effective in reducing SIB, particularly in the early stages of the intervention. Third, there must be an empirical determination of the time interval during which the behavior should not occur. The initial DRO value should be approximately equal to the mean value between occurrences of the target behavior as determined by a representative baseline period. Fourth, the DRO duration should be gradually increased to ensure frequent reinforcement until an acceptable rate of the target behavior is maintained. Fifth, the occurrence of the target behavior should be monitored in other settings to identify instances of behavior contrast. Finally, generalization of the absence of the target behavior to new situations should be systematically expanded into various settings. When this recommended protocol is followed, reduction of the target behaviors is usually quite rapid and tends to be maintained. If difficulties arise, look at whether the initial interval is too long or whether the interval without the behavior was increased too rapidly.

RELEVANT TARGET POPULATIONS

One advantage of DRO is that it is effective across a range of behaviors, from those that are minor annoyances to behaviors that create a severe social problem. The effectiveness of the procedure has been reported both individually and in groups, and with normal and challenged populations. The procedure is especially useful with individuals with severe language delays who display unacceptably high rates of inappropriate behavior. Successful reductions in behavior using a DRO schedule have been reported for unwanted behaviors such as sibling conflict at home, aggression, disruptive classroom misconduct, self-injurious behavior, vomiting, aggressive biting, food stealing, bruxism, trichotillomania, pica, distractible behavior, asthma, thumb sucking, and seizure-like behaviors. When properly carried out, DRO has been shown to be an effective, socially acceptable behavior reduction procedure.

COMPLICATIONS

It has been reported that food and praise were relatively ineffective when used in a DRO contingency for stereotypic behavior apparently maintained by automatic-positive reinforcement. Without the incorporation of extinction for the unwanted behavior, food and praise did not compete with reinforcement directly produced by the behavior.

Another complication may occur because the procedure requires accurate timing and observation. Whole-interval DRO is somewhat difficult to implement in situations such as classrooms where one adult is in charge of many individuals. Momentary DRO is easier to administer but is often not as effective. Another problem with DRO occurs because reinforcement is contingent on the nonoccurrence of a behavior. A specific appropriate behavior is not targeted for reinforcement. This may lead to the inadvertent reinforcement of other inappropriate behaviors. A constructive alternative is to make reinforcement contingent on the occurrence of an appropriate behavior (i.e., DRI). Finally, under a DRO-reset contingency, the child may learn to exhibit the inappropriate behavior immediately after the timer is set and, after the timer is reset, yet still receive reinforcement at nearly the same density, even if the appropriate behavior occurred. This is perhaps why it has been reported, on rare occasions, that the DRO contingency produced superstitious behavior.

—*Elliott Bonem*

See also: *Differential Reinforcement of Other Behavior (Vols. I & III), Operant Conditioning (Vols. I, II, & III), Schedule-Induced Behavior (Vol. III), Schedules of Reinforcement (Vols. I, II, & III), Skinner, Burrhus Frederic (Vols. I, II, & III)*

Suggested Readings

Bellack, A. S., & Hersen, M. (Eds.). (1990). *International handbook of behavior modification and therapy* (2nd ed.). New York: Plenum.

Iwata, B. A., Vollmer, T. R., Zarcone, J. R., & Rogers T. A. (1993). Treatment classification and selection based on behavioral function. In R. Van Houten & S. Axelrod (Eds.), *Behavior analysis and treatment* (pp. 101–125). New York: Plenum.

Lentz, F. E. (1988). Reductive procedures. In J. C. Witt, S. N. Elliott, & F. M. Gresham (Eds.), *Handbook of behavior therapy in education* (pp. 439–468). New York: Plenum.

Leslie, J. C., & O'Reilly, M. F. (1999). *Behavior analysis: Foundations and applications to psychology.* Amsterdam: Harwood Academic.

Poling, A. D., & Ryan, C. (1982). Differential-reinforcement-of-other-behavior schedules: Therapeutic applications. *Behavior Modification, 6,* 3–21.

Repp, A. C., & Deitz, S. M. (1974). Reducing aggressive and self-injurious behavior of institutionalized retarded children through reinforcement of other behaviors. *Journal of Applied Behavior Analysis, 7,* 313–325.

DISCRETE TRIAL THERAPY

DESCRIPTION OF THE STRATEGY

Discrete trial therapy is a specific form of teaching that places emphasis on the instructor providing a structure, specific context, and pacing to a teaching interaction. It requires an active response from the learner and thus is different from lecture-style instruction. It is discrete in that the various components that comprise a teaching-learning interaction are specified and choreographed into a systematic and replicable interaction. Related parameters for discrete trial procedures include massed versus spaced practice, level and type of prompting for response emission and error correction, reinforcement parameters (such as schedule, type, and amount), physical set-up of the learning environment, precise selection of learning materials/stimuli, intertrial interval duration, response selection and criteria for reinforcement (shaping parameters), and response generalization and maintenance. In contrast, most typical teaching/learning interactions are fluid in that many different stimuli are presented, and a wide range of responses are expected of the learner. In turn, teacher response to learner correct responding and incorrect responding may be variable in degree and type. Typical teaching lessons often have a theme and a set of goals, but the teaching/learning interaction is not highly choreographed, and moment-to-moment changes are the norm.

RESEARCH BASIS

The research base for discrete trial learning is extensive because discrete trial is simply a format for basic trial-and-error learning, also known as "three-term contingency" or "ABC" of learning. These refer to the sequence of antecedent, behavior, and consequence that may be used to describe the conditions under which most learning occurs. The manipulation of each of these three variables, alone and in combination, has been the subject of thousands of research studies across human and nonhuman populations. Thus, the impact of these variables on learning has become a truism, and reference may be made to the laws of learning. However, while the basic and applied research base is extensive, because there are so many variants to each of the three components, research continues to flourish as more and more sophisticated questions are addressed, particularly with respect to learning for special populations.

RELEVANT TARGET POPULATIONS AND EXCEPTIONS

As mentioned above, discrete trial therapy, given its basis in basic learning theory, has been applied extensively to both typical and atypical populations, reflecting a broad range of species and behavior topographies. This research has led to a depth of knowledge that has permitted direct applied application to human populations with special needs. The focus has tended to be with individuals with mental retardation and/or developmental disabilities. While such application has been occurring in a formal and broad manner since the early 1960s, a rapid increase was observed in the mid-1980s due to publication of a number of research outcome studies and program descriptions, all indicating previously unheard of treatment gains in children with autism using intervention programs incorporating discrete trial therapy as an essential component. While discrete trial therapy can be appropriately applied to both typical and atypical populations, its use for children with autism spectrum disorders has become pervasive within behaviorally oriented treatment programs and has found its way into nonbehavioral treatment programs although rarely labeled as discrete trial therapy under those circumstances. Thus, it is this breadth of use within the autism spectrum population that has created the term *discrete trial therapy* to connote its core importance and extensive application, in contrast to the more correct terms *discrete trial training* and *discrete trial teaching*. However, among the lay public, the terms *discretes* and *discrete trials* are also used, and often incorrectly, to indicate it is the full extent of the treatment program, rather than as simply a component (albeit an important one) of a treatment program.

COMPLICATIONS

Because discrete trial therapy is typically used with individuals with significant learning problems and impoverished repertoires, certain cautions arise. First, in presenting discrete trials, because of the precise manner in which stimuli are presented and prompts delivered that allow learning to take place where previously it did not occur, care must be exercised that the learner does not become overly dependant upon certain aspects of the procedure that are not beneficial in the long term. Such aspects are referred to as cue dependency, prompt dependency, and stimulus overselectivity.

Cue dependency is the limited range of response forms and/or the limited response to a range of similar stimuli. For example, in teaching the verbal label "table" in response to holding up pictures and asking "What is this?" cue dependency would be seen if the learner responded correctly to the specific picture used during discrete trial teaching but did not respond to a different picture of a table or a real table. That is, the learner formed an association of the label specific to the particular picture used, not the class of objects referred to as tables. This example illustrates the heart of a common clinical dilemma: Discrete trial procedures can be effective in teaching the atypical learner, but the learner characteristics that have made learning difficult can limit the impact of discrete trial procedures. In the above example, if many exemplars were used as the stimulus associated with the request "What is this?" then learning may not take place, as the task is too complex for the learner. As the task is adjusted, especially for severely impaired learner, to a simpler level such that the learner is able to make correct responses, then the problem of cue dependency may arise. Thus, assessment of cue dependency is a typical part of the use of discrete trial teaching.

Prompt dependency is a related problem. It is associated with the emission of a response in association with a prompt. Prompts are often used to assist the learner in responding and can take many forms. However, if prompts are used too routinely without programming intermittent use and differential reinforcement for unprompted responding, the learner can remain passive and respond only when the instructor provides a specific prompt. It may arise when disproportionate attention is given to promoting accurate and/or fast responding at the cost of nonprompted responding. This problem is conceptually related to cue dependency.

Stimulus overselectivity, in this context, refers to the use of a superfluous or irrelevant aspect of a stimulus to determine responding. An example would be that in showing a child a picture of mother and a picture of father and asking "Point to mother," the child appears to perform well, whereas in fact the child is responding to the picture because it has a slight curl on the lower left corner. Stimulus overselectivity is problematic in that it is often so subtle that it is difficult for the instructor to detect without a formal and systematic assessment procedure. It is also related to cue dependency in that an idiosyncratic aspect of the cue is attended to rather than what might be referred to as the commonly agreed important aspects. Proper ongoing assessment and evaluation can address these three problems, especially given an awareness of their prevalence with individuals with autism spectrum disorders.

CASE ILLUSTRATION

This is a highly abbreviated illustration of the factors influencing choice of goals and the decision to use discrete trial format with specific goals.

Brief History

"John," a 3-year and 8-month-old male, was classified as a "preschool child with a disability" based on the presence of atypical developmental patterns. These included lack of age-appropriate social skills, speech and language development, and severe maladaptive behavior. In addition, the family was finding it more and more difficult to manage John's behavior and was concerned about the slow progress he was making in achieving his developmental milestones. John began receiving itinerant speech services at home 2 hours a week for a period of 9 months prior to the intake interview. According to both "Mr. and Mrs. Jones" and the speech pathologist servicing John, this level of intervention had not resulted in any observable or functional change in his ability to communicate. Subsequent evaluations confirmed a diagnosis of autism.

Specific Development

John was aware of the response-consequence chain associated with his behavior and behaved consistent with his expectation of the consequences. This level of awareness enabled him to recognize when a consequence was altered (e.g., when an adult ignored instead of comforted him during a tantrum). In addition, John was differentially reactive to and aware of different individuals in his environment.

Attentive and concept formation skills include the following: When placed in close proximity to the teacher, John inconsistently demonstrated the ability to remain seated for approximately 5 minutes at a time. He had also been able to visually focus on stimulus materials and demonstrated an emerging level of environmental awareness. He would at times search for preferred objects. If these were not easily visible, however, his search was limited to visually scanning the immediate area and did not include moving items to look under or around obstacles in order to locate items. John could locate the source of sound by turning his head in the direction from which the sound was coming.

John's most interpretable form of communication was his behavioral and facial responses to situations. John would appear distressed and begin to engage in escape behaviors such as resisting teacher prompts and attempting to leave the instructional area when presented with a task that appeared to be unpleasant or distasteful to him. Likewise, an apparently enjoyable situation was most often met with a smile or physically approaching the situation. His ability to interpret receptive language was difficult to assess at this time, as he responded almost exclusively to events as opposed to the communication of others.

Of great concern were John's attentive skill deficits. He had demonstrated difficulty establishing eye contact in response to an instruction to "Look at me," responding to his name by turning toward the speaker, orienting to the teacher or materials upon request, and remaining seated when placed in a chair without the constant close proximity of an adult. Verbal and physical prompts were most often required to obtain the aforementioned behaviors and were quite often met with resistance and tantrums from John.

In concept formation skills, John had difficulty responding to a request to match one object, even when presented with a single object to match to. For example, when John was presented with a cup on the desk, handed a second cup, and asked to put them together or "match," he typically did not respond to this request and might react by throwing or mouthing the cup. It is unclear at this time whether his lack of responsivity was a visual discrimination deficit, attentive skill deficit, or a lack of comprehension of the direction. John did not respond to basic instructions, for example, "point to," "match," or "give me," and such a "learning to learn" vocabulary had to be established so that he was able to respond as instructed and therefore allow his teachers to assess with a greater degree of accuracy his absolute skill levels. In addition, self-stimulatory behavior interfered with most tasks that involve the use of objects or other manipulatives.

John's language comprehension as well as language expression was severely delayed. His babbling included only simple sounds or syllables. He did, however, have some emerging imitative ability. He could imitate a model of clapping (although inconsistently) but no other simple actions, for example, waving. John did not imitate single sounds upon request, change or stop his activity in response to his name, or follow functional directions, for example, "sit down." When he desired something, his typical response was to grab or reach for the object. John did not lead adults to desired activities or hand things to others for assistance (e.g., handing an empty cup for more juice). At that time, John had no verbal expressive language skills, although he did emit random sounds spontaneously.

Overview

John's overall functioning level was severely delayed and immature when compared to same-age peers. However, specific skills of relative strength included a select number of gross motor and self-help skills. Primary concerns included John's limited speech, receptive and expressive language, attentive skills, concept formation, age-appropriate self-help, and social skills. John's maladaptive behaviors were severe in intensity and in the level of interference with his daily activities.

The presence of aggressive, self-injurious, self-stimulatory, and noncompliant behaviors negatively impacted on teaching activities and significantly reduced the amount of exposure to the instruction he received. John required an extensive level of structure within a small group setting to maximize acquisition and retention of skills.

Goal Selection

Based upon the information obtained and direct observation, the following short-term goals were chosen (Note: this is not the full list of goals, but only the subset of goals relevant to this example). Each goal further required an individualized operational definition prior to creating a specific teaching program for each goal, which would specify precise parameters of instructional procedure.

Establishes eye contact in response to command "Look at me"

Establishes eye contact in response to name only

Orients to materials upon teacher request

Imitates single action

Opens and closes mouth

Imitates other specific facial movements

Emits sounds in presence of primary reinforcement

Emits multisyllabic vocalizations in response to verbal stimulation

Imitates long vowel sounds

Imitates short vowel sounds

Imitates consonants

Imitates C-V syllables with long vowels (me, foo, bo)

Imitates V-C syllables (om, it, up)

Imitates C-V words (me, bye, hi)

Touches body parts on request

Performs actions on request

Follows functional directions upon request

Points to an object or picture when instructed, given a single stimulus item

Points to correct object upon instruction, given a choice of two

Produces consonant-vowel combination in response to an object

Labels familiar objects with a single word/sign/symbol

Labels events using a single work/sign/symbol

Requests assistance

Remains seated in small group (2–3 children)

Matches to sample of one, given one identical object

Matches one object in an array of two

Discrete Trial Format Selection

Now, given the goals and the information on specific child characteristics, the above goals would be prioritized and sequenced rather than addressed simultaneously. Good candidates for discrete trial instruction that also would be high initial priorities that are a close match to the child's current repertoire and skill level are the following:

Establishes eye contact in response to command "Look at me"

Orients to materials upon teacher request

Imitates single action

Emits sounds in presence of primary reinforcement

Emits multisyllabic vocalizations in response to verbal stimulation

Points to an object or picture when instructed, given a single stimulus item

Matches to sample of one, given one identical object

Based upon ongoing evaluation of the specific format and instructional parameters, use of discrete trial format might be expanded to other goals or in turn might be further limited with other forms of instructional procedures assessed for the same goals. This is a highly dynamic process, and the use of a specific format such as discrete trials (and within that format the many specific parameters) is but one factor in a complex set of factors influencing programmatic intervention.

—Raymond G. Romanczyk
and Jennifer M. Gillis

See also: *Applied Behavior Analysis (Vols. I, II, & III), Operant Conditioning (Vols. I, II, & III), Skinner, Burrhus Frederic (Vols. I, II, & III)*

Suggested Readings

Anderson, S. R., Avery, D. L., DiPietro, E. K., Edwards, G. L., & Christian, W. P. (1987). Intensive home-based early intervention with autistic children. *Education and Treatment of Children, 10,* 352–366.

Anderson, S. R., & Romanczyk, R. G. (1999). Early intervention for young children with autism: Continuum-based behavioral models. *Journal of the Association for Persons With Severe Handicaps, 24,* 162–173.

Cooper, J. O., Heron, T. E., and Heward, W. L. (1987). *Applied behavior analysis.* Englewood Cliffs, NJ: Prentice Hall.

Lovaas, O. I. (1987). Behavioral treatment and normal educational and intellectual functioning in young autistic children. *Journal of Consulting and Clinical Psychology, 55,* 3–9.

Martin, G., & Pear, J. (1992). *Behavior modification: What it is and how to do it.* (4th ed.). Englewood Cliffs, NJ: Prentice Hall.

Maurice, C., Green, G., & Luce, S. C. (1996). *Behavioral intervention for young children with autism: A manual for parents and professionals.* Austin, TX: Pro-Ed.

DISCRIMINATION TRAINING

DESCRIPTION OF THE STRATEGY

Discrimination training involves the use of selective reinforcement and extinction to generate differential responding to two or more stimuli. Training automobile drivers to stop when the light is red and to go when the light is green is an example. The act of responding differentially to stimuli (e.g., different colored lights) is called *stimulus discrimination*. It is the goal of discrimination training to elicit stimulus discrimination.

The process of discrimination training within laboratory settings involves repeated trials in which two or more stimuli are presented (concurrently or sequentially) and the subject is provided an opportunity to obtain reinforcement, given the presentation of one but not the other. As a result of such training, responding will come to occur in the presence of the stimulus that signals the availability of reinforcement. That stimulus is often called the S+ or S^D (pronounced "ess dee"). The stimulus that signals the lack of reinforcement is often called the S– or S^D (pronounced "ess delta"). For example, during discrimination training, a 400-Hz tone might be consistently followed by the presentation of reinforcement, while a 600-Hz tone is not. In this case, the 400-Hz tone is the S+ or S^D and the 600-Hz tone is the S– or S^D.

Stimulus discrimination training often involves a graduated approach to reducing the stimuli that give rise to a certain response. To accomplish this, successively similar stimuli are presented, and responding to one type is reinforced, while responding to the other is not. In the above example, on subsequent trials reinforcement will continue to be given to responses that follow a 400-Hz tone. However, presentations that do not signal the availability of reinforcement may include not only 600-Hz tones but also 500-Hz tones and 450-Hz tones. In this example, training leads to the discrimination of stimuli that are increasingly similar and more difficult to discriminate.

Early experimental studies of discrimination training revealed a phenomenon referred to as *experimental neurosis*, in which experimental participants illustrated unusual behavior arising out of exposure to increasingly difficult discriminations. In a classic study, a dog was trained to salivate to a circle but not to ellipses. Over the course of repeated trials, the shape of the ellipses presented to the dog became more and more similar to that of a circle. As the discrimination became more difficult to make due to the increased similarity between the shapes, the dog began to display heightened levels of restlessness, agitation, and unprovoked aggressiveness—behaviors resembling anxiety or neurosis observed in humans. Pavlov explained this unusual behavior as arising from a conflict between cortical excitation and inhibition.

It was subsequently argued that the conditions giving rise to experimental neuroses in animals may resemble the nonlaboratory conditions that generate neuroses in humans. In particular, the experimental conditions were seen as resembling human environments in which it is difficult to identify conditions leading to reinforcement and those leading to no reinforcement or to punishment. Such unpredictability—arising from either randomness or stimulus discrimination failure—is thought to be an environmental condition leading to a subjective experience of anxiety and also overtly anxious and, perhaps, aggressive behavior.

There exist some situations in which one might wish to make stimulus discrimination difficult. This is the case when we want behavior to generalize. For instance, a store may not have camera coverage in every aisle, but would want that fact concealed from would-be shoplifters. Similarly, teachers want children to obey rules and to act toward others with courtesy in all situations—not just those in which training occurs or when the child is being supervised by an adult.

RESEARCH BASIS

A great deal of research illustrates discrimination training as a successful procedure for eliciting stimulus discrimination. The procedure has been used clinically as a means of generating socially appropriate and safe

behavior. With respect to the former, discrimination training occurs within classroom settings whenever a teacher systematically rewards children for speaking only after raising their hand and waiting to be called on. It also occurs when children are taught to wait their turn. Discrimination training involves teaching the child the environmental cue or set of cues that signal the appropriateness of engaging in some activity.

RELEVANT TARGET POPULATIONS AND EXCEPTIONS

Discrimination training has been widely used within the context of social skills training programs for children who display aggressiveness and impulsiveness and for adults and children with mental retardation. A form of discrimination training also occurs in traditional "talk therapies" with respect to differentiating emotions. For example, in cognitive therapy for depression, clients are asked to identify the occurrence of specific emotions and to differentiate them from other emotions. Subsequently, they are offered strategies for responding differentially, depending on the emotions they are experiencing. This represents a form of discrimination training.

COMPLICATIONS

Discrimination training involves the systematic presentation of the stimuli to be discriminated and provides feedback that is contingent upon differential responding. In some instances, it may be difficult to meet these conditions. For example, one may attempt to alter the behavior of an aggressive child by teaching him or her to discriminate between the neutral and positive behavior of peers and the aggressive behavior of peers. For such training to be successful, it is necessary that the child be exposed to situations that have real-world relevance. However, it may be difficult to establish training conditions that mirror real-world social contexts. Moreover, some individuals may continue to struggle to discriminate between subtle social, emotional, and environmental cues.

—*Paul S. Strand*

See also: *Differential Reinforcement of Other Behavior (Vols. I, II, & III), Operant Conditioning (Vols. I, II, & III), Schedule-Induced Behavior (Vol. III), Schedules of Reinforcement (Vols. I, II, & III), Skinner, Burrhus Frederic (Vols. I, II, & III)*

Suggested Readings

Bolling, M. Y., Kohlenberg, R. J., & Parker, C. R. (2000). Behavior analysis and depression. In M. J. Dougher (Ed.), *Clinical behavior analysis* (pp. 127–152). Reno, NV: Context Press.

Cavell, T. A. (2000). *Working with parents of aggressive children: A practitioner's guide.* Washington, DC: American Psychological Association.

Luiselli, J. K., & Cameron, M. J. (Eds.). (1998). *Antecedent control: Innovative approaches to behavioral support.* Baltimore: Paul H. Brookes.

Reese, H. W. (1968). *The perception of stimulus relations: Discrimination learning and transposition.* New York: Academic Press.

DRUG ABUSE PREVENTION STRATEGIES

Over the past three decades, several approaches to preventing alcohol, tobacco, and drug abuse in young people have been developed and implemented. Most of these prevention approaches take the form of programs designed to be implemented in middle or junior high schools because schools offer access to youth during the period of time when they typically initiate substance use. Traditionally, these programs have involved the dissemination of information about substance use and the negative health, social, and legal consequences of use and abuse. Despite the fact that simply providing students with factual information about drugs is ineffective in changing behavior, it remains the most commonly used approach to prevention. However, information dissemination approaches are slowly being replaced by more effective strategies that focus less on didactic instruction regarding the adverse health of drug abuse and more on interactive skills training techniques. The most effective programs teach children and adolescents social, cognitive, and behavioral skills using key principles of behavior modification and focus on how to apply these skills to the developmental challenges young people face, including the issue of drug use initiation.

DESCRIPTION OF THE STRATEGY

Over the past two to three decades, the focus of adolescent drug abuse prevention programming has shifted as knowledge concerning the etiology of drug abuse has accumulated. The most promising contemporary approaches are conceptualized within a theoretical framework based on the etiology of drug abuse and relevant psychological theories of human behavior. Effective prevention approaches can be grouped into two general categories: (1) social resistance approaches and (2) competence enhancement or "life skills" approaches.

Social Resistance Strategies

According to the social resistance skills approach, adolescent drug use results from a variety of social influences, including the direct modeling of drug use behavior, particularly that of peers, and persuasive advertising appeals and media portrayals encouraging alcohol, tobacco, and other drug use. Therefore, social influence programs focus extensively on teaching youth how to recognize and resist pressures to use drugs using a variety of resistance skills training exercises. The goal of these exercises is to have students learn ways to avoid high-risk situations where they are likely to experience pressure to smoke, drink, or use drugs, as well as acquire the knowledge, confidence, and skills needed to handle social pressure in these and other situations. These programs frequently included a component that makes students aware of pro-drug influences in the media, with an emphasis on the techniques used by advertisers to influence consumer behavior. Also, because adolescents tend to overestimate the prevalence of drug use, social resistance programs often attempt to correct normative expectations that nearly everybody smokes, drinks alcohol, or uses drugs. In fact, resistance skills training may be ineffective in the absence of clear social norms against drug use because adolescents are less likely to resist if the norm is to engage in drug use.

Competence Enhancement Strategies

A limitation of the social influence approach is that it assumes that young people do not want to use drugs but lack the skills or confidence to refuse social influences promoting use. For some youth, however, using drugs may not be a matter of yielding to peer pressure, but instead may have instrumental value; it may, for example, help them deal with anxiety, low self-esteem, or a lack of comfort in social situations. According to the competence enhancement approach, drug use is conceptualized as a socially learned and functional behavior that is the result of an interplay between social and personal factors. Drug use behavior is learned through a process of modeling, imitation, and reinforcement and is influenced by an adolescent's pro-drug cognitions, attitudes, and beliefs. These factors, in combination with poor personal and social skills, are believed to increase an adolescent's susceptibility to social influences in favor of drug use.

The most effective competence enhancement approaches to drug abuse prevention emphasize the teaching of generic personal self-management skills and social coping skills in combination with social resistance skills training. Examples of the kind of competence skills included in this prevention approach are decision-making and problem-solving skills, cognitive skills for resisting interpersonal and media influences, skills for enhancing self-esteem (goal-setting and self-directed behavior change techniques), adaptive coping strategies for dealing with stress and anxiety, general social skills (complimenting, conversational skills, and skills for forming new friendships), and general assertiveness skills. The most effective way to teach these skills is by using cognitive-behavioral skills training methods: instruction and demonstration, role playing, group feedback and reinforcement, behavioral rehearsal (in-class practice), and extended (out-of-class) practice through behavioral homework assignments.

RESEARCH BASIS

While evaluation research has clearly shown that information dissemination approaches to drug abuse prevention are ineffective in changing behavior, there have been many studies showing that social resistance skills programs and competence enhancement programs are generally effective. A comprehensive review of resistance skills studies published from 1980 to 1990 reported that the majority of prevention studies (63%) had positive effects on drug use behavior, with fewer studies having neutral (26%) or negative effects on behavior (11%); and several studies finding no effects had inadequate statistical power to detect program effects. Furthermore, several follow-up studies of social resistance skills interventions have reported positive behavioral effects lasting for up to 3 years. Longer-term follow-up studies have shown that these effects gradually decay over time, suggesting the need for ongoing intervention or booster sessions.

A number of evaluation studies have tested the efficacy of the competence enhancement or life skills approach to drug abuse prevention. These studies have demonstrated behavioral effects on smoking, alcohol, marijuana use, as well as the use of multiple substances and illicit drugs. The magnitude of these effects has typically been relatively large, with some studies showing reductions in drug use behavior in the range of 40% to 80%. Long-term follow-up data indicate that the prevention effects of these approaches can last for up to 6 years. Furthermore, recent studies have shown that competence enhancement approaches are effective with a broad variety of youth, including predominantly White samples in suburban and rural settings as well as predominantly Black and Hispanic samples in urban minority samples. Overall, the strongest behavioral effects across studies have been found when programs are delivered with high integrity by trained providers and when booster sessions are provided to reinforce the material after the initial intervention.

RELEVANT TARGET POPULATIONS

Contemporary programs are typically categorized into one of three types: *universal* programs focus on the general population, such as all students in a particular school; *selective* programs target high-risk groups, such as poor school achievers; and *indicated* programs are designed for youth already experimenting with drugs or engaging in other high-risk behaviors. The majority of school-based prevention programs are universal programs that focus on middle or junior high school children, and a smaller number of programs focus on elementary school children. The goal of these primary prevention programs is to prevent substance use before it begins by impacting risk factors associated with the early stages of drug use. By preventing drug use with younger populations (e.g., elementary and junior high school students), it is presumed that this will ultimately reduce the prevalence of drug abuse among these youth during later adolescence and early adulthood.

In addition, some drug prevention programs have been developed for high school and college-aged populations. Most of these are selective or indicated interventions that target students with poor academic records and those at high risk of dropping out of school, or those students who are already involved in drug abuse and other behavioral problems.

CASE ILLUSTRATION

This section describes an example of an effective universal drug abuse prevention program, called Life Skills Training (LST), which combines elements of both social resistance and competence enhancement approaches. The LST approach is a universal intervention in that it is designed for all individuals in a given setting rather than a selective or targeted intervention that is only for individuals at "high risk." The middle school version of LST is typically provided in school classrooms in fifteen to seventeen 45-minute sessions. In addition to the initial year of intervention, there are 2 years of booster intervention designed to reinforce the material covered during the first year, including 10 booster sessions in Year 2 and five sessions in Year 3. Below is a brief description of the major components of the LST program.

Program Components

Personal Self-Management Skills

The personal skills component of the LST program is designed to impact on a broad array of self-management skills. To accomplish this, the personal skills component contains material to (a) foster the development of decision making and problem solving (e.g., identifying problems, defining goals, generating alternative solutions, considering consequences), (b) teach skills for identifying, analyzing, and resisting media influences, (c) provide students with self-control skills for coping with anxiety (e.g., relaxation training) and anger/frustration (e.g., inhibiting impulsive reactions, reframing, using self-statements) and (d) provide students with the basic principles of personal behavior change and self-improvement (e.g., goal setting, self-monitoring, self-reinforcement).

Social Skills

The social skills component is designed to impact on several important social skills and enhance general social competence. This social skills component contains material designed to help students improve general interpersonal skills such as how to overcome shyness and how to give and receive compliments. This material emphasizes the teaching of (a) communication skills, (b) general social skills (e.g., initiating social interactions and conversational skills), (c) skills related to dating relationships, and (d) verbal and nonverbal assertive skills.

Drug-Related Information and Skills

This component is designed to impact on knowledge and attitudes concerning drug use, normative expectations, and skills for resisting drug use influences from the media and peers. The material contained in this component is similar to that contained in many psychosocial drug abuse prevention programs that focus on the teaching of social resistance skills. Included is material concerning the (a) short- and long-term consequences of drug use, (b) knowledge about the actual levels of drug use among adolescents and adults in order to correct normative expectations about drug use, (c) information about the declining social acceptability of cigarette smoking and other drug use, (d) information and class exercises demonstrating the immediate physiological effects of cigarette smoking, (e) material concerning media pressures to smoke, drink, or use drugs, (f) information concerning the techniques used in tobacco and alcohol advertisements to promote the use of these drugs, along with skills for resisting these influences, and (g) techniques for resisting direct peer pressure to smoke, drink, or use drugs.

Prevention Methods

The LST program is taught using cognitive-behavioral skills training, facilitated group discussion, classroom demonstrations, and traditional didactic teaching methods. Much of the material in the LST program is most effectively taught by facilitating group discussion and through skills training, although lecturing and conventional didactic teaching methods are appropriate for some of the material. Because the major emphasis of the LST program is on the teaching of general personal self-management skills, social skills, and drug resistance skills, the most important intervention method is skills training. The cognitive-behavioral skills in the LST program are taught using a combination of instruction, demonstration, behavioral rehearsal, feedback, social reinforcement, and extended practice in the form of behavioral homework assignments.

Instruction and Demonstration

The first step in the skills training process involves instruction and demonstration. Instruction involves explaining a particular skill to students in a careful step-by-step fashion, along with a clear explanation of when to use the skill. Demonstration involves showing students how to perform a particular skill. This can be done by the program provider, by videotape, or even by a member of the class who has already learned the skill being taught.

Behavioral Rehearsal

Once the skill has been explained and demonstrated by the LST provider, students are given the opportunity to practice the skill themselves through selected behavioral rehearsal scenarios. To practice the skills, students can take turns coming to the front of the classroom to participate in a brief role play that requires that they use the skill being taught. The class can also be divided into small groups, with the program provider circulating from group to group to observe the students practicing. The behavioral rehearsal scenarios are first described by the provider or a small group leader, and the exercises are kept as brief as possible (a minute or less each) so that as many students as possible can have a chance to participate.

Feedback

After students rehearse the skills being taught, they are provided with feedback concerning the strengths and weaknesses of their skills performance. The teacher or program provider conveys this information in a supportive manner so students understand what aspects of the skill they performed well and what needs improvement. It is important that students are given specific recommendations concerning how to improve. Emphasis is placed on constructive feedback designed to guide students as they strive to improve and "successively approximate" mastery of the skills being taught.

Social Reinforcement

Since the primary objective of the LST program is to reduce risk for drug abuse, the goal of the skills training is to improve the target skills and self-efficacy of each student. Therefore, students are assessed individually with respect to improvement over their own baseline levels, however low. During and after the behavioral rehearsal exercises, the teacher or LST program provider reinforces each student for one or two positive elements of his or her performance of the skill. Although at times this may be a challenge, the program provider can simply identify the most positive element of the student's performance.

Extended Practice

The purpose of extended practice is to provide opportunities for additional practice of the target skills outside the classroom, in an effort to promote skill development and utilization. This is accomplished through behavioral homework assignments, which may include tasks such as practicing a new technique for coping with anxiety once a day or using an assertive response in three different situations that arise during a particular week. In addition to providing opportunities for practice in general, extended practice is intended to facilitate the use of new skills in situations outside the classroom and encourage students to use these skills in their everyday lives.

In summary, the most effective contemporary strategies for prevention of drug abuse among children and adolescents focus less on didactic instruction about the adverse consequences of drug abuse and more on interactive skills training techniques that aim to enhance social, cognitive, and behavioral skills using key principles of behavior modification.

—Gilbert J. Botvin
and Kenneth W. Griffin

See also: *Behavioral Treatment of Cigarette Smoking (Vol. I), Behavioral Treatments for the Addictions (Vols. I & III), Controlled Drinking (Vol. III)*

Suggested readings

Hawkins, J. D., Catalano, R. F., & Miller, J. Y. (1992). Risk and protective factors for alcohol and other drug problems in adolescence and early adulthood: Implications for substance abuse prevention. *Psychological Bulletin, 112,* 64–105.

National Institute on Drug Abuse; National Institute of Health. *Preventing drug use among children and adolescents: A research-based guide.* Available: http://www.nida.nih.gov/Prevention/PREVOPEN.html.

Petraitis, J., Flay, B. R., & Miller, T. Q. (1995). Reviewing theories of adolescent substance use: Organizing pieces in the puzzle. *Psychological Bulletin, 117,* 67–86.

Sloboda, Z., & Bukoski, W. J. (Eds.). (2003). *Handbook of drug abuse prevention: Theory, science, and practice.* New York: Kluwer Academic.

E

EMPIRICALLY SUPPORTED TREATMENTS FOR CHILDHOOD DISORDERS

PROCESS, EVIDENCE, AND ISSUES

Empirically supported treatments refer to a subset of treatments for mental health problems that have met a specified set of criteria designed to increase confidence that a treatment will be effective for a specific problem. The identification of empirically supported treatments for mental health problems represents part of a larger movement within medical, educational, and social sciences designed to increase attention to the quality of evidence used to understand, evaluate, and select interventions to remedy or prevent specific problems. Within psychological science, the origins of a formalized process for the identification of empirically supported treatments had its roots largely in the Division of Clinical Psychology of the American Psychological Association. This group's Task Force on Promotion and Dissemination of Psychological Procedures (TFPD) produced the first set of guidelines for the evaluation of evidentiary support, and its initial and subsequent reports catalogued those treatments that had sufficient evidence based on these guidelines to be identified as "empirically validated."

A second group within the American Psychological Association, the Task Force on Psychological Intervention Guidelines (TFIG), outlined a broader template for determining the quality of evidence supporting psychosocial interventions. This group delineated criteria along two dimensions on which to evaluate the evidence supporting the use of a particular treatment, efficacy, and effectiveness (or clinical utility). Studies that provide evidence concerning efficacy establish whether or not a particular intervention works (e.g., reduces symptoms, increases functioning), and these studies are most often conducted under tightly controlled conditions (e.g., using random assignment and control groups, interventions that are well described and of fixed length, clearly specified inclusion and exclusion criteria, individuals with single disorders). Studies that provide evidence concerning effectiveness establish how well a particular intervention works in the environments and under the conditions in which treatment is typically offered (e.g., interventions of variable duration, individuals with multiple disorders).

CRITERIA USED TO ESTABLISH EFFICACY

Different groups reviewing treatments have established slightly different criteria for judging a treatment as efficacious; however, most groups have used a variation of the criteria established by the TFPD. This group defined two levels at which a treatment could be labeled empirically supported. The highest level of support was termed "well established." To be placed in the well-established category, a treatment had to have published evidence of demonstrated efficacy either (a) in a minimum of two good between-group design experiments, where the treatment was superior to pill or psychological placebo or to another treatment, (b) the treatment was equivalent to an already established treatment in two between-group design experiments with adequate sample size, or

(c) in a large series of controlled single-case experiments ($n > 9$) that compared the treatment to another treatment. In addition, the effects of the treatment had to have been demonstrated by at least two different investigators for a treatment to be judged well established. The second level of support was termed "probably efficacious." Treatments placed in this category had to have published evidence that demonstrated that the treatment was either (a) superior to a wait-list control group in two experiments, (b) equivalent to an already established treatment or superior to pill placebo, psychological placebo, or another treatment in a single experiment (or two experiments conducted by the same investigator), or (c) superior to pill placebo, psychological placebo, or another treatment in a small series of single-case design experiments ($n > 3$). For either category, treatments had to be conducted with a treatment manual or some other clear description of the treatment, and a clear description of the sample had to be provided.

CHILDHOOD TREATMENTS THAT ARE EMPIRICALLY SUPPORTED

It is beyond the scope of this entry to catalogue and describe all the treatments for childhood disorders that have been judged empirically supported. Noted below are those treatments that have been identified by a variety of working groups as meeting criteria for being an empirically supported treatment for disorders that are seen at high frequency in clinical settings. Empirically supported treatments for problems often seen in pediatric care settings (e.g., elimination disorders, pain) have also been identified (see suggested readings for more complete lists and descriptions). Although review groups have often used different variations of review criteria, treatments identified as empirically supported tend to be common across groups; however, classification of a treatment as well established or probably efficacious has sometimes differed. Treatments consistently categorized as well established are noted.

For children with mood disorders, both interpersonal psychotherapy (IPT) and cognitive behavior therapy (CBT) have demonstrated efficacy. CBT for depression focuses on teaching patients how their thoughts and actions relate to their mood and may include skill development in communication, problem solving, anger management, relaxation, and social skills. IPT focuses on problems in the patient's relationships with family and friends, major life transitions, and bereavement.

For children with anxiety disorders, CBT, exposure, modeling, reinforced practice, relaxation, and family anxiety management have demonstrated efficacy. CBT for anxiety includes a combination of techniques designed to change distorted thinking, recognize anxious thoughts, manage anxiety, and cope with anxiety-producing situations. CBT also includes techniques such as exposure, relaxation, and reinforced practice. Exposure involves systematic, often gradual, approach and confrontation with feared objects or situations. Modeling involves the demonstrations of nonfearful behavior in anxiety-producing situations. Reinforced practice represents a combination of exposure and modeling in which the patient is provided with rewards for confronting the feared object or situation. Family anxiety management combines CBT with explicit training of parents in dealing appropriately with their children's anxiety, and some variants include treatment focused on parents' own anxiety.

For children with conduct disorder or oppositional defiant disorder, parent training in various forms, including videotape training, multisystemic therapy (MST), problem-solving skills training (PSST), anger control therapy, assertiveness training, and rational emotive therapy (RET) have demonstrated efficacy. Of all these treatments, parent training has well-established efficacy. Parent training focuses on teaching effective discipline skills, including monitoring of specific behaviors, rewarding positive behaviors, and punishing or ignoring problem behaviors. MST is a multifaceted intervention approach designed to alter the different systems impacting the adolescent (e.g., family, peers, work, school, community). PSST involves teaching appropriate problem-solving strategies such as developing alternative solutions, evaluating consequences, and perspective taking through role play, modeling, practice, and feedback. Anger control therapy focuses on preventing anger and teaching alternative responses to anger-provoking situations through developing recognition of cues of anger, problem-solving skills training, relaxation, and teaching of appropriate responses. Assertiveness training teaches children to use assertive verbal responses in place of aggressive responses. RET involves teaching children to examine their beliefs, understand how these beliefs relate to situations and behavior, and develop more accurate beliefs and more adaptive strategies.

For children with attention-deficit/hyperactivity disorder, variants of behavior therapy, including parent training and behavioral classroom interventions, have well-established efficacy. Parent training is described above. Behavioral classroom interventions involve providing consultation with teachers regarding the use of structure and rules, appropriate contingencies, and communication with parents regarding specific child behavior (e.g., use of daily report cards).

CONSIDERATIONS OF EFFECTIVENESS

A consistent criticism of the movement to identify empirically supported treatments has been that the procedures and processes used in the type of studies required to establish efficacy are unlike the functioning of practice in typical clinical settings. Arguments leveled against the empirically supported treatment approach include the fact that patients in clinical settings are not randomly assigned to a treatment, often have comorbid disorders (i.e., more than one disorder), participate in treatment for varying lengths of time, may not meet diagnostic criteria for a disorder as defined by the *Diagnostic and Statistical Manual of Mental Disorders,* and may be more interested in improvement in outcome domains other than symptom reduction. Hence, opponents of the movement to identify empirically supported treatments argue that results of efficacy studies are of little relevance to clinical practice. Many opponents suggest that effectiveness studies, or studies of the treatments offered most often and with the type of clients typically seen in common clinical settings, are needed to provide the type of information that can guide clinical practice.

Efficacy and effectiveness are often treated as if they represent endpoints on the same continuum, with efficacy studies having high internal validity (i.e., precision that allows an attribution of causality to the independent variable) but low external validity (i.e., restrictions in design and eligibility of participants that limit generalizability of findings). Conversely, effectiveness studies are often viewed as having high external validity (i.e., results derived in more naturalistic contexts) but low internal validity (i.e., conducting research in a traditional clinical setting would not allow design features, like random assignment and fixed length treatment that enable specific causal statements).

Of course, internal validity and external validity are not the endpoints of a single continuum, and it is possible both to demonstrate causality and to provide information concerning generalizability in a single study. However, generalizability is only one facet of effectiveness. As outlined by the American Psychological Association's TFIG, there are at least three dimensions that influence how well a treatment with established efficacy may translate into effective clinical practice in more traditional settings. The first dimension outlined involved feasibility. Treatments with high levels of feasibility are those that are (a) acceptable to patients, (b) likely to be chosen by patients, (c) likely to have a high degree of patient compliance, and (d) easily disseminable to those in the practice community. The second dimension outlined involved generalizability. Treatments with a high degree of generalizability are those that (a) are robust across a variety of patient characteristics including cultural factors, gender, developmental factors, (b) are robust across a variety of therapist characteristics, (c) do not require an inordinate amount of specialized training or excessive time, and (d) provide similar effects across a variety of settings. The final dimension outlined included issues related to costs and benefits. For instance, a treatment may yield very positive results but be cost prohibitive because it requires a lot of time to complete, requires a high degree of specialized training or supervision for a therapist to conduct, or requires a specialized setting (e.g., inpatient care) to implement.

It is clear that information about a treatment along the dimensions of effectiveness is needed; however, efficacy studies are both required and informative for clinical practice in more traditional settings. Efficacy is a necessary but not sufficient condition for demonstrating the effectiveness of a psychosocial intervention. That is, establishing the efficacy of a treatment is only the first step in providing evidence required for informed selection of the treatment most appropriate for a particular patient. However, a treatment that does not yield a more potent response than no treatment or placebo in well-controlled clinical trials is unlikely to produce a potent response in less controlled clinical practice. Conversely, a treatment may have demonstrated efficacy in clinical trials but fail to yield similar results in clinical practice. Such a failure may be the result of difficulty in implementing the intervention in clinical settings, ease of dissemination, acceptability of the intervention to clients, or the increased heterogeneity of clinical populations and problems in clinical settings (e.g., comorbidity) compared to research settings. The question of whether or not the positive effects of interventions for children as demonstrated in efficacy studies will generalize to more typical clinical settings is an empirical question that, in most cases, has yet to be addressed. Some work, albeit mainly concerning treatment of adults, has been conducted using a "benchmarking" strategy in which effect sizes from less controlled studies in common practice settings are compared to effect sizes obtained in randomized controlled trial research.

ISSUES AND CONTROVERSIES IN EMPIRICALLY SUPPORTED TREATMENTS

A significant issue in identifying empirically supported treatments concerns the question of what constitutes the same treatment in research studies. One criterion for well-established treatments is replication by different research groups. However, studies designed to be exact replications of previous treatment outcome studies are rarely conducted. That is, seldom do independent investigators use the same treatment manual to treat the same population in different studies. Hence, the issue of when two approaches are sufficiently similar to be considered the same treatment needs to be addressed. For instance, does a study that evaluated a treatment for depression with children that involved self-monitoring, identifying problem thoughts, developing coping thoughts or problem-solving strategies, and accompanying behavioral exercises represent a replication of a study of a similar treatment protocol used with adolescents that included age-appropriate modifications in language, thematic areas, and complexity? Are two treatment manuals that employ the same cognitive-behavioral strategies for the treatment of anxiety descriptive of a single treatment if one manual includes 10 treatment sessions and the other manual includes 16 treatment sessions? If a very conservative strategy in defining treatments is employed, it is unlikely that many treatments would rise to the highest level of evidentiary support because strict replications are so rare. However, if liberal criteria in defining treatments are used, the benefit of specificity that the empirically supported treatments approach offers in terms of the identification of treatments is lost.

One creative solution to this issue was recently employed by the task force of the Child and Adolescent Mental Health Division of the Hawaii Department of Health, which was established to generate practice guidelines through the use of a multidisciplinary evaluation of psychosocial treatments for common disorders of childhood and adolescence based on reviews of studies in psychology, psychiatry, and related mental health disciplines. This group adopted a middle-ground strategy for the specification of a treatment (i.e., multiple variations of similar techniques were identified as a single treatment approach) and considered evidence of efficacy of variations of a treatment to imply that the approach was robust. Moreover, such a strategy was viewed as providing evidence along the effectiveness dimension inasmuch as some variation in treatment (e.g., cognitive-behavioral treatment of depression in children versus adolescents) speaks to generalizability of the treatment approach.

Another criticism of the empirically supported treatments approach has concerned the requirement that treatments be manualized or otherwise described in detail. Some opponents of manualized treatments argue that manuals limit the degree of flexibility required in clinical practice to adapt a treatment to an individual, reducing the clinician to a technician who applies treatment devoid of the "art" of clinical practice. Rather than suggesting that clinical practice is an art, a more apt analogy would be to identify clinical practice as part of a craft. That is, clinicians do engage in artful aspects of practice (e.g., establishing a positive therapeutic relationship), but they also need to apply foundational principles concerning human behavior and disorder. Basing those foundational principles on the science of clinical psychology and intervention seems better than basing them on nonverifiable factors such as approaches consistent with a favored theoretical orientation, a recently attended workshop, or accumulated personal experience. Moreover, whereas an idiographic approach to clinical practice is intuitively appealing, it ignores a large and consistent literature on human judgment and clinical prediction that indicates that all but the simplest of information is often misapplied in the individual case.

Within the context of treatment outcome research, manualization allows fidelity checks that provide the means of determining when results apply to an intervention. In the absence of a detailed description of the intervention being tested and a check that the intervention as delivered actually conformed to the description, there is no way to determine if results are applicable to that intervention approach. A treatment manual simply provides a means of specifying the intervention procedures conducted during the course of therapy. A manualized treatment can be as prescriptive as one that specifies session-by-session activities, or it can simply represent a codified framework for a treatment approach in which the clinician chooses which techniques to apply to what issue in what session. Many manuals are elaborated with examples of dialogue between therapist and patient, and describe means to deal with problems that may arise in the course of treatment. Treatment manuals provide the level of detailed description and standardization of a treatment that is required for replication, dissemination, and adequate training of therapists. Finally, concerns that the standardization of treatment associated with manualized treatments will reduce the effectiveness of psychosocial intervention have not been supported by research.

Critics of the empirically supported treatment approach also have noted that the majority of studies evaluating psychosocial interventions have investigated cognitive-behavioral interventions. In contrast, most surveys of clinical practitioners reveal that the majority of treatments used in clinical practice involve treatments other than those that could be classified as cognitive-behavior (e.g., psychodynamic, systems, eclectic). Whereas this situation partially reflects the focus of the treatment outcome literature, it highlights the fact that many interventions in use in a majority of clinical settings are lacking in strong empirical support, accentuating the need to subject these interventions to more rigorous empirical scrutiny. Whereas this process may support the efficacy of some additional treatments, a number of meta-analyses of studies examining treatment of childhood disorders have found that interventions that can be classified as cognitive-behavioral produce larger effects than other interventions.

Critics of the empirically supported treatments approach have noted that clinical trials research with children is often conducted with nonreferred populations, by persons in training, and using interventions of fixed duration. In contrast, clinical practice generally involves children referred by parents, schools, and the courts; treatment generally is conducted by professionals; and interventions are of varying length, depending on the severity and intractability of the problems, ability to pay, and commitment to treatment. The majority of these issues relate to the issue of generalizability as discussed earlier. Factors by which outcome research differs from typical clinical practice may impact an empirically supported treatment's effectiveness. However, such arguments suggest that these differences imply that an alternative treatment approach would be more effective. To date, there is no evidence to support such a suggestion.

One final criticism of the empirically supported treatments approach concerns the methodology of the reviews. That is, whereas criteria for the type of studies required to support treatment at different levels are well specified, issues such as definition of treatments, as discussed above, as well as specifics of the review methodology employed by different review groups have been questioned. For instance, some have noted that no review group has provided data on the reliability of judgments reached by review groups. Yet, the work of the review groups follows the transparent nature of science in general. That is, interested individuals can review the evidence cited in support of specific well-established or probably efficacious treatments because the work groups provide the evidence on which such judgments are made.

CONCLUSIONS

The findings of the various groups that have worked to identify empirically supported treatments are intended to be viewed more as descriptive than prescriptive. That is, whereas the findings of these groups can be seen as identifying psychosocial interventions with demonstrated efficacy, the findings are as much a statement about the current status of research on psychosocial interventions as they are a statement about the interventions. It is almost certainly true that there are interventions, both already in practice and yet to be developed, that will be demonstrated to be effective. However, these treatments have not yet been subjected to the type of empirical evaluation that would yield the level of required evidentiary support to be classified as empirically supported. Consequently, as more treatments are developed and studied, the number of treatments that are empirically supported is likely to grow. Additional research will also identify the limits of effectiveness for treatments currently classified as empirically supported. Despite changes in research required to provide better evidence for clinical practice, empirically supported treatments represent a good choice when compared to clinical procedures currently lacking in empirical support.

—*Christopher J. Lonigan*

See also: *Behavior Therapy With Children and Youth (Vol. II), Efficacy, Effectiveness and Patient-Focused Research (Vols. I & III), Private Practice of Behavior Therapy (Vol. I), Single-Case Research (Vols. I & III), Treatment Failures in Behavior Therapy (Vols. I & III)*

Suggested Readings

Chambless, D. L., & Hollon, S. D. (1998). Defining empirically supported therapies. *Journal of Consulting and Clinical Psychology, 66,* 7–18.

Chambless, D. L., & Ollendick, T. H. (2001). Empirically supported psychological interventions: Controversies and evidence. *Annual Review of Psychology, 52,* 685–716.

Chorpita, B. F., Yim, L. M., Donkervoet, J. C., Arensdorf, A., Amundsen, M. J., McGee, C., et al. (2003). Toward large-scale implementation of empirically supported treatments for children: A review and observations by the Hawaii Empirical Basis to Services Task Force. *Clinical Psychology: Science and Practice, 9,* 165–190.

Kazdin, A. E., & Weisz, J. R. (1998). Identifying and developing empirically supported child and adolescent treatments. *Journal of Consulting and Clinical Psychology, 66,* 19–36.

Lonigan, C. J., & Elbert, J. C. (Eds.). (1998). Special Issue on Empirically Supported Psychosocial Interventions for Children. *Journal of Clinical Child Psychology, 27,* 138–226.

Nathan, P. E., & Gorman, J. M. (Eds.). (2002). *A guide to treatments that work.* New York: Oxford University Press.

Spirito, A. (Ed.). (1999). Empirically supported treatments in pediatric psychology (Special Issue). *Journal of Pediatric Psychology, 24,* 87–174.

Task Force on Promotion and Dissemination of Psychological Procedures, Division of Clinical Psychology, American Psychological Association. (1995). Training in and dissemination of empirically validated psychological treatments: Report and recommendations. *The Clinical Psychologist, 48,* 3–23.

Task Force on Psychological Intervention Guidelines, American Psychological Association (1995). *Template for developing guidelines: Interventions for mental disorders and psychosocial aspects of physical disorders.* Washington, DC: American Psychological Association.

ERRORLESS COMPLIANCE TRAINING

DESCRIPTION OF THE STRATEGY

Errorless compliance training was developed to provide an alternative to traditional parent management training approaches for reducing antisocial responses in children. Conventional parent management training involves several components, including teaching parents to reward child prosocial behavior and to use decelerative consequences, such as time-out, following child oppositionality. Notwithstanding the demonstrated efficacy of such strategies, the use of consequences like time-out may at times be contraindicated, as some children demonstrate high levels of resistance to parent enforcement of the consequence, potentially resulting in parent-child confrontation and conflict. Given that much developmental research on parenting points to power assertive and coercive parenting styles as early antecedents to future antisocial child behavior, an effective intervention that reduces the need for physically enforced consequences could circumvent prospective negative outcomes.

Errorless compliance training, which can be completed in a parent group or individual format, offers management of child behavior without coercion. With this approach, each parent is asked to categorize a range of household requests into four compliance probability levels (Level 1: "almost always complies," Level 2: "usually complies," Level 3: "occasionally complies," or Level 4: "rarely complies") based on the current compliance of the child. From this list of parent-rated requests, the clinician selects six to eight requests from each probability level and includes them on an individualized data sheet for recording the results of the parent-conducted compliance assessment. Parents are then trained in request-delivery guidelines, including issuing requests only once in a polite but firm voice, using single rather than multiple component requests, and using the imperative rather than the interrogative. Parents are also taught how to record their child's response to the request (compliance or noncompliance). Parents deliver the 24 to 32 requests to their children over the next 2 weeks. This compliance assessment typically results in data on child compliance to about 5 to 10 repetitions of each of the requests. For each child, the clinician calculates the probability of compliance to each request and sequences the requests according to likelihood of child compliance. Requests are then divided into four probability levels, from Level 1 (high probability of compliance) to Level 4 (low probability of compliance).

Following this assessment of compliance probabilities, parents are trained in the use of treatment procedures, including reinforcing compliance (immediate, consistent, enthusiastic, and effective praise or other reinforcement), ignoring noncompliance (no punitive consequences, responding as though the request had never been delivered), and avoiding requests from subsequent levels (using gentle prompts to complete essential tasks that involve requests from succeeding levels). Treatment begins with parent delivery of a high density of Level 1 requests (e.g., "give me five," "turn on the television") over the course of several days. Considering the high likelihood of child compliance to these requests, parents are able to provide intensive praise and affection contingent on frequent prosocial child responses. With the greatly reduced probability of noncompliance, consequences such as time-out are unnecessary, and minor problem responses can typically be ignored. Lower compliance probability levels (Levels 2 through 4) are introduced sequentially over several weeks at a slow enough pace to ensure that children continue to comply at high levels, enabling parents to maintain profuse praise and acknowledgment for child cooperative behavior. When Level 4 requests (those that had been associated with severe noncompliance before treatment) are introduced by parents in the last phase of treatment, children typically continue to comply at high levels. By means of this graduated and positive process, substantial treatment effects are obtained without need for punishment or constraints.

Errorless compliance training has several advantages over more traditional forms of parent training. The graduated nature of the approach teaches children to tolerate demand without avoidance responses, greatly reduces the need for coercion, and enhances parent-child relations. The approach provides parents with an effective alternative to physical constraint of the child (which is often necessary when using time-out with highly oppositional children), making it well suited for use by parents who are at risk for maltreatment of their children. In addition, errorless compliance training allows parents to focus almost exclusively on child successes and capabilities rather than on their failings and problem responses, creating a warm and supportive child environment that can benefit child self-concept. Finally, the approach is relatively simple for parents to use, requiring them to learn only a small skill set to produce meaningful behavior change in their children. The approach is therefore suitable for parents with cognitive, physical, or emotional difficulties that make parenting and child behavior management a challenge.

RESEARCH BASIS

Errorless compliance training has received extensive empirical support in time-series designs evaluating process and outcomes of treatment. The intervention has been demonstrated effective with children with conduct difficulties, children with developmental disabilities, child witnesses and victims of family violence, and children of brain-injured parents. Studies have found evidence of generalization of effects to requests not included in treatment, improvement of nontargeted problem behaviors, and maintenance of effects several months after treatment completion. Parents typically perceive their children to be much more cooperative after treatment.

RELEVANT TARGET POPULATIONS AND EXCEPTIONS

This intervention has the potential to benefit any child population that demonstrates oppositional behavior in the face of demands presented by parents. Errorless compliance training may not be as effective with children whose behavior has a more biological etiology (e.g., impulsivity that is unaffected by environmental modifications), although the approach can augment pharmacological intervention for these children.

COMPLICATIONS

The most common difficulty encountered by clinicians using this approach is the inability of some parents to conceive of changing child behavior without the use of punitive or constraining consequences. Thus, some parents have dropped out of treatment, even after seeing positive results, because of beliefs that one must not "spare the rod" when disciplining children. Such parents may require extensive support and education on the benefits of parent-child warmth and on parent-child relationship difficulties that can ensue from excessive punishment.

It is also important to note that to date, all studies on errorless compliance training have used time-series methodologies, sometimes with small numbers of subjects. Thus, future investigation using randomized control trials could provide an evaluation of the effects of this intervention in comparison with more traditional parent management approaches.

—*Joseph M. Ducharme*

See also: *Behavioral Treatment in Natural Environments (Vols. I & III), Differential Reinforcement of Other Behavior (Vols. I, II, & III), Generalization (Vols. I, II, & III)*

Suggested Readings

Ducharme, J. M. (1996). Errorless compliance training: Optimizing clinical efficacy. *Behavior Modification, 20,* 259–280.

Ducharme, J. M., Atkinson, L., & Poulton, L. (2000). Success-based, non-coercive treatment of oppositional behavior in children from violent homes. *Journal of the American Academy of Child and Adolescent Psychiatry, 39,* 995–1003.

Ducharme, J. M., Spencer, T., Davidson, A., & Rushford, N. (2002). Errorless compliance training: Building a cooperative relationship between brain-injured parents at risk for maltreatment and their oppositional children. *American Journal of Orthopsychiatry, 72,* 585–595.

ESCAPE TRAINING

DESCRIPTION OF THE STRATEGY

Escape training is a procedure for maintaining or increasing the future likelihood of a behavior. Escape training is based on the principle of negative reinforcement, where termination or reduction of an aversive stimulus is made contingent upon the occurrence of a specific behavior. As a result, the individual or organism being trained becomes more likely to display the behavior in the presence of the aversive stimulus (i.e., the behavior is reinforced).

Escape training can lead to gradual yet long-lasting increases in the frequency of the trained behavior within the training context. To maximize effectiveness, the behavior should immediately lead to a termination of the aversive stimulus. Combining escape training with positive reinforcement-based procedures may lead to quicker, longer-lasting, and more generalized changes in the behavior.

RESEARCH BASIS

Research on escape training has been conducted with both animal and human populations. In the classic animal experiment, a rat is placed in a cage and an aversive stimulus, such as a bright light or mild electrical shock, is presented. A lever on the wall of the cage is attached to a switch that either reduces the intensity of or terminates the aversive stimuli. When the aversive stimulus is presented, the rat may display a variety of behaviors, until eventually it presses the lever and the aversive stimulus is terminated. Upon subsequent presentations of the aversive stimulus, the rat is more likely to press the lever, exclusive of other behaviors that do not terminate the aversive.

Human researchers have demonstrated the effectiveness of escape training in teaching a variety of behaviors, including self-administration of medication, compliance with dental and medical procedures, increased work productivity, and socially appropriate play behaviors. While some studies involve termination of an experimenter-introduced aversive, such as a loud buzzer, many studies employ the termination of naturally occurring aversive stimuli, such as unpleasant dental procedures or nonpreferred work activities. Studies frequently combine escape training with other procedures, such as differential reinforcement or extinction, both to maximize learning and ameliorate potential negative side effects of aversive-based procedures.

RELEVANT TARGET POPULATIONS AND EXCEPTIONS

Escape training can be effective with children and adults with a wide range of intellectual, medical, and behavioral functioning. Escape training has been used effectively with individuals diagnosed with autism and other pervasive developmental disorders, mild to severe mental retardation, disruptive behavior disorders, and simple phobias. Aversive-based procedures, particularly those employing artificially introduced aversives, should be used with caution when teaching individuals with histories of severe aggressive behavior, as the procedure may elicit aggression. Aversive procedures may be indicated when powerful positive reinforcement based procedures have proven ineffective, particularly when the client's health, or even life, is at risk.

COMPLICATIONS

Escape training is subject to the same caveats as are all aversive-based procedures. The introduction of aversive stimuli may elicit aggression. Individuals may avoid teaching environments (and teachers) associated with aversive stimuli. Behaviors taught through escape training may be less likely to generalize outside the teaching environment than those taught with positive reinforcement. In addition, it may be difficult to ensure that the aversive stimuli are always available and delivered or that they are terminated appropriately, thus reducing the effectiveness of the procedure.

In addition to the above-mentioned clinical complications, the use of escape training presents some ethical dilemmas. The use of aversives, particularly artificially introduced aversive stimuli, frequently goes against community standards for acceptable treatment, particularly when used with young children or individuals with severe disabilities. Aversive-based procedures are typically subject to more regulatory oversight than more positive procedures and thus require more clinical and administrative oversight. In addition, teachers and other personnel may be either less likely to administer or more likely to abuse aversive-based procedures.

—Dennis C. Russo and Jeffrey Skowron

See also: *Aversion Relief (Vols. I & III), Aversive Conditioning (Vol. II), Extinction and Habituation (Vol. III), Operant Conditioning (Vols. I, II, & III)*

Suggested Readings

Allen, K. D., Loiben, T., Allen, S. J., & Robert, T. (1992). Dentist-implemented contingent escape for management of disruptive child behavior. *Journal of Applied Behavior Analysis, 25,* 629–636.

Catania, A. C. (1998). *Learning.* Upper Saddle River, NJ: Prentice Hall.

Cooper, J. O., Heron, T. E., & Heward, W. L. (1987). *Applied behavior analysis.* Upper Saddle River, NJ: Prentice Hall.

EVENT RECORDING

Event recording is simply a procedure for recording the occurrence of a behavior of interest. Skinner recognized the importance of precise recording of data when he studied animal operant behavior in the Skinner box. In most cases, the data were whenever an animal pressed a bar or pecked a key. He devised an event recorder called the cumulative recorder for just this purpose. The cumulative recorder produced graphs similar to that seen in Figure 1. This device was composed of a roll of paper that moved at a constant speed with a pen traveling across the paper. Whenever a response was emitted, a circuit was completed and an ink pen jumped up a unit of distance while the paper in the recorder continued to move at a constant rate. Whenever the pen reached the edge of the paper (the top of the graph), it reset itself by traveling back to baseline (the bottom of the graph).

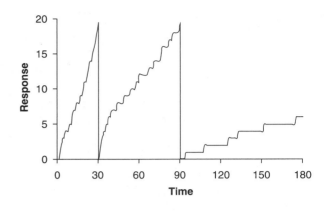

Figure 1   Representation of the output from a cumulative recorder

Skinner's event recorder had another pen that could also record when some preprogrammed experimenter initiated event occurred. Skinner's event recorder allowed him to study the rate of responding by examining the slope of the line generated. The steeper the slope, the higher the rate of behavior is.

HOW TO RECORD AN EVENT

While the cumulative recorder was an electromechanical device that automatically recorded animal behavior in the laboratory, the simplest kind of event recording is done by an observer making a tally mark on a piece of paper whenever the behavior of interest occurs. If all that is done is tallying the occurrence of a behavior over some observation period, the dependent measure is simply the frequency or number of behaviors. If the behavior is tallied on a piece of paper that has some indicator of not only the occurrence of the behavior but the time when it was observed, then the experimenter can study the rate of behavior along with its frequency. If other facets of the environment are noted, it may be possible to determine the relationship between the behavior of interest and possible controlling variables in the environment.

There are a number of pragmatic factors that make tallying each and every behavior difficult for an observer. If events occur very rapidly, are hard to discriminate, or do not have a discrete onset and offset, tally marks may produce inaccurate recordings. Often other recording strategies are used. There are times when not just the occurrence of an event is of interest.

Duration recording is when how long an event takes is recorded. If one is trying to establish positive behaviors such as exercise, then start and stop times of each episode of exercise are the parameters of interest. There may be circumstances where monitoring the duration is useful when one wants to decrease total time spent at some nonproductive activity such as total amount of time spent watching television.

Partial duration recording is used when there may not be a clear onset or offset of a behavior. A behavior is counted if it occurred at any time during a specified interval. For example, a teacher might record whether a particular child exhibited cooperative play behavior at any time during 5-minute intervals at recess. This method of event recording is not particularly precise, since the recording procedure doesn't allow one to distinguish between six episodes of cooperative play behavior or one episode that might have occurred during the interval. Since at least one behavior of interest occurred during the specified interval, a tally is recorded.

Whole interval recording sits in contrast with partial interval recording. For an event (a behavior) to be recorded as having occurred, it must last for the whole duration of the interval. For example, napping for a specified duration is counted only if the child is in bed for the entire specified interval.

Momentary time sampling is another procedure often used for high-frequency behavior. Behavior is recorded if the behavior is occurring at the moment a specified time interval elapses.

TECHNOLOGY AND EVENT RECORDING

The Skinner box and the cumulative recorder were sophisticated technologies for the times. Many important behavioral studies have been conducted using a research assistant and the paper and pencil tally method. Other simple tally methods have been used ranging from using a wrist golf counter to track how many cigarettes someone smokes to a stopwatch to measure the duration of tantrums a child exhibits. To add the element of time to behavioral observation strategies as simple as having a series of cooking timers go off to prompt observations have been used.

However, as technology advances, the scope of events considered important to scientists that are amenable to counting have greatly expanded, as has the sophistication of the equipment used to record the events of interest. While it is not possible to describe all the current technologies that could be used as event recorders, some examples illustrate how much the

field is advancing. In behavioral pharmacology studies, an investigator may be interested in studying the effects of a drug on the motor behavior of a rat. Making use of magnetic and optical sensors, it is now possible to continuously record the movement a lab animal makes under different conditions (doses of a drug). The total distance in all directions per unit time can now be measured as a response to the drug. It would be almost impossible for a human observer to accurately make these measurements efficiently. Responses previously considered unobservable are now measurable. For example, it is possible for physicians, neurophysiologists, and neuropsychologists to record the oxygen utilization of specific parts of the brain in response to a variety of stimuli using advanced computerized imaging technologies.

The simple advent of video recording technologies now allows a researcher to record and code complex chains of behaviors to study chains of behaviors that were previously too complicated to monitor accurately. Many dedicated microcomputer devices and software programs are available that can store a variety of codes that can be applied to what is observed on a video recorder. For example, it is possible to watch an interaction between a parent and child and at the end of each one's turn at interacting the recording can stop and prompt the observer to enter one or more of a list of potential codes indicating an event. The recording can be replayed as many times as needed to code all the behaviors each person exhibits.

Certainly, profoundly important interventions have resulted from simple event recording procedures combined with single-subject designs. However, the ability to code long chains of events allows for a variety of data analytic strategies to determine how sequences of behaviors can mutually influence each other. For example, it is possible to determine if a particular response by a parent increases, decreases, or has no effect on a child's behavior. Through sophisticated event recording and analysis strategies such as these, it is possible to tailor intervention strategies to particular dyadic interactions.

WHAT CONSTITUTES AN EVENT?

In the early days of event recording, what actually constituted the event was generally operationally defined. In the Skinner box, any response that completed a circuit was an event. In the case of rat responses, whenever a rat pressed a bar with sufficient pressure, a circuit was completed and the event recorder (the cumulative recorder) moved the pen up one unit on the paper record. It did not matter whether the bar press was exploratory behavior by the rat or under the control of some other experimental factor. Skinner developed the Skinner box to study the effects of reinforcement schedules on the rate and perseverance of behavior among other purposes.

When the application of operant principles moved from the laboratory to clinical and educational settings, the nature of the event still often remained easy to discriminate and record. In early research on the study of self-injurious behavior by researchers such as Sidney Bijou and later O. Ivar Lovaas, the target behavior of interest was often of a dramatic and distinct topography such as a child banging his or her head against a hard object like a wall, desk, or a self-delivered blow to the head. These behaviors presented little difficulty for an observer. When researchers noted one of these clearly identifiable behaviors, they used a pencil and a piece of paper or a mechanical counter. A pencil and paper were frequently a perfectly satisfactory event recorder. The meaningfulness of the event itself was in the topography of the behavior. When an autistic child banged his or her head against the wall or hit himself or herself, no one debated whether such an event should be considered injurious or whether it had occurred.

Recording events is not always so straightforward. In educational settings, researchers and applied behavior analysts often study behaviors that impede learning. Disruptive behaviors are a concern for teachers and students alike. If one were trying to record the occurrence of disruptive behaviors, the obvious question emerges: What does one mean by a disruptive behavior? In some cases, the topography (the form or appearance) of the behavior is clearly disruptive and can easily be discriminated and recorded by an observer. Loud talking or shouting without being recognized by the teacher is unambiguously disruptive to the classroom and would be recorded with little error. A researcher could create a list of discrete behaviors that should be counted as disruptive. The accuracy of the recording would be a function of how well the behaviors were defined and discriminated by the observers.

When behaviors are defined independently of the context in which they occur, they form a topographical class (e.g., disruptive behaviors). Some behaviors may be easily recognized while others less so. For example, if "bothering neighbors" is listed as a disruptive behavior, it may be difficult to know when that has occurred. If a child taps a neighbor on the shoulder, that is easy to record as an instance of bothering. It may be less clear whether prolonged staring at a neighbor is disruptive, since in reality it depends on whether the definition of the researcher is sufficiently clear.

The example of disruptive behavior raises a more complicated issue when considering event recording. While the researcher may define topographical behaviors as constituting instances of disruptive behavior, the real consideration is whether a behavior, regardless of whether it is on the list of behaviors of interest, actually disrupts the classroom. A student could engage in an entirely different behavior that appears topographically to be nondisruptive, such as withdrawing from classroom activities by putting his or her head down on the desk for extended periods. If this behavior caused the teacher to ask the student to reengage or distracted students around him or her, it could have as much disruptive function as talking out loud when not called upon. When behaviors are studied on the basis of what function they serve, rather than only their topography, they are counted as members of a functional class. This makes it much more difficult for an observer to be certain when a behavior of interest has occurred, since not only the occurrence or nonoccurrence must be noted but also whether the behavior functions in a particular manner. If functional classes are the object of study, then the observer must make the determination of the function rather than relying on the appearance of a behavior.

As long as behavior that was to be recorded was clearly distinguishable and the rule was that it should be counted each time it occurred, event recording occurred with relatively little error. The major sources of error were equipment failure if the events were mechanically recorded, or observer error due to inattention or distraction. Assuming observer errors were small and randomly distributed over time and events, this was not a very troubling source of error. This nonsystematic error affects the reliability of the data. For our purposes, reliability refers to the degree to which multiple observers agree on whether an event occurred or did not occur. Little attention was paid to reliability in the early days of behavioral observation when the topography of the target behavior was so unambiguous. When it became apparent that it was not always easy for observers to agree on some classes of behavior, researchers began to calculate elementary reliability statistics such as percent agreement rates between two observers [agreements/(agreements + disagreements) × 100]. When researchers depart from defining behaviors in terms of clear topography, reliability often decreases.

However, reliability of observations is not the only consideration to which a researcher must attend. The other issue important in data collection and analytic inference is that of elements of construct validity. A construct is a hypothetical explanation for how observations and measurement procedures work together to supply an explanation of some phenomenon of interest. Acting out or disruptiveness as an explanation for behavior is a construct. Constructs have generally been eschewed by behavior analysts, yet as behavioral principles are applied in more complex settings, it is inevitable that constructs will be used as explanations. To the extent that constructs are not well defined in terms of the relationship between putative causes and measurement or observational strategies, the science will suffer. There are many types of validity that relate to construct validity. Behavior analysts have concerned themselves primarily with two types of validity: face validity and social validity.

Face validity refers to the degree to which that which on the face of it properly reflects the construct. Though it has an intuitive appeal, face validity is the weakest test of construct validity. However, it is difficult to imagine face validity being absent in a valid construct. On the face of it, shouting and loud talking look like what one ought to mean when describing disruptive behavior. It is harder to determine if a smirk or a disrespectful tone of voice is part of the construct of disruptive behavior. Yet, until one has determined the scope of those measurement procedures that constitute the construct, the person functioning as an event recorder does not know whether or not to record a smirk as an instance of disruptive behavior.

The other form of validity with which behavior analysts have concerned themselves is social validity. Social validity refers to the favorable impact that targeted behavior change produces for the consumer of services when it occurs. There is little question that the impact of reducing self-injurious behavior has a positive impact on the consumer of services. Data recorded documenting the decrease in head banging stand on their own as documenting a benefit. As behaviors targeted for change are part of functional classes that have less obvious consumer advantage, what and how to record its occurrence becomes more difficult to demonstrate purely on the basis of counts.

ILLUSTRATION

An investigator is studying the degree to which specific behavioral parenting practices shape collaborative activities between siblings who are within 18 months of age of each other when both children are less than 5 years of age. The researcher conducts the following study. The investigator hypothesizes that ignoring collaborative behavior and reprimanding noncollaborative behavior interfere with collaborative child interactions, while praising collaborative interactions and modeling collaborative activities increase the likelihood of such behavior. Two observers are trained to continuously record the behaviors of interest. One observer records the presence or absence of collaborative interaction defined as nonconflictual touching, talking, or sharing while being within 3 feet of each other. Noncollaborative interaction is defined as the children engaging in conflictual or isolated behavior. The second observer codes the actions of each parent as either praising, ignoring, modeling, reprimanding, or other (undefined topography). During a three-evening baseline period, the parents are instructed to behave as they normally do. A 4-minute partial duration recording procedure is used for a 90-minute period. This allows the investigator to determine the rate of collaborative interaction and the frequency of how the parents behave. On the fourth night, the parents are shown a training film instructing them on how to positively attend to and model collaborative interactions and to decrease criticism and reprimands. The same event recording procedure is used for an additional three evening intervals. Two types of information are analyzed. First, the rate of collaborative interactions between the children is plotted for the three baseline evening periods and is noted to be stable. On the same plot, the parenting behaviors are plotted. On the fourth day, the parents' positive attending and modeling increase and the reprimanding and ignoring behavior decrease. The frequency of collaborative interaction between the children increases. Data collection continues for a total of 3 days with the new contingencies in place. At this point, the contingencies were reversed so that the parents returned to their normal behavior. The parents' and children's behavior were again recorded over a two-evening period, and the rate of collaborative interactions between the children returned to a lower level near the baseline. The positive contingencies were again reinstated and the collaborative interactions again increased. This study design (an A-B-A-B design) indicated that parental behavior exercised substantial behavioral control over the children's collaborative behavior. Had the event recording procedure included a continuous recording of activity with time information also recorded. thus allowing the exact order of parent and child behaviors to be recorded, a *lag sequential* analysis could have been used to permit a more sophisticated causal analysis of the role of the parents' contingent responding.

SUMMARY

In any scientific investigation, the collection of data is a critically important factor. If data are not collected accurately, then the data will reflect not only the phenomenon of interest but some degree of error as well. The more an observation is recorded with error, the more difficult it is to identify regularities in data. In its simplest form, there is a one-to-one correspondence between the occurrence of an event and the recording of the event. As the application of behavioral principles and the procedures of event recording move into more complex environments and address more complex systems, conceptual and measurement challenges will increasingly confront researchers.

—*William C. Follette*

See also: *Behavioral Assessment (Vols. I, II, & III), Motor Activity and Behavioral Assessment (Vols. I & III), Operant Conditioning (Vols. I, II, & III)*

Suggested Readings

Bakeman, R., & Gottman, J. M. (1997). *Observing interaction: An introduction to sequential analysis* (2nd ed.). New York: Cambridge University Press.

Ferster, C. B., & Skinner, B. F. (1957). *Schedules of reinforcement.* New York: Appleton-Century-Crofts.

Krauss, R. M., Morrel-Samuels, P., & Hochberg, J. (1988). VIDEOLOGGER: A computerized multichannel event recorder for analyzing videotapes. *Behavior Research Methods, Instruments & Computers, 20,* 37–40.

Skinner, B. F. (1938). *The behavior of organisms.* New York: Appleton-Century-Crofts.

Suen, H. K., & Ary, D. (1989). *Analyzing quantitative behavioral observation data.* Hillsdale, NJ: Erlbaum.

EXPOSURE AND RESPONSE PREVENTION

Exposure and response prevention (ERP) is a behavioral technique commonly used to treat anxiety disorders, including OCD, specific phobia, and PTSD among children and adolescents. In general, children with anxiety disorders have developed a fearful reaction to a nonthreatening situation or object, perhaps because of a chance association with a threatening or anxiety-provoking object. The lack of threat that the innocuous situation poses and the interference that the fear causes in the child's life makes the anxious response maladaptive. Over time, the child's anxiety may generalize to other situations or objects, further exacerbating the impact that the fear has on his or her life. To cope with this emotional distress, the child may develop unproductive behaviors, such as compulsive hand washing because of fears of germs and contamination, which the child associates with anxiety-reducing effects. Children also try to avoid the anxiety-provoking situation, further limiting their involvement in age-appropriate activities. With each episode of avoidance or escape, the child experiences a reduction in anxiety, which reinforces these avoidant responses. As long as the feared object is avoided, the child never has the opportunity to encounter the situation or object without anxiety.

The basic principle of exposure is to allow children to experience sustained contact with the feared object so that, over time, they learn that the object is not threatening and that they can successfully manage their emotional arousal in the future. With repeated and prolonged exposure, children learn that there are no negative consequences from exposure and that anxiety responses are reduced until they are eventually extinguished. In response prevention, children are prevented from avoiding the object or from engaging in any unproductive behaviors until the cycle of exposure-avoidance is broken and they can encounter the object without distress. While teaching children that the principles of ERP can assist with treatment, young children may not understand the theoretical underpinnings. Hence, treatment may be applied to younger children without explaining the principles.

ERP can be applied in different forms. For example, treatment can involve one long continuous exposure session or multiple shorter exposure sessions. Furthermore, there may be longer or shorter durations of time between each treatment session. It is unclear from the research literature what is the optimal number of exposure sessions. Other variations to treatment include the use of graduated versus intense exposure to the feared object. In the graduated exposure approach, the child ranks different anxiety-provoking situations in a hierarchical order from least to most anxiety provoking. Treatment begins with exposing the child to the least anxiety-provoking situation. Exposure to the feared object or situation may be in vivo or imagined by the child with the therapist's guidance. In vivo exposure produces more powerful effects because of the real-life applications. However, personal contact with the object or situation may be contraindicated in some situations, as in the case of abuse or where there is a risk of harm (e.g., petting a pit bull to overcome fear of the dog). Exposure to situations that the child imagines with the therapist's guidance may take longer to yield effects, but it is effective for situations in which live exposure is precluded. The therapist can help make the imagined scenes seem more realistic to the child by describing the scenes in vivid detail, perhaps including descriptions of the texture and sounds of objects. Guided imagery in which the therapist is actively involved in monitoring the child's level of anxiety in response to exposure and is also preventing the child from avoiding exposure helps to enhance treatment efficacy. The therapist may ask the child to describe in detail the scenes that are being imagined to ensure that the child is not avoiding anxiety-provoking scenes. As the child masters exposure to the situation without experiencing anxiety, then the child graduates to the next situation on the hierarchy until the child has been systematically desensitized to all the scenes.

In contrast to this sequential approach, the intense exposure approach involves exposing the child to the most anxiety-provoking situation on the hierarchy first and maintaining exposure until the child can tolerate the situation without distress. Graduated exposure tends to be preferred over intense exposure, however, because intense exposure may intensify the child's fear and subsequently cause the child to resist further treatment. The graduated approach also allows the child to learn techniques to overcome his or her anxiety. These techniques may involve muscle relaxation exercises and engaging in adaptive self-talk while learning to tolerate the situation or object.

ERP is effective for treating OCD, specific phobias, separation anxiety, and PTSD. In some cases,

ERP has been more effective than pharmacological treatments for OCD. Treatment gains may be more enduring with ERP because children learn adaptive coping skills in the process. Children and adolescents diagnosed with a specific phobia show significant improvement in as few as one or two sessions of exposure therapy, regardless of whether or not their parents participate in treatment. ERP also reduces children's separation anxiety and enhances their ability to function independently. Children and adolescents with PTSD also respond well to ERP, which is currently considered a necessary component of treatment for this disorder.

Developmental differences should be considered during the planning and implementation of ERP. For example, it is important to assess the child's level of cognitive functioning, social maturity, and his or her ability to maintain attention during treatment. Younger children may require more directions to focus on the treatment task than adolescents. Older children and adolescents may require more time discussing the impact that their symptoms have on their social functioning. Parents should be included in their children's treatment so that they can learn how to reinforce their children's successful treatment gains. Some argue that parental involvement may actually be counterproductive because the parents inadvertently reinforce the child's avoidant or unproductive ritualistic behaviors. Nevertheless, the parents need to be educated about the reinforcing effects of their behavior on their children and how they can reinforce their children's newly acquired adaptive coping skills.

Comorbid psychiatric disorders, especially externalizing disorders such as oppositional defiant disorder, can interfere with treatment. However, recent research suggests that neither externalizing behavior problems nor other anxiety disorders were related to treatment outcome for children and adolescents treated for OCD. Comorbid depressive symptoms, however, are associated with lower rates of success and interfere with the child's ability to focus and learn that the anxiety-provoking situation is not threatening. It is recommended, therefore, to treat the depressive symptoms to maximize the effect of ERP for anxiety-related disorders.

—*Laura Stoppelbein and Leilani Greening*

See also: *Exposure (Vols. I & III), Extinction (Vol. II), Foa, Edna B. (Vol. I), Relapse Prevention (Vols. I, II, & III)*

Suggested Readings

Berman, S. L., Weems, C. F., Silverman, W. K., & Kurtines, W. (2000). Predictors of outcome in exposure-based cognitive and behavioral treatments for phobic and anxiety disorders in children. *Behavior Therapy, 31,* 713–731.

March, J. S., & Mulle, K. (1998). *OCD in children and adolescents: A cognitive-behavioral treatment manual.* New York: Guilford Press.

Ost, L., Svensson, L., Hellstrom, K., & Lindwall, R. (2001). One-session treatment of specific phobias in youths: A randomized clinical trial. *Journal of Consulting and Clinical Psychology, 69,* 814–824.

EXTINCTION

DESCRIPTION OF THE STRATEGY

Extinction is a behavior modification procedure used to decrease the frequency with which a behavior occurs. The basic idea is a relatively simple one: If the reinforcer(s), positive or negative, maintaining a behavior are removed, the behavior will decrease. Extinction occurs often in daily life (e.g., a child stops pressing the buttons on a handheld video game shortly after the batteries run out) and is regularly used without explicit recognition (e.g., when children who reinforce each others' deviant behavior are placed in separate groups on a school field trip). In this entry we will focus on the explicit use of extinction to decrease problem behavior.

The use of extinction involves two steps. The first step is to determine the reinforcer maintaining the problem behavior. When possible, relevant functional assessment methodologies should be utilized. However, sometimes assessment of the reinforcer(s) maintaining the behavior must be done via naturalistic observation or, depending on the setting, caretaker descriptions during a clinical interview.

Once the reinforcer maintaining the problem behavior has been identified, the second step in implementing extinction is to stop the delivery of the reinforcer. In discontinuing the relationship between the problematic response and the reinforcer, it is important to note that the behavior of the person implementing the procedure will differ, depending on whether a positive reinforcer (e.g., tantrums result in the child getting what he or she wants) or negative reinforcer (e.g., tantrums result in the removal of parental demands) is maintaining the problem behavior. Discontinuing a positive reinforcer involves withholding it (e.g., no longer acquiescing to the child's wants), while discontinuing a negative reinforcer involves failing to remove it (e.g., maintaining the demands despite the tantrum).

RESEARCH BASIS

Extinction has been the focus of a great deal of nonhuman animal research and is receiving increased attention by applied researchers. Extinction is a component in many effective behavior change interventions, offering a nonpunishment-based method for decreasing problem behavior. As mentioned earlier, extinction involves identifying and discontinuing the reinforcer maintaining the problem behavior. In practice, however, extinction is often most effective when combined with reinforcement procedures. Most commonly, extinction is coupled with reinforcement of an alternative replacement behavior (e.g., tantrums are no longer reinforced, but the child may be reinforced for politely asking for things he or she desires such as juice or snacks), reinforcement of any other behavior (e.g., tantrums are no longer reinforced, but the child earns a quarter toward purchase of a small item at the end of the shopping trip for each 5-minute period that he or she is tantrum free), or noncontingent presentation of reinforcers (e.g., self-injury no longer produces attention, but the child is given attention every 30 seconds).

Extinction weakens performance of behavior but does not completely wipe out or erase prior learning. The weakening effect of extinction is generally gradual, requiring consistent implementation and a number of nonreinforced instances of the behavior for extinction to have its effects. No new behavior is directly trained via extinction; hence its frequent use in conjunction with reinforcement-based procedures. While combining extinction and reinforcement-based procedures often expedites the decline of the problem-behavior (and may help reduce some of the side effects of extinction discussed below), at times it is unclear whether the problem behavior has really been weakened or is simply not occurring because the alternative procedures have altered the opportunity or motivation to engage in the problem behavior. The concern is that the problem behavior will reoccur at the next available opportunity (e.g., when in a new setting) or when the motivational conditions change (e.g., when other reinforcers are not available). Thus, it appears important that, when possible, procedures are maintained across settings and that the alternative behaviors trained to replace those being extinguished are ones that are likely to produce consistent reinforcement across settings.

The extinction process may also be expedited when it is readily detectable to the child that conditions have changed. For instance, with a child who has sufficient receptive language skills, the procedure, and any incentives, can be described to the child. Of course, the verbal description must be backed up by consistent implementation across relevant settings.

RELEVANT TARGET POPULATIONS, TARGET BEHAVIORS, AND EXCEPTIONS

Extinction is most appropriate for behaviors maintained by identifiable and removable reinforcers. Because of the development of functional assessment methods that allow for the careful determination of the reinforcers maintaining many aberrant behaviors, much of the research on extinction comes from intervention studies attempting to reduce maladaptive behavior engaged in by some individuals with mental retardation, brain injury, autism, or other developmental disabilities. However, extinction can and has been incorporated in behavior modification and parent training interventions for reducing child problems like excessive whining or complaining, task refusal, and bedtime refusal. Parents learn to ignore whining and complaining and maintain expectations that the child comply with expected demands. Parents do not attend to, or wait progressively longer intervals to attend to, a child that is not settling at bedtime. Some parent training interventions teach parents to avoid power struggles, prolonged arguments, and extended tantrums by ignoring attention-getting responses of the child that often begin such aversive give-and-take sequences. (Positive attention, reinforcement for appropriate behavior, and other contingency management strategies are also incorporated as necessary.)

One circumstance where extinction appears inappropriate is with aberrant behavior that is automatically reinforcing (via its immediate sensory effects), because it can be very difficult to block or remove access to these reinforcers. Some researchers have developed ingenious, minimally invasive ways to stop the automatic sensory properties of some behaviors of developmentally disabled individuals, but this is very difficult to do. Another potential exception is with extreme self-injurious behavior or any other behavior that places the individual, or others, at significant danger or risk. Extinction takes some time to be effective, and it is not ethical to allow a behavior to continue that might cause significant bodily harm to the individual or to others. It is important to recognize that these may be the more extreme cases, as extinction has been employed effectively in the treatment of numerous self-injurious behaviors.

COMPLICATIONS

When using extinction, one must be aware of and be prepared for the possibility of an extinction burst (i.e., a temporary initial increase in frequency, duration, and/or intensity of the problem behavior) or extinction-induced aggression or agitation (i.e., an emotional reaction to the onset of extinction). It is important to be prepared for these side effects of extinction such that the procedure is not discontinued prematurely, unwittingly reinforcing escalation of the problem behavior. These side effects tend to dissipate relatively quickly and appear significantly less likely when reinforcement-based procedures are combined with extinction.

Because extinction often requires tolerating a short-term surge in the problem behavior, it may be difficult for some to implement. For example, it may be challenging for parents to allow their child to cry and fuss when extinguishing nighttime settling problems.

Finally, sometimes even when an extinction procedure appears to have been initially successful, the behavior seemingly spontaneously appears again. This is often temporary and happens upon initial reentry into a setting where extinction has occurred. However, if the reappearance of the problem behavior continues, it is necessary to once again examine the contingencies surrounding the behavior. Sometimes a source of reinforcement (e.g., other caretakers) was missed or multiple reinforcers are maintaining the behavior.

—Scott T. Gaynor and Amanda Harris

See also: *Exposure (Vols. I & III), Exposure and Response Prevention (Vol. II), Extinction and Habituation (Vols. I & III), Operant Conditioning (Vols. I, II, & III), Schedule-Induced Behavior (Vol. III), Schedules of Reinforcement (Vols. I, II, & III), Skinner, Burrhus Frederic (Vols. I, II, & III)*

Suggested Readings

Lerman, D. C., & Iwata, B. A. (1996). Developing a technology for the use of operant extinction in clinical settings: An examination of basic and applied research. *Journal of Applied Behavior Analysis, 29,* 345–382.

Lerman, D. C., Iwata, B. A., & Wallace, M. D. (1999). Side effects of extinction: Prevalence of bursting and aggression during the treatment of self-injurious behavior. *Journal of Applied Behavior Analysis, 32,* 1–8.

Martin, G., & Pear, J. (2003). Decreasing a behavior with extinction. In G. Martin & J. Pear, *Behavior modification: What it is and how to do it* (7th ed., pp. 58–72). Upper Saddle River, NJ: Prentice Hall.

Mindell, J. A. (1999). Empirically supported treatments in pediatric psychology: Bedtime refusal and night wakings in young children. *Journal of Pediatric Psychology, 24,* 465–481.

Williams, C. D. (1959). The elimination of tantrum behavior by extinction procedures. *Journal of Abnormal and Social Psychology, 59,* 269.

FACIAL SCREENING

The treatment of self-injurious behavior is often a daunting task for therapists working with autistic, mentally handicapped, and organically disabled children or adults. Numerous techniques such as overcorrection, time-out, water spray, aversive tickling, and contingent restraint have been used to try to suppress and eliminate self-injurious behaviors. The technique of facial screening has also been used and was the focus of several reviews and studies beginning in the 1970s and 1980s.

Facial screening is a procedure that involves visual occlusion, that is, covering an individual's face (usually with a terry cloth towel or opaque bib) for a specific amount of time as a consequence of self-injurious or other problem behavior. Theoretically, facial screening serves as a mild punisher. To employ the technique, the patient and the therapist sit in chairs closely facing each other. A bib or towel is placed or tied around the patient's neck and the therapist lifts the bib up and holds it over the patient's face as a consequence of the individual engaging in self-injurious behavior. Blindfolds have also been used. The length of time that the facial screen is applied is normally from 30 seconds to 1 minute, but longer time periods have been used.

The development of facial screening came about as an alternative to other types of contingent punishment because other punishments were either too aversive (e.g., shock therapy) or proved ineffective. One of the advantages of facial screening is that the patient is not subjected to any physical pain or danger (and thus eliminates the need for the therapist to apply a physical punisher in response to self-injurious behavior). Facial screening is thought to produce a rapid suppression of self-injurious behaviors in patients. It is also cost effective, portable, and relatively easy to use. A disadvantage of this technique is that it may be considered aesthetically unappealing. Care also needs to be taken to prevent accidents such as falls if blindfolds are used.

Although facial screening has received little current attention in the research literature, several case studies and single-case design experiments suggest that facial screening may be effective in reducing the occurrence of several types of self-injurious behaviors such as face slapping, hand clapping, thumb biting, and hair picking. It has also been shown to be effective in treating trichotillomania and compulsions but has been reported to be ineffective in the treatment of stereotypy. Because facial screening has been found to reduce self-injurious behaviors quickly, the effects of its use should be noticeable after its first few applications. Failure to decrease the number and/or frequency of the self-injurious behaviors after applying facial screening is thus usually indicative that facial screening may be an inappropriate technique for that specific individual.

—*Carl F. Weems and Natalie M. Costa*

See also: *Aversion Relief (Vols. I & III), Extinction and Habituation (Vol. III), Operant Conditioning (Vols. I, II, & III), Punishment (Vol. II)*

Suggested Readings

Demetral, G. D., & Lutzker, J. R. (1981). The parameters of facial screening in treating self-injurious behavior. *Behavior Research of Severe Developmental Disabilities, 1,* 261–277.

Horton, S. V. (1987). Reduction of disruptive mealtime behavior by facial screening. *Behavior Modification, 11,* 53–64.

Lutzker, J. R. (1978). Reducing self-injurious behaviour by facial screening. *American Journal of Mental Deficiency, 82,* 510–513.

Lutzker, J. R., & Wesch, D. (1983). Facial screening: History and critical review. *Australia and New Zealand Journal of Developmental Disabilities,* 9, 209–223.

FADING

DESCRIPTION OF THE STRATEGY

Fading is the gradual transfer of control from one stimulus to another. The procedure is useful when a stimulus or prompt exerts control over a desired response, and the goal is to shift that control to a different stimulus that occurs in the natural setting. The first step is to identify stimuli in the presence of which the target response occurs. Frequently, the response can be emitted in the presence of "prompts," stimuli that guide the response. The prompts could be physical, gestural, verbal, or modeled. The prompt could even be a general setting that evokes the behavior. Prompts facilitate correct performance and provide the opportunity for reinforcement. For example, a child may ride a two-wheel bicycle while a parent runs alongside and holds the handlebars with two hands, or a child with selective mutism may speak in the presence of his or her parents but not when the parents are absent. In each case, the target response occurs, but not in the desired natural setting.

The second step is to identify a stimulus in the presence of which the response should occur. To maintain the response, select a stimulus, or setting, that the child encounters in the natural environment. For example, the goal is for the child to ride the bicycle without the parent's physical prompt, and the goal is for the child with selective mutism to speak in the presence of the teacher at school.

Select an effective reinforcer and then implement the fading procedure. Start with the stimulus or prompt that currently has control over the behavior. The response is emitted and reinforced. Then successively remove, or fade, the prompt. Specific dimensions of the stimulus prompt or entire settings can be faded. For example, the parent may run alongside the bicycle holding a handlebar with one hand instead of two. Or the parent and the child with selective mutism

may visit the teacher in the classroom. While the three of them converse, the parent may momentarily step away a few feet while the teacher and child continue talking. In some cases, a new stimulus is gradually introduced or faded in. For example, the teacher may also gradually move closer to the child with selective mutism. Across many learning trials, the prompts that control the behavior are gradually faded away (or faded in) until the desired stimulus (i.e., the bicycle or the teacher in these examples) controls the response. Fading steps are gradual, so an advantage of fading is that children may learn to make the desired response in the presence of new stimuli without committing many errors. This is important because errors use time, prevent positive feedback, and can elicit emotional responses incompatible with learning.

RESEARCH BASIS

Although an abundance of research supports the effective use of fading, there is little research to guide the rate at which fading should be carried out. If there are too few steps or if the prompts are faded too quickly, then the child will make errors and the program may have to revert to earlier steps. Conversely, if there are too many steps or the fading is too slow, then the child may become dependent on the prompts.

RELEVANT TARGET POPULATIONS AND EXCEPTIONS

Fading is a procedure used in everyday situations as well as therapeutic settings. The procedure is useful in classrooms, in programs for children with developmental disabilities, and in therapy programs for children with anxiety disorders. For example, in systematic desensitization, the stimuli that elicit fear are gradually faded in. Programs that teach language to children with autism often begin with verbal or gestural prompts that are faded away.

COMPLICATIONS

A common error occurs when the program stops before the child emits the behavior in the final natural environment. For example, the procedure for teaching a child to ride a bicycle will require trials on pavement if that is where the child will be riding. The procedure for teaching the child to speak in the school may require the presence of classmates as well as the teacher.

—Jeffrey S. Danforth

See also: *Applied Behavior Analysis (Vols. I, II, & III), Generalization (Vols. I, II, & III), Guided Mastery (Vols. I & III), Operant Conditioning (Vols. I, II, & III)*

Suggested Readings

Deitz, S. M., & Malone, L. W. (1985). Stimulus control terminology. *The Behavior Analyst, 8,* 259–264.

Kaplan, J. S., & Carter, J. (1995). *Beyond behavior modification: A Cognitive-behavioral approach to behavioral management in the school* (3rd ed.). Austin, TX: Pro-Ed.

Kazdin, A. E. (2001). *Behavior modification in applied settings* (6th ed.). Belmont, CA: Brooks/Cole.

Martin, G., & Pear, J. (2003). *Behavior modification: What it is and how to do it* (7th ed.). Saddle River, NJ: Prentice Hall.

Spiegler, M. D. (1998). *Contemporary behavior therapy* (3rd ed.). Pacific Grove, CA: Brooks/Cole.

FEEDBACK

Feedback is a process in which information about a person's performance is presented back to the individual. Providing information to individuals about their performance can serve as a reinforcer and can also be used in conjunction with other reinforcers and is often used in behavior therapy both combined with other reinforcers and alone (i.e., independent of other reinforcers). When used with other reinforcers, feedback can inform the individual which behaviors are considered suitable responses by those providing reinforcement and thus which behavioral responses will result in presentation of the reinforcer. When feedback is used independent of other reinforcers, positive feedback can give information to individuals about various aspects of their behaviors and socially reinforce the individuals' performance of those particular behaviors.

Numerous advantages are related to the use of feedback. Feedback is relatively easy to use and can be used with several different types of client populations and across a variety of therapeutic settings (e.g., individual therapy setting, school, inpatient hospital). Feedback can also be implemented in a variety of ways (e.g., when a specific performance criterion has to be met or when numerous criteria have to be met). Presentation is also flexible with regard to deciding when to provide feedback (e.g., directly after the behavior, intermittently after the criterion behavior, or on various time schedules: hourly, daily, weekly, monthly, yearly).

Feedback is often used in designing and implementing treatment programs when other types of reinforcement prove difficult to implement. For example, reinforcement programs that rely heavily on the use of extrinsic reinforcers (e.g., money or a token economy) can be costly to implement or may make it difficult to provide the reinforcer immediately after the correct behavioral response. Programs based on feedback have the option to provide feedback without extrinsic reinforcers feedback alone and thus can be inexpensive and the feedback can be presented immediately. Feedback reinforcers such as praise reduce the cost and the complexity involved in delivering a reinforcement program based on tangible reinforcers. An illustration of this can be found in a study in which observational feedback was used to increase the integrity of a treatment for behavioral disorders being provided by teachers in a special education setting. The treatment consisted of teachers providing social reinforcers in response to child on-task behavior. However, the consistency of the teacher's implementation of the treatment was low. Observational feedback based on how well they implemented the treatment program was given to teachers, and this feedback considerably increased the integrity of the treatment. Although feedback is relatively easy to use and can be applied to a variety of populations, the effects may be weak and inconsistent relative to other types of reinforcers.

Another area in which feedback is involved is biofeedback. Biofeedback involves presenting information to individuals about the status of their physical processes. For example, presenting feedback about the individual's heart rate provides information about the individual's level of arousal. Theoretically, individuals can use this information to help modify or control their level of arousal. Biofeedback has been used with blood pressure, heart rate, skin conductance, muscle tension, and brain activity for the treatment of stress, anxiety, and a variety of other medical and psychological problems.

—*Carl F. Weems and Natalie M. Costa*

See also: *Behavioral Treatment in Natural Environments (Vol. I), Guided Mastery (Vols. I & III), Problem-Solving Therapy (Vol. I), Reinforcement (Vols. I & III), Social and Interpersonal Skills Training (Vol. II), Social Competence Treatment: Externalizing Disorders (Vol. II), Social Effectiveness Training (Vols. I & III), Social Skills Training (Vols. I & III), Video Feedback (Vols. I & III)*

Suggested Readings

Jones, K. M., Wickstrom, K. F., & Friman, P. F. (1997). The effects of observational feedback on treatment integrity in school-based behavioral consultation. *School Psychology Quarterly, 12,* 316–326.

Kazdin, A. E. (2001). *Behavior modification in applied settings* (6th ed.). Belmont, CA: Wadsworth.

Weems, C. F. (1998). The evaluation of heart rate biofeedback using a multi-element design. *Journal of Behavior Therapy and Experimental Psychiatry, 29,* 157–162.

Werts, M. G., Wolery, M., Holcombe-Ligon, A., Vassilaros, M. A., & Billings, S. S. (1992). Efficacy of transition-based teaching with instructive feedback. *Education and Treatment of Children, 15,* 320–334.

FIVE-STEP PROCEDURE FOR STEALING

DESCRIPTION OF THE STRATEGY

The prevalence of stealing among children presenting at clinical settings has been estimated as high as 60%, making it one of the more common problems brought to the attention of mental health professionals. Developmental studies show that stealing activity tends to reach an early peak around age 3 and a later one between the ages of 8 and 11. Beyond early childhood, stealing rarely presents as an isolated issue; its clinical importance derives in part from its association with a broader constellation of conduct problems. The longer stealing persists, the greater the risk that it will represent an early step on a developmental progression toward chronic and increasingly serious antisocial behavior, usually combined with academic and occupational underachievement. The potential costs of this problem, therefore, are borne not only by the children and their families but also by the entire community.

Efforts to reduce stealing must contend with the difficulty of identifying the perpetrator of a (usually) covert act. An additional obstacle to monitoring covert stealing is parents' frequent receptiveness to alternative explanations for their child's new possessions, such as finding, receiving a gift, or "borrowing." Negative consequences for stealing are, therefore, typically not reliably or promptly delivered. For these reasons, a common first step in intervening with children who steal is to transfer the burden of proof to the child: Anything in the possession of the child that does not clearly belong to him or her is presumed to be stolen. This strategy renders diversionary tactics on the part of the child ineffective, a lesson considered sufficiently important to outweigh the occasional unjust accusation that may result.

Behavioral interventions for children who steal have usually involved some combination of confessing to the victim of the theft, restitution (payment for or return of the stolen object), and sometimes additional punishment for stealing or rewards for alternative behavior. The procedure developed at our clinic incorporates a confession and apology to the victim, restitution (i.e., return or replacement of the stolen object), two levels of overcorrection, and praise for alternative behavior. We institute a "presumption of guilt," as described above: Children are given no more than a few minutes to explain the possession of any object unfamiliar to the parent or other authority figure, and if the adult is not convinced that the child came by it honestly, the child is treated as if the object were stolen. By way of explanation, children are told that because they have stolen before, people can no longer assume that they are behaving honestly, and they must now earn their trust by remaining above suspicion.

Step 1: Identifying Instances of Stealing

First, search the child's bedroom with the child present. We recommend an amnesty for any stolen items found during this first search: If the child assists in getting the object returned to its rightful owner, no further consequences, as described in Steps 2 to 5, are imposed. The amnesty is intended as a gesture of fairness to the child so as not to impose penalties the child was unaware of at the time the item was stolen. The child then starts the program with a clean slate and full awareness of the consequences for any further acts of stealing.

Parents are advised to exercise particular vigilance in monitoring their children's possessions, in maintaining a staunchly skeptical position when challenging them to explain the presence of unfamiliar items, and in delivering consequences. We usually do not advocate routine searches of children's bedrooms for unspecified stolen items once the program begins, believing that this places the parent in an extremely punitive role, carries the presumption of guilt too far, and is, in most cases, unnecessary for the detection of theft. Careful observation of children's activities that are normally visible to the parent will usually be sufficient to provoke suspicion where it is warranted. A child carrying unfamiliar objects, bestowing them on friends, spending money the parent was not aware of, not eating the lunch taken to school, or engaging in secretive activities are all examples of observable behavior that should prompt questioning of the child. Searches of the child's private space (without the child present) may prove necessary if the parent has reason to suspect a hidden object.

Step 2: Apology for Theft

When the child's explanation of suspicious circumstances is not satisfactory, the parent must insist upon a confession and apology to the victim of the theft. Parents are instructed to accompany the child on this mission (immediately, if possible) to supervise the apology and restitution. The child must directly state to the victim that he or she stole the object and has come to apologize. Refusal by the child to cooperate with any aspect of this procedure, including those to be outlined below, results in aversive consequences such as the suspension of all privileges (including television viewing, video games, participation in desired activities, play with friends) until the procedure is completed. Parents should be prepared by the clinician to deliver these consequences should the need arise.

Step 3: Return of the Stolen Item

If the stolen item has not been consumed or otherwise damaged, it is returned at the time of the apology. If no longer intact, the item is replaced as closely as possible with a new object purchased at the child's expense, or some other form of restitution may be negotiated with the victim. A child who has stolen a peer's lunch in school, for example, might offer to prepare a lunch for the classmate the following day. Parents are cautioned not to conduct these interactions themselves but rather to rehearse them with the child beforehand, and do no more than prompt when necessary to ensure that the child delivers the appropriate apologies and reparations. Clarification of parent and child roles in this process may be accomplished via role plays provided as part of the family's instruction in the intervention.

Step 4: Restitution + 100%

In addition to simple restitution, the child is required to pay the victim an amount of money equal to the value (i.e., replacement cost) of the stolen item. Children who do not possess sufficient funds of their own are provided with household tasks beyond their usual responsibilities, which they must complete in order to earn the money for restitution payments from their parents. Alternatively, the child may be required to perform chores for the victim of the theft, which the latter considers sufficient to substitute for financial restitution as outlined in Step 3 and/or Step 4. In an example from our clinic, the neighbor of a 6-year-old who had gained entry into her home and taken several objects agreed to have the child weed her gardens daily for a month in compensation.

Step 5: Role Reversal

As a further measure of overcorrection, the child is made to relinquish one of his or her own possessions of approximately equal value and, if possible, similar function to the stolen item. This last is intended to add a consequence that is both particularly salient (experiencing the loss of one's own possession) and logical (approximately reversing the roles of victim and perpetrator). The child should participate in selecting which among his or her possessions will be forfeited and should personally give it to the victim of the theft, with an explanation to the effect that "I need to learn what it feels like to lose one of my things too."

Testing the Effectiveness of the Intervention

We use a "baiting" strategy to monitor stealing behavior in the home. Items identified as possible targets of theft are purposely left around the house under circumstances designed to tempt the child. A known quantity of money, for example, labeled with an inconspicuous pencil mark, might be left in a parent's coat pocket or bedroom furniture. The child is informed that parents will be watching his or her behavior closely for stealing but is not forewarned of the baiting strategy. If the bait is stolen, the procedure outlined above is invoked. Instances in which the child successfully resists the bait become opportunities for praise, for example, "Congratulations! I accidentally left that dollar in my drawer and you did not take it. By not stealing things you used to take, you are beginning to show that you are growing up" (or, for older children, "earning back our trust," etc.). The child's success in remaining above suspicion under any conditions that previously occasioned stealing should be similarly rewarded.

RESEARCH BASIS

The intervention described herein is a variant of contingency contracting, which has accumulated substantial empirical support as a general strategy for managing the behavior of children and adolescents. Clear definition of target behaviors is a critical element in the effectiveness of behavioral contracting, to maximize predictability of consequences. Also important is the reliable provision of consistent, highly salient, and (for younger children especially) prompt contingencies that help children to discriminate between desirable and undesirable performances of target behaviors. Punishment or response cost procedures can be highly effective, though it is important that children have opportunities to earn positive reinforcement as well, in order to sustain a critical mass of positive exchanges between parents and children and to model and support inclusion of noncoercive influence strategies in their behavioral repertoire.

Overcorrection has been found to enhance the potency of many learning procedures and is often prescribed for those with learning problems or developmental delays. An overcorrection of 100%, or repaying twice the value of the stolen item, is typical of current recommendations. Overcorrection may take forms other than money, such as some specified amount of work around the house.

RELEVANT TARGET POPULATIONS AND EXCEPTIONS

The intervention outlined here has been used successfully with children aged 4 through adolescence. The developmental progression described earlier, by which stealing becomes incorporated into a repertoire of antisocial behaviors, characterized by increasing diversification and decreasing desistance over time, argues strongly for intervention during early to middle childhood.

As with all contingency contracting, the clinician must assess the ability and commitment of parents to follow through with the terms of the contract and with a minimum of extraneous responding (e.g., lecturing, physical punishment). Any of the following should serve as red flags to alert clinicians to potential obstacles: parents who are excessively moralistic or

punitive (more inclined to berate than to deliver predictable contingencies), highly stressful or chaotic lifestyles, or mental health problems (e.g., depression, substance abuse) that might interfere with the capacity of the parent to attend or respond to the child's behavior. Where any of these are present, more intensive intervention is likely to be required.

In addition, for more entrenched stealers or those who are also experiencing serious difficulties with peer relations or academic performance, the approach offered herein will likely need to be augmented with strategies targeting a broader spectrum of the child's environment.

COMPLICATIONS

Some parents demonstrate a reluctance to identify or acknowledge instances of stealing or to enforce the specified consequences. For some, failing to implement the intervention is part of a pattern of denying or minimizing the problem. Others express concerns about the intrusiveness of the intervention: the imposition of treatment without the child's consent, the presumption of guilt in identifying stolen items, searching of the child's private space under some circumstances, and deliberate baiting of the child to test the child's resistance to temptation. Whatever the source of their reluctance, the result is intermittent reinforcement of the stealing behavior, which builds resistance to extinction and undermines the credibility of the intervention. In such instances, more extensive instruction in child behavior management principles may be a prerequisite to successful use of the stealing intervention. We contend that the strong contingencies built into this program are necessary because of the developmental significance of stealing behavior, the frequent need to overcome a pattern of poorly specified and enforced contingencies in the household, and the increasing resistance of conduct problems to intervention as the child matures. The benefits of forestalling the development of more serious behavior patterns amply justify the restrictions imposed on the child by an effective treatment.

CASE ILLUSTRATION

The case of "Stephen Baker," a 9-year-old male, will be used to illustrate the procedure. According to his parents, Stephen had been surreptitiously taking toys from his friends' homes for about 2 years. They had been inclined to regard this stealing behavior as a passing phase, they said, until it had recently escalated to removing money from his parents' clothes and objects from his classmates' desks in school. Following the initial assessment, the clinician spent the next session explaining the intervention first to Stephen's parents and then to the child himself, after which he was asked to explain the procedure to his parents. Finally, the family was provided with a brief written outline of the steps to be followed upon discovery of stolen items. This process helps to establish a clear understanding of the intervention prior to its implementation.

Step 1: Identifying Stealing

In accordance with the clinician's instructions, Stephen accompanied his father to his bedroom upon arriving home that afternoon, where Mr. Baker searched through Stephen's closet, under the bed, in the bureau, and any other locations that offered opportunities for concealment. This search did not yield any contraband. A few days later, however, Stephen's mother found a video game cartridge, placed under some clothing in a bureau drawer, which she had not seen before. Stephen claimed that a friend who had become bored with the game had offered it to him, although he could not recall which of his friends was the original owner of the game. This story was not implausible to Mrs. Baker, for she knew that Stephen rapidly tired of his own game cartridges, but she insisted on confirmation from the alleged donor of the game. When Stephen protested that he simply could not remember the game's previous owner, Mrs. Baker replied that she had to assume that item was stolen.

Step 2: Apology

Stephen was reminded that until he was prepared to identify and apologize to the victim of the theft, he would lose all privileges. He would not be able to watch television, use his own video games, spend time with friends, or engage in any leisure activities away from home. The Bakers were advised to remain firm about the loss of privileges but not to engage in any other form of punishment, such as lecturing Stephen at length, restricting his movements within the house, or corporal punishment.

The next day after the suspension of his privileges, Stephen "remembered" where he had gotten the video game and acknowledged that its owner had perhaps "loaned" it to him and he had neglected to return it. Following the procedures outlined by the therapist, Mrs. Baker called the parents of the video game's rightful owner, explained the situation, confirmed that the game was indeed stolen, and asked if she and Stephen could speak with their son after school. Mrs. Baker then rehearsed with Stephen his apology for stealing the game and supervised his performance at the victim's home.

Step 3: Return

Given that the video game cartridge had not been damaged, restitution was accomplished by simply returning the game at the time of the apology.

Step 4: Restitution + 100%

Prior to visiting the victim's home that afternoon, Mrs. Baker told Stephen to call a local retailer of video games and ask the price of the game he had stolen from his friend. Stephen did not have the $29 price of the game readily available, so his mother informed him that she would supply this sum for restitution to his friend, but that he would have to repay her by contributing 2 hours each of the next four Saturdays to helping her clean the house.

Step 5: Role Reversal

As part of their preparation for visiting the victim's home, Mrs. Baker instructed Stephen to select one of his own video games to give to his friend so that Stephen would understand what it felt like to lose a possession like the one he had stolen. She reminded him that he must choose a game that was compatible with his friend's system, rather than one of his less expensive (and less favored) games.

When Stephen had carried out the above tasks, under his mother's observation, he was encouraged to consider how he felt right then and why it was important that he not steal anymore. Stephen's parents had been instructed to avoid excessive verbal punishment after the five steps had been completed, for the intervention is sufficiently punishing without undue nagging.

For the next month, Stephen's parents placed marked $1 bills in their bedroom furniture and left them in their clothing. Twice during the first 2 weeks, they discovered some of this money missing and found it in Stephen's possession. On each of these occasions, he was made to apologize, return twice the amount of money he stole (restitution + 100%), and lose an equivalent amount of his own money. At the end of the third week, his parents complimented Stephen on resisting the temptation to steal their money that week, adding that perhaps he was beginning to earn their trust. The baiting strategy was discontinued after the fourth week, reinstituted a month later as a follow-up check (none of it was stolen), and then stopped altogether unless further stealing was identified. Mr. and Mrs. Baker were advised to continue their close observation of Stephen's possessions for at least 2 more months and to relax their vigilance then only if no further episodes of stealing had been identified.

—*George C. Tremblay*
and Ronald S. Drabman

See also: *Applied Behavior Analysis (Vols. I, II, & III), Behavioral Treatment in Natural Environments (Vols. I & III), Overcorrection (Vols. I, II, & III)*

Suggested Readings

Azrin, N. H., & Weslowski, M. D. (1974). Theft reversal: An overcorrection procedure for eliminating stealing by retarded persons. *Journal of Applied Behavior Analysis, 7,* 577–581.

Barth, R. P. (1987). Assessment and treatment of stealing. In B. Lahey & A. Kazdin (Eds.), *Advances in clinical child psychology* (Vol. 10, pp. 137–170). New York: Plenum.

Loeber, R. (1990). Development and risk factors of juvenile antisocial behavior and delinquency. *Clinical Psychology Review, 10,* 1–41.

Loeber, R. (1991). Antisocial behavior: More enduring than changeable? *Journal of the American Academy of Child and Adolescent Psychiatry, 30,* 393–397.

Miller, G. E., & Klungness, L. (1986). Treatment of nonconfrontative stealing in school-age children. *School Psychology Review, 15,* 24–35.

Miller, G. E., & Klungness, L. (1989). Childhood theft: A comprehensive review of assessment and treatment. *School Psychology Review, 18,* 82–97.

Seymour, F. W., & Epston, D. (1989). An approach to childhood stealing with evaluation of 45 cases. *Australian and New Zealand Journal of Family Therapy, 10,* 137–143.

FLOODING

DESCRIPTION OF THE STRATEGY

"When you fall off a horse, you need to get right back on."

Everyday culture has long recognized the importance of exposing ourselves to things we fear in order to overcome those fears. Parents do this with children quite naturally; Mother nudges her reluctant toddler toward the other children in a playgroup, or Dad encourages his teen to "go for it" and try out for the diving team despite the intimidating height of the diving platform. Fears are simply part of everyday life, and being able to face them rather than avoid them is a crucial element of experiencing, learning, and living a full life. Obviously, using exposure to overcome fear isn't the best idea if the feared object or situation is actually harmful; entering the lion's den (in the literal sense) may not be the most effective method of reducing a fear of lions. The realistic possibility of being eaten by the lion outweighs any potential benefit of reduced fear. In addition, exposure may not be the most adaptive method of responding to a realistic danger; reducing fear may reduce a child's future caution in risky situations and increase the chance of being eaten by that lion (or one of his cousins) at a later date. In short, sometimes fear is a good thing, protecting us from danger. However, other times our fears are unreasonable, out of proportion to realistic danger, or excessive. While entering the lion's den may be unwise, being able to enter a friend's house to pet her gentle kitten is an important part of growing up.

Basics of Exposure-Based Treatment

The psychological literature contains many examples of treatments with demonstrated efficacy for helping individuals overcome unrealistic or excessive fears. Exposure-based techniques, or the psychological equivalent of "getting back on the horse," have proven quite useful in the treatment of phobias, obsessive-compulsive disorder, and other anxiety disorders in which avoidance plays a prominent role. Two major exposure-based techniques are systematic desensitization and flooding. These techniques share in common several ideas, including the notions that (a) fears develop because the individual anticipates (for any number of reasons) that contact with a particular object or event will result in some negative outcome, (b) by virtue of the anxiety being unrealistic or excessive, the feared negative outcome is also unrealistic or excessive, and would either not actually occur or would not be as catastrophic as anticipated, (c) escape or avoidance of the feared situation is reinforced when the anticipated negative outcome does not occur, and escape/avoidance becomes a conditioned response to both the feared stimulus and feelings of anxiety, and (d) successful treatment of excessive or unrealistic anxiety involves breaking the conditioned pairings of the feared stimulus and the anxious affect (stimulus → anxious affect) and avoidance/escape (stimulus → avoidance/escape) responses.

Where these techniques differ is in the specific ways in which exposure is accomplished and the mechanisms by which anxiety and avoidance are presumed to decline. For example, in systematic desensitization, the individual is first taught relaxation, a physiological response considered to be incompatible with anxiety (or anxiety-antagonistic), and then exposed to the feared object or situation. Using relaxation during exposure sessions is presumed to create a conditioned (relaxation) response to the target object/situation that is physiologically incompatible with the stimulus → anxiety response pairing. Relaxation should "displace" the anxiety such that there is now a conditioned stimulus → relaxation pairing. If the object/situation no longer evokes anxiety, there should be no further need for escape or avoidance. Then the individual can remain in contact with the feared stimulus to learn that it does not lead to the unrealistic feared negative outcome. Variants of systematic desensitization (e.g., distraction, cognitive coping) all emphasize the importance of exposure to the feared stimulus occurring during an anxiety-antagonistic state.

In contrast to systematic desensitization's focus on the stimulus → anxious affect pairing, flooding focuses more on the stimulus → escape/avoidance pairing. The individual is exposed to the feared stimulus and then required to remain in contact with it, without either cognitive or behavioral escape/avoidance, until the anxiety diminishes. This approach is based on the notion that anxiety, as a physiological state, cannot last indefinitely and that the individual will eventually habituate, or get used to, the stimulus and stop feeling anxious in its presence. In addition, because the anticipated negative outcome does not occur, the stimulus → escape/avoidance pairing is broken. However, perhaps the most critical aspect of flooding is the notion that "coping" strategies may actually serve to allow the individual to avoid truly experiencing the feared stimulus and may thus interfere with habituation and adaptive functioning. For example, cognitive distraction may allow the individual to avoid thinking about the feared stimulus and to

essentially "check out." This is fine if the stimulus is unlikely to ever occur at a time when the individual must be cognitively present (e.g., most surgical/dental procedures can be completed very successfully without the patient being aware of what is happening) but may not be adaptive in all situations.

Deciding to Use Flooding

The decision to use flooding versus systematic desensitization or some other treatment for child anxiety depends on several conceptual, practical, and ethical factors. First, the therapist should consider the function of coping for this child. In other areas of life, does the child use distraction, relaxation, or other coping techniques to "recharge" and prepare to tackle challenges or does the child tend to use them to check out and disengage? Certainly, a style of disengagement would interfere with exposure-based anxiety treatment and would argue strongly for the use of flooding over systematic desensitization.

Practical and ethical issues also should be considered. These include assessment of time available for treatment, skills and supports available to the child, and the likely reactions that children and their parents will have to flooding. For example, is there enough time to teach relaxation, an often time-intensive phase of treatment? Does the child have the skills (e.g., attention span, cognitive development) to use relaxation or cognitive coping effectively? If children are young or otherwise unable to use self-control strategies, do they have a parent or other support figure available to help guide relaxation or distracting or calming imagery? Will the parents view it as cruel to require that the child not run away from the feared stimulus? Will parents observe a child's distress after one session and discontinue treatment? Situations in which children are allowed to escape treatment prior to completion (i.e., habituation) can do more harm than good. For situations in which child and parent are willing to participate in exposure, and recognize that short-term anxiety may be distressing but that continued exposure until the anxiety dissipates is vital, flooding can be quite effective.

Planning and Implementing Flooding

Once the therapist, child, and parent(s) agree to proceed with flooding, the next step is to develop a detailed treatment plan. The therapist and family must identify and define specific aspects of the feared stimulus, much as journalists gather information: what, where, when, and how questions serve as useful guides. This information will be used to construct exposure experiences, and so the more detailed the better. For example, for a child who fears school, it is important to know whether the child fears the school building (e.g., is the child claustrophobic?), academic tasks (and if so, in what classes, for what reason—is it fear of being considered stupid by teachers or peers, fear of failing a class and needing to attend summer school?), social/relational aspects of school (is it a fear of being bullied, of talking to unfamiliar children?), or being away from home or parents? Once the feared school situation is identified, increasingly detailed questions might involve identifying specific environmental or sensory cues associated with the feared stimulus (e.g., who is present in the situation? What does the classroom or playground or lunchroom look like? How loud is it? Is the teacher smiling or frowning? Are the other children paying attention or ignoring, laughing or grimacing?).

Next, identifying and defining the child's fear response allows the therapist to incorporate this information into exposure experiences and to know what child responses provide cues about the child's anxious state. Again, details will help increase the effectiveness of flooding. For example, the therapist should identify how the child experiences and expresses his or her anxiety in terms of physiological responses (e.g., sweating, shaking), thoughts (e.g., self-doubts, difficulty concentrating or making sense), and behaviors (e.g., crying, running away, getting irritable and aggressive). Effective exposure should elicit these responses, particularly at the beginning of treatment when anxiety has not yet dissipated. It is also helpful to assess the typical intensity and duration of the child's anxiety response in order to have some idea of how distressing the exposure might be to the child and how long habituation might take.

Based on the practical and ethical issues outlined above, along with an understanding of the feared stimulus and the child's anxiety response, the therapist develops a plan of action for flooding treatment. The literature documents several variants of flooding, depending on the individual child's needs. For example, exposure can be provided in graduated versus intensive fashion. In graduated exposure, the therapist and child together develop a "fear hierarchy" in which encounters with the feared stimulus are rank-ordered from only mildly anxiety provoking (e.g., "only a little bit anxious; I would be nervous but probably wouldn't avoid it") to severely anxiety provoking (e.g., "the most anxious I have ever been; I would definitely avoid it"). Treatment begins with exposure to the lowest hierarchy item; for a child with a fear of dogs, this might be looking at a photo of a dog or looking at a dog in someone's backyard from the window of the house. Because the fear is mild, habituation to the situation will likely not take long and the child's anxiety should decrease to a minimum. This early and relatively easy success experience frequently increases the child's motivation to take the next hierarchy step. At each step, exposure continues until anxiety decreases (often to whatever level is considered manageable, with which the child could encounter the feared situation and still function adaptively). Usually, each step is repeated in therapy sessions or between-session practice until the child can reliably encounter the feared stimulus with only manageable anxiety. By the end of treatment, the child should have mastered all hierarchy steps and be able to encounter the most anxiety-provoking step without becoming unreasonably distressed or avoidant.

Intensive flooding, rather than following a hierarchical model, begins exposure at a much higher level of anxiety provocation and progresses rapidly (perhaps immediately) to the most intense levels of anxiety. Figuratively speaking, the child is dropped into the deep end of the pool and remains there (albeit with the therapist serving as lifeguard) until habituation has occurred. Obviously, this is typically much more distressing for the child, and habituation is likely to take much longer within each session. For many researchers and therapists, graduated flooding is preferred over intensive flooding due to its more "humane" nature, its greater acceptability to children and parents, and thus the greater likelihood that the clients will complete treatment. Perhaps the only compelling reasons to choose intensive flooding would be when the fear needs to be extinguished immediately (e.g., a child with a fear of flying needs to take an airplane flight within the next few days in order to participate in a life-saving surgery) or when the fear is really only debilitating at the highest levels.

Similarly, exposure can take place imaginally or in vivo (in real life). Imaginal exposure is exactly that—the child imagines himself or herself in the anxiety-provoking situation and remains in that scene until anxiety declines to the preset manageable level.

Typically, the therapist and child develop scenes together, including as many details as possible to ensure that they will elicit an anxiety response. During imaginal exposure, the therapist narrates the scene and may ask the child to help narrate or answer questions about the scene in order to confirm that the child is indeed experiencing the feared stimulus. The therapist also asks the child to indicate, using a previously defined rating scale, the level of anxiety the child is experiencing. Exposure continues until anxiety dissipates. Benefits of imaginal exposure include the ability to maintain control of a stimulus event that in real life may develop in unanticipated ways (e.g., a "friendly dog" stimulus may growl) and the ease of exposing the child to situations that may be difficult to engineer in real life. For example, airplane flights are expensive and imaginal exposure is a convenient way to practice boarding, taking off, landing, and so on.

Imaginal exposure is almost never conducted without combining it with in vivo exposure. After all, improving the child's ability to function effectively in everyday (real) life is the ultimate goal of treatment. In vivo exposure follows the same basic procedures as imaginal and involves the child looking at or interacting with the feared stimulus (e.g., petting a dog, giving a speech in front of others). Where possible, the therapist comments or asks the child to comment on anxiety-provoking aspects of the situation, again to ensure that the child is not avoiding mentally. As with imaginal exposure, the child remains in the situation until anxiety peaks (indicating true engagement vs. disengagement or avoidant coping) and then declines. Frequently, a child is first exposed to the feared situation imaginally and, after habituation, moves to in vivo exposure to the same situation.

RESEARCH BASIS

Research has demonstrated the utility of exposure-based techniques with anxious children. Although the necessity of a relaxation or other anxiety-antagonist component (i.e., systematic desensitization) is still the subject of debate, several investigators have demonstrated that exposure alone can lead to significant and meaningful reductions in child anxiety and avoidant behavior. What seems to be more important than the inclusion of an incompatible response is the exposure component. For example, relaxation alone has not shown the same effectiveness as exposure, either alone or along with relaxation. Most researchers seem to agree that a hierarchical or graduated approach to exposure is preferable, not only because it seems more humane and ethical but also because dropouts are minimized. Research also generally supports the notion that in vivo exposure (either alone or in combination with imaginal) is preferable to imaginal alone.

RELEVANT TARGET POPULATIONS AND EXCEPTIONS

Flooding is appropriate for children with anxiety disorders that involve an identifiable fear stimulus (e.g., phobias, obsessive-compulsive disorder) but may be less appropriate for children with more diffuse anxiety (e.g., generalized anxiety disorder). One distinct benefit of flooding over more cognitive treatments such as cognitive coping or anxiety management training is that it does not require the same level of attention span, cognitive ability, or self-motivation and is thus suitable for children who are relatively young or developmentally immature in these areas. However, imaginal flooding does require that the child have the attentional and cognitive ability to visualize details of the feared stimulus. Flooding is also more useful than systematic desensitization with action-oriented children who may be unable to sit still and focus on relaxation. However, for very young children (i.e., infants, toddlers), it may be preferable to give parents more responsibility for assisting the child's coping with anxiety-provoking situations by providing distraction or comfort. Finally, because of the effort required to participate in flooding and the distress that is part of the exposure sessions, a motivated child and parents are essential.

COMPLICATIONS

Even if flooding is the treatment of choice for a particular child, certain conditions can complicate the course of treatment or render flooding less effective. For example, even in motivated children, psychological conditions such as depression or extreme anxiety can lessen the child's ability to participate effectively in treatment. Depressed children may be unable to engage fully in exposure sessions or may fail to complete between-session exposure homework. Extremely anxious children may become "frozen" and incapacitated during exposure. In these situations, treatment of the depression or extreme anxiety (e.g., through alternative forms of psychological or pharmacological treatment) is indicated prior to flooding. Similarly, reluctant or nonsupportive caregivers may allow the child to escape the feared situations during exposure because they find it easier or less offensive to do this rather than to help the child work through his or her distress. Finally, many excessive or unrealistic fears still contain a kernel of realism (e.g., an airplane *could* crash), and cognitive interventions may be required to help children put their fears in perspective (e.g., yes, the airplane *could* crash, but the chance of this is lower than all sorts of things the child does not fear).

CASE ILLUSTRATION

"Sammy" was a 10-year-old boy brought to treatment by his parents because of an excessive fear of germs. Sammy avoided touching telephones, door knobs, papers, playground equipment, toys, and so on that he thought had been touched by other people, particularly children. Sammy did not have any known immune function problems or other conditions that might place him at increased risk for becoming ill from touching everyday objects. He reported knowing logically that his fear was unreasonable but still found himself unable to touch things comfortably. He would either avoid touching things entirely or would tremble and become dizzy and nauseous when forcing himself to touch things. Sammy was becoming increasingly embarrassed by his inability to "be like other kids" and was having increasing difficulty hiding his avoidance while interacting with peers. One of his treatment goals was to be able to play on a baseball team when the season started in 3 months.

During the assessment phase of treatment, Sammy and the therapist identified the range of anxiety-provoking stimuli and Sammy's anxiety response symptoms and agreed to focus on baseball-related situations. They then developed a 10-step fear hierarchy, ranging from a relatively mild fear stimulus of Sammy standing next to the equipment bag containing bats, balls, and so on belonging to his friend's baseball team (which Sammy rated as 3 on a 1–10 scale of anxiety) to a strongly anxiety-provoking situation involving Sammy picking up and using a bat (bare-handed) that he'd just seen a peer use after spitting on his hands (rated a 10). Sammy and the therapist developed detailed imaginal scenes for each hierarchy step, and they and Sammy's parents discussed pragmatics of arranging in vivo exposures at each step.

Treatment began with imaginal exposure to the first scene. Sammy had defined a rating of 3 as a

manageable level of anxiety—the highest level at which his discomfort would not be visible to others or interfere with his ability to participate in activities. Thus, a rating of 3 was used as the goal for ending each exposure session. However, because Sammy's first scene had been rated (prior to actual exposure) as a 3, the goal for this session was that Sammy's anxiety decline to a 1. Imaginal exposure involved having Sammy sit comfortably in a beanbag chair in a dimly lit room, close his eyes, and rate his preexposure anxiety (he rated it as 2). Then the therapist began narrating the exposure scene while Sammy envisioned it and occasionally responded to therapist prompts to note and describe aspects of the scene itself (e.g., the look, smell, etc. of the equipment bag, the heat of the day, the activity around him) and his anxiety experience (e.g., physical symptoms, anxious thoughts, anxiety rating). Over the course of 20 minutes, Sammy's anxiety rose to a 4 and gradually declined to 1.

Sammy was proud of his ability to imagine the first scene successfully, and was excited to complete his homework assignment of daily imaginal exposure to the same scene over the next week. Because of Sammy's facility with the exposure and motivation, he was allowed to do the homework relatively independently. He kept a log of his beginning, peak, and ending anxiety levels for each exposure session, as well as the duration of the session. His parents helped to remind him to complete and record his homework (he rarely needed reminding) and independently noted the duration of exposure (Sammy told them when he was going into his room to begin, as well as when he came out). The therapist made arrangements with Sammy and his parents to complete the same scene in vivo as the last homework assignment prior to the next session, contingent upon successful mastery of anxiety during imaginal sessions. For less competent or motivated families, or for more highly anxiety-provoking exposures, the therapist would have supervised the in vivo exposure at least the first time it was attempted.

As treatment progressed, Sammy moved smoothly and fairly rapidly through his hierarchy steps. For early steps, he was often able to master two steps a week—imaginal sessions became briefer as they were repeated two or three times, and in vivo scenes were completed with minimal difficulty. For later steps, a week or more was often required for each step, with three to four imaginal exposures plus three to four in vivo exposures required before Sammy's anxiety level was peaking at lower levels (e.g., 5/moderate vs. 8/extreme) and declining quickly. At the end of 10 weeks of treatment, Sammy was handling baseball equipment willingly, playing ball with family and friends, and could laugh when anyone suggested how germy the equipment might be. At that point, the therapist and Sammy focused on maintenance and preparation for his baseball tryouts in 2 weeks and made plans to apply exposure treatment to other germ concerns. Sammy had actually requested this and was looking forward to it. Sammy, his family, and the therapist all anticipated that the treatment gains for baseball-related fears would generalize to other fears and that treatment of these areas would proceed quickly and smoothly. In fact, some generalization had been noted already, with Sammy reporting that he had used the telephone at a friend's house with almost no anxiety and had pushed all the buttons on an elevator "just for fun" (a previously avoided activity).

—*Debora J. Bell*

See also: *Flooding (Vols. I & III), Foa, Edna B. (Vol. III), Imaginal Procedures (Vol. II), Stampfl's Therapist-Directed Implosive (Flooding) Therapy (Vols. I & III), Systematic Desensitization With Children and Adolescents (Vol. II)*

Suggested Readings

Barrios, B. A., & O'Dell, S. L. (1998). Fears and anxieties. In E. J. Mash & R. A. Barclay (Eds.), *Treatment of childhood disorders* (2nd ed., pp. 249–337). New York: Guilford Press.

Beidel, D. C., & Turner, S. M. (1998). *Shy children, phobic adults: Nature and treatment of social phobia.* Washington, DC: American Psychological Press.

Eisen, A. R., Kearney, C. A., & Schaefer, C. E. (1995). *Clinical handbook of anxiety disorders in children and adolescents.* Northvale, NJ: Jason Aronson Press.

March, J. S., & Mulle, K. (1996). Banishing obsessive-compulsive disorder. In E. Hibbs & P. Jensen (Eds.), *Psychosocial treatments for child and adolescent disorders* (pp. 82–103). Washington, DC: American Psychological Press.

Silverman, W. K., & Kurtines, W. M. (1996). *Anxiety and phobic disorders: A pragmatic approach.* New York: Plenum.

Svensson, L., Larsson, A., & Ost, L. (2002). How children experience brief-exposure treatment of specific phobias. *Journal of Clinical Child and Adolescent Psychology, 31,* 80–89.

Vasey, M. W., & Dadds, M. R. (2001). *The developmental psychopathology of anxiety.* New York: Oxford University Press.

FULL-SPECTRUM HOME TRAINING FOR SIMPLE BED-WETTING

DESCRIPTION OF THE STRATEGY

Regular bed-wetting of several times a week is a problem for about 1 of every 10 children from elementary school through high school. In first grade, about 15 of every 100 children wet the bed most nights. In high school, only about 1 of every 100 children continue to have the problem. Most bed-wetting will simply go away as a child matures physically in terms of bladder capacity and nervous system development. Bed-wetting is not generally a sign of psychological or emotional problems but is instead a problem of maturation and learning the proper sequence of behaviors to control the bladder during sleep. Most children learn this control without any special assistance by the time they are 4 years old. Some children fail to acquire this nighttime control, and many of them have an unknown genetic basis for this failure to acquire nighttime control. Those children who continue to have routine bed-wetting past age 4 may need special assistance to overcome the problem. The reason for treating the problem as opposed to just waiting for it to go away is that continued bed-wetting can interfere with a child's normal development and association with peers. Children who continue bed-wetting and do not get help may develop feelings of inferiority and embarrassment due to the fact that they are restricted in social activities.

Full-spectrum home training (FSHT) is a behavior therapy procedure for teaching a child how to overcome bed-wetting. The basic idea behind FSHT is that bed-wetting can continue due to many factors. FSHT was designed to address several of these major factors, and each part of the procedure was also selected for convenience of use by parents and children. The entire set of procedures that make up FSHT have been written into a manual that parents and children can follow under the guidance of a health care professional who understands basic principles of conditioning and learning.

FSHT consists of four components: (1) basic urine alarm training, (2) cleanliness training, (3) retention control training, and (4) overlearning. The components are presented in an integrated manual for parents to follow, and a behavioral contract between parents and children forms the basis for implementing the procedures.

Family Support Agreement

The behavioral contract between the child and parents is called a family support agreement. Like most child problems, correcting bed-wetting requires cooperation from the entire family. The most demanding part of FSHT is training a child to wake to the alarm. Many children need their parents' help to wake up. Parents have to be committed to waking the child and requiring the child to get out of bed to be fully awake. A family environment of cooperation and firm resolve is necessary. Children have to be ready to do the hard work of getting up whenever the alarm sounds and be mature enough to do so without having tantrums and defeating the whole process. The family support agreement is a behavioral contract procedure between parents and children designed to promote cooperation and to clarify family rules for assisting the child. Siblings are included in the family contract so that they will know how to help and what to avoid. In extended families and blended families, all are included in the contracting process if the child spends the night with those people. Consistency and follow-through in each household are needed for success.

The family support agreement covers all parts of the FSHT approach. Parents and children complete the family support agreement while a trainer illustrates what to do for each step.

Basic Urine Alarm Training and Cleanliness Training

The idea behind urine alarm training is to provide the child with a new opportunity to learn the active response needed to avoid wetting the bed. Most children learn this response without any assistance. We suspect they do this because they find the wet bed is noxious and it wakes them from a sound sleep. Children who get past 4 years old and who have not learned this response may get accustomed to the wet bed and sleep right through it without feeling anything. The urine alarm provides a new way to learn this response of stopping and then preventing altogether wetting during sleep. Eventually, children who use the urine alarm go from wetting to sleeping through the night without wetting and without even awakening. However, they have to go through the training to get to that final goal. Going through the training is difficult and means that the child will have to be awakened at first. This means work for the parents who must assist.

FSHT can be implemented with any urine alarm device. In the past 15 years, body-worn alarms have replaced the older bed pad alarms. Body-worn alarms use small alarm boxes that operate on hearing aid batteries, and the urine detection unit is typically placed in the child's underwear rather than on the bed. When even a very small amount of urine reaches the detection unit, a circuit is closed like a switch and the alarm sounds. The alarm is turned off when the detection unit is removed from the underwear and wiped dry.

These alarms are generally reliable and very convenient to use. However, they can lead parents to overlook the importance of full cleanliness training, which requires that the child remake the bed after each wetting episode. As children become more and more skilled at preventing bed-wetting, the amount they wet on the bed gets smaller and smaller. This is due to interrupting the stream sooner and sooner after wetting starts. As a result, some children can set off the alarm and never actually wet the sheets. Full cleanliness training requires that the bed be remade not only to provide appropriate consequences for bed-wetting but also to ensure that the child is fully awake after the alarm sounds.

Children follow the rule to get out of bed and stand up before turning off the alarm. Obviously, the entire process can be defeated if the child merely turns off the alarm and goes back to sleep. Parents follow the rule to never turn off the alarm for the child. The steps involved in remaking the bed are displayed on a wall chart (Daily Steps to a Dry Bed) placed in the child's room. The chart shows a record of progress, and the child colors the chart wet or dry for each day. Parents support a rule for the child to go through with the full procedure of remaking the bed even if the sheets are not wet. Some children are very deep sleepers and hard to train to awaken to the alarm. The child has to be awakened so that the child turns off the alarm. This may require having a parent share the room with the child for a short time. Training the child to awaken to the alarm is imperative. Giving parents an easy way to determine if their child is truly awake can help. Short-term memory checks such as choosing a password each night before bedtime or asking the child to spell a familiar word backwards will work.

The rationale for having the child take care of the wet bedclothes and bed linens is to have the child take responsibility for maintaining his or her own bed. This also relieves parents of the burden of doing this for the child. By taking active responsibility for keeping the bed made and cared for, the children learn a sense of pride in being grown up and solving problems for themselves with parent assistance rather than parent imposition. The aforementioned rules set forth in the family support agreement are there to ensure that the child and parent keep focused on the goals and the procedures.

In FSHT, the first goal of urine alarm training is for the child to achieve 14 consecutive dry nights. The professional assisting the child and parents needs to focus on reinforcing accomplishments during the urine alarm training. Children who wet multiple times each night get easily discouraged. These families need to understand that it will take 12 to 16 weeks as opposed to the average of 8 to 12 weeks for the child to get the first 14 consecutive dry nights. Also, multiple wettings mean multiple awakenings with all of the added work. For these children, their first goal is to get from multiple wettings to a single wetting each night.

Progress can be measured by the decreasing size of wet spots. This helps parents and children focus on the positive accomplishment of the child who is responding more readily to the alarm. As the size of the wet spot gets smaller and smaller, the child is learning to make the active avoidance response sooner and sooner. Dry nights are sure to follow. In focusing on the goal of attaining 14 consecutive dry nights, parents and children often need to be reminded of the overall picture. Even though a child may not have reached the 14-night goal, the child may have been 90% dry for the past 6 weeks. This can give the family a more positive perspective.

Many children enjoy the challenge of overcoming bed-wetting, and it is easy to engage their competitive spirit. Some bring their wall charts to each follow-up visit to show off their progress. Others set goals of beating the 42-day record for completing FSHT. So long as their goals are not outlandish and beyond reach, this energetic approach to getting rid of the problem is useful.

Parents often want to add other incentives to the FSHT program, and this is not a good idea. What can be helpful is to redirect this urge to teach the parents to use contingent praise for completion of various tasks. Praising children for their hard work of waking to the alarm, remaking the bed, and taking the soiled linens to the laundry is directly beneficial. Outcome-related rewards such as a new mattress or new bed upon completion of the program can be helpful.

Retention Control Training

This procedure is included in FSHT to increase the amount of fluid the child's bladder can hold before it reflexively contracts and produces the sensation of having to urinate. Due to hereditary factors and even habit, some children have low bladder capacities. This functional capacity can be altered by practicing holding larger and larger amounts of urine before giving in to the initial sensation to urinate. This can be practiced during the day and can help a child get to the 14 consecutive dry nights goal faster when using the urine alarm.

Retention control training is done once a day with a parent or older sibling assisting. Parents and children agree on a practice time spanning a 2-hour period when the child and the assistant can be together in the event the child has to urinate. The procedure begins by having the child drink a large quantity of water (12–16 oz.). The child finds the assistant when the child feels the urge to urinate, and the assistant starts timing the holding time. The child is given money for postponing urination for increasing amounts of time in a step-by-step fashion up to a 45-minute holding time. The total amount of money the child receives for reaching all 15 of the 3-minute incremented goals is $6.25. Children are encouraged to save the money in a prominent place to remind them of their success. Retention control training ends when the child attains the 45-minute goal, typically within 3 weeks.

Overlearning

Overlearning is the final component of FSHT and only begins once the child has attained 14 consecutive dry nights with the urine alarm. Overlearning is done to prevent relapse once the child has succeeded with the urine alarm. The chance of a relapse without overlearning is 4 out of 10. In contrast, the chance of relapse is less than 1 out of 10 if the child does overlearning. The benefit of doing overlearning far outweighs the time and effort to complete it.

Overlearning begins by determining a maximum amount of water. The maximum is 1 ounce for each year of age plus 2 ounces. For example, the maximum amount for an 8-year-old child is 10 ounces. Children then begin by drinking 4 ounces of water 15 minutes before bedtime. If they remain dry for two nights while drinking 4 ounces, the amount increases to

6 ounces. If they remain dry for two nights at 6 ounces, the water is increased to 8 ounces. The water increases continue in this fashion, 2 ounces more for every 2 consecutive dry nights, until the child's maximum is reached. The child continues to drink this maximum until 14 more consecutive dry nights are attained. In the event a child wets, and most do at least once, a simple rule is followed. The child goes back to whatever amount was consumed on the last dry night and continues with that amount until there are 5 dry nights in a row. If the child is not already at the maximum, the procedure continues as before, increasing by 2 ounces for every 2 dry nights. The goal remains 14 dry nights in a row during overlearning. Some children end up having all 14 of those dry nights at the maximum amount, but this is not required for the relapse prevention effect.

RESEARCH BASIS

Based on five randomized outcome trials, about three out of every four children treated with FSHT can be expected to stop bed-wetting by the end of the average of 12 weeks needed to complete the treatment. These outcomes were obtained under research protocol conditions where flexibility of procedures was highly constrained. These samples excluded children with clinically significant behavioral problems such as conduct disorder and ADHD. Single-parent households were represented in these data as were low-income families. However, the samples did not include families with marked marital discord or clinically significant family dysfunction. Although these sample characteristics limit the generalizability of findings, it also should be remembered that these samples are quite representative of bed-wetting children, most of whom do not have such additional problems.

At the 1-year follow-up, 6 out of every 10 children are permanently dry. In some studies, we obtained lower relapse rates in the range of 85% to 90% remaining permanently dry. These better long-term outcomes were from children who did the overlearning, where they increased nighttime drinking in 2-ounce increments adjusted for their age. That overlearning was described above. In other studies, overlearning was done in the original fashion of having children consume 16 ounces of water regardless of age. Recent evidence supports a consistent finding that slightly less than 10% of children relapse using the gradual overlearning procedure.

RELEVANT TARGET POPULATIONS AND EXCEPTIONS

The research evidence for saying that FSHT is an effective treatment has been based on monosymptomatic primary nocturnal enuresis (MPE) or simple bed-wetting. Almost all bed-wetting is of this type, with 85% being MPE. These children have no other physical symptoms or medical complications; they simply continued bed-wetting from birth and never had a period of 6 months or more of sustained nighttime continence. Furthermore, they also did not display other major behavior problems such as conduct disorder or ADHD.

COMPLICATIONS

As a general procedure, FSHT should not be started without first having a child examined by a medical doctor to rule out complicating factors. Most children will not have complicating factors, but it is a mistake to start FSHT if a child has a urinary tract infection. The infection should be treated first. If a child has daytime wetting in addition to nighttime wetting, the child needs a thorough medical evaluation. Daytime wetting needs to be corrected first and may require medical attention.

Children who have onset enuresis or secondary enuresis have a history of having been dry at night for 6 months or more. Sometimes they started wetting again at night when a stressful event occurred in their lives. These children need behavioral evaluation by a competent mental health professional. If they are not displaying behavior problems and problems of anxiety and if they have a cooperative family, they can be treated with FSHT. Otherwise, such additional problems need to be resolved before starting FSHT for the bed-wetting problem.

Given these limitations, there are still MPE children who do not respond to FSHT with success. Leaving aside cases where a child defeats the alarm device or where parents fail follow-through, there are still some 10% to 15% who do not respond even after 20 weeks. Information on such treatment failures is sorely lacking. Some may have problems with arousal and might benefit from behavioral or drug interventions to alter sleep patterns. Those who wet multiple times per night and never get to wetting once a night may have problems with concentrating urine and could benefit from taking antidiuretic hormone medications.

Some may have undiagnosed food and airborne allergies that complicate sleep and urination functions. Much more research is needed on those children who fail to respond. Fortunately, they are only a small proportion of MPE children.

CASE ILLUSTRATION

"Matthew" was an 8-year-old boy who was referred by his pediatrician, who had unsuccessfully treated him with antidiuretic hormone (DDAVP) and then with imipramine (Tofranil). Physical exam showed no medical complications, and developmental milestones were within normal limits. Matthew lived with both parents and his 14-year-old sister, Maggie. Both parents completed the child behavior checklist and indicated there were no additional problems for Matthew, who was described as an "A and B" student in third grade. Parents also indicated normal marital adjustment on the Locke Wallace Marital Adjustment Test.

Matthew wet the bed since birth, and the parents believed that he wet more than once per night. The family was seen in two 1-hour visits with all attending. Maggie agreed to supervise retention control training (RCT) in the afternoons, as both parents worked. The family completed the family support agreement, and RCT began after the first visit. At the second visit, the alarm procedures were demonstrated.

Matthew and Dad attended the third visit for half an hour. The RCT went well, with Matthew having completed the 33-minute goal. Review of the wetting record kept by parents showed that Matthew wet two times a night in the first week. The first wet typically occurred about 2 hours after bedtime (9 P.M.), with the second between 2 and 3 A.M. Matthew was reminded to drink fluid throughout the day with no restrictions, even at bedtime. Parents were told to make sure that at the first wetting episode, Matthew took the time to fully empty his bladder. This might prevent a second wetting.

Matthew and either Mom or Dad returned for a total of five more half-hour visits spaced from 2 to 4 weeks apart. By Week 4 of the alarm, Matthew was wetting only once a night between 2 and 3 A.M., and the size of that wet spot was decreasing. In Week 6 of the alarm, he had two consecutive dry nights. By Week 10 of the alarm, Matthew attained 14 dry nights in a row. Matthew and his family were very enthusiastic but also a bit afraid to start overlearning.

Matthew started overlearning by consuming 4 ounces of water just before bedtime. His maximum amount was 10 ounces. By Week 15 of the alarm, Matthew completed 14 dry nights in a row during overlearning. He was encouraged to accept sleepover invitations. The family was instructed that if wetting happened again, this would be typical. The only cause for alarm was if wetting happened twice within a 7-day period. In that case, they were instructed to call the clinic to review the circumstances. If wetting persisted twice within another 7-day period, the alarm would be introduced again until Matthew attained 14 consecutive dry nights on the second application of the alarm.

At 3-month follow-up, Matthew had wet once when the family was on vacation. He was otherwise dry and had spent the night away from home six times. At 6-month and 1-year follow-ups, Matthew remained completely dry at night. His parents reported that he had attended a 3-week Boy Scout camp without any problems and that he seemed to be more confident in himself.

—*Arthur C. Houts*

See also: *Applied Behavior Analysis (Vols. I, II, & III), Behavioral Treatment in Natural Environments (Vols. I & III), Bell and Pad Bladder Training (Vol. II), Classical Conditioning (Vols. I, II, & III), Overcorrection (Vols. I, II, & III), Retention Control Training (Vol. II)*

Suggested Readings

Houts, A. C. (1991). Childhood enuresis as a biobehavioral problem. *Behavior Therapy, 22*, 133–151.

Houts, A. C. (2003). Behavioral treatment for enuresis. In A. E. Kazdin & J. R. Weisz (Eds.), *Evidence-based psychotherapies for children and adolescents* (pp. 389–406). New York: Guilford Press.

Houts, A. C., Berman, J. S., & Abramson, H. (1994). The effectiveness of psychological and pharmacological treatments for nocturnal enuresis. *Journal of Consulting and Clinical Psychology, 62*, 737–745.

Houts, A. C., & Liebert, R. M. (1984). *Bed-wetting: A guide for parents and children*. Springfield, IL: Charles C. Thomas.

Mellon, M. W., & Houts, A. C. (1997). Home-based training for primary enuresis. In C. E. Schaefer & J. M. Briesmeister (Eds.), *Handbook of parent training* (2nd ed., pp. 60–79). New York: Wiley.

FUNCTIONAL ANALYSIS

In 1953, B. F. Skinner implicitly introduced the construct of a functional analysis of behavior by positing a causal chain consisting of an operation performed on the organism, a behavioral response by the organism, and some kind of stimulus that follows the behavior that affects the likelihood of the previous behavior being exhibited under the same or similar conditions. This way of construing behavior implied a notion of causality for a particular behavior. Functional analysis refers to a variety of ways of attempting to identify the causes of behavior with the goals of predicting, and controlling it once a proper understanding of the controlling variables occurs. Though Skinner speculated about a variety of complex human behaviors taking place in the natural environment, most of his actual analysis of behavior was confined to highly controlled laboratory situations where the presumed causal variables were well controlled, measured, manipulated, and recorded. In more contemporary times, functional analysis has been attempted in more complex environments where many factors can affect behavior. Humans, having more complex histories and behavioral repertoires, present a greater challenge when attempting to determine the cause of a behavior.

Applied psychologists face the task of understanding and often changing behavior in many situations, including schools, mental health institutions, clinical settings, families, organizations, and communities. Behavioral scientists must assume that behavior is determined by some factor rather than being random, or else it makes no sense to try to bring about change. The search for causal factors for behavior is conducted in a way similar to the traditional scientific method.

In the scientific method, observations about the phenomenon in question are made, hypotheses about factors that control the phenomenon are developed, experimental manipulations of important variables are made, and the observed results provide the data for a test of the hypothesis. If necessary, the hypotheses are modified, data are collected again, and the process goes through these iterations until a workable theory of causality is developed. This heuristic appeals to a variety of researchers, including behavioral scientists.

BEHAVIOR THEORY AND FUNCTIONAL ANALYSIS

A functional analysis relies on the principles and constructs of behavior theory. Behavior occurs in a context. Antecedents refer to those stimuli that precede a particular behavior of interest. When these antecedent stimuli set the occasion for when a particular response is likely to experience a consequence that affects the probability of that response occurring again, the antecedent is referred to as a discriminative stimulus. Generally, the discriminative stimulus precedes the behavior of interest, called the response, closely in time. When the response is emitted by the organism, if it is followed by a contingently delivered stimulus that alters the probability of that response occurring in the presence of the discriminative stimulus, then that consequence becomes an important factor to identify and control if one wishes to change the behavior of interest. If the contingent stimulus that follows the behavior increases the probability of the behavior in the presence of the same or similar circumstances, it is called a reinforcer. If the contingent stimulus decreases the probability of the behavior in the presence of the same or similar circumstances, it is called a punisher. This stimulus (antecedent), response (behavior), contingency (consequence) sequence is the unit that is studied in a functional analysis. It does not make sense to study any one of these three components in isolation of any of the others, because behavior can only be understood in the context in which it occurs. Functional analysis refers to the identification of the functional relationships between the discriminative stimuli, the behaviors of interests, and the contingencies (reinforcement and punishment) that affect rate or likelihood of behavior.

Functional Classes

In the simplest case, the discriminative stimulus, the behavior of interest, and the consequence may be easy to identify. A food-deprived pigeon in the presence of a lighted key pecks the key, and a pellet of food is delivered. When the key is not lighted, the food is not delivered, regardless of whether the key is pecked. When the key pecking is not followed by food pellets, the key pecking does not change from what it was when the pigeon first encountered the stimulus situation. By studying simple, well-controlled situations, Skinner was able to identify the principles of operant conditioning and the effects of different reinforcement schedules. From this work, Skinner believed it was possible to demonstrate causal control in determining the rate of target behavior, that is, perform a functional analysis.

Identifying control in the case of a simple antecedent, behavior, consequence situation proved possible. However, with organisms with more complex discrimination and behavioral repertoires, new issues emerged. One complexity was that the behavior of interest could no longer be understood as a simple repetitive response that always looks the same. Instead, behaviors could have very different topographies (forms) and still all have the same function and, therefore, be members of the same functional class. A functional class is the set of behaviors all under the same antecedent and contingent control, regardless of their form. This same notion applies to discriminative and reinforcing stimuli. Given that verbal organisms (humans) can transfer stimulus function to stimuli they have not directly experienced, the analysis can get very complex. For example, the stimulus of being refused a request for a date can function as a simple rebuff or be seen as part of a class of stimuli that suggest to people that they are worthless, terrible, or ugly, and people refusing the date could be responded to as if they were part of a class of people who were generally judgmental and condescending, when, in fact, neither of these inferences were correct. What is clear is that a functional analysis in a human whose reinforcement history is largely unknown and unknowable can be very difficult.

Functional Analysis Versus Functional Assessment

There has been little agreement on what is actually meant by the term *functional analysis*. The definition hinges on where one is in the process of the analysis, what one's goals are, and when one chooses to indicate that an adequate analysis has occurred. The analogy to the scientific method is again useful to consider. It is not uncommon to see the terms *functional analysis* and *functional assessment* used interchangeably. There is, however, an important conceptual distinction to be made. For clarity, functional assessment refers to the earlier stages of the scientific method, namely, the direct and indirect gathering of information and data leading to a hypothesis about what the controlling variables for a behavior might be. The term *functional analysis* refers to all the elements of the functional assessment *plus* the final steps in the scientific method analogy where the behavioral scientist actually tests the hypothesis by systematically varying the elements in the environment hypothesized to control the behavior. Data are gathered to establish whether or not when the hypothesized controlling variables are manipulated,

the target behavior changes as predicted. Just as with the scientific method, it is possible that the functional assessment, when tested, does not allow prediction or control of the behavior in question. In that case, an iterative process occurs where the assessment is repeated, a new conceptualization of the controlling variables is generated, and the hypothesized functional relationship is again empirically tested, and the functional analysis is again judged for adequacy. A functional assessment is a component of functional analysis, but a functional analysis goes beyond only hypothesizing to actually manipulating the environment and checking to see if subsequent behavior changes occur as predicted.

The Necessary Adequacy of a Functional Analysis

When Skinner was deriving operant principles in the laboratory using highly controlled conditions and animals, he was able to convincingly demonstrate what antecedent and contingent stimuli controlled the specified behavior of interest. In the less controlled world of human behavior, it is more difficult to demonstrate causality in the rigorous sense of the word. In most cases, the adequacy of the functional analysis is judged by whether it is sufficient to accomplish specific goals for the influence of behavior.

The impact of the functional analysis in clinical and applied settings had less influence than it might have if the procedures to conduct such an analysis had been more rigorously standardized. However, in 1997, federal amendments to the Individuals With Disabilities Education Act required that schools address student behavior problems to ensure that classrooms were conducive to learning for all students. In response to this law, efforts were made to develop guidelines for conducting functional assessments for classroom problems. The steps outlined for a functional assessment included an assessment of the adequacy of the conceptualization of the problem by using the assessment to plan an intervention, then intervene, collect data on the effectiveness of the intervention, and, if necessary, modify the assessment. The empirical testing of the functional assessment makes this procedure a functional analysis. With this federal mandate, attention has again returned to the importance of functional analysis as an important clinical and research tool.

The Meaning of *Causal* in a Functional Analysis

Though earlier it was mentioned that Skinner was able to demonstrate a form of causality in laboratory settings, he and others writing about functional analysis have generally not talked about causal relationships but rather functional relations between variables. A strict causal view implies that if one identifies a causal relationship, then effecting a change in the cause will necessarily produce an effect via some specific mechanism. This Aristotelian view of causality is not the focus of functional analysis. Rather, functional analysis in applied settings entails a much less strict view of what is required for the relationship between variables to be functionally useful. A functional relationship is more consistent with a successionist view of causality that recognizes that what one identifies as cause and effect is a reflection of the psychological processes of the observer and is related to where and how we look for causal explanations.

The simplest level of constraint in functional analysis is that for a functional relationship to exist, the two variables of interest must covary or change together. It is not strictly necessary for the functional analyst to know exactly what mechanism produces a change, only that the manipulation of certain antecedents or consequences reliably produce change in the behavior of interest. It may be that the change is produced through a third, unidentified variable that changes in response to whatever the functional analyst manipulates. In fact, one could get into an endless argument with other psychologists or scientists about whether changing a reinforcer "causes" a change in behavior, or whether the change is at a whole other level of analysis such as change in neurotransmitters leading to changes in membrane potentials followed by nerve impulses traveling down the spinal cord, and so on. Functional analysis concerns itself with identifying pragmatic functional relationships that allow for the prediction and influence of behavior.

This pragmatic argument shapes the kinds of variables that would be considered likely participants in a functional relationship. Human behavior as studied outside the laboratory generally occurs as complex chains where there is a stimulus followed by a response that can then serve as a stimulus for another response in the environment and so on. The search for functional relationships often focuses on identifying functionally important variables that have three characteristics.

First, the putative functional cause must reliably covary with the effect of interest in a temporal order that is consistent with a functional explanation. Second, the functionally important variable is in principle changeable. Third, when changed, the functionally important variable accounts for a clinically significant amount of variance in the behavior of interest. The temporal order component of these criteria refers to the fact that a change in a presumed causal variable must precede a change in that which it is presumed to control. The requirement that the causal variable be changeable is the result of the pragmatic nature of the behavior change agenda of a functional analysis. This focus on changeability does not mean that the functionally causal variable targeted for manipulation was the initial important event, only that it is now accessible and can be changed. For example, a person may have experienced a physical assault at a young age that led him or her to be distrustful in relationships and subsequently experience a series of failed relationships. While it may make sense to consider the initial assault as the cause of the subsequent relationship problems, a functional analysis would not focus on that historical fact because the assault cannot be changed. It is more likely that the functional analysis would focus on the resulting behaviors that are present in current relationships that lead to relationship failures, even if their initial cause was the assault. Current changeable behaviors could include classes of behaviors that function to communicate suspicion or mistrust, or instances of affective blunting that interfere with the formation of intimate relationships.

The last criterion—the functional relationship must account for a clinically significant proportion of the problematic behavior when changed—deserves additional explanation. In most noninstitutional settings, it is simplistic to think that any one behavior has a single cause or is maintained by a single consequence. Given the complexity of human learning, it is realistic to recognize that most functional analyses will only account for a portion of the variance observed in the class of target behaviors of interest. There are at least three implications of this supposition. First, one will be able to find evidence that multiple variables exhibit control over the target behavior, and those planning the intervention should choose to manipulate the variable(s) that account for the most variance using ethical, positive control strategies. The second implication is that any particular functional analysis is likely to be incomplete, meaning that even when one changes the hypothesized controlling variables, the result will be a change in the probability of the target behavior rather than a fully determined (100%) likelihood. The third implication is that a functional analysis done today may not be applicable tomorrow. In some ways, this last supposition is axiomatic, since people continue to learn each day. The point is that a subject is constantly interacting with his or her environment in ways that make more or less potent the influence of a previously important variable in the control of subsequent behavior. Though planned behavior change implies that behavior is determined rather than random, it is a moot point as to whether behavior is fully or partially determined by any particular system of variables, since the functional analyst could rarely expect to access or control any substantial portion of the likely important variables. That does not mean that interventions based on functional analyses cannot be powerful in bringing about large changes in behavior. It just means that to the extent many factors influence a particular class of target behaviors, the degree of influence will be lessened.

An often used example of the complexity of a functional analysis even in the relatively constrained environment of the classroom is discovering that a particular child's disruptive behavior is under the control of different contingencies under different circumstances (i.e., discriminative stimuli). A child may be disruptive when he or she is bored or when ignored or when he or she does not understand the materials being taught. The functional analyst has to evolve an analysis that recognizes that the same topographic class of disruptive behaviors is under the control of three different classes of discriminative stimuli and three different classes of contingent reinforcers. Thus, there are three different functional classes of disruptive behavior. While the iterative nature of a functional analysis should in principle identify these different contexts for the same apparent behavior, the complexity of the task is apparent.

Summary

While there has been a renewed interest in functional analysis and researchers are making significant progress on improving the methodologies for conducting such analyses, the enterprise remains complex. Functional analysts can choose to attempt an analysis using many different conceptualizations of where to look for sources of control. One person might consider the specific number of eye contacts made by a teacher as a measure of attention, while another might measure the number of verbal praise only when accompanied by a smile as a measure of the same controlling variable. Either or neither of the measures of attention might be adequate to achieve behavioral change. While the analysis of behavior using operant principles has frequently been shown to produce powerful, significant behavior change, there remain conceptual and methodological challenges as the practice of functional analysis advances.

CASE ILLUSTRATION

Consider a 5-year-old boy referred for evaluation because he was becoming increasingly disruptive with his parents at home. The therapist visited the home and observed the family interactions without commenting or intervening. After three evenings of being in the home and allowing the family to accommodate to his presence, he collected data on the frequency and conditions that precede and follow the behaviors of interest. The therapist noticed that when the child is quiet, the parents converse with each other or increasingly attend to their own end-of-day activities. When the child asked the parents to play, the parents frequently asked the child to wait until later. After a period of time, the child began to play in more dangerous ways such as playing with lamp cords, trying to get into kitchen drawers, or throwing his toys. Each time this happened, one of the parents stopped what he or she was doing and reprimanded the child, who then momentarily stopped what he was doing. The parent then returned to whatever he or she was doing. Soon the child emitted the disruptive behavior and again a parent intervened. This soon escalated into the child crying and the parents trying to calm him down.

The therapist hypothesized that the disruptive behavior occurred when the parents ignored the child's attempts to engage them in play and was reinforced by the attention the parents paid when the child was disruptive. While this might be counterintuitive, the hypothesis was that even aversive attention is preferable to being ignored. The therapist instructed the parents to respond to the child's request to play, regardless of what they were doing. The therapist collected data under these new conditions, and when the data were plotted, the disruptive behavior was observed to decrease to near zero, supporting the hypothesis that attention controls the child's disruptive behavior. To make certain the analysis was correct, the therapist instructed the parents to go back to the way they were behaving, that is, not attending to the child's request to play. Data were collected and the disruptive behavior again increased. The parents were again instructed to attend to the child's appropriate requests to play, and the disruptive behavior declined to zero again. This demonstrated that a useful functional analysis had occurred. To bring the child's behavior under appropriate control, the therapist taught the parents to reinforce the child's request for play on a variable reinforcement schedule so the child learned that not every request gets attention, but that requests generally lead to reinforcement. Other training principles were added to extend the time between when the child made the request and the parents reinforced it, so the child learned patience and the fact that not every request has to be reinforced in order to get access to adequate play time and attention.

—William C. Follette

See also: *Applied Behavior Analysis (Vols. I, II, & III), Descriptive and Functional Analyses (Vols. I & III), Operant Conditioning (Vols. I, II, & III)*

Suggested Readings

Cone, J. D. (1997). Issues in functional analysis in behavioral assessment. *Behavior Research and Therapy, 35,* 259–275.

Follette, W. C., Naugle, A. E., & Linnerooth, P. J. N. (2000). Functional alternatives to traditional assessment and diagnosis. In M. J. Dougher (Ed.), *Clinical behavior analysis* (pp. 99–125). Reno, NV: Context Press.

Gable, R. A., Quinn, M. M., Rutherford, R. B., Jr., Howell, K. W., & Hoffman, C. C. (1998). *Addressing student problem behavior: Part II. Conducting a functional behavioral assessment* (3rd ed.). Washington, DC: Center for Effective Collaboration and Practice.

Hanley, G. P., Iwata, B. A., & McCord, B. E. (2003). Functional analysis of problem behavior: A review. *Journal of Applied Behavior Analysis, 36,* 147–185.

Hayes, S. C., & Follette, W. C. (1992). Can functional analysis provide a substitute for syndromal classification? *Behavioral Assessment, 14,* 345–365.

Haynes, S. N. (1992). *Models of causality in psychopathology: Toward dynamic, synthetic and nonlinear models of behavior disorders.* New York: Macmillan.

Haynes, S. N., & O'Brien, W. H. (1990). Functional analysis in behavior therapy. *Clinical Psychology Review, 10,* 649–668.

Iwata, B. A., Wallace, M. D., Kahng, S., Lindberg, J. S., Roscoe, E. M., Conners, J., et al. (2000). Skill acquisition in the implementation of functional analysis methodology. *Journal of Applied Behavior Analysis, 33,* 181–194.

Skinner, B. F. (1953). *Science and human behavior.* New York: Free Press.

FUNCTION COMMUNICATION TRAINING

DESCRIPTION OF THE STRATEGY

Children and adults with developmental disorders often engage in behaviors that are extremely disruptive and occasionally dangerous to themselves and others. Aggression, self-injurious behavior, and other disruptive behaviors pose a serious threat to efforts to help these individuals lead more independent lives. Traditional behavioral approaches to treatment typically include a wide range of punishing consequences, including time-out from positive reinforcement, contingent restraint, overcorrection, and, in extreme cases, contingent electric shock. Although many of these interventions demonstrate effectiveness in the initial reduction of challenging behaviors, sustained and clinically relevant improvements are elusive.

Over the past several decades, researchers have studied the functions or reasons why these behaviors occur among persons with developmental disabilities. Several functions seem important, including attention from others, escape from demands, access to desired tangibles, and sensory stimulation. With our growing knowledge of the functions of these behaviors has come interventions that rely on this understanding for their design. The most heavily researched of these function-based approaches was developed in the mid-1980s and has been referred to as functional communication training (FCT). FCT specifically uses communication to reduce challenging behavior. This strategy includes assessing the variables maintaining the behavior to be reduced and providing the same consequences for a different behavior. It is assumed that if individuals can gain access to desired consequences more effectively with the new response, they will use this new response and will reduce their use of the undesirable response. Applying this logic to challenging behavior, one is able to teach individuals more acceptable behaviors that serve the same function as their problem behavior. So, for example, we could teach students to ask for attention in a classroom by saying, "Am I doing good work?" This would allow them to gain teacher attention in this appropriate way rather than in an inappropriate way such as through slapping their face.

The mechanism behind the success of FCT is assumed to rely on functional equivalence. In other words, behaviors maintained by a particular reinforcer (e.g., escape from work) are replaced by other behaviors if these new behaviors serve the same function and are more efficient at gaining the desired reinforcers. Using communication as the replacement behavior provides an added benefit because of its ability to recruit natural communities of the desired reinforcers. One effect of this view of behavior problems is that it suggests that these behaviors are not just responses that need to be reduced or eliminated. This perspective reminds us that attempting to eliminate these behaviors through some reductive technique would leave these individuals with no way of accessing their desired reinforcers and therefore you could anticipate that other maladaptive behaviors would take their place (also called "symptom substitution" or "response covariation").

To assess the function of a problem behavior, the antecedents and consequences of that behavior are identified. Once the purpose of a targeted behavior is understood, individuals can be taught to request the variables previously obtained by the challenging behavior. There are a number of functional assessment strategies that are useful for determining the function of behavior, including ABC charts, functional analyses, and a variety of rating scales. Most clinicians begin with informal observations and interviews of significant others but continue the process using multiple forms of assessment, including rating scales such as the Motivation Assessment Scale (MAS) and structured observations in the individuals' environment. Information from these functional behavioral assessments are used to design plans for reducing the behavior problems.

A functional analysis—manipulating aspects of the environment to assess behavior change—is frequently cited as the best method of determining the function of a behavior problem. However, there are also a number of issues to consider prior to conducting this type of assessment. One issue is accessibility to manipulation. There are certain influences that you cannot or would not manipulate or change in order to perform a functional analysis. Factors such as some illnesses, disrupted family life, and chromosomal aberrations can certainly affect behavior problems, but they cannot or should not be turned on and off in order to assess their influence.

Another concern involves the ethics of conducting a functional analysis. There are other influences that

you could manipulate, but you may not want to change if they will result in an increase in challenging behavior. In many instances, deliberately increasing a severe behavior problem in order to assess it (e.g., by reinforcing challenging behavior) can be questioned on ethical grounds. In these cases, assessment that does not involve manipulation (and subsequent increases in challenging behavior) would be recommended.

The type of response to encourage from the individual needs to be determined. If the individual already has some facility in one mode of communication (e.g., verbal, signing), then that mode should be considered for FCT. Usually, if an individual has been unsuccessful in learning to communicate effectively after extensive verbal language training, then the communication modality to be used should either be signing or symbolic. If the person has also been unsuccessful with sign language training (e.g., has not learned to sign or uses sloppy and incomprehensible signs), it is typically recommended that some type of symbolic communication training be used, at least initially. Symbolic communication training can involve the use of picture books, tokens with messages written on them, or other assistive devices (e.g., vocal output devices). This form of communication training has the advantage of being relatively easy to teach and is universally recognizable.

The environment is arranged to create opportunities for communication (e.g., putting an obstacle in the way of a person trying to open a door and prompting him or her to ask for assistance). This use of incidental teaching—arranging the environment to establish situations that elicit interest and that are used as teaching opportunities—is an important part of successful communication training. Using the person's interest in some interaction, whether it be a desire to stop working on a difficult task or to elicit the attention of an adult, is a very powerful tool in teaching generalized communication. As soon as possible, training trials are interspersed throughout the individual's day where appropriate. Generalization and maintenance of intervention effects may be facilitated by using the criterion environment (i.e., where you want the person to communicate) as the training environment. With the typical model of teaching skills in a separate setting (e.g., in the speech therapist's office), once the response is learned, you need to encourage the performance of that behavior in settings where you want it to occur (e.g., in the cafeteria). By beginning training in the natural or criterion setting, extensive programming for generalization is not necessary because it will be occurring where you want it to occur. In addition, obstacles to maintenance can be immediately identified when teaching in the criterion environment (e.g., are the consequences being provided in that setting going to maintain the new response?).

Teaching individuals to communicate as a replacement for their challenging behavior requires a range of sophisticated language training techniques. A multiphase prompting and prompt-fading procedure is used to teach the new communicative response. Prompts are introduced as necessary, then faded as quickly as possible. Some learners "negatively resist" attempts to teach important skills (e.g., individual screams and kicks), others "positively resist" (e.g., individual laughs and giggles instead of working), and still others "passively resist" (e.g., individual does not look at materials, makes no response). When an individual kicks, screams, and rips up work materials whenever they are presented, or passively ignores efforts to get them to attend to a task, teaching becomes a major challenge and learning becomes highly unlikely.

One procedure used for these types of problems is to teach the individual to request assistance (e.g., "Help me") or a brief break from work. Often the problem behaviors appear to be attempts to avoid or escape from unpleasant situations. It makes sense, then, that if the individual is taught to appropriately request assistance *and receives it,* then the task will seem easier and problem behaviors should be reduced. Similarly, if an individual has been working for some time on a task and is allowed to ask for a break *and receives it,* then this individual's problem behavior should also be reduced.

Reducing the individual's reliance on prompts begins by fading back on the most intrusive assistance being used. In the case of teaching a student to point to a picture book to make a request, one goes from a full physical prompt to partial prompts (e.g., just touching his or her hand), to gestural prompts (e.g., motioning to prompt his or her hands), to finally, only the verbal prompt "What do you want?" Throughout the individual's training, delayed prompting is used extensively. After several trials, clinicians intersperse a trial with a delayed prompt (i.e., we waited approximately 5 seconds) to see if the individual would respond without the next level of prompt. For example, if a student had been responding to just a touch of his or her hand to point to a picture, one would make a gesture as if the student was about to be prompted, and then wait 5 seconds.

It is recommended that one not wait until responding is extremely stable to move on to the next level of prompting. One should attempt to move to the next step if the individual is successful at a step for three to five consecutive responses. This is done in order to prevent the person from becoming prompt dependent (i.e., too reliant on prompts to respond). Training progresses quickly over several weeks to the point where the individual can communicate with no external prompting. As is typical in training, behavior improves most dramatically as soon as the individual begins to make requests without prompts. Once successful, intervention continues by introducing new communicative forms (e.g., requests for food, music, work), reintroducing work demands, expanding the settings in which communication is encouraged to include the whole day, and introducing new staff into the training program.

Recommendations are often made concerning environmental and curricula changes. For example, it can be useful to consider curricular changes for a student who is attempting to escape from academic tasks. However, it is wise to approach these types of changes with considerable caution. The fear is that we will create such an artificial environment that the student may not be able to adapt to new challenges or new environments. The goal of FCT is to teach the student a form of coping skill to be able to appropriately respond to new and unexpected situations (e.g., a new teacher, more difficult work). Therefore, environmental modifications should be viewed as a form of short-term prevention strategy rather than the main programmatic intervention.

RESEARCH BASIS

Empirical support for the success of functional communication training to reducing challenging behavior is growing. Numerous studies are now available demonstrating the effectiveness of this approach with a wide range of behaviors and individuals. Researchers are beginning to explore the boundaries of this intervention approach through the study of maintenance, the role of response efficiency, as well as a variety of other important parameters.

With growing evidence of the value of this intervention approach in reducing a variety of problem behaviors, it is important to evaluate how FCT compares with other interventions. One study, for example, compared the effectiveness of FCT with noncontingent reinforcement (NCR) on the multiple behavior problems of two children. This research established that both interventions initially reduced problem behaviors, but that the participants demonstrated a preference for FCT.

An important aspect of FCT—its usefulness outside of specially designed settings—has also been investigated. Several studies have found that not only can individuals be taught to communicate to reduce their behavior problems, but their requests can be adapted (at times using alternative communication systems) so that they are effective outside of school and with untrained community members. The research to date suggests that we can teach people with behavior problems ways of communicating that will be understood even by people who do not have training in the area of communication difficulties or intellectual disabilities.

RELEVANT TARGET POPULATIONS AND EXCEPTIONS

A variety of individuals with developmental disorders such as autistic disorder and mental retardation have been assisted with this approach. In addition, new research is exploring its use with children and adolescents with behavior disorders who do not also have developmental delays. Research on FCT has focused on severe challenging behaviors such as aggression and self-injurious behavior, stereotyped behavior, and a variety of communication disorders. Intervention has been conducted in group homes, schools, and vocational settings.

COMPLICATIONS

Several factors can limit the effectiveness of FCT as an intervention. For example, because of its reliance on communication, those individuals who are in environments that are relatively unresponsive to their needs and requests will often be frustrated in their attempts to gain access to preferred reinforcers. Therefore, major environmental modifications are sometimes required prior to any attempt to implement

FCT. Researchers have documented that the new more appropriate communicative response must be easier to use than the challenging behavior for replacement to occur (response efficiency). Individuals will continue to be disruptive if the requirements for communication are too difficult (e.g., required to speak in a full sentence versus a brief phrase). Similarly, if the new communicative response is seen as unacceptable in community settings, then others will not respond appropriately, and the desired consequences will not be obtained. Finally, if the trained response is not easily recognizable by significant others in the environment, then these other people will not respond, and challenging behavior will not be reduced. Efforts must be made to ensure that the communicative response is clear and unambiguous.

CASE ILLUSTRATION

"Michael" was a 7-year-old boy with diagnoses of autistic disorder and moderate mental retardation. He lived at home with his mother and 12-year-old brother and attended the neighborhood school. Michael could communicate basic requests (e.g., for food, bathroom) using a picture communication system but used it only with adults. Multiple times throughout the school day he would become upset and engage in a variety of disruptive behaviors. These behaviors included self-injury (e.g., face slapping and hand biting), aggression (e.g., pushing others away, grabbing clothing), and tantrums (e.g., screaming, running out of the classroom).

A variety of functional assessments were conducted, including observations in the classroom and a rating scale (Motivation Assessment Scale) completed by the teacher and teacher's aide. These assessments pointed to escape from academic demands as playing an important role in the maintenance of these behaviors. For example, if Michael was requested to complete a new task, he would become disruptive. A common consequence used at school was a time-out, where he was removed from the situation and placed in the corner of the room. This strategy seemed only to increase the frequency of his disruption.

FCT for Michael involved teaching him to respond to academic demands by requesting assistance. The rationale was for him to learn that rather than try to escape from new or difficult situations, he should request help. By requesting assistance and receiving it, this should make new and/or difficult tasks less aversive. Intervention began by sitting him at his desk and placing a task in front of him. Before he became disruptive, he was prompted to point to a new picture placed on his desk (two open hands held out, with the words "Help me" written underneath). Prompting occurs prior to any disruptive behavior so that the signal (discriminative stimulus) for the student's communication is eventually the difficult task and not an adult responding to the disruption. Once he pointed to the picture, the teacher would provide extra prompts—in essence, making the task easier. Over time, the prompts to point to the picture were faded until he pointed to the picture only when the task was placed on the desk. When he could request assistance without prompts, the picture was placed in his communication book, which was then made available to him on his desk.

Within a few days, Michael would spontaneously point to the picture for help when a new task was placed in front of him, and this generalized to outside the specific training setting. Simultaneously, Michael's disruptive behavior was significantly reduced. Whereas before he was disruptive at least 5 to 10 times per day, now this was reduced to once or twice per week. At first he asked for help using his picture during most tasks, even ones that were not new or difficult. Yet, after several weeks, the number of requests was reduced and his teachers were able to increase the number of new tasks they presented to him since he was rarely disruptive.

—*V. Mark Durand*

See also: *Applied Behavior Analysis (Vols. I, II, & III), Generalization (Vols. I, II, & III), Guided Mastery (Vols. I & III)*

Suggested Readings

Brown, K. A., Wacker, D. P., Derby, K. M., Peck, S. M., Richman, D. M., Sasso, G. M., et al. (2000). Evaluating the effects of functional communication training in the presence and absence of establishing operations. *Journal of Applied Behavior Analysis, 33,* 53–71.

Carr, E. G., & Durand, V. M. (1985). Reducing behavior problems through functional communication training. *Journal of Applied Behavior Analysis, 18,* 111–126.

Carr, E. G., Levin, L., McConnachie, G., Carlson, J. I., Kemp, D. C., & Smith, C. E. (1994). *Communication-based intervention for problem behavior: A user's guide for producing positive change.* Baltimore: Paul H. Brookes.

Durand, V. M. (1990). *Severe behavior problems: A functional communication training approach.* New York: Guilford Press.

Durand, V. M. (1999). Functional communication training using assistive devices: Recruiting natural communities of reinforcement. *Journal of Applied Behavior Analysis, 32,* 247–267.

Durand, V. M., & Carr, E. G. (1991). Functional communication training to reduce challenging behavior: Maintenance and application in new settings. *Journal of Applied Behavior Analysis, 24,* 251–264.

Durand, V. M., & Carr, E. G. (1992). An analysis of maintenance following functional communication training. *Journal of Applied Behavior Analysis, 25,* 777–794.

Durand, V. M., & Crimmins, D. B. (1992). *The Motivation Assessment Scale (MAS) administration guide.* Topeka, KS: Monaco & Associates.

Horner, R. H., & Day, H. M. (1991). The effects of response efficiency on functionally equivalent competing behaviors. *Journal of Applied Behavior Analysis, 24,* 719–732.

Kelley, M. E., Lerman, D. C., & Van Camp, C. M. (2002). The effects of competing reinforcement schedules on the acquisition of functional communication. *Journal of Applied Behavior Analysis, 35,* 59–63.

Luiselli, J. K. (1992). Assessment and treatment of self-injury in a deaf-blind child. *Journal of Developmental and Physical Disabilities, 4,* 219–226.

Wacker, D. P., Steege, M. W., Northup, J., Sasso, G., Berg, W., Reimers, T., et al. (1990). A component analysis of functional communication training across three topographies of severe behavior problems. *Journal of Applied Behavior Analysis, 23,* 417–429.

GENERALIZATION

DESCRIPTION OF THE STRATEGY

Generalization as an effect has been noted since researchers began discussing learning. Original experiments in classical conditioning found that animals conditioned to a particular tone would initially respond to similar tones. Operant conditioning has shown that an individual who is reinforced for a particular response is more likely to make that response in similar situations. Both these examples illustrate the general concept of generalization. Most often, during learning trials an organism learns not only to respond to the target stimuli but also to *not* respond to other, somewhat similar stimuli. This later phenomenon is discrimination, and it is unusual to see a description of generalization without a concomitant discussion of discrimination.

At the most basic level, all instances of learning may be considered generalization. In this most broad conceptualization, whenever an organism predicts that because a past behavior was reinforced the same behavior will be reinforced in the future, the organism shows generalization. Thus, according to this broad view, any instance of learning is generalization.

Most researchers, however, are not referring to the broad conceptualization when they discuss generalization. In general, when discussing generalization, researchers and practitioners are focusing on "one-many" generalization, also known as "stimulus generalization." Stimulus generalization refers to an organism responding to similar stimuli or situations in the same manner, albeit weaker, as it did to the original stimuli or situation.

Basic research with generalization has noted that generalization follows a predicted generalization gradient. For stimuli that are nearly identical to the original stimuli, the organism will respond in nearly the same way as it did to the original stimuli. Thus, in this instance the generalization gradient is flat, indicating that the response will be nearly as strong to similar stimuli as to the original stimuli, but the response gets somewhat weaker as the new stimulus deviates from the initial stimuli. In contrast, the greater the new stimuli differs from the initial stimuli, a more steep generalization gradient is noted. This means that the individual's response is likely to be weaker than the initial response, and the response becomes less strong the more the new stimuli differs. Learning theorists argue that what happens during generalization training is that the individual responds to a population of stimuli. Each population has a mean value for the response(s), and there is typically variability around the mean. Thus, the stimulus gradient follows a predictable pattern and can be seen for all types of stimuli, including visual and auditory stimuli, among others. In addition, this phenomena is observed during training using more basic stimuli (color hue, auditory pitch) and more complex phenomena (word learning). Overall, generalization is a robust phenomena that is observed among all organisms.

Studies conducted over many decades have shown the existence of generalization and the parameters affecting its acquisition for basic concepts. However, generalization has an important part in the applied literature as well. In this context, generalization is best described as the continued display of the behavior once the treatment program has been reduced or eliminated. The conceptualization of generalization within a treatment context indicates that there are two main aspects: (1) continuation of treatment effects after the elimination or reduction of the intervention and (2) presence of treatment effects in situations other than the one that was the focus of the intervention. Within the treatment literature, some authors have suggested that generalization and discrimination are so important to behavioral analysis that these principles should be primary and the investigation of *ways* in which behavior change is effected should be secondary.

Despite the importance of generalization in the applied literature, not all studies have generalization as the outcome goal. In fact, ABA studies are designed with the idea that generalization will *not* occur; otherwise, removal of the intervention and subsequent reduction or elimination of the treatment effect would not be predicted. Nevertheless, in most situations, generalization to other situations and across time without the continual influence of explicit and overt contingencies is the goal.

Most often the discussion of generalization focuses on stimulus generalization. As discussed, in its most basic form, stimulus generalization is when the individual responds to a stimulus or situation that is similar but not identical to the initial stimuli. However, other types of generalization exist, including generalization of setting (behavior changes to a different setting while the intervention remains in the training setting), time (maintenance of the behavior after the removal of the intervention), and response (production of a similar behavior than the one targeted for intervention). The goal is to have cross-setting generalization with response generalization that is maintained over time.

RESEARCH BASIS

Although generalization is arguably the primary outcome goal of behavioral interventions, little research has specifically focused on studying this phenomena. Nevertheless, over the last several decades, psychology has learned much in terms of the presence of generalization and the functional variables controlling generalization. For example, good generalization of treatment effect has been seen in the area of augmentative and alternate communication and social skills training. Behavior change strategies using prompting,

positive reinforcement, instructions, feedback, rehearsal, and modeling have also demonstrated generalization of treatment effects.

It is not surprising that reinforcement is strongly related to generalization. However, the schedule of reinforcement is important in determining whether the behavior will generalize. For example, continuous reinforcement is most effective in attempting to establish new behaviors, while intermittent reinforcement is thought to encourage generalization and maintenance. However, in the real world, continuous reinforcement is not often observed. Failure to provide the most effective schedule of reinforcement may contribute to the lack of generalization in some studies.

RELEVANT TARGET POPULATIONS AND EXCEPTIONS

Generalization applies to every human and nonhuman population for whom behavioral interventions work. Given that generalization is a fundamental aspect of all forms of learning, all organisms that have the ability to learn have the ability to generalize. Despite the ability for all individuals to generalize, factors can interfere with the generalization effect. Several meta-analyses have found generalization failure rates of approximately 16%. As noted, inappropriate reinforcement schedules may be partially to blame, as well as use of less effective methods in the initial training session. Other factors could include failure to attend to the relevant training stimuli. While research is pointing to specific variables linked to stimulus, setting, time, and response generalization, and while research shows that nearly all organisms should be able to generalize, the research shows that generalization is not always the case.

COMPLICATIONS

Complications typically include failure to generalize to situations where the behavior or response is desired or overgeneralization of behaviors to a broad number of barely similar situations. The most classic example of overgeneralization is the original Little Albert studies. In this infamous experiment, Albert was conditioned to fear a white rat by pairing the rat with an aversive, fear-inducing noise. Albert then reportedly generalized his fear to all white furry objects, including fur coats! However, most often, the main complication of behavioral interventions is the failure to generalize to other situations or without the presence of the treatment effect. As described above, generalization and maintenance have been very difficult to obtain. It is common for practitioners to obtain behavior change during the training sessions but, for the variety of reasons listed above, fail to see generalization across time and setting.

CASE ILLUSTRATION

"Roberto" was referred by his father, "Mr. G.," for a comprehensive assessment, and his mother, "Mrs. G.," also consented to testing. According to paternal and maternal report, Roberto was having behavioral difficulties at both homes, particularly with his younger brother and stepmother at his father's house and with talking back at his mother's house. In addition, Roberto was having problems at school, such as inattention, difficulty with school work, and variable grades.

Roberto was a 10-year, 2-month-old Hispanic boy in the seventh grade. His parents divorced when he was 3 years old and have shared custody since the divorce. Initially, Roberto spent half the week with one parent and half the week with the other, but this was changed, so he spent 1 week with his mother and 1 week with his father. His father brought Roberto to the first session and his mother brought him to the second session. While at his father's house, he lived with his father, stepmother, and 2-year-old half brother. While at his mother's house, he lived with his mother and 2-year-old half sister. Roberto's parents moved here from Belize 10 years ago, and Roberto was born in the United States. At his home, Roberto spoke Spanish, while at school he spoke English.

Maternal report indicated that Roberto was the product of an uncomplicated pregnancy but difficult delivery. Labor was induced, and due to complications, Roberto spent 9 days in NICU. Since then, he has been relatively healthy, and no other illnesses, injuries, or surgeries were reported.

Roberto had been attending elementary school for the last 2 years. Both parents reported that he was having problems at school, particularly with he conduct. Overall his grades were variable, although he had been on the A/B honor roll. According to his second grade teacher, Roberto was bright and a good worker when he "chose to be," but she felt that he did not always apply himself. She reported that he was in the accelerated math program and that he thrived on that challenge and competition.

Maternal, paternal, and teacher report indicated that Roberto was having significant behavioral problems at home and school. His teacher reported that he was more argumentative than last year and denied engaging in inappropriate behavior, even when it was obvious that he was guilty. He had also become much more defensive, especially when accused of an infraction. At home, Roberto argued, defied requests, and threw and hit things when angry. Mrs. G. reported that approximately 1 month ago, Roberto threw something at her while angry. Mr. G. is specifically concerned with Roberto's relationship with his stepmother and younger brother. According to Mr. G., Roberto often fought with his stepmother, and their relationship had been negative for the last year. Mrs. G. confirmed this and reported that although Roberto used to get along with his stepmother, he now reported that "she tells him what to do too much." Roberto reported during the interview that although she was nice in the beginning, now she "bugs" him a lot. He also indicated that he had a difficult time with his little brother.

Clinical Observations

Roberto arrived for testing neatly groomed and appropriately dressed. He was very polite, and good rapport was established. He presented with a flat affect but was friendly and conversed well with the examiner, often speaking thoughtfully and articulately. Overall, Roberto was very focused and persistent during testing. He persisted with items even when unsure of an answer and worked hard for every item. This style was evident for both the academic-oriented tasks and the more difficult affective and behavioral questionnaires. In general, Roberto was very calm and did not display any impulsivity during testing. No speech, motor, vision, or hearing problems were noted.

School Observation

As part of the current evaluation, Roberto was observed at his school for approximately 35 minutes, during which time his class was participating in an English assignment. Initially, he was working on his assignment, as were most of the students in his class. However, after approximately 15 minutes, his teacher began calling children to write correct answers on the board. In general, once the students began correcting their work and writing on the board, Roberto was inattentive. He initially raised his hand to participate, but within minutes he was distracted and no longer paying attention. Overall, Roberto displayed a flat affect during the entire period he was observed and did not interact with his peers.

Interpretation of Psychoeducational Results

Psychoeducational tests were administered to rule out any intellectual or achievement difficulties that might be contributing to Roberto's difficulties at school. On the K-BIT, Roberto obtained a Vocabulary Standard Score of 99, a Matrices Standard Score of 106, and a K-BIT IQ Composite Standard Score of 103 $\forall$ 7. On the PPVT, he obtained a Deviation Type Standard Score of 99, which is consistent with his obtained Vocabulary Standard Score on the K-BIT. The results of the present evaluation appear to be reliable and valid. On the WJ-III,TAch, Roberto obtained subtest and cluster scores in the Average to Above Average Range compared to other children his age. Overall, Roberto's achievement scores are commensurate with the current estimate of his intellectual ability.

Interpretation of Emotional and Behavioral Assessment

Roberto's emotional and behavioral functioning was assessed through rating scales completed by Roberto, his mother, his father, and his teacher. In addition, detailed interviews were conducted with all four informants.

The main areas of concern reported by Roberto, his mother, and his father are problems with argumentative, defiant, and hostile behaviors. Roberto's mother and father both report that Roberto frequently loses his temper, argues with adults, defies parental requests, deliberately annoys others, blames others for his mistakes, is touchy and easily annoyed by others, and is angry and resentful. Roberto's teacher reports seeing all these behaviors, although she did not report being as concerned with these behaviors as his parents. Roberto himself admitted that he loses his temper and argues with adults. Furthermore, he admitted that he is easily annoyed with others and often gets angry. These behaviors have worsened recently, particularly Roberto's habit of denying his guilt or "lying" when accused of a misbehavior. His teacher noted that he is quick to say that he did not do a particular behavior, even when there are witnesses to his misbehavior. His parents report that Roberto argues with his mother

and stepmother and frequently picks fights with his younger brother. Roberto's parents report that these behaviors are worsening and that he is beginning to engage in more severe problems of conduct, such as destroying others' property, physically hitting other people such as his brother, and taking things from others. Problems in these areas are supported by maternal and paternal BASC Conduct Problem and Aggression T-Scores and maternal PIC-R Delinquency T-Scores in the Clinically Elevated Range and paternal PIC-R Delinquency T-Scores and teacher BASC Conduct Problems T-Score in the At-Risk Range. Taken together, informant report indicates that these symptoms are more severe than would be expected from typical children and support a diagnosis of oppositional defiant disorder.

Diagnostic Impressions

Oppositional Defiant Disorder, 313.81

Treatment

Research suggests that the most effective treatment for oppositional defiant disorder and conduct problems is parent training; therefore, this approach was utilized with Roberto. As noted, Roberto's parents are divorced; however, since they have joint custody, it was decided that both parents needed parent training if the intervention was to be effective. Thus, it was decided that each parent would bring Roberto to treatment every other week, so that each parent was receiving two sessions a month, with Roberto receiving four.

For both parents, the initial session focused on describing parent training and listing in detail what would occur over the next several months. Both parents were informed that they would first learn to interact with Roberto in a more positive manner, learn the skills of praising and attending, and begin ignoring certain behaviors ("pick and choose their battles"). Then they would learn to give effective commands and begin initiating contingency management programs for use in their homes. Finally, they would learn time-out and other discipline techniques.

Once parent training began, each parent was repeatedly told the importance of consistency. Reinforcement schedules were described, and Roberto's parents learned that they could make the behaviors more entrenched if they eventually gave in to his demands or failed to follow through on their actions. Initial sessions focused on obtaining baseline information about how often noncompliant behaviors occurred, followed by an active attempt to decrease noncompliant behaviors and increase compliant behaviors. Each behavior was conceptualized as what Roberto would *do* to comply, rather that what he was not supposed to do. Roberto resisted these initial attempts to provide structure and track pertinent behavioral information, and he increased his oppositional and defiant behaviors. His parents had been warned that this might occur and were able to adhere to the parent training regimen. In Roberto's case, his parents had extreme difficulty adhering to the behavioral plan consistently; therefore, several sessions were spent problem solving ways to increase parental efficacy. The contingency management programs were nearly identical for both homes, and after much work, both parents were able to maintain roughly the same schedule for Roberto. Although the incentives varied by home (computer at his father's home, television at his mother's), each parent made a concerted effort to provide as similar a program as possible.

Generalization

The goal of the treatment program was to decrease Roberto's oppositional behaviors at both primary homes and at school. Since treatment was only occurring at the office, explicit steps were taken to ensure that generalization would occur. First, each parental session focused on *doing,* rather than just talking. For example, each parent sat with Roberto and the therapist and decided on which behaviors to target at home and at school. Similarly, after the therapist described more effective communication strategies, Roberto and his parent practiced the strategies in session. Second, explicit monitoring and tracking occurred at home and school. Each targeted behavior was monitored and tracked on a personalized chart, with appropriate consequences for positive and negative behaviors. Third, parental sessions focused on applying the techniques to novel situations (stores, grandparents' homes, etc.). Finally, toward the end of treatment, once Roberto was consistently engaging in compliant behaviors and had decreased the oppositional behaviors, active monitoring was decreased to more closely approximate a normal situation where intermittent reinforcement is desired.

Each of these steps was taken to increase the likelihood of generalization. Response generalization was encouraged by having the parents offer praise for all positive behaviors, including those not specifically targeted in session or on the behavior charts. In-session practicing, problem solving, and behavior charts at both home and school were used to increase setting generalization so that Roberto would exhibit appropriate behaviors in situations other than the therapist's office. Time generalization was fostered by decreasing the continuous reinforcement schedule, eliminating the behavior charts, and relying on environmental contingencies and parental praise instead of scheduled rewards. Due to the concerted effort to increase generalization, 8 months after the initiation of treatment, Roberto's behaviors were markedly improved both at home and at school.

—Persephanie Silverthorn
and Angela Walter Keyes

See also: *Applied Behavior Analysis (Vols. I, II & III), Generalization (Vols. I, II & III), Kazdin, Alan E. (Vols. I & III), Operant Conditioning (Vols. I, II & III)*

Suggested Readings

Freeland, J. T., & Noell, G. H. (2002). Programming for maintenance: An investigation of delayed intermittent reinforcement and common stimuli to create indiscriminable contingencies. *Journal of Behavioral Education, 11,* 5–18.

Mowrer, O. H. (1960). *Learning theory and behavior.* New York: Wiley.

Pfiffner, L. J., & McBurnett, K. (1997). Social skills training with parent generalization: Treatment effects for children with attention deficit disorder. *Journal of Consulting and Clinical Psychology, 65,* 749–757.

Rocca, J. V., & Gross, A. M. (1996). Report-Do-Report: Promoting setting and setting-time generalization. *Education and Treatment of Children, 19,* 408–424.

Schlosser, R. W., & Lee, D. L. (2000). Promoting generalization and maintenance in augmentative and alternative communication: A meta-analysis of 20 years of effectiveness research. *Augmentative and Alternate Communication, 16,* 208–226.

Stokes, T. (1992). Discrimination and generalization. *Journal of Applied Behavior Analysis, 25,* 429–432.

GENERALIZED CONDITIONED PUNISHER

DESCRIPTION OF THE STRATEGY

A generalized conditioned punisher is a stimulus that exerts a punishing effect because it has been associated with punishing stimuli. In contrast with unconditioned punishment, in which the stimulus is in itself punishing, conditioned punishers are stimuli that decrease the likelihood that a child will engage in a behavior as a result of learning. Furthermore, they have the additional property that their effectiveness does not depend upon a specific punisher, as the stimulus represents different punishers. There are thus three conditions that define generalized conditioned punishers: (1) the event must decrease the likelihood that a behavior will occur again (punishment), (2) the event must not be punishing in and of itself, but it must provide punishment through learning (conditioning), and (3) the event must be associated with two or more punishing events (generalization).

Generalized conditioned punishers are uncommon and are not widely employed in behavior modification programs. However, time-out from positive reinforcement, which is very commonly used in programs to manage child behavior, rely on similar mechanisms for punishment. In time-out programs, which emphasize time-out from positive reinforcement, the mechanism of action is negative punishment, in which a positively reinforcing stimulus is removed for a time in order to decrease the likelihood that a child will continue to engage in a particular behavior. Time-out is a generalized punisher in that the particular reinforcing stimulus changes, depending on the specific situation a child is involved in. For example, in one situation, the reinforcer may be parent attention, while in another it may be peer attention, or it may be participation in a reinforcing activity such as a sports game or recess. Time-out is a conditioned punisher because the behavior required by the time-out system is not necessarily punishing in and of itself, but it becomes punishing as a result of repeated trials as the child learns to associate time-out with the removal of reinforcing stimuli.

Punishers are used to decrease the likelihood that a child will engage in an undesired behavior (or engage in a desired behavior). As generalized conditioned punishers are associated with more than one particular undesired object or activity, they decrease the likelihood that an object or activity loses its punishing properties and allow more flexibility in applying punishing stimuli. For example, time-out can be used appropriately in nearly any context, regardless of the specific stimulus that is reinforcing a particular behavior. Therefore, the punishing stimulus need not be matched to a particular reinforcing stimulus, as long as it is matched to a specific behavior.

RESEARCH BASIS

Generalized conditioned punishers have not been studied within the context of laboratory or clinical settings. However, time-out and other specific types of generalized conditioned punishers have been included in treatment studies of children with externalizing disorders. The majority of treatments involving use of time-out are employed in parent training and child management programs. While some of these programs have established effectiveness through randomized trials, they do not usually include systematic evaluations of generalized conditioned punishers and their effectiveness compared to other types of punishers or reinforcement systems. Rather, generalized conditioned punishment systems such as time-out are usually evaluated as an integral part of an overall treatment package. A number of single-subject design studies have investigated the effects of time-out alone, and these studies indicate that time-out has a powerful suppressive effect on targeted behaviors.

—Greta M. Massetti and Gregory A. Fabiano

See also: *Applied Behavior Analysis (Vols. I, II & III), Generalization (Vols. I, II & III), Operant Conditioning (Vols. I, II & III)*

Suggested Reading

DiLorenzo, T. M. (1988). Operant and classical conditioning. In J. L. Matson (Ed.), *Handbook of treatment approaches in childhood psychopathology* (pp. 65–78). New York: Kluwer Academic Press.

GENERALIZED CONDITIONED REINFORCER

DESCRIPTION OF THE STRATEGY

A generalized conditioned reinforcer is a stimulus that exerts a reinforcing effect because it has been associated with reinforcing stimuli. In contrast with unconditioned reinforcement, in which the stimulus is in itself reinforcing, conditioned reinforcers are stimuli that have come to have value to an individual as a result of learning. Furthermore, generalized conditioned reinforcers are associated with many other reinforcers; their effectiveness does not depend upon a specific reinforcer, as the stimulus represents different reinforcers. There are thus three conditions that define generalized conditioned reinforcers: (1) the event must increase the likelihood that a behavior will occur again (reinforcement), (2) the event must not be reinforcing in and of itself, but it must provide reinforcement through learning (conditioning), and (3) the event must be associated with two or more reinforcing events (generalization).

Common types of generalized conditioned reinforcers are money and tokens. Token economy systems used in behavior modification programs thus employ generalized conditioned reinforcers, as receiving tokens as a consequence of performing a particular action is not initially reinforcing, but the tokens may be exchanged for an array of reinforcing objects or activities, such as candy or TV privileges. In addition, sticker charts commonly used in interventions with children also involve generalized conditioned reinforcers if accumulating a certain number of stickers is associated with several different kinds of reinforcers.

It is impractical to define a primary reinforcer for every behavior exhibited by an individual, and therefore generalized conditioned reinforcers are a highly effective and practical behavior modification procedure. Generalized reinforcers allow the use of less frequent reinforcement schedules, so that children are only reinforced when they have engaged in a behavior enough times to earn a desired object or activity. In addition, as generalized conditioned reinforcers are associated with more than one particular desired object or activity, they decrease the likelihood that an object or activity loses its reinforcing properties. For example, after repeated trials, an individual child may tire of watching one particular video if it is provided as the only reinforcer for a particular behavior. If the child is permitted to choose between a video and other desired activities, he or she is likely to find at least one of the activities reinforcing at the time.

RESEARCH BASIS

Generalized conditioned reinforcers have been studied within the context of laboratory settings. In addition, token economies, sticker charts, and other specific types of generalized conditioned reinforcers have been included in studies of treatments of individuals with developmental disabilities, externalizing and internalizing disorders, and in inpatient settings. The majority of treatments involving the use of token economies are employed in intensive treatment settings, such as residential programs. While some of these programs have established effectiveness through randomized trials, they do not usually include systematic evaluations of generalized conditioned reinforcers and their effectiveness compared to other types of reinforcers. Rather, generalized conditioned reinforcers are usually evaluated as part of an overall treatment package.

Older studies have compared the use of generalized conditioned reinforcers to other types of reinforcers. Studies indicate that stimuli that are generalized are more effective than nongeneralized stimuli. In addition, generalized conditioned reinforcers have greater resistance to extinction. These findings indicate that providing a choice of reinforcers leads to faster learning and lower rates of relapse than reinforcing every instance of a behavior or always providing the same reinforcer.

—Greta M. Massetti and Gregory A. Fabiano

See also: *Applied Behavior Analysis (Vols. I, II & III), Classical Conditioning (Vols. I, II & III), Generalization (Vols. I, II & III), Operant Conditioning (Vols. I, II & III)*

Suggested Readings

Comaty, J. E., Stasio, M., & Advokat, C. (2001). Analysis of outcome variables of a token economy system in a state psychiatric hospital: A program evaluation. *Research in Developmental Disabilities, 22,* 233–253.

Glynn, S. M. (1990). Token economy approaches for psychiatric patients: Progress and pitfalls over 25 years. *Behavior Modification, 14,* 383–407.

Kanger, F. H. (1960). Incentive value of generalized reinforcers. *Psychological Reports, 7,* 531–538.

GOAL SETTING

Goal setting was developed out of social-cognitive theory and involves an individual setting a standard for his or her performance, monitoring, and evaluating the performance against the standard. First, a task for improvement is identified. A goal for the task is then decided upon and recorded for the task. The goal can be set collaboratively with a therapist, teacher, or a parent. Alternatively, the child may set the performance goal. A time frame, or point at which performance will be evaluated, is identified. Goal achievement is evaluated, with the child examining present performance against the goal. For example, on-task behavior for math homework could be targeted. A goal for 10 math problems completed in 10 minutes could be negotiated. At the end of 10 minutes, the parent and child will evaluate if the goal has been met.

Goals can be graduated, or broken down into smaller steps, with more challenging standards set with successful goal attainment at the easier steps. Goals are thought to affect performance through direction of attention, energizing behavior, persistence during the task, and discovery and use of strategies relevant to the task. It also is hypothesized that in response to the monitoring, children will correct strategies and set goals that match their performance; therefore, performance and goal-setting ability will improve over time.

RESEARCH BASIS

While goal setting has been used in a variety of settings, research on goal setting with children has been limited. Often goal setting in children will be evaluated as part of a treatment package, which could include contingency management, anger control, or problem solving. Goal setting has been successful at improving both on-task behavior and accuracy of homework. In addition, adherence to a medical regimen has been an appropriate target for goal-setting interventions. Improvements in social behavior, disruptive behavior, and aggression also have been successfully targeted with treatments involving goal setting. Most commonly, goal setting is successfully utilized as an instructional technique in the classroom and has been found to improve the writing, arithmetic, and reading performance of students. Finally, goal setting has been identified as an acceptable treatment by parents.

COMPLICATIONS

Many studies included families that were highly motivated; therefore, goal setting with all individuals may not be effective. For academics, goal setting has been suggested for use in situations that have a consistent difficulty level. If the material has a variable difficulty level, the child will have more trouble setting appropriate goals, and the intervention may be unsuccessful. Both parents and children will need training on how to set appropriate goals that are challenging yet attainable. Goals that are not well defined, too difficult,

too easy, or set too far in the future will lead to an ineffective intervention.

—*Kellie A. Hilker*

See also: Behavioral Treatment in Natural Environments (Vols. I & III), Guided Mastery (Vols. I & III), Instructions (Vols. I & III), Problem-Solving Therapy (Vol. I), Reinforcement (Vols. I & III), Social and Interpersonal Skills Training (Vol. II), Social Competence Treatment: Externalizing Disorders (Vol. II), Social Effectiveness Training (Vols. I & III), Social Skills Training (Vols. I & III)

Suggested Readings

Kahle, A. L., & Kelley, M. L. (1994). Children's homework problems: A comparison of goal setting and parent training. *Behavior Therapy, 25,* 275–290.

Lochman, J. E., Burch, P. R., Curry, J. F., & Lampron, L. B. (1984). Treatment and generalization effects of cognitive-behavioral and goal-setting interventions with aggressive boys. *Journal of Consulting and Clinical Psychology, 52,* 915–916.

Locke, E. A., & Latham, G. P. (2002). Building a practically useful theory of goal setting and task motivation. *American Psychologist, 57,* 705–717.

Schafer, L. C., Glasgow, R. E., & McCaul, K. D. (1982). Increasing the adherence of diabetic adolescents. *Journal of Behavioral Medicine, 5,* 353–362.

GOOD BEHAVIOR GAME

The Good Behavior Game is a practical, straightforward method for managing disruptive behavior via rewarding children for engaging in on-task behaviors during instructional periods in elementary and younger middle school classroom settings. This program was first experimentally tested in 1969 by researchers at the University of Kansas, and several subsequent research studies substantiate its effectiveness.

Implementing the game is relatively easy, given that some preparatory time is allocated to becoming familiar with the main steps and identifying which classroom-accessible, effective reinforcers will be used for the "winning team." Prior to introducing the game to students, teachers must (a) determine during which daily instructional periods the game will be played, (b) identify specific negative behaviors to monitor via use of a "marking" procedure (i.e., "leaving one's seat," "talking-out behavior," and "other disruptive behavior"), and (c) select suitable rewards that can be given on a daily (e.g., less homework, extra recess time) and weekly and/or monthly basis (e.g., early dismissal on Friday, watching a preferred movie one afternoon, afternoon to complete projects usually assigned only as homework).

After these matters are settled, the game can be introduced and implemented via the following steps:

1. Introduce the Good Behavior Game to the class. Introduce the concept of playing a game to reward good behavior. A schedule should be prepared to indicate during which class instruction periods the game will be in effect and which behaviors will be monitored.

2. Inform the students that whenever a student engages in one of the targeted behaviors, the team to which that student belongs will receive a mark on the board. Explain that both teams may win if they earn no more than a set number of marks while the game is in effect. When the game is played for more than one instruction period, the maximum number of marks can be increased due to the lengthier "monitoring" period. If both teams exceed the maximum number of marks, the team with the lowest total number at the end of the day is the winner. If there is a tie, then both teams earn the reward. As the students and teacher become more practiced at playing the game, introduce challenges in which team(s) that accrue less than the maximum number of marks by the end of the week and/or month can win a presumably more difficult to attain highly desirable reward.

The Good Behavior Game is both effective for increasing on-task behavior and works well even with especially disruptive children, as the team that has such children can "vote" to not include them in the game. This provides an incentive to "stay in the game" and further promotes on-task behavior.

—*Shari K. Neul*

See also: *Applied Behavior Analysis (Vols. I, II & III), Behavioral Treatment in Natural Environments (Vols. I & III), Token Economy (Vols. I, II & III)*

Suggested Reading

Barrish, H. H., Saunders, M., & Wolf, M. M. (1969). Good Behavior Game: Effects of individual contingencies for group consequences on disruptive behavior in a classroom. *Journal of Applied Behavior Analysis, 2,* 119–124.

GRADUATED EXTINCTION

DESCRIPTION OF THE STRATEGY

Extinction is a term used to describe how a reinforced behavior becomes less frequent if reinforcement for that behavior is withdrawn. Eventually, if the behavior is not reinforced over a period of time, the behavior will cease. Extinction procedures are typically applied by removing a reinforcer in its entirety following a behavior (e.g., removing all attention from a tantrumming child). Graduated extinction is an application of the extinction principle that removes a reinforcer for a behavior in an incremental fashion or reduces the magnitude of reinforcement incrementally.

Graduated extinction is most widely used as an intervention for childhood sleep problems (e.g., refusal to go to sleep, frequent nighttime wakings). Two common variations of graduated extinction have been applied. In the first approach, a parent waits for longer periods of time over successive trials before attending to the child. In the other approach, a parent may attend to the child immediately but decrease the total amount of time spent attending to the child over successive interactions.

For example, if a child exhibits crying or noncompliant behavior at bedtime that is reinforced and maintained by adult attention, a parent may choose to implement a graduated extinction procedure. In such an approach, the parent would refrain from checking on the child for 5 minutes. The parent would then check on the child after 5 minutes regardless of whether the child was exhibiting negative behavior. After the first visit, the parent would then wait 10 minutes before checking on the child a second time. Once again, the parent would check on the child regardless of whether the child was crying or not. A third visit would not occur until 15 minutes later. Further visits would continue on 15-minute intervals until the child falls asleep. On subsequent nights, the time parents wait before the initial check is gradually lengthened from 5 minutes to increasingly longer time periods. In addition, the time between visits is also lengthened gradually. All visits throughout the procedure are short, and the focus is on minimizing disruption to help the child fall asleep faster. The procedure may be enhanced by setting a regular bedtime and establishing a bedtime routine.

RESEARCH BASIS

Graduated extinction for sleep problems has been investigated in single-subject multiple baseline studies as well as randomized, controlled, between-group studies. The majority of studies were conducted with infants or young children. Across studies, graduated extinction procedures were more effective than or equivalent to other behavioral interventions for sleep (e.g., extinction procedures). Compared to extinction, graduated extinction procedures result in better treatment compliance and less parental stress for nighttime wakings. As parents may be unwilling to completely ignore a child who appears to be in distress (e.g., wakes up in the middle of the night), parents may be more likely to comply with a graduated extinction procedure over an extinction procedure that requires complete ignoring. Because of this, some studies have found graduated extinction to be more palatable to parents than extinction, perhaps because the procedures permit the parent to "check" on the child periodically to ensure that the child is in no real distress.

Although not widely applied in the research literature to other behaviors it is possible that graduated extinction may be a helpful intervention for other problematic behaviors and may be preferred because it does not require absolute withdrawal of a reinforcing stimulus. Further research is needed to clarify this issue.

RELEVANT TARGET POPULATIONS AND EXCEPTIONS

The studies on graduated extinction have concentrated on children in infancy up to young childhood. Graduated extinction procedures might be used with older children or adults, but those age groups have not been studied. Graduated extinction is useful for cases where an abrupt extinction procedure may not be indicated (e.g., a parent who will not agree to completely ignore a child's crying because of a concern that the crying could indicate actual distress). Systematically planning the extinction schedule may help to prevent the unplanned reinforcement that occurs when a parent "gives in." Graduated extinction may not be appropriate for situations when a behavior needs to be eliminated immediately, such as aggressive or dangerous behavior.

COMPLICATIONS

Graduated extinction will not be effective if it is not possible to remove a reinforcer for the target behavior.

For example, in the case of bedtime crying maintained by parental attention, graduated extinction cannot be implemented if a parent is unwilling to ignore a crying child. Although some researchers have suggested that a graduated extinction procedure may exacerbate negative behavior at bedtime, controlled outcome studies do not support this contention. Similar to regular extinction procedures, it is necessary to ensure that the reinforcer for the targeted behavior is controlled. For example, if a graduated extinction procedure is being used to decrease bedtime problems, and an alternative caretaker is putting the child to bed, it is important to ensure that procedures are implemented consistently, regardless of who is putting the child to bed.

—*Greta M. Massetti and Gregory A. Fabiano*

See also: *Extinction (Vol. II), Extinction and Habituation (Vols. I & III), Operant Conditioning (Vols. I, II & III), Schedule-Induced Behavior (Vol. III), Schedules of Reinforcement (Vols. I, II & III)*

Suggested Readings

Ferber, R. (2002). *Solve your child's sleep problems.* New York: Simon & Schuster.

Kuhn, B. R., & Weidinger, D. (2000). Interventions for infant and toddler sleep disturbance: A review. *Child and Family Behavior Therapy, 22,* 33–50.

Lerman, D. C., & Iwata, B. A. (1996). Developing a technology for the use of operant extinction in clinical settings: An examination of basic and applied research settings. *Journal of Applied Behavior Analysis, 29,* 345–382.

Mindell, J. A. (1999). Empirically supported treatments in pediatric psychology: Bedtime refusal and night wakings in young children. *Journal of Pediatric Psychology, 24,* 465–481.

Reid, M. J., Walter, A. L., & O'Leary, S. G. (1999). Treatment of young children's bedtime refusal and nighttime wakings: A comparison of "standard" and graduated ignoring procedures. *Journal of Abnormal Child Psychology, 27,* 5–16.

Rickert, V. L., & Johnson, C. M. (1988). Reducing nocturnal awakening and crying episodes in infants and young children: A comparison between scheduled awakenings and systematic ignoring. *Pediatrics, 81,* 203–212.

GROUP CONTINGENCY

DESCRIPTION OF THE STRATEGY

A group contingency is a behavior modification strategy wherein consequences for a group are dependent upon the behavior of individuals in that group or the group as a whole. Group contingencies are commonly used when a number of individuals within a group are exhibiting a problem behavior, it is difficult to monitor a behavior either because of limited supervision resources or the behavior is covert, or an individual or group of individuals' problem behavior is wholly or partially maintained by attention or reinforcement from other group members. Group contingencies may be used to increase a desired behavior or decrease an undesired behavior, and they may utilize reward and/or punishment components.

Group contingencies have been generally divided into one of three categories: (1) a dependent group contingency, (2) an independent group contingency, and (3) an interdependent group contingency. In a dependent group contingency, the behavior of one or a few individuals within the group determines a group consequence. For example, if a child with aggression problems has no instances of physical fighting during recess, the entire class receives 5 extra minutes of recess time. In an independent group contingency, behavioral goals are applied to all children in a group, and consequences are applied to all children independent from each other. For instance, every child who has no instances of physical fighting during recess receives 5 extra minutes of recess time. In an interdependent group contingency, behavioral goals are established for the group, and consequences are applied based on the performance of the group as a whole. In this case, 5 extra minutes of recess time would be earned if there were no instances of physical fighting by any child in the class.

The hypothesized mechanism through which group contingencies work is the dependence of group consequences on behavior. By framing consequences in this way, peers within the group are invested in the group meeting the target goal and therefore decrease the frequency of reinforcement for behaviors incompatible with meeting the goal (e.g., laughing at a child disrupting the class) and help to monitor the group's progress toward the goal (e.g., reminding a child to follow rules so that the group meets the goal). In addition, an individual's desire to help a group of peers meet a goal may be an important antecedent to behavior change.

RESEARCH BASIS

Group contingencies have been studied within the context of regular and special education classrooms, workplaces, and communities. The majority of group contingency studies have been conducted in elementary classroom settings or other school-based settings such as the school cafeteria or recess playground. Group contingencies are also employed as components of more intensive, behavioral treatment packages (e.g., summer treatment programs, residential treatment settings) that have an established research basis, though the incremental benefit of group contingencies in these settings beyond the other behavior modification procedures employed has not been widely investigated.

Some studies have compared the use of group contingencies to individual contingencies and found beneficial effects of group contingencies. Comparisons of dependent, independent, and interdependent group contingencies yield somewhat mixed results, with some studies indicating there is no difference between the types of group contingency programs and others favoring one type over another. These different results likely reflect the heterogeneity in study populations, settings, and methodology employed in investigations of group contingencies. Overall, there is considerable support for group contingencies in the single subject and applied behavior analysis research literature, and most teachers rate group contingencies as acceptable interventions for use in their classrooms.

There are a number of areas where more research on group contingencies is needed. For example, the relative effects of using punishments versus rewards as the consequence for group contingencies has not been widely studied. Researchers must work to more clearly describe the similarities and differences between dependent, independent, and interdependent group contingencies and report the contexts and settings where each type of contingency is indicated. Finally, though a long-term outcome study of one type of group contingency exists, and reported positive outcomes for children introduced to a group contingency program, additional trials that include information on the maintenance of treatment gains are warranted.

RELEVANT TARGET POPULATIONS AND EXCEPTIONS

Relevant target populations include any group with two or more people. Group contingency procedures are especially efficient for modifying the behavior of a large group of individuals, or instances when supervision is limited.

Group contingencies are *not* appropriate in instances where the behavior is isolated to a single individual, and therefore better treated with an individual contingency, unless that behavior is in part reinforced by other members of the group (i.e., through peer attention or encouragement). Group contingencies are also not appropriate in instances where one or more members of the group are not capable of performing the required behavior (e.g., a group contingency for spelling words correctly may be inappropriate in a classroom where a child had a written language learning disability). Furthermore, the consequences of group contingencies must be carefully chosen, so that purposely undermining the group contingency as a means to gain attention is not more reinforcing than the reward. Finally, for covert aggressive behaviors (e.g., bullying, relational aggression), group contingencies may not be indicated if children are threatened or intimidated by the perpetrators for reporting instances of the targeted behavior.

COMPLICATIONS

Group contingencies are only effective insofar as the individuals within the group are (a) motivated to earn the reward and/or avoid the punishment and (b) able to exhibit the behaviors upon which the contingency is based. Group contingencies may require a reward menu to ensure that there is a desired positive consequence for each member of the group. In addition, group contingencies may be ineffective if one or more children are unable to meet the behavioral criteria set for the group. In these cases, the group criteria may need to be modified, or the criteria may be modified for an individual child or subgroup.

—*Greta M. Massetti and Gregory A. Fabiano*

See also: *Applied Behavior Analysis (Vols. I, II & III), Behavioral Contracting (Vols. I, II & III), Behavioral Treatment in Natural Environments (Vols. I & III), Token Economy (Vols. I, II & III)*

Suggested Readings

Abramowitz, A. J., & O'Leary, S. G. (1991). Behavioral interventions for the classroom: Implications for students with ADHD. *School Psychology Review, 20,* 220–234.

Kellam, S. G., Ling, X., Merisca, R., Brown, C. H., & Ialongo, N. (1998). The effect of the level of aggression in the first grade classroom on the course and malleability of aggressive behavior into middle school. *Development and Psychopathology, 10,* 165–185.

Lewis, T. J., Powers, L. J., Kelk, M. J., & Newcomer, L. I. (2002). Reducing problem behaviors on the playground: An investigation of the application of schoolwide positive behavior supports. *Psychology in the Schools, 39,* 181–190.

Litow, L., & Pumroy, D. K. (1975). A brief review of classroom group-oriented contingencies. *Journal of Applied Behavior Analysis, 8,* 341–347.

O'Leary, K. D., & Drabman, R. (1971). Token reinforcement programs in the classroom: A review. *Psychological Bulletin, 75,* 379–398.

Rohde, G., Jenson, W. R., & Reavis, H. K. (1992). *The tough kid book: Practical classroom management strategies.* Longmont, CO: Sopris West.

Speltz, M. L., Shimamura, J. W., & McReynolds, W. T. (1982). Procedural variations in group contingencies: Effects on children's academic and social behaviors. *Journal of Applied Behavior Analysis, 15,* 533–544.

Walker, H. M., Colvin, G., & Ramsey, E. (1995). *Antisocial behavior in school: Strategies and best practices.* New York: Brooks/Cole.

H

HABIT REVERSAL

DESCRIPTION OF THE STRATEGY

Habit reversal was developed by Nathan Azrin and Gregory Nunn in 1973 as a treatment for habit disorders (nervous habits and tics). Habit reversal is best characterized as a treatment package because it consists of multiple treatment components used in combination, typically in outpatient treatment settings, with adults or children with habit disorders. Habit reversal was originally developed to treat nervous habits and tics and modified a year later to treat stuttering.

Habit reversal has been shown to be effective in treating a wide variety of habit disorders. What characterizes each of these habit disorders is their repetitive nature. Habit behaviors occur repeatedly across situations and continue to occur in the absence of social reinforcement. Nervous habits, also called body-focused repetitive behaviors by some authors, consist of repetitive hand-to-head behaviors such as hair pulling or hair twirling, hand-to-mouth behaviors such as nail biting or thumb/finger sucking, hand-to-body behaviors such as skin picking or scratching, and oral behaviors such as mouth biting or teeth grinding. There are two types of tics: motor tics and vocal tics. Motor tics consist of rapid, repetitive, jerking movements of muscle groups (e.g., head jerking, facial grimacing, shoulder shrugging), and vocal tics consist of repetitive sounds and/or words spoken with no communicative function (e.g., throat clearing, grunting, swear words). Motor and vocal tics may be part of a diagnosable disorder such as Tourette's disorder. Stuttering involves disruption in the fluency or timing of speech such as word, syllable, or sound repetition, prolongation of word sounds, or blocking when attempting to speak.

There are four major components of the habit reversal procedure: awareness training, competing response training, habit control motivation, and generalization training.

Awareness Training

The goal of awareness training is to teach the child to become aware of each instance of the habit behavior or the immediate antecedents to the habit behavior. To accomplish this goal, a number of procedures are used.

First is *response description,* in which the child describes all of the behaviors involved in the habit. For example, if a child engages in hair pulling, the child would describe all of the movements involved in pulling a hair (e.g., raising the right hand to the scalp, feeling hairs with the fingertips, isolating a hair with the thumb and index finger, pulling the hair, rolling the hair between the thumb and index finger, and finally dropping the hair on the floor).

After describing the behavior, the child practices *response detection.* In this procedure, the therapist helps the child identify each instance of the habit behavior as it occurs in the session. For behaviors such as tics or stuttering that would naturally occur in session, the therapist engages the child in conversation and instructs the child to indicate each time the behavior occurs. For behaviors such as hair pulling, nail biting, or other nervous habits that typically occur only when the child is alone, the therapist has the child simulate the behavior in session and identify each occurrence of the behavior.

In the *early warning procedure,* the therapist works with the child to identify when the behavior is about to occur. For tics, the child might identify a physical sensation that typically precedes the occurrence of the tic. For nervous habits, the therapist might help the child identify the initial movements involved in the behavior (e.g., beginning to raise a hand to engage in hair pulling). For stuttering, the therapist may help the child identify the initial sound of a stutter to immediately recognize its occurrence.

In *competing response practice,* the child identifies a behavior that is incompatible with the habit behavior and engages in this behavior for a few minutes to heighten his or her awareness of the muscles involved in the habit behavior. For a motor tic, the competing response would involve tightening the muscles involved in the tic and holding the body part immobile. For a nervous habit involving the hands, the child might practice making a fist or grasping an object. For stuttering, the competing response is diaphragmatic breathing with a slight exhale before speaking.

The final awareness training procedure is *situation awareness training,* in which the therapist helps the child identify each of the situations in which the habit behavior is most likely to occur. For example, tics may be most likely to occur in stressful situations, nervous habits may be most probable when the child is alone at certain times, and stuttering may be most likely to occur with specific words or in specific evaluative situations.

Competing Response Practice

The next habit reversal procedure is competing response practice. As part of awareness training, the child identifies one or more competing responses that are physically incompatible with the habit behavior. In addition to being physically incompatible with the habit behavior, the competing response is a socially inconspicuous behavior that the child can engage in wherever and whenever the habit behavior occurs. The therapist instructs the child to engage in the competing response for 1 to 3 minutes contingent on the occurrence of the habit behavior or the antecedents to the habit behavior. If the child uses the competing response as instructed, the competing response will interrupt the incipient occurrence of the habit or prevent the occurrence of the habit.

The child practices the competing response in the treatment session with the guidance of the therapist.

Each time the habit behavior occurs in session and the child uses the competing response, the therapist provides praise. If the habit behavior occurs and the child fails to use the competing response, the therapist prompts the child to engage in the competing response. The child practices until he or she can successfully engage in the competing response to control the habit behavior without any further prompting from the therapist. For habits that typically occur only when the child is alone, the therapist instructs the child to simulate the habit behavior in session and to use the competing response contingent on its occurrence. The child practices using the competing response as he or she simulates the habit behavior in a variety of situations (e.g., pulling hair while sitting at the desk at school).

Once the child has demonstrated mastery of the competing response in the treatment session, the therapist instructs the child to use the competing response for 1 to 3 minutes contingent on the habit behavior or antecedents to the habit behavior outside the treatment session. To help motivate the child to use the competing response consistently outside the treatment sessions, the therapist utilizes habit control motivation procedures.

Habit Control Motivation

Three procedures are used to help increase the child's motivation to use the competing response to eliminate the habit behavior: habit inconvenience review, social support, and public display procedures. In *habit inconvenience review,* the therapist asks the child (and parent) to describe all the ways in which the habit behavior has caused inconvenience, embarrassment, or disruption in the child's life. After reviewing the negative aspects of the habit behavior, the child should be more motivated to carry out treatment procedures to change the behavior. In the *social support* procedure, the therapist enlists the help of a significant other (usually a parent) who helps the child control the habit behavior. Specifically, the social support person is instructed to (a) praise the child for using the competing response appropriately, (b) praise the child for the absence of the habit behavior in situations where the habit typically occurred before treatment, and (c) prompt the child to use the competing response if the child fails to use the competing response contingent on an instance of the habit behavior. Finally, in the *public display* procedure, the therapist instructs the child to demonstrate control of the habit behavior in session and in the presence of significant others in order to receive social reinforcement for controlling the habit.

Generalization Training

The final component of habit reversal, generalization training, is intended to promote the use of the competing response in all relevant situations outside the therapy sessions. To promote the successful use of the competing response, the therapist has the child practice it in session while providing social support. In addition, the child engages in *symbolic rehearsal* and imagines using the competing response successfully and controlling the habit behavior in everyday situations outside the therapy session.

RESEARCH BASIS

A large body of research has established the efficacy of habit reversal for eliminating or substantially decreasing a wide range of habit behaviors. In this research, habit reversal is implemented in one or a small number of outpatient sessions, and the habit behaviors are measured for weeks or months following treatment. In some studies, booster sessions are provided following the initial treatment sessions to maintain treatment gains.

Early research demonstrated the effectiveness of habit reversal for the treatment of nervous habits and tics and for the treatment of stuttering. Subsequently, researchers have evaluated habit reversal and variations of habit reversal using more rigorous research methods and have found similar results. Research has demonstrated the effectiveness of habit reversal for nervous habits, tics, and stuttering using single-subject designs and group designs. In addition, researchers have shown that habit reversal is superior to alternative treatments such as massed practice and to a placebo control group in the treatment of habit behaviors.

In addition to the basic demonstration of habit reversal as an effective procedure for a wide range of habit behaviors, researchers have also demonstrated the effectiveness of simplified versions for the procedure. Researchers have shown that the use of awareness training, competing response training, and social support is effective for the treatment of nervous habits, tics, and stuttering. Furthermore, researchers

have demonstrated the effectiveness of awareness training and competing response training alone, and some researchers have posited that these are the two essential ingredients of the habit reversal procedure.

RELEVANT TARGET POPULATIONS AND EXCEPTIONS

Habit reversal is an effective treatment for habit behaviors exhibited by adults, adolescents, and children. Habit reversal procedures have not been found to be successful with individuals with mental retardation or with very young children. A critical ingredient for success of habit reversal is the ability of the child to understand the treatment instructions, demonstrate the correct use of the procedures in session, and comply with the treatment procedures outside of therapy sessions in everyday environments where the habit behaviors are likely to occur. Therefore, habit reversal is most likely to be effective for those individuals who have the cognitive capacity to understand and comply with the procedures and who are motivated to change their behavior. Individuals with mental retardation or young children may lack the skills or motivation to use the procedure successfully.

COMPLICATIONS

The effectiveness of habit reversal is likely to be compromised when the individual receiving treatment does not want to change his or her behavior (e.g., a child or adolescent being required to attend treatment by a parent). As stated, habit reversal is also least likely to be effective with young children or individuals with intellectual disabilities. However, adjunct treatments may enhance the effectiveness of habit reversal in such cases. For example, a parent may provide tangible reinforcers for appropriate use of the competing response, may implement response cost when the child does not use the competing response as instructed, or may use physical guidance to ensure that the child uses the competing response at the appropriate times. Finally, habit reversal may be less effective or ineffective with some severe habit disorders in adolescents (e.g., hair pulling that meets the diagnostic criteria for trichotillomania), especially if there is a comorbid disorder such as depression. In such cases, other cognitive-behavioral interventions may be added to habit reversal to enhance its effectiveness.

CASE ILLUSTRATION

"Jennifer" was a 12-year-old in sixth grade. She engaged in hair pulling in which she reached up to her scalp just above her ear with her right hand, rubbed her fingertips in her hair, found an individual hair that "felt different," and pulled out the hair with her thumb and index finger. After rubbing it between her thumb and finger for a few seconds, she dropped the hair and repeated the behavioral chain. Jennifer pulled her hair almost exclusively while sitting on her sofa alone watching television in the evening or on the weekends. She reported that she did not engage in hair pulling at school, in any other public place, or in the presence of her parents, although they sometimes walked in the room as she was engaging in hair pulling. She occasionally pulled her hair in the car if she was in the back seat and her parents were not watching. Jennifer had a 1-inch-diameter spot of thinned hair on her scalp, and she and her mother spent time fixing her hair each morning so that the spot was not obvious to others. She had been pulling her hair "for a few years," although she could not identify a specific onset. She sought treatment because she thought "it was not normal" and wanted her hair to grow back before her classmates noticed.

Assessment information was collected from a behavioral interview with Jennifer and her mother and through self-monitoring. Jennifer estimated that she pulled 10 to 20 hairs each day before treatment. She did not report any negative emotion as an antecedent to hair pulling, and simply said that it was "a habit" that she often did it without thinking about it. She usually sat with her elbow on the arm of the sofa and her head resting on her hand. In this position, it took little effort to pull her hair. For self-monitoring, Jennifer recorded on a small tablet how many hairs she pulled each day. She kept the tablet on the table next to the sofa. In addition, once per day she and her mother looked in a mirror at the spot of thinned hair on her scalp and provided a numerical rating of the thickness of the hair. Using a 5-point rating scale, a rating of 1 meant that there was no hair in the area, 2 was little hair, 3 was a medium amount of hair, 4 was hair mostly grown back, and 5 meant that the hair was fully grown in the area. Just before treatment was implemented, Jennifer gave herself a rating of 2.5.

Habit reversal was implemented in one treatment session. Following the initial treatment session, Jennifer was scheduled to attend two more sessions where she and the therapist would review the treatment procedures and evaluate progress. One month later, a follow-up session was planned.

In the treatment session, Jennifer described and demonstrated the hair pulling movements without actually pulling a hair. Jennifer was instructed to simulate the hair pulling movements 10 times while sitting in the same position as she typically sat while pulling her hair at home. In the simulations of the hair pulling, the therapist instructed Jennifer to stop at various points in the movement to observe different stages of the behavior to heighten her awareness. Following awareness training, the therapist introduced the rationale for the competing response and Jennifer chose a number of competing responses that she could use while sitting on the sofa watching television. The competing responses included holding a Koosh Ball, holding on to the remote control, and sitting with her hands folded in her lap. Jennifer chose the Koosh Ball as her primary competing response and always had it available on the sofa when she sat down to watch television. In the session, Jennifer simulated the hair pulling movements and engaged in the competing response before she pulled a hair. In each simulation, she stopped herself at a different point in the movement (e.g., as she raised her hand from her lap, when her hand touched her scalp) and engaged in the competing response. In addition to instructions to use the competing responses, the therapist instructed Jennifer to sit in a different position on the sofa so that her hand was not resting on her head. Even though Jennifer did not pull her hair in the presence of her parents, the therapist enlisted her mother to serve as a social support person. The therapist instructed her mother to check on Jennifer at periodic intervals (every 10–15 minutes) while Jennifer watched television and to praise her when her hand was not touching her hair and when she was using the competing response. Her mother was also instructed to prompt Jennifer to use the competing response if she caught Jennifer with her fingers in her hair and not using the competing response. Her mother readily agreed to carry out the procedures.

In the second treatment session 1 week later, Jennifer reported that she had pulled only one hair on two different days and that, in response, she engaged in her competing response. On all other days, she occupied her hands with the cushball while watching television and prevented the hair pulling from occurring. On each occasion when she pulled her hair,

Jennifer was able to stop immediately and prevent further occurrences with the use of the competing response. Her mother reported that she had not caught Jennifer with her fingers in her hair any of the times she checked on her. After reviewing her self-monitoring data in this session, Jennifer simulated hair pulling and practiced her competing responses a few times. She brought her Koosh Ball to the session so she could practice holding the Koosh Ball as the competing response. The session was brief because Jennifer was using the competing response successfully and did not need further intervention.

Jennifer's mother called prior to her third scheduled appointment and cancelled the appointment, saying that Jennifer did not need to come in for the session. She reported on the phone that Jennifer had not pulled her hair in the preceding week and that she was successfully using her competing response. She was extremely pleased with Jennifer's progress (as was Jennifer) and scheduled an appointment 1 month later for a follow-up visit. She also called to cancel her 1-month follow-up visit. She reported that Jennifer was no longer pulling her hair, that she was using the competing response consistently, and that her hair was growing back. Jennifer and her mom rated Jennifer's hair growth with a 4 (hair mostly grown back) and were both confident that it was just a matter of time before their ratings would be a 5 (hair fully grown back). She declined an offer for another follow-up appointment.

—*Raymond G. Miltenberger*

See also: *Azrin, Nathan (Vols. I & III), Habit Reversal (Vols. I & III), Homework (Vols. I, II, & III), Overcorrection (Vol. II)*

Suggested Readings

Azrin, N. H., & Nunn, R. G. (1974). Habit reversal: A method of eliminating nervous habits and tics. *Behaviour Research and Therapy, 11,* 619–628.

Azrin, N. H., & Nunn, R. G. (1974). A rapid method of eliminating stuttering by a regulated breathing approach. *Behaviour Research and Therapy, 12,* 279–286.

Azrin, N. H., & Nunn, R. G. (1977). *Habit control in a day.* New York: Simon & Schuster.

Miltenberger, R. G. (2001). Habit reversal treatment manual for trichotillomania. In D. Woods & R. Miltenberger (Eds.), *Tic disorders, trichotillomania, and other repetitive behavior disorders: Behavioral approaches to analysis and treatment* (pp. 171–196). Norwell, MA: Kluwer.

Miltenberger, R. G., Fuqua, R. W., & Woods, D. W. (1998). Applying behavior analysis to clinical problems: Review and analysis of habit reversal. *Journal of Applied Behavior Analysis, 31,* 447–469.

Woods, D. W. (2001). Habit reversal treatment manual for tic disorders. In D. Woods & R. Miltenberger (Eds.), *Tic disorders, trichotillomania, and other repetitive behavior disorders: Behavioral approaches to analysis and treatment* (pp. 33–52). Norwell, MA: Kluwer.

Woods, D. W., & Miltenberger, R. G. (Eds.) (2001). *Tic disorders, trichotillomania, and other repetitive behavior disorders: Behavioral approaches to analysis and treatment.* Norwell, MA: Kluwer.

HABITUATION

Behavior is often categorized into two fundamental forms: respondent and operant behavior. Respondent behavior is often called elicited behavior because it occurs in reaction to events or stimuli in the environment and is demonstrable in all animals with a nervous system. Respondent behavior includes reflexes (i.e., sucking in an infant when its mother's nipple is presented) and more complex responses such as feeding or reproductive behaviors that are elicited by multiple stimuli in the environment.

Habituation is considered to be an example of the most basic change in behavior that results from experience (i.e., learning). Habituation is defined as a diminution or reduction in responding after repeated presentations of an unconditioned environmental stimulus, and is differentiated from extinction, which involves a reduction in responding to conditioned stimuli. Habituation helps to channel behavioral responses, potentially affected by a barrage of stimuli, by organizing these responses in relation to the most relevant environmental influences. Although thought to be mediated at the level of the shortest neural pathway that connects the sensory apparatus to the muscles involved in making a response (i.e., the reflex arc), habituation is often distinguished from reduced responding as a result of the sense organs becoming temporarily insensitive to stimulation or from muscles becoming incapacitated by fatigue.

The intensity of the eliciting stimulus and the frequency of its presentation affect habituation. In general, the weaker the intensity of the eliciting stimulus and the more frequently an eliciting stimulus is presented, the sooner the organism will habituate a response (i.e., learn not to respond). Habituation is also considered to be "stimulus specific" in that even a minor change in the characteristics of the eliciting stimulus will evoke a response of full strength.

Two types of habituation have been proposed to operate in different experimental conditions. A long-lasting form of habituation occurs when the eliciting stimulus is presented after long pauses (i.e., once daily). The response to the eliciting stimulus gradually becomes smaller in magnitude but is not completely suppressed. When the learning condition includes frequent presentation of the same eliciting stimulus (i.e., every 5 seconds), the response quickly diminishes and is eliminated. This form is often referred to as short-lasting habituation.

As a real-world example of habituation, consider a typical family with two parents and a year-old baby boy named Jack. Russell, the father, had suffered from allergies his whole life and had developed an extremely loud sneeze that has been reportedly heard by neighbors two doors down when it occurs. For those unfamiliar with Russell's sneeze, when it occurred, they would exhibit a rather intense startle response, immediately followed by a strong urge to seek cover. The victims would typically require a few deep breaths to calm themselves down once again. The behaviorally oriented observer, victimized by Russell's explosive-sounding sneeze, would soon recognize that he or she was the only person in the home exhibiting a pronounced startle response. Mary, Jack's mother, recalled that over the course of Jack's first few months of development, this same startle response would occur, followed by extended periods of crying. However, by the time Jack was 6 months old, he would barely interrupt his play when Russell sneezed. Jack had no longer reacted to his father's explosive-sounding sneeze and had habituated his startle response. It was as though Jack had learned that the loud sound was now generally an irrelevant stimulus in the environment.

—*Michael W. Mellon*

See also: *Classical Conditioning (Vols. I, II, & III), Extinction (Vol. II), Extinction and Habituation (Vols. I & III), Operant Conditioning (Vols. I, II, & III)*

Suggested Readings

Bijou, S. (1995). *Behavior analysis of child development.* Reno, NV: Context Press.

Domjan, M., & Burkhard, B. (1986). *The principles of learning and behavior* (2nd ed.). Belmont, CA: Brooks/Cole.

Donahoe, J., & Palmer, D. (1994). *Learning and complex behavior.* Boston: Allyn & Bacon.

HOME-BASED REINFORCEMENT

DESCRIPTION OF THE STRATEGY

As parents have the greatest amount of contact with their children, home-based reinforcement is often the treatment of choice for increasing desirable child behaviors. A key requirement for home-based reinforcement is that the target behavior be both observable and precisely defined. The behavior must be observable so that the parent can directly monitor it, and it must be precisely defined so the parent and child know exactly what behaviors will lead to reinforcement.

An essential component of home-based reinforcement is measurement of the target behavior. Before the intervention begins, measuring the frequency of the desired behavior provides a baseline. Once reinforcement is begun, continuous measurement of the frequency of the target can be used to gauge the success of the intervention.

Once the target behavior is defined and its baseline frequency recorded, a reinforcer is chosen. An appropriate reinforcer is typically chosen through consultation with the parent and child. A positive reinforcer should fill the following requirements: It is valuable to the child and is rarely, if ever, given to the child, and is available to be given by the parent as often as needed. To be used as a reinforcer, it must also be contingent, that is, it is given to the child *only* following the target behavior. In addition, it must be available so that it can be given to the child as close to the performance of the desired behavior as possible. Thus, the best reinforcers are those that are valuable and can be applied both consistently and contingently.

Once a reinforcer that can be administered both consistently and contingently is chosen, a schedule of reinforcement is chosen. The schedule may depend, in part, on how often the parent will be able to administer the reinforcer considering time, cost, and availability. While the child is acquiring the desired behavior, the child should be reinforced every time the behavior occurs. Once the behavior is established, the schedule of reinforcement most resistant to extinction is a variable-ratio schedule, in which the child is reinforced after a variable number of instances of the target behavior.

Token economies can be an important part of home-based reinforcement, especially when the reinforcer is large or unable to be given immediately after the exhibition of a behavior. Using tokens that add up to the reinforcer, either by using physical tokens or using checks on a behavioral chart, can facilitate the continuous reinforcement needed to help the child acquire the desired behavior. In addition, using tokens instead of the reinforcer can widen the choice of reinforcers. If the reinforcer most desired by the child is large, the parent can continuously reinforce the child with tokens to earn the large reinforcer.

Home-based reinforcement can also be used to reduce undesirable behaviors through differential reinforcement of incompatible behavior. Reinforcing a behavior that is impossible to engage in at the same time as the undesirable behavior may lead to a decrease in the undesirable behavior.

RESEARCH BASIS

Home-based reinforcement is a major component of parent training. Parent training has strong empirical support for its efficacy in the treatment of childhood behavior problems. Considerable evidence shows both that improvements in child behavior attained through parent training are maintained over time and that the effects of the intervention generalize to behaviors that were not originally targeted.

—*Timothy R. Stickle and Christopher Dehon*

See also: *Applied Behavior Analysis (Vols. I, II, & III), Behavioral Contracting (Vols. I, II, & III), Behavioral Treatment in Natural Environments (Vols. I & III), Token Economy (Vols. I, II, & III)*

Suggested Readings

Kazdin, A. E. (2001) *Behavior modification in applied settings* (6th ed.). Belmont, CA: Wadsworth.

McMahon, R. J., & Forehand, R. L. (2003). *Helping the noncompliant child* (2nd ed.). New York: Guilford Press.

HOMEWORK

DEFINITION

Homework in behavior therapy refers to a variety of treatment-related tasks that are completed between therapy sessions. The content of these assignments varies as a function of the behavioral targets of focus.

Typically, a treatment target is addressed in a session and the client is provided with the necessary skills to complete the task(s) that will be assigned for homework. A specific homework assignment is agreed upon between the client and the clinician, and a due date set, typically at a subsequent treatment session. In the subsequent session, the clinician and the client discuss the homework assignment, successes are praised, difficulties are discussed, failures are examined, and solutions are generated. One example of a homework assignment for depression is for the client to engage in one fun activity a week. In the session prior to the homework assignment, the clinician and client make a list of a number of these activities for the client to choose from, and after the homework is assigned, each subsequent session begins with a discussion of the activity completed between sessions. The focus of these discussions may focus on increasing the client's awareness that fun is possible and that the client has the power to engage in activities that improve his or her mood. Another example of homework is in behavioral parent training, where homework is primarily used to practice and generalize skills that have been modeled and role-played in the therapist's office to the home environment.

BENEFITS

Although the specific goals and proposed benefits to homework assignments vary, there are some general assumed benefits to all therapy homework assignments. One benefit is that homework is thought to aid in the generalization of positive treatment gains to the client's or family's everyday life and interactions. For example, a parent may appropriately use positive reinforcement when practicing with the therapist. This parent, however, may have trouble in applying positive reinforcement with a noncompliant and demanding child in the home. Homework assignments are designed to bridge the gap between the therapeutic environment and the client's home environment both during and after completion of treatment. In addition, homework is thought to increase client perceptions of self-efficacy. Through successful completion of homework assignments, it is intended to build confidence in the client's abilities to handle challenging, treatment-relevant situations independent of the clinician. A third proposed benefit is practice of newly acquired skills. Finally, homework assignments are designed to allow the coverage of more treatment in a shorter amount of time. With the recent increase of third-party payment for psychotherapy, there has been a push for briefer, more effective, and less expensive therapies, and homework is one method for including more treatment at lower cost.

RESEARCH BASIS

Generally, research indicates that homework adherence is associated with better treatment outcomes. Increased acceptance of the treatment rationale is associated with greater homework compliance, and homework appears to contribute unique variance to outcome. More research is needed to determine whether homework completion and better outcomes result from stronger client motivation or other factors associated with increased engagement in treatment.

—*Timothy R. Stickle and Andrew M. Terranova*

See also: *Habit Reversal (Vols. I, II, & III), Homework (Vols. I & III), Instructions (Vols. I & III)*

Suggested Readings

Addis, M. E., & Jacobson, N. S. (2000). A closer look at the treatment rationale and homework compliance in cognitive-behavioral therapy for depression. *Cognitive Therapy and Research, 24,* 313–326.

Beck, J. S. (1995). *Cognitive therapy: Basics and beyond.* New York: Guilford Press.

McMahon, R. J., & Forehand, R. L. (2003). *Helping the noncompliant child* (2nd ed.). New York: Guilford Press.

I

IMAGINAL PROCEDURES

DESCRIPTION OF THE STRATEGY

Imaginal procedures are primarily used in exposure therapies for children with anxiety problems but are also often used to assist in the development of coping skills for a variety of child problems through the use of role plays or imagery in relaxation training or cognitive restructuring. With respect to exposure therapy, imaginal exposure requires the child to confront the feared stimuli in a way that typically produces less anxiety than an in vivo or real-life exposure. Children are asked to imagine themselves at various degrees of confrontation with the feared object or situation. Typically, anxious children focus on threat in their environment. The anxious child overestimates the likelihood of threat, overestimates the consequences of the threat, and underestimates their ability to cope in the face of the feared stimulus. As a result of these interpretations, the child avoids the feared situation, and the anxiety is maintained, as the child is unable to experience evidence contrary to his or her beliefs. Imaginal exposure allows the child to, in a gradual way, face the feared stimulus. Imaginal exposure produces physiological reactions that mimic those experienced during in vivo exposure and hence is typically used as part of gradual exposure therapy. By repeatedly facing their fear, children learn that they are able to cope with the feared stimuli and their negative expectations are not as likely to occur as predicted. Consequently, children experience a reduction in their anxiety. Gradual exposure involves creating a list of ascending steps of exposure to the feared stimulus, beginning with the least fearful and culminating in in vivo exposure to the most feared situation or object. The exposure is repeated and prolonged until the child is less fearful of the situation. The aim is not to reduce all fear and anxiety completely, as some stimuli demand a degree of developmentally appropriate fear. For children, beginning the exposure hierarchy with an imaginal exposure allows them to practice their skills in a less anxiety-provoking situation than if they were to face the situation in real life.

Imaginal exposure differs somewhat from systematic desensitization. During systematic desensitization, the child imagines the feared stimulus (as described above) but does so following deep muscle relaxation. The purpose of this procedure is to pair the feared stimulus with the feeling of relaxation. In contrast, imaginal exposure requires children to experience anxiety when facing the feared stimuli. The children are provided with new information regarding their ability to cope in the face of anxiety and regarding their expectations of threat in the situation.

One of the benefits of imaginal exposure is the convenience of applying it in an office setting. The therapist and the child can conduct exposures within the therapy session in a controlled environment. For many childhood fears, direct exposure to the feared stimulus may be difficult or impossible. For example, in vivo exposure to death, trauma, cyclones, tidal waves, disease, violence, dentists, or electrical storms may prove expensive, impractical, or unethical. Using imaginal procedures, the therapist is able to allow the child to confront the feared stimulus when actual exposure is not possible.

The therapist may also find that imaginal exposure can be used when the child is experiencing difficulties recalling or accessing the cognitions and physiological reactions from past anxious experiences. If the therapist encourages the child to imagine the situation, the child may be in a better position to verbalize the experience and report anxious symptoms and the severity of the fear.

In addition to imaginal exposure for childhood fears and anxiety, imaginal procedures such as rehearsing an imagined event are often used as a method to reinforce skill development for a variety of child problems. Once a skill is taught, the therapist and child can make up a play or act out an imaginary scene in which they could use the new skill. Using tag-along techniques, the therapist can first act out the scene, and then on the next rehearsal the child's involvement can be gradually increased. The imaginal procedure allows the child to practice the skill in a less stressful environment and receive feedback from the therapist (the collaborative and support coach) regarding the use of the skill. With continued feedback and practice, the child is able to internalize the concepts, gaining confidence and a sense of self-efficacy with the skills, requiring less intervention from the therapist.

Covert modeling is another imaginal procedure used in skill development. Covert modeling involves the child imagining a model successfully performing the skill. For example, a child who is learning appropriate ways to express anger can imagine a child (model) responding assertively to a situation rather than aggressively. The client imagines a model in the middle of a video game responding to a request from the model's mother to clean up his or her bedroom: "Mom, I'm in the middle of a game. Would it be okay if I finished the game and then cleaned up my room?" Covert modeling has shown to be as effective as overt modeling. Some evidence has suggested that in combination with behavioral rehearsal, it may in fact be superior to overt modeling.

Imagery is often used to assist children in confronting anxiety-provoking situations such as using their favorite superhero or animal to help them face the situation. The Coping Cat and Coping Koala programs for the treatment of anxiety use an image of an animal that moves from being a fearful "scaredy cat" to being able to manage anxiety-provoking situations as a "coping cat." Imaginal characters have also been used in cognitive restructuring techniques with children. Children choose their favorite detective from

cartoons, television, video games, or movies to help them collect evidence for their unrealistic thoughts.

Relaxation therapies for children typically include imaginal exercises. For example, when teaching the difference between tense and relaxed muscles, the therapist can encourage children to imagine that they are a robot with stiff tense muscles and a jellyfish with very relaxed muscles. This imaginal exercise provides an opportunity for the therapist to reinforce the skill the child has learned. The therapist may also make use of other images throughout the relaxation. For example, children can be asked to imagine themselves in their favorite or peaceful place (commonly suggested places are a secluded beach or in their bed under a warm blanket). For children, this is a particularly useful method of teaching the relaxation skill.

RESEARCH BASIS

Few studies have systematically examined the use of imaginal exposure in children and adolescents. More often the efficacy of the technique is evaluated in conjunction with in vivo exposure. Cognitive-behavioral treatments for childhood anxiety, including imaginal exposure, have shown to be effective in reducing anxiety and fear. Separate parts of this treatment package, that is, imaginal exposure, have not been evaluated in controlled trials.

In adult studies, however, imaginal exposure has been shown to enhance the efficacy of in vivo exposure techniques, that is, a combination of imaginal and in vivo exposures is more effective than in vivo exposures alone. However, in vivo exposures have consistently been shown to be more effective in reducing fear in adults compared to imaginal exposure alone. This evidence suggests that imaginal exposures should be used in conjunction with direct exposure to maximize outcome.

RELEVANT TARGET POPULATIONS

The imaginal exposure technique is documented in manuals for the treatment of anxiety disorders such as generalized anxiety disorder, separation anxiety disorder, social phobia, obsessive-compulsive disorder, school refusal, panic disorder, specific phobias, and posttraumatic stress disorder.

The use of imagery, imaginal role plays, or covert modeling, however, can be included in interventions for a wide variety of child problems. The technique might be particularly useful for children who have difficulties implementing the skills being taught during therapy; such a child may require a great deal of imaginal practice before entering the situation.

COMPLICATIONS

One of the complications with imaginal exposure is that the therapist is not able to control the imaginal situation. The child could imagine anything and not necessarily what the therapist has instructed. This may potentially reduce the efficacy of the exposure. However, studies have indicated that participants are able to adhere to the instructions of imaginal procedures, and in most cases this is not likely to be a problem. Nevertheless, some children may have difficulties imagining the situation and may begin to think of something else not related to the feared situation. For children who have difficulty imagining the situation, additional cues or props may be required. Some studies have indicated that when clients are asked to elaborate on the scenario, outcome of the procedure is improved. For example, the child may require an audiotape of cues from the environment or the therapist and child may need to construct an elaborate story that the child reads aloud to allow the child to focus on the task at hand.

Some adult studies of posttraumatic stress have reported a temporary exacerbation of symptoms following imaginal exposure. This is likely to come about if the child continues to escape the imaginal exposure without a reduction in fear or a change in beliefs. Research on thought suppression suggests that attempting to escape or avoid thoughts leads to increased intrusions and anxiety. It is important to ensure that the child is taught skills to manage the exposure and reduce the likelihood of excessive escape and avoidance behavior. Nevertheless, most studies show that imaginal exposure is superior or equivalent to cognitive therapy alone in reducing PTSD symptoms in adults.

CASE ILLUSTRATION

"Tony," an 8-year-old boy, received treatment for severe fears of going to the dentist. Tony would begin to cry at the mention of the dentist and would experience severe temper tantrums when his parents talked about booking a dental checkup. Tony reported having stomachaches when he thought about the dentist and experienced a strong sensation "to get away." During the assessment, Tony reported that he was worried the dentist would use sharp instruments and hurt him. Tony had avoided going to the dentist for 3 years. His mother was concerned that he had a hole in his tooth and wanted to take him to the dentist but feared that it will be too stressful for him.

The therapist worked with Tony and his parents to build a hierarchy about going to the dentist. Given his extreme fear reaction regarding visiting the dentist, imaginal exposure to the feared situation was warranted to allow a more gradual exposure to the dentist. Also, repeated visits to the dentist would prove costly for the family. Tony built a hierarchy where the first four steps involve imaginal exposures only. Tony and the therapist determined which parts of the dentist would be the most and the least distressing. The most distressing parts included the sharp utensils being placed in his mouth and the experience of pain, while the least distressing parts were sitting in the chair and seeing the utensils.

For the first imaginal exposure, the therapist described a situation that caused moderate levels of anxiety in the child. The first step on the hierarchy, described below, was to imagine a visit to the dentist for a quick checkup with no interventions:

Therapist:	Tony, close your eyes and imagine you are walking into the dentist's office. You are wearing your favorite t-shirt. You notice the cool blue walls of the dentist's waiting room and a row of other children waiting their turn to see the dentist. You start to feel nervous. You can feel the butterflies in your stomach and your legs feel a little shaky.
	Tony, what is your SUDS [Subjective Units of Distress] rating on a scale of 1 to 10, where 10 is really scared, the most scared you could be, and 0 is you're not feeling worried at all.
Tony:	Three. A little worried.
Therapist:	Okay, a little worried. So, you say to yourself, "I can handle this. I know that this dentist is nice. I will be okay." You take a couple of deep breaths and remember to relax all the muscles in

your body. You think about what else you could to do help yourself feel less nervous. You see your favorite comic book on the coffee table and decide to sit down in the waiting room and read it. You notice the smell of the examination room wafting into the waiting area. It smells like the mouthwash they give you to rinse out your mouth. You hear your name called out by the dental nurse. "Tony?" You say, "Yes. I'm here." Your stomach makes a jump and you can feel your heart beating. Your legs feel shaky as you walk toward the dentist.

Tony, what is your SUDS rating now?

Tony: Five. Pretty worried!

Therapist: Okay, pretty worried. The dentist says, "Hello Tony. I haven't seen you for a long time. How about we just have a quick look at your teeth and then you can go. How does that sound?" You feel nervous and you have this strong feeling that you want to get out of the chair and run back to Mom. But then you remember your coping skills. You know that you can handle it. You think to yourself, "There were a lot of kids coming out of the examination room while I was waiting, and they were all okay. It probably won't be as bad as I think." You remember the reward Mom and Dad have planned for you if you can make it through the appointment. So you say to the dentist, "Okay." You move toward the chair and climb up into it. The chair is cold and covered in plastic that sticks to your legs. All of a sudden you see the tray of utensils. You notice the sharp pick that is used for finding holes in teeth. It has a pointy bit at the end. You notice the other tools as well. They look cold.

Tony, what is your SUDS rating now?

Tony: Six. Still pretty worried.

Therapist: Okay, still pretty worried! You can feel the sick feeling in your stomach. You know you need to stay in the chair until you don't feel as nervous. The dentist asks you

to open your mouth, but it feels like it is wired shut. You remember the skills you have to manage your worry. You remember to relax your muscles like a jellyfish so your mouth can open up. The dentist says, "Wider, wider." You open your mouth wider and feel the skin around your mouth stretch. The dentist says, "Good, Tony. Now I am going to have a quick look in your mouth. I will not be using any utensils, only my hands. Okay?"

You grunt, "Owkway!" with your mouth still open. You can see the dentist as she comes closer and the big bright light is shining over your face. The dentist moves in even closer and you can smell the rubber gloves on her fingers. The gloves taste kind of funny. She pokes around in your mouth and a second later says, "Okay, Tony. All done. Wash your mouth out with this." She hands you a cup of pink colored water. "Spit it out here." You wash your mouth out with the funny-tasting liquid and spit it out and watch it swirl down the drain. Your mouth feels fresh. You hop down from the chair and feel so proud of yourself. "I did it. I felt nervous about coming but did it anyway. Nothing bad happened. I was able to handle my worry. Now it is time for my reward!"

Tony, what is your SUDS rating now?

Tony: Zero!

The therapist and Tony discussed what they learned from the practice and then planned the next exposure. Tony decided that he wanted to practice the same exposure without the therapist's help. On the next rehearsal, Tony talked through and elaborated on the imaginal scenario. Once Tony developed confidence with the scenario, the difficulty of the exposure was increased. The next exposure involved the dentist using the dental instruments and causing mild discomfort in his mouth. Following habituation to the scenario of mild discomfort, Tony developed a story of increased difficulty involving moderate pain. In the next story, the dentist found a hole in his tooth and had to remove his tooth. The story involved feeling the pain but developing strategies to deal with it.

Tony completed a number of imaginal exposures for homework that involved writing out the stories and reading them aloud at home. Once Tony felt more comfortable with the imaginal exposures, he was ready to move on to the in vivo exposures. The in vivo exposures consisted of visiting the dentist to make an appointment for his sister, sitting in the dentist's chair while his sister received a checkup, practicing at home setting up a dentist's chair in the lounge room and having Mom brush his teeth, putting a toothpick in his mouth, visiting the dentist to make an appointment for himself, and, finally, visiting the dentist for his own checkup.

—Jennifer L. Hudson and Elizabeth Seeley Wait

See also: Cautela, Joseph R. (Vols. I & III), Covert Conditioning With Children and Adolescents (Vol. II), Covert Control (Vol. III), Covert Positive Reinforcement (Vols. I & III), Covert Reinforcer Sampling (Vol. III), Covert Sensitization Conditioning (Vols. I & III), Lazarus, A. A. (Vols. I & III), Self-Control Desensitization (Vol. III), Systematic Desensitization With Children and Adults (Vols. I, II, & III), Wolpe, Joseph (Vols. I & III)

Suggested Readings

Dadds, M., Bovbjerg, D. H., Redd, W. H., & Cutmore, T. R. (1997). Imagery in human classical conditioning. *Psychological Bulletin, 122,* 89–103.

Foa, E. B., Zoellner, L., Feeny, N. C., Hembree, E. A., & Alvarex-Conrad, J. (2002). Does imaginal exposure exacerbate PTSD symptoms? *Journal of Consulting and Clinical Psychology, 70,* 1022–1028.

Kendall, P. C. (2000). *Cognitive behavioral therapy for anxious children: Treatment manual* (2nd ed.). Ardmore, PA: Workbook.

Mash, E. J., & Barkley R. A. (Eds.). (1998). *Treatment of childhood disorders* (2nd ed.). New York: Guilford Press.

Rapee, R. M., Wignall, A., Hudson, J. L., & Schniering, C. A. (2000). *Evidence-based treatment of child and adolescent anxiety disorders.* Oakland, CA: New Harbinger.

IN VIVO DESENSITIZATION

DESCRIPTION OF THE STRATEGY

In vivo desensitization is a widely used, exposure-based strategy for the treatment of anxiety, fears, and phobias. This approach alone is a well-supported treatment of childhood fears and phobias; however, in vivo desensitization is often a component of cognitive-behavioral treatment packages. Other components used in conjunction with in vivo desensitization could include imaginal desensitization, contingency management, cognitive restructuring, and modeling.

In vivo means "in life," which refers to the presentation of the feared stimuli or situation. Thus, the child or adolescent is directly exposed to the feared object. This is in contrast to imaginal exposure, during which the child is instructed to imagine the feared stimulus in rich detail. Desensitization, also called counterconditioning or deconditioning, is developed from classical conditioning theory. From this perspective, feared objects or situations are classically conditioned stimuli. Desensitization involves pairing a response incompatible with anxiety (e.g., relaxation) with the conditioned stimulus until the fear response is eliminated.

Treatment using in vivo desensitization involves three steps. First, children are taught a behavior that is incompatible with the fear response. They could be taught progressive muscle relaxation (PMR). During PMR, children are taught to systematically tense and release their muscles. Throughout instruction of PMR, children are taught to recognize the difference between tension and relaxation. This skill is then practiced regularly by the children. Other relaxation methods could be taught, including deep breathing and imagery. Often, relaxation instructions need to be altered for the child or adolescent, depending on his or her abilities. Other inhibitory or incompatible activities can include hypnosis, games, edibles, humor, conversation, and therapist contact. These may be more appropriate for a younger child or a child with attention problems who would have difficulty maintaining the attention required to learn relaxation techniques.

Second, feared situations are chosen for exposure. This is based on a fear hierarchy developed with the child's input. A fear hierarchy is a list of anxiety-provoking situations arranged from least to most anxiety-provoking. The child also can rate each of the situations using a fear thermometer. A fear thermometer is a drawing of a thermometer that allows children to indicate how anxious or fearful a situation is for them on a scale from 0 to 10. Lower ratings on the thermometer indicate less anxiety and higher ratings indicate greater anxiety. Younger children may need to rely more on the therapist and parent to assist in the development of the fear hierarchy. A fear hierarchy typically includes numerous levels, usually between 15 and 25.

Last, the child is gradually exposed to the feared situations identified on the fear hierarchy. Each item of the fear hierarchy is paired with the incompatible behavior. The incompatible response, most likely relaxation, is used to manage the fear encountered by the child along each step of the hierarchy. Subjective Units of Distress (SUDS), or ratings of subjective distress felt by the child, can be used by the therapist and child to monitor the level of anxiety during the exposure task. For a younger child, fear thermometer ratings can be used to track level of anxiety. The child or adolescent will be exposed to the feared stimulus long enough for habituation to occur; therefore, the child will maintain exposure to the feared situation until the anxiety attenuates.

The exposure component of desensitization can vary across numerous dimensions. As discussed previously, exposure can be in vivo or imaginal. Also, prolonged exposure or graduated exposure could be employed. Prolonged exposure has a longer duration versus graduated, which will involve small steps while increasing exposure to more anxiety-provoking situations. Rate or pace is how rapidly the client is exposed. Several trials or exposure sessions may be presented in close proximity, which is often called massed exposure. In contrast, exposure sessions may be spaced over a number of weeks. Desensitization can occur in individual therapy sessions, as well as group therapy sessions. Finally, desensitization can occur with the therapist assisting during the exposure process, the clients conducting exposure on their own, or computer-presented exposure. The format chosen may depend on the nature of the fear or phobia and the individual's level of distress. For children, graduated exposure over a number of trials is most often employed.

The history of in vivo desensitization began in the early 1920s. Mary Cover Jones was one pioneer in the area of fear and phobia treatment. Jones and her treatment of a child named Peter paved the way for future case studies and research on exposure-based treatments of anxiety. She treated Peter's fear of rabbits using direct conditioning and modeling. Presentation of food and eating were chosen as incompatible behaviors to fear. Jones gradually paired the rabbit and food to countercondition the fear of the rabbit and successfully treated Peter's fear of the animal.

In the 1950s, systematic desensitization was officially formulated and evaluated by Joseph Wolpe. It was Wolpe who described in vivo desensitization as a systematic treatment technique and who made this therapeutic approach widely known. He developed this approach from the concept of reciprocal inhibition, or pairing of the feared stimulus with a response opposite of anxiety to reduce the anxiety response.

Even though in vivo desensitization is a component of an empirically evaluated psychological treatment package, parents and caregivers may utilize this approach informally to help reduce anxiety in their children. For example, a parent might encourage a child to "face his or her fears." The parent may gradually introduce a child to the feared object in a positive setting. One common example is having a child who is afraid of dogs approach a dog at a party.

The exact mechanism of change of in vivo desensitization is still unknown. Wolpe hypothesized that counterconditioning was responsible for the effectiveness of in vivo desensitization. Counterconditioning involved the replacement of an adaptive response (relaxation) for the maladaptive response (conditioned fear). Habituation and extinction are other proposed reasons for the success of in vivo exposure. For extinction to occur, the individual must not be allowed to escape the feared situation. Habituation occurs when the physiological arousal surrounding the anxiety-provoking stimulus subsides. Many theorists have argued that the habituation and extinction are the main components of in vivo desensitization that render this treatment approach effective. Thus, some have proposed that the relaxation is not a necessary component to anxiety treatment.

A cognitive explanation of the effectiveness of in vivo desensitization is a model involving a memory network. Specifically, children and individuals with fears and phobias have a memory network that consists of the details surrounding anxiety-provoking situations. Exposure creates a situation in which the memory network is activated; however, the negative outcomes expected do not occur. This new information is incorporated into the memory network. Thus, a correction in cognition occurs with a decrease in negative thoughts about the outcome of exposure to the feared situation. Others have suggested that as the child develops a sense of mastery during repeated exposure activities, an increase in self-efficacy occurs, improving the response to future feared situations.

RESEARCH BASIS

Numerous reports have demonstrated the effectiveness of in vivo desensitization to treat childhood phobias and fears. Loud noises, water, animals, high buildings, elevators, and darkness are examples of childhood fears that have been successfully targeted. In vivo desensitization has been effective in combination with other cognitive-behavioral strategies. For example, both school refusal and social anxiety have been successfully treated with in vivo desensitization in combination with other techniques.

In addition to individual treatment, research has supported in vivo desensitization as a component of cognitive-behavioral group treatments for anxious children and adolescents. For example, social phobia has been treated in a group format. Thus, this treatment approach has successfully been applied in both individual and group treatment formats.

For phobic disorders in children, in vivo desensitization has demonstrated superiority to vicarious approaches during which the child observes the model approach the feared situation. Also, in vivo desensitization has been shown to be more successful than computer-generated exposure activities. In addition, some researchers have found in vivo exposure to be more effective than imaginal exposure. Other research has suggested that for younger children (between approximately 5 to 10 years), in vivo desensitization is more effective. For older ages, both imaginal and in vivo desensitization may be equally effective for some feared situations. Finally, self-directed in vivo desensitization is less effective and can be difficult for clients; therefore, therapist involvement may be needed during the in vivo exposure. Some have found that a combination is successful using therapist-directed exposure during session and client-directed in vivo exposure as homework. In vivo desensitization can be effective in a minimal number of sessions for children with some phobias. Furthermore, treatment gains obtained with in vivo desensitization are shown to be maintained over time.

RELEVANT TARGET POPULATIONS AND EXCEPTIONS

Adults, adolescents, and children have all successfully been treated for a broad variety of phobias and anxiety disorders. For example, phobias targeted with children include fear of heights, animals, tests, injections, darkness, separation, school, water, and social situations. Desensitization can be used in a group format, with the child or adolescent contracting for the exposure he or she will accomplish between group sessions. In addition, parents may be involved with homework activities; for example, parents may be involved in delivering positive reinforcement for completion of an exposure task. Often, group treatments will include a separate group for the parents. Younger children may have more difficulty with imaginal exposure; therefore, in vivo exposure may be a better choice. This approach also has been modified for use with individuals with mental retardation and autism. Finally, it is thought that this procedure is more useful for highly anxious and avoidant children.

COMPLICATIONS

The most obvious barrier to in vivo desensitization is resistance to engage in the exposure tasks. This complication exists regardless of the age group of the clients. Further complicating this difficulty, many parents or guardians seek treatment for their children and adolescents. As one could imagine, a great deal of resistance for the exposure activities may be encountered from children and adolescents who may not understand the rationale for pursuing treatment. The therapist may need to provide reassurance that children will work up the hierarchy only after they expose themselves to the initial feared situations, or a therapist may initially use imaginal desensitization. Parental cooperation is important, especially since their child will experience an increase in distress during the exposure sessions.

Some have found this approach to be less useful with those individuals with mild anxiety; therefore, imaginal techniques or cognitive approaches may be a more successful alternative for these patients. In addition, there may be situations when in vivo exposure is not possible and another approach is needed. In these cases, imaginal desensitization or cognitive strategies may be more applicable as well.

When preparing for the exposure phase, it is crucial to construct the fear hierarchy so that the initial steps produce minimal distress. This will improve the chance of completion and success with the exposure activity. As patients move up the hierarchy, they will have a sense of mastery, therefore contributing to the future success of the entire fear hierarchy. In addition, a initial exposure session that results in a high level of anxiety may lead to reinforcement of the fear. The fear or phobia may become strengthened through negative reinforcement or escape from the situation. Subsequently, future avoidance will occur. Co-occurring psychological diagnoses or psychosocial stressors can create an obstacle to successful treatment. This could include an externalizing disorder or depression;

therefore, identifying treatment priorities for that individual child or adolescent should occur before treatment with in vivo desensitization can be undertaken.

CASE ILLUSTRATION

"Ann" was a 16-year-old female in the 10th grade. She presented with a long history of social difficulties. Both she and her mother reported that she has had few friends and relied mainly on a cousin for social contact. In addition, she reported numerous situations in class that were difficult for her, including answering questions in class and presenting oral reports. The classroom difficulties were beginning to negatively impact her grades. Her main concern or focus in social situations was that she would do something wrong and people would laugh at her or make fun of her. Ann was interviewed and completed self-rating measures of anxiety. At the time of assessment, Ann met criteria for social phobia. Because her cousin was graduating and would no longer be a ready source of social contact, Ann was motivated to undergo treatment for her anxiety in social settings.

Initially, she was provided education on the nature of anxiety and provided a rationale for in vivo desensitization. Ann was taught progressive muscle relaxation, imagery, and deep breathing. She practiced these skills as homework until she felt competent at achieving a relaxed state with ease. A fear hierarchy was developed with Ann. With the input of the therapist, she generated a list of various anxiety-provoking situations. She assigned ratings of distress anticipated in each of these situations and put the identified situations in order from least to most anxiety provoking. The fear hierarchy was then reviewed to ensure that the activities with lower ratings involved minimal anxiety, therefore setting the stage for initial success. Ann was required to contact each of the feared situations along the hierarchy. Because some of the situations in the fear hierarchy activity were not able to be conducted during session, Ann was required to conduct in-between therapy sessions. Ann and her mother were given extensive information on how to implement exposure in between sessions as homework. Contracts were developed with the therapist to assist with adherence to the in vivo desensitization homework. The activities mainly involved increasing contacts with peers and increasing verbalizations in class.

Subjective Units of Distress (SUDS) were used to assess Ann's fear throughout treatment. Specifically, SUDS ratings were monitored at both the onset and the completion of the exposure task.

Ann had little difficulty completing the initial in vivo exposure tasks on the fear hierarchy. As the exposure tasks elicited more distress, she began having difficulty with completing the tasks between sessions. The hierarchy was reviewed, and additional steps were added at the intermediate level. In time, Ann successfully completed in vivo exposure throughout the fear hierarchy, with significant improvement of symptoms of social anxiety and social functioning. At follow-up, she was involved in some socially oriented school activities, including choir.

—Kellie A. Hilker

See also: *Extinction (Vol. II), Extinction and Habituation (Vols. I & III), Lazarus, A. A. (Vols. I & III), Self-Control Desensitization (Vol. III), Systematic Desensitization (Vols. I, II, & III), Wolpe, Joseph (Vols. I & III)*

Suggested Readings

Barlow, D. H., Raffa, S. D., & Cohen, E. M. (2002). Psychosocial treatments for panic disorders, phobias, and generalized anxiety disorder. In P. E. Nathan & J. M. Gorman (Eds.), *A guide to treatments that work* (2nd ed., pp. 301–335). New York: Oxford University Press.

Barrios, B. A., & O'Dell, S. L. (1998). Fears and anxieties. In E. J. Mash & R. A. Barkley (Eds.), *Treatment of childhood disorders* (2nd ed., pp. 249–337). New York: Guilford Press.

Kendall, P. C., Flannery-Schroeder, E., Panichellie-Mindel, S. M., Southam-Gerow, M., Hennin, A., & Warman, M. (1997). Therapy for youths with anxiety disorders: A second randomized clinical trial. *Journal of Consulting and Clinical Psychology, 65,* 366–380.

King, N. J., Hamilton, D. I., & Ollendick, T. H. (1988). *Children's phobias: A behavioural perspective.* Chichester, UK: John Wiley & Sons.

Marsh, J. (Ed.). (1995). *Anxiety disorders in children and adolescents.* London: Guilford Press.

Ollendick, T. H., & King, N. J. (1998). Empirically supported treatments for children with phobic and anxiety disorders: Current status. *Journal of Clinical Child Psychology, 27,* 156–167.

Ollendick, T. H., King, N. J., & Yule, W. (Eds.). (1994). *International handbook of phobic and anxiety disorders in children and adolescents.* New York: Plenum.

Silverman, W. K., Ginsburg, G. S., & Kurtines, W. M. (1995). Clinical issues in treating children with anxiety and phobic disorders. *Cognitive and Behavioral Practice, 2,* 93–117.

L

LEMON JUICE THERAPY

Contingent lemon juice for the treatment of behavior problems when combined with positive reinforcement for desirable behaviors can produce immediate, positive, and enduring change of clinical significance when applied judiciously by trained personnel or family members. It can be applied quickly in brief, convenient time intervals, resulting in little interference with the child's activities and ensuring close supervision of treatment. However, as with all aversive procedures, contingent lemon juice should only be used when positive reinforcement and less restrictive approaches such as differential reinforcement of other behavior (DRO), overcorrection, and time-out have been tried unsuccessfully. Approval from ethical boards and the family is needed before initiating treatment, and staff and child care workers should agree that the aversive procedure is less harmful than providing no treatment at all because of the dangerousness of the child's behavior problem either to the child or others.

Contingent lemon juice has proven to be successful for treating behavior problems in children, including rumination, repetitive, and self-injurious behaviors. Children who were formerly found to be unresponsive to positive reinforcement, DRO, overcorrection, and time-out have responded successfully to contingent lemon juice therapy. Although most often reported to be successful for children and adolescents with mild and profound mental retardation, lemon juice therapy has also been found to be effective for treating such problems as unremitting rumination in infants as young as 6 months of age. Chronic rumination is a life-threatening behavior that involves regurgitation of food without nausea or distress. The food is then ejected or reswallowed.

Lemon juice therapy involves squirting 5 to 10 cubic centimeters of unsweetened lemon juice into the child's mouth using a medical syringe or spray bottle immediately upon the onset of the undesirable behavior problem. It is important to specify behaviorally the target behavior to ensure that the lemon juice is applied consistently by staff and others. Applications of the juice should be paired with the verbal reprimand, "No," so that verbal instructions will eventually obtain stimulus control over the response. The treatment sessions should be divided into observation blocks lasting a few minutes or seconds to obtain baseline and intervention data on treatment efficacy. For example, a 30-minute treatment session could be divided into 10-second observation blocks to collect baseline information on the number of times the target behavior occurs and then to document the number of incidents after treatment is initiated. Since not everyone finds lemon juice aversive, it is important to ensure the juice's punishing effect for each case before initiating treatment. Finally, treatment sessions should be scheduled when the target behavior such as rumination occurs to increase the opportunities to apply the contingency.

Research has revealed that contingent lemon juice can be more effective than DRO, time-out, DRO and overcorrection combined, mechanical restraints, overcorrection, water mist, and facial screening. The effects can be immediate, with a 50% reduction in the target behavior observed on the first day of treatment. Results are usually seen, on average, within 13 to 17 days, with near total suppression in 5 to 6 weeks. Success tends to be limited to the treatment setting, however, requiring that lemon juice be applied across settings, people, and situations to maximize the generalization of effects. It is important to ensure that lemon juice is applied consistently in these other settings and situations to maximize the opportunity for generalization. Treatment gains can be enduring, and there have been no reports of symptom substitution. Suppression of the target behavior is greater if DRO and positive reinforcement of desirable, incompatible behaviors are also applied. Relapses may occur after treatment is discontinued, but such reversals to pretreatment baseline levels can be addressed by reintroducing contingent lemon juice and verbal instructions for the child to refrain from engaging in the target behavior. In addition to effectively extinguishing behavior problems formerly found to be resistant to therapeutic approaches, there are anecdotal reports of collateral effects from therapy, including an increase in appropriate social behavior, smiling, and playing with others.

Side effects to treatment are possible, the most common being minor irritation in the interior of the mouth. The child may also rub excess lemon juice into his or her eyes and face, thereby causing further irritation. These risks can be reduced by wiping the child's face after each application. Children may also cough, spit, and physically resist the lemon juice applications. Although unpleasant, these reactions extinguish over the course of treatment as the target behavior improves and as the number of applications declines. Other side effects include aspirations of lemon juice into the child's lungs and the medical complications associated with this risk. This side effect can be avoided or minimized by keeping the child's head upright or down, not back, when injecting lemon juice into the child's mouth, thereby reducing the force with which the lemon juice strikes the inside of the mouth. Demineralization of dentition is also a risk factor because of the acidic ingredients in lemon juice. The therapist should consult a dentist about providing fluoride treatment during treatment to prevent this risk. Although not necessarily a side effect, children may adapt to and become habituated to the lemon juice. A more aversive stimulus such as Tabasco sauce would then be required to extinguish the target behavior. However, habituation can be overcome by alternating lemon juice with another citrus juice such as lime juice.

Some of the advantages to using contingent lemon juice are that it is generally safe, accessible, quick and easy to implement, requires minimal training, and there is little potential for misuse or abuse. The noxious taste of lemon juice is short lasting and discrete, and it is considered less aversive than Tabasco sauce. In addition, treatment can be topographically related to the behavior problems being treated, including biting, finger gnawing, or rumination. Staff and therapists generally tend to prefer contingent lemon juice over other aversive approaches such as aromatic ammonia or electric shock because of the lower risk for possible deleterious side effects.

—*Laura Stoppelbein and Leilani Greening*

See also: *Aversive Conditioning (Vol. II), Aversion Relief (Vols. I & III), Classical Conditioning (Vols. I, II, & III), Electrical Aversion (Vols. I & III), Operant Conditioning (Vols. I, II, & III)*

Suggested Readings

Gross, A. M., Wright, B., & Drabman, R. S. (1980). The empirical selection of a punisher for a retarded child's self-injurious behavior: A case study. *Child Behavior Therapy, 2,* 59–65.

Matson, J. L., Manikam, R., & Ladatto, J. (1990). A long-term follow-up of a recreate the scene, DRO, overcorrection and lemon juice therapy program for severe aggressive biting. *Scandinavian Journal of Behaviour Therapy, 19,* 33–38.

Paisey, T. J., & Whitney, R. B. (1989). A long-term case study of analysis, response suppression, and treatment maintenance involving life-threatening pica. *Behavioral Residential Treatment, 4,* 191–211.

Sajwaj, T., Libet, J., & Agras, S. (1989). Lemon juice therapy: The control of life-threatening rumination in a six-month-old infant. In D. Wedding & R. J. Corsini (Eds.), *Case studies in psychotherapy* (pp. 113–122). Itasca, IL: Peacock.

LIFE SKILLS TRAINING

DESCRIPTION OF THE STRATEGY

The term *life skills* refers to a broadly defined set of skills and competencies needed to survive and prosper in society. These skills range from such basics as bathing and dressing, include study, work, and leisure activities, and extend to maintaining interpersonal relationships and advanced problem-solving skills. Though many manualized therapies now include life skills components, life skills interventions are most commonly primary prevention strategies implemented in either a broadly targeted or universal manner. By increasing social competence, problem-solving skills, knowledge of risk factors, self-esteem, and communication skills, life skills interventions aim to decrease individuals' vulnerability to risk factors, thereby preventing the development of dysfunction, psychopathology, and other undesired outcomes such as drug use, smoking, and teen pregnancy.

The broader category of life skills has been grouped into domains and subdomains in a variety of different ways. Some of these taxonomies are driven by more global theoretical considerations. Most groupings, however, are tailored to a specific population of interest (e.g., developmentally disabled adults, delinquent youth). Despite differences in the conceptualization of the exact number and content of skill areas, all life skills models contain components in three main areas: (1) social skills, (2) problem solving, and (3) education. Social skills include such competencies as communication skills, interpersonal relationship skills, pro-social behavior, and understanding social expectations in different settings. Problem solving includes emotion regulation and self-control, decision-making skills, learning to access community resources, and working with others. Education, in its broadest definition, refers to any portion of a life skills program that focuses on increasing knowledge rather than teaching and honing a skill. The education component of a life skills training program may include information on health promotion, suicide prevention, substance abuse, preventing unwanted pregnancy, choosing a career, using public transportation, or proper hygiene, to name just a few of the possibilities.

Life skills training programs used as universal interventions seek to minimize the effects of a wide range of negative life events by enhancing the participant's ability to successfully cope with life stresses. Good communication skills, advanced problem-solving strategies, and knowledge of resources in the community and how to access them are viewed as powerful protective factors that serve to reduce the effects of the majority of risk factors and negative life events.

In more targeted life skills interventions, a particular outcome of interest, the risk factors associated with that outcome, and an at-risk population are identified. Next, a decision is made as to which skills, abilities, and knowledge are most likely to minimize those risk factors. Based on the characteristics of the at-risk population and practical limitations on intervention, a delivery method is selected. Finally, the skills training components are adapted to the specific needs of the targeted population (e.g., culture, geographic location), the method of delivery, and the exact skills and knowledge being taught.

Life skills interventions have most commonly been implemented in classroom settings either with populations deemed at risk or as universal prevention programs. As with other prevention and intervention programs targeting the prevention of negative outcomes in adolescence and adulthood, it is highly preferred to begin life skills interventions before or during pubertal onset rather than after (i.e., middle school rather than high school).

Life skills interventions have also been designed as adventure-based programs, outpatient psychoeducational groups, athletic programs, inpatient groups, and individual coaching sessions. After classroom-based delivery models, adventure based is the most common mode of delivery. The adventure programs (i.e., Outward Bound, Adventure Therapy) seek to enhance the efficacy of life skills training with the use of experiential learning techniques.

RESEARCH BASIS

Life skills training has been widely tested and empirically supported as both a universal and targeted prevention method. The most common application and empirically investigated target is substance abuse prevention. Though there has been some debate over the methodology of trials of specific life skills training packages as prevention programs targeting substance use, the majority of research has found life skills approaches to be generally efficacious. Other common outcomes that life skills training strategies are intended to prevent include suicide, teen pregnancy, eating disorders, obesity, delinquency, mental disorders, and general health problems.

Follow-up data in studies of life skills prevention trials generally support increased knowledge, retention of skills, increased internal locus of control, and increases in other desirable psychological characteristics. The positive outcomes have shown good retention for long periods, years in some cases. These gains in knowledge and skills, however, do not always translate to significant changes in the targeted behaviors or outcomes in groups receiving the intervention. For example, although a group at risk for depression that receives a life skills intervention may show an increased understanding of depression, ability to identify the onset of depressive symptoms, competence at formulating an effective plan for increasing their mood, and extensive knowledge of the family and community resources available to assist them in combating depression compared to an at-risk group not receiving the intervention, tests of differences in postintervention rates of depression between the two groups are often nonsignificant.

RELEVANT TARGET POPULATIONS AND EXCEPTIONS

Life skills training components are incorporated in many manualized and nonmanualized treatments for adults and children. As a stand-alone intervention, life skills training generally targets youth between late childhood and early adulthood. Life skills training is designed to teach the skills needed to be a successful adult in a complex society. By teaching these skills to adolescents and young adults in a timely manner, it is hypothesized that they will avoid many negative outcomes that might be arrived at through inadequate preparation for the challenges of adult life.

Within the noted conceptual framework, nearly all adolescents fall into at least one, and generally more than one, target population. Life skills training has been used with populations including, but not limited to, students at risk of dropping out of school, young adults deemed to have inadequate preparation for employment, prevention of drug, alcohol, and tobacco use, youth from disadvantaged (i.e., low socioeconomic status [SES]) households, language-impaired students, underachievers and marginalized racial, ethnic, and cultural groups, sexually active teenagers, and adolescents with low-self esteem and poor body image.

COMPLICATIONS

It is important to note that life skills training programs developed for one ethnic, racial, or cultural group ought not to be applied to another group in a cookbook fashion. For example, role playing is one of the most common techniques throughout skills training programs for both teaching and practicing new skills. Before a suicide prevention program developed on a white urban population is used on a Native American reservation, however, tribal taboos prohibiting pretending to kill or pretending to want to kill oneself

must be taken into account. Other factors such as acceptable levels of emotional expression within a community, fear of losing face, discomfort with revealing information about oneself or one's family, and differences between the ethnicity of the instructors and the participants should be taken into account when designing a skills training program for a specific population.

Much of the specialization of a skills training program occurs in the educational components. Care must be taken when adapting the educational components of a skills training curriculum that maladaptive behaviors not be normalized for an asymptomatic at-risk population. Such normalization may result in iatrogenic effects. For example, normalization of restrictive dieting or purging for a population of female college students with poor body image may well result in an increase of eating disordered behaviors.

The greatest complication with successful implementation of a skills training program lies in the selection of relevant risk factors and understanding how those risk factors relate to the outcome of interest. Risk factors relate to outcomes in a variety of ways, some causal and some not. Some risk factors are merely correlates of an outcome of interest and have no temporal precedence or understood pathway of direct effect on that outcome. Such risk correlates are a poor choice for intervention efforts. Some risk factors, which may be more easily assessed, may serve as proxies for true causal risk factors that are harder (or even impossible) to assess directly. Alternatively, a proxy risk factor may indicate the presence of a more global set of risk factors, in which case, targeting that proxy factor will likely miss the true causal process it represents. Some risk factors may serve moderating roles that affect the individual's response to treatment rather than playing a direct role in the development of the disorder or outcome targeted for prevention. Many risk factors may also be fixed and immutable to change, making efforts to target those factors futile. Finally, risk factors may work together or form independent chains of causal processes that lead indirectly to the outcome of interest, with each risk factor varying in its contribution and directness of impact on the development of a disorder or negative outcome. Broad approaches to intervention such as life skills training, if not carefully targeted and thoughtfully designed, may result in intervention efforts targeting fixed, proxy, and noncausal risk factors, which in turn results in the dilution of efficacy and the diversion of resources that might be more usefully employed in interventions that target true causal risk factors. Thus, life skills training interventions are best employed where the processes by which specific risk factors lead to negative outcomes are clearly understood and appropriately targeted. For example, inclusion criteria among participants in interventions might be employed to increase the likelihood of specific intervention effects. Overly general "broadband" approaches to prevention frequently result in the waste of time, money, and effort, with few resulting treatment effects.

CASE ILLUSTRATION

"Sam" was a bright, socially withdrawn, 12-year-old seventh grade boy who earned average to above-average grades in school. Sam had few friends, and he infrequently spent time with those few friends he did have. Although Sam did not meet diagnostic criteria for any anxiety disorders, his mother reported that both she and several members of her immediate family have received treatment for anxiety-related problems, including social anxiety. Sam spent more time with friends and earned all A's until he entered the seventh grade. His mother also reported that up until the seventh grade, Sam spent a great deal of time on his schoolwork and would become upset if he did not get every question and problem correct. Sam's schoolwork was done haphazardly and quickly. He had been observed being teased by older students, and responded with increased withdrawal and avoidance of groups of peers. Sam began to spend most of his free periods and lunch hours in the school library. In addition, Sam described schoolwork and striving for high grades as "too stressful," despite his stated desire to do well in school. Sam was viewed by his mother and his teachers as coping poorly with stress and as at risk for anxiety problems, poor school achievement, worsening peer relations, and depression.

Sam was entered into the school's peer group life skills training program. Students met biweekly with same age, gender, and grade peers. The program focused on prevention of anxiety, depression, and school-related problems through stress management and coping. This life skills approach was aimed at training students to cope not only with present-day stresses but also with high school and beyond, when demands increase and become more complex. The life skills program consisted of a sequence of an introduction to stress, and of teaching general and then specific coping, stress management, and social skills. After an educational approach, including the overview of stress and learning general coping and stress management skills, the program was based on a standard A-B-C cognitive behavioral model. The program focused on first identifying antecedents, that is, teaching students to recognize sources of stress. Once antecedents were identified and recorded, behaviors were observed and recorded. Behaviors were broadly defined as any behaviors performed in response to a stressful event and included cognitive (e.g., thoughts and attributions), physiological (bodily responses such as increased heart rate), and overt or voluntary levels of behavior. In addition, consequences that occurred during and after particular behaviors were predicted and then observed and recorded in between biweekly group meetings. Participants maintained a daily rating of stress using the Subjective Units of Distress Scale (SUDS).

Sam's specific skill training focused on applying coping and stress management strategies to his thoughts and behaviors about school achievement and his thoughts and behaviors about peer relationships. The problems were addressed separately, and Sam's school achievement was addressed first, because his SUDS ratings for schoolwork and worries were highest. After recording stress triggers, Sam identified behaviors such as social withdrawal and consequences of those behaviors such as having fewer friends and increased sadness. Sam was able to generate solutions by applying general skills already learned to the stress and subsequent withdrawal and sadness. As Sam began coping more effectively by challenging catastrophic cognitions and substituting study time for "escape reading," he began to see improvements in his grades. His teachers provided additional reinforcement through praise and increased attention in the classroom. As Sam's school achievement improved, he also noted stress from his self-imposed expectation of perfect scores on all assignments and tests. Again, previously learned strategies were applied. In this case, Sam engaged in behaviors incompatible with the stress trigger of perfect schoolwork, such as setting a goal of getting no more than two or three answers incorrect on his daily assignments. Finally, as his schoolwork SUDS ratings declined, Sam applied similar strategies to peer relationships. When withdrawal and avoidance of his peers were resisted and Sam substituted engagement with friends, additional improvements in mood, anxiety, and peer relationships followed.

—*Timothy R. Stickle and Neil M. Kirkpatrick*

See also: *Problem Solving Therapy (Vols. I & III), Social and Interpersonal Skills Training (Vol. II), Social Competence Treatment: Externalizing Disorders (Vol. II), Social Effectiveness Training (Vols. I & III), Social Skills Training (Vols. I & III)*

Suggested Readings

Botvin, G. J., & Kantor, L.W. (2000). Preventing alcohol and tobacco use through life skills training. *Alcohol Research & Health, 24,* 250–263.

Compas, B. E. (1993). Promoting positive mental health during adolescence. In S. G. Millstein, E. O. Nightingale, and A. C. Petersen (Eds.), *Promoting the health of adolescents: New directions for the twenty-first century.* Oxford, UK: Oxford University Press.

Gilchrist, L. D., Schinke, S. P., & Maxwell, J. S. (1987). Life skills counseling for preventing problems in adolescence. *Journal of Social Service Research, 10,* 73–84.

Kraemer, H. C., Stice, E., Kazdin, A., Offord, D., & Kupfer, D. (2001). How do risk factors work together? Mediators, moderators, and independent, overlapping, and proxy risk factors. *American Journal of Psychiatry, 158,* 848–856.

LaFromboise, T., & Howard-Pitney, B. (1995). The Zuni life skills development curriculum description and evaluation of a suicide prevention program. *Journal of Counseling Psychology, 42,* 479–486.

Moote, G. T., & Wodarski, J. S. (1997). The acquisition of life skills through adventure-based activities and programs: A review of the literature. *Adolescence, 32,* 143–167.

O. IVAR LOVAAS

Ole Ivar Lovaas was born on May 8, 1927, in Lier, Norway. He became interested in behavioral therapy as a result of his childhood experiences in Norway during World War II. He hoped that the destruction and cruelty displayed during the war were a result of the environment and not genetics. This eventually led to his research into behavioral treatment of autism.

Lovaas began his secondary education at Drammen Latinskole in Drammen, Norway. He completed the Examen Artium, the final examinations of upper secondary school in Norway, in 1947. He continued his education in the United States. In 1951, he received a bachelor of arts degree in social studies from Luther College in Decorah, Iowa. By 1958, he had received both his master's and doctoral degrees in psychology from the University of Washington in Seattle, where he was influenced by pioneers in applied behavior analysis with children, Donald M. Baer and Sidney W. Bijou.

After receiving his PhD, Lovaas became an acting assistant professor at the University of Washington. In 1961, he took a position as assistant professor at the University of California in Los Angeles and rose to associate professor in 1965. During this time, he collaborated with Baer and Bijou on such articles as "The Interaction Between Verbal and Nonverbal Behavior" in 1961 and "Experimental Procedures for Analyzing the Interaction of Symbolic Stimuli and Children's Behavior" in 1965. Lovaas quickly advanced to full professor in 1967.

The major contributions of Lovaas to the field of psychology derive from his work with children with autism. He was strongly influenced by the work of Charles Ferster, who, in 1961, was the first major behavior analyst to advocate the use of behavioral principles to solve the behavior problems exhibited by people with autism. For instance, in 1962, Ferster and Marian K. DeMyer demonstrated that simple behaviors in children with autism could be established using contingent reinforcement. In 1964, Montrose Wolf, Todd Risley, and Hayden Mees expanded Ferster's work with a classic study showing how a systematic program of reinforcement contingencies could be used to significantly improve the life of a young boy with autism. Lovaas built on these and similar works to develop a comprehensive curriculum for the treatment of autism based on empirically validated principles of learning. For instance, in a 1965 article, "Experimental Studies in Childhood Schizophrenia: Analysis of Self-Destructive Behavior," he demonstrated that self-injurious behavior could be reduced by reinforcement of an incompatible behavior, and in the 1969 article "Manipulation of Self-Destruction in Three Retarded Children," he demonstrated that self-injurious behavior could be immediately reduced by presenting electric shock contingent on self-injurious behavior.

The curriculum Lovaas developed is aimed at the reduction of self-stimulatory and aggressive behaviors and also targets the development of language, social behavior, play behavior, preacademic skills, and independent living skills. By implementing intensive, early, long-term treatment based on a behavioral approach, he found that individuals with autism could make significant improvements in functioning not possible with treatments based on psychodynamic theory or organic psychiatry. Indeed, at the time he began his work, autism, which was then known as childhood schizophrenia, was considered largely untreatable, and many people with autism were relegated to spending their entire lives in the back wards of state hospitals. Lovaas also showed that treatment gains could be significantly enhanced if the child returned from therapy to an environment with people familiar with behavioral principles who would continue contingency management at home or other natural settings. He demonstrated that gains could be maintained if treatments were specifically designed to generalize from the treatment setting to natural contingencies of reinforcement.

In addition to the development of a comprehensive behavioral treatment for autism, Lovaas contributed to the understanding of autism by studying the effects of stimulus overselectivity and self-stimulation on the development of autistic children. For instance, in a 1971 article, "Selective Responding by Autistic Children to Multiple Sensory Input," he demonstrated that subjects with autism were able to attend to only one sensory modality at a time. He called this "stimulus overselectivity" and concluded that this could interfere with the education of children with autism. In another 1971 article, "Response Latencies to Auditory Stimuli in Autistic Children Engaged in Self-Stimulatory Behavior," he demonstrated that when taught to approach a dispenser for reinforcement at the sound of a tone, mute subjects with autism waited a longer period to respond to the tone when engaged in self-stimulatory behavior than when not. Lovaas also conducted many studies to explore the variables that control verbal and nonverbal behavior and further contributed to the field of developmental disabilities through research on viable treatments for self-injurious behavior.

Although Lovaas has contributed greatly to the effective treatment of autism, his work has also been the focus of controversy. In the 1960s, Lovaas pursued therapies using aversive procedures that are no longer employed. For instance, in a 1969 article, "Pain and Punishment as Treatment Techniques," he reduced the self-stimulatory behavior in a 4-year-old boy with developmental delay by slapping him contingent on the problem behaviors, and eliminated the self-injurious behavior of a 7-year-old boy with mental retardation

by presenting contingent slapping and electric shock. Largely forgotten, however, is that psychology and psychiatry at the time offered no effective treatments for severe self-injurious and self-stimulatory behavior. In this vacuum, Lovaas was forced to search through available knowledge of behavior for methods that would achieve any positive results at all.

Given more recent discoveries, some by Lovaas himself, Lovaas has changed his views on aversives. Initially, in the absence of effective alternatives for quickly reducing some problem behaviors, he included the use of aversives in the comprehensive treatment program that he developed. Aversives are now excluded from the program. Even so, Lovaas has defended the judicious use of aversives for otherwise intractable or dangerous self- or other-directed aggressive and self-stimulatory behavior. Given that there remain some problems for which better solutions are not available, the alternative is to allow the behaviors to persist and reduce the chance of any possible functional living skills training.

Currently, Lovaas is professor emeritus at the University of California at Los Angeles. He maintains directorship positions at the Clinic for the Behavioral Treatment of Children at UCLA and also the Lovaas Institute for Early Intervention in Los Angeles. He continues his research into behavioral intervention in autism, and in his 2002 book *Teaching Individuals With Developmental Delays: Basic Intervention Techniques,* he details the changes in programming that have occurred since his original curriculum for early, intensive autism treatment was published in *Teaching Developmentally Disabled Children: The Me Book* in 1981.

—*Amy K. Drayton and James T. Todd*

See also: *Aversion Relief (Vols. I & III), Aversive Conditioning (Vol. II), Behavioral Treatment in Natural Environments (Vols. I & III), Electrical Aversion (Vols. I & III), Extinction (Vol. II), Extinction and Habituation (Vol. III), Operant Conditioning (Vols. I, II, & III), Reinforcement (Vols. I & III)*

Suggested Readings

Lovaas, O. I. (2002). *Teaching individuals with developmental delays: Basic intervention techniques.* Austin, TX: Pro-Ed.

Lovaas, O. I., Ackerman, A., Alexander, D., Firestone, P., Perkins, J., & Young, D. (1981). *Teaching developmentally disabled children: The me book.* Austin, TX: Pro-Ed.

Lovaas, O. I., & Favell, J. E. (1987). Protection for clients undergoing aversive/restrictive interventions. *Education and Treatment of Children, 10,* 311–325.

Lovaas, O. I., Litronick, A., & Mann, R. (1971). Response latencies to auditory stimuli in autistic children engaged in self-stimulatory behavior. *Behavior Research and Therapy, 9,* 39–49.

Lovaas, O. I., Schreibman, L., Koegel, R., & Rehm, R. (1971). Selective responding by autistic children to multiple sensory input. *Journal of Abnormal Psychology, 77,* 211–222.

Lovaas, O. I., & Simmons, J. Q. (1969). Manipulation of self-destruction in three retarded children. *Journal of Applied Behavior Analysis, 2,* 143–157.

M

MAINTENANCE

DESCRIPTION OF THE STRATEGY

Since the 1960s, the disciplines of applied behavior analysis (formerly known as behavior modification) and behavior therapy have developed a number of highly effective behavior-change strategies. Many of these strategies, most of which are based on the principles of operant or respondent conditioning, have been effectively disseminated such that they are now readily available to clinicians. A fundamental aspect of behavioral treatment, and perhaps its most important feature, is the *maintenance* of behavior change. Maintenance is defined as the continued performance of an appropriate target behavior (e.g., communication) or the continued reduction of a problem behavior (e.g., aggression) after treatment has been withdrawn. Maintenance can also be conceptualized as behavior that is resistant to extinction and thereby more likely to persist in the absence of reinforcement. A better understanding of maintenance may be illustrated by contrasting it with the related process of generalization.

There are two types of generalization: stimulus and response. *Stimulus generalization* occurs when a behavior learned under one set of circumstances (e.g., in an outpatient clinic with a therapist) occurs at other times, in novel settings, and/or in the presence of different people. For example, stimulus generalization is said to occur when an unassertive and shy child is taught by a therapist to be more socially assertive, and subsequently demonstrates those same skills at school with peers. When stimulus generalization occurs, the trained response occurs in different situations. Alternatively, *response generalization* occurs when different, but functionally similar, responses occur after training. For example, response generalization might occur when the child mentioned earlier uses assertive phrases that were not directly taught but are, nonetheless, equally effective in social situations. Both stimulus and response generalization are important considerations when changing behavior because it is frequently clinically advantageous for multiple variations of a target behavior to occur across a variety of situations. Although maintenance has sometimes been referred to as "temporal" generalization because it refers to the durability of behavior change over time, it is important to consider it apart from stimulus and response generalization because maintenance requires its own clinical strategies.

Successful behavior change is a prerequisite for maintenance. Obviously, if a behavior is not effectively changed, there will not be anything to maintain over time. Although generally very effective, most behavioral treatments cannot be continued indefinitely and thus must eventually be withdrawn. Of course, despite the withdrawal of some or all aspects of a treatment, behavior change still needs to be maintained. For example, a teacher who uses preferred snacks and toys to reinforce student compliance must at some point stop delivering those rewards. However, if the teacher abruptly withdrew treatment, compliance would likely worsen. Maintenance generally will not occur unless certain variables are addressed during the behavior-change process. In other words, maintenance must be explicitly programmed. Such programming can occur when behavior has already been changed or, better yet, during the behavior-change process before treatment has been withdrawn.

At least four strategies can be used to program maintenance. The first strategy, the use of indiscriminable contingencies, is actually a group of methods that produces a common goal: the gradual elimination of training contingencies such that the process is undetectable. The primary method by which this is accomplished is the use and thinning of intermittent reinforcement schedules. Behaviors that are intermittently, or periodically, reinforced (i.e., consequences are provided for some, but not all, of the behaviors) are generally more resistant to extinction (i.e., nonreinforcement) than behaviors that are continuously reinforced. Although it is generally recommended to first use continuous reinforcement when teaching a behavior, after it has been acquired the schedule can be gradually thinned, thus making the behavior more resistant to extinction. For example, a continuous schedule could first be thinned by reinforcing every other behavior, every third behavior, approximately every fifth behavior, and so on. In addition, the schedule might be further thinned until reinforcers are no longer delivered. A second method involves gradually increasing the delay between the behavior and its reinforcer. This can be used instead of or in addition to reinforcement-schedule thinning. For example, after a behavior has been taught using the immediate delivery of reinforcers, the time between the behavior and reinforcer could be gradually extended over time (e.g., from 1 to 60 seconds), possibly until the reinforcers are eventually removed altogether. A third method for creating an indistinguishable contingency is to gradually over time deliver the programmed consequence independent of (e.g., every 5 minutes) *and* contingent on the target behavior. Thus, the likelihood of the child receiving these consequences independent of the target behavior would eventually increase. However, one should take great care not to introduce response-independent reinforcers too quickly or the target behavior will likely extinguish. The three aforementioned methods for creating indistinguishable contingencies should always be incorporated with the use of natural reinforcers (described below) such that when programmed consequences are gradually removed, natural contingencies will remain to maintain the behavior. The fourth method for creating indistinguishable contingencies applies to the gradual withdrawal or thinning of treatments designed to reduce problem behavior. This is sometimes referred to as treatment fading. For example, with a differential reinforcement of other behavior (DRO) procedure, a reinforcer is delivered when a problem behavior has not occurred for a specified period of time. This time period can be gradually extended over time (e.g., from 5 to 30 minutes) such that the DRO treatment is easier to implement but still effective at maintaining the behavioral reduction. Thinning procedures have also been developed for several other reductive treatments, including functional communication training and noncontingent reinforcement.

The second strategy for programming the maintenance of behavior change is the introduction of reinforcers from the natural environment into the training situation. Before this strategy can be implemented, a clinician must identify the reinforcers that would maintain the target behavior in the natural environment. For example, the natural reinforcer for telling a joke is often laughter from the person to whom the joke is told. After natural reinforcers are identified, they can be incorporated into the training situation so that when the programmed reinforcers are withdrawn, the natural reinforcers will maintain the behavior. A common natural reinforcer that is included in many training programs is descriptive praise. A related method for programming maintenance is to select only target behaviors for training that reliably produce identifiable reinforcers in the natural environment. The outcome of this method is sometimes known as the "behavior trap" because the natural reinforcer is said to trap (i.e., maintain) the target behavior in the environment. For example, the programmed consequences (e.g., preferred foods, drinks, and toys) that are delivered in a toilet training program can be gradually withdrawn during training because the natural reinforcers of having dry pants, clean clothes, behaving like a "big boy" or "big girl," and so on will likely maintain the program's treatment gains. If a clinician has difficulty identifying a target behavior's natural reinforcers, the behavior of other individuals (e.g., parents, siblings) in the natural environment can be changed such that they will deliver explicit reinforcers for the target behavior.

A third strategy designed to promote maintenance is the use of booster treatment sessions to prevent the degradation of maintenance. Booster sessions are essentially brief refresher sessions that involve the continuation of treatment at a reduced level beyond what was delivered in the acute treatment period. Booster sessions are especially important with treatments whose effects are known to deteriorate over time (e.g., aversion therapy) and for children who are at a high risk for relapse (e.g., adolescents with substance abuse).

The fourth strategy for promoting maintenance is to teach the child self-management skills, such as self-monitoring (recording) and the ability to recruit reinforcers from others in the environment. With self-monitoring, the child records the frequency and/or intensity of each of the target behaviors (e.g., tics), perhaps in a diary. Parents and teachers can then access the record to determine, for example, whether a reinforcer should be delivered. In addition, self-monitoring on its own has been shown to produce therapeutic behavior change. However, the most useful function of self-monitoring for maintenance is that it provides children with a record of their behavior, which can prompt their recruitment of natural reinforcement from others. For example, a teacher might treat a young girl's attention-maintained disruptive behavior by teaching her to (a) monitor her own disruptions and (b) appropriately request attention when she refrains from being disruptive for 30 minutes. In this example, the girl can determine when the reinforcer should be delivered, which might produce better maintenance than a similar treatment in which data are collected and monitored by a busy teacher with many other duties. Under some circumstances, a child might also be taught to deliver his or her own consequences for appropriate behavior (i.e., self-reinforcement).

After a behavioral treatment has been removed and maintenance has been programmed, a *follow-up assessment* is used to periodically evaluate the durability of behavior change. Maintenance failures can be addressed by conducting booster treatment sessions as previously described or reevaluating the maintenance plan.

It is often important to consider one additional issue related to the aforementioned maintenance and follow-up strategies. Treatments that will be managed by individuals in the natural environment (e.g., family members), either from the beginning of treatment or at the beginning of the maintenance period, should have good *contextual fit* with the environment. In other words, the treatment should be acceptable to the contingency managers and require the lowest possible effort to increase the likelihood that it will be implemented with integrity.

RESEARCH BASIS

Unfortunately, relatively few studies have exposed specific maintenance strategies to rigorous experimental evaluation, which would include comparisons of behavioral maintenance under multiple conditions (e.g., delay to reinforcement vs. reinforcement schedule thinning). Instead, much of the research database on maintenance strategies is derived from their use in studies whose primary focus was behavioral treatment but nonetheless also included programs for maintenance. The four primary maintenance strategies discussed earlier (i.e., indiscriminable contingencies, natural reinforcers, booster treatments, self-management) continue to receive attention in the applied research literature, but the fact that they are often combined (e.g., both natural reinforcers and booster sessions are used) makes it difficult to evaluate the independent contributions of each strategy. In addition, it is common for several maintenance strategies to be employed along with a number of strategies to promote stimulus generalization. Unfortunately, it is unclear whether one or all of these variables are necessary for behavioral maintenance because few definitive comparisons of these strategies have been conducted.

The most frequently investigated topic relevant to maintenance is resistance to extinction. A number of variables can affect resistance to extinction, which often poses a difficulty for researchers, who, when studying one of these variables, must also adequately control for many others. Although intermittent reinforcement schedules generally appear to increase resistance to extinction and thus improve maintenance, a number of other variables such as reinforcer magnitude might also contribute to this finding. Nonetheless, there are a few well-documented findings in this area. When delays to reinforcement have been gradually extended, resistance to extinction appears to be enhanced. A similar outcome is likely when conditions are varied during training. Finally, recent studies on "behavioral momentum" from the basic literature indicate that the rate of reinforcement during training is positively correlated with the subsequent resistance of a behavior to extinction.

RELEVANT TARGET POPULATIONS AND EXCEPTIONS

Strategies designed to maintain treatment gains are somewhat unique because they are essentially relevant to every individual who receives clinical services in which behavior change is the desired outcome. There are presumably few, if any, circumstances in which one would desire a behavior to be changed during treatment but not have that behavior change maintain over time. Thus, maintenance programming is relevant to virtually all clinical populations and target behaviors.

COMPLICATIONS

Although there are complications associated with each maintenance strategy, a comprehensive account of them is beyond the scope of this entry. Instead, one primary complication of three common maintenance strategies will be discussed.

The main complication associated with the use of indiscriminable contingencies is the expertise required for their design and execution. The thinning of reinforcement schedules, extension of reinforcement delays, delivery of response-independent reinforcers, and schedule thinning of reductive procedures all require considerable expertise during their development. The systematic execution of these methods is designed to slowly and imperceptibly alter contingencies over time such that behavior is maintained while the treatment is withdrawn. If contingencies are changed too abruptly, the behavior change might reverse. In addition, despite our best efforts, these methods sometimes result in a minor worsening of the behavior. When this occurs, it is sometimes helpful to revert to an earlier version of the schedule before again proceeding through the progression. Such decisions can only be made during a maintenance plan that is being deliberately and precisely executed along with ongoing data collection for effective decision making.

The main complication when using natural reinforcers during training is their identification. It might be difficult to determine how a target behavior will contact naturally occurring reinforcers. If natural reinforcers cannot be identified, the environment will need to be amenable to the introduction of new contingencies for maintaining behavior change. In addition, as mentioned earlier, any maintenance procedure that is introduced into the natural environment must have a good contextual fit with that environment.

The main complication with self-management strategies is that although they are sometimes used to assist with the maintenance of another behavior, they too sometimes suffer from poor maintenance. Self-management strategies for children occasionally fail, especially when an adult does not reliably monitor their outcomes. In addition, self-management techniques might not be appropriate for some children with severe developmental disabilities for whom rules do not reliably affect their behavior.

CASE ILLUSTRATION

"Oliver" was a 6-year-old boy who attended a general education kindergarten class 5 days each week. Oliver's language skills were age appropriate and he responded well to questions and social initiations. In other words, if other children or adults asked Oliver a question, he was likely to answer. Oliver also played appropriately with a variety of toys and typically remained close by his peers during free-play periods in the classroom. However, he rarely directed verbal initiations toward his peers and, consequently, spent more time alone than with other children.

The school psychologist assigned to Oliver's school implemented social skills training that consisted of structured, dyadic peer-play sessions. At the beginning of treatment, Oliver was introduced to his peers in structured-play sessions with the school psychologist or teacher's aide present to facilitate the interactions. Sessions were 30 minutes in duration and included Oliver and one peer. Approximately three sessions were conducted each week. During sessions, Oliver was initially prompted to initiate social interactions (e.g., "Do you want to play with me?" "Do you like this toy?"). Successful initiations were reinforced by adult praise and the natural consequences of his peer (e.g., "Let's play." "I like that toy because it's fast."). As Oliver began to demonstrate successful social initiations, the adult reinforcers were gradually withdrawn, which gave him the opportunity to succeed independently with his peer. The adult then gradually stopped attending Oliver's sessions. These play sessions naturally became less structured when Oliver was able to independently initiate and play with his peer and was able to imitate his peer's appropriate social behaviors. At this point, additional peers were gradually introduced into sessions, which were then incorporated into naturally occurring playtimes. Follow-up assessments were conducted 1, 3, and 6 months after training had formally ended to evaluate maintenance of Oliver's social initiations.

The aforementioned treatment designed to enhance Oliver's social repertoire incorporated several strategies to promote maintenance, including the use of natural reinforcers via peers and the use of indiscriminable contingencies by thinning the adult's reinforcement schedule and gradually removing the adult from sessions. Finally, several follow-up assessments were conducted to evaluate the durability of Oliver's treatment gains. Had one of the assessments indicated a lack of maintenance, a booster treatment session could have been conducted.

—James E. Carr and Daniel B. Shabani

See also: *Applied Behavior Analysis (Vols. I, II, & III), Azrin, Nathan H. (Vols. I & III), Generalization (Vols. I, II, & III), Kazdin, Alan E. (Vols. I & III),*

Suggested Readings

Esveldt-Dawson, K., & Kazdin, A. E. (1998). *How to maintain behavior* (2nd ed.). Austin, TX: Pro-Ed.

Foxx, R. M. (1996). Twenty years of applied behavior analysis in treating the most severe problem behavior: Lessons learned. *The Behavior Analyst, 19,* 225–235.

Foxx, R. M., & Livesay, J. (1984). Maintenance of response suppression following overcorrection: A 10-year retrospective examination of eight cases. *Analysis and Intervention in Developmental Disabilities, 4,* 65–79.

Hanley, G. P., Iwata, B. A., & Thompson, R. H. (2001). Reinforcement schedule thinning following treatment with functional communication training. *Journal of Applied Behavior Analysis, 34,* 17–38.

LeBlanc, L. A., Hagopian, L. P., Maglieri, K. A., & Poling, A. (2002). Decreasing the intensity of reinforcement-based interventions for reducing behavior: Conceptual issues and a proposed model for clinical practice. *The Behavior Analyst Today, 3,* 289–300.

Lerman, D. C., & Iwata, B. A. (1996). Developing a technology for the use of operant extinction in clinical settings: An examination of basic and applied research. *Journal of Applied Behavior Analysis, 29,* 345–382.

Sarafino, E. P. (2001). *Behavior modification: Principles of behavior change* (2nd ed.). Mountain View, CA: Mayfield.

Stokes, T. F., & Baer, D. M. (1977). An implicit technology of generalization. *Journal of Applied Behavior Analysis, 10,* 349–367.

Stokes, T. F., & Osnes, P. G. (1989). An operant pursuit of generalization. *Behavior Therapy, 20,* 337–355.

Sulzer-Azaroff, B., & Mayer, G. R. (1991). *Behavior analysis for lasting change.* Orlando, FL: Harcourt Brace Jovanovich.

Whitaker, S. (2002). Maintaining reductions in challenging behaviours: A review of the literature. *British Journal of Developmental Disabilities, 48,* 15–25.

MANUALIZED BEHAVIOR THERAPY

DESCRIPTION OF THE STRATEGY

A child behavioral treatment manual provides explicit instructions and guidelines for assessing the problem and for delivering treatment procedures. While manuals vary a great deal in their level of specificity, the best manuals are disorder specific. In some instances, they include descriptions of the underlying theory of change on which the procedures or techniques are based.

Although treatment manuals have been used in behavior therapy since the late 1960s, the systematic use of therapy manuals became more popular after the 1995 report of the American Psychological Association's Task Force on Promotion and Dissemination of Psychological Procedures, which argued for collecting and disseminating empirically supported treatments, or ESTs. ESTs are treatments that have research supporting their efficacy or ability to show clear positive effects in well-controlled studies.

Detailed descriptions of treatment procedures are necessary for both treatment researchers and clinicians who use ESTs to ensure that treatments are delivered in the same way as the original study, or studies, that demonstrated the utility of the treatment. These descriptions of treatment protocols are referred to as manuals. Unfortunately, virtually all of the manualized treatments found by the Task Force to have empirical support are targeted toward adults. Despite the fact that manuals are often used in the conduct of behavior therapy with children and adolescents, most of these manuals have not been well described in the literature.

Theoretical Basis of Manualized Behavior Therapy

Behavior therapy is an orientation to clinical work that is aligned philosophically with an experimental approach to the study of human behavior. Behavior therapy adherents believe that problem behaviors seen in clinical settings can best be understood in light of principles derived from psychological experimentation and learning theory. Child behavior therapists rely on the scientific study of behavior and typically focus on overt behavior.

For the behavior therapist, behavior is assumed to be lawful and a function of specifiable antecedent, organismic, behavioral, and consequent conditions. In the initial stages of therapy, the therapist uses a functional, idiographic assessment to identify the conditions associated with the clients' problematic behaviors. This assessment leads directly to specific maladaptive behaviors, antecedents that lead to those behaviors, and consequences that follow the behaviors and serve to maintain them.

In behavior therapy, patients are taught new behaviors and skills to foster positive behavior change. Behavior therapists have developed standardized treatment strategies, based on behavior principles, to alter problematic behavior. The use of manuals to guide assessment and therapy standardizes treatment across therapists and clients with similar clinical presentations. As a practical matter, treatment manual applications are often tailored to the individual client.

History of Behavior Therapy and Applications for Children

Behavior therapy interventions for children have a short history. Early behavioral interventions for childhood psychopathology were drawn either directly from empirical research with animals during the 1960s or from adult interventions that had been developed using basic learning principles. Early behavior therapy research narrowly focused on the usefulness of conditioning and deconditioning fear and avoidant behaviors. Behavior problems in children were theorized to be a function of a deficient learning history, and early interventions focused on behavioral interventions to teach appropriate responses. Over time, researchers began to realize the complexity of the child's environment and how difficult it was to gain control of it.

As behaviorists looked for more effective interventions, the focus expanded to include the child's developmental status, the child's tendency to imitate others in his or her environment, the verbal mediation of consequences, and other factors such as gender, ethnicity, and family structure. Current interventions are examined for efficacy, effectiveness (how well treatment works in clinical settings), and for what works for whom and under what circumstances. Manualized behavior therapy has fueled this area of research.

RESEARCH BASIS

Usefulness of Manuals in Behavior Therapy

In the mid- to late-1960s, the first behavior therapy manuals were created to improve methodology in treatment research and ensure consistent treatment delivery. This consistency increased precision in outcome research. This standardization of methods paved the way for the empirical evaluation of treatment integrity. A published treatment manual makes it possible to determine whether a reported treatment actually was delivered as intended and as conducted in the original efficacy trials. Manuals can also better prepare practicing psychotherapists to handle more consistently situations in which they may not have had a great deal of experience.

Treatment outcome data suggest that using manualized treatment increases both cost effectiveness and time efficiency. When used in research, manuals facilitate the comparison of one therapy with other methods of treatment, such as pharmacological therapy. With all of the details of assessment and treatment provided, manuals also can be important in clarifying and comparing the many types or variants of therapy.

Empirically Supported Treatments and Manualized Behavior Therapy

As empirical clinical research has advanced, manuals have been integrated into behavioral therapies. The American Psychological Association's Task Force on ESTs listed treatments that had demonstrated efficacy across research trials. One criterion for inclusion in the list of ESTs is the availability of a treatment manual, and this has spurred the creation of more manuals. As new treatments develop and old ones are subjected to empirical scrutiny, the number of standardized treatments with treatment manuals continues to grow.

Manualized treatments are placed on the EST list based on demonstration of their efficacy in large-scale randomized clinical trials where clinical outcomes are compared with a placebo treatment, another form of therapy, or psychotropic medication. If a treatment demonstrates efficacy, it is listed as either "a well-established treatment" or "a probably efficacious treatment," depending on the number of well-controlled studies that have been published on its use. "Well-established treatments" have been found to produce superior outcomes when compared to a comparison group or another psychotherapy on at least two separate occasions by independent researchers. "Probably efficacious treatments," on the other hand, have been found to produce positive outcomes in a single study or by a single set of researchers. The majority of interventions that have been demonstrated to be well established or probably efficacious for childhood disorders are behavioral or cognitive-behavioral in nature.

RELEVANT TARGET POPULATIONS AND EXCEPTIONS

Manualized behavior therapy has been shown to be effective in the treatment of both internalizing and externalizing disorders in children and adolescents. Manualized behavior therapy has been found to be a well-established or probably efficacious treatment for children and/or adolescents for the following disorders: depression, childhood obesity, anxiety, specific phobia, generalized anxiety disorder, separation anxiety disorder, attention-deficit/hyperactivity disorder, oppositional defiant disorder, conduct disorder, encopresis, enuresis, trichotillomania, binge eating disorder, bulimia nervosa, and anorexia nervosa. However, the manualized treatments for most of these disorders have only one or two empirical investigations in their support. For some of the disorders for which empirically supported manualized treatments exist, such as eating disorders, there is empirical support for their use with adolescents and adults, but not with children.

The lack of empirically supported manuals for treatment of childhood disorders other than those listed above is largely due to the paucity of research on the efficacy and effectiveness of psychosocial therapies for children in general. Many treatments currently used in the treatment of childhood disorders have not been manualized, making it difficult to evaluate their efficacy. The existence of multiple (or comorbid) disorders in children has not been extensively examined, and there are few manualized behavior therapies for children with comorbid conditions.

CRITICISMS

Manuals can specify the nature of the treatment and articulate the details of therapy delivery. This ensures that researchers have precise and standardized clinical methods that can then be used in the evaluation of treatment efficacy. Nonetheless, the manualization of behavior therapy has not been without criticism. The major controversies are described in this section.

Length of Treatment

Health care policymakers have encouraged the development of brief treatments as well as the use of manualized treatments in an effort to minimize the cost of service delivery while still maintaining effective treatment. However, treatment manual protocols rarely specify fewer than 8 sessions, and for the treatment of both internalizing and externalizing conditions, some manuals call for more than 24 sessions. Most manuals include modules that build on knowledge and skills in a logical, cumulative sequence, such that skills acquired in any one session depend on those acquired in the previous session. Despite the solid logic behind the development and use of such manuals, their success is unknown when they are adapted in clinical settings where few treatment sessions are allowed or where treatment is often terminated by the child or the child's family without consulting with the therapist. Research must clarify whether manuals need to be simplified and adapted to the limited duration of therapy as it is routinely practiced or if current manualized treatments are generalizable to the typical clinical setting.

Process Variables

Recent research has shown that process variables, such as the therapeutic relationship, patient characteristics, and treatment motivation, can be important for successful implementation of behavioral treatment protocols, including those using manuals. Behavior therapy research has focused primarily on technique-oriented methods and has paid little attention to therapy process variables. Evidence that there can be variations in effectiveness across therapists, even when they use the same treatment manual, supports the importance of these factors.

Flexibility

Critics accuse manual-based treatment of emphasizing technique at the expense of individual problem analyses and individual tailoring of treatment. Proponents of manualized behavior therapy agree that manuals need to be flexible enough, and therapists adaptive enough, to deviate from standard protocols when events arise that interfere with the implementation of the manualized treatments. Consequently, treatment manuals are beginning to incorporate treatment flexibility. Many newer manuals describe an ordered sequence of treatment interventions but offer algorithms that allow the clinician to delay, accelerate, or drop techniques, depending on the particular client's needs and response to treatment. Others offer therapists a number of different treatment modules that can be adapted according to more general guidelines for setting and achieving treatment priorities, or create a principle-driven treatment with individualized interventions conducted within the overall framework of a treatment manual. This last approach seems best suited to behavior therapy. This approach allows clinical practice to continue to apply validated principles of behavior rather than fixed strategies. By using empirically derived decision rules to facilitate clinical judgment, treatment manuals can guide treatments tailored to the individual. This has been successfully demonstrated with some treatment manuals for child behavior problems.

Clinical Versus Research Applicability

Nearly all manuals are written by researchers. While treatment manuals have been found useful and efficacious in clinical research, a number of therapist, client, and context factors are typically not addressed in manual development. This leaves some psychologists with concerns about the clinical utility of treatment manuals. Many believe that the results from studies where manuals are tested in well-controlled settings are not generalizable to actual clinical settings. Furthermore, treatment manuals are commonly believed to be too unwieldy for clinical practice. Typically, manuals are written with sufficient detail to train therapists involved in empirical studies of the treatment. Most manuals are intended to provide checks of the accuracy of the treatment implementation. Therefore, much of the information included in manuals may not be relevant to practitioners seeking to use effective treatment planning and delivery strategies. This may make manuals seem user unfriendly to clinicians.

Others criticize manualized behavior therapy for not including more clinical setting illustrations, such as strategies for dealing with difficult clients and for handling procedural failures. These critics advocate increased attention to clinician end users in manual development and publication.

Proponents of manuals, however, argue that manuals can provide optimal approaches for guiding treatments in typical practice while they facilitate dissemination of scientifically supported treatments. Manuals have been created that cover all relevant aspects of treatment, including general therapeutic relationship principles, a focus on specific issues and techniques, and indications for when the planned treatment needs to be reexamined and altered. There currently are no viable alternatives to operationalizing

treatment considerations and strategies in some form of a manual for a psychologist who wants to develop, evaluate, or use empirically supported treatments.

CASE ILLUSTRATION

The following describes the use of a treatment manual for social skills training with a group of six junior high students. The students had been identified by school personnel as "loners"—socially isolated, having no or few friends, spending most of their time alone, and not involved in extracurricular events.

Social problem-solving skills and abilities were assessed by having students write the middle portion of stories for which they were given a beginning and an end. All students responded to the same four stories on seven different occasions: four different times during the 5 weeks prior to training, once following each of two treatment phases, and again at follow-up. Stories were rated on the number of steps the student described that were directed toward the stated outcome. Also, conversational skills were measured by quality ratings of audiotaped conversations for which students were randomly paired and instructed to spend 5 minutes "getting to know each other."

Group training consisted of eight 40-minute sessions conducted according to the manual designed by the researchers to guide therapists in intervention implementation. Sessions were held twice weekly for 4 weeks.

The first four training sessions focused on acquisition of problem-solving skills. Students were trained in component steps of problem-solving and then given practice in applying the learned steps to problems they or the therapists had suggested during session. Each of the four sessions targeted a different type of social interaction problem: (1) initiating an interaction with one other person, (2) participating in class and getting involved in group activities, (3) dealing with negative peer pressure and teasing, and (4) making requests of adults. The final four training sessions focused on improving four different sets of conversational skills: (1) listening skills, (2) talking about oneself, (3) initiating conversations, and (4) making requests of others. Each session began with a discussion of the skills for that session, followed by the leaders' modeling the skills. Each session ended with the students' practicing these skills with each other. Group leaders provided ongoing, corrective feedback and encouraged members of the groups to do the same.

This group treatment led to meaningful changes in some aspects of the students' behaviors. Students demonstrated enhanced skill in conversing with peers. Problem-solving skills and conversational skills both showed improvements in performance.

—Thomas W. Lombardo,
Emily Thomas-Johnson, and Karen A. Christoff

See also: *Barlow, David H. (Vols. I & III), Beck, Aaron, T. (Vols. I & III), Behavioral Approaches to Sexual Deviation (Vols. I & III), Behavioral Marital Therapy (Vols. I & III), Behavioral Treatments for Cigarette Smoking (Vols. I & III), Behavioral Treatments for the Addictions (Vols. I & III), Manualized Behavior Therapy (Vols. I & III)*

Suggested Readings

Chambless, D. L., & Hollen, S. D. (1998). Defining empirically supported therapies. *Journal of Consulting and Clinical Psychology, 66,* 7–18.

Chambless, D. L., Sanderson, W. C., Shoham, V., Bennett-Johnson, S., Pope, K. S., Crits-Christoph, P., et al. (1996). An update on empirically validated therapies. *The Clinical Psychologist, 49,* 5–18.

Eifert, G. H., Schulte, D., Zvolensky, M. J., Lejuez, C. W., & Lau, A. W. (1998). Manualized behavior therapy: Merits and challenges. *Behavior Therapy, 28,* 499–509.

Ollendick, T. H., & King, N. J. (2000). *Empirically supported treatments for children and adolescents.* In P. C. Kendall (Ed.), *Child and adolescent therapy* (pp. 386–423). New York: Guilford Press.

Weisz, J. R., & Hawley, K. M. (1998). Finding, evaluating, refining, and applying empirically supported treatments for children and adolescents. *Journal of Clinical Child Psychology, 27,* 206–216.

Zvolensky, M. J., & Eifert, G. H. (2002). Manualized behavior therapy. In M. Hersen & W. Sledge (Eds.), *Encyclopedia of psychotherapy* (Vol. 1, pp. 115–121). Boston: Academic Press.

MARKING TIME-OUT

Marking time-out is a specific application of time-out for use in circumstances that are unfavorable (e.g., in the car, grocery store) for punishing children's disruptive behavior in an effective or meaningful way. Children misbehave in public places for three reasons: (1) they learn that parents are reluctant to punish them in front of others, (2) they believe that parental threats or punishment will be forgotten before returning home, and (3) their self-control is compromised by the stimulation of public places and increased opportunity for misbehavior.

In our experience, marking time-out is very effective in controlling disruptive behavior in public. Children mark time for misbehavior until they are able to serve a time-out in the regular time-out setting at home. All that is required to use this procedure is a water-based marker and these steps:

1. Time-out must be established as a consistently used and reliable punisher in the home *prior to* implementing marking time-out.

2. Rules for appropriate behavior, opportunities to be rewarded for good behavior, and specific examples of unacceptable behaviors that would result in getting a mark should be discussed with the child prior to an outing. For instance, children who misbehave in the grocery store may be told, "If you do as you are told and stay with me and receive no marks, you may pick out a pack of gum at the checkout counter."

3. Each mark corresponds to one time-out period in the time-out area at home (e.g., 5 minutes for children under 5 years and 10 minutes for children over 5 years). Children should be told immediately why they are receiving a mark. Also explain that if a second mark is given, they will be taken home immediately, regardless of what the family may be doing. Then make it clear that they will be placed in time-out for two time periods.

4. Planning some practice trips is important to help parents feel comfortable and proficient in using the marking time-out procedure. Initially, practice using the procedure in relatively controlled circumstances where the child is likely to be disruptive (e.g., only placing nonperishable items in the shopping basket so that the cart can be left if the child needs to be taken home). Do *not* inform the child that these are practice trips.

Once ready, begin taking real trips and follow the above steps. When disruptive behavior occurs, mark the child's hand, provide the reason for the mark, and explain that the reward is now lost and time-out will occur once they return home. If negative behavior occurs again, mark a second time and immediately remove the child from the setting. If negative behavior occurs in the car ride home, mark these as well (when possible and safe) and implement the corresponding number of time-out periods. This can occur immediately once at home and/or during a favorite television show. Once the time-out periods are served, the marks are then washed off. Improvement in public behavior should be seen within a few weeks if all steps are followed and the procedure used consistently across situations.

—*Shari K. Neul and Ronald S. Drabman*

See also: *Behavioral Treatment in Natural Environments (Vols. I & III), Generalization (Vols. I, II, & III), Parent Training (Vol. II), Setting Events (Vols. I & III)*

Suggested Reading

Drabman, R. S., & Creedon, D. L. (1979). Marking time-out: A procedure for away from home disruptive behavior. *Child Behavior Therapy, 1,* 99–101.

MASSED PRACTICE

Learning typically occurs with repeated responses, such as in trial-and-error learning where correct responses are learned through the process of selective feedback and reward. Learning can also be structured so as to minimize errors in responding. It is in this context of repeated responding (i.e., the attempts of the learner to emit the correct response) that consideration is given to the number of responses that will be required in a given session or teaching lesson.

There are two basic forms of massed practice: positive massed practice and negative massed practice. Massed practice requires a relatively large number of responses to be emitted in a given time period. In positive massed practice, the purpose is to maximize learning of correct responses and to strengthen responding through repetition to high levels of consistently correct responses (mastery). Most typically, positive massed practice is used to develop motor skills. For example, when learning to play basketball, one of the first skills needed is the ability to quickly toss and catch the ball. Coaches often devote a significant amount of time during each practice for players to toss and catch rapidly and repeatedly for an extended period of time. This type of training is intended to develop automaticity of responding, that is, quick reflexive responses that do not require self-monitoring.

The second form, negative massed practice, is typically used to decrease behaviors. The target behavior is repeated as in positive massed practice, but with the goal of reducing the target behavior through fatigue and/or response inhibition. As an example, negative massed practice is used in the treatment of motor tics. The individual is encouraged to repeat the tic movement as much as possible in a short period of time.

There is much research on both positive and negative massed practice as it applies to motor learning, motor tics, procrastination and study habits, and language instruction, to name a few. In many research studies, a comparison of massed practice to distributed practice is explored. Distributed practice is when a response is practiced for a shorter time period than massed practice over a number of days or weeks. An alternative term for distributed practice that is often used is spaced practice. For example, a distributed practice schedule might be studying 1 hour each day for a week and a massed practice schedule might be studying 3 hours each day for a week. Interestingly, under certain circumstances, following a distributed practice schedule can result in better retention of the studied material. As in the previous example, distributed practice provides better results (more learning) for a continuous task, such as studying. Massed practice, on the other hand, has more success at learning of a discrete task, such as a motor movement.

It is important to emphasize that use of massed practice, as with any procedure used to affect learning, must take into consideration the specifics of the learner's current ability, specific limitations or restrictions in the teaching and criterion environment, and the specific nature of the behavior to be taught, strengthened, or reduced.

—*Raymond G. Romanczyk and Jennifer M. Gillis*

See also: *Classical Conditioning (Vols. I, II, & III), Generalization (Vols. I, II, & III), Operant Conditioning (Vols. I, II, & III)*

Suggested Readings

Baddeley, A., & Longman, D. J. A. (1978). The influence of length and frequency of training sessions on rate of learning to type. *Ergonomics, 21,* 627–635.

Chiara, L., Schuster, J., Bell, J., & Wolery, A. (1995). Small-group massed-trial and individually distributed trial instruction with preschoolers. *Journal of Early Intervention, 19,* 203–217.

Levine, M. D., & Ramirez, R. (1989). Contingent negative practice as a homebased treatment of tics and stuttering. In C. E. Schaefer & J. M. Briesmeister (Eds.), *Handbook of parent training: Parents as co-therapists for children's behavior problems* (pp. 38–59). New York: Wiley.

Peterson, A. L., Campise, R. L., & Azrin, N. H. (1994). Behavioral and pharmacological treatment for tic and habit disorders: A review. *Journal of Developmental and Behavioral Pediatrics, 15,* 430–441.

Yates, A. J. (1958). The application of learning theory to the treatment of tics. *Journal of Abnormal and Social Psychology, 56,* 175–182.

MODELING

DESCRIPTION OF THE STRATEGY

Modeling is said to occur when a child learns by observing others. A young boy "pretends" to smoke a cigarette like his father and get ready for work in the morning like his mother. Similarly, a teenager "swaggers" down the street like his or her favorite actor or actress. As noted early on by Albert Bandura, modeling is based on the principles of vicarious or observational learning. Research conducted within the broad framework of cognitive social learning theory, a theory pioneered by Bandura, shows that virtually all learning that results from direct experiences can also result from vicarious ones (i.e., as a function of observing the behavior of others and the consequences associated with that behavior). Children acquire new responses, both appropriate (e.g., dressing oneself, social skills, play a musical instrument) and inappropriate (e.g., hitting a sibling, being afraid of dogs), through observing others. In addition, Bandura described how previously acquired responses can be facilitated, inhibited, or disinhibited through vicarious learning or modeling procedures. For example, a girl who observes her older brother engage in fearful behaviors toward dogs may subsequently inhibit approach behavior toward dogs—something in the past that she seemed to do and enjoy. Likewise, a boy who is fearful of novel social situations and observes a close friend engage in nonfearful social interactions may disinhibit avoidant responses and subsequently engage in approach behavior to the previously feared situations. With fearful children, this disinhibiting effect is believed to play a particularly critical role. That is, as the child observes appropriate positive interaction with the feared stimuli without undue negative consequences, extinction of the fear is facilitated, thus making approach possible.

With modeling, it is important to distinguish between *learning* the response and subsequently *performing* the response. In the examples cited above, the child might learn the various responses vicariously but not actually exhibit them. For example, a girl might learn how to dress herself and brush her teeth by observing her parents each morning but, much to the dismay of her parents, not exhibit the dressing and care skills. The distinction between learning and performance has been demonstrated in many research studies. In one such study, preschool children observed a film in which a model exhibited verbal and physical aggression to a Bobo doll. For one group of children, the model was rewarded for aggressive behavior toward the doll, in a second group the model was punished for the same behavior, and for a third group the model received no consequences for the aggressive behavior. Although children in all three groups learned the aggressive response, children who observed the model being punished inhibited the response, whereas those who saw the model reinforced actively displayed the aggressive response. Of most interest here, those children in the group who saw the model neither punished nor reinforced learned the response, even though they initially failed to display aggressive behavior. However, they clearly had acquired the actual behaviors depicted in the film as evidenced when they were subsequently reinforced for display of those behaviors. They simply failed to display them until reinforced for doing so. Thus, consequences to the model during the vicarious learning *and* subsequently administered to the child determine whether the response is actually displayed. Such findings are the cornerstone for societal concerns about violence and other "inappropriate" behaviors depicted in films more broadly. Learning occurs but might not find its expression until a later point in time.

RELEVANT TARGET POPULATIONS AND EXCEPTIONS

Modeling procedures have been used in the treatment of many different types of behaviors, including the acquisition of language, the development of self-care, and the attainment of academic and social skills. Here their relevance to the treatment of fears and phobias will be highlighted, inasmuch as social skills training and modeling procedures in the treatment of aggressive behaviors are presented elsewhere in this volume.

Several different types of modeling have been employed in the treatment of childhood fears and phobias. *Videotape modeling* consists of having the child view a filmed version of a model (ideally a model with similar characteristics to the observing child) demonstrating successively greater interactions with the feared stimulus. For example, a boy afraid of dogs might observe another child on videotape enter a room with a dog on a leash at the other end of the room, walk halfway up to the dog and look at it, approach the dog closer, bend over, and let the dog sniff his hand, pet the dog, feed the dog a snack, and finally pick up the leash and walk the dog for a brief period of time. The same procedures are followed with *live modeling;* however, in this instance the child observes the interactions directly and in real life rather than on film. As a result, the child is in closer contact with the feared object and is able to more directly observe the subtle nuances of the model's approach behavior. The child is not, however, asked to interact directly with the feared object; rather, the child is simply requested to observe the model.

Participant modeling generally consists of three stages: observation of live modeling, therapist-guided interaction, and unaccompanied interaction. During the first stage, the therapist or model demonstrates gradually successive nonfearful but coping approaches toward the feared stimulus. For a dog-phobic child, this might entail the following successive steps: having the model walk toward the dog with an outreached hand, letting the dog sniff the model's hand, petting the dog on the back and then head, and sitting on the ground and playing with the dog. During this stage of live modeling, it is important that the child observe only positive consequences and appropriate coping skills. In the second stage, the therapist-model uses physical contact to guide the child through the behavioral approach tasks previously demonstrated. Continuing with the example of a dog-phobic child, this process might involve having the therapist hold the child's hand while the two of them approach the dog together, having the child place his or her hand on top of the therapist's hand while they pet the dog, and sitting next to the therapist on the ground while the therapist plays with the dog. During this stage, the therapist-model offers encouragement and support while physically assisting the child approach the feared stimulus. Finally, the third stage consists of the child performing the same behavioral approach tasks without physical assistance from the therapist-model. During this stage, the therapist would again accompany the child through the dog-approach and interaction tasks; however, the child would be requested to perform

these tasks alone. Furthermore, throughout these procedures, the child would be reinforced profusely or praised for initiating nonfearful approach and imitation behaviors.

RESEARCH BASIS

As noted above, modeling has been used primarily to treat children and adolescents with fears and/or phobic avoidance of specific stimuli. As indicated by Bandura, the goals of modeling are to reduce fear and facilitate new skill acquisition. Accordingly, modeling is often combined with other behavioral treatment strategies (e.g., reinforcement, sequential learning). Empirical studies employing modeling have been conducted with individuals of all ages, including children of preschool and early elementary school grades.

Although modeling procedures have been used with a diverse array of childhood fears, research is presently lacking regarding the long-term maintenance of treatment gains attained with this approach. In an early review, Thomas Ollendick and Jerome Cerny reported differential short-term outcomes (i.e., posttreatment with up to 1-year follow-up) with the various forms of modeling. The findings demonstrated the superiority of participant modeling over both live and filmed modeling. Efficacy for filmed modeling was reported to range from 25% to 50%, live modeling from 50% to 67%, and participant modeling from 80% to 92%. Based on these findings, childhood treatment of fears and phobias with participant modeling has received "well-established" status, according to the guidelines set forth by the Task Force for Promotion and Dissemination of Psychological Procedures, as reviewed recently by Chambless and Ollendick.

Ollendick and King have provided more extensive details of studies demonstrating the effectiveness of modeling, in general, and participant modeling in particular. To illustrate these findings, two prominent studies will be described and a third will be briefly mentioned. In an early study, 44 elementary school-age children identified as snake avoidant were treated. A 29-item behavioral avoidance task (BAT) was constructed, and only those children who were unable to hold a snake for a few seconds with gloved hands were selected for treatment. Children were matched based on their level of snake-avoidant behavior and randomly assigned to one of three groups. The modeling-only treatment group simply observed an adult and five peers demonstrate progressive interactions with a harmless snake. The participant modeling treatment group observed the same modeling procedures, were then assisted by the adult in completing the interactive tasks, and finally completed the interactions with the snake alone. The control group of children completed only the pre- and posttreatment BAT. At posttreatment, children from both the live modeling and participant modeling groups indicated less snake fearfulness than the control group. In addition, the children who were treated with participant modeling demonstrated superior gains than those in the live modeling group. At posttreatment, 80% of the children from the participant modeling treatment condition were able to complete the entire 29-item BAT compared with 53% of the children from the live modeling-only condition, and none of the control children.

In another early study, the superior efficacy of participant modeling to filmed modeling-only, participation-only, and a control condition was demonstrated. Forty African American boys (aged 5–12) who displayed water-avoidant behaviors were individually assessed using a 16-item BAT of progressively greater interactions in a swimming pool. Children were matched based on their level of water avoidance and randomly assigned to one of the four conditions. In the modeling-only treatment group, children observed a videotape of three peers modeling each of the approach behaviors from the BAT and then played a game with an adult model. The participation-only group of children viewed a neutral videotape and were subsequently accompanied to the pool by an adult who physically aided them in performing the behavioral approach tasks in the pool (but in the absence of modeling). The participant modeling group of children first viewed the videotape of peers performing the BAT task; subsequently, the group was physically assisted in completing the tasks by the adult. Finally, the control group of children viewed the neutral videotape and then played a game with an adult.

Results from this study revealed less fearfulness and greater involvement regarding water activities for the three treatment groups when individually compared to the control condition. Furthermore, greater changes were reported for children who received the participation component in their treatment as compared with those from either the modeling-only or control conditions. Finally, comparison of the participant modeling treatment and participation-only treatment revealed greater changes for the former, suggesting that the combination of modeling and assisted participation was superior to either of the conditions alone.

Presently, Ollendick and his colleague in Sweden (Professor Lars-Goran Ost) are undertaking an NIMH-funded project examining the relative effects of an intensive exposure-based intervention that combines participant modeling and reinforced practice. The study will enlist 120 phobic children in Virginia and 120 phobic children in Sweden. Early findings suggest the clear superiority of this treatment over an education/support treatment and a wait-list control condition.

CASE ILLUSTRATION

Prior to initiating treatment, fearful and avoidant children are assessed using a behavioral avoidance task (BAT). The BAT consists of predetermined and progressively intimate interactions with the feared stimulus or situation. The child's ability to progress through the tasks is assessed, and often the child is asked to indicate his or her subjective distress or discomfort (e.g., on a 0–8 scale) during each of the interactions. These tasks are then incorporated into treatment with the goal of having the child progress through the BAT without significant distress or anxiety. In addition, prior to treatment, children are frequently asked to report their overall level of fear on an instrument such as the Fear Survey Schedule for Children developed by Ollendick. This survey consists of 80 fear stimuli to which the children are asked to indicate whether their fear level is "none," "some," or "a lot." The stimuli include items such as "snakes," "dogs," "putting on a recital," "meeting new people," and "getting an injection." Thus, both fear in general and fear in particular are tapped by this measure.

"Jimmy" (11 years of age) was very afraid of dogs. His phobia developed following the observation of his mother being attacked by a large dog when the family was on an evening walk in the neighborhood. Jimmy and his father tried to pull the dog away, but they were only successful after considerable injury had occurred. His mother received lacerations on her right arm, shoulder, and face. Subsequently, they rushed her to the emergency room, where minor surgery was undertaken. Jimmy and his father were not injured in the attack.

Although Jimmy had apparently been fond of dogs prior to this attack and in fact played quite nicely with his grandmother's collie and his aunt and uncle's German shepherd, he developed a strong and persistent fear and aversion of dogs, even miniature ones. About 7 months following the incident, his parents brought him in to treatment. On the BAT, he was not able to open the door to a room where a dog was tethered at the other end. Moreover, he reported his distress level to be very high (7) on the 0 to 8 point scale. He also reported a high level of general fearfulness on the Fear Survey Schedule for Children (FSSC), with excessive fears of danger and death, as well as numerous animal fears. Since the event, it was reported that he also developed a sense of sadness and that he stopped doing many of the things he once enjoyed (e.g., playing with friends, riding his bicycle, going to the swimming pool). He met diagnostic criteria for major depressive disorder as well as specific phobia of dogs on the basis of the clinical interview. Of importance, his mother and father did not appear to be phobic of dogs, even though both had a newfound respect for them. They had tried numerous things to help him deal with his fear, but none of them seemed to work. He refused to go on walks with them and continued to seclude himself in his room. His phobia appeared primary and his depression to be a reaction to the avoidance and fear of dogs. His quality of life had become compromised.

Jimmy was treated with participant modeling and reinforced practice, and his parents were instructed in parenting strategies to help expose him to those situations that he was avoiding and to reinforce him upon those exposures. Treatment was conducted over 10 sessions, spread over a 4-month period of time. Initially, participant modeling was enacted with a small dog, then a midsize dog, and then a large dog. Sessions were conducted in the clinic, and then his parents were encouraged to conduct similar sessions outside the clinic at home and throughout the neighborhood. All parties were highly motivated to engage in treatment, given the level of interference and discord associated with the fear. At the end of treatment, Jimmy was readministered the BAT and was able to approach the dog, pet him, and take him for a walk in the clinic and on a street outside the clinic. His parents reported that he had begun to be more of his old self and that he had begun to do some of the activities he had avoided earlier in the summer (e.g., go to friends' homes, stay overnight, and go for walks with them).

Jimmy and his parents were followed up 1 and 2 years posttreatment. At both points in time, he failed to meet diagnostic criteria for either specific phobia or major depressive disorder. Although his parents bought him a dog about 10 weeks following treatment (a collie like his grandmother's) and he played appropriately and frequently with the dog, he remained generally fearful, as reported on the FSSC-R, and somewhat aloof and isolated. His parents reported that he had been seemingly "scarred" by the event—an observation with which the therapist agreed. They were advised that the healing process would take some time but to be encouraged by the significant gains he had made in therapy with their assistance. They were quite satisfied with the treatment outcome, as was Jimmy.

—*Thomas H. Ollendick and Amie E. Grills*

See also: *Behavioral Rehearsal (Vols. I, II, & III), Modeling (Vols. I & III), Role Playing (Vols. I, II, & III)*

Suggested Readings

Bandura, A. (1971). *Psychological modeling: Conflicting theories.* Chicago: Aldine-Atherton.

Chambless, D. L., & Ollendick, T. H. (2001). Empirically supported psychological interventions: Controversies and evidence. *Annual Review of Psychology, 52,* 685–716.

Ollendick, T. H. (1983). Reliability and validity of the revised Fear Survey Schedule for Children (FSSC-R). *Behaviour Research and Therapy, 21,* 685–692.

Ollendick, T. H., & Cerny, J. A. (1981). *Clinical behavior therapy with children.* New York: Plenum.

Ollendick, T. H., & King, N. J. (1998). Empirically supported treatments for children with phobic and anxiety disorders: Current status. *Journal of Clinical Child Psychology, 27,* 156–167.

MULTISYSTEMIC THERAPY

DESCRIPTION OF THE STRATEGY

Multisystemic therapy (MST) is a family- and community-based treatment of serious emotional and behavioral problems presented by adolescents. The development of this model began in the late 1970s, and today MST is a leading evidence-based treatment of serious antisocial behavior in youths, with programs transported to more than 30 states and 8 nations. This entry presents the keys to the effective outcomes achieved in randomized trials of MST, a summary of those outcomes, and the current thrust of MST-related research and dissemination efforts.

Several processes are critical to the success of MST.

Addresses Known Determinants of Problems

A wealth of longitudinal and correlational research has shown that serious antisocial behavior in adolescents (e.g., violence, substance abuse, criminal activity) is multidetermined. These influences can be conceptualized within a social-ecological conceptual framework. That is, antisocial behavior is influenced by the interplay of youth characteristics (e.g., cognitive skills, attitudes toward antisocial behavior) and aspects of the multiple systems in which the youth is embedded. The main systems and their influences include the family (e.g., discipline strategies, affective relations, parental psychopathology), peers (e.g., support of antisocial behavior), school (e.g., academic and social climates), family social network (e.g., social support, isolation), and neighborhood (e.g., criminal subculture).

A central clinical task of the MST therapist is to conduct a broad-based functional analysis to determine the most proximal predictors of the presenting problems identified by the family and other stakeholders (e.g., juvenile justice authorities, school officials). This analysis serves as the basis for initial clinical decision making. Thus, for example, if the main reason that a youth is able to steal cars at 2:00 A.M. with his friends is that his single-parent mother works a night shift or has a drug problem that compromises her ability to provide effective monitoring, the therapist might focus his or her attention on bringing additional monitoring resources (e.g., extended family) into the family and providing evidence-based substance abuse treatment for the parent. Subsequently, it would also be necessary to develop family-based strategies that disengage youths from deviant peers while supporting involvement with prosocial peer activities. Extensive descriptions of these and other MST-related intervention strategies are provided in published treatment manuals.

Provides Treatment Where the Problems Occur

MST programs use a home-based model of service delivery, and this model has several important features that contribute to favorable clinical outcomes and very high rates of treatment completion. First, therapists have caseloads of only four to six families per therapist, which allows the provision of intensive services needed to prevent expensive out-of-home placements. Second, to overcome barriers to service access (i.e., families of antisocial youths have high no-show rates for clinic-based services), therapists provide treatment in the home and other community locations (e.g., school). Third, conducting clinical assessments in the home provides more valid information for clinical decision making and for outcome measurement. Fourth, the provision of home-based services facilitates the treatment engagement process. And fifth, the thorny issue of treatment generalization is largely negated when changes are made where the actual problems have emerged.

Uses Evidence-Based Intervention Techniques

MST provides a comprehensive framework that incorporates empirically based treatments insofar as they exist. Thus, MST programs include cognitive-behavioral approaches, the behavior therapies, behavioral parent training, pragmatic families therapies, and certain pharmacological interventions that have a reasonable evidence base. As suggested by other assumptions noted in this section, however, these treatments are delivered in a considerably different context than is usual for these treatments. For example, consistent with the view that the caregiver is key to long-term outcomes, an MST cognitive-behavioral intervention would ideally be delivered by the caregiver under the consultation of the therapist. Similarly, the therapist would also be accountable for removing barriers to service access.

Intensive Quality Assurance to Support Treatment Fidelity and Youth Outcomes

The developers of evidence-based treatments have increasingly come to recognize that intensive and ongoing quality assurance protocols provide support that is critical for therapists to maintain fidelity to complex treatments and to facilitate the attainment of favorable client outcomes. MST quality assurance protocols extend across several levels. An organization manual and accompanying site assessments by MST transportability experts set the stage for the development of MST programs in practice settings. Principle-based treatment manuals set the parameters of MST interventions. A supervisory manual specifies clinical supervision from an on-site supervisor, and the focus of relatively intensive (i.e., 50 supervisor FTE for each MST team of 3–4 therapists) supervision is on supporting therapist fidelity to the treatment principles, developing therapist skills, and attaining youth outcomes. A consultation manual provides a second level of weekly clinical oversight with, again, the focus on treatment fidelity, youth outcomes, and therapist development. These manuals and processes occur within a context of rigorous hands-on training (e.g., a week of orientation, quarterly booster training) as well as an Internet-based fidelity feedback system. The value of this particular system has been the focus of considerable research.

Caregivers Play Pivotal Roles in Achieving Favorable Youth Outcomes

The caregiver is viewed as the key to obtaining positive long-term outcomes for the youth. Ideally, the caregiver is a parent, but another adult (e.g., grandparent, aunt, uncle, sibling) with an enduring emotional tie to the youth can serve in this role. Professional supports are introduced only after exhausting resources in the family's natural ecology. Paid professionals may genuinely care but invariably leave the youth's life for reasons such as professional advancement or termination of treatment. Thus, by focusing clinical resources on developing the caregiver's ability to parent effectively and strengthening the family's indigenous support system, treatment gains are more likely to be maintained.

RESEARCH BASIS

Based on recent reports from the U.S. Surgeon General, federal-level research entities, and leading reviewers, MST is regarded as an effective or highly promising treatment model. These conclusions are based on findings from seven published randomized trials, one published quasi-experimental study, and more than a dozen recently completed and ongoing randomized trials with youths presenting serious clinical problems.

With three randomized trials published in the 1990s, the most extensive empirical support for MST has been attained for the treatment of *youth violence*. Together, these studies demonstrated significant reductions in criminal activity by violent juvenile offenders for up to 4 years follow-up. An additional randomized trial with substance abusing juvenile offenders showed significant MST effects for reduced violent offending at a 4-year follow-up. Moreover, substantive reductions in incarceration and other out-of-home placements have led economic analysts to conclude that MST is a highly cost-effective strategy for the treatment of serious juvenile offenders at imminent risk of incarceration. Consistent with these findings, the clinical trials have demonstrated MST treatment effects for short-term outcomes such as improved family relations, improved parental functioning, and decreased youth symptomatology. Several large-scale multisite randomized trials are currently examining the effectiveness of MST programs that have been transported to real-world settings. Though not yet published, these studies are showing considerable variation in treatment effects per site.

Several trials have evaluated the effects of MST on the substance use of juvenile offenders and on offenders meeting diagnostic criteria for *substance abuse.* These studies have demonstrated short-term reductions in substance use as well as long-term (4 years) reductions in drug use based on biological indices. In addition, and consistent with findings from the aforementioned trials with violent juvenile offenders, MST has been effective at reducing rates of incarceration, and improvements in school attendance have been observed. Current research is examining the integration of contingency management, an evidence-based treatment of substance abuse, with MST, and such is proving to be a very potent intervention with this challenging clinical population.

Traditionally, MST has focused on treating serious antisocial behavior in adolescents. The success of this work, however, has led to efforts adapting MST for treating *serious emotional disturbance.* A recent randomized trial evaluated the effectiveness of MST as an alternative to the hospitalization of youths presenting psychiatric emergencies (i.e., homicidal, suicidal, psychotic). Results supported the effectiveness of MST at safely decreasing rates of hospitalization, reducing psychiatric symptoms, improving family functioning, increasing school attendance, and increasing consumer satisfaction. Favorable between-groups differences, however, dissipated by about 16 months postreferral. Current research is examining strategies to sustain treatment effects with such youths.

MST trials have been published with other challenging clinical populations as well. A small efficacy study with *juvenile sex offenders* was published more than a decade ago and has recently been replicated. These studies served as the foundation for a large effectiveness trial for juvenile sex offenders that has recently been funded. Similarly, a modest randomized trial of MST with *maltreated children* was published more than a decade ago, and this trial has also set the stage for a larger effectiveness trial that is currently in progress.

With the widespread dissemination in recent years of MST programs for treating antisocial behavior in adolescents, a major new emphasis of MST-related research has evolved. This research aims to determine the key components of the effective (i.e., capable of achieving favorable outcomes) transport of MST programs to real-world settings. As such, variables of interest extend beyond therapist and training characteristics to include factors associated with the organizations that house MST programs (e.g., organizational culture) as well as variables such as funding structures.

RELEVANT TARGET POPULATIONS AND EXCEPTIONS

MST is most appropriate for youths presenting serious clinical problems at high risk of costly out-of-home placement. The model is best validated for such youths and can produce cost savings when applied appropriately to this population. In addition, MST programs are currently only available for the treatment of serious antisocial behavior, as the model is best validated for such populations. If the aforementioned effectiveness trials with sexual offenders, maltreated youths, and youths with serious emotional disturbance are successful; MST adaptations for these populations will be made available to funders and providers of such services.

MST is not appropriate for treating emotional or behavioral problems of moderate severity for which simpler and less expensive evidence-based treatments are available (e.g., medication for attention-deficit/hyperactivity disorder, cognitive-behavioral treatment for moderate depression). Nor is MST appropriate for use with clinical populations that have not been the focus of successful randomized trials. Substantive evidence of positive effects is required before the model can be transported for a new clinical population.

CASE ILLUSTRATION

The typical MST case is a 15-year-old male chronic offender, with a single mother, a father in jail, and siblings in the criminal justice system. The youth's closest friends are also engaged in high rates of antisocial behavior. These youths are either performing poorly at school or have been expelled, and all live in high crime neighborhoods. Most important, the caregiver is having considerable difficulty monitoring, supervising, and structuring the adolescent.

As suggested earlier, the clinical team (therapist, supervisor, consultant) conducts a functional analysis of the key presenting problems, and treatment decisions are based on this analysis. For example, inept parenting can be associated with a variety of factors, including untreated parental mental health or substance abuse problems, high levels of stress (e.g., from working 60-hour weeks and caring for 6 children), low social support, lack of knowledge and competence in effective parenting, weak bonding with the child, and parental relationship problems (e.g., marital conflict). The therapist's task is to develop hypotheses about the key determinants and to design and implement interventions to test these hypotheses. If the interventions are successful, the hypotheses are supported. If interventions are unsuccessful, alternative hypotheses must be developed and tested. Thus, MST includes a recursive feedback system in which hypotheses, interventions, and outcomes are assessed continuously, with considerable access to supervisory and consultant (i.e., an MST expert) resources.

When the caregiver barriers to effective parenting have been removed and an indigenous support system (i.e., extended family, friends, neighbors) has been developed around the caregiver, he or she is in a much stronger position to effect change in most aspects of the youth's life. For example, the empowered caregiver can collaborate with (versus work against) teachers and principals in the development and implementation of behavioral and academic plans to improve the youth's functioning in school. Similarly, with therapist support, strategies for disengaging the youth from deviant peers can be developed and implemented. The ultimate goal of treatment is to empower families to address their children's difficulties independently or with indigenous supports. The relatively favorable long-term outcomes from clinical trials suggest that MST can be effective in this regard.

—Scott W. Henggeler
and Colleen A. Halliday-Boykins

See also: *Behavioral Treatment in Natural Environments (Vols. I & III), Generalization (Vols. I, II, & III), Guided Mastery (Vols. I & III), Parent Training (Vol. II), Social Competence Treatment: Externalizing Disorders (Vol. II)*

Suggested Readings

Henggeler, S. W., & Lee, T. (2003). Multisystemic treatment of serious clinical problems. In A. E. Kazdin and J. R. Weisz (Eds.), *Evidence-based psychotherapies for children and adolescents* (pp. 301–322). New York: Guilford Press.

Henggeler, S. W., Schoenwald, S. K., Borduin, C. M., Rowland, M. D., & Cunningham, P. B. (1998). *Multisystemic treatment of antisocial behavior in children and adolescents.* New York: Guilford Press.

Henggeler, S. W., Schoenwald, S. K., Rowland, M. D., & Cunningham, P. B. (2002). *Serious emotional disturbance in children and adolescents: Multisystemic therapy.* New York: Guilford Press.

Sheidow, A. J., Henggeler, S. W., & Schoenwald, S. K. (2003). Multisystemic therapy. In T. L. Sexton, G. Weeks, & M. Robbins (Eds.), *Handbook of family therapy: Theory, research, and practice* (pp. 303–322). New York: Brunner-Routledge.

NEGATIVE PRACTICE

Negative practice involves the repeated performance of a behavior with the goal of eliminating or reducing the occurrence of the behavior. The idea is that massed practice of the problem behavior creates fatigue or a similar aversive consequence and thus reduces the rates of the behavior in the future (similar to the process of positive punishment). Hull's concepts of reactive inhibition and conditioned inhibition have been used to explain the mechanism whereby negative practice produces reduction in rates of behavior. Specifically, the aversive consequence associated with performing a behavior repeatedly produces an inhibition of performing the behavior (i.e., reactive inhibition). In addition, because the aversive consequence occurs while practicing the particular behavior, the aversive consequence becomes associated with that behavior (i.e., conditioned inhibition).

Application of the technique involves having the individual perform the targeted problem behavior repeatedly with as little rest as possible. A critical goal for the therapist is determining the number or duration of the repeated performances of the behavior and the duration of rest periods. Theoretically, the greater the number of performances of the behavior, combined with the least amount of rest between performances of the target behavior, should produce the largest reduction or strongest elimination of the target behavior. Heuristics on which to base appropriate time periods for practice and rest may not be useful, and so the duration of the behavior and duration of rest periods should be tailored to the individual situation.

Negative practice has been used as a technique to eliminate small motor behaviors such as tics and nighttime teeth grinding. For example, the treatment of a facial tic with negative practice would require the client to repeatedly voluntarily perform the tic with minimal rest time. The rationale is that repeating the motor tic without being able to rest will produce fatigue and discomfort in the individual, thereby reducing the likelihood of future performance of the tic. Although tics are typically involuntary and negative practice requires an individual to voluntarily produce the tic, research has shown that repeated massed voluntary production of tics in the therapy session can result in a decline of involuntary tics outside the treatment session.

Research findings have been somewhat inconsistent with regard to the efficacy of negative practice across behaviors. Research has shown that negative practice has been effective in eliminating behaviors such as performance errors in piano or organ playing, spelling errors in typing and maze learning, pica, and teeth grinding. There is also some evidence that negative practice is helpful in treating Tourette's syndrome. However, negative practice appears to be less effective in treating problem behaviors that involve inhibition (e.g., speech blocking, stammering).

—*Carl F. Weems and Natalie M. Costa*

See also: *Classical Conditioning (Vols. I, II, & III), Generalization (Vols. I, II, & III), Operant Conditioning (Vols. I, II, & III), Overcorrection (Vol. II)*

Suggested Readings

Duker, P. C., & Nielen, M. (1993). The use of negative practice for the control of pica behavior. *Journal of Behavior Therapy and Experimental Psychiatry, 24,* 249–253.

Masters, J. C., Burish, T. G., Hollon, S. D., & Rimm, D. C. (1987). *Behavior therapy: Techniques and empirical findings* (3rd ed.). Orlando, FL: Harcourt Brace Jovanovich.

Storms, L. (1985). Massed negative practice as a behavioral treatment for Gilles de la Tourette's syndrome. *American Journal of Psychotherapy, 39,* 277–281.

Yates, A. J. (1959). Negative practice: A theoretical interpretation. *Australian Journal of Psychology, 11,* 126–129.

NEGATIVE REINFORCEMENT

DESCRIPTION OF THE CONCEPT

A negative reinforcer is a stimulus the withdrawal or escape from which, or the postponement, termination, or avoidance of which, increases the probability of (i.e., strengthens) responses that produce any of these events. Negative reinforcement (NR) is the descriptive label for the relationship between the stimulus, the events, and the change in probability. NR is a ubiquitous phenomenon, and examples of negatively reinforced behavior abound on every scale of human (and infrahuman) existence. Some small-scale examples include scratching irritated skin, pulling up the covers on a cold night, turning off an alarm, rolling up the car windows while driving on a dusty road, using mouthwash, moving away from the campfire, using sunscreen, visiting the bathroom before boarding an airplane, taking an antacid tablet for heartburn, and wearing galoshes. Large-scale examples include the field of preventive medicine (e.g., vaccinations, inoculations, hygienic maneuvers), disaster alert systems, flood prevention and control, key rituals in the great religions (e.g., circumcision, ablutions, penance), speed limits, and most aspects of the law. On a colloquial level, behavior whose purpose is the reduction or avoidance of unwanted experience is said to be negatively reinforced.

Despite its ubiquity and the long-standing and ready availability of its technical definition, NR is probably the most misunderstood concept in behavioral psychology and one of the most misunderstood in psychology at large. Relatedly, the most common misunderstanding is that NR involves punishment. For example, a story published in the *New Yorker* magazine described a punishing event as a negative reinforcer. When informed of the error, the editorial staff replied that a definition equating NR with punishment was so prevalent in journalism that it had become the de facto definition. Note, though, that this is true only in a colloquial context; the definition offered in this entry remains correct for NR in a technical context.

That NR is difficult to understand is because it involves the absence of events, and it is difficult to apprehend how the absence of an event can supply reinforcement. That NR is widely equated with punishment is due in part to the word *negative*. In NR, however, the word *negative* merely refers to any of a number of synonyms for escape or avoidance, not to the aversive quality of an experience or event. In fact, the word closest in meaning to the negative in NR is *minus*. Misconstruing NR with punishment also happens because the production of NR depends on aversive events, and the most intuitively accessible perspective on aversive events is that they punish (i.e., reduce the probability of) behaviors that bring them about (e.g., once burned, twice shy).

Research Basis

The research base of NR includes several lines of investigation and hundreds of studies. As a classic example, one of the earliest and abidingly most influential lines stems from the early 1950s and involves continuous avoidance or what has come to be called Sidman avoidance (named after Murray Sidman, the scientist who published the initial research). Most of the experiments involved laboratory animals, usually rats. Briefly, an animal was placed in a laboratory chamber equipped with a response lever and an electric shock delivery device. Two clocks were set to control shock delivery. The first clock timed a shock-shock (SS) interval, the time between shocks when the animal did not depress the lever. The delivery of a shock reset the SS clock to zero and started a new SS interval. The second clock timed a response-shock (RS) interval, the time shock was postponed when the lever was pressed. Each lever press reset the RS clock to zero. Under these experimental conditions, animals routinely learned the optimal number of lever presses to maintain a minimal number of shocks. Theoretically, the animal could postpone shock indefinitely, merely by regularly pressing the lever at RS intervals that were shorter than SS intervals. The illustrative point is that lever pressing was maintained not by what happened afterward but by what did not happen or by NR.

There are many variations on this theme. Initially, the relevant research involved only basic science demonstrations, but by the late 1960s research showing the applied implications of NR began to appear. Currently, a very large literature, composed of basic science experiments, applied science derivations, and a diverse array of clinically relevant reports and anecdotes, cogently shows the power and widespread availability of NR in the everyday life of human beings and, indeed, all sentient beings.

Clinical Implications

There are two salient clinically relevant features of NR-maintained behavior: slow inception and persistence.

Slow Inception

Because NR-maintained behavior fundamentally is behavior maintained by events that do not happen, it can be difficult to inaugurate. For example, the animals in Sidman avoidance experiments merely had to press a lever to postpone shocks. But their experience after pressing the lever would involve no immediately detectable differences, and thus regular pressing took some time to develop. Similarly, a broad array of health relevant, NR-maintained human behaviors involve no immediately detectable benefits. For example, receiving vaccinations, taking vitamins, or eating vegetables produce few salubrious short-term effects. However, contact with some of the aversive events that these behaviors usually prevent can expedite the learning process. For example, the line for a flu shot is usually long but rarely includes young children or even young adults. Young children typically have little or no knowledge of the flu and are usually more concerned about the pain of the shot than they are about being ill. Young adults have probably had the flu but survived it easily and thus are often more concerned about the inconvenience of receiving the shot than its preventive benefits. But the elderly have usually had experience with the debilitating effects of illnesses such as the flu and probably know (or know of) persons who have died or nearly died from it. Thus, they are usually more eager to receive the shot.

More generally, safety behaviors and preventive procedures are more likely to be established and maintained by artificially established consequences (e.g., rules, penalties) than by naturally occurring NR-type experiences. It simply takes too long for

natural consequences (i.e., NR) to shape some important health related behaviors.

Persistence

Once established, however, NR-maintained behavior can be very difficult to diminish or extinguish. Clinically relevant examples are abundant. Painful bowel movements (e.g., due to constipation) can establish a long-term pattern of stool withholding and toileting avoidance that inevitably leads to encopresis, fecal impaction, and even an enlarged colon. These events can then lead to further painful bowel movements and initiate a reciprocally perpetuating system. Frightening encounters with an animal (e.g., dog) can cause children and even adults to develop phobic levels of perpetual avoidance of large numbers or even classes of animals (e.g., all dogs). Experiencing panic away from home, regardless of the inaugurating event, can teach some people to never leave home (e.g., develop agoraphobia). The key (i.e., NR) result of these avoidant behaviors is that unpleasant experience (e.g., pain, fear) does not occur as long as the behaviors are maintained. And rather than function as an inducement to try something new, extended periods of successful avoidance tend to reinforce continuation of the avoidant pattern (e.g., "As long as I press this lever, I don't get shocked," says the rat).

In a more general sense, there is an emerging literature suggesting that a major portion of clinically significant concerns in human life involves an NR-pertinent construct called experiential avoidance. Specifically, experiential avoidance involves behavior maintained by the NR that results from the avoidance of experience perceived to be unpleasant. Although there is tremendous survival value in avoiding some unpleasant experiences (e.g., avoiding ingesting substances whose container is marked "poison"), in many other instances the avoidance is of experiences that, although potentially unpleasant, actually add to rather than subtract from the quality of a person's life. For example, the depressed person's limited activities are maintained by NR resulting from the avoidance of everyday activities that, although perceived by the person to be very unpleasant, are actually necessary for an unimpaired, healthful life (e.g., eating, dealing with people, especially strangers, working). The anxious person's limited repertoire is maintained by NR resulting from the avoidance of activities that, although perceived to be dangerous, are not just physically harmless but can actually be psychologically healthful (e.g., speaking to groups, being out in the open, approaching animals). There are many other examples. The fundamental point is that NR is a powerful element in many clinically relevant behaviors.

Clinical Applications

Although examples of clinical applications can readily be inferred from review of the material above, explication of at least one representative application may be necessary for a fuller understanding of the difficult concept of NR. A noteworthy example involves extreme self-injurious behavior (SIB) exhibited by individuals with developmental disabilities. The behavior is sometimes so extreme that bone structures can become misshapen and limbs can actually be torn from the body. Historically, a common assumption was that SIB was maintained by positive reinforcement, particularly attention. Because of its extraordinary and often grotesque presentation, SIB can be very hard to ignore, and thus attention for it had been universally present. Yet, some functional assessment techniques established by various investigators, most notably Brian Iwata and Edward Carr, have produced data showing that SIB is sometimes maintained by NR. From a slightly different and more colloquial perspective, SIB can sometimes be viewed as a primitive but powerful communication to stay away or, more generally, that the self-injurious person wants to avoid undesirable activities or unwanted attention. The discovery of the counterintuitive but nonetheless real fact that individuals exhibiting SIB may be doing so to avoid or escape something has resulted in major changes to SIB treatment programs. As one general example, when a functional assessment indicates that SIB has an avoidant or escapist function (i.e., is maintained by NR), therapists establish training programs that allow afflicted individuals access to NR (e.g., avoidance or escape) in return for initially small but increasingly larger amounts of the behaviors that previously led to SIB (e.g., interaction with staff, completion of tasks). Experimental analyses of such interventions routinely show an abrupt, clinically significant reduction in SIB.

There are myriad other examples of clinically relevant behavior maintained by NR, but those involving SIB are particularly useful here because the profound presentation of the target problem is emblematic of the potential power of NR in the establishment and maintenance of human behavior.

CASE ILLUSTRATION

NR presents special opportunities for clinicians seeking strong influences on behavior but who have limited access to events or objects that can be employed in a positive reinforcement application. This case example is a demonstration.

The client, "Tom," was a 14-year-old boy living at home with his natural parents and 8-year-old sister. His medical history was unremarkable. His psychiatric history included a diagnosis of attention-deficit/hyperactivity disorder (ADHD) for which he was receiving 36 milligrams of Concerta, a psychostimulant, every day. His educational history included strong test scores (e.g., high 90th percentile) but poor performance in school (failing in four topics and just passing in one). The parents had seen several counselors about their son's poor academic performance, but none of them had been able to improve Tom's grades either through direct counseling with him or recommendations made to his parents.

The initial assessment included meetings with Tom's parents, his schoolteacher and the principal, and his family physician. The assessment included a physical examination by the physician and a variety of tests and observations by the therapist. The tests included the Diagnostic Interview Schedule for Children (youth and parent versions), a computerized structured interview with a large ADHD section, and some paper-and-pencil behavior problem checklists (e.g., Eyberg Child Behavior Inventory) completed by the parents and teacher. The observations included home and school samples of behavior as well as Tom's behavior in the waiting room. The results of the physical exam showed the boy to be in good health and within normal limits for height and weight. The results of the tests and observations indicated only modest levels of inattentive, impulsive, and overactive behavior at home and school. A conference between the physician, teacher, principal, and therapist yielded a consensual conclusion that the primary problem involved Tom's failure to do his homework. The parents were aware that he did little homework but were unaware of the amount that had been routinely assigned but was not brought home. A discussion with Tom ended with his proclamation that he hated homework and was not going to bring it home, and even if he did, he was not going to do it. The parents reported having tried a variety of incentive systems to induce Tom to bring and do homework but none had worked. A homeschool program with a predominant NR component was then established. The physician agreed to monitor the medication and, along with the parents, felt that the current type and dose was probably helpful.

The initial part of the home program involved structured feedback and consequence systems for general aspects of Tom's behavior (e.g., motivational systems addressing chores and household rules, special time with parents, enhanced clarity of parental instructions, intensive effort to catch Tom in the act of behaving appropriately). A critical component for the homework part of the program was the establishment of a fixed 9:00 P.M. bedtime. Two NR-based components, both tied to avoidance of an even earlier bedtime, were then derived from the fixed bedtime. The first required that Tom bring enough work home to occupy him for 1 hour a night. The teacher agreed to supply the work. The penalty for not bringing the work home was a bedtime that began immediately after dinner (e.g., usually around 6:00 P.M.). The second component required that Tom either go to bed at 7:30 P.M. or sit at the kitchen table and do his homework for at least 1 hour. If he complied, he could then stay up until 9:00 and do what he pleased. On the first afternoon of the program, he brought home no work and was sent to bed right after dinner. He protested loudly on the way to his room, hitting walls, kicking the staircase banister, and destroying some personal possessions once in his room. The parents were undeterred and did not intervene. The next afternoon he brought home a large amount of work but refused to do it. He was sent to bed at 7:30, and although he again protested loudly, his display was solely verbal, and by 8:30 was pleading to be allowed to do his work. The following afternoon he again brought home a large amount of work, and at 7:30 he sat at the kitchen table and worked steadily for 70 minutes. The parents allowed him to stay up until 9:10. Similar results were subsequently regularly produced, and the program was kept in place for the entire final month of his school year. There were no more outbursts. On one occasion, he left his work at school but readily agreed to walk back to school and retrieve it before the teacher went home for the night. By the end of the school year, his grades had risen from their mostly failing level to two Bs, two Cs, and a D. The parents and teacher considered this a major success.

CONCLUSION

NR is a ubiquitous phenomenon that influences behavior not by what happens but by what does not happen. In colloquial terms, the purpose of a large amount of human behavior is to reduce, postpone, avoid, or escape unpleasant events. NR is the technical term for this purpose. A fuller understanding of the concept not only leads to a fuller understanding of a vast range of clinically relevant human behavior but also to a range of novel and powerful applications for that behavior.

—*Patrick C. Friman*

See also: *Aversion Relief (Vols. I & III), Electrical Aversion (Vols. I & III), Operant Conditioning (Vols. I, II, & III), Positive Reinforcement (Vol. II), Reinforcement (Vols. I & III)*

Suggested Readings

Catania, A. C. (1998). *Learning.* Upper Saddle River, NJ: Prentice Hall.

Hayes, S. C., Strosahl, K. D., & Wilson, K. G. (1999). *Acceptance and commitment therapy.* New York: Guilford Press.

Skinner, B. F. (1953). *Science and human behavior.* New York: Free Press.

NONCONTINGENT REWARD (REINFORCEMENT)

DESCRIPTION OF THE STRATEGY

Noncontingent reward (NCR)* is a procedure that, as its name suggests, involves delivering rewards independent of the occurrence of any specified behavior. Sometimes NCR is used to make a particular setting more attractive. That is, offering a high rate of rewards reinforces entering and staying in that setting. However, once in the setting, receipt of the rewards does not depend on engaging in any particular response and, in fact, may alter previously established patterns of behavior. Indeed, the most common and well-studied use of NCR is as a procedure for decreasing problem behavior. To illustrate, imagine a child diagnosed with autism who engages in self-injurious behavior (e.g., head banging), maintained by social reinforcement (i.e., the child receives attention following head banging). A typical NCR procedure to decrease head banging would involve the regular provision of attention regardless of head banging.

RESEARCH BASIS

The general description of the NCR procedure leaves unspecified a number of parameters that appear important to consider in employing NCR. The first is to decide the type of schedule according to which the rewards will be offered. Will they be continuously available, delivered at regular time intervals (a fixed-time schedule), or at irregular time intervals (a variable-time schedule)? Building on the above example, attention might be provided continuously, every 60 seconds, or at varying intervals averaging 60 seconds. Fixed-time schedules have been the most widely used to date, but all three varieties have been used effectively, with continuous reward often employed when the problem behavior is maintained by automatic/sensory reinforcement.

In addition to determining how rewards will be scheduled, the frequency or magnitude of reward delivery must be determined. Some, but not all, of the available research has shown that higher rates or magnitudes have led to greater reductions in problem behavior. Thus, the generally preferred strategy appears to be to begin the intervention using a relatively high rate/magnitude, which is gradually reduced after the problem behavior has declined.

There are a number of additional variations on the basic procedure that have been explored in the research literature and which a practitioner needs to consider. When possible, it appears generally preferable to use the reinforcer maintaining the problematic behavior (determined through a functional analysis) as the noncontingent reward. In the previous example, attention was maintaining head banging, and thus attention was chosen as the noncontingent reward. In addition, a decision has to be made whether to use NCR with or without extinction. For example, NCR could be introduced while continuing to provide attention following head banging, or head banging could be simultaneously put on extinction. Most interventions employ NCR and extinction; however, both NCR with and without extinction have demonstrated some efficacy, and studies directly comparing the two procedures have yet to reveal clear superiority of one over the other.

It is not always possible to identify the reinforcer(s) maintaining the problematic behavior, and even when identified, it is not always feasible to provide rewards that approximate the functional reinforcer (e.g., in the case of some automatic/sensory reinforcers). In such cases, one might have to use an arbitrary reward (e.g., food or toys) determined, when possible, on the basis of a preference assessment. Whether noncontingent delivery of arbitrary rewards is as useful in reducing problem behavior as using the reinforcer maintaining the behavior remains to be fully determined. That said, arbitrary rewards have been successfully used in several studies and appear most effective when a wide variety of high preference items are utilized.

The preceding describes important parameters for effectively using NCR but does not address why NCR is effective. Extinction is well known to decrease responding, so when extinction is incorporated into NCR, one potential reason for a decrease is readily apparent. However, the effective use of NCR without extinction points to the involvement of other processes. When the noncontingent reward presented is the same as the functional reinforcer maintaining the problem behavior, the decrease appears to be, at least partially, the result of changing an establishing operation—i.e., satiation. For example, by repeatedly providing noncontingent attention, the child becomes satiated (in everyday terms he or she no longer "wants" for attention), resulting in a reduction in behavior that has produced attention. In addition, the provision of a noncontingent reward degrades the response-reinforcer relationship. That is, prior to the NCR procedure, there exists a stronger relationship between the problem behavior and the reinforcer; however, when the reinforcer is provided noncontingently the relationship between the response and that reinforcer is weakened (in everyday terms, the child still "wants" for attention, but why do anything to get it when it is offered for "free"?). When arbitrary rewards are provided noncontingently, still other processes may be important. Making contact with or accessing the noncontingent rewards (e.g., preferred foods or toys) often requires engaging in responses that compete, at least somewhat, with the problem behavior and therefore may reduce its frequency. Finally, according to the matching law, the frequency of a response is determined by the rate of reinforcement for that response relative to all other sources of reinforcement (e.g., rate of head banging = reinforcement for head banging ÷ reinforcement for head banging + all other alternative sources of reinforcement). NCR, regardless of whether the reward is the same as the functional reinforcer or is arbitrary, because it increases the total amount of reinforcement in the environment, would be expected to decrease the behavior.

RELEVANT TARGET POPULATIONS, TARGET BEHAVIORS, AND EXCEPTIONS

Most of the research on NCR comes from intervention studies attempting to reduce maladaptive behavior engaged in by some individuals with mental retardation, brain injury, autism, or other developmental or cognitive impairments. The range of target behaviors for which NCR has been employed includes self-stimulation (e.g., head rocking, face rubbing, hand flapping), bizarre speech, disruptive classroom behavior, disruptive vocalizations, tantrums, and destructive behaviors (aggression, self-injury, property destruction). Based on these intervention studies, NCR appears to be a very promising procedure that is relatively easy to implement and offers a "positive" (i.e., nonpunishment-based) method for decreasing problematic behavior.

A limitation recognized in the current literature is that NCR studies typically utilize relatively short sessions (5–30 minutes). Thus, the utility of NCR during long sessions and its applicability as an ongoing intervention in the home, school, residential facility, and so on remains to be determined. In addition, NCR, especially when high rates or magnitudes of reward are used, may interfere with the concurrent learning of other adaptive responses. Thus, NCR may need to be discontinued, or the rates decreased, when focusing on teaching new or alternative behaviors.

NCR is not a response acquisition procedure. However, as mentioned earlier, NCR can be used to increase the attractiveness of a particular setting. For instance, if certain contexts have become so aversive that they are routinely avoided, no new learning or positive experiences can be encountered. Implementing NCR in that context can promote approach behaviors, setting the stage for new experiences and new learning. This logic has been used in parent/family interventions for children diagnosed with ADHD and oppositional defiant disorder (ODD). In these cases, parent-child relations have often become antagonistic, strained, and mutually coercive. One initial intervention strategy is to schedule a regular (e.g., 5 days/week), brief (e.g., 15 minutes) period of positive parental attention that is to occur regardless of the child's behavior that day and during which the child and a parent engage in an activity chosen and directed by the child (with the parent offering both contingent and noncontingent praise and approval). Providing these regular periods of noncontingent positive attention can improve parent-child relations and set the stage for subsequent contingency management interventions.

COMPLICATIONS

There are some potential complications in using NCR. When NCR and extinction are used together, there is the possibility that a temporary burst of the problematic responding will occur at the onset of extinction (i.e., an extinction burst). Because NCR offers rewards along with extinction, it appears to reduce the likelihood of such extinction-induced responding. However, during NCR, if there is an extinction burst or if the maladaptive target response has a high initial frequency, it is possible that the problematic behavior will occasionally occur closely in time with the noncontingent receipt of the reward, resulting in an accidental contingency providing intermittent reinforcement for the behavior. To guard against accidental contingencies of this sort, the practitioner can arrange for instances of the maladaptive target response to result in the next reward being cancelled or delayed for a brief time.

—Scott T. Gaynor and Dikla Eckshtain

***See also**: Noncontingent Reinforcement (Vols. I & III), Operant Conditioning (Vols. I, II, & III), Positive Reinforcement (Vol. II), Reinforcement (Vols. I & III)*

Authors' Note: The most appropriate terminology for identifying this procedure has been a source of debate. For the purposes of this entry we will use noncontingent reward, defining rewards as stimuli that would function as reinforcers if they were presented immediately following a response. However, the term most commonly applied in the literature is noncontingent reinforcement; hence its parenthetical inclusion in the title.

Suggested Readings

Carr, J. E., Coriaty, S., Wilder, D. A., Gaunt, B. T., Dozier, C. L., Britton, L. N., et al. (2000). A review of "noncontingent" reinforcement as treatment for the aberrant behavior of individuals with developmental disabilities. *Research in Developmental Disabilities, 21,* 377–391.

Goh, H., Iwata, B. A., & DeLeon, I. G. (2000). Competition between noncontingent and contingent reinforcement schedules during response acquisition. *Journal of Applied Behavior Analysis, 33,* 195–205.

Hagopian, L. P., Crockett, J. L., van Stone, M., DeLeon, I. G., & Bowman, L. G. (2000). Effects of noncontingent reinforcement on problem behavior and stimulus engagement: The role of satiation, extinction, and alternative reinforcement. *Journal of Applied Behavior Analysis, 33,* 433–449.

Lindberg, J. S., Iwata, B. A., Roscoe, E. M., Worsdell, A. S., & Hanley, G. P. (2003). Treatment efficacy of noncontingent reinforcement during brief and extended application. *Journal of Applied Behavior Analysis, 36,* 1–19.

Vollmer, T. R., Ringdahl, J. E., Roane, H. S., & Marcus, B. A. (1997). Negative side effects of noncontingent reinforcement. *Journal of Applied Behavior Analysis, 30,* 161–164.

OPERANT CONDITIONING

DESCRIPTION OF THE STRATEGY

Prior to the 1930s, behavioral psychology focused on the study of behaviors reliably elicited by unconditioned stimuli. In contrast to the study of classical (respondent) conditioning, in which an organism ("involuntarily") responds to its environment almost reflexively, the study of operant conditioning, in which an organism ("voluntarily") emits a behavior or acts/operates on its environment, proposed that consequences, or events following a behavior rather than antecedent eliciting events, change the probability of that behavioral occurrence. Popularized by the research and publications of B. F. Skinner, operant conditioning works according to a three-term contingency involving the following terms: (1) the circumstances under which the organism acts (stimulus/antecedent), (2) the emitted behavior, and (3) the consequences of the emitted behavior. Although Skinner admired Pavlov's studies of classical conditioning, he believed that this explanation of behavior was severely limited because most behaviors are not elicited by a known stimulus. Furthermore, he believed that describing the consequences of behavior more accurately and usefully explains behaviors.

Skinner's ideas on behavior were greatly influenced by E. L. Thorndike's studies of how nonreflexive animal behaviors may be modified according to experience. Skinner's theories followed in the wake of Thorndike's Law of Effect, which stated that response probability is increased by "satisfying" consequences and decreased by "annoying" consequences. In addition,

Charles Darwin's influence on Skinner's theory is evident in the parallels between the theory of natural selection and operant conditioning. In the same fashion that traits contributing to an organism's survival and species propagation are selected, consequences of available operant responses result in the strengthening or maintaining of some behaviors and the elimination or extinction of others.

Discussion of operant conditioning involves a closer examination of each of Skinner's three terms: stimulus/antecedent, behavior, and consequence. Because the most notable difference between operant conditioning and classical/respondent conditioning involves the role of behavioral consequences, this third term will be presented first. In operant conditioning, the consequences of an emitted behavior may either increase or decrease the probability of the event recurring in the future. Consequences may be divided into two distinct classes: reinforcers and punishers. Reinforcers are stimuli that follow a response, thereby increasing the probability that the response will recur in the future. Punishers are stimuli that follow a response and decrease the probability that the response will recur in the future.

Often mistakenly equated with rewards, reinforcers are not inherently pleasant and are context dependent (e.g., the candy bar that reinforces the hungry child may be punishing for the child who just ate a large dinner). Whereas rewards do not necessarily increase the probability that a response will recur in the future, reinforcers, by definition, must. Reinforcers may be categorized according to whether or not learning is required for them to increase response probability. Primary reinforcers are stimuli that are inherently reinforcing. Stimuli that meet biological needs (e.g., sexual gratification, food) are common examples. Generalized reinforcers are learned reinforcers that increase a wide variety of behaviors due to their cultural value (e.g., money, power, intelligence). Secondary reinforcers are stimuli that, while not inherently reinforcing, acquire the ability to increase response probability via pairing with primary or generalized reinforcers through classical conditioning (e.g., stickers used to reinforce good schoolwork). These objects are not inherently reinforcing, but through their association with other reinforcers such as intelligence, praise, and even money, they come to increase the probability of the events preceding reinforcement (e.g., studying, working hard).

The procedure of reinforcement can also be divided into two classes, depending upon whether a stimulus is added to or removed from the environment to increase the probability of future responding. Positive reinforcement occurs when a stimulus is added to the postresponse environment, increasing the future probability of the behavior preceding that stimulus (e.g., as a result of the teacher giving candy to the first child to raise his or her hand to answer a question, the child will be more likely to raise his or her hand to answer future questions). Negative reinforcement (relief reinforcement) occurs when a (unpleasant) stimulus is removed from the postresponse environment, increasing the future probability of that behavior preceding that stimulus. The most commonly cited example of negative reinforcement is putting up an umbrella to remove the rain. Another example of negative reinforcement is the child who notices that as a result of cleaning his or her room (behavior), the mother's incessant nagging (stimulus) ceases (is removed from the environment). As a result, the child is more likely to clean the room in the future because this response is known to eliminate an aversive stimulus.

Operant conditioning also allows for the consequences of a behavior to decrease the probability that that response will recur in the future; this procedure is known as punishment. In the same way that reinforcement procedures are distinguished based on the addition or removal of a stimulus, punishment is classified according to whether an aversive stimulus is added to or removed from the environment. A punisher is any event or object that, when presented following a behavior, decreases the probability that the response will recur in the future.

Positive punishment (Type I or presentation punishment) occurs when an aversive stimulus is added to the environment following a behavior, thereby decreasing the probability that the response will recur in the future. This type of punishment is also referred to as presentation punishment. A common example of positive punishment used with children is corporal punishment (spanking).

Negative punishment (Type II or penalty) occurs when a pleasant event or object is removed from the environment following a behavior, thereby decreasing the probability that the response will recur in the future. An example of negative punishment (Type II) is time-out. As a result of some undesired behavior, a reinforcing stimulus (e.g., playground) is removed, and the child is placed in an environment where behaviors are not reinforced.

Considerable inter- and intrasubject variability exists with regard to reinforcers and punishers. In general, high-quality (preferred reinforcers, detested punishers) stimuli delivered in close temporal proximity (i.e., quickly) to the behavior work best to modify behavior. Varying the ratio of responses required to obtain reinforcement and/or the time interval that must elapse in order to obtain reinforcement results in consistent response patterns or topographies. There are four simple reinforcement schedules: fixed ratio (FR), variable ratio (VR), fixed interval (FI), and variable interval (VI), which can be combined into concurrent or chained schedules. Ratio schedules are characterized by the first response after a specified number (FR) or, on average, number (VR) of responses (e.g., reinforcement delivered after every 12th response in FR 12 schedule) being reinforced. Ratio schedules are characterized by a postreinforcement pause followed by rapid responding. Interval schedules may also be either fixed (FI) or variable (VR) and are characterized by reinforcement of the first response after a scheduled period of time elapses. This schedule results in a scallop response topography where the postreinforcement pause is followed by slow responding, which gradually increases to a maximum just prior to the next reinforcer delivery.

It is easy to understand how schedules of reinforcement maintain responding. But what happens when reinforcement no longer follows the behavior? In operant conditioning, extinction (or cessation) of a behavior occurs when reinforcement no longer follows the response (e.g., attention-seeking behaviors in schoolchildren may cease when children in the class no longer laugh at them and the teacher stops calling attention to the misbehaving child), when behaviors are noncontingently reinforced (e.g., self-injurious behavior can be reduced or extinguished in children with mental retardation by providing them with deliberate and systematic attention when they are not being disruptive), and when behaviors are punished. Behaviors learned on intermittent and variable schedules of reinforcement are more resistant to extinction. During the extinction process, behaviors tend to increase in frequency as the individual attempts to obtain reinforcement; this is known as an extinction burst. In addition, it is not uncommon for behaviors to spontaneously recover after extinction. However, if reinforcement is not reinstated, the target behavior will eventually permanently disappear from the behavioral repertoire.

Returning to Skinner's three-term contingency, the second term, or the behavior to be changed or developed, is known as the target behavior. In some cases, individuals already exhibit the target behavior, so the goal is increasing the frequency. However, individuals often do not possess the target behavior in their repertoire, so the behavior must be shaped. Shaping is the reinforcement of successive approximations of the final, desired response. A common example of shaping occurs when children are taught to speak. An existing response (any vocalization) is initially reinforced. Later on, responses more closely approximating "mommy" are required (e.g., "mm," "ma," "ma-m," "mama") for the child to be reinforced.

Some behaviors are discrete, but others, such as "cleaning your room," consist of a sequence of responses. The behaviors of daily life can be thought of as chains of behaviors; chaining is defined as reinforcing the entire sequence of behaviors, rather than developing discrete behaviors through reinforcement. Similar to shaping, these complex behaviors can be developed by reinforcing successive approximations of the full behavioral chain. Chaining can be either forward, in which the behaviors are developed in the order of occurrence, or backward, in which the final behavior in the sequence is developed first. Although behavioral chains appear to be maintained by a single reinforcer, intermediate steps in the chain are believed to be conditioned reinforcers, signaling that the individual is one step closer to obtaining the final reinforcer.

Events or objects signaling the opportunity for reinforcement fall in the realm of Skinner's first term. Stimuli or antecedents, the events or objects that precede a behavior, fall into three classes: setting events, prompts, and discriminative stimuli (S^D). A setting or establishing event temporarily changes the value of the reinforcer, thereby increasing the likelihood that the behaviors necessary for reinforcement will be performed. Common examples of setting events include deprivation (of food, water, attention) and exposure to a (un)pleasant interaction. A prompt is a stimulus/event, directly associated with the target behavior, that guides or facilitates performance. Verbal instructions and physical assistance (e.g., physically assisting shoelace tying) are common examples of prompts. Finally, discriminative stimuli are events or stimuli that indicate the availability of a reinforcer. Common examples of S^Ds include a ringing telephone (signals that someone is on the other line) and the lights on a vending machine (signals that the machine is working and will deliver food or drink in exchange for some money). S^Ds come to exert stimulus control over a behavior, affecting whether or not the response is emitted. A common example of stimulus control occurs in a child whose parents anticipate and meet all needs and desires. Concerned about why the child does not speak in their presence but clearly expresses needs and desires at school, the parents are informed that their presence has stimulus control over the child's speaking because it signals that speaking is unnecessary to obtain reinforcement.

RESEARCH BASIS

Relevant research reveals several implications for operant conditioning procedures. Studies suggest that reinforcement-based learning is more effective at creating long-term behavior changes than punishment-based procedures. Punishment may be more effective at extinguishing behaviors in the short term, but because it does not teach alternative desirable behaviors, the passage of time often results in the return of previously punished behaviors. Reinforcement-based procedures add new, desirable behaviors to the behavioral repertoire; these behaviors will likely be maintained when placed on an intermittent schedule of reinforcement.

Many studies have highlighted the importance of heredity in operant conditioning. Early studies on the acquisition of "superstitious behavior" suggest that an organism's genes influence which behaviors are more likely to occur when the probability of reinforcement is low (interim behaviors) or high (terminal behaviors). Known as adjunctive behaviors, these interim behaviors, once believed to be purely "accidentally conditioned," may be innate behaviors that become highly probable when reinforcement is temporally distant. This concept may help explain why some individuals are more prone to develop unique "superstitious" behaviors, but more important, it also provides a rationale for why some people are more prone to develop functionally impairing (versus adaptive) anxiety-reducing behaviors.

An additional biological constraint on operant conditioning methods is known as instinctive drift. Research suggests that, over time, reinforced behaviors drift back to instinctive behaviors that characterize reinforcement-seeking in the natural environment. This principle has profound implications for treating behavior and substance abuse problems in children and adolescents who will return to their former peer group following treatment.

RELEVANT TARGET POPULATIONS

Although most of the early operant conditioning research was conducted with animals (e.g., Thorndike's cats and Skinner's pigeons), an extensive and convincing literature currently demonstrates the effective application of operant conditioning procedures in the treatment of a variety of behavioral problems across the lifespan. Most notably, operant-based interventions have been employed to treat childhood clinical problems via contingency contracting in parent training. Parents and children agree to participate in a program where specific three-term contingencies are applied to encourage behavior modification. Behaviors commonly treated in this fashion include anxiety, childhood eating disorders, conduct disorders, attention-deficit/hyperactivity disorder, and pain.

Extensive research also exists supporting the use of operant-based methods to treat autism and autistic spectrum disorders. Studies suggest that the repetitive speech patterns, known as echolalia, of children with autism can be reduced or eliminated, and appropriate social skills can be taught to these children. Additional demonstrated clinical applications involve children with mental retardation. These include increasing school attendance, teaching self-care, and reducing self-injurious behavior.

Another area where operant-based methods are commonly employed is the classroom. In addition to increasing attendance, a general use of operant methods is producing desired behaviors in problem children, while more classroom-specific behavioral modifications such as increasing reading and/or studying behaviors, individualized education programs, and teaching self-control have also been demonstrated. Token economy systems in which individuals earn tokens for performing specific behaviors that can be exchanged for primary reinforcers are often used to modify classroom behavior (or the behavior of any large group). Clearly, the applications of operant conditioning are far too numerous to list, but any number of applied behavioral analysis texts, journal articles on specific procedures, or treatment protocols will provide further details.

COMPLICATIONS

A common complication associated with operant-based strategies is inadequate assessment of the target behavior and the relevant antecedents and consequences. In developing a plan to shape desired behaviors and extinguish undesired ones, it is imperative that the function of the behavior be identified. Without proper knowledge of the behavioral function (e.g., sensory, attention-seeking, self-stimulatory), effective replacement behaviors that will satisfy the individual cannot be identified. In addition, without knowledge of what consequences are most or least likely to produce and maintain behavior change, operant conditioning will either be inefficient or ineffective. Functional behavior assessments and reinforcer assessments are commonly used to gain a proper understanding of the events producing and maintaining target behaviors.

Concerns regarding the use of operant conditioning and operant-based behavior modification methods have been seen in the social, ethical, and legal context. Legal and ethical concerns include the perceived loss of individual freedom (although behavioral modification does not aim to "control" but rather meet the goals of individuals, families, and society), misuse of reinforcement and aversive techniques, and the least-restrictive environment doctrine. Legal decisions have maintained that involuntarily confined populations (e.g., prisoners, psychiatric patients, institutionalized individuals with mental retardation) have certain rights, and these basic events and activities (e.g., balanced meals, regular exercise, access to television) cannot be used as reinforcers contingent upon behavior.

The use of aversive procedures has been hotly debated in the literature and in the courts. Cited problems with punishment include the following: punishment by itself rarely leads to the acquisition and maintenance of appropriate behavior; punishment affects only the response rate of behavior, whereas nonreinforcement results in extinction of target behaviors; punishment may lead to negative emotional states associated with the punisher or individual providing punishment, rather than the target behavior. It is the growing opinion of professionals that reinforcement is the preferred method to change behaviors, unless the target behavior is dangerous and requires immediate attention. Moreover, punishment is not used in isolation. That is, reinforcement for appropriate behaviors is always included when punishment is used to eliminate undesirable behaviors.

Should aversive techniques be the method of choice for changing the probability of target behaviors, the least-restrictive environment doctrine of treatment provisions calls for use of the least restrictive procedure to produce therapeutic change. This doctrine suggests that reinforcement (either positive or negative) should be attempted first, followed by successively more restrictive techniques (e.g., wearing a helmet, followed by restraints for head banging) until behavior is successfully modified.

CASE ILLUSTRATION

"Marie" was a 14-year-old Caucasian female client at a state-supported facility for people with mental retardation. Marie was blind and suffered from severely compromised hearing. She was functioning within the profound range of mental retardation and carried additional diagnoses of autism and stereotypic movement disorder. Marie engaged in severe self-injurious behaviors, including head banging, hitting her head and body (with fists), heel banging, skin picking, and toe popping. These behaviors were previously controlled through use of the Self-Injurious Behavior Inhibition System (SIBIS), a device that delivers electric shock to punish self-injurious behaviors, and pharmacotherapy. In addition to the ineffectiveness of the SIBIS, continued social pressure led the center to develop a different behavior modification program utilizing less restrictive punishing procedures. The goals of Marie's behavior modification plan included reducing the frequency and intensity of her self-injurious behavior to a level where she could be removed from intensive treatment (two- to three-on-one supervision) and attend a developmental classroom at school.

Marie's behaviors occurred with increased frequency around menstruation and when she was experiencing (frequently) an ear infection. These behaviors were also noted to increase when she returned to the institution from home, when she lost access to her preferred items, and when demands were placed on her. A functional behavioral analysis following a standard A-B-C model was performed in an effort to precisely define target behaviors and the conditions maintaining them. Functional assessment of Marie's SIB suggested that the primary functions of her behavior were self-stimulatory and escape/avoidance. A reinforcer assessment suggested that edibles (especially chocolate), tangibles (e.g., soft and/or vibrating toys), and stimulation (e.g., massages) were the most potent reinforcers for good behavior. Although no formal outcome measure was utilized, specialized data sheets were developed for the one-on-one staff member staying with Marie to document instances of SIB.

Because attempts to reinforce Marie's desired behaviors (e.g., "good hands") were unsuccessful, treatment involved a four-step punishment hierarchy for SIB. The consequences for SIB are as follows: verbal warning, stand up (from desk) for 1 minute (or until calm) and lose access to toys, walk (assisted by staff member) for 5 minutes, physical restraint. According to this program and the least-restrictive environment doctrine, Marie's consequences reset to verbal warning every 15 minutes, ensuring that physical restraint was not overused. This program utilized Type II (negative punishment) in Steps 2 to 4. During each of these steps, Marie's toys, sensory stimulation, and "alone time" were removed when she was made to stand up, walk with staff members, or be physically restrained. Type I (positive punishment) was also utilized in Steps 3 to 4 when an aversive stimulus (e.g., 5-minute walk or physical restraint on mat) was added to Marie's environment. It is important to note that verbal ("have good hands") and physical (gently holding down hands) prompts, as well as positive reinforcement ("I like the way you have good hands" and access to additional toys), were never abandoned throughout the program because they aided in teaching the appropriate desired behavior.

At the beginning of this program, Marie lost several pounds from all the walking she was doing during Step 3. She also had several months where she was physically restrained greater than 100 times. However, as Marie learned the behavioral contingencies, verbal warnings and standing up became the primary method of behavioral control. After approximately 6 months with this program, Marie's physical signs of SIB (e.g., bruising, scabs, callused knuckles, scarring) were visibly reduced, she no longer required intensive treatment (although she still required one-on-one supervision to implement her program), she was engaging in more on-task activities at school, data showed that her monthly restraints had dropped to fewer than 20, and she had gained back the lost weight. This combined (reinforcement and punishment) operant procedure was generally believed to be successful.

—*Hillary Hunt and Alan M. Gross*

See also: *Applied Behavior Analysis (Vols. I, II, & III), Functional Analysis (Vol. II), Operant Conditioning (Vols. I & III), Schedule-Induced Behavior (Vol. III), Schedules of Reinforcement (Vols. I, II, & III), Single-Case Research (Vols. I & III), Skinner, Burrhus Frederic (Vols. I, II, & III)*

Suggested Readings

Kazdin, A. E. (2001). *Behavior modification in applied settings* (6th ed.). New Haven, CT: Yale University Press.

LeBlanc, L. A., Le, L., & Carpenter, M. (2000). Behavioral treatment. In M. Hersen & R. Ammerman (Eds.), *Advanced abnormal child psychology* (2nd ed., pp. 197–218). Mahwah, NJ: Erlbaum.

O'Donohue, W. T. (2001). *The psychology of B. F. Skinner.* Thousand Oaks, CA: Sage.

Ollendick, T. H., Vasey, M. W., & King, N. J. (2001). Operant conditioning influences in childhood anxiety. In M. W. Vasey & M. R. Dadds (Eds.), *The developmental psychopathology of anxiety* (pp. 231–252). Blacksburg, VA: Virginia Polytechnic Institute and State University, Dept. of Psychology.

Platt, J. R. (1973). The Skinnerian revolution. In H. Wheeler (Ed.), *Beyond the punitive society; operant conditioning: Social and political aspects* (pp. 22–56). San Francisco: W. H. Freeman.

Walker, C. E., & Roberts, M. C. (1992). *Handbook of clinical child psychology* (2nd ed.). New York: John Wiley.

OVERCORRECTION

DESCRIPTION OF THE STRATEGY

Overcorrection is a procedure developed by Richard Foxx and Nathan Azrin for the treatment of aggressive, disruptive, and self-stimulatory behavior exhibited by children and adults with mental retardation and autism. Since its development in the early 1970s, overcorrection has been used effectively for numerous problem behaviors exhibited by children with and without disabilities and for a variety of problem behaviors exhibited by adults with disabilities. In the overcorrection procedure, the caregiver (parent, teacher, staff person) requires the child to engage in an effortful activity for a specified period of time (e.g., 5–20 minutes) contingent on the occurrence of the problem behavior. In most cases, the caregiver uses physical guidance to get the child to engage in the effortful activity. For example, in an early study by Foxx and Azrin, overcorrection was used to decrease self-stimulatory behaviors exhibited by children with mental retardation. When a child engaged in a self-stimulatory behavior, a staff member required the child to hold his or her hands for 15 seconds in each of five positions (together, above the head, straight out, behind the back, and into pockets). The child had to continue engaging in the series of hand movements for 5 minutes each time self-stimulatory behavior occurred.

Overcorrection decreases problem behavior through a positive punishment process. The procedure functions as a form of punishment by the application of aversive activities. Because the child has to engage in an aversive activity contingent on the occurrence of the problem behavior, the problem behavior is less likely to occur again in the future. Time-out from positive reinforcement (a negative punishment procedure) is also involved in overcorrection as the child is removed from reinforcing activities for an extended period of time while engaging in the overcorrection activities. Because the child loses the opportunity to engage in reinforcing activities contingent on the occurrence of the problem behavior, the problem behavior is less likely to occur in the future.

There are two forms of overcorrection involving two types of effortful activities, restitution and positive practice. Restitution and positive practice may be used individually or in combination as a consequence for a problem behavior.

Restitution

In the restitution procedure, the child has to correct the environmental disruption or damage caused by the problem behavior and restore the environment to an improved state. For example, if a child engages in tantrum behavior and throws a toy, the parent would require the child to pick up the toy and to pick up other toys in the room as well. Restitution is considered *over*correction because the corrective action goes beyond the disruption or damage caused by the problem behavior. Consider another example of a child who colors on a wall in the kitchen when he or she is angry at a parent. To implement the restitution procedure, the parent would have the child wash the wall on which he or she colored and wash an additional wall as well.

Positive Practice

In the positive practice procedure, the child has to engage in a correct form of relevant behavior contingent on the occurrence of the problem behavior and repeat the correct behavior a number of times for an extended period of time. For example, if a student makes careless errors on spelling tests, the teacher could implement positive practice by having the child write each misspelled word on a test 20 times. The positive practice procedure would make the child less likely to make careless errors. Consider another example of a 5-year-old child who wets his pants while playing in the backyard. Once the child had cleaned up and changed his clothes, the parents would implement positive practice by requiring the child to practice walking from the backyard to the toilet and standing in front of the toilet as if to urinate in the toilet. The child would have to repeat this correct behavior a number of times (e.g., 10–15 times) over a period of 10 to 15 minutes. In this case, the parents could also implement restitution along with positive practice. As soon as the parent becomes aware that the child has urinated in his clothes, the parent would require the child to go to the bathroom, undress, bathe himself, put on clean clothes, take his wet clothes to the laundry room, put the clothes in the washer, and clean up any mess caused by wetting his pants.

Considerations in the Use of Overcorrection

The child is required to engage in an effortful activity for an extended period of time as part of the restitution or positive practice procedure. Because the effortful activity is low-probability behavior (an aversive or nonpreferred activity), most children will not readily engage in the activity and may exhibit escape or avoidance behaviors when instructed to do so. Therefore, the caregiver typically must use physical guidance to get the child to engage in the effortful activity, at least initially. Once the parent has physically guided the child to engage in the restitution or

positive practice activity a number of times and the child learns that he or she cannot escape the activity, the child typically will begin to comply with the parents' instructions so that the use of physical guidance becomes unnecessary.

While implementing overcorrection, the caregiver must not accidentally reinforce the problem behavior with attention. The caregiver must simply state the nature of the problem behavior, instruct the child to engage in the restitution or positive practice activity, and provide physical guidance as needed. When using physical guidance, the caregiver must not provide attention in the form of explaining, scolding, nagging, repeating prompts, cajoling, or getting upset with the child. The procedure should be implemented in a calm, matter-of-fact way without the expression of negative emotion by the parent.

Because the use of physical guidance is usually required in the early stages of overcorrection, it is important that the caregiver has the physical ability to carry out the physical guidance with the child. The caregiver must anticipate that the child will resist physical guidance initially and must be certain that he or she can implement the procedure if resistance should occur. The caregiver must be certain that the physical guidance involved in the procedure is not reinforcing to the child in any way. If it is, the caregiver must change the way physical guidance is used or choose a procedure to address the child's problem behavior that does not require physical guidance (e.g., response cost). Finally, the caregiver must be certain that the physical guidance can be carried out without any harm to the child or to the caregiver. Consideration of these issues suggests that overcorrection is most appropriate for younger children, because it may be more difficult to use physical guidance successfully with older children or adolescents.

One final issue to consider before using overcorrection is whether a functional assessment has been conducted and whether functional, nonaversive interventions have been used to address the problem behavior. A functional assessment is used to identify the antecedents and consequences maintaining the problem behavior so that the antecedents and consequences can be modified in treatment. Functional treatments involve extinction (in which the reinforcer for the problem behavior is withheld), differential reinforcement (in which more desirable behaviors are reinforced to replace the problem behavior), and antecedent control procedures (in which antecedents are manipulated to prevent the problem behavior). In most cases, overcorrection will be used in conjunction with these functional interventions or when such interventions have been demonstrated to be ineffective in decreasing the problem behavior.

RESEARCH BASIS

Numerous research studies have demonstrated the effectiveness of overcorrection, showing that both restitution and positive practice are effective in decreasing problem behaviors exhibited by children with and without disabilities. Problem behaviors that have been effectively treated with overcorrection include self-injurious behaviors, self-stimulatory behaviors, aggressive behaviors, destructive behaviors, disruptive behaviors, out-of-seat behavior, toileting accidents, and noncompliance. The duration of overcorrection has varied from 1 minute to 30 minutes across studies, with shorter durations being as effective as longer durations. Overcorrection has been effective with younger and older children, children with normal intelligence, and children with disabilities such as mental retardation or autism. Overcorrection has also been effective with adults with mental retardation. Finally, some studies show that overcorrection can have an "educative" effect when a child is more likely to engage in a desirable behavior in order to escape or avoid the overcorrection activities. In such studies, the desirable behavior is negatively reinforced by the termination of the aversive activities.

RELEVANT TARGET POPULATIONS AND EXCEPTIONS

Overcorrection is most useful for younger children who engage in problem behaviors at home or in the classroom. Because the parent or teacher must physically guide the child through the restitution or positive practice activity, the child's size is an important factor to consider. Physical prompting or physical guidance is more likely to be successful with younger children and is more likely to be seen as acceptable for use with younger children. The exceptions would be children for whom the physical contact associated with physical guidance is reinforcing. If the physical contact is reinforcing, then overcorrection would not function as punishment and would not be likely to be an effective treatment for problem behaviors.

Overcorrection may be effective for some children (even older children) without the use of physical guidance if the child's behavior is under good instructional control (perhaps due to the prior use of physical guidance to enforce compliance). For such children, instructions to engage in the restitution or positive practice activity may be sufficient to get the child to engage in the activity contingent on the problem behavior.

COMPLICATIONS

There may be a number of complications in the use of overcorrection. First, the caregiver may not have the physical ability to physically guide the child through the overcorrection activity. Second, the caregiver may find the use of physical guidance associated with overcorrection to be unacceptable. Third, because the caregiver must engage the child in the overcorrection activity for an extended period of time contingent on the problem behavior, the caregiver may inadvertently reinforce the child's problem behavior with attention during the overcorrection procedure. Fourth, the physical contact associated with physical guidance may be reinforcing to the child. Finally, the use of overcorrection may be restricted in some settings. Because it is a punishment procedure, its use may be banned or limited by school, agency, or state rules and regulations. In some cases, rules or regulations may require the use of functional, nonaversive approaches before overcorrection can be considered.

CASE ILLUSTRATION

One common use of overcorrection is in a treatment package for daytime or nocturnal enuresis. The following case illustrates the use of overcorrection as part of a treatment package for nocturnal enuresis (bed-wetting).

"Sam" was a 5-year-old boy in a family of four (a 2-year-old sister and both parents). Sam was toilet trained at 3 years of age without complication but had continued to wet the bed at period intervals (1–3 times per week). After seeing a physician to rule out any medical problems, the parents implemented a treatment program with the following components under the instruction of a behavioral psychologist: (a) the parents limited Sam's fluid intake 1 hour before bed; he could only drink water if he was thirsty; (b) Sam urinated in the toilet just before going to bed; (c) a pad and buzzer were placed under Sam's sheets to detect urination in the bed; (d) Sam's parents woke him up one time before they went to bed at 11:00 P.M. and had him urinate in the toilet; (e) if Sam had a dry night, the parents provided substantial praise and intermittent tangible reinforcers; the parents also provided praise when Sam urinated in the toilet at night; (f) finally, the parents implemented restitution and positive practice overcorrection if Sam wet the bed at night.

When the buzzer sounded at night indicating that Sam had wet the bed, one parent went immediately to Sam's room, turned off the buzzer, and implemented restitution followed by positive practice. In the restitution procedure, the parent instructed Sam to go to the bathroom, remove his wet clothes, and get in the bathtub. The parent then turned on a warm shower and had Sam rinse himself. After Sam dried himself and put on clean pajamas, he had to take his wet clothes and put them in the laundry room, return to his room, remove his sheets, wipe off the plastic mattress cover, and take the sheets to the laundry room. The parent then instructed Sam to put the clothes and sheets in the washer, add detergent, and turn on the washer. When this was done, Sam had to get new sheets from the closet and make the bed under the parent's guidance.

Positive practice was implemented after the restitution activities were completed. In the positive practice procedure, the parent instructed Sam to practice getting out of bed and going to the bathroom. Sam was told to get in bed and pull the covers over himself as if asleep and then practice getting out of bed in the dark (a night light provided enough light to see), walking to the bathroom, and standing in front of the toilet as if to urinate. The parent instructed Sam to repeat this chain of behaviors 10 times. Once Sam completed the positive practice procedure, he could return to bed to go back to sleep.

Because the overcorrection procedure required substantial time and effort by the parent in the middle of the night, the therapist provided a careful rationale explaining the importance of using the procedure and the positive outcome that was likely (no more bed-wetting). The therapist helped the parents understand that they were already spending time dealing with bed-wetting in the middle of the night, and that although the overcorrection procedure required more time, in the end they would spend far less time as the bed-wetting was reduced and eliminated. The therapist also instructed the parents to implement the procedure in a calm and nonpunitive manner. The therapist told the parents to describe the procedure to Sam as a way for him to take responsibility for the bed-wetting and not as punishment for bed-wetting.

In the case of Sam, the parents used the overcorrection procedure for bed-wetting just five times in 4 weeks and then bed-wetting did not occur again. They kept the other procedures in place for a few more months (pad and buzzer under the sheets, no drinks before bed, reinforcement for dry nights, etc.) and then faded these procedures as Sam continued to be successful having dry nights.

—*Raymond G. Miltenberger*

See also: *Applied Behavior Analysis (Vols. I, II, & III), Aversion Relief (Vols. I & III), Azrin, Nathan H. (Vols. I & III), Habit Reversal (Vol. II), Overcorrection (Vols. I & III)*

Suggested Readings

Azrin, N. H., & Foxx, R. M. (1971). A rapid method of toilet training the institutionalized retarded. *Journal of Applied Behavior Analysis, 4,* 89–99.

Foxx, R. M., & Azrin, N. H. (1972). Restitution: A method of eliminating aggressive-disruptive behavior of retarded and brain damaged patients. *Behaviour Research and Therapy, 10,* 15–27.

Foxx, R. M., & Azrin, N. H. (1973). The elimination of autistic self-stimulatory behavior by overcorrection. *Journal of Applied Behavior Analysis, 6,* 1–14.

Foxx, R. M., & Bechtel, D. R. (1983). Overcorrection: A review and analysis. In S. Axelrod & J. Apsche (Eds.), *The effects of punishment on human behavior* (pp. 133–220). New York: Academic Press.

Marholin, D., Luiselli, J. K., & Townsend, N. M. (1980). Overcorrection: An examination of its rationale and treatment effectiveness. *Progress in Behavior Modification, 9,* 383–390.

Miltenberger, R. M., & Fuqua, R. W. (1981). Overcorrection: A review and critical analysis. *The Behavior Analyst, 4,* 123–141.

Ollendick, T. H., & Matson, J. L. (1978). Overcorrection: An overview. *Behavior Therapy, 9,* 830–842.

P

PAIN MANAGEMENT

DESCRIPTION OF THE STRATEGY

Although pain management has been an area of interest for psychologists for some time, it was only recently that pain in children and adolescents was recognized as a legitimate medical and psychological concern. Before then, pain in children was seen as a fleeting, behaviorally reflexive event that was not fully apprehended by children due to their developmental stage and lack of cognitive understanding. It is ironic, then, that behavioral and cognitive-behavioral interventions have proven so effective in pain management in children.

Assessment

Effective pain management begins with an accurate assessment of pain. This can be problematic, as many pain episodes are infrequent or occur only under specific circumstances. However, the clinician should consider at least five areas for assessment of pain—location, frequency, intensity, duration, and quality—and painfree periods. Pain *location* can be assessed by asking where on the child's body the pain occurs. The child should be asked to point to the pain, and the accompanying adult should be asked to verify this location. Pain *frequency* should be assessed on both the micro and macro level: Is the pain constant or transient? How often has it occurred during the past hour, day, and week? and When does it occur more often? Pain *intensity* is usually gauged with a visual analog scale for younger children or a verbal analog scale for

older children. The Whaley-Wong visual analog scale can range from 0 to 4 and have frowning and smiling faces as anchors. For older children, the analog scale usually ranges from 0 (no pain) to 10 (worst pain ever). Pain *duration* is assessed by inquiring how long pain occurs, once it begins, and what is associated with pain remittance. Pain *quality* is subjective, but certain descriptive terms are commonly employed, such as *burning*, *stabbing*, or *squeezing*. Children should be asked to describe the pain themselves first, and then prompted with these terms if necessary. Finally, how often and under what environmental and behavioral circumstances *painfree periods* occur should be assessed.

It is important to obtain multiple assessments in multiple settings in order to increase the likelihood of detecting patterns of pain as well as to assess for inter- and intrasubject variability. For instance, it is helpful to know if the child reports more pain than usual for his or her developmental age, if this pain is reported more at home than at school, and if this pain is reported more in the presence of Mom as opposed to Dad. Moreover, a good assessment will elucidate what type of pain the child is experiencing and will enable the clinician to target pain behaviors and symptoms effectively. It is apparent that multiple variables affect what type of intervention is chosen for pain; these multiple variables are not necessarily mutually exclusive, often operating in conjunction with each other. Therefore, an accurate assessment will consider these variables as overlapping and covariate.

For example, time of pain should be assessed. The clinician must know whether the pain is acute or chronic. While both acute and chronic pain can be treated with standard behavioral interventions such as distraction, as pain moves more into the chronic phase, more cognitive coping skills can be utilized. For example, a child with sickle-cell disease may experience pain crises only one or two times per year, but a child with chronic back pain resulting from an automobile accident may experience daily pain. An assessment of frequency and duration of pain will provide this information.

Another variable to consider during assessment is the origin of the reported pain. Pain resulting from disease (whether that disease is chronic or acute) should be differentiated from procedural pain. For example, a child with juvenile rheumatoid arthritis (JRA) will have a different pain experience than a child who has to get an antibiotic shot at the pediatrician's office. Obviously, frequency and duration of pain will co-vary with this variable. However, not all chronic pain is disease related. For example, a child with diabetes may experience frequent acute pain resulting from finger sticks.

Developmental aspects should also be taken into consideration. Older children report pain differently than younger children. Hence, different types of interventions can be utilized in varying degrees of intensity in order to achieve efficacy. In general, the clinician should follow guidelines similar to those put forward in the child clinical literature, that is, behavioral techniques for younger children, moving to more cognitive-behavioral with older adolescents. In other words, as a child gets older, behavioral techniques are still recommended, but cognitive coping skills begin to play a role in pain management.

Finally, the modality of the pain management intervention needs to be considered. Pain interventions can take place with the child or adolescent, with the parent/family/medical staff, or with both. Interventions aimed at a child's management of pain will necessarily be different from interventions designed to utilize the child's family to help with pain management, but these interventions should work in harmony toward the goal of pain management. In short, pain is not unidimensional, and therefore the conceptualization and management of pain is not unidimensional. Assessment techniques that focus on these variables will provide the clinician with appropriate targets for intervention.

Interventions

In general, clinicians should attempt to accomplish several basic steps in pain management. An accurate assessment of pain behaviors should reveal specific behaviors to target during intervention. The contingencies that hold these behaviors in place should be modified so that more adaptive behaviors will increase. These adaptive behaviors should be reinforced, and the targeted pain behaviors should be punished or ignored. And all this should be accomplished both with the child and any adults that significantly affect the child's environment, such as parents or nurses. In the following section, these specific steps will be discussed in greater detail.

Behavioral and cognitive-behavioral interventions have been shown to be the most effective in helping children and adolescents manage pain. These techniques are the same as are used in the treatment of other psychological disorders and need only mild accommodation to be effective in this specific population. Specifically, distraction is the standard first-line intervention for pain in children and adolescence. Children should be distracted by asking them to describe objects in their immediate surroundings (i.e., "What is that on TV?" or "Help me count how many pictures there are in this room") or by asking them to describe events from another time (i.e., "Tell me what you had for breakfast this morning" or "Tell me about your vacation"). Imagery is also recommended, though its use with younger children may be more difficult. Children can be trained to visualize a calm, soothing mental scene (such as the beach or their bedroom) and then prompted to "see" this image during their painful episode. Finally, progressive muscle relaxation (PMR) can be used to train children to tense and relax large muscle groups. As children attain these skills, they can then be prompted to relax during pain episodes. As children get older, they can be taught coping skills (such as positive self-statements) in addition to behavioral techniques.

As with most techniques used in child psychology, adults need to be included in the intervention for best results. This means teaching adults (parents, caregivers, nurses, etc.) techniques that can then be used with the child or adolescent. Adults should be advised to follow several guidelines: (a) reduce attention to pain behavior, within reason: after the initial assessment regarding pain intensity, frequency, duration, location, and so on these questions should not be asked again; also, responses to pain behavior should be reduced, and the child should be assisted in coping with pain, other than an initial prompt to practice self-skills; (b) normality should be encouraged: daily routines should be reinstated and maintained (school, chores, activities), and appropriate coping skills should be modeled by the adult with the child.

RESEARCH BASIS

The research shows that behavioral techniques (i.e., distraction and/or imagery) work better than cognitive techniques alone (i.e., positive self-statements). These findings offer key guidelines for the clinician's decision making regarding interventions. While most parents and other adults may feel that distraction is too "cold" for a child who is experiencing pain, and naturally feel inclined to engage in more emotion-focused, cognitive interventions, the research clearly demonstrates that distraction works best for reducing pain behaviors. Many adults naturally think that calming, soothing statements to a child in pain constitutes effective caregiving. However, these behaviors typically serve as positive reinforcement for the pain in children and can thereby extenuate and exacerbate the pain behaviors rather than reducing them. Distraction, as a primary intervention for pain management in children and adolescents, has been shown to be more efficacious at reducing pain intensity, frequency, and duration.

Research has also demonstrated that teaching children self-management techniques without using an adult to model and prompt these behaviors is not effective. These primarily cognitive techniques may have more efficacy with older children and adolescents as the target intervention group. However, younger children need an adult to prompt them to engage in these interventions. Hence, the clinician is encouraged to utilized caregivers or medical staff to help implement pain management techniques with younger children. As the child gets older, the clinician can move toward more self-directed interventions for the patient.

RELEVANT TARGET POPULATIONS AND EXCEPTIONS

All pain behaviors in children and adolescents can be treated with behavioral and cognitive-behavioral interventions. The clinical research literature is replete with examples of these techniques being used with a various pain linked to various sources. For example, studies have demonstrated the efficacy of these interventions using children and adolescents with JRA, cancer, HIV, sickle-cell disease, headache, burn patients, postsurgical pain, medical procedure pain, and invasive procedures. As stated earlier, these situations will be associated with pain that varies by intensity, frequency, duration, quality, and location. Behavioral interventions have been shown to be efficacious, especially when paired with caregiver or other adult implementation.

COMPLICATIONS

Since pain is a complex phenomenon, it can be difficult to assess and intervene upon, as has been discussed above. However, any attempt at pain management would be misguided and ultimately dangerous without consultation with a health care professional. Pain itself is adaptive, and often the child or adolescent can be experiencing pain that is symptomatic of a serious medical and physical concern. Attempts to minimize response to this sort of pain can prove harmful. For example, a 4-year-old girl standing on a stool recently fell and struck the back of her head on the edge of the kitchen counter. She cried only momentarily and then began playing with her sisters again. Over the course of the evening, she intermittently complained of head pain before returning to normal activity. Her father used distraction techniques successfully; however, when he was checking on her as she slept that night, he discovered that her pillowcase and the back of her head were bloody. She had a 2-inch laceration with a large extradural hematoma; her father realized he had not thought to check the back of her head. Since she had returned to normal activity so soon after the fall, her father assumed that her pain behaviors were exaggerated, when in fact they were adaptive. This case illustrates that pain management interventions can be very successful but should only be attempted when medically appropriate.

CASE ILLUSTRATION

"Sally" was a 6-year-old female who had been recently diagnosed with type 1 diabetes, previously known as insulin-dependent diabetes mellitus (IDDM). She had a 4-year-old sister and lived with both biological parents in a rural community. She was brought to the emergency department, where she was diagnosed and placed inpatient for stabilization and diabetes care education, following standard medical care. There was no history of chronic disease in her family and so no precedent for coping with medical procedures other than occasional doctor visits.

Sally was very resistant to the daily finger sticks and insulin injections that are required in the treatment for type 1 diabetes. She complained that they hurt and stated repeatedly that she did not want to "get stuck." Sally's mother was the primary caregiver during her hospital stay. Her mother reported that though she knew the finger sticks and insulin injections were part of diabetes care, she still had difficulty dealing with Sally's obvious pain.

Though minor in terms of overall invasiveness, finger sticks are nevertheless painful, due to the large number of nerve endings located on the human finger tip. Likewise, insulin injections are delivered with a hypodermic needle; these shots must be rotated about the torso and thighs so that the same delivery site is not used repeatedly. This can be problematic, as some individuals like to find "sweet spots" where they can give themselves a shot with less pain involved.

The initial assessment indicated that Sally was most distressed about the finger sticks. At first when the nurse would enter the room, she would become tearful, say "no, no" repeatedly, and look to her mother. She would allow the nurse to stick her finger, though. However, when the switch was attempted to get her mother to administer the finger stick, Sally engaged in these same resistant behaviors and began stalling and negotiating with her mother. Sally's mother would attempt to calm Sally before attempting the stick. This became problematic both for mother and for the medical staff, as it would often take the mother 30 to 60 minutes to obtain a finger stick. Sally's mother expressed concern about her ability to obtain a stick at home. Sally reported that the pain was intense but quickly subsided. Her main concern was the fact that this pain was going to be routine, a part of her regular day, from now own.

Interventions were focused on both Sally and her mother. Sally was taught to look away from her finger during the time of the stick and to try to whistle when she exhaled, utilizing distraction and deep breathing. Sally's mother was taught not to make any statements to Sally other than "look away and whistle"; she was specifically told not to make calming statements to Sally, but to quickly and efficiently engage in the behavior (i.e., administer the finger stick). When Sally was able to have her finger stuck within 1 minute of the initiation of the stick, she was rewarded with 15 minutes extra in the playroom on her hospital floor. After 2 days, this time interval was reduced to 30 seconds from initiation of the stick.

Sally responded well to her mother's cues to engage in distraction and deep breathing. Likewise, her mother (after some initial hesitancy) was able to refrain from calming statements and to administer the finger stick swiftly. Sally particularly enjoyed the reward of going to the playroom, and her nonresistant behaviors appeared to be rewarded by this. By the day of discharge, Sally offered minor resistance. She and her mother were able to generate a list of rewards that could be implemented at home to replace the time in the hospital playroom.

This case illustrates assessment and treatment of intense, brief, chronic, treatment-related pain in a young child. As Sally gets older, our plan is to engage her in more cognitive skills, demonstrating to her how she has learned over time to cope with a less than desirable medical condition.

—*T. David Elkin*

See also: *Behavioral Gerontology (Vols. I & III), Behavioral Medicine (Vol. I), Behavioral Pediatrics (Vol. II), Biofeedback (Vols. I, II, & III)*

Suggested Readings

American Academy of Pediatrics & the American Pain Society. (2001). The assessment and management of acute pain in infants, children, and adolescents. *Pediatrics, 108,* 793–797.

Dahlquist, L. M. (1999). Pediatric pain management. In M. C. Roberts & A. M La Greca (Eds.), *Clinical child psychology library.* New York: Kluwer Academic/Plenum.

Finley, G. A., & McGrath, P. J. (Eds.). (2001). *Progress in pain research and management.* Seattle, WA: IASP Press.

Kuppenheimer, W. G., & Brown, R. T. (2002). Painful procedures in pediatric cancer: A comparison of interventions. *Clinical Psychology Review, 22,* 753–786.

McGrath, P. A., & Hillier, L. M. (2002). A practical cognitive-behavioral approach for treating children's pain. In D. C. Turk & R. J. Gatchel (Eds.), *Psychological approaches to pain management: A practitioner's handbook* (2nd ed., pp. 534–552). New York: Guilford Press.

PARADIGMATIC BEHAVIOR THERAPY

Paradigmatic (psychological) behaviorism is a behavioral framework model that aids clinicians and researchers in the conceptualization of a variety of etiological and maintaining factors that might contribute to an individual's repertoire of behavior—both normal and pathological. The model, unlike single-factor models (e.g., learning theory, cognitive processing, biological factors, or genetic predisposition), delineates the interactive roles of multiple response domains (i.e., affective/physiological, covert/cognitive, and overt/motor) in the symptomatic presentation of individuals. In addition, the model allows one to conduct a clinical functional analysis and identify appropriate intervention strategies that are tailored to the individual's idiosyncratic presentation through function-treatment matching.

BACKGROUND OF THE MODEL

Arthur Staats proposed paradigmatic behaviorism in an attempt to provide order to the theoretical chaos that pervades present-day psychology and to thus achieve progress in building a body of conceptually consistent principles. The field of psychology consists of many problem areas, methods, and theories that have developed as relatively independent models, often at very different levels of analysis (e.g., operant learning principles vs. personality theory vs. cultural differences). In addition, the various fields of psychology have developed as if they are autonomous, with little interaction and cross-fertilization. The paradigmatic behavioral model integrates research from a variety of fields and from a variety of theoretical perspectives so as to provide a conceptually unified framework theory for psychology. The framework integrates multiple perspectives and levels of approach (e.g., biological and genetic factors, learning theory, cognitive processing, social and cultural influences) into a single multilevel model. Empirical findings and conceptual developments that are regarded as important in the single-factor models are adapted and integrated into the multilevel theory of the paradigmatic behavioral model. In addition, the more advanced and specifically human levels of functioning (e.g., language and thinking) are built upon and integrated with basic levels and principles of behavior (the physiological and conditioning bases of behavior).

FRAMEWORK OF THE MODEL

The general framework of the model and the basic principles are similar for each of the various psychological dysfunctions to which it might be applied; however, the specific processes and the interaction of these processes may differ somewhat for each dysfunction and ultimately should be based on empirical research. Relevant variables within the model are linked together in such a way as to allow sufficient flexibility to incorporate idiographic differences. The model consists of five critical elements: (1) original learning (historical antecedents), (2) unlearned genetic and biological vulnerability, (3) present situational factors, (4) psychological vulnerability, and (5) present symptomatic responses. A brief description of each of these elements follows, as these variables have been explicated more fully in previous works (see list of suggested readings). Examples of each of these variables as they apply to posttraumatic stress disorder (PTSD) is provided to demonstrate their usefulness in a clinical functional analysis.

Original Learning (Historical Antecedents)

In the paradigmatic model, original learning refers to an individual's past learning experiences. History, which is sometimes given short shrift in behavioral models, is an important contributor in this framework. Historical antecedents typically include age and developmental/medical history, socioeconomic status, individual and family history of psychopathology, educational level, and cultural and ethnic background. Additional factors relevant to a particular disorder, such as PTSD, would include prior trauma (including abuse and neglect, as well as accidents, disasters, combat, etc.), coping skills, and substance use and abuse, among others.

Unlearned Genetic and Biological Vulnerability

Unlearned genetic and biological vulnerabilities are the predispositions for certain disorders (e.g., anxiety disorders, depression, schizophrenia) as well as general physiological reactivity and high autonomic resting levels that might be related to conditionability. Individuals with PTSD may well have genetically based characteristics that increase the likelihood that under certain circumstances they will develop PTSD. In this manner, the paradigmatic behavioral model can incorporate aspects of a diathesis-stress approach.

Present Situational Factors

Current situational factors have an important place in the paradigmatic behavioral model. These factors include personal or interpersonal life events that cause stress (distress and eustress) for an individual, such as loss of resources and supports, separation from family, grief/bereavement, childbirth, and marriage or divorce. For individuals with PTSD, this may also include trauma-relevant and generalized stimuli, such as the smell of gasoline and loud noises in the case of PTSD resulting from a motor vehicle crash (MVC). These factors are stimuli that in the present situation can reevoke (as discriminative stimuli or occasion setters) aspects of prior situations, including thoughts, feelings, and motor behaviors.

Psychological Vulnerability

Original learning conditions result in the three basic behavioral repertoires (BBRs; emotional-motivational, language-cognitive, and motor repertoires) that can be understood at the level of personality. Individuals learn BBRs in a cumulative-hierarchical fashion in which learning one behavioral repertoire is a prerequisite for learning additional and more complex repertoires (consider the pivotal importance of such keystone behaviors as reading and social skills on the direction that further academic and social development can take). The process of learning BBRs begins with simple responses to environmental stimuli as an infant and progressively results in very complex BBRs that can affect an individual's experience of life situations, learning with respect to those situations, and the behavior displayed in those situations. Individuals with different BBRs may behave differently in the same situation, may experience the same situation in different ways, or may have different outcomes in the same situations. Moreover, their different behaviors may have differential impacts on their environment, which may act back and produce additional differences on them (the concept of reciprocal causation). Individuals with PTSD may have deficient or inappropriate behavioral repertoires in each of the three domains, such as overreactivity to noises, increased perception of threat, and avoidance of threat-related cues.

Present Symptomatic Responses

Present symptomatic responses or consequences are the "symptoms" that result from the cumulative and reciprocal interactions over time of the critical elements in the model. Symptoms that may be sufficient

to diagnose a disorder such as PTSD include avoidance of people, places, and reminders; substance abuse to manage arousal levels; hypervigilance and persistent perception of threat; and intrusive thoughts and nightmares. These symptomatic responses can be exacerbated (e.g., present situational stressors, biological predispositions) or moderated (e.g., good coping skills and social support) by other factors in the model.

Scotti and colleagues have identified two additional elements in the model that are particularly important for conceptualizing PTSD but that may have relevance to other disorders. These include (1) trauma learning and characteristics and (2) acquired biological vulnerability. Trauma learning refers to conditioning that occurs to features of the environment at the time of the event, generalized stimuli, and the individual's exposure to and role in (perceived and actual) the event. Acquired biological vulnerability includes the physical, physiological, and neurological changes that occur as a result of the traumatic event and subsequent behavior (e.g., neurotransmitter levels, size and functioning of the hypothalamus and other brain structures).

Individualized Treatment

Individuals who present to psychologists usually have unique sets of presenting problems. For example, an individual presenting with PTSD symptoms resulting from an MVC likely would have a different set of presenting problems than another person who was involved in an MVC of different severity or another type of trauma. Each trauma survivor has a unique learning history as well as unique biological and genetic vulnerabilities. Thus, treating all clients with a comprehensive treatment package is not always efficacious for a specific client's problems and may include superfluous aspects or fail to address idiosyncratic factors. In turn, the lack of treatments adjusted to the unique aspects of a client's problems may cause insensitivity to differences in people who have the same diagnostic label. Therapy based upon the paradigmatic behavioral model allows for function-treatment matching whereby identified factors within a clinical case analysis based upon the model can be specifically addressed and not left to the "blanket coverage" of treatment packages. The next section presents an application of the paradigmatic behavioral model as it would be utilized in a clinical case of PTSD based on research that fills in relevant aspects of the model.

CASE ILLUSTRATION

"Janice," age 9, and "Monica," age 12, were biological siblings who were living with "Tommy," age 48, and "Inez," age 47, during a trial period to evaluate the potential for adoption. They were involved in a motor vehicle collision when the sport utility vehicle in which they were riding overturned and struck a tree. Janice, who was riding on the side of the vehicle that struck the tree, experienced minor head trauma and a related worsening of her preexisting behavior problems. Monica, who was diagnosed with mild mental retardation prior to the accident, received only minor injuries to her abdomen as a result of the seatbelt. Within 1 month and continuing, Janice became resistant to entering the family vehicle, yelling and "pitching a fit." She exhibited hypervigilant and anxious behaviors when coaxed to ride in the car and also began having nightmares about cars and monsters. In addition, she was angry with and fought more often with her sister, whose behavior in the vehicle had distracted the driver and led to the accident. The potential adoptive parents had the children in their care for only 1 week prior to the accident. Tommy and Inez did not have children of their own and had little prior experience with children of these ages. As Tommy and Inez increasingly exhibited guilty feelings about the accident, they began to experience marriage problems and were unable to tolerate and patiently address the children's behavior. Inez utilized an inappropriate behavioral management strategy in dealing with the children, frequently yelling at the children and threatening to hit them. The children were returned to the adoption agency 4 months later, as the adoptive parents could not deal with the problems being exhibited by the children.

Although Janice and Monica were biological siblings, they had lived in separate foster care homes for approximately 5 years. One may suppose a relatively high degree of similarity in their biological and genetic predispositions, with vulnerabilities that included a family history of depression, mental retardation, and substance abuse. Their original learning and historical antecedents included a similar history of exposure to other traumatic events (i.e., sexual abuse by the biological father and neglect by both biological mother and biological father), a similar socioeconomic status while in foster care, and the same cultural and ethnic background, but very different levels of academic achievement and social and coping skills, as Janice was of average intelligence, while Monica functioned in the mild range of mental retardation.

The children's present symptomatic responses differed greatly. Monica appeared little affected by the accident. Janice, on the other hand, recalled the event and was angry with her sister for "causing" the accident. In addition, Janice blamed Monica for causing their return to the adoption agency and foster care. Thus, key aspects of the same accident (i.e., accident-related stimuli, type and extent of injury and blame) were experienced quite differently by these sisters and resulted in different outcomes and symptom expressions. Monica had few problems of note, with no discernible change from preaccident functioning; thus, she was not in need of treatment. Janice, however, was phobic of riding in cars and reported hypervigilance while in a car. Janice met criteria for PTSD and was treated using imaginal exposure and desensitization to trauma-related stimuli through toy play (e.g., toy cars and houses on a play mat depicting roads), followed by in vivo exposure (rides in the foster family car) and deep breathing relaxation, as needed.

CONCLUSION

The paradigmatic behavioral model equips researchers and clinicians with a framework that links together various perspectives and sources of data into a conceptually unified model. The model allows for a conceptualization of a variety of factors, both etiological and maintaining processes, that might contribute to an individual's psychopathology. In areas where limited research exists (e.g., treatment of PTSD in children), paradigmatic models likely will prove useful in advancing treatment outcome research in a more consistent and rapid fashion as several single-factor models are unified into a multilevel theory model and areas in need of additional research support are identified.

—*Beverly L. Fortson, Yi-Chuen*
Chen, and Joseph R. Scotti

See also: *Behavioral Treatment in Natural Environments (Vols. I & III), Behavior Therapy (Vol. II), Behavior Training (Vol. I), Manualized Behavior Therapy (Vols. I, II, & III)*

Suggested Readings

Eifert, G. H., & Evans, I. M. (Eds.). (1990). *Unifying behavior therapy: Contributions of paradigmatic behaviorism.* New York: Springer.

Eifert, G. H., Evans, I. M., & McKendrick, V. G. (1990). Matching treatments to client problems not diagnostic labels: A case for paradigmatic behavior therapy. *Journal* of Behavior, Therapy, & Experimental Psychiatry, 3, 163–172.

Scotti, J. R., Beach, B. K., Northrop, L. M. E., Rode, C. A., & Forsyth, J. P. (1995). The psychological impact of accidental injury: A conceptual model for clinicians and researchers. In J. R. Freedy & S. E. Hobfoll (Eds.), Traumatic stress: From theory to practice (pp. 181–212). New York: Plenum. [Modified and reprinted in Schultz, I. Z., & Brady, D. O. (Eds.). (2003). Psychological injuries at trial (CD-ROM). Chicago: American Bar Association Tort and Insurance Practice Section.]

Scotti, J. R., Ruggiero, K. J., & Rabalais, A. E. (2002). The traumatic impact of motor vehicle accidents. In A. M. La Greca, W. K. Silverman, E. M. Vernberg, & M. C. Roberts (Eds.), Helping children cope with disasters and terrorism (pp. 259–291). Washington, DC: American Psychological Association.

Staats, A. W. (1990). Paradigmatic behavior therapy: A unified framework for theory, research, and practice. In G. H. Eifert & I. M. Evans (Eds.), Unifying behavior therapy: Contributions of paradigmatic behaviorism (pp. 14–54). New York: Springer.

PARENT-CHILD INTERACTION THERAPY

DESCRIPTION OF THE STRATEGY

Parent-child interaction therapy (PCIT) treats disruptive behavior in preschool children using elements of relationship-enhancement and behavioral treatment approaches. As a form of parent training, PCIT is unique in its inclusion of the child in treatment and the in vivo coaching of the child's caregivers during treatment sessions. During coaching, the therapist observes the parent interacting with the child via a one-way mirror and provides guidance and feedback to the parent by speaking into a microphone that transmits the coaching to a receiver, called a bug-in-the-ear, worn by the parent like a hearing aid. In this way, parents receive encouragement and direction in parenting skills as they play with their child.

PCIT sessions are conducted once a week and are approximately 1 hour in length. Treatment is divided into two major phases: child-directed interaction (CDI) and parent-directed interaction (PDI). Each phase of treatment begins with a didactic session in which the relevant interaction skills are taught to the parents (typically without the child present). The didactic session is followed by a series of coaching sessions that continue until the parents have mastered the skills of that phase. Treatment is usually completed in about 12 to 14 sessions.

Child-Directed Interaction (CDI)

The first phase of PCIT, child-directed interaction (CDI), resembles traditional play therapy approaches. The focus is on strengthening the parent-child attachment, increasing positive parenting, and improving child social skills. CDI is presented first because children tend to become less angry and calmer during the CDI phase and thus accept the discipline component of PDI more readily. In addition, teaching CDI first allows parents to master these skills before implementing them simultaneously with the PDI skills.

During CDI, the parents learn to let the child lead a play situation by using the nondirective PRIDE skills (Praising the child, Reflecting the child's statements, Imitating the child's play, Describing the child behavior, and using Enthusiasm in the play) and refraining from the use of questions, commands, or criticisms. At the same time, they learn to ignore negative child behaviors. Using the PRIDE skills to attend to the child's positive behavior and actively ignoring any undesirable behavior provides a positive form of behavior management called differential social attention. Parents are asked to practice the CDI skills at home during daily 5-minute play sessions with their child. Therapists also review topics such as modeling appropriate behavior for children, the importance of social support, and additional information on behavior management with the parents, and provide supporting handouts.

During CDI coaching sessions, therapists coach by praising the parents' use of the PRIDE skills, making suggestions, and encouraging the parents. The therapists' first goal is to shape the parents' verbal behavior to help them reach the CDI mastery criteria, which are 10 behavioral descriptions, 10 reflective statements, 10 labeled praises, and no more than 3 questions, commands, or criticisms during a 5-minute period. Furthermore, therapists teach parents basic behavioral principles by pointing out the specific effects of their behaviors on the behaviors of their child. It is also through coaching that therapists model and encourage positive attitudes toward the child, reframe parent attributions, and convey appropriate developmental expectations.

Parent-Directed Interaction (PDI)

Once parents master the CDI skills, the therapist introduces the second phase, parent-directed interaction (PDI). PDI resembles clinical behavior therapy and focuses on limit setting, consistency, and fairness in discipline. PDI targets inappropriate child behaviors that are too harmful to be ignored and those that do not respond to differential social attention alone. During PDI, parents continue to give positive attention to appropriate behavior and to ignore inappropriate behavior. However, they are taught to direct the child's behavior when necessary with effective commands and specific consequences for compliance and noncompliance.

In PDI, parents learn to give *effective commands* as the first step in teaching their child to comply. Following this, the parents are taught to give a labeled praise if the child obeys the command or initiate the *time-out from positive reinforcement* procedure if the child disobeys. If the child does not obey within 5 seconds of a direct command, the parent issues a warning. If the child still does not obey, the child is escorted to a time-out chair with the direction, "Stay here until I tell you you can get up." Following a 3-minute interval, the child is given an opportunity to complete the initial command. If the child does not comply, the child is placed on the time-out chair for another 3-minute interval. Compliance with the initial command is followed by an acknowledgment and then another simple command. Compliance to this follow-up command is praised enthusiastically. A time-out room is used when the child gets off the time-out chair without permission, and as the family progresses in treatment, use of the time-out room decreases.

The therapist describes and role-plays the time-out procedure with the parents alone during the didactic session of the PDI phase and encourages the parents to review the steps of the procedure during the next week using handouts that are provided. The parents wait to use the PDI procedure with their child until the next treatment session, so that the therapist can coach them the first time they use it and provide emotional support if the parents find the procedure difficult. Parents are considered to have mastered the PDI skills when, during the 5-minute coding of parent-child interaction at the beginning of the session, at least 75% of parent commands are stated correctly and parents show 75% correct follow-through after their commands (labeled praise after obey and warning after disobey).

Throughout the PDI phase of treatment, the therapist guides the parents in applying the principles and procedures of CDI and PDI to their child's behavior at home and in other settings. Initially, parents are instructed to practice the PDI skills in brief 5- to 10-minute daily practice sessions after the daily CDI play session. Homework assignments proceed gradually until parents use the PDI procedure throughout the day whenever child compliance is important. Parents then are taught *house rules,* a variation of the PDI algorithm that is primarily used to deal with aggressive behavior, in which certain rules (e.g., no hitting) become "standing commands" that remain in effect. If the child violates these rules, a time-out from positive reinforcement is immediately instituted. In the last few sessions of treatment, therapists encourage parents to assume more responsibility for applying the principles to new situations and practice problem-solving future situations as their children become older. Treatment ends when parents show mastery of the CDI and PDI skills, rate their child's behavior within normal limits, and express confidence in their ability to use the PCIT skills to manage their child's behavior effectively.

RESEARCH BASIS

Research with children with disruptive behavior disorders shows that after PCIT, children's behavior falls into the normal range on measures of disruptive behavior. Weekly ratings by parents of the frequency of their child's behavior problems at home shows a gradual, steady decline during the course of treatment, which is matched by a steady decline in parents' self-ratings of parenting stress. At the end of treatment, parent-child interactions show that, in addition to cooperative child behavior, there are very significant increases in parental reflective listening and praise, closer physical proximity, and less sarcasm and criticism of the child. These changes observed in the parent-child interaction are reflected in improved parent ratings of the parent-child attachment, the behavior of siblings, the conflict and cohesion within the family, and the parents' locus of control, marital distress, and psychopathology. In addition, teacher ratings show significant decreases in disruptive behavior and increases in social competence at school, and direct observation in the classroom shows that treated children cannot be distinguished from untreated children at the end of treatment.

Several follow-up studies have demonstrated maintenance of gains for children and their families after PCIT. In the earliest follow-up study, 14 families were reassessed at 6 weeks after treatment completion and found to have maintained the significant pre- to posttreatment gains on observational measures of child compliance, parent-rating scale measures of disruptive behavior, internalizing problems, activity level, maternal stress, and child self-report of self-esteem. Thirteen of these families were seen again for 1-year follow-up, and 12 were seen for 2-year follow-up. For all parent report measures, very large effect sizes were found for comparisons of the pretreatment scores with the Year 1 and Year 2 follow-up scores. Observational measures of parent-child interaction showed more positive and fewer negative behaviors in the parents and children at both follow-up points as well, as evidenced by medium-to-large effect sizes.

More recently, another sample of families—including 23 who had dropped out of PCIT and 23 who had completed treatment—were contacted by telephone and mail to assess differences at a follow-up point averaging just under 20 months for both groups. Results indicated significantly poorer long-term outcomes for the dropout families, with rating scale measures of disruptive behavior and parenting stress at pretreatment levels. In contrast, for the children and families who completed treatment, these measures remained within the normal range over this period of time. Three years later, 23 families who completed treatment in that study participated in a similar follow-up. Now 6 to 12 years old, the children who completed PCIT continued to demonstrate maintenance of treatment gains on measures of disruptive behavior, still with very large effect sizes for the changes from pretreatment scores. Taken together, the follow-up studies suggest that PCIT can alter the developmental path of conduct-disordered behavior for the young children who complete this treatment.

RELEVANT TARGET POPULATIONS AND EXCEPTIONS

PCIT is designed for families of 3- to 6-year-olds with disruptive behaviors such as noncompliance, defiance, and aggression. Families from diverse cultural backgrounds and highly diverse socioeconomic situations have participated equally successfully in PCIT. Boys and girls younger than 3 or older than 6 may also benefit, although PCIT with these ages has not been empirically tested. The decision to use PCIT outside the standard age range must be clinically determined on a case-by-case basis. Issues to consider would include whether the child is able to understand spoken language, particularly simple commands, and whether the child's physical size or strength precludes being taken safely to a time-out chair against his or her will if needed. In some cases, a child unsuitable for PCIT in its entirety may benefit from CDI alone or in combination with another treatment.

PCIT may be used concurrently with other treatments, such as medication for children with significant ADHD symptoms. Other evidence-based treatments for personal or marital problems of parents may improve treatment success for their family. For children with noted peer difficulties, simultaneous involvement in a social skills training group may be appropriate.

COMPLICATIONS

Although PCIT is a manualized treatment, each family presents unique characteristics that shape the course of treatment progress and outcome. In some cases, parents may begin treatment with a premature focus on instituting a new form of punishment to manage their child's behavior. As a result, they may be impatient with the CDI phase, which alone does not usually decrease severe negative behavior to within the normal range. The rationale for mastering the CDI skills before instituting the PDI skills is presented during the initial didactic session to avert impatience. However, the therapist also may use the parents' eagerness to help motivate them to meet the CDI mastery criteria. In addition, the therapist may emphasize the improvements in parent ratings of disruptive behavior and in the child's responsiveness observed during CDI play to further encourage the parents.

Parents also may be resistant to using the skills taught in PCIT. Some parents feel that they already have a good relationship with their child and therefore place less importance on mastering the CDI skills. For parents who spend a significant amount of time playing with their child, instituting a 5-minute "special time" may seem redundant and ineffectual. Sometimes parents complain that they have used time-out before without success and express doubt that it will succeed. In these kinds of situations, the in-session coaching is targeted not only to encourage parents in the correct use of the skills but also to emphasize how the skills are affecting the child.

Highly aggressive children pose unique challenges as well. During the CDI phase of treatment, parents are coached to ignore most forms of disruptive behavior and to praise the child for prosocial behaviors. If physically aggressive or destructive behavior occurs, however, parents are encouraged to end the CDI special time. Most children respond to these contingencies because the CDI skills are so highly reinforcing. In the PDI phase of treatment, parents may be instructed to use a time-out room if the child becomes aggressive in response to the time-out on the chair.

Ideally, both parents attend all treatment sessions and implement the PCIT skills. Occasionally, however, one parent may be unable or unwilling to participate. We encourage reluctant parents at least to observe the teaching sessions so that they will have a general understanding of what is taking place, which may help to prevent sabotage due to mistrust or misunderstanding. Sometimes reluctant partners will respond to an invitation to participate once they recognize the positive changes in their child's behavior. If a second parent does not participate, however, one parent can learn the skills and change their child's behavior successfully, despite inconsistent behavior from another parent. Additional caregivers living in the home (e.g., grandparents, foster parents) are also encouraged to participate in treatment.

A final complication that may occur occasionally is when a child's behavior improves significantly at home but continues to be problematic at school. If this happens, parents may be encouraged to institute a daily school behavior "report card," with a sticker chart at home to provide monitoring and positive reinforcement for good behavior at school. The therapist may also meet with the child's teacher to determine ways in which PCIT strategies might be incorporated into the classroom.

CASE ILLUSTRATION

"Jake" was a 4½-year-old boy who was brought for treatment by his parents because they felt they had no control over his behavior. In addition, they were afraid that he would be kicked out of preschool due to escalating incidents of property destruction during angry outbursts. Jake's parents were also concerned about his difficulty getting along with other children, whom he "bossed around." During a structured diagnostic interview with his parents, their report of his behaviors met criteria for oppositional defiant disorder

(ODD), but not other commonly co-occurring disorders such as ADHD. On a screening measure of child development, his mother's responses suggested that Jake was delayed in social development (age equivalent = 2.5 years) and self-help skills (age equivalent = 3.5 years). On a follow-up screening measure of intellectual functioning, Jake performed in the average range. His mother's responses on the Eyberg Child Behavior Inventory (ECBI) yielded an intensity score of 152, which falls in the clinically significant range of disruptive behavior. Both parents were observed playing with Jake in structured parent-child interaction situations, and their behaviors were coded by the therapist. Jake's mother used many questions in an inadvertent attempt to control his behavior in the play. When Jake did not comply with her repeated requests to clean up the toys, she appeared angry, raised her voice, and threatened to take away a favorite toy, but Jake never obeyed. The interactions between Jake and his father were characterized by little warmth and almost no verbalization. When Jake disobeyed, his father simply repeated his command in a resigned tone of voice and gave no consequences for continued noncompliance. Based on this evaluation, Jake and his parents were offered PCIT to address his disruptive behaviors.

Jake's parents attended all treatment sessions together. During the CDI teaching session, both parents expressed a clear understanding of the principles and eagerness to begin practicing the PRIDE skills with Jake. They varied in their commitment to daily practicing, however, with rates between 2 and 6 days a week over 6 weeks of CDI. The therapist helped them determine an optimal time for regular practice and acknowledged their efforts to practice despite time constraints. Although they were never able to practice every day, their adherence improved, and they reported gradual improvements in Jake's behavior throughout CDI.

One obstacle during coaching was Jake's father's obvious discomfort in the play situation. Jake's father had described himself as shy and appeared tense during coaching sessions, which hindered his enthusiasm in the play. He complained of not knowing what to say and feeling silly playing with children's toys. In the earliest coaching sessions, the therapist offered phrases he could say to Jake as they played. Each time Jake's father repeated a modeled phrase or used a PRIDE skill spontaneously, the therapist praised him immediately to reinforce these new behaviors. The therapist also used frequent humor in coaching to help Jake's father relax and increase the enthusiasm in his interaction with Jake—and initially to help him gain perspective on Jake's reactions.

Jake's earliest reactions to his parents' use of the PRIDE skills were mostly sassy comments and repeated attacks with a toy bull on the figures his parents were holding. When his parents first ignored these behaviors, Jake escalated his negative attention seeking. His parents were responsive to coaching on differential social attention, however, and both parents, particularly his mother, learned to shift rapidly from ignoring to attending at Jake's slightest positive behavior. Jake gradually showed more reciprocal behavior during the CDI sessions, and his negative behaviors ceased altogether by the fifth CDI coaching session. It was also at the fifth coaching session that his parents met the CDI mastery criteria.

Both parents were eager to begin PDI and learn more effective discipline strategies. They again understood the principles and had positive expectations about implementing the skills with Jake. In the first PDI coaching session, Jake initially responded to time-out by refusing to stay on the chair and shouting hurtful comments. After consistent ignoring of his comments on the chair and three escape attempts that resulted in time-outs in the time-out room, Jake began obeying most commands even without a warning. On subsequent occasions when he required time-out from positive reinforcement, he stayed on the chair with little fuss.

Jake's parents continued to practice CDI approximately every other day and added PDI practice to their routine. They never missed a clinic session and were able to master the procedures quickly. Generalizing the skills to new situations was more challenging for them, though. In the last few sessions, the therapist emphasized problem-solving skills and generalization training. The parents brought a cushion with them to one session as a traveling time-out chair, and the therapist accompanied Jake and his parents to the hospital cafeteria and gift shop to coach them in public situations. Shortly before treatment ended, Jake's mother proudly reported that his teacher had commented on his improved school behavior. She also noted that he was able to play more cooperatively with his cousin on a recent visit.

At their last treatment session, Jake's mother's score on the ECBI Intensity Scale was 97, well below the clinical range for child disruptive behavior. Jake's parents' CDI and PDI skills had been at mastery criteria for several weeks before their final session. Perhaps the most remarkable change for this family was in the father-son interaction. During the final assessment observation, Jake and his father chatted animatedly about the barn they were constructing for the toy animals. Jake's mother, in the observation room with the therapist, said she would never have believed they could have become so close.

—*Sheila M. Eyberg and Melanie D. McDiarmid*

See also: *Behavioral Treatment in Natural Environments (Vols. I & III), Behavior Training (Vol. I), Manualized Behavior Therapy (Vols. I, II, & III), Parent Training (Vol. II)*

Suggested Readings

Bagner, D., & Eyberg, S. M. (2003). Father involvement in treatment. In T. H. Ollendick & C. S. Schroeder (Eds.), *Encyclopedia of clinical child and pediatric psychology.* New York: Plenum.

Brinkmeyer, M., & Eyberg, S. M. (2003). Parent-child interaction therapy for oppositional children. In A. E. Kazdin & J. R. Weisz (Eds.), *Evidence-based psychotherapies for children and adolescents.* New York: Guilford Press.

Eyberg, S. M., Funderburk, B. W., Hembree-Kigin, T. L., McNeil, C. B., Querido, J. G., & Hood, K. (2001). Parent-child interaction therapy with behavior problem children: One and two year maintenance of treatment effects in the family. *Child & Family Behavior Therapy, 23,* 1–20.

Herschell, A., Calzada, E. J., Eyberg, S. M., & McNeil, C. B. (2002). Clinical issues in parent-child interaction therapy. *Cognitive and Behavioral Practice, 9,* 16–27.

Herschell, A., Calzada, E. J., Eyberg, S. M., & McNeil, C. B. (2002). Parent-child interaction therapy: New directions in research. *Cognitive and Behavioral Practice, 9,* 9–16.

Hood, K. K., & Eyberg, S. M. (2003). Outcomes of parent-child interaction therapy: Mothers' reports on maintenance three to six years later. *Journal of Clinical Child and Adolescent Psychology, 32,* 430–441.

Nixon, R. D. V., Sweeney, L., Erickson, D. B., & Touyz, S. W. (2003). Parent-child interaction therapy: A comparison of standard and abbreviated treatments for opposition defiant preschoolers. *Journal of Consulting and Clinical Psychology, 71,* 251–260.

PARENT TRAINING

DESCRIPTION OF THE STRATEGY

Parent training is a widely used intervention for children with behavior problems. Unlike other child treatments, therapists who conduct parent training work directly with the parent to improve a child's functioning. It is assumed that by changing ineffective or maladaptive parenting practices, practitioners can indirectly help child clients.

Parent training began in the early 1960s as an attempt to teach parents the kind of behavior change techniques that professionals and paraprofessionals were using in schools, clinics, and hospitals. The assumption was that parents could alter controlling stimuli in the home in the same way that a trained behavior modifier might reengineer behavioral contingencies in a school classroom or a residential treatment facility. Because an important goal in parent training is for parents to learn ways to manage their child's misbehavior, this therapeutic strategy is also known as *behavior management training* or *parent management training*.

Common Features

A single, uniform approach to parent training does not exist, but most programs share a number of common features. Many of these features were first derived by Constance Hanf and later codified and empirically evaluated by Rex Forehand and Robert McMahon. The training usually follows an initial assessment and an opportunity to convey to parents a conceptual overview of the goals, process, and methods of parent training. As with other skill-building strategies, parent trainers use a combination of instruction, modeling, rehearsal, coaching, feedback, and homework to enhance parents' skills. Somewhat unique to parent training is the use of a bug-in-the-ear listening device to augment in-the-moment coaching. With this device, therapists can suggest responses, give reminders, and offer encouragement, all while the parents are interacting with their child. This kind of device has also been used to assess children's level of compliance: Therapists deliver a series of clearly worded commands to parents via the bug-in-the-ear, and these commands are then repeated aloud to the child. This procedure controls for the quality of parents' commands and allows for a more valid assessment of children's willingness to comply with simple, direct command.

The content of most parenting training programs includes two general sets of parenting techniques. One set is designed to *increase* the rate at which children perform behaviors that parents deem appropriate and

desirable. These techniques are based on the principle of positive reinforcement and include social reinforcement (e.g., praise, play, affection, attention), material rewards, and token economies. A second set of techniques is designed to *decrease* the likelihood that children will perform behaviors that are judged inappropriate or undesirable. Techniques designed to lower the rate of misbehavior include issuing clear commands, withdrawing social attention, taking away privileges, placing children in less reinforcing environments (i.e., time-out), and presenting children with aversive, punishing consequences.

Another common feature among parent training programs is the sequence of training. Typically, parents learn to use accelerative, reinforcement-based techniques before learning to use decelerating, punishment-based techniques. The first phase of training is sometimes referred to as child-directed interaction (CDI) or the child's game. The labels reflect the fact that the parent-child play sessions serve as the context for learning this first set of behavior management skills. Parents are trained to follow their child's lead during play and to attend to and contingently praise their child for appropriate behavior. Parents also learn to ignore their child's display of minor misbehaviors. The skills of contingent reinforcement are often extended beyond play to situations where the child's use of appropriate behavior is perhaps infrequent or inadequate. Sheila Eyberg and other proponents of parent-child interaction therapy (PCIT) have expanded this phase of training to ensure its equal emphasis with parent discipline and to highlight the importance of the affective quality of the parent-child relationship.

The second phase of training has been labeled parent-directed interaction (PDI) or the parent's game. Here parents learn to shift to a more controlling position in the dyad, signaling that shift both verbally and nonverbally. Parents learn to make eye contact, to use a firm voice, and to state clearly worded commands ("Marcus, brush your teeth now"). The authoritative use of commands is meant to replace vaguely worded instructions or tentative suggestions/questions that invite noncompliance from difficult children ("Marcus, don't you want to brush your teeth now?"). Parents also learn how to respond when children fail to comply with these commands or are engaging in other types of misbehavior. The recommended parental response might vary with the age of the child, but common to all programs is an emphasis on following through with stated commands and parents' use of nonviolent discipline. Some programs also train parents to warn children of the consequences that will follow if they fail to follow parents' requests. If that happens or if children commit acts that cannot be ignored (e.g., dangerous acts, aggressive behaviors), parents are then expected to impose swift, salient consequences.

The two most commonly recommended sanctions are time-out and response cost. *Time-out,* also known technically as time-out from reinforcement, involves removing children from a reinforcement-rich setting and placing them in a setting that offers little or no reinforcement. (Some parents confuse this procedure with the notion of children taking a time-out if upset or out of control.) *Response cost* refers to the fact that children's misbehavior essentially *costs* them something of value for a limited period of time. Typically, what is lost is a routine privilege (e.g., use of the phone), a prized possession (e.g., favorite video game), or an anticipated event (friend's party). Most parent training programs provide strict guidelines for how to administer time-out. These guidelines are meant to prevent the misapplication of time-out—an effective but sometimes demanding procedure to use. Commonly voiced recommendations are that (a) time-out last 1 minute for each year of the child's age, (b) the time-out area should be fairly devoid of reinforcement, and (c) parents not interact with children during time-out. Parents are also warned to expect strong protests from children when first using time-out (i.e., extinction bursts) and to be prepared to use additional sanctions (e.g., spanking, holding) if children try to escape from time-out.

Important Distinctions

Despite these common features, there are also some important distinctions among currently available parent training programs. For example, some programs cover in their curriculum areas of parenting that go beyond the two general skill areas noted earlier. For example, some programs emphasize parents' ability to closely track and record specific child behaviors before introducing the notion of contingent reinforcement. The importance of parental monitoring of children's whereabouts, activities, and peer associations is emphasized in other programs, particularly those targeting adolescent clients. Other programs address parents' knowledge of childhood development, their understanding of behavioral principles, or

their ability to engage in systematic problem solving. More recently developed approaches to parent training tend to include modules designed to enhance parents' ability to teach children, often through their use of mutual problem-solving dialogue. Finally, some programs have added features designed to help parents cope with stress, increase social support, or reduce marital conflict.

Parent training programs can also differ in the format used. The primary distinction here is whether parents are seen individually as part of a larger group. There are advantages and disadvantages to each approach. Working with an individual parent allows practitioners to customize training to fit the needs and preferences of that parent. Rather than relying on a standard training curriculum, practitioners can select topics and techniques that are most relevant. Ideally, a baseline period of assessment and a thorough functional analysis will guide the practitioner in this decision-making process. Another advantage to using an individualized training format is greater flexibility in the process of training. Instruction, modeling, rehearsal, coaching, feedback, and homework can all be varied to fit the needs and preferences of the parent involved. Certain examples, exercises, and assignments might be appealing to one parent but seem odd or inappropriate to another parent. Working with only one family also allows therapists to more readily assess the degree to which a parent has mastered a given skill before moving on to the next skill. A mastery-based approach is less likely when working with a group of parents; there the pace is often tied to a predetermined curriculum designed to address the needs of the "average" group member. When working one-on-one with a parent, therapists can quicken the pace if parents prefer it and are relatively competent from the start. For other parents, the therapist can slow the pace of training so as to prevent parents from feeling overwhelmed and to foster an emergent sense of self-efficacy. Finally, an individualized training format gives practitioners greater opportunity to consider a parent's willingness to implement targeted skills and to process a parent's resistance to various aspects of training. These are important therapeutic tasks that are made more difficult when practitioners are training an entire group of parents at the same time.

There are advantages, however, to a group-based parent training format. The most obvious advantage is the potential to help a wider number of struggling parents in less time with fewer resources. It is not uncommon for parent training groups to include as many as 6 to 8 parents, with some programs targeting even larger groups recruited from a single community or school. A less obvious advantage to the group format is that participants can sometimes contribute to the process of therapeutic change. Coparticipants can offer support and validation to a struggling parent, as well as praise and suggestions when a parent is attempting to use a new skill.

Another variation in parent training format is the medium by which information is imparted to parents. Traditionally, parents and parent trainers work together in a face-to-face manner, with parents having at least some opportunities to dialogue about issues of concern or clarification. In an effort to standardize and economize the process by which parents receive useful information, researchers have developed alternative formats. For example, Carolyn Webster-Stratton's videotaped series *The Incredible Years* uses brief vignettes and narrative instruction to cover a range of parenting skills and issues. Vignettes are used to illustrate parenting errors and to model more effective parenting behaviors. The entire series is often used in conjunction with a face-to-face group discussion format; however, it is also fully contained and can be self-administered by parents. Another example of researchers seeking to widen the dissemination of parent training is found in Matthew Sanders's Triple P program. Sanders and his colleagues have used prime-time television and other forms of mass communication to teach adaptive parenting skills to entire communities. There are even parent training programs that combine video with interactive computer technology. Parents are presented with specific situations and asked to choose the most effective response. Errors are met with depictions of the effective response. Technological advances in the formatting have allowed these programs to be used as tools for prevention as well as intervention.

RESEARCH BASIS

Parent training is one of the most heavily researched and empirically supported interventions available to practitioners working with children and families. Scores of researchers and over three decades of work have yielded an impressive body of knowledge. Recent estimates include over 100 parent training outcome studies involving more than 5,000 children. Today, parent training is the treatment of choice for children whose problem behavior includes aggression, temper tantrums, or noncompliance.

Outcome Studies

The early parent training outcome literature describes single-case studies offering clear support for training parents to use techniques based on operant and social learning principles. However, findings from early group outcome studies both supported and failed to support the short-term efficacy of parent training. Negative findings were believed to be the result of poorly trained or novice therapists, treatment formats that were too brief (e.g., only 8 to 10 weeks), or characteristics and risk factors of the participants. Subsequent studies were designed to broaden the conceptual and empirical underpinnings of parent-based interventions for child antisocial behavior (see below) and to improve the overall quality and rigor of behaviorally based parent training. Researchers conducted analogue training studies, developed detailed treatment manuals, and expanded their training curricula. They also focused intently on the goal of preventing later delinquency in young at-risk children, placing less emphasis on the treatment of serious antisocial behavior in older children and adolescents.

A more recent accounting found consistent support for parent training. In this meta-analysis, the immediate impact of parent training on children's level of problem behavior was examined in an original pool of 117 studies. The overall mean effect size was 86, indicating that children whose parents participated in parent training were, on average, functioning better than 81% of the children in the control group. Also, the mean effect size did not differ greatly across parent, teacher, and observer reports. These findings offer strong support for the value of parent training, especially when compared against no intervention. Less clear is the value of parent training compared to alternative treatments; families in control groups received an alternative treatment less than 25% of the time. It is also worth noting that comparisons were based on a small subset of studies because only 26 of the 117 studies met the study's inclusion criteria.

Of these 26 studies, about two thirds were based on individually administered parent training, the average number of sessions was just below 10, and the mean age of the target child was 6 years.

Compared to research on the short-term benefits of parent training, less is known about its long-term benefits. The vast majority of published outcome studies fail to provide follow-up data on the impact of parent training. Follow-up studies do exist, and these have ranged in duration from 1 to 14 years. The findings from these studies are also fairly consistent in reporting positive findings. The conclusions that can be drawn from these studies are limited, however, by a lack of comparison data from subjects who were left untreated or who received contrasting treatments. Some studies also suffer from differential rates of attrition between target and comparison subjects, although occasionally these differences indicate higher risk among the families who remained in the study. There have also been a few studies indicating that treatment gains were lost at follow-up, a finding that is usually attributed to significant levels of *insularity* (i.e., low income, social isolation, emotional distress) in the participating parents.

Research on the long-term impact of parent training is currently being pursued by several teams of researchers. Of particular interest is the degree to which parent training prevents the occurrence of clinically significant behavior problems during adolescence and early adulthood. This is an important question for those who use parent training as a tool for preventing later delinquency. At issue is whether difficult preschoolers are likely to improve without the benefit of parent training. One estimate is that less than half of all hard-to-manage preschoolers will meet criteria for a disruptive behavior diagnosis at age 13 years. Follow-up studies reporting the *clinical* significance of parent training outcomes generally find that between 50% and 70% of children benefit. The downside of this finding is that 30% to 50% of treated families failed to maintain clinically significant gains.

Some studies have examined the impact of parent training on children's behavior at school and on untreated siblings. There is currently stronger support for carryover effects to siblings than support for generalized effects to classrooms. Available findings have been inconsistent about school effects, with some studies reporting an improvement in school behavior, others finding a worsening of behavior, and still others indicating little or no change.

Parents who participate in parent training tend to rate the experience as very positive. Measures of consumer satisfaction reveal that parents prefer performance oriented (e.g., skill rehearsal exercises) and group discussion formats over formats that rely solely on the use of lectures, written material, or self-administered videotapes. As for specific behavioral techniques, parents typically rate rewarding good behavior and time-out as more useful than all other techniques. Rated as least useful to parents are ignoring and attending—techniques in which parents must inhibit their urges to control their child's behavior.

Process Studies

Process studies examine the role of hypothesized causal mechanisms in an intervention strategy. In the area of parent training, process studies test whether changes in parenting are related to changes in children's behavior. Conceivably, children whose behavior improves after their parents participate in parent training could be affected by factors that have little to do with changes in how they are parented. Despite the importance of these issues, there have been precious few studies of the causal process in parent training. Studies that have been conducted tend to support the role of improved parenting as a causal factor in treatment outcome. These studies have also revealed, however, that parent training is often a more complex enterprise than first conceived. One of the first process studies found that improvement in parents' use of monitoring was more predictive of treatment gains than improvements in discipline. Also, changes in parents' use of positive reinforcement and child-focused problem solving failed to predict posttreatment reductions in child antisocial behavior. Children of parents who improved both their use of discipline and monitoring were expected to gain the most; however, only 50% of parents improved their discipline, only 16% improved their monitoring, and only 10% improved on both discipline and monitoring. A subsequent reanalysis of these data revealed that posttreatment use of coercive behavior was above normative levels for most treated families and that families who failed to reach normative levels had children who were significantly more likely to be arrested and placed out of the home 2 years later.

More recent investigations lend additional support to the notion that posttreatment changes in parenting practices are responsible for later improvements in children's functioning. These studies are not without limitations, and nagging questions remain for future researchers. For example, how much change in parenting can be expected from parents whose children are highly coercive? What factors explain variability in parents' degree of change? How much change is needed before one sees a positive impact on children's problem behavior? Are some parenting practices more important to change than others? For how long are these changes needed?

Conceptual Studies

An important assumption underlying parent training is that parents have an appreciable impact on their child's development. Specifically, it is presumed that directly experienced contingencies and repeated observations of behavioral models lead children to acquire and perform behaviors that are reinforced and fail to acquire or suppress behaviors that are punished or extinguished. This behaviorally based model of parental influence has been challenged on three fronts. Developmental psychologists have long criticized behavioral models as inadequately capturing the natural unfolding of children's internal structures and abilities, which purportedly allow children to actively construct meaning out of their experiences. Behavior geneticists have questioned the importance of environmental influence generally and parents' influence specifically, given recent findings documenting the role of genetic endowment in human development. A third challenge is based on recent findings and theoretical arguments that nonfamilial inputs (e.g., peers, teachers, schools, media) exert a much greater impact on children's development than do parents. Interestingly, counterarguments to these challenges often cite findings from parent training outcome studies as clear evidence that altered parenting can lead to significant and lasting changes in child behavior.

Research on the conceptual underpinnings of parent training is extensive and spans more than three decades. Leading the way in this effort are Gerald Patterson and his colleagues at the Oregon Social Learning Center. Patterson's extensive observational research led to his proposing the coercion hypothesis to explain the relation between poor parenting and children's antisocial behavior. Proposed is a developmental process whereby children undergo "basic training" in antisocial behavior by parents who reinforce their children's use of coercive actions. Parents unwittingly engage in this coercive process because they are negatively reinforced for giving in or reacting harshly to children's aversive behavior. Key to this process is the power of escape conditioning: Behaviors that lead reliably and quickly to the cessation of aversive stimuli are likely to be repeated time and again. Over time, both parent and child come to rely on coercive influence strategies that can only work if escalated in intensity and frequency, thereby leading to more aggression and other forms of antisocial behavior.

Patterson's coercion hypothesis was recently revised to reflect the perspective of the matching law. A major tenet of the matching law is that behavior is not simply a function of the rewards that accrue to that behavior; rather, it is a function of rewards accruing to that behavior *relative* to the rewards accruing to alternative behaviors. Thus, the rate at which two children display aggressive behavior can be drastically different despite identical consequences if there are differences in the consequences for nonaggressive behavior. Empirical studies informed by the matching law and intraindividual analyses reveal that coercive behavior used by conduct problem children is more effective than noncoercive behavior in terminating conflicts with parents. The opposite is generally true for control children.

Complementing Patterson's coercion hypothesis is Robert Wahler's social continuity hypothesis. Whereas Patterson's work has focused on children's use of coercion to escape parental demands, Wahler's research has investigated why conduct problem children initiate coercive behavior. Wahler and his colleague Jean Dumas proposed that high rates of coercive behavior represented an attempt by conduct problem children to escape the inherent discomfort of unpredictable family environments. Said differently, conduct problem children initiate a large proportion of coercive exchanges with parents in order to generate greater predictability. Extending this notion, Wahler argued that conduct problems arise from an absence of continuity or predictability in children's relationships with important others—particularly parents. Children whose relationships lack predictability tend to generate it through coerciveness, but this short-term strategy interferes with the development of skills needed for social continuity in the long run. Thus, a preschooler who engages in disruptive behavior at home might continue such behavior at school, but in both contexts coercion interferes with the acquisition of skills necessary for generating more stable and satisfying relationships later in life.

The insights and findings generated by the coercion and the social continuity hypotheses have important implications for parent training, but existing parent training programs have been slow to incorporate these developments. This delay is due, in part, to questions about how to apply these recent advances. As noted earlier, parent training began as an effort to impart to parents basic techniques used by trained behavior modifiers working in educational or treatment settings. As a result, there has been a greater emphasis on short-term reductions in misbehavior than on children's long-term socialization. More research is needed to determine how the mechanisms for achieving long-term socialization differ from the mechanisms for achieving children's short-term compliance. Particularly relevant are recent developmental studies indicating that some children are far less responsive to parental discipline. If corroborated in future studies, these findings suggest that parent trainers will need to adopt a more idiographic and developmental perspective if they are to help struggling parents socialize their difficult children.

RELEVANT TARGET POPULATIONS AND EXCEPTIONS

Parent training is most appropriate for children whose problem behaviors meet criteria for oppositional defiant disorder (ODD). These children are using defiance, tantrums, and other forms of coercion to influence their parents. As such, they are at risk for adopting coercion as a dominant influence strategy and for further progression down an antisocial pathway. Left untreated, many of these children are at risk for adding to their repertoire physical aggression and covert rule breaking, behaviors that signal a conduct disorder diagnosis. Parent training is ideally suited for preventing this developmental worsening. It should be noted, however, that parents who are multiply stressed, economically disadvantaged, or psychologically impaired are likely to benefit less from parent training. Also, the vast majority of research in this field has been conducted on samples of nonminority children, often exclusively boys.

Parent training is certainly indicated for children with conduct disorder, but as the severity and duration of antisocial behavior increases, practitioners are advised to combine parent-based interventions with other treatment components. For example, there is empirical support for adding child-focused skills training that addresses aggressive children's deficiencies in social information processing, social problem solving, interpersonal skills, and affect regulation. As conduct children move into adolescence, they come increasingly under the influence of deviant peers, a phenomenon that is itself predictive of school dropout, delinquent behavior, and substance use. Parent training is still useful, but also needed are interventions designed to impact multiple systems (family, peer, school).

Parent training has also been adapted for use with other clinical populations, especially those children whose symptoms include behavioral excesses that are highly disruptive or harmful to self and others (e.g., attention-deficit/hyperactivity disorder, autism, Asperger's syndrome). The role of parent training in the treatment of children with ADHD has shifted recently. Parent training is often recommended for parents of ADHD children, either alone or in combination with medication. Recently, however, there is a growing recognition that parent training is more accurately viewed as an adjunct to medication except for those ADHD children whose coexisting conduct problems greatly increase their risk for later maladjustment. Parent training has also been used to help parents who have a history of maltreating their children. There is less research on this application of parent training, but the most effective programs appear to be those that are theory driven and well implemented. A notable concern when working with physically abusive parents is the means by which parents enforce time-out. The concern is that spanking and other forms of physical discipline (e.g., holding) could lead to excessive hostility and further occurrences of physical aggression. For maltreating parents, response cost procedures that can be implemented without force and with less reliance on children's cooperation are often preferred over time-out.

COMPLICATIONS

Several risk variables have been linked empirically with a poor response to parent training. These include both characteristics of the child (e.g., severity of problem behavior) and characteristics of the parent (e.g., depression and antisocial traits). Maternal depression is particularly important because it has been shown to be a better predictor of mothers' ratings of child behavior than independent observations of the child's level of disruption. Also implicated are stressful family circumstances (e.g., divorce, marital strife, poverty, social isolation) that can disrupt parenting practices. The risk variables that predict a poor response to parent training also predict which families are most likely to drop out of therapy. The percentage of parents who drop out has been estimated to be around 30%, with the likelihood increasing as the number of child, parent, and family risk factors increases. Some researchers have suggested that parent training is inadequate to meet the needs of parents who are multiply stressed. Several have attempted to bolster the impact of parent training by adding treatment components that address such issues as depression, marital discord, and social isolation. Results generally support these add-ons, but the outcomes are not uniformly positive.

Parent training is more than "training parents," and the complications that arise often stem from a tendency for practitioners to forget this important caveat. Parents of antisocial children often feel defeated, incompetent, and resentful. At times, their inclination is to resist attempts to change how they parent, although the reasons for this resistance are not clear. Having suffered "a thousand defeats," struggling parents doubt whether an alternative and more effective way to interact with their child is even possible. They might bring an earnest desire to know what will work, but they also have a strong sense of what will not work. To suggest otherwise is to risk defensiveness, yea-saying, dropping out, or some other form of resistance. Managing this risk requires a working alliance that does not rest solely on the assumption that skill deficits are the single, primary cause of mutual coercion and child conduct problems. The more practitioners appreciate the challenge of parenting a difficult child and the more they understand parents as individuals, the more effective they will be in helping them.

CASE ILLUSTRATION (INCLUDES BEHAVIORAL ASSESSMENT)

"Marcus" was a 6-year-old boy who was brought to the clinic after having been suspended from school for the second time in a month. Marcus had committed a number of "offenses," including taking things from other children's desks, damaging others' artwork, and pushing and hitting other boys during playground disputes. Marcus's mother, "Ms. J.," was concerned about her son but also angry with the school because she now had to make arrangements to take off work while her son was home from school. It was learned that Marcus lived with two older half-siblings, neither of whom had a history of problem behavior. Ms. J. reported that Marcus's father was a convicted felon with whom the family now had little or no contact. Interview, observation, and behavioral rating scales led to a diagnosis of conduct disorder and ruled out

ODD and ADHD. The possibility of the latter diagnosis was raised by Ms. J. because her nephew had recently been placed on medication for ADHD and had responded well. Ms. J. was hopeful for a similar treatment scenario.

The therapist in this case was faced with the challenge of (a) understanding the difficulties associated with parenting Marcus, (b) improving Ms. J.'s current parenting practices, and (c) avoiding whatever resistance might follow from Ms. J. learning that her son was not ADHD. In an effort to establish a working alliance, the therapist in this case spent considerable time learning about the struggle Ms. J. faced and affirming her constructive efforts. The therapist also referred Ms. J. to a local pediatrician for possible medication for Marcus. This referral was followed, however, by a consult with the pediatrician about the fact that Marcus did not meet diagnostic criteria for ADHD, questions about whether medication might still be helpful, the importance of being supportive to this mother's efforts, and the expectation that successful intervention would require working directly with Ms. J. on her parenting.

Ms. J. was pleased with this first step but soon returned with additional concerns about Marcus's behavior at home and school. He was being aggressive toward his sisters and peers and defiant with teachers. At that point, the therapist began to explore with Ms. J. the specific strategies she was using to manage her son's behavior. It was learned that Ms. J. was fairly inconsistent with him, letting things slide when she was tired or in a particularly good mood or reacting harshly when he fought loudly with his sisters or got in trouble at school. She described the quality of their relationship in positive terms, pointing to specific occasions when they set out on their own for special times together. It appeared, therefore, that Ms. J. was failing to appreciate the mixed messages she was giving her son about which behaviors were appropriate and which were not.

The therapist asked Ms. J. if she could narrow her disciplinary focus to one or two specific behaviors, especially behaviors that were coercive or antisocial in nature. Ms. J. identified hitting his sisters as the target behavior. The therapist then discussed with Ms. J. the goal of raising the cost of Marcus hitting his sisters relative to the cost of his using other behaviors for resolving conflict. The therapist and Ms. J. worked together to generate parenting strategies (disciplinary and nondisciplinary) that could be used to shift the reinforcement contingencies surrounding this one behavior. For Ms. J., the challenge was twofold: (1) allow Marcus and his sisters to engage in sometimes loud but nonviolent arguments without punishment or criticism and (2) respond consistently and firmly to those occasions when Marcus did resort to aggression with his sisters. Establishing and implementing this initial plan illustrated the process by which Ms. J. slowly learned that parenting her son would require a plan of discipline that was selective, effective, and sustainable.

—*Timothy A. Cavell*

See also: *Applied Behavior Analysis (Vols. I, II, & III), Behavioral Contracting (Vols. I & III), Behavioral Treatment in Natural Environments (Vols. I & III), Manualized Behavior Therapy (Vols. I, II, & III), Parent-Child Interaction Therapy (Vol. II)*

Suggested Readings

Brestan, E. V., & Eyberg, S. M. (1998). Effective psychosocial treatments of conduct-disordered children and adolescents: 29 years, 82 studies, and 5,272 kids. *Journal of Clinical Child Psychology, 27,* 180–189.

Cavell, T. A., & Strand, P. S. (2002). Parent-based interventions for aggressive, antisocial children: Adapting to a bilateral lens. In L. Kuczynski (Ed.), *Handbook of dynamics in parent-child relations.* Thousand Oaks, CA: Sage.

Forehand, R. L., & McMahon, R. J. (1981). *Helping the non-compliant child: A clinician's guide to parent training.* New York: Guilford Press.

Forgatch, M. S., & DeGarmo, D. S. (1999). Parenting through change: An effective prevention program for single mothers. *Journal of Consulting and Clinical Psychology, 67,* 711–724.

Hembree-Kigin, T., & McNeil, C. B. (1995). *Parent-child interaction therapy.* New York: Plenum.

Patterson, G. R., Reid, J. B., & Dishion, T. J. (1992). *Antisocial boys: A social interactional approach.* Eugene, OR: Castalia.

Wahler, R. G. (1994). Child conduct problems: Disorders in conduct or social continuity? *Journal of Child and Family Studies, 3,* 143–156.

Webster-Stratton, C., & Herbert, M. (1994). *Troubled families—problem children.* New York: John Wiley.

PEER INTERVENTION

DESCRIPTION OF THE STRATEGY

Clinicians have increasingly recognized the potential of peers as effective agents of behavioral change in children. A considerable body of research conducted over the past three decades has convincingly demonstrated that the peer group exerts strong influences on the acquisition and refinement of a wide range of skills, most notably social skills and academic competencies. Given their important role as teachers across a wide range of skills and settings, peers are a natural choice for treatment agents and can be equally or more effective than adults. Peer intervention strategies focus on using children's interactions with age mates as a means of teaching new skills through modeling, providing opportunities for skill usage, and improving upon already established competencies. Targets have been wide-ranging. Teaching social skills, increasing rates of peer interaction, decreasing disruptive classroom behavior, and remediating academic deficiencies are some examples.

Peer intervention can be split into two broad categories: indirect and direct peer approaches. Indirect approaches capitalize on naturally occurring contingencies to increase appropriate social and academic behaviors. Particular strategies falling in this category include the use of group reinforcement and peer modeling. *Group reinforcement* involves using the responses of the peer group as naturally occurring reinforcement for socially appropriate behaviors. Peer attention is an often-used example. A child who is behaving in a socially competent way will receive attention and acceptance from the peer group. For example, a student who is sharing toys with the other children in the classroom will receive praise and attention from the peers around him or her. This positive attention, in turn, will increase the likelihood of using socially appropriate behavior in the future. In contrast, if a child is behaving in an unacceptable manner, the group might ignore the child and the behavior, resulting in behavioral change. For example, children who react with a tantrum when they do not get what they want might be ignored by the peer group. *Peer modeling* is another indirect strategy that entails using competent peers as exemplars of adept behavior. With a strong empirical basis in the work of Bandura, the rationale for using peers as prototypes is that after target children are exposed to models of skilled behavior, they are likely to acquire new competencies, altering their own behavior to match that which they have observed. Children are more likely to imitate a peer they perceive as receiving reinforcement and less likely to emulate behavior of a peer who has been punished for a behavioral transgression. In somewhat more direct variations, sometimes using prompts and reinforcement, peers have served as coping models in treatments addressing a whole range of presenting concerns from specific phobias to compliance with painful medical procedures. Overall, indirect peer intervention strategies use peers in a subtle way to increase or decrease particular behavior patterns.

The direct peer approach, in contrast, utilizes peers in a more immediate manner to enhance children's social competence and academic behaviors. Direct peer interventions include peer proximity techniques, direct peer prompting and reinforcement, and peer initiation strategies. The *peer proximity approach* is based on the premise that placing skilled peers with target children will allow for the natural transmission of skills from one child to another. Furthermore, these children are more likely to use newly acquired skills when surrounded by a peer group that facilitates and reinforces their use. Accordingly, children with behavioral problems are simply placed with more socially competent peers. The socially skilled companions are often instructed to play with the target child, engage the child in play, and teach the child how to play. *Peer prompting and reinforcement* involve, as the name implies, teaching peers to prompt and reinforce the responses of target children. A prompt is defined as a directive to engage in an activity (e.g., "Why don't you get on the swing and I'll push you"), and reinforcement comes subsequently during the interaction (e.g., "I like to play with you"). *Peer initiation,* however, is the most frequently used intervention for promoting social interaction among target children. Using this approach, socially competent peers are instructed to both initiate social interactions and to respond to initiations from children with behavioral problems. Social initiation may include asking a child to play, suggesting an idea for an activity, or providing assistance with something. Direct peer intervention techniques can be used with either a single peer or within the context of multiple peers.

RESEARCH BASIS

The research shows immediate and substantial treatment effects for the use of peer intervention, but with some differential efficacy across treatment strategies. Specifically, large-scale reviews of the treatment literature suggest that peer initiation and prompt/reinforcement interventions have comparatively stronger effects on positive behavior changes than do proximity interventions. In terms of the indirect strategies, empirical work demonstrates significant effects of both peer modeling and reinforcement strategies. As suggested, researchers have demonstrated that children are likely to imitate peers whom they perceive as the recipients of reinforcement from fellow classmates. Similarly, in terms of reinforcement interventions, peer attention has empirical support as a useful tool for modifying disruptive classroom behavior. Specifically, the withdrawal of peer attention has been demonstrated to reduce disruptive and inappropriate behavior in the classroom. Interestingly, several studies report concurrent social gains by the competent children who serve as peer-intervention agents.

Despite such short-term success and the fact that these types of intervention are often touted for their hypothesized ability to enhance generalization, the generalization and long-term stability of these effects are less clear. In terms of generalization of new skills to nonintervention settings, the findings are inconsistent. Regardless of the strategy that is employed, some researchers find cross-setting generalization, whereas others do not. Overall, it seems that socially competent and responsive peers must be present in order for skills to generalize to new settings. The same kind of mixed evidence exists regarding the maintenance of treatment effects across time. It should be noted that ambiguities regarding generalization and maintenance of effect exist not only for peer intervention techniques but for most social skills training approaches in general.

RELEVANT TARGET POPULATIONS

Children benefiting from peer interventions generally suffer from social skills deficits, social withdrawal, behavioral disorders, or academic deficiencies.

These kinds of interventions are shown to be useful with populations of children ranging in age from early preschool through adolescence. Moreover, peer intervention techniques are demonstrated to be effective with special populations, including autistic and mentally retarded children. Although peer interventions have been used almost entirely with children, there is some evidence to suggest that these kinds of strategies may also be useful with alternative populations, including developmentally mentally disabled adults and the elderly.

COMPLICATIONS

Practically speaking, peer-mediated intervention, particularly in its more direct forms, seems best suited for clinicians working in settings, such as school and treatment programs, in which they can more readily recruit and utilize groups of children. For the individual clinician in a private practice, the practical obstacles are many. For example, identifying and recruiting more competent peers while balancing needs for client confidentiality may not be possible. Likewise, gaining the consent of larger groups of peers without bringing unwanted attention to the target child is difficult if not impossible. Furthermore, the clinician must obtain consent from the other child(ren)'s parents to be included as part of the intervention. As is easy to imagine, it may be difficult for a clinician to provide incentive to parents of a normally adjusted, socially competent student to have their child participate in the psychological treatment of another child in the classroom.

An issue of particular concern to participating parents, schools, and Institutional Review Boards is the possibility of negative consequences for the more socially and academically skilled peer. Past research on group therapies with behaviorally disordered adolescents has demonstrated that peers often can reinforce negative behavior in other children. In other words, it is possible that the direction of influence will not simply flow from the socially competent peer to the target child. Instead, it may be that the target child negatively impacts the behavior of the skilled peer. To shield against these kinds of negative outcomes, peer interventions must be closely monitored both by the clinician and the other adults in the children's environment. Indeed, when these kinds of interventions are executed appropriately, it is often found to be beneficial to the participating peer.

CASE ILLUSTRATION

"Bobby" was a 9-year-old boy enrolled in the third grade who lived with both parents, an older brother, and a younger sister. After beginning elementary school, Bobby became increasingly socially withdrawn in the classroom. He spent most of his free time at school playing alone, removing himself from group activities, and physically placing himself in the corner or in remote regions of the playground. Most notably, Bobby did not speak and would only respond softly when questions were posed directly to him. As a result, Bobby's classmates did not befriend him and did not include him in class activities either at recess or after school. At that time, Bobby did not identify any children as friends and spent most of his time either playing alone or occasionally with his siblings.

At the time of intake, a thorough behavioral assessment was performed to determine the nature of Bobby's problems in the school setting. A classroom observation was done in which rates of interaction with both peers and teachers were noted and his withdrawing behaviors were identified. Furthermore, both Bobby's teachers and parents completed behavioral rating scales. These procedures converged with interview findings to suggest significant social withdrawal and skills deficits. Assessment results further suggested that Bobby's social problems were becoming worse over time and that neglect by his classmates was leading to increased levels of social withdrawal in the classroom.

In addition to social skills training, treatment involved a combination of peer-mediated interventions. First, a socially skilled peer was identified by Bobby's teacher. Consent was obtained from that student's parents, and Bobby was paired with the peer in the classroom. This classmate was instructed to teach and model ways that Bobby could both join, as well as initiate, group activities. Furthermore, Bobby's peer teacher provided instruction to Bobby on starting conversations with other children and reinforced Bobby with praise and attention when he successfully initiated conversations on his own. Moreover, the selected peer was instructed to engage Bobby in activities frequently throughout the day (e.g., "How about we play kickball at recess?") and to provide Bobby with reinforcement (e.g., "Sure, it will be fun to play a game together later") when he asked the child to engage in social activities. Spending increased amounts of time with a socially skilled peer allowed Bobby to practice some of the social skills he was simultaneously learning in the context of skills training and thereby generalize these skills from the therapy to the class setting.

After 2 months, a follow-up classroom observation was conducted, and behavioral rating scales were readministered to Bobby's parents and teachers to determine the effectiveness of the intervention. These assessments indicated that Bobby began initiating interactions with other children in the classroom, played and talked more frequently with other children throughout the school day, isolated himself less often, and joined in group activities. As Bobby's repertoire of social skills increased, his social withdrawal began to decrease and, accordingly, his social acceptance within the classroom improved.

—Douglas W. Nangle,
Karen R. Zeff, and Michelle S. Rivera

See also: *Applied Behavior Analysis (Vols. I, II, & III), Behavioral Contracting (Vols. I, II, & III), Behavioral Treatment in Natural Environments (Vols. I & III)*

Suggested Readings

Bandura, A. (1977). *Social learning theory.* Oxford, UK: Prentice Hall.

Foot, H. C., Morgan, M. J., & Shute, R. H. (1990). *Children helping children.* New York: John Wiley.

Foster, S. L., Kendall, P. C., & Guevremont, D. C. (1988). Cognitive and social learning theories. In J. L. Matson (Ed.), *Handbook of treatment approaches in childhood psychopathology: Applied clinical psychology* (pp. 79–117). New York: Plenum.

Kelly, J. A. (1982). *Social skills training: A practical guide for interventions.* New York: Springer.

Mathur, S. R., & Rutherford, R. B. (1991). Peer-mediated interventions promoting social skills of children and youth with behavioral disorders. *Education and Treatment of Children, 14,* 227–243.

Odom, S. L., & Strain, P. S. (1984). Peer-mediated approaches to promoting children's social interaction: A review. *American Journal of Orthopsychiatry, 54,* 544–557.

Strain, P. S., Cooke, T. P., & Apolloni, T. (1976). The role of peers in modifying classmates' social behavior: A review. *Journal of Special Education, 10,* 351–356.

Topping, K., & Stewart, E. (Eds.). (1998). *Peer-assisted learning.* Mahwah, NJ: Erlbaum.

Wahler, R. (1967). Child-child interactions in free field settings: Some experimental analyses. *Journal of Experimental Child Psychology, 5,* 109–113.

PHARMACOTHERAPY

DESCRIPTION OF THE STRATEGY

Pharmacotherapy as a treatment modality for children and adolescents is a relatively young discipline that is based more on the collective experiences of clinicians than on empirical verification of the effects of various classes of psychoactive medications on children's psychiatric disorders. Because of the paucity of empirical data, pharmacotherapy was regarded as the treatment of last resort in this population until the mid-1990s. Indeed, clinicians did not consider it during initial treatment formulation until all other treatment modalities had been tried.

The situation today, however, is somewhat different. Although there are still few empirically based studies on the use of psychotropic drugs in the treatment of childhood disorders, pharmacotherapy is considered, along with other treatment modalities, an integral part of a treatment plan. Like any other single modality treatment, pharmacotherapy is limited in scope because it focuses on only one aspect of the child. Given that children develop in an interactional biological, psychological, social, and cultural matrix, effective interventions must be multimodal, multifocused, and interdisciplinary in nature.

A comprehensive psychiatric assessment is necessary before a child or adolescent can be considered for pharmacotherapy. The assessment provides the basis for determining the child's psychopathological condition, indications for treatment, and the nature of the proposed treatment. It is multidimensional and interdisciplinary, incorporating assessments of the child's symptoms and functioning across multiple domains, as well as an evaluation of his or her family history and physical and cultural environment. Typically, a baseline assessment includes (a) the source of and reason for referral, including the target symptoms that may be the focus of treatment, (b) history of the presenting symptoms, (c) psychiatric history and current mental status, (d) developmental and medical history, (e) family and education/school history, and (f) an evaluation of cultural context of the family (e.g., determine if the family has any specific religious, spiritual, or cultural beliefs that may interact with the child's psychiatric treatment in general and psychopharmacological treatment in particular).

In general, the psychiatrist's goal is to understand the presenting problems or symptoms at the highest level of diagnostic sophistication that can be achieved based on a comprehensive interdisciplinary assessment. There are four levels of diagnostic sophistication: (1) symptomatic, which includes isolated symptoms (e.g., auditory hallucinations) that provide an indication of a possible diagnosis (e.g., psychotic disorder not otherwise specified), (2) syndromic, which includes the constellation of signs and symptoms that have been present for a given time, and standardized inclusionary and exclusionary criteria can be used to derive a diagnosis (e.g., depression), (3) pathophysiologic, which includes structural or biochemical changes that indicate the diagnosis (e.g., an individual presenting with anxiety, depression, or manic excitement, weakness, excessive sweating, tremors, and, in some cases, with disturbances of thought and cognition may have elevated thyroid function tests that suggest a diagnosis of hyperthyroidism, and (4) etiologic, in which the diagnosis is based on known causative factors.

With children, most psychiatric diagnoses are at the symptomatic and syndromic levels of sophistication because we currently do not have a thorough understanding of the pathophysiology or etiology of many childhood disorders. Thus, it is not uncommon to find wide variability in treatment outcomes in children diagnosed with the same syndrome because they have similar presentations but substantially different underlying mechanisms. This means that at times we treat children's behavioral symptoms or psychiatric disorders without fully appreciating the biological and genetic underpinnings or how these factors transact with the children's physical, psychosocial, and cultural environments.

The clinical formulation follows the standard biopsychosocial model, which means that biological, psychological, and social factors are integrated into a comprehensive framework for understanding the child's symptomatic and syndromic presentation. Once the relevant data are gathered, the clinician synthesizes the information and reaches a working diagnosis. However, before a psychiatric diagnosis is finalized, any general medical conditions that may account for the child's problems are ruled out. In addition, it is critical that deviation from the normal range of development is considered. Furthermore, a child may have symptoms of multiple conditions and all relevant diagnoses are considered (e.g., attention-deficit/hyperactivity disorder [ADHD] and learning disorders).

In the clinical formulation for pharmacotherapy, the clinician pays particular attention to signs and symptoms associated with psychiatric disorders that are biologically based. These disorders are potentially responsive to psychotropic agents. The clinician obtains much of this information from a descriptive, phenomenological assessment of the child's feelings, emotions, and behaviors, which provides important insights on the child's disorder(s). Because the same signs and symptoms occurring at different ages may be indicative of different disorders, information on the clinical course helps the clinician to place the disorder

in a specific developmental context. For example, attention and concentration problems may be indicative of ADHD at ages 5 or 6 but of a mood disorder at 15 or 16. The clinician uses all of this information to formulate a treatment plan that includes pharmacotherapy as well as psychosocial and psychoeducational interventions, because pharmacotherapy alone is rarely sufficient for complete recovery. Medication provides symptomatic relief, allowing the child to function more fully at school and home and in the community. Furthermore, medication usually relieves the child's symptoms of psychiatric illness, but it does not address the vulnerability to its recurrence because the environmental and constitutional stressors that gave rise to the illness are not affected by the medication.

RESEARCH BASIS

Until very recently, children were thought of as little adults in terms of pharmacotherapy. Drugs and dosages were extrapolated from the adult research literature to treat childhood disorders. Pharmacotherapy was based more on the trial-and-error experiences of individual clinicians than on evidence-based practice derived from randomized controlled trials. Indeed, in the United States, the Food and Drug Administration (FDA) has not formally approved many of the drugs currently used by physicians to treat childhood disorders. Using drugs not approved by the FDA is called "off-label" use and sometimes leads to questionable medication management practices.

With the passage of the FDA Modernization Act in 1997, drug companies were encouraged to conduct pediatric studies of psychotropic agents. In 1998, the FDA passed regulations mandating that drug companies assess the safety and efficacy of new drugs intended for use by children. In addition, the National Institute of Mental Health began sponsoring large multicenter research studies with the Research Units on Pediatric Psychopharmacology (RUPP) grants. While the evidence-based research data on the safety and efficacy of drugs for treating childhood disorders are currently very limited, these recent national efforts should increase our knowledge substantially in the near future.

RELEVANT TARGET POPULATIONS AND EXCEPTIONS

The target patient populations for pharmacotherapy are defined by the presumed etiology of the presenting problems of children and adolescents. Additional factors that define these populations include empirical evidence from randomized controlled trials, other well-controlled treatment outcome research, and, to a lesser extent, clinical case studies. When clearly implicated in the etiology of the disorder, or the presenting problem, psychobiology and neurobiology may provide rational targets for pharmacological interventions.

Following a complete diagnostic assessment, medication is prescribed adjunctively within an interdisciplinary psychosocial and psychoeducational plan. Pharmacotherapy is used only when a child has a medication-responsive psychiatric diagnosis or there is a behavioral-biological rationale for the treatment. For example, aggression associated with an identifiable psychiatric illness (e.g., psychotic disorder, mood disorder, or mental disorder due to a general medical condition) may be controlled when the underlying disorder is treated with medication, but instrumental or predatory aggression, which is associated with low levels of autonomic nervous system arousal and intended to extract resources from the environment in a planned and premeditated fashion, may not be responsive to medication.

The major classes of medications used with children include the antipsychotics, antidepressants, antimanics, anxiolytics, and stimulants. In children, the antipsychotics are used mainly in the treatment of psychotic disorders, as well as other behavioral symptoms such as agitation, aggression, self-injury, tics, and stereotypies. Psychotic disorders (e.g., schizophrenia) present with positive (or productive) symptoms (e.g., delusions and hallucinations) and negative (or deficit) symptoms (e.g., blunting or flattening of affect, poverty of speech and thought, lack of motivation, poor self-care, and social withdrawal). There are two main classes of antipsychotics: the older or typical agents and the newer agents, referred to as novel or atypical. Positive symptoms respond well to both typical and atypical antipsychotics, but negative symptoms respond better to atypicals. The typical antipsychotics are divided into high-potency (or low-dosage) and low-potency (or high-dosage). Among the typicals, haloperidol and pimozide are the drugs of choice for treating children with Tourette's disorder. Clozapine, an atypical agent, is particularly useful in treating refractory schizophrenia in adolescence. The atypical agent risperidone is useful in treating some symptoms associated with pervasive developmental disorders.

Several different types of antidepressants are used for treating children and adolescents with psychiatric disorders. Tricyclic antidepressants (e.g., imipramine, amitriptyline, desipramine, nortriptyline) have been used extensively to treat nocturnal enuresis, obsessive-compulsive disorder, ADHD, and anxiety disorders (e.g., school phobia, separation anxiety). Tricyclic antidepressants are no longer considered first-line drugs because of the clinical concern over their cardiovascular safety profile. A new generation of antidepressants, called selective serotonin reuptake inhibitors (SSRIs, e.g., fluoxetine, paroxetine, sertraline, fluvoxamine, and citalopram), with much safer side effect profiles has been introduced. They are clearly effective for the treatment of depressive and obsessive-compulsive disorders and are probably effective for selective mutism, school phobia, and separation anxiety. Other antidepressants, such as venlafaxine, nefazodone, trazodone, mirtazapine, and bupropion, are beginning to be used with children and adolescents. Their effectiveness with specific disorders has yet to be established, with the exception of bupropion, which has proven efficacy in the treatment of ADHD.

Lithium carbonate is the main antimanic drug used with children, with the anticonvulsants carbamazepine and valproic acid used as alternative antimanic agents. Lithium carbonate is currently indicated for the treatment of bipolar disorder, aggression, impulsivity, and temper tantrums in children. The drug works reasonably well in children with behavior problems that are characterized by impulsivity, aggressiveness, rage, or emotional lability. However, clinicians are cautioned that most of this understanding comes from clinical experience and not from double-blind, placebo-controlled studies. Carbamazepine and valproic acid are indicated for bipolar disorder and as an adjunct treatment in refractory major depressive disorders.

Antianxiety agents, also called anxiolytics, are used to treat the various anxiety disorders seen in children (e.g., separation anxiety disorder, panic disorder, agoraphobia, school phobia, and generalized anxiety disorder). Benzodiazepines are the most notable agents. They are also known as sedative-hypnotics because they act as sedatives in low doses, as anxiolytics at moderate doses, and as hypnotics in high doses. In general, sedatives reduce daytime activity, temper excitement, and generally calm the child, and hypnotics produce drowsiness and facilitate the onset and maintenance of sleep. High-potency benzodiazepines (e.g., clonazepam, alprazolam, lorazepam) are used in the treatment of anxiety disorders and as adjuncts in the treatment of refractory psychosis and mania, severe agitation, Tourette's disorder, severe insomnia, and major depressive disorder with anxiety. Buspirone, an atypical anxiolytic, is also used for anxiety disorders and as an adjunct in the treatment of refractory obsessive-compulsive disorder and for treating aggressive behaviors in children with mental retardation and autism.

Stimulants are probably the most widely used psychotropic drugs with children. The most commonly used stimulants include dextroamphetamine, methylphenidate, and magnesium pemoline. They are indicated for ADHD, ADHD with comorbid disorders, ADHD in children with developmental disabilities, and as adjunctive therapy for refractory depression. Generally, stimulants are effective in controlling the symptoms of ADHD, especially hyperactivity, impulsivity, distraction, and inattention. Furthermore, they are effective in improving parent-child interactions, peer relationships, academic productivity, and classroom behavior. Stimulants minimally affect academic achievement, but they do enhance performance on measures of vigilance, impulse control, fine motor coordination, and reaction time.

COMPLICATIONS

All medications used to treat psychiatric disorders generally have adverse effects. The issue is whether, on balance, the benefits of using psychotropic drugs to treat the disorder outweigh the adverse effects associated with them. Typically, the benefits outweigh the costs, but there are definite risks involved in using drugs for treating childhood disorders. For example, most drugs can cause weight gain, some by as much as 30% to 40% in less than a year, and excessive weight gain is a risk factor for type 2 diabetes.

Certain adverse effects are associated with the different classes of drugs. For example, even when effective, the typical antipsychotic medications may produce Parkinsonian signs (e.g., muscle stiffness, gait disturbance, and tremors), abnormal muscle contractions, drowsiness and sedation, and anticholinergic side effects (e.g., dry mouth, constipation, urinary retention, and blurred vision). Other side effects include other movement disorders as well as cardiovascular and hematological adverse effects. The antimanic drug lithium has the potential to induce central

nervous system confusional state, gastrointestinal disturbance, and kidney problems. The anxiolytic agents, such as benzodiazepines, have the short-term problem of sedation that may interfere with learning and can cause drug dependency in the longer term. Furthermore, anxiolytic agents may cause irritability and aggressiveness. The most frequently reported adverse effects of stimulants include insomnia, decreased appetite, weight loss, abdominal pain, and headaches.

When using medications for the adjunctive treatment of childhood disorders, clinicians carefully monitor medical, physical, behavioral, and cognitive side effects. They use data on the intended and adverse effects of medication to revise the child's treatment plan so that the smallest effective dose can be prescribed.

CASE ILLUSTRATION

"Monica" was a 15-year-old who had been a well-behaved young lady until about 4 months ago, when she began displaying behavior problems. These included verbal outbursts, irritability, changes in mood, grandiosity, and hyper-episodes (e.g., not sleeping for several days, excessive shopping). Furthermore, both her parents and teachers reported increasing oppositional behaviors at home and at school. A few weeks prior to seeing her family physician, Monica began smoking and drinking alcohol, activities that she had abhorred before. Her family physician noted that these were common problems of adolescence, and with parental support and understanding, she would gradually grow out of it.

As Monica's behavior worsened, it reminded her father that his younger brother had exhibited similar behaviors during his teen years that necessitated treatment with lithium before he got better. Thus, he arranged a psychiatric consultation for Monica. The psychiatric assessment suggested that Monica met some of the signs and symptoms of bipolar disorder and had a paternal family history of bipolar disorder and maternal family history of depression and alcohol abuse. Her parents maintained that until the last 4 or 5 months, Monica was a completely different child. The psychiatrist suggested a provisional diagnosis of bipolar disorder and prescribed her a daily dose of lithium that was maintained at steady-state serum levels between 0.9 and 1.1 mEq/L.

Most of Monica's signs and symptoms were resolved within 6 to 8 weeks of pharmacotherapy. She was referred for cognitive-behavioral therapy with the following goals: increasing her knowledge of bipolar disorder and its treatment, teaching her cognitive behavioral skills for coping with psychosocial stressors and related problems, facilitating compliance with pharmacological and cognitive behavioral interventions, self-monitoring the occurrence and severity of her symptoms, and seeking professional help when necessary. Monica is back on track with her life and knows what to do about her disorder.

—Nirbhay N. Singh and Mohamed Sabaawi

See also: *Agras, W. S. (Vols. I & III), Behavioral Approaches to Schizophrenia (Vol. III), Behavioral Medicine (Vols. I & III), Behavioral Pediatrics (Vol. II), Cognitive-Behavioral Approach to Bipolar Disorder (Vol. III), Intensive Behavior Therapy Unit (Vols. I & III), Pharmacotherapy and Behavior Therapy (Vols. I & III), Psychoneuroimmunology (Vols. I & III)*

Suggested Readings

Jensen, P. S., Bhatara, V. S., Vitiello, B., Hoagwood, K., Feil, M., & Burke, L. B. (1999). Psychoactive medication prescribing practices for U.S. children: Gaps between research and clinical practice. *Journal of the American Academy of Child and Adolescent Psychiatry, 38,* 557–565.

Singh, N. N., & Ellis, C. R. (2000). Pharmacological therapies. In T. H. Ollendick (Ed.), *Comprehensive clinical psychology: Vol. 5. Children and adolescents: Clinical formulation and treatment* (pp. 267–293). Oxford, UK: Pergamon.

Weisz, J., & Jensen, P. S. (1999). Efficacy and effectiveness of child and adolescent psychotherapy and psychopharmacology. *Mental Health Services Research, 1,* 125–157.

Wolraich, M. L. (2003). The use of psychotropic medications in children: An American view. *Journal of Child Psychology and Psychiatry, 44,* 159–168.

Zito, J., Safer, D. J., DosReis, S., Gardner, J. F., Boyles, M., & Lynch, F. (2000). Trends in the prescribing of psychotropic medication to preschoolers. *Journal of the American Medical Association, 283,* 1025–1030.

POINT SYSTEM

A point system is a behavior change program that involves the delivery of points to a child for appropriate behaviors and the taking away of points for inappropriate behavior. The purpose of a point system is to strengthen desired behaviors that are not occurring frequently enough and to decrease the occurrence of behaviors that are undesirable. The points are delivered (or removed) immediately after the desired (or undesired) behavior occurs. The points are then traded or exchanged at some later point in time for rewards.

When using a point system, the giving or taking away of points is typically governed by a predetermined set of guidelines. First, points are earned when the child demonstrates specific, desirable target behaviors. The program must clearly define these behaviors that will earn or lose points. Clearly defining these behaviors is important so that the child knows what is expected and so that the parent or teacher implementing the program knows when to deliver (or remove) points.

Second, the program must define how many points each behavior earns. Initially, the program may specify that the child earns a point every time he or she demonstrates a target behavior. Later, as the child improves and the frequency of the desired behavior increases, the individual running the point system may alter the program such that more occurrences are necessary before a point is earned.

Third, the rewards that are to be used must be clearly specified. With a point system, the points themselves are not rewarding; rather, points acquire value when the child experiences the fact that earned points may be traded in for valuable rewards. The rewards are most commonly objects, activities, and privileges that are valued by the child. Common rewards might include snacks or drinks, toys or novelties, activities such as painting, reading with a parent, or playing videogames, and privileges such as staying up late, eating out, or renting a video. The effectiveness of a point system depends heavily on the fact that these rewards do indeed provide motivation for the child to increase the desired and decrease the undesired behaviors. If the rewards are not providing motivation to improve behavior, the individual running the point system typically must reassess the value of the rewards and include alternative items.

Finally, the individual implementing the point system must clearly designate the value of each reward. That is, the program must include an exchange rate that specifies the number of points that must be spent to "buy" each reward that is available. In addition, a predetermined schedule is usually arranged identifying the specific time each day when points can be traded for rewards that are available. It is common practice to include a wide variety of rewards with a range of values. A point system that clearly provides the child with experiences that teach that more points gets better rewards will help generate the motivation that is important to the success of the program.

Some point systems, but not all, include guidelines requiring the child to lose points (i.e., response cost) for certain undesirable target behaviors. Adding a response cost component to a point system is usually reserved for situations in which one or more undesirable behaviors actually interfere with the development of the desired behaviors. If a response cost component is to be added, the specific behaviors that will lose points must be clearly identified and the points lost for an occurrence of each behavior must be established. Typically, more severe behaviors result in more significant point losses.

Research has shown the point system to be an effective intervention procedure to increase desirable behavior such as compliance, social skills, coping skills, and negotiating skills. It has also been shown to be effective in increasing medical treatment adherence in children. When used with a response cost component, it has been found to effectively reduce undesirable behaviors that compete with more desired behaviors. Point systems have proven effective in working with children ages 7 and up and have been used to address problems in both home and school settings. However, it should be noted that the concept of trading points for desired goods may be too complex for individuals who are severely cognitively impaired. Specialized training and/or alternative procedures may be warranted in this case.

Although point systems have a wide variety of applications across different problems, ages, and settings, some challenges may arise in implementing a point system. For example, ensuring initial success can be important for developing motivation. Making it too difficult to earn or spend points can render a point system ineffective. Initially, it should be relatively easy to earn and spend points, and the child must be provided with multiple opportunities for success from the beginning of the program. Specifically, items should be "priced" such that they may be earned with very few points. This early success will motivate the child to work for points, perhaps building momentum to greater levels of behavior change and success. If early success is not achieved, the program is likely to fail. Another common pitfall is that adults assume that what is reinforcing for one child is reinforcing for the target child. It is critical to assess those items that will motivate the target child to change his or her behavior. Finally, including a response cost component can be problematic if the "cost" (i.e., number of points lost) is set so high that the child is often without any points at all. Although a response cost may be helpful to decrease undesirable behaviors, having opportunities to experience success (i.e., trading in points for desired items) is a critical learning component in a point system.

CASE ILLUSTRATION

An 8-year-old student with attention-deficit/hyperactivity disorder often spoke out of turn when the teacher was asking questions and often left his seat without permission during independent seat work. In addition, his comments were, at times, rude, and his behavior when out of seat, at times, included touching and poking others in the class. A point system was implemented in which the student could earn a point for raising his hand and waiting for permission to talk and a point for leaving his seat only when given specific permission to leave. He lost half a point each time he was rude or touched inappropriately. The student was allowed to buy prizes (chosen from a "treasure box" containing some of his favorite things, including diesel trading cards, various small toys, and miniature-sized candy bars) two different times during the day with the points he had earned. Points were recorded on a small dry-erase board on the wall next to the student's desk. The point system rules were posted on the dry-erase board. When points were earned, his teacher marked a point and offered specific praise describing the behavior that earned the point. When he lost half a point, his teacher would mark the point loss and point to the rules posted on the dry-erase board. As the student gradually increased the frequency of the desired behaviors, the point system exchange rate was occasionally changed so that items cost more. Later, the original problem behaviors were removed from the point system and improvements were maintained with teacher praise alone.

—*Keith D. Allen and Richard J. Cowan*

See also: *Applied Behavior Analysis (Vols. I, II, & III), Azrin, Nathan H. (Vols. I & III), Contingency Management (Vol. II), Token Economy (Vols. I, II, & III)*

Suggested Readings

Ayllon, T., & Azrin, N. (1968). *The token economy: A motivational system for therapy and rehabilitation.* New York: Appleton-Century-Crofts.

Christophersen, E. R. (1994). *Pediatric compliance: A guide for the primary care physician.* New York: Plenum.

Christophersen, E. R., & Mortweet, S. L. (2001). *Treatments that work with children: Empirically supported strategies for managing childhood problems.* Washington, DC: American Psychological Association.

Hutton, J. B. (1983). How to decrease problem behavior at school by rewarding desirable behavior at home. *Pointer, 27*, 25–28.

Phillips, E. L., Phillips, E. A., Fixsen, D. L., & Wolf, M. M. (1971). Achievement place: Modification of the behaviors of pre-delinquent boys within a token economy. *Journal of Applied Behavior Analysis, 4*, 45–59.

POSITIVE PRACTICE

Positive practice involves the repeated practice of a desired behavior and is considered one of the two components of overcorrection (the other component is restitution and involves correcting the effects of an inappropriate behavior). Overcorrection is a behavior modification technique that has been used with a variety of patient populations for numerous types of behaviors. Overcorrection involves requiring an individual to engage in "positive" behaviors that correct a problem in the same situation or context as the problem behavior, and the positive behaviors are logically linked to the problem behavior. For example, a child who purposefully knocks a plate of food out of the hands of a classmate in the lunch line might be made to repeatedly serve food to his or her classmates as a consequence.

Positive practice overcorrection is used when the purpose is to develop new and appropriate behaviors to replace a problem behavior. The technique requires that (a) the individual repeatedly practice a positive, functional, and appropriate behavior, as a consequence of performing a problem behavior and (b) the appropriate behavior is incompatible with the problem behavior. The use of appropriate and incompatible behaviors serves an educational purpose and differentiates positive practice from other types of punishment (i.e., other types of punishment reduce the rates of the problem behavior; however, positive practice reduces the problem behavior and theoretically develops an appropriate behavior in its place).

Positive practice has been utilized to treat a variety of problem behaviors such as antisocial behavior, self-injurious behavior, self-stimulatory behavior, school phobia, and tics. Four procedural characteristics have been identified that aid in the implementation of overcorrection and its components. First, the techniques of overcorrection need to be directly related to the problem behavior. For example, if a child repeatedly doesn't make his or her bed and/or purposely messes up the bed, then an appropriate positive practice behavior for the child to engage in would be to require the child to make the bed and also make everyone else's bed in the family. Second, positive practice methods are most useful when employed immediately following the problem behavior. Third, the individual needs to actively perform the positive behaviors. Finally, the duration of time that the individual is required to engage in the appropriate behavior needs to be for a fairly extended period. The length of time used in past studies has ranged from 48 seconds to 2 hours, depending on the type of behavior.

When using positive practice, rapid and dramatic effects have been shown for numerous problem behaviors. Positive practice has been effective in changing behavior even after other techniques such as time-out, reprimands, reinforcement, and physical restraint have proven ineffective. Research suggests that the use of positive practice is often more palatable than other types of punishment for those having to implement the technique such as therapists and staff workers. Disadvantages of overcorrection do exist. These include the complexity of the technique, the time and effort required to implement the technique, the numerous variations of the technique, and the possibility that the individual may come to think of the appropriate behavior as a punishment.

—*Carl F. Weems and Natalie M. Costa*

See also: *Applied Behavior Analysis (Vols. I, II, & III), Aversion Relief (Vols. I & III), Azrin, Nathan H. (Vols. I & III), Overcorrection (Vols. I, II, & III)*

Suggested Readings

Cannon, S. B. (1983). A clarification of the components and the procedural characteristics of overcorrection. *Educational and Psychological Research, 3*, 11–18.

Kolko, D. J., Ayllon, T., & Torrence, C. (1987). Positive practice routines in overcoming resistance to the treatment of school phobia: A case study with follow-up. *Journal of Behavior Therapy and Experimental Psychiatry, 18*, 249–257.

MacKenzie-Keating, S. E., & McDonald, L. (1990). Overcorrection: Reviewed, revisited, and revised. *The Behavior Analyst, 13*, 39–48.

POSITIVE REINFORCEMENT

DESCRIPTION OF THE STRATEGY

A positive reinforcer is a stimulus (e.g., item, event, experience) the presentation of which, or contact with which, increases the probability of (i.e., strengthens) responses that produce the presentation or contact. Positive reinforcement (PR) is the descriptive label for the relationship between the stimulus, the presentation or contact, and the change in probability. The increase in probability (or strengthening) that defines reinforcement refers to measurable changes in the dimensions of behavior (e.g., rate, duration, magnitude). PR is a ubiquitous phenomenon, and examples of positively reinforced behavior abound on every scale of human (and infrahuman) existence. Some small-scale examples include button pressing that produces desired results (e.g., elevator arrives), work that produces wages, study that produces high grades, comportment that produces praise, exercise that produces improved health and appearance, dressing that produces admiring glances, and gardening that produces attractive landscaping. Large-scale examples include higher education, theft, selling, investing, and capitalism itself. Relatedly, the range of events that can exert a PR influence is extraordinarily broad. Colloquially, any events that have even a remote possibility of being preferred over other available events have the potential to be positive reinforcers, and behavior whose purpose is the production of, or contact with, these events is said to be positively reinforced.

Despite a fairly straightforward definition that is widely available in textbooks and research literature, PR is often misunderstood and the word *reinforce* and its cognates misused. A common misunderstanding is that the words *reinforce* and *reward* are interchangeable. Colloquially, they may be, but technically, they are not. A reward is a reinforcer only if its presentation strengthens the behavior that produces the reward. That rewards do not always have such an effect is often used to criticize the concept of reinforcement and, indeed, operant theory itself (more on it below). This criticism is misplaced, however, because reinforcers, by definition, are consequential events that increase the probability of (i.e., strengthen) the behaviors that produce them. If events do not have a strengthening effect on behavior, they may still be rewards, but they are not reinforcers. Another common misunderstanding is that the word *positive* in PR refers to a quality of the reinforcing event, meaning pleasant or something preferred. Although reinforcers are often pleasant or preferred, the word *positive* refers to something that has been added (e.g., presented, obtained, contacted) and not to a quality. A common misuse of the term *positive reinforcement* involves statements that pertain to

reinforcing persons (e.g., "I reinforced him for doing his chore"). PR refers to the strengthening of behavior, not persons. Persons can be rewarded, but they cannot be reinforced.

Historically, PR emerged from and was actually a primary predicate of the operant learning tradition and the work of B. F. Skinner, arguably the most influential psychologist of the 20th century. Although facts pertaining to PR were available long before Skinner, he organized the most pertinent ones, incorporated them with new facts generated by his own experiments, and developed what has come to be known as operant learning theory.

RESEARCH BASIS

Generally, PR research involves the study of the relationships between manipulations of antecedent and consequent environmental events and the behavioral responses affected by the manipulations (although there are myriad variations on that theme). Notably, the research base for PR is probably the largest for a single concept in all of psychology. There are two major scientific journals (*The Journal of the Experimental Analysis of Behavior* and *The Journal of Applied Behavior Analysis*) devoted almost solely to the study of reinforcement (and most of it on PR). In addition, there are thousands of published scientific papers, emanating from multiples fields of scientific inquiry, reporting experimental preparations that directly or indirectly pertain to PR. Early PR research was conducted with laboratory animals in highly controlled environments, but as early as the mid-1960s, PR researchers began reporting experiments involving persons. Soon thereafter, the applied implications of PR were explored in earnest, and since then, PR has been a partial or primary topic in scientific papers, too numerous to count, pertaining to almost all aspects of human life. Given the enormity of the research base, a comprehensive account of PR would not fit into several large books, not to mention the few pages available here. Thus, this entry will merely note a few salient areas of PR research, specifically, the distinction between behavior conditioned by consequences (e.g., PR) and behavior conditioned by antecedents and some variables that influence the effectiveness of PR.

Consequent Versus Antecedent Conditioning

Among the most important of B. F. Skinner's contributions was an empirically based conceptual distinction between behavior conditioned by consequences (e.g., PR) and behavior conditioned by antecedents (i.e., by classical conditioning). The former are referred to as operants and the latter as respondents. Confusion between the two can occur because, despite the essential role of consequences in PR, full understanding of the concept also requires consideration of the events that precede reinforced behavior (antecedents). The emphasis on antecedents, however, brings to mind classically conditioned behavior or behavior that is elicited by antecedent events (e.g., ringing bell elicits salivation). But operant behavior is actually emitted in the presence of antecedents and not elicited by them. Operant behavior has more of a volitional quality (although volition is not part of the definition), whereas respondent behavior has a more reflexive quality. In operant behavior, the antecedent sets the occasion for a response that operates on the environment (thus the term *operant*) to produce reinforcing consequences (e.g., light turns green, pressing the gas pedal is emitted, forward progress is attained), but in respondent behavior the antecedent evokes or elicits a response (thus the term *respondent*).

Influences on the Effectiveness of PR

Research on PR has generated a large number of variables that influence its effectiveness, and the more salient ones are relativity, contingency, timing, schedule, and rules. Actually, all of these can be incorporated into a superordinate variable, context, but the scope of PR research ranges from a macro contextual focus down to a micro focus on subelements of the other variables (e.g., effects of a tightly defined PR schedule). A brief description of some of the major variables will be provided here.

Relativity

PR is a relative concept. For example, events involving the necessities of life such as eating, drinking, or procreating can have powerfully reinforcing functions, but not under all circumstances. The preferences and needs of individuals change (often dramatically) in accord with changes in antecedent environmental conditions, and thus the effects of PR-based applications often fluctuate with circumstances. For example, food can be a powerful reinforcer if a person is hungry, but it can quickly lose this power when the person is full. In addition, experiences that are reinforcing for some persons can be punishing for others (e.g., deep water for swimmers versus non-swimmers). There are many other examples.

Contingency

Most of the research on PR emphasizes the importance of a contingent relationship between response and consequences. Generally, contingency refers to a dependency between reinforcers and the responses that produce them; as dependency decreases, so too does the influence of reinforcing consequences. For example, the value of preventive medicine is hard to overestimate, and yet the use of, faith in, and support for curative and rehabilitative medicine is vastly greater. This is largely due to the obvious dependency (i.e., contingency) between procedures that cure or rehabilitate and healthful outcomes and the subtle and at times virtually undetectable dependency between preventive procedures and healthful outcomes.

Timing

"Timing is everything," or so it is said. In the study of PR, the saying is mostly if not entirely true, and generally, maximally effective PR requires a minimal temporal distance between response and reinforcer; immediate delivery is optimal. The relationship between timing and contingency should not be overlooked. For example, time is the primary element obscuring contingencies between preventive medicine and healthful outcomes. The benefits of a curative procedure are almost immediately apparent, whereas the benefits of a preventive procedure may take years to emerge.

Schedule

The importance of the schedule of PR is hard to overestimate. All reinforcers are delivered (or contacted) according to a schedule, and the primary dimensions used to establish it include rate of response (a reinforcer for a defined number of responses) and interval between responses (a reinforcer for a response emitted after a set amount of time has passed). There are other dimensions such as duration or intensity, but they can be incorporated into the defining properties of the response for which PR is scheduled. There are two primary types of schedules derived from the two primary dimensions: continuous (a reinforcer is delivered for each target response) and intermittent (a reinforcer is delivered only after a set number of responses have been emitted or amount of time has passed). And there are numerous secondary subtypes of schedules, the most common of which are fixed interval, fixed rate, variable interval, and variable rate, and each exerts a characteristic effect upon behavior. In addition, these subtypes can be combined into complex multiple schedules. Because PR strengthens behavior, it seems logical that the more frequently a behavior is reinforced, the stronger it would become and thus that continuous PR would be the most effective schedule. This is not always the case, however. The effects of continuous PR can quickly deteriorate, especially if response rates are high and the scheduled reinforcer is consumable (e.g., food, water) or an event whose reinforcing properties include novelty (e.g., bird watching). In addition, behavior maintained by continuous PR is much more susceptible to experimental manipulations such as abrupt withdrawal of PR (i.e., extinction). For additional information on schedules consult the book by Charles Ferster and B. F. Skinner listed in the suggested readings.

Rules

Over the last three decades, it has become increasingly apparent that verbal behavior (e.g., language) can powerfully influence the effectiveness of PR. Simply and colloquially stated, things said about PR can influence its effects. B. F. Skinner labeled behavior brought about or influenced by things said "rule-governed behavior," and he defined rules as contingency-specifying stimuli. In more general terms, rule-governed behavior is behavior influenced by language. The profound role such behavior plays in human life is underscored by the minimal role it plays in animal life. For example, the statement "Don't eat that food, it's poisoned" would diminish the reinforcing properties of the food for virtually all language-able persons and for virtually no animals. More generally, rules (e.g., language) can strongly influence a person's susceptibility to stimuli deployed as potential reinforcers.

CLINICAL IMPLICATIONS

Behaviors, not persons, are the target consideration in the analysis of PR, and, in principle, most human behavior is susceptible to its influence. In addition, although clinical concerns involve a dauntingly large and diverse category, they can productively be reduced to two subcategories of behavior: excesses and deficits. Said slightly differently and more colloquially, clinical concerns involve behavior that occurs either too much or too little. For example, alcoholism involves behavior that occurs too much and selective mutism involves behavior that occurs too little. From the perspective of excesses and deficits, PR has implications for virtually all clinical concerns. The obvious implications are for behavior that occurs too little. By definition, PR strengthens behavior, and a hallmark of strengthened behavior is an increase in its rate. Therefore, PR can be applied to behavior that occurs too little in order to increase its occurrence. Less straightforward but nonetheless real are clinical implications of behavior that occurs too much. Two options are to reduce the PR for the behavior or to supply PR for an incompatible alternative. There are many other examples.

PR also has powerful implications for clinical assessment. Understanding problem behavior is the logical first step in attempts at remedy, and, correspondingly, determining the role of PR in the maintenance of the problem behavior can be a major step in understanding the problem. Sometimes the role of PR is obvious. When asked why he robbed banks, the notorious thief Willie Sutton said "because that is where the money is." In many cases, however, the role of PR is subtler. For example, its role in cigarette smoking is widely misunderstood. Most people believe nicotine is the reinforcer that maintains smoking, but clinical assessment of smoking indicates that nicotine is but one of many forms of PR that support it. For example, smokers take breaks from work to meet with other workers and smoke. The breaks and contacts can be powerful reinforcers. As another example, when children steal, the ostensible operating PR is procurement of the thing stolen. In some cases, however, the actual operating PR is the impression the theft makes on peer witnesses. There are a vast number of other examples that reveal the extraordinary range of the clinical implications of PR.

CLINICAL APPLICATIONS

The extensive clinical implications of PR have led to an extraordinary array of clinical applications, ranging in complexity from simple PR delivery for isolated noncomplex responses (e.g., pick up the block, receive candy) to multilevel PR systems that incorporate many different types of reinforcers and methods for enhancing effectiveness (e.g., token economies in residential care). In fact, the extent of clinical applications is so broad that it is virtually impossible to determine where it begins and ends. PR is employed to solve behavior problems (excesses or deficits) across virtually all fields whose primary purpose is the provision of some type of human service ranging from education to penal systems.

The ubiquity of applications of PR does not mean the concept is without controversy, and yet most of the criticism stems from fundamental misunderstandings. For example, one major controversy involves the belief that use of external reinforcers (e.g., stickers) with children undermines their intrinsic motivation. Review of the extensive literature on this topic, however, reveals that the misunderstanding referred to earlier in the entry—mistaking rewards for reinforcers—is at the heart of the critical argument. In addition, researchers making the case against PR rarely incorporate any of the methods to increase its effectiveness described earlier. Assessments of whether something used as a reward is actually a reinforcer are not conducted, strict contingencies are not established, rewards are withdrawn without explanation, and rewards promised are not delivered. Rather than a convincing case against clinical application of PR, the critical literature is a valuable source of information on ineffective ways of using it.

Another source of controversy or at least concern is when PR seems not to work. Actually, this concern too involves some misunderstanding because, technically, PR is an operational concept, and if it is "not working," it is not actually PR. But in many clinical cases, PR is very difficult to establish, and these give rise to the notion that PR does not always work. One often effective strategy in such cases is to review the methods for ways to improve a PR-based program.

CASE EXAMPLE

"Alex" was a 10-year-old boy living in a behaviorally oriented residential care program. Alex was so frequently disruptive that the program began a termination plan that would result in his referral to a more restrictive facility. A brief reprieve was provided, accompanied by a request for behavioral assessment of the disruption and a new treatment plan. Alex's primary problem was a high rate of arguing that frequently led to aggressive interactions with peers. His behavior assessment focused on identifying sources of reinforcement, maintaining that arguing and his treatment plan focused on teaching him to interact more appropriately with peers. The assessment included two major components: (1) unobtrusive observations of Alex interacting with peers in his home with special attention on antecedents and consequences, and (2) an experimental manipulation of consequences for arguing. The assessment indicated that Alex was most at risk for arguing when more than 11 minutes passed without direct attention from staff. Arguments, however, were routinely followed almost immediately by staff attention, albeit typically negative. These findings suggested that staff attention was functioning as PR for arguing and that its delayed delivery produced a characteristic increase in rate. Subsequent experimental manipulations of staff attention for arguing supported these suggestions. Subsequent related changes in Alex's program included at least 30 seconds of staff attention at least every 8 minutes and requiring staff to direct all attention to Alex's adversaries whenever arguments occurred. Arguing reduced to near zero rates, prosocial behaviors increased in frequency, and at 3-month follow-up, Alex's placement was still maintained.

CONCLUSION

PR is one of the most widely studied and applied concepts in all of psychology. Unfortunately, it is also widely misunderstood and misapplied. Accurate understanding is dependent on strict variations of its technical definition (e.g., events produced by behavior that increase its probability). Effective application is dependent on the extent that known methods for increasing effectiveness are incorporated into the application. Fuller understanding of the concept could lead to fuller understanding of and better solutions for many of the aberrant aspects of human behavior.

—*Clinton Field and Patrick C. Friman*

See also: *Differential Reinforcement of Other Behavior (Vols. I, II, & III), Operant Conditioning (Vols. I, II, & III), Reinforcement (Vols. I & III), Schedules of Reinforcement (Vols. I, II, & III), Skinner, Burrhus Frederic (Vols. I, II, & III)*

Suggested Readings

Catania, C. A. (1998). *Learning* (4th ed.). Englewood Cliffs, NJ: Prentice Hall.

Ferster, C. B., & Skinner, B. F. (1957). *Schedules of reinforcement.* New York: Appleton-Century-Crofts.

Skinner, B. F. (1969). Contingencies of reinforcement: A theoretical analysis. In R. M. Elliot, K. MacCorquodale, G. Lindzey, & K. E. Clark (Series Eds.), *The century psychology series.* New York: Appleton-Century-Crofts.

PREMACK PRINCIPLE

DESCRIPTION OF THE STRATEGY

By the time the average undergraduate student has completed his or her college career, chances are that he or she has been exposed to the Premack principle virtually dozens of times in the formal classroom setting. Classes such as Learning, Child Development, and Behavior Modification are sure to have brought the student into contact with one of the most universally recognized principles in the field of behavior change. And yet, even prior to embarking on that college career, it is a certainty that most students had been exposed to the Premack principle in a less formal manner—through its application to them by parents, teachers, and perhaps other authority figures seeking to elicit a desired behavior. When a parent withholds a child's playtime with friends until the child has completed homework, the Premack principle is employed. When a parent withholds time on the computer until the child has straightened his or her room, the Premack principle is employed.

The Premack principle states that it is possible to use a high probability behavior, that is, a behavior one regularly chooses to engage in, in order to reinforce participation in a low probability behavior, i.e., a behavior one does not regularly choose to engage in.

David Premack first introduced this concept in the mid-1960s to account for results found in a new experimental procedure he had developed in his research with rats. In Premack's research, a rat was first placed in a box that allowed it to run on a wheel or drink water from a spout as freely as it wanted. Baseline data were collected on the amount of time the rat spent engaging in each behavior. In a second phase, the rat was required to engage in a specified amount of one activity (e.g., drinking) in order to gain the other activity (running). Then the contingencies were reversed, that is, the rat was required to engage in running in order to get drinking. Premack found that when a behavior was more probable (occurred more often than the other behavior) during the initial baseline phase, it could be used to increase (beyond baseline levels) the probability that the less frequent behavior would occur.

Based on this work, Premack suggested that reinforcement can involve contingency between behaviors, blurring the line between response (behavior) and reinforcer. Whereas response and reinforcer were historically thought of as two distinct, separate classes, Premack defined them by their function in a particular situation and their relative probabilities in that situation. A behavior can act as a reinforcer for other behaviors that are lower in probability *and* can be a reinforceable behavior when contingent on other more probable behaviors. In practice, basing contingencies on the probabilities of behaviors should increase the ability to predict the effectiveness of a reinforcer. If we know that a child freely chooses to draw pictures more often than read books, then we know that the former is more likely an effective reinforcer compared to the latter *and* that it may even be used to reinforce the latter. Furthermore, the strength of any reinforcer is based on the relative disparity in probability between it and the instrumental behavior. If reading books and playing on the computer are relatively equally enjoyable activities for a child, neither is likely to be a strong reinforcer for the other. However, if reading books is highly preferred to playing on the computer, then, under the Premack principle, its possible role as a reinforcer for computer time is more certain.

Although the Premack principle is almost exclusively discussed as it relates to reinforcement, in theory it has applications to the use of contingent punishment as well. Specifically, less probable behaviors can be used to reduce the likelihood of more probable but undesirable behaviors if their introduction is made contingent upon engaging in the more probable behavior.

RESEARCH BASIS

The original research upon which Premack based his theory is described above, and a great deal of the literature to be found on this topic is based on research with animals, most notably rats and monkeys. Premack's original paradigm, that is, a paired baseline phase preceding contingency phases, is still a popular framework for research in this area. Although research published within the decade following Premack's original work was largely supportive of predictions based on the principle, work published between that time and the present has been more equivocal.

Premack's work led him to conclude that difference in probability was sufficient to establish reinforcement.

However, some studies suggest otherwise. What seems to be at the heart of this debate is whether the frequency of a behavior represents its true probability of occurring, since the former can be influenced by a variety of constraints in the environment (e.g., the availability of peers with whom to play). Extending this debate even further, some have questioned whether response probability is an appropriate measure of *preference* at all. In recent years, the Premack principle has been examined in comparison to competing theories, often with mixed results.

One competing theory, response deprivation, posits that a contingent behavior (e.g., playing outside) will serve to reinforce an instrumental behavior (e.g., completing one's chores) if, and only if, by engaging in a baseline amount of the instrumental behavior, a person is consequently deprived of the baseline amount of the contingent behavior. In other words, if a person (or animal) is unable to engage in an activity as much as he or she would like (as suggested by a baseline measure of how much the person chooses an activity when given free choice), then the opportunity to engage in that activity can serve as a reinforcer. The response deprivation theory is really a modification of the Premack principle, which suggests that a person's optimal level for each activity factors into whether or not that activity can serve as a reinforcer. In general, comparison research has been kinder to response deprivation than to the Premack principle.

Empirical examination of the Premack principle can be found across a variety of social science literature, with the majority of this focused on its role in interventions. Industrial/organizational psychology reflects published work on the application of the Premack principle in the workplace, for example, as a means of increasing worker productivity. Developmental psychology reflects published work on the principle's application with developmentally delayed individuals, for example, increasing on-task behavior in the classroom. The field of pediatrics reflects published work on the application of Premack to treatment compliance, and so on.

RELEVANT TARGET POPULATIONS

As indicated above, research efforts have often employed animals, particularly rats and monkeys, to test the strength and limits of the Premack principle. Animals have also been considered a population for the application of Premack as well. Dog trainers claim to use the Premack principle with dogs when they train first and have a play session later. But technically,

the Premack principle, as commonly taught in education settings, would not apply to dogs because the principle implies self-management and understanding of what is in one's best interest.

The principle is most popularly discussed in its application to children. Teacher and parent training manuals and workshops regularly tout the application of Premack, even if not in name. There is also a significant amount of literature on the use of Premack with individuals with developmental disabilities. Although Premack is not a "treatment" per se, it is regularly used in intervention programs. The principle has obvious applications within token economies (e.g., in the classroom, in hospital wards), particularly for those who refuse tangible rewards. It is typically less costly than interventions built around object-based reinforcers. In addition, it is regularly used in work settings as a means of shaping worker productivity.

COMPLICATIONS

Experiments on the Premack principle suggest that reinforcers cannot be defined independently of the responses that they reinforce. In Premack's original work with rats, drinking reinforced running when drinking was more probable than running, but running reinforced drinking when the probabilities were reversed. The conclusion to be drawn is that *reinforcers are relative and not absolute*, and that their important properties are based on the responses for which they provide an opportunity. In practice, this means that a therapist, business manager, and so on must have extensive a priori knowledge of the relative behavior probabilities of the individuals or groups with whom they are attempting intervention. Historically, attempts to gather this information would be focused on the frequency of occurrence; however, as indicated above, there are questions about whether frequency is an appropriate index of probability.

Some research suggests that the principle does not always hold true. Specifically, research appears to indicate that deprivation (relative to baseline probability) of the contingent behavior is necessary to create conditions for reinforcement. Thus, although a behavior (playing outside) is more probable than another (doing homework), it will not serve as a reinforcer if the individual is able to play outdoors as often as he or she would freely choose. The "response deprivation" modification to the principle focuses more on the optimal level for each activity as a key in determining a behavior's reinforcing qualities.

CASE ILLUSTRATION

A successful college professor discovered early on in her career that activities that she enjoyed and regularly engaged in were becoming a distraction from making progress toward tenure. "Dr. Lee" spent time each day reading her e-mail, surfing the Internet, reading the newspaper, and watching television. Although she had a strong preference for these activities, she was not regularly attending to more necessary but less preferred activities such as preparing her lectures, organizing her office, and writing manuscripts.

After delivering a lecture to her undergraduate learning class on reinforcement, which included some discussion of the Premack principle, Dr. Lee decided to create a probability hierarchy for herself in order to shape her own professional productivity. Over a 3-week period, Dr. Lee monitored her activities (without modifying them) and kept a diary of her daily activities along with a rating of how much she enjoyed each activity. She then created the brief hierarchy that follows, from her most probable behaviors to her least probable behaviors:

1. Watching television

2. Reading e-mail

3. Reading the newspaper

4. Surfing the Internet

5. Taking a walk

6. Cooking for friends

7. Cleaning her office

8. Reading journal articles

9. Writing manuscripts

10. Preparing lectures

Dr. Lee then created a daily schedule in which she did not allow herself to watch television or read the newspaper unless she had first spent an equivalent amount of time reading journal articles, writing professional papers, or preparing lectures. Dr. Lee continued to collect data on her activities over the next 3 weeks. After the new schedule had been in place for 3 weeks, Dr. Lee reviewed her work productivity. She found that during this period she had read 100% more journal articles than previously, she had completed a manuscript, which had been sent to a journal for review, and she was now several weeks ahead in her lecture preparation, rather than completing lectures the night before class. Although Dr. Lee's system involved the initial deprivation of certain activities, for example, watching television, her increased productivity at work allowed her to enjoy her preferred activities, when she earned them, without the guilt and worries that had previously plagued her.

—*Brian Rabian*

See also: *Contingency Management (Vol. II), Differential Reinforcement of Other Behavior (Vols. I, II, & III), Operant Conditioning (Vols. I, II, & III), Positive Reinforcement (Vol. II), Reinforcement (Vols. I & III)*

Suggested Readings

Allison, J. (1989). The nature of reinforcement. In S. B. Klein, B. Stephen, & R. R. Mowrer (Eds.), *Contemporary learning theories: Instrumental conditioning theory and the impact of biological constraints on learning* (pp. 13–39). Hillsdale, NJ: Erlbaum.

Charlop, M. H., Kurtz, P. F., & Casey, F. G. (1990). Using aberrant behaviors as reinforcers for autistic children. *Journal of Applied Behavior Analysis, 23,* 163–181.

Danaher, B. C. (1974). Theoretical foundations and clinical applications of the Premack principle: Review and critique. *Behavior Therapy, 5,* 307–324.

Klatt, K. P., & Morris, E. K. (2001). The Premack principle, response deprivation, and establishing operations. *The Behavior Analyst, 24,* 173–180.

Konarski, E. A., Johnson, M. R., Crowell, C. R., & Whitman, T. L. (1981). An alternative approach to reinforcement for applied researchers: Response deprivation. *Behavior Therapy, 12,* 653–666.

Mazur, J. E. (1975). The matching law and quantifications related to Premack's Principle. *Journal of Experimental Psychology: Animal Behavior Processes, 1,* 374–386.

Premack, D. (1963). Prediction of the comparative reinforcement values of running and drinking. *Science, 139,* 1062–1063.

Timberlake, W., & Allison, J. (1974). Response deprivation: An empirical approach to instrumental performance. *Psychological Review, 81,* 146–164.

PROBLEM-SOLVING TRAINING

DESCRIPTION OF THE STRATEGY

Children face problems every day, and some have more difficulties evaluating and coming up with viable solutions than others. Problem solving is a behavioral strategy that aids in the identification and definition of challenging situations, as well as the generation, selection, and activation of potentially effective responses. Clearly defining a problem situation and generating multiple solutions can enhance the likelihood that an effective response will emerge. Children with effective problem-solving skills are accepted by their peers, able to communicate effectively, and are cautious decision makers. In contrast, problem-solving deficits have been linked to many child and adolescent problems, including academic failure, school dropout, substance use, conduct problems, teenage pregnancy, and peer rejection. Thus, these skills are important for adaptive functioning.

Consistent with these findings, problem-solving training (PST) is based on the assumption that addressing relevant skills deficits will lead to some amelioration of a targeted clinical concern and that an individual's problem-solving ability can be enhanced by skills training. For example, PST can reduce impulsive behavior, replacing it with skills that allow the child to systematically generate and consider several more adaptive choices. The therapist's role in PST is to assist the client in defining the problem, generating alternatives, and learning how to evaluate and choose the best course of action for a specific problem. In addition, the therapist helps the client enact the chosen strategy through role playing, modeling, and addressing possible pitfalls prior to the problem solving attempt.

Although PST has evolved into several types of therapies, including interpersonal cognitive problem solving (ICPS), behavioral problem solving (BPS), social problem solving (SPS), and cognitive problem-solving skills training (PSST), the basic tenets of the treatments are quite similar. The following steps have been identified as key components in the remediation of problem-solving deficits:

1. General orientation and noticing feeling cues: Initial reactions to problem situations are often emotional rather than intellectual. Children can be overwhelmed by this emotional response, leading to impulsive reactions when carefully thought-out responses would be more adaptive. Thus, it is important for the child to learn feeling cues in order to assess the situation and determine that there is a problem to be solved. The therapist's role is to assist the child in expanding his or her emotions vocabulary and ask questions to focus the child on his or her emotional state.

2. Problem definition: Once the child has moved away from an emotional, reactive state, it is important that the child is able to define all aspects of the problematic situation. Problems are often ambiguous, making it very difficult for some children to articulate what is problematic about the situation. To assist in problem identification, the therapist should encourage the child to put the problem into words and consider that the problem can be seen from other viewpoints. Although such perspective taking can be difficult, it is important for children to be able to look at the problem from different angles, which may, in turn, allow for the generation of more effective strategies.

3. Generation of alternatives: Thinking of a variety of possible solutions (i.e., brainstorming) is the core of PST. The subsequent goal of this stage is to produce a range of potential responses from which an effective solution is chosen. Some children are more flexible thinkers than others, and it is not unusual for children who have problem-solving deficits to become stuck and only generate extreme solutions. Thus, during this phase, it is important to reserve judgment about the effectiveness of possible solutions and to continually encourage the child to generate a variety of responses. Furthermore, it is useful for the therapist to write down all of the generated solutions to help model organized thinking, behaving, and problem solving for the child.

4. Decision making: When deciding on a plan of action, it is important to consider the likely short- and long-term consequences of each possible response. The therapist's role is to ask questions that will help the child think carefully about the consequences for each course of action. After each possibility is examined, the therapist should read the list back to the child in order to demonstrate that there are in fact several options that the child can pursue. A course of action is then agreed upon by the child and the therapist. The therapist must be cognizant that the client may lack skills necessary to successfully execute some of the options, even if a chosen solution may be the most successful in solving the problem. If needed skills are lacking, another option should be considered while the child is taught the necessary skills. Once a choice has been made, the therapist assists the child in producing specific tactics for implementing the chosen response. Role-playing the chosen plan can help the child rehearse the skills, as well as identify possible pitfalls that can be addressed prior to the actual problem-solving attempt.

5. Verification: After a plan of action is chosen, the child attempts to solve the problem using the agreed-upon solution. The therapist and child should discuss the outcome in detail in order to determine if the response is effective in dealing with the problem. If the effort does not lead to successful problem resolution, the therapist and child start the process again until an effective means of problem solving is reached. Children often have a difficult time learning from past actions, and it is important for them to learn that problem solving is a process.

In sum, the child client is taught how to utilize a step-by-step approach to problem solving that increases flexibility in thinking and reduces impulsive responses that are less adaptive. Therapists play an active role in the skills training process by modeling the steps of problem solving within session, providing verbal cues that encourage the child to use the skills, and delivering feedback and praise that reinforces the correct use of skills. Thus, the child and therapist work as a team in order to enhance the child's problem-solving skills.

RESEARCH BASIS

Social problem solving (SPS), a particular approach focusing on social situations, is an often-studied application. SPS has been associated with improvements in peer functioning across numerous domains. For instance, SPS has resulted in improved role-taking abilities, prosocial orientation, group functioning in the classroom, and peer cooperation. Children who have participated in SPS are less withdrawn as evidenced by more frequent engagement with the peer group. SPS has also been successfully used to facilitate leadership training in adolescence. Despite these gains, enhancement of SPS skills has not been consistently linked with increased acceptance by the peer group. This may be in part due to methodological constraints. Specifically, short follow-up assessments are unable to measure gradual improvements in peer acceptance, which is more common than rapid changes after an intervention.

PST has also been used in the treatment of externalizing disorders with impressive results. In most cases, PST is a component of a larger treatment package, such as Lochman's Anger Management Training. Findings indicate that PST decreases impulsive, aggressive, and antisocial behavior at home, at school,

and in the community, and that these gains are maintained up to 1 year after intervention. In addition, treatment effects have been found for both inpatient and outpatient children. There are also findings indicating that combining PST with parent training where the parents are taught strategies to manage their child's behaviors (e.g., positive reinforcement, providing time-out) may be more beneficial than PST alone. Specifically, the combined treatment led to more marked gains as compared to the single treatments in areas of child aggression and antisocial behavior. Furthermore, the combined treatment led to a reduction in parent stress and family dysfunction, which are additional risk factors for children. Despite these encouraging results, questions remain whether improved problem solving is responsible for these changes in behaviors, since skill acquisition has not been consistently correlated with child behavioral adjustment.

Likewise, based on children's self-report, success has been found with internalizing concerns such as depression, loneliness, and social anxiety. However, it is unclear if the improvements were generalized to the home environment, since parent ratings did not differentiate between children who had received the treatment from those who had not. Discrepant findings may be due to the fact that children are more accurate reporters of internalizing symptoms as compared to outside observers (e.g., parents or teachers). In addition, most of the improvements were observed at a 1-year follow-up rather than immediately after the intervention. Thus, the acquisition of problem-solving skills may precede changes in behavior.

RELEVANT TARGET POPULATIONS AND EXCEPTIONS

PST is a component of most behavioral treatments and has been used successfully with children of most ages, from preschool to adolescence. The training programs have been used to target several behavior problems, including aggression, anger management difficulties, antisocial behaviors, impulsivity, off-task behaviors in the classroom, peer relationship difficulties, and coping with divorce, depression, and anxiety. Thus, the target population is quite large due to the applicability of PST to most age groups and a variety of adjustment problems.

Although PST can be used with most children, the program appears to benefit some children more than others. PST seems to be more effective in changing younger children's social behavior as compared to adolescents. Furthermore, at-risk children benefit more from the training than better-adjusted children, suggesting that problem solving is less effective when used as a preventative intervention. Despite this finding, children with several comorbid diagnoses who demonstrate academic delays, and who come from families with significant levels of impairment (e.g., parent psychopathology, family discord, coercive parenting), show less gains as compared to children without these additional risk factors.

COMPLICATIONS

Although there is considerable evidence that PST is effective, there are several questions that remain. Many researchers do not assess changes in cognitive processes; thus, it is unclear if PST results in acquisition of cognitive skills. When cognitive processes are measured, it is still uncertain if this change mediates or is responsible for changes in behavior. Findings indicate that problem-solving skill improvements often do not have a significant relationship with child adjustment and changes in behavior. For instance, it has been found that neither skill acquisition nor problem-solving ability is related to outcome, and that IQ was the single best predictor of adjustment. It should be noted that longer treatment programs lead to more social and behavioral gains. Thus, social-cognitive skills may be learned fairly quickly, but behavioral application may require longer interventions.

Another difficulty is that children with problem-solving deficits often generate as many solutions as other children but produce less effective strategies, or they choose maladaptive courses of action. As such, the rationale that generating several options increases the likelihood of choosing an adaptive response does not appear to be supported. In response, some clinicians do not focus exclusively on the number of solutions generated but consider quality as well. For instance, multiple aggressive solutions to a social problem would not be reinforced. Other clinicians choose to encourage as many solutions as possible in the generation phase and focus on evaluation afterwards.

CASE ILLUSTRATION

"Kathy" was an 11-year-old girl who lived with her divorced mother. Her father had limited contact with

her. After her parents' divorce, Kathy evidenced difficulties managing her anger, often verbally lashing out at her mother. She had also become angrier at school, leading to many fights with her friends. Distressed about the problems with her family and peers, Kathy started to feel hopeless. Her schoolwork began to suffer, and she withdrew from several activities. Her mother became concerned and referred her for treatment.

During the intake, her mother completed the Child Behavior Checklist (CBCL). A functional analysis was conducted to determine the circumstances that maintained Kathy's angry outbursts, and the Children's Depression Inventory (CDI) was administered. In addition, Kathy completed measures of problem-solving skills, including the Means-Ends Problem-Solving measure (MEPS) and the Awareness of Consequences Test (ACT).

Three phases of treatment were followed: an introduction to PST and goal setting, problem-solving skills acquisition, and behavioral application of learned skills. During the first phase, the rationale for problem-solving training was explained to Kathy and her mother. Kathy felt that PST would help her learn adaptive skills for modulating her anger, which would ultimately improve her feelings of sadness and hopelessness. Goals of reducing her anger outbursts with her family and peers were established.

The next phase consisted of learning step by step the problem-solving skills. Several teaching aids were used, including a poster listing the problem-solving skills and cue cards that Kathy took home. In addition, Kathy used cognitive rehearsal in order to assess what she would be thinking in problematic situations, helping her identify triggers and define the problem. The skills were practiced in session through question-and-answer and role-playing activities. For example, Kathy was having a difficult time responding to teasing without yelling at her peers. After generating several options, Kathy and the therapist agreed that she should walk away in order to cool off. This scenario was role-played in session. After this phase, Kathy once again completed the MEPS and ACT in order to assess the acquisition of key cognitive skills.

The behavioral application phase began after the needed skills were acquired. Each week, Kathy and her therapist would discuss a problem that Kathy needed help solving, eventually choosing a course of action. Kathy would try the chosen alternative during the week, and then the outcome would be discussed in session. For instance, Kathy tried walking away from her peers when they were being mean, which allowed her to calm down rather than yell at them. When discussed in session, Kathy realized that she was able to avoid a negative confrontation that would have further damaged her relationship with her friends and could possibly have gotten her into trouble. After several months of behavioral application, Kathy's mother completed the CBCL, and Kathy completed the CDI, the MEPS, and the ACT. Social-cognitive gains were maintained, and significant improvements were observed in her anger management, social interactions, and depressive symptoms.

*—Douglas W. Nangle,
Jessica M. Matthews, and Elizabeth J. Shepherd*

See also: *Problem-Solving Therapy (Vols. I & III), Social and Interpersonal Skills Training (Vol. II), Social Competence Treatment: Externalizing Disorders (Vol. II), Social Effectiveness Training (Vols. I & III), Social Skills Training (Vols. I & III)*

Suggested Readings

D'Zurilla, T. J. (1986). *Problem-solving therapy: A social competence approach to clinical intervention.* New York: Springer.

D'Zurilla, T. J., & Goldfriend, M. R. (1971). Problem solving and behavior modification. *Journal of Abnormal Psychology, 78,* 107–126.

Elias, M. J., & Tobias, S. E. (1996). *Social problem solving: Interventions in the schools.* New York: Guilford Press.

Haley, J. (1987). *Problem solving therapy* (2nd ed.). San Francisco: Jossey-Bass.

Hops, H., & Lewinsohn, P. M. (1995). A course for the treatment of depression among adolescence. In K. D. Craig & K. S. Dobson (Eds.), *Anxiety and depression in adults and children* (pp. 230–245). Thousand Oaks, CA: Sage.

Larson, J., & Lochman, J. E. (2002). *Helping schoolchildren cope with anger: A cognitive-behavioral intervention.* New York: Guilford Press.

Spivack, G., Platt, J. J., Jr., & Shure, M. (1976). *The problem solving approach to adjustment.* San Francisco: Jossey-Bass.

PROMPT

A *prompt* is a behavioral strategy that is used to promote the production of a target behavior that is to be increased. Prompts also may be used to promote the cessation of an undesirable behavior (i.e., while teaching a replacement behavior) or to promote maintenance and generalization of a behavior. Once the appropriate behavior occurs, reinforcement can be provided. There are several ways in which a prompt can be delivered, including verbal, auditory, written, gestural, or physical forms. Verbal, auditory, written, and gestural prompts are thought to be the least intrusive to the individual learning the new behavior, whereas physical prompts typically are considered the most intrusive.

Research has demonstrated that prompts are useful for promoting desirable behavior in many individuals with a wide range of presenting concerns. For example, prompts have been used in teaching skills to children with autism and other developmental disabilities, in teaching children with anxiety disorders to use anxiety reduction strategies, in behavioral parent training programs aimed to improve child noncompliance and disruptive behavior, and in classroom settings with children with behavioral (e.g., attention-deficit/hyperactivity disorder) or academic problems. Prompts are useful not only when individuals are motivated to change their behavior (e.g., a child who wants to stop nail biting but does not always realize when the behavior is occurring) but also when behavior change is motivated by a third party. In this instance, prompts promote the occurrence of desirable behaviors so that reinforcement may be provided.

Parents may use verbal prompts when teaching children polite manners. For example, when a parent says, "Remember to say thank you," they are using a verbal prompt. Similarly, other auditory cues may be used to prompt a behavior. For example, parents may implement the technique of setting a timer and using the timer buzzer as a prompt to provide specific praise to a child who is behaving appropriately. Other, yet similar, prompts may be written or visual. For example, a child who has difficulty getting items together to take to school each morning may benefit from a written prompt such as a checklist of necessary items taped to the door. This way, each day before leaving the house, the child walks up to the door and sees the visual prompt, which serves as a cue for the child to make sure all items have been collected before leaving for school. Gestural prompts include the use of body movements that are designed to promote the occurrence of the desirable behavior. Parent-training programs implement the use of gestural prompts when teaching children to comply with instructions. For example, when parents give instructions to put a toy away in a box, they are taught to point from the toy to the box, hence implementing the use of a gestural prompt. Finally, physical prompts are used when other, less intrusive prompting strategies have been ineffective at promoting the desirable behavior. For example, a hand-over-hand, physical prompt may be used to teach personal hygiene and hand-washing skills to a child. Once an individual has acquired the target behavior, prompts can be faded. This means that the level of intensity of the prompt is decreased gradually until the desired behavior occurs independently.

—Alisa B. Bahl-Long

See also: Behavioral Treatment in Natural Environments (Vols. I & III), Differential Reinforcement of Other Behavior (Vols. I, II, & III), Operant Conditioning (Vols. I, II, & III)

Suggested Readings

Kazdin, A. E. (2001). *Behavior modification in applied settings* (6th ed.). Belmont, CA: Wadsworth.

Rathvon, N. (1999). *Effective school interventions: Strategies for enhancing academic achievement and social competence.* New York: Guilford Press.

PUBLIC POSTING

Public posting is a strategy, often used in classroom settings, in which publicly displayed charts, pictures, or posters are used to increase appropriate academic or other classroom behaviors. Currently, these goals are achieved by placing emphasis on desirable and appropriate behaviors. Historically, however, public posting strategies were used to record inappropriate behavior (e.g., teachers writing the names of children who misbehaved on the blackboard). The success of public postings is based on the assumption that public display of appropriate instances of behavior either reinforces these behaviors or provides the opportunity for reinforcement by others.

Public postings may be displayed in a variety of formats, depending on the targeted behaviors. In addition, public postings may be used to address individual child behavior or group (i.e., whole-classroom) behavior. Typically, information is displayed on charts that track daily progress. However, public posting strategies used in conjunction with whole-classroom

behavior management programs may track progress over brief, discrete periods of time.

For example, one strategy used to improve academic class averages is to publicly display individual grades (without names), as well as the calculated daily class average. This may be used for daily quiz grades, number of completed worksheet problems, writing and language performance, and so on. Another use of public posting is to improve desirable classroom behaviors, such as class participation, attendance, and prosocial behaviors. Some interventions designed to address classwide behavior management endorse the use of public posting of appropriate behaviors for brief periods of time, allowing the individual or group of individuals to earn reinforcers for appropriate behaviors multiple times each day. Hence, the public posting of points earned (e.g., smiley faces, stars) refers to a designated period of time only.

Several components enhance the success of public postings. The system must be in a conspicuous place that is visible to the targeted individuals. Also, the information posted must be meaningful to those who will be viewing it. By including a goal-setting component, criteria (that may change over time as the targeted behavior improves) are set to guide student performance. Finally, posting of data must be as immediate as possible, and the postings must elicit positive reinforcement. It is important to note that the most effective public posting systems are combined with praise and immediate performance feedback.

—Alisa B. Bahl-Long and Stacy B. Fried

See also: Behavioral Treatment in Natural Environments (Vols. I & III), Positive Reinforcement (Vol. II), Reinforcement (Vols. I & III)

Suggested Readings

McNeil, C. B. (2001). *Tough class discipline kit.* Longmont, CO: Sopris West.

Rathvon, N. (1999). *Effective school interventions: Strategies for enhancing academic achievement and social competence.* New York: Guilford Press.

Rhode, G., Jenson, W. R., & Reavis, H. K. (1992). *The tough kid book: Practical classroom management strategies.* Longmont, CO: Sopris West.

Wolfe, L. H., Heron, T. E., & Goddard, Y. L. (2000). Effects of self-monitoring on the on-task behavior and written language performance of elementary students with learning disabilities. *Journal of Behavioral Education, 10,* 49–73.

PUNISHMENT

"Nature, if not God, has created man in such a way that he can be controlled punitively. . . . The need for punishment seems to have the support of history, and alternative practices threaten the cherished valued of freedom and dignity."

Burrhus Frederic Skinner (1971 p. 75)

DESCRIPTION OF THE STRATEGY

In colloquial terms, punishment has moral overtones: an unpleasant thing done to people who "deserve" to be punished due to violations of laws or social norms. From a behavioral perspective, punishment has a neutral and operational definition that is not necessarily linked to the hedonic value of the stimuli involved or the intent of the punishment. Punishment is defined as an operation or environmental change that, when made contingent on behavior, reduces the probability or likelihood of that behavior in the future. In other words, certain results or consequences of behavior, whether caused by or coincidental with the behavior, serve to decrease the probability of that behavior in the future. This process is called punishment in behavioral terminology. There is no judgment as to whether the punishment was deserved or the outcome was beneficial, but rather punishment is a process whereby the rate of behavior is reduced. The term *punishment* can describe both the *procedure* involving the delivery of a punisher and the *effect* that results from the operation (i.e., decrease in responding).

Punishment can occur either by the introduction of a stimulus contingent upon a behavior or by the termination of an ongoing stimulus situation. The term *positive punishment* describes the process of adding or presenting a punishing stimulus after a behavior or response has been performed. Generally, these stimuli are considered to be aversive or unpleasant. The presentation of an aversive stimulus is the most familiar form of punishment, and it corresponds most closely with the layperson's concept of punishment. All animal species need punishment in the behavioral sense, as it serves to teach the organism which behaviors lead to pain, discomfort, or danger and to avoid those dangers in the future. Touching a hot stove, even if accidental, results in a more careful approach to the stove in the future. Without this learning mechanism,

organisms would be doomed to repeat behaviors that may result in discomfort, injury, or even death.

Punishment can also occur when an ongoing stimulus situation is terminated contingent upon a response or behavior. This process is called *negative punishment*. The ongoing stimulus situation is usually assumed to be positive, pleasant, or enjoyable so that its termination is unpleasant. For example, a teenage boy enjoying his date accidentally calls her by another girl's name. The date becomes upset and, perhaps, asks to be taken home, thereby turning the pleasant interaction between boy and date into an unpleasant one. The boy is less likely to call his date by another name in the future as a result of her reaction (a consequence of his behavior), and therefore the process of punishment has taken place. Behaviorally defined, if a contingent reduction in reinforcement density leads to a decrease in the rate of a behavior, the behavior can be said to have been punished. Negative punishment forms the basis for common punishment techniques, such as time-out or grounding, that will be discussed later.

Positive Punishment

Therapeutically, positive punishment is generally used to decrease the occurrence of behaviors that may be dangerous to the individual or to others and should be combined with a reinforcement-based program designed to teach other more appropriate behaviors. These interventions usually involve the planned introduction of an aversive or unpleasant stimulus upon the occurrence of a predefined behavior. The most effective punishers are those that can be delivered immediately. As in the process of reinforcement, immediate delivery of the punishing stimulus is important, and delays in the presentation can dramatically reduce the effectiveness of the punisher or render it ineffective altogether. In addition, a punisher is more effective if it is resistant to having its intensity reduced or if the punisher can be avoided altogether by the behavior of the person being punished. For example, one technique for reducing unwanted behavior has been to squirt sour lemon juice into the mouth of a person contingent upon an undesired behavior. Clamping the mouth shut or physically resisting the lemon juice application can serve to reduce the amount of lemon juice in the mouth or avoid it altogether, thereby reducing its effectiveness as a punisher. An effective punishing stimulus should have unpleasant effects that are short lived. Lingering unpleasant effects may be associated with behavior that is actually desired, thereby inadvertently reducing it, or the effectiveness of subsequent applications for the target behavior may be reduced because the person is still experiencing the last application. As in the example of contingent lemon juice, once in the mouth, the unpleasant sensation may linger, making further applications less aversive, as they do not serve to increase the unpleasantness beyond what is already experienced.

Examples of punishing consequences that have been reported in therapeutic interventions using positive punishment range from mild verbal reprimands to contingent electric shock, and include aversive or unpleasant agents such as the lemon juice mentioned above, water mist sprayed to the face, aromatic ammonia (smelling salts) applied under the nose, pinching, and visual screening. The application of contingent electric shock is often perceived as the strongest and least acceptable punishing stimulus. However, there is substantial evidence supporting its rapid and dramatic effectiveness for treating severe self-injurious behavior and aggression. The assumption is that contingent electric shock may the most effective punisher based on its intensity. Given the above-stated requirements for an effective punisher, it may be that electric shock is effective based more on the properties of shock itself rather than the intensity. First, it can be delivered immediately and without personal contact if a remote-controlled device designed for use with humans is utilized. In addition, the person cannot escape from or reduce the intensity of the shock based on their behavior. If the duration of the shock is brief and if kept to as low an intensity as possible, the sensation disappears with the termination of the shock. The Self-Injurious Behavior Inhibiting System or SIBIS is an example of a device that was designed for use with humans. It has a number of electrical safeguards and uses standard 9-volt batteries to power its components. A mild electric shock can be delivered to the subject instantly, the shock lasts only 0.2 second, and is at an intensity that causes only a startle reaction with mild discomfort. Immediacy of delivery, short duration with nonlingering effects, and the inability of the person to reduce or avoid the shock make electric shock an effective punisher at lower intensities than often assumed and accounts for its superiority over other forms of punishers that do not have these qualities.

The above discussion of positive punishment referred to techniques in which a specific stimulus is contingently introduced in order to decrease the frequency of a behavior. Another approach is called overcorrection and involves requiring the person engaging in undesirable behavior to perform another set of behaviors contingent upon the undesirable behavior. Overcorrection is often not thought of as punishment, as it seems to be more of a teaching procedure, but because it reduces the future probability of the undesired behavior, it is by definition punishment. There are two types of overcorrection: *restitution* consists of requiring the individual to correct the environmental effects of the inappropriate behavior (e.g., apologizing, cleaning a room), and *positive practice* involves repeated practice of an alternative and appropriate behavior (e.g., writing an incorrect spelling word correctly 100 times). Restitution and positive practice can be combined or used separately.

Negative Punishment

As discussed earlier, the adjective *negative* refers to how the punishment comes about and does not have an evaluative meaning. The reduction in the rate of behavior is produced by a contingent reduction or termination of an ongoing positively reinforcing situation rather than by the contingent introduction of an aversive stimulus, as is the case with positive punishment.

The most common application of negative punishment is commonly called *time-out,* but the full name of the procedure is time out from positive reinforcement. Contingent upon a specified target behavior or behaviors, all sources of possible reinforcement are removed. This is commonly accomplished by sending a child to his or her room or to sit on a chair, based on inappropriate behavior. The assumption is that the child's room or being made to sit on a chair in an uninteresting part of the house will functionally reduce the child's access to reinforcing stimuli (e.g., toys, TV, social interaction) and therefore serves as a time-out from positive reinforcement. This is referred to as exclusionary time-out. If the source of reinforcement is primarily social, it may not be necessary to physically exclude the individual from others if others in the environment can withhold social interaction contingent upon inappropriate behavior. This is called inclusionary time-out. In both procedures, the effectiveness of the procedure depends on two factors. First, the ongoing situation (time-in) must be reinforcing to the individual, and second, there must be a dramatic reduction in reinforcement density imposed. An already bored child will not learn much by being removed to another boring situation contingent upon behavior. Similarly, a child who is sent to his or her room where there are toys, games, and so on may not learn to reduce the rate of the targeted inappropriate behavior.

Response cost is another negative punishment procedure and involves the *loss* of positive reinforcers such as tokens, points, or rewards as a consequence of the occurrence of a behavior. The procedure entails a penalty or a fine of some sort. Response cost is often used as a component of a positive reinforcement program (e.g., token economy), in which conditioned reinforcers are delivered for some desired behaviors and removed following inappropriate ones.

RESEARCH BASIS

There is strong research evidence for the effectiveness of punishment procedures in the therapeutic reduction of undesirable behaviors. The research has used primarily single-case designs rather than large *N*-group comparisons and has investigated punishment alone and in combination with reinforcement procedures.

For the reduction of severe and physically dangerous behaviors, research suggests that contingent electric shock is capable of producing rapid and dramatic reductions in targeted behaviors. Despite widely held beliefs, there is little research evidence for negative side effects from contingent electric shock treatment; indeed, the empirical evidence documents more positive than negative side effects.

It has been shown that the immediate delivery of a punishing stimulus coupled with the inability of the person receiving the punishment to reduce it or avoid it produces the greatest therapeutic results. In addition, treatments that combine punishment with positive reinforcement to teach appropriate alternative behaviors are the most effective. Continuous punishment (punishing every occurrence of the target behavior) is most effective for initial suppression of the behavior, and there is disagreement about whether intermittent punishment can be used to reduce the recovery of the behavior if the punisher cannot be administered on each occasion of the behavior. There is no substantial evidence suggesting that punishment leads to aggression by the person being punished. This phenomenon, called elicited aggression, has been demonstrated in animal research but only under very specific conditions that are not usually in effect when punishment is used with humans.

RELEVANT TARGET POPULATIONS AND EXCEPTIONS

Most commonly, the therapeutic use of punishment has been investigated with typically developing children and in the population of individuals with mental retardation or developmental disabilities. Because these populations are vulnerable to abuse, misuse and overuse of punishment was not uncommon, and a strong antiaversive, antipunishment advocacy movement arose beginning in the late 1980s. As a result of this movement, there has been a significant decrease in the inappropriate use of punishment and a dramatic reduction in research on punishment techniques. However, there are many appropriate uses of punishment, and its systematic inclusion into overall treatment programs can produce significant therapeutic results. Care must be taken to ensure the rights of individuals subjected to punishment, and this is accomplished by utilizing strong oversight committees, advocacy groups, or legally appointed guardians.

COMPLICATIONS

Opponents of punishment argue that punishment dehumanizes individuals and results in side effects worse than the original behavior. However, as stated above, there is little empirical evidence for negative side effects of elicited aggression when using punishment. Terms such as *dehumanization* are subjective, and there is much room for disagreement on the relative benefits of treatment versus the potential for misuse or abuse. In addition, because punishment can produce very dramatic and rapid effects, some argue that its success itself can lead to an overreliance on it to the exclusion of positive reinforcement procedures or environmental changes that may also be therapeutic. Careful and intense monitoring of punishment programs is needed by trained professionals to guard against these complications.

CASE ILLUSTRATION

"Jim" was a 14-year-old male with a diagnosis of autism, severe mental retardation, and Tourette's syndrome with a history of aggressive behaviors. Over a period of 3 months, Jim had drastically reduced his food intake, resulting in a 35-pound weight loss in the absence of any medical explanations. This prompted a referral to a behavioral feeding program.

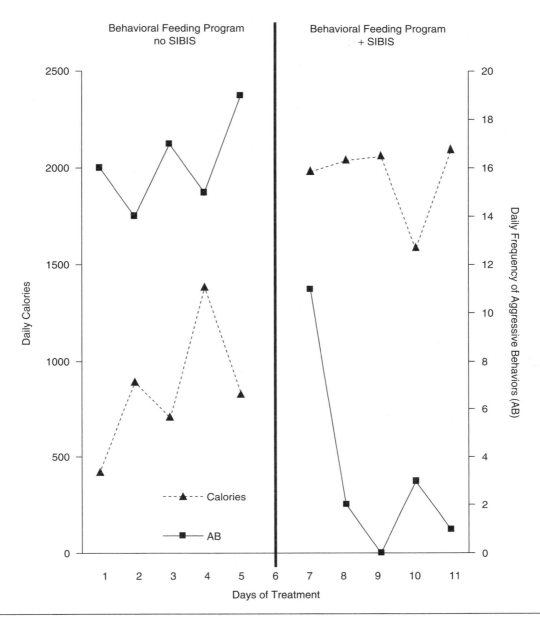

Figure 1   Frequency of aggressive behavior (AB) and daily calories consumed

Upon referral, and following a thorough behavioral history that failed to identify precise factors that triggered Jim's food refusal and subsequent weight loss, it was decided to admit Jim to a medical hospital for a behavioral feeding program to promote weight gain and increase the variety of his diet. The behavioral plan involved the following components: manipulation of hunger to increase acceptance of nonpreferred items, positive and negative reinforcement of eating, and extinction (by ignoring) of inappropriate (spitting, throwing, and

expelling food) and aggressive (biting, kicking, hitting) behaviors.

Functional assessment throughout the first 5 days of treatment indicated that inappropriate and aggressive behaviors were most likely maintained by escape from eating or nursing interventions (blood draws, bathing). These behaviors were extremely difficult to extinguish and were compromising his relationship with the medical staff. Jim's aggressive and inappropriate behaviors were blocking the effectiveness of the feeding treatment intervention, thereby impacting his overall heath and nutrition. For these reasons, it was deemed necessary to address his aggressive behaviors that could not be ignored (severe physical aggression and spitting in caregiver's face) by using contingent electric shock as administered by the SIBIS to decrease interfering behaviors. SIBIS was introduced on Day 6 and used contingently to treat aggressive behaviors throughout the remaining feeding interventions at mealtime only.

As seen on Figure 1, the introduction of the punishment component to the ongoing positively based feeding intervention produced large decreases in severe and long-standing aggressive behaviors and significant improvements in Jim's eating behaviors. This resulted in adequate weight gain and nutritional status. In addition, he began to exhibit a number of positive behaviors such as increased sociability and communication with staff, which in return resulted in positive reinforcement from staff who had avoided him for fear of his aggressive kicking and spitting. Positive side effects clearly outnumbered negative side effects. He was discharged after 10 days of treatment eating an adequate and nutritionally balanced diet and with his aggressive behaviors essentially eliminated. The use of punishment in this case speeded treatment, resulted in the return of natural reinforcers in his environment, and made it possible to eliminate his nutritional deficits.

—Thomas R. Linscheid and Sarah-Jeanne Salvy

See also: *Aversion Relief (Vols. I & III), Aversive Conditioning (Vol. II), Behavioral Treatment in Natural Environments (Vols. I & III), Goldiamond, Israel (Vols. I & III), Operant Conditioning (Vols. I, II, & III), Overcorrection (Vols. I, II, & III), Schedule-Induced Behavior (Vol. III), Skinner, Burrhus Frederic (Vols. I, II, & III)*

Suggested Readings

Kazdin, A. E. (2001). *Behavior modification in applied settings* (6th ed.). Belmont, CA: Wadsworth.

Lerman, D. C., & Vorndran, C. M. (2002). On the status of knowledge for using punishment: Implications for treating behavior disorders. *Journal of Applied Behavior Analysis, 35*, 431–464.

Linscheid, T. R. (1993). The development and evaluation of the Self-Injurious Behavior Inhibiting System: A personal perspective. In R. Van Houten & S. Axelrod (Eds.), *Behavior analysis and treatment* (pp. 345–365, xvii, 388). New York: Plenum.

Maag, J. W. (2001). Rewarded by punishment: Reflections on the disuse of positive reinforcement in schools. *Exceptional Children, 67*, 173–186.

Mulick, J. A. (1990). Ideology and punishment reconsidered. *American Journal on Mental Retardation, 95*, 173–181.

Saadeh, W., Rizzo, C. P., & Roberts, D. G. (2002). Spanking. *Clinical Pediatrics, 41*, 87–88.

Stein, M. T., & Perrin, E. L. (1998). Guidance for effective discipline: American Academy of Pediatrics Committee on Psychosocial Aspects of Child and Family Health. *Pediatrics, 101*, 723–728.

R

REGULATED BREATHING

Regulated breathing is a behavior therapy technique that involves an effort to slow an individual's breathing rate to below the usual rate and to install a regular breathing rhythm. Regulated breathing therapies, or "relaxed breathing" therapies, are commonly used in combination with other relaxation techniques for reducing physiological tension and arousal and for treating a variety of stress-related conditions. Research has demonstrated the effectiveness of regulated breathing as a part of treatment packages that have addressed conditions such as panic, headaches, chronic pain, asthma, hypertension, and irritable bowel syndrome, as well as for a number of anxiety-related disorders, including stuttering, sports performance anxiety, and panic disorder. In addition, regulated breathing techniques have been used effectively with children, adolescents, and adults involved in relaxation training as treatment for the various stress and anxiety-related conditions.

The notion behind the need for regulated breathing is that improper breathing can result in chronically altered levels of carbon dioxide in the blood. Carbon dioxide is considered to be a vital gas that must be maintained at certain levels in the blood to regulate the chemical (pH) balance in the blood. Too little or too much carbon dioxide can result in physiological distress (i.e., tension). It is believed that regulated breathing then helps reestablish metabolic balance and therefore produces relaxation. It is also true, however, that individuals who are working to regulate their breathing are performing voluntary actions that may serve as a source of distraction from anxious or distressing thoughts. This too may help calm an individual and reduce arousal. Either way, regulated breathing is thought to result in relaxation and to reduce or stop emotional distress.

Diaphragmatic breathing is the most common type of regulated breathing that is taught. The diaphragm is the major muscle involved in breathing. It sits underneath the lungs. For an individual to inhale, the diaphragm must contract and descend, expanding the belly. This allows the lungs to fill. There are other muscles around the chest that also assist with breathing by expanding the ribs and raising the chest and shoulders, making room for air to fill the lungs. Diaphragmatic breathing involves focusing on breathing with the diaphragm and minimizing the use of chest breathing muscles. The goal is often to slow respiration by 50% below typical breathing rates. The method consists of slow, deep, abdominal inhalations for a few seconds, followed by slow exhalations. Clients are often asked to count slowly and silently while practicing, aiming for 6 to 8 breaths per minute, which is significantly less than the 12 to 15 breaths per minute typical for most people. Therapists often place a large book or telephone directory on the abdomen to provide feedback to the individual regarding the use of a proper breathing technique. The weight of the book provides continuous feedback and helps increase and maintain awareness about the use of the diaphragm when breathing.

Paced respiration is another regulated breathing technique that involves inhaling and exhaling at a predetermined rate, usually with the help of some external pacing device such as a metronome. The metronome, or other pacing device, helps the client breathe at a slow preset rhythm. In teaching either diaphragmatic breathing or pace respiration, the focus on breathing is typically just one component of a treatment designed to reduce distress and produce relaxation. Regulated breathing is usually used in combination with other techniques such as relaxing specific muscle groups (e.g., progressive muscle relaxation), reciting mantras (meditative techniques), or techniques designed to alter or replace distressing thoughts.

Although teaching regulated breathing techniques typically does not involve the use of specialized equipment, there are several feedback systems that are readily available and easily used. Strain gauges are stretchable tubes that wrap around the abdomen or chest. These sensors detect the degree of expansion during inhalation, allowing for monitoring and feedback about breathing patterns. Trainers may also attach a small temperature monitor just below the nostrils to detect changes in temperature of inhaled and exhaled air. A computer-based display depicts temperature peaks (exhalation) and valleys (inhalation) to the client, who then strives to produce temperature curves of about the same size and duration.

Regulated breathing appears relatively straightforward, and many practitioners commonly use regulated or relaxed breathing techniques for reducing tension and arousal and for treating stress-related disorders. However, some experts caution against employing these methods without a strong understanding of breathing physiology and measurement. Slowing the rate of breathing may improve metabolic balance, but it may also create further imbalance and generate breathing complications that heighten rather than relieve tension and distress. Nevertheless, regulated breathing is rarely used alone, and when used in combination with other relaxation therapies, behavioral therapies, or stress management techniques, it can be an important source of positive influence on overall physiological and psychological well-being.

CASE ILLUSTRATION

A 6-year-old boy presented with recurrent headache activity. He had been evaluated by neurology, and standard attempts at medical intervention had proven ineffective. Assessment suggested that the headaches were stress related and occurred most frequently during school days in the afternoon. The boy was taught to use relaxation as a means of controlling stress. Relaxation was achieved using diaphragmatic breathing,

a regulated breathing technique. Using a mirror, the instructor taught the boy to observe and notice the differences between upper chest breathing and lower abdominal or diaphragmatic breathing. A book was placed on the boy's stomach to help amplify and provide feedback about changes in the diaphragm when breathing; the boy was to observe the book raising when breathing in and lowering when breathing out. Daily 10- to 15-minute practices of slow, deep diaphragm breathing by the boy were combined with his use of the breathing technique whenever headache onset was first noticed. Over 2 to 3 weeks, his headache activity gradually reduced in frequency and intensity.

—*Keith D. Allen and Richard J. Cowan*

See also: *Applied Relaxation and Tension (Vol. III), Biofeedback (Vols. I, II, & III), Breathing Retraining (Vol. I), Cue-Controlled Relaxation (Vols. I & III), Progressive Muscular Relaxation (Vols. I & III), Relaxation Strategies (Vol. III), Relaxation Training With Children (Vol. II)*

Suggested Readings

Fried, R. (2000). Breathing as a clinical tool. In David I. Mostofsky and David H. Barlow (Eds.), *The management of stress and anxiety in medical disorders* (pp. 100–118). Boston: Allyn & Bacon.

Schwartz, M. S. (1995). Breathing therapies. In Mark S. Schwartz & Associates (Eds.), *Biofeedback: A practitioner's guide* (2nd ed., pp. 248–287). New York: Guilford Press.

Woods, D. W., Twohig, M. P., Fuqua, R.W., & Hanley, J. M. (2000). Treatment of stuttering with regulated breathing: Strengths, limitations, and future directions. *Behavior Therapy, 31,* 547–568.

REINFORCED PRACTICE

Reinforced practice is one of several different types of "exposure" procedures that are used in the treatment of fears and phobias. Exposure-based treatments for fears and phobias typically involve requiring the individual to confront, for prolonged periods, a real or imagined version of the feared object or situation. Reinforced practice, in particular, involves rewarding an individual for remaining in the presence of a feared stimulus for progressively longer periods of time. Initially, the individual remains in the presence of the feared object for short, "tolerable" periods. Gradually, the expectations are increased, and rewards are only delivered for increasingly longer periods of time in the presence of that object or situation. Important elements of reinforced practiced include (a) gradual and repeated practice in approaching the object of fear or anxiety, (b) providing rewards for gains in the length of time exposed, and (c) providing feedback to the individual about measurable progress. Early uses of reinforced practice tended to rely solely on the praise of the therapist as a reward for treatment gains. However, praise alone may not be sufficient as a reward for many individuals, and more recent approaches to reinforced practice have emphasized the use of tangible rewards (i.e., treats, prizes, activities).

Numerous studies over the past 30 years have been conducted on the use of exposure-based treatments in general, demonstrating effectiveness in reducing fears and anxieties. Specific studies of reinforced practice have demonstrated its effectiveness with adults and children alike. Reports suggest effectiveness with children as young a 4 years of age. A wide variety of fears and anxieties have been treated, including fear of heights, fear of the darkness, fear of snakes, fear of storms, fear of open spaces, fear of closed spaces, fear of dental procedures, and fear of people.

Using reinforced practice can present some challenges, depending upon the nature of the fear or phobia. Although some forms of exposure therapy involve the individual simply imagining the distressing situation, reinforced practice requires the use of the actual feared object or situation. This can present a difficult obstacle in some cases. In addition, some fears and phobias can be especially challenging to solve due to well-established and long-standing avoidance behaviors that are resistant to treatment. Thus, reinforced practice, by itself, may not be adequate to address some complicated fears and phobia. Indeed, reinforced practice is often used in combination with other treatments such as relaxation. Finally, children are not always good reporters of their own thoughts and feelings, making it difficult to determine how much they can tolerate in establishing the criteria for rewards.

CASE ILLUSTRATION

A 5-year-old boy reported being afraid of the dark and would refuse to enter any room in which the light was not on. At night, the boy insisted that the light be on in his room, disrupting the sleep of a brother who shared the room. Treatment using a reinforced practice procedure involved placing the boy in his room,

with the light out, and shutting the door, telling him that he should exit when he felt the least bit afraid. He was told that he would have the chance to practice and that he could earn prizes (chosen from a box with various inexpensive prizes such as gum, candy, stickers, matchbox cars, pens, etc.) each time he stayed longer than his previous time. Feedback about the length of time in the room was displayed using a plastic "thermometer" with a sliding gauge that could be moved to show that he had spent more or less time in the room. Each increase in time was met with praise and a prize selection. Practice sessions occurred twice daily, in the evening, with a maximum of five practice trials each session. Treatment was terminated after the boy could remain alone in his dark room for 5 minutes across two successive sessions. The boy continued sleeping with the light on until Day 4, when he entered his dark room at bedtime and, without turning the light on, went to bed.

—Keith D. Allen and Richard J. Cowan

See also: *Differential Reinforcement of Other Behavior (Vols. I, II, & III), Operant Conditioning (Vols. I, II, & III), Positive Reinforcement (Vol. II), Reinforcement (Vols. I & III)*

Suggested Readings

Allen, K. D., Stark, L. J., Rigney, B. A., Nash, D., & Stokes, T. F. (1988). Reinforced practice during restorative dental treatment. *Journal of Dentistry for Children, 55,* 273–277.

Barrios, B. A., & O'Dell, S. L. (1998). Fears and anxieties. In E. J. Mash & R. A. Barkley (Eds.), *Treatment of childhood disorders* (2nd ed.; pp. 249–337). New York: Guilford Press.

Leitenberg, H., & Callahan, E. J. (1973). Reinforced practice and reduction of different kinds of fears in adults and children. *Behavior Research and Therapy, 11,* 19–30.

REINFORCER SAMPLING/ASSESSMENT

DESCRIPTION OF THE STRATEGY

Reinforcer sampling and assessment are procedures that guide—or serve as a component of—a variety of behavioral interventions. These procedures emerged from the field of behavior analysis and are easy for teachers, caregivers, and other providers to use. To define briefly, *reinforcer sampling* involves making freely available (i.e., administering noncontingently) a portion of a potential reinforcer (e.g., a taste of candy, movie preview) to increase the likelihood that the relevance and strength of the reinforcer will be maximized when it is made available contingently. *Reinforcer assessment* refers to the observation-driven or interview-based measurement of the relative strength of stimuli/events with regard to their reinforcing effects on behavior. These procedures are described in more detail below.

Reinforcer Sampling

A child's prior experience with an event or stimulus may influence the effect that the event or stimulus has on the child's behavior. For example, a child who has never tasted a particular piece of candy may be relatively uninfluenced by the statement "I will give you a piece of this candy if you share your toys with your brother." If the child is first given a taste of the candy, however, the child may be more inclined to share with his or her brother when this contingency is stated. Researchers have also noted that prior experience with an event or stimulus in one context may not carry over into other contexts. Thus, it is important that sampling of the reinforcer(s) occurs in a setting that is as similar as possible to that in which the reinforcer will later be made contingently available.

On a larger scale, reinforcer sampling procedures can serve several of the same purposes that are served by reinforcer assessment procedures (described below). That is, when a range of reinforcers are made freely (i.e., noncontingently) available for sampling, providers and caretakers will have an opportunity to observe the relative strength of each reinforcer as measured by how often and for how long the child comes into contact with each type of reinforcer. For example, when a series of activities are made freely available for sampling (e.g., listening to music, eating ice cream, playing a game), some children may engage in certain activities more often than other activities. Some activities/events may not be approached at all, indicating to observers that those events— relative to events that are more frequently approached— may be relatively weak reinforcers.

Reinforcer Assessment

Interventions designed to decrease undesirable and increase desirable behavior require knowledge about which stimuli have reinforcing or punishing effects on a child's behavior. For one child, a mother's attention may have strong reinforcing effects, whereas for another child, mother's attention may be a weak reinforcer relative to a certain type of candy, playing with the dog, or playing with neighborhood friends. Thus, the success of a well-designed intervention may largely be dependent on whether the most appropriate reinforcers have been selected for a particular child. To increase the likelihood that a 5-year-old will share a toy with his or her sister, for example, a parent might model sharing and also try to shape the child's sharing behavior by reinforcing successive approximations of sharing. However, if the parent then attempts to reinforce any instance of actual sharing with a nonreinforcing or weakly reinforcing stimulus, the child may not continue to share with the sister. Even more problematic, negative attention can have reinforcing effects for some children, and it is not unusual for a parent to give negative attention to a child who is not complying with requests. Thus, if a parent attempts to reinforce sharing with a nonreinforcing stimulus, and then responds with negative attention when the child fails to comply with additional requests to share, the parent may in effect *decrease* the child's likelihood of sharing, despite using a procedure that is generally effective in managing behavior.

Researchers and clinicians have developed a variety of strategies for conducting reinforcer assessments that aim to assess the relative strength (i.e., effectiveness as compared to other possible reinforcers) of a particular reinforcer or pool of potential reinforcers. For example, *reinforcer menus* have been used to give children the opportunity to select from a pool of potential reinforcers. Reinforcer menus can take the form of actual lists of potential reinforcers from which the child can select, or they can involve physically presenting to the child a tray of several different stimuli from which the child can select directly (e.g., candy, chips, stickers, and other alternatives). The use of reinforcer menus helps clinicians and caretakers to identify stimuli that can have relatively strong or weak reinforcing effects on behavior for a particular child. It is sometimes necessary to manipulate reinforcer menus (i.e., remove items from or add items to menus) when certain stimuli are never selected by the child or if one or two stimuli are almost always selected (thereby precluding assessment of the relative strength of a sufficient range of potential reinforcers).

Reinforcer surveys are another widely used method for conducting reinforcer assessments with children, adolescents, parents, and adults. These surveys can be used for a range of purposes (e.g., to guide an intervention that encourages appropriate vs. disruptive behavior, healthy vs. depressive behavior, or approach vs. avoidance behavior) but tend to be used by clinicians and providers to serve specific purposes for different populations. For example, clinicians using these surveys usually do so as a guide for addressing disruptive behavior of young children or depressive behavior of adults. Thus, for younger children, these surveys (e.g., Children's Reinforcement Survey Schedule) aim to identify specific stimuli/activities that a child reports liking to have (e.g., "Do you like stuffed toy animals?"), do (e.g., "Do you like coloring?"), or eat (e.g., "Do you like raisins?" "Do you like milk?"). For adolescents, these surveys (e.g., Adolescent Reinforcement Survey Schedule, School Reinforcement Survey Schedule) tend to place relatively less emphasis on tangible and edible reinforcers and greater emphasis on activities (e.g., "Going places with my friends," "Going places with my brother and/or sister," "Dating"). Reinforcer surveys for adults (e.g., Pleasant Events Schedule, Reinforcement Survey Schedule) place the greatest amount of emphasis on healthy activities (e.g., going to a movie, visiting friends, sewing, beachcombing).

Information gathered via reinforcement surveys, reinforcer menus, and other methods of reinforcer assessment or sampling can provide critical guidance to clinicians and caretakers. A child who is noncompliant but is observed (via reinforcer assessment/sampling procedures) to actively seek positive or negative maternal attention would likely respond well to an intervention that focuses on the level of attention that is provided for compliant versus noncompliant behavior. An adolescent who reports feeling depressed would likely respond well to an intervention that increases the regularity with which pleasurable activities occur, with pleasurable activities being identified on the basis of adolescents' reported frequency and desirability of events listed on the Pleasant Events Schedule.

RESEARCH BASIS

Several studies have evaluated *reinforcer sampling* procedures. The first and perhaps most influential studies were conducted by Ayllon and Azrin in the late 1960s with psychiatric inpatients. A token economy system was used in an inpatient facility such that patients were given tokens when they exhibited certain forms of desirable behavior. Patients were permitted to exchange these tokens for one of many potentially reinforcing events that were made contingently available to them (i.e., they had to earn tokens to engage in these activities) on a daily or weekly basis (e.g., listening to music, going for a walk outdoors). Yet Ayllon and Azrin noticed that certain events were rarely used by patients even though earlier evaluations suggested that these events were effective reinforcers. They then conducted several experiments in which patients "sampled" the reinforcing conditions of activities before deciding whether to use their token to do the activity, whereas standard facility procedures did not include a sampling component. For example, instead of patients being asked *inside* the facility whether they would like to use one token in exchange for going on a walk outdoors, patients were asked to line up *outdoors* before being asked whether they wanted to exchange a token for the activity. Remarkably, patients were more likely to use a token to go on a walk when they lined up outside (i.e., thereby sampling some of the reinforcing conditions of the activity) before making this decision. Similar findings were revealed for other activities, such as listening to music and watching a movie, suggesting that these procedures can maximize the *effectiveness* of a wide range of reinforcers.

The utility of *reinforcer assessment* procedures has been demonstrated in a wide range of settings and with several different populations. Structured assessment of the relative strength of a range of reinforcers is particularly useful when the primary goal of treatment is to restore or improve upon schedules of positive reinforcement for the child by changing the quality, level, and/or range of reinforcing stimuli that are made accessible as contingencies for behavior. In particular, observation-driven and interview-based assessment of reinforcers has been used successfully in studies with children and adolescents who have developmental disabilities or exhibit disruptive or depressive or, to a lesser extent, fearful behavior.

RELEVANT TARGET POPULATIONS AND EXCEPTIONS

Reinforcer sampling and assessment can be used with virtually any clinical population. However, whereas the research literature in reinforcer sampling and assessment is fairly well developed in the area of developmental disabilities, in psychiatric inpatient settings, and with adults who report depressed mood, relatively less research is available concerning the use of these procedures to treat other populations. In particular, the literature presently includes little information about the evidence base supporting these procedures for children and adolescents who present to outpatient settings with disruptive behavior, depressed mood, fearful responding, or a variety of other clinical problems.

It is important to note also that, particularly for young children seen for treatment in outpatient settings, clinicians should fully educate and enlist the assistance and cooperation of parents while working within their household rules. Ultimately, parents are the ones who make the rules regarding whether or not they allow their children to have, eat, or do certain things. Thus, it is important for clinicians to avoid using reinforcer sampling without reviewing the specifics of this strategy and the reinforcer(s) to be sampled with the child's parent. This ensures that a clinician does not permit a child to sample a certain piece of candy or game, for example, that the child is restricted from using at home. Also, by fully educating parents regarding the use of these behavioral techniques, parents will quickly learn how to adapt them to different contexts and settings and will be able to apply them to children of different ages with the use of more age-appropriate reinforcers.

COMPLICATIONS

Complications can arise when reinforcers are sampled but parents fail to follow through with contingencies after stating that reinforcers will be made available contingent upon specified behavior. That is, if the parent states a contingency and the child exhibits the specified behavior, the parent should follow through with the reinforcement contingency. Similarly, if the contingency is stated and the specified behavior is not exhibited, the parent should withdraw access to the reinforcer for an appropriate period of time.

Complications also can arise when, in the context of conducting reinforcer assessments, clinicians and caretakers indiscriminately apply the reasoning that "activities that are identified as pleasurable or desirable should be used as reinforcers" without giving adequate consideration to the risk associated with

access to these reinforcers. For example, events can be reported by adolescents to be "pleasurable" but simultaneously can be unhealthy when they significantly increase the risk for potentially dangerous conditions such as substance use, risky sexual behavior, or other physically or psychologically threatening events. Thus, when reinforcers are assessed, clinicians and caretakers should be cautious about balancing the strength and effectiveness of the reinforcer with the potential health risk associated with access to the reinforcer.

CASE ILLUSTRATION

Because most of the case illustrations available in the literature on reinforcer assessment/sampling involve psychiatric inpatient populations or children with developmental disabilities, an attempt is made here to illustrate two different populations to which these procedures can be applied. First, the use of reinforcer sampling with a 6-year-old boy with disruptive behavior is described. Next, the use of reinforcer assessment with a 16-year-old girl with depressed mood is illustrated.

Reinforcer Sampling

A father observed that his 6-year-old son, "Mark," had been increasingly noncompliant with relatively simple and infrequent requests during the past several weeks. One of the more frustrating instances of noncompliance was occurring on a daily basis: Requests to come to the dinner table were ignored by Mark until the father physically guided him to the table. The father wanted to change this behavior, and a variety of contingencies were considered that might motivate his son to come to the dinner table when requested to do so. Remembering that he had recently purchased a new game that had not yet been given to Mark, the father initially contemplated introducing it through the contingency system for coming to the table when prompted. However, being familiar with behavioral principles, he recognized that Mark's lack of prior experience using the game might play a significant role in determining whether an opportunity to use the game would motivate compliance. For this reason, in the middle of the following afternoon, the new game was given to Mark and was made temporarily freely available to him. As expected, Mark clearly enjoyed playing the game and did not get bored with it after a short time playing. Later that day, with the reinforcer having been sampled, Mark's father stated the following contingency as dinnertime approached: "If you come to the table now, you can play this game after dinner is over." Unexpectedly, on this occasion Mark again ignored this request, perhaps "testing" whether his father would follow through. However, because the father *did* follow through by withdrawing access to the game after dinner, Mark complied with his father's request with little hesitation on each subsequent day that the contingency was reintroduced at dinnertime.

Reinforcer Assessment

"Amanda," age 16 years, presented to an outpatient clinic with depressed mood. Results of an initial intake assessment revealed that a variety of environment stressors coincided with the onset of her depressed mood several weeks earlier. These stressors included the recent divorce of her parents and the recent relocation of a close friend to a different city. Furthermore, self-report assessment of Amanda's daily and weekly routine over the past several weeks revealed that she gradually had been engaging in considerably fewer "pleasurable" activities and had increasingly begun to isolate herself socially. Recognizing the relation between Amanda's activity level and mood, the clinician administered a reinforcement survey to identify a range of reinforcing life events that might be integrated into Amanda's weekly routine. Amanda identified a variety of healthy life events (e.g., going to the movies, phoning certain friends regularly, spending time with other friends) that she and her parent agreed could be integrated into her weekly routine. The clinician enlisted the help of Amanda's parent to ensure that Amanda was regularly prompted to engage in certain activities. These activities were gradually (re)introduced into Amanda's schedule, first with low frequency and with easier activities (e.g., phoning a particular friend twice per week) and later with more difficult activities (e.g., enroll in an extracurricular activity at school). As Amanda gradually began to increase the number and regularity of pleasurable/reinforcing activities in which she engaged, she reported reductions in depressed mood. Furthermore, because the activities in which she engaged were naturally reinforced by her social environment, her increased activity level persisted over time with minimal clinician contact, as did her healthier mood.

—*Kenneth J. Ruggiero and Ron Acierno*

See also: Behavioral Assessment (Vols. I, II, & III), Covert Reinforcer Sampling (Vol. I), Operant Conditioning (Vols. I, II, & III), Positive Reinforcement (Vol. II), Reinforcement (Vols. I & III)

Suggested Readings

Ayllon, T., & Azrin, N. H. (1968). Reinforcer sampling: A technique for increasing the behavior of mental patients. *Journal of Applied Behavior Analysis, 1,* 13–20.

Ayllon, T., & Azrin, N. (1968). *The token economy: A motivational system for therapy and rehabilitation* (pp. 88–103). New York: Appleton-Century-Crofts.

Cautela, J. R., & Kastenbaum, R. A. (1967). Reinforcement survey schedule for use in therapy, training, and research. *Psychological Reports, 20,* 1115–1130.

Kazdin, A. E. (1977). *The token economy: A review and evaluation* (pp. 157–158). New York: Plenum.

Lejuez, C. W., Hopko, D. R., & Hopko, S. D. (2001). A brief behavioral activation treatment for depression: Treatment manual. *Behavior Modification, 25,* 255–286.

Lewinsohn, P. M., & Libet, J. (1972). Pleasant events, activity schedules, and depression. *Journal of Abnormal Psychology, 79,* 291–295.

MacPhillamy, D., & Lewinsohn, P. M. (1971). *The pleasant events schedule.* Eugene, OR: University of Oregon.

Spiegler, M. D., & Guevremont, D. C. (1993). *Contemporary behavior therapy* (2nd ed., pp. 105–137). Pacific Grove, CA: Brooks/Cole.

RELAPSE PREVENTION

DESCRIPTION OF THE STRATEGY

Behavior therapists and clinical researchers have long recognized relapse prevention as an essential area of focus in the treatment of clinical problems. Relapse prevention strategies are defined as treatment procedures that aim to protect patients from the realistic threat that their clinical problems will recur or return to pretreatment levels. Behavior therapists historically have used the term *relapse prevention* vis-à-vis treatment of substance use problems, although this term also applies to a wide range of clinical problems, such as eating disorders, anxiety, depression, disruptive behavior, and sexual offending with some terminological modifications. For example, interventions for anxiety disorders include relapse prevention strategies that are designed to prevent what is frequently called *renewal, reinstatement,* or *return* of fear. Also, procedures described as addressing the *generalization* or *maintenance* of outcomes across time and settings relate to relapse prevention in important ways.

Behavioral interventions have been developed to treat children with a broad range of clinical problems, and many of these interventions commonly are delivered effectively in outpatient therapy settings. Despite the success of such interventions, however, risk of relapse may remain high when a child's experience with the *natural environment* does not change in meaningful ways throughout the course of treatment. For example, parents may learn and successfully role-play behavior management strategies for disruptive behavior in the clinic setting, but if parents fail to use such strategies reliably at home, it is unlikely that any short-term improvements in the child's disruptive behavior will be maintained over time. For a more traditional example, consider a substance-abusing adolescent who is temporarily placed in a restrictive environment, "successfully" treated, and then returned to an environment that might include permissive caretakers and regular contact with peers who use and encourage use of substances. Unless efforts are made to facilitate changes within the peer network, and unless parents learn strategies that enable them to exercise greater control over the adolescent's behavior, risk of relapse for this adolescent is likely to be high.

Behavior therapists use a variety of clinical techniques that can reduce risk of relapse. Techniques discussed here include functional assessment, identification of risk factors, psychoeducation, skills training, and behavioral rehearsal. *Functional assessment* helps clinicians identify the wide range of contextual cues or antecedents (e.g., situations, events, people) that are associated with the targeted behavior, as well as reinforcing or punishing consequences that typically follow such behavior. Identifying the antecedents and consequences for targeted behavior across multiple settings and contexts prepares clinicians to guide changes in the way the child relates to and experiences the natural environment. With such changes in effect, the natural environment is more likely to sustain improvements in behavior that occur as a function of treatment.

The *identification of risk factors* can occur in the context of functional assessment and entails the identification of factors that are associated with risk for returning to pretreatment behavior patterns. Factors are identified in collaboration with the child and family and may include risk factors that are present in the external environment (e.g., socializing with unsafe people) and/or correlates at the level of the individual (e.g., increased heart rate, muscle tension). Coping skills are developed to promote functional and safe ways of responding when these factors are recognized in the natural environment.

Psychoeducation refers to a range of techniques that therapists use throughout treatment to educate children and parents about the problem behavior and correct inaccurate interpretations (e.g., of events, situations, or behavior) that may be associated with relapse. For example, educating parents about relatively normal artifacts of behavior management strategies (e.g., extinction bursts, spontaneous recovery) can promote adherence to such strategies. Relapse prevention also is promoted by providing realistic interpretations of problem behavior after treatment has been completed. For example, helping substance-abusing children and parents distinguish between a "lapse" (a brief return to use) and "relapse" (a return to pretreatment use patterns) can foster a rapid return to nonproblem behavior patterns after short-term errors in judgment. Likewise, educating parents and children about the accurate appraisal of danger (e.g., the probability of harm) and the relation between avoidance and other forms of fearful responding can help prevent a return of fear.

Skills training involves teaching children and parents skills that are designed to alleviate behavioral, verbal-cognitive, or affective deficits that are associated with the targeted problem. Common skills training components include emotion identification (e.g., teaching the child to identify various physiological reactions that relate to fearful responding, such as rapid heart rate and sweating), coping skills (e.g., relaxation training), problem-solving skills, and communication/social skills, among others. Skills training is particularly important for relapse prevention because augmentation of general and broad-based skills can provide children with tools to cope with various circumstances that occur outside the therapy context and after therapy has ended. Parent-focused strategies typically entail behavior management exercises that reduce the frequency of the child's problematic behavior and increase the frequency of alternative, more desirable forms of behavior.

Behavioral rehearsal refers to the practicing of skills (e.g., coping skills, social skills) in situations that resemble those in the natural environment but where the clinician can provide feedback to enhance skill acquisition. For example, clinicians often provide opportunities to practice assertiveness and social skills by role-playing these skills during the session. The probability of relapse is decreased particularly when behavioral rehearsal is repetitive and closely mimics situations that the child encounters in the natural environment.

The extent to which sessions are arranged and spaced apart may also have important effects on relapse prevention. For some clinical problems, research has shown that long-term treatment effects can be improved in part by using a "stepped" approach to treatment termination in which more intense or restrictive treatments are followed by less intense methods. In this way, treatment is faded out gradually, thereby gradually transferring the responsibility for treatment maintenance from the clinician to the family and other sources of support. For example, common approaches in inpatient settings are to graduate children first to a day program and then to an outpatient program. In outpatient programs, relapse prevention can be affected by gradually spacing sessions from weekly to biweekly meetings and, finally, to monthly (i.e., "booster" or follow-up) sessions.

RESEARCH BASIS

The effectiveness of various relapse prevention techniques has not been widely researched among children. However, data from clinical research and human and animal laboratory experiments provide suggestions regarding the use of specific treatment procedures that are likely to reduce relapse. Taken together, these substantive literatures point to both *patient* and *treatment* factors that can influence the probability of relapse following treatment, and therefore deserve attention from clinicians.

Among *patient factors,* individuals with especially severe and/or chronic behavior problems are at increased risk for relapse. For example, studies have found that when anxiety-related (especially phobic) problems are targeted in treatment, individuals with particularly high physiological reactivity during fear-cue exposure prior to the start of treatment are more likely to exhibit a return of fear following treatment. Children and adolescents with weak social and family support networks are also at risk for a return of clinical problems following treatment. Several *treatment factors* are also associated with relapse prevention following treatment. Inconsistent treatment attendance and adherence, which hinders the effectiveness of the treatment itself, is associated with a return of clinical problems following treatment. Relapse prevention is enhanced when interventions are delivered across multiple settings and situations, when there is repeated practice, and when treatments are conducted using in vivo situations that closely approximate high-risk situations in the environment. Moreover, when exposure-based treatments for anxiety are used, relapse prevention is enhanced for cases in which fear habituation occurs within each session, the individual is not distracted during exposure, and fear intensity is not too high or too low.

RELEVANT TARGET POPULATIONS AND EXCEPTIONS

Relapse prevention efforts are applicable to virtually any clinical population, and comprehensive treatment for any clinical problem should incorporate strategies that guard against the recurrence of presenting problems. However, whereas the research literature in relapse prevention is fairly well developed in the area of substance use problems, relatively less research is available concerning relapse prevention for other clinical problems. Furthermore, the literature presently offers insufficient guidance in the use of evidence-based strategies for relapse prevention with children and adolescents.

It is important to note also that, particularly for young children, relapse prevention efforts do not necessitate the full understanding, awareness, or involvement of the child. Because the primary focus is on the child's natural environment, strategies to prevent relapse frequently emphasize the social environment of the child (e.g., parents, teachers, siblings) rather than the child specifically. This emphasis on the social network enhances the likelihood that the child's natural environment will sustain improvements in clinical problems that initially brought him or her into treatment.

COMPLICATIONS

A variety of complications can arise when behavior therapists attempt to prevent relapses of clinical problems. An adolescent who responds well to substance abuse treatment may encounter social circumstances or stressful events that were unanticipated by the clinician or adolescent, which may put the adolescent at risk for relapse. A child who is provided with successful treatment following a serious car accident may later be involved in a second accident that produces a return to pretreatment levels of accident-related anxiety and distress. Comorbidity also may be associated with increased likelihood of relapse. For example, a rape-victimized adolescent with comorbid substance abuse and posttraumatic stress disorder (PTSD) may be successfully treated for substance abuse, but unless successful treatment also is provided for PTSD, risk for substance abuse relapse may be high when the adolescent encounters strong reminders of his or her victimization.

Clearly, it would be inefficient and unproductive for clinicians to attempt to address all of the many ways in which clinical problems can reemerge following successful treatment. For this reason, relapse prevention efforts frequently focus on the most common and preventable circumstances under which relapse can occur. However, behavior therapists also use psychoeducation and related techniques to teach children and their caretakers to manage situations in which clinical problems appear to have reemerged. For instance, when clinicians *predict* potential complications, such as a child's disruptive behavior potentially reemerging in a new situation or that a child may attempt new forms of disruptive behavior while the parent works to extinguish other forms, parents are better prepared to manage these situations when they arise. Clinicians' anticipation of complications also is likely to have the effect of building the parents' confidence in the clinician's knowledge and also may improve their willingness to adhere to treatment recommendations. Furthermore, behavior therapists often provide parents with an understanding of the *principles* supporting the treatment procedures they are using, which allows parents to apply these principles to new forms of problem behavior and across multiple settings.

CASE ILLUSTRATION

"Kelly" was a 16-year-old girl who was raped and physically assaulted by a coworker several weeks before presenting for treatment. In the weeks leading up to treatment, she regularly experienced nightmares about her victimization, had difficulty falling and staying asleep nearly every evening, and experienced intense fear, panic, and distress in the presence of victimization-related cues. She engaged in various patterns of victimization-related avoidance in an attempt to control these reactions, such as avoiding people, places, situations, and conversations that reminded her of the assault. In addition, Kelly reported having frequent suicidal thoughts, was having considerable difficulty concentrating in school, and recently had discontinued her involvement in various social and extracurricular activities.

In the context of the clinical interview, a comprehensive functional assessment was conducted to identify the range of antecedents (setting events, discriminative stimuli) and consequences associated with the clinical problems Kelly reported. Assessment of antecedents led to an enhanced awareness of the range and nature of conditioned stimuli that produced Kelly's fearful responding. Such information, in turn, was used to develop a fear hierarchy that guided the exposure-based component of treatment. Initially, exposure-based treatment was conducted in an outpatient therapy setting on a weekly basis, with Kelly recounting her victimization in considerable detail. After a handful of these sessions, Kelly reported significant decreases in her frequency and intensity of nightmares, sleep difficulties, and fear in the presence of assault-relevant cues.

Despite the significant gains Kelly had made in treatment, the clinician recognized that she might experience a return of fear upon encountering a particularly salient cue or set of cues in the natural environment. For this reason, the clinician extended exposure exercises outside the therapy setting. Specifically, in vivo exposure to realistically nondangerous settings and cues was used to increase the likelihood that Kelly's gains would be maintained in the natural environment. In addition, the clinician provided education with regard to the adaptive nature of fear, the protective functions it serves, and the distinction between fearful responding to dangerous versus nondangerous situations. It was communicated to Kelly that, following the completion of treatment, she might encounter nondangerous situations in the future that lead her to respond fearfully. The clinician described that this is common among victims of traumatic events and explained how Kelly could respond effectively to future fear-eliciting (but nondangerous) situations by applying her knowledge about reducing fear through exposure (or approach/acceptance). Examples were used to ensure that Kelly could differentiate realistically dangerous from nondangerous situations.

At this point in treatment, assessment results revealed sustained improvements in the area of fearful responding and general distress. However, Kelly continued to spend little time outside the classroom with peers and doing extracurricular activities that she previously enjoyed. These observations raised questions about the heightened risk of relapse that may coincide with elevations in depressed mood. To address this issue, the clinician discussed with Kelly and her parents ways in which they might ensure that Kelly had increased contact with peers outside the classroom setting. Once Kelly reestablished regular contact with her peers outside the classroom setting, she elected also to reenroll in two extracurricular activities. This increased engagement in pleasurable activities coincided with further reductions in depressed mood. At this stage of treatment, improvements in fearful responding had been maintained, and Kelly reported significant reductions in depressed mood while denying suicidal thoughts. By targeting fearful responding and comorbid clinical problems through psychoeducation and at the level of the natural environment, the clinician had made efforts to reduce risk of relapse following treatment.

—*Kenneth J. Ruggiero and Steven R. Lawyer*

See also: *Generalization (Vols. I, II, & III),*
Relapse Prevention (Vols. I & III), Treatment
Failures in Behavior Therapy (Vols. I & III)

Suggested Readings

Bouton, M. E. (2000). A learning theory perspective on lapse, relapse, and the maintenance of behavior change. *Health Psychology, 19,* 57–63.

Bry, B. H., & Krinsley, K. E. (1992). Booster sessions and long-term effects of behavioral family therapy on adolescent substance use and school performance. *Journal of Behavior Therapy & Experimental Psychiatry, 23,* 183–189.

Carroll, K. M. (1996). Relapse prevention as a psychosocial treatment: A review of controlled clinical trials. *Experimental and Clinical Psychopharmacology, 4,* 46–54.

Fox, J. J., & McEvoy, M. A. (1993). Assessing and enhancing generalization and social validity of social-skills interventions with children and adolescents. *Behavior Modification, 17,* 339–366.

Gunther, L. M., Denniston, J. C., & Miller, R. R. (1998). Conducting exposure treatment in multiple contexts can prevent relapse. *Behaviour Research and Therapy, 36,* 75–91.

Hiss, H., Foa, E. B., & Kozak, M. J. (1994). Relapse prevention program for treatment of obsessive-compulsive disorder. *Journal of Consulting and Clinical Psychology, 62,* 801–808.

Irvin, J. E., Bowers, C. A., Dunn, M. E., & Wang, M. C. (1999). Efficacy of relapse prevention: A meta-analytic review. *Journal of Consulting and Clinical Psychology, 67,* 563–570.

Landrum, T. J., & Lloyd, J. W. (1992). Generalization in social behavior research with children and youth who have emotional or behavioral disorders. *Behavior Modification, 16,* 593–616.

Marlatt, G. A., & Gordon, J. R. (Eds.). (1985). *Relapse prevention: Maintenance strategies in the treatment of addictive behaviors.* New York: Guilford Press.

RELAXATION TRAINING IN CHILDREN

DESCRIPTION OF THE STRATEGY

Relaxation training (RT) refers to a variety of techniques and procedures used to reduce stress-related behavioral or physiological problems in children. Hypothesized to decrease both emotional and somatic reactions to stress, RT is often classified as an emotion-focused coping strategy, in contrast to more problem-focused strategies geared toward resolving and managing stressful events. Two of the more common variants of RT used with children are progressive muscle relaxation (PMR) and imagery-based relaxation (IBR).

Conceptualized as a sensory approach to relaxation, PMR attempts to directly influence somatic reactions to stress by helping children identify their own bodily sensations associated with tension and consciously relax muscles of the body on demand. To facilitate the recognition of stress-related bodily states, PMR incorporates a series of exercises that systematically instruct children to tense and relax various muscle groups in the body. Although the number and location of muscle groups used during PMR may vary, common muscle groups employed include toes, legs, hands, arms, chest, shoulders, stomach, forehead, cheeks, eyes, and nose.

Special attention should be given to preparing the child for PMR. Using developmentally appropriate language, PMR is typically introduced by explaining that the muscles in your body tighten up when you are nervous, upset, angry, or in pain, while they are loose when you are relaxed, happy, or having fun. RT is then framed as an educational strategy geared toward teaching how to recognize when the muscles of the body are tight and when they are loose. Children are then informed that the overall goal of the procedure is to (a) enable them to tell when they are tense and (b) relax their muscles by themselves when nervous, upset, angry, or in pain.

After presenting this rationale and clarifying any questions or concerns about the procedure, it is advisable for the therapist to model the procedure. While demonstrating how to tense and relax various muscle groups, the therapist encourages the child to ask questions so as to provide clarity on any ambiguous points. Modeling may also help alleviate any inhibitions that the child may have in assuming the bodily postures required during PMR.

After modeling PMR, the therapist instructs the child to get into a relaxed position, sitting upright in a chair or couch with the feet flat on the floor and the arms and hands at the side or in the lap. Instructions are also given to close the eyes, although it is occasionally necessary to allow highly anxious or apprehensive children to keep their eyes open during initial sessions. Deep-breathing strategies (e.g., party blower, paced counting, or blowing bubbles) are commonly incorporated into PMR as a means to further relax the child.

Once the child appears relaxed, the therapist systematically instructs the child to tense and relax various muscle groups. Age-appropriate analogies for tensing and relaxing each muscle group are often used to enhance the appeal of the process. Animals and objects such as cats, flies, mud, and lemons have been used in this manner. For example, the child is told to pretend that a fly is on the tip of the nose for several seconds, then instructed to wiggle the nose in order to get rid of it. In tensing and relaxing the arms, the child may be told to pretend to squeeze half of a lemon in each hand for several seconds and then drop it to the ground. In addition to increasing the appeal of PMR, the use of such analogies may also facilitate a better understanding of the bodily postures required during the exercises.

Although initially conducted during supervised therapeutic sessions, the bulk of PMR occurs outside therapy during homework assignments. Depending on the child's age and/or level of functioning, these practice sessions may be completed individually or under the supervision of a parent. The child or parent is instructed to locate a quiet place at home and practice PMR at that location two to three times a day, with an emphasis placed on allocating enough time (i.e., 15 to 20 minutes) to complete the majority of muscle groups covered during therapeutic sessions. To facilitate these

homework sessions, the therapist typically equips the child or parent with an audiotape that describes the procedure as well as an exercise sheet that lists the positions focused on during therapy and provides check boxes to record the muscles groups practiced by the child on a daily basis.

While PMR attempts to influence somatic stress reactions by directly targeting bodily muscles, IBR takes a more indirect approach to stress management by targeting children's cognitions. As a cognitive strategy to stress reduction, IBR utilizes two types of therapeutic techniques: emotive and guided imagery. With emotive imagery, the therapist instructs the child to imagine a scene that elicits anxiety-inhibiting emotions such as excitement, pride, joy, and affection. Frequently reported emotive images may include a child's favorite superhero or professional athlete. The child is then asked to close his or her eyes and imagine a sequence of events that are similar to those in the child's everyday life (e.g., playing with peers or watching TV with family members), except that the child's favorite superhero or alter ego is woven into the story line. The superhero then accompanies the child through events or situations that may be causing the child distress.

Guided imagery involves instructing a child to imagine a relaxing scene while the therapist describes elements and sensations of that scene in order to help reduce anxiety. Common themes utilized in these guided journeys included beaches, parks, and enchanted forests. During such exercises, children are often instructed to imagine themselves as an animal, such as a bird or butterfly, so that the elements of the scene can be constructed by having the child fly through various aspects of the peaceful location. As with PMR, children are encouraged to practice IBR at home through the use of an audiotape and worksheet.

While PMR has traditionally been associated with RT, the use of IBR with children as a form of RT has been growing. For example, PMR is frequently implemented in conjunction with other treatment procedures, most notably systematic desensitization and biofeedback. With systematic desensitization, PMR is used to induce a deep state of relaxation that is hypothesized to compete with the anxiety that occurs when the therapist guides a child through a graded series of increasingly aversive situations. More recently, therapists have begun using variants of systematic desensitization that incorporate IBR, especially in cases where PMR has been found to be developmentally unsuitable or too demanding for the child. While it is common for both forms of RT to be included in other treatment packages such as systematic desensitization, the use of PMR or IBR as the sole treatment for a variety of childhood disorders has become more frequent. Furthermore, recent variants of RT have incorporated both procedures into a single treatment package aimed at maximizing the development of coping behavior through the use of both somatic and cognitive elements.

RESEARCH BASIS

As a stand-alone treatment, RT has been applied to a variety of clinical problems, with a great deal of evidence suggesting that RT may be beneficial in reducing somatic and psychological symptoms associated with stress as well as in helping children cope with emotional responses that often accompany illness or medical procedures. The majority of these studies have focused on the usefulness of RT in secondary prevention (i.e., in reducing somatic or psychological symptoms associated with a preexisting condition). In this line of research, controlled studies indicate that PMR may be beneficial in reducing the severity of asthmatic attacks, in decreasing the frequency of migraine headaches, and in managing recurrent pain associated with certain medical conditions. Case studies and quasi-experiments have also reported the effectiveness of PMR in treating insomnia, seizure disorders, coprolalia associated with Tourette's syndrome, symptoms of hyperactivity, and childhood phobias. As a more recent variant of RT, IBR's efficacy as an RT is still questionable, but support for the technique is growing. Some research has indicated that IBR is effective in treating childhood phobias and in helping children prepare for and recover from medical procedures, although far more clinical research is needed in this area. Several studies have indicated that RT is more effective when it is used to augment other forms of treatment, which may explain the frequent use of PMR and/or IBR in conjunction with other therapies. With this said, the aforementioned research suggests that there are cases in which RT may be as sufficient as a stand-alone treatment.

In addition to secondary prevention, research has also investigated the efficacy of RT when it is applied in primary prevention programs (i.e., programs geared toward enhancing children's coping skills in everyday situations to help prevent the occurrence of emotional and somatic problems). For example, RT is commonly applied in school-based prevention programs along with additional elements such as games, exercises in concentration, and discussion groups. Research shows that RT applied in the context of these programs can lead to positive outcomes such as reductions in anxiety and hyperactivity. Although these results are promising, many of these studies fail to isolate individual elements of the prevention programs (games, relaxation), leaving questions regarding the exact mechanisms of action. With this in mind, research focusing specifically on the efficacy of RT as a primary prevention method indicates that the application of either PMR or IBR has positive short-term effects (such as increases in positive mood and physical well-being), although similar states of relaxation can be achieved by presenting children with nontension-producing stories. Furthermore, extended and intensified training in RT fails to demonstrate significant improvements in relaxation over neutral stories, raising questions about the long-term impact of RT in primary prevention.

RELEVANT TARGET POPULATIONS AND EXCEPTIONS

RT represents a cost-effective, straightforward intervention that has the potential to benefit any child who is experiencing stress caused by environmental or physiological problems. Some clinicians have reported difficulty in applying RT with hyperactive children, noting difficulties in maintaining high levels of cooperation during training. Due to the cognitive requirements of IBR, younger children have had difficulty benefiting from this form of RT. Therefore, PMR may be preferable with younger children. As alluded to earlier, RT may also be used concurrently with other treatments, such as medications (for children experiencing stress related to pain) or behavioral techniques aimed at reducing phobic responses (e.g., systematic desensitization, biofeedback).

COMPLICATIONS

Using RT requires a high level of attention to the relaxation instructions. As noted above, this may be difficult with highly active children. In such cases, the attainment of effective relaxation skills may require an extensive investment of time and effort by the child, therapist, and parent. Mastering relaxation procedures also requires practice outside the therapy room. Therefore, compliance with homework assignments is fundamental to the process. Treatment gains have also been associated with extended training and additional environment supports (e.g., parent involvement and training) when RT is used in secondary prevention. Enlisting the cooperation of parents as additional treatment supports has proved difficult in some instances.

CASE ILLUSTRATION

"Craig" was a 10-year-old boy who was referred by his primary physician due to reoccurring headaches. He was accompanied to the therapy session by his parents, who expressed concern regarding the impact that these headaches may have had on his social and academic development. Craig's parents indicated that he often has difficulty engaging his peers in social situations, noting several instances where Craig was reluctant to initiate conversation or play with other children. They also noted that Craig has had difficulty concentrating during classroom activities and homework when the headaches occur. During the clinical interview, Craig was talkative and cooperative, freely answering the therapist's questions. He was able to report that the majority of his headaches occur while at school, primarily during lunch and recess. Due to the social nature of these situations and his parent's interview, follow-up questions addressed the extent of his peer network. Craig was unable to name any close friends. He also reported frequent teasing by other members of his class. The therapist hypothesized that the headaches may be related to anxiety experienced in social situations. In accordance with the literature, it was decided that Craig might benefit from progressive muscle relaxation. Before leaving the session, Craig was given a data sheet to record the frequency of his headaches.

The first session following the initial intake focused on presenting the rationale for PMR as well as addressing any questions or concerns that Craig or his parents might have about the procedure. During the course of the session, the therapist modeled PMR in order to provide a concrete example of how to tense and relax the various muscle groups as well as to help normalize the bodily positions for Craig. Craig and his parents were also informed of the importance of practicing PMR outside the therapy session on a regular basis. Craig and his parents agreed to devote

time outside the therapy session to practicing PMR. They were instructed to locate a good place and time for Craig to practice the procedure before the next session. Craig was also instructed to continue keeping track of his headaches on a daily basis.

Over the next seven sessions, Craig was trained in PMR. While sitting in a chair in the therapy room with his eyes closed, the therapist directed Craig to systematically relax muscles in the toes, legs, stomach, back, shoulders, arms, jaw, nose, eyes, and forehead. When tensing each group, Craig was instructed to hold the position for 5 seconds and then to relax for 10 seconds. With each muscle group, the therapist used age-appropriate examples to increase the saliency of the procedure. Given Craig's history of headaches, particular attention was given to helping Craig master relaxing the muscles in the face. Following the first session, Craig was given an audiotape copy of the relaxation instructions as well as an exercise sheet to document his practice sessions. Craig's parents reported assisting Craig in these homework assignments, and his weekly exercise sheet indicated that he regularly practiced these exercises before school and after school.

By the third session, Craig's skills in PMR had improved significantly. To facilitate the application of these skills outside the therapy room, Craig's parents were asked to enlist the help of Craig's primary teacher in setting aside a place for Craig to practice PMR before lunch and recess. By the fifth session, Craig reported that he was regularly practicing relaxation before lunch and recess, as well as continuing to practice before and after school. He also reported a marked improvement in the frequency and intensity of his headaches, which was reflected in his headache data sheet. By the seventh session, Craig appeared to have mastered the fundamental body movements required of PMR. After a conversation with Craig and his parents, it was mutually decided to terminate therapy.

—*William Sharp and Alan M. Gross*

See also: *Applied Relaxation and Tension (Vol. III), Biofeedback (Vols. I, II, & III), Breathing Retraining (Vol. I), Cue-Controlled Relaxation (Vols. I & III), Progressive Muscular Relaxation (Vols. I & III), Relaxation Strategies (Vol. III)*

Suggested Readings

Christophersen, E. R., & Mortweet, S. L. (2001). *Treatments that work for children.* Washington, DC: American Psychological Association.

Hiebert, B., Kirby, B., & Jaknavorian, A. (1989). School-based relaxation: Attempting primary prevention. *Canadian Journal of Counselling, 23*, 273–287.

King, N. J., Heyne, D., Gullone, E., & Molloy, G. N. (2001). Usefulness of emotive imagery in the treatment of childhood phobias: Clinical guidelines, case examples and issues. *Counseling Psychology Quarterly, 14*, 95–101.

Klein-Hessling, J., & Lohaus, A. (2002). Benefits and interindividual differences in children's responses to extended and intensified relaxation training. *Anxiety, Stress, and Coping, 15*, 275–288.

Lohaus, A., & Klein-Hessling, J. (2003). Relaxation in children: Effects of extended and intensified training. *Psychology and Health, 18*, 237–249.

Richter, N. C. (1984). The efficacy of relaxation training with children. *Journal of Abnormal Child Psychology, 12*, 319–344.

Zaichkowsky, L. B., & Zaichkowsky, L. D. (1984). The effects of a school-based relaxation training program on fourth grade children. *Journal of Clinical Child Psychology, 13*, 81–85.

RESEARCH DESIGNS

INTRODUCTION

Scientific research involves the systematic investigation of events of interest so as to increase our understanding of those events. As applied to cognitive behavior therapy and behavior modification with children and adolescents, scientific research often consists of inquiry that improves our knowledge of childhood psychopathology and the variables that impact the development, maintenance, and treatment of disordered behavior. To conduct research in a rigorous way, investigators use specific methods of selecting participants, arranging experimental conditions, and gathering and analyzing data. These methods are referred to as research designs. Various experimental, quasi-experimental, and correlational designs are used in research on child behavior modification and cognitive behavior therapy. Selection of an appropriate design depends on several variables, including the goals of research, the topic under investigation, characteristics of participants such as age, ethical and practical considerations, and a host of other factors. Prior to discussing some of the specific designs that are most commonly used when conducting research on cognitive behavior therapy and behavior modification with children and adolescents, information about the goals and categories of research is presented.

GOALS OF RESEARCH

Scientific inquiry can occur for many different reasons. The design that one selects depends on the goal of conducting the research. In this section, the goals of research in the context of conducting investigations on cognitive behavior therapy and/or behavior modification with children are discussed. Psychological research focused on other issues will likely have other goals, which are beyond the scope of this entry.

One common goal of psychological research on cognitive behavior therapy and behavior modification is to identify treatments that work for specific disordered behavior and emotion patterns. In other words, it is important to document that a particular treatment is effective in ameliorating a specific problematic response, as compared to no treatment. As a related goal, investigators are often interested in determining the number/percentage of youngsters with a given problem who respond positively to a specific intervention. Accomplishing this goal is important in improving the understanding of the likelihood of treatment effectiveness for any given patient, which has important clinical implications. For example, if researchers determine that only 25% of a given population of children with a particular disorder respond positively to an intervention, then clinicians may not wish to devote a large amount of time to learning and then implementing the approach, particularly if there are other interventions that have been proven to be effective for a larger percentage of the population.

Third, researchers are often interested in determining which intervention is most effective with a given clinical population. To accomplish this goal, researchers can compare the impact of two or more types of treatment for a clinical problem and determine which produces the best outcomes. For example, investigators may wish to compare the use of exposure-based treatment, medication, and a combination of exposure-based treatment and medication to treat social phobia in adolescents. Fourth, investigation of the variables that influence the effectiveness of treatment is important. Evaluating the variables that impact treatment—such as age of the youngster, comorbid problems, or family involvement, to name a few—helps clinicians determine whether optimal conditions exist to use a particular intervention with a client.

Fifth, researchers might be interested in investigating the mechanisms that produce change as part of a treatment. Because treatments for psychological conditions typically include multiple components, investigators may wish to determine which treatment components are the most essential to success in order to streamline the intervention. Doing so can increase the cost effectiveness of intervention. Studies attempting to accomplish this goal are often referred to as dismantling studies, whereby individual components of a treatment package are isolated and their relative influence on the clinical problems is determined.

CATEGORIES OF RESEARCH DESIGNS

Efficacy Versus Effectiveness Studies

Treatment efficacy research refers to investigations conducted on intervention strategies using a high degree of control over all aspects of the study. In this type of research, the investigator carefully selects participants who fit a clear, narrowly defined set of criteria and implements the intervention in a prescribed, regimented way in a very controlled setting. In efficacy studies, participants are screened for comorbid conditions, and only those with the particular condition of interest are to be included in the study. Researchers then implement a standardized protocol for each participant, with essentially no variation to account for individual differences. Research involving children with separation anxiety disorder who have no comorbid conditions utilizing a standardized, manualized 8-week treatment program would be an example of efficacy research. This type of research is advantageous when investigating whether particular methods of intervention produce desired outcomes for specific problems.

In contrast, treatment effectiveness research involves investigating the impact of an intervention in typical clinical settings with typical clients who may have one or more comorbid conditions, rather than in controlled setting with very well-selected participants. When conducting clinical effectiveness research, the participants are generally referred for treatment rather than carefully screened and selected, and the intervention is implemented without many of the rigorous safeguards used in efficacy research. Continuing the example provided when discussing efficacy research, effectiveness research might involve applying a manualized treatment to all children who present to an outpatient mental health clinic with separation anxiety disorder. No attempts would be made to screen out children with comorbid conditions, and while a treatment manual may be available for use, treatment providers may not be mandated to follow strict guidelines for implementation.

Both efficacy and effectiveness studies are important in behavior modification and cognitive behavior therapy with children and adolescents. The former allow for a better understanding of which treatments are likely to be successful for particular types of presenting problems. Furthermore, efficacy research provides estimates as to the number of children with particular conditions that are likely to respond successfully and generates data that are useful for analyzing variables that may be related to treatment success or failure. Effectiveness studies expand on the findings of efficacy research by addressing how well interventions work in real-world settings. This type of research can be very helpful for determining the generality of results from efficacy studies. For instance, suppose efficacy research demonstrates that Treatment A is effective with children who have separation anxiety disorder. Effectiveness research might show that Treatment A has diminished, although still positive, effects when children present with comorbid conduct problems, thus helping establish the parameters of the intervention.

Intersubject Versus Intrasubject Research

Research methods can vary depending on whether they involve intersubject versus intrasubject analyses. Intersubject research involves investigating variation across subjects. The goal of this type of research is typically to learn about the aggregate, or mean, occurrence of a specified variable. Therefore, such research typically involves comparing groups of individuals on relevant dimensions. An example of intersubject research with childhood populations might be comparing the outcomes of 50 children diagnosed with attention-deficit/hyperactivity disorder (ADHD) who were treated with parent management training (PMT) to the outcomes of 50 children of similar age and gender also diagnosed with ADHD who were treated with PMT *plus* stimulant medication. By comparing the aggregate of the data collected on targeted clinical problems (e.g., tantrums), researchers can determine which intervention (i.e., PMT alone versus PMT plus stimulant medication) produced the greatest impact.

Intrasubject research involves investigating variation within subjects. In other words, repeated samples of an individual's performance may be taken multiple times across several conditions, resulting in the ability to determine whether differences in performance exist across conditions. Research using intrasubject analysis can include either comparing repeated measurements of the variable of interest demonstrated by one person, and comparing that across conditions, or may involve comparisons of aggregate data obtained from a group of individuals all exposed to the same conditions. Since intrasubject research has been extensively used in cognitive-behavioral approaches to treatment, they will be discussed in more detail in the section on single-subject designs.

Experimental Versus Correlational Research

Research designs can also be distinguished by whether they provide information about experimentally determined relationships between the independent variable and dependent variable, or whether the results allow only for a determination of the strength of association (i.e., correlation) between different variables. In the first type of investigation (experimental), the investigator must be able to directly manipulate an independent variable (e.g., psychological treatment) so as to observe its impact on the dependent variable (e.g., clinical problem). Furthermore, the design must include a method by which to compare levels of the dependent variable during treatment and nontreatment conditions, so as to determine whether any differences exist. As such, it is necessary, but not sufficient, for the investigator to have tight control over all aspects of the study so as to eliminate sources other than the independent variable that might account for changes in the dependent variable.

In the second type of research (correlational), the goal is to evaluate the strength of association between two or more variables. This type of research may be most appropriate when it is not feasible (e.g., ethical, practical) to directly manipulate experimental conditions so as to observe changes in the dependent variables of interest. For example, it would be clearly unethical to expose children to various levels and types of child abuse so as to evaluate the impact of such experiences on emotional and behavioral well-being. Instead, to conduct such an investigation, one would need to obtain a sample of children who, through their unfortunate experiences, have experienced varied levels of exposure to such events, and then assess the degree to which the experiences are associated (i.e., correlated) with particular behavioral or emotional profiles. While this type of research does not allow for a determination of the causal role of abuse, it may be the only way to investigate certain aspects of children's lives.

SINGLE-SUBJECT DESIGNS

Single-subject designs (SSDs) are valuable for completing intrasubject research, in that their use is based primarily on demonstrating experimental control through replication of the impact of an independent variable on a case-by-case basis rather than by aggregation of obtained data across cases. When using SSDs, the individual serves as his or her own control, and performance is compared across different conditions. Given the nature of SSDs, they are particularly useful for experimental research designed to evaluate the impact of particular interventions on the behavior of an individual. In this way, their use is well suited for analyzing the relationship between particular independent variables and changes in dependent variables.

The various SSDs available share three important features. First, they involve repeated observation of the phenomena of interest, typically across time in standardized conditions. Specifically, observation of the dependent variable occurs multiple times (e.g., over several hours of a day or days of a week) across a minimum of two conditions: baseline (i.e., pretreatment) and treatment. Second, SSDs have in common the use of methods that involve replication of the experimental effect. Thus, with the exception of multiple baseline designs (see below for discussion of how this is accomplished using these types of designs), each participant in single-subject research is repeatedly exposed to baseline and treatment conditions. With each demonstration of changes in the dependent variable as a function of removing or adding the independent variable, one's confidence in the causal relationship between the two increases. Third, SSDs typically have in common the practices of changing only one variable at a time in order to observe the impact of that change on the phenomena of interest. For example, if a researcher was investigating effective interventions for treating nighttime bed-wetting, the investigator would want to introduce only one intervention (e.g., the urine alarm) at the start of the treatment phase. If more than one variable is changed, then it becomes impossible to determine which variable is operative in terms of producing change in the dependent variable.

SSDs can be divided into two distinct categories: withdrawal designs and stage-process designs. Each is discussed next.

Withdrawal Designs

Withdrawal designs typically involve a minimum of two phases (i.e., A, or baseline, and B, or treatment). The underlying strategy employed to demonstrate experimental control using the various withdrawal designs is the repeated introduction and withdrawal of the treatment. That is, after observing the dependent variable under baseline conditions, experimenters then implement a treatment phase. Take a child who engages in noncompliance as an example. After establishing the typical rate of noncompliance to adult instructions, the experimenter may then teach the parent a new method of giving instructions (i.e., simple, one-step instructions). Assuming a change in the dependent variable in the desired direction (that is, noncompliance decreases and compliance increases), the treatment is then withdrawn (i.e., return to baseline condition). If the removal of the treatment condition produces a return to baseline rates of the dependent variable, then experimental control over that variable has been demonstrated. Such a design is often referred to as an A-B-A design. In child behavior modification and cognitive-behavioral therapy research, withdrawal designs typically involve a return to the treatment condition so as to end the experiment in the condition that produces desired outcomes in targeted clinical phenomena. This type of withdrawal design (i.e., the A-B-A-B design) is perhaps the most common form of withdrawal design used in research.

Multiple variations of the simple principle of changing from baseline to treatment conditions exist, allowing flexibility in how one demonstrates experimental control of the independent variable over the dependent variable. For example, assume a situation in which it would not be ethical to sustain pretreatment conditions so as to establish base rates of the dependent variable (e.g., the child behavior of interest is dangerous to self or others, the behavior problem can no longer be tolerated by care providers). In this situation, the investigator may wish to use a B-A-B design, whereby the intervention is implemented immediately so as to (hopefully) improve the targeted behavioral disturbance as fast as possible. Or, assume

a situation in which the investigator is interested in determining the relative effects of adding a second treatment component to an existing one. To accomplish this, an A-B-BC-B-BC design could be used. In this scenario, the C represents a second treatment component, and the investigator would be able to evaluate the change that is produced in the dependent variable by adding this component to the first intervention. To demonstrate this, consider the example provided earlier regarding increasing child compliance. After establishing rates of compliance under normal (i.e., A) conditions, the investigator teaches the care provider to give simple, direct one-step commands (i.e., B). While this might result in some increase in child compliance, perhaps the desired outcome was not achieved. As a result, the care provider is taught to also provide specific, labeled praise contingent upon compliance (i.e., C). The rate of compliance is then assessed when the combined treatment is in place (i.e., BC phase). After establishing the new rate of compliance, the second treatment is removed so as to evaluate whether rates of compliance return to levels previously obtained under the first treatment condition alone. Assuming a return to previous rates, the combined treatment could then be reintroduced so as to reestablish improved child compliance.

Stage-Process Designs

Although the flexibility of withdrawal designs allows their use in many research situations, there are conditions that prevent their appropriateness. For example, in some situations it may be unethical to withdraw a treatment (e.g., following elimination of a targeted behavior that produces serious harm to self or others) or perhaps the treatment produces lasting and "irreversible" change in behavior (i.e., once a child has been taught to read through intervention, removing the intervention will likely not result in the elimination of learned reading skills). In these situations, use of stage-process designs may be appropriate. Multiple stage-process designs exist, including multielements designs, multiple baseline designs, and changing criterion designs.

The multielements design (also referred to as the simultaneous treatment design or the alternating treatments design) differs from other SSDs in that multiple conditions (i.e., baseline and treatment conditions, two or more treatment conditions) are conducted in rapid succession, with the order of presentation typically determined through random selection and compared against each other. For example, perhaps baseline conditions are in effect on one day, treatment conditions the next, and so forth.

With the multielements design, often there are three phases: baseline, comparison (rapid alternation between two or more conditions), and the use of the effective intervention. In some situations, however, the baseline might not be necessary. This may be particularly true if one of the comparison conditions is a baseline condition. One treatment condition is judged to be superior if it produces data patterns in the expected direction at a level that is greater than other conditions. Another component of the multielements design is that an equal number of sessions of each condition should be conducted. To ensure discriminated responding across conditions, researchers often pair separate but salient stimuli with each condition. This design may be particularly useful if the investigator is comparing interventions that have an immediate effect and when the dependent measure is particularly sensitive to changes in stimulus conditions (i.e., reversible).

A second type of stage-process design is the multiple baseline design. There are three types of multiple baseline designs: (1) multiple baseline across behaviors, (2) multiple baseline across persons, and (3) multiple baseline across settings. With the multiple baseline design across behaviors, the investigator evaluates the impact of an intervention across different behaviors emitted by the same person. As such, this is a within-subjects design. The intervention is applied sequentially to the different (presumably) independent behaviors. The second design—multiple baseline across persons—involves the evaluation of the impact of a particular intervention across at least two individuals *matched,* according to relevant variables, who are presumed to be exposed to identical (or at least markedly similar) environments. Finally, with the multiple baseline across settings design, a particular intervention is applied sequentially to a single participant or group of participants across independent environments (e.g., home and school).

Technically, there must be at least two separate dimensions (i.e., behaviors, persons, or settings) present to utilize a multiple baseline design, although convention suggests a minimum of three or more. Multiple baseline designs are characterized by the presence of only two conditions: baseline and treatment.

Treatment is introduced in such a way that one is able to evaluate experimental control of the independent variable. With these designs, the baseline condition is extended for increasing lengths of time as the intervention is introduced with the other dependent variables. Thus, these designs are particularly useful for studying irreversible effects, because replication is achieved without withdrawal and reintroduction of the independent variable. Experimental control is inferred based on the comparison of nontreated dependent variables as compared to the treated variables and thus is not demonstrated directly.

The changing criterion design is characterized by the presence of only one baseline and one treatment phase. However, implementation of the treatment condition involves the sequential introduction of different performance goals. In other words, the treatment phase is applied until the targeted dependent variable achieves a specified level of performance. At that time, the goal (i.e., criterion) of performance is altered and the intervention continues until the behavior again achieves the desired level. Changes in the criterion occur until the dependent measure is occurring at the desired terminal level. As such, the changing criterion design is particularly well suited for situations in which the investigator is interested in evaluating shaping programs that are expected to result in increases or decreases in the dependent measure (e.g., increase amount of seatwork a student will complete prior to needing a break). Evaluation of the intervention as the causal agent occurs through two comparisons: between the occurrence of the dependent measure during baseline and treatment, and between the occurrence of the dependent measure across the different levels of the intervention. If the dependent variable changes in the desired direction only when the criterion changes, then the investigator can have confidence in the controlling nature of the independent variable.

GROUP DESIGNS

In contrast to single-subject designs that focus primarily on idiographic approaches to researching human phenomena, group designs take a decidedly nomothetic approach to understanding general laws and principles of human behavior. In this way, group designs involve comparing aggregated data from two or more groups exposed to different experimental conditions. Group designs may be used when conducting correlational or experimental research. Two general categories of group designs exist: between-groups comparison designs and within-groups comparison designs. Each is explored next, followed by a discussion of other group designs that are based on the general methods of between-groups and within-groups designs.

Between-Groups Comparison Designs

Between-groups comparison designs involve investigating how different groups of individuals perform when exposed to some form of experimental manipulation. At their most basic, between-group designs involve two groups: an experimental group (i.e., typically exposed to a treatment, or independent variable) and a control group (i.e., typically exposed to no experimental manipulation). An important hallmark of such designs is group equivalence on important variables (e.g., gender, age, type and/or level of pathology), so that experimenters can be confident that any differences between groups is due to experimental conditions instead of preexisting differences in group members. Equivalence is achieved either through random assignment of participants to groups or through matching group members based on their presentation of specific characteristics hypothesized to be important to the investigation. As an example of matching, investigators researching the difference between juvenile sex offenders and nonoffending delinquent peers in terms of emotional and/or behavioral health might match participants based on age, history of abuse, and presence of psychopathology, all of which have been shown in research to correlate with emotional and behavioral outcomes. If group equivalence is achieved, either through random assignment or matching, any differences between the groups on the dependent variables being investigated are presumed to be the result of the differences in experimental conditions to which the group members were exposed.

Several different between-group comparison designs have been described in the literature. Perhaps the most common version of this type of design is the pretest-posttest control group design. This design typically includes two groups (i.e., an experimental group that is exposed to an intervention and a control group that is not), with participants randomly assigned to groups. Participants of both groups are tested both prior to the treatment (i.e., pretest) and following treatment (i.e., posttest). For members of the control group, posttest assessment typically occurs once the amount of time has passed that it took to implement the treatment with the members of the experimental group. This design is particularly popular in treatment research, because the format allows for an assessment in the changes of psychological symptoms in the presence and absence of treatment, and any difference in the amount of change between groups can be attributed to the independent variable.

The posttest-only control group design is another between-groups comparison design available for researchers investigating cognitive behavior therapy and behavior modification with children. This design is essentially the same as the pretest-posttest control group design, with one major exception. With this design, no assessment is conducted prior to implementing the treatment with the experimental group. The posttest-only design is practical when it is not feasible to conduct pretest assessment. Examples of situations that might preclude utilizing pretest assessment include a concern that exposing participants to pretest measures will sensitize them to aspects of the experiment and thus skew any results, or when it is too expensive or time-consuming due to a large sample size.

Factorial design is another example of between-group comparison designs and is used when the investigator is interested in assessing the influence of two or more independent variables, or two or more levels/variations of one independent variable. For example, perhaps an investigator is interested in evaluating a classroom-based reinforcement program for sustained attention to task for children diagnosed with ADHD. However, the investigator may not be sure of the optimal level of treatment. Using a factorial design, the investigator could compare three versions of the same treatment (i.e., hourly reward, daily reward, weekly reward) to see which most effectively increases attention to task. When using a factorial design, as many levels and independent variables as is desired may be used to address the question at hand. In this way, use of the factorial design can be an economical means of conducting research.

Within-Groups Comparison Designs

While between-group comparison designs are useful because of their flexibility and statistical power (i.e., the probability of detecting an effect of treatment when it occurs), at times their use may be precluded due to practical difficulties related to creating group equivalence. Moreover, certain research questions are best answered by exposing the same individuals to different experimental conditions (i.e., conditions containing different independent variables or conditions with different levels of the same independent variable). In these situations, use of within-groups comparison designs, sometimes referred to as repeated measures designs, may be appropriate. Several within-groups designs exist, including within-groups design to assess multiple levels of one independent variable, pretest-posttest within-groups designs, and factorial within-groups designs. Each is discussed next.

Investigators are often interested in assessing the differing amount of influence of various levels of one independent variable on the dependent variable of interest. While this is possible to do with between-groups designs, the number of participants required for statistical power increases with each level of the independent variable. Continuing the example provided earlier, assume the researcher is interested in investigating the influence of three levels of a reinforcement program for attention problems in children with ADHD. If it is determined that 60 participants are needed in each group for the test to be powerful, then the total number of participants needed would be 180 (i.e., 60 × 3 groups). If obtaining this large number of participants is not feasible, then using a within-groups design is an appropriate alternative.

To use a within-groups comparison design to assess the influence of different levels of the independent variable, all participants would be exposed to each variation of the experimental condition, and measures of the dependent variable(s) would occur at least one time in each variation. Investigators would then compare the obtained measures of the dependent variable(s) across the different levels of the independent variable so as to determine which level had the greatest impact.

Another type of within-groups design is the pretest-posttest within-groups design. Using this approach, a pretest is given to all participants to measure the dependent variable(s). Following the pretest, all participants are exposed to an experimental condition that contains only one independent variable (or one level of an independent variable). Following this, the posttest is given so as to reassess the dependent variable(s). Although this type of design might be beneficial in certain situations (e.g., smaller-scale programs, unethical to create a control group that is

not exposed to treatment), it lacks safeguards against internal validity because of the lack of a control group. In other words, it does not allow one to determine if other extraneous variables accounted for any changes in the dependent variable.

The factorial within-group design is similar to the between-groups factorial design in that it involves an examination of two or more independent variables, or two or more levels of the same independent variable, in the same experiment. Furthermore, as with the between-groups version, the number or level of independent variables is theoretically only limited by the feasibility of the study itself. It differs from the between-groups version in that each participant is exposed to the different independent variables.

Other Group Designs

Mixed designs blend aspects of between-groups and within-groups comparison designs. One example of a category of a mixed design is the counterbalanced designs. These designs are used to eliminate the influence of order effects on the dependent variable, which are inherent with within-groups designs. Counterbalanced designs involve ensuring that order effects are distributed equally across groups with approximately an equal number of participants in each group receiving the treatment conditions in the same order. Using the example of using various levels of reinforcement to increase attention to task, counterbalancing might look like the following: Group 1 exposure order is Level 1, Level 2, and Level 3; Group 2 exposure order is Level 2, Level 3, Level 1; and Group 3 exposure order is Level 3, Level 1, Level 2. Counterbalanced designs include either complete counterbalancing (i.e., all potential variations of the order of presenting the independent variable are used) or incomplete counterbalancing (i.e., ensuring that a portion of all possible orders of presentation are presented to roughly an equivalent number of participants).

A mixed factorial design involves combining between-groups and within-groups comparisons into the same investigation. Using this design, there is both a between-groups comparison and a within-groups comparison. For example, perhaps the investigator completing the study described above on increasing attention to task is interested in the influence of gender on treatment effectiveness. The participants would be divided based on gender (i.e., male versus female is the between-group comparison). In addition, within each group, participants would be exposed to different levels of the reinforcement program. Using this design, the investigator can analyze the influence of gender, levels of reinforcement, and the interaction of gender and levels of reinforcement on attention to task.

To research the ways in which youth change over time, such as when investigating developmental pathways for psychological conditions, experimenters often rely on research designs that allow for gathering data over extended periods of time when children are at different ages. Two different types of designs are commonly used for this type of research: cross-sectional and longitudinal designs. Cross-sectional designs involve studying children at different ages at the same point in time and comparing them against each other. For example, a researcher interested in the behavioral expression of ADHD across childhood might compare groups of children who are 5, 10, and 15 years of age on several measures of inattention, distractibility, and impulsivity/hyperactivity. As such, this is a between-groups comparison design. Using a longitudinal approach, the same set of individuals is studied over an extended period of time. Continuing from the example provided with cross-sectional research, a longitudinal approach would involve assessing the same group of children at ages 5, 10, and 15 and comparing the resulting data within the group across time. Thus, longitudinal research is typically considered a type of within-groups comparison design.

SUMMARY

Various research designs exist to assist investigators in analyzing phenomena of interest. Many common research designs were highlighted, within the context of conducting research on child cognitive behavior therapy and behavior modification, including single-subject and group comparison designs. Other research methodologies exist, including meta-analytic approaches and qualitative analyses. Experimenters investigating childhood disorders need to select the design that is most appropriate to the experimental question and goals of the research being conducted, taking into account various pragmatic constraints.

In addition to being familiar with the various designs available, it is important for researchers to be knowledgeable about other aspects of conducting scientific research. These include, but are not necessarily limited to, ethical considerations, legal requirements for conducting research with human participants, and

threats to internal and external validity and methods of reducing these threats. By attending to these and related issues, investigators can further the understanding of cognitive-behavioral and behavior modification approaches to the assessment and treatment of childhood psychopathology.

—*Kurt A. Freeman and Eric J. Mash*

See also: *Computer-Based Data Collection (Vols. I & III), Computers and Data Assessment (Vols. I & III), Efficacy, Effectiveness, and Patient-Focused Research (Vols. I & III), Empirically Supported Treatments for Childhood Disorders (Vol. II), Evaluating Behavior Plans (Vol. III), Informed Consent (Vols. I & III), Single-Case Research (Vols. I & III)*

Suggested Readings

Bailey, J. S., & Burch, M. R. (2002). *Research methods in applied behavior analysis.* Thousand Oaks, CA: Sage.

Barlow, D. H., & Hersen, M. (1984). *Single case experimental designs: Strategies for studying behavior change* (2nd ed.). New York: Pergamon.

Kazdin, A. E. (Ed.). (2003). *Methodological issues and strategies in clinical research* (3rd ed.). Washington, DC: American Psychological Association.

Kazdin, A. (2003). *Research design in clinical psychology* (4th ed.). Needham Heights, MA: Allyn & Bacon.

Kendall, P. C., Butcher, J. N., & Holmbeck, G. N. (Eds.). (1999). *Handbook of research methods in clinical psychology* (2nd ed.). New York: Wiley.

Kratochwill, T. R., & Levin, J. R. (1992). (Eds.). *Single-case research design and analysis: New directions for psychology and education.* Hillsdale, NJ: Erlbaum.

Mash, E. J., & Krahn, G. (1999). Research strategies in child psychopathology. In M. Hersen & R. T. Ammerman (Eds.), *Advanced abnormal child psychology* (2nd ed., pp. 101–130). Hillsdale, NJ: Erlbaum.

Thomas, J. C., & Hersen, M. (2003). *Understanding research in clinical and counseling psychology.* Mahwah, NJ: Erlbaum

RESPONSE BLOCKING

DESCRIPTION OF THE STRATEGY

Response blocking refers to physically preventing a maladaptive behavior from occurring. Examples of maladaptive behavior include self-injury (e.g., eye poking), pica, aggression, throwing objects, loud clapping, inappropriate touching, and mouthing (i.e., placing one's mouth on inedible surfaces). Typically, a clearly visible motor response is required for response blocking to be used. In many cases, maladaptive behaviors are maintained by sensory reinforcement or a desire for tactile, auditory, visual, or other stimulation. As a result, maladaptive behaviors often become habitual, automatic responses that are not easily self-controlled. Response blocking is often utilized, therefore, as a means of preventing a maladaptive response and providing feedback to the person that the behavior has occurred. Because maladaptive behaviors can also be maintained by attention, tangible reinforcement, and escape from aversive situations, however, these factors must be considered carefully as well when designing a response-blocking intervention.

Response blocking is typically conducted by a teacher or other person who works closely with a client in situations where a maladaptive behavior is most likely to occur. As a first step, the behavior in question is operationally defined so that occurrences of the behavior may be accurately targeted. The behavior and its definition should be specific, motorically based, and clear to those who will engage in response blocking. Ideally, teachers and relevant others are trained to observe and accurately record the maladaptive behavior. In addition, they are taught the specific response-blocking gesture that will be used to prevent the maladaptive response as well as ways of addressing untoward consequences (e.g., aggression).

Following this training procedure, a baseline period is implemented to record frequency, severity, duration, latency, and other relevant factors of the maladaptive behavior. Care should be taken to note times when the behavior is most common as well as its common antecedents (e.g., extended work time, frustration, hunger). In this way, response blocking can be used at selected times of the day rather than the entire day. However, if the maladaptive behavior is truly automatic and reinforced by sensory consequences, then response blocking may be necessary for extended periods of time.

Following baseline, response blocking and any accompanying treatments (e.g., functional communication training) begin. The person conducting the response blocking procedure typically places himself or herself near the client, often in a sitting position, and interacts with the client in some way. In many cases, response blocking is integrated with educational programs but can be used in self-care, recreational, or other situations as well. Whenever the client begins to engage in the maladaptive behavior, the teacher physically blocks the behavior from occurring. For example, a client who picks up an inedible substance and begins to place it in his or her mouth may be prevented from doing so by a teacher who blocks the mouth and gently guides the hand away. In many cases, this preventive behavior can be accompanied by verbal feedback to enhance the effect (e.g., "Remember, you do not eat lint"). In general, the procedure is conducted in a matter-of-fact and quick manner so as not to further reward the maladaptive behavior via attention.

During the response-blocking phase, the teacher or an independent observer records the frequency or other relevant factors of the maladaptive behavior. The data are then examined over time to see if the procedure is effective and whether it needs modification. In the case of pica, for example, it is possible that a simple touch of the hand is necessary to prevent the response. In other cases, a more forceful blocking of the maladaptive response is necessary.

The final phase of response blocking involves fading. In this phase, the teacher continues to block the response but does so in a less intrusive way (e.g., shadowing a person's hand). If treatment gains are maintained, then less intrusive blocking continues until very little physical intervention is necessary. Indeed, response blocking may progress to the point where only verbal feedback is necessary to arrest the maladaptive behavior. Eventually, of course, one final goal is for the person to control the maladaptive behavior himself or herself without external control or feedback. Another final goal is to generalize treatment effects from the initial training setting to more naturalistic settings and to other persons.

RESEARCH BASIS

The behavior analysis literature is rich with single-case experimental designs that support the effectiveness of response blocking for treating various maladaptive behaviors. Response blocking has been evaluated as a single procedure and as a component of a larger treatment protocol. In most cases, the procedure is supplemented with other interventions for people with developmental disorders, such as differential reinforcement of other behavior, punishment, and functional communication training.

RELEVANT TARGET POPULATION

Response blocking is primarily used for people with maladaptive behaviors with severe developmental disorders such as severe or profound mental retardation, autism, and neurological impairment. However, it could be useful as well for any clinical population (e.g., schizophrenia) that engages in maladaptive motor behavior (e.g., perserverations).

COMPLICATIONS

A key drawback of response blocking is that it is extremely labor intensive, requiring a teacher to physically block a high-frequency maladaptive behavior for extended periods of time. As a result, response blocking may be reserved for times when the behavior is most frequent or for intermittent times during the day. Another key drawback of the procedure is that initial success may decline when the physical blocking is faded or withdrawn. This often occurs with entrenched behaviors that have been reinforced over long periods of time. In this case, very gradual fading, lengthy extensions of response blocking, prosthetic devices (e.g., goggles, helmets), or some combination with other treatment procedures may be necessary.

CASE ILLUSTRATION

"Alan" was a 17-year-old male with severe mental retardation in a large residential facility. Over the past 15 months, Alan had begun to scratch his arm repeatedly to the point that serious damage was occurring. A functional analysis indicated that the behavior was due to sensory reinforcement. Baseline measures revealed that most of the scratching occurred prior to lunch and dinner and following educational and self-care tasks. As a result, a combination of procedures was used. Alan's scratching was prevented by having a staff member gently move his hand away from the arm area that was most often damaged. In addition, Alan was presented with a choice of meals and allowed to play video games (a competing response) prior to lunch and dinner. Treatment reduced scratching by 90% in 3 weeks, and gains were maintained even following fading of the response-blocking component.

—Christopher A. Kearney,
Lisa Linning, and Krisann Alvarez

See also: *Exposure (Vols. I & III), Extinction (Vol. II), Extinction and Habituation (Vols. I & III), Response Prevention (Vols. I & III)*

Suggested Readings

Carr, J. E., Dozier, C. L., Patel, M. R., Adams, A. N., & Martin, N. (2002). Treatment of automatically reinforced object mouthing with noncontingent reinforcement and response blocking: Experimental analysis and social validation. *Research in Developmental Disabilities, 23,* 37–44.

Hagopian, L. P., & Adelinis, J. D. (2001). Response blocking with and without redirection for the treatment of pica. *Journal of Applied Behavior Analysis, 34,* 527–530.

Kelley, M. E., Lerman, D. C., & Van Camp, C. M. (2002). The effects of competing reinforcement schedules on the acquisition of functional communication. *Journal of Applied Behavior Analysis, 35,* 59–63.

MacDonald, J. E., Wilder, D. A., & Dempsey, C. (2002). Brief functional analysis and treatment of eye poking. *Behavioral Interventions, 17,* 261–270.

RESPONSE COST

DESCRIPTION OF THE STRATEGY

Response cost is a special case of a punishment procedure that involves taking away desirable possessions, points, tokens, or privileges in planned, incremental steps following the occurrence of an undesirable behavior or failure to meet a specific goal. That is, behaving inappropriately or in an undesirable manner *costs* the individual something they already possess or privileges they currently enjoy and expect to have access to in the future. Technically, the cost component of the procedure is referred to as a "loss of reinforcers"— which means that individuals lose something they value or consider desirable and currently possess—and the procedure results in a reduction in or weakening of behavior following the removal of a positive stimulus. Its end goal, as with all punishment procedures, is to reduce the frequency and/or strength of maladaptive or undesirable behavior. Common examples of response cost include introducing monetary fines for inappropriate behavior (speeding in an automobile, filing a delinquent income tax return) and losing points or tokens used to access special privileges in a classroom (e.g., as part of an ongoing classroom incentive system or token economy).

Punishment is a frequently misunderstood technical term. For example, many parents complain that their children don't respond to punishment or that punishment is ineffective. Both statements are inaccurate. Punishment is defined as the reduction in behavior following the introduction of an aversive stimulus or removal of a positive stimulus. Thus, if an undesirable behavior shows no reduction in frequency or strength following the introduction of an aversive stimulus or removal of a positive stimulus, then the procedure fails to meet the definition as punishment. In these situations, the intended stimulus (either presentation of an aversive or removal of a positive) is not an effective punisher. At first glance, this definitional nuance may appear trivial, but it is an important distinction because many people assume that if some event or stimulus is aversive to them personally, it must be aversive to everyone. Clearly, this is not the case. There is considerable variability with respect to what individuals regard as aversive. For example, consider the extreme case of children who engage in self-injurious behavior by chronically slamming their head against hard surfaces or an adult with a masochistic personality.

Response cost differs procedurally from other common forms of punishment. Punishment may involve (a) the presentation of an aversive stimulus (e.g., a light swat on the buttocks for running out into the street without looking for cars), (b) removing the individual from a situation or setting that is desirable (referred to as time-out from reinforcement), and (c) removing a positive stimulus, as is the case with response cost. All three variations of punishment result in a decrease in or weakening of behavior but use different processes to accomplish this goal. Traditional punishment introduces an aversive stimulus following an undesirable or inappropriate behavior. Time-out removes the individual from an otherwise positive or reinforcing situation or setting. And response cost takes away reinforcers that have already been earned or are in the person's possession. Thus, response cost is similar to other forms of punishment in that it reduces or weakens a behavior, but is unique in the manner by which it accomplishes this goal—by taking away items, activities, and privileges that are considered desirable by an individual following an incidence of inappropriate or undesirable behavior.

One of the most intriguing aspects of response cost is that it can affect a wide range of desirable behaviors if programmed with these goals in mind. For example, response cost can be used as part of a broader behavioral program to increase children's ability to pay attention in the classroom. In this situation, children might earn points on an ongoing basis for paying attention and lose points for not paying attention. Earned points are subsequently exchanged for extra time playing learning games or other special activities in the classroom at the end of the academic session.

A host of other positive behaviors are likely to accrue in this scenario owing to the combined response cost-positive reinforcement program. Attentive children are less likely to be out of their seats, annoying others, and acting impulsively and more likely to complete academic assignments. These behavioral changes have a high probability of translating into additional benefits, such as improved learning for children receiving contingent response cost, as well as for other children in the classroom who benefit indirectly from a less disruptive environment that is more conducive to learning.

Extant research related to response cost focuses primarily on its use as a treatment intervention. The procedure, however, is also used judiciously in other scientific works to investigate a wide range of phenomena. For example, researchers interested in operant conditioning principles incorporate the procedure into experimental protocols to examine how particular punishment techniques affect behavior being maintained under different schedules of reinforcement (i.e., to better understand underlying principles of behavior). Response cost procedures are also invoked to investigate a wide range of phenomena that may be better accounted for by individual differences in motivation. Investigations of behavioral inhibition (i.e., the ability to withhold a previously reinforced response when signaled to do so by some external cue such as a tone), for example, use response cost contingencies to examine whether motivational factors underlie the typically poor response inhibition in children with attention-deficit/hyperactivity disorder (ADHD). If poor inhibitory performance is observed despite the imposition of response cost procedures scheduled to punish such behavior (and by extension, improve inhibitory performance), this would render a motivational explanation unlikely and support the notion of response inhibition deficits.

RESEARCH BASIS

Extant research provides strong support for the use of response cost when used as part of a more comprehensive treatment approach. The majority of published research describes various uses and modified applications of the procedure in regular education classrooms, usually combined with an ongoing reinforcement program or token economy. For example, when response cost principles are introduced as part of a classroom lottery, elementary school-age boys exhibit rapid and significant reductions of inappropriate and disruptive behavior and concomitant increases in attention and scholastic productivity.

Research consistently reveals that response cost is significantly more effective than no intervention for reducing a wide range of inappropriate classroom behaviors, including clear reductions in verbal and physical incidences of aggressive behavior. The procedure is also used with special populations of children, such as those placed in special education classrooms or with learning disabilities. Both populations show clear benefit from a combined response cost-positive incentive program, including enhanced ability to pay attention for longer intervals, and improved scholastic performance.

Response cost is also more effective than positive reinforcement alone in improving on-task (attentive) behavior and academic performance in school-age children and as an effective management technique for regulating the behavior of children with ADHD in particular. Other research findings reveal that the technique, when coupled with a positive incentive program, is as or more effective than carefully adjusted doses of psychostimulant medication such as Ritalin (i.e., the most widely used treatment for ADHD) for improving attentive behavior, reducing teacher ratings of disruptive behavior, and increasing daily academic work productivity.

Other applications of response cost noted in the literature include using the technique to increase (a) time spent playing the piano at home, (b) compliance in completing household chores in a timely manner, and (c) homework completion. It is also commonly used in institutional settings (e.g., inpatient units) as a component of a broader token economy or positive incentive system for reducing inappropriate behavior and improving adaptive behavior. Note in the above examples that changes in behavior are nearly always related to increases in appropriate behavior rather than to decreases in inappropriate behavior, which appears contradictory to the definition of punishment (i.e., a reduction in behavior). This seeming contradiction is easily resolved, however, by carefully considering the specific stimulus used and how it is applied to produce behavior change. In the above examples, 1 minute of outside playtime might be taken away following each interval exceeding 15 seconds in which a child is not practicing the piano or completing chores or homework. This clearly meets the criteria of punishment (i.e., the removal of a positive stimulus) as long as access to outdoor play is viewed as a desirable activity

by the child. When children decrease their time off-task (the actual behavior being punished), they typically engage in more productive forms of behavior such as playing the piano and completing homework and chores—hence, the noted increases in behavior represent indirect results of the procedure.

RELEVANT TARGET POPULATIONS AND EXCEPTIONS

Response cost is traditionally reserved for situations in which positive incentive systems and procedures have already been tried and resulted in limited or no success, when rapid behavior change is warranted owing to safety concerns and for special target populations supported by extant research. Relevant target populations currently include children with ADHD, children with learning disability (particularly those who experience problems maintaining attention), children in special classrooms for emotional/behavioral problems (particularly those with externalizing behavior problems), and psychiatric inpatient units. Behavior problems common to each of these populations include difficulty concentrating (staying on-task, in educational vernacular), low rates of academic assignments completed on a daily basis, capricious behavior, and poor compliance with verbal requests and instructions.

There are exceptional cases and situations in which response cost and other forms of punishment may be inappropriate. Very young children and those with impaired cognitive functioning (e.g., individuals with schizophrenia, autism, or mental retardation) may not understand the contingent relationships between their behavior and the loss of reinforcers. Individuals with particular handicapping conditions that limit their ability to meet performance criteria also represent cases in which response cost procedures are inappropriate, unless they can accommodate the individual's disability. Individuals with a history of becoming highly emotional or agitated with minimal provocation, such as adolescents and adults with explosive personality disorder and some children with mental retardation and concomitant explosive tendencies, represent additional exceptions because of the tendency of response cost (and punishment techniques more generally) to evoke emotional responding.

COMPLICATIONS

The most frequent complications associated with response cost include the (a) potential to lose points too quickly, (b) mismanagement of the procedure by overly enthusiastic or callous adults, (c) potential of evoking emotional behavior, and (d) tendency to focus on reductions in inappropriate behavior to the exclusion of strengthening adaptive functioning.

Losing points too quickly is a common complication of response cost. Many individuals, and younger children in particular, will simply give up and stop trying following rapid point loss. This is particularly true in situations in which there is no opportunity to gain additional points for appropriate behavior. The complication can usually be avoided by programming a positive incentive program such that points are awarded on a fixed or variable schedule of reinforcement (i.e., as opposed to providing all possible points initially) while limiting the number of points that can be lost within a given period of time to match the reinforcement schedule. The program should be modified whenever point loss exceeds point gains. That is, the opportunity of rewards should always exceed the possibility of losing them. Invoking these types of contingent relationships also helps to reduce the likelihood of misusing the procedure by well-meaning but overly zealous adults.

Response cost, as with most forms of punishment, has the potential to invoke emotional responding and aggression following point loss. Emotional responding, in turn, may result in additional punishment, leading to a spiraling sequence of punishment and undesirable behaviors. These situations can be largely avoided by (a) combining response cost with an ongoing positive incentive system, (b) closely monitoring emotional reactions to point loss, and (c) ensuring that the opportunity to earn points always exceeds the possibility of losing points.

A final complication related to the use of response cost concerns the tendency to rely exclusively on the procedure for behavioral control. Response cost, like all punishment procedures, decreases, weakens, or eliminates undesirable behavior but does not directly teach or strengthen adaptive behavior. A child who spends less time off-task must possess or be taught the requisite skills by which to learn, and individuals who exhibit decreases in disruptive or aggressive behavior must still learn how to interact appropriately with their peers.

CASE ILLUSTRATION

"George" was a 9-year-old, third grade, Caucasian male with a protracted history of classroom behavior problems beginning shortly after entering the first grade. He experienced significant difficulty paying attention to academic assignments or classroom instruction for more than a few minutes at a time, disturbed other children, was capricious, and was frequently out of his seat. A comprehensive diagnostic evaluation at the community mental health clinic revealed that George met diagnostic criteria for ADHD. George's mother consulted with the mental health center, her son's pediatrician, and relevant school personnel before deciding on a course of therapy for her son. Following a 1-week baseline assessment period (i.e., no intervention), George received three dosages (morning and early afternoon) of a commonly prescribed psychostimulant medication (Ritalin) consisting of 5 milligrams, 10 milligrams, and 15 milligrams, each for a 2-week time interval. He exhibited clear and immediate improvement in his ability to remain attentive (on-task) during academic assignments, completed significantly more academic assignments on a daily basis, and was less disruptive in the classroom and at school in general, with the highest rates of combined improvements occurring during the 10-milligram weeks.

The medication regimen was discontinued after the 6-week trial period and, following a second baseline condition, replaced by an in-class, combined incentive-response cost intervention for the ensuing 4 weeks. In this unique application, response cost was coupled with positive reinforcement to create the Attentional Training System (ATS), which consists of student and teacher modules. A base unit is placed on the child's desk and assigns one point for each minute the child is on-task. The classroom teacher uses a lightweight, handheld, wireless control unit and monitors the child's behavior from anywhere in the room, which facilitates concomitant involvement in other instructional activities (e.g., working with other children in small groups in the classroom). Unlike other conventional classroom behavioral systems, the teacher does nothing if the child is on-task (i.e., the child is automatically awarded one point per minute by the ATS), and activates a button on the handheld unit if the child is off-task. Pushing the button causes a red light to illuminate on the child's unit and signals the child that a point has been deducted from the accumulated total. A counter on the front of the child's unit shows the total number of accumulated points earned throughout the academic session to enable children to monitor their own progress.

George and the classroom teacher received their respective modules and detailed instructions concerning the ATS. The ATS was programmed such that George earned one point for each minute that he remained attentive to his academic assignments or teacher instruction and lost one point following each occasion in which the classroom teacher noticed that he was off-task. Points were traded in at the conclusion of each academic assignment throughout the day for access to special activities available within the classroom (i.e., each point earned 1 minute of access to special activities). George's favorite special activity incentives included playing learning games on the computer and drawing with colored markers. Implementation of the ATS resulted in clear and sustained increases in attentive behavior, assignment completion, and reduced disruptiveness in the classroom over the 4-week period. Positive effects, however, did not generalize to situations outside the classroom. George continued to experience behavior problems during recess and other activities that occurred away from the classroom in which the ATS was inoperative.

A final, 1-week baseline phase was scheduled following the discontinuation of the response cost procedure to facilitate comparisons of the two treatments with no intervention. The final baseline (no intervention) period also allowed the treatment team to determine whether any gains associated with response cost were maintained following its discontinuation (i.e., treatment maintenance effects). Inspection of the data revealed that George reverted back to his initial baseline levels of behavior and academic performance after a few days of no treatment. This finding was largely expected and is consistent with results obtained from highly controlled treatment outcome studies involving psychostimulant and behavioral treatments (i.e., neither is associated with sustained gains following the withdrawal of active treatment).

George's mother elected to have her son continue with the response cost treatment for the remainder of the school year but switched him to a 10-milligram psychostimulant regimen the following year, owing to inconsistent use of the behavior management procedure by the new classroom teacher.

—*Mark D. Rapport and Gezim Begolli*

See also: *Applied Behavior Analysis (Vols. I, II, & III), Azrin, Nathan H. (Vols. I & III), Operant Conditioning (Vols. I, II, & III), Positive Reinforcement (Vol. II), Punishment (Vol. II), Reinforcement (Vols. I, II, & III)*

Suggested Readings

Gresham, F. M. (1979). Comparison of response cost and time-out in a special education setting. *Journal of Abnormal Child Psychology, 13*, 199–208.

Hallahan, D. P., Tarver, S. G., Kauffman, J. M., & Graybeal, I. L. (1978). Selective attention abilities of learning disabled children under reinforcement and response cost. *Journal of Learning Disabilities, 11*, 39–47.

Kazdin, A. E. (1972). Response cost: The removal of conditioned reinforcers for therapeutic change. *Behavior Therapy, 3*, 533–546.

Little, L. M., & Kelley, M. L. (1989). The efficacy of response cost procedures for reducing children's noncompliance to parental instructions. *Behavior Therapy, 20*, 525–534.

McSweeny, A. J. (1978). Effects of response cost on the behavior of a million persons: Charging for directory assistance in Cincinnati. *Journal of Applied Behavior Analysis, 11*, 47–51.

Rapport, M. D., Murphy, H. A., & Bailey, J. S. (1980). The effects of a response cost treatment tactic on hyperactive children. *Journal of School Psychology, 18*, 98–111.

Rapport, M. D., Murphy, H. A., & Bailey, J. S. (1982). Ritalin versus response cost in the control of hyperactive children: A within-subject comparison. *Journal of Applied Behavior Analysis, 15*, 205–216.

Reynolds, L. K., & Kelly, M. L. (1997). The efficacy of a response-cost based treatment package for managing aggressive behavior in preschoolers. *Behavior Modification, 21*, 216–230.

Witt, J. C., & Elliot, S. N. (1982). The response cost lottery: A time efficient and effective classroom intervention. *Journal of School Psychology, 20*, 155–161.

RESTITUTION

Restitution is a corrective procedure that consists of both restoring and improving the environmental effects of an inappropriate or undesired behavior. Essentially, the individual who engages in the unwanted behavior is required to not only correct but also improve the environmental consequences of that behavior. For example, a child who throws food on the wall may be required to clean the entire wall in addition to the spot on the wall where the food was thrown.

Restitution is one component of a larger set of aversive procedures referred to as overcorrection. Generally, overcorrection consists of two components: restitution and positive practice. The primary distinction between these two procedures is a topographical one. In restitution, the corrective behavior is directly related to, and as such, is topographically identical to, the undesired behavior, as can be seen from the example provided above. Since the corrective behavior is directly related to the unwanted behavior, it is assumed that restitution aids in the learning process by helping the individual to realize the effort required to restore the environment. Conversely, positive practice consists of repeatedly engaging in an appropriate behavior that usually is incompatible with the unwanted behavior that is to be suppressed. Positive practice is an educative procedure in that it provides the individual with the opportunity to engage in the appropriate behavior.

Since it was initially used to decrease aggressive behavior in a severely retarded female, restitution has been used successfully in a variety of clinical, educational, and institutional settings for a wide range of behaviors. Restitution has been effective in decreasing aggressive behavior, toileting accidents, and tantrums and has been shown to be effective at increasing the use of table manners.

From a practical perspective, restitution can be difficult. Because restitution requires that the environment not only be restored but also be improved from prebehavior conditions, restitution requires adequate staff to ensure that this actually occurs. Staff members are needed to oversee behaviors and to provide the prompts that might be needed to ensure that restitution actually takes place. Providing these prompts can be problematic if the client resists or becomes aggressive. If physical force is required, alternative techniques may need to be considered.

As mentioned, clients may have to be prompted or physically guided, at least in the early stages of the procedure, for restitution to be effective. Thus, the supervision required is a consideration. The individual overseeing the procedure must make sure that restitution is being carried out and that the prompts needed are delivered in a constructive way. The financial realities of treatment settings may make this requirement difficult to meet. A number of studies have shown that restitution was effective but had to be terminated because the procedure required too much staff and supervision.

Finally, restitution is not appropriate for all types of behaviors, as some behaviors do not lend themselves to restitution. For example, many self-stimulatory and self-injurious behaviors have no clear environmental consequences that can be corrected. In these situations, positive practice may be a viable alternative.

Although there are a number of practical considerations inherent in using restitution, the procedure has often led to rapid and long-lasting behavior change. The primary advantage of restitution from a learning theory perspective is that the corrective action is directly related to the consequences of the behavior. This quality makes restitution a powerful procedure for achieving behavior change.

—Kevin J. Armstrong
and Christopher M. Browne

See also: *Aversion Relief (Vols. I & III), Electrical Aversion (Vols. I & III), Extinction and Habituation (Vol. III), Operant Conditioning (Vols. I, II, & III), Punishment (Vols. II & III), Response Cost (Vol. II)*

Suggested Reading

Foxx, R. M., and Azrin, N. H. (1972). Restitution: A method for eliminating aggressive disruptive behavior of retarded and brain damaged patients. *Behavior Research and Therapy, 10,* 15–27.

RETENTION CONTROL TRAINING

DESCRIPTION OF THE STRATEGY

Retention control training (RCT) is a daytime treatment procedure for nocturnal enuresis (i.e., bed-wetting) designed to increase functional bladder capacity (e.g., how much urine an individual can retain before voiding). Often described as an operant procedure, RCT involves encouraging increased fluid intake while reinforcing urine retention for successively longer periods of time. The procedure is based on findings that enuretic children urinate more frequently during the day, demonstrate strong urges to urinate at low bladder pressures, and possess functionally smaller bladder capacities than nonenuretic children. RCT attempts to modify this lack of bladder control by instructing enuretics to systematically refrain from urination under increasing bladder dilation cues.

RCT typically commences following an initial baseline assessment. Common baseline measures employed during this phase include bed-wetting frequency, maximum functional bladder capacity (MBC), and average length of urine retention. Bed-wetting frequency is recorded by having the parent check for nighttime wetting on an hourly or nightly basis. MBC and average length of urine retention are obtained by instructing parents to use what is known as a water-loading procedure on a daily or weekly basis. This procedure consists of four primary steps. First, the child is sent to the toilet and instructed to urinate, if possible. Upon return, the child is giving a large quantity of fluid to drink (up to 500 ml) and asked to report when the initial urge to void occurs. Following this initial urge, the child is instructed to refrain from voiding until it becomes uncomfortable. At that time, the child is sent to the toilet with a measuring jug or graduated glass beaker. Parents are instructed to record the total time that voiding was postponed (i.e., from the initial urge to void to the indication that the urge to void was uncomfortable) and the amount of urine voided into the jug or beaker. MBC is obtained by dividing the total amount of urine voided by the number of the water-loading procedures conducted, while the average length of urine retention is calculated by averaging the total postponement time.

Following this formal assessment of enuretic behaviors, treatment begins by instructing parents to encourage increased fluid intake and to reinforce urine postponement. Urine retention is typically reinforced through tangible rewards, such as toys and candy, or parental attention, such as praise or games. Using these reinforcers, the child's retention period is gradually shaped by systematically increasing the length of retention necessary for reinforcement. Depending on the child's baseline measures, the retention criteria may start as low as a few minutes, increasing in 1- to 5-minute blocks. Maximum retention length is typically determined based on the child's reaction to the treatment (e.g., persistence of enuretic behaviors), with documented retention intervals reaching as high as 45 minutes. In addition to retention, RCT may also incorporate physical exercises aimed at increasing the child's control over actual urine flow. Such exercises typically require the child to practice stop-and-go patterns of urination, during which the child ceases and resumes voiding a number of times.

Although initially developed as a stand-alone treatment for enuresis, retention control training is often combined with other behavioral interventions. For example, a multicomponent treatment approach known as the full-spectrum home training makes use of a urine alarm (e.g., an apparatus consisting of a pad the child sleeps upon, a signal such as a loud noise or flashing light for waking the child, and a circuit that is completed and triggers the signal in the presence of fluid), RCT with monetary rewards, self-monitoring of wet/dry nights, and cleanliness training. Combining RCT with other enuretic treatment approaches allows for treatment flexibility and the creation of personalized treatment programs, although the application of such packages increases the treatment demands on both the parent and child.

RESEARCH BASIS

The efficacy of RCT as the primary method of treating nocturnal enuresis is questionable. Early research reported that RCT increased bladder capacity while decreasing both diurnal and nocturnal voiding. More recent research has failed to replicate these initial findings. Current studies indicate that RCT is effective in normalizing enuretic bladder capacity and may decrease diurnal urination but is generally ineffective in reducing nocturnal bed-wetting. These findings suggest that functional bladder capacity is not a prerequisite for nocturnal dryness. With this said, some studies have suggested that the incorporation of RCT with other treatment approaches may improve outcome levels and decrease relapse rates.

RELEVANT TARGET POPULATIONS AND EXCEPTIONS

Combined with other treatment approaches, this intervention has the potential to benefit most enuretic children. As with other behavioral treatments, RCT may not be as effective with children whose enuresis has a more biological etiology. A thorough medical screening should precede treatment to rule out diseases of the urinary tract such as cystitis and pyelonephritis. Although traditionally applied to enuresis, RCT may be applicable with other urinary difficulties. One promising line of research has suggested that RCT may be beneficial for the treatment of excessive urinary urgency (e.g., excessive frequency and urgency of voiding).

COMPLICATIONS

With the responsibility of administering RCT placed primarily in the hands of the parents, clinicians have encountered problems with treatment compliance. Some parents may require extensive support and training to ensure proper implementation. Some parents find the treatment to be aversive, thus increasing treatment noncompliance.

—*William Sharp and Alan M. Gross*

See also: *Behavioral Treatment in Natural Environments (Vols. I & III), Bell and Pad Bladder Training (Vol. II), Classical Conditioning (Vols. I, II, & III), Full-Spectrum Home Training for Simple Bed-Wetting (Vol. II)*

Suggested Readings

Doleys, D. M. (1977). Dry-bed training and retention control training: A comparison. *Behavior Therapy, 8,* 541–548.

Mellon, M. W., & McGrath, M. L. (2000). Empirically supported treatments in pediatric psychology: Nocturnal enuresis. *Journal of Pediatric Psychology, 25,* 193–214.

Miller, P. M. (1973). An experimental analysis of retention control training in the treatment of nocturnal enuresis in two institutional adolescents. *Behavior Therapy, 4,* 288–294.

RITUAL PREVENTION

DESCRIPTION OF THE STRATEGY

Ritual prevention is a technique typically used for curbing compulsive behaviors in those with obsessive-compulsive disorder (OCD). Obsessions are ruminative, bizarre thoughts that create distress, and compulsions are behaviors performed after an obsession to lower distress. An example would be a person obsessed with thoughts of contamination and who compulsively washed his or her hands frequently throughout the day.

Ritual prevention involves some stoppage of the compulsion either via a client's self-control or with a therapist's help. Ritual prevention is typically used in conjunction with other procedures such as somatic control exercises, cognitive restructuring, and exposure. Initially, clients with OCD are taught to control aversive physical sensations such as trembling or hyperventilation. Cognitive restructuring is also employed to help clients fully explore alternative and more realistic explanations for events.

Following the development of somatic and cognitive control strategies, a client with OCD is generally exposed to his or her obsession by establishing a situation that triggers the thought. For example, a therapist may ask a client with contamination obsessions to plunge his or her hand into dirt or ask a client with checking obsessions to check the oven once and then leave the house to meet the therapist several miles away. With exposure comes ritual prevention, which involves not allowing the client to engage in the compulsion (e.g., hand washing, returning to the house to check the oven). As the client refrains from the compulsion, he or she practices somatic and cognitive control strategies and should eventually realize that anxiety will decrease without the need for compulsive behavior. Contemporary exposure/ritual prevention protocols for OCD indicate that a client should eventually practice these techniques as independently as possible.

RESEARCH BASIS

Many single-case experimental and large between-group studies have empirically supported the use of ritual prevention for OCD. Ritual prevention is not highly effective, however, when separated from exposure-based assignments.

RELEVANT TARGET POPULATION

Ritual prevention has been developed and used primarily for people with OCD. In particular, the procedure is useful for those with hand washing, checking, ordering, counting, and other compulsions that involve clearly defined motor behavior. However, ritual prevention has also been used to successfully treat people with bulimia nervosa.

COMPLICATIONS

Ritual prevention is less useful in cases where people with OCD have very severe obsessions and compulsions, are unable or unwilling to attempt the procedures independently of a therapist, and/or utilize mental compulsions such as praying or repeating words silently. Clients must fully understand the rationale behind this technique for it to be useful.

CASE ILLUSTRATION

"Amanda" was a 17-year-old female who presented to a specialized outpatient therapy clinic for OCD. At the time of her referral, Amanda was checking mirrors at school for any cracks that could lead to bad luck. In particular, she believed that if she did not check for cracks, terrible events would happen. She checked for several hours per day, which precluded her ability to attend classes and concentrate on her schoolwork. Following training in somatic and cognitive control strategies, Amanda was instructed to check a mirror at school only once per class period. This allowed her some release of tension while simultaneously reducing her checking behavior. Initially, Amanda was escorted by the therapist or a school official to ensure that she was not checking mirrors beyond her approved schedule. Although her anxiety spiked at first, Amanda was shown that her anxiety did eventually diminish independent of checking and that terrible events had not occurred. Amanda's schedule of checking was eventually reduced to once every 2 hours and then gradually longer. After a period of 5 weeks, Amanda's checking behavior diminished substantially.

—Christopher A. Kearney,
Jennifer Vecchio, and Kelly Drake

See also: *Exposure (Vols. I & III), Foa, Edna B.*
(Vols. I & III), Relapse Prevention
(Vols. I, II, & III), Response Blocking (Vol. II)

Suggested Readings

Franklin, M. E., Abramowitz, J. S., Kozak, M. J., Levitt, J. T., & Foa, E. B. (2000). Effectiveness of exposure and ritual prevention for obsessive-compulsive disorder: Randomized compared with nonrandomized samples. *Journal of Consulting and Clinical Psychology, 68,* 594–602.

Overholser, J. C. (1999). Cognitive-behavioral treatment of obsessive-compulsive disorder. *Journal of Contemporary Psychotherapy, 29,* 369–382.

ROLE PLAYING

Role playing is broadly defined as any instance or situation in which one deliberately acts out or assumes a particular character or role. In behavior therapy, role playing refers to widely accepted therapeutic techniques in which participants act out specific behavioral roles. The enactments provide material that can be targeted by interventions, with the goals of modifying behavior, expanding awareness, or changing attitudes. The therapist often plays the role of antagonist, while the client usually plays himself or herself. Because role playing allows one to overcome inhibitions and act out the inner self in a spontaneous, creative way, this process is widely used and accepted as an intervention for children.

Although there are many variations of the technique, role plays often involve acting out either hypothetical situations or circumstances that the child actually faces. The therapist may begin with imaginal situations and then gradually, as rapport is built and the child becomes accustomed to role playing, move to real-life situations (e.g., peer interactions). Hypothetical scenarios should generally be close to real-life situations. Role playing can be effective for children because the child becomes an active participant in the treatment process. Through active involvement, children feel as if they have some control in the therapeutic process and often enjoy these activities. The child's enjoyment not only makes therapy more engaging for the child but also decreases the likelihood of resistance.

Role-playing adaptive behaviors is important in the amelioration of behavioral and psychological difficulties. Through role playing, the child can learn and practice in a safe environment. Not only is the child an active participant, but the therapist also plays an active role by fully experiencing and reinforcing progress. By practicing various situations that the child may face, the child is taught that he or she has choices in behaviors and is expected to generate his or her own possibilities for actions. The child is then faced with the consequences of these choices. Through this process, adaptive behaviors are learned and practiced.

Many empirical studies suggest that role playing is an effective therapeutic intervention for children. Not only is role play effective for teaching children coping strategies and social skills but it also is influential in treating children with pervasive difficulties. For example, research suggests that role play techniques can be effective for treating sexually abused children and children with language delays.

Both specific role-play techniques and general terminologies grew out of the initial endeavors toward developing role theory. The emergence of role playing as a therapeutic intervention in the 20th century was eventually extended to behaviorally oriented interventions for children. Currently, behavioral role-play activities are utilized in a broad range of settings with diverse populations. Role playing is frequently used as an intervention for child inpatient and outpatient therapy, in group settings, and in correctional environments. Because role-play techniques are effective for children across multiple settings, they are widely used by teachers and counselors with various clinical orientations.

—Jeffrey L. Kibler and Katherine M. Dollar

See also: Behavioral Rehearsal (Vols. I, II, & III), Modeling (Vols. I, II, & III), Role Playing (Vols. I & III)

Suggested Readings

Brooks, A. R., & Benjamin, B. J. (1989). The use of structured role play therapy in the remediation of grammatical deficits in language delayed children: Three case studies. *Journal of Children's Communication Development, 12*, 110–128.

Kipper, D. A. (1996). The emergence of role playing as a form of psychotherapy. *Journal of Group Psychotherapy, Psychodrama and Sociometry, 49*, 99–119.

Yardley-Matwiejczuk, K. A. (1997). *Role play: Theory & practice.* Thousand Oaks, CA: Sage.

S

SCHEDULES OF REINFORCEMENT

DESCRIPTION OF THE STRATEGY

The rate at which learning occurs varies according to the consequences that follow a behavior, and such consequences can occur on various "schedules." Consequences that follow a behavior and strengthen the likelihood that the behavior will be performed again in the future are referred to as reinforcers. Reinforcers, ideally, are delivered following an appropriate, or desirable, behavior, and the frequency and conditions by which they occur will yield changes in the behaviors performed by a child. Indeed, much of the variability observed in children's behavior can be explained by differences in schedules of reinforcement.

Schedules of reinforcement can be defined according to two basic parameters: (1) ratio versus interval and (2) fixed versus variable. Ratio schedules provide reinforcement based on a number of behaviors, whereas interval schedules deliver reinforcement following behavior that occurs after the passage of a given interval of time. With fixed schedules, reinforcers are delivered after an exact number of responses or an exact interval of time, whereas with variable schedules, the rate at which reinforcement is delivered occurs according to an average number of responses or average intervals of time.

If the two parameters of ratio versus interval and fixed versus variable are crossed, almost any schedule of reinforcement can be classified into one of the four types: fixed ratio, variable ratio, fixed interval, or variable interval.

Under fixed ratio (FR) schedules of reinforcement, a reinforcer is delivered when a target response has been emitted a specified number of times. FR schedules require that reinforcers are delivered consistently following the same number of responses, and that the counting of responses required for the delivery of a reinforcer begins after the previous reinforcer has been provided. Under FR schedules, the time interval between reinforcers will necessarily vary, as the interval depends on the number of responses displayed.

A special case of the FR schedule is that in which the ratio of responses to reinforcers is 1:1. Specifically, an FR 1 schedule ("1" meaning delivery of a reinforcer after one response) is called a "continuous" schedule of reinforcement. Schedules requiring more than one response for a reinforcer are called "intermittent" schedules. Although continuous schedules will yield a higher rate of new response acquisition, intermittent schedules are typically more effective in producing a stable or consistent pattern of behavioral responding. In the natural environment, FR schedules are relatively rare, as reinforcers are not typically delivered in a consistent manner after exactly the same number of responses has been emitted. One example of an FR schedule is household chores, for which the child is provided with a reinforcer upon the completion of a set number of tasks.

Under a variable ratio (VR) schedule of reinforcement, the number of responses that the child must emit before a reinforcer is delivered varies around a set number. For example, on a VR 50 schedule, a reinforcer would be delivered after an average of 50 responses but would not always be delivered after precisely 50 responses.

VR schedules occur fairly commonly, such that in many circumstances it is difficult to predict when one's efforts will lead to a reinforcer. When rewards are unpredictable, the child must continue to exert effort at a steady rate. VR schedules are often observed in the social interactions of children, such that when children attempt to initiate play with their peers, some overtures will be reinforced by acceptance, whereas other invitations will be declined. Another example of a VR schedule is free throws with a basketball, such that the child must make a variable number of shots before one goes in.

Under fixed interval (FI) schedules, reinforcers are delivered only when the response occurs after a given period of time, such that a specific interval of time must elapse after the target behavior is produced in order for the reinforcer to be delivered. For example, an FI 5 schedule denotes that the first response emitted 5 minutes or more after the previous reinforcer will be reinforced. Common examples of FI schedules include an allowance, such that many children who do chores are provided with a monetary reward at the end of each week, or recess, such that at the same time each day, children who participate in school are rewarded with time to engage in play activities.

Finally, variable interval (VI) schedules are those under which the frequency of reinforcement varies around an average interval of time. For example, under a VI 15 schedule, a reinforcer would be delivered after an average interval of 15 seconds had elapsed following the production of the target behavior. Naturally occurring VI schedules in the environment include waiting in line for the water fountain, such that the average amount of time the child will have to wait in line before being reinforced with a drink varies around some average interval. Similarly, although a family might eat dinner at approximately the same time each evening, the precise time that dinner occurs will most likely vary around a set average.

Not all schedules fall into these four categories. For example, a schedule under which no reinforcer is delivered is called extinction. When a behavior is placed on an extinction schedule, behaviors that previously occurred with great frequency occur with reduced frequency. Particularly when following a continuous schedule of reinforcement, extinction will ultimately result in a rapid reduction in behavioral responding. However, before a behavior is extinguished, an initial increase in the behavior is sometimes observed, which is referred to as an "extinction burst," which typically drops off with continued extinction.

One variation of extinction is noncontingent reinforcement (NCR), in which reinforcers are administered according to a predetermined time schedule, rather than delivered contingently upon a desired target behavior. NCR weakens the association between the inappropriate target behavior and the reinforcer by providing the child with a reinforcer independent of the inappropriate behavior. Thus, the child's motivation to display the inappropriate behavior in order to obtain the reinforcer is greatly reduced, leading the child to produce desired behaviors at a greater frequency.

Some schedules involve the simultaneous consideration of two behaviors. For example, differential reinforcement of other behavior (DRO) schedules are typically applied when addressing behavioral excesses rather than behavioral deficits, such that the goal of the intervention would be to decrease the display of a problematic high-frequency behavior while simultaneously increasing the display of a low-frequency desired behavior. For example, in using a DRO schedule to reduce the frequency of whining, instances of whining are placed on an extinction schedule, and reinforcers are delivered contingently upon instances of talking pleasantly.

Various schedules of reinforcement will result in different effects on the rate and frequency of the desired behavioral response. For example, when a child is acquiring a new behavioral response, learning typically occurs most efficiently under a very high rate of reinforcement, such that a reinforcer is delivered very frequently or after only a small number of target responses have been emitted. However, variable schedules will ultimately result in behavioral responses that are most resistant to extinction. For example, if a parent is interested in teaching a child to say "Please" before every request, the parent would initially deliver a reinforcer to the child following every utterance of "Please." However, once such a response was established, the parent would place the child on variable ratio schedule, whereby reinforcement was delivered on only a percentage of the occasions on which the child emitted the desired response. This example illustrates that, once a new behavior is emitted at a constant rate, the ratio of responses to reinforcers can be increased, such that more behaviors or a longer interval of time is required before a reinforcer will be delivered. Such practices are referred to as stretching the ratio or schedule thinning. To determine the optimal point at which a schedule has been "thinned," the consistency of the behavioral responding must be examined closely.

RESEARCH BASIS

Research has shown that variations in schedules of reinforcement will yield changes in the child's behavioral responding and that each type of schedule is associated with a typical pattern and rate of response. Children reinforced on an FR schedule will generally produce behaviors at a high rate, with the rate of response production corresponding to the rate of reinforcement. However, after each reinforcer is delivered, the child will pause, yielding what is termed a "postreinforcement" pause. As the number of responses required is increased, the pauses following reinforcer will increase.

VR schedules typically yield higher rates of responding than do FR schedules, primarily because children in VR conditions never know with certainty how many responses are required for the delivery of reinforcement. The overall pattern of responding in a VR schedule also depends on the number of responses required to attain a reinforcer. If an average of 50 responses is required for a reinforcer, a child might continue to respond if a reinforcer is delivered after 45 or 55 responses but might stop emitting the desired response once the number of responses required goes beyond a certain number. Unlike FR schedules, VR schedules typically do not yield a postreinforcement pause.

FI schedules typically result in relatively stable pauses following each delivered reinforcer and an increase in responding once the time interval has elapsed. Similar to FR schedules, a postreinforcement pause will be observed when behaviors are maintained under an FI schedule. Another typical response pattern observed under FI schedules is the production of few or no responses immediately following reinforcement.

Finally, VI schedules yield higher rates of responding than do FI schedules, although the rates of responding under a VI schedule are typically not as high as those observed under FR and VR schedules. Similar to the pattern of responding observed under VR schedules, response patterns observed under VI schedules also do not involve postreinforcement pauses. Under a VI 5 schedule, reinforcers are delivered after intervals of an average length of 5 minutes

have passed following the performance of the target behavior. Thus, when the behavior is placed on an extinction schedule, it will take much longer for the child to realize that his or her behavior is not being reinforced than if he or she had acquired the behavior under an FI 5 schedule; because the child is uncertain of precisely when reinforcement will occur, the child will continue to respond in the hopes of receiving a reinforcer.

RELEVANT TARGET POPULATIONS AND EXCEPTIONS

Reinforcement is a universal and ubiquitous component of learning that spans gender, age, and culture. As the behavioral treatment literature has demonstrated, practically any child exhibiting a behavioral deficit can benefit from the provision of reinforcement on a specific schedule, given sufficient aptitude or physical skill to learn the behavior.

COMPLICATIONS

Schedules of reinforcement play a large part in determining how successful a specific reinforcer will be in eliciting the desired response. For example, if the schedule on which reinforcers are being delivered is too lean, the child will become frustrated and cease responding; conversely, if the schedule is too rich, the child will not have sufficient incentive to continue to respond or the response will not generalize to contexts with leaner schedules. The reinforcers being delivered must also be desirable to the child, such that the child is motivated to display the desired responses. Moreover, in many cases the child might already be receiving reinforcers that have not yet been made contingent upon the target behavior; if such items or events are delivered according to a schedule of reinforcement, the child can learn to emit the target response in order to receive items that are of value to him or her.

The extent to which the target behavior is discrepant from the child's baseline behavior must also be examined. If the target behavior is complex, the child might be incapable of producing the desired response spontaneously. In such instances, approximations of the behavior must be reinforced until the target behavior is mastered.

The consistency with which a schedule can be followed must also be considered. For example, particular schedules might lend themselves better to specific behaviors or settings. In a large classroom, a teacher might find it easiest to provide reinforcement on a VI schedule, such that the delivery of reinforcers is not contingent upon the display of particular behaviors, which might be particularly difficult to notice consistently in a busy classroom. Conversely, behaviors that occur very infrequently might be learned most efficiently under an FR 1 schedule, thus strengthening the association between the desired response and the reinforcer. If reinforcers are delivered after too long a delay, the child will not learn to associate the reinforcer with the target response.

Finally, many behaviors are initially acquired under continuous schedules of reinforcement but then maintained under intermittent schedule. One of the risks associated with such schedule thinning is ratio strain, or the effect of increasing the ratio of reinforcers to responses too quickly. If the ratio strain is too great (i.e., increasing the ratio from FR 2 to FR 10), the child can cease to emit the target behavior altogether.

CASE ILLUSTRATION

"James" was a 5-year-old boy attending a regular education kindergarten class. During classroom instruction, James was unable to stay seated at his desk. He frequently walked around the room, talked with his peers, stood over the shoulders of students at their desks, and tapped his teacher on the back to request her attention. James was unable to complete any of his assignments and frequently elicited negative attention from his classmates and teacher. However, when James's teacher or the educational assistant aide returned him to his seat, they would talk for several seconds with James, pat him on the shoulder, physically sit him down in his chair, and frequently pause to help with his assignment at his desk.

A behavioral analysis revealed that the antecedents of James's behavior pertained primarily to situations in which students were required to sit at their desks and complete assignments independently. The primary target behaviors identified included leaving his seat, distracting other students, and interrupting his teacher. Consequences of James's behaviors included escape from having to complete his assignments, being spoken to by his classmates, being reprimanded by his teacher, and receiving attention and assistance with his work.

Given that James's inability to remain seated during periods of classroom instruction appeared to be reinforced by the attention that he was receiving from his teacher and peers, it was suggested to the teacher and the aide that they provide James with attention contingent upon remaining seated that would be delivered on a VI 60" schedule. Specifically, James was required to remain in his seat for an average duration of 60 seconds before positive attention was provided. A VI schedule was chosen over a VR or an FI schedule because the teacher reported she would have difficulty delivering reinforcers contingent upon a specific behavior or in accordance to a fixed duration of time in the context of the busy classroom. A variable interval of 60 seconds was selected, given that observations indicated that James was able to remain in his seat for an average duration of 90 seconds before leaving his seat to walk around the classroom. It was hypothesized that a VI 60" schedule would require James to stay at his desk for a long enough period of time to experience a reinforcer. Finally, positive attention was chosen as the reinforcer, given that James appeared to respond very well to the attention he received from the teacher and the aide when he was returned to his desk and frequently sought out the attention of these individuals while they were assisting other students with their work.

On the first day of implementing the VI 60" schedule, James was observed to leave his desk on five occasions before the appropriate time had elapsed. On these occasions, James was returned to his desk by the teacher or aide who had been instructed to only say to James "Please stay here; I'll be back to check on you in 1 minute." On the second day of the schedule, James was observed to leave his seat only three times, and after one week of providing James with attention on the VI 60" schedule, James was able to remain seated for the full interval between reinforcers throughout the instructional periods. The teacher and aide were then requested to begin thinning the schedule of reinforcement, such that James would receive the attentional reinforcer after longer and longer variable intervals. The intervals were increased gradually from 60 seconds, to 90 seconds, and then to 2 minutes. After 6 weeks, James was able to remain seated at his desk without individual attention from the teacher for an average duration of 5 minutes, a duration that was relatively typical among his classmates. Follow-up assessment further revealed that James was finishing his assignments with the same rate of completion and accuracy as his classmates and that his relationships with his classmates had improved. James's teacher reported that James's ability to spend an increased amount of time at his desk during instructional periods greatly reduced the amount of strain on her time with respect to assisting her students in the classroom.

—*Bruce F. Chorpita and Sarah E. Francis*

See also: *Operant Conditioning (Vols. I, II, & III), Positive Reinforcement (Vol. II), Reinforcement (Vols. I & III), Schedule-Induced Behavior (Vol. III), Schedules of Reinforcement (Vols. I & III), Skinner, Burrhus Frederic (Vols. I, II, & III), Token Economy (Vols. I, II, & III),*

Suggested Readings

Bijou, S. W. (1996). Reflections on some early events related to behavior analysis of child development. *The Behavior Analyst, 19,* 49–60.

Bowman, L. G., Fisher, W. W., Thompson, R. H., & Piazza, C. C. (1997). On the relation of mands and the function of destructive behavior. *Journal of Applied Behavior Analysis, 30,* 251–265.

Chance, P. (1988). *Learning and behavior* (2nd ed.). Belmont, CA: Wadsworth.

Fattu, N. A., Mech, E. V., & Auble, D. (1955). Partial reinforcement related to "free" responding in extinction with pre-school children. *Journal of Experimental Education, 23,* 365–368.

Ferster, C. B., & Skinner, B. F. (1957). *Schedules of reinforcement.* New York: Appleton-Century-Crofts.

Lalli, J. S., Casey, S. D., & Kates, K. (1997). Noncontingent reinforcement as treatment for severe problem behavior: Some procedural variations. *Journal of Applied Behavior Analysis, 30,* 127–137.

Lerman, D. C., Iwata, B. A., Shore, B. A., & Kahng, S. W. (1996). Responding maintained by intermittent reinforcement: Implications for the use of extinction with problem behavior in clinical settings. *Journal of Applied Behavior Analysis, 29,* 153–171.

Luiselli, J. K., & Reisman, J. (1980). Some variations in the use of differential reinforcement procedures with mentally retarded children in specialized treatment settings. *Applied Research in Mental Retardation, 1,* 277–288.

O'Reilly, M., Lancioni, G., & Taylor, I. (1999). An empirical analysis of two forms of extinction to treat aggression. *Research in Developmental Disabilities, 20,* 315–325.

Ramasay, R., Taylor, R. L., & Ziegler, E. W. (1996). Eliminating inappropriate classroom behavior using a DRO schedule: A preliminary study. *Psychological Reports, 78,* 753–754.

SELF-INJURY AND SUICIDE

DESCRIPTION OF THE STRATEGY

Self-injurious thoughts and behaviors in children and adolescents represent an enormous public health concern around the world. In the United States, for example, completed suicide is currently the sixth leading cause of death among children (5–14 years) and the third leading cause of death among adolescents and young adults (15–24 years). Nonfatal self-injurious behaviors are even more common. Approximately 20% of high school students report seriously considering suicide, and 9% report making an actual suicide attempt in the previous 12 months. Moreover, up to 40% of adolescents in the community and 60% of adolescent psychiatric inpatients report engaging in self-mutilative behavior. Despite the high prevalence and serious physical and psychological damage associated with these behaviors, information about effective evaluation and treatment practices is limited.

The evaluation and treatment of self-injurious behaviors is often hindered by a failure to carefully distinguish among and assess the different self-injurious constructs of interest. For instance, what does it mean to say a child or adolescent is suicidal? The following nomenclature has been recommended by researchers to clarify such issues. *Suicide* refers to death from a self-inflicted injury in which the individual *intended* to die. *Suicide attempt* refers to potentially self-injurious, but currently nonfatal, behavior in which the individual *intended* to die. *Suicidal ideation* refers to self-reported thoughts of making a suicide attempt. *Self-mutilative behavior* refers to intentional destruction of one's own body tissue in which there is *no intent* to die. Evaluation of self-injurious thoughts and behaviors should include the collection of data related to each of these constructs.

Evaluation should also focus on factors known to be associated with self-injurious thoughts and behaviors. Self-injurious thoughts and behaviors are multi-determined events, and etiological factors will vary somewhat from case to case; however, research has identified several variables associated with increased risk. These include the presence of a mood disorder, particularly with hopelessness and anhedonia; a substance use disorder; a psychotic disorder; anxiety and agitation; difficulties with problem solving and cognitive flexibility; and a previous history of self-injurious behaviors, particularly previous suicide attempts. The evaluation should also include an examination of the degree of planning of and preparation for self-injurious behavior. In addition, the individual's ability to implement any identified plan should be taken into consideration (e.g., does the individual have access to a firearm, pills, sharp object, or other means of self-injury?).

Cognitive-behavioral treatment strategies for modifying self-injurious thoughts and behaviors center on reducing the frequency of these thoughts and behaviors, as well as on modifying correlates or risk factors that are present that might play a role in the generation or maintenance of self-injurious thoughts and behaviors. Perhaps the most common component in cognitive-behavioral treatments for self-injurious thoughts and behaviors is a focus on improving interpersonal problem-solving skills. This typically involves teaching the individual several steps for identifying problems, generating potential solutions, evaluating the probable consequences associated with each solution, choosing and implementing a solution, and engaging in self-evaluation.

Cognitive-behavioral treatments for self-injurious thoughts and behaviors also typically emphasize improving emotion regulation and distress tolerance skills. It is believed that those who resort to self-injury often do so to relieve distress due to an inability to inhibit impulsive responding to provocative events. Thus, alternative, more adaptive skills for relieving or tolerating distress and for inhibiting impulsive responding are taught and practiced. Emotion regulation skills taught in such treatments include identifying and labeling emotions (both positive and negative), expressing emotions (both verbally and nonverbally), and engaging in pleasurable activities. Distress tolerance skills include engaging in distraction and relaxation exercises. Consistent with the cognitive-behavioral approach, throughout each of these components there is also an emphasis on self-monitoring of the individual's thoughts, behaviors, and emotions and special attention to the antecedents and consequences of the self-injurious thoughts and behaviors.

Cognitive-behavioral treatments are also aimed at relieving the psychiatric symptoms that may be contributing to the self-injurious thoughts and behaviors, such as those mentioned above. Most cognitive-behavioral treatments for self-injurious thoughts and behaviors also stress the importance of careful and continuous evaluation of self-injurious thoughts and behaviors, as well as an emphasis on the importance of facilitating treatment attendance and adherence.

RESEARCH BASIS

There is a growing body of research on psychosocial treatments aimed at decreasing suicidal ideation and suicide attempts. Overall, several brief cognitive-behavioral treatment packages have demonstrated some success at decreasing suicidal ideation as well as depressed mood and negative cognitions, but not suicide attempts. These treatments vary in structure and content; however, most include a problem-solving skills training component. One long-term treatment package, dialectical behavior therapy (DBT), had demonstrated success in reducing the frequency of suicide attempts and hospitalization time. DBT included a problem-solving skills training component as well as components focused on teaching emotion regulation, distress tolerance, and interpersonal communication skills. Unfortunately, this treatment had no effect on reducing suicidal ideation compared to a treatment-as-usual condition. To date, no treatment packages or techniques have satisfied the criteria for empirically supported treatment status for reducing suicidal ideation, suicide attempts, or self-mutilative behaviors.

It is notable that research on the treatment of self-injurious thoughts and behaviors has focused almost exclusively on adult populations. Few treatment studies have attempted to address self-injurious thoughts and behaviors in child and adolescent samples, and there are currently no empirically supported treatments for this group.

RELEVANT TARGET POPULATIONS AND EXCEPTIONS

Self-injurious thoughts and behaviors occur across all diagnostic, developmental, and socioeconomic groups and are thus relevant to all populations. Nevertheless, research has identified factors associated with increased risk of self-harm thoughts and behaviors. In terms of developmental level, rates of self-mutilation, suicidal ideation, suicide attempts, and completed suicide, all increase significantly as children transition into adolescence. For example, the rate of completed suicide increases sixfold during the transition from early (10–14 years) to late (15–19 years) adolescence.

Those with an identified psychiatric diagnosis are at greatly increased risk of self-harm. Although a psychiatric diagnosis obviously is not required for a child or adolescent to engage in self-injurious thoughts or behaviors, research has demonstrated that most individuals who engage in self-injurious thoughts or behaviors (whether death is intended or not) have a diagnosable psychiatric disorder at the time. Those diagnosed with a mood disorder, psychotic disorder, substance use disorder, and conduct disorder are at particularly high risk.

In terms of gender, among children and adolescents, girls report suicidal ideation and self-mutilation at a higher rate than boys and make suicide attempts approximately twice as often as boys. However, adolescent boys are approximately four to five times more likely to die by suicide than girls, perhaps as a function of the more lethal methods of self-harm typically employed by boys (e.g., firearms and jumping) compared to girls (e.g., overdose).

COMPLICATIONS

A number of factors can complicate the evaluation and treatment of self-injurious thoughts and behaviors. Perhaps the greatest difficulty involves the reliability and validity of risk-assessment throughout the course of treatment. Introducing uncertainty into the evaluation process is the low agreement among informants in the assessment of self-injurious thoughts and behaviors. Children/adolescents, parents, teachers, and clinicians often disagree as to whether self-injurious thoughts and behaviors are present, and if so, to what degree. Another complicating factor is the rapidity and unpredictability with which self-injurious thoughts and behaviors often occur. Such events often occur impulsively and with little warning. It is not uncommon for a child or adolescent to fail to inform a parent, friend, or clinician that a stressor has occurred or that self-injury is being contemplated, planned, or implemented.

These complications and the associated risk of self-harm can be minimized by frequent and thorough assessment of key constructs. Such assessment always should draw from multiple informants (i.e., involve the child/adolescent, parents, teachers, and clinician) and measurement methods (i.e., interview, rating scale, observation).

CASE ILLUSTRATION

"Donna" was a 13-year-old African American girl who was brought to an emergency room by her mother after Donna reportedly ingested 20 aspirin tablets. After receiving medical intervention in the emergency room, Donna was admitted to an adolescent psychiatric inpatient unit where she stayed for 3 days before being discharged and referred to a child and adolescent outpatient clinic for psychosocial treatment.

Donna presented to the outpatient clinic with her mother 1 day after discharge from the hospital. Donna and her mother were interviewed together and separately. The diagnostic interview was guided by a semi-structured diagnostic measure. In addition, Donna's mother completed several rating scales relevant to psychiatric diagnosis as well as aspects of Donna's past history and current risk of self-injurious thoughts and behaviors. With Donna and her mother's consent, the clinician also contacted her current teacher and school guidance counselor, who provided historical information via telephone and completed several rating scales via postal mail, and her inpatient treatment team, which provided detailed records of her inpatient assessment and treatment. In addition to the diagnostic interview, Donna completed several self-report and clinician-administered rating scales focused on past history and current risk of self-injurious thoughts and behaviors, including the Children's Depression Inventory, the Beck Hopelessness Scale for Children, the Scale for Suicidal Ideation, the Suicide Intent Scale, and the Functional Assessment of Self-Mutilation. In addition, Donna participated in a clinical interview focused on obtaining information about her history of self-injurious thoughts and behaviors and current risk of self-harm.

Evaluation data yielded several inconsistent findings. Donna's mother, teachers, and inpatient treatment team reported that this was Donna's first episode of suicidal ideation and her first suicide attempt. Donna's report on the clinical interview was consistent with this. However, Donna indicated on the self-report rating scales that she had made two previous suicide attempts (both by overdose, neither reported or requiring medical intervention) and that she had contemplated suicide on many occasions in the past, suggesting a higher risk for future suicide attempt than previously assumed. Donna denied a history of contemplating or engaging in self-mutilative behavior.

Follow-up assessment of Donna's suicidal ideation and suicide attempts revealed that most episodes of suicidal ideation and all three suicide attempts were immediately preceded by verbal arguments with her mother in which Donna was told she would be "thrown out of the house" if she continued to disobey her mother's commands. Donna reported that she contemplated and attempted suicide as a way to escape from her situation and from the intense, negative affect she experiences when arguing with her mother because she could not think of any other way to improve her feelings or her situation.

Treatment focused immediately on ensuring Donna's safety throughout the treatment period. The clinician met with Donna and her mother to develop a plan for safety, which included reaching an agreement about the focus and structure of treatment and the importance of honesty and adherence to the treatment program, the generation of a list of "go to" people Donna could approach if she began to experience thoughts of self-harm, and a discussion of how and under what circumstances Donna and her mother should seek immediate professional assistance. Donna and her mother also received psychoeducation about self-injurious thoughts and behaviors, particularly about their course and effects of current treatment approaches, and Donna received instruction in self-monitoring of thoughts, feelings, and self-injury related thoughts and behaviors. Donna began self-monitoring practices immediately to facilitate continuous assessment of the antecedent and consequent events related with her self-injurious thoughts and behaviors.

Given Donna's difficulties generating alternative, adaptive solutions to her problems, treatment focused on improving her problem-solving skills. She was taught basic steps for identifying problems, generating alternative solutions, evaluating the probable consequences of each solution, and selecting and implementing a solution. She practiced these problem-solving steps with her clinician both verbally and in role-play situations. She was also assigned problem-solving situations for homework in which she was required to practice her problem-solving steps in real-life situations.

Given Donna's difficulties with affect regulation and distress tolerance, she was taught emotion regulation and distress tolerance skills. These focused on teaching Donna to identify and label her emotions and to communicate these effectively to others. Donna also learned to tolerate negative affective states via the use of exposure exercises as well as through practicing relaxation techniques.

In addition, Donna was taught and practiced interpersonal communication skills to improve her ability to effectively and assertively communicate her thoughts and feelings to her mother as well as to others around her. For instance, Donna and her clinician practiced basic conversational skills and discussed and role-played the use of empathy, validation, compromising, and collaborative problem-solving in sessions. Donna later used these skills in homework assignments with her mother, teachers, and friends.

Donna did not make any additional suicide attempts over the course of treatment, although she did experience brief periods of suicidal ideation on several occasions. However, in the context of her strong treatment attendance and adherence, she demonstrated increasing abilities for affect regulation, distress tolerance, and interpersonal communication. Donna also developed an impressive ability to generate proactive, adaptive solutions to problems she had with her mother and other people around her, which decreased the frequency with which she considered suicide a solution to her problems.

—*Matthew K. Nock*

See also: *Coping With Depression (Vols. I & III), Problem-Solving Therapy (Vols. I & III), Social and Interpersonal Skills Training (Vol. II), Social Competence Treatment: Externalizing Disorders (Vol. II), Social Effectiveness Training (Vols. I & III), Social Skills Training (Vols. I & III)*

Suggested Readings

Brent, D. A., & Poling, K. (1997). *Cognitive therapy treatment manual for depressed and suicidal youth.* Pittsburgh, PA: University of Pittsburgh, Services for Teens at Risk.

Linehan, M. M. (1993). *Cognitive-behavioral treatment of borderline personality disorder.* New York: Guilford Press.

Miller, A. L., & Glinski, J. (2002). Youth suicidal behavior: Assessment and intervention. *Journal of Clinical Psychology, 56,* 1131–1152.

Nock, M. K., & Kazdin, A. E. (2002). Examination of cognitive, affective, and behavioral factors and suicide-related outcomes in children and young adolescents. *Journal of Clinical Child and Adolescent Psychology, 31,* 48–58.

O'Carroll, P. W., Berman, A. L., Maris, R. W., Moscicki, E. K., Tanney, B. L., & Silverman, M. M. (1996). Beyond the Tower of Babel: A nomenclature for suicidology. *Suicide & Life Threatening Behavior, 26,* 237–252.

Prinstein, M. J., Nock, M. K., Spirito, A., & Grapentine, W. L. (2001). Multi-method assessment of suicidality in adolescent psychiatric inpatients: Preliminary results. *Journal of the American Academy of Child and Adolescent Psychiatry, 40,* 1053–1061.

Rudd, M. D., Joiner, T., & Rajab, M. H. (2001). *Treating suicidal behavior: An effective, time-limited approach.* New York: Guilford Press.

SELF-INSTRUCTION TRAINING

DESCRIPTION OF THE STRATEGY

Self-instruction training is an evidenced-based treatment strategy usually employed as part of a cognitive-behavioral intervention. In self-instruction training, emphasis is placed on teaching the individual a variety of self-statements that would be used by the individual to either control his or her behavior or perform certain tasks.

The theoretical base for self-instruction training was derived from Lev Vygotsky's and Aleksandr Luria's work in the late 1950s on the functional relationship between language and behavior. Vygotsky theorized that as children internalize verbal commands, they take a critical step toward voluntary control of their own behavior. Luria, Vygotsky's student, elaborated on this theory by proposing that children undergo two developmental shifts concerning language and behavior. According to Luria, children's behaviors are initially under the control of others' verbalization, particularly parents. The first developmental shift takes place when children gain verbal control over their own behavior through overt verbalizations. The verbal control initially experienced by children is mainly impulsive, and speech is used as a physical stimulus that can either inhibit or promote behaviors. The second developmental shift takes place by age 5 or 6 years when children begin control over their behavior through their own covert verbalizations. The shift from overt to covert verbal control also signals a shift from impulsive to semantic verbal control. When children acquire covert verbal control, they also begin to view speech as a carrier of symbolic meaning and acquire internal self-regulating speech.

Early support for this position theory can be drawn from research studies conducted in the 1970s. These studies examined the ability of impulsive preschool children to resist distractions and delay self-gratification through the use of self-generated verbal strategies (e.g., self-instructions and self-praise). Results indicated children were unable to come up with self-instructions to help themselves cope with distractions on their own. However, if the children were provided with specific self-instructions from the experimenters, they were able to improve resistance to distractions.

Similar to Luria, researchers also proposed that children's private speech followed a developmental hierarchy. The lowest level consisted of self-stimulatory private speech (e.g., animal noises, singing, repeating words). The second level, similar to Jean Piaget's collective monologue, consisted of outer-directed private speech (e.g., speech directed to inanimate objects and self-narration of children's own activities). The third level consisted of inward-directed or self-guided private speech (e.g., self-instructions). The final level consisted of external manifestations of inner speech characterized by inaudible mutterings. The inner speech of impulsive children was considered immature and proposed to consist of self-stimulatory private speech (Level 1).

Results from research studies showed that impulsive children used similar amounts of inner-directed private speech (Level 3) as nonimpulsive children. Also, impulsive children used more self-stimulating (Level 1) and outer directed private speech (Level 2). Similarly, a majority of verbalization emitted by aggressive children consisted of immature self-stimulating private speech (Level 1).

Other researchers applied the concept of private speech to young children's problem-solving abilities and proposed that impulsive and hyperactive children did not process information efficiently because they used feedback in a trial-and-error fashion during problem-solving tasks. Impulsive and hyperactive children possessed difficulties in (a) comprehending the task or problem, (b) accessing mediators needed to complete task, and (c) producing mediators that did not guide behavior. The interventions formulated to address these three deficiencies contained discrete steps, each aimed at addressing each deficiency and improving task.

Donald Meichenbaum and Joseph Goodman drew from these theories on the private speech of children in their formulation of self-instruction procedures. Their application of self-instruction training is as follows: The clinician breaks up the task (e.g., completing a school assignment) in discrete steps and teaches performance-relevant skills to the child. The clinician begins by first modeling the desired behavior while narrating the self-instructions (cognitive modeling). The self-instructions used are focused on the specifics of the task, including (a) problem definition and approach (strategy used to solve problem), (b) focusing of attention, (c) selection of a solution, and (d) self-reinforcement for the desired outcome or coping statement for an undesirable outcome. Next, the clinician narrates the self-instructions while the child performs the desired behavior (overt, external guidance). In the next step, the child whispers the self-instructions while performing the desired behavior (covert, self-instruction). Finally, the child uses private speech in the form of self-instructions to guide his or her performance of the desired behavior (covert, self-instruction). This conceptualization of self-instruction training has been used alone or as a part of a cognitive-behavioral intervention to treat a range of disorders.

RESEARCH BASIS

Self-instruction training has been used to treat a variety of child (e.g., fears, impulsivity) and adult (e.g., schizophrenia, social phobia) problems. Studies in the 1970s and early 1980s generally used self-instruction training exclusively; more recently, self-instruction training has been used as part of cognitive-behavioral treatment programs that also include a variety of other therapeutic techniques, such as problem solving and relaxation training. Self-instruction training has been shown to have limited success on its own; however, as a component of a cognitive behavioral treatment program, self-instruction training has been shown to have efficacy. When self-instruction training has been compared to other active treatments, however, no significant differences have been found.

Child Nighttime Fears

Self-instruction training has been used to treat young children's fear of the dark. Results from these studies showed that children were able to tolerate less illumination and stay in the dark longer by using competence self-statements ("I am a brave boy [girl]. I can take care of myself"). However, the use of self-instruction did not generalize to other situations. The investigator suggested that children may make greater improvements if they were reminded to use the self-instruction in other situations. When relaxation, positive imagery, self-monitoring, and contingency management were added to competence self-statements, nighttime fears for all child participants decreased relative to pretreatment. Also, for most of the children, the fears were no longer present at 1-year follow-up. These findings suggest that a more comprehensive approach has greater efficacy than self-instruction training alone.

Child Behavior Problems

Self-instruction training has been shown to be efficacious relative to a control group for decreasing disruptive behavior and increasing educational performance. For example, the Think Aloud program is a 13-session training program for aggressive elementary schoolboys. This program applied the techniques of Meichenbaum and Goodman to a group format.

The first four steps used in the training program were consistent with Meichenbaum and Goodman's formulation and included (1) problem identification:

What is my problem?; (2) problem approach/strategy: How can I do it?; (3) focusing attention: Am I using my plan?; and (4) self-reinforcement for correct performance or coping statement for incorrect performance. A final step was added: (5) evaluation of task performance: How did I do? The five steps were first modeled by the therapist, and later the verbalizations were prompted by the therapist and then slowly faded. Children who participated in the Think Aloud program showed improvements in psychoeducational measures relative to a control group.

Hyperactive and Impulsive Children

Despite some evidence for efficacy with disruptive children, self-instruction training has generally not been found to improve either academics or classroom behavior among impulsive and hyperactive children. When self-instruction training was employed as part of a cognitive-behavioral treatment program, children showed improvements in self-control and hyperactivity as rated by teachers. However, when the intervention program was compared to a nonspecified group treatment condition, both conditions showed significant improvements, suggesting that neither treatment was superior.

Treatment Following Life Changes for Children

One study was found that used self-instruction training along with other techniques (e.g., relaxation, imagery, cognitive correction) as part of a treatment program aimed at helping young children adjust to family changes (e.g., divorce, death of a parent). Findings indicated that the program was useful in reducing cognitive distortions.

RELEVANT TARGET POPULATIONS

Although self-instruction training has been used to treat a variety of problems in children, the area most frequently addressed with this strategy includes difficulties associated with externalizing disorders such as impulsive and disruptive behavior. Despite this focus, there is little empirical support for the use of self-instruction training for reducing impulsive and disruptive behaviors. The most favorable results concerning self-instruction training are from studies that have included self-instruction training as part of a cognitive-behavioral intervention to treat phobic disorders in children. One example of how self-instruction training can be used as part of a cognitive-behavioral treatment program to treat children with phobic disorders is described in the case illustration.

COMPLICATIONS

As mentioned earlier, self-instruction training often includes the use of coping statements. In the area of phobias and anxiety disorders, there is some evidence that the use of coping statements may elevate anxiety. Some researchers have cautioned, however, that positive cognitions in the form of coping statements may even negatively affect performance. Coping statements may interfere with, or consume, resources related to information processing, thereby interfering with task performance. This view is supported by research findings showing that anxious children report significantly more coping and negative self-talk than nonanxious children.

Despite these concerns, some researchers have suggested that coping self-statements may be useful as a short-term treatment strategy to reduce the negative cognitions reported by children and their parents. This may be due to qualitative differences between self-talk at initial assessment and self-talk as part of a self-instruction treatment strategy. The self-talk of children at the initial assessment may not be functionally useful in reducing anxiety and improving performance; however, self-talk conducted under the supervision of a clinician may become more functionally useful in reducing anxiety and increasing task performance because the self-talk tends to become more focused and strategic.

CASE ILLUSTRATION

"David," a 10-year-old African American boy, was referred to a child anxiety disorders specialty clinic by one of his teachers. He refused to participate in group activities or talk in front of the class, and he had few friends. His mother reported that her son was very shy and feared that other children would pick on him if he made a mistake. Similar to his mother, David reported that the reason he avoided speaking in front of class and working in groups was because he feared he would be picked on by other children if he made a mistake. David was assessed using a diagnostic structured interview and received a diagnosis of social phobia. David began cognitive-behavioral treatment, which included self-instruction training.

Treatment initially focused on breaking the desired task (e.g., working in a group) into discrete steps. These steps included (a) sitting in a group without talking, (b) introducing himself in a group, (c) making one contribution during the group activity, (d) making at least three contributions during the group activity, and (e) making at least five contributions during the group activity.

The desired behaviors during these tasks were first modeled by the therapist in the clinic. The therapist narrated the self-statements during the task. These self-statements covered the following areas: (a) problem identification: "I want to join the group"; (b) problem approach/strategy: "I am going to sit in the group"; (c) focusing attention: "I need to pay attention to my task"; (d) self-reinforcement for correct performance or coping statement for incorrect performance: "I was not able to sit in the group, I did a good job" or "Although I was not able to sit in the group, I made progress toward my goal because I approached the group."

The therapist next narrated the self-instructions while David performed the desired behavior in the clinic. In the final two steps, the therapist's instructions were faded, and David practiced the desired behavior first in the clinic and then in the classroom. David whispered the self-instructions while performing the desired behavior and finally used private speech in the form of self-instructions to guide his performance while in the group.

—*Barbara Lopez and Wendy K. Silverman*

See also: *Instructions (Vols. I & III), Meichenbaum, Donald H. (Vols. I & III), Self-Control Therapy (Vols. I & III), Self-Monitoring (Vols. I, II, & III), Self-Statement Modification (Vols. I & III)*

Suggested Readings

Meichenbaum, D. (1977). *Cognitive behavior modification, an integrative approach.* New York: Plenum.

Silverman, W. K., & Kurtines, W. M. (1996). *Anxiety and phobic disorders: A pragmatic approach.* New York: Plenum.

SELF-MONITORING

DESCRIPTION OF THE STRATEGY

Self-monitoring is an assessment and intervention technique that has been widely used over the past several decades in the treatment of children. Self-monitoring, along with self-evaluation and self-reinforcement, is considered one form of self-control or self-regulation. Self-monitoring can be defined as a child's assessment of whether or not a target behavior occurred, followed by a self-recording of the event. In effect, the child must observe occurrences of his or her own behavior and then record the occurrences of the behavior upon a self-monitoring device. Self-monitoring is characterized by frequent data collection, typically in the form of self-graphing or the completion of checklists. It is a desirable assessment and intervention technique because it is considerably less intrusive than other approaches, and it enables the child to participate actively in the treatment process. As such, the child can then take some responsibility in the resulting changes in behavior.

Self-monitoring can take several forms, the most common of which requires that the child record data on a checklist immediately after the target response has been emitted. For example, following the completion of a math problem, a student could be required to refer to a checklist of reminders. After placing a plus or a minus next to each reminder, the student might then be required to correct those steps for which a minus was scored. Another approach is for the child to self-record following some time interval during which the target response could have occurred, such as at the conclusion of a class period. A teacher or parent might also arrange for the presentation of auditory stimuli at random intervals that signal the child to observe his or her own behavior and self-record. For example, a student might be required to ask the question, "Was I paying attention?" each time a tone is emitted from a tape recorder. The student could then be required to place a check in a "yes" or "no" column after each tone on a piece of paper. Other devices such as handheld computers or daily diaries can also be used to self-record. It is most desirable for the child to self-record immediately following the emission of the target response rather than relying upon his or her retrospective recall.

Self-monitoring is a frequently used assessment technique in the field of behavioral medicine, where it has been applied to a number of pediatric problems, including diabetes, enuresis or bed-wetting, fingernail biting, thumb sucking, trichotillomania or hair pulling, and obesity. As an assessment technique, self-monitoring can be used to teach children to identify the status of their medication. A child who is able to monitor the effects of medication can inform parents, teachers, and pediatricians of the time course over which their

medication ceases to work, as well as of any adverse side effects. The advantages of self-monitoring as an assessment technique include the fact that parents and teachers do not have to rely exclusively upon their own observations of the target behavior. Specific information can also be obtained that cannot be readily obtained from other traditional assessment methods, such as covert emotions and precipitating conditions. Thus, it may be more feasible to have the child collect data on his or her own behavior, particularly when the target behaviors are personal for the child (such as bedwetting) or are covert responses that cannot be readily observed by others (such as depressive thoughts).

The procedure is more commonly used as an intervention strategy and is often effective in improving a number of areas of academic performance, such as speech production, writing comprehension, and mathematic computations. It may also be an appropriate intervention for reducing a number of behaviors that are of clinical concern, including thumb sucking, fingernail biting, trichotillomania, reports of hallucinations, depressive thoughts, and vocal or motor tics. Advantages of self-monitoring as an intervention include the fact that observing and evaluating one's own behavior are important skills that will aid the child later in life, and the child's own self-management may enable parents or teachers to devote time toward other responsibilities.

The intervention is seldom an effective strategy by itself. Positive reinforcement for the target response is also typically necessary for the intervention to have lasting effects upon behavior. For example, in addition to a student's use of a checklist to monitor accuracy in his or her math problems, the student's teacher might deliver a token or some other incentive at the end of the class period for every math problem completed correctly. To further increase the child's participation in the intervention, the teacher might teach the child to self-reinforce. It is often desirable to begin with self-monitoring alone and then introduce a positive reinforcement contingency once the child has gained some control over his or her behavior. While treatment packages consisting of self-monitoring and positive reinforcement are effective, it is difficult to determine whether changes in behavior are attributable to self-monitoring, positive reinforcement, or both, in the absence of a component analysis. Such treatment packages are, however, generally more effective than reinforcement of the target response alone. This may be due in part to the stimulus control over behavior that is provided by the checklists.

Self-monitoring is most effective when the target response is a specific, active response, as opposed to a more general pattern of behavior. For example, requiring a student to monitor the amount of homework completed as opposed to on-task behavior is likely to be more effective in enhancing the student's productivity. It is also important that the child is motivated to self-monitor. The provision of positive reinforcement for self-monitoring is likely to improve the likelihood that the child will follow through on the intervention. Finally, it is not necessary that the child be accurate in his or her self-monitoring for the intervention to be effective, yet for the intervention to be maximally effective, the child's accuracy should be ensured. It may be necessary for a parent or teacher to reinforce the child's accuracy; the child is most likely to be accurate with such a contingency in place.

RESEARCH BASIS

Research has shown that children are capable of monitoring behaviors related to certain medical conditions, including their medication status and certain dietary practices. Children with attention-deficit/hyperactivity disorder (ADHD), for example, have been taught to self-monitor the dosage levels of dextroamphetamine and were able to do so even after an extended time period had elapsed since taking the medication. Research has shown that even very young children are capable of some form of self-monitoring, often following lengthy instruction and with ongoing supervision. For example, a very young child with enuresis may well become proficient at placing a telephone call to a receptionist at a clinic to report the occurrence or nonoccurrence of bed-wetting after waking each morning. With children under the age of 4, it is typically most desirable to have a parent or other caregiver perform the monitoring.

Considerable research has shown that as an intervention, the effects of self-monitoring alone are not likely to be maintained. For example, self-monitoring has proven effective in reducing the repetitive throat clearing of a child with Tourette's disorder, but the reduction was only temporary until a differential reinforcement for low-rate behavior (DRL) contingency was introduced. It has also been shown that self-monitoring is most effective in enhancing academic performance when the target response is a specific, active response, such as spelling word accuracy, as opposed to some more general, passive pattern of behavior, such as

attending to the teacher. In fact, it has been shown that when students are given the opportunity to choose to self-monitor a specific, active response or a more general behavior pattern, students will demonstrate a preference for monitoring the active response.

Conflicting results have been obtained from studies addressing the necessity of the child's accuracy in self-monitoring interventions. While some studies have shown that the intervention will be most effective when the child is, in fact, accurate, a number of studies have shown that changes in behavior will nonetheless be established when the child makes errors in self-recording. It is most desirable for the child to self-monitor accurately. Studies have shown that the best way to sustain a child's accuracy is to provide positive reinforcement for doing so. Moreover, regardless of the age of the child, the target response must be clearly defined so as to ensure his or her accuracy.

RELEVANT TARGET POPULATIONS AND EXCEPTIONS

As either an assessment technique or as a component of an intervention package, self-monitoring can be used with a number of different populations of children. Much research has focused upon its efficacy with children with such disorders as learning disability, ADHD, mental retardation, and Tourette's disorder. It can also be used to reduce various habits demonstrated by children with or without disabilities and may be beneficial for use with juvenile offenders. Self-monitoring was not traditionally used with children with internalizing disorders such as childhood anxiety or depression, but it is becoming more widely used for children with these and other psychiatric disorders, including obsessive-compulsive disorder.

Caution should be exercised depending upon the age of the child and his or her cognitive abilities. While even children between the ages of 4 and 6 years have proven capable of relatively simple forms of self-monitoring, considerable instruction and supervision will be necessary for young children. The same is true for the use of self-monitoring with children with severe or profound mental retardation or psychotic symptoms. In the event that it appears a child lacks the skills to self-monitor, even with instruction and supervision, efforts should be made to choose a more appropriate treatment alternative or to have a trained adult perform the monitoring.

COMPLICATIONS

The efficacy of self-monitoring is limited by several methodological barriers. First, self-monitoring treatment packages often produce reactive behavior change. In other words, the child's behavior may be affected by his or her awareness of the assessment procedure. One explanation is that the response of self-recording reminds the child of the external contingencies of reinforcement that are either sustaining occurrences or nonoccurrences of the target response, thus increasing the salience of the relationship between the response and its consequence. Reactivity has been observed given minimal levels of accuracy in self-recording and may even occur over the course of training a child, before the intervention has even been implemented. The presence of the self-monitoring device itself (i.e., checklists) has also been suggested to prompt behavior change during self-monitoring. Finally, the presence of an adult observer may produce reactivity, particularly if the child knows he or she is recording. Whatever the theoretical explanation for the reactivity, it is clear that the reactive nature of the procedure makes it difficult to determine the agent responsible for changes in the child's behavior.

Second, depending upon the target response, a child could conceivably falsify his or her data. This may be particularly problematic when the target behavior is socially undesirable or embarrassing for a child or when the target behavior is known to be harmful for the child, such as cigarette smoking or eating foods forbidden by diet. For this reason, it is important that high-magnitude, strongly preferred reinforcers be provided contingent upon accurate self-monitoring. Third, some target behaviors are likely to occur outside the child's awareness, such as nail biting or hair twirling. The presentation of auditory signals at random intervals to occasion the child's observation of his or her own behavior, followed by self-recording, is one way to circumvent this problem.

CASE ILLUSTRATION

"David" was a 10-year-old male diagnosed with ADHD. He was in the fifth grade and exhibited difficulties staying on task and completing in-class assignments. As a result, he was performing poorly academically and his parents and teachers were concerned about his ability to be successful in junior high school in the coming years. David's problems were most evident in his math class, in which the completion of in-class assignments was a daily requirement. David could seldom remain focused for more than 3 to 4 minutes during this period of time, and he often provoked other students after a few moments of working. David was generally accurate on the problems that he did complete, but his failure to complete entire assignments was contributing to his failing grade.

A functional assessment of David's disruptive behavior was conducted, and it was found that while David's peers typically provided no consequences for his behavior, he was regularly reprimanded by the teacher and teacher's aide. Thus, assessment results showed that David's disruptive behavior was maintained by teacher attention. A treatment package consisting of (a) extinction of David's disruptive behavior, (b) self-monitoring of math problems completed, and (c) intermittent reinforcement of the completion of math problems was implemented. First, David's teachers were instructed to refrain from reprimanding David for his disruptive behavior and to hence withhold any attention for this behavior. Second, David's teacher provided him with a small cassette tape recorder to keep at his desk, which presented a series of auditory beeps at random intervals throughout the 30-minute work period. Beeps were presented anywhere from 1 to 30 seconds apart, every 15 seconds, on the average. David was instructed to ask himself "Am I doing my assignment?" each time a beep was presented. He was then to check a box on a sheet of paper taped to his notebook following each beep, either a box reading "Yes, I am working" or a box reading "No, I am not working." At the end of each 30-minute math period, David was allowed to self-reinforce and select from a menu of potential reinforcers, including extra minutes of recess, running office errands, or listening to his Walkman for a few minutes, depending how many times he had checked the "Yes, I am working" box. Initially, the criterion was set very low, and David was allowed to self-reinforce following fewer than 10 marked boxes. This criterion was gradually increased, and eventually David was successfully completing more than 20 "Yes, I am working" boxes during each period. The time between the beeps presented on the tape recorder was gradually increased as well, to the point where only one beep per minute was presented. Third, because attention from David's teachers had been shown to be an effective reinforcer, he was provided with verbal praise from his teachers contingent upon the number of math problems completed per period. Initially the required number was set low, so that David only had to complete 1 or 2 problems per period for verbal praise, but the required number was gradually increased to approximately 10 problems.

This procedure was effective in making David's disruptive behavior nonfunctional and also increased his on-task behavior and productivity. His parents were able to implement the treatment package at home so as to increase David's homework productivity. Treatment effects were maintained at 1-month follow-up.

—*Ruth Anne Rehfeldt*

See also: *Instructions (Vols. I & III), Meichenbaum, Donald H. (Vols. I & III), Self-Control Therapy (Vols. I & III), Self-Instruction Training (Vol. II), Self-Monitoring (Vols. I & III), Self-Statement Modification (Vols. I & III),*

Suggested Readings

Ardoin, S. P., & Martens, B. K. (2000). Testing the ability of children with attention deficit hyperactivity disorder to accurately report the effects of medication on their behavior. *Journal of Applied Behavior Analysis, 33,* 593–610.

Dunlap, L. K., & Dunlap, G. (1989). A self-monitoring package for teaching subtraction with regrouping to students with learning disabilities. *Journal of Applied Behavior Analysis, 22,* 309–314.

Hallahan, D. P., & Sapona, R. (1983). Self-monitoring of attention with learning-disabled children: Past research and current issues. *Journal of Learning Disabilities, 16,* 616–620.

Harris, K. (1986). Self-monitoring of attentional behavior versus self-monitoring of productivity effects on on-task behavior and academic response rate among learning disabled children. *Journal of Applied Behavior Analysis, 19,* 417–423.

Peterson, L., & Tremblay, G. (1999). Self-monitoring in behavioral medicine: Children. *Psychological Assessment, 11,* 458–465.

Sainato, D. M., Strain, P. S., Lefebvre, D., & Rapp, N. (1990). Effects of self-evaluation on the independent work skills of preschool children with disabilities. *Exceptional Children, 56,* 540–549.

Shapiro, E., & Cole, C. L. (1999). Self-monitoring in assessing children's problems. *Psychological Assessment, 11,* 448–457.

SELF-PRAISE

Self-praise is the use of positive statements made to oneself after exhibiting an appropriate behavior that one desires to increase. Such self-statements increase the probability that the target behavior will occur in the future (i.e., reinforce the behavior). Self-praise is one method of self-reinforcement, and, like other self-reinforcement strategies, it typically is used within the context of self-monitoring procedures.

One of the advantages of self-praise as a reinforcement procedure is that the individual controls the delivery of the praise. Hence, no other individuals need to be present to monitor and/or deliver the reinforcer after the target behavior has occurred. Because individuals are praising themselves, the reinforcers are available to individuals in all situations. In addition, self-praise can be delivered immediately after the occurrence of the target behavior, thus minimizing the delay of reinforcement. Self-praise also can be a useful reinforcement procedure for behaviors that are not easily observed by others or that are "private" behaviors (e.g., thoughts, self-statements).

One example of the use of self-praise would be in the case of a child who wants to increase the frequency of tooth brushing. After brushing his or her teeth, the child might say, "Nice job cleaning my teeth!" to himself or herself, regardless of who is present. Another example in which self-praise could be used is in increasing attention to academic tasks. That is, a child may engage in self-praise following the completion of a certain number of math problems by saying "Great job finishing those five questions. Way to stay focused!" Self-praise strategies also are often used by individuals to reinforce their use of habit-reversal behaviors (e.g., self-praising after clasping hands to prevent nail biting), social skills behaviors (e.g., self-praising after engaging in rehearsed behaviors in real-life situations), and anxiety reduction procedures (e.g., self-praising after using relaxation procedures in anxiety-provoking situations).

The advantages of self-praise (i.e., the individual controls the reinforcer) also may be reasons for concern when considering the use of self-praise as a reinforcement procedure. For self-praise to be effective, individuals must be motivated to change their behavior and to self-praise after the occurrence of the target behavior. In addition, individuals must be able to recognize when they have exhibited praiseworthy behaviors. Often, it may be difficult for someone to observe the delivery of the self-praise. As a result, it may be difficult to determine if the self-praise is being delivered. In addition, the use of verbal praise is a conditioned reinforcer, as opposed to a primary reinforcer. The effectiveness of the use of self-praise alone may be limited if not used in combination with other, primary reinforcers or additional reinforcement procedures.

—*Alisa B. Bahl-Long*

See also: *Instructions (Vol. III), Meichenbaum, Donald H. (Vols. I & III), Positive Reinforcement (Vol. II), Reinforcement (Vols. I & III), Self-Statement Modification (Vols. I & III), Self-Control Therapy (Vols. I & III), Self-Monitoring (Vols. I, II, & III)*

Suggested Reading

Kazdin, A. E. (2001). Self-control techniques. In A. E. Kazdin, *Behavior modification in applied settings.* Belmont, CA: Wadsworth.

SENSORY EXTINCTION

DESCRIPTION OF THE STRATEGY

Since the late 1970s, a procedure referred to as sensory extinction has provided clinicians with a tool for addressing certain problematic behaviors of individuals with disabilities. The term *sensory extinction*, coined by Arnold Rincover, refers to masking or removing the sensory effects of an undesirable behavior in order to reduce or eliminate the behavior. Sensory extinction procedures have been used to address proprioceptive, visual, auditory, and tactile forms of stimulation produced by undesirable behavior (e.g., clicking and grinding sound produced by clenching teeth). The procedure operates on the basic principle of extinction, which means that when a behavior no longer produces the outcome that was maintaining it or keeping it going (e.g., reinforcement), the behavior will stop.

Individuals with developmental disabilities and autism frequently exhibit high levels of self-stimulatory behavior, many of which can be self-destructive (e.g., self-injurious behavior). The functional analysis procedures developed in the 1980s provide a tool for clinicians and researchers to determine what environmental factors might influence these unusual human behaviors. The most commonly identified factors that maintain behavior are social interactions with others, escape or termination of unpleasant events, access to highly preferred items and activities, and specific sensory experiences produced directly by the behavior referred to as automatic reinforcement.

The term *automatic reinforcement* is used to describe behavior that is not affected by social experiences with others. Instead, these behaviors occur because something about the behavior itself produces a desirable physical or sensory experience. For example, people may drum their fingers in time to music because they enjoy the sound it makes or the feeling it produces. One might also twirl a lock of hair because of the tactile experience (i.e., feeling of hair on the skin) or the proprioceptive experience (i.e., feeling of movement) twirling produces. A person with an itch will scratch in order to produce the specific physical sensation of cessation of the itch. Each of these behaviors is considered self-stimulatory because the behavior occurs in order to produce a sensation rather than to effect a social experience with another person.

When behavior is maintained by its own sensory consequences, the physical experience the behavior produces is always available. Children with autism who wave their fingers in front of their face because they like the visual stimulation that is produced always have the option to engage in that behavior. The ubiquitous nature of the reinforcer often leads to situations where a child will engage in the self-stimulatory behavior instead of interacting with others or participating in learning experiences. Thus, behaviors maintained by automatic reinforcement can dramatically limit a child's skills and experiences, making these some of the most important behaviors to treat.

Sensory extinction procedures require the clinician to generate hypotheses about the sensory impact of a behavior and to find creative ways to interrupt the connection between the behavior and the sensory experience it produces. There are three typical means for creating this interruption. First, sensory extinction may take the form of environmental alteration in such a way that the behavior no longer produces the sensory experience. In Rincover's first demonstration of the procedure, a child incessantly spun a plate on a table in order to produce an unusual sound. Sensory extinction was implemented by carpeting the top of the table to muffle the sound. The child could still spin the plate, but engaging in the behavior no longer produced the desired effect (i.e., extinction). He subsequently stopped spinning the plate.

A second common sensory extinction procedure involves the use of some type of applied equipment that masks the sensory experience of the behavior. For example, researchers have treated children who twirl objects and their fingers incessantly by administering a vibrator to the back of their hands. The vibration masked the proprioceptive experience that the initial twirling produced. Protective equipment such as padded helmets to address head banging, hand mitts to address hand mouthing, and eye goggles to address eye poking are other examples of this application of sensory extinction.

A final procedure often described as sensory extinction is response blocking. Response blocking involves a person rather than equipment actively preventing the completion of the response. This procedure, though often effective in reducing behavior, has drawbacks as an intervention. First, the procedure requires constant monitoring and effort on the part of the care provider. When caregivers cannot be vigilant, the problematic behavior is likely to return. Second, response blocking should probably not be called an extinction procedure because the problem behavior is not actually allowed to occur, and if it does occur, due to a procedural error (i.e., the person misses a block), then the reinforcer occurs as well.

RESEARCH BASIS

Three initial studies were conducted by Arnold Rincover in the 1970s when he developed the procedure. Since then, different authors have published approximately 20 papers, including applications of the procedure and conceptual comments about the procedure. Published experiments have been conducted exclusively with individuals with developmental disabilities and autism. The most commonly treated repetitive behaviors are hand mouthing and finger stereotypies (e.g., tapping, twirling objects), but extremely dangerous behaviors such as head banging and eye poking have also been treated with sensory extinction procedures.

In one study, an individual with severe head banging was treated with sensory extinction in the form of a padded helmet. The helmet allowed the individual to strike his head but masked the sensation that had previously been produced and prevented injury. In another study, researchers effectively treated an individual who forcefully put his fingers in his eye sockets with sensory extinction by using protective goggles, so that bringing the finger to the eye no longer produced the same visual and physical sensation or injury. In each instance, the sensory extinction procedure produced clear beneficial effects. In summary,

several experiments support the finding that sensory extinction procedures can be used to treat behaviors that range from mild stereotypies to very severe self-injury. These studies also indicate that the procedures are only effective when the important sensory feature of the behavior can be identified. However, it can be difficult to identify the relevant sensory feature for all behaviors. This concern and other complications are covered in the section on complications.

RELEVANT TARGET POPULATIONS AND EXCEPTIONS

Sensory extinction procedures are most commonly used with individuals with autism and individuals with severe mental retardation. When behaviors are either physically dangerous (e.g., self-injurious behavior) or occur so often that they interfere with learning opportunities (e.g., stereotypies), it may be appropriate to use a sensory extinction procedure. Other children with high rates of self-stimulatory behavior may also benefit from creative application of these procedures, such as young children who suck their thumbs or children with attention-deficit/hyperactivity disorder (ADHD) who fidget constantly.

COMPLICATIONS

Several issues complicate the use of sensory extinction procedures. Sensory extinction procedures are only expected to work if a behavior occurs completely independent of social consequences. Many behaviors that appear via casual observation to be maintained by automatic reinforcement are actually occurring to produce environmental events such as interactions with others or escape from unpleasant situations. Therefore, a thorough functional analysis should precede the use of any sensory extinction procedure.

Another complication with implementation of sensory extinction involves problems with identifying exactly which sensory experience is the important one for a given behavior. For example, if people constantly put their hands in their mouths, the important sensory experience might be the feeling of something in the mouth or it might be the feeling of moisture on the skin. A sensory extinction procedure that involved putting a glove on the hand would work if the important sensation was the feeling of moisture on the skin, because putting the hand in the mouth would no longer produce that feeling. However, if the important sensation was the feeling of something in the mouth, we would expect people to put the gloved hand in their mouths. New assessment procedures have been developed to assist with identification of the relevant sensory reinforcers for behaviors maintained by automatic reinforcement (the reader is directed to the review by Linda LeBlanc and colleagues included in the suggested readings).

Two other complications involve individual rights. Individuals who engage in a behavior in order to produce a certain sensation obviously enjoy that sensation, and sensory extinction will eliminate their access to it. A good clinician should have the following objectives when treating such behavior: elimination of the problem behavior and creation of a safe, socially acceptable means of producing the individuals desired sensation. The second concern is perhaps the most troubling complication. It is possible that many sensory extinction procedures do not actually work through extinction processes but instead work via punishment processes. A series of studies have attempted to determine whether the use of protective equipment and response blocking works via sensory extinction or punishment. One study determined that the effects of protective mitts on hand mouthing were probably due to punishment rather than extinction when the mitts were applied as a consequence each time hand mouthing occurred. A second study investigating this issue determined that response blocking functioned as extinction rather than punishment for eye poking in an individual with profound disabilities. Given the controversy over the use of punishment procedures with individuals with disabilities, additional research must be conducted to determine which behavioral process is in effect with blocking procedures. The individual clinician should be careful when implementing this procedure and should monitor for the most common side effects of punishment such as extreme emotional behavior and aggression.

CASE ILLUSTRATION

"John" was a 4-year-old nonverbal male diagnosed with autism. He was referred for a high frequency of finger flicking on hard surfaces, including tables, walls, wood furniture, and specific toys and most objects. During a behavioral interview, his parents reported an increase in finger flicking over the past several months. The behavior occurred almost constantly and interfered with John's interactions with other children and his functional toy play. The

parents' initial attempts at blocking the response resulted in intense tantrums and aggression. John's mother also tried ignoring the finger flicking, but no reduction occurred.

A functional analysis was conducted to determine the variables maintaining John's finger-flicking behavior. John was placed in four different situations to determine which ones produced the highest levels of finger flicking. In one condition (social attention), a person asked him to stop whenever he flicked. In a second condition (escape from demands), ongoing tasks were removed if he flicked. In a third condition (alone), John was alone in a room with low stimulation. In the final condition (control), he was able to interact with toys and with a person and no demands were presented.

The results of the functional analysis indicated that John's finger flicking behavior was consistently high across all conditions, suggesting that flicking was maintained by automatically produced sensory stimulation. John's finger flicking produced both auditory stimulation and tactile stimulation. His parents indicated that John flicked many different surfaces and often cocked his head as if he was listening to the sound. Based on this report and direct observation of John, the clinician hypothesized that the auditory sensation was an important aspect of the behavior. Therefore, the sensory extinction procedure was directed at the auditory experience produced by finger flicking.

Sensory extinction in the form of environmental alteration could not be easily implemented because the behavior occurred across settings on almost any surface. Therefore, equipment was applied to mask the sensory experience of John's finger-flicking behavior. At home, John's parents were instructed to place thin mittens on John's hands to be worn throughout the day except when toileting, eating, or bathing. The parents blocked any attempts to remove the mittens.

As finger flicking decreased, the mittens were systematically reduced in size and thickness and eventually replaced with bandages on the ends of John's fingers. Ultimately, John's finger flicking was reduced to near zero rates without any hand coverage at all. As a supplement to sensory extinction, various means of auditory stimulation were made available to John throughout the day. He was given headphones and musical toys to provide a more appropriate means of accessing enjoyable sounds.

—*Linda A. LeBlanc, Christine M. Bennett, and Rachael A. Sautter*

See also: *Applied Behavior Analysis (Vols. I, II, & III),
Functional Analysis (Vol. II), Generalization
(Vols. I, II, & III), Guided Mastery (Vols. I & III),
Operant Conditioning (Vols. I, II, & III),
Skinner, Burrhus Frederic (Vols. I, II, & III)*

Suggested Readings

Iwata, B. A., Pace, G. M., Cowdery, G. E., & Miltenberger, R. G. (1994). What makes extinction work: An analysis of procedural form and function. *Journal of Applied Behavior Analysis, 27,* 131–144.

LeBlanc, L. A., Patel, M. R., & Carr, J. E. (2000). Recent advances in the assessment of aberrant behavior maintained by automatic reinforcement in individuals with developmental disabilities. *Journal of Behavior Therapy & Experimental Psychiatry, 31,* 137–154.

Lovaas, I., Newsom, C., & Hickman, C. (1987). Self-stimulatory behavior and perceptual reinforcement. *Journal of Applied Behavior Analysis, 20,* 45–68.

Mazaleski, J. L., Iwata, B. A., Rodgers, T. A., Vollmer, T. R., & Zarcone, J. R. (1994). Protective equipment as treatment for stereotypic hand mouthing: Sensory extinction or punishment effects? *Journal of Applied Behavior Analysis, 27,* 345–355.

Rincover, A. (1978). Sensory extinction: A procedure for eliminating self-stimulatory behavior in developmentally disabled children. *Journal of Abnormal Child Psychology, 6,* 299–310.

Rincover, A. (1985). Sensory extinction: Some answers and questions. *Behavior Therapist, 8,* 177–178.

Smith, R. G., Russo, L., & Le, D. D. (1999). Distinguishing between extinction and punishment effects of response blocking: A replication. *Journal of Applied Behavior Analysis, 32,* 367–370.

SHAPING

DESCRIPTION OF THE STRATEGY

It is often desirable for clients to acquire new ways of responding, that is, to expand their behavioral repertoire. Shaping is a procedure for teaching children to do new things. When using the shaping procedure, new behaviors are constructed from the bottom up. The procedure starts with a response that the child is already able to do, and works step-by-step from this response to the goal behavior. Each small step along the way is reinforced, and once a step is accomplished, an additional small requirement is added. This gradual building process facilitates motivation and progress and continues until the goal is reached.

Technical Description

Shaping involves differentially reinforcing responses that successively approximate a terminal response class resulting in new and/or more complex and elaborated behaviors. The basic behavioral principles operating in shaping are reinforcement and extinction, which when used in combination, such that only a certain class of responses is reinforced while others are not, is referred to as differential reinforcement. For example, when coloring with crayons, children must acquire responses of adequate force to produce marks on paper. One set of responses, those involving sufficient force to produce color, is reinforced, while responses of insufficient force produce no reinforcement.

In differential reinforcement, the response requirement for reinforcement is generally relatively stable. For instance, a certain class of forces, once established, will almost always produce color on paper. How, though, is the response class established? Here is where shaping enters the picture. Shaping involves a sequence of differential reinforcements where the provision of, or the amount of, reinforcement is linked to the progression of responding. As performances that more and more closely resemble the ultimate performance are established, previous steps in the sequence no longer produce reinforcement (or produce less reinforcement than current and subsequent steps). To illustrate, imagine teaching a child who failed to learn to color. First, the child might be reinforced with food for holding or grasping a crayon. Then, holding the crayon with the tip touching the paper would be required for reinforcement. Next, some small movement of the crayon on the paper with enough force to produce faint color would be required. Finally, only movements of the crayon that produced solid color would be reinforced. Notice in the coloring example the interaction between an arbitrary reinforcer and a naturally occurring reinforcer. Early responses in the sequence were reinforced by food; however, as shaping progressed, the natural contingency between using adequate force and seeing color on the paper could also begin to reinforce appropriate responding along the force dimension. That is, too much force would result in the crayon breaking, too little force would produce no, or only faint, color, while a range of forces produced the clear sight of color.

It is important to note that shaping is involved in the acquisition of many responses but is often not recognized as such because it is occurring naturally or in the context of the child's interaction with a social environment that is effective in intuitively shaping behavior. For instance, when a child first responds to the letter *W* by saying "double cue," caretakers may provide praise but later will require the child to more closely approximate "double you" before praise is given. When the child begins to string letters together and first utters "a-b-c-d-e-c-d-e," the parents may praise the partially correct response. However, soon such praise will be reserved for only more extended correct utterances. The programmed use of shaping in clinical settings is simply a formal extension of the process that is occurring in a less formal, but no less influential, manner across many domains during development.

Clinical Description

When using shaping clinically, five basic steps can be identified. The first two steps occur before the shaping procedure is actually initiated.

The first step is to conduct a thorough baseline assessment to determine how the problem relates to a deficit in the content/form, duration/amount, force/intensity, or latency of some aspect of the child's behavioral repertoire. In some cases, an apparent deficit is due to a lack of opportunities to respond or to existing contingencies that reinforce incomplete or weak responding (e.g., when a caretaker withdraws a demand at the first sign of resistance or intervenes at the first sign of difficulty). Shaping can still be employed in such situations; however, altering the antecedent conditions or changing the existing contingencies will greatly facilitate the process.

Once the problem has been identified as involving a deficient response repertoire, the second step is to identify a reinforcer (or set of reinforcers) that can be used in shaping the response. Depending on the clinical situation, one could employ a formal preference assessment, where across several trials the child chooses between two or more potential reinforcers offered simultaneously, to determine the reinforcers that are likely to be most effective. Alternatively, therapists can often make educated guesses based on information from caretakers or their knowledge of the client. In some cases, trial and error during the shaping process may be required. In all cases, it is worth remembering that a reinforcer is defined based on its function (its response contingent immediate presentation increases future responding), and that an effective reinforcer at one time may not be effective at a later time. When possible, it is desirable to arrange the shaping procedure so that the ultimate control of the response will be by naturally occurring or conventional social reinforcers (e.g., praise).

The third step is to define the class of behavior in which the client would ultimately, at the end of the shaping intervention, be able to engage. When possible, it is useful to be as specific as possible when identifying what constitutes the terminal response class and what does not. Finally, when possible, it is important to specify what will define learning of the terminal behavior. It is important to remember that saying a behavior is now part of a client's repertoire is merely to say that the client emits the behavior. Speaking of a client's repertoire is an abstraction; the new behavior does not exist somewhere within the client in a place called the repertoire. As such, it is not enough to simply observe the terminal behavior once, discontinue the procedure, and conclude that the performance is now part of the client's repertoire. Instead, it is important to specify, to the extent possible, what indicates a successful conclusion for this particular client (e.g., when asked by a teacher or parent, the child can say the entire alphabet accurately across 10 consecutive occasions, with each occurrence taking less than 10 seconds to complete).

The fourth step is to identify an initial behavior that the child currently emits with some frequency and that shares as many features as possible with the terminal response. Reinforcement occurs after a response and increases the future likelihood of that response class. If a relevant response is never emitted, reinforcement cannot be received. Thus, the initial response chosen must be maintained currently at some minimal frequency. That said, one need work backward from the terminal behavior only far enough to find a relevant response that is already being emitted prior to implementing the shaping procedure. However, it is possible that you will need to begin the procedure with an extremely basic response class such as simply orienting, vocalizing, or touching. Once the initial behavior is identified and its frequency increased, it is then time to increase the threshold for reinforcement by requiring that the client emit a behavior that more closely resembles the terminal response.

These behaviors that more and more closely resemble the terminal response are considered intermediate steps. The fifth step in using shaping is to identify responses that might constitute intermediate steps between the current response and the final performance. In other words, what behaviors will be established along the path to the final performance? As each one is mastered, the criterion for reinforcement is increased to include the next intermediate behavior. This gradual process continues until the final performance is achieved. It is often helpful for the practitioner to outline a possible list of component steps in advance. Such a list is useful in making sure that the practitioner is fully familiar with the dimensions of response class of interest and provides the practitioner with a crude assessment of how far the client has to progress to achieve the terminal behavior and how long the intervention might take. Once the list of potential intermediate steps is complete, however, it is useful to remind oneself of the maxim "The client is always right." In other words, proceed according to the child's behavior, not the list.

The strategy can be summarized as follows:

1. Assess to determine the appropriate role of shaping in the intervention.

2. Determine the reinforcers.

3. Identify the terminal response class.

4. Identify and then implement differential reinforcement for the initial response.

5. Identify and then implement differential reinforcement progressively across the intermediate responses until the terminal response is reached.

RESEARCH BASIS

The available research suggests that shaping is often most effectively used in combination with manipulations of antecedent conditions. There are several reasons why this is so. First, a response cannot be reinforced until it occurs. Thus, shaping requires identification of a response that the child is currently engaging in that can be used as the starting point. However, rather than simply waiting for this initial response (e.g., grasping a crayon in teaching coloring) to spontaneously occur, the practitioner may need to alter the environment (e.g., by placing the child in a high chair with many crayons before the child, but no other toys), model the desired response (e.g., by demonstrating to the child picking up the crayon) or provide a physical or vocal prompt (e.g., by guiding the child's hand to the crayon or by asking the child to pick up the crayon) to make the response more likely. Once the response occurs, reinforcement can then be delivered. Prompting and modeling are provided as necessary at the initiation of each new step but are then gradually withdrawn (i.e., faded) such that before progressing to the next step, the response is performed without the prompt. This combined approach appears to expedite the learning process and ensures that the child receives a relatively high rate of reinforcement while making relatively few errors.

The second reason shaping is often combined with manipulation of antecedents is that for many responses, not only the occurrence, but also the timing and/or placement of the response, is important. In these instances, shaping is combined with stimulus discrimination procedures. Here the developing response class that is targeted via the shaping procedure is only reinforced in the presence of a discriminative stimulus (and not in its absence). For instance, in teaching a child to color, only marks of sufficient force (the behavior that is being shaped) that occur on paper (the discriminative stimulus) are reinforced, while attempts to mark on walls, tables, clothing, and so on are not reinforced.

Finally, putting it all together, discriminative stimuli, prompts, and shaping are often simultaneously used. In teaching a child to label (i.e., tact) an apple, the child is shown an apple (the discriminative stimulus), the practitioner provides a vocal prompt "apple," and the child says "appa," which is reinforced. Before concluding, the child's responding will need to more closely approximate standard usage of "apple" (the terminal response) and occur without the formal prompt and only in the presence of apples (and not, say, bananas).

RELEVANT TARGET POPULATIONS, TARGET BEHAVIORS, AND EXCEPTIONS

Shaping is most well recognized as a component of applied behavior analysis interventions, which have been widely used in the treatment of children with mental retardation, brain injury, autism, or other developmental disabilities. The range of target behaviors for which shaping (in combination with prompts and/or discriminative stimuli) has been used is quite large, and includes prerequisite skills for learning (e.g., remaining seated, making eye contact, speaking with sufficient voice volume), language skills (e.g., speech acquisition), social skills (e.g., sharing, attending to others and getting others' attention, shaking hands), motor skills (e.g., coordinated hand movements), self-care skills (e.g., self-feeding, toileting, contact lens use), life skills (telephone use, bed making), and other adaptive behaviors (e.g., school attendance). This list further illustrates how shaping can be employed across response dimensions, including different topographies, forces/intensity levels, and amounts/durations.

Shaping is also often used as a component of treatment with more traditional outpatient populations (e.g., those often diagnosed with learning disorders, attention-deficit/hyperactivity disorder [ADHD], depression, anxiety, or oppositional behavior). These children generally have established functional verbal repertoires and are often somewhat older. As such, aspects of shaping (i.e., treatment goals targeting progressive improvements) are often used in conjunction with verbal instructions specifying relevant natural and/or any added contingencies, what is to be done, and when it should occur. For instance, as part of the treatment for a child diagnosed with separation anxiety disorder, the child might be told that he or she will receive stickers on a chart (that when completed can be exchanged for a larger reward) for greater and greater periods of time playing with a babysitter, or alternative caretaker, in the absence of the primary caretaker. Similarly, when therapeutic homework practice is sequenced well, it encourages the client to engage in a challenging behavior but does not request so much as to lead to failure. Shaping can also occur directly in the clinical setting, such as when the therapist attempts to reinforce small improvements as they are observed in session. For instance, reinforcing increasingly assertive behaviors emitted by a generally inhibited adolescent.

An enormous variety of response classes can be, and are, developed and refined via formal and informal shaping. However, there are some limitations to what shaping can accomplish. First, shaping applies to operant, not respondent, behavior. As such, while a snake-phobic child might be gradually taught snake-handling skills and to hold a snake for progressively longer intervals, accompanying decreases in emotional responses (e.g., anxiety) are not the result of shaping, but respondent extinction. Second, for shaping to be effective, the child must have the prerequisite physical capabilities for engaging in the terminal response. There also appears to be a pragmatic upper

limit as to what typical shaping procedures can produce. For instance, we would be unlikely to be able to routinely shape children to develop the basketball skill of Michael Jordan. This pragmatic upper limit appears determined by a number of factors, including (but not limited to) child physical characteristics, the current state of knowledge in shaping, and the amount and duration of shaping for one particular response class compared to others.

COMPLICATIONS

A primary complication associated with shaping involves the failure to make progress toward the terminal behavior. In determining the rate of progress, it must be recognized that even though the steps may seem logical, straightforward, and nicely sequenced to the practitioner, that does not mean that the child will progress as such. Rather, progress may at times appear erratic and better characterized as periods of fast forward and then rewind. In the former, it is important not to discontinue shaping too early when the terminal behavior may be especially fragile. In the latter, it may be important to temporarily move back to an established step. In addition, there are times when progress plateaus. When there is a sustained lack of progress, the practitioner may be advancing too rapidly or in too large increments. As such, breaking the intermediate levels down into smaller steps or adding prompts can help remedy the problem.

The need for creative adjustments during the procedure might also reflect the difference between the contingency described by the practitioner and the functional contingency experienced by the child. That is, even though the practitioner may be very clear about what behavior produced the reinforcer, the contingency experienced by the child may be different. This is most likely when there is a delay between the response and the reinforcer such that the child may emit some other behavior prior to reinforcer delivery. In addition, there may be a loss of reinforcer effectiveness. For instance, if food reinforcement is being used, the child may become satiated over the course of a long training session. Given concerns about reinforcer timing and effectiveness, when possible, it is useful to arrange the procedure such that control can be by, or transferred to, natural reinforcers or conventional social reinforcers, which do, or can, immediately follow the response and may be less likely to lose their effectiveness.

There are two additional potential complications that warrant mention. First, there are times when it is difficult to implement shaping because other incompatible response classes may be automatically reinforcing or unable to be put on extinction. For instance, it would be difficult to reinforce coloring if breaking the crayons or throwing the crayons is very reinforcing. These alternative behaviors are incompatible with coloring, and the reinforcement they produce is readily available and difficult to put on extinction, because in order to color, the child must have access to the crayons. Modeling, verbal, and physical prompts, along with other contingency management strategies, may be required in these situations. A second complication involves the maintenance and generalization of the shaped behavior. Training in the natural setting where the behavior is to occur, using natural or conventional social reinforcers that will be maintained after training, and establishing fluent performance before discontinuing shaping, can facilitate maintenance and generalization.

CASE ILLUSTRATION

"Deb" was a 13-year-old female diagnosed as moderately mentally retarded. She lived with her parents and attended a special education classroom at the public middle school. Deb's parents always had a difficult time getting Deb to complete a morning hygiene routine (e.g., taking a shower, brushing teeth, putting on deodorant, applying lotion to arms and legs, and combing/brushing hair). Now that she was entering adolescence, it was more important socially, and for encouraging her development of independence, that she routinely engage in this class of hygienic behaviors. Assessment materials suggested that Deb has the relevant physical skills to complete the routine, as she could complete each specific response on separate occasions (e.g., she might brush her teeth but do none of the others). In addition, she appeared able to sequence the responses that are part of a behavioral chain (e.g., the component responses in taking a shower or brushing her teeth). However, simply posting a list of what she was to accomplish each morning and attempting to reinforce completion of the entire routine have not been effective interventions. Thus, Deb's noncompliance appeared, at least in part, a result of a response amount deficit—too much was being asked of her.

Based on a preference assessment in which Deb was presented with a series of two items and asked to choose one, glitter pens were identified as especially reinforcing for her. Thus, a reinforcement procedure was implemented in which Deb earned stickers toward the purchase of new glitter pens. In addition, in an attempt to make the hygiene behaviors as naturally reinforcing as possible, Deb was taken to a local retail store with her parents and allowed to select the toothpaste and brush, deodorant, shampoo, lotion, and hair brush and comb of her choice.

Deb's parents defined the terminal response class as completion of an established hygiene repertoire consisting of the following: taking a shower, brushing teeth, putting on deodorant, applying lotion to arms and legs, and combing/brushing hair. Baseline assessments revealed that Deb typically managed to do at least one, occasionally two, of these behaviors, but never completed all of them independently. Thus, an intervention was developed in which each morning Deb would be prompted to look at the list of responses and to select one or more to complete in order to earn a sticker. Completion of any one of the responses was considered as meeting the initial response requirement. The intermediate responses were defined as completing two to four items.

After completing the initial response requirement on three consecutive days, the criterion for reinforcement was increased and Deb was prompted each morning to independently complete two or more of the responses to earn a sticker. From that day on, Deb earned the sticker only after completing two responses (completing one behavior was no longer reinforced). After three successful days, the response requirement was again increased, and Deb was prompted each morning to independently complete three or more of the responses to earn a sticker. This process continued until Deb consistently completed all five items of the morning routine. At this point, prompting Deb to look at the list was faded to increase her independent engagement in the routine. In addition, as she progressed through the procedure, her parents, extended family, school staff, and therapists praised relevant aspects of her appearance to attempt to facilitate transfer to the natural outcome of good hygiene and conventional social reinforcers. It is hoped that over time these reinforcers will come to maintain the routine, and use of the stickers can be gradually withdrawn.

—*Scott T. Gaynor and Jean Clore*

See also: *Applied Behavior Analysis (Vols. I, II, & III), Functional Analysis (Vol. II), Generalization (Vols. I, II, & III), Guided Mastery (Vols. I & III), Operant Conditioning (Vols. I, II, & III), Skinner, Burrhus Frederic (Vols. I, II, & III)*

Suggested Readings

Cooper, J. O., Heron, T. E., & Heward, W. L. (1987). *Applied behavior analysis*. Columbus, OH: Merrill.

Malott, R.W., Malott, M. E., & Trojan, E. A. (2000). *Elementary principles of behavior* (4th ed.). Upper Saddle River, NJ: Prentice Hall.

Martin, G., & Pear, J. (2003). *Behavior Modification: What it is and how to do it* (7th ed.). Upper Saddle River, NJ: Prentice Hall.

Skinner, B. F. (1953). *Science and human behavior*. New York: Free Press.

BURRHUS FREDERIC SKINNER

When Burrhus Frederic (B. F.) Skinner passed away on August 18, 1990, of leukemia at the age of 86, he left behind a 60-year legacy of research and writing that fundamentally reshaped psychology. Combining the inductive positivism of the 17th-century philosopher Francis Bacon, the pragmatic progressivism of John Dewey and Charles Pierce, the experimental biology of Jacques Loeb, the precision of Ivan Pavlov, and the behaviorism of John B. Watson, Skinner's version of behaviorism remains one of the most conceptually complete and powerful systems in 20th-century psychology. For Skinner, behavior is a lawful and orderly phenomenon that should be studied using the same techniques and measurement systems employed by the other sciences. He insisted that psychological explanations should describe relationships between physical events rather than ascribing observed behavior to inferred nonphysical mental or cognitive events, which Skinner called "mental fictions." He argued strongly for the direct practical application of the principles of behavior derived from the science of behavior. Skinner's methodological advances have become foundational to research in many areas of psychology, including animal behavior, behavioral pharmacology, developmental disabilities treatment, human and nonhuman language, and even large-scale social change.

Skinner was born on March 20, 1904, in Susquehanna, Pennsylvania. Intensely curious and skilled with tools, Skinner was also a talented student. A favorite of teacher Mary Graves, she introduced the teenaged Skinner to literature and science. Skinner attended Hamilton College to study literature—graduating in 1926. Unsuccessful as a writer, a reference to John B. Watson by philosopher Bertrand Russell led Skinner to Watson's 1924 *Behaviorism*. Transfixed by the idea of an objective psychology of behavior based on the work of Watson and Pavlov, Skinner enrolled in the psychology program at Harvard in 1928.

Skinner arrived at Harvard knowing little psychology beyond Watson and Pavlov. His mentor, physiologist William Crozier, a student of radical biologist Jacques Loeb, emphasized the study of the "organism as a whole" and approached scientific discovery as a form of engineering. Both become features of Skinner's system. Skinner eventually developed techniques for studying "contingencies of reinforcement." He proposed an unconventional dissertation that argued for viewing the reflex as a descriptive relationship between observable events rather than the manifestation of invisible nervous activity.

In 1936, Skinner moved to the University of Minnesota, where he completed *The Behavior of Organisms: An Experimental Analysis* published in 1938. *The Behavior of Organisms* formalized the distinction between operant behavior (behavior controlled by its consequences) and respondent behavior (reflexive behavior controlled by the properties of antecedent eliciting stimuli). Not as successful at the time as Clark Hull's superficially similar approach based on inferred internal drives, Skinner's work nevertheless attracted the attention of a group of young researchers and established Skinner as an important new figure in psychology.

In the 1940s, during World War II, Skinner worked on a secret project to produce a missile guided by pigeons housed inside. The system passed its technical tests but was never used. The discovery of "shaping"—producing desired behavior by reinforcing successive approximations—was a side benefit of the project. Drafty Minnesota houses inspired Skinner to construct an enclosed, temperature-controlled crib for a second daughter. The "baby tender" has been mistaken for an experimental chamber and inspired erroneous tales that Skinner experimented on his children. In 1945, Skinner moved to the University of Indiana.

Postwar disillusionment inspired Skinner to write the 1948 utopian novel *Walden Two*. The characters in *Walden Two* lived in small, highly planned, egalitarian, self-sustaining communities. Appropriate and useful behavior was established by the sophisticated application of behavioral principles. Careful design ensured the availability of much free time for the residents of Walden Two to indulge their artistic, intellectual, and social interests.

Skinner's interest in applying his principles of behavior to humans inspired a series of works on human language, presented as Harvard's William James Lectures in 1948. A 1945 precursor, "The Operational Analysis of Psychological Terms," emphasized the importance of including "private events," such as thinking and feeling, in a complete analysis of behavior. Skinner stayed at Harvard and in 1953 published *Science and Human Behavior,* a textbook that consisted of analyses of a wide range of human social issues in behavioral terms.

During the 1950s, Skinner's concern for his daughters' education led to "programmed instruction" and the "teaching machine," precursors to today's computer-based instruction. In programmed instruction, tasks were broken down into small steps, each of which could be easily learned and immediately reinforced. Skinner's William James Lectures were eventually worked into a 1957 book, *Verbal Behavior,* an analysis of language in terms of the principles of behavior. A popular but highly misinformed 1959 critique of *Verbal Behavior* by linguist Noam Chomsky set back the functional analysis of language for years. Eventually, the ideas in *Verbal Behavior* formed the basis of the most successful methods of establishing language in nonverbal persons. Also in 1957, Charles Ferster and Skinner published *Schedules of Reinforcement*—a compendium of data on schedules of reinforcement. In 1958, the *Journal of the Experimental Analysis of Behavior* was established to disseminate basic research in the Skinnerian tradition.

In the 1960s, behavior analysis grew rapidly. The successful application of basic reinforcement principles to a wide variety of human behavior problems established "applied behavior analysis." A new APA Division, Division 25, Experimental Analysis of Behavior, was founded in 1965. The *Journal of Applied Behavior Analysis* was founded in 1968. The field of applied behavior analysis revolutionized the treatment of many previously intractable behavior problems, developmental disabilities, autism, severe mental illness, and even animal behavior.

In 1971, Skinner's controversial book *Beyond Freedom and Dignity* argued that traditional aversive methods of behavior control had become ineffective against unforeseen problems such as worldwide pollution, nuclear war, and overpopulation. The benefits of freedom might be lost unless the world abandoned mentalistic assumptions about behavior. *Beyond Freedom and Dignity* was misunderstood as advocating totalitarian methods. In 1974, Skinner published *About Behaviorism* to correct common misconceptions about behaviorism.

Throughout the 1970s and 1980s, Skinner was officially retired but continued to publish prolifically. A three-volume autobiography detailed his life and had sufficient scope to serve well as an overview of the history of behavior analysis. In 1974, the Association for Behavior Analysis (ABA) was founded, and in 1978 initiated another journal, *The Behavior Analyst.* The 1983 book *Enjoy Old Age* suggested a variety of behavioral strategies to reduce problems associated with advancing age. Skinner took on the growing field of cognitive psychology, characterizing it as a kind of "scientific creationism" in which every behavior could be "explained" simply by inventing unverifiable, unobservable mental processes with exactly the properties needed to account for the observed responding. Diagnosed with leukemia in 1989, Skinner continued work but curtailed his schedule while blood transfusions held the disease temporarily at bay. On August 10, 1990, just 10 days before he passed away, Skinner presented his final address to the American Psychological Association. A master of behavioral self-management, Skinner worked even on the day of his death on August 18, 1990.

—*James T. Todd and Kelly J. Sandor*

See also: *Applied Behavior Analysis (Vols. I, II, & III), Azrin, Nathan H. (Vols. I & III), Behavioral Treatment in Natural Environments (Vols. I & III), Operant Conditioning (Vols. I, II, & III), Single-Case Research (Vols. I & III), Skinner, Burrhus Frederic (Vols. I & III)*

Suggested Readings

Catania, A. C., & Harnad, S. (Eds.). (1983). *The selection of behaviour: The operant behaviour of B. F. Skinner: Comments and consequences.* New York: Cambridge University Press.

Skinner, B. F. (1953). *Science and human behavior.* New York: Macmillan.

Skinner, B. F. (1957). *Verbal behavior.* New York: Appleton-Century-Crofts.

Skinner, B. F. (1968). *Technology of teaching.* New York: Appleton-Century-Crofts.

Skinner, B. F. (1971). *Beyond freedom and dignity.* New York: Knopf.

Skinner, B. F. (1974). *About behaviorism.* New York: Knopf.

Skinner, B. F., & Vaughan, M. E. (1983). *Enjoy old age: A program of self management.* New York: W. W. Norton.

Todd, J. T., & Morris, E. K. (Eds.). (1994). *Modern perspectives on B. F. Skinner and contemporary behaviorism.* Westport, CT: Greenwood Press.

SOCIAL AND INTERPERSONAL SKILLS TRAINING

DESCRIPTION OF THE STRATEGY

Since the 1970s, social skills training has been widely used to assist children with impaired social competence. This strategy focuses on teaching the interpersonal skills necessary for successful social interactions and relationships. Social skills training is designed to improve the verbal and nonverbal behaviors related to interpersonal effectiveness and peer acceptance, as well as others' judgment or impression. The underlying assumption behind this approach is that social skills are learned behaviors that can be taught to children using structured teaching methods.

Numerous social skills programs are available for children and adolescents. The specifics of these programs differ, based on the population for which the treatment was designed (e.g., socially anxious, impulsive, or oppositional children). The basic social skills intervention components, however, are similar and include teaching skills such as initiating and maintaining conversations, listening to others, inviting someone to get together, assertion, aggression control, moral reasoning, and social perspective taking. Training also focuses on teaching nonverbal skills such as making eye contact, smiling, appearing relaxed, and limiting fidgeting. Within training sessions, these skills are taught to the child and repeatedly practiced until a criterion for skill mastery is met.

There are five core components of social skills training: (1) assessment, (2) direct instruction, (3) modeling, (4) conducting role plays and practice, and (5) corrective feedback and additional practice. The assessment involves understanding the factors responsible for a child's social difficulties. It may be helpful to observe peer interactions in a natural environment or in a role play or simulated situation. Another common method is to obtain teacher and parent reports of social behavior with peers in school and at home. At the conclusion of training, social skills and interpersonal relatedness are reassessed through behavioral observation and vis-à-vis teacher-, parent-, and child-ratings to ensure that treatment gains have generalized to the child's social environment.

Skills training begins with direct instruction by the therapist. The child is taught the "rules" of social interaction, as well as the importance and rationale of the behavior. For example, when teaching a child to initiate conversations, the therapist might review the appropriate settings for starting conversations (e.g., when sitting next to someone, standing in line in the cafeteria), as well as different strategies for successful initiation (e.g., smiling, commenting on something going on in the environment). Next, the therapist models the skill. This technique involves the therapist demonstrating the appropriate behavior to the child. In many instances, family members or peers can act as helpful models. The child then role-plays the modeled skill with others and receives constructive feedback to incorporate into future interactions. Practice on a skill should be continued until the child demonstrates mastery across a variety of situations. Another particularly effective way to practice skills is through coached play, whereby the therapist observes a child interacting with a peer and provides immediate feedback and coaching to the child about his or her behavior. Homework is assigned between sessions so that the child further practices the skills in the child's natural environments.

Contingency management can be helpful for enhancing motivation for practice, maintaining new behaviors, and generalizing learned skills. It involves the use of consequences to reward appropriate, adaptive behaviors and reduce undesirable ones. This might involve, for example, ignoring a child when the child interrupts as opposed to providing praise and attention when the child speaks in turn. In addition, a reticent child may receive a sticker and praise after approaching a peer. Contingency management techniques may also assist in improving a child's performance on individual skills through, for example, providing praise for speaking louder or increasing eye contact.

Social skills training can also involve social problem solving, which focuses on training broad-based thought processes that apply to a range of situations. This approach guides children in identifying difficult situations, generating a range of possible responses, predicting probable outcomes of each response, and then selecting the response most likely to result in a positive outcome. For example, children who are frequently bullied might identify places where they have an increased probability of being bullied (e.g., on the playground), derive several potential responses (e.g., stay near a teacher during recess, assert themselves), predict the bullies' response (e.g., less likely to tease in presence of a teacher, get beat up if they assert themselves), and then behave accordingly. In essence, this approach aims at teaching children coping skills that can be used to determine the most adaptive behavior in a variety of situations.

The various social skill components can be used alone or in combination. In guiding one's decision about the use of specific techniques, it has been suggested that different skill deficits or problem areas may demand different techniques. For example, modeling and coaching may be most useful when a child is acquiring a particular skill, whereas contingency management techniques may assist in enhancing a child's performance (e.g., speaking louder, increasing eye contact, proximity to another person), improving motivation, or eliminating an undesirable behavior (e.g., biting or hitting another child, interrupting others during conversation). Certain approaches may also work better with particular age groups. Role playing is often used with older children, given their greater cognitive abilities, whereas coaching is a large component of training with elementary aged and less mature children.

RESEARCH BASIS

Studies have evaluated various social skills programs in a wide range of populations, including children who are depressed, anxious, developmentally delayed, and have disruptive behavior problems. Since the populations for which these strategies are used can be very impaired, skills training is often one component in a multifaceted treatment plan. Overall, social skill training interventions are viewed as effective short-term interventions for enhancing children's social deficits. These interventions have demonstrated improvements on laboratory measures relative to control conditions but have often failed to replicate such positive effects in natural settings. In addition, few studies have documented long-term changes in social competency as measured by teacher and peer report. Finally, differences have been found in the effectiveness of this intervention as a function of child characteristics. For example, social skills training tends to work better for preschoolers and adolescents as compared to elementary children.

Due to questions regarding the clinical significance of research outcomes, clinical researchers have suggested procedures to facilitate generalization, namely "generalization facilitators." Some strategies include (a) training across stimuli common to the environment (e.g., at school), (b) rewards for engaging in the skill (e.g., stickers, movie or fast-food passes), (c) teaching behaviors that are likely to be maintained by naturally occurring consequences (e.g., participating in enjoyable interactions), and (d) incorporating prosocial, popular, or outgoing peers within the treatment approach to provide opportunities to practice acquired social skills in a natural setting.

RELEVANT TARGET POPULATIONS AND EXCEPTIONS

Social skills training is often used as one component of comprehensive treatment programs for various childhood problems. Children with externalizing problems such as attention-deficit/hyperactivity disorder (ADHD), conduct disorder, and oppositional defiant disorder often have social competency deficits (e.g., impulsivity, aggressiveness), which can lead to negative interpersonal interactions and peer rejection. Social skills training has been found to be useful in reducing levels of impulsiveness, aggressiveness, and oppositionality and increasing rates of positive, prosocial behaviors such as playing cooperatively, expressing emotions, and reading social cues.

Social skills training can also be helpful for children with internalizing disorders, such as depression and anxiety, by enhancing the quality of social interactions. Depression in children is often associated with a lack of environmental rewards such as enjoyable peer interactions. Training depressed children to be more socially adept can assist them in obtaining more social reinforcement and in increasing their social activity level. In addition, anxious children and adolescents tend to be shy or reticent. Therefore, enhancing their ability to enter groups, start and maintain conversations, use appropriate nonverbal behavior, and assert themselves is helpful in increasing the frequency and quality of their social contact. This strategy is particularly relevant when treating social anxiety disorder; behavioral treatment programs for this disorder include a substantial social skills training component that is often conducted in a group format.

Finally, social skills training may be beneficial with higher-functioning autistic children and youth with Asperger's disorder and Rett's disorder. Somewhat different from the typical approach, skills training within this population involves relatively extensive prompting and reinforcement to engage in prosocial behavior, in addition to the skills typically used (e.g., modeling, coaching). Skills generally focused upon within this population include making eye contact, initiating play, sharing, and nonaggressive behavior.

COMPLICATIONS

Numerous issues may interfere with the provision of effective social skills interventions. Problems may include familial conflict (e.g., parent-child conflict, child abuse), negative peer group influences (e.g., gang activity, bullies), disruptive behavior problems, substance abuse problems, and limited cognitive abilities. In addition, many youth, particularly adolescents, are often referred for psychological services involuntarily. Not surprisingly, this creates difficulty in eliciting accurate information and establishing rapport. Some children, particularly shy and withdrawn youth, may also be hesitant to engage in generalization exercises due to social anxiety and fear of negative evaluations. Homework exercises may also be unsuccessful due to the stability of peer rejection or other unforeseeable events (e.g., attempts at initiating a conversation with an unfamiliar peer are ignored). Finally, given that many social interactions occur quickly (e.g., answering a question in class, talking to a peer), children must practice frequently in order to become proficient in learned skills. Naturally, getting children to practice can be a difficult task and often requires parental collaboration in order to devise a contingency management system to reward practice.

Issues within the clinical setting may also complicate treatment. It may be difficult to simulate peer social interactions within an office setting, particularly when therapy consists of one-on-one interactions with an adult. Therapists also may not be knowledgeable about the social norms of the child's age group. Given this, some have suggested using school-based interventions in a group format to enhance the generalizability of social skills interventions. Such an approach also addresses the issue of not having peers of comparable age to the child, also likely to be a problem in clinic-based treatment.

CASE ILLUSTRATION

"Andrew" was a 9-year-old boy who was experiencing significant peer rejection. He complained of having few friends, being teased frequently, and engaging in few social activities. Andrew's teacher and parents corroborated this report and further noted that he had difficulty relating socially to others. For example, Andrew had difficulty reading social cues (e.g., interrupting others), was awkward when approaching/interacting with other children, and overly submissive (e.g., did not stand up for himself).

Given that the treatment goal was to improve Andrew's socialization skills and peer acceptance, it was important for the assessment to include multiple sources of information. First, reports from Andrew's teacher suggested that he was frequently teased and exhibited more "unskilled" behaviors (e.g., interrupting others during conversation) than other same-aged children. Second, Andrew's parents rated him as having problems approaching and socializing with other children. Third, Andrew reported that although he had several friends, he was frequently left out of activities and rarely invited to other children's homes. Finally, the therapist noted that Andrew had difficulty reading social cues, often speaking out of turn, making poor eye contact, and interrupting others.

Treatment initially involved coaching and practicing adaptive communication techniques such as voice volume, smile, eye contact, and appropriate physical closeness. Proficient use of these skills was reinforced through therapist praise. The second session introduced good and bad times and places to try to make friends. For example, Andrew was encouraged to approach children on the playground but to avoid initiating conversations during class time. Following Andrew's repeated practice of these tasks within session, which involved incorporating feedback from his therapist, a series of real-life practices was assigned. Andrew was instructed to approach a familiar peer and initiate a conversation. Following these assignments, Andrew discussed his performance with the therapist and what areas still needed improvement.

The next several sessions focused on teaching and practicing rules of etiquette for initiating conversations or attempting to join a group of children at play. For example, Andrew, who had difficulty choosing an appropriate time to participate in a conversation, was instructed to wait for a pause before commenting about the activity or environment. Initially, Andrew was somewhat hesitant to approach peers. To address this, a reinforcement schedule was implemented in which his teachers provided him with a favorite candy for each attempt.

As Andrew became more skilled at interacting with friendly, nonaggressive peers, treatment shifted to addressing the frequent teasing that he experienced. Although some children are able to respond to teasing through humor or assertion, Andrew generally possessed poor conflict management skills that might motivate bullies to continue aggressing upon him. As such, Andrew was taught to respond to teasing neutrally or through mild humor. To illustrate, in response to being called a "toothpick," Andrew responded by saying "So what?" in a neutral, unemotional tone of voice. Subsequent sessions addressed methods of asserting himself when appropriate, as well as a strategy for avoiding physical fights with bullies. Such techniques include staying out of "high-risk" environments (e.g., engaging with bullies without adult supervision), staying near friends, and not antagonizing bullies.

Treatment was concluded with a graduation party and ceremony for Andrew. Postassessment using a combination of teacher-, parent-, and self-report questionnaires suggested that Andrew's socialization skills had improved significantly. For example, his teacher noted that he rarely blurted out responses during class and was engaging in other improved interpersonal skills (e.g., playing with children). Furthermore, Andrew and his teacher noted that Andrew was teased less frequently, and Andrew stated that he had scheduled several play dates in the immediate future. Despite these gains, however, Andrew's teacher reported that he was relatively often excluded from peers' games. Follow-up assessment 3 months later revealed that although Andrew was not universally accepted by his peers, there was no decline in Andrew's social skills and that levels of teasing were not significantly greater than that experienced by other children.

—*Eric A. Storch and Carrie Masia-Warner*

See also: *Problem-Solving Therapy (Vols. I & III), Social Competence Treatment: Externalizing Disorders (Vol. II), Social Effectiveness Training (Vols. I & III), Social Skills Training (Vols. I & III)*

Suggested Readings

Beidel, D. C., Turner, S. M., & Morris, T. L. (2000). Behavioral treatment of childhood social phobia. *Journal of Consulting & Clinical Psychology, 68,* 1072–1080.

Elliott, S. N., & Gresham, F. M. (1993). Social skills interventions for children. *Behavior Modification, 17,* 287–313.

Elliott, S. N., Gresham, F. M., & Heffer, R. W. (1987). Social skill interventions: Research findings and training techniques. In C. Maher & J. E. Zins (Eds.), *Psychoeducational interventions in the schools: Methods and procedures for enhancing student competence* (pp. 141–159). Elmsford, NY: Pergamon Press.

Forman, S. G. (1993) *Coping skills interventions for children and adolescents.* San Francisco: Jossey-Bass.

Frankel, F., Cantwell, D. P., & Myatt, R. (1996). Helping ostracized children: Social skills training and parent support for socially rejected children. In E. D. Hibbs & P. S. Jensen (Eds.), *Psychosocial treatments for child and adolescent disorders: Empirically based strategies for clinical practice.* Washington, DC: American Psychological Association.

Gresham, F. M., & Elliot, S. N. (1984). Assessment and classification of children's social skills: A review of methods and issues. *School Psychology Review, 13,* 292–301.

Masia, C. L., Klein, R. G., Storch, E. A., & Corda, B. (2001). School-based behavioral treatment for social anxiety disorder in adolescents: Results of a pilot study. *Journal of the American Academy of Child and Adolescent Psychiatry, 40,* 780–786.

Sheridan, S. M., & Walker, D. (1999). Social skills in context: Considerations for assessment, intervention, and generalization. In C. R. Reynolds & T. B. Gutkin (Eds.), *The handbook of school psychology* (3rd ed., pp. 686–708). New York: John Wiley.

Spence, S. H., Donovan, C., & Brechman-Toussaint, M. (2000). The treatment of childhood social phobia: The effectiveness of a social skills training-based, cognitive-behavioral intervention, with and without parental involvement. *Journal of Child Psychology and Psychiatry, 41,* 713–726.

SOCIAL COMPETENCE TREATMENT

DESCRIPTION OF THE STRATEGY

Interpersonal difficulties are considered one of the hallmark qualities of children with attention-deficit/hyperactivity disorder (ADHD), oppositional defiant disorder (ODD), and conduct disorder (CD). Children with these disorders, collectively referred to as externalizing disorders, are rated more negatively by peers on sociometric measures and are more likely to experience peer rejection. Thus, peer relationships are an important target of comprehensive treatment for externalizing disorders. For over 30 years, researchers have investigated and disseminated treatment packages targeting the social competence of children with externalizing disorders. Social competence treatments (SCT) for these children focus on teaching and reinforcing the use of adaptive social skills and social problem-solving strategies during interactions with peers and adults across settings. Two broad classes of SCT for children with externalizing disorders include social skills training (SST) and social problem-solving training (SPST).

SST interventions aim to remediate the basic social skills knowledge and performance deficits of children with externalizing disorders by teaching and reinforcing the use of appropriate social skills (e.g., communication, cooperation, participation, validation) during interactions with peers and adults. The rationale for this approach is based on literature suggesting that (a) deficits in social skill knowledge and application underlie the social incompetence of children with externalizing disorders and (b) social skills can be learned through instruction and practice.

In contrast with SST, SPST focuses on modifying deficits in social cognitive processes (e.g., encoding and interpreting social cues, social problem solving) that have been shown to mediate the inappropriate social behavior of children with externalizing disorders. SPST interventions teach children with externalizing disorders to (a) recognize errors in their social information processing, (b) cope with stressful interactions using self-talk and perspective taking strategies, and (c) utilize more appropriate problem-solving strategies when conflicts arise with others. For example, anger coping programs were developed from the theory that anger-eliciting stimuli are not the cause or sole determinant of aggressive responses. Rather, children may respond aggressively to perceived provocation by peers because they misperceive the stimuli (e.g., inaccurately attributing hostile intent to others) and utilize immature coping strategies (e.g., aggression) to control their responses to the stimuli. Taking an alternative approach, problem-solving skills programs focus on deficits in social problem solving and teach children to identify the problem, generate multiple solutions, evaluate alternatives, and select adaptive solutions. In sum, anger coping and problem-solving interventions focus on teaching children with externalizing problems to recognize their cognitive biases and to utilize coping and problem-solving strategies that facilitate more appropriate responses to others.

SST and SPST programs for children with externalizing disorders tend to include most, if not all, of the following instructional components to develop and reinforce knowledge and use of proper social skills and social problem-solving strategies: didactic instruction, group discussion, role play, modeling, in vivo play experience, coaching, social reinforcement, contingency management, and homework. Teachers or therapists implementing SST or SPST programs use didactic instruction to introduce a social skill or problem-solving strategy by describing the skill and providing multiple examples. To illustrate, a typical SST session might begin with the therapist defining cooperation and providing examples of how children can cooperate with others at home, school, and on the playground. The therapist also engages the children in a discussion regarding the importance of the skill and further elicits examples from the children about how the skill can be used in interactions with others.

Role play is used to model both positive and negative examples of the social skill or social problem-solving strategy. For example, the therapist might role-play with a coleader or a child an example of participation by describing and acting out a scenario in which children actively and appropriately participate in a board game. Role play is a useful technique for describing visually what is meant by a particular skill, demonstrating how to use a particular skill in a real-life context, and to further elicit discussion among the children.

Social skills and social problem-solving strategies are also taught to the children via modeling. For example, group leaders model proper use of social skills during all of their interactions with one another and the children. By modeling skills taught during the session (e.g., cooperating with children by following the rules of a board game), therapists provide the children with multiple opportunities to learn by watching others apply the skills. In addition to therapist modeling, skills taught in SPST programs are often modeled in videotaped vignettes or through the use of puppets. The videotaped vignettes depict several positive and negative examples of children using each of the social skills and social problem-solving strategies taught during treatment sessions. The vignettes are used to generate discussion among the children regarding how the skills presented in the videotapes may generalize to situations in their own lives. Puppets are particularly effective to teach skills, generate group discussion, and reinforce the use of skills during sessions of SPST programs with younger children.

Two important components of SCT programs, particularly SST, are coaching and social reinforcement. Following a brief group discussion, therapists may utilize the majority of time coaching each child or groups of children on the use of appropriate social skills during ecologically valid, in vivo play activities (e.g., board games, sports). Coaching is used to prompt children to use the social skills presented during the initial group discussion. Coaching allows group leaders to tailor SST to address the individual needs of each child in a group.

Social reinforcement and contingency management are used in conjunction with coaching to provide immediate feedback to children regarding their social behavior in the context in which it occurs. For example, therapists may provide praise, privileges, and/or tangible prizes to children who use social skills and give neutral feedback and/or remove privileges or rewards from children who exhibit negative social behaviors. Many researchers believe that social reinforcement and contingency management are essential components of SST, suggesting that without it, children would not otherwise be motivated to change their social behavior. Moreover, gains in social competence may only generalize beyond the treatment setting if important adults (e.g., parents, teachers) in the child's environment model and consistently reinforce socially appropriate behavior.

In addition, homework assignments are given to children in both SST and SPST programs to encourage using the social skills and social problem-solving strategies at home, school, and other social settings. Both programs place an emphasis on assigning and reviewing homework because these assignments encourage children to practice the skills taught through experience in situations beyond the treatment session. SCT homework assignments sometimes require parents and teachers to track the frequency of positive and negative social behaviors and to provide reinforcement for the children's use of adaptive social and social problem-solving skills at home and at school. Tracking is used to monitor the children's progress toward reaching attainable goals for social behavior across settings and to encourage parental and teacher involvement in the treatment.

Aside from the differences in theory and treatment focus between SST and SPST, the methods used by SST and SPST programs to treat the social impairments of children with externalizing disorders largely overlap. The only significant difference between SST and SPST programs used to treat children with externalizing disorders is the length of treatment. Although both programs typically include 1 weekly session lasting from 60 to 120 minutes, SPST programs generally range in length from 12 to 24 sessions, while SST programs typically include 8 to 12 sessions.

RESEARCH BASIS

A recent meta-analytic review assessing the overall efficacy of SCT for children with social impairments found the effects of SCT on posttreatment parent and teacher ratings of child social impairment to be small in magnitude ($d = 0.199$). Similarly, an earlier meta-analysis of SCT interventions concluded that children viewed as most needing the treatment (i.e., children with externalizing disorders) were the least likely to respond favorably, based on parent and teacher ratings of social behavior. Moreover, studies suggesting significant post-SCT improvement in social skills or social problem solving often do not assess for long-term maintenance of gains in social functioning. Thus, evidence supporting the use of SCT for children with social impairment, particularly children with externalizing behavior disorders, is mixed at best.

Two newly developed, multimodal SST interventions for children with ADHD and ODD have demonstrated stronger treatment effects across home and school settings than those reported in the meta-analyses referred to previously. For both of these SST interventions, a parent group met concurrently to discuss ways to reinforce their child's use of appropriate social skills in order to maintain treatment gains over time and across settings. Relative to a SST-only group and a wait-list control group, both studies reported that children with ADHD and ODD in the SST + parental involvement condition demonstrated moderate to very large effects on parent and teacher reports of social skills knowledge, social skills performance, and overall behavior. Thus, teaching and encouraging parents to reinforce their child's use of appropriate social skills appears to result in larger improvements in the social behavior of children with externalizing disorders than those achieved with SST-only interventions.

Similarly, research has also examined the incremental benefit of adding parent involvement to SPST interventions for children with externalizing disorders. One well-controlled study suggests that children with ODD and CD randomly assigned to an SPST intervention with concurrent behavioral parent training exhibited significantly greater improvements in social skill performance, social problem solving, and overall behavior as rated by parents and teachers at postintervention and 1-year follow-up compared to children who received SPST alone or children whose parents received BPT only. In sum, results of these studies support the utility of combining SST or SPST with parental involvement and reinforcement to enhance the effects of these interventions on the social behavior of children with ADHD, ODD, and/or CD.

Intensive, multimodal programs such as the summer treatment program (STP) were developed specifically to address the peer difficulties experienced by children with externalizing disorders, particularly ADHD. The STP includes both SST and SPST components that are practiced, modeled, and reinforced in the context of ecologically valid activities, including academic classrooms and recreational settings. Parents and community school teachers are also instructed to provide instruction and reinforcement for use of appropriate social and social problem-solving skills in the home and school settings in order to enhance maintenance and generalization of the intensive 8-week program. Many studies have demonstrated very large effects of the STP on measures of the social functioning of children with externalizing disorders. The magnitude of these effects far exceeds those that have been documented using traditional clinic-based approaches. However, to date, no study has specifically dismantled this program to evaluate the incremental benefit of SST and SPST components.

RELEVANT TARGET POPULATIONS AND EXCEPTIONS

The behavioral excesses of children diagnosed with ADHD, ODD, and CD are often associated with profound impairments in their social functioning. Research suggests that school-age children presenting with problems of inattention, hyperactivity, impulsivity, adult-directed defiance, aggression, and other conduct problems often have pervasive social skills knowledge *and* performance deficits and are likely to be disliked and rejected by their peers. Knowledge of the degree and pervasiveness of the social problems for children with ADHD, ODD, and CD is concerning, because research has shown that children with poor peer relations, especially those with externalizing behavior problems, are at a significant risk for continued interpersonal difficulties and other social problems as adolescents (e.g., dropping out of school,

juvenile delinquency) and adults (e.g., being laid off from work, imprisonment).

COMPLICATIONS

Although intervening at an early age appears crucial, equally as important, if not more important, is choosing an SCT program that is developmentally appropriate for the child. In order for children to demonstrate improved social behavior as a result of SCT, skills must be transmitted to children in a manner that is easily comprehendible and affords them the opportunity to practice the skills in relevant social contexts. Thus, considering the multitude of SCT programs available, it is important to choose one that best fits the developmental level and presenting problems of the child.

Moreover, because social impairment is chronic, treatment should also be chronic. Owing to the prevailing thought in the SCT literature that insufficient positive reinforcement across settings contributes to the chronic social impairment of children with ADHD, ODD, and CD, current research emphasizes the need to incorporate parents and teachers as reinforcing agents for social behavior at home and school in order to facilitate generalized effects across these settings. Current and future research in this area is exploring the benefit of using siblings and peers at school as agents of change for social behavior of children with externalizing disorders.

CASE ILLUSTRATION

Ten children were referred by their mothers to participate in an SST program conducted at a university ADHD clinic in the spring of 2002. The children were largely comprised of Caucasian (60%) males (80%) between the ages of 6 and 12 ($M = 9$) from middle-class households (M family income = $31,500). Each of the children presented with social behavior problems across settings with peers and adults. A multiinformant (e.g., parent and teacher), multimethod (e.g., questionnaires, semistructured interview) assessment was used to examine whether children met criteria for ADHD, ODD, and CD and the degree to which their behavioral excesses resulted in social impairment across multiple settings. Based on this assessment, all children met *DSM-IV* criteria for ADHD; 60% were diagnosed with comorbid ODD and 20% were diagnosed with CD.

Fifty percent of the children were prescribed stimulant medication to help manage their ADHD symptoms.

The SST program in which these children were enrolled met weekly for eight 2-hour sessions. Each session included 15 to 20 minutes of didactic instruction by a therapist, group discussion, and instructor-led role play to improve the children's knowledge of how to listen to others, compliment others, help, share, follow directions, ignore provocation, and make appropriate complaints. During the next 60 minutes of each session, children were coached by the therapist to use skills taught during interactions with children while playing board games. Social reinforcement (i.e., praise) was used to reward children for actively participating in group discussions and for using good social skills with children during the board game activities. A response-cost contingency management system was used to manage the rate of negative behaviors (e.g., disrespect toward others, disobedience) exhibited by children during the sessions. Children exhibiting negative behaviors lost points for each negative behavior. Children who lost fewer than a predetermined number of points were rewarded with 15 minutes of computer time at the end of each session. Children who exceeded the set number of points were not permitted to use the computer and instead spent the time writing down ways they could use good social skills at home and at school during the upcoming week. Consistent with literature supporting the incremental benefit of parent involvement in social skills programs, mothers participated in a concurrent group that focused on reinforcing their children's use of social skills at home and school.

Changes in social skill knowledge and performance were assessed using (a) child-reports of their use of social skills in hypothetical situations in which they were asked to solve a problem with peers, siblings, and adults and (b) parent-report questionnaires assessing rates of social skill performance at home and with peers. In addition, mothers were asked to report posttreatment changes in social impairment with peers and rates of being ignored and rejected by peers. Mothers reported improvements in child cooperation at home and social impairment with peers. Moreover, children demonstrated improvement in using positive social behaviors to solve problems with siblings, peers, and adults. To enhance generalization of these gains to other settings in which these children experience social impairment, it is recommended that teachers, coaches, scout leaders, and other adults be trained in behavioral principles so that they may also reinforce appropriate social behavior.

—*Brian T. Wymbs and Andrea M. Chronis*

See also: *Problem-Solving Therapy (Vols. I & III), Social and Interpersonal Skills Training (Vol. II), Social Effectiveness Training (Vols. I & III), Social Skills Training (Vols. I & III)*

Suggested Readings

Frankel, F., Myatt, R., Cantwell, D. P., & Feinberg, D. T. (1997). Parent-assisted transfer of children's social skills training: Effects on children with and without attention-deficit hyperactivity disorder. *Journal of the American Academy of Child and Adolescent Psychiatry, 36,* 1056–1064.

Kavale, K. A., Mathur, S. R., Forness, S. R., Rutherford, R. G., & Quinn, M. M. (1997). The effectiveness of social skills training for students with emotional or behavioral disorders: A meta-analysis. In T. E. Scruggs & M. A. Mastropieri (Eds.), *Advances in learning and behavioral disabilities* (Vol. 11, pp. 1–26). Greenwich, CT: JAI Press.

Kazdin, A. E., Siegel, T. C., & Bass, D. (1992). Cognitive problem-solving skills training and parent management training in the treatment of antisocial behavior in children. *Journal of Consulting and Clinical Psychology, 60,* 733–747.

Lochman, J. E., Whidby, J. M., & FitzGerald, D. P. (2000). Cognitive-behavioral assessment and treatment with aggressive children. In P. C. Kendall (Ed.), *Child and adolescent therapy: Cognitive-behavioral procedures.* New York: Guilford Press.

Pelham, W. E., & Bender, M. E. (1982). Peer relationships in hyperactive children. In K. Gadow & I. Bailer (Eds.), *Advances in learning and behavioral disabilities* (pp. 365–436). Greenwich, CN: JAI Press.

Pelham, W. E., Fabiano, G. A., Gnagy, E. M., Greiner, A. R., & Hoza, B. (2005). Comprehensive psychosocial treatment for ADHD. In E. Hibbs and P. Jensen (Eds.), *Psychosocial treatments for child and adolescent disorders: Empirically based strategies for clinical practice* (2nd ed.). Washington, DC: American Psychological Association.

Pfiffner, L. J., Calzada, E., & McBurnett, K. (2000). Interventions to enhance social competence. *Child and Adolescent Psychiatric Clinics of North America, 9,* 689–709.

Pfiffner, L. J., & McBurnett, K. (1997). Social skills training with parent generalization: Treatment effects for children with attention deficit disorder. *Journal of Consulting and Clinical Psychology, 65,* 749–757.

Webster-Stratton, C., & Hammond, M. (1997). Treating children with early-onset conduct problems: A comparison of child and parent training interventions. *Journal of Consulting and Clinical Psychology, 65,* 93–109.

Webster-Stratton, C., Reid, J., & Hammond, M. (2001). Social skills and problem-solving training for children with early-onset conduct problems: Who benefits? *Journal of Child Psychology and Psychiatry, 42,* 943–952.

SOMATIC CONTROL STRATEGIES

DESCRIPTION OF THE STRATEGY

Somatic control strategies refer to techniques one can use to manage aversive physiological symptoms that may interfere with functioning. Such physiological symptoms include shaking, trembling, hyperventilation, rapid heartbeat, muscle tension, and "butterflies" or nervousness in the stomach, among others. Controlling or managing these symptoms may lead as well to the amelioration of related problems such as sleep disturbance, difficulty driving, and embarrassment in social situations. Somatic control strategies are most commonly used for people with anxiety disorders and related conditions but can be useful as well for people with other mental or physical conditions that involve high levels of physiological arousal or pain. The procedures are also used in many cases as preparation for advanced exposure-based techniques. Somatic control strategies often involve progressive muscle relaxation, breathing retraining, applied tension, and other procedures.

Progressive Muscle Relaxation

Progressive muscle relaxation can be conducted in many ways, although one of the most common involves a tension-release model. In this procedure, a client is instructed to sit in a comfortable chair in a therapist's office and try to relax as much as possible. The lights may be dimmed with the goal of providing as relaxed an environment as possible. The therapist then asks the client to concentrate on his or her voice to the exclusion of other distractions. During the procedure, described completely by the therapist, the voice should be kept even and smooth to promote a sense of calm.

The initial target of progressive muscle relaxation can vary but often involves the hands. The client is instructed to ball one of his or her hands into a fist. The client is then told to squeeze the fist as tightly as possible, with care taken with long fingernails or any physical condition (e.g., arthritis) the client may have. The fist is held tightly for 5 to 10 seconds, after which the client is instructed to quickly release the fist and allow the hand to fall limp. After a period of several seconds, the client is again instructed to ball his or her hand into a fist and hold it tightly for 5 to 10 seconds. The therapist should carefully examine the client's

hand to see if it is indeed tightly held and instruct the client to squeeze harder if necessary. Following the second period of tension, the client is again asked to let go quickly of the fist and allow the hand to feel limp. The process is repeated with the other hand. At this point, the therapist may wish to help the client understand the difference between a tense fist and a loose hand and the accompanying sensations. As the hand falls limp after tension, for example, most people report sensations of relaxed muscles, warmth, and tinginess. This should be shown to the client as different from sensations of tension, tightness, and pain.

Following this initial procedure, the therapist may instruct the client to tense and release additional muscle groups. A common second target is the arms, which may be twisted and tensed and released individually or together. Again, the procedure is to have the client tense for 5 to 10 seconds and release quickly to feel the relaxation. Intermittently throughout the progressive muscle relaxation procedure, the therapist praises the client for his or her effort and expresses the belief that the client will become a good relaxer. In addition, the client is reminded periodically during the process to focus on the difference between tensed and relaxed muscles, a difference not always recognized in people with anxiety disorders or chronic tension.

Targets of relaxation next include the shoulders, face, jaw, stomach, legs, and feet. With respect to the shoulders, the client is instructed to raise his or her arms over the head and stretch the arms as far as possible toward the ceiling. If the client can stretch his or her arms backward past the head, this may be encouraged as well. With respect to the face, the client is instructed to squeeze muscles around the eyes, nose, cheeks, and other areas, being careful if wearing contact lenses. With respect to the jaw, the client is instructed to clench his or her jaw muscles or teeth tightly before releasing. With respect to the stomach, the client is instructed to bring his or her stomach inward and as close to the spine as possible. This is recommended for clients who have "butterflies" in the stomach but not for those who experience nausea when anxious or in pain. With respect to the legs and feet, the client is instructed to tense by pushing the feet or toes toward the floor. At the end of the exercise, the client is encouraged to sit comfortably and try to relax his or her entire body, focusing on any areas of tension that remain and working to ease the muscles in that area.

The relaxation procedure in its entirety lasts about 25 minutes. Following this in-session procedure, which is often audiotaped, the client is instructed to practice the relaxation at least twice per day and during any times when he or she feels most stressed. Special attention is given to those muscle groups that seem most problematic. In addition, the therapist generally reviews progress in this area from session to session and helps the client identify and remediate any muscle tension that remains. As therapy continues, the client generally practices the relaxation more independently.

Breathing Retraining

Another somatic control exercise is breathing retraining, which is particularly useful for people who breathe shallowly or who hyperventilate when anxious or otherwise aroused. Breathing retraining focuses mostly on diaphragmatic breathing, or breathing deeply into the lungs and against the diaphragm (as opposed to chest breathing by simply expanding the rib cage). For children, this is done by asking them to inhale slowly through their nose, hold their breath for about a second, and exhale slowly out of their mouth with pursed lips. This can be done several times in a row each session for about 5 minutes. For added effect, children can press their fingers into their ribcage as they inhale. If a person has trouble breathing in this way, he or she may be asked to lie on a couch or the floor. Youth are generally encouraged to count aloud slowly (i.e., 1, 2, 3, 4) as they inhale and exhale so that both breathing processes are similar in length.

For young children, imagery during the procedure can be helpful. For example, a child can imagine a tire being inflated and deflated as they inhale and exhale. Another common image is to have a child picture a hot air balloon that needs air as fuel. The child is encouraged to think of himself or herself as the balloon filling up with fuel and rising, then gradually releasing air to return to the ground. These analogies are useful because children often understand the consequences of too much and too little air in tires and balloons.

As with progressive muscle relaxation, breathing retraining can be used during stressful situations in daily life. In fact, breathing retraining is often preferred by clients over muscle relaxation because it is portable, easier to do without other people taking notice, and less time-consuming. In many treatment protocols for anxiety disorders, however, progressive muscle relaxation and breathing retraining are administered together because the breathing enhances the effects of the muscle relaxation.

Applied Tension

Another somatic control exercise commonly used for an anxiety disorder, but which involves an increase in muscle tension, is applied tension. For most people with specific phobias (e.g., of heights), panic attacks and increased physiological arousal are the norm when they come into contact with their phobic stimulus. Most commonly, these people experience accelerated heart rate and blood pressure and may require the procedures discussed above. However, for people with a specific phobia of blood, injections, or injury, a decrease in blood pressure and reduced blood flow to the brain is a common symptom. This vasovagal response and the subsequent fainting that it often produces eventually becomes, in many cases, the very event that people fear even more than blood or the needle itself.

To address this peculiar specific phobia, one method that has been developed is applied tension. Although various forms of applied tension exist, a common method is to first have the client identify physical sensations that warn him or her that fainting may soon occur. Examples include lightheadedness, weakness in the limbs, or temperature changes. Whenever the client feels as though fainting is imminent, applied tension procedures are used.

In a therapy session, the client is usually instructed to sit in a comfortable chair and imagine feelings of faintness. An imaginal scene may be presented to enhance this process. When the client feels faint or can vividly imagine fainting, he or she is instructed to tense various muscles around the neck, shoulders, back, chest, and legs. The stomach is often left relaxed so the person can practice diaphragmatic breathing. The muscles are generally tensed all at once for 10 to 30 seconds or until the person feels that his or her face is flushed. The person is then instructed to fully relax his or her body and practice diaphragmatic breathing for at least 30 seconds. The process is then repeated.

Over time, the person practices applied tension several times a day and at times when he or she is most at risk for fainting. The optimal level of tension and relaxation is specific to each client, so practice to find the best individual strategy is recommended. As with other somatic control methods, applied tension serves partially as a prelude to exposure-based techniques where a person gradually approaches a feared stimulus. In later sessions, however, unlike progressive muscle relaxation and breathing retraining, applied tension is usually faded.

Other Methods

Although progressive muscle relaxation and breathing retraining are commonly used in therapy to lower tension, other somatic control strategies are available and may be preferable for some clients. Common examples include meditation, hypnosis, and pharmacotherapy. Some clients prefer to meditate and are able to successfully lower their arousal level when doing so. Therapists can thus utilize meditation in lieu of other somatic control strategies mentioned above. In addition, some clients respond best to hypnosis or focused arousal away from muscle tension, although hypnosis is generally dependent on therapist inducement and therefore not portable in many daily life situations.

Pharmacotherapy may also be used as a somatic control strategy in certain situations. Classes of drugs most utilized in this regard include anxiolytics, sedatives, and antidepressants. More specifically, benzodiazepine drugs are commonly used to reduce physiological arousal and include clonazepam (Klonopin), chlordiazepoxide (Librium), diazepam (Valium), lorazepam (Ativan), alprazolam (Xanax), triazolam (Halcion), and oxazepam (Serax). Pharmacotherapy is sometimes recommended as an adjunctive treatment for people with severe levels of fear or anxiety that initially prevent a full engagement in exposure-based treatment. Most protocols for treating anxiety disorders recommend a gradual weaning of pharmacological agents prior to the end of therapy.

RESEARCH BASIS

The concept of somatic control strategies has been discussed in the literature for decades as a way of countering excessive physiological arousal. Tension-release exercises to reduce muscle tension were formalized in the 1930s, for example, and later refined as part of the growing literature on systematic desensitization. In this procedure, typically used to treat specific phobias, a three-step procedure is generally adopted. First, the client learns to control his or her somatic symptoms. Second, the therapist and client develop a fear and avoidance hierarchy of 5 to 10 situations that range from least to most anxiety-provoking in nature. Third, the client is gradually exposed to these situations, using somatic control exercises to assist approach and eventual habituation to the stimulus (e.g., dog). The process is largely based on the premise of classical conditioning, or learning by association. Essentially, a fearful person learns to associate relaxation, an incompatible response to fear, with the previously phobic stimulus. Many studies over several decades have documented the effectiveness of systematic desensitization and somatic control strategies for different clinical populations.

In more advanced treatment protocols for anxiety disorders, progressive muscle relaxation and breathing retraining are used in conjunction with other procedures. In many cases, somatic control strategies are learned with cognitive control strategies (e.g., cognitive restructuring) as methods of controlling and managing one's anxiety. Earlier sessions of therapy are often devoted to learning and perfecting these strategies in session and in real-life situations. Later sessions of therapy are often devoted to incorporating these somatic and cognitive control strategies into exposure-based practices that vary in type and level of difficulty. These strategies are meant to facilitate exposure and act as coping methods so that one can fully habituate to a phobic stimulus.

RELEVANT TARGET POPULATIONS

Somatic control exercises are most commonly used for people with anxiety disorders, especially panic disorder and agoraphobia, specific and social phobias, generalized anxiety disorder, and acute stress and posttraumatic stress disorder. From a diagnostic perspective, the exercises can also be used for any problem that involves high levels of tension or physiological arousal, such as adjustment disorder or substance-related disorder. As mentioned earlier, applied tension is specifically used for persons with blood-injection-injury phobia. Somatic control exercises are also useful for those with medical problems exacerbated by stress. This is especially true for painful conditions such as those related to cancer, burns, and other maladies. In addition, progressive relaxation has been utilized in several studies as a component for treating insomnia or related sleep disturbances.

Stress management is also recommended for people with Type A personalities or those who find themselves in demanding and frequently upsetting life circumstances. Stress management techniques often include relaxation or meditation or medication as key components along with proper diet, sleep hygiene, general exercise, and attitude change. Of course, somatic control strategies can also be used by anyone who finds himself or herself in a stressful situation (e.g., first date) where physiological arousal needs to be reduced.

COMPLICATIONS

A main complication of somatic control exercises is that they will not be effective if a particular client does not practice the procedures and use them in key situations. In this case, obstacles to treatment must be fully addressed. In addition, the procedures may have to be modified or simplified for people or children with limited cognitive or motor abilities or for those who worry that the procedures will lead to social embarrassment. Furthermore, several studies indicate that somatic control exercises on their own are not highly effective in treating people with anxiety disorders. Instead, the exercises seem most useful in conjunction with exposure-based practices. Even in more general stress management programs, somatic control strategies are recommended as only one component of many for reducing stress.

CASE ILLUSTRATION

"Claire" was a 13-year-old multiracial female who presented to a university-based clinic (with her parents) for severe test and oral presentation anxiety. Claire had entered middle school just 2 months earlier and was still adjusting to rapid changes in classes, workload, student diversity, and type of classroom assignments. Although typically a very good student, Claire seemed a bit overwhelmed by the frequency of tests in her classes and by a new requirement in her English class, oral presentations.

During the assessment, Claire and her parents indicated that the girl had always been socially anxious to a moderate degree and tended to stay with a few close friends. Thus, her introversion was at odds with standing alone in front of a large classroom of students and speaking on a given topic. Claire's anxiety about tests and oral presentations had progressed to the point where she had begun to skip certain classes at school and was now experiencing declining grades.

Claire's treatment involved a combination of somatic and cognitive control strategies with exposure-based practices in session and in real life. During the first four sessions, Claire was instructed how to ease her muscle tension and control her breathing in such a way as to lower her considerable physiological arousal. In addition, her thoughts in key anxiety-provoking situations were explored, and her perfectionistic tendencies and worries about catastrophic events (e.g., complete humiliation) were addressed.

In the next four sessions of therapy, Claire was instructed to practice different academically oriented tasks in the therapist's office. These included practice tests sent from her teachers as well as oral presentations on topics assigned by the therapist. During each practice, Claire was instructed to use her somatic and cognitive control strategies before, during, and after the task. Ratings of anxiety were taken throughout each exposure and revealed increased habituation over time. Indeed, Claire reached a point quickly where she was able to take practice tests and give oral presentations with little difficulty in session. Distractions were later added to her exposures (e.g., larger audience, more snickering, more noise), but she became adept at handling these as well.

The final four sessions of therapy involved exposures in real life, or in vivo, situations. Claire was required to take makeup and regularly scheduled tests at school and complete her oral presentations. She experienced little problem with the examinations but had substantial anxiety during her initial oral presentation. Although that presentation did not go well, Claire saw that the consequences were not terrible (e.g., no one laughed). Her remaining oral presentations, while not excellent, were completed without avoidance.

—Christopher A. Kearney,
Kelly Drake, and Lisa Linning

See also: *Applied Relaxation and Tension (Vol. III), Biofeedback (Vols. I, II, & III), Breathing Retraining (Vol. I), Cue-Controlled Relaxation (Vols. I & III), Panic Control Treatment (Vols. I & III), Progressive Muscular Relaxation (Vols. I & III), Relaxation Strategies (Vol. II), Relaxation Training With Children (Vol. II)*

Suggested Readings

Carlson, C. R., & Hoyle, R. H. (1993). Efficacy of abbreviated progressive muscle relaxation training: A quantitative review of behavioral medicine research. *Journal of Consulting and Clinical Psychology, 61,* 1059–1067.

Kearney, C. A., & Albano, A. M. (2000). *When children refuse school: A cognitive-behavioral therapy approach/therapist's guide.* San Antonio, TX: Psychological Corporation.

Kendall, P. C. (2000). *Cognitive-behavioral therapy for anxious children: Therapist manual.* Ardmore, PA: Workbook.

Lohaus, A., Klein-Hebling, J., Vogele, C., & Kuhn-Hennighausen, C. (2001). Psychophysiological effects of relaxation training in children. *British Journal of Health Psychology, 6,* 197–206.

Means, M. K., Lichstein, K. L., Epperson, M. T., & Johnson, C. T. (2000). Relaxation therapy for insomnia: Nighttime and daytime effects. *Behaviour Research and Therapy, 38,* 665–678.

Ollendick, T. H., & Cerny, J. A. (1981). *Clinical behavior therapy with children.* New York: Plenum.

Ost, L. G., & Sterner, U. (1987). Applied tension: A specific behavioural method for treatment of blood phobia. *Behaviour Research and Therapy, 25,* 25–30.

Stetter, F., & Kupper, S. (2002). Autogenic training: A meta-analysis of clinical outcome studies. *Applied Psychophysiology and Biofeedback, 27,* 45–98.

Taylor, S. (2001). Breathing retraining in the treatment of panic disorder: Efficacy, caveats, and indications. *Scandinavian Journal of Behaviour Therapy, 30,* 49–56.

SPONTANEOUS RECOVERY

Spontaneous recovery is typically defined in relation to "habituation" or the learning to "not respond" to irrelevant environmental stimuli. Spontaneous recovery refers to the reemergence of a previously habituated response. The reappearance of a habituated response occurs following a period of time in which the eliciting stimulus is no longer presented. Spontaneous recovery is a defining characteristic of the "short-lasting" type of habituation in which the eliciting stimulus is presented frequently (i.e., every 5 seconds). If a long period of time (i.e., 24 hours) has elapsed since the last presentation of the eliciting stimulus, and the stimulus is presented once again, the previously habituated response will reoccur and with nearly the same response strength as demonstrated in the initial presentation. The concept of spontaneous recovery is also used in describing the reemergence of previously extinguished conditioned responses in a classical conditioning paradigm and also operant responses. In these instances, the organism seems to have forgotten that the eliciting stimuli were irrelevant (i.e., respondent conditioning) or that the responses were no longer reinforced (i.e., operant conditioning).

As a real-world example of spontaneous recovery of a previously extinguished operant response, consider 6-month-old Jack. Jack had acquired a rather obnoxious behavior of repeatedly throwing his spoon on the floor during mealtimes. His dutiful parents would immediately pick up the spoon, give it back to Jack, and urge him not to do it again. Being quite frustrated by this behavior, Jack's parents consulted a behaviorally oriented child psychologist who immediately recognized how the parents had actually strengthened Jack's spoon throwing behavior. The parents were giving Jack much attention after throwing the spoon along with returning it to him. The child psychologist advised the parents to not return the spoon once it was on the floor and to generally ignore Jack for 60 seconds after it was thrown. The parents observed that over the course of the next week, Jack stopped throwing his spoon altogether. However, shortly thereafter, Jack's aunt Jan came to visit and was quite excited about having a chance to feed Jack and spend some "quality time" with him. At the first meal, Jack immediately threw his spoon on the floor and his Aunt Jan returned it to him with a big smile on her face and with many comments about how cute Jack was. Jack repeatedly threw his spoon on the floor for the rest of that meal and for every meal that Aunt Jan attended. Jack's spoon-throwing behavior "spontaneously recovered" after his parents had successfully extinguished this response in him. Jack's parents insisted that Aunt Jan attend the next visit with the behaviorally oriented child psychologist to learn the error of her ways.

—*Michael W. Mellon*

See also: *Applied Behavior Analysis (Vols. I, II, & III), Extinction (Vol. II), Extinction and Habituation (Vols. I & III), Operant Conditioning (Vols. I, II, & III), Schedule-Induced Behavior (Vol. III), Schedules of Reinforcement (Vols. I, II, & III), Skinner, Burrhus Frederic (Vols. I, II, & III)*

Suggested Readings

Bijou, S. (1995). *Behavior analysis of child development.* Reno, NV: Context Press.

Domjan, M., & Burkhard, B. (1986). *The principles of learning and behavior* (2nd ed.). Belmont, CA: Brooks/Cole.

Donahoe, J., & Palmer, D. (1994). *Learning and complex behavior.* Boston: Allyn & Bacon.

SPORT SKILL TRAINING

DESCRIPTION OF THE STRATEGY

Readers of a large volume concerned with behavior modification and cognitive therapy may find sport skill training a curious entry. To clarify, sport skill training (SST) is defined as the application of behavioral training principles to skill acquisition in sports settings. Behavioral training principles include the use of state-of-the-art teaching techniques, including, but not limited to, modeling, role play, feedback, and generalization planning. Although behavioral techniques have been used for the sole purpose of improving athletic skills, this entry will focus on sport-related efforts to facilitate the performance of behaviors providing increased social acceptance.

Interventions that promote social acceptance through skill acquisition can be divided into athletic and interpersonal approaches. Athletic skill-based programs promote social acceptance by enhancing athletic performance. These interventions may be thought of as existing on a continuum from general to sport-specific. For example, developing good hand-eye coordination or excellent physical conditioning might be considered general athletic skills, while learning to hit a baseball is relatively sport-specific. Presumably, children who perform well athletically would be more likely to gain social acceptance. On the other hand, only a few children will excel in any given athletic competition, and not all children who are good athletes are judged to be socially competent. For the above reason, contemporary efforts to promote social acceptance through athletics utilize sports as a context for developing interpersonal skills, in addition to promoting athletic competence.

Interpersonal behaviors exhibited in sports settings can be thought of as important in facilitating social acceptance. For example, the term *good sport* suggests that a child is likely to follow the rules of the game and conform to social expectations for reciprocity (e.g., if you pass the ball to me, I'll pass it to you) that are common to all team sports. Sports-specific social behaviors might include giving a high five to a teammate following a hit or home run or knowing the postgame rituals associated with a given sport (e.g., lining up and shaking hands at the conclusion of an ice hockey game). In our research, we have grouped the above behaviors under the umbrella of "good sportsmanship."

Historical trends in behavioral research and therapy have also influenced the development of sport skill intervention models. Throughout the 1970s, behavioral and cognitive-behavioral therapists became dissatisfied with relatively short-term, circumscribed changes in behavior. Predictably, researchers began to evaluate procedures for producing the maintenance and generalization of socially valid changes in behavior. For example, many early social skills programs were conducted in groups outside the context in which behavior change was expected (e.g., the classroom or schoolyard). Many of these studies sought to increase "eye contact" or "social entry behaviors." Generally, there was little long-term follow-up (i.e., evaluation of maintenance) and little evidence that changes persisted outside training settings (i.e., generalization). Similarly, it was uncertain whether changes in these behaviors resulted in meaningful improvement in peer acceptance or friendship formation (i.e., social or treatment validity).

Whether applied to athletic or interpersonal skills, behavioral skills training typically begins with the selection of the target skill. The selection of target behaviors frequently requires a distinction be made between skill or performance (motivation)-based deficits in behavior. Thus, skills assessment is a generic feature of behavioral approaches. Assessment can take the form of interviews or rating scales, although performance of the skill in the setting would generally be preferred. Ideally, the practitioner combines multiple sources of information to best determine the needs of a given individual.

Following selection of the skill (whether athletic or interpersonal) and a determination of skill or performance needs related to demonstration of the behavior, the intervention can proceed. If a skill deficit is observed, then the intervention will begin with a clear demonstration (modeling) of the appropriate behavior. Efforts will be made to demonstrate the desired behavior in as realistic a manner as possible. Following the modeling phase, the participant should be given ample opportunities to practice the skill along with feedback regarding the quality of the performance (role play with feedback).

The final phase of the intervention, designing consequences for performance of the behavior, plays an important role in facilitating generalization and maintenance of the behaviors, whether the problem was initially conceptualized as a skill or a performance (motivation) deficit. Ideally, the consequences that arise from performance of the behavior should produce their own social or material reinforcers. For example, the routine display of "good sportsmanship" should produce sufficient social reinforcement in the setting to maintain socially appropriate behavior. Unfortunately, many social settings (e.g., the classroom) provide insufficient opportunities for either skill acquisition or skill development. Even assuming a child has developed an appropriate repertoire of social skills, some settings provide insufficient reinforcement for appropriate social behavior. It has been argued by many that the sports setting provides an ideal environment to develop and monitor change in social behavior. Moreover, because many children find physical activity and athletic competition to be highly rewarding in their own right, they exhibit less resistance to training efforts.

RESEARCH BASIS

Both behavioral and pharmacological interventions have been incorporated in SSTs in order to improve performance, to decrease negative behaviors, and to increase the child's enjoyment and interest in sports. The research literature suggests that SST may result in enhanced sportsmanship, self-esteem, game knowledge, and social competence.

As noted above, early research examined the relationship between athletic skill and social status for school-age children. Descriptive research suggests that in less structured sports environments (e.g., physical education classes, sandlot games), the most competent players are typically designated captains, and teammates are systematically chosen according to ability. Children picked last are not only considered the least skilled but are also rated least popular. To compound these problems, children who struggle in sports are often assigned nonintegral positions (e.g., right field in baseball or a blocker in football) that limit opportunities for practice and social recognition, further reducing the likelihood of skill enhancement and social acceptance. Children frequently relegated to nonintegral positions generally become disinterested, report feeling rejected, and ultimately choose to withdraw from sports participation. This rejection has led several investigators to examine the role sports plays in self-esteem and self-efficacy. The extent to which a child "values" sports may mediate the negative impact however; thus, devaluing sports and sports participation may be adaptive for some children.

The correlation between skill and social acceptance resulted in the creation of a number of protocols targeting improvements in athletic skill proficiency as a means of enhancing peer relations. Peer ratings (i.e., sociometric ratings) of "favorite or least favorite playmate" or "most popular" peers frequently serve as

outcome measures in these protocols. Correlational studies also suggest that both physical competence and peer acceptance are related to the development of cognitive, social, and emotional functioning of children.

RELEVANT TARGET POPULATIONS

SST has been utilized with girls and boys of diverse ethnicity and socioeconomic status. Behavioral interventions have been tailored to address a number of specific problems arising in sports settings, ranging from decreasing aggression to improving dribbling performance. Recently, researchers have begun to utilize SST with children in clinical settings. One example is work with children diagnosed with attention-deficit/hyperactivity disorder (ADHD). Same-age peers often exclude children diagnosed with ADHD and other disruptive behavior disorders from recreational activities because of failure to follow rules, failure to pay attention to the game, skills deficits, aggressiveness, or some combination of these factors. A few studies have evaluated the influence of methylphenidate (Ritalin) on sports performance and social behavior. Medication has been found to decrease negative social behaviors and improve attention and game awareness; however, gains in prosocial behaviors have not been as readily observed.

Successful behavioral interventions have employed contingent praise and token economies to reinforce the occurrence of prosocial behavior. The token economy-based protocols have included other behavioral techniques such as modeling and mastery-oriented learning procedures in addition to more common features of token systems (e.g., immediate token delivery followed by exchange for secondary rewards). It should be noted that in many cases, combined pharmacological and behavioral interventions have been found to be superior to either alone. However, single-case studies suggest exceptions to this oft-stated maxim. When synergy between behavioral and pharmacological treatments has been observed, the phenomenon may be attributed to medication-induced reductions in impulsivity and hyperactivity that render environmental contingencies more salient.

COMPLICATIONS

Several practical challenges confront mental health professionals seeking to utilize SST with their clients. First, less structured sports (e.g., soccer, relative to baseball) without clear "breaks in the action" make identification of specific measurable target behaviors, implementing contingencies, delivering feedback, and data collection difficult. Much of the recent sports training research has been included in intensive summer treatment programs. These programs often have small staff-to-child ratios and other controls that may poorly reflect the conditions existing in organized athletics in community settings (e.g., Little League), much less informal playground activities. Moreover, because of limited resources, therapeutic sports camps are likely to be insufficient in number or size to accommodate existing clinical needs.

Perhaps most important, it remains to be seen if improving competence, awareness, attention, and sportsmanship in athletic settings results in clinically meaningful gains in the child's natural social environment. Both pharmacological and psychosocial interventions lack evidence of generalization and maintenance beyond training settings. The impact of pharmacological interventions, while frequently impressive in the short-term, appears far less compelling when long-term outcome is evaluated. Similarly, enhancements in performance arising from behavioral interventions has diminished after discontinuation of incentives. To address this shortcoming, psychosocial interventions should design their interventions with generalization in mind. Research has shown that generalization can be maximized by promoting contact with naturally occurring sources of support (e.g., teaching a child to recruit feedback or praise) and, wherever possible, by conducting training in the setting in which skills are needed. Admittedly, efforts to promote generalization and maintenance of social skills in sports settings are in their infancy.

CASE ILLUSTRATION

"Brady" was a 6-year-old male attending first grade at a public elementary school. He had previously been diagnosed with ADHD, and his parents were pleased with his increase in classroom attentiveness following the combined treatment of stimulant medication, classroom behavior management strategies, and a school-home note. On the other hand, Brady and his parents continued to express concerns regarding peer relationships at home and school. Most notably, Brady was excluded from playing with most of the other children during recess because he "hated" soccer and

kickball, the two most common recess activities at his school. Brady's parents enrolled him on a T-ball team in the community; however, they withdrew him from participation because he reportedly did not pay attention during practice and was disruptive to his teammates.

The assessment of sports skills occurred at the beginning of a summer treatment program for children diagnosed with ADHD. The assessment centered around skills related to kickball, because this activity was known to the children and provided sufficient structure for training in a camp setting for young children. On the first day of assessment, Brady attempted to answer five key questions about the rules of the game (i.e., where to run, number of strikes, number of balls, number of outs, and how to make an out) and one question regarding how much he liked kickball (i.e., "Point to the face that shows how you feel about kickball"). Brady answered all of the rule questions incorrectly and then pointed to the "sad face," indicating that he did not like kickball. Brady also participated in a kicking drill in which he kicked 40% of slow-paced pitches and 10% of medium-paced pitches within the field of play. During several baseline games in the first week, Brady assumed the "ready position" (a skill taught on the first day of camp) during 33% of the pitches while playing in the field, and he did so only following the coaches' verbal prompts to the team. Finally, Brady demonstrated sportsmanlike behavior (e.g., cheering for a teammate) during 0% of the pitches and demonstrated disruptive behavior (e.g., playing with sticks) during 45% of the pitches.

During the second day of camp, a limited number of rules were reviewed verbally, and the children were required to demonstrate knowledge of the rules nonverbally (e.g., run to the correct base after striking the ball) and verbally (e.g., Answer "3" when asked "How many strikes is an out?"). Three consecutive correct responses were received for each question. Follow-up checks for rule knowledge continued during the beginning of several subsequent practices. During the second week of camp, training in kicking began. Athletically based skill training began with Brady kicking a still ball within the field of play 10 times in a row. Training continued with Brady running forward to kick a still ball and then progressed (via modeling, guided compliance, shaping, and fading assistance) until he could successfully kick a medium-paced ball within the field of play 10 times in a row (the mastery criterion). By the end of the second week, Brady demonstrated mastery. Following the achievement of intermediate goals along the way to mastery, Brady frequently chose from a "prize box" containing small toys (e.g., cars, pencils) and activity coupons (e.g., staying up 10 minutes late) previously identified by Brady and his parents as powerful incentives.

During the second week, Brady's attentiveness (i.e., as measured by assuming the "ready position") and sportsmanlike behavior continued to be low, and his disruptive behavior continued to occur at a relatively high rate. In an attempt to increase attentive behavior, a counselor (standing just outside the field of play) inserted tokens into a can each time Brady assumed the ready position while saying, "You get a token for being ready." After the game, tokens were exchanged for items selected from the prize box. With the use of tokens, Brady's attentive behavior quickly increased. During the third week, sportsmanlike behavior also increased after the application of a token economy. Interestingly, disruptive behavior significantly declined during the second and third week of camp, despite the fact that disruptions were never directly targeted for reduction.

By the end of the month-long summer camp, Brady demonstrated increases in rule knowledge, athletic skill, attentiveness, and sportsmanlike behavior while also demonstrating significant reductions in disruptive behavior. On the last day of camp, Brady answered the question regarding how much he liked kickball by pointing to the "happy face." Anecdotally, his father reported that Brady frequently came home sharing stories and "statistics" following each day's kickball game. During the final week of camp, several efforts were made to promote the generalization of skills to other settings. For example, tokens were delivered intermittently, games were played in different settings, and on one day soccer was played instead of kickball. Brady's parents also participated in a training session in which they were encouraged to (a) incorporate several aspects of the camp-based training in special home-based practices, (b) enroll Brady in a recreational team sport of his choice, and (c) create a "sport-home note" in which the coach could rate his attentive and sportsmanlike behavior during practices and games. During the end of the summer, Brady's parents enrolled him in a soccer camp, and they indicated this experience was much more enjoyable than his previous experience on the T-ball team. Brady's parents reported he looked forward to recess once school started, and he usually enjoyed playing sports with the other children. Also, during the second grade,

Brady developed a close friendship with another boy at his school who was in his soccer camp.

—*David Reitman, Stephen D. A. Hupp, and Patrick M. O'Callaghan*

See also: *Problem-Solving Therapy (Vol. I & III), Social and Interpersonal Skills Training (Vol. II), Social Competence Treatment: Externalizing Disorders (Vol. II), Social Effectiveness Training (Vols. I & III), Social Skills Training (Vols. I & III)*

Suggested Readings

Allen, K. D. (1998). The use of an enhanced simplified habit-reversal procedure to reduce disruptive outbursts during athletic performance. *Journal of Applied Behavior Analysis, 31,* 489–492.

Frankel, F., Myatt, R., Cantwell, D. P., & Feinberg, D. T. (1997). Parent-assisted transfer of children's social skills training: Effects on children with and without attention-deficit hyperactivity disorder. *Journal of the American Academy of Child and Adolescent Psychiatry, 36,* 1056–1064.

Hupp, S. D. A., & Reitman, D. (1999). Improving sports skills and sportsmanship in children diagnosed with attention-deficit hyperactivity disorder. *Child and Family Behavior Therapy, 21,* 35–51.

Hupp, S. D. A., Reitman, D., Northup, J., O'Callaghan, P., & LeBlanc, M. (2002). The effects of delayed rewards, tokens, and stimulant medication on sportsmanlike behavior with ADHD-diagnosed children. *Behavior Modification, 26,* 148–162.

Pelham, W. E., McBurnett, K., Harper, G., Milich, R., Clinton, J., Thiele, C., et al. (1990). Methylphenidate and baseball playing in ADD children: Who's on first? *Journal of Consulting and Clinical Psychology, 58,* 130–133.

Reitman, D., Hupp, S. D. A., O'Callaghan, P., Gulley, V., & Northup, J. (2001). The influence of a token economy and stimulant medication on attentive and disruptive behavior during sports with children diagnosed with ADHD. *Behavior Modification, 25,* 305–323.

Sharp, T., Brown, M., & Crider, K. (1995). The effects of a sportsmanship curriculum intervention on generalized positive social behavior of urban elementary school students. *Journal of Applied Behavior Analysis, 28,* 401–416.

Weiss, M. R., & Duncan, S. C. (1992). The relationship between physical competence and peer acceptance in the context of children's sport participation. *Journal of Sport and Exercise Psychology, 14,* 177–191.

STICKER/STAR CHART

A sticker or star chart is a behavior change program that involves the delivery of a sticker or star to a child as a reward for engaging in an appropriate or desired behavior. The sticker or star is typically placed on a chart that is visible to the child. The chart commonly displays descriptions of the specific behaviors that have been identified for improvement. Sticker/star charts are typically designed to increase the frequency of desired behaviors by rewarding desired behaviors that do not occur frequently enough. For example, behaviors identified for improvement might include doing chores, completing homework, remembering to brush teeth, and so on. However, sticker/star charts may also be used to decrease the frequency of undesired behaviors by rewarding other behaviors that interfere with the undesirable ones. For example, sticker/star charts might be used to reward a child for squeezing a "stress ball" rather than chewing on his or her fingernails or to reward using the toilet before bed to reduce nighttime wetting.

Stickers/stars are thought to be rewarding to children because (a) the stickers/stars themselves are attractive, interesting, or novel, (b) the stickers/stars are delivered along with praise and recognition, or (c) the stickers/stars can be exchanged for some other type of tangible reward (e.g., candy) or activity (e.g., staying up late). In addition, the chart itself may contribute to the success of the behavior change program because it may serve as a visual reminder to the child of things they need to work on and of past successes. Sticker/star charts may be effective for any or all of these reasons. Indeed, research has demonstrated sticker/star charts to be effective in increasing desirable behaviors such as appropriate social behavior, work completion, and chore completion. In addition, research has shown the sticker/star chart to be an effective behavior change program for decreasing undesirable behaviors such as thumb sucking, lip biting, bed-wetting, and soiling. Although a sticker/star chart program may be used effectively for most preschool and school-aged children (up to age 12), it is most commonly used for children under age 7 where the stickers themselves and the praise associated with delivery are often adequate for holding the child's attention and motivation. Given that the effectiveness of a sticker/star chart behavior change program depends heavily upon the stickers/star to provide the child with motivation to change behavior, older children may need for the stickers/star to be paired with other tangible rewards and privileges. As a result, once the child is above age 7, it may be beneficial to consider the use of alternative behavior change programs such as a point system.

CASE ILLUSTRATION

A 5-year-old girl was learning to brush her teeth on a regular basis, without reminders. Her mother posted a chart by the bathroom mirror that said "BRUSH TEETH" and had a small picture of the child brushing her teeth. Colorful stickers of her favorite cartoon characters were delivered each morning and night that she remembered to brush. Each sticker delivery was accompanied by praise and hugs.

—*Keith D. Allen and Richard J. Cowan*

See also: *Applied Behavior Analysis (Vols. I, II, & III), Azrin, Nathan H. (Vol. I & III), Public Posting (Vol. II), Token Economy (Vols. I, II, & III)*

Suggested Readings

Baldwin, J. D., & Baldwin, J. I. (1998). *Behavior principals in everyday life* (3rd ed.). Upper Saddle River, NJ: Prentice Hall.
Clark, L. (1996). *SOS: Help for parents.* Bowling Green, KY: Parents Press.

STIMULUS CONTROL

DESCRIPTION OF THE STRATEGY

Stimulus control broadly refers to the ability of stimuli in the environment to influence behavior and, in the narrower sense, is a moniker for a self-control technique used to ameliorate certain types of behavior problems. In its broader scientific usage, the term describes the controlling relationship that develops between stimuli and behavior through association. For example, myriad stimuli in the environment are associated with the desire to eat: olfactory sensations (the smell of freshly baked bread), sights (a billboard of pizza with the extras), sounds (the clink of cutlery in a restaurant), and, of course, countless tastes. In these examples, the desire to eat is cued through its past association with stimuli previously associated with eating such that their presence now makes the behavior (in this case, eating) more likely to occur. That is, the probability of eating increases in the presence of these stimuli and usually decreases in their absence. This controlling nature of environmental stimuli over the behavior of organisms is referred to as *stimulus control*.

Stimulus control, by necessity, involves the ability to discriminate among stimuli in the environment, and organisms come under their control when the organisms behave differently in the presence of different stimuli. For example, safe drivers stop when confronted with a red traffic signal and accelerate in the presence of a green light. Coming under *control* of the traffic signal does not imply an absence of choice—one could elect to run the red light—it merely reflects a probabilistic statement concerning the likelihood of behaving in a particular manner in the presence of different traffic signals.

Factors that influence the ability of stimuli to affect behavior include the (a) potency of the stimulus, (b) reliability of the stimulus, (c) time parameters associated with the stimulus, and (d) economic costs associated with the stimulus. Stimulus potency reflects how desirable a particular stimulus is to an organism. For example, for some adolescents, tickets to a Snoop Dogg concert might be considered more desirable (i.e., more potent in influencing our behavior) than tickets to an art gallery but may also depend on the reliability and trustworthiness of the ticket provider. The influence of temporal parameters or time factors is readily observed in everyday situations. Near-term stimuli typically exert greater influence over behavior relative to delayed stimuli. For example, tickets for a concert scheduled for next year may have minimal influence on behavior, whereas a concert occurring in the next few weeks might prompt a quick visit to the local event's Web site with credit card in hand. Finally, economic cost influences the strength of a stimulus. There are limits to what people will pay (in time or money) to attend a concert, regardless of the performer.

Stimulus control as a clinical intervention or strategy is used to address three primary types of behavior problems that stem from maladaptive stimulus control: (1) behavior that is not under the control of stimuli when such control is desirable, (2) behavior under the control of inappropriate stimuli, and (3) undesirable behavior under the control of stimuli. Children who fail to follow their parents' instructions illustrate a type of behavior that is not under the control of verbal stimuli when such control is desirable. The therapeutic goal in this situation is to increase the child's responsiveness to the parent's verbal instructions. Other behaviors are under the control of inappropriate stimuli such as the eating behavior of some obese children. The sight of food (candy bars on the racks adjacent to checkout lanes in grocery stores) or cues that signal the sight of food (e.g., golden arches), rather than actual hunger, control eating. The focus of therapy in these cases is to reduce the control that

seeing food or food cues exerts on eating. Finally, undesirable behaviors under the control of stimuli include ecumenical health problems such as cigarette smoking. In this case, the behavior of smoking is cued by a wide variety of stimuli because the behavior has been repeatedly associated with these cues. For example, smoking by youths is usually associated with observing friends smoking, such that the behavior has a much higher probability of occurring in their presence. The therapeutic goal in this case is to weaken and eventually eliminate the control these stimuli exert on behavior (e.g., by restricting social activities with friends who smoke to situations and places that do not permit smoking, such as organized sport activities and dance clubs that ban smoking).

Stimulus control strategies nearly always require a therapist to serve as a consultant to the client and explain the basic principles, techniques, and applications of stimulus control and its relation to existing behavior problems—that behavior does not occur extemporaneously but is under lawful stimulus control. Both internal (e.g., states of deprivation ranging from loneliness to starvation) and external (contact with external cues) stimuli obtained from interviewing the client are examined to piece together a comprehensive picture of potentially controlling stimuli that contribute to maintaining unwanted behavior, or stimuli that are not associated with behavior when such an association is desirable. If the behavior is under inappropriate stimulus control, therapeutic exercises are scheduled to weaken and eliminate the controlling nature of these stimuli (if the effect is undesirable) or strengthen the relationship in situations in which appropriate stimulus control is lacking. It is the client, however, who traditionally applies the procedures using a variety of self-control and self-monitoring techniques, although there are exceptions (e.g., clients who are incapable of understanding cause-and-effect relationships or are unable to exert control over their behavior).

RESEARCH BASIS

Stimulus control, as a therapeutic technique, addresses myriad problems associated with maladaptive stimulus control. Extant research concerning the therapeutic benefits associated with stimulus control interventions indicates that the technique can be used to successfully treat protracted health problems such as insomnia, obesity, smoking, alcoholism, and drug dependence. Novel applications have also proved useful for improving studying behavior and teaching language and other academic skills to children who are intellectually or emotionally challenged. Other applications involving stimulus control have proven successful in modifying problematic behavior in elderly institutionalized patients, inappropriate arousal in sexual offenders, and ameliorating or eliminating ruminative thinking, compulsive spending, psychotic speech, and self-injurious behavior in affected individuals.

Specific applications and outcomes related to stimulus control interventions in the clinical literature are too numerous to detail, but an emblematic summary provides an overview of the wide range of health and behavior problems that are addressed by the technique. Published literature reviews indicate that stimulus control is an essential element in behaviorally oriented weight reduction programs that produce and maintain significant weight reduction in children and adolescents. The technique also plays a central role in behavior programs that produce significant reductions in immediate and long-term illicit drug use among adolescent drug users. Some of the more novel applications involving stimulus control include (a) reducing littering in cities and on national highways by utilizing special trash receptacles, (b) using response contingent music to reduce disruptive bus riding behavior in an 8-year-old profoundly retarded female, and (c) incorporating specific visual stimuli on restaurant placemats to facilitate social and educational dialogue among family members. Stimulus control consisting of sleep restriction therapy (i.e., consolidating sleep into a limited block of time) is more effective than commonly prescribed hypnotic drugs for adults with a protracted history of insomnia (i.e., difficulty falling asleep), and therapeutic effects observed during treatment persist at follow-up. Chronic worriers report significant reductions in daily worries and feelings of tenseness relative to untreated adults following the introduction of a stimulus control treatment package that involves learning to limit worry thoughts to a specific time of the day and replace worry thoughts with nonworry thoughts at other times during the day. Establishing, strengthening, or weakening the association between human behavior and environmental stimuli is the sine qua non in each of the aforementioned examples. This may be accomplished by (a) introducing a new stimulus into the existing environment, as is the case with the trash receptacle, music, and restaurant placemats, (b) restricting which stimuli are present when behavior is emitted (e.g., programs designed to improve sleep and study habits or lessen anxiety), or (c) weakening the preexisting association between behavior and stimuli, as is the case with weight reduction and drug treatment programs.

RELEVANT TARGET POPULATIONS AND EXCEPTIONS

Stimulus control is used to address a nearly unlimited range of behavior, health, and social problems across the age spectrum, in regular and special education classrooms, at home and at work, in inpatient and outpatient mental health facilities, and by means of state and nationally sponsored programs throughout the country. Although desired change occurs as a function of strengthening or weakening the association between specific stimuli and behavior, the most potent and widely used applications of stimulus control require the investment of individual effort and a desire to achieve change (e.g., weight loss and smoking cessation programs). Human volition, however, is not requisite for success. Large-scale institutions such as libraries, and small-scale establishments such as coffeehouses, establish environments highly conducive to particular types of behavior (e.g., muted speech, reading), and programs geared toward improving the environment (e.g., reduced littering) or strengthening adaptive functioning in children do not require participant endorsement or individual resolve. Applications involving stimulus control for children, for example, include targeting specific behaviors for diminution such as excessive weight and self-injurious behavior, or focusing on strengthening behaviors such as studying, communication and reading skills, compliance with adult instructions, and myriad classroom behaviors.

There are very few instances in which stimulus control therapy might be considered inappropriate if applied following standard ethical guidelines. Individuals do, however, vary in their readiness and ability to apply and monitor stimulus control therapeutic techniques. In these cases, additional support or complementary therapy is introduced to achieve desired outcomes (e.g., youth weight loss and smoking cessation programs).

COMPLICATIONS

Several factors must be considered to avoid or minimize possible complications associated with applications of stimulus control. Strengthening or weakening behavior by introducing, eliminating, or altering stimuli in the environment requires careful deliberation and scrutiny. The inadvertent inclusion of inappropriate stimuli or failure to include appropriate stimuli, for example, may establish undesirable associations that are difficult to disassociate at a later point in time. Particular scrutiny is warranted in clinical applications of the technique owing to the vulnerability and idiosyncratic nature of some individuals. For example, stimulus control techniques are frequently incorporated as one component of a comprehensive behavioral plan for reducing self-injurious behavior in children. Applications with high-risk children require close scrutiny and monitoring, however, because self-injurious behavior may initially worsen before coming under appropriate control. In a similar vein, if too few cues are associated with eating in a weight loss program, some individuals may suffer from malnutrition. Complementary therapy and related health information are nearly always required in these applications to promote an all-around healthy lifestyle.

Other complications may arise owing to differences in opinion concerning what constitutes desirable and undesirable behavior, and applications of the technique must avoid infringing on human values and rights. Consent to treat forms and complementary information are traditionally used to address these concerns. Finally, initiation of treatment may overlook preexisting causal factors that may be directly relevant to long-term outcome and ultimate health. For example, stimulus control programs are frequently developed to treat children with diurnal enuresis, and positive results can occur (i.e., decreased urinary incontinence) despite the presence of an underlying bladder infection.

CASE ILLUSTRATION

"Thom Jr.," an 8-year-old male, was brought to a university outpatient client by his mother owing to worsening behavior problems related to completing his homework. His difficulties had become particularly troublesome in recent months and contributed to a drop in grades on his past two report cards and increasing arguments with his mother.

A careful history of Thom's homework problems was obtained, with particular emphasis on detailing both internal and external stimuli associated with his study habits and argumentativeness with his mother. Historical review of Thom's homework difficulties revealed an onset coinciding with entry into the third

grade and a gradual worsening over the past 6 months. A functional analysis revealed that Thom experienced no problems concentrating while engaged in particular types of activities. For example, he was able to watch movies on weekend nights and cartoons on Saturday morning for extended periods of time without difficulty. He was also able to persevere on other, nonacademically oriented tasks and particularly enjoyed playing video games and building things with his Legos set. Additional information was obtained to determine when and where Thom tended to complete his daily homework. Thom's mother revealed that her son was permitted to complete his homework anytime after school, as long as it was done before dinner at 7 P.M. He frequently sat on the floor in the family's living room and completed his assignments on a coffee table. At other times, he sat at the kitchen counter or attempted to complete his homework at a desk in his bedroom. Thom's teenage brother, Matt, frequently worked on the kitchen computer while playing MP3 music files or watching television at these times, although he usually kept the sound reasonably low so as not to interfere with his brother's homework. Thom's mother was typically busy preparing dinner or chatting with her mother on the telephone while Thom completed homework. At other times, she would actively engage him in conversation, asking him questions about his day. An analysis of internally produced stimuli (i.e., thought or covert speech) that occurred on a regular basis whenever Thom sat down to work on his homework revealed that his thoughts quickly changed from his homework to daydreaming about skateboarding or playing outside with his friends. He revealed that he experienced difficulty concentrating, particularly when faced with "boring" and lengthy assignments such as the dreaded 50-problem math sheets his classroom teacher seemed to enjoy assigning on a near daily basis.

Prior to initiating therapy, Thom's mother was asked to keep a detailed, daily activity log concerning Thom's homework behavior. A 15-minute continuous log was created to cover the time corresponding with Thom's arrival home from school until dinner each evening. She worked with the therapist to develop a simple behavioral code of usual behaviors and activities that occurred during this time frame, and these were included at the bottom of each of the log's pages. For example, an "OUT" code was used to indicate that Thom was outside playing, whereas a "BRO" code indicated that he was engaged with his brother in some manner (e.g., talking, teasing, fighting). A secondary coding scheme was included in the log to indicate where Thom was located in the house during each 15-minute observation period. A kitchen timer was used to signal each 15-minute interval. Scrutiny of the log during the 2-week (no treatment) period revealed that Thom tended to wait until just before dinnertime to complete his homework and worked in one of three places—his bedroom, at the kitchen counter, or at the living room table. He completed approximately 20% of his homework on a daily basis and argued with his mother one to two times each day. The arguments were nearly always instigated by his mother's nagging him to begin his homework and the long-term consequences of not doing so.

The basic principles, techniques, and application of stimulus control were explained to Thom's mother to enable her to understand that behavior does not occur extemporaneously but is under lawful stimulus control. A combined stimulus control and incentive protocol was created and refined during the ensuing week. It was decided that the alcove adjacent to the kitchen would serve as the designated homework completion setting and that homework could only be completed in this setting. Thom's bedroom desk was moved to this location. Two homework times were designated. The first was a 15-minute session immediately after school and the second was scheduled for 6 P.M. each day. Two sessions were scheduled to break up the lengthy nature of the assignments because most children Thom's age are unable to concentrate and remain engaged in academic activity for more than 20 to 30 consecutive minutes. The 6 P.M. session was also scheduled to accommodate Thom's daily after-school activities (i.e., baseball, karate) and to provide him with a break from academics before it turned dark each day. Thom's older brother was permitted to use the kitchen computer during the designated homework time but had to plug his headset into the speaker outlet, which effectively silenced the external speakers. Thom's mother signed a simplified contract to continue completing the daily activity log, to either place the telephone on mute or handle all calls in a separate room, and to not engage Thom in conversation during the homework time. If Thom completed all of his assigned homework during the 6 P.M. session, he was allowed to go outside and play or engage in a desirable inside activity of his choosing until dinnertime. Thom's study alcove was decorated with pictures that he associated with *smart people*. For example, posters of Einstein, George Lucas, Steven Spielberg, and Data (*Star Trek* fame) were selected. Additional items were selected by Thom's mother that she associated with thinking ($E = mc^2$), motivation (e.g., "Just Do It!"), and perseverance (e.g., picture of Yoda, the Jedi master).

Thom accompanied his mother to the final baseline session and actively participated in the discussion of the home study plan. Although many therapists work solely with the parent, others have found that actively soliciting children's opinions and cooperation facilitates treatment outcome. The therapist discussed the basics of stimulus control with Thom and established realistic expectations for the first 2 weeks. Thom was told to initially expect some difficulty concentrating and completing assignments but that these difficulties would gradually lessen over the ensuing 2 weeks as his ability to concentrate strengthened.

Inspection of the daily log coupled with discussion during the first weekly treatment session revealed no infractions of the contract and moderate improvement in homework completion. When queried, Thom reported being able to sit down at the two study times without any difficulty, but that it was hard to concentrate after about 5 minutes. He daydreamed about playing with his friends and baseball and completed approximately 50% of his daily academic assignments during the first week. He was praised for sitting down each day at the agreed upon time and attempting to complete his homework. Thom complained, however, that his mother continued to nag him on several occasions during the week. His mother admitted to nagging despite agreeing to abandon this strategy but did not believe that Thom would complete his homework without at least minimal prompting. A chart was created to track the occurrence of daily nagging and placed on the kitchen refrigerator. Thom agreed to place sad face stickers on the chart to correspond to the number of nags each day and a happy face sticker on the chart for each nagfree day.

Thom greeted the therapist enthusiastically following the second week of stimulus control therapy. He completed over 75% of his assignments during the first 2 days of the week and 100% of his assignments the past 3 days. He was very pleased with himself and reported that it was easier to concentrate at his home study center during the past week. He successfully completed all homework assignments during the ensuing 2 weeks and earned additional free time before dinner on several days. Inspection of the nag chart revealed a clear reduction in his mother's reminders, with a corresponding reduction in daily arguments. Thom's mother enjoyed receiving a daily happy face from her son. Some slippage was noted during the fifth week, and Thom admitted to bringing his Game Boy into the study area and playing games instead of working during part of the study time. He agreed to leave the gaming device in the kitchen and use it as an additional incentive for completing his assignments. The ensuing months revealed a highly consistent pattern of daily homework completed, coupled with significantly fewer arguments with his mother. Thom reported that he no longer experienced any difficulties concentrating. He was able to sit down and work for 30 consecutive minutes without day-dreaming. Thom's improved study behavior was reflected in two domains—he earned better grades on his quarterly report card and his interactions with his mother were much more positive at home.

—*Mark D. Rapport and Thomas M. Timko Jr.*

See also: *Operant Conditioning (Vols. I, II, & III), Schedule-Induced Behavior (Vol. III), Schedules of Reinforcement (Vols. I, II, &III), Skinner, Burrhus Frederic (Vols. I, II, & III)*

Suggested Readings

Azrin, N. H., Acierno, R., Kogan, E. S., Donohue, B., Besalel, V. A., & McMahon, P. T. (1996). Follow-up results of supportive versus behavioral therapy for illicit drug use. *Behavior Research and Therapy, 34,* 41–46.

Borklovec, T. D., Wilkinson, L., Folensbee, R., & Lerman, C. (1983). Stimulus control applications to the treatment of worry. *Behavior Research and Therapy, 21,* 247–251.

Carr, E. G., Newsom, C. D., & Binkoff, J. A. (1976). Stimulus control of self-destructive behavior in a psychotic child. *Journal of Abnormal Child Psychology, 4,* 139–153.

DeGrandpre, R. J., & Bickel, W. K. (1993). Stimulus control and drug dependence. *Psychological Record, 43,* 651–666.

Haddock, C. K., Shadish, W. R., Klesges, R. C., & Stein, R. J. (1994). Treatments for childhood and adolescent obesity. *Annals of Behavioral Medicine, 16,* 235–244.

Halle, J. W., Baer, D. M., & Spradlin, J. E. (1981). Teachers' generalized use of delay as a stimulus control procedure to increase language use by handicapped children. *Journal of Applied Behavior Analysis, 14,* 389–409.

Martin, G. L. (1982). Thought-stopping and stimulus control to decrease persistent disturbing thoughts. *Behavior Therapy and Experimental Psychiatry, 13,* 215–220.

McClusky, H. Y., Milby, J. B., Switzer, P. K., Williams, V., & Wooten, V. (1991). Efficacy of behavioral versus triazolam treatment in persistent sleep-onset insomnia. *American Journal of Psychiatry, 148,* 121–126.

Quinsey, V. L., & Chaplin, T. C. (1984). Stimulus control of rapists' and non-sex offenders' sexual arousal. *Behavioral Assessment, 6,* 169–176.

STIMULUS DISCRIMINATION TRAINING

Stimulus discrimination training is a strategy that is used to teach an individual to engage in particular behaviors in the presence of certain situations, events, or stimuli. Specifically, this is a procedure in which a response is trained to occur in the presence of a particular stimulus and to not occur in the presence of other stimuli. When a response is trained to occur in a particular situation, this situation or stimulus is referred to as a discriminative stimulus, or S^D. When a response is trained to not occur in a given situation, this situation or stimulus is referred to as S^p, or S-delta. Hence, during training, the behavior is reinforced when it occurs in the presence of a discriminative stimulus and is not reinforced when the discriminative stimulus is not present. It is important to note that a discriminative stimulus signals the availability of the reinforcer for the designated behavior, but it does not *cause* the behavior to occur. Rather, the behavior is more likely to occur because it has been reinforced in the past in the presence of the discriminative stimulus.

It is helpful to use an everyday experience to understand stimulus discrimination training. When a person approaches a traffic light, he or she responds differently depending on the color of the light. In the presence of a red light, the person pushes the brake pedal because this behavior has been reinforced in the past. However, in the presence of other color lights, pushing the brake pedal does not occur. Pushing the brake pedal in the presence of a red light is reinforced (e.g., safely arriving at the destination), but pushing the brake pedal in the presence of other stimuli (e.g., a green light) is not reinforced (and likely is punished by others honking or yelling at the driver).

Many examples of child behavior are impacted by stimulus discrimination training. Often, parents report that children act differently depending on the adults present or on the setting (e.g., the child is more compliant with one parent than the other or behaves more appropriately in one class than in another). These differences likely are due to stimulus discrimination training. That is, the child has learned that some behaviors are more likely to elicit reinforcement in certain situations or in the presence of certain adults, whose presence may be conceptualized as discriminative stimuli.

Stimulus discrimination training also is involved in traditional academic education. For example, if a child responds "4" in the presence of the question "What is 2 + 2," the behavior of saying "4" will be reinforced, but saying "4" will not be reinforced in the presence of the question "What is 2 + 5?" Accordingly, the child is trained to discriminate between those stimuli that do and do not signal the availability of reinforcement for the response "4." This same explanation can be applied to learning in many other capacities.

—*Alisa B. Bahl-Long*

See also: *Operant Conditioning (Vols. I, II, & III), Schedule-Induced Behavior (Vol. III), Schedules of Reinforcement (Vols. I, II, & III), Skinner, Burrhus Frederic (Vols. I, II, & III)*

Suggested Readings

Kazdin, A. E. (2001). *Behavior modification in applied settings* (6th ed.). Belmont, CA: Wadsworth.

Miltenberger, R. G. (2003). *Behavior modification* (3rd ed.). Belmont, CA: Wadsworth.

Rathvon, N. (1999). *Effective school interventions: Strategies for enhancing academic achievement and social competence*. New York: Guilford Press.

SYSTEMATIC DESENSITIZATION WITH CHILDREN AND ADOLESCENTS

DESCRIPTION OF THE STRATEGY

Since the 1950s, systematic desensitization has been a primary behavioral intervention used for a variety of fear- and anxiety-based difficulties experienced by children and adolescents. Developed by Joseph Wolpe, systematic desensitization is premised on the assumption that fear responses cannot simultaneously exist in the presence of a competing response. This basic principle is referred to as *reciprocal inhibition*. In essence, responses that are incompatible or inhibitory to anxiety (e.g., relaxation, a state of calm) are created and compete with the fear response. Because of their incompatibility, both responses cannot coexist, and the anxiety decreases. Through repeated pairings of the inhibitory response with the anxiety-provoking stimuli, the connection between the feared stimuli and the anxiety response is diminished, a process known as counterconditioning. Fear and anxiety are the most typical presenting problems for which systematic desensitization is utilized.

Systematic desensitization involves three separate components, including (1) relaxation training, (2) the creation of an anxiety or fear hierarchy, and (3) the systematic presentation of the fear hierarchy while the child is in a relaxed state. The implementation of systematic desensitization follows these three components and consists of two phases. In the first phase, the child is taught relaxation strategies. Most frequently, progressive muscle relaxation is utilized. This component of training can take anywhere from 3 to 10 sessions; the primary goal is for the child to attain a deep state of relaxation. Relaxation tapes are often created so that the child can practice on a regular basis in the home context. To facilitate the acquisition of skills, parents are often trained to coach their children in the relaxation procedures and to reinforce their children's efforts. For children who have difficulty learning and utilizing progressive muscular relaxation, alternative means of achieving a relaxed state can be introduced, such as diaphragmatic breathing exercises, imagery exercises, or autogenic training.

Simultaneous to the relaxation training, an anxiety or fear hierarchy is created. The construction of a fear hierarchy essentially involves the creation of a number of different fear-related scenarios that approximate the target fear or anxiety-provoking situation. Children are asked to help create descriptions of different situations that produce different levels of anxiety, fear, or tension. These scenes are then rank ordered from least anxiety provoking to most anxiety provoking. For example, a child with a fear of receiving shots may begin by first creating an imaginal scene that involves driving past the doctor's office. The next scene may involve walking into the doctor's office with the child's parent, but not having an appointment. A third scene might involve going to the doctor's office with the child's parent for an appointment that would not involve a shot. A fourth scene might involve seeing a needle and watching a friend or sibling receive a shot, and so on. A final scene in the hierarchy might involve actually receiving multiple shots at the doctor's office. In addition to the feared scenes, the child is also asked to identify one scene that is relaxing and nonanxiety provoking (e.g., playing computer games, reading a book).

Once the fear hierarchy has been completed and it is apparent that the child can engage in the requisite imaginal activities, the second phase of treatment is initiated. The child begins the first treatment session of this phase by engaging in deep relaxation. Once that state is obtained, the child is then asked to briefly imagine a scene from the hierarchy that is considered to be the least tension or anxiety provoking. Once the child has successfully engaged in imaginal exposure three to four times to this scene without significant anxiety, he or she is then exposed to a subsequent hierarchy scene. Anywhere from one to four different scenes can be presented per session, depending on the child's response. Scenes are typically presented for about 10 to 15 seconds each time. Should the child begin to experience anxiety or tension, he or she is requested to raise the right index finger. At that time, the therapist instructs the child to imagine his or her relaxation scene and assists the child in utilizing relaxation skills. Once the child has returned to a state of relaxation, the scene from the hierarchy is presented again. Should the child not be able to successfully engage in imaginal exposure without tension on two consecutive opportunities, the therapist directs the child to move back down the hierarchy to a less anxiety-provoking scenario. The child is then asked to reinitiate the imaginal process, and then moves again up to the hierarchy until he or she is able to successfully remain relaxed during exposure to the most anxiety-provoking scene in the hierarchy.

RESEARCH BASIS

Research evidence exists that supports the use of systematic desensitization in the successful treatment of phobias, fears, and anxiety. Notably, the majority of this research involves case studies and single-subject designs, and unfortunately most of these studies have evaluated systematic desensitization in combination with other treatments. Only on rare occasions has the efficacy of this procedure been evaluated with controlled treatment studies using random assignment. Because of the lack of controlled studies, systematic desensitization has been deemed "probably efficacious" rather than "well established" according to standards created for empirically supported treatments. Indeed, additional research is needed to examine the efficacy and effectiveness of systematic desensitization, especially given the widespread clinical acceptance of this approach.

Notwithstanding the relative lack of a strong research base, some authors have tentatively identified those factors that may influence the clinical effectiveness of systematic desensitization. Such factors include the child's willingness to or ability to successfully engage in relaxation, age of child (9 years and above), compliance with homework assignments, motivational level of parent and child, and skill at imagery. Clinicians should be mindful of such factors as treatment is undertaken.

RELEVANT TARGET POPULATIONS AND EXCEPTIONS

Systematic desensitization has been used to treat a wide variety of anxiety disorders, including generalized anxiety disorder, specific phobia, social phobia, school refusal or phobia, posttraumatic stress disorder, panic disorder, and selective mutism. In addition, this procedure has been utilized to target a wide variety of specific fears (i.e., test anxiety, darkness, blood, heights, food swallowing, motion sickness) and painful medical procedures. Notably, systematic desensitization has been used as well with individuals with mild to moderate levels of developmental disabilities and cognitive impairments. Thus, systematic desensitization has witnessed wide acceptance among clinicians for treating childhood anxiety disorders, fears, and phobias. Notably, this procedure is often used in combination with other behavioral and cognitive-behavioral interventions (e.g., covert conditioning, modeling, in vivo desensitization) and is integrated readily into treatment "packages."

Systematic desensitization procedures may not be recommended for extremely young children (i.e., under the age of 4 or 5), and some researchers have expressed concerns about the use of this procedure with children under the age of 9. For younger children, it may be difficult to have them engage in the imagery process itself. Some research does exist to support the use of shaping procedures as a means of teaching individuals how to successfully engage in imagery. Picture cards, video models, and audiotapes have also been used to facilitate the acquisition of vivid images.

To the extent that parents are equivocal in their support of this treatment procedure, success is also less likely and clinicians may choose an alternative therapeutic approach. Developing relaxation skills typically requires home-based practice that is most successful when parents are positively involved and committed to the intervention. In addition, if parents express reluctance to have their child experience the anxiety associated with imagining the fear hierarchy, the child may be less likely to engage in the process and may experience anticipatory anxiety that could interfere with the intervention.

COMPLICATIONS

In some cases, the level of fear or anxiety is sufficiently high that the child is unable to actively engage in either the relaxation component of training or the creation of the fear hierarchy. In those cases, supportive therapy, reassurance, or even medication management as a final resort may be in order. Teaching the parents strategies for ameliorating the child's fear can also be helpful before beginning systematic desensitization proper.

It is also notable that some children appear to be unable to achieve a state of deep relaxation, or they report subjective distress (fears of losing control) in their attempt to relax. Slow shaping procedures may be in order for these individuals, or use of alternative means of relaxation, that is, listening to their favorite music on tape, hypnosis.

CASE ILLUSTRATION

"Tonya" was a 10-year-old girl who presented to the clinic with a fear of dogs. Tonya was an only child and came from a family with no pets. Her mother reported that Tonya had limited exposure to dogs growing up, as neither close friends nor extended family members had dogs. Tonya and her family had recently moved to a new home where neighborhood dogs were common. While meeting a neighbor and his dog, the exuberant dog jumped up on Tonya and knocked her down. This startled Tonya, and she wanted no further contact with the dog. Later in the week, Tonya was outside in her yard when this dog got into an altercation in front of Tonya's house with another neighborhood dog. Tonya reported being frightened by the sounds of the dogs fighting as well as the response of the adults (i.e., yelling at the dogs, yelling at Tonya to get in the house).

Tonya began avoiding being outside and refused to walk near the neighbor's house. To get to school, she was required to walk past this house as well as several other homes with large dogs. Tonya subsequently began asking her parents to drive her to school. When being driven to school was not possible, she began

reporting stomach pains and headaches and requested to stay home. At times her parents allowed her to stay home, while at other times they required her to go to school. On the days Tonya did go to school, she was observed to run down the middle of the street when passing those homes with dogs. Other fears reported during the intake included fear of the dark and fear of fire. These fears had not interfered with Tonya's daily routine and were reported as being only mildly disturbing.

According to her teacher, Tonya had several close friends and was continuing to perform above grade level despite recently missing school. However, Tonya's teacher did report concerns that if Tonya continued to miss school, her grades would drop. She also reported frequent comments by Tonya about not wanting to walk home and concerns about dogs getting loose in her neighborhood.

Treatment began by teaching Tonya relaxation skills. A brief rationale was given to Tonya and her mother regarding the need to learn relaxation skills, and a description of what to expect was provided. A large overstuffed reclining chair was utilized, as Tonya preferred to sit and recline during this procedure rather than lie on a couch. A script was used to guide Tonya in progressive muscle relaxation (e.g., "Imagine a dinosaur is about to step on your stomach; make it hard"). She was able to demonstrate adequate engagement in the task, and no difficulties with relaxation were noted. An audiotape of the procedure was made during the session and given to Tonya and her mother to take home. It was agreed to have Tonya practice the skills for about 10 to 15 minutes twice a day by listening to the tape once each night before she went to sleep and once each afternoon prior to doing her school homework. Three subsequent sessions were spent on practice, with the script being phased out and Tonya internalizing the relaxation process. Tonya was successfully able to do this and became proficient at inducing a relaxed state on command. It was indicated that Tonya was practicing on average about once daily with her relaxation tape. While this was less than the twice daily recommendation, her development of the skills indicated that this was sufficient.

In addition to the relaxation skill training, time was also spent developing a fear hierarchy specific to dogs. Thirteen different situations were generated, ranging from seeing a picture of a dog (very little anxiety) to walking past a house with a dog locked inside (moderate anxiety) to petting multiple dogs in a small space, including the dog who knocked Tonya over and got into the fight (high anxiety). In addition, an anxiety-free scene also was selected. Tonya identified reading a book on her bed as her relaxing situation. Time was spent practicing imagining this scene as part of the relaxation training. Tonya was able to verbally describe the scene and reported feelings of relaxation when she imagined herself in the scene.

Given Tonya's quick mastery of relaxation skills, desensitization began during Session 5. Tonya was asked to spend about 5 minutes relaxing in the recliner and indicate when she was in a relaxed state by raising her right index finger. The therapist then presented the scene from the fear hierarchy with the lowest anxiety level and asked Tonya to imagine the scene as vividly as possible. Tonya was able to successfully imagine this scene (viewing a picture of a large dog) on three consecutive tries without any distress and was able to move up the hierarchy to the next scene (imagining being inside her house and seeing a dog in the fenced yard several houses down the street). Tonya experienced anxiety at this point and was instructed to imagine her relaxation scene. After several minutes of relaxation, she was again asked to imagine the scene from her fear hierarchy. This time she was successful and was able to imagine the scene three consecutive times without distress. Six subsequent sessions involved Tonya imagining additional scenes. Each scene was presented until she was able to visualize it for 10 to 15 seconds without anxiety on three consecutive occasions. As Tonya approached the higher end of the hierarchy, she had more difficulty imagining the scenes without anxiety and had two occasions where she had to return to previously mastered scenes. However, with minimal prompting to imagine her relaxation scene, she was able to successfully advance through the hierarchy. Upon completion of all the identified scenes, Tonya described a willingness to play with and pet dogs and reported no concerns about being around dogs she was acquainted with or who were with their owners. She had resumed walking to school on a daily basis, and her somatic complaints decreased. Tonya did report some minor fears of dogs fighting and of walking past houses where unknown, unrestrained dogs lived. As this fear was considered appropriate due to safety considerations, Tonya's overall progress in therapy was considered a success.

—*Larry L. Mullins and Sharon M. Simpson*

See also: *Lazarus, A. A. (Vols. I & III), In Vivo Desensitization (Vol. II), Paul, Gordon L. (Vols. I & III), Self-Control Desensitization (Vol. III), Systematic Desensitization (Vols. I & III), Wolpe, Joseph (Vols. I & III)*

Suggested Readings

Koeppen, A. S. (2002). Relaxation training for children. In C. E. Schaefer & D. Cangelosi (Eds.), *Play therapy techniques* (2nd ed., pp. 295–302). Northvale, NJ: Jason Aronson.

Morris, R. J., & Kratochwill, T. R. (1998). Childhood fears and phobias. In R. J. Morris & T. R. Kratochwill (Eds.), *The practice of child therapy* (3rd ed., pp. 91–131). Boston: Allyn & Bacon.

Ollendick, T. H., & King, N. J. (2000). Empirically supported treatments for children and adolescents. In P. C. Kendall (Ed.), *Child and adolescent therapy: Cognitive-behavioral procedures* (2nd ed., pp. 386–425). New York: Guilford Press.

Powers, S. W. (2000). Behavior therapy with children. In C. E. Walker & M. C. Roberts (Eds.), *Handbook of clinical child psychology* (3rd ed., pp. 825–839). New York: Wiley.

Wolpe, J. (1995). Reciprocal inhibition: Major agent of behavior change. In W. T. O'Donohue & L. Krasner (Eds.), *Theories of behavior therapy: Exploring behavior change* (pp. 23–57). Washington, DC: American Psychological Association.

T

TASK ANALYSIS

DESCRIPTION OF THE STRATEGY

Many everyday responses are really sequences of small units of behavior. A sequence of such responses is a behavioral chain. Although the chain of responses may appear to be one unit of behavior, most behaviors are really a complex series of responses. For example, responses such as getting dressed, completing homework, and completing an algebra problem consist of a sequence of responses, not just one response.

When teaching a behavioral sequence, it is often advantageous to break down the chain of responses into precise individual components, in their proper order. This procedure is called task analysis, subdividing a response into individual, discrete, and orderly steps. The complex target behavior is thus broken down into the specific sequence of behavior components that make up the target behavior. Each step is defined in operational terms.

After a target response is identified, a task analysis identifies the component steps of the target behavior. For each step that is identified, the instructor must consider the action the child must perform and the stimuli (cues) that control initiation and completion of each step. That is, what stimuli in the environment indicate when to start a step, and what stimuli in the environment indicate when the step is completed. Sometimes, the persons responsible for program design do not have the experience necessary to define the essential steps of a task. Effective strategies that help identify the details of each step include (a) observing children who already perform the target behavior well and/or (b) seeking advice about the subject matter from people with knowledge in the specific area. Ultimately, a task analysis must be approached from the perspective of the child and the responses they are required to perform.

Task analysis is an important part of effective programming. Identifying the component responses in concrete steps is consistent with good behavioral programming and has a number of advantages. First, task analysis requires identification of a concrete behavioral objective. Second, rather than starting with what may appear to be an unwieldy or complicated goal, the program is initiated with small trainable steps that can be easily achieved and thus reinforced. Each step becomes a goal that is described in observable and measurable terms. As a result, one can teach specific responses regardless of how complex the terminal behavior is. Third, after a sequence of responses is identified, shaping can be used to teach the final product. The therapist/teacher presents differential reinforcement to the child for successful completion of the first component of the response. After the first component is mastered, the criterion for reinforcement is increased to include the first and second components of the behavior, and so on. Task analysis facilitates differential reinforcement of responses as they successively approximate the final outcome. Fourth, discrete steps with operational definitions make it possible to assess systematically the progress a child is making toward the desired outcome behavior. Task analysis allows formulation of goals into identifiable units that can be monitored individually by both the trainer and the child. Finally, task analysis is amenable to other behavioral procedures such as presenting rules to the child with an operational description and reasons for the desired response, modeling, rehearsal, constructive feedback, and prompt fading.

RESEARCH BASIS

There is a large published research base demonstrating the utility of task analysis. The range of successful applications exemplifies the broad utility of the procedure. Task analysis has been used with child populations and problem areas so diverse that the following examples are merely illustrative. Task analysis has been used to train a wide range of academic skills to schoolchildren, football skills to youth, and parent training skills to families of children with disruptive behavior disorders. The procedure has been used to help children with mental retardation learn how to use first aid, prepare food, and safely walk across the street. It has been used to assist adolescents with traumatic brain injury learn how to avoid hazards in the home. Furthermore, several published curricula programs provide task analyses for teaching a wide range of skills.

RELEVANT TARGET POPULATIONS AND EXCEPTIONS

Task analysis is relevant to all settings where learning takes place. This would include therapy settings, schools, health settings, vocational programs, and sports training. Task analysis is relevant to all child target populations. That task analysis is a common procedure in business and work settings speaks to the ubiquitous relevance of the procedure. Nonetheless, most of the published outcome research focuses on education and therapy for individuals with developmental disabilities.

COMPLICATIONS

The essential element of task analysis is to break the behavior steps into small, trainable units. Although there are published curricula programs that provide task analyses for teaching a wide range of skills, there is little research to help guide the trainer on a case-by-case basis. The unit of analysis selected for individual components is identified on a case-by-case basis, taking into consideration many variables: (a) the developmental age of the child, (b) the range of the steps the child is able to learn, (c) the child's current skill level, (d) the physical capabilities of the child, (e) the complexity of the desired response, (f) the degree of

proficiency needed for success, (g) the child's previous skills and experience, and (h) the settings and circumstances where the target behavior is required. Some situations may require that a target behavior be broken into many small units of behavior, whereas in other situations, the target behavior may be broken into just a few steps. For example, when teaching a child with mental retardation to set a dinner table, the first step might be to "take four plates out of the cupboard and put them on the countertop" and the second step might be to "take the plates to the table." For a typical 10-year-old child, the first step might be to "put the plates around the table." Such requirements could change as the setting changes. It is essential that component steps are clearly distinct from one another, but to date there is no rubric to guide the trainer through an individual task analysis. We do not have a simple procedure for dividing novel behavior that takes into consideration all of the potential variables delineated above. In cases where task-analyzed curricula are available for defined populations, the task analyses will most likely require refinement on an individual basis.

—*Jeffrey S. Danforth*

See also: *Applied Behavior Analysis (Vols. I, II, & III), Manualized Behavior Therapy (Vols. I, II, & III), Operant Conditioning (Vols. I, II, & III)*

Suggested Readings

Danforth, J. S. (1998). The behavior management flow chart: A component analysis of behavior management strategies. *Clinical Psychology Review, 18,* 229–257.

Johnson-Martin, N., Attermeier, S., & Hacker, B. (1990). *The Carolina curriculum for preschoolers with special needs.* Baltimore: Paul H. Brookes.

Jonassen, D., Hannum, W., & Tessmer, M. (1989). *Handbook of task analysis procedures.* New York: Praeger.

Kazdin, A. E. (2001). *Behavior modification in applied settings* (6th ed.). Belmont, CA: Brooks/Cole.

Martin, G., & Pear, J. (2003). *Behavior modification: What it is and how to do it* (7th ed.). Saddle River, NJ: Prentice Hall.

Sulzer-Azaroff, B., & Mayer, G. R. (1994). *Achieving educational excellence: Behavior analysis for school personnel.* San Marcos, CA: Western Image.

THOUGHT STOPPING

DESCRIPTION OF THE STRATEGY

Thought stopping is a cognitive strategy wherein individuals are taught to take control of negative, intrusive thoughts and replace them with neutral or positive thoughts. The concept behind thought stopping addresses the issue of negative cognitions serving a reinforcing effect and leading to further negative thoughts and maladaptive thinking and behavior. Thought stopping therefore operates by interfering with the reinforcing pattern and replacing the learned behavior with a more adaptive behavior. Individuals are thus reinforced for the effort to stop their negative thoughts by becoming engaged in more positive, adaptive cognitive strategies.

Thought stopping is a commonly used cognitive strategy in cognitive-behavioral treatment of both children and adults. It is most frequently applied in situations when individuals' cognitive strategies are characterized by negativistic cognitions and high levels of maladaptive thinking strategies. In such situations, it is often the case that the negative thoughts either serve a reinforcing function or result in a reinforcing activity for the individual, thereby increasing the likelihood that the negative thoughts will be maintained and will recur. For example, children with obsessive-compulsive disorder (OCD) may experience intrusive thoughts of contamination, and such thoughts are not abated until they wash their hands. The relief that is brought about by the hand-washing behavior serves to reinforce the intrusive thoughts of contamination. If children are taught to stop the intrusive thoughts, they may be able to avoid the reinforcing compulsive behavior.

Two thought-stopping techniques are commonly used: simple thought stopping and thought replacement. In simple thought stopping, the individual is taught strategies to recognize and stop negative cognitions. Thought replacement strategies involve teaching individuals to shift thinking to neutral or positive thoughts when they experience negative, intrusive thoughts. In this approach, positive cognitions replace negative cognitions, which are mutually exclusive, and therefore prevent the short-term recurrence of the negative thoughts.

When instructing children to use thought-stopping techniques, children are taught to follow a step-by-step sequence. Children are first taught to identify negative, intrusive thoughts and to be able to notice them each time they occur. As children become proficient at identifying intrusive thoughts, they are often taught a simple strategy for arresting the cognitive process. This usually involves teaching children to visualize a stop sign while saying or thinking the word *Stop*. Children may then be instructed to replace the intrusive thought with a more adaptive thought. The replacement thought may either involve restructuring the negative cognition, or it may be an unrelated thought involving a pleasant activity or situation for the child. Children may also be taught adaptive self-statements to help them manage the negative emotions that often accompany negative thoughts. For example, youths with binge-eating problems can be taught to identify cravings for food or thoughts about food and eating. The youths can then begin using the visualization technique consistently every time they think of food. They may then proceed to repeat a coping statement to themselves such as "I don't need to eat to feel good right now." The more consistently the thought-stopping procedure is applied, the more likely it is to have an impact on the recurrence of negative thoughts.

RESEARCH BASIS

Thought stopping has been extensively studied as part of treatment programs for stress management, anxiety, insomnia, depression, smoking cessation, binge eating and other addictive behaviors, OCD, and simple phobias. The majority of treatment approaches involving thought stopping are designed for adult populations. However, treatment studies for anxiety disorders in children have employed thought-stopping techniques. Thought stopping has also been employed as part of treatment packages for pain management in pediatric cancer patients. In these programs, children with cancer are taught to use different adaptive coping strategies, including thought stopping, to manage acute pain and anxiety. Such programs have a well-established research basis as a whole, although the incremental benefit of thought-stopping procedures has not been studied. In addition, thought stopping as an independent treatment strategy has not been studied in child populations.

There are a number of areas where more research on thought stopping is needed. For example, the relative effects of using simple thought stopping versus thought replacement has not been studied. In addition, the most effective approaches to helping children identify maladaptive thoughts that would be subject to thought stopping have not been identified. While some studies have indicated that thought stopping techniques are not as effective as exposure and response prevention for obsessive-compulsive behaviors, the integration of different strategies to address problems across different situations and in different contexts has not been explored systematically.

RELEVANT TARGET POPULATIONS AND EXCEPTIONS

Relevant target populations include any individual for whom negative, intrusive, and/or maladaptive cognitions are implicated in presenting problems. Thought-stopping procedures are especially efficient for modifying the maintenance of negative cognitive strategies, particularly with respect to internalizing problems. In addition, thought stopping may be an effective tool in a treatment package for addictive behaviors such as binge eating.

COMPLICATIONS

Thought stopping is only effective insofar as individuals are able to (a) identify intrusive, negative thoughts that should be targeted through thought stopping and (b) consistently employ thought-stopping strategies when experiencing such intrusive, negative thoughts. If efforts to stop intrusive thoughts continue to be reinforced through the original maintenance systems (e.g., individuals continue to engage in compulsions *after* attempting thought stopping for obsessions), thought stopping will not be effective and may in fact work to further reinforce negative thoughts. Thought stopping may require the integration of cognitive coping strategies, such as positive self-statements, to reinforce efforts to stop intrusive thoughts. Finally, research suggests that thought stopping for complex presentations (such as OCD) may be ineffective in isolation and is likely best presented as one potential strategy in a comprehensive treatment package.

—Greta M. Massetti and Gregory A. Fabiano

See also: *Lazarus, A. A. (Vols. I & III), Thought Stopping (Vols. I & III), Wolpe, Joseph (Vols. I & III)*

Suggested Readings

Butterfield, W. H., & Cobb, N. H. (1994). Cognitive-behavioral treatment of children and adolescents. In D. K. Granvold (Ed.), *Cognitive and behavioral treatment: Methods and applications* (pp. 65–89). Belmont, CA: Wadsworth.

Dangel, R. F., Deschner, J. P., & Rasp, R. R. (1989). Anger control training for adolescents in residential treatment. *Behavior Modification, 13,* 447–458.

Jenike, M. A. (1983). Obsessive compulsive disorder. *Comprehensive Psychiatry, 24,* 99–115.

Ross, D. M. (1984). Thought-stopping: A coping strategy for impending feared events. *Issues in Comprehensive Pediatric Nursing, 7,* 83–89.

Zelter, L. (1994). Pain and symptom management. In D. J. Bearison & R. K. Mulhern (Eds.), *Pediatric psychooncology: Psychological perspectives on children with cancer* (pp. 61–83). New York: Oxford University Press.

3-5-10-15 METHOD FOR SPELLING

DESCRIPTION OF THE STRATEGY

The 3-5-10-15 method, also known as the write-say method, is a classroom-based procedure designed to improve children's academic performance in key areas such as spelling. The technique is based on the premise that some children, particularly those with learning disorders, benefit from feedback to two or more sensory modalities (e.g., sight, hearing, and touch). In essence, the technique is designed to improve upon traditional forms of learning such as simple memorization and studying.

The procedure begins by evaluating a child's spelling performance over a period of at least 2 weeks. During this time, a teacher and relevant others assess the child by assigning to the child 10 spelling words on a Monday morning and testing the child on these words the Friday afternoon of that week. The words should be those typical of a particular child's grade level. During the week, the child is instructed to study the words as he or she normally would. This may involve, for example, a predetermined study time in class or memorization at home. The child's performance on the Friday tests serves as the baseline measure. The 3-5-10-15 technique is typically used when a child is failing or clearly not performing to his or her expected level with respect to spelling or when it is determined that a child would significantly benefit from added procedures.

Following baseline, the child is again given a list of 10 words (always different ones from week to week) on a Monday morning. At some point during that morning, the child is allotted a specific amount of time (e.g., 30–60 minutes) to study the words. At some point in the afternoon, the child is given a practice spelling test in which the teacher verbally presents a word and the child writes it on paper. Immediately following the test, the teacher and student examine the test and mark any misspelled words. The child is then instructed to write all misspelled words three times while saying the word aloud. This allows the child to see the word, hear himself or herself speak the letters in sequence, and physically feel how the letters and words are formed. In this way, feedback is provided to multiple sensory modalities. The child is then instructed to take the words home for further study.

The following day, Tuesday, the child is given a second practice test in the afternoon, using the same words assigned from the day before. This practice test may or may not be preceded by a regular spelling study time in the morning. Again the test is administered and the teacher and student examine it afterward for errors. This time, any misspelled word is rewritten and said aloud five times. Again, this is later followed by home-based study.

The procedure for Wednesday is identical except that misspelled words are rewritten and said aloud 10 times. The procedure for Thursday is also identical except that misspelled words are rewritten and said aloud 15 times. Following a final study period on Friday morning, the child is given a formal spelling test (i.e., one that will count toward his or her spelling grade) that afternoon. Immediate feedback to the child regarding his or her performance is recommended. The entire procedure is repeated the following Monday with a new list of words.

The 3-5-10-15 spelling procedure may be modified as necessary. For example, a child may be allowed to begin his or her study of new words on a Friday afternoon, giving him or her lead time toward Monday's practice test. Also, the 3-5-10-15 spelling procedure can be shortened if needed by eliminating the Monday practice test (i.e., a Tuesday to Thursday-based 5-10-15 procedure). All remaining aspects of the procedure should remain similar.

RESEARCH BASIS

The 3-5-10-15 procedure has been successfully used to increase spelling scores in various youth. Several studies of individuals and small groups have been conducted to provide empirical support. However, the studies are not completely comparable, given that variations in the procedures were used (i.e., different study times and strategies, number of words tested). Still, the procedure does seem effective for most youth and, in one study, increased spelling scores by a mean of 50.7% at posttreatment following an intervention lasting at least 3 weeks. A related study has also shown the procedure to be useful for teaching multiplication tables and problems.

RELEVANT TARGET POPULATION

The 3-5-10-15 method for spelling has been primarily used for children with learning disorders, particularly those with deficits in spelling. However, youth with subclinical learning problems as well as those with more substantial developmental disabilities may benefit as well. The procedure has been used for youth at the elementary as well as high school levels.

COMPLICATIONS

In general, the 3-5-10-15 procedure requires the presence of basic skills such as writing, sight, hearing, understanding letters and words, and following teacher instructions. Modifications in the procedure may be made as necessary if a child has significant deficits in these areas, although such modifications have not been empirically evaluated. The procedure can be complicated as well by insufficient teacher time, frequent changes in schedules or other variables at school, lack of child motivation, and distractions. In some cases, the procedure may need to be supplemented by a contingency management program to provide incentives for a child's on-task behavior.

CASE ILLUSTRATION

"Ethan" was a 7-year-old multiracial male in second grade who was having significant problems with respect to reading and spelling. In particular, his writing was very slow and he continued to lack full command of his letters and their proper sequencing in various words. As a result, his mean score on twice-a-month spelling tests was 30%. Following consultation with his parents, Ethan's teacher recommended a more accelerated and intensive approach that combined increased study time, a home- and school-based contingency management procedure, and the 3-5-10-15 technique. The process began in January of the academic year and continued for 8 weeks. Following this time, Ethan's mean scores on his spelling tests increased to 50%. The number of words were then reduced to seven per week, after which Ethan's scores improved to 60%. A trial of five words per week did not reveal any significant difference in testing scores, so the number of words fluctuated between five and seven for the remainder of the academic year, depending on the length and difficulty of the words. At the end of the year, Ethan's mean score on his spelling tests was 67%.

—Christopher A. Kearney,
Krisann Alvarez, and Jennifer Vecchio

See also: *Applied Behavior Analysis (Vol. II), Attention-Training Procedures (Vol. II), Behavior Management for Improving Academic and Classroom Behavior (Vol. II), Good Behavior Game (Vol. II), Write-Say Method (Vol. II)*

Suggested Readings

Graham, S., & Freeman, S. (1986). Strategy training and teacher vs. student-controlled study conditions: Effects on LD students' spelling performance. *Learning Disability Quarterly, 9,* 15–22.

Kearney, C. A., & Drabman, R. S. (1993). The write-say method for improving spelling accuracy in children with learning disabilities. *Journal of Learning Disabilities, 26,* 52–56.

Lombardo, T. W., & Drabman, R. S. (1985). Teaching LD children multiplication tables. *Academic Therapy, 20,* 437–442.

Singh, N. N., Farquhar, S., & Hewett, A. E. (1991). Enhancing the spelling performance of learning disabled students. *Behavior Modification, 15,* 271–282.

TIME-OUT

DESCRIPTION OF THE STRATEGY

Time-out refers to a discipline procedure used with preadolescent children. During a time-out, the child is denied access to one or more classes of positive reinforcement for a brief period, usually 2 to 10 minutes, contingent upon a specific coercive behavior, such as noncompliance or aggression. When first introduced into the child clinical literature in the 1960s, the more apt but awkward expression "time-out from positive reinforcement" was used, since the procedure resembled one used to suppress mistakes by laboratory animals engaged in various operant tasks. Unlike a simple extinction procedure, the animal's mistake resulted in a brief electrical blackout or the temporary discontinuation of reinforcement for a previously reinforced operant. Different lab animals engaged in different learning paradigms consistently adjusted their behavior to avoid these brief periods of "time-out from positive reinforcement." For children, the classes of reinforcers unavailable during time-out generally include attention and toys. To prevent the child from seeking and obtaining attention and toys during the time-out interval, the child's mobility is invariably restricted. For example, Johnny and his little sister get into a physical fight over a toy; mother immediately pronounces that "There is no fighting in this house; you both go to time-out." Each child is then quickly escorted to a chair placed against a wall in the family room and told, "Stay there and be quiet." The process sounds rather simple and commonplace. Nevertheless, using time-out with clinically deviant children has proven to be more difficult than it sounds and has even stirred some controversy, since some would prefer to treat deviant children without the use of punishment of any kind.

Time-outs vary by at least the following five parameters: (1) positive reinforcers denied, (2) location, (3) duration, (4) release rules, and (5) maintenance. Each parameter can vary quantitatively or qualitatively, producing different time-out protocols.

The Positive Reinforcers Denied

In all published time-out routines, the child is ignored by available social agents (i.e., parents, teachers, siblings, and/or peers), thereby denying access to the positive reinforcer of attention from adults or other children. If a chair time-out location is selected, object access (e.g., toys) is denied in addition to attention. In contrast, most room time-outs allow limited object access, reducing the denied positive reinforcers to attention and objects outside the room. Both chair and room time-outs restrict the child's mobility to a specific time-out location, thereby preventing responses that could access attention and objects, not to mention an endless variety of activity reinforcers available to a child with unstructured free time. Therefore, two classes of positive reinforcers, attention and objects, are removed and/or restricted during time-out, and one response class, mobility, is blocked during time-out. Note that a simple extinction procedure (e.g., ignoring a pouting child) does not restrict a child's mobility and would not be considered a time-out procedure. Restriction to a specific location for a short period of time is considered a defining component of a time-out.

Time-Out Location

Children have been required to stand in corners or sit on chairs placed against a wall, in a corner, or behind a moveable screen. Such time-outs are often referred to as "exclusion time-outs," since the child is excluded from activities but not removed from the social context. Bedrooms and other rooms located in homes, schools, and residential centers are referred to as "isolation time-outs," since the child is removed from the social context. In public settings, parents can escort the child from the problem setting and find a relatively private place to sit or stand for exclusion time-out, remaining beside the child at all times. Even more private locations (e.g., public restrooms or the parked family car) are sought if isolation is needed to manage intense resistance to exclusion time-outs in public.

Time-Out Duration

Minimum time-out durations have ranged from 10 seconds to 3 hours in the published literature, but most clinical studies report using 2- to 10-minute durations. Some association with age seems to influence time-out duration decisions. Two-minute time-outs are common for preschoolers, whereas 5 to 10 minutes is common for middle childhood.

Time-Out Release Rules

Many time-out protocols extend time-out conditions beyond the minimum duration if the child continues to tantrum or otherwise make noise in time-out. A 10- to 60-second quiet rule is common prior to termination of time-out conditions. Consequently, a child facing a 2-minute time-out might well spend 5 or even 10 minutes during initial time-out exposures prior to calming down sufficiently to meet the 10-second quiet rule. A quiet rule is an extinction procedure. All crying and noise making is ignored, and time-out conditions enforced, thereby preventing any reinforcement (i.e., attention or time-out release) for crying or noise making. Indeed, the child is negatively reinforced for calming down by release from time-out.

Time-Out Maintenance

Children tend to escape from time-out if given the opportunity. Children will avoid time-out by inhibiting misbehavior (e.g., aggression) and by complying with instructions and warnings that might lead to time-out for continued noncompliance. Therefore, like the lab animals in the operant literature, time-out appears to be an aversive condition for young children. Escape efforts are predictable and take the form of tantrums, verbal demands, and motoric efforts to leave time-out chairs or break down barriers. Consequently, some mechanism to inhibit or prevent escape from time-out conditions is specified by the protocol. Room time-outs, the first used in the child clinical literature, can be maintained by simply holding the door shut for the required period. Chair time-outs, in contrast, pose a

more difficult problem. Tantrums and noise making can be ignored during chair time-outs, but motoric escape cannot. Punishing escape efforts from chair time-outs has proven controversial, since a procedure more aversive than the chair time-out conditions must be devised to motivate inhibition of escape. The original formulation dating back to the late 1960s was a spanking, once on the child's buttocks with the adult's hand. The shortcomings of spanking (e.g., temporary pain, might become abusive, models aggression, etc.), however, were apparent to many, spawning an array of modern-day options. A 1-minute room time-out can be used to enforce chair time-outs. The child is told, "Since you won't sit on your chair, you must go to your room." After 60 seconds, the child is returned to the time-out chair and given another opportunity to remain. Another alternative to spanking is a brief restraint, called the "two-chair hold" procedure. Escape following an initial warning results in a 45-second hold from behind on a different chair; the child is then returned to the time-out chair with a reduced requirement to remain for only 5 additional seconds. Time-out duration is gradually increased thereafter. Three additional enforcement procedures have been mentioned in the literature but inadequately studied to date: fines, privilege losses, or work chores.

RESEARCH BASIS

The parameters of time-out protocols have been studied off and on for three decades. See the reviews by Harris and MacDonough in the suggested readings. A summary of findings for each parameter follows.

Positive Reinforcers Denied

The author is unaware of any experimental manipulations of attention, objects, or mobility. Instead, theoretical interest has focused on the relative density of available response options and positive reinforcers during time-in, compared to time-out. It is widely accepted that time-in response options and reinforcers need to exceed those during time-out to achieve the time-out suppression effect. The foundation laboratory work with animals always adhered to this principle.

Time-Out Location

Again, no definitive study exists contrasting isolation with exclusion forms of time-out. Ideas about time-out location center around the reinforcers denied, the principle of least restrictive treatment, and developmental issues. Room time-outs allow limited object access but minimize inadvertent attention access (e.g., from a sibling or irritated parent) that might occur during chair time-outs. Exclusionary time-outs have always been considered less restrictive than isolation time-outs, since the child remains in the social context. Chair time-outs might be safer for young children (2–5 years), since the child is always visually monitored by a caregiver.

Time-Out Duration

Empirical work has established that time-outs less than 1 minute are generally ineffective. Countless studies have used 2-minute or 5-minute time-outs with preadolescent children to good effect. It is difficult to empirically justify a time-out longer than 5 minutes. Contrast effects have been found, indicating that longer time-outs may actually degrade the effectiveness of shorter time-outs and therefore should be avoided. Should middle childhood referrals have longer time-outs than preschoolers? The author is not aware of an empirical test.

Time-Out Release Rules

Quiet contingencies are associated with less noise-making during time-out. The impact of quiet rules on time-out suppression, however, is mixed. It appears that a clinician could release a tantrumming child from time-out to reinforce nonescape without attenuating the time-out effect, as long as a minimum time-out duration has been achieved. The adventitious reinforcement of noisemaking can be temporarily tolerated.

Maintenance

Experimental contrasts with disobedient preschoolers have found that spanking and 60-second room back-ups are equally effective, which thereby favors the room back-up protocol on the grounds of potential adverse side effects associated with spanking. The two-chair hold routine is effective but has not been experimentally compared to the spanking or room back-up options. Almost nothing is known empirically about strategies for middle childhood that include fines, privilege loss, and work chores. One might naively argue for a classic room time-out procedure

for all children, given the problems with maintaining chair time-out conditions. The counterargument is that isolation time-outs are more restrictive, not available in many important community settings, and possibly risky for preschool children who might accidentally injure themselves when angry and unmonitored in a bedroom with a shut door.

The inclusion of time-out protocols (i.e., punishment) in the treatment of coercive children continues to provoke controversy (see the McNeil article). Early empirical studies using randomized assignment to positive-only strategies versus those that included time-out for noncompliance repeatedly demonstrated the necessity of including a time-out component, at least for noncompliant children. Noncompliance appears to be motivated by task avoidance. Consequently, an all-positive approach to treatment is flawed, since it permits negative reinforcement for noncompliance in the form of task avoidance. One must either use time-out for noncompliance or pursue an endless quest for highly valued, idiosyncratic, satiation-resistant positive reinforcers to induce child compliance. Theoretically, the child would have to perceive the positive reinforcers for cooperation to be of greater magnitude than the negative reinforcement inherent in task avoidance. The author finds the latter approach socially invalid and infeasible. Furthermore, since noncompliance is a foundation response for oppositional defiant disorder and conduct disorder, it would be difficult to treat any of these children without a time-out component in the treatment package.

RELEVANT TARGET POPULATIONS AND EXCEPTIONS

Time-out has generally been used to suppress coercive behavior in preadolescent children. Coercive behaviors are presumed to be intentional, aversive actions displayed by a deviant or unsocialized child to affect the behavior of social agents. Any number of frustrators could be presented by a social agent that might set the occasion for reinforcement of child coercion. A child's learning history with a specific social context and agent might well include both positive and negative reinforcement for coercion. For example, tantrums, aggression, noncompliance, and rude talk may all, at one time or another, have effectively resulted in the removal of frustrators by social agents. These agents are simply responding to the aversiveness of the child and attempting to reduce that unpleasantness in any way possible. The behavioral trap is obvious and unfortunate for both the child and the agent. The child gets positively or negatively reinforced for coerciveness, at least some of the time, and the agent gets negatively reinforced for whatever stops the child's coercion. Unfortunately, the "whatever" can include an array of child management mistakes, any one of which might mollify the child or prevent coerciveness in the short run, but none of which seem helpful for the long-run task of socializing the child. For example, to avoid or escape from child coerciveness, social agents might give in to the child's unreasonable demands, withdraw reasonable instructions, inhibit subsequent reasonable instructions, abuse the child, or even work diligently to prevent the child from experiencing any distress. If one compounds such processes over the course of thousands of trials across several years in multiple contexts, the child is very likely to be diagnosed with disruptive behavior NOS, oppositional defiant disorder, or conduct disorder at some point in the future. Consequently, it has been this large response class of coerciveness that so often finds child clinicians recommending a time-out procedure as a part of the treatment package. Time-out attempts to block all reinforcers coerced by the child's aversiveness. Subsequently, coercive actions (e.g., child aggression, noncompliance, tantrums, rude talk) no longer elicit a partial schedule of positive or negative reinforcement. Rather, coercion is yielding no reinforcers at all for a brief but specific period. Theoretically, coercion should eventually cease altogether if time-out is combined with treatment components that promote prosocial alternatives to coercion (e.g., positive reinforcement for play, cooperation, or rule following; social skill building programs). See Patterson in the suggested readings for a thorough explication of coercion theory.

Time-out procedures have no known utility for reducing covert misbehaviors that occur beyond the home or school (e.g., stealing, fire setting, vandalism, truancy). Furthermore, there is no evidence that time-out is germane to the treatment of internalizing disorders, which may include behaviors that are topographically similar to coercion (e.g., tantrums) but serve a different function, such as escape from a fear-inducing setting. Developmental limitations are also apparent. Time-outs are not generally recommended for infants or adolescents. Infants' limited behavioral repertoire and nascent intentionality preclude the use of standard time-out routines. A 10-minute withdrawal of toys, attention, and mobility is not likely to influence a teenager except to irritate him or her for being treated like a younger child.

COMPLICATIONS

Time-out resistance can be sufficiently aversive that parents, teachers, or clinicians may abandon the time-out routine. Predicting time-out resistance is easy; the more defiant the child, the greater the likelihood of escape efforts. Managing time-out resistance is difficult. If a room time-out is used, the child may physically resist the adult escort and/or violently attack the door and/or destroy property once placed in the room. If a chair time-out is used, punishing escape efforts is no easy feat. Spanking, the 1-minute room time-out, or the two-chair hold procedure are all emotionally demanding routines. For middle childhood referrals (i.e., 7–12-year-olds), very little empirical work exists to guide the clinician to more age-appropriate time-out enforcement routines, such as fines, privilege losses, and/or work chores. It is the author's opinion that when treatment failures are documented for preadolescent externalizing disorder youth, time-out resistance is a contributing factor to that failure. The good news is that time-out enforcement procedures with 2- to 7-year-old children are effective. As long as the clinician monitors and adjusts the protocol as needed, time-out resistance quickly abates. Specifically, escape efforts decline from the first to second time-out, and, by the end of four weeks of parent-child interaction therapy, are virtually absent. The yield is important. A successful time-out protocol establishes a noncorporal punishment procedure that effectively suppresses intentional misbehavior and concurrently calms the child down. The time-out protocol successfully replaces spanking, grabbing, shaking, screaming at, threatening, demeaning, or otherwise abusing the coercive child.

Efforts to attenuate time-out resistance through modeling and awareness training have failed to reduce initial resistance in clinic-referred, overtly noncompliant children. Therefore, supporting parents, teachers, and staff members during initial time-outs and adjusting those procedures on the spot seems essential. Given the child's reaction to time-out, the supervising clinician can switch enforcement procedures (60-second room backup or traditional room time-out or two-chair hold routine), reduce the time-out duration, reduce or abandon a quiet rule, gradually shape time-out duration or quiet rules, introduce parent or clinician proximity, or alter the post-time-out tasks. These are among the many nuances of the time-out protocol considered by experienced child clinicians when faced with intense time-out resistance.

CASE ILLUSTRATION

"Sean's" mother was referred to the Psychology Clinic by the family's pediatrician for apparent "problems of conduct." Sean was a 5-year-old male residing with his 18-month-old sister and a single-parent, working-class mother. The mother reported that Sean "was very stubborn," displayed tantrums when told "no," hit or pushed his infant sister when she got in his way, ran off in stores, and would not remain in bed at nighttime. A Child Behavior Checklist profile indicated elevations on the Aggressive Behavior Scale and the Oppositional Defiant Problem Scale (both T-scores over 70). Sean and his mother were observed interacting in two standardized clinic analogs for 10 minutes each: Play (sometimes called the Child's Game) and Clinic Task (toy cleanup). The Play data revealed a maternal frequency of 6.2 commands + questions + criticism per minute; the Clinic Task data indicated a compliance ratio of 4%, a contingent praise ratio of 0%, and a vague/repeated instruction ratio of 82%. Sean's mother tracked daily frequencies of aggression and tantrums in the home for 1 week, revealing 2.6 fights and 4.3 tantrums per day. Sean met *DSM-IV* criteria for oppositional defiant disorder. Parent-child interaction therapy (PCIT) was recommended.

During the third week of PCIT, time-out was introduced to suppress noncompliance with instructions. The time-out procedure was modeled for Sean. A doll was sent to the time-out chair for defiance to a warning. The therapist asked Sean what happened and why, providing answers for him, since Sean refused to talk. The doll resisted time-out to show Sean the mistakes and "smart things" to do if sent to time-out (i.e., "stay there and be quiet"). The therapist then provided Sean's mother with a bug-in-the-ear device to allow communication while the therapist was in the observation room. When the therapist left, Sean immediately started demanding to go home but defied his mother's request to help clean up. The first time-out ensued. It was awful! Sean had to be sent to the backup room three times before staying on the time-out chair, and 8 minutes later he finally calmed down to meet a reduced quiet rule of 2 seconds. He refused to leave time-out when told he could, choosing to pout instead. His mother was prompted to ignore pouting, and Sean left the chair 20 seconds later. He disobeyed again right away, but his second time-out was considerably toned down (no escapes and quiet within 4 minutes). Sean then proceeded to obey 10 tasks in a row (the standard criterion), complaining the entire time. A phone check that evening indicated that Sean had been sent to time-out once, and needed a room back-up, but did quiet down within 5 minutes. Phone checks were discontinued after Sean's mother reported he had remained in time-out without an escape effort. At the next clinic visit, Sean's home record card for the week indicated two time-outs per day for defiance and a room backup/chair time-out ratio of 1 to 3. Home record cards collected 1 month later indicated zero room backups and only three time-outs for the whole week. Sean's reaction to time-out was typical of this class of referrals.

—Mark W. Roberts

See also: *Applied Behavior Analysis (Vols. I, II, & III), Behavioral Treatment in Natural Environments (Vols. I & III), Operant Conditioning (Vols. I, II, & III), Positive Reinforcement (Vol. II), Punishment (Vols. II & III), Reinforcement (Vols. I & III)*

Suggested Readings

Harris, K. R. (1985). Definitional, parametric, and procedural considerations in time-out interventions and research. *Exceptional children, 52,* 279–288.

Leitenberg, H. (1965). Is time-out from positive reinforcement an aversive event? A review of the experimental evidence. *Psychological Bulletin, 64,* 428–441.

MacDonough, T. S., & Forehand, R. (1973). Response-contingent time out: Important parameters in behavior modification with children. *Journal of Behavior Therapy and Experimental Psychiatry, 4,* 231–236.

McNeil, C. B., Clemens-Mowrer, L., Gurwitch, R. H., & Funderburk, B. W. (1994). Assessment of a new procedure to prevent timeout escape in preschoolers. *Child & Family Behavior Therapy, 16,* 27–35.

McNeil, C. B., Clemens-Mowrer, L., Gurwitch, R. H., & Funderburk, B. W. (1994). Author's response to Lutzker's evaluation. *Child and Family Behavior Therapy, 16,* 37–46.

Patterson, G. R. (1982). *Coercive family process.* Eugene, OR: Castalia.

Powers, S. W. (1990). Adjusting chair timeout enforcement procedures for oppositional children. *Behavior Therapy, 21,* 257–271.

Roberts, M. S. (1988). Enforcing chair timeouts with room timeouts. *Behavior Modification, 12,* 353–370.

Roberts, M. W. (1982). Resistance to timeout: Some normative data. *Behavioral Assessment, 4,* 237–246.

Wolf, M., Risley, T., & Mees, H. (1964). Application of operant conditioning procedures to the behavior problems of an autistic child. *Behaviour Research & Therapy, 1,* 305–312.

TOKEN ECONOMY

DESCRIPTION OF THE STRATEGY

A token economy is a treatment procedure based on the principles of operant conditioning. The primary goal of the token economy is to increase and maintain appropriate behavior, although a response-cost procedure is sometimes added to reduce problem behavior. The basic premise of the token economy is fairly straightforward—children earn "tokens" (e.g., points) for appropriate behavior and, at a later time, exchange the tokens for "backup" reinforcers (e.g., extended recess time). With an added response-cost component, children would also lose tokens for engaging in problem behavior. Although response-cost procedures are frequently implemented within token economies, it is beyond the scope of this entry to address the topic in sufficient detail. Therefore, this entry will be devoted to the token economy as a reinforcement system.

The token economy is based on the principle of *generalized conditioned reinforcement*. Within the system, tokens, which are inherently neutral items, are paired during the exchange with backup reinforcers. Through this pairing, tokens eventually function as conditioned reinforcers for appropriate behavior. The term *generalized* is used to refer to the child's ability to purchase a wide variety of backup reinforcers with tokens.

The token economy is a popular treatment system due to its many benefits, one of which is the ability of tokens to bridge the gap between the time a behavior occurs and when the backup reinforcer is eventually delivered. Another important benefit is that the use of tokens, which represent a variety of backup reinforcers, can prevent the satiation that sometimes occurs in single-reinforcer programs. In addition, the token economy is useful because it specifies a number of target behaviors for change and can easily be used to manage the behavior of a group of children.

Despite the apparent simplicity of the token economy, its design and execution require considerable planning and attention to detail. When designing a token economy, at least five factors should be considered, including (1) identifying and defining target behaviors, (2) selecting tokens, (3) selecting backup reinforcers, (e) establishing the exchange system, and (f) programming for maintenance. These factors are discussed in detail below.

Identifying and Defining Target Behaviors

One of the first tasks in the development of a token economy is selecting target behaviors to include in the system. Target behaviors should be observable, reasonable in number, and relevant to the clinical/educational goals of the children. In addition, the children should generally be capable of performing the behaviors, although they will obviously do so at frequencies that are less than optimal. If children are not already able to perform the target behaviors, an additional teaching strategy must also be used. Token economies designed for groups of children typically include target behaviors that are relevant to most, if not all, of the members of the group. Finally, the target-behavior list should be reviewed with each child before the system is implemented.

Selecting Tokens

Tokens are tangible items such as points, poker chips, coupons, and tally marks on a wall chart. They should be safe (e.g., not able to be swallowed), age appropriate, impossible to counterfeit, and durable. Tokens should not be highly preferred (e.g., baseball cards) because at some point they will need to be given away for a backup reinforcer. In addition, storage of the tokens needs to be considered. One should decide whether children are capable of keeping the tokens they earn (until the exchange) or whether they will be kept in another location such as in a clear plastic piggy bank on the teacher's desk.

Selecting Backup Reinforcers

The power of the token economy is primarily based on its backup reinforcers; thus, they should be selected carefully. Common backup reinforcers include highly preferred tangible items (e.g., toys, snacks) and activities (e.g., miniature golf, choosing a story for the reading group). There should be a wide variety of backup reinforcers, which can be posted on a backup-reinforcer "menu." Including a sufficient number of backup reinforcers on the menu and regularly updating them help ensure that children remain motivated to earn them. Backup reinforcers can be identified by surveying the children, observing their interactions in the natural environment, and conducting stimulus preference assessments. Finally, items and activities on the menu should generally be unavailable outside of the token economy.

Establishing the Exchange System

The token economy works by creating a balanced ratio of exchange between the worth of target behaviors (i.e., the number of tokens delivered for their performance) and the price of backup reinforcers (i.e., the number of tokens required to obtain them). Before the token economy is implemented, each target behavior and backup reinforcer must be assigned a token value. When assigning these values, it is important to consider how often a particular behavior might be expected to occur, as well as the highest frequency at which a backup reinforcer should be delivered. The more important behaviors should have higher token values than their less important counterparts. Similarly, the highest preference backup reinforcers should be relatively expensive within the economy. A token economy with an unbalanced exchange ratio might result in too few appropriate behaviors and/or the delivery of too many backup reinforcers. Keep in mind that it is common for a token economy's exchange ratio to be adjusted during the first few weeks of implementation.

Tokens should be delivered immediately following every target behavior, at least during the initial stages of the system. This means that within the first few hours of the program, children might have acquired a number of tokens to spend. When developing the system, it is important to determine at what point exchanges will be allowed. Common exchange times are at lunch, at the end of the day, and at the end of the week. For the sake of program management, it is not recommended to allow children the opportunity to exchange tokens at any time. If the exchange period is too frequent, children might spend frequently instead of saving for higher preference backup reinforcers. If the exchange period is too infrequent, the tokens might not function as effective conditioned reinforcers. In addition, tokens should have an expiration date (e.g., tokens not spent at the end of the week are returned to the central bank) to prevent hoarding, which could undermine the effectiveness of the economy.

Programming for Maintenance

The token economy is a highly artificial system; thus, at some point it will need to be withdrawn. Before implementing the token economy, or at least in its early stages, one should develop a plan for the maintenance of its target behaviors in the absence of the system. Common procedures for programming maintenance within a token economy include pairing praise (e.g., a natural consequence) with token delivery, delivering tokens on an intermittent schedule, increasing the delay between target behavior and token delivery, and increasing the delay between exchange opportunities. Level systems can also be used to gradually eliminate a token economy from an environment. For older children, the token economy can also be a way to teach money management skills by, for example, incorporating in the maintenance plan characteristics of a bank account such as using checkbook registers to keep track of earnings.

RESEARCH BASIS

In the 1960s, Teodoro Allyon and Nathan Azrin developed and conducted the first systematic research on the token economy. The authors originally designed the procedure for institutionalized psychiatric patients. Since the 1960s, there have been hundreds of studies published on the token economy, most of which were designed to evaluate its effectiveness with a variety of populations, settings, or behaviors. Research generally indicates that the token economy can be used effectively with a wide range of populations across the lifespan. The token economy is also effective for individuals, as well as groups (e.g., a classroom of students). In addition, the token economy has been demonstrated effective in home, school, institutional, and occupational settings. The token economy has been used to maintain a variety of behaviors, including social skills, classroom skills, personal-care skills, and academic skills, among others. Token economies that incorporate response cost have also been demonstrated effective in managing problem behavior, including aggression, disruption, and noncompliance, among others.

Several studies have demonstrated the failure of a token economy to effectively change behavior. However, these failures were frequently the result of suboptimal implementation of the token economy, rather than an inherent flaw with the procedure itself.

This issue of treatment integrity is described further in the Complications section below.

Research has also evaluated the long-term effectiveness of the token economy because some early studies indicated that behavior change did not maintain after the token economy was removed. However, the results of subsequent studies have shown that, with advanced planning, maintenance strategies such as those described earlier can greatly improve the durability of a token economy's treatment gains.

RELEVANT TARGET POPULATIONS AND EXCEPTIONS

Since its inception, clinicians and researchers have effectively used the token economy with a wide range of populations and behaviors across a variety of settings. With regard to specific populations, the token economy has been effectively implemented with children diagnosed with learning disabilities, conduct disorder, mental retardation, and autism, among other conditions. Despite such widespread applicability, there are several learner characteristics that might render the token economy ineffective. First, if a child does not have the ability to physically exchange a token for a backup reinforcer or attend to the exchange, the token might not become a conditioned reinforcer. Second, a token economy might not be appropriate with children for whom few reinforcers have been identified. Third, some children might verbally refuse to participate in the token economy. However, this problem can typically be remedied by (a) including the child in the development of the system (e.g., selecting behaviors, tokens, and backup reinforcers), (b) allowing the child to view other children successfully participating in the program, and (c) ignoring protests and restricting access to backup reinforcers outside the token economy.

In addition to considering whether a token economy is appropriate for a specific child or group of children, it is also important to consider its appropriateness as a behavior management system for the person who plans to implement it. Along with his or her regularly scheduled duties, the implementer of a token economy must be able to establish and adjust the exchange ratio, consistently monitor behavior and appropriately deliver tokens, keep track of token earnings, and manage periodic exchanges. However, if the system is well designed and capably implemented, and the few learner characteristics mentioned earlier are considered, the token economy should prove to be an effective behavior-change strategy.

COMPLICATIONS

Because of its complexity, a number of events can adversely affect the token economy. However, many of these can be anticipated and thus prevented. These events can be classified into two main areas: problems that occur during the development of the token economy and problems that arise after its implementation.

When developing a token economy, it is essential that the defining factors mentioned earlier are carefully considered such that target behaviors are properly defined, sufficient backup reinforcers are identified, tokens are not able to be counterfeited, an adequate exchange ratio is established, and so on. These are the prerequisites for an effective token economy, and if they are not adequately designed, the system might be compromised. It is also important to address two additional issues. First, the token economy should have strong administrative support from the individuals who are ultimately responsible for the environment in which it is implemented. For example, a teacher who implements a classroom-based token economy should have the support of the school principal. Similarly, a token economy conducted in a residential treatment facility should be adequately supported by the facility's administrators. Such support is important for at least two reasons. First, additional expenses might be incurred when implementing a token economy (e.g., the cost of backup reinforcers). Second, the token economy, although highly effective, is essentially a simulated environment based on effective reinforcement. Some individuals might consider such a system too unnatural or even describe its contingencies as bribery. These opinions might at some point undermine the support of the program. If these opinions were those of an administrator, the token economy obviously might be jeopardized. However, if implemented consistently, the token economy can be a very effective way to manage behavior. Consequently, it is important that the person implementing the token economy be assisted and encouraged by his or her supervisors.

After a token economy has been implemented, the most common obstacle to its effectiveness is poor treatment integrity. In other words, if the token economy is not implemented properly, then it obviously cannot be expected to function in an optimal manner.

Common treatment integrity problems include failure to deliver tokens on the predetermined schedule (e.g., after every target behavior), failure to adjust the economy when it becomes unbalanced (e.g., when children begin hoarding tokens), failure to update the backup-reinforcer menu, and allowing access to the backup reinforcers outside the token economy. Many of these problems occur for two reasons. First, the token economy requires consistent effort to implement, which can be difficult when someone has other duties to which he or she needs to attend. Second, when a token economy results in initial success, the individual responsible for the system might perceive that because things have improved, the program can be relaxed. However, one of the reasons the token economy works is that because of its precision, specific behaviors are effectively reinforced. Treatment integrity needs to be maintained in a token economy so that it remains a successful reinforcement system.

CASE ILLUSTRATION

"Ms. Andrews" was the teacher of a small, self-contained classroom for preadolescents who were unable to participate in general education because of problem behaviors associated with "emotional" disorders. Although each student already had an individualized behavior plan for his or her most troublesome behaviors (e.g., aggression), many of them also failed to exhibit a number of classroom behaviors that are important for academic success. For example, it was not uncommon for students to skip class, arrive to class late, refuse to participate, and fail to turn in homework. Consequently, Ms. Andrews requested special consultation with the school's behavior management specialist, "Mr. Garcia."

Mr. Garcia suggested that Ms. Andrews develop and implement a token economy in her classroom because it is an effective way to manage the behavior of a group of children who exhibit similar behavioral deficits. He shared with her a book on how to design an effective token economy and met with her on a regular basis to help her design the system. Together they developed a list of target behaviors for which the students could earn tokens. These behaviors included arriving to class on time, participating in class discussions, and turning in assignments, among others. Ms. Andrews posted on a wall in the classroom the list of target behaviors along with a clear definition for each or them. She then discussed the list with her students and teacher assistants, carefully explaining each

behavior and answering all their questions. Ms. Andrews made a few minor adjustments to the list based on the discussion.

Ms. Andrews then developed a classroom "store," in which students could exchange their tokens for backup reinforcers. Ms. Andrews observed the students during free time for 1 week and noted the items and activities in which the students most frequently engaged. She also asked the students what items they would like to have available in the store. After obtaining a small token-economy budget from the school's principal, Ms. Andrews stocked the store with a variety of backup reinforcers.

Ms. Andrews and Mr. Garcia considered several types of tokens for the system and eventually decided to use points that would be recorded by her in a notebook, as well as by the students at their desks. They then assigned a specific point value to each target behavior and a specific cost to each backup reinforcer, taking care to establish a balanced economy. They also decided to allow students to visit the store at the end of each school day. Students could purchase something from the store at that time or "bank" their points for later use. However, all points expired at the end of the week to prevent hoarding. Thus, students began each week with a zero balance.

In addition to the token economy, Mr. Garcia developed for Ms. Andrews a simple data collection and graphing form to allow her to track the target behaviors of each student. Ms. Andrews used the form for 2 weeks before the token economy was implemented to identify students' "baselines" so she could objectively determine whether the token economy resulted in behavioral improvement.

Finally, Ms. Andrews met with her students and teacher assistants on a Friday afternoon to explain the details of the token economy. The target behaviors, point values, backup reinforcers, data collection, and exchange times were carefully discussed. The token economy was implemented the next Monday morning.

After implementing the token economy for 1 month, Ms. Andrews observed substantial improvements in her students' behaviors, including a small but noticeable increase in attendance. In addition, students generally seemed to like the program. One unexpected problem occurred when several students were observed rushing through their homework assignments so they could earn points for turning them in; thus, the accuracy of their work was poor. After identifying the problem, Ms. Andrews changed the definition of the target behavior by adding a requirement that the assignment also earn a grade of C or better. This change seemed to adequately address the problem. Students continued to turn in their homework assignments more often than before, but the quality of the work had improved.

After a successful first month, Ms. Andrews scheduled bimonthly meetings with Mr. Garcia to discuss a variety of issues, including how to adjust the economy, how to update the store, and how to eventually remove the token economy while maintaining behavior change.

—James E. Carr, Tawnya J. Fraizer,
and Jonathan P. Roland

See also: Azrin, Nathan H. (Vols. I & III), Behavioral Treatment in Natural Environments (Vols. I & III), Contingency Management (Vol. II), Differential Reinforcement of Other Behavior (Vols. I, II, & III), Operant Conditioning (Vols. I, II, & III), Parent Training (Vol. II), Positive Reinforcement (Vol. II), Reinforcement (Vols. I & III), Response Cost (Vol. II), Token Economy (Vols. I & III)

Suggested Readings

Ayllon, T. (1999). *How to use token economy and point systems* (2nd ed.). Austin, TX: Pro-Ed.

Ayllon, T., & Azrin, N. (1968). The token economy: A motivational system for therapy and rehabilitation. New York: Appleton-Century-Crofts.

Ayllon, T., & Milan, M. A. (2002). Token economy: Guidelines for operation. In M. Hersen & W. H. Sledge (Eds.), *Encyclopedia of psychotherapy* (pp. 829–833). San Diego, CA: Academic Press.

Cooper, J. O., Heron, T. E., & Heward, W. L. (1987). *Applied behavior analysis.* Columbus, OH: Merrill.

Kazdin, A. E. (1982). The token economy: A decade later. *Journal of Applied Behavior Analysis, 15,* 431–445.

Kazdin, A. E., & Bootzin, R. R. (1972). The token economy: An evaluative review. *Journal of Applied Behavior Analysis, 5,* 343–372.

Thibideau, S. F. (1998). *How to use response cost* (2nd ed.). Austin, TX: Pro-Ed.

TRANSFER OF STIMULUS CONTROL

DESCRIPTION OF THE STRATEGY

Transfer of stimulus control (TSC) is a behavioral treatment technique that has been found to be a useful treatment with a range of childhood behavior issues, particularly with childhood autistic spectrum disorders, developmental disabilities, and classroom management situations. TSC is firmly based in learning theory and procedures. The majority of clinical research utilizing TSC techniques is in the areas of elimination disorders, child management issues, and improving spelling skills.

TSC is the transference of one target behavior-eliciting stimulus (the primary stimulus) to a new target behavior-eliciting stimulus (secondary stimulus). TSC is utilized when a primary stimulus cannot be used effectively due to a change in persons or settings. The transfer from the primary stimulus to the secondary stimulus occurs via a temporal pairing of the primary and secondary stimulus, coupled with the gradual fading of the primary stimulus. This accomplishes the transference of the primary stimulus to the secondary stimulus such that the target behavior is successfully elicited by the secondary stimulus. For example, a mother (who has successful compliance control over her child) may come into a classroom where her child is exhibiting a low level of compliance to teacher commands. The mother will provide the majority of commands interspersed by teacher commands. The mother's commands are the primary stimulus; the teacher's commands are the secondary stimulus. The ratio of maternal commands to teacher commands (primary to secondary stimulus) is slowly reversed until the teacher is providing the majority of commands. Thus, teacher commands—which were unsuccessful in gaining child compliance prior to the introduction of TSC—will now yield the desired level of child compliance. TSC of the target behavior of child compliance from maternal commands to teacher commands would be considered successfully completed.

RESEARCH BASIS

TSC utilizes a classical conditioning paradigm. The founder of classical conditioning, Ivan Pavlov (1849–1936), was a Russian physiologist. His original work was on gastric physiology. During his work in 1903, he observed that the subjects of his experiments, dogs, often began salivating *prior* to his placement of food into their mouths. Pavlov concluded that after repeated pairings of walking toward the dogs with giving them food, the animals became conditioned to salivate, without receiving the food. Pavlov knew that food was a primary stimulus for eliciting salivation behavior in dogs. He theorized that the repeated pairing of the primary stimulus (food) with the secondary stimulus (his walking with food to the dogs) had created a TSC from a primary (food) to a secondary (walking toward dogs) controlling stimulus. He called this elicited salivation behavior to his walking a "conditioned response."

Pavlov took this observation and completed a line of experiments that supported his theory of classical conditioning. His most famous experiment was pairing a bell to food, thus creating a conditioned response in his subjects to respond to a bell by salivating. This experiment is the classical conditioning basis for stimulus control. Pavlov showed that there are stimuli that can be classically conditioned to act as stimulus control in eliciting a response or behavior in animals.

John B. Watson (1878–1958), an academician and founder of behaviorism, was familiar with Pavlov's work with classical conditioning of animals. Watson believed that he could apply the same conditioning techniques to humans. In 1920, Watson, along with his graduate student Elizabeth Raynor, completed a series of experiments now called The Little Albert Experiments. In these experiments, Watson and Raynor studied whether (a) humans worked under the same classical conditioning laws as animals, (b) classical conditioning procedures could condition emotional responding behaviors, and (c) classical conditioning techniques could lead to stimulus generalization. Stimulus generalization occurs when a behavior that is emitted in the presence of a high probability antecedent stimulus is also emitted in the presence of other similar stimuli.

Watson and Raynor had classically conditioned a toddler, "Little Albert," to elicit a conditioned fear of white mice. Then they utilized other objects very similar to white mice (e.g., white furry objects). Little Albert showed fear and anxiety responses to other objects similar to the conditioned fear of white mice. Thus Watson and Raynor utilized a stimulus generalization paradigm to elicit anxiety and fear responses from Little Albert. These studies provided evidence that classical conditioning laws held for humans as well as animals. In addition, their work showed that emotional states, such as fear and anxiety, as well as physiological processes, could be conditioned. Last, the studies supported the phenomena of stimulus generalization and the concept of a generalization gradient.

A generalization gradient shows the relationship between the probability of a response and the stimulus value. The stimulus value describes the phenomena that the more a new stimulus differs from the original discriminative stimulus, the fewer number of responses will be emitted in the presence of the new stimulus. For example, Little Albert would exhibit a high probability of fear behavior to a white mouse yet a lower probability of a furry object eliciting the fear response behavior, and a very low probability of exhibiting a fear response to a black furry object.

TSC primarily utilizes classical conditioning procedures; however, operant learning may also be involved in interventions. On occasion, a behavior therapist will need to create a primary stimulus prior to the creation of a secondary stimulus. For example, the behavioral therapist may need to create successful child compliance in the home, under maternal commands, before it can be transferred to the school, under teacher commands. The behavior therapist will utilize operant procedures to create a primary controlling stimulus of compliance to maternal commands in the home before engaging in the TSC in the classroom.

The majority of clinical research has centered on the utilization of TSC in parental or classroom child management issues and elimination skill development (e.g., urinating, bowel movements) in autistic spectrum children. In addition, TSC has been a useful behavioral technique for teaching daily living skills, reduction of self-injurious behavior, and development of communication skills to autistic spectrum children. Last, a data set has developed in the area of utilizing TSC in the development of spelling mastery in children.

TARGET POPULATIONS

TSC can be across two variables: (1) transfer across setting and (2) transfer across people. Transfer across settings is utilized in situations where the therapist has a parent who is able to elicit a behavior, given an eliciting controlling stimulus in one setting, such as at home, but the controlling stimulus is not feasible in another setting, such as church. For example, parents who utilize a loud "1-2-3" as a discriminative stimulus, or controlling stimulus, in the home environment to have their young child comply with a command may find it inappropriate to utilize the loud discriminative stimulus during a church service. Therefore, the behavior therapist may want to begin utilizing transfer of control from a verbal "1-2-3" to a hand signal such as one finger-two fingers-three fingers. The behavior therapist would have the parent make this transfer via fading procedures in the home.

Transfer across people is utilized when the behavior therapist observes a high probability target behavior occurring with one individual, yet the eliciting stimulus only yields a low probability target behavior when a second individual administers it. The goal in this situation is to transfer the stimulus control of one individual to another individual, thereby eliciting a high probability of a target behavior being emitted. For example, a student may exhibit a high probability of compliance with his or her parents' commands but exhibit a low rate of probability of compliance with a teacher's commands. The behavior therapist would therefore have the teacher and a parent work together in the classroom to transfer stimulus control from the parents' commands to the teacher's commands. This could be accomplished by the parental commands gradually being faded out while a corresponding increase in teacher's commands was put in place.

TSC can be used in any situation where a high probability antecedent stimulus is available, and the behavior therapist wishes to install a more appropriate eliciting stimuli that, however, has a low probability of eliciting the target behavior. For example, TSC has been utilized in academic areas as a technique to increase spelling skills in children. Other target behaviors that have been changed by TSC techniques are reduction of fear and anxiety, efficient transitions between activities in school, and reduction of food refusal.

CASE ILLUSTRATION

"Bobby S.," a 7-year-old diagnosed with profound mental retardation, was referred to a behavior therapist for assistance in gaining and utilizing appropriate toileting behaviors. Bobby S. had recently been placed at a day-care setting by his parents to increase his daily self-care habits. Bobby S. had never developed urinary continence. His parents hoped that the day-care staff could train Bobby in appropriate toileting behaviors. Bobby had never exhibited appropriate urination into a toilet bowl. Instead, he would urinate in his diapers. The behavior therapist observed Bobby's behavior and correctly analyzed that Bobby's diapers were serving as the eliciting stimulus for the target behavior of urination. Thus, a TSC across settings intervention (diapers to sitting on toilet) was developed and implemented.

Five steps were implemented. First, Bobby had to learn to urinate while sitting on the toilet with his diaper on. Thirty-minute training sessions were held twice per day at times when staff members observed the highest frequency of urinary incontinence for Bobby. Operant conditioning was used during the first step to increase Bobby's urination behavior while sitting on the toilet, albeit with diapers on.

Once Bobby accomplished a high probability of sitting on the toilet and engaging in urination, the TSC could be completed. This consisted of four additional steps: (1) Bobby sat on the toilet and urinated while wearing a diaper, (2) a 1-inch hole was cut in the center of Bobby's diaper and he urinated in the toilet while wearing this modified diaper, (3) a 3-inch hole was cut in the center of Bobby's diaper and he urinated in the toilet while wearing this further modified diaper, and (4) the final step called for Bobby to urinate while sitting on the toilet but in the absence of wearing a diaper at all. Each step was continued until Bobby successfully urinated in the toilet at a rate of 90% of the time.

The above procedure incorporated both operant and classical conditioning techniques. As a result, Bobby was able to increase urinary continence and appropriate toileting behavior in 90% of elimination episodes.

—*Jonathan Weinand and J. Scott Allen Jr.*

See also: *Behavioral Treatment in Natural Environments (Vols. I & III), Generalization (Vols. I, II, & III), Operant Conditioning (Vols. I, II, & III), Schedule-Induced Behavior (Vol. III), Schedules of Reinforcement (Vols. I & III)*

Suggested Readings

Auguston, E. M., & Dougher, M. J. (1997). The transfer of avoidance-evoking functions through stimulus equivalence classes. *Journal of Behavior Therapy, 28,* 181–191.

Dube, W. V., Moniz, D. H., & Gomes, J. F. (1995). Use of computer and teacher-delivered prompts in discrimination training with individuals who have mental retardation. *American Journal on Mental Retardation, 100,* 253–261.

Luiselli, J. K. (1996). A transfer of stimulus control procedure applicable to toilet training programs for children with developmental disabilities. *Child and Family Behavior Therapy, 18,* 29–35.

Ray, K. P., Skinner, C. H., & Watson, S. T. (1999). Transferring stimulus control via momentum to increase compliance in a student with autism: A demonstration of collaborative consultation. *School Psychology Review, 28,* 622–627.

Stromer, R. S., MacVey, H. A., Howell, S. R., McVay, A. A., & Flusser, D. (1996). Teaching computer-based spelling to individuals with developmental and hearing disabilities: Transfer of stimulus control to writing tasks. *Journal of Applied Behavior Analysis, 29,* 25–42.

VICARIOUS CONDITIONING

Vicarious conditioning can be defined as learning by observing the reactions of others to an environmental stimulus that is salient to both the observer and the model. The saliency of the stimulus is characterized by its relevance (e.g., fear relevance) and ability to produce emotional arousal. Vicarious conditioning is a particularly important process in observational learning. One effect of vicarious conditioning may be increased imitation of the model by the observer, in that observers imitate successful models. The greater the positive reinforcement of the model's reaction, the more the observer tends to imitate those responses. It is reasonable to suppose that the primary way vicarious conditioning works is through the assumption on the part of the observer that "If I do that, I will get rewarded (or punished) too." There are four primary factors that are thought to impact the magnitude of vicarious conditioning: (1) attention to critical features of the stimulus and model's reactions, (2) memory of the modeled behaviors, (3) practice of the modeled behaviors, and (4) incentives or punishment associated with the modeled behaviors. However, other factors that likely play a role include the model's status, goal setting, and perceived self-efficacy.

The mechanisms involved in the vicarious conditioning of emotional responses are similar to those of direct classical conditioning and involve the organism attempting to detect the causal structure of its environment. However, the distinction between vicarious conditioning and classical conditioning has been based on findings (e.g., with phobic patients) that suggest that many people with intense fears have no known traumatic conditioning history with regard to the object of their fear. This has led to the speculation that many fears and phobias are acquired vicariously, that is, simply through observing someone else behave fearfully with some object or in a certain situation.

In the study of human fear origins, children and adolescents have attributed the onset of their fears to vicarious and instructional factors, although these indirect sources of fear were often combined with direct conditioning experiences. Boys report more direct and vicarious conditioning sources than girls do, and vicarious and instructional sources are endorsed more frequently by children than adolescents. Albert Bandura's Bobo doll experiments have received the most attention with regard to the study of vicarious conditioning in children. His research demonstrated that kindergartners who observed a video of a female experimenter beating up a blowup doll would mimic the experimenter almost exactly when subsequently allowed free play in a room with toys that included a blowup doll. This study was important because it demonstrated that children would modify their behaviors without first being rewarded for the target behavior.

Research of laboratory-reared rhesus monkeys, which do not show an innate fear of snakes, has demonstrated that observation of a wild monkey reacting fearfully to a snake will produce a fear of snakes in the lab monkeys. The fears occurred when the lab monkeys were later assessed alone and were enduring. This vicarious acquisition of fear for monkeys was evident even when the monkeys watched the model on a video. This suggests that the model does not have to be physically present to exert an influence on the observer. Further research suggests that the monkeys can be inoculated against the vicarious fear conditioning. Laboratory monkeys that are first exposed to a model that is not afraid of snakes are unaffected by the fearful models.

What is known about vicarious conditioning suggests that modeling can be used in behavioral treatments. Modeling in therapy can lead to desirable behaviors and help prevent undesirable behaviors. In some cases, the therapist, serving as the model, carries out a desired activity. Alternatively, the therapist can show the patient a successful model. Modeling tends to work best in therapy with very young children. Children who are afraid of animals can learn to be less afraid by watching a model that is not afraid of the animal—live models work better than videos in such cases. With regard to inoculating at-risk children against acquiring future problems with excessive fear, exposing a young child of a phobic parent to a non-fearful model may be protective.

The potential benefits of vicarious conditioning are not limited to behavior therapy for fear or other anxiety-provoking situations. Humans naturally learn vicariously how to successfully perform activities in a variety of domains. In part, this is how we learn to interact with peers, perform activities of daily living or work-related activities, care for children, and comfort someone who is in distress, among other tasks. The fact that we learn through what we observe highlights the importance of parents and teachers in the development of children and adolescents. In short, the content of what key developmental figures convey is important, but the overt behaviors of teachers and caregivers also play a primary role in the learning of adaptive behavior. The importance of vicarious conditioning for everyday activities has been demonstrated through behavioral treatments for individuals who are deficient in such activities—children with severe developmental delays can learn basic skills such as dressing themselves by observing videotaped models.

Criticisms of therapies that utilize modeling are primarily based on human error. Some clinicians speculate that letting the therapist determine the activities that represent adaptive behavior leaves too much room for subjectivity. This view posits that the therapist is subject to bias based on their beliefs, opinions, and feelings, among other factors. It may, therefore, be advisable for therapists to seek assistance from other professionals or from documented standards of treatment when conceptualizing appropriate model activities for a therapy based on vicarious conditioning.

—*Jeffrey L. Kibler and Daniel T. Shea*

See also: *Behavioral Rehearsal (Vols. I, II, & III), Modeling (Vols. I, II, & III), Role Playing (Vols. I, II, & III)*

Suggested Readings

Bandura, A. (1969). *Principles of behavior modification.* New York: Holt, Rinehart & Winston.

Berger, S. (1962). Conditioning through vicarious instigation. *Psychological Review, 69,* 450–466.

Mackintosh, N. (1983). *Conditioning and associative learning.* New York: Oxford University Press.

Marks, I. (1987). *Fears, phobia, and rituals: Panic, anxiety, and their disorders.* New York: Oxford University Press.

McNally, R. (1987). Preparedness and phobias: A review. *Psychological Bulletin, 101,* 282–303.

Mowrer, O. H. (1960). *Learning theory and the symbolic processes.* New York: John Wiley.

VICARIOUS EXTINCTION

Vicarious extinction is a form of modeling in which a previously reinforced behavior is eliminated by withdrawal of consequences applied to a model. It is generally used within a therapeutic context as a method of reducing anxiety or fear but can also be used to eliminate other unwanted emotions or behaviors. Extinction refers to the elimination of all response-maintaining reinforcers; after these reinforcers are eliminated, so is the undesired response. Vicarious extinction involves the individual observing another person performing the behavior without incurring the maintaining consequences.

For example, "Ryan" is an 8-year-old boy who is afraid of dogs. To eliminate this fear, Ryan's therapist has him view other children playing with a dog. The interaction has no adverse consequences. Furthermore, the positive consequences (i.e., immediate fear reduction) associated with avoidance do not occur. After witnessing the absence of aversive consequences, Ryan's fear is diminished, and he is able to approach a dog. Vicarious extinction has just taken place. Studies have also shown that increasing the diversity of stimuli decreases fear. For example, Ryan would be more likely to experience a reduction in anxiety after seeing several models interacting with several different dogs, rather than observing one model interacting with one dog.

The observation of a model is central to vicarious extinction. Modeling is part of social learning theory, which holds that learning, or changes in behavior, can come about through observation. In vicarious extinction, individuals learn through observing models that engaging in a behavior does not necessarily lead to the expected outcomes.

Although it is used in therapy, vicarious extinction can occur in everyday life as well. Simply by observing others interacting without fear and without the anticipated consequences, an anxious person's own fear can be reduced. Studies have shown that children with phobias who observe peers interacting with their feared stimuli—without incurring negative consequences—demonstrate stable and generalized avoidance reduction. This can be accomplished with a wide range of fears, from specific phobias to social avoidance.

Vicarious extinction can be accomplished through a variety of means. For instance, live or symbolic models can be used. That is, models can be observed directly (live) or can be observed on tape (symbolic). Whether the model is symbolic or live does not appear to affect treatment outcome. Symbolic modeling is sometimes preferred, as it allows an additional degree of control over the feared situation. Taped interactions can be carefully screened for the presence of unintended consequences, while live modeling involves a small degree of risk, as consequences are occasionally unpredictable.

Additional types of modeling in vicarious extinction for the treatment of anxiety involve the presence or the absence of fear. A mastery model displays no fear at all and engages in the behavior competently and calmly. Conversely, a coping model displays initial fearfulness but gradually becomes less fearful and more competent as the behavior is performed.

—*Laura D. Seligman and Lisa A. Wuyek*

See also: *Behavioral Rehearsal (Vols. I, II, & III), Exposure (Vols. I & III), Exposure and Response Prevention (Vol. II), Extinction (Vol. II), Extinction and Habituation (Vols. I & III), Modeling (Vols. I, II, & III)*

Suggested Readings

Bandura, A., Grusec, J. E., & Menlove, F. L. (1967). Vicarious extinction of avoidance behavior. *Journal of Personality and Social Psychology, 5,* 16–23.

Bandura, A., Grusec, J. E., & Menlove, F. L. (1968). Factors determining vicarious extinction of avoidance behavior through symbolic modeling. *Journal of Personality and Social Psychology, 8,* 99–108.

Hersen, M., & Van Hasselt, V. B. (Eds.). (1987). *Behavior therapy with children and adolescents: A clinical approach.* New York: John Wiley.

Hill, J. H., Liebert, R. M., & Mott, D. E. (1968). Vicarious extinction of avoidance behavior through films: An initial test. *Psychological Reports, 22,* 192.

VICARIOUS PUNISHMENT

Vicarious punishment occurs when the tendency to engage in a behavior is weakened after having observed the negative consequences for another engaging in that behavior. This is a form of observational learning as described by social learning theory. According to Albert Bandura's social learning theory, observers change their behavior based on viewing the behavior of another person (often referred to as a "model"). In vicarious punishment, an observer views a model experiencing a negative outcome—either the application of an aversive consequence or the removal of a desired consequence—for emitting a behavior, and as a result the observer is less likely to exhibit the behavior. The observer infers the likelihood of punishment for himself or herself, which decreases the probability that he or she will engage in the behavior.

A motorist who observes another driver being pulled over and ticketed for speeding and, as a result, decreases his or her own speed is demonstrating the effects of vicarious punishment, as is a child who observes a classmate losing privileges for talking in class and then decreases his or her disruptive behavior in the classroom.

The degree to which the observer is likely to change his or her behavior depends on a number of variables. People are more likely to learn from models that sustain their attention, such as those who are high in stature, desirability, attractiveness, likeability, and successfulness. The characteristics of the observer and the observed situation must be such that the observer is able to retain the information observed regarding the consequences of the model's behavior. Moreover, the observer must possess the skills, both physical and cognitive, to change the behavior in question. In addition, the motivation of the observer must be considered. An observer's motivation for a behavior is often influenced by his or her perception of the utility of that behavior to them.

Similar to many traditional behaviorists, Bandura believed that punishment, whether vicarious or direct, does not work as well as reinforcement to change one's behavior or extinction procedures. More specifically, Bandura asserted that vicarious punishment, like direct punishment, might result in the unintended consequences of general inhibition, socially undesirable behaviors, and avoidance of the punishing agent.

—Laura D. Seligman
and Heidi Bechtoldt Baldacci

See also: *Aversion Relief (Vols. I & III), Behavioral Rehearsal (Vols. I, II, & III), Modeling (Vols. I & III), Punishment (Vols. II & III), Role Playing (Vols. I, II, & III)*

Suggested Readings

Bandura, A. (1977). *Social learning theory.* Englewood Cliffs, NJ: Prentice Hall.

Bandura, A. (1986). *Social foundations of thought and action: A social cognitive theory.* Englewood Cliffs, NJ: Prentice Hall.

VICARIOUS REINFORCEMENT

Vicarious reinforcement more generally falls under the rubric of social learning and modeling theory procedures. These procedures are often called observational learning or, more simply, modeling. As with simple reinforcement procedures, vicarious reinforcement involves the alteration of environmental consequences to increase the probability of the occurrence of a given behavior. Unlike other reinforcement procedures, however, *vicarious* reinforcement does not involve direct application of consequences to the individual whose behavior is targeted for change; rather, learning takes place when an individual observes the consequences that result from another's behavior.

Vicarious reinforcement, like more straightforward reinforcement procedures, can either involve the addition of desirable stimuli (i.e., positive reinforcement) or the removal of aversive stimuli (i.e., negative reinforcement). Examples from everyday life include the adolescent who starts smoking because he or she sees a friend's social status increase when smoking or children who learn to complete their chores because they notice that their older siblings receive attention from parents for finishing all their chores.

A good example of the use of vicarious reinforcement procedures in treatment comes from pediatric psychology and the preparation of children for painful medical procedures. After teaching a child various coping skills, the child observes a model undergoing a painful medical procedure and successfully uses the coping strategies to reduce the pain, thereby making it more likely that the child will employ the coping skills again in the future.

Vicarious reinforcement operates on the principle that the individual who receives the direct reinforcement changes, as does the individual who observes the behavior change. This is especially evident in school or social settings for young children and teenagers. Children are easily influenced by their peers and often engage in inappropriate behaviors based on peer pressure. An example of this would be a child acting out in class and getting attention from his or her classmates. Therefore, another child who observed this disruptive behavior would be more likely to act out in class to also receive positive reinforcement from his or her peers. Close proximity or interrelatedness between the two individuals may lead to greater vicarious reinforcement influence. For example, a child would be less influenced by a stranger of the same age and more influenced by a close friend or classmate.

However, some studies have suggested that in certain situations, individuals show little evidence of vicarious reinforcement. They may observe positive or negative reinforcement applied to others, but this does not influence their perceptions or behaviors, because the consequences are not naturally reinforcing for them. For example, a child who answers questions in class may receive attention and praise from a teacher for participating in classroom discussion. However, a child who has a phobia of public speaking or is afraid of being judged will not be vicariously reinforced by increased attention from the teacher.

Other studies have suggested that when vicarious reinforcement occurs, its effects may last for a limited time (i.e., a couple of days). Other studies have found that attempts at vicarious reinforcement may have the unintended consequence of implicitly punishing the observer. For example, if two employees are typically punctual for meetings and one receives praise for the punctuality while the other simply observes the praise, the employee who is not directly praised may decrease his or her punctuality rather than increase it.

Despite some inconsistent conclusions, vicarious reinforcement has been demonstrated to be successful in combination with existing treatments. Vicarious effects can be useful if incorporated into an intervention with direct consequences. For example, a program may incorporate direct and vicarious consequences with a gradual shift from direct consequences in the beginning to vicarious consequences near the end of the treatment.

—*Laura D. Seligman and Sarah J. Hildebrand*

See also: *Behavioral Rehearsal (Vols. I, II, & III), Modeling (Vols. I, II, & III), Role Playing (Vols. I, II, & III), Vicarious Conditioning (Vol. II)*

Suggested Readings

Bandura, A. (1971). Vicarious and self-reinforcement processes. In R. Glaser (Ed.), *The nature of reinforcement.* New York: Academic Press.

Bandura, A. (1977). *Social learning theory.* Englewood Cliffs, NJ: Prentice Hall.

Bandura, A., Ross, D., & Ross, S. A. (1972). Vicarious reinforcement and imitative learning. *Journal of Abnormal and Social Psychology, 67,* 601–607.

VIRTUAL REALITY THERAPY WITH CHILDREN

DESCRIPTION OF THE STRATEGY

Virtual reality is a medium of human-computer interaction that is more than just a multimedia interactive display, as the user is no longer simply an external observer of an image but becomes an active participant within a computer-generated, three-dimensional virtual world. Efforts to create this experience of presence or immersion in the virtual environment include multisensory stimuli involving visual, auditory, and kinesthetic. To illustrate the importance of a sense of presence, imagine seeing a photograph of the Grand Canyon, or even a videotape of the Grand Canyon. One can get a sense of it but wouldn't feel present at the Grand Canyon. With virtual reality, one feels present in the virtual environment.

The setup for most virtual reality uses includes a computer to run the software program and a viewing system. The software programs are virtual environments created by computer programmers and graphic designers. The viewing system can be a series of large screens surrounding the user in a room, also known as a "cave." Most applications in psychiatry and psychology, however, use a helmet-like head-mounted display consisting of display screens for each eye. With advances in technology, it is possible to show slightly different images in each eye, producing a stereoscopic display, which can add a sense of visual depth. There are often headphones, sometimes incorporating directional sound. A position tracker and sensor is used to pick up head movements and change the display in real time so that the user's view changes in a natural way with head and body movements. Finally, the user can navigate physical movement within the virtual environment through a handheld puck, similar to a joystick. Other props or devices can also be used, such as an actual railing that corresponds to a virtual railing, or a subwoofer embedded in the base of the chair or mounted below the chair to produce vibrations consistent with the sounds of the virtual environment. In all the environments, the patient experiences only computer-generated audio and visual stimuli while real-world stimuli are shut out. The therapist communicates with the patient with a microphone connected through the computer to the headphones.

Virtual reality is frequently used as a medium for exposure therapy to treat anxiety disorders. Examples of some of these applications include a virtual glass elevator and atrium building with catwalks for people with the fear of heights. In this environment, the user can control movement by opening and closing the elevator doors, ascending and descending throughout the building, and walking across a catwalk, able to look both up and down in the atrium. The next application was a virtual window seat in the passenger cabin of a commercial airplane used for people with the fear of flying. The program begins with the airplane engines off, then engines on, then taxiing to the runway, then taxiing down the runway, takeoff, flying in both calm and turbulent weather, and landing. The passenger hears engine noises, the landing gear, the bells signifying the fasten seat belts sign, flight attendant and pilot announcements, thunder and rain during turbulence, and tires screeching upon landing. In addition, a virtual thunderstorm environment is used for people with a fear of thunderstorms. It consists of a living room with a large picture window. The sky starts off blue with birds chirping and, as the therapist directs, darkens to gray and ominous and develops into a lightning and thunderstorm. The patient sits in a chair in front of the window and can view the weather outside and hears the thunderclaps. These three environments—heights, flying, and thunderstorms—are suitable for treating children and adults.

Current virtual environments used to treat posttraumatic stress disorder (PTSD) are primarily designed for adults. For example, virtual Vietnam War environments have been specifically designed for helping veterans. Users are instructed in imaginal exposure to their most traumatic Vietnam memories while immersed in Vietnam stimuli. The therapist attempts to match the virtual stimuli to what the patient is describing. More recently, a virtual twin towers environment was created using film clips of the terrorist attacks of 9/11. This has been used with residents of New York City who have suffered from PTSD symptoms as a result of witnessing the attacks. Based on the success of these applications, it is likely that additional trauma-related environments will be developed, such as missile attacks and suicide bombings or natural disasters such as earthquakes, that will have applicability to both children and adults.

Another environment currently used primarily for adults is the virtual audience designed for people with a fear of public speaking. In this environment, the user is in a computer-generated room with a virtual podium, upon which the text of his or her speech may be downloaded. A handheld puck, similar to a joystick, is used to scroll forward or backward through their notes on the virtual podium. Directly in front of the user is a computer-generated curtain. When the curtain opens, a virtual audience appears, comprised of 5 individuals seated around a conference table (small audience) or of 35 individuals seated in an auditorium (large audience). The virtual audience consists of live videos of actual people embedded within the virtual environment. During exposure therapy, the therapist controls the audience's reactions, including looking interested, bored, neutral, and applauding. This specific environment has somewhat limited applicability to children, because the audience is comprised only of adults. Creating a similar school classroom environment could be used to help children and adolescents overcome anxiety related to classroom presentations, one aspect of social anxiety in children.

In all the virtual environments used to treat anxiety disorders, patients use a SUDS (Subjective Units of Distress/Discomfort Scale) ranging from 0 to 100 to rate anxiety, in which 0 indicates no anxiety and 100 indicates panic level anxiety to rate their anxiety approximately every 5 minutes, as in standard in vivo or imaginal exposure therapy. As in standard exposure therapy, they are encouraged to approach the situation, then remain at that level until their anxiety decreases, then to gradually increase the exposure. This is repeated until they can approach everything in

the virtual environment without undue anxiety. For several problems, virtual reality exposure is a component of a comprehensive treatment program, and treatment may also include training in anxiety management techniques.

Two other areas in which virtual reality environments are being used primarily with children are for assessment of attention-deficit/hyperactivity disorder (ADHD) and pain distraction. For ADHD assessment, a virtual classroom with multiple distractions allows the evaluator to assess the extent to which a child is able to attend to the teacher's instruction while at the same time observing the manner in which the child is impacted by the surrounding distractions. This type of virtual reality environment provides a format for a classroom observation without leaving the therapist's office.

The idea of using virtual reality for distraction from painful medical procedures makes sense because of its immersive properties and therefore its ability to distract. Instead of focusing on the pain or anxiety, the participant is able to be a participant in a computer-generated 3-dimensional virtual world. Several environments have been created for this use.

RESEARCH BASIS

Very little has been published in the area of virtual reality applications for children. A few case studies have demonstrated the benefit of virtual reality as a distracter for pain management. One research group found that virtual reality distraction relieved children's anxiety associated with chemotherapy. Another group determined that virtual reality was a more effective distraction than video games during burn patient wound care procedures based on lower pain and anxiety ratings and patients' decreased need for pain medication. Another case study followed a pediatric patient during four consecutive appointments for oncology treatments and compared baseline ratings with virtual reality used with and without a headset. The findings from this study revealed that virtual reality distraction with the headset resulted in significantly lower pulse ratings during the procedure. Finally, a controlled pilot study was conducted in which 59 children between the ages of 7 and 19 were randomly assigned to one of three distractions (no distraction control group, virtual reality without the headset, and virtual reality with the headset). Findings suggest that virtual reality may be a useful tool for distraction during painful medical procedures as evidenced by lower pulse rate and lower reports of pain by nurses.

RELEVANT TARGET POPULATION

Virtual reality has primarily been used with adults with anxiety disorders, although it is likely to be equally effective in helping children confront phobic objects and situations as well. Research in this area suggests that any disorder in which standard exposure therapy would be appropriate could also be treated in virtual reality. As a very visual and auditory presentation, people without visual or auditory impairments capable of seeing and hearing the virtual reality are appropriate.

Another target population includes patients undergoing medical procedures. Virtual reality has been tested more extensively in this area among children, though it could also benefit adults.

COMPLICATIONS

Although it is rare, simulator sickness has been noted with virtual reality. In its extreme form, users can become nauseous and get sick. In milder cases, users can get a headache or feel slightly altered perception after using virtual reality. With better resolution in head-mounted displays, the problem of simulator sickness has become almost nonexistent. During medical procedures, virtual reality equipment could get in the way in crowded procedure rooms. In addition, some procedures are performed while the patient is prone, which makes head tracking more complicated.

As with any computer application, computer glitches can interfere with the proper running of a program. The most formidable obstacle to virtual reality is the time, expertise, and expense of constructing appropriate virtual environments and the expense of the hardware.

CASE ILLUSTRATION, INCLUDING BEHAVIORAL ASSESSMENT

"Brian" was an 8-year-old Caucasian male diagnosed with acute lymphocytic leukemia (ALL). He was diagnosed 2 years prior to participation in this single-case design study and had received more than 10 previous port accesses for his oncology treatment. This case study used an A-B-C-A sequence during four consecutive clinic appointments. During the control condition (A), medical treatment was delivered as usual. For the virtual reality without the headset condition (B), Brian played with the virtual reality habitat by watching it on a computer monitor, similar to a computer video game. In the virtual reality with the headset condition (C), Brian participated in the virtual program immersively through a headset. Finally, the control condition (A) was used during his final visit to assess any lasting benefit of the virtual reality distraction intervention. During each condition, Brian's pulse was monitored before, during, and after the procedure, and the researcher observed pain-related behaviors in him. Also, pain and anxiety ratings were obtained from Brian, parent, and nurse.

On self-report measures, neither Brian nor his parents reported any internalizing or externalizing behavior problems, including anxiety, depression, and oppositional behavior. Based on the researcher's behavioral observation of pain during these four sessions, only during the virtual reality with the headset condition (C) were fewer pain-related behaviors observed. During the other three conditions, an equal number of pain behaviors were observed. Brian's, parent's, and nurse's ratings of pain and anxiety revealed the lowest ratings during the (C) condition in which the headset was used with virtual reality, although Brian reported lower anxiety during the nonheadset condition (B). Finally, pulse was measured as more than 30 beats per minute lower in the virtual reality headset condition (C).

Overall, these results suggest a benefit for using virtual reality distraction during painful medical procedures. In fact, the benefit of reduced pain, anxiety, and pulse rate continued in the final control session (A), suggesting the possibility that the benefit of reduced distress during the medical procedure was maintained even when the distraction was not used. Although the generalizability of these results is limited, this study provides a basis for further testing of virtual reality as a distraction.

—*Barbara O. Rothbaum and Elana Zimand*

See also: Systematic Desensitization (Vols. I & III), Systematic Desensitization With Children and Adolescents (Vol. II), Virtual Reality Therapy (Vols. I & III)

Suggested Readings

Anderson, P. L., Rothbaum, B. O., & Hodges, L. (2001). Virtual reality: Using the virtual world to improve quality of life in the real world. *Bulletin of the Menninger Clinic Supplement, 65,* 4–17.

Gershon, J., Anderson, P., Graap, K., Zimand, E., Hodges, L., & Rothbaum, B. O. (2002). Virtual reality exposure therapy in the treatment of anxiety disorders. *Scientific Review of Mental Health Practice, 1,* 78–83.

Gershon, J., Zimand, E., Lemos, R., Rothbaum, B. O., & Hodges, L. (2003). *Use of virtual reality distracter for painful medical procedures with pediatric cancer: A case study.* Manuscript submitted for publication.

Gershon, J., Zimand, E., Pickering, M., Lemos, R., Rothbaum, B. O., & Hodges, L. (2003). *A pilot study of virtual reality as a distraction during an invasive medical procedure for children with cancer.* Manuscript submitted for publication.

Hoffman, H. G., Doctor, J. N., Perterson, D. R., Carrougher, G. J., & Furness, T. A. (2000). Virtual reality as an adjunctive pain control during burn wound care in adolescent patients. *Pain, 85,* 305–309.

Schneider, S., & Workman, M. (1999). Effects of virtual reality on symptom distress in children receiving chemotherapy. *Cyberpsychology & Behavior, 2,* 125–134.

Wolitzky, K., Fivush, R., Zimand, E., Hodges, L., & Rothbaum, B. O. (2003). *Coping with cancer: Relations among parent and child coping, anxiety and distress, and effectiveness of virtual reality during invasive medical procedures.* Manuscript submitted for publication.

Zimand, E., Anderson, P. L., Gershon, J., Graap, K., Hodges, L. F., & Rothbaum, B. O. (2002). Virtual reality therapy: Innovative treatment for anxiety disorders. *Primary Psychiatry, 9,* 51–54.

WATER MISTING

Water misting is an aversive punishment technique that involves spraying a light mist of water in the client's face, contingent on presentation of the undesired behavior. As a behavior change technique, water misting has several advantages. First, it is relatively easy to carry out. There is little need for training, and the mist can be delivered quickly and easily. Second, although there is relatively little discomfort, water misting has been shown to effectively suppress behavior. Finally, water misting is generally more socially acceptable than other punishment procedures such as electric shock or the presentation of aromatic ammonia.

The use of water mist has generally been reserved for self-stimulatory and self-injurious behaviors (SIB) that cannot be managed through the use of nonaversive techniques. These behaviors are persistent and highly resistant to change. The use of contingent water misting developed as a result of an effort to identify techniques that were not only effective in suppressing these behaviors but were also safe and ethically acceptable. While it is clear that electric shock does not meet these criteria, several other techniques, including aromatic ammonia, lemon juice, shaving cream, and Tabasco sauce, which have generally been regarded as less intrusive than electric shock, have been the subject of similar concern by researchers. Water misting represents an important improvement in this regard. It has been shown to be effective in reducing SIB, self-stimulatory behavior, stereotypical responding, and pica. Perhaps as important, water mist is more likely to be considered ethically and socially acceptable.

As with any punishment procedure, undesirable side effects may result from the use of water mist. Potential side effects of water mist, and punishment more generally, include emotional reactions such as crying, anger, avoidance of the punisher or the punishing situation, and aggression against the punisher. In addition to these reactions, the individual receiving the water mist may learn through modeling that punishment is an effective way to get others to comply. There is also the likelihood that the use of punishment will be reinforced in the staff member who uses it. Finally, careful consideration should go into how the water misting program will be removed. For these reasons, it is important that the use of water misting (or any aversive consequence) always be combined with reinforcement. Although less desirable than antecedent control and reinforcement techniques for a number of reasons, punishment can be an effective behavior change strategy when other approaches can't be used successfully. When administered judiciously in conjunction with reinforcement, water misting is one of the safest and most effective means of modifying behavior with punishment.

—*Kevin J. Armstrong and Christopher M. Browne*

See also: *Aromatic Ammonia (Vol. II), Aversive Conditioning (Vol. II), Aversion Relief (Vols. I & III), Electrical Aversion (Vols. I & III), Facial Screening (Vol. II), Lemon Juice Therapy (Vol. II), Punishment (Vols. II & III)*

Suggested Readings

Bailey, S. L., Pokrzywinski, J., & Bryant, L. E. (1983). Using water mist to reduce self-injurious and stereotypic behavior. *Applied Research in Mental Retardation, 4,* 229–241.

Fehr, A., & Beckwith, B. E. (1989). Water misting: Treating self-injurious behavior in a multiply handicapped, visually impaired child. *Journal of Visual Impairment & Blindness, 83,* 245–248.

Friman, P. C., Cook, J. W., & Finney, J. W. (1984). Effects of punishment procedures on the self-stimulatory behavior of an autistic child. *Analysis & Intervention in Developmental Disabilities, 41,* 39–46.

Singh, N. N., Watson, J. E., & Winton, A. S. W. (1986). Treating self-injury: Water mist spray versus facial screening or forced arm exercise. *Journal of Applied Behavior Analysis, 19,* 403–410.

JOHN BROADUS WATSON

John Broadus Watson (1878–1958) is widely acknowledged to be the founder of behaviorism—an objective, natural science approach to psychology and one of the most important developments in the history of psychology. Yet, beyond a paragraph or two in textbooks, Watson is barely visible in modern psychology. What does appear is often more caricature than history—fragments of academic folklore introduced, only to be dismissed as components of an allegedly ill-conceived diversion on a journey to some supposedly superior viewpoint. A legitimate examination of Watson's work shows him to be a sophisticated scientist who fused functionalist psychology, pragmatism (America's homegrown philosophy), Russian studies of the reflex, and experimental physiology into a philosophy of psychology still flourishing almost a century later. Watson's lifespan developmental approach to all behavior rejected a simplistic nature-nurture dichotomy, emphasized combining laboratory analyses with observational studies of organisms in their natural environments, dismissed Ernst Haeckel's discredited recapitulation theory (despite its foundational role in most other developmental psychologies), and strongly advocated the application of scientific findings to social problems. Watson insisted that psychology could become truly successful only by replacing its religious and philosophical preconceptions with the methods of science. He was among the first to argue for the cognitive precocity of newborn infants, question the quality of empirical evidence for prevailing racist and sexist assumptions about inheritance of intelligence, argue for accurate and frank sex education to prevent the spread of sexually transmitted diseases, reject the prejudice of inevitable cognitive decline with aging, and state that abnormal behavior might be the result of an abnormal behavioral history rather than being a manifestation of a disordered mind. Watson's view of emotional development still provides the conceptual basis of the dominant therapies for anxiety disorders.

An excellent student despite a chaotic childhood, Watson graduated in 1899 from Furman University in Greenville, South Carolina. From Furman, he went to the University of Chicago to study philosophy with John Dewey. Attracted instead by psychology and biology, Watson's 1903 dissertation, *Animal Education: An Experimental Study on the Psychical Development of the White Rat,* correlated with the growth of the rat's nervous system, was a lifespan developmental analysis of the relationship between learning ability and brain myelinization in rats. Infant rats exhibited considerable learning ability despite incomplete brain development. Extrapolating, Watson argued that infant humans, like infant rats, possessed considerable unrecognized early learning ability. This prebehaviorist work clearly showed the combined influences of the functionalist psychologist James Angell, experimental physiologist Henry Donaldson, embryologist Jacques Loeb, and pragmatist philosopher John Dewey.

Eclectic in his choice of research topics throughout his career, Watson was best known in these early years for studies of the role of sensory abilities in learning. His most important work in retrospect was an extensive, multiyear ethological study of the instinctual and learned behavior of seabirds. Watson showed an impressive talent and insight as an ethologist years before the discipline had a name. Through this work, he adopted a view on the relative importance of nature and nurture similar to Sigmund Freud's: An understanding of adult behavior requires the knowledge of innate capabilities combined with an appreciation of the immense power of early experience.

Watson remained at Chicago until 1908, when he was hired by Johns Hopkins University as its youngest full professor. In 1913, Watson introduced behaviorism with a pair of articles. The now obscure "Image and Affection in Behavior" was a technical piece on the nature of sensations written for the structuralist audience. The better-known "Psychology as the Behaviorist Views It" outlined the failures of structuralism and functionalism in psychology and introduced behaviorism as an objective, natural science of behavior with a fundamentally progressive, pragmatic agenda. Its "theoretical goal" was the decidedly practical "predication and control of behavior." Although "Psychology as the Behaviorist Views It" was almost exclusively concerned with human behavior, including a lengthy footnote on the nature of thinking, it was written from the perspective of an animal psychologist whose extrapolations to human psychology were necessarily theoretical. In 1913, Watson lacked a specific mechanism of behavior change to back up his theory and had done no research with humans.

Watson's popular 1914 textbook, *Behavior: An Introduction to Comparative Psychology,* revealed both his impressive knowledge of research in animal behavior and his initial failure to recognize the broad implications of Pavlov's work. This failure would be rectified in 1916 when Watson described Pavlovian conditioning in his presidential address to the American Psychological Association. Pavlov had provided the much-needed behavioral mechanism to complement the theoretical aspects of behaviorism. At the same time, Watson's research shifted from non-humans to human infants, where he concentrated on unlearned behavior and emotional development. He continued to espouse a kind of ethological approach combining laboratory and observational studies informed by an interactionist viewpoint: It is impossible to fully understand the behavior of organisms, including humans, without understanding their unlearned behavioral capabilities. Here he saw too much conjecture and too little research. Watson argued strongly that there was little good evidence supporting the inheritance of behavioral tendencies such as criminality. Even so, he also never claimed that all behavior was learned. Watson's oft-quoted "give me a dozen healthy infants" statement from the 1924 book *Behaviorism* seems to be the final word of an uncompromising environmentalist. However, it was really a rhetorical device to introduce a discussion of the failure of early 20th-century hereditarians to produce evidence for their views. Watson did believe experience was a better place to look to explain behavior. Yet, rather than rejecting the influence of genetics on behavior, he believed that the relative importance of learning over instinct in humans was itself an inherited, adaptive characteristic.

Contrary to academic folklore, which asserts that behaviorists deny emotions, beginning in 1917 Watson became an acknowledged authority on emotions when he introduced his theory that complex emotional reactions in humans arise via classical conditioning from newborns' unlearned reactions of fear, rage, and love. His most famous experiment in this area, "Conditioned Emotional Reactions," was an attempt to demonstrate the transfer of an innate startle response from a loud noise to a rat using Pavlovian conditioning. A film of the study made by Watson himself suggests that the conditioning, if produced at all, was quite weak. Even so, "Conditioned Emotional Reactions" remains the most cited study in the history of psychology. In 1924, Mary Cover Jones, working with Watson, showed that a fear response could be unconditioned by gradually reintroducing the fear-eliciting object while preventing the emotional response. Now known as systematic desensitization, this technique has been refined to become one of the most successful and empirically validated forms of therapy for a wide variety of behavior problems, including emotional disorders, phobias, and obsessive-compulsive disorders.

In 1920, Watson was dismissed from Johns Hopkins for an affair with a student, but he subsequently prospered in the field of advertising. He continued promoting behaviorism through popular books such as *Psychology from the Standpoint of a Behaviorist* in 1919 and *Behaviorism,* magazine articles, and even radio broadcasts. Pavlovian conditioning, considerably simplified, became a compelling mechanism to account for behavior. Child-care advice, often Watson's own views dressed in behavioristic terms, appeared in *Harpers, McCalls,* and *Cosmopolitan. Psychological Care of Infant and Child,* a 1928 book of much exaggerated influence, is remembered primarily for the rather Freudian idea that excessive emotional attachment to children by parents breeds overdependence in adulthood. Not commonly remembered are Watson's strong warnings against the use of corporal punishment, advice about the relative harmlessness of masturbation, and advocacy of an open approach about sexual issues—the final item being derived from a series of studies of the value of sex education for preventing venereal disease.

Watson ceased publishing broadly in 1930, and the Watsonian behaviorism did not gain many adherents. The neo-behaviorisms of Clark Hull, Edwin Guthrie, and Edward Tolman focused on conditioning and learning per se. B. F. Skinner, in contrast, rejected Watson's mechanistic, stimulus-response approach but emulated his strong advocacy of application of behavioral principles to human behavior problems. Eventually, the successful application of behavioral principles derived from the work of Skinner to developmental disabilities in the 1950s reinvigorated a purely behavioral approach to child development that had been missing from behaviorism since the 1930s. Consistent with its progressive and pragmatic roots, applied behavior analysis, using primarily operant principles, exists along with the Pavlovian-derived behavior therapy, associated with Joseph Wolpe and others, which can trace its ancestry to the work of Watson and Mary Cover Jones.

—James T. Todd

See also: Historical Antecedents of Behavior Modification and Therapy (Vols. I & III), Operant Conditioning (Vols. I, II, & III)

Suggested Readings

Buckley, K. W. (1989). *Mechanical man: John Broadus Watson and the beginnings of behaviorism.* New York: Guilford Press.

Morris, E. K., & Todd, J. T. (1998). Watsonian behaviorism. In W. O'Donohue & R. F. Kitchener (Eds.), *Handbook of behaviorism.* (pp. 15–69). San Diego, CA: Academic Press.

Todd, J. T. & Morris, E. K. (Eds.). (1994). *Modern perspectives on John B. Watson and classical behaviorism.* Westport, CT: Greenwood Press.

Watson, J. B. (1919). *Psychology from the standpoint of a behaviorist.* Philadelphia: Lippincott.

Watson, J. B. (1930). *Behaviorism* (Rev. ed.). New York: People's Institute.

WRITE-SAY METHOD

The write-say method is a behavioral strategy designed to improve academic performance in children. It has typically been used to improve spelling accuracy or to teach basic math facts such as multiplication tables. It is most effective in teaching material that requires rote memorization. It has been used to teach material to children with and without learning disabilities, as well as children with mental retardation. For spelling, the write-say method requires that the child write the spelling word on a sheet of paper after the teacher has spoken the word aloud. If the child spells the word accurately, the next word is spoken aloud and the child writes the new word. However, if the word is misspelled, the child is required to pronounce the word and each letter with the teacher while rewriting the word. This process is repeated 3 to 10 times and occurs before moving on to a new word.

Several researchers have demonstrated the effectiveness of the procedure in teaching spelling to children with and without learning disabilities. For instance, one study required that children say the spelling word out loud, then write the word and say the word, check the word, trace the word and say the word, and finally write the word from memory. This study strategy was compared to a group of children who were allowed to study the spelling words by any strategy they chose. After only 30 minutes of study, the children who were required to study using the write-say procedure scored significantly higher than children who studied via other strategies.

For math, the write-say procedure involves rewriting a math problem a specified number of times if answered incorrectly. The method also involves saying the answers to problems aloud and verbally identifying mistakes. Researchers have successfully used the write-say procedure to teach multiplication tables to children with learning disabilities. In one study, children were required to rewrite a multiplication table five times if they answered incorrectly. Furthermore, they were required to say the answers out loud and state what their mistakes were. This procedure was used to teach math problems involving multiplication by 2 through 9. Success rates improved from 43% to 77%, demonstrating the effectiveness of the procedure in teaching certain basic math facts.

In general, there are many variations in the way the write-say procedure can be implemented, but all variations share in common immediate feedback to multiple sensory modalities (i.e., auditory and visual) for incorrect answers. Several researchers have concluded that it is the dual sensory approach in combination with immediate feedback that is the mechanism of improved performance. This may be particularly true for children with learning disabilities because of the fact that deficits in one sensory modality (e.g., visual processing) may be compensated for by a stronger sensory modality (e.g., auditory processing). Other researchers have pointed out that the aversive nature of rewriting problems many times may serve as a motivator to improve performance. Most of the research involving the write-say procedure has demonstrated its effectiveness in improving the accuracy of immediate recall of material, although at least one study has demonstrated the effectiveness of the procedure in improving delayed recall of spelling accuracy. In general, the procedure has proven to be more consistently effective in teaching basic academic facts than more traditional approaches (e.g., simple memorization).

—*Heather Applegate*

See also: *Behavioral Neuropsychology (Vols. I & III), Behavioral Treatment in Natural Environments (Vols. I & III), Behavior Management for Improving Academic and Classroom Behavior (Vol. II), Generalization (Vols. I, II, & III), 3-5-10-15 Method for Spelling (Vol. II)*

Suggested Readings

Graham, S., & Freeman, S. (1986). Strategy training and teacher vs. student-controlled study conditions: Effects on LD children's spelling performance. *Learning Disability Quarterly, 9,* 15–22.

Kearney, C. A., & Drabman, R. S. (1993). The write-say method for improving spelling accuracy in children with learning disabilities. *Journal of Learning Disabilities, 26,* 52–56.

Lombardo, T. W., & Drabman, R. S. (1985). Teaching LD children multiplication tables. *Academic Therapy, 20,* 437–442.

Matson, J. L., Esveldt-Dawson, K., & Kazdin, A. E. (1982). Treatment of spelling deficits in mentally retarded children. *Mental Retardation, 20,* 76–81.

Ormrod, J. E., & Jenkins, L. (1989). Study strategies for learning spelling: Correlations with achievement and developmental changes. *Perceptual and Motor Skills, 68,* 643–650.

Bibliography

Abramowitz, A. J., & O'Leary, S. G. (1991). Behavioral interventions for the classroom: Implications for students with ADHD. *School Psychology Review, 20,* 220–234.

Adams, C. D., & Drabman, R. S. (1996). Improving morning interactions: Beat-the-buzzer with a boy having multiple handicaps. *Child & Family Behavior Therapy, 17,* 13–26.

Addis, M. E., & Jacobson, N. S. (2000). A closer look at the treatment rationale and homework compliance in cognitive-behavioral therapy for depression. *Cognitive Therapy and Research, 24,* 313–326.

Albano, A. M., & Morris, T. L. (1998). Childhood anxiety, obsessive-compulsive disorder, and depression. In J. J. Plaud & G. H. Eifert (Eds.), *From behavior theory to behavior therapy.* Needham Heights, MA: Allyn & Bacon.

Alexander J. F., & Parsons, B.V. (1982). *Functional family therapy.* Monterey, CA: Brooks/Cole.

Allan, R. W. (1998). Operant-respondent interactions. In W. O'Donohue (Ed.), *Learning and behavior therapy.* Needham Heights, MA: Allyn & Bacon.

Allen, K. D. (1998). The use of an enhanced simplified habit-reversal procedure to reduce disruptive outbursts during athletic performance. *Journal of Applied Behavior Analysis, 31,* 489–492.

Allen, K. D., Loiben, T., Allen, S. J., & Robert, T. (1992). Dentist-implemented contingent escape for management of disruptive child behavior. *Journal of Applied Behavior Analysis, 25,* 629–636.

Allen, K. D., Stark, L. J., Rigney, B. A., Nash, D., & Stokes, T. F. (1988). Reinforced practice during restorative dental treatment. *Journal of Dentistry for Children, 55,* 273–277.

Allison, J. (1989). The nature of reinforcement. In S. B. Klein, B. Stephen, & R. R. Mowrer (Eds.), *Contemporary learning theories: Instrumental conditioning theory and the impact of biological constraints on learning* (pp. 13–39). Hillsdale, NJ: Erlbaum.

Altmeyer, B. K., Williams, D. E., & Sams, V. (1985). Treatment of severe self-injurious and aggressive biting. *Journal of Behavior Therapy and Experimental Psychiatry, 16,* 159–167.

American Academy of Pediatrics & the American Pain Society. (2001). The assessment and management of acute pain in infants, children, and adolescents. *Pediatrics, 108,* 793–797.

Ammerman, R. T., Hersen, M., & Last, C. G. (1999). *Handbook of prescriptive treatments for children and adolescents* (2nd ed.). Needham Heights, MA: Allyn & Bacon.

Anderson, C. M., & Long, E. S. (2002). Use of a structured descriptive assessment methodology to identify variables affecting problem behavior. *Journal of Applied Behavior Analysis, 35,* 137–154.

Anderson, P. L., Rothbaum, B. O., & Hodges, L. (2001). Virtual reality: Using the virtual world to improve quality of life in the real world. *Bulletin of the Menninger Clinic Supplement, 65,* 4–17.

Anderson, S. R., & Romanczyk, R. G. (1999). Early intervention for young children with autism: Continuum-based behavioral models. *Journal of the Association for Persons With Severe Handicaps, 24,* 162–173.

Anderson, S. R., Avery, D. L., DiPietro, E. K., Edwards, G. L., & Christian, W. P. (1987). Intensive home-based early intervention with autistic children. *Education and Treatment of Children, 10,* 352–366.

Andrasik, F., & Lords, A. O. (2003). Biofeedback. In L. Freeman (Ed.), *Mosby's complementary and alternative medicine (CAM): A research-based approach* (2nd ed.). Philadelphia: Elsevier Science.

Ardoin, S. P., & Martens, B. K. (2000). Testing the ability of children with attention deficit hyperactivity disorder to accurately report the effects of medication on their behavior. *Journal of Applied Behavior Analysis, 33,* 593–610.

Asmus, J. M., Wacker, D. P., Harding, J., Berg, W. K., Derby, K. M., & Kocis, E. (1999). Evaluation of antecedent stimulus parameters for the treatment of escape-maintained aberrant behavior. *Journal of Applied Behavior Analysis, 32,* 495–513.

Attanasio, V., Andrasik, F., Burke, E. J., Blake, D. D., Kabela, E., & McCarran, M. S. (1985). Clinical issues in utilizing biofeedback with children. *Clinical Biofeedback and Health, 8,* 134–141.

Auguston, E. M., & Dougher, M. J. (1997). The transfer of avoidance-evoking functions through stimulus equivalence classes. *Journal of Behavior Therapy, 28,* 181–191.

Axelrod, S. (1998). How to use group contingencies. In R. V. Hall & M. L. Hall (Series Eds.), *How to manage behavior series.* Austin, TX: Pro-ed.

Axelrod, S., & Hall, R. V. (1999). *Behavior modification: Basic principles* (2nd ed.). Austin, TX: Pro-ed.

Ayllon, T. (1999). *How to use token economy and point systems* (2nd ed.). Austin, TX: Pro-Ed.

Ayllon, T., & Azrin, N. (1968). *The token economy: A motivational system for therapy and rehabilitation* (pp. 88–103). New York: Appleton-Century-Crofts.

Ayllon, T., & Azrin, N. H. (1968). Reinforcer sampling: A technique for increasing the behavior of mental patients. *Journal of Applied Behavior Analysis, 1,* 13–20.

Ayllon, T., & Milan, M. A. (2002). Token economy: Guidelines for operation. In M. Hersen & W. H. Sledge (Eds.), *Encyclopedia of psychotherapy* (pp. 829–833). San Diego, CA: Academic Press.

Azrin, N. H., & Foxx, R. M. (1971). A rapid method of toilet training the institutionalized retarded. *Journal of Applied Behavior Analysis, 4,* 89–99.

Azrin, N. H., & Nunn, R. G. (1973). Habit-reversal: A method of eliminating nervous habits and tics. *Behaviour, Research, and Therapy, 11,* 619–628.

Azrin, N. H., & Nunn, R. G. (1974). A rapid method of eliminating stuttering by a regulated breathing approach. *Behaviour Research and Therapy, 12,* 279–286.

Azrin, N. H., & Nunn, R. G. (1974). Habit reversal: A method of eliminating nervous habits and tics. *Behaviour Research and Therapy, 11,* 619–628.

Azrin, N. H., & Nunn, R. G. (1977). *Habit control in a day.* New York: Simon & Schuster.

Azrin, N. H., & Weslowski, M. D. (1974). Theft reversal: An overcorrection procedure for eliminating stealing by retarded persons. *Journal of Applied Behavior Analysis, 7,* 577–581.

Azrin, N. H., Acierno, R., Kogan, E. S., Donohue, B., Besalel, V. A., & McMahon, P. T. (1996). Follow-up results of supportive versus behavioral therapy for illicit drug use. *Behavior Research and Therapy, 34,* 41–46.

Baddeley, A., & Longman, D. J. A. (1978). The influence of length and frequency of training sessions on rate of learning to type. *Ergonomics, 21,* 627–635.

Baer, D. M. (1981). A flight of behavior analysis. *The Behavior Analyst, 4,* 85–91.

Baer, D. M., Wolf, M. M., & Risley, T. R. (1968). Some current dimensions of applied behavior analysis. *Journal of Applied Behavior Analysis, 1,* 91–97.

Baer, R. A., Detrich, R., & Weninger, J. M. (1988). On the functional role of the verbalization in correspondence training procedures. *Journal of Applied Behavior Analysis, 21,* 345–356.

Bagner, D., & Eyberg, S. M. (2003). Father involvement in treatment. In T. H. Ollendick & C. S. Schroeder (Eds.), *Encyclopedia of clinical child and pediatric psychology.* New York: Plenum.

Bailey, J. S., & Burch, M. R. (2002). *Research methods in applied behavior analysis.* Thousand Oaks, CA: Sage.

Bailey, S. L., Pokrzywinski, J., & Bryant, L. E. (1983). Using water mist to reduce self-injurious and stereotypic behavior. *Applied Research in Mental Retardation, 4,* 229–241.

Bakeman, R., & Gottman, J. M. (1997). *Observing interaction: An introduction to sequential analysis* (2nd ed.). New York: Cambridge University Press.

Baldwin, J. D., & Baldwin, J. I. (1998). *Behavior principals in everyday life* (3rd ed.). Upper Saddle River, NJ: Prentice Hall.

Bandura, A. (1969). *Principles of behavior modification.* New York: Holt, Rinehart & Winston.

Bandura, A. (1971). Vicarious and self-reinforcement processes. In R. Glaser (Ed.), *The nature of reinforcement.* New York: Academic Press.

Bandura, A. (1971). *Psychological modeling: Conflicting theories.* Chicago: Aldine-Atherton.

Bandura, A. (1977). *Social learning theory.* Englewood Cliffs, NJ: Prentice Hall.

Bandura, A. (1977). Self-efficacy: Towards a unifying theory of behavioral change. *Psychological Review, 84,* 191–215.

Bandura, A. (1986). *Social foundations of thought and action: A social cognitive theory.* Englewood Cliffs, NJ: Prentice Hall.

Bandura, A., Grusec, J. E., & Menlove, F. L. (1967). Vicarious extinction of avoidance behavior. *Journal of Personality and Social Psychology, 5,* 16–23.

Bandura, A., Grusec, J. E., & Menlove, F. L. (1968). Factors determining vicarious extinction of avoidance behavior through symbolic modeling. *Journal of Personality and Social Psychology, 8,* 99–108.

Bandura, A., Ross, D., & Ross, S. A. (1972). Vicarious reinforcement and imitative learning. *Journal of Abnormal and Social Psychology, 67,* 601–607.

Barkley, R. A. (1997). *Defiant children* (2nd ed.). New York: Guilford Press.

Barlow, D. H., & Hersen, M. (1984). *Single case experimental designs: Strategies for studying behavior change* (2nd ed.). New York: Pergamon.

Barlow, D. H., Raffa, S. D., & Cohen, E. M. (2002). Psychosocial treatments for panic disorders, phobias, and generalized anxiety disorder. In P. E. Nathan & J. M. Gorman (Eds.), *A guide to treatments that work* (2nd ed., pp. 301–335). New York: Oxford University Press.

Baron, G., & Cautela, J. (1983). Imagery assessment with normal and special needs children. *Imagination, Cognition, and Personality, 3,* 17–30.

Barrios, B. A., & O'Dell, S. L. (1989). Fears and anxiety. In E. J. Mash & R. A. Barkley (Eds.), *Treatment of childhood disorders.* New York: Guilford Press.

Barrios, B. A., & O'Dell, S. L. (1998). Fears and anxieties. In E. J. Mash & R. A. Barclay (Eds.), *Treatment of childhood disorders* (2nd ed., pp. 249–337). New York: Guilford Press.

Barrish, H. H., Saunders, M., & Wolf, M. M. (1969). Good Behavior Game: Effects of individual contingencies for group consequences on disruptive behavior in a classroom. *Journal of Applied Behavior Analysis, 2,* 119–124.

Barth, R. P. (1987). Assessment and treatment of stealing. In B. Lahey & A. Kazdin (Eds.), *Advances in clinical child psychology* (Vol. 10, pp. 137–170). New York: Plenum.

Bateson, G., Jackson, D. D., Haley, J., & Weakland, J. (1956). Toward a theory of schizophrenia. *Behavioral Science, 1,* 251–264.

Beck, A. T. (1970). Cognitive therapy: Nature and relation to behavior therapy. *Behavior Therapy, 1,* 184–200.

Beck, J. S. (1995). *Cognitive therapy: Basics and beyond.* New York: Guilford Press.

Beck, R., & Fernandez, E. (1998). Cognitive-behavioral therapy in the treatment of anger. *Cognitive Therapy and Research, 22,* 63–74.

Becker, R. E., Heimberg, R. G., & Bellack, A. S. (1987). *Social skills training treatment for depression.* New York: Pergamon Press.

Beidel, D. C., & Turner, S. M. (1998). *Shy children, phobic adults: Nature and treatment of social phobia.* Washington, DC: American Psychological Press.

Beidel, D. C., Turner, S. M., & Morris, T. L. (2000). Behavioral treatment of childhood social phobia. *Journal of Consulting and Clinical Psychology, 68,* 1072–1080.

Bell, K. E., & Stein, D. M. (1992). Behavioral treatments for pica: A review of empirical studies. *International Journal of Eating Disorders, 11,* 377–389.

Bellack, A. S., & Hersen, M. (Eds.). (1990). *International handbook of behavior modification and therapy* (2nd ed.). New York: Plenum.

Bellack, A. S., & Hersen, M. (Eds.). (1998). *Behavioral assessment: A practical handbook.* Boston: Allyn & Bacon.

Bellack, A. S., & Hersen, M. (Eds.). (1998). *Behavioral assessment: A practical handbook* (3rd ed.). Boston: Allyn & Bacon.

Berger, S. (1962). Conditioning through vicarious instigation. *Psychological Review, 69,* 450–466.

Berkowitz, R. I., & Stunkard, A. J. (2002). Development of childhood obesity. In T. A. Wadden & A. J. Stunkard (Eds.), *Handbook of obesity treatment* (pp. 515–531). New York: Guilford Press.

Berman, S. L., Weems, C. F., Silverman, W. K., & Kurtines, W. (2000). Predictors of outcome in exposure-based cognitive and behavioral treatments for phobic and anxiety disorders in children. *Behavior Therapy, 31,* 713–731.

Bijou, S. (1995). *Behavior analysis of child development.* Reno, NV: Context Press.

Bijou, S. W. (1996). Reflections on some early events related to behavior analysis of child development. *The Behavior Analyst, 19,* 49–60.

Bijou, S. W., & Baer, D. M. (1978). *Behavior analysis of child development.* Englewood Cliffs, NJ: Prentice Hall.

Blum, N., & Friman, P. C. (2000). Behavioral pediatrics: The confluence of applied behavior analysis and pediatric medicine. In J. Carr and J. Austin (Eds.), *Handbook of applied behavior analysis* (pp. 161–186). Reno, NV: Context Press.

Blum, N., Williams, G., Friman, P. C., & Christophersen, E. R. (1995). Disciplining young children: The role of reason. *Pediatrics, 96,* 336–341.

Bolling, M. Y., Kohlenberg, R. J., & Parker, C. R. (2000). Behavior analysis and depression. In M. J. Dougher (Ed.), *Clinical behavior analysis* (pp. 127–152). Reno, NV: Context Press.

Bond, F. W., & Dryden, W. (2002). *Handbook of brief cognitive behaviour therapy.* New York: John Wiley.

Borklovec, T. D., Wilkinson, L., Folensbee, R., & Lerman, C. (1983). Stimulus control applications to the treatment of worry. *Behavior Research and Therapy, 21,* 247–251.

Botvin, G. J., & Kantor, L.W. (2000). Preventing alcohol and tobacco use through life skills training. *Alcohol Research & Health, 24,* 250–263.

Boutin, M. E., & Nelson, J. B. (1998). The role of context in classical conditioning: Some implications for cognitive behavioral therapy. In W. O'Donohue (Ed.). *Learning and behavior therapy.* Needham Heights, MA: Allyn & Bacon.

Bouton, M. E. (2000). A learning theory perspective on lapse, relapse, and the maintenance of behavior change. *Health Psychology, 19,* 57–63.

Bowman, L. G., Fisher, W. W., Thompson, R. H., & Piazza, C. C. (1997). On the relation of mands and the function of destructive behavior. *Journal of Applied Behavior Analysis, 30,* 251–265.

Brem, C. (1993). *A comprehensive guide to child psychotherapy.* Needham Heights, MA: Allyn & Bacon.

Brent, D. A., & Poling, K. (1997). *Cognitive therapy treatment manual for depressed and suicidal youth.* Pittsburgh, PA: University of Pittsburgh, Services for Teens at Risk.

Brestan, E. V., & Eyberg, S. M. (1998). Effective psychosocial treatment of conduct-disordered children and adolescents: 29 years, 82 studies, 5275 children. *Journal of Clinical Child Psychology, 27,* 180–189.

Brinkmeyer, M., & Eyberg, S. M. (2003). Parent-child interaction therapy for oppositional children. In A. E. Kazdin & J. R. Weisz (Eds.), *Evidence-based psychotherapies for children and adolescents.* New York: Guilford Press.

Brooks, A. R., & Benjamin, B. J. (1989). The use of structured role play therapy in the remediation of grammatical deficits in language delayed children: Three case studies. *Journal of Children's Communication Development, 12,* 110–128.

Brown, K. A., Wacker, D. P., Derby, K. M., Peck, S. M., Richman, D. M., Sasso, G. M., et al. (2000). Evaluating the effects of functional communication training in the presence and absence of establishing operations. *Journal of Applied Behavior Analysis, 33,* 53–71.

Bry, B. H., & Krinsley, K. E. (1992). Booster sessions and long-term effects of behavioral family therapy on adolescent substance use and school performance. *Journal of Behavior Therapy & Experimental Psychiatry, 23,* 183–189.

Buckley, K. W. (1989). *Mechanical man: John Broadus Watson and the beginnings of behaviorism.* New York: Guilford Press.

Butterfield, W. H., & Cobb, N. H. (1994). Cognitive-behavioral treatment of children and adolescents. In D. K. Granvold (Ed.), *Cognitive and behavioral treatment: Methods and applications* (pp. 65–89). Belmont, CA: Wadsworth.

Cannon, S. B. (1983). A clarification of the components and the procedural characteristics of overcorrection. *Educational and Psychological Research, 3,* 11–18.

Carlson, C. R., & Hoyle, R. H. (1993). Efficacy of abbreviated progressive muscle relaxation training: A quantitative review of behavioral medicine research. *Journal of Consulting and Clinical Psychology, 61,* 1059–1067.

Carr, E. G., & Durand, V. M. (1985). Reducing behavior problems through functional communication training. *Journal of Applied Behavior Analysis, 18,* 111–126.

Carr, E. G., Levin, L., McConnachie, G., Carlson, J. I., Kemp, D. C., & Smith, C. E. (1994). *Communication-based intervention for problem behavior: A user's guide for producing positive change.* Baltimore: Paul H. Brookes.

Carr, E. G., Newsom, C. D., & Binkoff, J. A. (1976). Stimulus control of self-destructive behavior in a psychotic child. *Journal of Abnormal Child Psychology, 4,* 139–153.

Carr, J. E., Coriaty, S., Wilder, D. A., Gaunt, B. T., Dozier, C. L., Britton, L. N., et al. (2000). A review of "noncontingent" reinforcement as treatment for the aberrant behavior of individuals with developmental disabilities. *Research in Developmental Disabilities, 21,* 377–391.

Carr, J. E., Dozier, C. L., Patel, M. R., Adams, A. N., & Martin, N. (2002). Treatment of automatically reinforced object mouthing with noncontingent reinforcement and response blocking: Experimental analysis and social validation. *Research in Developmental Disabilities, 23,* 37–44.

Carroll, K. M. (1996). Relapse prevention as a psychosocial treatment: A review of controlled clinical trials. *Experimental and Clinical Psychopharmacology, 4,* 46–54.

Catania, A. C. (1998). *Learning.* Upper Saddle River, NJ: Prentice Hall.

Catania, A. C., & Harnad, S. (Eds.). (1983). *The selection of behaviour: The operant behaviour of B. F. Skinner: Comments and consequences.* New York: Cambridge University Press.

Cautela, J. R. (1982). Covert conditioning in children. *Journal of Behavior Therapy and Experimental Psychiatry, 13,* 209–214.

Cautela, J. R. (1983). The self-control triad. *Behavior Modification, 7,* 299–315.

Cautela, J. R. (1986). Covert conditioning and the control of pain. *Behavior Modification, 10,* 205–217.

Cautela, J. R., & Kastenbaum, R. A. (1967). Reinforcement survey schedule for use in therapy, training, and research. *Psychological Reports, 20,* 1115–1130.

Cautela, J. R., & Kearney, A. J. (1986). *The covert conditioning handbook.* New York: Springer.

Cautela, J. R., & Kearney, A. J. (1993). *Covert conditioning handbook.* Pacific Grove, CA: Brooks Cole.

Cavell, T. A. (2000). *Working with parents of aggressive children: A practitioner's guide.* Washington, DC: American Psychological Association.

Cavell, T. A., & Strand, P. S. (2002). Parent-based interventions for aggressive, antisocial children: Adapting to a bilateral lens. In L. Kuczynski (Ed.), *Handbook of dynamics in parent-child relations.* Thousand Oaks, CA: Sage.

Chambless, D. L., & Hollen, S. D. (1998). Defining empirically supported therapies. *Journal of Consulting and Clinical Psychology, 66,* 7–18.

Chambless, D. L., & Ollendick, T. H. (2001). Empirically supported psychological interventions: Controversies and evidence. *Annual Review of Psychology, 52,* 685–716.

Chambless, D. L., Sanderson, W. C., Shoham, V., Bennett-Johnson, S., Pope, K. S., Crits-Christoph, P., et al. (1996). An update on empirically validated therapies. *The Clinical Psychologist, 49,* 5–18.

Chance, P. (1988). *Learning and behavior* (2nd ed.). Belmont, CA: Wadsworth.

Chandler, L. K., & Dahlquist, C. M. (2002). *Functional assessment: Strategies to prevent and remediate challenging behavior in school settings.* Upper Saddle River, NJ: Prentice Hall.

Charlop, M. H., Kurtz, P. F., & Casey, F. G. (1990). Using aberrant behaviors as reinforcers for autistic children. *Journal of Applied Behavior Analysis, 23,* 163–181.

Chiara, L., Schuster, J., Bell, J., & Wolery, A. (1995). Small-group massed-trial and individually distributed trial instruction with preschoolers. *Journal of Early Intervention, 19,* 203–217.

Chorpita, B. F., Yim, L. M., Donkervoet, J. C., Arensdorf, A., Amundsen, M. J., McGee, C., et al. (2003). Toward large-scale implementation of empirically supported treatments for children: A review and observations by the Hawaii Empirical Basis to Services Task Force. *Clinical Psychology: Science and Practice, 9,* 165–190.

Christophersen, E. R. (1982). Behavioral pediatrics. *Pediatric Clinics of North America, 29*(2).

Christophersen, E. R. (1994). *Pediatric compliance: A guide for the primary care physician.* New York: Plenum.

Christophersen, E. R., & Friman, P. C. (2003). Elimination disorders. In R. Brown (Ed.), *Handbook of pediatric psychology in school settings* (pp. 467–487). Mahwah, NJ: Erlbaum.

Christophersen, E. R., & Mortweet, S. L. (2001). *Treatments that work with children: Empirically supported strategies for managing childhood problems.* Washington, DC: American Psychological Association.

Christophersen, E. R., & Mortweet, S. L. (2001). *Treatments that work for children.* Washington, DC: American Psychological Association.

Christophersen, E. R., & Mortweet. S. L. (1999). *Treatments that work with children.* Washington, D.C.: American Psychological Association.

Christophersen, E. R., Finney, J. W., & Friman, P. C. (Eds.). (1986). Prevention in primary care. *Pediatric Clinics of North America, 33*(4).

Ciminero, A. R., Calhoun K. S., & Adams, H. E. (Eds.). (1986). *Handbook of behavioral assessment* (2nd ed.). New York: John Wiley.

Clark, L. (1996). *SOS: Help for parents.* Bowling Green, KY: Parents Press.

Comaty, J. E., Stasio, M., & Advokat, C. (2001). Analysis of outcome variables of a token economy system in a state psychiatric hospital: A program evaluation. *Research in Developmental Disabilities, 22,* 233–253.

Compas, B. E. (1993). Promoting positive mental health during adolescence. In S. G. Millstein, E. O. Nightingale, and A. C. Petersen (Eds.), *Promoting the health of adolescents: New directions for the twenty-first century.* Oxford, UK: Oxford University Press.

Cone, J. D. (1997). Issues in functional analysis in behavioral assessment. *Behavior Research and Therapy, 35,* 259–275.

Cooper, J. O., Heron, T. E., & Heward, W. L. (1987). *Applied behavior analysis.* Columbus, OH: Merrill.

Corbett, L. O., & Corbett, N. J. (1996). Covert conditioning in behavioral medicine. In J. R. Cautela & W. Ishaq (Eds.), *Contemporary issues in behavior therapy: Improving the human condition* (pp. 23–43). New York: Plenum.

Craighead, L. W., Craighead, W. E., Kazdin, A. E., & Mahoney, M. J. (1994). *Cognitive and behavioral interventions: An empirical approach to mental health problems.* Boston: Allyn & Bacon.

Craighead, W. E., Meyers, A. W., & Craighead, L. W. (1985). A conceptual model for cognitive-behavior therapy with children. *Journal of Abnormal Child Psychology, 13,* 331–342.

Crone, D. A., & Horner, R. H. (2003). Building positive behavior support systems in schools: Functional behavioral assessment. New York: Guilford Press.

Culbert, T. P., & Banez, G. A. (2003). Pediatric applications other than headache. In M. S. Schwartz & F. Andrasik (Eds.), *Biofeedback: A practitioner's guide* (3rd ed., pp. 696–724). New York: Guilford Press.

D'Zurilla, T. J. (1986). *Problem-solving therapy: A social competence approach to clinical intervention.* New York: Springer.

D'Zurilla, T. J., & Goldfriend, M. R. (1971). Problem solving and behavior modification. *Journal of Abnormal Psychology, 78,* 107–126.

Dadds, H. R. (1995). *Families, children and the development of dysfunction.* Thousand Oaks, CA: Sage.

Dadds, M. R., & Barrett, P. M. (1996). Family processes in child and adolescent anxiety and depression. *Behaviour Change, 13,* 231–239.

Dadds, M., Bovbjerg, D. H., Redd, W. H., & Cutmore, T. R. (1997). Imagery in human classical conditioning. *Psychological Bulletin, 122,* 89–103.

Dahlquist, L. M. (1999). Pediatric pain management. In M. C. Roberts & A. M. La Greca (Eds.), *Clinical child psychology library.* New York: Kluwer Academic/Plenum.

Danaher, B. C. (1974). Theoretical foundations and clinical applications of the Premack principle: Review and critique. *Behavior Therapy, 5,* 307–324.

Danforth, J. S. (1998). The behavior management flow chart: A component analysis of behavior management strategies. *Clinical Psychology Review, 18,* 229–257.

Dangel, R. F., Deschner, J. P., & Rasp, R. R. (1989). Anger control training for adolescents in residential treatment. *Behavior Modification, 13,* 447–458.

Day, R., Rea, J., Schussler, N., Larsen, S., & Johnson, W. (1988). A functionally based approach to the treatment of self-injurious behavior. *Behavior Modification, 12,* 565–589.

Deacon, J. R., & Konarski, E. A. (1987). Correspondence training: An example of rule-governed behavior? *Journal of Applied Behavior Analysis, 20,* 391–400.

Deblinger, E., Stauffer, L. B., & Steer, R. A. (2001). Comparative efficacies of supportive and cognitive behavioral group therapies for young children who have been sexually abused and their nonoffending mothers. *Child Maltreatment, 6,* 332–343.

Deffenbacher, J. L. (1999). Cognitive-behavioral conceptualization and treatment of anger. *JCLP/In Session: Psychotherapy in Practice, 55,* 295–309.

DeGrandpre, R. J., & Bickel, W. K. (1993). Stimulus control and drug dependence. *Psychological Record, 43,* 651–666.

Deitz, S. M. (1977). An analysis of programming DRL schedules in educational settings. *Behavior Research and Therapy, 15,* 103–111.

Deitz, S. M., & Malone, L. W. (1985). Stimulus control terminology. *The Behavior Analyst, 8,* 259–264.

Demetral, G. D., & Lutzker, J. R. (1981). The parameters of facial screening in treating self-injurious behavior. *Behavior Research of Severe Developmental Disabilities, 1,* 261–277.

DiLorenzo, T. M. (1988). Operant and classical conditioning. In J. L. Matson (Ed.), *Handbook of treatment approaches in childhood psychopathology* (pp. 65–78). New York: Kluwer Academic Press.

Dobson, K. S. (2001). *Handbook of cognitive-behavioral therapies* (2nd ed.). New York: Guilford Press.

Doleys, D. M. (1977). Dry-bed training and retention control training: A comparison. *Behavior Therapy, 8,* 541–548.

Domjan, M., & Burkhard, B. (1986). *The principles of learning and behavior* (2nd ed.). Belmont, CA: Brooks/Cole.

Donahoe, J., & Palmer, D. (1994). *Learning and complex behavior.* Boston: Allyn & Bacon.

Drabman, R. S., & Creedon, D. L. (1979). Beat the buzzer. *Child Behavior Therapy, 1,* 295–296.

Drabman, R. S., & Creedon, D. L. (1979). Marking time-out: A procedure for away from home disruptive behavior. *Child Behavior Therapy, 1,* 99–101.

Dube, W.V., Moniz, D. H., & Gomes, J. F. (1995). Use of computer and teacher-delivered prompts in discrimination training with individuals who have mental retardation. *American Journal on Mental Retardation, 100,* 253–261.

Ducharme, J. M. (1996). Errorless compliance training: Optimizing clinical efficacy. *Behavior Modification, 20,* 259–280.

Ducharme, J. M., Atkinson, L., & Poulton, L. (2000). Success-based, non-coercive treatment of oppositional behavior in children from violent homes. *Journal of the American Academy of Child and Adolescent Psychiatry, 39,* 995–1003.

Ducharme, J. M., Spencer, T., Davidson, A., & Rushford, N. (2002). Errorless compliance training: Building a cooperative relationship between brain-injured parents at risk for maltreatment and their oppositional children. *American Journal of Orthopsychiatry, 72,* 585–595.

Duker, P. C., & Nielen, M. (1993). The use of negative practice for the control of pica behavior. *Journal of Behavior Therapy and Experimental Psychiatry, 24,* 249–253.

Dunlap, L. K., & Dunlap, G. (1989). A self-monitoring package for teaching subtraction with regrouping to students with learning disabilities. *Journal of Applied Behavior Analysis, 22,* 309–314.

Durand, V. M. (1990). *Severe behavior problems: A functional communication training approach.* New York: Guilford Press.

Durand, V. M. (1999). Functional communication training using assistive devices: Recruiting natural communities of reinforcement. *Journal of Applied Behavior Analysis, 32,* 247–267.

Durand, V. M., & Carr, E. G. (1991). Functional communication training to reduce challenging behavior: Maintenance and application in new settings. *Journal of Applied Behavior Analysis, 24,* 251–264.

Durand, V. M., & Carr, E. G. (1992). An analysis of maintenance following functional communication training. *Journal of Applied Behavior Analysis, 25,* 777–794.

Durand, V. M., & Crimmins, D. B. (1992). *The Motivation Assessment Scale (MAS) administration guide.* Topeka, KS: Monaco & Associates.

Eifert, G. H., & Evans, I. M. (Eds.). (1990). *Unifying behavior therapy: Contributions of paradigmatic behaviorism.* New York: Springer.

Eifert, G. H., Evans, I. M., & McKendrick, V. G. (1990). Matching treatments to client problems not diagnostic labels: A case for paradigmatic behavior therapy. *Journal of Behavior, Therapy, & Experimental Psychiatry, 3,* 163–172.

Eifert, G. H., Schulte, D., Zvolensky, M. J., Lejuez, C. W., & Lau, A. W. (1998). Manualized behavior therapy: Merits and challenges. *Behavior Therapy, 28,* 499–509.

Eisen, A. R., Kearney, C. A., & Schaefer, C. E. (1995). *Clinical handbook of anxiety disorders in children and adolescents.* Northvale, NJ: Jason Aronson Press.

Elias, M. J., & Tobias, S. E. (1996*). Social problem solving: Interventions in the schools.* New York: Guilford Press.

Elliott, S. N., & Gresham, F. M. (1993). Social skills interventions for children. *Behavior Modification, 17,* 287–313.

Elliott, S. N., Gresham, F. M., & Heffer, R. W. (1987). Social skill interventions: Research findings and training techniques. In C. Maher & J. E. Zins (Eds.), *Psychoeducational interventions in the schools: Methods and procedures for enhancing student competence* (pp. 141–159). Elmsford, NY: Pergamon Press.

Ellis, A. (1973). *Humanistic psychotherapy: The rational-emotive approach.* New York: Julian Press.

Epstein, L. H., Myers, M. D., Raynor, H. A., & Saelens, B. E. (1998). Treatment of pediatric obesity. *Pediatrics, 101,* 554–570.

Ervin, R. (2002). School based interventions for ADHD. In K. Lane, F. Gresham, & T. O'Shaughnessy (Eds.), *Interventions for students with or at-risk for emotional and behavior disorders.* Needham Heights, MA: Allyn & Bacon.

Esveldt-Dawson, K., & Kazdin, A. E. (1998). *How to maintain behavior* (2nd ed.). Austin, TX: Pro-Ed.

Eyberg, S. M., Funderburk, B. W., Hembree-Kigin, T. L., McNeil, C. B., Querido, J. G., & Hood, K. (2001). Parent-child interaction therapy with behavior problem children: One and two year maintenance of treatment effects in the family. *Child & Family Behavior Therapy, 23,* 1–20.

Eysenck, H. J. (1952). The effects of psychotherapy: An evaluation. *Journal of Consulting Psychology, 16,* 319–324.

Fattu, N. A., Mech, E. V., & Auble, D. (1955). Partial reinforcement related to "free" responding in extinction with pre-school children. *Journal of Experimental Education, 23,* 365–368.

Fehr, A., & Beckwith, B. E. (1989). Water misting: Treating self-injurious behavior in a multiply handicapped, visually impaired child. *Journal of Visual Impairment & Blindness, 83,* 245–248.

Feindler, E. L. (1995). An ideal treatment package for children and adolescents with anger disorders. In H. Kassinove (Ed.), *Anger disorders: Definition, diagnosis, and treatment* (pp. 173–194). New York: Taylor & Francis.

Feindler, E. L., & Ecton, R. B. (1990). Anger control training for temper control disorders. In E. L. Feindler & G. R. Kalfus (Eds.), *Adolescent behavior therapy handbook* (pp. 351–371). New York: Springer.

Feindler, E. L., & Guttman, J. (1994). Cognitive-behavioral anger control training for groups of adolescents: A treatment manual. In C. W. LeCroy (Ed.), *Handbook of child and adolescent treatment manuals* (pp. 170–199). New York: Lexington Books.

Ferber, R. (2002). *Solve your child's sleep problems.* New York: Simon & Schuster.

Ferster, C. B., & Skinner, B. F. (1957). *Schedules of reinforcement.* New York: Appleton-Century-Crofts.

Finley, G. A., & McGrath, P. J. (Eds.). (2001). *Progress in pain research and management.* Seattle, WA: IASP Press.

Foa, E. B., Zoellner, L., Feeny, N. C., Hembree, E. A., & Alvarex-Conrad, J. (2002). Does imaginal exposure exacerbate PTSD symptoms? *Journal of Consulting and Clinical Psychology, 70,* 1022–1028.

Follette, W. C., Naugle, A. E., & Linnerooth, P. J. N. (2000). Functional alternatives to traditional assessment and diagnosis. In M. J. Dougher (Ed.), *Clinical behavior analysis* (pp. 99–125). Reno, NV: Context Press.

Foot, H. C., Morgan, M. J., & Shute, R. H. (1990). *Children helping children.* New York: John Wiley.

Forehand, R. L., & McMahon, R. J. (1981). *Helping the non-compliant child: A clinician's guide to parent training.* New York: Guilford Press.

Forgatch, M. S., & DeGarmo, D. S. (1999). Parenting through change: An effective prevention program for single mothers. *Journal of Consulting and Clinical Psychology, 67,* 711–724.

Forman, S. G. (1993). *Coping skills interventions for children and adolescents.* San Francisco: Jossey-Bass.

Foster, S. L., Kendall, P. C., & Guevremont, D. C. (1988). Cognitive and social learning theories. In J. L. Matson (Ed.), *Handbook of treatment approaches in childhood psychopathology: Applied clinical psychology* (pp. 79–117). New York: Plenum.

Fox, J. J., & McEvoy, M. A. (1993). Assessing and enhancing generalization and social validity of social-skills interventions with children and adolescents. *Behavior Modification, 17,* 339–366.

Foxx, R. M. (1996). Twenty years of applied behavior analysis in treating the most severe problem behavior: Lessons learned. *The Behavior Analyst, 19,* 225–235.

Foxx, R. M., & Azrin, N. H. (1972). Restitution: A method of eliminating aggressive-disruptive behavior of retarded and brain damaged patients. *Behaviour Research and Therapy, 10,* 15–27.

Foxx, R. M., & Azrin, N. H. (1973). The elimination of autistic self-stimulatory behavior by overcorrection. *Journal of Applied Behavior Analysis, 6,* 1–14.

Foxx, R. M., & Bechtel, D. R. (1983). Overcorrection: A review and analysis. In S. Axelrod & J. Apsche (Eds.), *The effects of punishment on human behavior* (pp. 133–220). New York: Academic Press.

Foxx, R. M., & Livesay, J. (1984). Maintenance of response suppression following overcorrection: A 10-year retrospective examination of eight cases. *Analysis and Intervention in Developmental Disabilities, 4,* 65–79.

France, R., & Robson, M. (1997). *Cognitive behavioral therapy in primary care: A practical guide.* Bristol, PA: Jessica Kingsley.

Frankel, F., Cantwell, D. P., & Myatt, R. (1996). Helping ostracized children: Social skills training and parent support for socially rejected children. In E. D. Hibbs & P. S. Jensen (Eds.), *Psychosocial treatments for child and adolescent disorders: Empirically based strategies for clinical practice.* Washington, DC: American Psychological Association.

Frankel, F., Myatt, R., Cantwell, D. P., & Feinberg, D. T. (1997). Parent-assisted transfer of children's social skills training: Effects on children with and without attention-deficit hyperactivity disorder. *Journal of the American Academy of Child and Adolescent Psychiatry, 36,* 1056–1064.

Franklin, M. E., Abramowitz, J. S., Kozak, M. J., Levitt, J. T., & Foa, E. B. (2000). Effectiveness of exposure and ritual prevention for obsessive-compulsive disorder: Randomized compared with nonrandomized samples. *Journal of Consulting and Clinical Psychology, 68,* 594–602.

Freeland, J. T., & Noell, G. H. (2002). Programming for maintenance: An investigation of delayed intermittent reinforcement and common stimuli to create indiscriminable contingencies. *Journal of Behavioral Education, 11,* 5–18.

Freeman, K. A., & Miller, C. O. (2003). Behavioral case conceptualization for children and adolescents. In M. Hersen (Ed.), *Clinical behavior therapy: Adults and children.* New York: John Wiley.

Fried, R. (2000). Breathing as a clinical tool. In David I. Mostofsky and David H. Barlow (Eds.), *The management of stress and anxiety in medical disorders* (pp. 100–118). Boston: Allyn & Bacon.

Friman, P. C., & Blum, N. J. (2003). Behavioral pediatrics: Primary care behavioral pediatrics. In M. Hersen and W. Sledge (Eds.), *Encyclopedia of psychotherapy* (pp. 379–399). New York: Academic Press.

Friman, P. C., & Jones, K. M. (1998). Elimination disorders in children. In S. Watson & F. Gresham (Eds.), *Handbook of child behavior therapy* (pp. 239–260). New York: Plenum.

Friman, P. C., Cook, J. W., & Finney, J. W. (1984). Effects of punishment procedures on the self-stimulatory behavior of an autistic child. *Analysis & Intervention in Developmental Disabilities, 41,* 39–46.

Gable, R. A., Quinn, M. M., Rutherford, R. B., Jr., Howell, K. W., & Hoffman, C. C. (1998). *Addressing student problem behavior: Part II. Conducting a functional behavioral assessment* (3rd ed.). Washington, DC: Center for Effective Collaboration and Practice.

Garb, H. N. (1996). *Studying the clinician: Judgment research and psychological assessment.* Washington, DC: American Psychological Association.

Gershon, J., Anderson, P., Graap, K., Zimand, E., Hodges, L., & Rothbaum, B. O. (2002). Virtual reality exposure therapy in the treatment of anxiety disorders. *Scientific Review of Mental Health Practice, 1,* 78–83.

Gershon, J., Zimand, E., Lemos, R., Rothbaum, B. O., & Hodges, L. (2003). *Use of virtual reality distracter for painful medical procedures with pediatric cancer: A case study.* Manuscript submitted for publication.

Gershon, J., Zimand, E., Pickering, M., Lemos, R., Rothbaum, B. O., & Hodges, L. (2003). *A pilot study of virtual reality as a distraction during an invasive medical procedure for children with cancer.* Manuscript submitted for publication.

Gilbert, C., & Moss, D. (2003). Biofeedback. In D. Moss, A. McGrady, T. Davies, & I. Wickramasekera (Eds.), *Handbook of mind body medicine for primary care* (pp. 109–122). Thousand Oaks, CA: Sage.

Gilchrist, L. D., Schinke, S. P., & Maxwell, J. S. (1987). Life skills counseling for preventing problems in adolescence. *Journal of Social Service Research, 10,* 73–84.

Glynn, S. M. (1990). Token economy approaches for psychiatric patients: Progress and pitfalls over 25 years. *Behavior Modification, 14,* 383–407.

Goh, H., Iwata, B. A., & DeLeon, I. G. (2000). Competition between noncontingent and contingent reinforcement schedules during response acquisition. *Journal of Applied Behavior Analysis, 33,* 195–205.

Goldfield, G. S., Raynor, H. A., & Epstein, L. H. (2002). Treatment of pediatric obesity. In T. A. Wadden, &

A. J. Stunkard (Eds.), *Handbook of obesity treatment* (pp. 532–555). New York: Guilford Press.

Goldfried, M. R., Decenteceo, E. T., & Weinberg, L. (1974). Systematic rational restructuring as a self-control technique. *Behavior Therapy, 5,* 247–254.

Grace, N., Spirito, A., Finch, A. J., & Ott, E. S. (1993). Coping skills for anxiety control in children. In A. J. Finch, M. W. Nelson, & E. S. Ott (Eds.), *Cognitive-behavioral procedures with children and adolescents: A practical guide* (pp. 257–288). Boston: Allyn & Bacon.

Graham, S., & Freeman, S. (1986). Strategy training and teacher vs. student-controlled study conditions: Effects on LD students' spelling performance. *Learning Disability Quarterly, 9,* 15–22.

Green, G. (2001). Behavior analytic instruction for learners with autism: Advances in stimulus control technology. *Focus on Autism and Other Developmental Disabilities, 16,* 72–85.

Greenspan, S. I. (1981). *The clinical interview of the child.* New York: McGraw-Hill.

Gresham, F. M. (1979). Comparison of response cost and time-out in a special education setting. *Journal of Abnormal Child Psychology, 13,* 199–208.

Gresham, F. M. (1998). Social skills training with children: Social learning and applied behavioral analytic approaches. In T. S. Watson & F. S. Gresham (Eds.), *Handbook of child behavior therapy* (pp. 475–497). New York: Plenum.

Gresham, F. M., & Elliot, S. N. (1984). Assessment and classification of children's social skills: A review of methods and issues. *School Psychology Review, 13,* 292–301.

Griest, D. L., & Wells, K. C. (1983). Behavioral family therapy with conduct disorders in children. *Behavior Therapy, 14,* 37–53.

Gross, A. M., Wright, B., & Drabman, R. S. (1980). The empirical selection of a punisher for a retarded child's self-injurious behavior: A case study. *Child Behavior Therapy, 2,* 59–65.

Guevremont, D. C., Osnes, P. G., & Stokes, T. F. (1986). Programming maintenance after correspondence training interventions with children. *Journal of Applied Behavior Analysis, 19,* 215–219.

Gunther, L. M., Denniston, J. C., & Miller, R. R. (1998). Conducting exposure treatment in multiple contexts can prevent relapse. *Behaviour Research and Therapy, 36,* 75–91.

Guthrie, E. R. (1952). *The psychology of learning.* New York: Harper.

Haddock, C. K., Shadish, W. R., Klesges, R. C., & Stein, R. J. (1994). Treatments for childhood and adolescent obesity. *Annals of Behavioral Medicine, 16,* 235–244.

Hagopian, L. P., & Adelinis, J. D. (2001). Response blocking with and without redirection for the treatment of pica. *Journal of Applied Behavior Analysis, 34,* 527–530.

Hagopian, L. P., Crockett, J. L., van Stone, M., DeLeon, I. G., & Bowman, L. G. (2000). Effects of noncontingent reinforcement on problem behavior and stimulus engagement: The role of satiation, extinction, and alternative reinforcement. *Journal of Applied Behavior Analysis, 33,* 433–449.

Haley, J. (1987). *Problem solving therapy* (2nd ed.). San Francisco: Jossey-Bass.

Hall, R. V., & Hall, M. L. (1998). How to use time-out (2nd ed.). In R. V. Hall & M. L. Hall (Series Eds.), *How to manage behavior series.* Austin, TX: Pro-ed.

Hallahan, D. P., & Sapona, R. (1983). Self-monitoring of attention with learning-disabled children: Past research and current issues. *Journal of Learning Disabilities, 16,* 616–620.

Hallahan, D. P., Tarver, S. G., Kauffman, J. M., & Graybeal, I. L. (1978). Selective attention abilities of learning disabled children under reinforcement and response cost. *Journal of Learning Disabilities, 11,* 39–47.

Halle, J. W., Baer, D. M., & Spradlin, J. E. (1981). Teachers' generalized use of delay as a stimulus control procedure to increase language use by handicapped children. *Journal of Applied Behavior Analysis, 14,* 389–409.

Hanley, G. P., Iwata, B. A., & McCord, B. E. (2003). Functional analysis of problem behavior: A review. *Journal of Applied Behavior Analysis, 36,* 147–185.

Hanley, G. P., Iwata, B. A., & Thompson, R. H. (2001). Reinforcement schedule thinning following treatment with functional communication training. *Journal of Applied Behavior Analysis, 34,* 17–38.

Harris, K. (1986). Self-monitoring of attentional behavior versus self-monitoring of productivity effects on on-task behavior and academic response rate among learning disabled children. *Journal of Applied Behavior Analysis, 19,* 417–423.

Harris, K. R. (1985). Definitional, parametric, and procedural considerations in time-out interventions and research. *Exceptional children, 52,* 279–288.

Hawkins, J. D., Catalano, R. F., & Miller, J. Y. (1992). Risk and protective factors for alcohol and other drug problems in adolescence and early adulthood: Implications for substance abuse prevention. *Psychological Bulletin, 112,* 64–105.

Hayes, S. C., & Follette, W. C. (1992). Can functional analysis provide a substitute for syndromal classification? *Behavioral Assessment, 14,* 345–365.

Hayes, S. C., Strosahl, K. D., & Wilson, K. G. (1999). *Acceptance and commitment therapy.* New York: Guilford Press.

Haynes, S. N. (1992). *Models of causality in psychopathology: Toward dynamic, synthetic and nonlinear models of behavior disorders.* New York: Macmillan.

Haynes, S. N., & Heiby, E. M. (Eds.). (2003). *Behavioral assessment.* New York: Wiley.

Haynes, S. N., & O'Brien, W. H. (1990). Functional analysis in behavior therapy. *Clinical Psychology Review, 10,* 649–668.

Haynes, S. N., & O'Brien, W. H. (2000). *Principles and practice of behavioral assessment.* New York: Kluwer.

Hembree-Kigin, T. L., & McNeil, C. B. (1995). *Parent-child interaction therapy.* New York: Plenum.

Henggeler, S. W., & Lee, T. (2003). Multisystemic treatment of serious clinical problems. In A. E. Kazdin and J. R. Weisz (Eds.), *Evidence-based psychotherapies for children and adolescents* (pp. 301–322). New York: Guilford Press.

Henggeler, S. W., Melton, G. B., & Smith, L. A. (1992). Family preservation using multisystemic therapy: An effective alternative to incarcerating serious juvenile offenders. *Journal of Consulting and Clinical Psychology, 60,* 953–961.

Henggeler, S. W., Schoenwald, S. K., Borduin, C. M., Rowland, M. D., & Cunningham, P. B. (1998). *Multisystemic treatment of antisocial behavior in children and adolescents.* New York: Guilford Press.

Henggeler, S. W., Schoenwald, S. K., Rowland, M. D., & Cunningham, P. B. (2002). *Serious emotional disturbance in children and adolescents: Multisystemic therapy.* New York: Guilford Press.

Herbert, M. (2003). *Typical and atypical development: From conception to adolescence.* Oxford, UK: BPS-Blackwell.

Herbert, M., & Wookey, J. (2003). *Managing disruptive behavior: The Child-Wise approach.* Chichester, UK: Wiley.

Herschell, A., Calzada, E. J., Eyberg, S. M., & McNeil, C. B. (2002). Clinical issues in parent-child interaction therapy. *Cognitive and Behavioral Practice, 9,* 16–27.

Herschell, A., Calzada, E. J., Eyberg, S. M., & McNeil, C. B. (2002). Parent-child interaction therapy: New directions in research. *Cognitive and Behavioral Practice, 9,* 9–16.

Hersen, M. (2002). *Clinical behavior therapy: Adults and children.* New York: John Wiley.

Hersen, M., & Van Hasselt, V. B. (Eds.). (1987). *Behavior therapy with children and adolescents: A clinical approach.* New York: John Wiley.

Hiebert, B., Kirby, B., & Jaknavorian, A. (1989). School-based relaxation: Attempting primary prevention. *Canadian Journal of Counselling, 23,* 273–287.

Hill, J. H., Liebert, R. M., & Mott, D. E. (1968). Vicarious extinction of avoidance behavior through films: An initial test. *Psychological Reports, 22,* 192.

Hiss, H., Foa, E. B., & Kozak, M. J. (1994). Relapse prevention program for treatment of obsessive-compulsive disorder. *Journal of Consulting and Clinical Psychology, 62,* 801–808.

Hoffman, H. G., Doctor, J. N., Perterson, D. R., Carrougher, G. J., & Furness, T. A. (2000). Virtual reality as an adjunctive pain control during burn wound care in adolescent patients. *Pain, 85,* 305–309.

Hood, K. K., & Eyberg, S. M. (2003). Outcomes of parent-child interaction therapy: Mothers' reports on maintenance three to six years later. *Journal of Clinical Child and Adolescent Psychology, 32,* 430–441.

Hops, H., & Lewinsohn, P. M. (1995). A course for the treatment of depression among adolescence. In K. D. Craig & K. S. Dobson (Eds.), *Anxiety and depression in adults and children* (pp. 230–245). Thousand Oaks, CA: Sage.

Horner, R. H., & Day, H. M. (1991). The effects of response efficiency on functionally equivalent competing behaviors. *Journal of Applied Behavior Analysis, 24,* 719–732.

Horton, S. V. (1987). Reduction of disruptive mealtime behavior by facial screening. *Behavior Modification, 11,* 53–64.

Houts, A. C. (1991). Childhood enuresis as a biobehavioral problem. *Behavior Therapy, 22,* 133–151.

Houts, A. C. (2003). Behavioral treatment for enuresis. In A. E. Kazdin & J. R. Weisz (Eds.), *Evidence-based psychotherapies for children and adolescents* (pp. 389–406). New York: Guilford Press.

Houts, A. C., & Liebert, R. M. (1984). *Bed-wetting: A guide for parents and children.* Springfield, IL: Charles C. Thomas.

Houts, A. C., Berman, J. S., & Abramson, H. A. (1994). The effectiveness of psychological and pharmacological treatments for nocturnal enuresis. *Journal of Consulting and Clinical Psychology, 62,* 737–745.

Hudson, A., Vincent, J., Wilks, R., & Drabman, R. (1986). "Beat the Buzzer" for early morning dawdling: Two case illustrations. *Behaviour Change, 2,* 136–142.

Hupp, S. D. A., & Reitman, D. (1999). Improving sports skills and sportsmanship in children diagnosed with attention-deficit hyperactivity disorder. *Child and Family Behavior Therapy, 21,* 35–51.

Hupp, S. D. A., Reitman, D., Northup, J., O'Callaghan, P., & LeBlanc, M. (2002). The effects of delayed rewards, tokens, and stimulant medication on sportsmanlike behavior with ADHD-diagnosed children. *Behavior Modification, 26,* 148–162.

Hutton, J. B. (1983). How to decrease problem behavior at school by rewarding desirable behavior at home. *Pointer, 27,* 25–28.

Irvin, J. E., Bowers, C. A., Dunn, M. E., & Wang, M. C. (1999). Efficacy of relapse prevention: A meta-analytic review. *Journal of Consulting and Clinical Psychology, 67,* 563–570.

Israel, A. C., & O'Leary, K. D. (1973). Developing correspondence between children's words and deeds. *Child Development, 44,* 577–581.

Iwata, B. A., Pace, G. M., Cowdery, G. E., & Miltenberger, R. G. (1994). What makes extinction work: An analysis of procedural form and function. *Journal of Applied Behavior Analysis, 27,* 131–144.

Iwata, B. A., Smith, R. G., & Michael, J. L. (2000). Current research on the influence of establishing operations on behavior in applied settings. *Journal of Applied Behavior Analysis, 33,* 411–418.

Iwata, B. A., Vollmer, T. R., Zarcone, J. R., & Rogers, T. A. (1993). Treatment classification and selection based on behavioral function. In R. Van Houten & S. Axelrod (Eds.), *Behavior analysis and treatment* (pp. 101–125). New York: Plenum.

Iwata, B. A., Wallace, M. D., Kahng, S., Lindberg, J. S., Roscoe, E. M., Conners, J., et al. (2000). Skill acquisition in the implementation of functional analysis methodology. *Journal of Applied Behavior Analysis, 33,* 181–194.

Jenike, M. A. (1983). Obsessive compulsive disorder. *Comprehensive Psychiatry, 24,* 99–115.

Jensen, P. S., Bhatara, V. S., Vitiello, B., Hoagwood, K., Feil, M., & Burke, L. B. (1999). Psychoactive medication prescribing practices for U.S. children: Gaps between research and clinical practice. *Journal of the American Academy of Child and Adolescent Psychiatry, 38,* 557–565.

Johnson-Martin, N., Attermeier, S., & Hacker, B. (1990). *The Carolina curriculum for preschoolers with special needs.* Baltimore: Paul H. Brookes.

Jonassen, D., Hannum, W., & Tessmer, M. (1989). *Handbook of task analysis procedures.* New York: Praeger.

Jones, K. M., Wickstrom, K. F., & Friman, P. F. (1997). The effects of observational feedback on treatment integrity in school-based behavioral consultation. *School Psychology Quarterly, 12,* 316–326.

Jones, M. C. (1924). The elimination of children's fears. *Journal of Experimental Psychology, 7,* 382–390.

Jones, R. S., & Baker, L. J. (1990). Differential reinforcement and challenging behaviour: A critical review of the DRI schedule. *Behavioural Psychotherapy, 18,* 35–47.

Kahle, A. L., & Kelley, M. L. (1994). Children's homework problems: A comparison of goal setting and parent training. *Behavior Therapy, 25,* 275–290.

Kanfer, F. H., & Gaelick-Buys, L. (1991). Self-management methods. In F. H. Kanfer & A. P. Goldstein (Eds.), *Helping people change* (pp. 305–360). New York: Pergamon Press.

Kanger, F. H. (1960). Incentive value of generalized reinforcers. *Psychological Reports, 7,* 531–538.

Kaplan, J. S., & Carter, J. (1995). *Beyond behavior modification: A Cognitive-behavioral approach to behavioral management in the school* (3rd ed.). Austin, TX: Pro-Ed.

Kavale, K. A., Mathur, S. R., Forness, S. R., Rutherford, R. G., & Quinn, M. M. (1997). The effectiveness of social skills training for students with emotional or behavioral disorders: A meta-analysis. In T. E. Scruggs & M. A. Mastropieri (Eds.), *Advances in learning and behavioral disabilities* (Vol. 11, pp. 1–26). Greenwich, CT: JAI Press.

Kazdin, A. (2003). *Research design in clinical psychology* (4th ed.). Needham Heights, MA: Allyn & Bacon.

Kazdin, A. E. (1972). Response cost: The removal of conditioned reinforcers for therapeutic change. *Behavior Therapy, 3,* 533–546.

Kazdin, A. E. (1977). *The token economy: A review and evaluation* (pp. 157–158). New York: Plenum.

Kazdin, A. E. (1982). The token economy: A decade later. *Journal of Applied Behavior Analysis, 15,* 431–445.

Kazdin, A. E. (2000). *Psychotherapy for children and adolescents.* New York: Oxford University Press.

Kazdin, A. E. (2001). *Behavior modification in applied settings,* (6th ed.). Belmont, CA: Wadsworth.

Kazdin, A. E. (2001). Self-control techniques. In A. E. Kazdin, *Behavior modification in applied settings.* Belmont, CA: Wadsworth.

Kazdin, A. E. (Ed.). (2003). *Methodological issues and strategies in clinical research* (3rd ed.). Washington, DC: American Psychological Association.

Kazdin, A. E., & Bootzin, R. R. (1972). The token economy: An evaluative review. *Journal of Applied Behavior Analysis, 5,* 343–372.

Kazdin, A. E., & Weisz, J. R. (1998). Identifying and developing empirically supported child and adolescent treatments. *Journal of Consulting and Clinical Psychology, 66,* 19–36.

Kazdin, A. E., Siegel, T. C., & Bass, D. (1992). Cognitive problem-solving skills training and parent management training in the treatment of antisocial behavior in children. *Journal of Consulting and Clinical Psychology, 60,* 733–747.

Kearney, C. A., & Albano, A. M. (2000). *When children refuse school: A cognitive-behavioral therapy approach/therapist's guide.* San Antonio, TX: Psychological Corporation.

Kearney, C. A., & Drabman, R. S. (1993). The write-say method for improving spelling accuracy in children with learning disabilities. *Journal of Learning Disabilities, 26,* 52–56.

Keenan, K. (2000). Emotion dysregulation as a risk factor for child psychopathology. *Clinical Psychology: Science and Practice, 7,* 418–434.

Kellam, S. G., Ling, X., Merisca, R., Brown, C. H., & Ialongo, N. (1998). The effect of the level of aggression in the first grade classroom on the course and malleability of aggressive behavior into middle school. *Development and Psychopathology, 10,* 165–185.

Kelley, M. E., Lerman, D. C., & Van Camp, C. M. (2002). The effects of competing reinforcement schedules on the acquisition of functional communication. *Journal of Applied Behavior Analysis, 35,* 59–63.

Kelley, M. L. (1990). *School-home notes: Promoting children's classroom success.* New York: Guilford Press.

Kelly, J. A. (1982). *Social skills training: A practical guide for interventions.* New York: Springer.

Kendall, P. C. (1991). *Child and adolescent therapy: Cognitive-behavioral procedures.* New York: Guilford Press.

Kendall, P. C. (1992). *Coping cat workbook.* Ardmore, PA: Workbook.

Kendall, P. C. (2000). *Cognitive-behavioral therapy for anxious children: Therapist manual.* Ardmore, PA: Workbook.

Kendall, P. C., & Braswell, L. (1993). *Cognitive-behavioral therapy for impulsive children.* New York: Guilford Press.

Kendall, P. C., & Treadwell, K. R. H. (1996). Cognitive-behavioral treatment for childhood anxiety disorders. In E. O. Hibbs and P. S. Jensen (Eds.), *Psychosocial treatments for child and adolescent disorders: Empirically based strategies for clinical practice* (pp. 23–42). Washington, DC: American Psychological Association.

Kendall, P. C., Butcher, J. N., & Holmbeck, G. N. (Eds.). (1999). *Handbook of research methods in clinical psychology* (2nd ed.). New York: Wiley.

Kendall, P. C., Chansky, T. E., Friedman, M., Kim, R., Kortlander, E., Sessa, F. M., & Siqueland, L. (1991). Treating anxiety disorders in children and adolescents. In P. C. Kendall (Ed.), *Child and adolescent therapy: Cognitive-behavioral procedures* (pp. 131–164). New York: Guilford Press.

Kendall, P. C., Chansky, T. E., Kane, M. T., Kim, R., Kortlander, E., Ronan, K. R., et al. (1992). *Anxiety disorders in youth: Cognitive-behavioral interventions.* Needham Heights, MA: Allyn & Bacon.

Kendall, P. C., Chu, B., Gifford, A., Hayes, C., & Nauta, M. (1998). Breathing life into a manual: Flexibility and creativity with manual-based treatments. *Cognitive & Behavioral Practice, 5,* 177–198.

Kendall, P. C., Flannery-Schroeder, E., Panichellie-Mindel, S. M., Southam-Gerow, M., Hennin, A., & Warman, M. (1997). Therapy for youths with anxiety disorders: A second randomized clinical trial. *Journal of Consulting and Clinical Psychology, 65,* 366–380.

Khalsa, S. S. (1996). *Group exercises for enhancing social skills and self-esteem.* Sarasota, FL: Professional Resource Exchange.

King, N. J., Hamilton, D. I., & Ollendick, T. H. (1988). *Children's phobias: A behavioural perspective.* Chichester, UK: John Wiley & Sons.

King, N. J., Heyne, D., Gullone, E., & Molloy, G. N. (2001). Usefulness of emotive imagery in the treatment of childhood phobias: Clinical guidelines, case examples and issues. *Counseling Psychology Quarterly, 14,* 95–101.

Kipper, D. A. (1996). The emergence of role playing as a form of psychotherapy. *Journal of Group Psychotherapy, Psychodrama and Sociometry, 49,* 99–119.

Klatt, K. P., & Morris, E. K. (2001). The Premack principle, response deprivation, and establishing operations. *The Behavior Analyst, 24,* 173–180.

Klein-Hessling, J., & Lohaus, A. (2002). Benefits and interindividual differences in children's responses to extended and intensified relaxation training. *Anxiety, Stress, and Coping, 15,* 275–288.

Koegel, L. K., Koegel, R. L., & Dunlap, G. (1996). *Positive behavioral support: Including people with difficult behavior in the community.* Baltimore: Paul H. Brookes.

Koegel, R. L., Dunlap, G., Richman, G. S., & Dyer, K. (1981). The use of specific orienting cues for teaching discrimination tasks. *Analysis and Intervention in Developmental Disabilities, 1,* 187–198.

Koeppen, A. S. (1974). Relaxation training for children. *Elementary School Guidance and Counseling,* October, 14–21.

Koeppen, A. S. (2002). Relaxation training for children. In C. E. Schaefer & D. Cangelosi (Eds.), *Play therapy techniques* (2nd ed., pp. 295–302). Northvale, NJ: Jason Aronson.

Kolko, D. J., Ayllon, T., & Torrence, C. (1987). Positive practice routines in overcoming resistance to the treatment of school phobia: A case study with follow-up. *Journal of Behavior Therapy and Experimental Psychiatry, 18,* 249–257.

Konarski, E. A., Johnson, M. R., Crowell, C. R., & Whitman, T. L. (1981). An alternative approach to reinforcement for applied researchers: Response deprivation. *Behavior Therapy, 12,* 653–666.

Kraemer, H. C., Stice, E., Kazdin, A., Offord, D., & Kupfer, D. (2001). How do risk factors work together? Mediators, moderators, and independent, overlapping, and proxy risk factors. *American Journal of Psychiatry, 158,* 848–856.

Kratchowill, T. R., Bergan, J. R., Sheridan, S. M., & Elliot, S. N. (1998). Assumptions of behavioral consultation: After all is said and done, more has been done than said. *School Psychology Quarterly, 13,* 63–80.

Kratochwill, T. R., & Levin, J. R. (1992). (Eds.). *Single-case research design and analysis: New directions for psychology and education.* Hillsdale, NJ: Erlbaum.

Krauss, R. M., Morrel-Samuels, P., & Hochberg, J. (1988). VIDEOLOGGER: A computerized multichannel event recorder for analyzing videotapes. *Behavior Research Methods, Instruments & Computers, 20,* 37–40.

Kuhn, B. R., & Weidinger, D. (2000). Interventions for infant and toddler sleep disturbance: A review. *Child and Family Behavior Therapy, 22,* 33–50.

Kuppenheimer, W. G., & Brown, R. T. (2002). Painful procedures in pediatric cancer: A comparison of interventions. *Clinical Psychology Review, 22,* 753–786.

La Vaque, T. J., Hammond, C., Trudeau, D., Monastra, V., Perry, J., Lehrer, P., et al. (2002). Template for developing guidelines for the evaluation of the clinical efficacy of psychophysiological interventions. *Applied Psychophysiology and Biofeedback, 27,* 273–281.

LaFromboise, T., & Howard-Pitney, B. (1995). The Zuni life skills development curriculum description and evaluation of a suicide prevention program. *Journal of Counseling Psychology, 42,* 479–486.

Lalli, J. S., Casey, S. D., & Kates, K. (1997). Noncontingent reinforcement as treatment for severe problem behavior: Some procedural variations. *Journal of Applied Behavior Analysis, 30,* 127–137.

Lancioni, G. E., & Smeets, P. M. (1986). Procedures and parameters of errorless discrimination training with developmentally impaired individuals. *International Review of Research in Mental Retardation, 14,* 135–164.

Landrum, T. J., & Lloyd, J. W. (1992). Generalization in social behavior research with children and youth who have emotional or behavioral disorders. *Behavior Modification, 16,* 593–616.

Lange, A. J., & Jakubowski, P. (1976). *Responsible assertive behavior.* Champaign, IL: Research Press.

Laraway, S., Snycerski, S., Michael, J., & Poling, A. (2003). Motivating variables and terms to describe them: Some further refinements. *Journal of Applied Behavior Analysis, 36,* 407–414.

Larson, J. D., Calamari, J. E., West, J. G., & Frevert, T. A. (1998). Aggression management in the residential setting: Integration of a cognitive-behavioral component. *Residential Treatment for Children and Youth, 15,* 1–9.

Larson, J., & Lochman, J. E. (2002). *Helping schoolchildren cope with anger: A cognitive-behavioral intervention.* New York: Guilford Press.

LeBlanc, L. A., Hagopian, L. P., Maglieri, K. A., & Poling, A. (2002). Decreasing the intensity of reinforcement-based interventions for reducing behavior: Conceptual issues and a proposed model for clinical practice. *The Behavior Analyst Today, 3,* 289–300.

LeBlanc, L. A., Le, L., & Carpenter, M. (2000). Behavioral treatment. In M. Hersen & R. Ammerman (Eds.), *Advanced abnormal child psychology* (2nd ed., pp. 197–218). Mahwah, NJ: Erlbaum.

LeBlanc, L. A., Patel, M. R., & Carr, J. E. (2000). Recent advances in the assessment of aberrant behavior maintained by automatic reinforcement in individuals with developmental disabilities. *Journal of Behavior Therapy & Experimental Psychiatry, 31,* 137–154.

LeCroy, C. W. (1994). *Handbook of child and adolescent treatment manuals.* New York: Free Press.

Leitenberg, H. (1965). Is time-out from positive reinforcement an aversive event? A review of the experimental evidence. *Psychological Bulletin, 64,* 428–441.

Leitenberg, H., & Callahan, E. J. (1973). Reinforced practice and reduction of different kinds of fears in adults and children. *Behavior Research and Therapy, 11,* 19–30.

Lejuez, C. W., Hopko, D. R., & Hopko, S. D. (2001). A brief behavioral activation treatment for depression: Treatment manual. *Behavior Modification, 25,* 255–286.

Lentz, F. E. (1988). Reductive procedures. In J. C. Witt, S. N. Elliott, & F. M. Gresham (Eds.), *Handbook of behavior therapy in education* (pp. 439–468). New York: Plenum.

Lerman, D. C., & Iwata, B. A. (1996). Developing a technology for the use of operant extinction in clinical settings: An examination of basic and applied research. *Journal of Applied Behavior Analysis, 29,* 345–382.

Lerman, D. C., & Vorndran, C. M. (2002). On the status of knowledge for using punishment: Implications for treating behavior disorders. *Journal of Applied Behavior Analysis, 35,* 431–464.

Lerman, D. C., Iwata, B. A., & Wallace, M. D. (1999). Side effects of extinction: Prevalence of bursting and aggression during the treatment of self-injurious behavior. *Journal of Applied Behavior Analysis, 32,* 1–8.

Lerman, D. C., Iwata, B. A., Shore, B. A., & Kahng, S. W. (1996). Responding maintained by intermittent reinforcement: Implications for the use of extinction with problem behavior in clinical settings. *Journal of Applied Behavior Analysis, 29,* 153–171.

Leslie, J. C., & O'Reilly, M. F. (1999). *Behavior analysis: Foundations and applications to psychology.* Amsterdam: Harwood Academic.

Levine, M. D., & Ramirez, R. (1989). Contingent negative practice as a homebased treatment of tics and stuttering. In C. E. Schaefer & J. M. Briesmeister (Eds.), *Handbook of parent training: Parents as co-therapists for children's behavior problems* (pp. 38–59). New York: Wiley.

Lewinsohn, P. M., & Libet, J. (1972). Pleasant events, activity schedules, and depression. *Journal of Abnormal Psychology, 79,* 291–295.

Lewis, T. J., Powers, L. J., Kelk, M. J., & Newcomer, L. I. (2002). Reducing problem behaviors on the playground: An investigation of the application of schoolwide posi-

tive behavior supports. *Psychology in the Schools, 39,* 181–190.

Lindberg, J. S., Iwata, B. A., Roscoe, E. M., Worsdell, A. S., & Hanley, G. P. (2003). Treatment efficacy of noncontingent reinforcement during brief and extended application. *Journal of Applied Behavior Analysis, 36,* 1–19.

Linehan, M. M. (1993). *Cognitive-behavioral treatment of borderline personality disorder.* New York: Guilford Press.

Linscheid, T. R. (1993). The development and evaluation of the Self-Injurious Behavior Inhibiting System: A personal perspective. In R. Van Houten & S. Axelrod (Eds.), *Behavior analysis and treatment* (pp. 345–365, xvii, 388). New York: Plenum.

Litow, L., & Pumroy, D. K. (1975). A brief review of classroom group-oriented contingencies. *Journal of Applied Behavior Analysis, 8,* 341–347.

Little, L. M., & Kelley, M. L. (1989). The efficacy of response cost procedures for reducing children's noncompliance to parental instructions. *Behavior Therapy, 20,* 525–534.

Lochman, J. E., & Dodge, K. A. (1994). Social-cognitive processes of severely violent, moderately aggressive, and non-aggressive boys. *Journal of Child Clinical Psychology, 62,* 366–374.

Lochman, J. E., Burch, P. R., Curry, J. F., & Lampron, L. B. (1984). Treatment and generalization effects of cognitive-behavioral and goal-setting interventions with aggressive boys. *Journal of Consulting and Clinical Psychology, 52,* 915–916.

Lochman, J. E., Whidby, J. M., & FitzGerald, D. P. (2000). Cognitive-behavioral assessment and treatment with aggressive children. In P. C. Kendall (Ed.), *Child and adolescent therapy: Cognitive-behavioral procedures.* New York: Guilford Press.

Locke, E. A., & Latham, G. P. (2002). Building a practically useful theory of goal setting and task motivation. *American Psychologist, 57,* 705–717.

Lockwood, K., & Bourland, G. (1982). Reduction of self-injurious behavior by reinforcement of toy use. *Mental Retardation, 20,* 169–173.

Loeber, R. (1990). Development and risk factors of juvenile antisocial behavior and delinquency. *Clinical Psychology Review, 10,* 1–41.

Loeber, R. (1991). Antisocial behavior: More enduring than changeable? *Journal of the American Academy of Child and Adolescent Psychiatry, 30,* 393–397.

Lohaus, A., & Klein-Hessling, J. (2003). Relaxation in children: Effects of extended and intensified training. *Psychology and Health, 18,* 237–249.

Lohaus, A., Klein-Hebling, J., Vogele, C., & Kuhn-Hennighausen, C. (2001). Psychophysiological effects of relaxation training in children. *British Journal of Health Psychology, 6,* 197–206.

Lombardo, T. W., & Drabman, R. S. (1985). Teaching LD children multiplication tables. *Academic Therapy, 20,* 437–442.

Lonigan, C. J., & Elbert, J. C. (Eds.). (1998). Special Issue on Empirically Supported Psychosocial Interventions for Children. *Journal of Clinical Child Psychology, 27,* 138–226.

Lovaas, I., Newsom, C., & Hickman, C. (1987). Self-stimulatory behavior and perceptual reinforcement. *Journal of Applied Behavior Analysis, 20,* 45–68.

Lovaas, O. I. (1987). Behavioral treatment and normal educational and intellectual functioning in young autistic children. *Journal of Consulting and Clinical Psychology, 55,* 3–9.

Lovaas, O. I. (2002). *Teaching individuals with developmental delays: Basic intervention techniques.* Austin, TX: Pro-Ed.

Lovaas, O. I., & Favell, J. E. (1987). Protection for clients undergoing aversive/restrictive interventions. *Education and Treatment of Children, 10,* 311–325.

Lovaas, O. I., & Simmons, J. Q. (1969). Manipulation of self-destruction in three retarded children. *Journal of Applied Behavior Analysis, 2,* 143–157.

Lovaas, O. I., Ackerman, A., Alexander, D., Firestone, P., Perkins, J., & Young, D. (1981). *Teaching developmentally disabled children: The me book.* Austin, TX: Pro-Ed.

Lovaas, O. I., Koegel, R. L., & Schreibman, L. (1979). Stimulus overselectivity in autism: A review of research. *Psychological Bulletin, 86,* 1236–1254.

Lovaas, O. I., Litronick, A., & Mann, R. (1971). Response latencies to auditory stimuli in autistic children engaged in self-stimulatory behavior. *Behavior Research and Therapy, 9,* 39–49.

Lovaas, O. I., Schreibman, L., Koegel, R., & Rehm, R. (1971). Selective responding by autistic children to multiple sensory input. *Journal of Abnormal Psychology, 77,* 211–222.

Luce, S. C., Delquadri, J., & Hall, R. V. (1980). Contingent exercise: A mild but powerful procedure for suppressing inappropriate verbal and aggressive behavior. *Journal of Applied Behavior Analysis, 13,* 583–584.

Luciano-Soriano, M. C., Molina-Lobos, F. J., & Gomez-Becerra, I. (2000). Say-do report training to change chronic behaviors in mentally retarded subjects. *Research in Developmental Disabilities, 21,* 355–366.

Luiselli, J. K. (1992). Assessment and treatment of self-injury in a deaf-blind child. *Journal of Developmental and Physical Disabilities, 4,* 219–226.

Luiselli, J. K. (1996). A transfer of stimulus control procedure applicable to toilet training programs for children with developmental disabilities. *Child and Family Behavior Therapy, 18,* 29–35.

Luiselli, J. K., & Cameron, M. J. (Eds.). (1998). *Antecedent control: Innovative approaches to behavioral support.* Baltimore: Paul H. Brookes.

Luiselli, J. K., & Reisman, J. (1980). Some variations in the use of differential reinforcement procedures with mentally retarded children in specialized treatment settings. *Applied Research in Mental Retardation, 1,* 277–288.

Lutzker, J. R. (1978). Reducing self-injurious behaviour by facial screening. *American Journal of Mental Deficiency, 82,* 510–513.

Lutzker, J. R., & Wesch, D. (1983). Facial screening: History and critical review. *Australia and New Zealand Journal of Developmental Disabilities, 9,* 209–223.

Maag, J. W. (2001). Rewarded by punishment: Reflections on the disuse of positive reinforcement in schools. *Exceptional Children, 67,* 173–186.

MacDonald, J. E., Wilder, D. A., & Dempsey, C. (2002). Brief functional analysis and treatment of eye poking. *Behavioral Interventions, 17,* 261–270.

MacDonough, T. S., & Forehand, R. (1973). Response-contingent time out: Important parameters in behavior modification with children. *Journal of Behavior Therapy and Experimental Psychiatry, 4,* 231–236.

Mace, C. F., & Roberts, M. L. (1993). Factors affecting selection of behavioral interventions. In J. Reichle & D. P. Wacker (Eds.), *Communicative alternatives to challenging behavior: Integrating functional assessment and intervention strategies* (3rd ed., pp. 113–133). Baltimore, MD: Paul H. Brookes.

MacKenzie-Keating, S. E., & McDonald, L. (1990). Overcorrection: Reviewed, revisited, and revised. *The Behavior Analyst, 13,* 39–48.

Mackintosh, N. (1983). *Conditioning and associative learning.* New York: Oxford University Press.

MacPhillamy, D., & Lewinsohn, P. M. (1971). *The pleasant events schedule.* Eugene, OR: University of Oregon.

Malott, R. W., Whaley, D. L., & Malott, M. E. (1991). *Elementary principles of behavior* (2nd ed.). Englewood Cliffs, NJ: Prentice Hall.

Malott, R.W., Malott, M. E., & Trojan, E. A. (2000). *Elementary principles of behavior* (4th ed.). Upper Saddle River, NJ: Prentice Hall.

March, J. S. (1995). Cognitive-behavioral psychotherapy for children and adolescents with OCD: A review and recommendation for treatment. *Journal of the American Academy of Child and Adolescent Psychiatry, 34,* 7–18.

March, J. S., & Mulle, K. (1996). Banishing obsessive-compulsive disorder. In E. Hibbs & P. Jensen (Eds.), *Psychosocial treatments for child and adolescent disorders* (pp. 82–103). Washington, DC: American Psychological Press.

March, J. S., & Mulle, K. (1998). *OCD in children and adolescents: A cognitive-behavioral treatment manual.* New York: Guilford Press.

March, J. S., and Mulle, K. (1996). Banishing OCD: Cognitive-behavioral psychotherapy for obsessive-compulsive disorders. In E. O. Hibbs and P. S. Jensen (Eds.), *Psychosocial treatments for child and adolescent disorders: Empirically based strategies for clinical practice* (pp. 83–102). Washington, DC: American Psychological Association.

March, J. S., Franklin, M., Nelson, A., & Foa, E. (2001). Cognitive-behavioral psychotherapy for pediatric obsessive-compulsive disorder. *Journal of Clinical Child Psychopathology, 30,* 8–18.

March, J. S., Mulle, K., & Herbel, B. (1994). Behavioral psychotherapy for children and adolescents with obsessive-compulsive disorder: An open trial of a new protocol-driven treatment package. *Journal of the American Academy of Child and Adolescent Psychiatry, 33,* 333–341.

Marholin, D., Luiselli, J. K., & Townsend, N. M. (1980). Overcorrection: An examination of its rationale and treatment effectiveness. *Progress in Behavior Modification, 9,* 383–390.

Marks, I. (1987). *Fears, phobia, and rituals: Panic, anxiety, and their disorders.* New York: Oxford University Press.

Marlatt, G. A., & Gordon, J. R. (Eds.). (1985). *Relapse prevention: Maintenance strategies in the treatment of addictive behaviors.* New York: Guilford Press.

Marsh, J. (Ed.). (1995). *Anxiety disorders in children and adolescents.* London: Guilford Press.

Martin, G. L. (1982). Thought-stopping and stimulus control to decrease persistent disturbing thoughts. *Behavior Therapy and Experimental Psychiatry, 13,* 215–220.

Martin, G., & Pear, J. (1992). *Behavior modification: What it is and how to do it.* (4th ed.). Englewood Cliffs, NJ: Prentice Hall.

Martin, G., & Pear, J. (2003). Decreasing a behavior with extinction. In G. Martin & J. Pear, *Behavior modification: What it is and how to do it* (7th ed., pp. 58–72). Upper Saddle River, NJ: Prentice Hall.

Mash, E. J., & Barkley R. A. (Eds.). (1998). *Treatment of childhood disorders* (2nd ed.). New York: Guilford Press.

Mash, E. J., & Krahn, G. (1999). Research strategies in child psychopathology. In M. Hersen & R. T. Ammerman (Eds.), *Advanced abnormal child psychology* (2nd ed., pp. 101–130). Hillsdale, NJ: Erlbaum.

Masia, C. L., Klein, R. G., Storch, E. A., & Corda, B. (2001). School-based behavioral treatment for social anxiety disorder in adolescents: Results of a pilot study. *Journal of the American Academy of Child and Adolescent Psychiatry, 40,* 780–786.

Masters, J. C., Burish, T. G., Hollon, S. D., & Rimm, D. C. (1987). *Behavior therapy: Techniques and empirical findings* (3rd ed.). Orlando, FL: Harcourt Brace Jovanovich.

Mathur, S. R., & Rutherford, R. B. (1991). Peer-mediated interventions promoting social skills of children and youth with behavioral disorders. *Education and Treatment of Children, 14,* 227–243.

Matson, J. L., & Keyes, J. B. (1988). Contingent reinforcement and contingent restraint to treat severe aggression and self-injury in mentally retarded and autistic adults. *Journal of the Multihandicapped Person, 12,* 141–153.

Matson, J. L., & Ollendick, T. H. (1988). *Enhancing children's social skills: Assessment and training.* New York: Pergamon Press.

Matson, J. L., Esveldt-Dawson, K., & Kazdin, A. E. (1982). Treatment of spelling deficits in mentally retarded children. *Mental Retardation, 20,* 76–81.

Matson, J. L., Manikam, R., & Ladatto, J. (1990). A long-term follow-up of a recreate the scene, DRO, overcorrection and lemon juice therapy program for severe aggressive biting. *Scandinavian Journal of Behaviour Therapy, 19,* 33–38.

Matthews, B., Shute, R., & Rees, R. (2001). An analysis of stimulus overselectivity in adults with autism. *Journal of Intellectual & Developmental Disability, 26,* 161–176.

Maurice, C., Green, G., & Luce, S. C. (1996). *Behavioral intervention for young children with autism: A manual for parents and professionals.* Austin, TX: Pro-Ed.

Mazaleski, J. L., Iwata, B. A., Rodgers, T. A., Vollmer, T. R., & Zarcone, J. R. (1994). Protective equipment as treatment for stereotypic hand mouthing; Sensory extinction or punishment effects? *Journal of Applied Behavior Analysis, 27,* 345–355.

Mazur, J. E. (1975). The matching law and quantifications related to Premack's Principle. *Journal of Experimental Psychology: Animal Behavior Processes, 1,* 374–386.

McClusky, H. Y., Milby, J. B., Switzer, P. K., Williams, V., & Wooten, V. (1991). Efficacy of behavioral versus triazolam treatment in persistent sleep-onset insomnia. *American Journal of Psychiatry, 148,* 121–126.

McConaghy, N. (1994). Paraphilias and gender identity disorders. In M. Hersen and R. T. Ammerman (Eds.), *Handbook of prescriptive treatments for adults* (pp. 317–346). New York: Plenum.

McGrath, P. A., & Hillier, L. M. (2002). A practical cognitive-behavioral approach for treating children's pain. In D. C. Turk & R. J. Gatchel (Eds.), *Psychological approaches to pain management: A practitioner's handbook* (2nd ed., pp. 534–552). New York: Guilford Press.

McKee, W., & Witt, J. (1990). Effective teaching: A review of instructional and environmental variables. In T. Gutkin & C. R. Reynolds (Eds.), *The handbook of school psychology.* New York: John Wiley & Sons.

McMahon, R. J., & Forehand, R. L. (2003). *Helping the noncompliant child: Family-based treatment for oppositional behavior* (2nd ed.). New York: Guilford Press.

McNally, R. (1987). Preparedness and phobias: A review. *Psychological Bulletin, 101,* 282–303.

McNeil, C. B. (2001). *Tough class discipline kit.* Longmont, CO: Sopris West.

McNeil, C. B., Clemens-Mowrer, L., Gurwitch, R. H., & Funderburk, B. W. (1994). Assessment of a new procedure to prevent timeout escape in preschoolers. *Child & Family Behavior Therapy, 16,* 27–35.

McNeil, C. B., Clemens-Mowrer, L., Gurwitch, R. H., & Funderburk, B. W. (1994). Author's response to Lutzker's evaluation. *Child and Family Behavior Therapy, 16,* 37–46.

McSweeny, A. J. (1978). Effects of response cost on the behavior of a million persons: Charging for directory assistance in Cincinnati. *Journal of Applied Behavior Analysis, 11,* 47–51.

Means, M. K., Lichstein, K. L., Epperson, M. T., & Johnson, C. T. (2000). Relaxation therapy for insomnia: Nighttime and daytime effects. *Behaviour Research and Therapy, 38,* 665–678.

Meichenbaum, D. (1977). *Cognitive-behavior modification: An integrative approach.* New York: Plenum.

Mellon, M. W., & Houts, A. C. (1997). Home-based training for primary enuresis. In C. E. Schaefer & J. M.

Briesmeister (Eds.), *Handbook of parent training* (2nd ed., pp. 60–79). New York: Wiley.

Mellon, M. W., & McGrath, M. L. (2000). Empirically supported treatments in pediatric psychology: Nocturnal enuresis. *Journal of Pediatric Psychology, 25,* 193–214.

Mellon, M. W., and Houts, A. C. (1998). Home-based treatment for primary enuresis. In C. E. Schaefer and J. Briesmeister (Eds.), *Handbook of parent training: Parents as co-therapists for children's behavior problems* (Rev. ed.). New York: Wiley.

Miller, A. L., & Glinski, J. (2002). Youth suicidal behavior: Assessment and intervention. *Journal of Clinical Psychology, 56,* 1131–1152.

Miller, G. E., & Klungness, L. (1986). Treatment of nonconfrontative stealing in school-age children. *School Psychology Review, 15,* 24–35.

Miller, G. E., & Klungness, L. (1989). Childhood theft: A comprehensive review of assessment and treatment. *School Psychology Review, 18,* 82–97.

Miller, P. M. (1973). An experimental analysis of retention control training in the treatment of nocturnal enuresis in two institutional adolescents. *Behavior Therapy, 4,* 288–294.

Miltenberger, R. G. (2001). *Behavior modification: Principles and procedures* (2nd ed.). Belmont, CA: Wadsworth.

Miltenberger, R. G. (2001). Habit reversal treatment manual for trichotillomania. In D. Woods & R. Miltenberger (Eds.), *Tic disorders, trichotillomania, and other repetitive behavior disorders: Behavioral approaches to analysis and treatment* (pp. 171–196). Norwell, MA: Kluwer.

Miltenberger, R. G. (2001). Positive punishment procedures. In R. G. Miltenburger, *Behavior modification: Principles and procedures* (2nd ed., pp. 343–360). Belmont, CA: Wadsworth.

Miltenberger, R. G. (2003). *Behavior modification* (3rd ed.). Belmont, CA: Wadsworth.

Miltenberger, R. G., Fuqua, R. W., & Woods, D. W. (1998). Applying behavior analysis to clinical problems: Review and analysis of habit reversal. *Journal of Applied Behavior Analysis, 31,* 447–469.

Miltenberger, R. M., & Fuqua, R. W. (1981). Overcorrection: A review and critical analysis. *The Behavior Analyst, 4,* 123–141.

Mindell, J. A. (1999). Empirically supported treatments in pediatric psychology: Bedtime refusal and night wakings in young children. *Journal of Pediatric Psychology, 24,* 465–481.

Minuchin, S. (1974). *Families and family therapy.* Cambridge: Harvard University Press.

Moote, G. T., & Wodarski, J. S. (1997). The acquisition of life skills through adventure-based activities and programs: A review of the literature. *Adolescence, 32,* 143–167.

Morris, E. K., & Todd, J. T. (1998). Watsonian behaviorism. In W. O'Donohue & R. F. Kitchener (Eds.), *Handbook of behaviorism.* (pp. 15–69). San Diego, CA: Academic Press.

Morris, R. J., & Kratochwill, T. R. (1998). Childhood fears and phobias. In R. J. Morris & T. R. Kratochwill (Eds.), *The practice of child therapy* (3rd ed., pp. 91–131). Boston: Allyn & Bacon.

Mowrer, O. H. (1956). Two-factor learning theory reconsidered, with special reference to secondary reinforcement and the concept of habit. *Psychological Review, 63,* 114–128.

Mowrer, O. H. (1960). *Learning theory and behavior.* New York: Wiley.

Mowrer, O. H. (1960). *Learning theory and the symbolic processes.* New York:Wiley.

Mueller, M. M., Wilczynski, S. M., Moore, J. W., Fusilier, I., & Trahant, D. (2001). Antecedent manipulations in a tangible condition: The effects of stimulus preference on aggression. *Journal of Applied Behavior Analysis, 34,* 237–240.

Mueser, K. T., & Glynn, S. M. (1999). *Behavioral family therapy for psychiatric disorder.* New York: New Harbinger.

Mulick, J. A. (1990). Ideology and punishment reconsidered. *American Journal on Mental Retardation, 95,* 173–181.

Mulick, J., Hoyt, P., Rojahn, J., & Schroeder, S. (1978). Reduction of a "nervous habit" in a profoundly retarded youth by increasing toy play. *Journal of Behavior Therapy and Experimental Psychiatry, 9,* 381–385.

Muris, P., Meesters, C., & Melick, M. V. (2002). Treatment of childhood anxiety disorders: A preliminary comparison between cognitive-behavioral group therapy and a psychological placebo intervention. *Journal of Behavior Therapy and Experimental Psychiatry, 33,* 143–158.

Nathan, P. E., & Gorman, J. M. (Eds.). (2002). *A guide to treatments that work.* New York: Oxford University Press.

National Institute on Drug Abuse; National Institute of Health. *Preventing drug use among children and adolescents: A research-based guide.* Available: http://www.nida.nih.gov/Prevention/PREVOPEN.html.

Nelson, W. M., III & Finch, A. J., Jr. (1996). Managing anger in youth: A cognitive-behavioral intervention approach. In P. C. Kendall (Ed.), *Child and adolescent therapy: Cognitive-behavioral procedures* (2nd ed.). New York: Guilford Press.

Nixon, R. D. V., Sweeney, L., Erickson, D. B., & Touyz, S. W. (2003). Parent-child interaction therapy: A comparison of standard and abbreviated treatments for opposition defiant preschoolers. *Journal of Consulting and Clinical Psychology, 71,* 251–260.

Nock, M. K., & Kazdin, A. E. (2002). Examination of cognitive, affective, and behavioral factors and suicide-related outcomes in children and young adolescents. *Journal of Clinical Child and Adolescent Psychology, 31,* 48–58.

Noell, G. H. (2003). Functional assessment of school-based concerns. In M. L. Kelley, D. Reitman, and G. H. Noell (Eds.), *Practitioner's guide to empirically based measures of school behavior* (pp. 37–61). New York: Kluwer Academic/Plenum.

Noell, G. H., & Witt, J. C. (1996). A critical re-evaluation of five fundamental assumptions underlying behavioral consultation. *School Psychology Quarterly, 11,* 189–203.

Noell, G. H., Gresham, F. M., & Duhon, G. (1998). Fundamental agreements and epistemological differences in differentiating what was said from what was done in behavioral consultation. *School Psychology Quarterly, 13,* 81–88.

Novoco, R. (1979). The cognitive regulation of anger and stress. In P. C. Kendell & S. C. Hollon (Eds.), *Cognitive-behavioral interventions: Theory, research and procedures* (pp. 241–285). New York: Academic Press.

O'Brien, W. H. (1995). Inaccuracies in the estimation of functional relations using self-monitoring data. *Journal of Behavior Therapy and Experimental Psychiatry, 26,* 351–357.

O'Brien, W. H., & Haynes, S. N. (1995). A functional analytic approach to the assessment and treatment of a child with frequent migraine headaches. *In Session: Psychotherapy in Practice,1,* 65–80.

O'Carroll, P. W., Berman, A. L., Maris, R. W., Moscicki, E. K., Tanney, B. L., & Silverman, M. M. (1996). Beyond the Tower of Babel: A nomenclature for suicidology. *Suicide & Life Threatening Behavior, 26,* 237–252.

O'Donohue, W. T. (2001). *The psychology of B. F. Skinner.* Thousand Oaks, CA: Sage.

O'Donohue, W. T., & Henderson, D. A. (Eds.). (2001). *A history of the behavioral therapies: Founders' personal histories.* Reno, NV: Context Press.

O'Leary, K. D., & Drabman, R. (1971). Token reinforcement programs in the classroom: A review. *Psychological Bulletin, 75,* 379–398.

O'Reilly, M., Lancioni, G., & Taylor, I. (1999). An empirical analysis of two forms of extinction to treat aggression. *Research in Developmental Disabilities, 20,* 315–325.

Odom, S. L., & Strain, P. S. (1984). Peer-mediated approaches to promoting children's social interaction: A review. *American Journal of Orthospsychiatry, 54,* 544–557.

Ollendick, T. H. (1983). Reliability and validity of the revised Fear Survey Schedule for Children (FSSC-R). *Behaviour Research and Therapy, 21,* 685–692.

Ollendick, T. H., & Cerny, J. A. (1981). *Clinical behavior therapy with children.* New York: Plenum.

Ollendick, T. H., & King, N. J. (1998). Empirically supported treatments for children with phobic and anxiety disorders: Current status. *Journal of Clinical Child Psychology, 27,* 156–167.

Ollendick, T. H., & King, N. J. (2000). Empirically supported treatments for children and adolescents. In P. C. Kendall (Ed.), *Child and adolescent therapy: Cognitive-behavioral procedures* (2nd ed., pp. 386–425). New York: Guilford Press.

Ollendick, T. H., & Matson, J. L. (1978). Overcorrection: An overview. *Behavior Therapy, 9,* 830–842.

Ollendick, T. H., King, N. J., & Yule, W. (Eds.). (1994). *International handbook of phobic and anxiety disorders in children and adolescents.* New York: Plenum.

Ollendick, T. H., Vasey, M. W., & King, N. J. (2001). Operant conditioning influences in childhood anxiety. In M. W. Vasey & M. R. Dadds (Eds.), *The developmental psychopathology of anxiety* (pp. 231–252). Blacksburg, VA: Virginia Polytechnic Institute and State University, Dept. of Psychology.

Ormrod J. E., & Jenkins, L. (1989). Study strategies for learning spelling: Correlations with achievement and developmental changes. *Perceptual and Motor Skills, 68,* 643–650.

Osnes, P. G., Guevremont, D. C., & Stokes, T. F. (1986). If I say I'll talk more then I will. *Behavior Modification, 10,* 287–299.

Ost, L. G., & Sterner, U. (1987). Applied tension: A specific behavioural method for treatment of blood phobia. *Behaviour Research and Therapy, 25,* 25–30.

Ost, L., Svensson, L., Hellstrom, K., & Lindwall, R. (2001). One-session treatment of specific phobias in youths: A randomized clinical trial. *Journal of Consulting and Clinical Psychology, 69,* 814–824.

Overholser, J. C. (1999). Cognitive-behavioral treatment of obsessive-compulsive disorder. *Journal of Contemporary Psychotherapy, 29,* 369–382.

Paisey, T. J., & Whitney, R. B. (1989). A long-term case study of analysis, response suppression, and treatment maintenance involving life-threatening pica. *Behavioral Residential Treatment, 4,* 191–211.

Paniagua, F. A., & Baer, D. M. (1982). The analysis of correspondence training as a chain reinforceable at any point. *Child Development, 53,* 786–798.

Paniagua, F. A., & Black, S. A. (1990). Management and prevention of hyperactivity and conduct disorders in 8–10-year-old boys through correspondence training procedures. *Child and Family Behavior Therapy, 12,* 23–56.

Patterson, G. R. (1982). *Coercive family process.* Eugene, OR: Castalia.

Patterson, G. R., Reid, J. B., & Dishion, T. J. (1992). *Antisocial boys: A social interactional approach.* Eugene, OR: Castalia.

Paunovic, N. (1999). Exposure counterconditioning (EC) as a treatment for severe PTSD and depression with an illustrative case. *Journal of Behavior Therapy and Experimental Psychiatry, 30,* 105–117.

Pavlov, I. P. (1927). *Conditioned reflexes* (G. V. Anrep, Trans.). London: Oxford University Press.

Pelham, W. E., & Bender, M. E. (1982). Peer relationships in hyperactive children. In K. Gadow & I. Bailer (Eds.), *Advances in learning and behavioral disabilities* (pp. 365–436). Greenwich, CN: JAI Press.

Pelham, W. E., Fabiano, G. A., Gnagy, E. M., Greiner, A. R., & Hoza, B. (2005). Comprehensive psychosocial treatment for ADHD. In E. Hibbs and P. Jensen (Eds.), *Psychosocial treatments for child and adolescent disorders: Empirically based strategies for clinical practice* (2nd ed.). Washington, DC: American Psychological Association.

Pelham, W. E., McBurnett, K., Harper, G., Milich, R., Clinton, J., Thiele, C., et al. (1990). Methylphenidate and baseball playing in ADD children: Who's on first? *Journal of Consulting and Clinical Psychology, 58,* 130–133.

Persel, C. S., Persel, C. H., Ashley, M. J., & Krych, D. K. (1997). The use of noncontingent reinforcement and contingent restraint to reduce physical aggression and self-injurious behaviour in a traumatically brain-injured adult. *Brain Injury, 11,* 751–760.

Persons, J. B., & Tompkins, M. A. (1997). Cognitive-behavioral case formulation. In T. D. Eells (Ed.), *Handbook of psychotherapy case formulation* (pp. 314–339). New York: Guilford Press.

Peterson, A. L., Campise, R. L., & Azrin, N. H. (1994). Behavioral and pharmacological treatment for tic and habit disorders: A review. *Journal of Developmental and Behavioral Pediatrics, 15,* 430–441.

Peterson, L., & Tremblay, G. (1999). Self-monitoring in behavioral medicine: Children. *Psychological Assessment, 11,* 458–465.

Petraitis, J., Flay, B. R., & Miller, T. Q. (1995). Reviewing theories of adolescent substance use: Organizing pieces in the puzzle. *Psychological Bulletin, 117,* 67–86.

Pfiffner, L. J., & McBurnett, K. (1997). Social skills training with parent generalization: Treatment effects for children with attention deficit disorder. *Journal of Consulting and Clinical Psychology, 65,* 749–757.

Pfiffner, L. J., Calzada, E., & McBurnett, K. (2000). Interventions to enhance social competence. *Child and Adolescent Psychiatric Clinics of North America, 9,* 689–709.

Phillips, E. L., Phillips, E. A., Fixsen, D. L., & Wolf, M. M. (1971). Achievement place: Modification of the behaviors of pre-delinquent boys within a token economy. *Journal of Applied Behavior Analysis, 4,* 45–59.

Platt, J. R. (1973). The Skinnerian revolution. In H. Wheeler (Ed.), *Beyond the punitive society; operant conditioning: Social and political aspects* (pp. 22–56). San Francisco: W. H. Freeman.

Poling, A. D., & Ryan, C. (1982). Differential-reinforcement-of-other-behavior schedules: Therapeutic applications. *Behavior Modification, 6,* 3–21.

Powers, S. W. (1990). Adjusting chair timeout enforcement procedures for oppositional children. *Behavior Therapy, 21,* 257–271.

Powers, S. W. (2000). Behavior therapy with children. In C. E. Walker & M. C. Roberts (Eds.), *Handbook of clinical child psychology* (3rd ed., pp. 825–839). New York: Wiley.

Premack, D. (1963). Prediction of the comparative reinforcement values of running and drinking. *Science, 139,* 1062–1063.

Prins, P. J. M., & Ollendick, T. H. (2003). Cognitive change and enhanced coping: Missing mediational links in cognitive behavior therapy with anxiety-disordered children. *Clinical Child and Family Psychology Review, 6,* 87–105.

Prinstein, M. J., Nock, M. K., Spirito, A., & Grapentine, W. L. (2001). Multi-method assessment of suicidality in adolescent psychiatric inpatients: Preliminary results. *Journal of the American Academy of Child and Adolescent Psychiatry, 40,* 1053–1061.

Quinsey, V. L., & Chaplin, T. C. (1984). Stimulus control of rapists' and non-sex offenders' sexual arousal. *Behavioral Assessment, 6,* 169–176.

Rachman, S. J., & Teasdale, J. (1969). *Aversion therapy and behavior disorders: An analysis.* Coral Gables, FL: University of Miami Press.

Rakos, R. F. (1991). *Assertive behavior: Theory, research and training.* London: Routledge.

Ramasay, R., Taylor, R. L., & Ziegler, E. W. (1996). Eliminating inappropriate classroom behavior using a DRO schedule: A preliminary study. *Psychological Reports, 78,* 753–754.

Rapee, R. M., Wignall, A., Hudson, J. L., & Schniering, C. A. (2000). *Evidence-based treatment of child and adolescent anxiety disorders.* Oakland, CA: New Harbinger.

Rapp, J. T., Miltenberger, R. G., Galensky, T. L., Roberts, J., & Ellington, S. A. (1999). Brief functional analysis and simplified habit reversal of thumb sucking in fraternal twin brothers. *Child & Family Behavior Therapy, 21,* 1–17.

Rapport, M. D., Murphy, H. A., & Bailey, J. S. (1980). The effects of a response cost treatment tactic on hyperactive children. *Journal of School Psychology, 18,* 98–111.

Rapport, M. D., Murphy, H. A., & Bailey, J. S. (1982). Ritalin versus response cost in the control of hyperactive children: A within-subject comparison. *Journal of Applied Behavior Analysis, 15,* 205–216.

Rathvon, N. (1999). *Effective school interventions: Strategies for enhancing academic achievement and social competence.* New York: Guilford Press.

Ray, K. P., Skinner, C. H., & Watson, S. T. (1999). Transferring stimulus control via momentum to increase compliance in a student with autism: A demonstration of collaborative consultation. *School Psychology Review, 28,* 622–627.

Reese, H. W. (1968). *The perception of stimulus relations: Discrimination learning and transposition.* New York: Academic Press.

Reid, M. J., Walter, A. L., & O'Leary, S. G. (1999). Treatment of young children's bedtime refusal and nighttime wakings: A comparison of "standard" and graduated ignoring procedures. *Journal of Abnormal Child Psychology, 27,* 5–16.

Reitman, D., Hupp, S. D. A., O'Callaghan, P., Gulley, V., & Northup, J. (2001). The influence of a token economy and stimulant medication on attentive and disruptive behavior during sports with children diagnosed with ADHD. *Behavior Modification, 25,* 305–323.

Repp, A. C., & Deitz, S. M. (1974). Reducing aggressive and self-injurious behavior of institutionalized retarded children through reinforcement of other behaviors. *Journal of Applied Behavior Analysis, 7,* 313–325.

Reynolds, L. K., & Kelly, M. L. (1997). The efficacy of a response-cost based treatment package for managing aggressive behavior in preschoolers. *Behavior Modification, 21,* 216–230.

Rhode, G., Jenson, W. R., & Reavis, H. K. (1992). *The tough kid book: Practical classroom management strategies.* Longmont, CO: Sopris West.

Richman, D. M., Wacker, D. P., Cooper-Brown, L. J., Kayser, K., Crosland, K., Stephens, T. J., et al. (2001). Stimulus characteristics within directives: Effects on accuracy of task completion. *Journal of Applied Behavior Analysis, 34,* 289–312.

Richter, N. C. (1984). The efficacy of relaxation training with children. *Journal of Abnormal Child Psychology, 12,* 319–344.

Rickert, V. L., & Johnson, C. M. (1988). Reducing nocturnal awakening and crying episodes in infants and young children: A comparison between scheduled awakenings and systematic ignoring. *Pediatrics, 81,* 203–212.

Rincover, A. (1978). Sensory extinction: A procedure for eliminating self-stimulatory behavior in developmentally disabled children. *Journal of Abnormal Child Psychology, 6,* 299–310.

Rincover, A. (1985). Sensory extinction: Some answers and questions. *Behavior Therapist, 8,* 177–178.

Risly, T. R., & Hart, B. (1968). Developing correspondence between the nonverbal and verbal behavior of preschool children. *Journal of Applied Behavior Analysis, 1,* 267–281.

Roberts, M. S. (1988). Enforcing chair timeouts with room timeouts. *Behavior Modification, 12,* 353–370.

Roberts, M. W. (1982). Resistance to timeout: Some normative data. *Behavioral Assessment, 4,* 237–246.

Roberts, M. W. (1982). The effects of warned versus unwarned time-out procedures on child noncompliance. *Child and Family Behavior Therapy, 4,* 37–53.

Roberts, M. W. (1985). Praising child compliance: Reinforcement or ritual? *Journal of Abnormal Child Psychology, 13,* 611–629.

Roberts, M. W., & Powers, S. W. (1988). The compliance test. *Behavioral Assessment, 10,* 257-271.

Roberts, M. W., Hatzenbuehler, L. C., & Bean, A. W. (1981). The effects of differential attention and timeout on child noncompliance. *Behavior Therapy, 12,* 93–99.

Roberts, M. W., McMahon, R. J., Forehand, R., & Humphreys, L. (1978). The effect of parental instruction-giving on child compliance. *Behavior Therapy, 9,* 793–798.

Rocca, J. V., & Gross, A. M. (1996). Report-Do-Report: Promoting setting and setting-time generalization. *Education and Treatment of Children, 19,* 408–424.

Rogers-Warren, A., & Baer, D. M. (1976). Correspondence between saying and doing: Teaching children to share and praise. *Journal of Applied Behavior Analysis, 9,* 335–354.

Rohde, G., Jenson, W. R., & Reavis, H. K. (1992). *The tough kid book: Practical classroom management strategies.* Longmont, CO: Sopris West.

Rojahn, J., McGonigle, J. J., Curcio, C., & Dixon, M. J. (1987). Suppression of pica by water mist and aromatic ammonia: A comparative analysis. *Behavior Modification, 11,* 65–74.

Ronen, T. (1998). Linking developmental and emotional elements into child and family cognitive-behavioural therapy. In P. Graham (Ed.), *Cognitive-behaviour therapy for children and families* (pp. 1–17). New York: Cambridge University Press.

Rose, S. D. (1998). *Group therapy with troubled youth: A cognitive-behavioral interactive approach.* Thousand Oaks, CA: Sage.

Ross, D. M. (1984). Thought-stopping: A coping strategy for impending feared events. *Issues in Comprehensive Pediatric Nursing, 7,* 83–89.

Rudd, M. D., Joiner, T., & Rajab, M. H. (2001). *Treating suicidal behavior: An effective, time-limited approach.* New York: Guilford Press.

Ruth, W. J. (1996). Goal setting and behavior contracting for students with emotional and behavioral difficulties: An analysis of daily, weekly, and total goal attainment. *Psychology in the Schools, 33,* 153–158.

Saadeh, W., Rizzo, C. P., & Roberts, D. G. (2002). Spanking. *Clinical Pediatrics, 41,* 87–88.

Sainato, D. M., Strain, P. S., Lefebvre, D., & Rapp, N. (1990). Effects of self-evaluation on the independent work skills of preschool children with disabilities. *Exceptional Children, 56,* 540–549.

Sajwaj, T., Libet, J., & Agras, S. (1989). Lemon juice therapy: The control of life-threatening rumination in a six-month-old infant. In D. Wedding & R. J. Corsini (Eds.), *Case studies in psychotherapy* (pp. 113–122). Itasca, IL: Peacock.

Sanders, M. R., & James, J. E. (1983). The modification of parent behavior: A review of generalization and maintenance. *Behavior Modification, 7,* 3–27.

Sarafino, E. P. (2001). *Behavior modification: Principles of behavior change* (2nd ed.). Mountain View, CA: Mayfield.

Schafer, L. C., Glasgow, R. E., & McCaul, K. D. (1982). Increasing the adherence of diabetic adolescents. *Journal of Behavioral Medicine, 5,* 353–362.

Schlosser, R. W., & Lee, D. L. (2000). Promoting generalization and maintenance in augmentative and alternative communication: A meta-analysis of 20 years of effectiveness research. *Augmentative and Alternate Communication, 16,* 208–226.

Schneider, S., & Workman, M. (1999). Effects of virtual reality on symptom distress in children receiving chemotherapy. *Cyberpsychology & Behavior, 2,* 125–134.

Schreibman, L. (1975). Effects of within-stimulus and extra-stimulus prompting on discrimination learning in autistic children. *Journal of Applied Behavior Analysis, 8,* 91–112.

Schreibman, L., Charlop, M. H., & Koegel, R. L. (1982). Teaching autistic children to use extra-stimulus prompts. *Journal of Experimental Child Psychology, 33,* 475–491.

Schroeder, S. R., Rojahn, J., Mulick, J. A., & Schroeder, C. S. (1990). Self-injurious behavior. In J. L. Matson (Ed.), *Handbook of behavior modification with the mentally retarded* (2nd ed., pp. 141–180). New York: Plenum.

Schwartz, M. S, & Andrasik, F. (Eds.). (2003). *Biofeedback: A practitioner's guide* (3rd ed.). New York: Guilford Press.

Schwartz, M. S. (1995). Breathing therapies. In Mark S. Schwartz & Associates (Eds.), *Biofeedback: A practitioner's guide* (2nd ed., pp. 248–287). New York: Guilford Press.

Scotti, J. R., & Meyer, L. H. (1999). *Behavioral intervention: Principles, models, and practices.* Baltimore: Paul H. Brookes.

Scotti, J. R., Beach, B. K., Northrop, L. M. E., Rode, C. A., & Forsyth, J. P. (1995). The psychological impact of accidental injury: A conceptual model for clinicians and researchers. In J. R. Freedy & S. E. Hobfoll (Eds.), *Traumatic stress: From theory to practice* (pp. 181–212). New York: Plenum. [Modified and reprinted in Schultz, I. Z., & Brady, D. O. (Eds.). (2003). *Psychological injuries at trial* (CD-ROM). Chicago: American Bar Association Tort and Insurance Practice Section.

Scotti, J. R., Ruggiero, K. J., & Rabalais, A. E. (2002). The traumatic impact of motor vehicle accidents. In A. M. La Greca, W. K. Silverman, E. M. Vernberg, & M. C. Roberts (Eds.), *Helping children cope with disasters and terrorism* (pp. 259–291). Washington, DC: American Psychological Association.

Seymour, F. W., & Epston, D. (1989). An approach to childhood stealing with evaluation of 45 cases. *Australian and New Zealand Journal of Family Therapy, 10,* 137–143.

Shapiro, E. S. (1996). Interventions for academic problems II: Specific skill areas. In E. Shapiro (Ed.), *Academic skills problems: Direct assessment and intervention* (2nd ed., pp. 146–167). New York: Guilford Press.

Shapiro, E. S., & Kratochwill, T. R. (Eds.). (2000). *Behavioral assessment in schools: Theory, research, and clinical foundations* (2nd ed., pp. 3–15). New York: Guilford Press.

Shapiro, E., & Cole, C. L. (1999). Self-monitoring in assessing children's problems. *Psychological Assessment, 11,* 448–457.

Sharp, T., Brown, M., & Crider, K. (1995). The effects of a sportsmanship curriculum intervention on generalized positive social behavior of urban elementary school students. *Journal of Applied Behavior Analysis, 28,* 401–416.

Sheidow, A. J., Henggeler, S. W., & Schoenwald, S. K. (2003). Multisystemic therapy. In T. L. Sexton, G. Weeks, & M. Robbins (Eds.), *Handbook of family therapy: Theory, research, and practice* (pp. 303–322). New York: Brunner-Routledge.

Sheridan, S. M., & Walker, D. (1999). Social skills in context: Considerations for assessment, intervention, and generalization. In C. R. Reynolds & T. B. Gutkin (Eds.), *The handbook of school psychology* (3rd ed., pp. 686–708). New York: John Wiley.

Shukla, S., & Albin, R. W. (1996). Effects of extinction alone and extinction plus functional communication training on covariation of problem behaviors. *Journal of Applied Behavior Analysis, 29,* 565–568.

Sidman, M. (1960). *Tactics of scientific research.* New York: Basic Books.

Silverman, W. K., & Kurtines, W. M. (1996). *Anxiety and phobic disorders: A pragmatic approach.* New York: Plenum.

Silverman, W. K., Ginsburg, G. S., & Kurtines, W. M. (1995). Clinical issues in treating children with anxiety and phobic disorders. *Cognitive and Behavioral Practice, 2,* 93–117.

Singh, N. N., & Ellis, C. R. (2000). Pharmacological therapies. In T. H. Ollendick (Ed.), *Comprehensive clinical psychology: Vol. 5. Children and adolescents: Clinical formulation and treatment* (pp. 267–293). Oxford, UK: Pergamon.

Singh, N. N., & Singh, J. (1984). Antecedent control of oral reading errors and self-corrections by mentally retarded children. *Journal of Applied Behavior Analysis, 17,* 111–119.

Singh, N. N., Farquhar, S., & Hewett, A. E. (1991). Enhancing the spelling performance of learning disabled students. *Behavior Modification, 15,* 271–282.

Singh, N. N., Watson, J. E., & Winton, A. S. W. (1986). Treating self-injury: Water mist spray versus facial screening or forced arm exercise. *Journal of Applied Behavior Analysis, 19,* 403–410.

Skinner, B. F. (1938). *The behavior of organisms.* New York: Appleton-Century-Crofts.

Skinner, B. F. (1953). *Science and human behavior.* New York: Macmillan.

Skinner, B. F. (1957). *Verbal behavior.* New York: Appleton-Century-Crofts.

Skinner, B. F. (1968). *Technology of teaching.* New York: Appleton-Century-Crofts.

Skinner, B. F. (1969). Contingencies of reinforcement: A theoretical analysis. In R. M. Elliot, K. MacCorquodale, G. Lindzey, & K. E. Clark (Series Eds.), *The century psychology series.* New York: Appleton-Century-Crofts.

Skinner, B. F. (1971). *Beyond freedom and dignity.* New York: Knopf.

Skinner, B. F. (1974). *About behaviorism.* New York: Knopf.

Skinner, B. F., & Vaughan, M. E. (1983). *Enjoy old age: A program of self management.* New York: W. W. Norton.

Slifer, K. J., Babbit, R. L., & Cataldo, M. D. (1995). Simulation and counterconditioning as adjuncts to pharmacotherapy for invasive pediatric procedures. *Developmental and Behavioral Pediatrics, 16,* 133–141.

Slifer, K. J., Koontz, K. L., & Cataldo, M. F. (2002). Operant-contingency-based preparation of children for functional magnetic resonance imaging. *Journal of Applied Behavior Analysis, 35,* 191–194.

Sloboda, Z., & Bukoski, W. J. (Eds.). (2003). *Handbook of drug abuse prevention: Theory, science, and practice.* New York: Kluwer Academic.

Smith, R. G., & Iwata, B. A. (1997). Antecedent influences on behavior disorders. *Journal of Applied Behavior Analysis, 30,* 343–375.

Smith, R. G., Russo, L., & Le, D. D. (1999). Distinguishing between extinction and punishment effects of response blocking: A replication. *Journal of Applied Behavior Analysis, 32,* 367–370.

Speltz, M. L., Shimamura, J. W., & McReynolds, W. T. (1982). Procedural variations in group contingencies: Effects on children's academic and social behaviors. *Journal of Applied Behavior Analysis, 15,* 533–544.

Spence, S. H., Donovan, C., & Brechman-Toussaint, M. (2000). The treatment of childhood social phobia: The effectiveness of a social skills training-based, cognitive-behavioral intervention, with and without parental involvement. *Journal of Child Psychology and Psychiatry, 41,* 713–726.

Spiegler, M. D. (1998). *Contemporary behavior therapy* (3rd ed.). Pacific Grove, CA: Brooks/Cole.

Spiegler, M. D., & Guevremont, D. C. (1993). *Contemporary behavior therapy* (2nd ed., pp. 105–137). Pacific Grove, CA: Brooks/Cole.

Spirito, A. (Ed.). (1999). Empirically supported treatments in pediatric psychology (Special Issue). *Journal of Pediatric Psychology, 24,* 87–174.

Spivack, G., Platt, J. J., Jr., & Shure, M. (1976). *The problem solving approach to adjustment.* San Francisco: Jossey-Bass.

Spreat, S., Lipinski, D., Hill, J., & Halpin, M. E. (1986). Safety indices associated with the use of contingent restraint procedures. *Applied Research in Mental Retardation, 7,* 475–481.

Staats, A. W. (1990). Paradigmatic behavior therapy: A unified framework for theory, research, and practice. In G. H. Eifert & I. M. Evans (Eds.), *Unifying behavior therapy: Contributions of paradigmatic behaviorism* (pp. 14–54). New York: Springer.

Stallard, P. (2002). Cognitive behaviour therapy with children and young people: A selective review of key issues. *Behavioural and Cognitive Psychotherapy, 30,* 297–309.

Steen, P., & Zuriff, G. (1977). The use of relaxation in the treatment of self-injurious behavior. *Journal of Behavior Therapy and Experimental Psychiatry, 8,* 447–448.

Stein, M. T., & Perrin, E. L. (1998). Guidance for effective discipline: American Academy of Pediatrics Committee on Psychosocial Aspects of Child and Family Health, *Pediatrics, 101,* 723–728.

Stetter, F., & Kupper, S. (2002). Autogenic training: A meta-analysis of clinical outcome studies. *Applied Psychophysiology and Biofeedback, 27,* 45–98.

Stokes, T. (1992). Discrimination and generalization. *Journal of Applied Behavior Analysis, 25,* 429–432.

Stokes, T. F., & Baer, D. M. (1977). An implicit technology of generalization. *Journal of Applied Behavior Analysis, 10,* 349–367.

Stokes, T. F., & Osnes, P. G. (1989). An operant pursuit of generalization. *Behavior Therapy, 20,* 337–355.

Storms, L. (1985). Massed negative practice as a behavioral treatment for Gilles de la Tourette's syndrome. *American Journal of Psychotherapy, 39,* 277–281.

Strain, P. S., Cooke, T. P., & Apolloni, T. (1976). The role of peers in modifying classmates' social behavior: A review. *Journal of Special Education, 10,* 351–356.

Stromer, R. S., MacVey, H. A., Howell, S. R., McVay, A. A., & Flusser, D. (1996). Teaching computer-based spelling to individuals with developmental and hearing disabilities: Transfer of stimulus control to writing tasks. *Journal of Applied Behavior Analysis, 29,* 25–42.

Suen, H. K., & Ary, D. (1989). *Analyzing quantitative behavioral observation data.* Hillsdale, NJ: Erlbaum.

Suinn, R. M. (1990). *Anxiety management training.* New York: Plenum.

Sukhodolsky, D. G., Solomon, R. M., & Perine, J. (2000). Cognitive-behavioral, anger-control intervention for elementary school children: A treatment-outcome study. *Journal of Child and Adolescent Group Therapy, 10,* 159–170.

Sulzer-Azaroff, B., & Mayer, G. R. (1991). *Behavior analysis for lasting change.* Orlando, FL: Harcourt Brace Jovanovich.

Sulzer-Azaroff, B., & Mayer, G. R. (1994). *Achieving educational excellence: Behavior analysis for school personnel.* San Marcos, CA: Western Image.

Svensson, L., Larsson, A., & Ost, L. (2002). How children experience brief-exposure treatment of specific phobias. *Journal of Clinical Child and Adolescent Psychology, 31,* 80–89.

Swenson, C. C., & Brown, E. J. (1999). Cognitive behavioral group treatment for physically abused children. *Cognitive and Behavioral Practice, 6,* 212–220.

Task Force on Promotion and Dissemination of Psychological Procedures, Division of Clinical Psychology, American Psychological Association. (1995). Training in and dissemination of empirically validated psychological treatments: Report and recommendations. *The Clinical Psychologist, 48,* 3–23.

Task Force on Psychological Intervention Guidelines, American Psychological Association (1995). *Template for developing guidelines: Interventions for mental disorders and psychosocial aspects of physical disorders.* Washington, DC: American Psychological Association.

Taylor, S. (2001). Breathing retraining in the treatment of panic disorder: Efficacy, caveats, and indications. *Scandinavian Journal of Behaviour Therapy, 30,* 49–56.

Thibideau, S. F. (1998). *How to use response cost* (2nd ed.). Austin, TX: Pro-Ed.

Thomas, J. C., & Hersen, M. (2003). *Understanding research in clinical and counseling psychology.* Mahwah, NJ: Erlbaum.

Thorpe, G. L., & Olson, S. L. (1997). *Behavior therapy: Concepts, procedures, and applications.* Needham Heights, MA: Allyn & Bacon,

Timberlake, W., & Allison, J. (1974). Response deprivation: An empirical approach to instrumental performance. *Psychological Review, 81,* 146–164.

Todd, J. T. & Morris, E. K. (Eds.). (1994). *Modern perspectives on John B. Watson and classical behaviorism.* Westport, CT: Greenwood Press.

Todd, J. T., & Morris, E. K. (Eds.). (1994). *Modern perspectives on B. F. Skinner and contemporary behaviorism.* Westport, CT: Greenwood Press.

Topping, K., & Stewart, E. (Eds.). (1998). *Peer-assisted learning.* Mahwah, NJ: Erlbaum.

Touchette, P. E., & Howard, J. S. (1984). Errorless learning: Reinforcement contingencies and stimulus control transfer in delayed prompting. *Journal of Applied Behavior Analysis, 17,* 175–188.

Vasey, M. W., & Dadds, M. R. (2001). *The developmental psychopathology of anxiety.* New York: Oxford University Press.

Vickers, B. (2002). Cognitive behaviour therapy for adolescents with psychological disorders: A group treatment programme. *Clinical Child Psychology and Psychiatry, 7,* 249–262.

Vollmer, T. R., Ringdahl, J. E., Roane, H. S., & Marcus, B. A. (1997). Negative side effects of noncontingent reinforcement. *Journal of Applied Behavior Analysis, 30,* 161–164.

Vollmer, T. R., Roan, H. S., Ringdahl, J. E., & Marcus, B. A. (1999). Evaluating treatment challenges with differential reinforcement of alternative behavior. *Journal of Applied Behavior Analysis, 32,* 9–23.

Von Bertalanffy, L. (1968). *General systems theory.* Harmondsworth, UK: Penguin.

Wacker, D. P., Steege, M. W., Northup, J., Sasso, G., Berg, W., Reimers, T., et al. (1990). A component analysis of functional communication training across three topographies of severe behavior problems. *Journal of Applied Behavior Analysis, 23,* 417–429.

Wahler, R. (1967). Child-child interactions in free field settings: Some experimental analyses. *Journal of Experimental Child Psychology, 5,* 109–113.

Wahler, R. G. (1994). Child conduct problems: Disorders in conduct or social continuity? *Journal of Child and Family Studies, 3,* 143–156.

Walker, C. E., & Roberts, M. C. (1992). *Handbook of clinical child psychology* (2nd ed.). New York: John Wiley.

Walker, C. E., Kenning, M., & Faust-Campanile, J. (1989). Enuresis and encopresis. In E. J. Mash & R. A. Barkley (Eds.), *Treatment of childhood disorders.* New York: Guilford Press.

Walker, H. M., Colvin, G., & Ramsey, E. (1995). *Antisocial behavior in school: Strategies and best practices.* New York: Brooks/Cole.

Waters, T. L., Barrett, P. M., & March, J. S. (2001). Cognitive-behavioral family treatment of childhood obsessive-compulsive disorder. *American Journal of Psychotherapy, 55,* 372–388.

Watson, J. B. (1919). *Psychology from the standpoint of a behaviorist.* Philadelphia: Lippincott.

Watson, J. B. (1930). *Behaviorism* (Rev. ed.). New York: People's Institute.

Watson, J. B., & Rayner, R. (1920). Conditioned emotional reactions. *Journal of Experimental Psychology, 3,* 1–14.

Watson, T. S., & Steege, M. (2003). *Conducting school-based functional behavioral assessments: A practitioner's guide.* New York: Guilford Press.

Webster-Stratton, C., & Hammond, M. (1997). Treating children with early-onset conduct problems: A comparison of child and parent training interventions. *Journal of Consulting and Clinical Psychology, 65,* 93–109.

Webster-Stratton, C., & Herbert, M. (1994). *Troubled families—problem children.* New York: John Wiley.

Webster-Stratton, C., Reid, J., & Hammond, M. (2001). Social skills and problem-solving training for children with early-onset conduct problems: Who benefits? *Journal of Child Psychology and Psychiatry, 42,* 943–952.

Weems, C. F. (1998). The evaluation of heart rate biofeedback using a multi-element design. *Journal of Behavior Therapy and Experimental Psychiatry, 29,* 157–162.

Weiss, M. R., & Duncan, S. C. (1992). The relationship between physical competence and peer acceptance in the context of children's sport participation. *Journal of Sport and Exercise Psychology, 14,* 177–191.

Weisz, J. R., & Hawley, K. M. (1998) Finding, evaluating, refining, and applying empirically supported treatments for children and adolescents. *Journal of Clinical Child Psychology, 27,* 206–216.

Weisz, J., & Jensen, P. S. (1999). Efficacy and effectiveness of child and adolescent psychotherapy and psychopharmacology. *Mental Health Services Research, 1,* 125–157.

Werts, M. G., Wolery, M., Holcombe-Ligon, A., Vassilaros, M. A., & Billings, S. S. (1992). Efficacy of transition-based teaching with instructive feedback. *Education and Treatment of Children, 15,* 320–334.

Whitaker, S. (2002). Maintaining reductions in challenging behaviours: A review of the literature. *British Journal of Developmental Disabilities, 48,* 15–25.

White, G. W., Mathews, R. M., & Fawcett, S. B. (1989). Reducing risk of pressure sores: Effects of watch prompts and alarm avoidance on wheelchair push-ups. *Journal of Applied Behavior Analysis, 22,* 287–295.

Williams, C. D. (1959). The elimination of tantrum behavior by extinction procedures. *Journal of Abnormal and Social Psychology, 59,* 269.

Wisniewski, L., & Marcus, M. D. (1998). Childhood obesity. In V. B. Van Hasselt & M. Hersen (Eds.), *Handbook of psychological treatment protocols for children and adolescents* (pp. 179–201). Mahwah, NJ: Erlbaum.

Witt, J. C., & Elliot, S. N. (1982). The response cost lottery: A time efficient and effective classroom intervention. *Journal of School Psychology, 20,* 155–161.

Wolery, M., Gast, D. L., Kirk, K., & Schuster, J. (1988). Fading extra-stimulus prompts with autistic children using time delay. *Education and Treatment of Children, 11,* 29–44.

Wolf, M., Risley, T., & Mees, H. (1964). Application of operant conditioning procedures to the behavior problems of an autistic child. *Behaviour Research & Therapy, 1,* 305–312.

Wolfe, D. A., Kelly, J. A., & Drabman, R. S. (1981). "Beat the Buzzer": A method for training an abusive mother to decrease recurrent child conflicts. *Journal of Clinical Child Psychology, 10,* 114–116.

Wolfe, L. H., Heron, T. E., & Goddard, Y. L. (2000). Effects of self-monitoring on the on-task behavior and written language performance of elementary students with learning disabilities. *Journal of Behavioral Education, 10,* 49–73.

Wolitzky, K., Fivush, R., Zimand, E., Hodges, L., & Rothbaum, B. O. (2003). *Coping with cancer: Relations among parent and child coping, anxiety and distress, and effectiveness of virtual reality during invasive medical procedures.* Manuscript submitted for publication.

Wolpe, J. (1958). *Psychotherapy by reciprocal inhibition.* Stanford, CA: Stanford University Press.

Wolpe, J. (1990). *The practice of behavior therapy* (4th ed.). New York: Pergamon Press.

Wolpe, J. (1995). Reciprocal inhibition: Major agent of behavior change. In W. O'Donohue & L. Kransner (Eds.) *Theories of behavior change: Exploring behavior change.* Washington, DC: American Psychological Association.

Wolpe, J., & Plaud, J. J. (1997). Pavlov's contributions to behavior therapy: The obvious and the not so obvious. *American Psychologist, 52,* 966–972.

Wolraich, M. L. (2003). The use of psychotropic medications in children: An American view. *Journal of Child Psychology and Psychiatry, 44,* 159–168.

Woods, D. W. (2001). Habit reversal treatment manual for tic disorders. In D. Woods & R. Miltenberger (Eds.), *Tic disorders, trichotillomania, and other repetitive behavior disorders: Behavioral approaches to analysis and treatment* (pp. 33–52). Norwell, MA: Kluwer.

Woods, D. W., & Miltenberger, R. G. (1995). Habit reversal: A review of applications and variations. *Journal of Behavior Therapy and Experimental Psychiatry, 26,* 123–131.

Woods, D. W., & Miltenberger, R. G. (1996). A review of habit reversal with childhood habit disorders. *Education and Treatment of Children, 19,* 197–214.

Woods, D. W., & Miltenberger, R. G. (Eds.). (2001). *Tic disorders, trichotillomania, and other repetitive behavior disorders: Behavioral approaches to analysis and treatment.* Norwell, MA: Kluwer.

Woods, D. W., Twohig, M. P., Fuqua, R.W., & Hanley, J. M. (2000). Treatment of stuttering with regulated breathing: Strengths, limitations, and future directions. *Behavior Therapy, 31,* 547–568.

Yardley-Matwiejczuk, K. A. (1997). *Role play: Theory & practice.* Thousand Oaks, CA: Sage.

Yates, A. J. (1958). The application of learning theory to the treatment of tics. *Journal of Abnormal and Social Psychology, 56,* 175–182.

Yates, A. J. (1959). Negative practice: A theoretical interpretation. *Australian Journal of Psychology, 11,* 126-129.

Yucha, C., & Gilbert, C. (in press). *The clinical efficacy of biofeedback and neurofeedback.* Wheat Ridge, CO: Association for Applied Psychophysiology and Biofeedback.

Zaichkowsky, L. B., & Zaichkowsky, L. D. (1984). The effects of a school-based relaxation training program on fourth grade children. *Journal of Clinical Child Psychology, 13,* 81–85.

Zaichkowsky, L. B., Zaichkowsky, L. D., & Yeager, J. (1986). Biofeedback-assisted relaxation training in the elementary classroom. *Elementary School Guidance & Counseling, 20,* 261–267.

Zelter, L. (1994). Pain and symptom management. In D. J. Bearison & R. K. Mulhern (Eds.), *Pediatric psychooncology: Psychological perspectives on children with cancer* (pp. 61–83). New York: Oxford University Press.

Zimand, E., Anderson, P. L., Gershon, J., Graap, K., Hodges, L. F., & Rothbaum, B. O. (2002). Virtual reality therapy: Innovative treatment for anxiety disorders. *Primary Psychiatry, 9,* 51–54.

Zito, J., Safer, D. J., DosReis, S., Gardner, J. F., Boyles, M., & Lynch, F. (2000). Trends in the prescribing of psychotropic medication to preschoolers. *Journal of the American Medical Association, 283,* 1025–1030.

Zvolensky, M. J., & Eifert, G. H. (2002). Manualized behavior therapy. In M. Hersen & W. Sledge (Eds.), *Encyclopedia of psychotherapy* (Vol. 1, pp. 115–121). Boston: Academic Press.

Index

ABC charts and scatterplots, 1119-1123
case illustration, 1120-1123
description of, 1119-1120
limitations of, 1120
research basis of, 1120
target populations for, 1120
See also **Behavioral assessment; Descriptive and functional analysis; Functional analysis; Functional behavioral assessment of problem behavior**
ABCT (Alcohol Behavioral Couple Treatment) protocol, 559
Abstinence violation effect, 480
Abt Associates, 1469
Academic interventions, 1123-1125
applied behavior analysis and, 1124
behavioral interventions and, 1123-1124
components of, 1124-1125
education crisis and, 1123
effective models of, 1124
instructional practices in, 1124
intervention packages, models of, 1125
teacher role in, 1124
See also **Academic learning time; Behavior management for improving academic and classroom behavior; Direct instruction; Error correction; Pacing; Task analysis**
Academic learning time (ALT), 1125-1127
allocated time and, 1125
case illustration, 1126-1127
complications with, 1126
description of, 1125-1126
engaged time and, 1125
research basis of, 1126
success rate and, 1125-1126
target population for, 1126
See also **Active student responding; Opportunity to respond**
Academic Performance Rating Scale, 792
Acceptance and commitment therapy (ACT), 1-5, 20, 539
behavior change, commitment to, 5
cognitive diffusion, mindfulness and, 4
emotional/cognitive control, problems of, 3-4

language use, metaphor/paradox and, 2-3, 4
literality, context of, 1-2
reason-giving, experiential control and, 2
self vs. action, distinction between, 4
solutioning system, confrontation of, 2-3
values work in, 5
willingness exercises, struggle acceptance and, 4-5
See also **Cognitive behavior therapy; Motivational enhancement therapy; Motivational interviewing; Relational frame theory**
Achenbach Child Behavior Checklist, 1170, 1173
Acquisition, 1127-1131
case illustration, 1130
complications with, 1129-1130
developmental readiness and, 1129-1130
end-of-acquisition, determination of, 1128-1129
errorless teaching procedures and, 1130
instructional strategy selection of, 1130
research basis of, 1129
steady-state vs. transition-state behaviors and, 1128
strategy, description of, 1127-1129
target population for, 1129
See also **Errorless learning; Mastery learning; Phases of learning; Shaping to teach new behaviors**
Actigraphy, 389
Active student responding, 1131-1132
data collection process for, 1132
instructional effectiveness and, 1132
methods in, 1131-1132
research on, 1132
See also **Academic learning time; Choral responding; Opportunity to respond**
Active supervision, 1132-1135
case illustration, 1134-1135
complications with, 1134
positive behavior support and, 1134
research basis of, 1133-1134
strategy, description of, 1132-1133
target populations for, 1134
teacher proximity, student behavior and, 1133
See also **Precorrection; Schoolwide discipline**
Acute stress disorder (ASD), 596, 597
Adaptive information processing (AIP) model, 297

Addiction. *See* Alcoholism; **Behavioral approaches to gambling**; **Behavioral treatment for the addictions**; Substance abuse disorders
Adler, A., 244
Adolescent anger management, 653-657
  case illustration, 655-656
  research basis of, 654-655
  strategy, description of, 653-654
  target populations for, 655
  See also **Anger**; **Anger management**; **Behavioral treatment for aggression in couples**
Aggregation principle, 1210-1211
Agoraphobic Cognitions Questionnaire, 441
Agras, W. Stewart, 5-6
  See also **Applied behavior analysis**; **Barlow, David H.**; **Single-case research**
Alcohol Behavioral Couple Treatment (ABCT), 559
Alcoholism:
  aversion relief and, 40
  community reinforcement method and, 42
  See also **Behavioral treatments for the addictions**; **Controlled drinking**
Alcohol Use Disorders Identification Test, 221
Allison, J., 474
Allyon, T., 34, 41, 537, 594, 983, 1076
American Counseling Association (ACA), 338
American Medical Association (AMA), 280, 281
American Psychological Association (APA), 36, 96, 338, 442, 585
Americans with Disabilities Act, 1508
Anger management, 6-11
  anger activation links and, 8
  case illustration, 10-11
  cognitive-behavioral therapy and, 7-8
  comorbid disorders and, 10
  complications with, 9-10
  institutionalized clients, 9-10
  leverage for change and, 7
  provocation hierarchy scenarios and, 8
  relapse prevention and, 8-9
  research basis of, 9
  stress inoculation approach to, 7, 8, 9
  target populations for, 9
  treatment strategies, description of, 6-9
  See also **Adolescent anger management**; **Behavioral contracting**; **Coverant control**; **Cue-controlled relaxation**
Anger treatment, 7
Anorexia nervosa, 6, 264-265
Antecedent, 1135-1137
  antecedent events, functions of, 1135-1136
  description of, 1135
  interventions and, 1136
  operant relations and, 1135-1136

respondent relations and, 1135
  See also **Antecedent control procedures**; **Applied behavior analysis**; **Consequence**; **Functional behavioral assessment of problem behavior**; **Operant conditioning**
Antecedent, behavior, consequence (ABC) charts. *See* AABC charts and scatterplots
Antecedent control procedures, 657-662
  antecedent conditions, aversiveness of, 659
  case illustration, 661
  challenging behaviors, reduction approaches to, 657-660
  complications with, 661
  consequence control procedures and, 658-659
  development of, 658
  differential reinforcement of alternative behavior and, 658
  extinction and, 658
  law of effect and, 657
  punishment and, 658-659
  reinforcer effectiveness and, 660
  reinforcer frequency and, 659-660
  research basis of, 660-661
  strategy, description of, 657-660
  target populations for, 661
  See also **Behavioral analytic approach to gambling**; **Behavioral treatment in natural environments**; **Changes in behavior**; **Stimulus control**
Anti-social personality disorder (ASPD), 1227
Anxiety/anger management training (AMT), 11-14
  case illustration, 13-14
  complications with, 13
  research basis of, 12
  strategy, description of, 11-12
  target populations for, 12-13
  See also **Relaxation strategies**; **Role playing**; **Social effectiveness training**
Anxiety disorders, 2, 6, 28
  aversion relief and, 40
  geriatric clients and, 111, 112
  spouse-aided therapy and, 559, 560
  See also **Exposure**
Anxiety Disorders Interview Schedule (ADIS), 363, 550
Anxiety management training (AMT), 510, 662-666
  case illustration, 665-666
  complications with, 664-665
  relaxation training and, 663
  research basis of, 664
  strategy, description of, 662-664
  target populations for, 664
  See also **Anxiety/anger management training**; **Barlow, David H.**; **Cognitive-behavior therapy: Child clinical applications**; **Foa, Edna B.**; **Stress inoculation training**

Anxiety responses, 28
  fainting, 29-30
  fighting, 29
  flight, 29
  freezing, 28-29
Anxiety Sensitivity Index, 441
**Applied behavior analysis (ABA),
    14-23, 666-674, 1124, 1137-1143**
  adult populations and, 19-20
  behavioral assessment and, 17
  behavior therapy and, 15-17
  case illustrations of, 22-23
  challenging behavior, management of,
    1140-1141
  cognitions, causal role of, 16
  community-based applications of, 20-21
  community psychology/injury prevention case
    example, 23
  complex behavior, analysis of, 672-673
  complication with, 21
  conclusions/implications of, 673-674
  data systems in, 673
  description/theoretical assumptions of,
    666-667, 1137-1138
  developmental disabilities and, 20
  education applications of, 1137-1141
  ethical considerations in, 1142-1143
  experimental design for, 19
  extinction and, 669
  fading and, 1139
  functional approach to, 16-17
  institutionalized adult/self-injury case
    example, 22
  instructional strategies and, 1138-1139
  misconceptions/myths about, 1141-1142
  model description, 14-15
  natural contexts and, 672
  next-generation therapies and, 20
  outpatient psychotherapy case example, 22-23
  outpatient settings and, 20
  practice implications, 19, 671-673
  principles of, 667-671
  punishment-based procedures and, 18, 669-670
  reinforcement-based procedures and, 17-18, 667-669
  selectionist model and, 16
  shaping/chaining behaviors and, 668-669, 1139
  skill vs. performance deficits and, 18-19
  stimulus control and, 17, 670-671
  target behavior selection and, 671
  target populations for, 21
  theoretical/philosophical elements of, 15
  tool skills and, 1139
  See also **Baer, Donald M.; Function-based support;
    Goldiamond, Israel; Kazdin, Alan E.; Positive**
**behavior support; Schedules of reinforcement;
    Skinner, Burrhus Frederic**
Applied relaxation and tension, 23-27
  case illustration of, 27
  complications with, 26-27
  research basis of, 25-26
  strategy, description of, 23-25
  target populations for, 26
  See also **Anxiety management; Applied tension;
    Relaxation strategies**
Applied tension, 27-32
  anxiety experience, responses to, 28-29
  case illustration, 31
  complications with, 31
  research basis of, 30
  strategy, description of, 27-30
  target populations for, 30
  See also **Anxiety management; Applied relaxation
    and tension; Breathing retraining**
Archival records, 1143-1147
  behavior management, school records and, 1144
  case illustration, 1145-1146
  complications with, 1144-1145
  confidentiality issues and, 1145
  description of, 1143-1144
  institutional idiosyncrasies and, 1145
  research data and, 1144
  target population for, 1144
  See also **Behavioral assessment; Functional
    behavioral assessment of problem behavior**
Aromatic ammonia, 674-675
  See also **Aversion relief; Classical conditioning;
    Extinction and habituation; Punishment**
Arousal systems:
  anger management and, 8
  See also **Arousal training**
Arousal training, 32-33
  cognitive-behavioral treatment regimes and, 33
  male erectile disorder and, 32
  panic disorder and, 32
  See also **Marshall, William L.; Masturbatory
    retraining; Orgasmic reconditioning**
Assertiveness training (AT), 675-679
  case example, 677-679
  complications with, 677
  research basis of, 676
  strategy, description of, 675-676
  target populations for, 677
  See also **Behavioral marital therapy; Behavioral
    treatment for aggression in couples; Social
    competence treatment: Externalizing disorders;
    Social effectiveness training; Social and
    interpersonal skills training; Social skills
    training**

Assertive Self-Statement Test (ASST), 526
**Association for Advancement of Behavior Therapy
    (AABT), 33-37**, 184, 188, 310, 331, 698
    contributors to, 33-34
    current work/views and, 35-36
    early influences on, 33
    future plans/directions for, 36-37
    history of, 34-35
    organizational overview, 33
    See also **Applied behavior analysis; Behavior
        therapy; Franks, Cyril M.**
Association for Applied Psychophysiology and
    Biofeedback (AAPB), 753-754
Association for Behavior Analysis (ABA), 331, 1037
Association for the Treatment of Sexual Abusers, 367
Attentional Training System (ATS), 1005, 1006
**Attention-deficit/hyperactivity disorder (ADHD),
    1147-1148**
    interventions for, 1147-1148
    parent-mediated strategies and, 1147
    self-management and, 1147
    See also **Attention training procedures;
        Pharmacotherapy; Pharmacotherapy and
        behavior therapy; Self-management; Social
        skills instruction; Teaching students self-control**
Attention training procedures, 679-683
    case illustration, 682-683
    complications with, 681-682
    extra-stimulus prompting and, 680-681
    research basis of, 681
    stimulus overselectivity and, 679
    strategy, description of, 679-681
    target populations for, 681
    within-stimulus prompting and, 679-680
    See also **Behavioral assessment; Behavior therapy
        and neuropsychology; Private events**
**Augmentative and alternative
    communication (AAC), 1148-1149**
    complications with, 1149
    research basis of, 1149
    selection techniques and, 1149
    strategy, description of, 1148-1149
    symbol display techniques and, 1148-1149
    symbolic representation and, 1148
    target populations for, 1149
    See also **Functional communication training**
Autism Diagnostic Observation Checklist (ADOS), 1150
Autism spectrum disorders, 1149-1154
    adulthood, preparations for, 1153
    communication/speech/language and, 1151
    diagnosis of, 1150-1151
    discrete trial approach and, 1152
    educational settings and, 1152-1153
    incidence, increase of, 1151

    naturalistic behavioral approach and, 1153
    play activities, deficits in, 1151
    social interaction, deficits in, 1151
    support services and, 1152
    See also **Applied behavior analysis; Discrete trial
        instruction; Discrete trial therapy; Functional
        communication training; Lovaas, O. Ivar;
        Pivotal response training for autism**
Autistic Diagnostic Interview (ADI), 1150
Autogenic training (AT), 37-38, 486
    complications with, 38
    research basis of, 38
    strategy, description of, 37-38
    target populations for, 38
    See also **Classical conditioning; Mindfulness
        meditation; Relaxation strategies**
Automatic Thoughts Questionnaire (ATQ), 526
Aversion relief, 39-40
    research basis of, 39-40
    stategy, description of, 39
    target populations for, 40
    See also **Aromatic ammonia; Electrical aversion;
        Emmelkamp, Paul M. G.; Extinction and
        habituation; Relaxation strategies**
Aversive conditioning, 683-685
    case illustration, 685
    complications with, 684-685
    research basis of, 683-684
    strategy, description of, 683
    target populations for, 684
    See also **Aversion relief; Avoidance training;
        Electrical aversion; Operant conditioning**
Avoidance training, 686
    See also **Aversion relief; Aversive conditioning;
        Electrical aversion; Extinction and habituation;
        Operant conditioning**
Awareness of Consequences Test (ACT), 971
Azrin, Nathan H., 34, **40-42**, 207, 325, 537, 594, 873,
    928, 983, 1076
    See also **Habit rehearsal; JobClub method; Token
        economy**

Baer, Donald M., 41, **687-688**, 1349, 1350
    See also **Applied behavior analysis; Azrin, Nathan
        H.; Behavioral treatment in natural
        environments; Correspondence training;
        Operant conditioning; Single-case research**
Bain, J. A., 591
Bandura, A., 45, 346, 719, 768, 908, 1085, 1137, 1508
Bank Street model, 1469
Barlow, David H., **43-45**, 92, 188, 537
    See also **Agras, W. Stewart; Behavior training; Panic
        control treatment**
Barrett, P., 702

Baseline, 1155-1156
See also **Behavioral assessment; Research designs;**
    Single case research; Single-subject design
Bateson, G., 719
Baucom, D. H., 120
Beat the buzzer, 689-690, 693
    complications with, 690
    research basis of, 689
    strategy, description of, 689
    target populations for, 689
    See also **Behavioral treatment in natural**
        environments; Good behavior game; Positive
        reinforcement; Reinforcement; Setting events
Beck, Aaron T., 45-46, 92, 188, 195, 199, 203, 204, 245,
    559, 587, 621, 768, 775
    See also **Child clinical applications; Cognitive-behavioral**
        approach to bipolar disorder; Cognitive-behavior
        therapy
Beck Anxiety Inventory, 46
Beck Depression Inventory, 46, 68, 206, 441
Beck Hopelessness Scale, 46
Beck, J., 245
Beck Self-Concept Test, 46
Beck Youth Inventories of Emotional and Social
    Impairment, 46
Becker, Wesley, 1156-1160, 1468
    See also **Applied behavior analysis; Direct**
        Instruction; Project Follow Through and Direct
        Instruction
Bed-wetting. *See* **Bell and pad bladder training;**
    Full-spectrum home training for simple
    bed-wetting; Retention control training
Beginning reading, 1160-1165
    automaticity/fluency, phonological code and, 1161-1162
    case illustration, 1164-1165
    comprehension skills, 1163-1164, 1163 (figure)
    description of, 1160-1164
    phonemic awareness and, 1161
    phonics and, 1161
    research basis of, 1164
    target populations for, 1164
    vocabulary development and, 1162-1163
    See also **Becker, Wesley; Beginning reading**
        instruction; Direct Instruction; Dynamic
        indicators of basic early literacy skills;
        Engelmann, Siegfried
Beginning reading instruction, 1165-1170
    big-idea focus of, 1165-1166
    case illustration, 1168-1169, 1169 (figure)
    conspicuous instruction and, 1166
    description of, 1165-1167
    instructional scaffolding in, 1166-1167
    practice opportunities, feedback and, 1167
    research basis of, 1167

target population for, 1168
    See also **Beginning reading; Learning disabilities**
Behavior activation (BA), 46-51
    behavioral avoidance and, 47
    case illustration, 49-50
    complications with, 49
    research basis of, 48
    strategy, description of, 46-48
    target populations for, 49
    See also **Homework; Manualized behavior therapy;**
        Motor activity and behavioral assessment
Behavioral analytic approach to supervision, 63-67
    behavior change principles and, 63, 64
    behavior-consequence relationships and, 65
    bug-in-the-ear procedure, 66
    clinical behavior analysis and, 63-65
    natural vs. arbitrary reinforcement and, 64-65
    response discrimination and, 65, 66
    rule-governed behavior and, 65, 66
    strategy, description of, 63
    supervision process and, 65-66
    treatment coding systems and, 63
    See also **Applied behavior analysis; Behavioral**
        consultation; Behavioral contracting
Behavioral approaches to gambling, 67-72
    anxiety reduction and, 70
    aversive stimuli and, 67
    behavior completion theory and, 67-68
    case illustration, 71-72
    complications with, 70-71
    false cognitions and, 68
    habituation and, 67
    intention-to-treat evaluation and, 69
    relapse prevention and, 68
    research basis of, 68-70
    strategy, description of, 67-68
    target populations for, 70
    See also **Behavioral treatment for the addictions;**
        Behavioral treatment of cigarette smoking;
        Self-control
Behavioral approaches to schizophrenia, 72-78
    antipsychotic medications and, 72
    case illustration, 77-78
    cognitive-behavioral therapy and, 74-75
    cognitive remediation and, 75-76
    social skills training and, 72-74
    strategy, description of, 72
    token economies and, 76-77
    See also **Bellack, Alan S.; Role playing; Social skills**
        training
Behavioral approaches to sexual deviation, 78-82
    arousal reduction/redirection, 80
    assessment/testing processes in, 78-79
    case illustration, 81-82

cognitive restructuring, 79
cognitive skills training, 80
complications with, 81
emotional recognition skills and, 80
group treatment and, 79
masturbatory reconditioning, 80
problem-solving approach, 79-80
relapse preventions and, 80
relationship deficits and, 80
research basis of, 80-81
strategies, description of, 78, 79-80
substance abuse choices and, 80
target populations for, 81
See also **Electrical aversion; Masturbatory
    retraining; Orgasmic reconditioning**
Behavioral Approach Test (BAT), 189
Behavioral Assertiveness Test-Revised (BAT-R), 494
Behavioral assessment, 82-90, 704-711, 1170-1173
case illustration, 1172-1173
causal functional relations, identification methods,
    88-90, 709-710
causation issues, 83, 84, 705, 706
complications with, 1172
contexts of behaviors and, 83, 84, 704-705, 1172
definition/specification of behaviors/causes, 84-85
empiricism concept and, 83, 704
environmental determinism and, 83, 704
experimental manipulations, observation of, 89-90, 710
features of, 1171-1172
frequency of, 1172
functional analysis of behavior problems,
    85-86, 706-707
goals/applications of, 84-86, 705-707
hypothetico-deductive method in, 83, 704
individual differences, sensitivity to, 83, 705
interviewing and, 86, 707-708, 1171
marker-variable strategy and, 89, 709-710
measurement dimensions, 85
multiple assessments, concurrent
    administration of, 89, 710, 1171
natural context-behavior interactions,
    observations of, 89, 710, 1172
observations and, 86-87, 708, 1171
problems/causes, functional relations of, 84
questionnaires and, 87, 708-709, 1170-1171
record/permanent product review and, 1171
replacement behaviors and, 1171-1172
research basis of, 1172
sampling methods and, 88, 709
self-monitoring and, 87, 708
self-report questionnaires/rating scales and,
    87, 708-709
social system context and, 84, 705
strategy, description of, 82-84, 704-705, 1170-1172

target populations for, 1172
temporal considerations, 83-84, 705
theoretical foundations of, 1170
See also **Behavioral assessment interviews; Behavior
    rating scales; Behavior therapy and
    neuropsychology; Direct observation; Functional
    analysis; Motor activity and behavioral
    assessment; Progress monitoring; Virtual reality
    therapy**
Behavioral assessment interviews, 1173-1176
case illustration, 1175-1176
complications with, 1175
intervention development/implementation and, 1174
research basis of, 1174-1175
semistructured questions in, 1173-1174
strategy, description of, 1173-1174
structured questions in, 1173
subjective nature of, 1174, 1176
target populations for, 1175
unstructured questions in, 1174
See also **Behavioral assessment; Behavioral
    interview; Function-based support; Positive
    behavior support**
Behavioral case formulation, 90-102
behavior antecedents/consequences and, 93-94
case illustration, 96-101, 100-101 (figures)
complications with, 96
data collection methods in, 90-91
functional assessment, behavior context and, 92-93
hypotheses development, 94-95
hypotheses testing/revising, 95
observational assessment phase of, 90-94
research basis of, 95-96
scientific method and, 90, 91 (figure)
strategy, description of, 90-95
target behaviors, identification/
    description of, 91-94
target populations for, 96
treatment planning, 94-95
See also **Applied behavior analysis; Behavioral
    assessment; Case conceptualization**
**Behavioral consultation, 102-106, 711-714,
    1176-1180**
accountability of staff and, 105
adherence to behavioral protocols and, 104-105
assumptions in, 1176-1177
business/industry applications of, 103
case illustration, 105-106, 713-714, 1179
complications with, 104-105, 713, 1178-1179
educational systems applications of, 103, 713
research basis of, 102-103, 712-713, 1177-1178
stages in, 1177
strategy, description of, 102, 711-712, 1176-1177
target populations for, 103-104, 713, 1178

See also **Behavioral assessment; Behavioral assessment interviews; Behavioral consultation; Functional behavioral assessment of problem behavior; Private practice of behavioral treatment; Problem-solving consultation model**

Behavioral contracting, 17-18, 20, **106-110, 715-719, 1180-1182**
case illustration, 109-110, 717-718
client involvement in, 109, 1181
complications with, 108-109, 717, 1181-1182
contingencies in, 107, 1180
development/implementation of, 1180-1181
research basis of, 107-108, 716, 1181
strategy, description of, 106-107, 715-716, 1180-1181
target populations for, 108, 716-717, 1181
weight control interventions and, 167-168
See also **Behavioral consultation; Behavioral marital therapy; Behavior management; Contingency management; Evaluating behavioral plans; Positive reinforcement; Premack principle**

Behavioral dimensions, 1182-1185
consistency, 1185
duration/endurance, 1183-1184
efficiency, 1184
functional dimensions, 1184-1185
interresponse time, 1184
intraresponse time, 1184
latency, 1183
locus, 1182-1183
operant-to-operant/response-to-response interval, 1184
physical dimensions, 1182-1183
rate/frequency, 1183
shape/form/topographical features, 1182
social acceptability, 1185
temporal dimensions, 1183-1184
See also **Behavioral assessment; Rate and frequency**

Behavioral family therapy (BFT), **719-723**
case illustration, 721-722
complications with, 721
research basis of, 720-721
strategy, description of, 719-720
target populations for, 721
See also **Behavioral contracting; Behavioral marital therapy; Behavioral treatment in natural environments; Compliance training**

Behavioral fluency, **1185-1188**
case illustration, 1188
complications with, 1187-1188
description of, 1185-1186
endurance/resistance to distraction and, 1187
learning stages and, 1186
research/experiential basis of, 1186-1187
retention/maintenance and, 1187
skills applications/ combinations and, 1187

See also **Behavioral rehearsal; Phases of learning; Positive reinforcement; Reinforced practice**

Behavioral gerontology, **110-114**
aggressive behavior and, 113
anxiety disorders and, 111, 112
behavioral medicine and, 111-112
case illustration, 114
complications with, 113-114
dementia and, 113
dependency, functional decline and, 111
depression and, 112
disruptive vocalizations and, 113
incontinence treatments, 112
memory/cognition deficits and, 111
pain treatment and, 111
paranoia and, 112-113
psychopathology and, 112-113
research basis of, 110
self-care behaviors and, 110
sleep disturbances and, 111-112
social skills training and, 110
strategy, description of, 110
wandering risk, 113
See also **Behavoral treatment in natural environments; Cognitive behavior therapy with religious beliefs and practices; Hersen, Michel**

Behavioral group therapy with children and youth, **723-727**
assessment in groups and, 724
case illustration, 726-727
complications with, 726
effective treatment, principles of, 724-725, 725 (table)
modes of intervention, 725-726
research basis of, 726
strategy, description of, 723-726
target populations for, 726
See also **Behavioral group work; Group behavioral therapy for depression; Social competence treatment: Externalizing disorders; Social effectiveness training; Social and interpersonal skills training; Social skills training**

Behavioral group work, **114-118**
assessment in groups and, 115
case illustration, 117-118
cohesion and, 115
complications with, 117
goals of treatment and, 115-116, 116 (table)
interventions in, 116
problems, resolution of, 116
research basis of, 116
strategy, description of, 114-116
target populations for, 116-117
weight control interventions and, 168

See also **Behavioral family therapy**; **Behavioral marital therapy**; **Coercive cycles in families**
Behavioral interview, 727-731
case illustration, 729-730
complications with, 729
research basis of, 728
strategy, description of, 727-728
target populations for, 728-729
See also **Behavioral assessment**; **Dialectical behavior therapy**; **Multimodal behavior therapy**
Behavioral marital therapy (BMT), 118-122
assessment procedures in, 119
case illustration, 121-122
complications with, 121
interventions in, 119-120
research basis of, 120
strategy, description of, 118-119
target populations for, 120-121
See also **Behavioral family therapy**; **Behavioral group work**; **Coercive cycles in families**
Behavioral medicine, 6, 123-136
behavior therapy and, 125-126
biofeedback and, 124-125
cancer chemotherapy, anticipatory nausea and, 131-132
case illustrations, 134-135, 135 (table)
clinical applications of, 127-133
cognitive-behavioral therapy and, 125
depression and, 133
exercise and, 127, 133
future directions of, 133-134
geriatric clients and, 111-112
history of, 123-124
holistic approaches and, 124
hypertension and, 132-133
hypnosis and, 126-127
insomnia and, 131
irritable bowel syndrome and, 130-131
obesity and, 129
pain reduction and, 125, 127-129
relaxation therapy and, 126
self-monitoring and, 1024
smoking cessation and, 129-130
strategy, description of, 123
stress reduction and, 127
treatment compliance and, 132
treatment modalities in, 124-127
urinary/fecal incontinence and, 130
See also **Behavioral treatment for the addictions**; **Behavioral treatment of cigarette smoking**; **Behavioral weight treatment control therapy with children**; **Satiation**
Behavioral momentum, 1189-1190
complications with, 1190
research basis of, 1189

strategy, description of, 1189
target populations for, 1189-1190
See also **Extinction**; **Maintenance**; **Positive reinforcement**; **Schedules of reinforcement**; **Task interspersal**
Behavioral objectives, 1190-1194
case illustration, 1192-1194
complications with, 1192
conditions/performance standards and, 1193
goal, determination of, 1192-1193
identification of behaviors, 1193
research basis of, 1191, 1191-1192 (tables)
sequencing process and, 1193-1194
strategy, description of, 1190-1191
target populations for, 1192
See also **Behavioral contracting**; **Individualized education program**; **Long-term objectives**; **Short-term objectives**; **Task analysis**
Behavioral observations (event/interval), 1194-1198
controlled presentation/opportunity recording, 1195
duration recording, 1196
event-based recording, 1194-1196
frequency recording, 1194
latency recording, 1196
momentary interval recording, 1197-1198
partial interval recording, 1197
permanent product recording, 1194-1195
time-based interval recording, 1196-1198
trials to criterion recording, 1195-1196
whole interval recording, 1197
See also **Baseline**; **Behavioral assessment**; **Behavioral dimensions**
Behavioral parent training (BPT), 720
Behavioral pediatrics (BP), 731-739
bedtime problems, 732-733
behavioral influences and, 735-737
biological influences and, 733-735
biology-behavior interaction and, 737
case illustration, 737-738
functional encopresis and, 733-735
nocturnal enuresis, biofeedback and, 736-737
pharmacotherapy and, 738
strategy, description of, 731-733
See also **Applied behavior analysis**; **Behavioral consultation**; **Behavioral medicine**; **Bell and pad bladder training**; **Memory rehabilitation after brain injury**; **Psychoneuroimmunology**
Behavioral problem-solving (BPS), 969
Behavioral rehearsal, 739-742, 1198-1200
case illustration, 741-742, 1199-1200
complications with, 740-741, 1199
drug abuse prevention and, 815
relapse prevention and, 986-987
research basis of, 740, 1198

strategy, description of, 739-740, 1198
target populations for, 740, 1199
See also **Behavioral fluency; Massed practice;**
    Modeling; Role playing
Behavioral social work, 136-140
    child welfare and, 138-139
    community mental health and, 138
    health care work and, 137-138
    home-based behavioral interventions, 138
    school-based behavioral interventions, 139
    social work perspective and, 136-137, 139
    strategy, description of, 136
    See also **Behavioral treatment in natural**
        environments; Home-based reinforcement;
        Systems of care
Behavioral sport psychology, 140-145
    behavior modification principles and, 143-144
    complications with, 143
    developmental phases, procedural emphases
        and, 143-145
    mental skills training and, 144-145
    metapostulates in, 140-141
    overt vs. covert behaviors and, 142
    research basis of, 140-143
    strategy, description of, 140
    See also **Cue-controlled relaxation;**
        Self-instruction; Sports skills training
Behavioral treatment for aggression in
    couples, 145-146
    complications with, 146
    research basis of, 146
    strategy, description of, 145-146
    target populations for, 146
    See also **Behavioral group therapy with children**
        and youth; Behavioral marital therapy;
        Behavior management
Behavioral treatment of cigarette smoking, 155-160
    biobehavioral model of smoking and, 155-156
    case illustration, 158-159
    complications with, 157-158
    research basis of, 156-157
    strategy, description of, 156
    target populations for, 157
    See also **Behavioral treatment for the addictions;**
        Competing response training; Positive behavior
        support
Behavioral treatment of insomnia, 160-164
    case illustration, 163-164
    cognitive therapy and, 161
    complications with, 163
    pharmacologic interventions and, 162
    relaxation-based interventions and, 161
    research basis of, 162
    sleep hygiene education and, 161-162

sleep restriction therapy and, 161
stimulus control therapy and, 160
strategy, description of, 160-162
target populations for, 162-163
treatment formats in, 162
See also **Applied relaxation and**
    tension; Biofeedback; Fading
Behavioral treatment of minorities, 164-167
    complications with, 166
    research basis of, 165-166
    strategy, description of, 164-165
    target populations for, 166
    See also **Cultural differences in cognitive therapy;**
        Peer intervention; Peer tutoring
Behavioral treatment in natural
    environments, 151-155
    case illustration, 154-155
    complications with, 153-154
    research basis of, 152
    strategy, description of, 151-152
    target populations for, 152-153
    See also **Bell and pad bladder training; Classroom**
        management; Contextualism
Behavioral treatments for the addictions, 147-151
    case illustration, 149-150
    community reinforcement approach and, 148
    complications with, 149
    contingency management and, 148
    coping/refusal skills and, 147
    functional analysis of behavior and, 147
    pharmacotherapy and, 148-149
    psychosocial issues and, 147-148
    relapse prevention and, 148
    research basis of, 149
    seemingly irrelevant decisions and, 147
    strategy, description of, 147-149
    target populations for, 149
    See also **Behavioral contracting; Behavioral**
        treatment of cigarette smoking;
        Operant conditioning
Behavioral weight control therapy with
    children, 742-746
    case illustration, 746
    complications with, 745-746
    meal planning and, 743
    physical activity and, 743-744
    problem-solving training and, 744
    reinforcement/shaping and, 743
    research basis of, 744
    self-monitoring and, 743
    social support and, 744
    stimulus control and, 743
    strategy, description of, 742-744
    target populations for, 745

See also **Behavioral group work; Group behavioral therapy for depression; Social competence treatment: Externalizing disorders; Social effectiveness training; Social and interpersonal skills training; Social skills training**

Behavioral weight control treatments, 167-171
case illustration, 170-171
complications with, 169-170
components of interventions and, 167-168
philosophy of treatment and, 167
research basis of, 168-169
strategy, description of, 167-168
target populations for, 169
See also **Behavioral medicine; Behavioral weight control therapy with children; Homework**

Behavioral working alliance, 171-175
case illustration, 174
complications with, 173
disruptions in, 172
engagement sessions and, 171
nonengagement sessions and, 171-172
research basis of, 173
strategy, description of, 171-173
target populations for, 173
termination phase and, 172-173
See also **Behavioral assessment; Behavior rating scales; Role playing**

Behavior Analysis Follow-Through project, 103
Behavior-analytic view. *See* **Applied behavior analysis**
Behavior Evaluation Strategy and Taxonomy (BEST) software, 210-212
Behavior intervention planning (BIP), 1200-1204
case illustration, 1204
complications with, 1203
description of, 1200-1203
evaluation plan and, 1202-1203
implementation plan and, 1202
research basis of, 1203
support plan and, 1200-1202, 1201 (figure)
target populations for, 1203
See also **Behavioral treatment in natural environments; Competing response training; Descriptive and functional analysis; Functional analysis; Functional behavioral assessment of problem behavior; Positive behavior support**

Behaviorism. *See* **Applied behavior analysis**
Behavioristic psychodrama, 51
Behavior management, 1204-1208
case illustration, 1207-1208
complications with, 1206-1207
contingencies and, 1205
effectiveness of, 1205
implementation process, 1206

objections to, 1205-1206
research basis of, 1206
strategy, description of, 1204-1206
target populations for, 1206
See also **Behavior management for improving academic and classroom behavior; Classroom management; Contingencies in educational settings; Differential reinforcement; Effective learning environments; Extinction; Function-based support; Good behavior game; Positive reinforcement; Precorrection; Response cost; Single-subject design; Time-out; Token economy**

Behavior management for improving academic and classroom behavior, 690-698
accelerative procedures and, 693
antecedent interventions, setting and, 691-692
consequence interventions and, 692
considerations in, 697
functional assessment, treatment-assessment link and, 691
group contingencies and, 695-696
home-based procedures and, 696-697
overcorrection and, 694-695
reductive procedures and, 693-694
self-management techniques and, 697
teacher attention and, 692-693
See also **Applied behavior analysis; Behavioral treatment in natural environments; Motor activity and behavioral assessment; Token economy**

Behavior modification. *See* **Applied behavior analysis; Historical antecedents of behavior modification and therapy; Sazrin, Nathan H.**

Behaviorology, 175-176
See also **Behavior therapy theory; Operant conditioning; Schedules of reinforcement**

Behavior rating scales, 1208-1212
advantages of, 1209
aggregation principle and, 1210-1211
bias of response and, 1210
case illustration, 1211
complications with, 1210-1211
error variance and, 1210
research basis of, 1209-1210
strategy, description of, 1208-1209
target populations for, 1210
See also **Behavioral assessment; Early-risk screening; Functional behavioral assessment of problem behavior**

Behavior rehearsal, 51-52
complications with, 52
research basis of, 51
strategy, description of, 51

target populations for, 51-52
See also **Modeling**; **Role playing**; **Social skills instruction**
Behavior support plan (BSP), 1141
Behavior therapy, 15, 698-704
applied behavior analysis and, 15-17
behavioral excesses/deficits and, 699
developmental issues and, 703
exposure-based interventions and, 700
family anxiety management, 702
medical/disease model and, 698
naturalistic interventions and, 702-703
operant-based approaches and, 700-701
respondent-based approaches and, 699-700, 701
respondent/operant approaches, integration of, 701
social effectiveness therapy for children, 701-702
strategy, description of, 698-699
systematic desensitization and, 700
treatment programs in, 701-702
See also **Behavioral approaches to gambling**; **Behavioral approaches to schizophrenia**; **Behavioral family therapy**; **Behavior therapy theory**; **Dialectical behavior therapy**; **Multimodal behavior therapy**
Behavior therapy and neuropsychology, 52-56
case illustration, 54-55
complications with, 54
research basis of, 53
strategy, description of, 52-53
target populations for, 53-54
See also **Behavioral assessment**; **Behavioral gerontology**; **Behavioral medicine**
Behavior therapy theory, 56-60
cognitive basis of, 59
explanatory bases of, 56
functional analytic basis of, 57-58
learning theory/memory and, 56-57
network theories and, 59
reciprocal inhibition basis of, 58-59
See also **Applied behavior analysis**; **Behavioral case formulation**; **Behavioral therapy**
Behavior training, 60-63
case illustration, 62-63
complications with, 62
extinction and, 60
operant conditioning and, 60, 61
punishment and, 60
reinforcement and, 61
research basis of, 60-61
strategy, description of, 60
target populations for, 61-62
token economy and, 60
See also **Cognitive behavior therapy**; **Homework**; **Social skills training**

Bellack, Alan S., 176-178
See also **Behavioral approaches to schizophrenia**; **Behavioral treatment in natural environments**; **Social skills training**
Bell and pad bladder training, 746-750
case illustration, 749, 750 (figure)
complications with, 748-749
research basis of, 747-748
strategy, description of, 746-747
target populations for, 748
See also **Behavioral treatment in natural environments**; **Biofeedback**; **Classical conditioning**; **Full-spectrum home training for simple bed-wetting**; **Operant conditioning**; **Retention control training**
Bereiter-Engelmann preschool, 1156, 1157, 1468
Bergin, A., 196
Bergson, H., 1233
Bernstein, D. A., 24
BEST (Behavior Evaluation Strategy and Taxonomy) software, 210-212
Bibliotherapy, 178-179
See also **Homework**; **Instructions**; **Manualized behavior therapy**
Bijou, S., 1326
Billingsley, F., 1353
Binge-eating disorder, 6, 263
Biofeedback, 124-125, 179-182, 486, 750-756
biofeedback therapists and, 752-753, 755
cancer chemotherapy, anticipatory nausea and, 131-132
case illustrations, 181, 755-756
complications with, 180-181, 754-755
computer interface for, 179-180
electromyographic biofeedback, 128, 129, 130
general approach to, 751
hypertension and, 132-133
operations in, 751
pain management and, 111, 125, 127-129
physiological processes in, 180
relaxation promotion modalities and, 181, 751-752
research basis of, 180, 753-754, 753 (table)
strategy, description of, 179-180, 750-753
target populations for, 180, 181 (table), 754
urinary/fecal incontinence and, 130, 736-737
See also **Applied relaxation and tension**; **Behavioral medicine**; **Behavioral pediatrics**; **Pharmacotherapy and behavior therapy**; **Progressive muscular relaxation**; **Relaxation strategies**; **Relaxation training with children**
Bipolar mood disorder, 7
antimanic agents and, 957
See also **Cognitive-behavioral approach to bipolar disorder**

Bladder control. *See* **Bell and pad bladder training;
    Full-spectrum home training for simple
    bed-wetting; Retention control training**
Blanchard, E. B., 124
Body mass index (BMI), 169, 745
Body Sensations Questionnaire, 441
Borderline personality disorder (BPD), 257, 259, 260
Borkovec, T. D., 24
Boys' Town, 702
Brain injuries:
    behavior therapy/neuropsychology and, 53-54
    See also **Memory rehabilitation after
        traumatic brain injury**
Breathing retraining, 182
    See also **Panic control treatment; Progressive
        muscular relaxation; Relaxation strategies**
Breathing techniques. *See* **Regulated breathing**
Brown, T., 44
Brown v. Board of Education, 1367
Buckley Amendment, 1145
Bulimia nervosa, 6, 263-264
Bureau of Education for the Handicapped (BEH), 1355
Burgess, A., 281
Bushell, D., Jr., 103

CALM (Counseling for Alcoholics' Marriages)
    project, 559-560
Cancer treatments, 131-132
Carnap, R., 435
Carnine, D., 1293
Carr, E., 1326, 1330
Case conceptualization, 757-761
    case illustration, 760-761
    complications with, 759-760
    components of, 757-758
    information gathering methods in, 758-759
    research basis of, 759
    strategy, description of, 757-759
    target populations for, 759
    See also **Behavioral case formulation; Behavioral
        treatment in natural environments; Operant
        conditioning; Single-case research**
Cautela, Joseph R., 43, 183-185, 227, 235, 797
    See also **Coverant control; Covert rehearsal; Covert
        sensitization conditioning**
Center for Advanced Study in the Behavioral
    Sciences, 353
Center for Mental Health Services (CMHS), 1558, 1603
Center for Stress and Anxiety Disorders, 44
Cerny, J. A., 908
Chaining, 1213-1216
    applied behavior analysis and, 668-669, 1139
    case illustration, 1215-1216
    complications with, 1215

correspondence training and, 791
errorless learning and, 1297-1298
examples of, 1213
research basis of, 1215
steps in, 1213-1214
strategy, description of, 1215
target populations for, 1215
variables in, 1214-1215
See also **Fading; Shaping to teach
    new behaviors; Task analysis**
Chambless, D. L., 908
Changing criterion designs, 1216-1217
    advantages of, 1217
    experimental control and, 1216
    steps in, 1216-1217
    See also **Applied behavior analysis;
        Research designs; Single case research;
        Single-subject design; Task analysis**
Chappell, M. N., 126
Character education, 1217-1218
    development of, 1217
    effectiveness evaluations of, 1218
    instructional strategies in, 1217
    values clarification/moral reasoning
        movements and, 1217
    See also **Social competence; Social and
        interpersonal skills training; Social skills
        instruction; Social skills training**
Checklist for Autism in Toddlers (CHAT), 1150
Child abuse, 11
Child behavior:
    behavioral social work and, 138-139
    behavior contracting and, 108
    behavior training and, 62
    See also **Behavioral group therapy with children
        and youth; Behavioral pediatrics; Behavioral
        weight control therapy with children;
        Cognitive-behavior therapy: Child
        clinical applications**
Child Behavior Checklist (CBCL), 971
Child Behavior Checklist Scales, 782
Child Study Center, 353
Child welfare services, 138-139
Childhood Autism Rating Scale (CARS), 1150
Childhood disorders. *See* **Empirically supported
    treatments for childhood disorders**
Children's Depression Inventory (CDI), 971
Child's Game, 779, 780
Chomsky, N., 1037
Choral responding, 1131, 1218-1219, 1404
    research basis of, 1219
    strategy, description of, 1218-1219
    See also **Active student responding;
        Opportunity to respond**

Chore and allowance program for children, 761-763

creation of, 761-762, 762 (table)

guidelines for, 762

money management/investment concepts and, 763, 763 (table)

See also **Behavioral contracting; Behavioral treatment in natural environments; Extinction and habituation**

Cigarette smoking. *See* **Behavioral treatment of cigarette smoking; Smoking cessation programs**

Clark-Beck Obsessive-Compulsive Inventory, 46

Classical conditioning, 123, 185-186, 763-767

behavioral discrepancy and, 186

behavior change and, 185-186

case illustration, 765-767

complications with, 765

contiguity and, 186

research basis of, 764-765

stimuli/responses in, 185

strategy, description of, 763-764

target populations for, 765

utility of, 186

See also **Behavioral weight control therapy with children; Covert sensitization conditioning; Electrical aversion; Historical antecedents of behavior modification and therapy; Pavlov, Ivan P.**

Classroom behavior. *See* **Behavior management for improving academic and classroom behavior; Classroom management**

Classroom management, 1219-1222

coceptual framework of, 1219

evaluative processes in, 1221

instructional alignment and, 1220

instruction-reinforcement linkages and, 1220-1221

planning process for, 1221-1222

proactive strategies in, 1219-1220

punishment, role of, 1221

spatial organization and, 1220

See also **Behavior management; Behavior management for improving academic and classroom behavior; Good behavior game; Positive reinforcement; Social skills instruction**

Classwide peer tutoring (CWPT), 1147, 1222-1223

case study, 1223

features of, 1222

research basis of, 1222

strategy, description of, 1222

See also **Active student responding; Behavior management; Classroom management; Cross-age tutoring; Mainstreaming; Peer intervention**

Clinical behavior analysis, 20

Coalition for Evidence-Based Policy, 1306

Code of Ethics and Standards of Practice, 1303

Coercive cycles in families, 1224-1226

anitsocial behaviors and, 1225

contingencies of negative reinforcement, 1225-1226

intervention/prevention programs for, 1226

long-term outcomes for, 1224

negative reinforcement, dyadic coercion process and, 1224-1225

See also **Home-based reinforcement; Negative reinforcement; Positive reinforcement**

Cognitive-behavioral approach to bipolar disorder, 198-203

case illustration, 202

cognitive-behavioral model and, 199, 199 (figure)

integrative model, treatment phases and, 200-201, 200 (figure)

research basis of, 201-202

strategy, description of, 198-199

See also **Cognitive-behavior therapy; Cognitive restructuring; Coping with depression; Eating disorders**

Cognitive-behavior therapy: Child clinical applications, 767-775, 818

case illustration, 772-774

client characteristics and, 772

developmental differences and, 770-771

limitation/complications with, 770-772

research basis of, 769-770

skill generalization and, 772

strategy, description of, 767-769

systemic influences and, 771

therapeutic techniques/procedures and, 768-769

treatment complexity and, 770

treatment manual limitations and, 772

See also **Cognitive-behavioral approach to bipolar disorder; Cognitive-behavior therapy; Cognitive-behavior therapy with religious beliefs and practices; Cognitive restructuring; Self-instruction training**

Cognitive-behavior therapy (CBT), 6, 186-195

anger management/treatment and, 7-9

assessment process in, 189-190

behavioral experiments and, 191

behavioral medicine applications, 125

brain injury and, 53

case illustration, 193-194

clinical interviews and, 189

cognitive restructuring and, 190-191

complications with, 75

depression treatment and, 45-46

direct behavioral observation and, 189

exposure-based techniques and, 191, 192 (table)

historical/conceptual foundations of, 187-188

intimate partner violence and, 146

monitoring diaries and, 189

pain relief, older adults and, 111
problem-solving strategies and, 192-193
protocols in, 193, 194 (table)
psychoeducation and, 190
psychological problems, factors in, 188-189
relaxation/meditation-based strategies and, 192
research basis of, 74
self-report scales and, 189-190
social/communication skills training and, 192
strategies used in, 190-193
strategy, description of, 74, 186-187
structure of, 190
target populations for, 74-75
See also **Beck, Aaron T.**; **Behavioral approaches to sexual deviation**; **Behavioral working alliance**; **Behavior training**; **Cognitive-behavior therapy: Child clinical applications**; **Coping with depression**; **Treatment compliance in cognitive behavior therapy**
Cognitive-behavior therapy with religious beliefs and practices, 195-198
disturbance-associated beliefs and, 197-198
doctrinal authority and, 198
empirical therapeutic tests and, 196
religious values and, 196
strategies, description of, 195-196
See also **Behavioral treatment of minorities**; **Cognitive-behavior therapy**; **Cognitive restructuring**
Cognitive control, 2
geriatric clients and, 111
insomnia and, 161
problem of, 3-4
Cognitive diffusion techniques, 4
Cognitive problem-solving skills training (PSST), 969
Cognitive-processing therapy (CPT), 598
Cognitive remediation therapy (CRT):
complications with, 76
research basis of, 76
strategy, description of, 75-76
target populations for, 76
Cognitive restructuring, 203-207, 775-777
case illustrations, 205-206, 776-777
cognitive-behavior therapy and, 190-191
complications with, 205, 776
research basis of, 204-205, 775-776
strategy, description of, 203-204, 775
target populations for, 205, 776
See also **Beck, Aaron T.**; **Cognitive-behavioral approach to bipolar disorder**; **Cognitive-behavior therapy**; **Cognitive-behavior therapy: Child clinical applications**; **Cognitive-behavior therapy with religious beliefs and practices**;

Coleman, J. C., 1355
Cole v. Greenfield-Central Community Schools, 1244
Collaborative empiricism, 46
Communication skills training:
cognitive-behavior therapy and, 192
See also **Augmentative and alternative communication**; **Function communication training**
Community mental health services, 138
Community reinforcement approach (CRA), 148
Competing response training (CRT), 207-208, 777-779
awareness training and, 207
competing response practice and, 207-208
complications with, 208, 778
research basis of, 208, 778
strategy, description of, 207-208, 777-778
target populations for, 208, 778
See also **Azrin, Nathan H.**; **Differential reinforcement of other behavior**; **Habit reversal**; **Operant conditioning**
Complementary-alternative medicine (CAM), 123-124
Compliance training, 779-783
case illustration, 782-783
Child's Game/Parent's Game and, 779, 780
complications with, 781-782
parent-child interaction therapy and, 779, 780, 781, 782
research basis of, 781
strategy, Description of, 779-781
target populations for, 781
See also **Behavioral contracting**; **Behavioral treatment in natural environments**; **Contingency management**; **Differential reinforcement of other behavior**; **Generalization**; **Time-out**
Computer-based data collection, 208-215
access to, 209-210
advantages of, 211
BEST (Behavior Evaluation Strategy and Taxonomy) software and, 210-212
case illustration, 213-215
coding system definition/development of, 209
complications with, 213
data analysis capabilities of, 212
data collection capabilities of, 211-212
direct observational data in real time and, 209
education research and, 213-214
general features of, 211
multiple discrete measures and, 209
research basis of, 212-213
sequential analysis and, 214-215
strategy, description of, 208-210
target populations for, 213
time-based analysis and, 215
See also **Behavioral assessment**; **Computers and behavioral assessment**

Computer-driven instruction, 1404

Computerized TSBC/SRIC Planned-Access observational Information System, 427

Computers and behavioral assessment, 216-218

complications with, 217-218

ecological momentary assessment and, 216

efficacy research, 216-217

interviewing and, 216

strategy, description of, 216

target populations for, 217

See also **Behavioral assessment; Computer-based data collection**

Conditioning, 14-15

Conduct disorders (CD), 6, 818, 1226-1228

anti-social behavior patterns and, 1227

childhood vs. adulthood onset, 1227

definition of, 1226-1227

developmental stages and, 1227

interventions for, 1227

severity assessment, 1227

See also **Behavioral treatment for aggression; Behavior management; Behavior rating scales; Early-risk screening; Preventing escalated behavior; Social competence treatment: Externalizing disorders**

Conner's Teacher Rating Scale, 792

Connor's Behavior Rating Scales, 1170, 1173

Consequence, 1228-1229

assessment/intervention planning and, 1228-1229

behavioral occurrences, evaluation of, 1228

role/function of, 1228

See also **Antecedent; Applied behavior analysis; Negative reinforcement; Operant conditioning; Positive reinforcement; Punishment; Reinforcement**

Consultation analysis record (CAR), 1177

Contextual fit, 1229-1233

case illustration, 1232

description of, 1229-1231

focus person variables and, 1230

key stakeholder variables and, 1230

positive behavior support and, 1229-1231

research basis of, 1231

setting/system variables and, 1230-1231

target populations for, 1231

See also **Behavior intervention planning; Contextualism; Generalization; Maintenance; Person-centered planning; Systems of care; Wraparound**

Contextualism, 218-219

world hypothesis and, 1233-1234

See also **Acceptance and commitment therapy; Behavioral case formulation; Behavioral treatment in natural environments**

Contextualism and behavior analysis, 1233-1235

controversy about, 1235

worldview, contextualism and, 123-1235

See also **Applied behavior analysis; Contextual fit; Contextualism; Person-centered planning; Positive behavior support**

Contingencies in educational settings, 1235-1240

case illustration, 1239-1240

dependent group-oriented contingencies, 1239

independent group-oriented contingencies, 1237-1238

individual contingencies, 1236-1237

interdependent group-oriented contingencies, 1238-1239

research basis of, 1236

strategies, description of, 1235-1236

See also **Antecedent; Behavioral treatment for aggression; Consequence; Contingency management; Operant; Operant conditioning; Positive reinforcement; Punishment; Stimulus control**

Contingency management, 783-788, 1147

baseline measurement and, 784-785

case illustration, 787

complications with, 786-787

contingency contracting and, 785

group contingencies and, 785

management plan, implementation of, 785-786

parent training and, 786

reinforcer assessment and, 784

research basis of, 786

strategy, description of, 783-786

target populations for, 786

See also **Applied behavior analysis; Azrin, Nathan H.; Operant conditioning; Single-case research; Skinner, Burrhus Frederic**

Contingent exercise, 788-789

case illustration, 789

complications with, 788

research basis of, 788

strategy, description of, 788

See also **Aversion relief; Behavioral treatment in natural environments; Operant conditioning**

Contingent restraint, 789-790

See also **Aversion relief; Behavioral treatment in natural environments; Operant conditioning**

Continuity hypothesis, 46

Controlled drinking, 219-222

abstinence/nonabstinence goals and, 219-220

case illustration, 221-222

complications with, 221

harm reduction model and, 221

pharmacological treatment and, 220

relapse prevention and, 220

research basis of, 220-221

strategy, description of, 219-220
target populations for, 221
See also **Behavioral medicine; Behavioral
    treatments for the addictions; Self-control**
Coping Cat program, 768-769, 882
Coping with depression (CWD), 223-226
    case illustration, 225
    complications with, 225
    manualized treatment in, 224-225
    pharmacological approach and, 224
    research basis of, 224-225
    strategy, description of, 223
    target populations for, 223-224
    See also **Beck, Aaron T.; Cognitive-behavior
        therapy; Cognitive restructuring; Group
        behavioral therapy for depression**
Coping skills:
    anger management and, 8
    anxiety-arousal and, 11
    blood pressure/flow increase, 30
    See also **Behavior activation; Self-control
        desensitization**
Corporal punishment, 1240-1245
    ban on, 1241, 1244
    court actions on, 1241, 1244
    description of, 1240
    public school systems and, 1240-1241,
        1242-1243 (table)
    supportive arguments, 1241, 1244
    See also **Ethical issues regarding behavior
        management in the schools;
        Punishment; Schoolwide discipline;
        Suspension; Zero tolerance**
Correction/overcorrection/positive practice
    procedure, 42
Correspondence training, 790-793
    case illustration, 792
    chaining procedures and, 791
    complications with, 792
    modeling and, 790-791
    research basis of, 791
    strategy, description of, 790-791
    target populations for, 791-792
    See also **Behavioral case formulation; Behavioral
        treatment in natural environments; Setting
        events; Stimulus control**
Council for Exceptional Children, 1303
Counseling for Alcoholics'
    Marriages (CALM) project, 559-560
Counterconditioning, 793-796
    case illustration, 795-796
    complications with, 795
    research basis of, 794
    strategy, description of, 793-794

target populations for, 794
    See also **Classical conditioning; Paul, Gordon L.;
        Systematic desensitization; Wolpe, Joseph**
Couple therapy. *See* **Behavioral marital therapy;
    Behavioral treatment for aggression in couples;
    Spouse-aided therapy**
Coverant control, 226-228
    complications with, 228
    research basis of, 227
    strategy, description of, 226-227
    target populations for, 227
    See also **Covert positive reinforcement; Covert
        rehearsal; Covert sensitization conditioning**
Cover Jones, M., 620, 699-700, 767, 886, 1093, 1094
**Covert conditioning with children and adolescents,
    796-800**
    case illustration, 799-800
    complications with, 799
    functional behavior analysis and, 797-798
    procedures in, 797
    research basis of, 798
    strategy, description of, 796-798
    target populations for, 798-799
    See also **Cautela, Joseph R.; Classical conditioning;
        Covert control; Covert positive reinforcement;
        Covert reinforcer sampling; Covert sensitization
        conditioning; Imaginal procedures**
Covert positive reinforcement, 228-231
    complications with, 230
    research basis of, 229
    strategy, description of, 228-229
    target populations for, 229-230
    See also **Coverant control; Cover rehearsal;
        Covert reinforcer sampling**
Covert rehearsal, 231-232
    complications with, 232
    research basis of, 231-232
    strategy, description of, 231
    target populations for, 232
    See also **Covert sensitization conditioning;
        Self-control; Self-control desensitization**
Covert reinforcer sampling, 232-235
    complications with, 234
    research basis of, 233-234
    strategy, description of, 232-233
    target populations for, 234
    See also **Covert control; Covert positive
        reinforcement; Covert rehearsal**
**Covert sensitization conditioning,
    39, 40, 235-241**
    case illustration, 239-240
    complications with, 238-239
    research basis of, 237-238
    strategy, description of, 235-237

target populations for, 238
See also **Covert control; Covert rehearsal; Covert reinforcer sampling**
Craske, M., 44, 188
Cross-age tutoring, 1245-1248
case illustration, 1247
complications with, 1247
implementation steps, 1247
research basis of, 1246
strategy, description of, 1245-1246
target populations for, 1246
See also **Active student responding; Behavior management; Classroom management; Mainstreaming; Modeling; Peer intervention**
Cruickshank, W. M., 1352, 1355
Cue-controlled relaxation, 241-244
case illustration, 243-244
complications with, 243
research basis of, 242-243
strategy, description of, 241-242
target populations for, 243
See also **Applied relaxation and tension; Relaxation training with children; Social skills instruction**
Cultural differences in cognitive therapy, 244-248
case illustration, 246-247
cognitive schemas and, 245, 246
complications with, 245-246
research basis of, 245
strategy, description of, 244-245
See also **Behavioral treatment of minorities; Peer intervention; Peer tutoring**
Curriculum-based assessment (CBA), 1248-1251
dynamic indicators of basic skills and, 1250
general outcome measurement and, 1249-1251
mastery monitoring and, 1248-1249, 1249 (table), 1250
research basis of, 1250-1251
See also **Behavioral assessment; Dynamic Indicators of Basic Early Literacy Skills (DIBELS); Progress monitoring**

Dadds, M., 702
Darwin, C., 57, 58, 532
Data collection. *See* **Computer-based data collection**
Davison, Gerald D., 249-250, 621
See also **Association for Advancement of Behavior Therapy; Relaxation strategies; Systematic desensitization**
Dawn Project, 1559
Deci, E., 1508
Deffenbacher, J., 510
Delusions, 6, 9

Dementia, 113
aggressive behavior and, 113
disruptive vocalizations and, 113
wandering and, 113
Depression:
behavior function and, 16-17
exercise and, 133
geriatric clients and, 112
reinforcement-based treatments and, 20
spouse-aided therapy and, 559, 560-561
See also **Beck, Aaron T.; Behavior activation; Coping with depression; Group behavioral therapy for depression**
Depression-Arkansas (D-ARK) Scale, 225
Deprivation, 1253-1254
strategy, description of, 1253
target populations for, 1253-1254
See also **Establishing operations; Preference and reinforcer identification; Satiation; Schedules of reinforcement**
Derogatis Symptom Checklist-90, 68
Descartes, R., 196
Descriptive and functional analysis, 250-256
behavior change and, 251
case illustration, 254-255, 255 (table), 256 (figure)
complications with, 253-254
descriptive analysis and, 251-252
functional analysis, 252-253
research basis of, 253
strategy, description of, 250-251
target populations for, 253
See also **Functional analysis; Functional analytic psychotherapy**
Detention, 1254-1256
complications with, 1255-1256
origins of, 1255
procedural steps in, 1254-1255
research basis of, 1255
strategy, description of, 1254-1255
target populations for, 1255
See also **Classroom management; Ethical issues regarding behavior management in the schools; Punishment; Schoolwide discipline; Zero tolerance**
Developmentally disabled clients:
applied behavior analysis and, 20
behavior training and, 62
Dewey, J., 1233, 1234
Diagnostic and Statistical Manual (DSM-IV), 85, 165, 268, 330, 363, 1150, 1226
Dialectical behavior therapy (DBT), 20, 256-261, 1018
case illustration, 260
complications with, 259-260
research basis of, 259

strategy, description of, 256-257
target populations for, 259
treatment strategies, 258-259
treatment structure/stages, 257-258
See also **Therapeutic relationship**; **Trauma management therapy**; **Treatment failures in behavioral treatment**
DIBELS Oral Reading Fluency (DORF), 1277
DIBELS. See **Dynamic Indicators of Basic Early Literacy Skills (DIBELS)**
Differential reinforcement (DR), 1256-1257
See also **Differential reinforcement of incompatible behavior**; **Differential reinforcement of low rates of behavior**; **Differential reinforcement of other behavior**; **Extinction**; **Positive reinforcement**; **Stimulus control**
Differential reinforcement of alternative behavior (DRA), 1141, 1256
Differential reinforcement of incompatible behavior (DRI), 794, **801-803**, 1256
complications with, 802
research basis of, 801-802
strategy, description of, 801
target populations for, 802
See also **Differential reinforcement of other behavior**; **Operant conditioning**; **Schedule-induced behavior**; **Schedules of reinforcement**; **Skinner, Burrhus Frederic**
Differential reinforcement of low rates of behavior (DRL), **803-804**, 1256, 1257
complications with, 804
strategy, description of, 803
treatment efficacy, target populations and, 803-804
See also **Differential reinforcement of other behavior**; **Operant conditioning**; **Schedule-induced behavior**; **Schedules of reinforcement**; **Skinner, Burrhus Frederic**
Differential reinforcement of other behavior (DRO), **261-262**, 658, 669, **804-806**, 1256-1257, **1257-1261**
case illustration, 1260-1261
complications with, 806, 1260
interval length and, 1258
interval variations and, 1258-1259
reinforcers, selection of, 1259
research basis of, 805, 1259
schedules of, 1257-1258
strategy, description of, 804-805, 1257-1259
target behaviors, selection of, 1258
target populations for, 805, 1259-1260
See also **Antecedent control procedures**; **Competing response training**; **Differential reinforcement**; **Differential reinforcement of incompatible behavior**; **Differential reinforcement of low rates of behavior**; **Operant conditioning**; **Reinforcement**; **Schedule-induced**

behavior; Schedules of reinforcement; **Skinner, Burrhus Frederic**
DiNardo, P., 44
Direct behavioral consultation (DBC), 1178
Direct instruction (DI), 1157-1160, 1261-1263, 1292
lesson format and, 1262
research basis of, 1262-1263
sequential instruction, prioritized objectives and, 1261-1262
strategies/procedures in learning and, 1262
strategy, description of, 1261
target populations for, 1263
See also **Becker, Wesley**; **Direct instruction mathematics**; **Engelmann, Siegfried**; **Project Follow Through and Direct Instruction**
Direct instruction mathematics, 1263-1266
case illustration, 1265-1266
complications with, 1265
instructional scaffolding and, 1264
research basis of, 1264-1265
strand structure and, 1263-1264
strategy, description of, 1263-1264
target populations for, 1265
See also **Becker, Wesley**; **Direct instruction**; **Engelmann, Siegfried**
Direct Instruction System for Teaching Arithmetic and Reading (DISTAR), 1261
Direct Instruction System for Teaching and Remediation (DISTAR), 1261, 1292
Direct observation, 15, 1266-1269
behavioral assessment and, 86-87, 708
behavioral case formulation and, 90-91
case illustration, 1269, 1270 (figure)
cognitive-behavior therapy and, 189
complications with, 1269
defining behaviors and, 1266-1267
description of, 1266-1268
descriptive analysis and, 251-252
dimensions of behavior, identification of, 1267
recording process, 1267
reporting process, 167-168, 1268 (figures)
research basis of, 1268
target populations for, 1268-1269
See also **Behavioral assessment**; **Functional behavioral assessment of problem behavior**
Discrete trial instruction, 1269-1274
applied behavior analysis and, 1272
between-trial interval and, 1271
case illustration, 1273-1274
complications with, 1273
incidental teaching and, 1273
objectives in, 1272
practice opportunities and, 1272
progress tracking in, 1272
research basis of, 1272

strategy, description of, 1269-1272

student response in, 1271

target populations for, 1272-1273

See also **Applied behavior analysis; Autism spectrum disorders; Direct instruction; Discrete trial therapy; Discrimination training; Lovaas, O. Ivar; Reinforcement**

Discrete trial therapy, 806-810

case illustration, 808-810

complications with, 807-808

research basis of, 806-807

strategy, description of, 806

target populations for, 807

See also **Applied behavior analysis; Operant conditioning; Skinner, Burrhus Frederic**

Discrimination training, 810-812, 1274-1276

classroom/community settings and, 1275-1276

complications with, 811

experimental neurosis and, 811

home electronics equipment and, 1276

personal/instructional materials, management of, 1275

public restrooms, selection of, 1276

public transportation, utilization of, 1276

research basis of, 811

strategy, description of, 810-811, 1274-1275

target populations for, 811

text decoding and, 1275

A Discrimination training, *See also* **Differential reinforcement; Differential reinforcement of other behavior; Discrimination training; Extinction; Operant conditioning; Reinforcement; Schedule-induced behavior; Schedules of reinforcement; Skinner, Burrhus Frederic; Stimulus control; Stimulus discrimination**

Diseases:

anxiety/anger and, 11

See also **Behavioral medicine; Psychoneuroimmunology**

DISTAR, 1261, 1292

Domestic abuse, 11

Drug abuse prevention strategies, 812-815

case illustration, 814-815

competence enhancement strategies and, 812-813

research basis of, 813

social resistance strategies and, 812

strategy, description of, 812-813

target populations for, 813

See also **Behavioral treatment of cigarette smoking; Behavioral treatments for the addictions; Controlled drinking**

Durand, M., 1330

Dynamic Indicators of Basic Early Literacy Skills (DIBELS), 1166, 1276-1279, 1564

case illustration, 1279

complications with, 1279

core components of early literacy and, 1277

description of, 1276-1278

instructional decision-making and, 1277

intervention planning/implementation and, 1277-1278

outcome review and, 1278

progress monitoring and, 1277

research basis of, 1278

target populations for, 1278-1279

See also **Beginning reading; Beginning reading instruction; Behavioral assessment; Progress monitoring**

Dynamic Indicators of Basic Skills (DIBS), 1250

Dysfunctional Styles Questionnaire (DSQ), 526

Early risk screening for school-related behavior disorders, 1281-1286

empirical support for, 1282

multiple gating approaches to, 1283-1284

obstacles to, 1281-1282

referral process, behavioral standards and, 1282-1283

systematic screening for behavior disorders procedure and, 1284-1286, 1285 (figure)

teacher ratings strategy, 1282

traditional screening approaches, 1283

utility of, 1286

See also **Behavioral assessment; Conduct disorders**

Eating disorders, 6, 263-267

anorexia nervosa, 264-265

bulimia nervosa, 263, 264

case illustration, 266-267

cognitive-behavioral therapy and, 263

complications with, 266

exposure techniques and, 264

psychoeducation techniques and, 263-264

research basis of, 265

strategy, description of, 263-265

target populations for, 265-266

See also **Behavioral medicine; Behavioral pediatrics**

Ecological momentary assessment (EMA), 216

Education for All Handicapped Children Act (EAHCA), 139, 1368, 1461

Education of the Handicapped Act (EHA), 1368

Education Resources Information Center (ERIC), 1222

Effective learning environments, 1286-1290

competent learner repertoires, development of, 1287-1288

contingencies of reinforcement and, 1286-1287

repertoire development example, 1288-1290

See also **Behavior management for improving academic and classroom behavior; Positive reinforcement; Schoolwide discipline**

Efficacy, effectiveness, and patient-focused research, 267-275

assessment strategies in, 273-274

control conditions, selection of, 269-271

interventions, delivery of, 272-273
limitations of, 274
participants, Selection of, 268-269
patient-focused research and, 274
strategy, description of, 267-268
treatment or control conditions,
    patient assignment to, 271-272
See also **Empirically supported treatment for
    childhood disorder**; **Evidence-based practice**;
    Manualized behavioral therapy
Ego psychology, 59
Eisler, R., 558
Electrical aversion, 275-284
alcoholism treatment and, 280-281
case illustration, 283-284
complications with, 282
gambling and, 280
research basis of, 276-281
sexual preference conversion and, 276-280, 282
strategy, description of, 275-276
target populations for, 281-282
See also **Masturbatory retraining**; **Orgasmic
    reconditioning**; **Treatment failures
    in behavioral treatment**
Ellis, Albert, 45, 188, 195, 203, 463-464,
    587, 621, 768, 775
Emmelkamp, Paul M. G., 284-286, 305
See also **Exposure**; **Extinction and habituation**;
    Flooding
Emotional control, 2, 3-4
**Empirically supported treatments for childhood
    disorders, 817-822**
attention-deficit/hyperactivity disorder and, 819
conduct disorder/oppositional defiant disorder
    and, 818
controversies/issues in, 820-821
effectiveness measures and, 819-820
efficacy criteria and, 817-818
mood disorders and, 818
process/evidence and, 817
See also **Behavioral group therapy with children and
    youth**; **Efficacy, effectiveness and patient-focused
    research**; **Private practice of behavioral
    treatment**; **Single-case research**; **Treatment
    failures in behavior therapy**
Engelmann-Becker direct instruction model,
    1157, 1468
Engelmann, Siegfried, 1156, 1261, 1263, **1290-1294**
See also **Becker, Wesley**; **Direct instruction**; **Direct
    instruction mathematics**; **Project Follow
    Through and Direct Instruction**
Environment:
control over, 3
reinforcement contingency, 6

Erectile dysfunction, 32, 62
See also **Squeeze technique**
Erofeeva, M. N., 793
Error correction, 1294-1296
correct response opportunities and, 1295
factors in, 1295
procedural steps in, 1294-1295
See also **Direct instruction**; **Errorless learning**;
    Mastery learning; **Overcorrection**
Errorless compliance training, 822-824
complications with, 823
research basis of, 823
strategy, description of, 822-823
target populations for, 823
See also **Behavioral treatment in natural
    environments**; **Differential reinforcement
    of other behavior**; **Generalization**
Errorless learning, 1130, **1296-1299**
assumptions in, 1296
chained responses and, 1297-1298
constant time delay procedure and, 1298
efficiency of learning and, 1296
graduated guidance procedure and, 1298-1299
least prompts system and, 1297-1298
most-to-least prompting procedure and, 1299
progressive time delay procedure and, 1298
response prompting strategies and, 1297-1299
simultaneous prompting procedure and, 1298
stimulus modification procedures and,
    1296-1297
See also **Direct instruction**; **Error correction**;
    Fading; **Time delay instructional procedure**
Escape training, 824-825
See also **Aversion relief**; **Aversive conditioning**;
    Extinction and habituation; **Operant
    conditioning**
Establishing operations (EOs), 1299-1302
competition between, 1301
description of, 1299-1300, 1300 (figure)
negative reinforcement and, 1300-1301
positive reinforcement and, 1300
utility of, 1301-1302
See also **Deprivation**; **Satiation**; **Setting events**;
    Sleep deprivation
**Ethical issues regarding behavior management
    in the schools, 1302-1306**
case illustration, 1305
complications with, 1304-1305
goal-setting and, 1303
intervention strategies and, 1303
problem behavior, definition of, 1302-1303
research basis of, 1303-1304
strategy, description of, 1302-1303
target populations for, 1304

See also **Contextual fit; Contextualism and behavior analysis; Corporal punishment; Evidence-based practice; Informed consent; Mainstreaming; Person-centered planning; Punishment; School emergency procedures; Self-determination**

Evaluating behavioral plans, 286-288
  comprehensive strategies and, 287-288
  data reliability/accuracy and, 288
  episodic severity vs. severity over time and, 287, 287 (table)
  label selection and, 286
  quality of life measures and, 287
  rate measures and, 286
  response occurrence measures and, 286-287
  strategy, description of, 286
  See also **Behavioral contracting**

Event recording, 825-829
  construct validity and, 828
  cumulative recorder output, 825, 825 (figure)
  duration recording and, 825-826
  error and, 829
  event, definition of, 826-828
  illustration of, 828-829
  methodology in, 825-826
  observational reliability and, 827-828
  partial duration recording and, 826
  social validity and, 828
  technology in, 826
  whole interval recording and, 826
  See also **Behavioral assessment; Motor activity and behavioral assessment; Operant conditioning**

Evidence-based practice, 1306-1311
  description of, 1306-1309
  dissemination of evidence, 1309
  evaluation of evidence, 1308-1309
  indicated intervention, 1310
  interventions, conceptual organization of, 1309-1310
  professional organization involvement, 1306, 1307 (table)
  review of evidence, 1306, 1308
  school-based applications, 1306-1309
  selected intervention, 1309-1310
  universal intervention, 1309
  See also **Applied behavior analysis; Contextual fit; Empirically supported treatments for childhood disorders; Ethical issues regarding behavior management in the schools; Single-subject design; Treatment failures in behavior therapy**

Evolution theory, 57, 58
Explanation process, 1, 2
Exposure, 288-292, 700, 842-843
  case illustration, 291-292
  cognitive-behavior therapy and, 191, 192 (table)
  complications with, 291

research basis of, 290
strategy, description of, 288-290
target population for, 290-291
See also **Exposure and response prevention; Extinction; Flooding**

Exposure and response prevention (ERP), 664, 829-831
  applications of, 829, 830
  comorbid psychiatric disorders and, 830-831
  developmental differences and, 830
  intense exposure approach and, 830
  principles of, 829-830
  sequential exposure approach and, 830
  See also **Exposure; Extinction; Foa, Edna B.; Relapse prevention**

Extinction, 60, 831-833, 1311-1314
  applied behavior analysis and, 669
  case illustration, 1313
  complications with, 832, 1312-1313
  consequence control procedure of, 658
  research basis of, 831-832, 1312
  strategy, description of, 831, 1311-1312
  target populations/behaviors for, 832, 1312
  See also **Differential reinforcement; Differential reinforcement of other behavior; Exposure; Exposure and response prevention; Extinction and habituation; Graduated extinction; Maintenance; Operant conditioning; Reinforcement; Schedule-induced behavior; Schedules of reinforcement; Sensory extinction; Skinner, Burrhus Frederic; Spontaneous recovery**

Extinction and habituation, 292-296
  aversive therapy and, 294, 295
  case illustration, 296
  classical conditioning and, 292
  classical extinction and, 292-294, 294-295
  complications with, 295-296
  counterconditioning and, 293
  habituation-based therapies and, 293-294, 295
  operant conditioning and, 294
  operant extinction and, 294, 295
  research basis of, 294-295
  strategy, description of, 292-294
  target populations for, 295
  See also **Exposure; Extinction; Negative reinforcement**

Eyberg Child Behavior Inventory, 782
Eyberg, S. M., 945
Eye movement desensitization and reprocessing (EMDR), 296-301
  adaptive information processing model and, 297
  case illustration, 300
  complications with, 299
  research basis of, 298-299

strategy, description of, 296-298
target populations for, 299
therapeutic approach, phases in, 298
See also **Exposure**; **Manualized
    behavioral therapy**; **Modeling**
Eysenck, H., 34, 56, 187, 330, 331, 621, 698
Eysenck Personality Questionnaire, 68

Facial screening, 835-836
See also **Aversion relief**; **Extinction and habituation**;
    Operant conditioning; **Punishment**
Fading, 836-837, 1139, 1315-1317
description of, 1315
guidelines for, 1316-1317
least-to-most/most-to-least prompting and, 1316
prompt hierarchy and, 1315-1316
See also **Applied behavior analysis**; **Differential
    reinforcement**; **Discrimination training**;
    Generalization; **Guided mastery**; **Operant
    conditioning**; **Prompting**; **Stimulus control**;
    Transfer of stimulus control
Failures in treatment. See **Treatment failures
    in behavior therapy**
Falk, J., 499
Family anxiety management, 702
Family Educational Rights and Privacy
    Act (FERPA), 1145
Family therapy. See **Behavioral family therapy**
FAPE. See Free appropriate public education
Fear avoidance hierarchy (FAH), 773
FEAR plan, 768-769
Fear Questionnaire, 441
Feedback, 837-838
See also **Behavioral treatment in natural
    environments**; **Guided mastery**; **Problem-solving
    therapy**; **Reinforcement**; **Social competence
    treatment: Externalizing disorders**; **Social
    effectiveness training**; **Social and interpersonal
    skills training**; **Social skills training**; **Video
    feedback**
FERPA. See Family Educational Rights and Privacy
    Act (FERPA)
Ferster, C., 64, 1037
Fight-or-flight response, 28, 293-294
First Step to Success, 1309-1310
Fisher, R. A., 533
Five-step procedure for stealing, 838-842
apology for theft, 839
case illustration, 840-842
complications with, 840
instances of stealing, identification of, 838-839
intervention effectiveness test, 839-840
research basis of, 840
restitution, replacement cost and, 839

return of stolen item, 839
role reversal and, 839
strategy, description of, 838-840
target populations for, 840
See also **Applied behavior analysis**; **Behavioral
    treatment in natural environments**;
    Overcorrecton
Flooding, 303-306, 700, 764-765, **842-847**
case illustration, 305-306, 846-847
choice of, 843
complications with, 305, 845-846
exposure-based treatment and, 842-843
planning/implementation of, 843-845
research basis of, 303-305, 845
strategy, description of, 303, 842-843
target populations for, 305, 845
See also **Emmelkamp, Paul M. G.**; **Extinction**; **Foa,
    Edna B.**; **Imaginal procedures**; **Stampfl's
    therapist-directed implosive (flooding) therapy**;
    **Systematic desensitization with children and
    adolescents**
Foa, Edna B., 285, **306-309**
Follow Through. See **Project Follow Through and
    Direct Instruction**
Forehand, R. L., 945
Foster-family-based treatment, 702
Foxx, R. M., 928
Franks, C., 187, 188, **309-311**, 621
See also **Association for Advancement of Behavior
    Therapy**; **Classical conditioning**; **Pavlov, Ivan P.**
Free appropriate public education (FAPE),
    1370-1371, 1554
Freud, Sigmund, 244, 329-330, 397
Friedman, R. M., 1555
**Full-spectrum home training for simple
    bed-wetting (FSHT), 847-851**
case illustration, 851
complications with, 850-851
family support agreement and, 848
overlearning and, 849-850
research basis of, 850
retention control training and, 849
strategy, description of, 847-850
target populations for, 850
urine alarm/cleanliness training and, 848-849
See also **Applied behavior analysis**; **Behavioral
    treatment in natural environments**; **Bell and
    pad bladder training**; **Classical conditioning**;
    Overcorrection; **Retention control training**
Functional analysis, 851-856, 1317-1322
adequacy demands on, 853
behavior theory and, 852-855
case illustration, 855-856, 1320-1321,
    1321 (figure)

causality, definition of, 854-855
complications with, 1320
foundational principles of, 851-852
functional assessment and, 853
functional classes and, 852-853
methodological improvements and, 855
research basis of, 1319-1320
strategy, description of,
      1317-1319, 1318 (table)
target populations for, 1320
See also **Applied behavior analysis; Descriptive
      and functional analysis; Functional behavioral
      assessment of problem behavior; Functional
      relation; Function-based approach to behavior
      support; Functions of behavior; Operant
      conditioning**
**Functional analytic psychotherapy (FAP),
      20, 64, 311-315, 539**
case illustration, 314-315
clinically relevant behaviors and, 312
combined treatments and, 313
complications with, 314
research basis of, 313-314
strategy, description of, 311
target populations for, 314
therapeutic strategies in, 312-313
See also **Behavioral analytic approach to
      supervision; Descriptive and functional
      analysis; Functional analysis**
**Functional behavioral assessment of
      problem behavior, 1322-1329**
case illustration, 1327-1328
complications with, 1327
data collection procedures in, 1324-1326
outcomes of, 1322-1324
research basis of, 1326
strategy, description of, 1322-1326
target populations for, 1326-1327
See also **Descriptive and functional analysis;
      Functional analysis; Functional relation;
      Function-based approach to behavior support;
      Functions of behavior; Testable hypothesis**
Functional behavior assessments (FBA), 1140, 1141,
      1200, 1302, 1322
**Functional communication training (FCT),
      856-860, 1329-1332**
behavior assessment and, 857
case illustration, 859-860, 1330-1332
communication environment and, 857-858
communication skills and, 858, 1329
complications with, 859, 1330
research basis of, 858-859, 1330
strategy, description of, 856-858, 1329
target populations for, 859, 1330

See also **Applied behavior analysis;
      Augmentative and alternative communication;
      Functions of behavior; Generalization; Guided
      mastery; Positive behavior support; Speech and
      language disorders**
Functional relation, 1332-1333
case illustration, 1333, 1333 (figure)
research basis of, 1332-1333
strategy, description of, 1332
See also **Descriptive and functional analysis;
      Functional analysis; Functional behavioral
      assessment of problem behavior; Function-based
      approach to behavior support; Testable
      hypothesis**
**Function-based approach to behavior
      support, 1333-1339**
conceptual logic/theory behind, 1334-1335, 1335 (figure)
definition of, 1334
practices/processes of, 1335-1338, 1337 (figure)
supporting systems for, 1338-1339
See also **Descriptive and functional analysis;
      Functional analysis; Functional behavioral
      assessment of problem behavior; Functional
      relation; Functions of behavior; Negative
      reinforcement; Positive behavior support;
      Positive reinforcement; Schoolwide discipline;
      Setting event; Stimulus control**
Functions of behavior, 1340-1341
classes of, 1340
nonassociative learning and, 1340
operant conditioning and, 1340-1341
respondent conditioning and, 1340
See also **Descriptive and functional analysis;
      Functional analysis; Functional behavioral
      assessment of problem behavior; Function-based
      approach to behavior support**

Gamblers Anonymous, 70
Gambling. See **Behavioral approaches to gambling**
Garcia v. Miera, 1244
General case programming, 1343-1347
case illustration, 1346
instructional universe and, 1343-1344
research basis of, 1345
sequencing of teaching examples and, 1345
skill instruction and, 1345
stimulus/response variation, examples of, 1344-1345
strategy, description of, 1343-1345
target populations for, 1345-1346
testing, novel probe examples and, 1345
See also **Applied behavior analysis; Discrimination
      training; Fading; Generalization; Phases of
      learning; Stimulus; Stimulus control; Transfer
      of stimulus control**

Generalization, 317-319, 861-865, 1347-1350
behavioral processes and, 318
case illustration, 863-865
complications with, 862-863, 1349-1350
habit reversal and, 875
research basis of, 862, 1347-1349
social skills instruction and, 1539
strategy, description of, 861-862
target populations for, 862
variables and, 317
See also **Applied behavior analysis; Behavioral treatment in natural environments; Discrimination training; Fading; General case programming; Kazdin, Alan E.; Operant conditioning; Phases of learning; Stimulus; Stimulus control; Transfer of stimulus control**
Generalized anxiety disorder (GAD), 11, 12, 44, 206
Generalized conditioned punisher, 865-866
research basis of, 866
strategy, description of, 865-866
See also **Applied behavior analysis; Generalization; Operant conditioning**
Generalized conditioned reinforcer, 866-867
research basis of, 867
strategy, description of, 866-867
See also **Applied behavior analysis; Classical conditioning; Generalization; Operant conditioning**
General Outcome Measurement (GOM), 1249-1251
Genetic history, 91-92
Gerontology. *See* **Behavioral gerontology**
Goal setting, 867-868
complications with, 868
research basis of, 868
strategy, description of, 867-868
See also **Behavioral treatment in natural environments; Guided mastery; Instructions; Problem-solving therapy; Reinforcement; Social competence treatment: Externalizing disorders; Social effectiveness training; Social and interpersonal skills training; Social skills training**
Goldfried, M. R., 45, 508, 775
Goldiamond, Israel, 319-320
See also **Azrin, Nathan H.; Behavioral assessment**
Good behavior game, 868-869, 1238
See also **Applied behavior analysis; Behavioral treatment in natural environments; Token economy**
Goodman, J., 1021
Gordon, J., 476
Graduated extinction, 869-870
complications with, 870
research basis of, 870

strategy, description of, 869
target populations for, 870
See also **Extinction; Extinction and habituation; Operant conditioning; Schedule-induced behavior; Schedules of reinforcement**
Gratification, 479
Group behavioral therapy for depression, 320-323
complications with, 322
research basis of, 322
strategy, description of, 321-322
target populations for, 322
See also **Coping with depression; Evidence-based practice; Manualized behavioral therapy**
Group contingency, 870-872
complications with, 872
research basis of, 871
strategy, description of, 870-871
target populations for, 871-872
See also **Applied behavior analysis; Behavioral contracting; Behavioral treatment in natural environments; Token economy**
Group research designs, 997-998
between-groups comparison designs, 998
cross-sectional/longitudinal designs, 1000
mixed designs, 999
mixed factorial design, 999-1000
within-groups comparison designs, 998-999
Group therapies. *See* **Behavioral group therapy with children and youth; Behavioral group work; Group behavioral therapy for depression**
Guided discovery process, 46
Guided imagery, 486, 830, 990
Guided mastery, 323-324
complications with, 324
independent functioning and, 324
research basis of, 324
strategies in, 323-324
target populations for, 324
See also **Behavior activation; Behavioral treatment in natural environments; Virtual reality therapy**
Gun Free Schools Act, 1607
Guthrie, E. R., 793, 1093
Guttman, N., 1347, 1348

Habit rehearsal, 41
Habit reversal, 207-208, **325-328**, 777, **873-877**
awareness training and, 873-874
case illustration, 326-327, 876-877
competing response practice and, 874
complications with, 326, 875
generalization training and, 875
habit control motivation and, 874-875
research basis of, 326, 875
strategy, description of, 325-326, 873-875

target populations for, 326, 875
See also **Applied behavior analysis; Azrin, Nathan H.; Homework; Overcorrection**
Habituation, 877-878
See also **Classical conditioning; Extinction; Extinction and habituation; Operant conditioning**
Hall v. Tawney, 1244
Hanf, C., 779, 945
Haring, Norris Grover, 1351-1354, 1380
See also **Applied behavior analysis; Learning disabilities; Operant conditioning; Positive reinforcement; Precision teaching; Token economy; Trend line**
Hart, B., 1361
Hartmann, H., 59
Harvard Counseling for Alcoholics' Marriages (CALM) project, 559-560
Head Start, 1157, 1291, 1292
Herrnstein, R. J., 1340
Hersen, Michel, 328-329, 537, 558
See also **Association for Advancement of Behavior Therapy; Single-case research; Social skills training**
Hewett, Frank M., 1354-1358
See also **Applied behavior analysis; Learning disabilities; Operant conditioning; Positive reinforcement; Precision teaching; Token economy; Trend line**
Historical antecedents of behavior modification and therapy, 329-331
behavior therapy alternative and, 330-331
diagnosis/therapy, criticisms of, 330
remote antecedents, 329-330
strategy, description of, 329
See also **Behavior therapy theory; Kantor's behaviorism; Skinner, Burrhus Frederic**
Holistic approaches, 124, 719
Home-based reinforcement, 878-879
research basis of, 879
strategy, description of, 878-879
See also **Applied behavior analysis; Behavioral contracting; Behavioral treatment in natural environments; Token economy**
Homebuilders program, 703
Homework, 331-335, 879-880
benefits of, 879-880
case illustration, 334-335
considerations in, 334
research basis of, 332-334, 880
strategy, description of, 331-332, 879
target populations for, 334
See also **Behavioral treatment in natural environments; Behavior rehearsal; Habit reversal; Instructions; Manualized behavior therapy**
Horvath, A. O., 174
Hull, C., 439, 574, 619, 1093, 1347
Hypertension, 6, 132-133
Hypnosis, 126-127, 486

IEP. *See* **Individualized education program**
Imagery-based relaxation (IBR), 989, 990-991
Imaginal procedures, 881-885
case illustration, 883-885
complications with, 883
covert modeling and, 882
research basis of, 882
strategy, description of, 881-882
target populations for, 882-883
See also **Cautela, Joseph R.; Covert conditioning with children and adolescents; Covert control; Covert positive reinforcement; Covert reinforcer sampling; Covert sensitization conditioning; Lazarus, Arnold Allan; Self-control desensitization; Systematic desensitization; Wolpe, Joseph**
Implosive therapy. *See* **Stampfl's therapist-directed implosive (flooding) therapy**
Impulse control dysfunctions, 7
Impulse control. *See* **Attention-deficit/hyperactivity disorder (ADHD)**
Incidental teaching, 1359-1363
case illustration, 1362-1363
complications with, 1362
confirmation/contingent access and, 1360
initiation of teaching episodes and, 1359-1360
practical advantages of, 1360
prompts and, 1360
research basis of, 1360-1361
response and, 1360
strategy, description of, 1359-1360
target populatons for, 1361-1362
See also **Autism spectrum disorder; Discrete trial instruction; Discrimination training; Prompting; Shaping to teach new behaviors; Stimulus control**
Inclusive education programs, 1152
Incontinence issues. *See* **Bell and pad bladder training; Full-spectrum home training for simple bed-wetting**
Individualized education program (IEP), 1363-1367
case illustration, 1366-1367
content of, 1364-1365
description of, 1363-1366
eligibility for, 1364
issues/errors in, 1365-1366
review/revision of, 1365

special factors, consideration of, 1365
team members in, 1364
See also **Individuals with Disabilities Education Act;**
     Long-term objective; Mainstreaming; Person-
     centered planning; Short-term objectives;
     Wraparound
Individuals with Disabilities Education Act (IDEA),
     853, 1281, 1322, 1363, **1367-1373**, 1461, 1479
components of, 1368-1369
comprehensive system of personnel development
     and, 1369
evaluation of, 1373
federal legislation and, 1368
free appropriate public education and, 1370-1371, 1554
funding requirements and, 1369
history of, 1367-1368
least restrictive environment and, 1371-1372
parent participation and, 1373
procedural safeguards and, 1372
protection in evaluation and, 1370
zero reject principle and, 1369-1370
See also **Individualized education program; Long-**
     term objectives; Mainstreaming; Short-term
     objectives
Informed consent to treatment, 337-339
acquisition of, 338-339
legal/ethical bases of, 337-338
strategy, description of, 337
See also **Behavior therapy theory;**
     Electrical aversion; Punishment
Ingraham v. Wright, 1241-1242
Initial sound fluency (ISF), 1277
Insomnia. *See* **Behavioral treatment of insomnia;**
     Sleep behaviors
Institute of Education Sciences, 1123
Instructions, 339-340
complications with, 340
strategy, description of, 339
target populations for, 339-340
See also **Direct instruction; Feedback;**
     Homework
Intensive behavior therapy unit (IBTU),
     340-342
case illustration, 341-342
complications with, 341
research basis of, 341
strategy, description of, 340-341
target populations for, 341
See also **Applied behavior analysis;**
     Behavioral approaches to schizophrenia;
     Token economy
Interdisciplinary Committee on Youth
     Mental Health Care, 1306, 1308
International Classification of Disease, 165

International Society for Augmentative
     and Alternative Communication (ISAAC), 1149
Interpersonal cognitive problem-solving (ICPS), 969
Interpersonal therapy, 6, 818
Interviewing:
behavioral assessment interviewing, 86, 707-708
behavioral case formulation and, 91
cognitive-behavior therapy and, 189
computerized interviews, 216
See also **Behavioral assessment interviews;**
     Behavioral interview; Motivational
     interviewing
Intimate partner violence (IPV), 145-146
In vivo desensitization, 885-888
case illustration, 888
complications with, 887-888
research basis of, 886-887
strategy, description of, 885-886
target populations for, 887
See also **Extinction; Extinction and habituation;**
     Lazarus, Arnold Allan; Self-control
     desensitization; Systematic desensitization;
     Wolpe, Joseph
Irrational Beliefs Test (IBT), 526
Irritable bowel syndrome (IBS), 130-131

Jacobson, E., 450, 574, 576, 620
Jacobson, N. S., 47
James, W., 767, 1037, 1233
Job Club method, 41, 343-344
complications with, 344
research basis of, 344
strategy, description of, 343-344
target populations for, 344
See also **Applied behavior analysis;**
     Azrin, Nathan H.; Homework
Johnson, B., 196
Juniper Gardens Children's Project, 1125, 1222

Kalish, H. I., 1347, 1348
Kamin, L., 186
Kanfer, Frederick H., 345-346
See also **Behavioral assessment;**
     Self-management; Self-monitoring
Kanner, Leo, 1150
Kantor, J. R., 215, 347-348, 439
Kantor's interbehaviorism, 346-353
contemporary contributions of, 350-352
contributions of, 346-348, 350-352
description of, 348-350
field systems approach and, 347-348, 349
scientific thought, historical analysis of, 348
See also **Behavior therapy; Behavior**
     therapy theory; Skinner, Burrhus Frederic

Kazantzis, N., 333
Kazdin, Alan E., **353-354**
  See also **Applied behavior analysis; Association for Advancement of Behavior Therapy; Behavioral assessment**
Kegel, A. H., 130
Kendall, P. C., 768
Keogh, B., 1357
Kiecolt-Glaser, J. K., 457, 459
King, N. J., 908
Kirk, S., 1377
Koenig, C. H., 1547
Kohlenberg, R. J., 64, 311, 313, 539, 588
Krasner, L., 34, 536

Lam, D. H., 201
Lang, P., 575, 578, 579, 621
Language:
  deictic relations, 4
  non-linear use, metaphor/paradox and, 2-3, 4
  relational frame theory and, 1-2
  See also **Speech and language disorders;**
    Verbal reason-giving
Law of effect, 657, 923
Lazarus, Arnold Allan, 34, 35, 45, 57, 187, 350, **355-356**, 578, 619, 621
  See also **Multimodal behavior therapy; Systematic desensitization; Wolpe, Joseph**
Learned helplessness, **1375-1377**
  cognition and, 1375-1376
  complications with, 1376-1377
  contingency and, 1375
  description of, 1375-1376
  guidelines for teachers and, 1377
  intervention strategies for, 1376
  passive behaviors and, 1376
  See also **Cognitive behavior therapy; Contingencies in educational settings; Self-determination; Self-management; Social Skills instruction; Teaching students self-control**
Learning disabilities (LD), **1377-1379**
  description of, 1377-1378
  future research directions and, 1378
  intraindividual differences model and, 1378
  research basis of, 1378
  response to instruction model and, 1378
  See also **Haring, Norris Grover; Individuals with Disabilities Education Act; Problem-solving consultation model**
Learning theory:
  behavior therapy and, 56-57
  habituation/sensitization and, 237
  See also **Social skills training**
Learning trial, 1131

Least restrictive environment, 1371-1372, 1387
Lemon Juice therapy, **889-890**
  advantages to, 890
  research basis of, 889-890
  risks of, 890
  strategy, description of, 889
  See also **Aversion relief; Aversive conditioning; Classical conditioning; Electrical aversion; Operant conditioning**
Levy, R. L., 332
Lewinsohn, Peter M., 321, **356-357**, 559
  See also **Behavioral assessment; Cognitive-behavior therapy; Setting events**
Liberty, K., 1353
Liebowitz Social Anxiety Scale, 434
Life Attitudes Schedule, 356
Life event issues, 92
Life skills training (LST), 814, **890-894**
  case illustration, 893-894
  complications with, 892-893
  prevention methods in, 814-815
  research basis of, 891-892
  strategy, description of, 814, 890-891
  target populations for, 892
  See also **Problem-solving therapy; Social competence treatment: Externalizing disorders; Social effectiveness training; Social and interpersonal skills training; Social skills training**
Lindsley, Ogden R., 34, 1185, 1250, **1379-1381**, 1433, 1475
  See also **Applied behavior analysis; Behavioral assessment; Precision teaching; Rate and frequency; Skinner, Burrhus Frederic; Standard celeration chart**
Literal meaning, 1-2
Lochman's Anger Management Training, 970
Locke Wallace Marital Adjustment Test, 861
Logan, P., 1567
Long-term care, 103, 104-105
Long-term objectives, **1381-1382**
  advantage of, 1382
  outcome measures and, 1382
  short-term objectives and, 1382
  strategy, description of, 1381-1382
  work time allowance decisions and, 1382
  See also **Behavioral contracting; Behavioral objectives; Individualized education program; Individuals with Disabilities Education Act; Short-term objectives**
Lovaas, O. Ivar, 41, **894-896**, 1355, **1382-1385**
  See also **Applied behavior analysis; Autism spectrum disorders; Aversion relief; Aversive conditioning; Behavioral treatment in natural environments; Discrete trial instruction; Discrete trial therapy;**

Electrical aversion; Extinction; Extinction
    and habituation; Operant conditioning;
    Punishment; Reinforcement
Lovitt, T., 1250, 1353
Luria, A., 526, 1021

Mahoney, M., 35, 188, 768
Mainstreaming, 1387-1389
    assumptions of, 1387-1388
    case illustration, 1388-1389
    implementation quality and, 1388
    least restrictive environment and, 1387
    research basis of, 1388
    strategy, description of, 1387-1388
    See also Effective learning environments;
        Individuals with Disabilities Education Act
Maintenance, 897-901, 1389-1392
    behavior-change process and, 897-898
    case illustration, 900-901, 1392
    common stimuli and, 1391
    complications with, 900, 1392
    functional skills teaching and, 1390
    generalization and, 897
    loosely controlled training and, 1390-1391
    multiple exemplars and, 1390
    natural reinforcers, incorporation of, 1390
    performance maintenance, 1389
    reinforcement schedules, modification of, 1391
    research basis of, 899, 1390
    self-management skills and, 1391
    strategy, description of, 897-899, 1389-1390
    target populations for, 899-900, 1391-1392
    See also Applied behavior analysis; Azrin,
        Nathan H.; Extinction; Generalization; Kazdin,
        Alan E.; Phases of learning; Schedules of
        reinforcement; Self-management
Major depressive disorder (MDD), 224
Male erectile disorder, 32, 62
Mand, 65
Manualized behavior therapy, 359-365, 901-905
    behavior therapy and, 361, 902
    case illustrations, 363-365, 904-905
    contemporary issues on, 361-363
    criticisms of, 903-904
    empirically supported therapies, treatment manual use
        and, 360-361, 901, 902
    future directions of, 363
    historical context of, 359-363
    panic disorder and, 364
    research basis of, 902
    strategy, description of, 364-365, 901-902
    target populations for, 903
    theoretical basis of, 901-902

    treatment manuals, implementation rationale, 359-360
    See also Barlow, David H.; Beck, Aaron T.;
        Behavioral approaches to sexual deviation;
        Behavioral marital therapy; Behavioral
        treatment for cigarette smoking; Behavioral
        treatments for the addictions; Dialectical
        behavior therapy; Homework; Role playing
MAPS (McGill Action Planning System), 1413
Marion County Office of Family and
    Children (MCOFC), 1558-1559
Marker-variable measures, 89, 709-710
Marking time-out, 905-906
    See also Behavioral treatment in natural
        environments; Generalization;
        Parent training; Setting events
Marks, Isaac M., 187, 365-366, 575
    See also Exposure; Flooding;
        Response prevention
Marlatt, A., 476
Marriage. See Behavioral marital therapy
Marrs, R., 179
Marshall, William L., 366-367
    See also Arousal training; Masturbatory
        retraining; Squeeze technique
Massachusetts Gambling Screen, 68
Massed practice, 906-907
    See also Classical conditioning; Generalization;
        Operant conditioning
Mastery learning, 1393
    See also Acquisition; Direct instruction;
        Phases of learning
Mastery monitoring approach, 1248-1249,
    1249 (table), 1250
Masturbatory retraining, 80, 367-368
    research basis of, 367-368
    strategy, description of, 367
    See also Marshall, William L.; Orgasmic
        reconditioning; Squeeze technique
MATCH. See Motivational enhancement therapy;
    Project MATCH
Mattis, S., 773
McCrady, B., 559, 560
McGill Action Planning System (MAPS), 1413
McMahon, R. J., 945
Mead, G. H., 1234
Means-Ends Problem-Solving (MEPS) measure, 971
Meditation, 192, 486
Meichenbaum, Donald H., 35, 45, 188, 368, 526, 570,
    768, 775, 1021
    See also Cognitive-behavior therapy;
        Self-monitoring; Self-statement modification
Melissa Institute for Violence Prevention and for the
    Treatment of Victims of Violence, 368

Memory rehabilitation after traumatic brain injury, 368-370
  complications with, 370
  research basis of, 369
  strategy, description of, 368-369
  See also **Behavioral assessment; Generalization; Instructions**
Metropolitan Achievement Test, 1158
Michael, J., 21
Miller, G., 767
Miller, N., 124, 180
Mills v. Board of Education, 1367, 1368
Miltenberger, Raymond G., 370-372
  See also **Applied behavior analysis**
Mindfulness meditation, 4, 372-375
  complications with, 375
  research basis of, 374-375
  strategy, description of, 372-374
  target populations for, 375
  See also **Autogenic training; Classical conditioning; Relaxation strategies**
Minnesota Multiphasic Personality Inventory, 166
Minority populations. *See* **Behavioral treatment of minorities**
Mobility Inventory, 441
Modeling, 73, 375-379, 907-910
  case illustrations, 378-379, 909-910
  complications with, 378
  correspondent training and, 790-791
  covert modeling, 227
  group intervention and, 725
  participant modeling and, 908
  research basis of, 377, 908-909
  social skills instruction and, 1538
  strategy, description of, 375-377, 907
  target populations for, 377-378, 907-908
  videotape modeling and, 907-908
  See also **Behavioral rehearsal; Peer tutoring; Role playing; Social skills training**
Moral philosophy, 437
Morse, W., 1355
Mortality rates, 11
Motivational enhancement therapy (MET), 379-383
  case illustration, 381-383
  complications with, 381
  Project MATCH and, 380
  research basis of, 381
  strategy, description of, 379-381
  target populations for, 381
  See also **Behavioral case formulation; Motivational interviewing**
Motivational interviewing (MI), 383-389
  case illustration, 387-388

complications with, 387
  guiding principles of, 384-385
  research basis of, 385-386, 386 (figure)
  strategy, description of, 383-385
  target populations for, 386-387
  See also **Behavioral case formulation; Motivational enhancement therapy**
Motivation Assessment Scale, 859
Motor activity and behavioral assessment, 389-393
  behavioral assessment and, 389
  case illustration, 392
  complications with, 392
  initial assessment/diagnosis and, 390-391
  medical diseases and, 390
  outcome evaluation and, 391
  process evaluation and, 391
  psychological/behavioral disorders and, 390
  research basis of, 391-392
  sleep disorders and, 390-391
  strategy, description of, 389-391
  target populations for, 392
  See also **Applied behavior analysis; Behavioral assessment**
Mowrer, O. H., 564, 747, 764
Multimodal behavior therapy, 393-396
  assessment/intervention methods in, 393-396
  BASIC I. D. assessments and, 394
  bridging and, 394-395
  firing order, tracking of, 395-396
  strategy, description of, 393
  See also **Behavioral assessment; Lazarus, Arnold A.**
Multimodal communication. *See* **Augmentative and alternative communication (AAC)**
Multisystemic therapy (MST), 818, 910-914
  caregiver role in, 912
  case illustration, 913-914
  evidence-based interventions and, 911, 1310
  problem-context-based service and, 911
  problem determinants and, 911
  quality assurance and, 911-912
  research basis of, 912-913
  strategy, description of, 910-912
  target populations for, 913
  See also **Behavioral treatment in natural environments; Generalization; Guided mastery; Parent training; Social competence treatment: Externalizing disorders**
Myofascial pain dysfunction (MPD) syndrome, 129

NAEP. *See National Assessment of Educational Progress (NAEP)*
National Alliance for Research on Schizophrenia and Depression (NARSAD), 177

National Assessment of Educational
    Progress (NAEP), 1123
National Association of School Psychologists, 1303
National Association for the Study of
    Obesity (NAASO), 169
National Center for Education Statistics, 1123
National Health Examination surveys (NHES), 745
National Heart, Lung, and Blood Institute (NHLBI), 169
National Institute on Alcohol Abuse and Alcoholism
    (NIAAA), 219, 220, 380
National Institute of Child Health
    and Human Development, 1166
National Institute for Direct Instruction (NIFDI), 1294
National Institute on Drug Abuse (NIDA), 178
National Institute of Education (NIE), 1159
National Institutes of Health (NIH), 44
National Reading Panel, 1166, 1167, 1277, 1306
National Research Council, 1164, 1167
National Research Panel, 1164, 1167
Natural language paradigm (NLP), 1419
NCLB. *See* No Child Left Behind (NCLB) Act of 2001
Negative cognitions, 3-4, **397-399**
    complications with, 398-399
    research basis of, 398
    strategy, description of, 397
    target populations for, 398
    threats to self and, 4
    See also **Cognitive-behavior therapy; Self-
        monitoring; Self-statement modifications**
Negative practice, **915-916**
    See also **Classical conditioning; Generalization;
        Operant conditioning; Overcorrection**
Negative reinforcement (NR), 39, **916-919**, **1395-1398**
    case illustration, 918-919, 1397-1398
    clinical applications of, 918
    complications with, 1397
    concept, description of, 916-918
    establishing operations and, 1300-1301
    persistence of, 917-918
    process, description of, 1395-1397
    research basis of, 916-917, 1397
    slow inception of, 917
    target populations for, 1397
    See also **Aversion relief; Coercive cycles in families;
        Electrical aversion; Escape training; Negative
        reinforcement; Operant conditioning; Positive
        reinforcement; Reinforcement**
Network behavior therapy theory, 59
Neuropsychiatric Institute (NPI) School, 1355, 1357
Neuropsychological Educational Approach to
    Remediation (NEAR), 75-76
Neuropsychology. *See* **Behavior therapy and
    neuropsychology**
No Child Left Behind (NCLB) Act of 2001, 1123

Noncontingent reinforcement (NCR), **399-401**
    complications with, 400-401
    research basis of, 400
    strategy, description of, 399-400
    target populations for, 400
    See also **Behavior management; Behavior therapy;
        Behavior therapy theory**
**Noncontingent reinforcement as a treatment for
    problem behavior in the classroom**, **1398-1400**
    case illustration, 1399-1400
    complications with, 1399
    description of, 1398-1399
    target populations for, 1399
    See also **Functional relation; Noncontingent
        reinforcement; Noncontingent reward;
        Reinforcement; Stimulus control**
Noncontingent reward (reinforcement), **919-922**
    complications with, 921
    research basis of, 920-921
    strategy, description of, 919-920
    target populations for, 921
    See also **Noncontingent reinforcement;
        Operant conditioning; Positive
        reinforcement; Reinforcement**
Nonsense word fluency (NWF), 1277
Noonberg, A. R., 124
Nunn, R. G., 41, 42, 207, 325, 873

Obesity, 6
    behavioral medicine and, 129
    behavior training and, 62
    body mass index and, 169, 745
    protein sparing modified fasts and, 744
    See also **Behavioral weight control therapy
        with children; Behavioral weight
        control treatments**
Observation. *See* **Direct observation**
Obsessive-compulsive disorder, 6
    aversion relief and, 40
    cognitive-behavior therapy and, 187
    computerized behavioral assessment and, 217
    See also **Exposure; Response prevention; Ritual
        prevention; Thought-stopping**
O'Farrell, T., 559
Ollendick, T. H., 908
Olton, D. S., 124
Operant, **1401**
    See also **Operant conditioning; Response
        class theory; Skinner, Burrhus Frederic**
Operant conditioning, 123, **403-407**,
    923-928, **1401-1403**
    academic/social behaviors and, 1402
    case illustrations, 406-407, 927-928
    complications with, 406, 926-927

consequence stimuli and, 1402
educational settings and, 1403
research basis of, 404-406, 925-926
respondent conditioning and, 1402-1403
strategy, description of, 403-404, 923-925
target populations for, 406, 926
taxonomy of, 404 (table)
See also **Applied behavior analysis; Behavioral treatment in natural environments; Behavior therapy theory; Consequence; Discrimination training; Functional analysis; Operant conditioning; Response class theory; Schedule-induced behavior; Schedules of reinforcement; Single-case research; Skinner, Burrhus Frederic; Stimulus control**
Opportunity to respond, 1403-1405
definition of, 1403
instructional methods and, 1404-1405
rates of, 1403-1405
See also **Active student responding; Choral responding; Direct instruction; Discrimination training**
Oppositional defiant disorder (ODD), 818, 950, 1227
Oral reading fluency measure, 1277
Oregon Adolescent Depression Project, 357
Oregon Safe Schools Survey, 1494
Oregon Social Learning Center, 719, 949
Organic brain disorders, 7
Organizational behavior management (OBM), 407-411
case illustration, 410-411
complications with, 409-410
research basis of, 408
strategy, description of, 407-408
target populations for, 409
See also **Behavioral consultation; Behavior management; Behavior management for improving academic and classroom behavior**
Orgasmic reconditioning (OR), 411-416
case illustration, 415-416
complications with, 414-415
research basis of, 413-414
strategy, description of, 411-413
target populations for, 414
See also **Barlow, David H.; Behavioral approaches to sexual deviation; Masturbatory retraining**
Öst, L. G., 30
Outward Bound, 891
Overcorrection, 416-417, 928-931
application, considerations in, 929-930
case illustration, 930-931
complications with, 930
positive practice procedure and, 929
research basis of, 416-417, 930
restitution procedure and, 928-929

strategy, description of, 416, 928-930
target populations for, 417, 930
See also **Applied behavior analysis; Aversion relief; Azrin, Nathan H.; Competing response training; Error correction; Habit reversal**
Overholser, J. C., 25

Pacing, 1407-1408
APacing, *See also* **Active student responding**
Pain management, 933-936
biofeedback and, 125, 127-129
case illustration, 935-936
complications with, 935
headache disorders, 127-128
interventions for, 934-935
lower-back pain, 128
myofascial pain dysfunction syndrome, 129
pain assessment and, 933-934
research basis of, 935
strategy, description of, 933-935
target populations for, 935
See also **Behavioral gerontology; Behavioral medicine; Behavioral pediatrics; Biofeedback**
Panic control treatment (PCT), 188, 419-422
behavioral avoidance and, 421-422
cognitions and, 420-421
physical sensations and, 420
strategy, description of, 419-420
See also **Evidence-based practice; Guided mastery; Relaxation training with children**
Panic control treatment for adolescents (PCT-A), 773
Panic disorder (PD), 44
arousal training and, 32
manualized behavior therapy and, 364
Paradigmatic behavior therapy, 936-940
case illustration, 939
current situational factors and, 937-938
development of, 937
framework of, 937-938
individualized treatment and, 938-939
original learning and, 937
present symptomatic responses and, 938
psychological vulnerability and, 938
unlearned genetic/biological vulnerability and, 937
See also **Behavioral treatment in natural environments; Behavior therapy; Behavior training; Manualized behavior therapy**
Paradoxical intention, 422-424
research basis of, 423
strategy, description of, 422-423
target populations for, 423
See also **Assertiveness training; Behavioral momentum; Motivational enhancement therapy**

Paranoia, 112-113
PARC (Pennsylvania Association
    for Retarded Citizens), 1367, 1368
Parent-child interaction therapy (PCIT),
    779, 780, 781, 782, **940-944**
    case illustration, 943-944
    child-directed interaction and, 940
    complications with, 942-943
    parent-directed interaction and, 941
    research basis of, 941-942
    strategy, description of, 940-941
    target populations for, 942
    See also **Behavioral treatment in natural**
        environments; Behavior training;
        Manualized behavior therapy;
        Parent training
Parenting skills:
    behavior training and, 62
    parent training programs, 720, 786
    See also **Behavioral family therapy; Compliance**
        training; Errorless compliance training
Parent management training (PMT), 786
Parent training, 944-952
    case illustration, 951-952
    complications with, 950-951
    conceptual studies of, 949-950
    features of, 945-946
    outcome studies of, 947-948
    process studies of, 948-949
    programs, distinctions among, 946-947
    research basis of, 947-950
    strategy, description of, 944-947
    target populations for, 950
    See also **Applied behavior analysis; Behavioral**
        contracting; Behavioral treatment in natural
        environments; Manualized behavior therapy;
        Parent-child interaction therapy
Participant observations, 87
PATH (Planning Alternative Tomorrows
    with Hope), 1413
Patterson, G., 719-720, 779, 949
Paul, Gordon L., 424-427, 621
    See also **Token economy**
Pavlov, Ivan P., 33, 123, 185, 292, 403,
    427-428, 574, 619, 763-764, 767, 793,
    1079-1080, 1340, 1347
    See also **Classical conditioning**
Peer-directed instruction, 1404
Peer intervention, 952-955
    case illustration, 954-955
    classwide peer tutoring, 1147
    complications with, 954
    research basis of, 953
    strategy, description of, 952-953
    target populations for, 953

See also **Applied behavior analysis; Behavioral**
    contracting; Behavioral treatment in natural
    environments
Peer-pairing interventions, 703
Peer tutoring, 1408-1412
    case illustration, 1410-1411
    failure, analysis of, 1410
    features of, 1408
    implementation of, 1409-1410
    instructional content and, 1409
    monitoring and, 1409
    pacing and, 1409
    reinforcement and, 1410
    strategy, description of, 1408
    theoretical foundation of, 1408-1409
    training and, 1409
    tutor-tutee matching, 1409
    See also **Classwide peer tutoring;**
        Cross-age tutoring; Peer intervention
Penn State Worry Questionnaire, 206, 441
Pennsylvania Association for Retarded Citizens (PARC) v.
    Commonwealth of Pennsylvania, 1367, 1368
Pepper, S., 1233, 1234
Personality assessment system, 82
Person-centered planning (PCP), 428-430,
    1203, **1412-1415**
    case illustration, 1414
    collaborative activity of, 429, 1413
    developmental disabilities and, 430, 1415
    empirical support for, 429-430, 1415
    information frames in, 1413-1414
    philosophical root of, 430, 1415
    positive behavior support and, 429, 1415
    rationale for, 429, 1414-1415
    strategy, description of, 428-429, 1412-1414
    See also **Contextual fit; Contextualism;**
        Individualized education program; Individuals
        with Disabilities Education Act; Multisystemic
        therapy; Positive behavior support; Wraparound
Pharmacotherapy, 955-959, 1147
    antianxiety agents and, 957-958
    antidepressants and, 957
    antimanic agents and, 957
    case illustration, 958-959
    complications with, 958
    research basis of, 956
    stimulants and, 958
    strategy, description of, 955-956
    target populations for, 956-958
    See also **Agras, W. Stewart.; Behavioral approaches**
        to schizophrenia; Behavioral medicine;
        Behavioral pediatrics; Cognitive-behavioral
        approach to bipolar disorder; Intensive behavior
        therapy unit; Pharmacotherapy and behavior
        therapy; Psychoneuroimmunology

Pharmacotherapy and behavior therapy, 430-434
  alternatives to, 6
  case illustration, 433-434
  complications with, 433
  research basis of, 431-432
  strategy, description of, 430-431
  target populations for, 432-433
  See also **Multimodal behavior therapy;**
    Multisystemic therapy; Systems of care
Phases of learning, 1416-1417
  acquisition, 1416
  adaptation, 1416-1417
  application, 1416
  fluency-building, 1416
  overlapping phases, 1417
  See also **Acquisition; Behavioral fluency;**
    Generalization; Maintenance
Phillips, E. L., 1352
Phillips, J., 346
Philosophical aspects of behaviorism, 434-439
  behaviorism, types of, 434-437
  causality/freedom and, 438-439
  moral philosophy and, 437
  private events and, 435-437
  strategy, description of, 434
  theory/application and, 437-438
  See also **Applied behavior analysis; Behavior therapy**
    theory; Paradigmatic behavior therapy
Phobias, 6, 11
  aversion relief and, 39-40
  See also **Applied tension**
Phoneme segmentation fluency (PSF), 1277
Piaget, J., 1021, 1469
Pivotal response training, 1417-1421
  case illustration, 1420-1421
  complications with, 1419-1420
  discrete trial training and, 1417-1418
  motivation and, 1418
  multiple-cue instruction and, 1419
  overselective responding and, 1418-1419
  research basis of, 1419
  stimulus variation and, 1418
  strategy, description of, 1417-1419
  target populations for, 1419
  See also **Autism spectrum disorders; Discrete trial**
    instruction; Speech and language disorders
Pleasant Events Schedule, 356
Point system, 959-961
  case illustration, 960
  strategy, description of, 959-960
  target populations for, 960
  treatment efficacy, 960
  See also **Applied behavior analysis; Aversion relief;**
    Azrin, Nathan H.; Contingency management;
    Overcorrection; Token economy

Positive behavior interventions and supports (PBIS), 1509
Positive behavior support (PBS), 1134, 1203, 1302,
    1421-1428
  applications of, 1423
  classroom applications of, 1425
  complex community environments and, 1427
  complications with, 1427-1428
  comprehensive/longitudinal implementation of, 1427
  contextual fit and, 1229-1231
  definition of, 1421-1422
  features of, 1422
  foundations of, 1422-1423
  functional behavioral assessment and, 1326
  functional communication training and, 1330
  group-/systems-level applications, 1427-1428
  individual students and, 1423-1424
  measurement complications and, 1428
  novel context populations and, 1428
  research basis of, 1425-1426
  rule-governed behavior and, 1484-1485
  schoolwide applications of, 1424-1425,
    1484, 1497-1498, 1499 (table)
  target populations for, 1426-1427
  See also **Applied behavior analysis; Functional**
    behavioral assessment of problem behavior;
    Function-based approach to behavior support;
    Person-centered planning
Positive behavior support teams (PBSTs),
    1497-1498, 1499 (table)
Positive peer reporting, 1428-1430
  complications with, 1429
  research basis of, 1429
  strategy, description of, 1428-1429
  target populations for, 1429
  See also **Classwide peer tutoring; Cross-age tutoring;**
    Group contingency; Peer intervention; Peer
    tutoring
Positive practice, 961
  See also **Applied behavior analysis; Aversion relief;**
    Azrin, Nathan H.; Overcorrection
Positive reinforcement, 961-966, 1430-1433
  case illustration, 965, 1432-1433
  clinical applications of, 964-965
  clinical implications of, 964
  complications with, 1432
  consequent vs. antecedent conditioning and, 962-963
  effectiveness, factors in, 963-964
  establishing operations and, 1300
  research basis of, 962-964, 1431-1432
  strategy, description of, 961-962, 1430-1431
  target populations for, 1432
  See also **Consequence; Differential reinforcement of**
    other behavior; Generalized conditioned
    reinforcer; Negative reinforcement; Operant
    conditioning; Positive reinforcement;

Reinforcement; Schedules of reinforcement;
Skinner, Burrhus Frederic; Stimulus control;
Vicarious reinforcement
Positive school climate. *See* **Active supervision**
Posttraumatic stress disorder (PTSD), 11, 12
    adaptive information processing model and, 297
    counterconditioning and, 794
    eye movement desensitization and
        reprocessing, 298-299
    network behavior therapy and, 59
    virtual reality therapy and, 1087-1088
    See also **Trauma management therapy; Virtual**
        reality therapy
Precision teaching, 1433-1437
    data display standard, 1435-1436, 1435 (figure)
    direct observation and, 1434
    empirical tradition and, 1433-1434
    frequency measure and, 1434
    instructional tactics, validation of, 1436-1437
    IS/DOES terminology and, 1436, 1436 (table)
    principles of, 1433-1436, 1435 (figure), 1436 (table)
    research basis of, 1437
    See also **Behavioral assessment; Contingencies**
        in educational settings; Haring,
        Norris Grover; Lindsley, Ogden R.;
        Phases of learning; Rate and frequency;
        Standard celeration chart; Trend line
Precorrection, 1437-1441
    anticipating problem behaviors and, 1437
    case illustration, 1440, 1440 (table)
    correction-precorrection relationship, 1438, 1438 (table)
    implementation steps for, 1438-1440
    instructional tool of, 1438
    social behaviors, management of, 1440
    See also **Antecedent; Antecedent control procedures;**
        Behavioral fluency; Behavioral rehearsal;
        Classroom management; Consequence;
        Prompting; Social skills instruction
Preference and reinforcer identification, 1441-1444
    applications of, 1443-1444
    choice assessments and, 1442
    description of, 1441
    free operant preference assessment, 1443
    multiple stimulus preference assessments, 1442-1443
    preference assessments and, 1441-1443
    reinforcer assessments, 1443
    See also **Behavioral assessment; Contextual fit;**
        Person-centered planning; Positive
        reinforcement; Reinforcer sampling/assessment
Premack principle, 966-968, 1444-1445
    case illustration, 968
    complications with, 967
    quidelines for, 1444-1445
    research basis of, 966-967

strategy description of, 966
    target populations for, 967
    See also **Behavioral contracting; Contingency**
        management; Differential reinforcement;
        Differential reinforcement of other behavior;
        Operant conditioning; Positive reinforcement;
        Reinforcement; Rules; Schedules of
        reinforcement
Preventing escalated behavior: Strategies for defusing
    problem behavior, 1445-1449
    agitation and, 1446-1447
    disrespectful behavior and, 1446
    limits-testing and, 1447-1448
    off-task behavior and, 1445
    rule violations and, 1445-1446
    teacher response and, 1448
    See also **Anger management; Antecedent control**
        procedures; Behavior management; Chaining;
        Classroom management; Precorrection;
        Relaxation strategies; Self-management
PRIDE skills, 940
Principles for Professional Ethics, 1303
Private events, 435-437, 439-440
    acceptance and commitment therapy and, 1, 3-4
    complications with, 440
    research on, 439-440
    strategy, description of, 439
    target populations, 440
    See also **Autogenic training; Cognitive restructuring;**
        Establishing operations
Private practice of behavioral treatment, 440-444
    advertising and, 443
    behavioral assessments and, 441
    court testifying and, 444
    ethical issues and, 442-443
    research basis of, 442
    supervision in, 443
    teaching duties and, 443
    therapeutic relationships and, 441
    treatment manuals and, 441-442
    See also **Behavior consultation; Manualized behavior**
        therapy
Private speech, 195-196
Problem-solving consultation model, 1449-1454
    case illustration, 1452-1454, 1452-1454 (figures)
    complications with, 1451-1452
    research basis of, 145-1451
    strategy, description of, 1449-1450
    See also **Behavioral consultation; Positive**
        behavior support; Problem-solving
        therapy; Program evaluation
Problem-solving skills training (PSST), 818, 969
Problem-solving therapy (PST), 444-449
    alternatives, generation of, 446

case illustration, 447-448
cognitive-behavior therapy and, 192-193
complications with, 447
decision-making and, 446
problem definition/formulation and, 446
problem orientation and, 445-446
research basis of, 446-447
solution implementation/verification, 446
strategy, description of, 444-446
supervised practice and, 446
target populations for, 447
See also **Homework**; **Problem-solving consult model**; **Problem-solving training**
Problem-solving training, 968-972
case illustration, 971-972
complications with, 971
research basis of, 970
strategy, description of, 968-970
target populations for, 970-971
See also **Problem-solving therapy**; **Social competence treatment: Externalizing disorders**; **Social effectiveness training**; **Social and interpersonal skills training**; **Social skills training**
Program evaluation, 1454-1459
case illustration, 1457-1459
description of, 1454-1456
evaluability assessment and, 1457
logic modeling and, 1456-1457
process of, 1455-1456
professional standards in, 1457
theories/beliefs and, 1456
See also **Behavioral assessment**; **Problem-solving consultation model**; **Progress monitoring**; **Research designs**; **Single-case research**
Programmed instruction, 1459-1461
complications with, 1461
description of, 145-1460
research basis of, 1460
target populations for, 1460-1461
See also **Behavioral assessment**; **Direct instruction**; **Operant conditioning**; **Opportunity to respond**; **Precision teaching**; **Shaping to teach new behavior**; **Stimulus control**
Progressive muscular relaxation, 126, 449-453
case illustration, 451-452
clinical assessment and, 449-450
complications with, 451
muscle groups and, 452
relaxation training in children and, 989-990
research basis of, 450-451
scripted procedures, examples of, 452
strategy, description of, 449
target populations for, 451

See also **Applied relaxation and tension**; **Relaxation training with children**; **Self-management**
Progress monitoring, 1461-1468
case illustration, 1466-1468, 1467 (figures)
conceptual foundations of, 1462
current functioning, description of, 1464-1465
decision-making planning and, 1465-1466
description of, 1462
goal statements, preparation of, 1465
graphic display of data and, 1465
measurement strategy, selection of, 1463-1464
problem behaviors, selection/definition of, 1462-1463
program evaluation and, 1462
Web-based/software programs and, 1466
See also **Behavioral assessment**; **Curriculum-based assessment**; **Direct observation**; **Dynamic indicators of basic early literacy skills**
Project Follow Through and Direct Instruction, 1157-1160, 1292-1293, **1468-1470**
description of, 1468
direct instruction and, 1468-1469
evaluation research design and, 1469
follow-along research and, 1469
See also **Becker, Wesley**; **Direct instruction**; **Engelmann, Siegfried**
Project MATCH, 380
Prolonged-exposure therapy (PE), 597-598
Prompt, 972-973
See also **Behavioral treatment in natural environments**; **Differential reinforcement of other behavior**; **Operant conditioning**
Prompting, 1470-1471
See also **Antecedent**; **Discrimination training**; **Fading**; **Prompt**; **Stimulus control**; **Time delay**
Propst, R., 196
Provocation hierarchy scenarios, 8
Psychodrama, 51
Psychodynamic assessment system, 82
Psychodynamic therapies, 64
Psychoeducational strategies:
anger management and, 7
cognitive-behavior therapy and, 190
eating disorders and, 263-264
problem of immediate gratification and, 479
See also **Coping with depression**
Psychoneuroimmunology (PNI), 453-462
acquired immunity and, 454
acute stress and, 456-457
behavioral interventions and, 459-461
cancer and, 458, 460
chronic stress and, 457
conditioned alterations, immune system and, 455-456
future directions in, 461-462

healthy individuals, behavioral interventions
    and, 459-460
HIV/AIDS and, 458-459, 460-461
immune activity, measurement of, 454-459
immune system overview, 453-454
innate immunity and, 453-454
strategy, description of, 453
stress, impacts on immunity, 456-459
stress, physiology of, 456
wound healing and, 457-458
See also **Behavioral pediatrics**; **Early risk
    screening**; **Memory rehabilitation
    after traumatic brain injury**
Psychopathological clients, 9, 112-113
Psychosomatic disorders, 6
Psychotherapy, 46
Psychotropic medication. See **Pharmacotherapy
    and behavior therapy**
PsycINFO database, 502
Public posting, 973
See also **Behavioral treatment
    in natural environments**; **Positive
    reinforcement**; **Reinforcement**
Punishment, 18, 60, **974-978**, **1471-1474**
applied behavior analysis and, 669-670
aversive conditioning and, 1472-1473
behavior reduction procedure and, 1471-1472
case illustration, 976-978, 977 (figure), 1474
complications with, 976
consequence control procedure of, 658-659
ethical issues in, 1473
negative punishment, 975-976
positive punishment, 974-975
reinforcement and, 474-475
research basis of, 976
response cost methods, 1472
strategy, description of, 974-976, 1471-1473
target populations for, 976, 1473-1474
time-out and, 1472
See also **Applied behavior analysis; Aversion relief;
    Aversive conditioning; Behavioral treatment in
    natural environments; Consequence; Ethical
    issues regarding behavior management in the
    schools; Generalized conditioned reinforcer;
    Goldiamond, Israel; Operant conditioning;
    Overcorrection; Positive practice; Response
    cost; Schedule-induced behavior; Skinner,
    Burrhus Frederic; Time-out; Vicarious
    punishment**

Quine, W. V., 436

Rachman, S. J., 34, 187, 575, 591, 619
Radical behaviorism, 20

Rapee, R., 44, 188
Rate and frequency, 1475-1476
description of, 1475-1476
research basis of, 1476
target populations for, 1476
See also **Behavioral assessment**; **Behavioral
    dimensions**; **Precision teaching**; **Skinner,
    Burrhus Frederic**; **Standard celeration chart**
Rating scales. See **Behavior rating scales**
Rational-emotive behavior therapy (REBT), 195, 196,
    203-204, 245, **463-472**, 775
adjuncts to treatment and, 466-467
basic approach of, 464
beliefs, types of, 467
childhood disorders and, 818
complex analysis and, 465-466
disputation process and, 466
disputation style and, 469-470
disputation, systemization of, 467-469
emotional bonds, necessity of, 467
functional/dysfunctional emotions and
    behaviors and, 465
irrational/rational beliefs and, 464
philosophic change and, 466
practitioner style and, 466
strategy, description of, 463-464
treatment sequence summary, 470-471
See also **Behavior therapy**; **Negative cognitions**;
    Social skills instruction
Raynor, E., 1080
Reading Mastery and Language for Learning
    series, 1468
Reading. See **Beginning reading**;
    Beginning reading instruction
Reason-giving, 1, 2
Reciprocal inhibition principle, 58-59
Reciprocity counseling program, 41-42
Recontextualization of behaviors, 1
Regulated breathing, 42, **979-980**
case illustration, 980
complications with, 980
diaphragmatic breathing, 979
feedback systems for, 980
paced respiration, 979-980
See also **Applied relaxation and tension**;
    Biofeedback; **Breathing retraining**;
    Cue-controlled relaxation; **Progressive
    muscular relaxation**; **Relaxation strategies**;
    Relaxation training with children
Reinforced practice, 980-981
case illustration, 981
complications with, 981
research basis of, 981
strategy, description of, 980-981

See also **Differential reinforcement of other behavior;**
     Operant conditioning; Positive reinforcement;
     Reinforcement
Reinforcement, 6, 17-18, 20, **472-476**
    applied behavior analysis and, 667-669
    behavioral analysis of, 475
    behavioral discrepancy and, 473-474
    differential reinforcement of alternative
         behavior, 1141
    experimental analysis of, 472
    implications of, 475-476
    natural vs. arbitrary reinforcement, 64-65
    punishment and, 474-475
    reinforcement principle, related formulations of, 474
    reinforcer, temporal relations with, 472-473
    strategy, description of, 472
    weight control and, 167, 743
    See also **Applied behavior analysis; Coverant**
         control; Covert positive reinforcement;
         Schedules of reinforcement; Vicarious
         reinforcement
Reinforcement Survey Schedule, 232-233
Reinforcer sampling/assessment, 981-985
    assessment procedures, 982-983
    case illustration, 984-985
    complications with, 984
    menus in, 982
    research basis of, 983
    sampling procedures, 982
    strategy, description of, 981-983
    surveys in, 983
    target populations for, 983-984
    See also **Behavioral assessment; Covert reinforcer**
         sampling; Operant conditioning; Positive
         reinforcement; Reinforcement
Relapse prevention (RP), 476-483, 985-989
    abstinence violation effect and, 480
    behavioral rehearsal and, 986-987
    case illustrations, 482-483, 988-989
    cognitive distortions and, 478-479
    complications with, 482, 987-988
    high-risk situations and, 478
    maintenance/aftercare and, 481
    outcome expectancies and, 479-480
    planning for, support groups and, 480-481
    problem of immediate gratification and, 479
    research basis of, 481, 987
    risk factors, identification of, 986
    seeming irrelevant decisions and, 477, 479
    social skills deficits and, 480, 986
    strategy, description of, 476-479, 985-987
    target populations for, 481-482, 987
    See also **Generalization; Schedules of reinforcement;**
         Treatment failures in behavior therapy

Relational frame theory (RFT), 1-2, **483-485**
    deictic relations and, 4
    derived stimulus relations and, 484
    strategy, description of, 483-484
    verbal problem-solving abilities and, 484-485
    See also **Behavioral family therapy; Contextualism;**
         Functional relation
Relaxation strategies, 6, **485-489**
    anxiety/anger management and, 11-12, 13
    assessment methods and, 487
    behavioral medicine applications, 126
    behavioral relaxation training and, 487
    biofeedback and, 486
    breathing training and, 487
    case illustration, 488-489
    cognitive-behavior therapy and, 192
    complication with, 488
    insomnia and, 161
    meditation and, 486
    progressive relaxation and, 485-486
    research basis of, 487-488
    strategy, description of, 485-487
    target populations for, 488
    verbal induction procedures and, 486
    See also **Anxiety/anger management training;**
         Applied relaxation and tension;
         Cue-controlled relaxation; Relaxation
         strategies; Self-management
Relaxation training (RT) in children, 989-993
    case illustration, 992
    complications with, 991-992
    imagery-based relaxation and, 990-991
    progressive muscle relaxation and, 989-990
    research basis of, 991
    strategy, description of, 989-991
    target populations for, 991
    See also **Applied relaxation and tension;**
         Biofeedback; Breathing retraining;
         Cue-controlled relaxation; Progressive
         muscular relaxation; Relaxation strategies
Religious beliefs/practices. *See* **Cognitive behavior**
     therapy with religious beliefs and practices
Reparative therapy, 276-280, 282
Rescorla, R., 185, 186
Research designs, 993-1000
    between-groups comparison designs, 998
    categories of, 994-995
    cross-sectional/longitudinal designs, 1000
    efficacy vs. effectiveness studies, 994
    experimental vs. correlational research, 995
    goals of research and, 993-994
    group designs, 997-1000
    intersubject vs. intrasubject research, 994-995
    mixed designs, 999-1000

single-subject designs, 995-997
stage-process designs, 996-997
withdrawal designs, 996
within-groups comparison designs, 998-999
See also **Computer-based data collection;
Computers and behavioral assessment;
Efficacy, effectiveness, and patient-focused
research; Empirically supported treatments
for childhood disorders; Evaluating behavioral
plans; Informed consent; Single-case research;
Single-subject design**
Respiratory diseases, 11
Response blocking, 1000-1002
case illustration, 1002
complications with, 1002
research basis of, 1001
strategy, description of, 1000-1001
target population for, 1001-1002
See also **Exposure; Extinction; Extinction
and habituation; Response prevention**
Response class theory, 1476-1479
behavioral allocation and, 1478
case illustration, 1479
complications with, 1479
description of, 1476-1477
functional equivalence and, 1478
matching law and, 1477-1478
research basis of, 1477
response classes, covariation and, 1477-1478
response efficiency/intensity,
measurement of, 1478
target populations for, 1478-1479
See also **Functional relation; Stimulus control**
Response cost, 1002-1006, 1472, 1480-1483
case illustration, 1005-1006, 1482
complications with, 1004-1005, 1481
guidelines for, 1481
implementation steps of, 1480
research basis of, 1003-1004, 1481
strategy, description of, 1002-1003, 1480-1481
target populations for, 1004, 1481
token economies and, 1480
See also **Applied behavior analysis; Azrin, Nathan
H.; Operant conditioning; Positive
reinforcement; Punishment; Reinforcement;
Token economy**
Response prevention, 489-493
case illustration, 492-493
complications with, 491-492
research basis of, 490-491
strategy, description of, 489-490
target populations for, 491
See also **Extinction and habituation; Massed
practice; Preventing escalated behavior**

Response prompting strategies, 1297
chained responses and, 1297-1298
constant time delay procedure, 1298
graduated guidance procedure, 1298-1299
least prompts system, 1297-1298
mean-to-least prompting procedure, 1299
progressive time delay procedure, 1298
simultaneous prompting procedure, 1298
Restitution, 1006-1007
See also **Aversion relief; Electrical aversion;
Extinction and habituation; Operant
conditioning; Punishment; Response cost**
Retention control training (RCT), 1007-1009
complications with, 1008-1009
research basis of, 1008
strategy, description of, 1007-1008
target populations for, 1008
See also **Behavioral treatment in natural
environments; Bell and pad bladder training;
Classical conditioning; Full-spectrum home
training for simple bed-wetting**
Rincover, A., 1028
Risley, T. R., 41, 1349, 1350, 1361
Ritual prevention, 1009-1010
case illustration, 1009-1010
complications with, 1009
research basis of, 1009
strategy, description of, 1009
target populations for, 1009
See also **Exposure; Foa, Edna B.;
Relapse prevention; Response blocking**
Road rage, 10
Rogers, C., 244
Role playing, 73, 493-497, 1010-1011
adolescent anger management and, 654
behavioral rehearsal and, 741
case illustration, 495-496
complications with, 495
research basis of, 494
role reversal and, 494
social skills training and, 495, 1538
strategy, description of, 493-494
target populations for, 494-495
See also **Augmentative and alternative
communication; Behavioral rehearsal; Modeling**
Role Play Test (RPT), 494
Rorschach test, 82
Rule-governed behavior, 1483-1487
applications of, 1483-1485
augmental behavior and, 1483
clinical psychology practice and, 1486-1487
description of, 1483-1485
pliance behavior and, 1483
positive behavior support and, 1484-1485

relational responding and, 1485-1486
tracking behavior and, 1483
See also **Contingencies in educational settings;**
    Relational frame theory; Schoolwide discipline;
    Teaching schoolwide expectations
Rules, 1487-1488
    appropriate behavior,
        acknowledgment of, 1487-1488
    communication of expectations and, 1487
    expectations, definition of, 1487
    inappropriate behaviors and, 1488
    See also **Rule-governed behavior; Schoolwide**
        discipline; Teaching schoolwide expectations
Ryle, G., 435

Salter, A., 620, 621
Sampling:
    behavioral assessment and, 88, 709
    duration sampling, 88
    event sampling, 88
    interval sampling, 88
    real-time sampling, 88
    setting sampling, 88
    subject sampling, 88
    See also **Reinforcer sampling/assessment**
Santa Monica Learning Center, 1357-1358
Saslow, G., 346
Satiation, 1489-1490
    complications with, 1489-1490
    strategy, description of, 1489
    target populations for, 1489
    See also **Deprivation; Establishing**
        operations; Setting event
Satiation therapy, 80
Scale for Suicide Ideation, 46
Schedule-induced behavior, 499-501
    adjunctive behavior and, 499-500
    compulsive responding and, 500
    induced responding, measurement of, 499
    strategy, description of, 499
    See also **Applied behavior analysis;**
        Schedules of reinforcement
Schedules of reinforcement, 501-504,
    1013-1017, 1490-1493
    application of, 1492-1493
    case illustrations, 504, 1016-1017
    complications with, 503-504, 1015-1016
    differential reinforcement of other
        behavior schedules and, 1014
    fixed ratio schedules and, 1013, 1491-1492
    noncontingent reinforcement, 1014
    positive/negative reinforcement and, 501
    ratio/interval contingencies and, 1490-1491
    research basis of, 502-503, 1015

schedule contingencies, 1490-1492
strategy, description of, 501-502, 1013-1015, 1490
target populations for, 503, 1015
variable ratio schedules and, 1013-1014, 1491-1492
See also **Applied behavior analysis; Extinction;**
    Maintenance; Operant conditioning;
    Positive reinforcement; Reinforcement;
    Rules; Schedule-induced behavior;
    Skinner, Burrhus Frederic
Schiefelbush, R. L., 1352
Schizophrenia, 6, 9
    behavioral contracting and, 108
    behavior training and, 62
    cognitive model of, 46
    See also **Behavioral approaches to schizophrenia**
School emergency procedures, 1493-1496
    academic achievement focus and, 1495
    action response plan and, 1495-1496
    community coordination and, 1494
    emergency response, follow-up steps and, 1496
    emergency situations, identification of, 1493-1494
    guiding principles for, 1494
    physical environment and, 1494
    prerequisites for, 1494-1495
    proactive schoolwide discipline plans and, 1494-1495
    school/district policy and, 1493
    staff/student training and, 1495
    See also **Positive behavior support; Schoolwide**
        discipline
School Situation Questionnaires, 792
Schoolwide discipline, 1496-1506
    antisocial behaviors, contributory factors in, 1499-1500
    need for, 1496-1497
    parental involvement in, 1502
    positive behavior support teams and, 1497-1498,
        1499 (table)
    positive consequences, rule-following and, 1503,
        1504 (table)
    program development/implementation and, 1505-1506
    punishment, serious infractions and,
        1503-1504, 1504 (table)
    rule development/communication and, 1500-1502
    staff development/support and, 1504-1505
    student success teams and, 1498-1499, 1499 (table)
    See also **Contingency management; Positive behavior**
        support; Positive reinforcement; Rules; Social
        and interpersonal skills training; Social skills
        instruction; Social skills training; Teaching
        schoolwide expectations
Schultz, I. H., 37
Science Research Associates (SRA), 1292, 1468
Scientific method, 90, 91 (figure)
Scott, J., 201
Second Step, 1309

Seeming irrelevant decisions (SIDs), 477, 479
Seeming unimportant decisions (SUDs), 479
Selectionist model, 16
Self-assessment, 1506-1508
    case illustration, 1507
    description of, 1506
    requirements of, 1506
    research basis of, 1507
    target populations for, 1507
    See also **Generalization; Goal setting;**
        Self-control; Self-instruction training;
        Self-management; Self-monitoring;
        Social skills instruction
Self-awareness, 4
Self-care behaviors, 110
Self-control, 504-508
    behavioral targets of, 504-505
    case illustration, 507-508
    choice-based model and, 506
    complications with, 507
    intervention modalities of, 505-506
    research basis of, 506-507
    self-regulation and, 505
    strategy, description of, 504-506
    target populations for, 507
    See also **Kanfer, Frederick H.; Self-management;**
        Self-monitoring; Teaching students self-control
Self-control desensitization (SCD), 508-512
    case illustration, 510-512
    complications with, 510
    coping skills model and, 509
    research basis of, 509-510
    strategy, description of, 508-509
    target populations for, 510
    See also **Self-control therapy; Self-management;**
        Systematic desensitization
Self-control therapy, 512-516
    case illustration, 515
    complications with, 514
    research basis of, 514
    strategy, description of, 512-514
    target populations for, 514
    See also **Self-control; Self-management;**
        Self-monitoring
Self-determination, 1508-1511
    case illustration, 1510-1511
    complications with, 1510
    positive behavior interventions and supports, 1509
    research basis of, 1509
    strategy, description of, 1508-1509
    target populations for, 1509-1510
    See also **Goal setting; Person-centered planning;**
        Self-control; Self-instruction training;
        Self-management; Self-monitoring; Self-praise;
        Teaching students self-control

Self-efficacy, 51, 52, 73
    See also **Guided mastery**
Self-help approaches, 61, 178-179
Self-injurious behavior (SIB), 789, 805, 1399
    facial screening and, 835
    negative reinforcement and, 918
    water misting technique and, 1091
Self-Injurious Behavior Inhibiting System (SIBIS), 975
Self-injury and suicide, 1017-1020
    case illustration, 1019-1020
    cognitive-behavioral treatments for, 1018
    complications with, 1019
    research basis of, 1018
    strategy, description of, 1017-1018
    target populations for, 1018-1019
    See also **Coping with depression; Problem-solving**
        therapy; Social competence treatment:
        Externalizing disorders; Social effectiveness
        training; Social and interpersonal skills training;
        Social skills training
Self-instruction, 1511-1513
    case illustration, 1512-1513
    complications with, 1512
    research basis of, 1512
    strategy, description of, 1511-1512
    target populations for, 1512
    See also **Generalization; Maintenance; Self-control;**
        Self-instruction training; Self-management;
        Self-monitoring; Self-praise; Teaching students
        self-control
Self-instruction training, 1020-1023
    case illustration, 1023
    child behavior problems and, 1022
    child nighttime fears and, 1022
    complications with, 1023
    hyperactive/impulsive children, 1022
    life changes for children and, 1022
    research basis of, 1022
    strategy, description of, 1020-1021
    target populations for, 1022-1023
    See also **Instructions; Meichenbaum, Donald H.;**
        Self-control therapy; Self-monitoring;
        Self-statement modification
Self-management, 516-521,
        1147, **1513-1515**
    awareness of behaviors and, 1513-1514
    case illustration, 520-521, 1515
    complications with, 520, 1515
    drug abuse prevention and, 814
    generalization of skills and, 1514
    ineffective natural contingencies
        and, 516-517
    performance management contingencies
        and, 517
    research basis of, 519, 1514

steps of, 517-519
strategy, description of, 516-519, 1513-1514
target populations for, 520, 1514
See also **Generalization; Goal setting; Maintenance;
Self-assessment; Self-control; Self-control
therapy; Self-instruction; Self-instruction
training; Self-management; Self-monitoring;
Self-praise; Self-statement modification;
Teaching students self-control**
Self-management therapy (SMT), 512-514
Self-monitoring, 87, 521-526, 1023-1027
assessment strategy of, 87, 522-523, 708
behavioral case formulation and, 91
behavioral weight control and, 167
case illustrations, 525, 1026-1027
complications with, 525, 1026
eating disorders and, 263
monitoring diaries and, 189
research basis of, 524, 1025
self-control, development of, 1573-1574
strategy, description of, 521-524, 1023-1025
target populations for, 524-525, 1025
treatment strategy of, 523-524
weight control treatments, 743
See also **Behavioral assessment; Instructions;
Kanfer, Frederick H.; Meichenbaum,
Donald H.; Self-control; Self-control therapy;
Self-instruction training; Self-monitoring;
Self-statement modification**
Self-monitoring attention (SMA), 1574
Self-monitoring performance (SMP), 1574-1575
Self-praise, 1027-1028
See also **Instructions; Meichenbaum,
Donald H.; Positive reinforcement;
Reinforcement; Self-control therapy;
Self-monitoring; Self-statement modification**
Self-reinforcement, 1575
external self-reinforcement and, 1575-1576
internal self-reinforcement and, 1576
Self-reports, 15, 87
behavioral assessment and, 87, 708-709
behavioral case formulation and, 91
self-report standardized scales, 189-190
Self-statement modification (SSM), 526-527
complications with, 527
research basis of, 527
strategy, description of, 526-527
target populations for, 527
See also **Cognitive-behavior therapy; Cognitive-
behavior therapy: Child clinical applications;
Meichenbaum, Donald H.**
Seligman, M. E. P., 1375
Sensitization:
covert sensitization, 227
See also **Covert sensitization conditioning**

Sensory extinction, 1028-1031
automatic reinforcement and, 1028
case illustration, 1030
complications with, 1029-1030
research basis of, 1029
strategy, description of, 1028-1029
target populations for, 1029
See also **Applied behavior analysis;
Functional analysis; Generalization;
Guided mastery; Operant conditioning;
Skinner, Burrhus Frederic**
Setting events, 527-528, 1301, 1515-1516
See also **Applied behavior analysis;
Deprivation; Establishing operations;
Satiation; Stimulus control**
Severe emotional disturbances (SED), 1557-1558
Sexual deviation:
covert sensitization conditioning and, 235-237, 238
See also **Behavioral approaches to sexual
deviation; Orgasmic reconditioning**
Sexual dysfunction:
anxiety research and, 44
behavior training and, 62
reciprocal inhibition principle and, 58
Shadowing, 528-532
case illustration, 531
complications with, 531
research basis of, 530
strategy, description of, 528-530
target populations for, 530-531
See also **Behavioral assessment;
Social skills training**
Shaping, 743, 1031-1036
applied behavior analysis and, 1139
case illustration, 1035
clinical description of, 1032-1033
complications with, 1034-1035
research basis of, 1033
strategy, description of, 1031-1033
target populations/behaviors for, 1033-1034
technical description of, 1031-1032
See also **Applied behavior analysis;
Functional analysis; Generalization;
Guided mastery; Operant conditioning;
Skinner, Burrhus Frederic**
Shaping to teach new behaviors, 1516-1519
backward chaining and, 1519
case illustration, 1519
shaping, description of, 1516-1517
stimulus response chaining and, 1518-1519
task analysis and, 1518
variable vs. fixed outcome shaping and, 1517-1518
See also **Differential reinforcement; Fading;
Positive reinforcement; Prompting;
Shaping; Stimulus control**

Shelton, J. L., 332
Sherrington, C., 574, 620
Short-term objectives, 1519-1520
   advantages/disadvantages of, 152
   long-term objectives and, 1520
   setting objectives, 1520
   strategy, description of, 1519-1520
   See also **Behavioral contracting;**
      Behavioral objectives; Behavior
      intervention planning; Individualized
      education program; Long-term objectives
Show-that-I-can tasks (STIC), 769
Sidman, M., 21, 533
Simplified habit reversal. *See* **Competing**
   response training
Simulated Social Interaction Test (SSIT), 494
Simulus generalization, 292
Single-case research, 532-540
   behavioral interventions and, 536-539
   brain dysfunction and, 538-539
   chemical dependencies and, 537-538
   data analysis in, 535-536
   designs of, 533-535
   developmental disorders/learning
      disabilities and, 538
   early history of, 532-533
   obsessive-compulsive disorder and, 527
   systematic desensitization and, 537
   token economies and, 536-537
   See also **Behavioral case formulation;**
      Single-subject design
Single-subject design (SSD), 995-996, 1520-1526
   a-b design, 1522-1523
   adapted alternating treatments design and, 1526
   alternating treatments design, 1525-1526
   changing criterion design, 997
   data display graphs in, 1522
   description of, 1520-1522
   independent/dependent variables, functional
      relationships between, 1522
   internal/external validity and, 1521
   intervention comparison research and, 1525-1526,
      1525-1526 (figures)
   intervention effectiveness research and, 1522-1524,
      1523 (figures)
   multielements design, 996-997, 1524
   multiple baseline design, 997
   multitreatment design and, 1525
   replication typology in, 1521-1522
   social validity and, 1522
   stage-process design, 996-997
   time-lagged strategy and, 1524
   withdrawal/reversal design, 996, 1523-1524
   See also **Changing criterion designs**

Single-subject research design. *See* **Single-subject design**
Skinner, Burrhus Frederic, 21, 34, 58, 140, 175, 215,
   294, 311, 330, 403, 436, 439, 473, 505, **540-545,**
   658, 698, 765, 767, 783, 851, 923, **1036-1037,**
   1137, 1340, 1476, **1526-1532**
   See also **Applied behavior analysis; Azrin, Nathan**
      H.; Behavioral objectives; Behavioral treatment
      in natural environments; Kantor's
      interbehaviorism; Operant; Operant
      conditioning; Pavlov, Ivan P.; Programmed
      instruction; Rate and frequency;
      Single-case research; Stimulus control
Skinner, C., 1567
Sleep behaviors, 62
   geriatric clients and, 111-112
   insomnia, behavioral medicine and, 131
   See also **Behavioral treatment of insomnia**
Sleep deprivation, 1532-1535
   alcohol/caffeine/tobacco and, 1534
   animal models of, 1532
   bed-wetting and, 1533
   behavioral observations and, 1534-1535
   bensodiazepines and, 1534
   disabled population and, 1532
   future research/interventions, 1535
   insomnia, 1533
   medication and, 1534
   melatonin and, 1534
   narcolepsy, 1533
   physiological measures/methodology and, 1535
   sleep apnea, 1533
   sleep walking and, 1533-1534
   See also **Establishing operations;**
      Functional behavioral assessment
      of problem behavior; Setting event
Sleep hygiene education, 161-162
Sleep restriction therapy, 161
SMART treatment criteria, 95
Smoking cessation programs:
   behavioral medicine and, 129-130
   behavior training and, 62
   See also **Behavioral treatment**
      of cigarette smoking
Social competence, 1535-1538
   emotional/behavioral disorders and, 1536
   school setting, social-behavioral expectations
      and, 1537
   social skills and, 1536
   social skills deficits, classification of, 1537
   theoretical/empirical foundations of, 1536
   See also **Generalization; Mastery learning; Phases of**
      learning; Problem-solving training; Self-control;
      Self-management; Social competence treatment:
      Externalizing behavior; Social effectiveness

training; Social and interpersonal skills training; Social skills instruction; Social skills training; Teaching schoolwide expectations

Social competence treatment: Externalizing disorders, 1041-1045
case illustration, 1044-1045
complications with, 1044
research basis of, 1043-1044
strategy, description of, 1041-1043
target populations for, 1044
See also **Problem-solving therapy; Social effectiveness training; Social and interpersonal skills training; Social skills training**

Social effectiveness training (SET), 546-551
case illustration, 550-551
children and, 701-702
complications with, 549-550
exposure therapy and, 548
programmed practice and, 548
psychoeducational sessions in, 547
research basis of, 548-549
social phobia assessment strategy, 546-547
social skills tr-548aining and, 547
strategy, description of, 546-548
target populations for, 549
teatment components in, 547-548
See also **Behavior rehearsal; Modeling; Social skills training**

Social Interaction Self-Statement Test (SISST), 526

Social and interpersonal skills training, 1038-1041
case illustration, 1040-1041
complications with, 1040
research basis of, 1039
strategy, description of, 1038-1039
target populations for, 1039-1040
See also **Problem-solving therapy; Social competence treatment: Externalizing disorders; Social effectiveness training; Social skills training**

Social justice values, 137
Social Learning Program, 427
Social Phobia and Anxiety Inventory (SPAI), 547
Social problem-solving (SPS), 969, 970

Social skills instruction (SSI), 1538-1541
case illustration, 1540-1541
complications with, 1540
generalization training and, 1539
modeling and, 1538
performance feedback and, 1538-1539
research basis of, 1539-1540
role-playing and, 1538
strategy, description of, 1538-1539
target populations for, 1540

See also **Direct instruction; Phases of learning; Problem-solving training; Self-control; Self-management; Social competence; Social competence treatment: Externalizing disorders; Social effectiveness training; Social and interpersonal skills training; Social skills training; Teaching schoolwide expectations; Teaching students self-control**

Social Skills Rating Scale, 1170

Social skills training (SST), 61-62, **551-558**
anxiety reduction methods and, 556
behavior rehearsal/feedback and, 553-554
case illustration, 77-78, 558
change programming and, 554
cognitive-behavior therapy and, 192
cognitive restructuring and, 555
complications with, 74, 557-558
drug abuse prevention and, 814
generalization/maintenance and, 555
geriatric clients and, 110
homework assignments and, 554-555
instructions in, 553
model presentation and, 553
research basis of, 73, 556
strategy, description of, 72-73, 551-556
target populations for, 73, 556-557
See also **Behavioral treatment in natural environments; Bellack, Alan S.; Social and interpersonal skills training; Social skills training**

Social-verbal context, 1, 2
Social work. *See* **Behavioral social work**
Society for Behavioral Medicine, 6
Society of Clinical Psychology, 363
Sociocultural factors, 93
Socratic dialogue process, 46
Solyom, L., 40

Somatic control strategies, 1046-1050
applied tension and, 1047-1048
breathing retraining and, 1047
case illustration, 1049
complications with, 1049
pharmacotherapy and, 1048
progressive muscle relaxation and, 1046-1047
research basis of, 1048
strategy, description of, 1046-10458
target populations for, 1048-1049
See also **Applied relaxation and tension; Biofeedback; Breathing retraining; Cue-controlled relaxation; Panic control treatment; Progressive muscular relaxation; Relaxation strategies; Relaxation training with children**

South Oaks Gambling Screen, 68
Specificity hypothesis, 46

Speech and language disorders, 1541-1545
   complications with treatment, 1544-1545
   description of, 1541-1543
   expressive language disorder, 1542
   mixed expressive-receptive language disorder, 1542
   phonological disorder, 1542
   practical difficulties of, 1543
   regulated breathing intervention and, 1544-1545
   research basis of, 1543-2544
   stuttering, 1542-1543
   See also **Augmentative and alternative communication; Beginning reading; Functional behavioral assessment**
Spelling. *See* **3-5-10-15 method for spelling; Write-say method**
Spielberger State-Trait Anxiety Inventory, 68
Spontaneous recovery, 1050
   See also **Applied behavior analysis; Extinction; Extinction and habituation; Operant conditioning; Schedule-induced behavior; Schedules of reinforcement; Skinner, Burrhus Frederic**
Sport psychology. *See* **Behavioral sport psychology; Sport skill training**
Sport skill training (SST), 1050-1054
   case illustration, 1053-1054
   complications with, 1052-1053
   research basis of, 1052
   strategy, description of, 1050-1052
   target populations for, 1052
   See also **Problem-solving therapy; Social competence treatment: Externalizing disorders; Social effectiveness training; Social and interpersonal skills training; Social skills training**
Spouse-aided therapy, 558-563
   anxiety disorders and, 559, 560
   case illustration, 562
   complications with, 562
   conjoint interpersonal therapy and, 559
   contingency management and, 561-562
   depression and, 559, 560-561
   research basis of, 560-562
   strategy, description of, 558-560
   substance use disorders and, 559-560, 561
   target populations for, 562
   See also **Behavioral treatment in natural environments; Flooding; Squeeze technique; Systematic desensitization**
Squeeze technique, 563-564
   research basis of, 563-564
   strategy, description of, 563
   See also **Behavioral treatment in natural environments; Orgasmic reconditioning; Spouse-aided therapy**

SRI International, 1469
Staats, A., 937
Stampfl's therapist-directed implosive (flooding) therapy, 564-569
   case illustration, 568-569
   complications with, 568
   fear/avoidance unlearning and, 565
   implosive therapy strategy and, 565-566
   research basis of, 567-568
   stimulus cue categories and, 567
   strategy, description of, 564-567
   symptom maintenance and, 565
   target populations for, 568
   treatment instructions and, 566-567
   See also **Flooding; Systematic desensitization**
Standard Behavior Chart, 1353
Standard celeration chart, 1435, 1435 (figure)
Standard celeration chart system (SCS), 1545-1548
   benefits of, 1547
   complications with, 1547-1548
   description of, 1545-1546, 1546 (figure)
   discoveries made from, 1547
   research basis of, 1547
   target populations for, 1547
   See also **Baseline; Behavioral assessment; Precision teaching; Rate and frequency; Skinner, Burrhus Frederic; Trend line; Visual analysis of graphic data**
State-Trait Anxiety Inventory, 441
Stealing. *See* **Five-step procedure for stealing**
Steely, D., 1293
Stevenson, T. I., 125
Sticker/star chart, 1054-1055
   See also **Applied behavior analysis; Azrin, Nathan H.; Public posting; Token economy**
Stimulus control, 17, 1055-1060, 1548-1552
   applied behavior analysis and, 670-671
   case illustration, 1058-1060, 1551-1552
   complications with, 1057-1058, 1551
   educational settings and, 1549
   establishing operations and, 1550
   fears/phobias and, 1549-1550
   insomnia and, 160
   research basis of, 1056-1057, 1550
   strategy, description of, 1055-1056, 1548-1550
   target populations for, 1057, 1550-1551
   weight control and, 167, 743
   See also **Attention training procedures; Operant conditioning; Schedule-induced behavior; Schedules of reinforcement; Skinner, Burrhus Frederic; Transfer of stimulus control**

Stimulus discrimination training, 1060-1061
    See also **Operant conditioning; Schedule-induced behavior; Schedules of reinforcement; Skinner, Burrhus Frederic**
Stimulus modification procedures, 1296-1297
Stokes, T. F., 1349
Stress inoculation training (SIT), 7, 8, 9, 569-573
    case illustration, 572
    complications with, 571-572
    research basis of, 571
    stages in, 570
    strategy, description of, 569-570
    target populations for, 571
    trauma management therapy and, 597
    See also **Anxiety/anger management training; Cue-controlled relaxation; Mindfulness meditation**
Stress reduction, 127
Stroul, B. A., 1555
Structural Profile Inventory (SPI), 395
Structured Clinical Interview for Diagonosis (SCID), 268
Student Risk Screening Scale (SRSS), 1282
Student success teams (SSTs), 1498-1499, 1499 (table)
Subjective Units of Distress (SUD) scale, 292, 298, 598, 614
Substance abuse disorders, 9, 93
    behavioral contracting and, 108, 109
    behavior training and, 62
    community reinforcement method and, 42
    spouse-aided therapy and, 559-560, 561
    See also Alcoholism; **Behavioral treatments for the addictions; Drug abuse prevention strategies;** Smoking cessation programs
Suicide:
    behavioral contracting and, 108
    dialectical behavior therapy and, 257
    inventories of, 46
    See also **Self-injury and suicide**
Suicide Intent Scale, 46
Suinn, Richard M., 510, 573-574
    See also **Anxiety/anger management training; Association for Advancement of Behavior Therapy; Behavioral consultation**
Supervision. *See* **Behavioral analytic approach to supervision**
Suspension, 1552-1555
    alternative schools and, 1554
    complications with, 1555
    disabled students and, 1554
    duration of, 1553
    free appropriate public education and, 1554
    guidelines for, 1555
    high- vs. low-suspensions schools, 1555
    procedure for, 1553

research basis of, 1554-1555
    strategy, description of, 1552-1554
    target populations for, 1555
    See also **Corporal punishment; Detention; Ethical issues regarding behavior management in the schools; Individuals with Disabilities Education Act; Negative reinforcement; Punishment; Schoolwide discipline; Zero tolerance**
Symbolic representation. *See* **Augmentative and alternative communication**
Systematic desensitization (SD), 508-509, 537, 574-582, 700
    analogue experiments and, 579
    animal studies and, 577-578
    assessment modes/purpose and, 575-576
    case illustration, 580-582
    clinical reports on, 578
    complications with, 580
    controlled experiments in, 578-579
    graded visualization, relaxation and, 577
    hierarchy construction and, 576-577
    relaxation training and, 576
    research basis of, 577-579
    strategy, description of, 574-577
    target populations for, 579-580
    See also **Classical conditioning; Relaxation strategies; Systematic desensitization with children and adolescents**
Systematic desensitization with children and adolescents, 1061-1064
    case illustration, 1063-1064
    complications with, 1063
    research basis of, 1062
    strategy, description of, 1061-1062
    target populations for, 1062-1063
    See also **In vivo desensitization; Lazarus, Arnold Allan; Paul, Gordon L.; Self-control desensitization; Systematic desensitization; Wolpe, Joseph**
Systematic rational restructuring (SRR), 775
Systematic screening for behavior disorders (SSBD) procedure, 1284-1286, 1285 (figure)
Systems of care, 1555-1559
    case illustration, 1558-1559
    complications with, 1558
    research basis of, 1556-1557
    services within, 1556 (figure)
    strategy, description of, 1555-1556
    target populations for, 1557-1558
    values/guiding principle, r, 1557 (table)
    See also **Contextual fit; Person-centered planning; Wraparound**
Szasz, T., 330

Task analysis, 1065-1066, 1561-1565
  backward chaining and, 1563-1564
  case illustration, 1564-1565
  chains of behavior and, 1562, 1563
  complications with, 1066, 1564
  research basis of, 1066, 1563-1564
  shaping process and, 1562
  strategy, description of, 1065-1066, 1561-1563
  target populations for, 1066, 1564
  See also **Applied behavior analysis; Chaining;
    Discrimination training; Manualized behavior
    therapy; Operant conditioning; Programmed
    instruction; Shaping to tneach new behaviors;
    Stimulus control**
Task Force on Empirically Supported Interventions in
    Clinical Psychology, 1306
Task Force on Evidence-Based Interventions in School
    Psychology, 1306, 1308
Task Force on Promotion and Dissemination of
    Psychological Procedures (TFPD), 817, 901, 908
Task Force on Psychological Intervention Guidelines
    (TFIG), 817
Task interspersal, 1565-1568
  case illustration, 1567-1568
  complications with, 1567
  research basis of, 1565-1566
  strategy, description of, 1565
  target populations for, 1567
  See also **Behavioral momentum;
    Shaping to teach new behaviors**
Taylor, J. G., 591
Teacher Rating Scale, 792
Teaching-family model, 702
Teaching schoolwide expectations, 1569-1572
  appropriate behavior, acknowledgment of, 1569-1570
  behavioral expectations, development of, 1569
  case illustrations, 1571-1572
  complications with, 1570-1571
  description of, 1569-1570
  inappropriate behaviors and, 1570
  research basis of, 1570
  rule identification and, 1569
  target populations for, 1570
  teaching process and, 1569
  See also **Positive reinforcement; Rules;
    Schoolwide discipline; Social and
    interpersonal skills training; Social
    skills instruction; Social skills training**
Teaching students self-control, 1572-1576
  cognitive model of self-control and, 1573
  mechanisms of self-control, 1573
  operant model of self-control and, 1573
  self-control, definition of, 1572-1573
  self-evaluation and, 1575

  self-monitoring skills and, 1573-1575
  self-reinforcement and, 1575-1576
  See also **Self-assessment; Self-control;
    Self-management; Social competence;
    Social and interpersonal skills training**
Temporomandibular joint (TMJ) syndrome, 129
Termination, 583-586
  case illustration, 586
  complications with, 585-586
  research basis of, 584-585
  strategy, description of, 583-584
  target populations for, 585
  See also **Behavioral case formulation;
    Behavioral consultation;
    Behavioral working alliance**
Testable hypothesis, 1576-1578
  intervention development and, 1578
  maintaining consequences and, 1577
  problem behavior and, 1577
  research basis of, 1577-1578
  setting events and, 1577-1578
  strategy, description of, 1576-1577
  triggering antecedents and, 1577
  See also **Antecedent; Consequence; Contingencies in
    educational settings; Descriptive and functional
    analysis; Establishing operations; Functional
    analysis; Functional behavioral assessment of
    problem behavior; Functional relation;
    Function-based approach to behavior support;
    Functions of behavior; Negative reinforcement;
    Positive reinforcement; Response class theory;
    Setting event; Stimulus control**
Therapeutic relationship, 586-590
  case illustration, 589-590
  complications with, 589
  research basis of, 588
  strategy, description of, 586-588
  target populations for, 588-589
  See also **Behavioral case formulation; Treatment
    compliance in cognitive behavior therapy;
    Treatment failures in behavior therapy**
Therapist Client Rating Scale, 589
Thorndike, Edward L., 294, 428,
    657, 767, 923, 1340
Thoughts:
  control attempts and, 2
  negative thoughts, threat of, 3-4, 16
  See also **Coverant control; Thought-stopping**
Thought-stopping (TS), 590-594, 1066-1068
  case illustration, 592-593
  cognitive alternative to, 592
  complications with, 591-592, 1068
  research basis of, 591, 1067
  strategy, description of, 590-591, 1066-1067